Less managing. More teaching. Greater learning.

INSTRUCTORS...

Would you like your **students** to show up for class **more prepared**?
(Let's face it, class is much more fun if everyone is engaged and prepared...)

Want an **easy way to assign** homework online and track student **progress**?
(Less time grading means more time teaching...)

Want an **instant view** of student or class performance?
(No more wondering if students understand...)

Need to **collect data and generate reports** required for administration or accreditation?
(Say goodbye to manually tracking student learning outcomes...)

Want to **record and post your lectures** for students to view online?
(The more students can see, hear, and experience class resources, the better they learn...)

With **McGraw-Hill's** *Connect,*™

INSTRUCTORS GET:

- Simple **assignment management**, allowing you to spend more time teaching.

- **Auto-graded** assignments, quizzes, and tests.

- **Detailed visual reporting** where student and section results can be viewed and analyzed.

- Sophisticated **online testing** capability.

- A **filtering and reporting** function that allows you to easily assign and report on materials that are correlated to learning objectives and Bloom's taxonomy.

- An easy-to-use **lecture capture** tool.

- The option to **upload course documents** for student access.

MODERN ADVANCED
ACCOUNTING
IN CANADA

EDITION

Murray W. Hilton, FCA
University of Manitoba

Darrell Herauf, CPA, CA, CGA
Carleton University

**McGraw-Hill
Ryerson**
Connect. Learn. Succeed.

Modern Advanced Accounting in Canada
Seventh Edition

ISBN-13: 978-0-07-105152-1
ISBN-10: 0-07-105152-X

4 5 6 7 8 9 0 CTPS 1 9 8 7 6 5

Printed and bound in China

Care has been taken to trace ownership of copyright material contained in this text; however, the publisher will welcome any information that enables it to rectify any reference or credit for subsequent editions.

Director of Product Management: *Rhondda McNabb*
Product Manager: *Keara Emmett*
Executive Marketing Manager: *Joy Armitage Taylor*
Product Developer: *Amy Rydzanicz*
Supervising Editor: *Cathy Biribauer*
Senior Product Team Associate: *Christine Lomas*
Photo/Permissions Researcher: *Robyn Craig*
Copy Editor: *Julie van Tol*
Proofreaders: *Rohini Herbert, Rodney Rawlings*
Production Coordinator: *Scott Morrison*
Cover and Inside Design: *Liz Harasymczuk*
Composition: *Laserwords Private Limited*
Cover Photo: © *Howard Sandler/Dreamstime.com*
Printer: *CTPS*

Library and Archives Canada Cataloguing in Publication Data

Hilton, Murray W.
    Modern advanced accounting in Canada / Murray W. Hilton, Darrell Herauf.—7th ed.

Includes index.
ISBN 978-0-07-105152-1

    1. Accounting—Canada—Textbooks. I. Herauf, Darrell II. Title.
HF5635.H486 2013   657'.046   C2012-906472-6

About the Authors

MURRAY W. HILTON, FCA

Murray Hilton holds the rank of Senior Scholar at the University of Manitoba where he has continued to teach in the MBA programs since his retirement in 2002. For 35 years he was Professor of Accounting at the university's Asper School of Business, teaching graduate and undergraduate courses in financial accounting. A Chartered Accountant with business degrees from the University of Saskatchewan and Oregon State University, he has published five advanced accounting books. In addition, he has been active in university and faculty administration, having previously served as Head of the Department of Accounting and Finance and as Director of the Master of Accountancy Program. He is currently the Director of the Centre for Accounting Research and Education. Murray has also been very involved in the accounting profession, teaching CA and CMA courses for many years, and serving on numerous national and provincial committees of both accounting bodies. He has on two separate occasions been a member of the National Examination Board of the Society of Management Accountants of Canada. In 1991, he received the FCA designation from the Institute of Chartered Accountants of Manitoba, and in 1994 he was made an honorary member of the Society of Management Accountants of Manitoba. For relaxation, he enjoys reading, golfing, and fishing.

DARRELL HERAUF, CPA, CA, CGA

Darrell Herauf teaches graduate and undergraduate courses in financial and managerial accounting at the Eric Sprott School of Business, Carleton University. A Chartered Accountant and a Certified General Accountant with a business degree from the University of Saskatchewan, this co-author of *Modern Advanced Accounting in Canada* is also the author of testbanks for several financial accounting textbooks. He is the recipient of numerous teaching awards, and participates on many committees at the university. Darrell has been involved in professional accounting education at the Institute of Chartered Accountants of Ontario for over 25 years in a variety of roles, including teaching, developing case/program material, and serving as a member of the Examinations subcommittee. For more than 25 years, he has been involved with the Certified General Accountants Association of Canada as national examiner, course author, and consultant. For relaxation, he enjoys cycling and skating.

Contents in Brief

Contents

CHAPTER 7
(A) Intercompany Profits in Depreciable Assets
(B) Intercompany Bondholdings   349

Preface

Welcome to the seventh edition of *Modern Advanced Accounting in Canada*. This book's well-deserved reputation for being the most current, concise, and technically accurate advanced accounting text on the market has not only been maintained but has been improved upon in this new edition. This edition is 100 percent compliant with International Financial Reporting Standards (IFRSs), not only with regard to the typical advanced accounting topics of business combinations and foreign currency transactions, but also for the topics studied in intermediate accounting and other courses. It also contains the reporting requirements for private enterprises and not-for-profit organizations. All of the extracts from financial statements are now taken from Canadian entities.

The book reflects standards that are expected to be in effect as of January 1, 2014, based on standards approved by the IASB or based on exposure drafts that were outstanding as of December 31, 2012. We have made every effort to illustrate and explain the requirements of the current standards at the time of publication, anticipating how these might change, what the effects of the changes will be, and what they will mean to the industry, professionals, and students.

We have also continued the presentation of advanced accounting topics that has been so well received by such a large number of instructors and students. Emphasis on the direct approach of preparing consolidated financial statements along with the "building block" development of the basics of consolidations has been maintained and strengthened. The working-paper approach is illustrated in Chapters 3 through 5, either in the body of the chapter or in the appendices.

Finally, as requested by instructors on behalf of their students, the following enhancements to problem material have been made in this edition:

- At least one new case has been added to each chapter to encourage critical thinking and classroom discussion. There are now five to seven cases in each chapter.

- All of the web-based problems have been changed to Canadian companies. These problems involve the analysis and interpretation of the recently published financial statements of public companies and not-for-profit organizations.

- One new self-study problem has been added to ten chapters, such that each chapter now has two self-study problems.

- The questions and/or solutions have been revised for approximately 55 percent of the end-of-chapter cases and problems.

- Finally, even more problems and questions can be found online for additional study on Connect.

New Features

- The financial statement disclosure examples in the body of each chapter have been changed to Canadian companies and to more recent years. The IFRS disclosure requirements are summarized, each followed by a real-life example from a public company or a not-for-profit organization.

- A new section on Analysis and Interpretation of Financial Statements has been added for each chapter. These sections compare the impact of different reporting methods on key financial ratios and illustrate and explain the interrelationship of financial statements.

- The following new IFRSs have been explained and applied in the appropriate chapters of the text: IFRS 10: Consolidated Financial Statements, IFRS 11: Joint Arrangements, IFRS 12: Disclosure for Interests in Other Entities, and IFRS 13: Fair Value Measurement.

- The titles and format of financial statements as traditionally used by Canadian companies are used in the illustrations throughout the body of the text, on the assumption that many Canadian companies will continue to use the same titles and format as used in the past. In the self-study problems and end-of-chapter material, both the format suggested by the IASB and the traditional format of Canadian companies are used.

- Major reorganization has occurred in Chapters 3, 4, 11, and 12. Substantial revisions have been made in eight chapters.

The following sections are provided at the end of all relevant chapters:

- *ASPE Differences.* This section highlights the differences in GAAP between accounting standards for private enterprises (ASPE) and IFRSs. There are sufficient illustrations throughout the text for the user of the text to know and apply both sets of GAAP.

- *U.S. GAAP Differences.* This section highlights the differences in GAAP between IFRSs and U.S. GAAP. Since the IASB and the FASB are working to merge their standards over the next few years, it is important to know where the differences lie so that we can anticipate where changes in IFRSs are likely to be made.

- Each chapter's *Summary* includes the following:
  - *Significant Changes in GAAP in the Last Three Years.* This section summarizes the major changes in GAAP since the publication of the sixth edition of the text.
  - *Changes Expected in GAAP in the Next Three Years.* This section summarizes the changes expected in IFRSs in the next few years, based on the projects currently on the IASB's work plan.

ORGANIZATION

Chapter 1 begins with an overview of the conceptual framework for financial reporting. Most of this material was previously contained in the prologue. The remainder of the chapter presents a survey of international accounting practices. It includes a listing of major countries requiring or permitting the use of IFRSs for listed companies. Some of the major differences between IFRSs and U.S. GAAP are identified, and the convergence project between the FASB and the IASB to harmonize their accounting standards is described. Some of the major differences between IFRSs and ASPE are identified. A new self-study problem on U.S. GAAP differences has been added.

Chapter 2 commences with an overview of the CICA pronouncements that make up the "big picture." Readers are encouraged to revisit this big picture many times as consolidation topics are developed in later chapters so that they do not lose sight of the forest as they examine the myriad of details that make up the trees. The chapter continues with a comprehensive example to illustrate the fair value, cost, and equity methods of reporting investments in equity securities, and it concludes with two self-study problems that compare these different reporting methods. Coverage of the comprehensive example could be postponed until after Chapter 4 without breaking continuity or could be omitted altogether if it is felt that adequate coverage has occurred in previous intermediate accounting courses. The new standards on Fair Value Measurement (IFRS 13) and Financial Instruments: Classification and Measurement (IFRS 9) are briefly described.

Chapter 3 describes two forms of business combinations and three methods that have been proposed or used to account for business combinations. The direct and working-paper methods are used to illustrate the acquisition method of accounting for a business combination. The new definition of control is discussed and used as the criterion for preparation of consolidated financial statements. A new section on reporting depreciable assets is added. Reverse takeovers are covered in an appendix.

Chapter 4 examines the preparation of consolidated financial statements for non–wholly owned subsidiaries at the date of acquisition. The direct method is used in the body of the chapter and the working-paper method is used in the appendix. Four theories of consolidation are discussed and illustrated. All four theories are currently or have recently been required under Canadian GAAP. Accounting for contingent consideration and bargain purchases are also illustrated.

Chapter 5 covers the preparation of consolidated financial statements subsequent to the date of acquisition when the parent uses the cost method in its internal records. The amortization and impairment of the acquisition differential is explained and illustrated, including an application of the effective interest method. A new appendix on goodwill impairment is added. The parent's journal entries under the equity method are summarized. Ten basic steps in the preparation of consolidated statements are introduced and form the foundation for the consolidation topics in the chapters that follow. The direct approach is used in the body of the chapter. Appendix B illustrates the working-paper approach for the same examples used throughout the chapter.

Chapter 6   discusses and illustrates the accounting for intercompany revenues and expenses, as well as intercompany unrealized profits or losses in inventory and land. The revenue recognition, matching, and historical cost principles are used to explain the rationale for consolidation adjustments associated with the holdback and realization of intercompany profits. The consolidation adjustments when the entities use the revaluation model for reporting land are described in the appendix.

Chapter 7   discusses the elimination of intercompany profits in depreciable assets, the recognition of gains or losses resulting from the elimination of intercompany bond-holdings, and the related income tax adjustments that are required. Two self-study problems are presented using the direct approach and involving the effective interest method for bond amortization. The consolidation adjustments when the entities use the revaluation model for reporting depreciable assets are described in the appendix.

Chapter 8   discusses the preparation of the consolidated cash flow statement and such ownership issues as subsidiaries with preferred shares, step purchases, reduction of parent's interest, and indirect holdings. In all situations, the direct approach is used. The chapter concludes with two self-study problems involving changes in ownership and preferred shares.

Chapter 9   examines other consolidation reporting issues, including special-purpose entities, deferred income taxes and business combinations, and segment disclosures. The accounting for joint arrangements is illustrated both under the equity method in the body of the chapter and under proportionate consolidation in the appendix. A new self-study problem on deferred income taxes pertaining to business combinations has been added.

Chapter 10   introduces the topic of foreign currency and four different perspectives in which currencies can be viewed. Foreign currency transactions are discussed, as are the concepts of hedging and hedge accounting. The handling of foreign currency gains and losses is illustrated, as are the accounting for fair value and cash flow hedges. The appendix describes how discounting can be applied when determining the fair value of a forward contract.

Chapter 11   concludes the foreign currency portion of the text by examining and illustrating the translation and subsequent consolidation of subsidiaries whose functional currency is the same as the parent's (i.e., integrated subsidiary) and whose functional currency is not the same as the parent's (self-sustaining subsidiary). The reporting of exchange gains and losses from the translation of self-sustaining subsidiaries in other comprehensive income is also illustrated. A new self-study problem has been added to illustrate the preparation of consolidated financial statements after translating the foreign operations under both the temporal and current-rate methods.

Chapter 12   discusses in depth the 13 not-for-profit sections in the *CICA Handbook*. The chapter concludes with a comprehensive illustration of the required journal entries and the preparation of financial statements using both the deferral method and the restricted fund method. Appendix 12A provides a real-life example of the deferral method by reproducing the financial statements of the United Way/Centraide Ottawa. Appendix 12B provides a comprehensive outline of the PSAB reporting requirements for federal, provincial, and local governments.

CONNECT

McGraw-Hill Connect™ is a web-based assignment and assessment platform that gives students the means to better connect with their coursework, with their instructors, and with the important concepts that they will need to know for success now and in the future.

With Connect, instructors can deliver assignments, quizzes, and tests online. Nearly all the problems from the text are presented in an auto-gradeable format and tied to the text's learning objectives. Instructors can edit existing questions and author entirely new problems; track individual student performance—by question, assignment, or in relation to the class overall—with detailed grade reports; and integrate grade reports easily with Learning Management Systems (LMS) such as WebCT and Blackboard.

By choosing Connect, instructors are providing their students with a powerful tool for improving academic performance and truly mastering course material. Connect allows students to practise important skills at their own pace and on their own schedule. Importantly, students' assessment results and instructors' feedback are all saved online, so students can continually review their progress and plot their course to success.

Connect also provides 24/7 online access to an eBook—an online edition of the text—to aid them in successfully completing their work, wherever and whenever they choose.

Key Features

Simple Assignment Management

With Connect, creating assignments is easier than ever, so you can spend more time teaching and less time managing.

- Create and deliver assignments easily with selectable end-of-chapter questions and testbank material to assign online.
- Streamline lesson planning, student progress reporting, and assignment grading to make classroom management more efficient than ever.
- Go paperless with the eBook and online submission and grading of student assignments.

Smart Grading

When it comes to studying, time is precious. Connect helps students learn more efficiently by providing feedback and practice material when they need it, where they need it.

- Automatically score assignments, giving students immediate feedback on their work and side-by-side comparisons with correct answers.
- Access and review each response; manually change grades or leave comments for students to review.
- Reinforce classroom concepts with practice tests and instant quizzes.

Instructor Library

The Connect Instructor Library is your course creation hub. It provides all the critical resources you'll need to build your course, just how you want to teach it.

- Assign eBook readings and draw from a rich collection of textbook-specific assignments.
- Access instructor resources, including ready-made PowerPoint presentations and media to use in your lectures.
- View assignments and resources created for past sections.
- Post your own resources for students to use.

eBook

Connect reinvents the textbook learning experience for the modern student. Every Connect subject area is seamlessly integrated with Connect eBooks, which are designed to keep students focused on the concepts key to their success.

- Provide students with a Connect eBook, allowing for anytime, anywhere access to the textbook.
- Merge media, animation, and assessments with the text's narrative to engage students and improve learning and retention.
- Pinpoint and connect key concepts in a snap using the powerful eBook search engine.
- Manage notes, highlights, and bookmarks in one place for simple, comprehensive review.

Instructor Resources

The following instructor resources are available online on Connect:

- **Solutions Manual:** This manual, prepared by the author, contains complete solutions to all the text's end-of-chapter review questions, cases, problems, and web-based problems.
- **Computerized Test Bank:** This test bank contains over 1,000 multiple-choice, true/false, and problem questions. Each test item is coded for level of difficulty and learning objective.
- **Microsoft® PowerPoint® Presentations:** These slides cover key concepts found in each chapter using outlines, summaries, and visuals.

Superior Learning Solutions and Support

The McGraw-Hill Ryerson team is ready to help you assess and integrate any of our products, technology, and services into your course for optimal teaching and learning performance. Whether it's helping your students improve their grades, or putting your entire course online, the McGraw-Hill Ryerson team is here to help you do it. Contact your Learning Solutions Consultant today to learn how to maximize all of McGraw-Hill Ryerson's resources!

For more information on the latest technology and Learning Solutions offered by McGraw-Hill Ryerson and its partners, please visit us online: **www.mcgrawhill.ca/he/solutions**.

Acknowledgements

This text includes the thoughts and contributions of many individuals, and we wish to express our sincere appreciation to them. First and foremost, we thank all the students in our advanced accounting classes, from whom we have learned so much. In many respects, this text is an outcome of the learning experiences we have shared with our students. Second, we wish to thank the technical checkers, Shari Mann, Ingrid McLeod-Dick, and Stephen Spector. The accuracy of the text is due in large part to their efforts. We also wish to thank the following colleagues for their invaluable advice:

Talal Al-Hayale, *University of Windsor*
Kiran Bisnauth, *Seneca College*
Chuck Campbell, *University of British Columbia*
Bill Dawson, *University of Western Ontario*
Pauline Downer, *Memorial University of Newfoundland*
Elizabeth Hicks, *Mount Saint Vincent University*
Stuart Jones, *University of Calgary*
Stephen Jussey, *Algoma University*
Michael Khan, *University of Toronto*
Deirdre Taylor, *Ryerson University*

Thanks also to the Canadian Institute of Chartered Accountants for granting permission to reproduce material from the *CICA Handbook* as well as questions from the Uniform Final Examinations (UFEs), and to the Certified General Accountants of Canada and the Certified Management Accountants for their permission to reproduce questions adapted from past examinations. Thank you to Peter Secord of St. Mary's University for all of his case contributions.

We are very grateful to the staff at McGraw-Hill Ryerson: Director of Product Management Rhondda McNabb, Product Manager Keara Emmett, Product Developers Amy Rydzanicz and Chris Cullen, and Supervising Editors Cathy Biribauer and Kara Stahl, who applied pressure in a gentle but persistent manner when we strayed from the project's schedule. Thanks also to Copy Editor Julie van Tol and Proofreaders Rohini Herbert and Rodney Rawlings, whose technical expertise was necessary to carry the project to its end.

And finally, we are grateful to our families for all of their support and encouragement.

Murray Hilton   *Darrell Herauf*
Asper School of Business   *Sprott School of Business*
University of Manitoba   *Carleton University*

A Survey of International Accounting

LEARNING OBJECTIVES

After studying this chapter, you should be able to do the following:

LO1 Describe the conceptual framework for financial reporting.

LO2 Identify factors that can influence a country's accounting standards.

LO3 Identify the role that the IASB intends to play in the establishment of uniform worldwide accounting standards.

LO4 Identify the direction that the FASB intends to follow for public companies.

LO5 Describe how accounting standards in Canada are tailored to different types of organizations.

LO6 Analyze and interpret financial statements to assess the impact of different accounting methods on key financial statement ratios.

LO7 Identify some of the differences between IFRS and ASPE.

INTRODUCTION

Welcome to advanced accounting. We wish you a prosperous learning experience. We will study three major accounting topics: consolidations, foreign currency transactions and operations, and not-for-profit and government organizations. The topics are presented and illustrated in accordance with the generally accepted accounting principles (GAAP) that are expected to be in effect in Canada as of January 1, 2014. You may have had some exposure to these topics in your previous accounting courses. We will build on this prior knowledge and the conceptual framework studied in intermediate accounting while we develop a thorough understanding of these selected topics.

Prior to the 1990s, the study of accounting principles in Canada focused on the *CICA Handbook - Accounting* (hereafter referred to as *CICA Handbook* or *Handbook*) and involved very little, if any, thought or discussion of accounting standards in other parts of the world. But since then, rapid changes have taken place throughout the world, and even more drastic changes are coming. Canadian companies now view the entire world as their marketplace; not only are they exporting their products to more countries than ever before, but they are also establishing factories and offices in foreign locations. Companies that used to raise capital strictly in their home countries are now finding that capital markets are available to them

Canadian companies are now able to raise capital resources on the world's marketplace.

around the world. Because their shares trade on stock exchanges, they are often required to prepare financial reports using accounting principles of countries other than Canada. Many accounting firms have offices throughout the world, and there are abundant opportunities for their Canadian staff members to transfer to these offices. With all these changes taking place, an accounting education that takes a narrow, parochial view is clearly inadequate. Canadian students of accounting need to be fully aware of what is happening in the rapid movement toward worldwide accounting standards, and it is imperative that the textbooks of today address this topic.

Before embarking on the study of the major topics in this book, we will review the role of accountants and the objectives of reporting. Then, we will survey the accounting principles and practices used in a sample of other countries. It is hoped that this exposure to other countries' standards will help us understand the future direction of standards in our own country.

LO1 THE CONCEPTUAL FRAMEWORK FOR FINANCIAL REPORTING

Professional accountants provide a variety of services ranging from accounting to tax planning to assurance to business consulting. In this course, we will focus on financial accounting; that is, providing general-purpose financial information to external users such as investors and creditors. These users usually have limited financial resources to invest in an entity. They wish to invest where they can earn the highest return with the lowest amount of risk. The general-purpose set of financial statements (balance sheet, income statement, cash flow statement, and notes to the financial statements) will be used by the external users to help them make their resource allocation decisions and to assess the stewardship of management. The general-purpose reports are not the only source of information used for decision making but provide a good starting point.

In most cases, users want to receive the general-purpose financial statements prepared in accordance with generally accepted accounting principles (GAAP) because by following these principles, the information is relevant, reliable, understandable, and comparable. However, there are times when users may want or require special-purpose financial reports that do not follow GAAP. For example, entities may need to prepare non–GAAP-based statements for legislative or regulatory purposes, or for contract compliance. Or, a prospective lender may want to receive a balance sheet with assets reported at fair value rather than historical cost. As accountants, we are able to provide financial information in a variety of formats or using a variety of accounting policies because we have the skills and abilities to produce this information. If we do provide fair-value-based financial statements, we cannot say that the statements were prepared in accordance with GAAP. We would simply state that the statements were prepared in accordance with the policies described in the notes to the financial statements.

GAAP encompass broad principles and conventions of general application, as well as rules and procedures that determine accepted accounting practices at a particular time. The process of developing GAAP is political. Both preparers and users of financial statements have an opportunity to comment on a proposal for a new accounting standard before it becomes generally accepted. If a new requirement is preferred by the preparers but not accepted by users, it is unlikely to become part of GAAP. Therefore, as we study existing accounting practices and proposed changes, we need to continually evaluate whether information provided by a reporting entity will satisfy users' needs.

In most cases, the users of the financial statements have access to information about the entity in addition to that provided in the financial statements. For example, the owner of a private company may also be the manager and would have intimate knowledge of the company. In such cases, the owner/manager may place less reliance on the financial statements than outside investors in public companies do. In other situations, the owner may not understand the financial reporting for complex transactions such as business combinations. In both of these situations, the owners may feel that the costs of complying with some of the complex sections of the *Handbook* are not worth the benefit. They may prefer to issue more simplified statements. The Canadian Institute of Chartered Accountants (CICA) recognized this difference in users' needs. In 2002, differential reporting was incorporated in the *Handbook* whereby qualifying enterprises could choose to apply differential reporting options and still be in compliance with GAAP. In 2011, these differential options were eliminated and replaced with a *Handbook* that is now segregated into different parts for different types of organizations.

> Financial statements should cater to the needs of the users.

> The *Handbook* is divided into different parts to cater to different types of reporting entities.

The *CICA Handbook* is an authoritative document in Canada because many legal statutes require its use. For example, companies incorporated under the Canada Business Corporations Act and certain provincial Companies Acts are required to prepare financial statements in accordance with the *CICA Handbook*. Publicly traded companies are required to submit financial statements that comply with GAAP to the securities commissions under which they are registered.

The *CICA Handbook* provides the accounting and reporting requirements as well as explanations and guidance for most transactions and events encountered by an entity. When an entity following International Financial Reporting Standards (IFRSs) encounters transactions or events that are not explicitly addressed by the standards, the entity should adopt accounting practices that are consistent with the spirit of the IFRSs and consistent with the financial statement concepts. These concepts are described in the "The Conceptual Framework for Financial Reporting," which is a document found just prior to the IFRSs in Part I of the *Handbook*. Entities that are reporting under Accounting Standards for Private Enterprises (ASPE) should adopt accounting practices that are consistent with Section 1000: Financial Statement Concepts, in Part II of the *Handbook*.

The financial statement concepts describe the principles and assumptions underlying the preparation of financial statements. They are very important parts of GAAP because they provide the framework for the development and issuance of other financial accounting standards. The main items included in this document are as follows:

- The objective of general-purpose financial reporting
- Qualitative characteristics of useful financial information
- Underlying assumptions
- Definition, recognition, and measurement of the elements of financial statements

You will probably recognize most of the concepts and remember studying them in your intermediate accounting courses. If you can explain the accounting practices learned there in terms of these basic concepts, you should have no trouble applying these concepts in the new situations we will encounter in this course. If you do not understand or cannot explain accounting requirements in terms of these basic concepts, it is never too late to start. As you study the accounting

> All accounting practices should be able to be traced back to and supported by the conceptual framework.

requirements in this course, try to understand them in terms of the basic concepts and principles that the *Handbook* describes.

By gaining a broad understanding of the logic and basic principles behind the accounting requirements, you will develop confidence and be able to apply these basic principles in a wide variety of situations. Rather than simply accepting accounting practices or memorizing specific requirements in the *Handbook,* you will begin to understand the logic of the requirements and evaluate whether these are consistent with the basic financial statement concepts. You will soon realize that most of the requirements in accounting can be understood, developed, and derived from these basic principles and concepts. Then, in turn, you will be able to use professional judgment to apply these basis principles to whatever situation you may encounter.

Professional Judgment

Lots of judgment is involved when preparing financial statements.

Judgment is the ability to make a decision in situations where the answer is not clear-cut. Professional judgment is the ability to make decisions for issues encountered by professionals in carrying out their day-to-day responsibilities. Judgment is a skill developed over many years of study and learning from one's experiences. Professional judgment is derived from knowledge and experience in the profession. It is not something that is learned from rote or memorization of requirements or answers to certain problems. It often involves making choices between meaningful alternatives and the ability to understand the consequences of one's actions.

In the preparation of financial statements, there are three main areas where judgment needs to be applied. First, accounting policies such as when to recognize revenue and whether or not to consolidate a special-purpose entity involve making a decision after considering various methods. The method adopted for a particular company must be appropriate for that company based on its existing situation. For example, if Company A is selling to customers with poor credit history and without obtaining any security for the receivables from these customers, it would be appropriate to recognize revenue when cash is received. If competitors were selling to customers with very high credit ratings, it would be appropriate for them to recognize revenue when the goods are delivered. The professional judgment of an accountant will take these factors into consideration and recognize that although one method is appropriate for the competitors, another may be more appropriate for Company A.

Judgment is involved when adopting accounting policies, making estimates and writing the notes to the financial statements.

Second, judgment is involved in making accounting estimates of many kinds. What is the estimated useful life of property, plant, and equipment? What is the recoverable amount for goodwill? Will a forward contract be effective as a hedge of expected sales for the next three years? The answers to these questions are not clearly defined. In the classroom, we are usually provided with this information, but in the real world, we must gather data and make our own assessment. Whether we feel that the company can continue as a going concern or not would likely have a material difference on the valuation of goodwill and the bottom line on the income statement.

Third judgment is involved in deciding what to disclose and how to disclose it in the notes to the financial statements. For example, in disclosing a contingent liability resulting from a lawsuit, the company could simply say that it has been sued but no provision is made in the financial statements because it feels that the lawsuit has no merit. Or, it could provide details of the lawsuit and give some probabilities of different outcomes in the note.

Is there too much latitude in accounting? Do the financial statements ever portray the complete facts? One could argue that there is no latitude because accountants are not free to randomly select any reporting method. They must represent faithfully what really happened and what really exists using the generally accepted conceptual framework. If the revenue has been earned, then the revenue should be recognized. If the expenditure will provide a future benefit, then the cost of the expenditure should be recognized as an asset. Latitude is necessary so that the accountant can choose the methods to reflect the real situation. If the requirements are written too rigidly, companies may be forced to use methods that do not reflect their own situations.

If accountants take their jobs seriously and have high ethical standards, they will present the financial statements as reliably as possible by using appropriate accounting policies, by making the best estimates possible, and by making honest and forthright statements in the notes to the financial statements. They will use judgment to fairly present the financial position and financial performance of the entity. Otherwise, the individual accountants and the entire accounting profession will lose credibility.

Financial statements should present what really happened during the period: that is, they should tell it how it is.

In this course, we will have an opportunity to develop our judgment skills and to exercise judgment through the use of cases. The cases provide realistic scenarios where conflicts exist and choices must be made. The answers are not usually clear-cut. In fact, different valid answers can be defended. For these cases, it is how you support your recommendation that is important, as opposed to what your final recommendation is. You will need to apply basic principles and use judgment to come up with an answer that "tells it how it is" as accurately as possible. In so doing, you will be developing the skills required of a professional accountant.

A Survey of International Accounting

GAAP have varied in the past from country to country around the world. If a detailed study had been made of the accounting practices used by every country in the world, it would probably have concluded that very few countries used exactly the same standards for external financial reporting purposes. Some comparisons would have yielded minor differences; others would have shown substantial ones. Differences existed in terminology and style of presentation, as well as in methods of measurement and disclosure.

In past years, the variety of accounting principles being used throughout the world was large.

Differences in measurement ranged from departures to the historical cost principle to varying standards within the historical cost model. A variety of methods existed worldwide for measuring and reporting inventories, research and development costs, fixed assets, leases, computer software, and deferred income taxes. Income-smoothing devices varied from country to country. In Canada and the United States, GAAP allowed little opportunity to smooth income, while in other countries income-smoothing devices were allowed under GAAP or were encouraged by government regulation. This was often accomplished by setting up reserves, which are special equity accounts, and using them to transfer amounts to and from the statement of comprehensive income as needed. Inadequate disclosures often masked the real effect on yearly income measurements.

Asset revaluations have long been acceptable in many countries. Circumstances for these revaluations range from price-level-adjusted historical costs, used to counteract distortions resulting from very high inflation rates, to the regular or periodic adjustment of asset measurements to current replacement costs. Even under historical costs, great variations have existed in yearly measurements. The accounting for the asset of goodwill, which arises as a result of one company

Asset revaluations have been a common practice in many countries.

buying another business, is a prime example. Practices included the immediate write-off of purchased goodwill to equity, capitalization with amortization over greatly varying periods, capitalization without amortization (thus, leaving it on the balance sheet forever), and capitalization and write-off to income only when there was evidence of impairment.

Not only were there differences in measurement, but there were often also differences in the presentation and description of elements in financial statements. For example, in many countries, long-term assets were, and continue to be, presented before current assets on the balance sheet, and shareholders' equity appears before liabilities.

Information disclosed is often more voluminous in other countries than that required in Canada.

Examples of areas where disclosure differences still exist are segment reporting, reporting financial forecasts, shareholder and environmental disclosures, and other value-added information. While many foreign multinational companies disclose the lines of business they are in and the geographical area in which they operate, there is still inconsistency in the level of detail provided. While the provision of financial forecasts is not common in North America, some companies in Europe do provide this information. Foreign companies often provide voluminous disclosures about their shares, shareholders' rights, and changes in shareholders' equity. Finally, while this is not required by accounting standards, multinational companies are increasingly providing information about environmental safety and protection issues and the ways in which they have added value to society by their distributions to owners, creditors, employees, and governments.

Differences in accounting standards have always existed, but they have been receiving greater attention in recent years because of the many changes taking place in the world economy. For example, the dismantling of the former Soviet empire has been accompanied by a shift from controlled to market-driven economies, and most of the countries in Europe have joined together to form the European Union (EU). The North American Free Trade Agreement allows the free flow of goods and services among Canada, the United States, and Mexico, and this agreement may soon be expanded to include some countries in South America.

Technology has improved the global flow of information.

In the midst of all this, there have been major advances in computer and communication technology that are dramatically improving the global flow of information and changing how business activities are conducted. As a result, foreign currencies now trade 24 hours a day in the world's financial centres. Accompanying this shift toward a global marketplace has been substantial growth in the size and number of multinational corporations. This growth has been achieved to a great extent by takeovers and mergers, often financed through the capital markets of *many* countries. Not only has there been a shift to a global marketplace for goods and services, but there has also been a shift toward a global capital market. Many of the world's stock exchanges now list foreign companies. There is also considerable activity involving mergers of stock exchanges from different parts of the world.

With such a global capital market comes the need to provide the suppliers of capital with useful accounting information. Fragmented accounting principles seriously compromise comparability, which is one of the key concepts associated with information usefulness. To counter this, securities regulators in foreign countries often require foreign companies listed on their stock exchanges either to prepare financial statements in accordance with their domestic accounting standards or to prepare reconciliations from foreign to domestic standards. For example, foreign companies listed on U.S. stock exchanges are required by the Securities and

Exchange Commission (SEC) to prepare reconciliations of net income measured in accordance with foreign GAAP to net income in accordance with U.S. GAAP, unless they use the IFRSs issued by the International Accounting Standards Board (IASB). Prior to the adoption of IFRSs in 2011, Canadian companies that were listed on U.S. stock exchanges also had to prepare these reconciliations. Exhibit 1.1 provides an extract from the 2010 financial statements of Encana Corporation, a leading North American natural gas producer. It shows the reconciliation of net income from Canadian GAAP to U.S. GAAP.

The SEC requires foreign companies to reconcile their earnings to U.S. GAAP unless they use IFRSs.

It is important to note that Encana's net income under Canadian GAAP was substantially different from net income under U.S. GAAP. The main difference in the Encana example is the impairment test for property, plant, and equipment. Under U.S. GAAP, future cash flows were based on the average price this past year and were discounted at 10%. Under Canadian GAAP, the future cash flows were based on forecast pricing and were not discounted. The extract below is only a small portion of Note 21. The entire note is seven pages long. It provides narrative explanations of the main reasons for the difference in net income and provides condensed financial statements under U.S. GAAP. With such a significant difference in net income and such extensive note disclosure, it is little wonder that there is pressure to develop one high-quality, worldwide accounting standard. These requirements substantially increase a company's costs of preparing financial statements. Investment analysts and other users then incur further additional costs when interpreting financial statements prepared under different standards. Because of these problems, many countries in the world have either recently adopted, or are seriously considering adopting IFRSs. However, there still are many countries that have not adopted IFRSs and may not ever do so. In order to fully understand the issues and how changes may occur in the future, we must first examine the major causes of differences in GAAP between countries.

Encana reported a significant difference between net earnings under Canadian GAAP and net earnings under U.S. GAAP.

The reconciliation of net income from a foreign country's GAAP to U.S. GAAP is very costly to prepare.

EXHIBIT 1.1	Extracts (in Part) from Encana's 2010 Financial Statements			

For the years ended December 31	*Note*	*2010*	*2009*	*2008*
Net Earnings—Canadian GAAP		$ **1,499**	$ 1,862	$ 5,944
Less:				
Net Earnings from Discontinued Operations – Canadian GAAP		**—**	32	(555)
Net Earnings from Continuing Operations – Canadian GAAP		**1,499**	1,830	6,499
Increase (Decrease) in Net Earnings from Continuing				
Operations under U.S. GAAP:				
Revenues, net of royalties		**—**	—	—
Operating	D ii), H	**(7)**	(16)	(46)
Depreciation, depletion and amortization	B, D ii)	**1,234**	(10,926)	(1,755)
Administrative	D ii)	**(3)**	22	(27)
Interest, net	A	**—**	—	(3)
Foreign exchange (gain) loss, net	G	**35**	128	—
Stock-based compensation – options	C	**—**	—	2
Income tax expense (recovery)	E	**(415)**	3,378	695
Net Earnings (Loss) from Continuing Operations – U.S. GAAP		**2,343**	(5,584)	5,365
Net Earnings (Loss) from Discontinued Operations – U.S. GAAP		**—**	32	(555)
Net Earnings (Loss) – U.S. GAAP		$ **2,343**	$ (5,552)	$ 4,810

Source: http://www.sec.gov/Archives/edgar/data/1157806/000110465911007980/a11-4497_240f.htm#introduction_143230 Page 46.

L02 Factors That Can Influence a Country's Accounting Standards

Many factors can influence a country's accounting standards. Usually, there is not one dominant factor. The following five factors can affect standards.

The Role of Taxation   In some countries, income tax has a minimal effect on how net income is measured for financial reporting. For example, in Canada and the United States, companies often report net incomes on their operating statements that are substantially different from the taxable incomes they report on their tax returns. This has led to the GAAP concept of inter-period tax allocation. However, in some countries where such differences exist, full tax allocation has not always been used.

> Accounting income and taxable income are virtually the same in some countries.

In other countries, taxation has a profound effect on how accounting income is measured. Accounting income will not differ much from taxable income if a country's tax statutes state that expenses must be recorded on the income statement if they are to be allowed as a deduction on the tax return. In countries where this is the case, the result is often the use of extreme conservatism in accounting measurements on the part of companies trying to keep their incomes as low as possible within the law. Germany and Japan are examples of countries whose tax laws have strongly influenced GAAP. In the United States, while taxable income and accounting income are different numbers, one area where consistency is required is the costing of inventory. If LIFO (last in, first out) is to be used for tax purposes, it must also be used for financial reporting.

> Highly developed capital markets often result in the development of quality accounting standards.

The Level of Development of Capital Markets   In countries where publicly traded debt and equity securities play a substantial role in the financing of business activities, accounting and disclosure standards tend to be much more extensive than in countries where this is not the case. This is because highly developed public capital markets tend to have fairly sophisticated investors who demand current and useful information from those who have received their capital. Canada, the United Kingdom, and the United States all have highly developed capital markets and strong accounting and disclosure standards. In countries where business financing tends to be private rather than public, there is less reliance on extensive accounting standards because the private suppliers of capital can demand and receive the information they need directly from the "consumers" of such capital. Japan is a prime example; there, corporate capital needs have been supplied by very large private suppliers, such as banks. However, it should be noted that when Japan's economy took a severe dive in the 1990s, many of Japan's major banks incurred massive loan losses that nearly bankrupted them; this was cited as a major contributor to the Japanese recession. Germany and Switzerland also have very large banks that satisfy much of the capital needs of business. Historically, a large number of businesses in Mexico were state owned, but in the 1990s, a change to private ownership resulted in a shift to financing through private and public capital markets.

> Code law systems specify what individuals and corporations can do, while common law systems specify what cannot be done.

Differing Legal Systems   Two different kinds of legal system are in existence today: code law systems and common law systems. Code law systems, which originated with the Roman Empire, contain very detailed statutes that govern a wide range of human activities. In general, they specify what individuals and corporations *can* do. Common law systems have less-detailed statutes and rely on the court system to interpret statutes and thus establish precedents through case law. In general, they specify what individuals and corporations *cannot* do (i.e., what is illegal).

In many common law countries, governments tend to take a hands-off approach to the setting of accounting standards. While there may be statutes requiring that companies make information available to the providers of capital, the *type* of information required is left to the private sector. In the United States, the SEC, which administers securities legislation, has given the right to develop accounting standards to a private group, the Financial Accounting Standards Board (FASB). In Canada, the *CICA Handbook* pronouncements constitute the accounting standards required by the provincial and federal Companies Acts and the Ontario Securities Commission (OSC). The United Kingdom also uses a private standard-setting body.

In code law countries such as Germany, France, and Japan, the private sector is involved only in an advisory capacity, and accounting standards are reflected in legal statutes, often as protection for creditors and other capital suppliers. It should not be surprising to note that tax law also heavily influences accounting standards in these countries.

> In Germany, France, and Japan, accounting standards are set by legal statutes.

Ties between Countries   Political and economic ties between countries have historically had some effect on accounting standards. For example, the accounting standards and professional accounting organizations of countries that were once colonies are often patterned after those of the "home" country. There have been strong similarities between the standards of India, South Africa, Australia, New Zealand, and Malaysia and those of Great Britain. During their early development, Canadian accounting standards were influenced by Great Britain's, but in later years, this influence shifted away from Britain to the United States due to the very strong economic ties that developed between those two countries. The formation of the European Union has certainly had an effect on the accounting standards used by its member countries. We will see more of this later.

Inflation Levels   The historical cost model, which implicitly assumes a relatively stable unit of measure, is used by many countries. However, the model is not useful when inflation rates are very high. Countries that have experienced high inflation rates often make financial reporting adjustments to counteract the effects of inflation. These adjustments involve price-level-adjusted statements, or a shift from historical costs to current-value accounting, or both. Many countries in South America that experienced inflation rates of 1,000% or more per annum in the 1980s and 1990s adopted inflation-based accounting. Inflation in most of these South American countries is now more reasonable and inflation accounting has been discontinued. Mexico used price-level accounting because of high inflation rates from 1983 to 2007. Canada, the United States, and the United Kingdom all experimented with the supplemental reporting of price level and current-value information in the 1970s when the inflation rate approached 20%. The experiment was not successful because of the high cost of providing such information and the general lack of comprehension on the part of financial statement users. All three countries abandoned the experiment when inflation declined.

> High inflation rates often result in departures from historical cost measurements.

Toward Accounting Harmonization and Convergence

A truly global economy will require some sort of harmonized accounting standards if it is to function properly. Three organizations that have been working

> The European Union, the IASB, and the FASB have been working toward accounting harmonization.

toward accomplishing this objective are the European Union, the IASB, and the FASB. The role of these three organizations is discussed next.

The European Union   In 1957, six European countries signed the Treaty of Rome, thereby establishing a common market for goods and services and common institutions for economic development. Originally called the European Economic Community, it is now called the European Union (EU), which had 27 members at the end of 2012.[1] A major goal of the EU is the promotion of the free flow of goods, labour, and capital among member countries. In 1998, in order to establish a common economic policy for the area, a European central bank was established, which subsequently issued a common currency called the *euro*.

> The use of the euro as a common currency in the European Union has not been a resounding success.

The intent was that the currencies of the member nations would be gradually phased out with full adoption of this common currency. As of January 1, 2013, only 17 members have complied.[2] Both Sweden and Denmark held referendums in which their citizens voted to reject the adoption of the euro. The government of the United Kingdom, sensing that a referendum would be defeated, decided to wait until such time that the public mood has changed. A major reason for rejection by these three countries was the fact that they did not wish to individually relinquish their ability to determine economic policy. It was also observed that each country's economy had performed much better than many of the other EU member countries that had switched their currencies, such as Germany, Italy, and France.

The credit crisis in Europe in 2011 and 2012 put much strain on the euro and the EU. Greece and Spain received conditional bailouts from the EU in attempts to avoid the complete collapse of the EU. Harsh austerity measures had to be taken by many of the member countries. Time will tell whether the euro and the European Union will survive.

> The EU has attempted to harmonize accounting standards used by its member countries.

The European Union has also attempted to harmonize the accounting principles used by its member countries by issuing "directives." In order to minimize conflict with the legal reporting requirements of certain of its member nations, these directives often allowed many alternative reporting practices. This is particularly true with respect to the first accounting directive. The second directive, issued in 1983, requiring the presentation of consolidated financial statements, has had a major impact on the accounting of many countries where consolidation was not previously a common practice. While flexibility appears to be contrary to the concept of harmonization, the adoption of the directives has, nevertheless, caused major changes to the accounting practices of some of its members.

L03   **The IASB**   The IASB became operational in 2001 as a result of a major restructuring of its former organization, which was called the International Accounting Standards Committee (IASC). This committee, based in London, England, was formed in 1973 by an agreement between the professional accounting bodies of 10 countries with the purpose of establishing worldwide accounting principles. The founding members came from Australia, Canada, France, Germany, Japan, Mexico, Netherlands, United Kingdom, Ireland, and United States. Over the years, the membership grew such that it represented more than 140 accounting

100 countries. It should be pointed out, however, that membership in the organization did not translate into the adoption of its standards, and the number of countries actually using IASC standards was a much lower number. Initially, many of the standards issued by the IASC were characterized by the number of acceptable alternatives that were permitted, but in the early 1990s, efforts were made to eliminate many of these alternatives. This initiative was partially successful, but it left a number of standards still allowing alternative treatments. Given that some of the board members came from countries whose accounting standards are reflected in legal statutes, it is understandable that the removal of alternatives can be a tricky political process requiring compromise. Notwithstanding this difficulty, achieving worldwide accounting uniformity will depend greatly on eliminating alternative accounting practices.

IASs often allow alternative accounting treatments.

Note that standards issued by the original IASC were issued in numerical order with the prefix IAS, while subsequent standards issued by the IASB were also issued numerically with the prefix IFRS. In future, we will refer to the current collection of international financial reporting standards as IFRSs. For a complete list of IFRSs, see the Table of Contents for Part I of the *CICA Handbook*.

In March 2001, a major restructuring of the IASB was completed, and the board adopted the following major objectives:

The IASB hopes to develop a single set of high-quality, global accounting standards that will be adopted by countries around the world.

- To develop a single set of high-quality, global accounting standards that require transparent and comparable information in general-purpose financial statements

- To cooperate with various national accounting standard setters in order to achieve convergence in accounting standards around the world

A dictionary meaning of the term *converge* is "to approach" or "to tend to meet." The hope of the board is that the appropriate national bodies will adjust their individual standards in such a way that the essence of the IASB standard is achieved, even though the exact wording is not adopted.

The IASB is now located in London, England, and has 16 members from 13 countries. The members are chosen more for their expertise than for geographical representation. However, nine of the members are expected to have formal liaison responsibilities with major national standard-setting bodies but must not be actual members of such national bodies. Presumably such a liaison will be instrumental in harmonizing the national standards of a very important group of countries with those of the IASB.

The number of countries adopting international standards has rapidly increased in recent years. Some of the increase has come from the adoption by those countries that previously had no standards but, because of a shift to a market economy, required new forms of financial reporting. Most of the increase has come from initiatives of the EU and the standard setters from Australia and New Zealand. (These initiatives are fully discussed in the next section.) As of December 2012, more than 100 countries required IFRSs for publicly traded companies, required IFRSs for some companies, or permitted IFRSs to be used by some companies. However, there are still some countries that do not permit the use of IFRSs. See Exhibit 1.2 for a selection of major countries in each of these categories. We expect that the number of countries requiring the use of IFRSs will continue to grow.

Companies in over 100 countries are now using IFRSs.

EXHIBIT 1.2	Use of IFRSs by Major Countries — December 2012		
IFRSs Required for All Domestic Listed Companies			
Argentina	European Union		
Australia	France	Korea	South Africa
Brazil	Germany	Mexico	Russia
Canada*	Italy	New Zealand	Turkey

Other Countries	Status
China	National standards substantially converged with IFRSs
India	Convergence process ongoing
Indonesia	Converging with IFRS
Japan	Permitted for some international companies
Saudia Arabia	Banks and insurance companies listed on the Saudi Stock Exchange must use IFRSs
United States	Not permitted for domestic listed companies

*Some rate regulated companies have been exempted from applying IFRSs and are using U.S. GAAP
Source: http://www.ifrs.org/Use-around-the-world/Pages/Use-around-the-world.aspx

Initiatives from the European Union, Australia, and New Zealand

A major development toward the convergence or harmonization of accounting standards throughout the world occurred in 2002 when the European Union issued a directive stating that effective January 1, 2005, all European companies whose shares trade on stock exchanges would be required to prepare their consolidated financial statements in accordance with IFRSs. Two other important developments occurred when Australia switched over to IFRSs in 2005, and New Zealand switched in 2007. It should be noted that while these developments brought 29 countries into the international standards arena, the methods used to do so were different.

Public companies in the EU as well as in Australia have been using IFRSs since 2005.

The standards boards of both Australia and New Zealand issued new domestic standards that were "equivalent to" IFRSs. In Australia's case, it was announced in 2002 that the Australian Accounting Standards Board intended to issue new standards that would essentially be the same as IFRSs, effective for all Australian business entities (public or private and incorporated or unincorporated). The issue of new standards was essential because Australian corporate law requires financial reports to comply with Australian accounting standards. The standards issued were not identical to IFRSs. In some instances, the new Australian standards restricted the use of the optional provisions allowed in some international standards and in other cases required additional disclosures when international disclosure requirements did not match existing Australian ones. The standards board also indicated that it intends to issue additional standards to cover areas that are purely domestic and not covered by IFRSs.

In the EU situation, the directive did not require each of the 27 member countries to change their domestic accounting standards but, rather, required all publicly traded companies located in EU countries to prepare their financial statements in accordance with IFRSs. The member states were not all required to issue new standards in such a short period of time but were expected to do so later. Keep in mind that the accounting standards of France and Germany are set by legislation, and changes to legislation are not made quickly.

The EU changeover affected more than 8,000 companies.

The EU directive resulted in more than 8,000 listed companies implementing international standards in their 2005 financial reports. In their document,

Observations on the Implementation of IFRS[3], Ernst and Young provided an overview of how some large multinationals reported their 2005 results using IFRSs. In general, the study concluded that the changeover was successful, even though many companies found that they had to make significant changes in their measurement and disclosure practices.

Because IFRSs do not require uniform presentation of the financial statement elements and descriptions, many companies were able to maintain previous presentations that were unique to their particular country. While this helps comparability from a domestic point of view, consistency and comparability are compromised from an international point of view when terminology differences are not understood.

In many cases, it was noted that the IFRS statements were far more complex than those based on national standards. Overall, the 2005 statements were 20 to 30% longer than the prior year's statements and contained far more notes than in prior years. The study questioned whether the overall usefulness of the financial information had been compromised as a result.

The study concluded that because IFRSs are broad based, extensive judgment is required in their application, and if judgment is not used on a consistent basis by the preparers of the financial statements in each of the EU countries, comparability could be, and probably is, severely compromised.

It should be noted that when IFRSs were adopted by the EU, Australia, and New Zealand, some tailoring of the standards for local conditions was done. For example, the EU standards related to IAS 39: Financial Instruments—Recognition and Measurement are not the same as the IASB standards. As a result, companies must disclose in their financial statements whether they are following the IASB standards or some sort of modified standards. Unless otherwise stated, when we refer to IFRSs in this textbook, we will always be referring to the standards published by the IASB.

> *Significant changes to corporate reporting were the result of the switch to IFRSs.*

IFRSs versus U.S. GAAP

> **L04**

Accounting principles in the United States are set by the FASB, which is a private organization. FASB's pronouncements are rule based and far more detailed than IFRSs, which are often described as principle-based standards requiring greater application of professional judgment by the preparers and auditors of financial statements. (U.S. public accounting firms have often indicated their support for the rule-based FASB over principle-based standards.)

> *FASB's statements are considered to be rule based, while IFRSs are principle based.*

While the FASB has often indicated its support for a single set of global accounting standards, it has also stated its belief that its standards are the best in the world and therefore should be used as a benchmark by the IASB. This argument somewhat lost its thrust with the accounting scandals associated with companies such as Enron and WorldCom. Despite this setback, FASB still carries a lot of clout, and its cooperation with the IASB is imperative if the goal of common, worldwide standards is to be met.

In September 2002, the IASB and the FASB signed the Norwalk Agreement, in which they each acknowledged their commitment to the development of high-quality, compatible accounting standards that could be used for both domestic and cross-border financial reporting. They pledged to use their best efforts (a) to make their existing financial reporting standards fully compatible as soon as is practicable and (b) to coordinate their future work programs to ensure that once achieved, compatibility is maintained.

> *The FASB and the IASB have been trying to converge their standards since 2002.*

The FASB has already revised a number of its standards to be fully consistent with IFRSs.

As part of the Norwalk Agreement, the two boards identified areas where differences could be eliminated in the short term by selecting existing standards from either the IASB or the FASB as the high-quality solution. This project was called the *Short Term Convergence Project*. By the end of 2009, the FASB issued new or amended standards to converge with IFRSs in the following areas:

- *Inventory costs:* Recognize idle facilities costs, excessive spoilage, double freight, and rehandling costs as current-period expenses.
- *Asset exchanges:* A non-monetary exchange of similar assets must apply the general rules for asset exchange and does not receive special treatment.
- *Accounting changes:* Reporting the cumulative effect of a change in accounting principle in the current-period net income is no longer permissible; retrospective adjustment is now required.
- *Financial instruments:* Require the reporting entity to measure a wide range of financial assets and liabilities at fair value.
- *Business combination:* In-process research and development could be recognized as an asset at the date of acquisition and tested for impairment thereafter.
- *Subsequent events:* The period for subsequent events ends when the financial statements are "available to be issued."

In a reciprocal fashion, the IASB issued new or amended standards to converge with the FASB for borrowing costs and segment reporting.

After much deliberation, the IASB and the FASB issued new but slightly different standards on a joint project on business combinations.

In 2006, the FASB and the IASB issued a memorandum of understanding (MOU) setting out the milestones of the FASB-IASB joint work program. The first joint project on business combinations has been completed, and both boards issued new standards in 2007/2008. Unfortunately, the standards issued by the two boards are not exactly the same, even though the project was carried out jointly with the goal of convergence. This underlies a key aspect of convergence. The process of attempting to dissect and eliminate every possible difference that may be experienced in practice is very costly and time consuming, if not impossible. A more effective approach focuses on aligning the general principles and overall methodologies. This is further illustrated in other converged standards such as operating segments and borrowing costs. Although the general principles and overall methodology of these standards are converged, there are still a few differences in the detail. This is an example of the politicization of the standard setting process. We may have been overly optimistic in expecting that convergence would eliminate all differences.

The SEC now allows foreign registrants to use IFRSs instead of U.S. GAAP for reporting on U.S. stock exchanges.

Given that companies from the EU had to report under IFRSs, and given that progress was being made on converging IFRSs and U.S. GAAP, there was increasing pressure from the EU to allow its companies to use IFRSs when reporting on American exchanges. As a result, the SEC made a monumental decision to change the requirements for foreign registrants. Commencing in November 2007, foreign registrants could use IFRSs in preparing their financial statements without reconciling them to U.S. GAAP. In order to qualify for this exemption, a foreign private issuer's financial statements must fully comply with the IASB's version of IFRSs, with one exception. The exception relates to foreign private issuers that use the version of IFRSs that includes the European Commission's special rules on financial instruments, which has been referred to as a "carve-out for IAS 39." The SEC has permitted such issuers to use that version in preparing their financial statements for a two-year period, as long as reconciliation to the

IASB's version of IFRSs is provided. After the two-year period, these issuers had to either use the IASB's version of IFRSs or provide reconciliation to U.S. GAAP.

Barrick Gold Corporation, a Canadian company, is the gold industry leader. It has a portfolio of 26 operating mines and advanced exploration and development projects located across five continents, and large land positions on some of the world's most prolific and prospective mineral trends. Prior to the adoption of IFRSs in 2011, Barrick, which is listed on a number of U.S. stock exchanges, chose to prepare its financial statements in accordance with U.S. GAAP. When Barrick adopted IFRSs in 2011, it had to apply most of the new accounting policies on a retrospective basis; that is, adjust retained earnings at the beginning of 2010 as if the new policies had always been applied. Then, it had to provide reconciliation from U.S. GAAP to IFRSs for 2010 to show the impact of changing to IFRSs and to make the 2010 figures comparable to 2011. Exhibit 1.3 is an extract from Barrick's 2011 financial statements. See Self-Study Problem 1 for another example of reconciliation between U.S. GAAP and IFRSs.

> Barrick reported numerous items where there was a difference between U.S. GAAP and IFRSs.

EXHIBIT 1.3 | **Extracts (in Part) from Barrick's 2011 Financial Statements**

The following is a reconciliation of the company's total equity reported in accordance with US GAAP to its total equity under IFRS at the transition date of January 1, 2010:

(millions of US$)	Ref	Capital Stock	Retained Earnings (Deficit)	Accumulated Other Comprehensive Income (AOCI)	Other	Non-controlling Interests	Total Equity
As reported under US GAAP		$ 17,390	$ (2,382)	$ 55	$ —	$ 484	**$ 15,547**
IFRS 1 Exemptions							
Deemed cost election for Barrick Energy	Note 3A (ii)	—	(166)	—	—	—	**(166)**
Reset of pension plan actuarial losses	Note 3A (iv)	—	(37)	37	—	—	**—**
Reset of cumulative translation losses	Note 3A (v)	—	(141)	141	—	—	**—**
IFRS Policy impacts							
Capitalized production phase stripping costs	(i)	—	408	—	—	—	**408**
Capitalized exploration and evaluation costs	(ii)	—	160	—	—	50	**210**
Reversal of past impairments	(iii)	—	55	—	—	—	**55**
Changes in capitalized interest	(iv)	—	(125)	—	—	—	**(125)**
Changes in PER	(v)	—	(101)	—	—	—	**(101)**
Bifurcation of senior convertible debt	(vi)	—	(31)	—	143	—	**112**
Exclusion of time value changes in fair value of options designated as hedging instruments	(vii)	—	(33)	33	—	—	**—**
Reclassification of hedge gains to related asset	(viii)	—	—	(20)	—	—	**(20)**
Tax effect of IFRS changes		(6)	(119)	(14)	—	(12)	**(151)**
Others, net		8	(23)	—	—	—	**(15)**
As reported under IFRS		$ 17,392	$ (2,535)	$ 232	$ 143	$ 522	**$ 15,754**

Source: http://www.sec.gov/Archives/edgar/data/756894/000119312511115614/dex991.htm Page 70.

The reconciliation of equity from one GAAP to another GAAP is very costly to prepare.

It is important to note that total equity under U.S. GAAP was different from total equity under IFRSs. The above extract is only a small portion of Note 3. The entire note is more than four pages long. It provides reconciliations for net income, other comprehensive income, and shareholders' equity, and provides narrative explanations of the main reasons for the differences.

New standards have been issued by the IASB and the FASB on joint projects undertaken under the updated MOU.

In September 2008, the FASB and the IASB signed an updated MOU that sets out priorities and milestones to be achieved on major joint projects by 2011. The boards acknowledged that although considerable progress has been made on a number of designated projects, achievements on other projects have been limited for various reasons. There were differences in views over issues of agenda size and project scope, over the most appropriate approach, and about whether and how similar issues in active projects should be resolved consistently. In April 2009, the leaders of the G20 countries called on FASB and the IASB to work urgently to achieve a single set of high-quality global accounting standards. The following table lists the major joint projects of the updated MOU and the status as at December 31, 2012.

STATUS OF JOINT PROJECTS BETWEEN IASB AND FASB

Joint Project	Project Completed?	Standards Converged?	Status
Consolidation	Yes	Yes	New standards, IFRS 10 & IFRS 12, effective 2013
Leases	No	Not yet	New exposure draft issued in 2012
Liabilities and equity	No	Not yet	Paused until completion of other major projects
Fair value measurement guidance	Yes	Yes	New standard, IFRS 13, effective 2013
Post-employment benefits (including pensions)	Yes	Yes	Amended IAS 19, effective 2013
Financial statement presentation	Partially	Yes for OCI	Amended IAS 1 for presentation of OCI, effective 2012
		No for others	IASB staff has prepared draft of position paper
Revenue recognition	No	Not yet	Issued re-exposure draft in 2011
Derecognition	Yes	Yes	Amended IFRS 7
Financial instruments	Partially	Yes	Classification and measurement of financial assets and liabilities in IFRS 9, effective 2015
		No	Major differences still outstanding and being debated
Joint ventures	Yes	Yes	New standard, IFRS 11, effective 2013

Progress has been slow in converging U.S. GAAP and IFRSs.

Although some progress was made on these major projects, it has been slow, and there is still considerable work to be done. The project on financial instruments is the most troublesome. The two boards' efforts to improve and achieve convergence of their standards have been complicated by differing imperatives that pushed their development timetables out of alignment. The IASB has been replacing its financial instrument requirements in a phased approach, whereas the FASB has been developing a single comprehensive proposal. Those differing development timetables and other factors have contributed to the boards reaching differing conclusions on a number of important technical issues. Each board will publish its proposals along with those of the other board as a way of giving interested parties the opportunity to compare and assess the relative merits of both boards' proposals. The boards will consider together the comment letters and other feedback they receive in an effort to reconcile differences in ways that foster improvement and convergence. The projects for leases and revenue recognition are still being worked on jointly. However, getting consensus from stakeholders is proving to be difficult. A second exposure draft was issued on revenue recognition late in 2011 and on leases in 2012.

If and when these joint projects are completed, attention will be directed to other areas. These joints projects were the priority items identified by the two boards in 2006. There are still hundreds of differences between U.S. GAAP and IFRSs. The Big Four accounting firms have all published documents comparing IFRSs and U.S. GAAP. Many of these documents are available on their websites. Exhibit 1.4 lists some of these differences in areas that may have

By identifying differences between U.S. GAAP and IFRSs, we can identify the standards that are most likely to change in the next few years.

EXHIBIT 1.4	Some Key Differences between IFRSs and U.S. GAAP

Accounting Item	IFRSs	U.S. GAAP
Conceptual Framework	Framework provides authoritative guidance, and the concepts are applied when there is no standard or interpretation that specifically applies to a transaction, other event, or condition	Concepts provide guidance for development of future standards but are not authoritative in and by themselves
Inventory		
Costing method	LIFO cannot be used	LIFO can be used
Lower of cost or market	Net realizable value is used for market value	Market value is replacement cost but not greater than net realizable value and not less than net realizable value less normal profit margin
Property, Plant, and Equipment		
Revaluation option	Can be revalued to fair value with adjustment to OCI and with depreciation based on revalued amount	Must be measured at cost less accumulated depreciation
Componentization of depreciation	Must split asset into major components and depreciate over lives of separate components	Do not need to split capital assets into major components when calculating depreciation expense

(continued)

EXHIBIT 1.4   **(continued)**

Asset Impairment

Test for impairment when indicators require it	Asset's carrying amount exceeds the higher of its (1) value in use (discounted expected future cash flows) and (2) fair value less costs of disposal	Asset's carrying amount exceeds the undiscounted expected future cash flows from the asset
Subsequent reversal of an impairment loss	Required if indicators change	Not allowed

Research and Development Costs

Development costs	Capitalized if certain criteria are met	Expensed immediately (except computer software development)

Leases

Recognition of gain on sale and leaseback on an operating lease	Recognized immediately	Amortized over the lease term

Revenue Recognition

Contingencies associated with price	Recognize revenue using probabilities to calculate an expected value	Recognize revenue only when contingency is resolved
Customer loyalty programs	Defer revenue until performance criterion is met related to loyalty award	Either defer as under IFRS or recognize revenue on delivery of main goods while accruing the cost of delivering the loyalty award

been studied in previous courses. Other differences will be listed in the U.S. GAAP "Differences" section at the end of each chapter in this text. If all of these standards are to be converged over the next few years, we can expect many changes. By noting these differences, we can get a sense of what standards may change.

With the movement to IFRSs as the international standard, and due to the high cost of reconciling to and from U.S. GAAP, there is increasing pressure on the SEC to allow U.S. domestic issuers to prepare financial statements in accordance with IFRSs. In a significant step toward that objective, in 2008, the SEC issued a roadmap for possible adoption of IFRSs by domestic issuers as early as 2014.

In 2008, the SEC released a roadmap for possible adoption of IFRSs by U.S. public companies by 2014.

In the roadmap, the SEC acknowledges that IFRSs have the potential to become the global set of high-quality accounting standards and sets out the seven milestones shown below that, if achieved, could lead to mandatory adoption of IFRSs.

Milestones 1–4 identified the following issues that needed to be addressed before mandatory adoption of IFRS:

1. Improvements in accounting standards (i.e., IFRSs).

2. Funding and accountability of the International Accounting Standards Committee Foundation.

3. Improvement in the ability to use interactive data (e.g., XBRL) for IFRS reporting.

4. Education and training on IFRSs in the United States.

Milestones 5–7 identified the transition plan for mandatory use of IFRSs.

In July 2012, the SEC staff issued a report on the IFRS work plan. The report summarized the SEC's efforts in advancing the potential adoption of IFRSs in the U.S. and noted some key findings as follows:

- The standards that are issued by the IASB are generally perceived to be of high quality by the global financial reporting community, but there are areas that are not addressed by IFRSs that may be important to the U.S. marketplace, including accounting for the extractive industries, insurance, and rate-regulated entities.

- The IFRS Interpretations Committee (IFRS IC) should do more to address practice issues on a timely basis.

- The IASB should consider placing greater reliance on national standard setters to assist with individual projects.

- Global application of IFRSs and cooperation among regulators could be improved with an objective to reduce diverse practices.

- The overall design of the governance structure of the IFRS Foundation appears to strike a reasonable balance of providing oversight of the IASB while supporting its independence; however, additional mechanisms such as maintaining an active FASB to endorse IFRSs may be necessary to protect the U.S. capital markets.

- The IFRS Foundation has made progress in developing a funding mechanism that is broad based, compelling, open ended, and country specific. However, more needs to be done to reduce reliance on voluntary contributions from the large accounting networks and to obtain a funding mechanism for the U.S. portion of the IASB budget.

- U.S. investors' current understanding of IFRSs varies significantly.

> In 2012, the SEC issued a report that commented positively on the work done by the IASB in developing high quality standards but that much more must be done to satisfy the SEC.

The SEC staff invited constituents to provide feedback on its final report but did not specify a submission deadline. Additional analysis and consideration will need to be done before the Commission would make any decision. The next steps and timing of future action were not announced by the staff or the Commission. Therefore, it is still not known if and when the U.S. will adopt IFRSs for use by public companies in the United States.

> As of January 2013, the SEC has not made a commitment as to when, if ever, it would allow U.S. companies to report in accordance with IFRSs.

Where Is Canada Going?

L05

Prior to 2000, the *CICA Handbook* did not have separate parts for public versus private corporations. Most sections applied equally to all entities. In 2002, differential reporting was introduced into the *Handbook*. Under differential reporting, qualifying entities could choose between different accounting policies for selected sections of the *Handbook*. It allowed qualifying entities to adopt simpler and less costly policies. This was the first step to customizing accounting standards for different types of entities. At the end of 2012, there were five parts of the *CICA Handbook*. The following table indicates to whom the different parts apply and the effective dates:

Part #	Applicable to	Name for Standards	Effective Date*
I	Publicly accountable entities	IFRSs	January 1, 2011, with some exceptions
II	Private enterprises	ASPE	January 1, 2011
III	Not-for-profit organizations		January 1, 2012
IV	Pension plans		January 1, 2011
V	All entities not yet using other parts	Pre-Changeover GAAP	Until new parts adopted

*The standards are effective for fiscal periods beginning on or after the dates indicated in the table.

The next few sections describe a bit of the history behind the development of different standards for different entities and the choices available for these entities in applying the different parts of the *CICA Handbook.*

GAAP for Publicly Accountable Enterprises   Public companies seemed to be moving toward American accounting standards when in 1998 the CICA announced that it would work with the FASB to harmonize the accounting standards of the United States and Canada, at the same time encouraging the IASB in its efforts to develop global accounting standards.

At one time, Canada intended to harmonize its standards with those of the United States.

The concept of harmonization would probably have proven to be a fairly difficult one because Canadian accounting standards tend to be broad based, while American standards tend to be based on detailed rules. This problem was alleviated when the CICA's position changed in 2006 with the announcement of the adoption of a strategic plan that would see the harmonization of the *CICA Handbook* with IFRSs for publicly accountable enterprises. A publicly accountable enterprise (PAE) is defined as an entity other than a not-for-profit organization or a government or another entity in the public sector that

Canadian publicly accountable enterprises had to report under IFRSs starting in 2011.

(i)   has issued, or is in the process of issuing, debt or equity instruments that are, or will be, outstanding and traded in a public market (a domestic or foreign stock exchange or an over-the-counter market, including local and regional markets), or

(ii)   holds assets in a fiduciary capacity for a broad group of outsiders as one of its primary businesses.

Banks, credit unions, insurance companies, securities brokers or dealers, mutual funds, and investment banks typically meet the second of these criteria. Other entities may also hold assets in a fiduciary capacity for a broad group of outsiders because they hold and manage financial resources entrusted to them by clients, customers, or members not involved in the management of the entity. However, if an entity does so for reasons incidental to one of its primary businesses (as, for example, may be the case for some travel or real estate agents, or cooperative enterprises requiring a nominal membership deposit), it is not considered to be publicly accountable.

Harmonization was chosen instead of the simple adoption of the international standards because security regulations and federal and provincial Companies Acts require financial reporting to be in accordance with Canadian GAAP. Because of this requirement, Part I of the *CICA Handbook* now contains standards that are the same as IFRSs. Rather than always referring to Part I of the *Handbook*, we will simply refer to IFRSs. Commencing in 2011, Canadian publicly accountable enterprises had to report under IFRSs.

Part I of the *CICA Handbook* contains the IFRSs.

The IFRSs were quite similar to Canadian standards prior to the adoption of the international standards because they are based on similar conceptual frameworks and reach similar conclusions. However, there were many differences in the detailed requirements. IFRSs often allow for optional treatments and in some instances allow or require the use of fair values in financial statement measurements, whereas Canadian standards did not

IFRSs allow the use of fair values and optional treatments to a greater degree than pre-changeover Canadian GAAP (Part V of the *CICA Handbook*).

often allow optional treatments and tended to require more historical cost measurements.

Much time, energy, and resources had to be devoted to identify the differences and prepare for the changeover to international standards. In 2010, the entities had to gather data for reporting under both pre-changeover Canadian GAAP and IFRSs because their 2011 statements had to present both the current year and comparative amounts for the previous year under IFRSs.

Disclosure Requirements   The disclosure requirements when adopting IFRSs for the first time are quite extensive. The following summarizes the main disclosures required by IFRS 1:

- Reconciliations of its equity reported in accordance with previous GAAP to its equity in accordance with IFRSs for both of the following dates:
  - the date of transition to IFRSs; and
  - the end of the latest period presented in the entity's most recent annual financial statements in accordance with previous GAAP.
- Reconciliation to its total comprehensive income in accordance with IFRSs for the latest period in the entity's most recent annual financial statements.
- Sufficient detail to enable users to understand the material adjustments to the statement of financial position, statement of comprehensive income and statement of cash flows.

Reconciliations of equity and comprehensive income had to be provided when a Canadian company adopted IFRSs for the first time.

Exhibit 1.5 is an extract from the financial statements for Kinross Gold Corporation, a Canadian company engaged in gold mining and related activities. It shows the impact on the company's Canadian GAAP balance sheet as a result of adopting IFRSs. It shows the adjustments in dollar values and the changes in classification and account titles on the balance sheet. A similar reconciliation was provided for the statement of operations. Explanations of the impact of the adjustments were provided in the explanatory notes following the reconciliations.

The balance sheet presentation under IFRSs is very similar, but not exactly the same, as the presentation under pre-changeover Canadian GAAP.

GAAP for Private Enterprises   In the 1970s, there was considerable discussion in Canada of Big GAAP versus Little GAAP. The question was as follows: Should there be different standards for big companies and for little companies?

It was argued that accounting standards were becoming increasingly complex and that a small company's costs of preparing its financial statements in compliance with the standards were greater than the benefits received by the users of such statements. Hence, small companies should be granted some sort of relief from having to use complex and hard-to-understand standards. Counter arguments suggested that the concept of fair presentation and comparability could not be achieved with different sets of standards, and the dividing line between big and small would be too arbitrary to be useful. After much study and discussion, the concept of Big GAAP/Little GAAP was abandoned.

The cost-benefit constraint is used when determining whether a private enterprise can use simpler reporting methods.

In the meantime, the issuance of new, complex financial reporting standards continued, and the last straw, so to speak, was the issuance of both the section on presentation and disclosure of financial instruments and the exposure draft on the

EXHIBIT 1.5 | **Extracts (in Part) from Kinross 2011 Financial Statements**

KINROSS'S GOLD CORPORATION
RECONCILIATION OF CONDENSED CONSOLIDATED BALANCE SHEET
At January 1, 2010

(Unaudited and expressed in millions of United States dollars)

CDN GAAP Accounts	*CDN GAAP*	*IFRS Adjustments*	*Re-classifications*	*IFRS*	*IFRS Accounts*
Assets					Assets
Current assets					Current assets
Cash, cash equivalents and short-term investments	$ 632.4	$ —	$ (35.0)	$ **597.4**	Cash and cash equivalents
Restricted Cash	24.3	—	—	**24.3**	Restricted cash
		—	35.0	**35.0**	Short-term investments
Accounts receivable and other assets	135.5	—	—	**135.5**	Accounts receivable and other assets
Inventories	554.4	—	—	**554.4**	Inventories
Unrealized fair value of derivative assets	44.3	—	—	**44.3**	Unrealized fair value of derivative assets
	1,390.9	—	—	**1,390.9**	
					Non-current assets
Property, plant, and equipment	4,989.9	(153.2)	—	**4,836.7**	Property, plant, and equipment
Goodwill	1,179.9	—	—	**1,179.9**	Goodwill
Long-term investments	292.2	16.3	(150.7)	**157.8**	Long-term investments
		—	150.7	**150.7**	Investments in associates and Working interest
Unrealized fair value of derivative assets	1.9	—	—	**1.9**	Unrealized fair value of derivative assets
Deferred charges and other long-term assets	158.4	—	—	**158.4**	Deferred charges and other long-term assets
	$8,013.2	$ (136.9)	$ —	**$7,876.3**	

CDN GAAP Accounts	CDN GAAP	IFRS Adjustments	Re-classifications	IFRS	IFRS Accounts
Liabilities					**Liabilities**
Current liabilities					Current liabilities
Accounts payable and accrued liabilities	$ 312.9	$ (0.9)	$ (24.4)	$ 287.6	Accounts payable and accrued liabilities
			24.4	24.4	Current tax payable
Current portion of long-term debt	177.0	—	—	177.0	Current portion of long-term debt
Current portion of reclamation and remediation obligations	17.1	—	—	17.1	Current portion of provisions
Current portion of unrealized fair value of derivative liabilities	131.0	83.6	—	214.6	Current portion of unrealized fair value of derivative liabilities
	638.0	82.7	—	720.7	
					Non-current liabilities
Long-term debt	515.2	(39.4)	—	475.8	Long-term debt
		169.0	279.5	448.5	Provisions
		77.2	212.8	290.0	Unrealized fair value of derivative liabilities
Other long-term liabilities	543.0	—	(492.3)	50.7	Other long-term liabilities
Future income and mining taxes	624.6	(390.3)	—	234.3	Deferred tax liabilities
	2,320.8	(100.8)	—	2,220.0	
Non-controlling interest	132.9	—	(132.9)	—	
Common shareholders' equity					**Equity**
Common share capital and common share purchase warrants	6,448.1	(68.8)	—	6,379.3	Common shareholders' equity
					Common share capital and common share purchase warrants
Contributed surplus	169.6	(62.2)	—	107.4	Contributed surplus
Accumulated deficit	(838.1)	97.5	—	(740.6)	Accumulated deficit
Accumulated other comprehensive loss	(220.1)	1.7	—	(218.4)	Accumulated other comprehensive loss
	5,559.5	(31.8)	—	5,527.7	
		(4.3)	132.9	128.6	Non-controlling interest
	5,559.5	(36.1)	132.9	5,656.3	
	$8,013.2	$ (136.9)	$ —	$7,876.3	

Source: http://www.sec.gov/Archives/edgar/data/701818/000104746911004489/a2203873zex-99_1.htm Page 100.

related measurement issues in the early 1990s. The issue of different standards was revisited by a CICA task force, but this time in relation to public versus non-public companies. The task force considered two basic approaches:

- A non-GAAP approach whereby non-public companies could use accounting policies completely separate from GAAP. An example is the use of cash-basis reporting instead of the required accrual basis. This approach was abandoned mainly because provincial and federal Companies Acts require companies to prepare financial statements in accordance with the CICA Handbook.

Companies were following GAAP when they adopted differential reporting options.

- A GAAP approach. This was looked at from two perspectives: full differentiation and partial differentiation. Full differentiation would encompass two distinct sets of GAAP, somewhat similar to the accounting for non-profit organizations and governments (discussed in Chapter 12). Partial differentiation encompasses one set of accounting standards with different treatments. This latter approach was adopted in 2002 when Section 1300, Differential Reporting, was issued and certain sections of the *CICA Handbook* were amended to allow optional treatments.

Section 1300 allowed a qualifying enterprise to select which reporting options it would apply when it prepared its financial statements. The differential reporting options allowed were contained in individual *Handbook* sections, and only a few sections contained such options.

Section 1300 was a part of the *Handbook* and was considered a primary source of GAAP. When a company adopted one or more of the differential reporting options, it was still considered to be following GAAP.

In 2006, when the decision was made by the Accounting Standards Board (AcSB) to adopt IFRSs for publicly accountable enterprises commencing in 2011, a CICA task force was established to revisit the question of what standards should be applied to private companies. The task force considered three different approaches:

- A non-GAAP approach, whereby private companies could use a more simplified method of reporting than what was presently required under differential reporting.

- A GAAP approach based on requirements being developed by IASB for small and medium-sized enterprises.

- A GAAP approach by developing a separate part of the *CICA Handbook* dedicated solely to private enterprises.

Part II of the CICA Handbook contains GAAP for private enterprises.

After much discussion and input from interested stakeholders, in 2009, the Canadian AcSB chose the third approach. These standards are included in Part II of the *Handbook* and are referred to as Accounting Standards for Private Enterprises (ASPE). A private enterprise is defined as a profit-oriented enterprise that

(a) has not issued, and is not in the process of issuing, debt or equity instruments that are, or will be, outstanding and traded in a public market (a domestic or foreign stock exchange or an over-the-counter market, including local and regional markets), and

(b) does not hold assets in a fiduciary capacity for a broad group of outsiders as one of its primary businesses.

The standards are available to any private enterprise. No size threshold or other barriers such as unanimous consent by shareholders or other users will be imposed. The standards stand alone (i.e., private enterprises applying them are not required to refer to standards applicable to publicly accountable enterprises).

Private enterprises may adopt either ASPE (Part II) or IFRSs (Part I). Whichever set of standards is adopted, it must be the whole package. It is not possible to apply certain standards from ASPE and others from IFRSs.

Private enterprises can either report under IFRSs or ASPE.

Some private companies may choose to follow GAAP for public companies for the following reasons:

- The company may be of a similar size to certain public companies, and the users of its financial statements may insist on IFRSs so that the company can be compared with other public companies.
- The company may be planning to go public in the near future.
- A parent company uses IFRSs.

Prior to 2009, the IASB did not have any special standards for private enterprises. In response to strong international demand from both developed and emerging economies for a rigorous and common set of accounting standards for smaller and medium-sized businesses, the IASB developed a separate set of standards for use by small and medium-sized entities (SMEs), which are estimated to represent more than 95% of all companies. The *IFRS for SMEs* is a self-contained standard of about 230 pages (about 10% the size of IFRSs for public companies) tailored to the needs and capabilities of smaller businesses. Many of the principles for recognizing and measuring assets, liabilities, income, and expenses for the IFRSs required for public companies have been simplified, topics not relevant to SMEs have been omitted, and the number of required disclosures has been significantly reduced. To further reduce the reporting burden for SMEs, revisions to the IFRSs for SMEs will be limited to once every three years.

The IASB has also developed a self-contained set of standards for small and medium-sized businesses.

The *IFRS for SMEs*

- provides improved comparability for users of financial statements,
- enhances the overall confidence in the accounts of SMEs and
- reduces the significant costs involved in maintaining standards on a national basis.

For now, Canada has developed and will maintain its own standards for private enterprises. Canadian public companies cannot use *IFRS for SMEs*. It is possible that it could adopt *IFRS for SMEs* sometime in the future.

For the next ten chapters, we will concentrate on IFRSs throughout the main body of each chapter. At the end of each chapter, we will summarize the main differences in the standards for private enterprises as compared with the standards for publicly accountable enterprises. To avoid information overload, we will not compare the Canadian standards for private enterprises to the IFRSs for SMEs.

GAAP for Not-for-Profit Organizations

Prior to segmentation of the *CICA Handbook* into five parts, the *Handbook* had a series of sections, the 4400 series, dedicated to not-for-profit organizations (NFPOs). Many of the other *Handbook* sections were also applicable to NFPOs. With the adoption of IFRSs for public companies and ASPE for private enterprises, a decision had to be made as to how to service the NFPOs.

In December 2008, the AcSB and the Public Sector Accounting Board (PSAB) jointly issued an Invitation to Comment, *Financial Reporting by Not-For-Profit Organizations*. In December 2010, the final standards for NFPOs were released.

As part of this process, the not-for-profit (NFP) sector was divided into two sectors: the government NFP sector and the non-government NFP sector. The government NFP sector includes NFPOs that are controlled by the government. They have a choice to follow either the 4200 series of the CICA Public Sector Accounting (PSA) Handbook or the PSA Handbook without the 4200 series. The non-government NFP sector includes NFPOs that are not controlled by the government. They have a choice to follow either IFRSs (which do not currently contain any standards specifically tailored for NFPOs) or Part III of the *CICA Handbook*. An NFPO applying Part III of the *Handbook* also applies the standards for private enterprises in Part II, to the extent that the Part II standards address topics not addressed in Part III.

> Non-government NFPOs can either report under IFRSs or Part III of the *CICA Handbook*, combined with relevant sections from Part II of the Handbook.

Part III carries forward the 4400 series of sections from the pre-changeover *Handbook*, largely without change. Five new sections were added. They contain relevant material from Part II that the AcSB deemed necessary to clarify their applicability to NFPOs.

The accounting standards for NFPOs will be discussed and illustrated in Chapter 12.

GAAP for Government and Other Government Organizations   All levels of government should follow the *PSA Handbook.* Government business enterprises are expected to follow IFRSs. Other government organizations can either follow IFRSs or the *PSA Handbook.* The accounting standards for government entities are summarized in the appendix for chapter 12.

> Cautionary Note: Unless otherwise stated, assume that IFRSs should be applied when answering end-of-chapter material.

The following table summarizes the standards required or allowed for different types of Canadian organizations:

Type of Organization	Standards Required or Allowed
Publicly accountable organization	IFRSs (Part I)
Private enterprise	IFRSs (Part I) or ASPE (Part II)
Non-governmental NFPO	IFRSs (Part I) or Standards for NFPOs (Part III)
Governmental NFPO	*PSA Handbook* with 4200 series or 4200 series in PSA Handbook
Government	*PSA Handbook*
Government business enterprise	IFRSs (Part I)
Other government organization	IFRSs (Part I) or *PSA Handbook*
Pension plan	Standards for Pension Plans (Part IV)

> The entity should specify in the notes to the financial statements the part of the *Handbook* being used for reporting purposes.

By using the above noted standards, the organization is considered to be following GAAP. In choosing between the various options, the organization would consider the needs of the users of their financial statements and the comparability of the organization with counterparts in the private or the public sector. In the notes to the financial statements, the set of standards being used should be explicitly stated.

L06   ## ANALYSIS AND INTERPRETATION OF FINANCIAL STATEMENTS

We have seen many examples in this chapter of differences in accounting and reporting practices. U.S. GAAP is different from IFRSs. ASPE is different from IFRSs. The CICA *Public Sector Accounting (PSA) Handbook* is different from Parts I,

II, or III of the *CICA Handbook.* With all of these differences, is there an opportunity for a company to manipulate its financial statements by choosing policies to produce desirable results? Do financial analysts know that these choices exist in accounting? Do they understand the impact of the different accounting methods on the financial statements?

These questions point out the importance of disclosing accounting policies in the notes to the financial statements. This will allow users to determine whether or not the same policies are being used by different entities and whether adjustments must be made to make the statements comparable from one entity to the next.

At the end of every chapter, there is a section on analysis and interpretation of financial statements. It reminds the reader that different accounting methods will have an impact on the financial statements. In turn, the different methods will have an impact on the ratios used by analysts in evaluating an entity. As preparers and users of financial statements, we should understand the impact of accounting methods on the financial statements.

> Different accounting methods have different impacts on key financial statement ratios.

In this text, we will focus on the following key ratios:

Ratio	Formula	What is measured
Current ratio	Current assets / Current liabilities	Liquidity; i.e., ability to pay short term obligations as they come due
Debt-to-equity ratio	Total debt / Shareholders' equity	Solvency; i.e., ability to pay all debt as it comes due
Return on assets	Income before interest & taxes / Total assets	Profitability of assets
Return on equity	Net income / Shareholders' equity	Profitability of owners' investment

These ratios have been covered in previous courses in accounting. They are summarized above for ease of reference. When asked to indicate the impact on these ratios, be sure to always consider and/or comment on the impact on both the numerator and denominator. For the denominator for the return ratios, it is more appropriate to use average balances for the year because the assets or equity likely changed during the year. However, many analysts use balances at the end of the year because it is simpler. To make the expectations clear for the end-of-chapter problems, we will use average in the ratio—that is, return on average equity—when we want you to use average of opening and closing balances in your calculation. If we simply use return on equity, you should use the balance at the end of the year in your calculation of the ratio.

> When determining the impact on ratios of changes in reporting methods, we must consider the impact on both the numerator and the denominator.

See Self-Study Problem 2 for a good illustration of the impact of accounting policies on key financial ratios.

ASPE DIFFERENCES

L07

Some of differences between IFRSs and ASPE in topics discussed in intermediate accounting are listed in Exhibit 1.6.

> ASPE sometimes allow a choice between different reporting methods.

EXHIBIT 1.6	Some Key Differences between IFRSs and ASPE

Accounting Item	IFRSs	ASPE
Disclosure	Very extensive for many items, especially financial instruments, post-employment benefits, and segment reporting	Moderate for financial instruments and post-employment benefits, and no disclosure for segments
Impaired loans	Discount future cash flows using original discount rate	Discount future cash flows using current rate of interest
Property, plant, & equipment		
Revaluation option	Can be revalued to fair value with adjustment to OCI and with depreciation based on revalued amount	Must be measured at cost less accumulated depreciation
Asset impairment		
Test for impairment if indicator requires	Asset's carrying amount exceeds the higher of its (1) value in use (discounted expected future cash flows) and (2) fair value less costs of disposal	Asset's carrying amount exceeds the undiscounted expected future cash flows from the asset. If so, write asset down to fair value.
Subsequent reversal of impairment loss	Required if indicators change	Not allowed
Development costs	Capitalize if certain criteria are met	Choice between capitalize, if criteria met, or expense
Post-employment benefits		
Actuarial gains/losses	Recognize immediately in OCI	Recognize immediately in net income
Income taxes	Set up deferred income taxes as applicable	Choice between taxes payable or future income tax methods
Interest capitalization	Capitalize if certain criteria are met	Choice between capitalize or expense
Compound financial instrument	Allocate between debt and equity	Can choose to allocate a nominal amount to equity
Preferred shares in tax planning arrangement	Assess whether debt or equity	Record as equity unless redemption demanded

SUMMARY

The diversity among the accounting principles in use throughout the world has long been viewed as a major stumbling block toward achieving the desired goal of a truly global capital market. The IASB has attempted to narrow this diversity by issuing a set of international standards, with the intent that they will be adopted worldwide. While a great deal of progress has been made, the goal of global harmonization and/ or convergence has not yet been fully reached. Over 100 countries have adopted these standards, but the United States is still not on board. The United States is lobbying the IASB to incorporate some of the American standards in IFRSs as a condition for their adoption of IFRSs. However, there is often a clash between the rule-based standards used in the United States and the more principle-based approach used in IFRSs. Even if this problem is solved, absolute comparability of financial information on a worldwide basis is still going to be difficult to achieve. There is a problem of consistency in the interpretation of the standards by preparers of financial statements because these standards are broad based and require professional judgment. An additional problem is created by the fact that some countries are adopting IFRSs but are making certain modifications and still calling them IFRSs. Other countries are adding additional home-grown standards to their own standards to make them more comparable with IFRSs. Readers of the financial statements of companies from these countries will have to understand where the differences lie if they wish to make realistic comparisons with companies in other countries.

Canadian public companies were required to adopt IFRSs starting in 2011, and Canadian private enterprises were required to adopt ASPE starting in 2011. The standards for NFPOs were modified slightly and were effective in 2012. Needless to say, a great deal is changing. Lots of work was required to change over to the new standards. Further changes can be expected over the next few years as IFRSs and U.S. GAAP converge.

Significant Changes in GAAP in the Last Three Years

1. Publicly accountable enterprises made the transition to and started reporting under IFRSs.

2. Differential reporting was withdrawn for private enterprises on the adoption of ASPE.

3. FASB has announced that IFRSs may be required by U.S. companies by 2016.

Changes Expected in GAAP in the Next Three Years

1. The format and structure of financial statements may change to present a cohesive relationship between the various statements. There would be separate sections for operating, investing, and financing activities in each of the balance sheet, statement of comprehensive income, and cash flow statement. The classification of assets and liabilities in the balance sheet would determine the classification of any related income or expense in the statement of comprehensive income, and any related cash flows in the cash flow statement. There may be further disaggregation of assets and liabilities into current and non-current and then according to the measurement basis used. There would be further disaggregation of expenses by function and then by nature. Discontinued operations and income taxes would be presented separately in each of the statements.

2. The SEC will announce a framework for transitioning to IFRSs for U.S. companies.

3. The definitions of assets and liabilities may change to focus more on rights and obligations and to eliminate the reference to past events. The when and how of use of the various measurement bases may be clarified.

SELF-STUDY PROBLEM 1

LO4, 6   Hyde Ltd. is an EU-based company that prepares its consolidated financial statements in accordance with IFRSs. Its profit in Year 3 was $1,000,000, and shareholders' equity at December 31, Year 3, was $8,000,000.

Hyde wishes to list its shares on a U.S. stock exchange. Although no longer required to do so, Hyde has decided to provide a U.S. GAAP reconciliation voluntarily, and has engaged you to reconcile profit and shareholders' equity to a

U.S. GAAP basis. You have identified the following five areas in which Hyde's accounting principles differ from U.S. GAAP:

1. Inventory—lower of cost or market
2. Property, plant, and equipment—measurement subsequent to initial recognition
3. Research and development costs—capitalization of development costs
4. Sale and leaseback transaction—gain on sale
5. Property, plant, and equipment—impairment

Hyde provides the following information with respect to each of these accounting differences.

Inventory

At the end of Year 3, inventory had a historical cost of $20,000, a replacement cost of $18,000, a net realizable value of $19,000, and a normal profit margin of 20% of cost.

Property, Plant, and Equipment

Hyde acquired equipment at the beginning of Year 2 at a cost of $250,000. The equipment has an estimated useful life of 10 years and an estimated residual value of $50,000 and is being depreciated on a straight-line basis. At the beginning of the current year, the equipment was appraised and determined to have a fair value of $320,000; its estimated useful life and residual value did not change. The company uses the allowed alternative treatment in IAS 16 to periodically revalue the equipment at fair value subsequent to acquisition. The revaluation adjustment goes through OCI.

Research and Development Costs

Hyde incurred research and development costs of $100,000 in Year 3. Of this amount, 60% related to development activities subsequent to the point at which criteria indicating that the creation of an intangible asset had been met. As of year-end, development of the new product had not been completed.

Sale and Leaseback

In January Year 1, Hyde realized a $150,000 gain on the sale and leaseback of an office building. The lease is accounted for as an operating lease and the term of the lease is five years.

Property, Plant, and Equipment

Hyde owns machinery on December 31, Year 3, with a carrying amount of $20,000, an estimated salvage value of $2,000, and an estimated remaining useful life of 10 years. On that date, there is an indication that the machinery may be impaired. The machinery is expected to generate future cash flows of $22,500 and has an estimated fair value, after deducting costs to sell, of $18,000. The present value of expected future cash flows is $18,600.

Required:

Prepare a schedule reconciling IFRS profit and IFRS shareholders' equity to a U.S. GAAP basis. Ignore income taxes.

SOLUTION TO SELF-STUDY PROBLEM 1

Hyde Ltd. Reconciliation from IFRSs to U.S. GAAP

Profit under IFRSs	$1,000,000
Adjustments:	
Additional write-down of inventory to replacement cost (Note 1)	(1,000)
Reversal of additional depreciation on revaluation of equipment (Note 2)	10,000
Reversal of deferred development costs (Note 3)	(60,000)
Amortization of deferred gain on sale and leaseback (Note 4)	30,000
Reversal of impairment loss (Note 5)	1,400
Profit under U.S. GAAP	$ 980,400
Shareholders' equity under IFRSs	$8,000,000
Adjustments:	
Additional write-down of inventory to replacement cost (Note 1)	(1,000)
Reversal of revaluation surplus on equipment (Note 2)	(90,000)
Reversal of accumulated depreciation on revaluation of equipment (Note 2)	10,000
Reversal of deferred development costs (Note 3)	(60,000)
Reversal of gain on sale and leaseback in Year 1 (Note 4)	(150,000)
Accumulated amortization of deferred gain on sale and leaseback (Year 1–Year 3) (Note 4)	90,000
Reversal of impairment loss (Note 5)	1,400
Shareholders' equity under U.S. GAAP	$7,800,400

Notes:

1. **Inventory** In accordance with IAS 2, the company reports inventory on the statement of financial position at the lower of cost ($20,000) and net realizable value ($19,000). As a result, it reported inventory on the December 31, Year 3, statement of financial position at its net realizable value of $19,000, and profit reflected a loss on write-down of inventory of $1,000.

   Under U.S. GAAP, the company reports inventory at the lower of cost or market, with market defined as replacement cost ($18,000) but not greater than net realizable value ($19,000), and not less than net realizable value less a normal profit ($19,000 − 20% × $20,000 = $15,000). In this case, inventory would be written down to replacement cost. A $2,000 loss would be included in Year 3 profit.

   U.S. GAAP profit is $1,000 less than IFRS profit. U.S. GAAP retained earnings are lower by the same amount.

2. **Property, Plant, and Equipment** Under IAS 16, depreciation expense on equipment in Year 2 was $20,000 ([$250,000 − $50,000]/ 10 years), resulting in a carrying amount of $230,000 at the end of Year 2. The equipment was then revalued upward to its fair value of $320,000 at the beginning of Year 3. The journal entry to record the revaluation was as follows:

Dr. Equipment—net	90,000	
Cr. OCI—revaluation surplus		90,000

   The accumulated revaluation surplus is reported as a separate component of shareholders' equity. In Year 3, depreciation expense was $30,000 ([$320,000 − $50,000]/9 years). Under U.S. GAAP, the company reported depreciation expense of $20,000 in both Year 2 and Year 3. The additional depreciation under IFRSs causes IFRS-based profit in Year 3 to be $10,000 lower than U.S. GAAP-based profit. The revaluation surplus caused IFRS-based shareholders' equity to be $90,000 higher than U.S. GAAP shareholders' equity. This is partially offset by the $10,000 additional depreciation in Year 3 under IFRSs, which resulted in retained earnings being $10,000 lower under IFRSs than under U.S. GAAP.

3. **Research and Development Costs** Under IAS 38, $40,000 of research and development costs would be expensed in Year 3, and $60,000 of development costs would be capitalized as an intangible asset.

Under U.S. GAAP, research and development expense of $100,000 would be recognized in determining Year 3 profit.

IFRS-based profit and retained earnings in Year 3 would be $60,000 higher than U.S. GAAP-based profit. Because the new product had not yet been brought to market, there was no amortization of the deferred development costs under IFRSs in Year 3.

4. **Sale and Leaseback** Under IAS 17, the entire gain of $150,000 on the sale and leaseback was recognized in profit in Year 1. This resulted in a $150,000 increase in retained earnings in that year.

Under U.S. GAAP, the gain on the sale and leaseback is recognized in profit over the life of the lease. With a lease term of five years, $30,000 of the gain would be recognized in Year 3, and $30,000 of the gain would have been recognized in each of Year 1 and Year 2, resulting in a cumulative amount of retained earnings of $90,000 at the end of Year 3.

In Year 3, U.S. GAAP profit would be $30,000 higher than IFRS-based profit, and shareholders' equity under IFRS was $60,000 higher than under U.S. GAAP at December 31, Year 3.

5. **Property, Plant, and Equipment** Since there is an indication that the asset may be impaired, an impairment test must be performed. Under IAS 36, an asset is impaired when its carrying amount exceeds its recoverable amount, which is the higher of (1) its value in use (present value of expected future cash flows) and (2) its fair value less costs of disposal. The machinery had a carrying amount of $20,000, and its value in use was $18,600, which is more than the fair value less cost to sell of $18,000. An impairment loss of $1,400 ($20,000 − $18,600) would have been recognized in determining Year 3 profit, with a corresponding reduction in retained earnings under IFRSs.

Under U.S. GAAP, an impairment occurs when an asset's carrying amount exceeds its undiscounted expected future cash flows. In this case, the expected future cash flows are $22,500, which is higher than the machinery's carrying amount, so no impairment occurred under U.S. GAAP.

SELF-STUDY PROBLEM 2

L04, 6   Jia Ltd. is a Canadian company listed on the TSX. One of its subsidiaries, Ian Ltd., is listed on the NYSE. Ian prepares its financial statements in accordance with U.S. GAAP for reporting on the NYSE. Ian's financial statements must be converted to

IFRSs and then consolidated with Jia's financial statements for reporting on the TSX. For its Year 4 financial statements, Ian reported the following in accordance with U.S. GAAP:

Net income	$1,500	Total debt	$12,600
Current assets	6,800	Total shareholders' equity	10,900
Current liabilities	5,400		

You have identified the following four areas where Ian's accounting policies have differences between U.S. GAAP and IFRSs:

1. Revenue recognition
2. Inventory costing
3. Depreciation expense
4. Patent impairment loss

The controller at Ian provides the following information with respect to each of these accounting differences:

Revenue Recognition

Ian introduced a customer loyalty program in Year 4. In its U.S. GAAP statements, it reported revenue under this program of $7,600 in Year 4, and accrued a current liability for costs related to this program of $770 at the end of Year 4. Under IFRSs, Ian would not accrue any liability but would have to defer revenue of $1,980 at the end of Year 4. The deferred revenue would be expected to be earned within one year.

Inventory

Ian used LIFO for reporting under U.S. GAAP and needs to convert to average costing for reporting under IFRSs. The value of Ian's inventory under these two costing methods was as follows:

	LIFO	Average
December 31, Year 3	$1,200	$1,500
December 31, Year 4	1,200	1,560

Depreciation

Ian depreciated its property, plant, and equipment on a group basis for U.S. reporting purposes but must refine the calculation of depreciation under IFRSs to separate items of property, plant, and equipment into significant components and depreciate each component over its own useful life. The carrying amount of Ian's depreciable property, plant, and equipment under these two depreciation methods was as follows:

	Group	Components
December 31, Year 3	$9,000	$8,600
December 31, Year 4	8,250	7,810

Patents

Ian owns a number of patents and depreciates them over their useful lives, ranging from 3 to 7 years. The patents are checked for impairment on an annual basis. Relevant values pertaining to these patents were as follows:

	Dec 31, Yr3	Dec 31, Yr4
Carrying amount before impairment	$6,000	$4,800
Undiscounted future cash flows	6,100	4,930
Value in use	5,870	4,770
Fair value	5,800	4,380

The CEO is concerned about the impact of converting Ian's financial statements from U.S. GAAP to IFRSs on the following metrics: current ratio, debt-to-equity ratio, and return on total shareholders' equity.

Required:

(a) Calculate the three ratios first using U.S. GAAP and then using IFRSs. Prepare a schedule showing any adjustments to the numerator and denominator for these ratios. Ignore income taxes.

(b) Explain whether Ian's liquidity, solvency and profitability look better or worse under IFRSs after considering the combined impact of the four areas of difference.

SOLUTION TO SELF-STUDY PROBLEM 2

Ian Ltd. Reconciliation from U.S. GAAP to IFRSs:

Description	Net Income	Current Assets	Current Liabilities	Debt	Equity
Per U.S. GAAP	$1,500	$6,800	$5,400	$12,600	$10,900
Revenue recognition	(1,210)[1]		1,210[1]	1,210[1]	(1,210)[1]
LIFO to average	60[2]	360[3]			360[3]
Group to component	(40)[4]				(440)[5]
Impairment loss reversed	100[6]				(30)[7]
Per IFRSs	$410	$7,160	$6,610	$13,810	9,580

		U.S. GAAP	IFRS
Current ratio	Current assets	$\dfrac{6,800}{5,400} = 1.26$	$\dfrac{7,160}{6,610} = 1.08$
	Current liabilities		
Debt to equity	Debt	$\dfrac{12,600}{10,900} = 1.16$	$\dfrac{13,810}{9,580} = 1.44$
	Equity		
Return on total equity	Net income	$\dfrac{1,500}{10,900} = 13.76\%$	$\dfrac{410}{9,580} = 4.28\%$
	Total equity		

Notes:

Net income captures the change in equity during one period; i.e., Year 4. Equity is the difference between assets and liabilities at a point in time; i.e., end of Year 4. It also captures the cumulative effect of net income and dividends for all years. The other items above are balance sheet items at the end of Year 4.

1. Current liabilities at end of the year increased by $1,210 (1,980 − 770)

2. Costs of goods sold for the year decreased by $60 (1,560 − 1,200) − (1,500 − 1,200)

3. Current assets at end of the year increased by $360 (1,560 − 1,200)

4. Depreciation expense for the year increased by $40 (9,000 − 8,250) − (8,600 − 7,810)

5. Assets at end of the year decreased by $440 (8,250 − 7,810)

6. No impairment under U.S. GAAP because undiscounted future cash flows exceed net book value. Under IFRS, impairment loss is excess of carrying amount over recoverable amount, which is higher of value in use and fair value. Accumulated impairment loss decreased during the year by $100 (6,000 − 5,870) − (4,800 − 4,770). Therefore, impairment loss reversal during the year was $100.

7. (a) Assets decreased at end of the year by $30 (4,800 − 4,770)

   (b) The current ratio decreased, which means that liquidity looks worse under IFRS.

      The debt-to-equity ratio increased, which means that solvency looks worse under IFRSs.

      The return on total equity decreased, which makes profitability look worse under IFRSs.

REVIEW QUESTIONS

LO1	1.	Explain if and when it may be appropriate for an accountant to prepare financial statements that are not in accordance with GAAP.
LO2, 4	2.	Why is it important to supplement studies of Canadian accounting principles with studies of the accounting practices used in other countries?
LO2	3.	In what manner has there been a shift toward a global capital market in recent years?
LO2	4.	List the factors that have influenced the accounting standards used in a particular country.
LO2	5.	What role does the stage of development of a country's capital markets have on the direction taken by the country's accounting standards?
LO2	6.	In what way has the level of inflation influenced the accounting standards of a particular country?
LO3	7.	In what manner does the balance-sheet format used by companies in other countries differ from the format used by Canadian companies?
LO4	8.	Identify some of the financial statement items where U.S. GAAP is different from IFRSs.
LO3	9.	What is the goal of the IASB?
LO4	10.	What does the FASB-IASB convergence project expect to achieve? How will it be carried out?
LO3	11.	What evidence is there that IASB pronouncements are becoming acceptable throughout the world?
LO5	12.	Describe the extent of harmonization or convergence of accounting standards for publicly accountable enterprises in Canada with the standards published by the IASB.
LO3, 4	13.	Explain why complete comparability on a worldwide basis is going to be difficult to achieve despite a switchover to IFRSs.
LO4	14.	Briefly explain why the Canadian AcSB decided to create a separate section of the *CICA Handbook* for private enterprises.
LO4	15.	Briefly explain why a Canadian private company may decide to follow IFRSs for public companies, even though it could follow GAAP for private companies.

CASES

Case 1-1
LO1, 4

In this era of rapidly changing technology, research and development (R&D) expenditures represent one of the most important factors in the future success of many companies. Organizations that spend too little on R&D risk being left behind by the competition. Conversely, companies that spend too much may waste money or not be able to make efficient use of the results.

In the United States, all R&D expenditures are expensed as incurred. However, expensing all R&D costs is not an approach used in much of the world. Firms using IFRSs must capitalize development costs as an intangible asset when they can demonstrate

(a) the technical feasibility of completing the intangible asset so that it will be available for use or sale;

(b) its intention to complete the intangible asset and use or sell it;

(c) its ability to use or sell the intangible asset;

(d) how the intangible asset will generate probable future economic benefits—among other things, the entity can demonstrate the existence of a market for the output of the intangible asset or for the intangible asset itself or, if it is to be used internally, the usefulness of the intangible asset;

(e) the availability of adequate technical, financial, and other resources to complete the development and to use or sell the intangible asset; and

(f) its ability to measure reliably the expenditure attributable to the intangible asset during its development.

Required:

(a) Using basic accounting principles as a guide, provide arguments to support
  (i) the IASB approach for reporting R&D costs, and
  (ii) the FASB approach for reporting R&D costs.

(b) In your opinion, which approach should become the sole worldwide standard? Briefly explain.

Case 1-2
LO1

You are examining the consolidated financial statements of a European company, which have been prepared in accordance with IFRSs. You determine that property, plant, and equipment is revalued each year to its current replacement cost, income and equity are adjusted, and the notes to the financial statements include the following items as a part of the summary of significant accounting policies:

- Tangible fixed assets are measured at replacement cost, less accumulated depreciation. The replacement cost is based on valuations made by internal and external experts, taking technical and economic developments into account and supported by the experience gained in the construction of plant assets throughout the world.

- Valuation differences resulting from revaluation are credited or debited to equity, where it is applicable, after deduction of an amount for deferred tax liabilities.

- Depreciation based on replacement cost is applied on a straight-line basis in accordance with the estimated useful life of each asset.

The provisions of IFRSs permit the use of alternatives to historical cost in the valuation of assets. IAS 16 specifically notes that as an allowed alternative treatment to historical cost:

Subsequent to initial recognition as an asset, an item of property, plant, and equipment shall be carried at a revalued amount, being its fair value at the date of the revaluation less any subsequent accumulated depreciation and subsequent accumulated impairment losses. Revaluations should be made with sufficient regularity such that the carrying amount does not differ materially from that which would be determined using fair value at the balance sheet date.

The auditor of the company has expressed his opinion on the financial statements and concluded that they present a "true and fair view."

The use of replacement cost accounting is a departure from the historical cost principle and represents a fundamental difference in the approach to financial reporting in this country compared with the United States. The debate as to the relative importance of relevance and reliability is one that surfaces often in the study of international accounting issues. Many countries are very strict as to the use of historical cost for all valuations and in the computation of income and often allow reductions from historical cost (such as with the application of the lower of cost or market requirement), but not increases. Others are very flexible in the choice of permissible approaches, while still others are very strict in that particular alternatives to historical cost (such as replacement cost or general price-level-adjusted amounts) must be used.

Required:

(a) Can any alternative to historical cost provide for fair presentation in financial reports, or are the risks too great? Discuss.

(b) Discuss the relative merits of historical cost accounting and replacement cost accounting. Consider the question of the achievement of a balance between relevance and reliability and the provision of a "true and fair view" or "fair presentation" in financial reporting.

(c) Financial statements are now beyond the comprehension of the average person. Many of the accounting terms and methods of accounting used are simply too complex to understand just from reading the financial statements. Additional explanations should be provided with, or in, the financial statements, to help investors understand the financial statements. Briefly discuss.

(adapted from a case developed by Peter Secord, St. Mary's University)

Case 1-3
LO1, 4, 5, 6

John McCurdy has recently joined a consultant group that provides investment advice to the managers of a special investment fund. This investment fund was created by a group of NFPOs, all of which have endowment funds, and rather than investing their resources individually, they have instead chosen a pooled approach whereby a single fund invests their moneys and distributes the earnings back to them on an annual basis. The board of directors of the investment fund, made up of members from each of the NFPOs, meets periodically to review performance and to make investment decisions.

John has been following the fortunes of Ajax Communications Corporation for a number of years. Ajax is a Canadian company listed on the TSX. At the beginning of this past year, Ajax acquired 60% of the shares of Waqaas Inc., a U.S. company, which was and continues to be listed on the NYSE. Ajax must decide whether to prepare financial statements for Waqaas in accordance with IFRSs or U.S. GAAP for reporting to the SEC.

As a starting point, John asked for and received the following comparison of financial statement information under U.S. GAAP and IFRSs from the controller at Waqaas (in millions of dollars):

	U.S. GAAP U.S. dollars	IFRSs U.S. dollars
Income statement		
Total revenue	$3,388.9	$2,611.9
Operating income	89.1	329.1
Income before extraordinary items	14.9	199.4
Net income	(66.2)	199.4
Balance sheet		
Total current assets	$ 862.1	$1,360.7
Investments	233.1	59.2
Property, plant, and equipment, net	889.9	1,866.5
Deferred income taxes	50.3	47.6
Intangibles, net	1,016.4	5,473.0
Other assets	90.8	265.1
Total assets	$3,142.6	$9,072.1

Working with this list, John's next step will be to determine why there is such a difference in the numbers.

Required:

(a) As John McCurdy, outline the initial approach that you will take in order to determine the reasons for the differences in the numbers.

(b) List some of the obvious items that need resolution, and indicate some of the possible causes of the discrepancies.

(c) In your opinion, which GAAP best reflects economic reality? Briefly explain.

(adapted from a case developed by Peter Secord, St. Mary's University)

Case 1-4
LO1, 5, 6, 7

Roman Systems Inc. (RSI) is a Canadian private company. It was incorporated in Year 1 by its sole common shareholder, Marge Roman. RSI manufactures, installs, and provides product support for its line of surveillance cameras.

Marge started the company with a small investment. For Years 7 through 9, the company grew rapidly. Most of the expansion was funded through debt financing. The rapid growth is attributable to several large contracts signed with banks for the installation of security camera systems at their branches.

RSI has a June 30 year-end. You, the CA, are with the firm of Sylvain and Charest, Chartered Accountants (SC). Your firm has performed the audit of RSI since its incorporation and prepares RSI's corporate tax returns and those of Marge Roman and her family.

Marge Roman called you in April Year 12 to inform you that she plans to take RSI public within the next year. Marge is negotiating with several underwriters, but no deal is in place yet. She plans to highlight the company's revenue growth in its annual press release publicizing its year-end results. Marge wants to show strong revenue growth to attract investors.

During the telephone conversation, Marge asked you and the partner on the audit to meet with her some time in early June to discuss and resolve potential issues related to the June 30 audit of RSI. In prior years, financial statements were issued in September, but this year the deadline for finalizing the financial statements will likely be in early August. Marge agreed that you would perform your interim audit procedures based on RSI's results as at April 30, Year 12.

It is now June Year 12. The planning and interim work for the fiscal Year 12 audit has been completed. A summary of items noted in the April 30, Year 12, interim financial statements as a result of work done to date is included in Exhibit I.

You are about to leave for the day when the partner in charge of the account comes into your office and announces that he has just received a call from Marge and she would like to meet with him within the next few days. He asks you to prepare a memo discussing the financial reporting issues arising from the interim audit work and any other matters that he should raise at the meeting. Ignore any additional audit procedures that should be considered as a result of the issues raised during the interim audit.

Required:

Prepare the memo.

EXHIBIT I

NOTES FROM THE INTERIM AUDIT

General

Pre-tax earnings for the period ended April 30, Year 12, were $1,375,000. For the fiscal years Year 11 and Year 10, RSI recorded pre-tax earnings of $435,000 and $325,000, respectively.

Marge Roman has received a valuation report valuing the company at $12 million. Shareholders' equity as at April 30, Year 12, consisted of:

100 common shares (voting)	$100
Retained earnings	$9,159,000

New Software

The company has been using a standard general ledger software package originally installed in Year 6 by a local computer consulting firm and upgraded annually.

In January Year 12, RSI hired BBC to oversee the implementation of a new third-party package. In March Year 12, RSI began converting its financial reporting system. The new general ledger software was installed in parallel with the old software and went live on April 1, Year 12.

The new general ledger software has been used to generate RSI's financial results since April 1, Year 12. Starting July 1, Year 12, the old system will no longer be used in parallel.

To date, RSI has been invoiced $720,000 by BBC. These costs have all been capitalized in the April 30, Year 12, financial statements. The invoices show the following services and costs:

Initial review and recommendations	$110,000
Cost of new software	200,000
Implementation work	120,000
Training work	225,000
Monthly support fee (April)	25,000
Other consulting (to April 30)	40,000
	$720,000

(continued)

In addition, as at April 30, Year 12, RSI also capitalized $70,000 related to the salaries of four employees who have worked on the accounting software project since January 1, Year 12. As a result of these individuals being pulled out of their regular jobs to handle the problem, RSI had to hire two additional employees.

The costs will be amortized beginning on July 1, Year 12, on a straight-line basis over three years. RSI intends to treat approximately $135,000 of carrying amount for the old software as part of the cost of the new software by reallocating this balance.

Revenues

During fiscal Year 11, total product revenue was $18.2 million and maintenance contract revenue was $5.6 million. For the period ended April Year 12, product revenue was $13.2 million, and maintenance contract revenue was $5.2 million.

RSI recognizes product revenue when shipment and installation take place. It is RSI's standard practice to request a customer sign-off for any installation work. The installation crew normally gets sign-off on the day of installation. During interim work for fiscal Year 12, it was noted in the audit file that approximately $640,000 of revenue recognized in April Year 12 related to work installed and invoiced in April, but customer sign-off was obtained only in early May. Such situations have not caught anyone's attention in previous years. RSI explained that it had recently hired new service technicians who were unfamiliar with the policy of customer sign-off and, accordingly, had to send technicians back to the client days after the installation was completed to get the sign-offs.

Maintenance contract revenues relate to one-year agreements that RSI signs with customers wanting product support. During the year, the company changed its revenue recognition policy on maintenance contracts to recognize revenue based on estimated costs incurred on the contract. Revenue is recognized as follows: 25% in each of the first two months of the contract and 5% in each subsequent month. This allocation is based on a study done by RSI in Year 10, which showed that the costs incurred on the contracts are mostly incurred in the first two months, during which RSI sends out a technician to perform preventive maintenance. The preventive maintenance reduces the number of future service calls and, therefore, overall costs.

ABM Business

As a result of RSI's strong relationship with its financial institution and Marge's desire to diversify RSI's product line, RSI began selling "Automated Bank Machines" (ABMs) in fiscal Year 12. The machines are purchased from a large electronic equipment manufacturer that is responsible for ongoing maintenance of the ABMs. RSI sells the ABMs to restaurants, bars, and clubs at margins of 5%. The sales revenue is included as product revenue.

The standard ABM sales agreement states that for a three-year period from the date of sale, RSI receives 40% of the transaction fee charged to customers using the machine, in addition to the sales revenue. A further 40% of the fee is payable to the financial institution for managing the cash in the machines, and the remaining 20% is remitted to the machine owners. The transaction fee charged to customers using an ABM is normally $1.50, and is set by the financial institution. RSI is not responsible for stocking the ABM with cash or emptying the cash machine. The financial institution performs all cash management duties and remits to RSI, at month-end, a statement showing money owed to RSI for its share of the transaction fee. A day later, the funds are deposited directly into RSI's main bank account.

A total of 2,830,000 ABM transactions were processed in Year 12 for a total fee of $4,245,000. RSI has booked transaction-fee revenue of $4,245,000 and an expense of $2,547,000 related to the fees, attributable to the financial institution and the machine owners.

Debentures

In January Year 12, RSI needed long-term financing and issued to a third-party venture capitalist $2,500,000 of debentures maturing in 10 years, with interest at 7.35%.

(continued)

The debentures are included as long-term debt in the accounts. The debentures are convertible at the option of the holder, at a rate of one voting common share for every $5 of debenture, if RSI issues shares to the public. If RSI does not issue shares to the public before June 30, Year 13, the debentures are repayable upon demand.

Accounts Receivable

Review of the aging of accounts receivable at April 30, Year 12, showed an amount of $835,000 in the over-120-day category. According to RSI's collection department, the balance relates to payments withheld by one of RSI's largest customers, Mountain Bank. RSI had contracted to install security cameras at all of its branches. The work was performed in August Year 11, a customer sign-off was received at each branch, and invoices were sent in early September. Mountain Bank refused to pay individual invoices. It wants to pay the total of all invoices in one payment.

In October Year 11, a few branches of Mountain Bank contacted their head office and requested that no payment be made to RSI until certain corrections were made to the angles at which the cameras were installed. Although not required to do so under its agreement with Mountain Bank, RSI fixed the problems, as Mountain Bank is one of its largest customers.

On June 1, Year 12, $450,000 was received. Mountain Bank asserts that some work remains to be done at 5 to 10 sites and is withholding final payment until it is completely satisfied. All amounts related to the contract are recorded as revenues. Internal reports reveal that it takes a service person approximately one hour to fix the problems at each branch. No significant materials costs have been incurred for the follow-up visits.

(CICA adapted)

Case 1-5
LO1, 5, 6

Minink Limited (ML) is a subsidiary of a large public company, federally incorporated 50 years ago. Until this year, ML's corporate structure consisted of three operating divisions and a corporate head office. Senior management receives financial reports on each division on a monthly basis. Bonuses are awarded annually to divisional managers based on the growth in net income on a year-over-year basis.

The corporate head office oversees the divisions and provides financial, payroll, legal, and administrative services. Corporate head office charges the divisions one-half of the cost of providing these services and absorbs the other half.

The Ladium Extraction Division (Extraction) mines ladium, a metal used in many industrial chemical processes. This division also performs the first stage in the refining process. The Ladium Processing Division (Processing) buys ladium from Extraction and further refines the metal before selling it to customers in North and South Americas. Both stages of the refining process cause airborne pollutants whose levels the government regulates (see Exhibit II for new legislation).

Processing's operations were sold to Donaz Integrated Limited (DIL) effective August 15, Year 4. An integral part of this sale is a long-term contract for Extraction to supply ladium to DIL. The negotiations leading up to the sale lasted nearly a year. An agreement was finally reached after DIL threatened to break off negotiations. Two offers were made by DIL, summarized in Exhibit III. ML management favoured the second offer but accepted the first offer under pressure from its parent company. The balance sheet of Processing

EXHIBIT II

HIGHLIGHTS OF NEW LEGISLATION ON EMISSIONS

New legislation to be implemented on January 1, Year 5, imposes a quota, or limits, on total annual emissions of sulphur by the mining industry in Canada. Each company in the mining industry, depending on its level of production, will annually be allocated a portion of the fixed, industry-wide quota. All companies will be required to file documents certifying actual emission and production levels for each calendar year.

At the beginning of each calendar year, the government will grant companies "pollution rights" that represent their portion of the annual sulphur emission quota. The rights will be valid for that year only. A company exceeding its own pollution rights (i.e., emitting more sulphur than it is allowed to emit) will have to buy pollution rights from other companies to make up the difference. On the other hand, a "clean company" (one emitting less sulphur than the amount permitted) will be allowed to sell its unused pollution rights. The big mining companies gained this compromise on the grounds that business should be allowed to find the least costly, most efficient way of meeting an annual target. "Dirty" companies will have until March 31 of the following year to purchase pollution rights from clean companies. Companies that violate the legislation will be subject to heavy fines or closure.

The government's objective is to give mining companies an incentive to invest in the innovative technology needed to reduce their current sulphur emission levels. Over time, the government will lower the emission levels for the industry; therefore, fewer pollution rights will be granted.

EXHIBIT III

LETTER CONCERNING SALE OF LADIUM PROCESSING DIVISION

May 2, Year 4

Mr. I. P. Labigne
President and Chief Executive Officer
Minink Limited

Dear Mr. Labigne,

For nearly a year now, we have been negotiating the purchase price of the operating assets of Minink Limited's Ladium Processing Division and the related long-term ladium supply contract. Following our telephone conversation yesterday, this letter confirms that Donaz Integrated Limited is not prepared to continue these negotiations.

We require a fax confirming acceptance of one of our two offers by midnight on May 4, Year 4. Our offers are summarized as follows, within the context of the detailed Purchase and Sale Agreement already agreed to:

1) $398.6 million for the operating assets of the division and $3,450/tonne adjusted annually for inflation as the price for ladium under the long-term supply contract.
2) $97.1 million for the operating assets of the division and $4,100/tonne adjusted annually for inflation as the price for ladium under the long-term supply contract.

I look forward to receiving your response by the deadline.

Yours sincerely,
Ms. S.N. Wong, CA
Vice-President, Finance and Chief Financial Officer
Donaz Integrated Limited

EXHIBIT IV

LADIUM PROCESSING DIVISION BALANCE SHEET
July 31, Year 4
(unaudited, in thousands of dollars)

	Year 4	Year 3
Accounts receivable	$ 51,223	$ 47,228
Inventories*	23,454	21,460
Prepaid expenses	4,002	5,103
Production equipment, net*	17,846	18,105
Buildings, net*	18,010	19,385
	$ 114,535	$ 111,281
Accounts payable and accruals	$ 19,123	$ 18,614
Advance from corporate head office	14,569	12,665
Divisional equity	80,843	80,002
	$ 114,535	$ 111,281

*Included in Purchase and Sale Agreement with Donaz Integrated Limited

at July 31, Year 4, is found in Exhibit IV, and selected information on Extraction is in Exhibit V.

The third division is the Mining Equipment Division (Equipment) which designs, builds, and sells sophisticated mining equipment. During Year 4, Equipment built six Crushones. Crushones are a new breed of open-pit mining machines

EXHIBIT V

LADIUM EXTRACTION DIVISION
SELECTED INFORMATION
(in thousands of dollars)

Year 4/5 Fiscal Year Budget	
Sales (volume 84,000 tonnes @ $3,700 per tonne)	$310,800
Variable cost of sales ($3,400 per tonne)	285,600
Contribution margin	25,200
Expenses	
Head office charges	3,100
Fixed costs	9,610
	12,710
Divisional income before taxes	$ 12,490

Additional information:

1. This budget was prepared on the basis that the Extraction Division would sell its ladium to the Processing Division.
2. When annual volumes exceed 90,000 tonnes, variable ladium extraction costs increase by $562/tonne on the additional volume. New extraction equipment with a useful life of 5 years must also be purchased, at a cost of approximately $58 million, to handle annual volumes over 85,000 tonnes.
3. The carrying amount of Extraction's equipment and buildings that are dedicated to ladium extraction at July 31, Year 4, was $76 million.

that have a very high output relative to capital cost. The provincial government agreed to fund 90% of the total production costs of $165.46 million. In return, the provincial government is entitled to 90% of the net proceeds on sale of the Crushones. Management expects that due to the nature of these machines, ML may have to wait several years to sell the Crushones that have been built. As of late July Year 4 the six Crushones were included in inventory and measured at their production cost of $165.46 million.

ML is the largest subsidiary of its parent and its financial statements are material to its parent's financial statements. The parent company has reported losses for the past few years, and the price of its shares has dropped. The parent company plans to issue additional shares in the near future.

The request for proposal for the audit of ML and its parent company for the year ended August 31, Year 4, resulted in the appointment of your firm, Douglas & Co., Chartered Accountants (DC). DC has already sent out an engagement letter to ML and corresponded with the previous auditors, who said they knew of no reason why DC should not accept the engagement. You, the CA, have been selected as the audit senior for the assignment. The manager in charge of the audit has requested that you prepare a memo covering the major accounting issues arising from this year's audit of ML.

It is now early August Year 4. Ian Kao, the audit partner, has met with the CFO of ML who is in charge of coordinating the external audit. The partner's notes from these meetings are summarized in Exhibit VI.

Required:

Prepare the memo requested by the audit manager.

EXHIBIT VI

NOTES FROM DISCUSSIONS WITH ML'S CFO

1. In February Year 4, ML started to receive $3 million per month from the provincial government to help fund research and development (R&D) into new mining techniques. ML has recorded these funds as revenue. R&D work will commence in September Year 4.
2. The Purchase and Sale Agreement with DIL specifies that Extraction must sell between 102,000 and 124,000 tonnes of ladium per year to DIL at the agreed price. The price for any sales beyond this range will be agreed upon at the time the order is made. Extraction is not permitted to sell to any other party. The duration of the agreement is 9 years from the closing of the sale.
3. Selling costs for the disposal of Processing are expected to amount to $6.7 million.
4. In response to public pressure to reduce pollution and protect the environment, the Canadian government will require all companies in the mining industry to maintain emissions at or below levels prescribed under the new legislation by allocating pollution rights.

    In June Year 4, ML purchased equipment that will reduce emission levels below the prescribed level. ML will therefore be able to sell pollution rights to other companies when the new legislation comes into effect. The equipment purchased by ML was more expensive than other equipment it could have purchased that would have reduced emissions only to the level prescribed for Year 5. Management wants to know how to account for the pollution rights.

(CICA adapted)

PROBLEMS

Problem 1-1
LO4, 5, 6

IAS 16, "Property, Plant, and Equipment" requires assets to be initially measured at cost. Subsequently, assets may be carried at cost less accumulated depreciation, or they can be periodically revalued upward to current value and carried at the revalued amount less accumulated depreciation. If revalued, the adjustment is reported in other comprehensive income. Subsequent depreciation is based on the revalued amount. U.S. GAAP does not allow assets to be revalued at an amount exceeding historical cost less accumulated depreciation.

ABC Ltd. lists its shares on an exchange that allows it to report either in accordance with U.S. GAAP or by using IFRSs. On January 1, Year 1, it acquired an asset at a cost of $10 million, which will be amortized on a straight-line basis over an estimated useful life of 20 years. On January 1, Year 3, the company hired an appraiser, who determined the fair value of the asset (net of accumulated depreciation) to be $12 million. The estimated useful life of the asset did not change.

Required:

(a) Determine the depreciation expense recognized in Year 2, Year 3, and Year 4 under
   (i) the revaluation treatment allowed under IAS 16, and
   (ii) U.S. GAAP.
(b) Determine the carrying amount of the asset under the two different sets of accounting requirements at January 2, Year 3; December 31, Year 3; and December 31, Year 4.
(c) Summarize the differences in profit and shareholders' equity over the 20-year life of the asset using the two different sets of accounting requirements. Assume that future appraisals indicated that the fair value of the asset was equal to carrying amount.

Problem 1-2
LO4, 5, 6

Fast Ltd. is a public company that prepares its consolidated financial statements in accordance with IFRSs. Its net income in Year 2 was $200,000, and shareholders' equity at December 31, Year 2, was $1,800,000.

Fast lists its shares on a U.S. stock exchange. Although no longer required to do so, Fast has decided to voluntarily provide a U.S. GAAP reconciliation. You have identified the following four areas in which Fast's accounting principles differ from U.S. GAAP.

1. Fast Company gathered the following information related to inventory that it owned on December 31, Year 2:

Historical cost	$100,000
Replacement cost	95,000
Net realizable value	98,000
Normal profit margin as percentage of cost	20%

2. Fast incurred research and development costs of $500,000 in Year 1. Thirty percent of these costs were related to development activities that meet the criteria for capitalization as an intangible asset. The newly developed product was brought to market in January Year 2 and is expected to generate sales revenue for 10 years.

3. Fast sold a building to a bank at the beginning of Year 1 at a gain of $50,000 and immediately leased the building back for a period of five years. The lease is accounted for as an operating lease.

4. Fast acquired equipment at the beginning of Year 1 at a cost of $100,000. The equipment has a five-year life with no expected residual value and is depreciated on a straight-line basis. At December 31, Year 1, Fast compiled the following information related to this equipment:

Expected future cash flows from use of the equipment	$85,000
Present value of expected future cash flows from use of the equipment	75,000
Fair value (net selling price), less costs to dispose	72,000

Required:

(a) Determine the amount at which Fast should report each of the following on its balance sheet at December 31, Year 2, using (1) IFRSs and (2) U.S. GAAP. Ignore the possibility of any additional impairment or reversal of impairment loss at the end of Year 2.
   (i) Inventory
   (ii) Research and development
   (iii) Deferred gain on lease
   (iv) Equipment

(b) Prepare a reconciliation of net income for Year 2 and shareholders' equity at December 31, Year 2, under IFRSs to a U.S. GAAP basis.

Problem 1-3
LO5, 6, 7

Harmandeep Ltd. is a private company in the pharmaceutical industry. It has been preparing its financial statements in accordance with ASPE. Since it has plans to go public in the next 3 to 5 years, it is considering changing to IFRSs for the current year. It wishes to adopt policies that will maximize the return on shareholders' equity. Based on the draft financial statements prepared in accordance with ASPE, its net income for Year 5 is $400,000, and its shareholders' equity at December 31, Year 5 is $3,500,000.

Harmandeep has engaged you to reconcile net income and shareholders' equity from ASPE to IFRSs. You have identified the following five areas for which IFRSs differs from ASPE:

1. Impaired loans—original versus market rate of interest
2. Interest costs—capitalize versus expense
3. Actuarial gains/losses—recognize immediately or defer and amortize
4. Compound financial instrument—debt versus equity components
5. Income taxes—future income tax method or taxes payable method

Harmandeep provides the following information with respect to each of these accounting differences.

Impaired Loans

One of Harmandeep's debtors is in financial difficulty and defaulted on its loan payment during the year. The outstanding balance on this loan receivable at the end of Year 5 was $220,000. Harmandeep agreed to accept five annual payments of $50,000 with the first payment due at December 31, Year 6, as a full settlement of the loan. The original interest rate on the loan was 8%. The market rate of interest for this type of loan is 6%. No adjustment has been made for the impairment of the loan receivable.

Interest Costs

Interest

Harmandeep arranged a loan of $800,000 to finance the construction of a warehouse. $400,000 was borrowed on March 1, Year 5, and another $400,000 was borrowed on October 1, Year 5. The loan is repayable over 5 years with an interest rate of 6%, with the first payment due on September 30, Year 6. The warehouse was nearly complete at the end of Year 5. No interest has been accrued on the loan at the end of Year 5.

Interest cost aen cur

Actuarial Gains/Losses

Harmandeep instituted a defined benefit pension plan in Year 3. The first actuarial evaluation, which was done as at June 30, Year 5, indicated an actuarial gain of $150,000. The expected average remaining service life of the employee workforce was 15 years at the time of the actuarial evaluation. The actuarial gain has not yet been recognized in the preliminary financial statements.

Compound Financial Instrument

Harmandeep issued bonds for proceeds of $1,000,000 on December 31, Year 5. The bonds are convertible into common shares at any time within the next five years. The bonds would have been worth only for $950,000 if they did not have the conversion feature. The proceeds on the bonds have been recognized as long-term debt in the preliminary financial statements.

Income Tax

Harmandeep's income tax rate has been and is expected to continue at 40%. Assume that any adjustments to accounting income for the above items are fully deductible or taxable for tax purposes. The preliminary financial statements reflect the tax payable method of accounting for income taxes. If the future income tax method were adopted, future tax liabilities should be set up for $300,000 at the end of Year 4 and $340,000 at the end of Year 5.

Required:

Prepare a schedule to convert net income and total shareholders' equity from the preliminary financial statements amounts to amounts under ASPE and IFRSs. Where accounting choices exist, choose policies that minimize return on total shareholders' equity under ASPE and maximize return on total shareholders' equity under IFRSs.

Problem 1-4
LO5, 6, 7

Andrew Ltd. is a large private company owned by the Andrew family. It operates a number of ski resorts in a very competitive industry. Its main competition comes from a couple of public companies. Andrew has been using ASPE in the past but has come under pressure from its bank to convert to IFRSs. Its bank is particularly concerned with the debt to equity ratio and the return on total shareholders' equity.

Andrew reported the following on its preliminary Year 6 financial statements in compliance with ASPE:

Net income	$3,000	Total debt	$25,200
		Total shareholders' equity	21,800

You have identified four areas where Andrew's accounting policies could have differences between ASPE and IFRSs. Where choices exist under ASPE, Andrew has adopted allowable policies that maximize net income and shareholders' equity.

The controller at Andrew provides the following information for the four areas:

Intangible Assets

Andrew owns a number of intangible assets and depreciates them over their useful lives, ranging from 3 to 7 years. The patents are checked for impairment on an annual basis. Relevant values pertaining to these patents were as follows:

	Dec 31, Yr5	Dec 31, Yr6
Carrying amount before impairment	$12,000	$9,800
Undiscounted future cash flows	12,100	9,840
Value in use	11,700	9,400
Fair value	11,600	8,600

Property, Plant, and Equipment

Andrew acquired equipment at the beginning of Year 4 at a cost of $1,250. The equipment has an estimated useful life of 10 years, an estimated residual value of $50, and is being depreciated on a straight-line basis. At the beginning of Year 6, the equipment was appraised and determined to have a fair value of $1,090; its estimated useful life and residual value did not change. The company could adopt the revaluation option in IAS 16 to periodically revalue the equipment at fair value subsequent to acquisition.

Research and Development Costs

Andrew incurred research and development costs of $200 in Year 6. Of this amount, 40% related to development activities subsequent to the point at which criteria indicating that the creation of an intangible asset had been met. As of year-end, development of the new product had not been completed.

Redeemable Preferred Shares

In Year 4, Andrew issued redeemable preferred shares to the original founders of the company in exchange for their previously held common shares as part of a tax planning arrangement. The preferred shares were assigned a value of $100 and have been reported in shareholders' equity in the preliminary financial statements. The common shares, which had a carrying amount of $100, were cancelled. The preferred shares would be classified as long-term debt under IFRSs and would need to be reported at their redemption value of $1,800.

The CEO is concerned about the impact of converting Andrew's financial statements from ASPE to IFRSs.

Required:

(a) Calculate the two ratios first using ASPE and then using IFRSs. Prepare a schedule showing any adjustments to the numerator and denominator for these ratios. Ignore income taxes.

(b) Explain whether Andrew's solvency and profitability look better or worse under IFRSs after considering the combined impact of the four areas of difference.

WEB-BASED PROBLEMS

Note: The annual reports of companies listed on U.S. stock exchanges can be accessed through the SEC's EDGAR system at www.sec.gov/edgar.shtml. Under this system, one can search by company name, country, SIC code, etc. The annual report is labelled as Form 20-F or Form 40-F. The annual reports of companies listed on the Toronto Stock Exchange (TSX) can be accessed at http://www.sedar.com or through the investor relations section of the company's website.

Web Problem 1-1
LO4, 6

Access the 2011 annual report for China Mobile Limited, which is a company incorporated in China and listed on the NYSE. Answer the questions below. Round ratios to two decimal points. For each question, indicate where in the financial statements you found the answer and/or provide a brief explanation.

(a) In what currency are the financial statements presented?
(b) GAAP from what country or jurisdiction was used in preparing the financial statements? See the notes to the financial statements.
(c) Is there a reconciliation of net income as reported to net income under U.S. GAAP? If so, identify the three major differences. If not, explain why the reconciliation was not provided.
(d) Calculate the current ratio for each of the last two years. Did the liquidity position of the company improve or weaken during the year? Briefly explain.
(e) Calculate the total debt to equity ratio for each of the last two years. Did the solvency position of the company improve or weaken during the year? Briefly explain.
(f) Did income increase or decrease from the previous year? What item on the income statement had the biggest impact on the change in income?

Web Problem 1-2
LO4, 6

Access the 2012 annual report for Dr. Reddy's Laboratories Limited, which is a company incorporated in India and listed on the NYSE. Answer the same questions as in Problem 1. For each question, indicate where in the financial statements you found the answer, and/or provide a brief explanation.

Web Problem 1-3
LO4, 6

Access the 2012 annual report for Toyota Motor Corporation, which is a company incorporated in Japan and listed on the NYSE. Answer the same questions as in Problem 1. For each question, indicate where in the financial statements you found the answer, and/or provide a brief explanation.

Web Problem 1-4
LO4, 6

Commencing in 2007, foreign companies that were using IFRSs did not have to reconcile their reported profit to profit under U.S. GAAP. Access the 2011 and 2010 annual reports for Cenovus, a Canadian oil company. Answer the questions below for each of the two years. Round ratios to two decimal points. For each question, indicate where in the financial statements you found the answer, and/or provide a brief explanation.

(a) In what currency are the financial statements presented?
(b) GAAP from what country or jurisdiction was used in preparing the financial statements?

(c) What was the percentage difference in reported net earnings under Canadian GAAP versus net earnings under U.S. GAAP?

(d) What three items, other than income taxes, caused the biggest change in net earnings between the two different GAAPs?

(e) If a reconciliation to U.S. GAAP were not provided, how would a financial analyst deal with this situation when comparing Cenovus to another company reporting under U.S. GAAP?

(f) What was the percentage difference in reported net earnings under Canadian GAAP versus net earnings under IFRSs?

(g) What three items, other than income taxes, caused the biggest change in net earnings between the two different GAAPs?

Web Problem 1-5
LO4, 6

Commencing in 2007, foreign companies that were using IFRSs did not have to reconcile their reported shareholders' equity to shareholders' equity under U.S. GAAP. Access the 2011 and 2010 annual reports for Goldcorp Inc., a Canadian gold producer. Answer the questions below for each of the two years. Round percentages to one decimal point. For each question, indicate where in the financial statements you found the answer, and/or provide a brief explanation.

(a) In what currency are the financial statements presented?

(b) GAAP from what country or jurisdiction was used in preparing the financial statements?

(c) What was the percentage difference between the reported shareholders' equity under Canadian GAAP and shareholders' equity under U.S. GAAP?

(d) What three items caused the biggest change in shareholders' equity between the two different GAAPs?

(e) If a reconciliation to U.S. GAAP were not provided, how would a financial analyst deal with this situation when comparing Goldcorp to another company reporting under U.S. GAAP?

(f) What was the percentage difference in reported shareholders' equity under Canadian GAAP versus shareholders' equity under IFRSs?

(g) What three items caused the biggest change in shareholders' equity between the two different GAAPs?

Investments in Equity Securities

LEARNING OBJECTIVES

After studying this chapter, you should be able to do the following:

LO1 Describe the broad relationship between all the relevant standards from Part I of the *CICA Handbook* that make up the "big picture."

LO2 Distinguish between the various types of equity investments measured at fair value.

LO3 Prepare journal entries to account for investments under the cost and equity methods.

LO4 Evaluate relevant factors to determine whether an investor has significant influence over an investee.

LO5 State the main disclosure requirements related to an investment in associate.

LO6 Analyze and interpret financial statements involving investments in equity securities.

LO7 Identify some of the differences between IFRSs and ASPE for investments in equity securities.

INTRODUCTION

Rogers Communications Inc. is a diversified public Canadian communications and media company with annual revenues in excess of $12 billion. It has operations in three segments—wireless, cable, and media. The wireless segment includes 100% interests in Fido Solutions Inc. and Rogers Communications Partnership, which operates both the wireless and cable businesses. The media segment includes the wholly owned subsidiary Rogers Media Inc. and its subsidiaries, including Rogers Broadcasting (which owns a group of 55 radio stations), the CityTV television network, the Sportsnet channels, and Canadian specialty channels, including Outdoor Life Network and CityNews Channel; Digital Media, which provides digital advertising solutions to over 1,000 websites; Rogers Publishing, which produces more than 50 consumer, trade, and professional publications; and Rogers Sports Entertainment, which owns the Toronto Blue Jays Baseball Club and Rogers Centre. Media also holds ownership interests in entities involved in specialty television content, television production, and broadcast sales.

Such ownership structures are hardly uncommon in the business world; corporate as well as individual investors frequently acquire ownership shares of both domestic and foreign businesses. These investments can range from a few shares to the acquisition of 100% control. There are many different methods of reporting

There are many different methods for reporting investments in equity securities.

these investments, ranging from fair value to cost-based approaches. Unrealized gains can be recognized in net income or in other comprehensive income.

Over the next eight chapters, we will examine various methods of reporting investments in equity securities. The focus is on investments, where one firm possesses either significant influence or control over another through ownership of voting shares. Transactions between these non–arm's-length entities require special scrutiny and special accounting procedures. We will begin our journey by reviewing the requirements for reporting equity investments, and then spend considerable time in preparing consolidated financial statements in increasingly complicated situations.

LO1 # EQUITY INVESTMENTS—THE BIG PICTURE

Equity investments are investments in shares of another company.

This is the first of eight chapters that make up a single accounting topic. This topic can be represented by the following question: How should a Canadian company report, in its financial statements, an investment in the shares of another company?

There are two main categories of equity investments: strategic and nonstrategic. For strategic investments, the investor intends to establish or maintain a long-term operating relationship with the entity in which the investment is made and has some level of influence over the strategic decisions of the investee company. The level of influence varies among full control, joint control, and significant influence. For nonstrategic investments, the investor is hoping for a reasonable rate of return without having the ability to play an active role in the strategic decisions of the investee company.

The methods of reporting equity investments have changed significantly over the past 10 years. Prior to 2005, these investments were typically reported at some cost-based amount. The investments were written down if there was impairment in value. However, the investments were not written up to reflect increases in value; gains were only reported when the investments were sold.

In 2005, IAS 39: Financial Instruments—Recognition and Measurement was introduced for the reporting of nonstrategic investments. For the first time, it was possible to report certain investments at fair value, regardless of whether fair value was higher or lower than the cost-based amounts. This was part of a trend to report more and more assets at fair value on the basis that fair value is more relevant information. The unrealized gains and losses were reported either in net income or in a new category of income called *other comprehensive income (OCI)*. When the investments were sold, the unrealized gains and losses were removed from OCI and reported in net income; that is, the unrealized gains were recycled through net income.

There is a trend in financial reporting to measure more assets at fair value on an annual basis.

After a few years of reporting these nonstrategic investments at fair value with gains and losses reported either in net income or other comprehensive income, both preparers and users of the financial statements started to complain about the different reporting options under IAS 39. They felt that the financial statements were getting too complicated and that IAS 39 was difficult to understand, apply, and interpret. They urged the International Accounting Standards Board (IASB) to develop a new standard for the financial reporting of financial instruments that was principle based and less complex. Although the Board amended

IAS 39 several times to clarify requirements, add guidance, and eliminate internal inconsistencies, it had not previously undertaken a fundamental reconsideration of reporting for financial instruments.

In 2009, the IASB introduced a new accounting standard for nonstrategic investments, International Financial Reporting Standard (IFRS) 9: Financial Instruments—Classification and Measurement. IFRS 9 established principles for the financial reporting of financial assets and financial liabilities that will present relevant and useful information to users of financial statements for their assessment of the amounts, timing, and uncertainty of an entity's future cash flows. It has replaced and superseded the classification and measurement standards that are in IAS 39. It will be mandatorily effective for fiscal periods beginning on or after January 1, 2015, but early adoption is permitted. In this text, we will focus on IFRS 9.

Starting in 2015, nonstrategic investments in private companies must be reported at fair value.

IFRS 9 requires that all nonstrategic equity investments be measured at fair value, including investments in private companies. Under IAS 39, investments that did not have a quoted market price in an active market and whose fair value could not be reliably measured were reported at cost. This provision no longer exists under IFRS 9. However, in limited circumstances, cost may be an appropriate estimate of fair value.

The IASB recognizes that measuring all investments in equity instruments at fair value will impose additional costs on preparers. In the IASB's view, these costs are justified by improved and useful decision-making information about equity investments for users of financial statements. Measuring all investments in equity instruments in the same way would also simplify the accounting requirements and improve comparability.

IFRS 9 no longer refers to and does not have any specific provisions for available-for-sale (AFS) investments; in effect, the AFS investment disappears as a separate category of equity investments. However, on initial recognition, an entity can elect to present the fair value changes on an equity investment that is not held for short-term trading in OCI. This concept is similar to that previously applied to AFS investments. One significant change is that the gains or losses are cleared out of accumulated OCI and transferred directly to retained earnings, and never ~new change~ recycled through net income.

Available-for-sale investments are being phased out as a separate category of investments.

In 2011, the IASB introduced a new accounting standard, IFRS 13: Fair Value Measurement. It replaced the fair value measurement guidance previously contained in individual IFRSs with a single, unified definition of fair value and a framework for measuring it. It also states the required disclosures about fair value measurements. Fair value is defined as the price that would be received to sell an asset or paid to transfer a liability in an orderly transaction between market participants at the measurement date (i.e., an exit price). It would reflect the highest and best use for a nonfinancial asset.

In 2011, the IASB issued an amendment to IAS 1: Presentation of Financial Statements. Entities must now group items presented in OCI in two categories— those that will be recycled through net income and those that will not be recycled through net income. If the items are presented before tax, then the tax related to each of the two groups of OCI items must be shown separately.

Exhibit 2.1 summarizes the reporting methods for equity investments. It would be easier if only one method was used for all investments, but such is not the case under current standards. The rationale for the different methods will be

EXHIBIT 2.1	**Reporting Methods for Investments in Equity Securities**	
Type of Investment	**Reporting Method**	**Reporting of Unrealized Gains**
Strategic investments		
Significant influence	Equity method	Not applicable
Control	Full consolidation	Not applicable
Joint control through joint venture	Equity method	Not applicable
Nonstrategic investments		
FVTPL (fair value through profit or loss)	Fair value method	In net income
Other – elect FVTOCI (fair value through OCI)	Fair value method	In other comprehensive income

discussed as the methods are introduced throughout the text. It is important that you try to understand the rationale because that will make it easier to remember which method to apply to which situation. There is always a danger that in attempting to absorb a large amount of new material, you will concentrate on the details to the point of losing sight of the big picture. It is very important that you do not lose sight of the forest when you study the trees.

Before proceeding with our examination of the "trees," it would be useful to look at this "forest." The question posed at the beginning of this section provides a path into the forest. The accounting principles involved with that question are contained in numerous standards and interpretations issued by the IASB. We will use a summarized balance sheet to illustrate the question, and then outline the possible answers that are contained in the IASB standards.

The balance sheet of J Company Ltd. follows:

J COMPANY LTD.

BALANCE SHEET

Miscellaneous assets	$ XXX	Liabilities	$ XXX
Investment in shares of K Corporation	**XXX**	Shareholders' equity	
		Common shares	XXX
		Retained earnings	XXX
	$ XXX		$ XXX

Dollar amounts have been omitted from the statement because our focus is only on the reporting of the "Investment in shares of K Corporation."

Five IFRSs are directly related to providing an answer to this question, while eight other IFRSs and one interpretation must also be considered. A brief summary of the provisions contained in these sections is presented next.

Directly Related IFRSs

1. IFRS 10: Consolidated Financial Statements If J Company controls K Corporation, then J Company is called a *parent company* and K Corporation

---

Always try to understand the forest before looking at the trees.

Cautionary Note: At the time of writing this seventh edition, there were a number of exposure drafts outstanding on topics relevant to this course. This text has incorporated these exposure drafts on the basis that the latest proposals will be approved and required as of January 1, 2015, or earlier. We will use Connect (www.mcgrawhillconnect.ca) to keep you informed of any deviations from what is in the text and what finally ends up in the *CICA Handbook*. In addition, this text uses the requirements for IFRSs that have been approved even though they may not yet be effective because early adoption is typically allowed for IFRSs once they have been approved.

Consolidated financial statements are prepared when one company controls another company.

is called a *subsidiary*, and GAAP require the preparation of consolidated financial statements by J Company. This involves removing the investment in K Corporation from J Company's balance sheet and replacing it with the assets and liabilities from the balance sheet of K Corporation. This process is illustrated in Chapters 3 through 9.

An investor controls an investee when it is exposed, or has rights, to variable returns from its involvement with the investee and has the ability to affect those returns through its power over the investee. In other words, J Company can determine the key operating and financing policies of K Company. Control is generally presumed if J Company's investment consists of a majority of the voting shares of K Corporation. But as we will see in later discussions,[1] control can exist with smaller holdings and does not necessarily exist with all majority holdings.

> Control is the power to direct the activities of another entity to generate variable returns.

2. IAS 28: Investments in Associates and Joint Ventures

This standard describes the financial reporting requirements for investments in associates, that is, investments where the investor has significant influence over the investee and sets out the requirements for the application of the equity method when accounting for investments in associates and joint ventures. *Significant influence* is defined as the power to participate in the financial and operating policy decisions of the investee, but it is not control or joint control of those policies. IAS 28 indicates that an investment of 20% or more of the voting shares of K Corporation, without control or joint control being present, would be presumed to be a significant influence investment, unless there is evidence to the contrary.

If J Company's investment is one of significant influence, it must be reported by the equity method. Thus, the investment is initially recorded at cost, and adjusted thereafter to include J Company's pro rata share of the earnings or losses of K Corporation, adjusted for the acquisition differential[2] and the elimination and subsequent recognition of all unrealized intercompany profits and losses that occur as a result of transactions between the two companies. Dividends received from K Corporation are recorded as a reduction of the investment. The accounting for significant influence investments will be illustrated in later sections of this chapter and in Chapters 5 through 8.

> The equity method is used when the investor has significant influence over the investee.

3. IFRS 11: Joint Arrangements

If the investment is not one of the two just described, it may possibly be a joint arrangement, if the following general provisions of this standard are satisfied. For a joint arrangement to exist, the owners (the venturers) must have made a contractual arrangement that establishes joint control over the venture. Under such joint control, the venturers are exposed, or have the rights, to variable returns from their involvement with the investee and have the ability to affect those returns through their power over the investee. No single venturer is able to unilaterally control the venture.

Under this standard, J Company Ltd. (the venturer) reports its investment in K Corporation Ltd. (the venture) by using the equity method when K Corporation is a joint venture. Some other types of joint arrangements will be reported using proportionate consolidation. Accounting for joint arrangements is illustrated in Chapter 9.

> The equity method is required when the investor has joint control over a joint venture.

4. IFRS 9: Financial Instruments—Classification and Measurement

IFRS 9 requires that all nonstrategic equity investments be measured at fair value, with

> All nonstrategic investments must be measured at fair value at each reporting date.

the fair value changes reported in net income. However, an entity can elect on initial recognition to present the fair value changes on an equity investment that is not held for short-term trading in OCI. The dividends on such investments must be recognized in net income. The gains or losses are cleared out of accumulated OCI and transferred directly to retained earnings. Accounting for fair value investments will be illustrated later in this chapter.

IFRS 9 also indicates when and how hedge accounting can be used to ensure that gains and losses on a hedged item are reported in income in the same period in which they occurred. In Chapters 10 and 11, we will illustrate fair value hedges, cash flow hedges, and hedges of net investments in foreign operations.

5. IFRS 12: Disclosure of Interests in Other Entities   IFRS 12 contains the disclosure requirements related to investments in associates, joint arrangements, non-controlled structured entities, and subsidiaries. It establishes disclosure objectives that require an entity to disclose information that helps users

- understand the judgments and assumptions made by a reporting entity when deciding how to classify its involvement with another entity,
- understand the interest that non-controlling interests have in consolidated entities, and
- assess the nature of the risks associated with interests in other entities.

Disclosure requirements related to the different types of investments will be described in each chapter of this text.

Other Related IFRSs

The remaining eight important IFRSs and one interpretation are directly related to the five standards that were just outlined. They are discussed briefly below.

A parent company does not have to issue consolidated financial statements if its parent issues consolidated financial statements.

6. IAS 27: Separate Financial Statements   IAS 27 states that a parent is not required to present consolidated financial statements for external reporting purposes if it is itself a subsidiary of another entity, and the ultimate or any intermediate parent of the parent does produce consolidated financial statements available for public use that comply with IFRSs. If the parent meets these conditions, it *can* (but is not required to) present separate financial statements as its only financial statements to external users. When an entity prepares separate financial statements, it shall account for investments in subsidiaries either at cost or fair value. Separate financial statements are described further in Chapter 3.

A business combination can occur indirectly by buying shares or directly by buying the net assets of another company.

7. IFRS 3: Business Combinations   A business combination is a transaction or other event in which an acquirer obtains control of one or more businesses. J Company Ltd. usually obtains *control* over the net assets of K Corporation by either

(a) investing in the voting shares of K Corporation (a parent–subsidiary relationship) or

(b) purchasing the net assets of K Corporation (not a parent–subsidiary relationship).

Business combination accounting is explained in Chapter 3.

8. IFRS 8: Operating Segments Consolidated financial statements often result in the aggregation of the statements of companies in diverse businesses located in countries throughout the world. Disaggregation into operating segments and disclosures about products, geographical areas, and major customers is required by this standard in order to improve the information content of the consolidated statements. Segment disclosures are discussed in Chapter 9.

Segment disclosures provide a breakdown of the aggregated information into various operating and geographical segments.

9. IAS 1: Presentation of Financial Statements This standard states that a complete set of financial statements comprises the following statements:

(a) Financial position as at the end of the period

(b) Comprehensive income for the period

(c) Changes in equity for the period

(d) Cash flows for the period

The statement of comprehensive income comprises a section for profit or loss and a section for other comprehensive income.

IAS 1 requires reporting enterprises to differentiate between profit as traditionally reported on the income statement and OCI. OCI includes unrealized gains and losses on certain equity investments and exchange gains and losses related to certain hedges of foreign currency transactions and types of foreign operations, which will be illustrated in Chapters 10 and 11.

Cautionary Note:
Although the titles stated in item 9 are recommended, they are not mandatory. Many Canadian companies now use and will likely continue to use the titles of *balance sheet* (rather than *statement of financial position*) and *income statement* (rather than *statement of profit or loss*). In this textbook, we will use both sets of titles. We will also vary the ordering of assets, liabilities, and shareholders' equity. In some cases, current assets will appear first and shareholders' equity will appear last. In other cases, long-term assets will be followed by current assets and shareholders' equity will precede liabilities on the credit side of the statement of financial position. Both formats are acceptable under IAS 1. In the problems and illustrations that do not involve OCI, we will focus only on the statement of profit or loss (i.e., the income statement), rather than the statement of comprehensive income, and on a statement of retained earnings, rather than preparing a complete statement of changes in equity.

10. IAS 12: Income Taxes The provisions of this standard add some complexity to the measurements associated with business combinations and consolidated financial statements. These provisions are discussed in Chapters 6 and 9.

11. IAS 21: The Effects of Changes in Foreign Exchange Rates This standard deals with the translation of the financial statements of foreign investees, subsidiaries, and joint ventures, and with the translation of transactions denominated in foreign currencies.

Provisions of this section apply if

(a) K Corporation was located in a foreign country and/or prepared its financial statements in a foreign currency, or

(b) J Company Ltd. had borrowings or lendings and/or export and import activities denominated in foreign currencies.

Chapters 10 and 11 examine the accounting concepts involved here.

12. IAS 36: Impairment of Assets This standard describes the impairment tests to be applied to all assets. We will primarily apply the standard to investments in associates, goodwill, and other intangible assets. This topic is discussed in Chapter 5.

13. IAS 38: Intangible Assets IFRS 3: Business Combinations outlines the procedures for measuring the identifiable assets acquired, liabilities assumed, and goodwill acquired in a business combination. IAS 38 provides additional

Foreign transactions and foreign financial statements must be translated to the entity's presentation currency.

guidance regarding the identifiable assets by detailing the various intangible assets that might have been acquired. This topic is discussed in Chapter 3.

14. IFRIC 16: Hedges of a Net Investment in a Foreign Operation   This interpretation provides guidance in applying IAS 21. We will discuss this topic further in Chapter 11.

[L02]

INVESTMENTS MEASURED AT FAIR VALUE

Unrealized gains and losses are reported in net income for FVTPL investments.

IFRS 9 deals with two types of equity investments: fair value through profit or loss (FVTPL) and fair value through OCI (FVTOCI). FVTPL investments include investments held for short-term trading. These investments are classified as current assets on the basis that they are actively traded and intended by management to be sold within one year. FVTPL investments are initially measured at fair value and subsequently measured at fair value at each reporting date. The unrealized gains and losses are reported in net income along with dividends received or receivable.

Unrealized gains and losses are reported in OCI for FVTOCI investments.

FVTOCI investments are equity investments that are not held for short-term trading and those for which management, on initial acquisition, irrevocably elects to report all unrealized gains and losses in OCI. These investments are classified as current or noncurrent assets, depending on how long company managers intend to hold on to these shares. They are initially measured at fair value and subsequently remeasured at fair value at each reporting date. The unrealized gains and losses are reported in OCI. Dividend income is reported in net income as the dividends are declared. The cumulative unrealized gains or losses are cleared out of accumulated OCI and transferred directly to retained earnings. The transfer to retained earnings would usually occur when the investment is sold or derecognized but could be transferred at any time.

Illustration   On January 1, Year 1, Jenstar Corp. purchased 10% of the outstanding common shares of Safebuy Company at a cost of $95,000. Safebuy reported net income of $100,000 and paid dividends of $80,000 for the year ended December 31, Year 1. The fair value of Jenstar's 10% interest in Safebuy was $98,000 at December 31, Year 1. On January 10, Year 2, Jenstar sold its investment in Safebuy for $99,000. The following table presents Jenstar's journal entries for the above-noted transactions under FVTPL, AFS under IAS 39, and the option under IFRS 9 to designate at FVTOCI. It ignores income tax and assumes that accumulated OCI for the FVTOCI investment is transferred to retained earnings when the investment is sold.

	FVTPL	AFS	FVTOCI
Jan. 1, Year 1			
Investment in Safebuy	95,000	95,000	95,000
Cash	(95,000)	(95,000)	(95,000)
To record the acquisition of 10% of Safebuy's shares			
Dec. 31, Year 1			
Cash (10% × 80,000)	8,000	8,000	8,000
Dividend income	(8,000)	(8,000)	(8,000)
Receipt of dividend from Safebuy			

	FVTPL	AFS	FVTOCI
Dec. 31, Year 1			
Investment in Safebuy (98,000 − 95,000)	3,000	3,000	3,000
Unrealized gains (reported in net income)	(3,000)		
OCI − unrealized gains		(3,000)	(3,000)
To record investment at fair value			
Jan. 10, Year 2			
Cash	99,000	99,000	99,000
Investment in Safebuy	(98,000)	(98,000)	(98,000)
Gain on sale (reported in net income)	(1,000)		
OCI—gain on sale		(1,000)	(1,000)
Record sale of investment			
Jan. 10, Year 2			
OCI—reclassification to net income		4,000	
Accumulated OCI—reclassification to retained earnings			4,000
Gain on sale (reported in net income)		(4,000)	
Retained earnings—gain on sale of FVTOCI investments			(4,000)
Clear OCI/Accumulated OCI to net income/retained earnings			

The investment is reported at fair value at each reporting date under all three methods of reporting. The credit side of the entry is shown in brackets.

There are two options for reporting OCI—a single-statement format and a two-statement format. In the single-statement format, all items of income and expenses are reported in the section for net income, which is then immediately followed by OCI items, and, finally, by the total of comprehensive income for the period. In the two-statement format, the statement of profit or loss (or income statement) is separate, and it is then followed by the statement of comprehensive income, which starts with net income and then displays the other comprehensive income items and provides the final total of comprehensive income. In either case, net income is added to retained earnings as in the past, and OCI is added to accumulated other comprehensive income (AOCI). Retained earnings and AOCI must be reported as separate components of shareholders' equity. We will illustrate the presentation of OCI and the components of shareholders' equity in Chapters 10 and 11.

Accumulated other comprehensive income is not included in retained earnings but is included as a separate component of shareholders' equity.

INVESTMENTS NOT MEASURED AT FAIR VALUE

When investments are not reported at fair value, they are usually reported using the cost method or the equity method. The next two subsections describe when these methods are used and illustrate how to apply them.

L03

Cost Method of Reporting an Equity Investment

The cost method is used under IFRSs in the following situations:

The cost method is used for external reporting and internal recording purposes.

- *For investments in controlled entities.* This is an option when the reporting entity prepares separate-entity financial statements in addition to or instead of consolidated financial statements. This situation will be discussed further in Chapter 3.

- For *available-for-sale investments that do not have a quoted market price in an active market and whose fair value cannot be reliably measured.* This requirement is specified in IAS 39 and is available until 2015, if the reporting entity does not adopt IFRS 9 early.

- For *a parent company's internal accounting records prior to preparing consolidated financial statements.* This situation will be discussed further in Chapter 5.

The cost method is allowed under Accounting Standards for Private Enterprises (ASPE) for equity investments that are not quoted in an active market.

The investment must be written down when there is impairment.

Under the cost method, the investment is initially recorded at cost. The investor's share of the dividends declared is reported in net income. The investment is reported at original cost at each reporting date unless the investment becomes impaired. Impairment losses are reported in net income. When the investment is sold, the realized gains or losses are reported in net income.

Prior to 2009, a liquidating dividend was treated by the investor as a reduction in the investment account. A liquidating dividend occurred when the cumulative amount paid out as dividends, since acquisition of the investment was greater than the cumulative net incomes earned by the investee since acquisition. Since dividends are a company's method of distributing earnings to its owners, it follows that a company cannot distribute as income more than it has earned. When it does so, it is really returning part of the original investment to its owners.

A liquidating dividend is now reported as dividend income under the cost method.

Even though it may be conceptually more appropriate to treat a liquidating dividend as a return of capital, the costs and complexities involved in determining whether or not the dividend is a liquidating dividend are often greater than the benefit. Accordingly, IAS 27 was changed in 2009 to require that all dividends be recognized in net income regardless of whether or not they were liquidating dividends.

Using the same data as in the previous illustration, Jenstar would make the following journal entries under the cost method:

Jan. 1, Year 1

Investment in Safebuy	95,000	
Cash		95,000

To record the acquisition of 10% of Safebuy's shares

Dec. 31, Year 1

Under the cost method, income is recognized when dividends are received or receivable.

Cash	8,000	
Dividend income		8,000

Receipt of dividend from Safebuy

Jan. 10, Year 2

Cash	99,000	
Investment in Safebuy		95,000
Gain on sale (reported in net income)		4,000

Record sale of investment

L04 Equity Method of Reporting an Equity Investment

An associate is an entity over which the investor has significant influence.

An investment in an associate is an investment in the voting shares of a corporation that permits the investor to exercise significant influence over the strategic operating and financing policies of the investee. However, it does not establish control or joint control over that investee. Note that the criteria for this type of investment require only the *ability* to exercise significant influence; there is no requirement to show that such influence is actually being exercised in a particular situation.

The following conditions are possible indicators that significant influence is present and that the investee is an associate:

(a) Representation on the board of directors or equivalent governing body of the investee

(b) Participation in policy-making processes, including participation in decisions about dividends or other distributions

(c) Material transactions between the investor and the investee

(d) Interchange of managerial personnel

(e) Provision of essential technical information

IAS 28 suggests that holding 20–50% of voting shares may indicate the presence of significant influence, but it also states that a holding of this size does not necessarily mean that such influence exists. The following scenarios will illustrate this.

> A guideline (not a rigid rule) in determining significant influence is holding 20–50% of voting shares.

Given that A Company owns 60% of the voting shares of C Company (probably a control investment), does B Company's holding of 30% of C Company's shares indicate that B Company has a significant influence investment? Not necessarily. If B Company were unable to obtain membership on the board of directors of C Company or participate in its strategic policy-making because of A Company's control, it would be difficult to conclude that B Company has significant influence. In such a situation, B Company's holding would be considered a non-strategic investment. Would this situation be different if B Company were allowed membership on C Company's board of directors?

> When one investor has control, other investors usually do not have significant influence.

IAS 28 indicates that a substantial or majority ownership by another investor would not necessarily preclude an investor from exercising significant influence. In other words, another company's control investment in C Company does not mean that B Company's 30% investment in C Company can never be considered a significant influence. Determination of significant influence depends on the particular circumstances and the use of judgment.

On the other hand, is it possible to have significant influence with less than 20%? Normally, an investment of less than 20% would not allow the investor to elect any members to the board of directors of the investee corporation; because of this, it probably cannot exert any influence on the decision-making processes of that company. However, 20% is only a guideline, and an examination of the facts may suggest some other type of investment. For example, if the investee's shares are widely distributed, and all the other shareholders hold very small blocks of shares and display indifference as to the make-up of the board of directors, an investment of less than 20% may be considered a significant influence investment. This could certainly be the case if some of the remaining shareholders gave the investor proxies to vote their shares.

> When an investor has less than 20% of the voting shares, it usually does not have significant influence.

From all these discussions and examples, it should be obvious that considerable professional judgment is required in determining whether an investor has significant influence. In later chapters, when we discuss the criteria used to determine whether a particular investment establishes control over an investee, we will also conclude that considerable professional judgment is required.

When an investor has significant influence, the investment should be reported by the equity method. The basic concept behind the equity method is that the investor records its proportionate share of the associate's income as its own income and reduces the investment account by its share of the associate's dividends declared.

[L04]   Illustration of Equity Method Basics

We return to the example of the Jenstar and Safebuy companies. All the facts remain the same, including the 10% ownership, except that we assume this is a significant influence investment. Using the equity method, Jenstar's journal entries would be as follows:

Jan. 1, Year 1

Investment in Safebuy	95,000	
Cash		95,000
To record the acquisition of 10% of Safebuy's shares		

Income is recognized based on the income reported by the associate, and dividends are reported as a reduction of the investment account.

Dec. 31, Year 1

Investment in Safebuy (10% × 100,000)	10,000	
Investment income		10,000
10% of Safebuy's Year 1 net income		
Cash (10% × 80,000)	8,000	
Investment in Safebuy		8,000
Receipt of dividend from Safebuy		

The equity method picks up the investor's share of the changes in the associate's shareholders' equity.

Under the equity method, the investor's investment account changes in direct relation to the changes taking place in the investee's equity accounts. The accounting objective is to reflect in the investor's financial statements the financial results arising from the close relationship between the companies. The equity method is effective at achieving this. Because the investor is able to influence the associate's dividend policy, dividends could end up being paid in periods during which the investee was suffering considerable losses. The cost method of reporting would reflect investment income, whereas the equity method would report investment losses during these periods.

The equity method provides information on the potential for future cash flows.

The equity method reflects the accrual method of income measurement. As the investee earns income, the investor accrues its share of this income. The associate is not obligated to pay out this income as a dividend on an annual basis. The investor can expect to get the dividend at a later date or to sell its shares at a higher value if the income is not paid out as a dividend. Therefore, the equity method does provide useful information about the future cash flow potential from the investment.

Additional Features Associated with the Equity Method

The previous example illustrated the basic concepts of the equity method. Besides these fundamentals, the following features are relevant for this course:

- The accounting for other changes in associate's equity
- Acquisition costs greater than carrying amount
- Unrealized intercompany profits

- Changes to and from the equity method
- Losses exceeding the balance in the investment account
- Impairment losses
- Gains or losses on sale of the investment
- Held for sale
- Disclosure requirements

Other Changes in Associate's Equity   In accounting for an investment by the equity method, IAS 28 requires that the investor's proportionate share of the associate's discontinued operations, other comprehensive income, changes in accounting policy, corrections of errors relating to prior-period financial statements, and capital transactions should be presented and disclosed in the investor's financial statements according to their nature.

Companies report certain items separately on their statements of comprehensive income so that financial statement users can distinguish between the portion of comprehensive income that comes from continuing operations and the portion that comes from other sources such as discontinued operations and other comprehensive income. Retrospective adjustments of prior-period results and capital transactions are shown as separate components of retained earnings or are disclosed in the footnotes.

> The investor's statement of comprehensive income should reflect its share of the investee's income according to its nature and the different statement classifications.

Example   A Company owns 30% of B Company. The statement of comprehensive income for B Company for the current year is as follows:

B COMPANY
STATEMENT OF COMPREHENSIVE INCOME

Sales	$500,000
Operating expenses	200,000
Operating income before income tax	300,000
Income tax	120,000
Net income from operations	180,000
Loss from discontinued operations (net of tax)	40,000
Net income	140,000
Other comprehensive income (net of tax)	10,000
Comprehensive income	$150,000

Upon receiving this statement of comprehensive income, A Company makes the following journal entry to apply the equity method:

Investment in B Company (30% × 150,000)	45,000	
Discontinued operations − investment loss (30% × 40,000)	12,000	
Other comprehensive income (30% × 10,000)		3,000
Investment income (30% × 180,000)		54,000

> The investor's shares of income from continuing operations, discontinued operations, and other comprehensive income are reported separately.

All three income items, which total $45,000, will appear on A Company's statement of comprehensive income. The investment loss from discontinued operations and the other comprehensive income items require the same presentation as would be made if A Company had its own discontinued operations or other comprehensive income items. Full footnote disclosure is required to indicate that these particular items arise from an investment in associate accounted for by the equity method. Materiality has to be considered because these items do not require special treatment in A Company's statement of comprehensive income if they are not material from A Company's point of view, even though they are material from B Company's perspective.

Many accounting procedures required for consolidated purposes are also required under the equity method.

Many of the accounting procedures for the application of the equity method are similar to the consolidation procedures for a parent and its subsidiary. Furthermore, the concepts underlying the procedures used in accounting for the acquisition of a subsidiary are also adopted in accounting for the acquisition of an investment in an associate. The next two sections briefly describe procedures required in applying the equity method that are equally applicable under the consolidation process. In this chapter, we will describe the procedures very generally. We will discuss these procedures in more detail in later chapters when we illustrate the consolidation of a parent and its subsidiary.

Acquisition Costs Greater than Carrying Amounts   In the previous examples, we recorded Jenstar's initial investment at its cost, but we did not consider the implications if this cost was different from the carrying amount of Safebuy's net assets at the time of the acquisition. We now add a new feature to equity method reporting by considering the difference between the amount paid for the investment and the investor's share of the carrying amount of the associate's net assets.

The investor's cost is usually greater than its share of the carrying amount of the associate's net assets.

Companies' shares often trade at prices that are different from their carrying amount. There are many reasons for this. The share price presumably reflects the fair value of the company as a whole. In effect, it reflects the fair value of the assets and liabilities of the company as a whole. However, many of the company's assets are reported at historical cost or cost less accumulated amortization. For these assets, there will be a difference between the fair value and the carrying amount. Some of the company's value may be attributed to assets that are not even reported on the company's books. For example, the company may have expensed its research and development costs in the past but is now close to patenting a new technology. This technology could have considerable value to a prospective purchaser, even though there is no asset recorded in the company's books. Last but not least, the company's earnings potential may be so great that an investor is willing to pay an amount in excess of the fair value of the company's identifiable net assets.[3] This excess payment is referred to as goodwill.

The difference between the investor's cost and the investor's percentage of the carrying amount of the associate's identifiable net assets is called the *acquisition differential*. The investor allocates this differential to specific assets and liabilities of the associate, and then either depreciates the allocated components over their useful lives or writes down the allocated component when there has been impairment in its value. This process of identifying, allocating, and amortizing the acquisition differential will be illustrated in later chapters.

Unrealized Profits   As we will see in later chapters, consolidated financial statements result from combining the financial statements of a parent company with the financial statements of its subsidiaries. The end result is the financial reporting of a single economic entity, made up of a number of separate legal entities. One of the major tasks in this process is to eliminate all intercompany transactions—especially intercompany "profits"—so that the consolidated statements reflect only transactions with outsiders. The basic premise behind the elimination is that, from the point of view of this single accounting entity, "you cannot make a profit selling to yourself." Any such "unrealized profits" from intercompany transfers of inventory (or other assets) must be held back until the specific assets involved are sold to outside entities or used in producing goods or providing services to outsiders.

> Consolidated statements should reflect only the results of transactions with outsiders.

In the case of a significant influence investment, any transactions between the investor and the associate (they are related parties) must be scrutinized so that incomes are not overstated through the back-and-forth transfer of assets. From an accounting perspective, any transfer is acceptable provided that both parties record the transfer at the value at which it is being carried in the records of the selling company. However, if the transfer involves a profit, a portion of that profit must be held back on an after-tax basis in the investor's equity method journal entries. When the asset in question is sold outside or consumed by the purchaser, the after-tax profit is realized through an equity method journal entry, again made by the investor. The entries under the equity method to account for unrealized and realized profit from intercompany transactions will be discussed and illustrated in detail in Chapters 6 and 7.

> Profits from intercompany transactions must be eliminated until the assets are sold to outsiders or used in producing goods or providing services to outsiders.

Changes to and from the Equity Method   The classification of investments will change as the particular facts change. An investment may initially be FVTPL and subsequently change to one of significant influence. This could happen if additional shares were acquired. Once significant influence has been achieved, a switch from the previous way of reporting is made on a prospective basis. The carrying amount of the FVTPL investment, which would be the fair value of the investment, becomes its new cost. If circumstances change, significant influence may also be achieved without additional shares being acquired, in which case the equity method would commence. For example, the holdings of a large block of investee shares by another company could prevent an investor from exercising significant influence. But if that other company sells its block on the market, the investor's previous FVTPL investment may now amount to significant influence. See Part A of Self-Study Problem 1 for an example of changing from FVTPL to the equity method on a prospective basis.

> Changes in reporting methods are accounted for prospectively if they are changed because of a change in circumstance.

When an investment changes from significant influence to FVTPL, the equity method ceases to be appropriate and the fair value method takes its place, also on a prospective basis. On this date, the investor shall measure at fair value any investment the investor retains in the former associate. The investor shall recognize in net income any difference between

(a) the fair value of any retained investment and any proceeds from disposing of the part interest in the associate, and

(b) the carrying amount of the investment at the date when significant influence is lost.

If an investor loses significant influence over an associate, the investor must account for all amounts recognized in other comprehensive income in relation to that associate on the same basis as would be required if the associate had directly disposed of the related assets or liabilities. When the investor sells its investment in the associate, it is, in effect, selling its proportionate share of the assets and liabilities of the associate. Therefore, if a gain or loss previously recognized in other comprehensive income by an associate would be reclassified to net income on the disposal of the related assets or liabilities, the investor reclassifies the gain or loss from accumulated other comprehensive income to net income (as a reclassification adjustment) when it loses significant influence over the associate. For example, if an associate had reported other comprehensive income on a cash flow hedge and the investor loses significant influence over the associate, the investor must reclassify to net income the gain or loss previously recognized in OCI in relation to that hedge. If an investor's ownership interest in an associate is reduced, but the investment continues to be an associate, the investor must reclassify to net income only a proportionate amount of the gain or loss previously recognized in OCI.

When an investment changes from significant influence to control, the preparation of consolidated statements commences, again on a prospective basis. The concepts relating to this particular situation will be discussed at length in later chapters.

| If an investor guaranteed an investee's obligations, the investor could end up reporting its investment as a liability rather than an asset. |

Losses Exceeding the Balance in the Investment Account   A question arises as to the appropriate accounting when an investor's share of an associate's losses exceeds the carrying amount of the investment. There are two possible ways to treat this. The investor could reduce the investment account to zero and recommence the use of the equity method when its share of associate's earnings exceeds its share of losses. Alternatively, the investor could continue to accrue losses, even though they result in a negative balance in the investment account. IAS 28 provides some guidance on this issue. After the investor's interest in the associate is reduced to zero, additional losses are provided for, and a liability is recognized, *only* to the extent that the investor has incurred legal or constructive obligations or made payments on behalf of the associate. The investor would have an obligation if it guaranteed certain liabilities of the associate or if it committed to provide additional financial support to the associate. If a liability is not reported, the investor resumes recognizing its share of those profits only after its share of them equals the share of losses not recognized.

| Other long-term interests in the associate may have to be written down when the associate is reporting losses. |

If the investor has other long-term interests in the associate over and above its equity investment, these other assets may also have to be written down. Such items may include preference shares and long-term receivables or loans but do not include trade receivables, trade payables, or any long-term receivables for which adequate collateral exists. Losses recognized under the equity method in excess of the investor's investment in ordinary shares are applied to the other components of the investor's interest in an associate in the reverse order of their seniority (i.e., priority in liquidation). Accordingly, an investment in preferred shares should be written down before a long-term note receivable because the preferred share becomes worthless before a note receivable. In other words, the note receivable has priority over the investment in preferred shares in the event that the associate is liquidated.

Impairment Losses   If there is an indication that the investment may be impaired, the investment is tested for impairment in accordance with IAS 36, as a single asset, by comparing its recoverable amount (higher of value in use and fair value less costs of disposal) to its carrying amount. In determining the value in use of the investment, an entity estimates

(a) its share of the present value of the estimated future cash flows expected to be generated by the associate, including the cash flows from the operations of the associate and the proceeds on the ultimate disposal of the investment, or

(b) the present value of the estimated future cash flows expected to arise from dividends to be received from the investment and from its ultimate disposal.

If the recoverable amount is less than the carrying amount, the investment is written down to the recoverable amount. The impairment loss is not allocated to goodwill or any other assets underlying the carrying amount of the investment because these underlying assets were not separately recognized. If the recoverable amount increases in subsequent periods, the impairment loss can be reversed.

Gains and Losses on Sale of Investments When all the shares that make up a long-term investment are sold, the gain (loss) is shown on the income statement and is calculated as the difference between the sale proceeds and the carrying amount of the investment. When only some of the shares are sold, the gain is calculated using the average carrying amount of the investment. Formulas such as first in, first out (FIFO), last in, first out (LIFO), or specific identification are not permitted. If a portion of a significant influence or a control investment is sold, a re-evaluation must be made to determine whether the previous classification is still valid.

Average cost should be used in determining any gain or loss when an investor sells part of its investment.

Held for Sale Investments in associates that meet the criteria to be classified as held for sale should be measured at the lower of carrying amount and fair value less costs of disposal, and should be reported as current assets. An entity shall classify an investment in associate as held for sale if its carrying amount will be recovered principally through a sale transaction rather than through continuing use. For this to be the case, the asset must be available for immediate sale in its present condition, subject only to terms that are usual and customary for sales of such assets, and its sale must be highly probable. For the sale to be highly probable, the appropriate level of management must be committed to a plan to sell the asset, and an active program to locate a buyer and complete the plan must have been initiated. Further, the asset must be actively marketed for sale at a price that is reasonable in relation to its current fair value. In addition, the sale should be expected to qualify for recognition as a completed sale within one year from the date of classification, and actions required to complete the plan should indicate that it is unlikely that significant changes to the plan will be made or that the plan will be withdrawn.

Presentation and Disclosure Requirements Investments in associates shall be classified as noncurrent assets. The investor's share of the profit or loss of such associates and the carrying amount of these investments must be separately disclosed. In addition, the following summarizes the main disclosures required in IFRS 12 for investments in associates:

L05

(a) Nature of the entity's relationship with the associate and the proportion of ownership interest or participating share held by the entity

(b) Fair value of investments in associates for which there are published price quotations

The fair value of an investment in associate should be disclosed when it is readily available.

(c) Summarized financial information of associates, including the aggregated amounts of assets, liabilities, revenues, and profit or loss

(d) Unrecognized share of losses of an associate, both for the period and cumulatively, if an investor has discontinued recognition of its share of losses of an associate

(e) Nature and extent of any significant restrictions on the ability of associates to transfer funds to the entity in the form of cash dividends, or to repay loans or advances made by the entity

(f) Contingent liabilities incurred relating to its interests in associates

Aecon Group Inc. is a publicly traded construction and infrastructure-development company incorporated in Canada. Aecon and its subsidiaries provide services to private and public sector clients throughout Canada and on a selected basis internationally. It reported numerous construction projects under the equity method in its 2011 financial statements. Excerpts from these statements, which applied the disclosure requirement in IAS 28 rather than IFRS 12, are presented in Exhibit 2.2. Much of the disclosure provided under IAS 28 would also be required under IFRS 12.

EXHIBIT 2.2 | **Extracts (in Part) from Aecon's 2011 Financial Statements**

5. Summary of Significant Accounting Policies

5.24 Associates
Entities in which the Company has significant influence and which are neither subsidiaries nor joint ventures are accounted for using the equity method of accounting. Under the equity method of accounting, the Company's investments in associates are carried at cost and adjusted for post-acquisition changes in the net assets of the investment. Profit or loss reflects the Company's share of the results of these investments. The consolidated statements of comprehensive income include the Company's share of any amounts recognized by associates in other comprehensive income. Where there has been a change recognized directly in the equity of the associate, the Company recognizes its share of that change in equity.

The financial statements of the associates are generally prepared for the same reporting period as the Company, using consistent accounting policies. Adjustments are made to bring into line any dissimilar accounting policies that may exist in the underlying records of the associate. Adjustments are made in the consolidated financial statements to eliminate the Company's share of unrealized gains and losses on transactions between the Company and its associates.

The Company discontinues the use of the equity method from the date on which it ceases to have significant influence, and from that date accounts for the investment in accordance with IAS 39, "*Financial Instruments: Recognition and Measurement*" (its initial costs are the carrying amount of the associate on that date), provided the investment does not then qualify as a subsidiary or joint venture.

14. Construction Projects Accounted for Using the Equity Method
The Company performs some construction projects through non-consolidated entities. The Company's participation in construction project entities where the Company exercises significant influence (i.e., associates), but does not control or jointly control the entity, are accounted for using the equity method.

The Company's share of assets, liabilities, revenues, and expenses of construction project entities accounted for using the equity method is as follows (in 000s):

(continued)

EXHIBIT 2.2   *(continued)*

	December 31 2011	December 31 2010
Assets	$ 25,337	$ 26,950
Liabilities	(7,406)	(15,077)
Net investment in construction projects accounted for using the equity method	$ 17,931	$ 11,873

Revenue and expenses for the year ended were as follows:

	December 31 2011	December 31 2010
Revenue	$ 84,253	$ 53,794
Expenses	(70,195)	(53,389)
Share of profits before income taxes	$ 14,058	$ 405

Information on the income, assets, and liabilities of the associates must be disclosed.

ANALYSIS AND INTERPRETATION OF FINANCIAL STATEMENTS   **LO6**

In this chapter, we have used the Jenstar example to illustrate five different methods for reporting equity investments. Exhibit 2.3 presents financial data (ignoring income tax) for Jenstar for Year 1. The data for the investment in and investment income from Safebuy for each method below has been taken from the previous examples earlier in this chapter. All other data is now being given so that we can see the impact of the accounting policy choice on three key financial ratios.

EXHIBIT 2.3   Impact of Reporting Methods on Key Financial Ratios (in 000s)

	Cost	Equity	FVTPL	IAS 39 AFS	IFRS 9 FVTOCI
Investment income	$ 8	$ 10	$ 11	$ 8	$ 8
Other income	67	67	67	67	67
Net income	75	77	78	75	75
OCI	0	0	0	3	3
Comprehensive income	$ 75	$ 77	$ 78	$ 78	$ 78
Investment in Safebuy			$ 98		
Other current assets	$ 300	$ 300	300	$ 300	$ 300
Current assets	300	300	398	300	300
Investment in Safebuy	95	97		98	98
Other noncurrent assets	700	700	700	700	700
Total assets	$1,095	$1,097	$1,098	$1,098	$1,098
Current liabilities	$ 250	$ 250	$ 250	$ 250	$ 250
Noncurrent liabilities	400	400	400	400	400
Total liabilities	650	650	650	650	650
Accumulated OCI	75	77	78	78	78
Other shareholders' equity	370	370	370	370	370
Total shareholders' equity	445	447	448	448	448
Liabilities & shareholders' equity	$1,095	$1,097	$1,098	$1,098	$1,098
Current ratio	1.20	1.20	1.59	1.20	1.20
Debt-to-equity ratio	1.461	1.454	1.451	1.451	1.451
Return on equity	16.85%	17.23%	17.41%	16.74%	16.74%

The FVTPL investment must be shown as a current asset, whereas the other investments could be current or noncurrent, depending on management's intention.

The FVTPL investment shows the best liquidity and profitability.

The following observations are made on the data in Exhibit 2.3:

- The current ratio is highest for the FVTPL method because the investment in Safebuy is shown as a current asset. Therefore, the FVTPL method shows the best liquidity.

- The last three methods show the lowest debt-to-equity ratio (and the best solvency) because equity is the highest under these three methods.

- The return on equity is highest for the FVTPL ratio because net income, rather than comprehensive income, is typically used as the numerator for this equity. Therefore, the FVTPL method shows the best profitability even though AFS and FVTOCI show the same comprehensive income as the FVTPL method.

Although the reporting methods show different values for liquidity, solvency, and profitability, the real economic situation is exactly the same for the five different methods. See Self-Study Problem 2 for another example, to compare the accounting for the different methods of reporting. This example shows that the timing of reporting income is different but the cumulative results are the same. If this is so, which method best represents the real economic situation? This is a question we should ask as we study different accounting and reporting methods throughout the course. Many of the end-of-chapter problems ask this question and give you an opportunity to express your own opinion.

L07   ## ASPE DIFFERENCES

As mentioned in Chapter 1 and as we have seen in this chapter, most of the discussion in this textbook deal with IFRSs. Starting in this chapter and in each subsequent chapter, we will have a section at the end on Canadian accounting standards for private enterprises, which we will refer to as ASPE. In this section, the differences in the reporting requirements for private entities for the topics discussed in the chapter will be summarized. Detailed illustrations will not be provided.

Section 3051: Investments of Part II of the *CICA Handbook* has different standards for a private enterprise than for a publicly accountable enterprise. The following excerpts from Section 3051 outline the main requirements for significant influence investments:

> Under ASPE, investments in associates can be reported using the cost method, equity method, or at fair value.

- An investor that is able to exercise significant influence over an investee should make an accounting policy choice to account for the investment using either the equity method or the cost method. An investor should account for all investments within the scope of this section using the same method.

- When an investee's equity securities are traded in an active market, the cost method cannot be used. Under such circumstances, the investment should be accounted for using the equity method or at fair value, with changes in fair value recorded in net income.

- The investments in and income from companies subject to significant influence, and other investments accounted for at cost, should be reported separately.

ASPE is also quite different for financial instruments. The following excerpts from Section 3856: Financial Instruments of Part II of the *CICA Handbook* outline the main requirements for nonstrategic investments:

- Nonstrategic investments in equity instruments that are quoted in an active market should be reported at fair value, and any changes in fair value should be reported in net income.
- Nonstrategic investments in equity instruments that are not quoted in an active market should be reported at cost less any reduction for impairment, and the impairment losses should be reported in net income.
- An entity may irrevocably elect to measure any equity investment at fair value by designating that fair value measurement shall apply.
- Other comprehensive income does not exist under ASPE.

> Under ASPE, nonstrategic equity investments should be reported at cost unless the value of the investment is quoted in an active market or the entity elects to report at fair value.

U.S. GAAP DIFFERENCES

U.S. GAAP and IFRSs are essentially the same for investments in associates. The minor differences are summarized as follows:

1. Whereas IFRSs require that the time between reporting dates of the investor and associate must not be more than three months and that the reporting entity must adjust for any significant intervening transactions, U.S. GAAP state that the time between reporting dates generally should not be more than three months and the reporting entity must disclose the effects of (and may adjust for) any significant intervening transactions.

2. Whereas IFRSs require that the accounting policies of the investor and associate conform, the SEC staff does not require policies to conform, provided that policies are in accordance with U.S. GAAP.

3. Losses in excess of the investor's interest in the associate should continue to be recognized when the associate is imminently expected to return to profitability.

> There are some minor differences between U.S. GAAP and IFRSs for reporting investments in associates.

> **Cautionary Note:** When answering the end-of-chapter material for Chapters 2 through 11, assume that IFRSs are to be applied unless otherwise stated.

SUMMARY

FVTPL and FCTOCI investments and most AFS investments are reported at fair value. Dividends from these investments are reported in income when they are declared. Unrealized gains and losses are reported in net income for FVTPL investments and in OCI for FVTOCI and AFS investments. If a quoted market price in an active market is not available for the AFS investments, these investments are reported using the cost method. AFS investments will cease to exist as an investment category when IFRS 9 becomes mandatory on January 1, 2015, or when a reporting entity chooses to adopt IFRS 9 early.

An investment where the investor is able to significantly influence the operations of the investee is called an *investment in associate* and must be accounted for using the equity method, as described in IAS 28. This requires the investor to record its share of any changes in the shareholders' equity of the investee, adjusted for the amortization of the acquisition differential and the holdback and realization of profits from the intercompany sale of assets.

Significant Changes in GAAP in the Last Three Years

1. The effective date for IFRS 9 has been changed from January 1, 2013, to January 1, 2015, with early adoption permitted. Under IFRS 9, all nonstrategic equity investments must be measured at fair value, with changes in fair value reported in net income; however, an entity can irrevocably elect on initial recognition to report the fair value changes on an equity investment that is not held for short-term trading in other comprehensive income.

2. IFRS 10 replaced certain components of IAS 28 and SIC 12; IFRS 11 replaced IAS 31 and SIC 13; and IRFS 12 replaced the disclosure requirements previously listed in IAS 28 and 31.

3. IFRS 13 is a new standard on fair value measurement. It replaces the fair value measurement guidance that was previously contained in individual IFRSs with a single, unified definition of fair value and a framework for measuring fair value. It also states the required disclosures about fair value measurements. It includes guidance to determine fair value measurement in inactive or illiquid markets. *Fair value* is defined as the price that would be received to sell an asset or paid to transfer a liability in an orderly transaction between market participants at the measurement date (i.e., an exit price). It would reflect the highest and best use for non financial assets.

Changes Expected in GAAP in the Next Three Years

No major changes are expected in the next three years for the topics discussed in this chapter.

SELF-STUDY PROBLEM 1

Part A
LO2, 3

On January 1, Year 5, High Inc. purchased 10% of the outstanding common shares of Lowe Corp. for $192,000. From High's perspective, Lowe was a FVTPL investment. The fair value of High's investment was $200,000 at December 31, Year 5.

On January 1, Year 6, High purchased an additional 25% of Lowe's shares for $500,000. This second purchase allowed High to exert significant influence over Lowe. There was no acquisition differential on the date of the 25% acquisition.

During the two years, Lowe reported the following:

	Profit	Dividends
Year 5	$200,000	$120,000
Year 6	270,000	130,000

Required:

Prepare High's journal entries with respect to this investment for both Year 5 and Year 6.

Part B   The following are summarized income statements for the two companies for Year 7:

	High Inc.	Lowe Corp.
Operating income before income taxes	$750,000	$340,000
Income tax expense	300,000	140,000
Net income before discontinued operations	450,000	200,000
Loss from discontinued operations (net of tax)	—	20,000
Net income	*$450,000	$180,000

*The net income of High does not include any investment income from its investment in Lowe.

Lowe paid no dividends in Year 7.

Required:

(a) Prepare the journal entries that High should make at the end of Year 7 with respect to its investment in Lowe.

(b) Prepare High's income statement for Year 7, taking into consideration the journal entries in part (a).

SOLUTION TO SELF-STUDY PROBLEM 1

The 10% purchase should be accounted for under the fair value method. High's journal entries during Year 5 are as follows:

Investment in Lowe	192,000	
Cash		192,000
Purchase of 10% of shares of Lowe		
Cash (10% × 120,000)	12,000	
Dividend income		12,000
Investment in Lowe (200,000 − 192,000)	8,000	
Unrealized gain on FVTPL investment		8,000

The 25% purchase in Year 6 changes the investment to one of significant influence, which is accounted for prospectively under the equity method.
The journal entries in Year 6 are as follows:

Investment in Lowe	500,000	
Cash		500,000
Purchase of additional 25% of shares of Lowe		
Investment in Lowe (35% × 270,000 profit)	94,500	
Investment income		94,500
Cash (35% × 130,000 dividends)	45,500	
Investment in Lowe		45,500

Part B   (a)   Applying the equity method, High makes the following journal entries in Year 7:

Investment in Lowe (35% × 180,000)	63,000	
Discontinued operations—investment loss, (35% × 20,000)	7,000	
Investment Income (35% × 200,000)		70,000

(b)

HIGH INC.
INCOME STATEMENT
Year Ended December 31, Year 7

Operating income	$750,000
Investment income*	70,000
Income before income taxes	820,000
Income tax expense	300,000
Net income before discontinued operations	520,000
Discontinued operations − investment loss (net of tax)*	7,000
Net income	$513,000

*A footnote would disclose that these items, in whole or in part, came from a 35% investment in Lowe, accounted for using the equity method.

SELF-STUDY PROBLEM 2

LO2, 3, 6   On January 1, Year 1, Joshua Corp. purchased 20% of the outstanding ordinary shares of Deng Company at a cost of $950,000. Deng reported profit of $900,000 and paid dividends of $600,000 for the year ended December 31, Year 1. The market value of Joshua's 20% interest in Deng was $990,000 at December 31, Year 1. On June 30, Year 2, Deng paid dividends of $350,000. On July 2, Year 2 Joshua sold its investment in Deng for $1,005,000. Deng did not prepare financial statements for Year 2 until early in Year 3.

Required:

(a) Prepare the journal entries for Joshua Corp. for Years 1 and 2 for the above-noted transactions under the following reporting methods: cost, equity, FVTPL, and FVTOCI.

(b) Prepare a schedule to show the profit, OCI, comprehensive income, and change in retained earnings for Joshua for Year 1, Year 2, and the total of the changes for Years 1 and 2 under the four methods.

(c) Prepare a schedule to compare the change in cash with change in profit, comprehensive income, and retained earnings for Joshua for the sum of the two years under the four methods.

(d) Comment on the similarities and differences in financial reporting for the four methods.

SOLUTION TO SELF-STUDY PROBLEM 2

(a) Credit entries are noted in brackets.

	Cost	Equity	FVTPL	FVTOCI
Jan. 1, Year 1				
Investment in Deng	950,000	950,000	950,000	950,000
Cash	(950,000)	(950,000)	(950,000)	(950,000)
To record the acquisition of 20% of Deng's shares				
Dec. 31, Year 1				
Investment in Deng (20% × 900,000)		180,000		
Investment income		(180,000)		
Accrue share of profit				
Cash (20% × 600,000)	120,000	120,000	120,000	120,000
Dividend income	(120,000)		(120,000)	(120,000)
Investment in Deng		(120,000)		
Receipt of dividend from Deng				
Investment in Deng (990,000 − 950,000)			40,000	40,000
Unrealized gains (reported in profit)			(40,000)	
OCI				(40,000)
To record investment at fair value				
June 30, Year 2				
Cash (20% × 350,000)	70,000	70,000	70,000	70,000
Dividend income	(70,000)		(70,000)	(70,000)
Investment in Deng		(70,000)		
Receipt of dividend from Deng				
July 2, Year 2				
Cash	1,005,000	1,005,000	1,005,000	1,005,000
Investment in Deng	(950,000)	(940,000)	(990,000)	(990,000)
Gain on sale (reported in profit)	(55,000)	(65,000)	(15,000)	
OCI–unrealized gains				(15,000)
Record sale of investment				
Accumulated OCI–reclassification to retained earnings				55,000
Retained earnings				(55,000)
Clear accumulated OCI to retained earnings				

(b)

(in $000s)	Cost			Equity			FVTPL			FVTOCI		
	YR1	YR2	Total	YR1	YR2	Total	YR1	YR2	Total	YR1	YR2	Total
Profit	120	125	245	180	65	245	160	85	245	120	70	190
OCI										40	15	55
Comprehensive income	120	125	245	180	65	245	160	85	245	160	85	245
Change in retained earnings	120	125	245	180	65	245	160	85	245	120	125	245

(c)

(in $000s)	Cost	Equity	FVTPL	FVTOCI
Cash received				
Dividends in Year 1	120	120	120	120
Dividends in Year 2	70	70	70	70
Sales proceeds in Year 2	1,005	1,005	1,005	1,005
Total cash received	1,195	1,195	1,195	1,195

(continued)

Cash paid for investment	950	950	950	950
Change in cash	245	245	245	245
= Change in profit	245	245	245	190
= Change in comprehensive income	245	245	245	245
= Change in retained earnings	245	245	245	245

(d)

Similarities

– Change in cash is the same for all methods.
– Profit for the two years in total is the same for the first three methods and comprehensive income is the same for all methods.
– Change in retained earnings for the two years in total is the same for all methods.
– Change in cash is equal to change in profit for the two years in total for the first three methods.
– Change in cash is equal to change in comprehensive income for the two years in total for all methods.
– Change in cash is equal to change in retained earnings for the two years in total for all methods.

Differences

– Timing of income recognition is different.
– Gains from appreciation go through profit for first three methods but never get reported in profit for the FVTOCI investment.

REVIEW QUESTIONS

LO1   1. How is the concept of a business combination related to the concept of a parent–subsidiary relationship?

LO2   2. Distinguish between the financial reporting for FVTPL investments and that for investments in associates.

LO2   3. What is the difference between a "control" investment and a "joint control" investment?

LO1   4. What is the purpose of IFRS 8 on Operating Segments?

LO2, 4   5. What criteria would be used to determine whether the equity method should be used to account for a particular investment?

LO3   6. The equity method records dividends as a reduction in the investment account. Explain why.

LO4   7. The Ralston Company owns 35% of the outstanding voting shares of Purina Inc. Under what circumstances would Ralston determine that it is inappropriate to report this investment using the equity method?

LO3   8. Because of the acquisition of additional investee shares, an investor may need to change from the fair value method for a FVTPL investment to the equity method for a significant influence investment. What procedures are applied to effect this accounting change?

LO3 9. An investor uses the equity method to report its investment in an investee. During the current year, the investee reports other comprehensive income on its statement of comprehensive income. How should this item be reflected in the investor's financial statements?

LO3 10. Ashton Inc. acquired a 40% interest in Villa Corp. at a bargain price because Villa had suffered significant losses in past years. Ashton's cost was $200,000. In the first year after acquisition, Villa reported a loss of $700,000. Using the equity method, how should Ashton account for this loss?

LO3 11. Able Company holds a 40% interest in Baker Corp. During the year, Able sold a portion of this investment. How should this investment be reported after the sale?

LO5 12. Briefly describe the disclosure requirements related to an investment in an associated company.

LO6 13. Which of the reporting methods described in this chapter would typically report the highest current ratio? Briefly explain.

LO7 14. How should a private company that has opted to follow ASPE report an investment in an associate?

LO2 15. How will the investment in a private company be reported under IFRS 9, and how does this differ from IAS 39?

CASES

Case 2-1
LO2, 3, 4

Hil Company purchased 10,000 common shares (10%) of Ton Inc. on January 1, Year 4, for $345,000, when Ton's shareholders' equity was $2,600,000, and it classified the investment as a FVTPL security. On January 1, Year 5, Hil acquired an additional 15,000 common shares (15%) of Ton for $525,000. On both dates, any difference between the purchase price and the carrying amount of Ton's shareholders' equity was attributed to land. The market value of Ton's common shares was $35 per share on December 31, Year 4, and $37 per share on December 31, Year 5. Ton reported net income of $500,000 in Year 4 and $520,000 in Year 5, and paid dividends of $480,000 in both years.

The management of Hil is very excited about the increase in ownership interest in Ton because Ton has been very profitable. Hil pays a bonus to management based on its net income determined in accordance with GAAP.

The management of Hil is wondering how the increase in ownership will affect the reporting of the investment in Ton. Will Hil continue to classify the investment as FVTPL in Year 5? What factors will be considered in determining whether the equity method should now be used? If the equity method is now appropriate, will the change be made retroactively? They would like to see a comparison of income for Year 5 and the balance in the investment account at the end of Year 5 under the two options for reporting this investment. Last but not least, they would like to get your opinion on which method should be used to best reflect the performance of Hil for Year 5.

Required:

Respond to the questions raised and the requests made by management. Prepare schedules and/or financial statements to support your presentation.

Case 2-2
LO2, 4, 7

Floyd's Specialty Foods Inc. (FSFI) operates over 60 shops throughout Ontario. The company was founded by George Floyd when he opened a single shop in the city of Cornwall. This store sold prepared dinners and directed its products at customers who were too busy to prepare meals after a long day at work. The concept proved to be very successful, and more stores were opened in Cornwall. Recently, new stores were opened in five other Ontario cities. Up to the current year, the shares of FSFI have been owned entirely by Floyd. However, during this year, the company suffered severe cash flow problems, due to too-rapid expansion exacerbated by a major decline in economic activity. Profitability suffered and creditors threatened to take legal action for long-overdue accounts. To avoid bankruptcy, Floyd sought additional financing from his old friend James Connelly, who is a majority shareholder of Cornwall Autobody Inc. (CAI), a public company. Subsequently, CAI paid $950,000 cash to FSFI to acquire enough newly issued shares of common stock for a one-third interest.

At the end of this year, CAI's accountants are discussing how they should properly report this investment in the company's financial statements.

One argues for maintaining the asset at original cost, saying, "What we have done is to advance money to bail out these stores. Floyd will continue to run the organization with little or no attention to us, so in effect we have lent him money. After all, what does anyone in our company know about the specialty food business? My guess is that as soon as the stores become solvent, Floyd will want to buy back our shares."

Another accountant disagrees, stating that the equity method is appropriate. "I realize that our company is not capable of running a specialty food company. But the requirements state that ownership of over 20% is evidence of significant influence."

A third accountant supports equity method reporting for a different reason. "If the investment gives us the ability to exert significant influence, that is all that is required. We don't have to actually exert it. One-third of the common shares certainly give us that ability."

Required:

How should CAI report its investment? Your answer should include a discussion of all three accountants' positions.

Case 2-3
LO2, 4, 6

Magno Industries Ltd., a public company, is a major supplier to the automotive replacement-parts market, selling parts to nearly every segment of the industry. Magno has a September 30 year-end.

During January Year 5, Magno acquired a 13% interest in the common shares of Grille-to-Bumper Automotive Stores, and in June Year 5 it acquired an additional 15%. Grille-to-Bumper is a retail chain of company-owned automotive replacement parts stores operating in most Canadian provinces. Its shares are not traded in an active market. Grille-to-Bumper has a December 31 year-end and, despite being profitable each year for the last 10 years, has never paid a dividend. While

Magno occasionally makes sales to Grille-to-Bumper, it has never been one of its major suppliers.

After the second acquisition of Grille-to-Bumper's shares, Magno Industries contacted Grille-to-Bumper to obtain certain financial information and to discuss mutual timing problems with respect to financial reporting. In the initial contact, Magno found Grille-to-Bumper to be uncooperative. In addition, Grille-to-Bumper accused Magno of attempting to take it over. Magno replied that it had no intention of attempting to gain control but rather was interested only in making a sound long-term investment. Grille-to-Bumper was not impressed with this explanation and refused to have any further discussions regarding future information exchanges and the problems created by a difference in year-ends.

At the year-end of September 30, Year 5, Magno's management expressed a desire to use the equity method to account for its investment.

Required:

(a) What method of accounting would you recommend Magno Industries use for its investment in Grille-to-Bumper Automotive common shares? As part of your answer, discuss the alternatives available.

(b) Why would the management of Magno want to use the equity method to account for the investment, as compared with other alternatives that you have discussed?

(c) Are there any circumstances under which the method you have recommended might have to be changed? If so, how would Magno Industries account for such a change?

Case 2-4
LO3

Canadian Computer Systems Limited (CCS) is a public company engaged in the development of computer software and the manufacturing of computer hardware. CCS is listed on a Canadian stock exchange and has a 40% non-controlling interest in Sandra Investments Limited (SIL), a U.S. public company that was de-listed by an American stock exchange due to financial difficulties. In addition, CCS has three wholly owned subsidiaries.

CCS is audited by Roth & Minch, a large public accounting firm. You, the CA, are the audit manager responsible for the engagement.

CCS has a September 30 fiscal year-end. It is now mid-November, Year 11, and the year-end audit is nearing completion. CCS's draft financial statements are included in Exhibit I. While reviewing the audit working papers (see Exhibit II), you identify several issues that raise doubts about CCS's ability to realize its assets and discharge its liabilities in the normal course of business.

After you have reviewed the situation with the engagement partner, he asks you to prepare a memo for his use in discussing the going-concern problem with the president of CCS, and suggests that you look to IAS 1 for guidance. Your memo should include all factors necessary to assess CCS's ability to continue operations. You are also to comment on the accounting and disclosure implications.

Required:

Prepare the memo requested by the partner.

(CICA adapted)

EXHIBIT I

CANADIAN COMPUTER SYSTEMS LIMITED
EXTRACTS FROM CONSOLIDATED BALANCE SHEET
As at September 30
(in thousands of dollars)

	Year 11	Year 10
Assets		
Current assets		
Cash	$ 190	$ 170
Accounts receivable	2,540	1,600
Inventories, at the lower of cost and net realizable value	610	420
	3,340	2,190
Plant assets (net of accumulated depreciation)	33,930	34,970
Property held for resale	1,850	1,840
Other assets	410	420
	$39,530	$39,420
Liabilities		
Current liabilities		
Demand loans	$ 1,150	$ 3,080
Accrued interest payable	11,510	10,480
Accounts payable	2,500	2,100
Mortgages payable due currently because of loan defaults	21,600	21,600
Long-term debt due within one year	290	1,780
Debt obligation of Sandra Investments Limited	50,000	55,420
	87,050	94,460
Long-term debt	26,830	21,330
Other long-term liabilities	250	330
	114,130	116,120
Contributed Capital and Deficit		
Contributed capital		
Issued:		
261 9% cumulative, convertible, preferred shares	10	10
1,000,000 Class B preferred shares	250	250
10,243,019 Common shares	100,170	100,010
	100,430	100,270
Deficit	(175,030)	(176,970)
	(74,600)	(76,700)
	$ 39,530	$39,420

CANADIAN COMPUTER SYSTEMS LIMITED
EXTRACTS FROM CONSOLIDATED STATEMENT
OF OPERATIONS AND DEFICIT
For the years ended September 30
(in thousands of dollars)

	Year 11	Year 10
Sales		
Hardware	$ 12,430	$ 19,960
Software	3,070	3,890
	15,500	23,850
Other income	1,120	–
	16,620	23,850

(continued)

EXHIBIT I   *(continued)*

Expenses		
Operating	10,240	15,050
Interest	4,590	4,690
General and administrative	2,970	4,140
Depreciation	2,400	3,630
Provision for impairment in plant assets	—	2,220
	20,200	29,730
Loss before the undernoted items	(3,580)	(5,880)
Loss from Sandra Investments Limited	(2,830)	(55,420)
Loss before discontinued operations	(6,410)	(61,300)
Gain (loss) from discontinued operations	8,350	(4,040)
Net income (loss)	1,940	(65,340)
Deficit, beginning of year	(176,970)	(111,630)
Deficit, end of year	$(175,030)	$(176,970)

EXHIBIT II

EXTRACTS FROM AUDIT WORKING PAPERS

1. Cash receipts are collected by one of CCS's banks. This bank then releases funds to CCS based on operating budgets prepared by management. Demand loans bearing interest at 1% over the bank's prime rate are used to finance ongoing operations. The demand loans are secured by a general assignment of accounts receivable and a floating-charge debenture on all assets.

2. CCS accounts for its interest in SIL using the equity method. As a result of SIL's recurring losses in prior years, the investment account was written off in Year 9. In Year 10, CCS recorded in its accounts the amount of SIL's bank loan and accrued interest, as CCS guaranteed this amount. During Year 11, CCS made debt payments of $5.42 million and interest payments of $1.8 million on behalf of SIL. In October Year 11, SIL issued preferred shares in the amount of US$40 million, used the proceeds to pay down the bank loan, and was re-listed on the stock exchange. Interest expense on the debt obligation in Year 11 totalled $2.83 million and has been included in the income statement under "Loss from Sandra Investments Limited."

3. Current liabilities include mortgages payable of $21.6 million due currently. They have been reclassified from long-term debt because of CCS's failure to comply with operating covenants and restrictions. The prior year's financial statements have been restated for comparative purposes.

4. Long-term debt is repayable over varying periods of time. However, the banks reserve the right to declare the loans due and payable upon demand. The loan agreements require CCS to obtain advance approval in writing from the bank if it wishes to exceed certain limits on borrowing and capital expenditures. The agreements also prohibit the sale of certain plant assets, payment of dividends, and transfer of funds among related companies without prior written approval. One loan of $15 million was in default at September 30, Year 11.

5. During the year, CCS issued common shares to the directors and officers to satisfy amounts owing to them totalling $160,000. New equity issues are being considered for the Year 12 fiscal year.

6. On November 10, Year 11, a claim related to a breach of contract was filed against one of the company's subsidiaries in the amount of $3.7 million, plus interest and costs of the action. Management believes that this claim is without merit. However, if any amounts do have to be paid as a result of this action, management believes that the amounts would be covered by liability insurance.

7. In Year 11, operating expenses include $1 million in development costs relating to a computer software program. Sales of this software are expected to commence in Year 12.

Case 2-5
LO2, 7

"The thing you, the CA, have to understand is how these stage plays work. You start out with just an idea, but generally no cash. That's where promoters like me come in. First, we set up a separate legal entity for each play. Then, we find ways of raising the money necessary to get the play written and the actors trained. If the play is a success, we hope to recover all those costs and a whole lot more, but cash flow is the problem. Since less than half of all plays make money, you cannot get very much money from banks.

"Take my current project, *Penguins in Paradise*. You only have to look at the cash inflows (Exhibit III) to see how many sources I had to approach to get the cash. As you can see, most of the initial funding comes from the investors in the Penguins in Paradise Limited Partnership (PIP). They put up their money to buy units in the limited partnership. One main reason a partnership is used is to let them immediately write off, for tax purposes, the costs of producing the play.

"Some investors do not want to invest the amount required for a partnership unit. So, for them, we structure the deal a little differently. Instead of buying a unit in the partnership, they buy a right to a royalty—a percentage of future operating profits (i.e., gross revenue less true operating expenses). In this way, these investors get an interest in the play without being in the partnership. Since they do not have a vote at the partnership meetings, they are more concerned about their risks. However, we agreed that PIP would get term insurance on my life in case I get hit by a truck!

"Funding the play is not that easy. The money that the investors put up is not enough to fund all the start-up costs, so you have to be creative. Take reservation fees, for example. You know how tough it is to get good seats for a really hot play. Well, PIP sold the right to buy great seats to some dedicated theatre-goers this year for next year's performance. These amounts are non-refundable, and the great thing is that the buyers still have to pay full price for the tickets when they buy them.

EXHIBIT III

PENGUINS IN PARADISE (A LIMITED PARTNERSHIP)
SUMMARY OF CASH FLOWS

For the period ended December 31, Year 1
(in thousands of dollars)

Cash inflows	
Investor contributions to limited partnership	$5,000
Sale of royalty rights	1,000
Bank loan	2,000
Sale of movie rights	500
Government grant	50
Reservation fees	20
	8,570
Cash outflows	
Salaries and fees	3,500
Costumes and sets	1,000
Life insurance	10
Miscellaneous costs	1,250
	5,760
Net cash inflows	$2,810

"Consider the sale of movie rights. Lots of good plays get turned into movies. Once the stage play is a success, the movie rights are incredibly expensive. My idea was to sell the movie rights in advance. PIP got a lot less money, but at least we got it up front when we needed it.

"The other sources are much the same. We received the government grant by agreeing to have at least 50% Canadian content. We also negotiated a bank loan with an interest rate of 5% a year plus 1% of the gross revenue of the play, instead of the usual 20% interest a year. Even my fee for putting the deal together was taken as a percentage of the operating profits, so just about everybody has a strong interest in the play's performance.

"As you know, I know nothing about accounting, so I need you to put together a set of financial statements. I will need you to certify that they are in accordance with GAAP for enterprises such as *Penguins in Paradise* because the investors and the bank require this. Since everybody else has taken an interest in the play in lieu of cash, I would like you to consider doing the same for your fees."

When you, the CA, discussed this conversation with a partner in your office, he asked you to prepare a memo addressing the major accounting implications of the client's requests.

Required:

(a) Prepare the memo to the partner.
(b) Briefly discuss how the following three investor groups would classify and account for their investment:
  (i) Investor in Limited Partnership units
  (ii) Investor in royalties
  (iii) Investor in movie rights

(CICA adapted)

Case 2-6
LO2, 4

Michael Metals Limited (MML) has been a private company since it was incorporated under federal legislation over 40 years ago. At the present time (September, Year 5), ownership is divided among four cousins, each of whom holds 25% of the 100 outstanding common shares of MML. Each shareholder obtained the shares from his or her parents, who formed and operated the company for many years.

The owners have decided to offer the business for sale over a period of years. Laser Investments Limited (LIL), a public company holding shares of companies in a number of other businesses, has been given the opportunity to acquire 46.67% of MML immediately, and the balance over the next five years. The proposal is to purchase 70 shares now as follows:

		Percentage
Obtain 33.33% by purchasing 50 new shares of MML	50	33.33%
Acquire one-fifth of the shares held by each cousin, reducing		
their shares from 25 to 20 each	20	13.34%
	70	46.67%

The other 80 shares would be acquired at a rate of four per year from each cousin for five years. The purchase price of the 80 shares would be tied to MML's profitability as measured by accounting standards for private enterprises (ASPE).

The board of directors of LIL is interested in pursuing the investment in MML. The proposed purchase price of the initial 70 shares is to be partially based on the financial statements for fiscal Year 5 and for future years. The board of directors of LIL has asked its advisors, Bouchard and Co., Chartered Accountants, to assist it in evaluating the proposed purchase. Jules Bouchard, the partner in charge of the engagement, has asked you, the CA, to prepare a memo discussing (1) all relevant business considerations pertaining to the purchase so that he can discuss the issues with the board of directors and (2) how LIL should report its investment in MML if it were to proceed with the purchase of 70 shares.

MML has always been a scrap-metal dealer, primarily of iron and copper. In recent years, it has also dealt in lead, brass, aluminum, and other metals. Scrap iron is acquired from a variety of sources (e.g., old automobiles, appliances, and spoilage during manufacturing processes) and is sorted, compacted, and sold to steel mills. Much of the scrap copper is coated electrical wiring, which has to be stripped of the insulation coating and then chopped into pieces. The copper wire pieces are stored in barrels, which are about one metre high. In summary, a limited amount of processing is needed to convert the purchased scrap into saleable products.

Most of the scrap arrives at MML's storage yards on trucks, which are weighed both loaded and empty in order to determine the physical quantities of scrap on the truck. Some of the scrap is kept indoors, but most is kept outdoors in several large piles in different yard locations. MML's property is protected by tall wire fences and monitored by security cameras 24 hours a day.

To be successful in this industry, a scrap dealer has to buy at low prices and store the processed or unprocessed scrap until metal prices are high. Sometimes, quantities of some grades of metal have to be stored for several years. When selling prices are stable, the purchase price has to be sufficiently low that a profit can be made after processing costs have been incurred.

MML tends to operate at its maximum bank line of credit, as it is generally short of cash. MML's maximum line of credit is 70% of its receivables and 50% of its inventory.

Your client arranged for you to have access to all of MML's accounting records and the auditors' working papers. MML's fiscal year-end is June 30. From the accounting records and auditors' working papers, you and your staff have assembled the information provided in Exhibit IV.

Required:

Prepare the memo.

(CICA adapted)

EXHIBIT IV

INFORMATION GATHERED BY CA FROM MML'S ACCOUNTING RECORDS AND AUDITORS' WORKING PAPERS

1. From audit working paper reviews:

   a. Most of the processing equipment and the buildings are old and almost fully depreciated. The company's land was purchased many years ago. As a result, inventory often represents two-thirds of the balance sheet assets, and receivables are close to one-fifth of assets in most years. Total assets vary between $25 and $32 million from year to year. Accounts receivable turnover can be anywhere between 1.5 and 4 times per year.

   (continued)

EXHIBIT IV   *(continued)*

b. Perpetual records are limited to estimates of quantity because the quality of the scrap, the amount of insulation on wires, and a variety of other factors affect how much saleable metal will result from a bulk purchase of scrap.

c. A seller of scrap seldom knows how much it weighs. MML usually quotes a price per unit, but does not inform the seller of the weight until the delivery truck has been weighed at MML's yard. MML's auditors are suspicious that MML reduces weights before calculating the amount payable.

d. The auditors visit MML's yard and offices three times per year to conduct an interim audit, to attend the physical inventory count, and to carry out year-end substantive audit procedures.

2. MML owns 40% of a joint venture, Green Environmental Limited (GEL), a waste disposal company. The other 60% is owned by the spouses of the four cousins who own MML. All of MML's waste is handled by GEL, and MML purchases scrap iron and wire from GEL.

3. MML deals with a Japanese trading company that allows lengthy credit terms and uses letters of credit stating that MML does not have to pay for five or six months. A substantial amount of MML's metal purchases are from various sites that are owned by the Japanese company.

4. The truck weigh scales produce weigh tickets that can be attached to receivable and payable invoices. However, no numerical ticket sequence exists to account for all tickets that have been printed. Receiving records are handwritten in a loose-leaf book.

5. Approximately 15% of sales invoices have to be adjusted for weight discrepancies between what was shipped and what the customer claims to have received. On average, the reductions are approximately 20% of the invoice amount.

6. The perpetual inventory weight records appear to have been adjusted each year to whatever the physical inventory count indicated.

7. In recent years, the after-tax profits of MML have ranged between $1.2 and $3 million, after management bonuses.

8. MML maintains two vacation homes, one in Florida and one in Barbados. These homes are usually occupied by suppliers and customers of MML, free of charge.

9. Accounts receivable and inventory are pledged as security to MML's bank. In addition, the bank has a general security agreement against all other assets, and has limited personal guarantees from the shareholders.

10. Revenue is usually recognized on shipment of the metal. Adjustments for weight discrepancies are made as they become known to MML.

11. MML's management has been considering expansion because one competitor is nearing retirement and wants to sell his company. In recent years, MML has purchased from, and sold to, this competitor. MML has also borrowed inventory from and loaned inventory to this competitor.

12. Some purchases of scrap are acquired on a conditional basis. MML pays the supplier only after it has determined the quality of metal that the scrap yielded when processed.

PROBLEMS

Problem 2-1
LO2, 3

PART A

On January 1, Year 5, Anderson Corporation paid $650,000 for 20,000 (20%) of the outstanding shares of Carter Inc. The investment was considered to be one of significant influence. In Year 5, Carter reported profit of $95,000; in Year 6, its profit was $105,000. Dividends paid were $60,000 in each of the two years.

Required:

Calculate the balance in Anderson's investment account as at December 31, Year 6.

PART B

Now assume that on December 31, Year 6, Anderson lost its ability to significantly influence the operating, investing, and financing decisions for Carter when another party obtained sufficient shares in the open market to obtain control over Carter. Accordingly, the investment in Carter was reclassified as a FVTPL investment. The fair value of the Carter shares was $35 per share on this date.

In Year 7, Carter reported profit of $115,000 and paid dividends of $50,000. On December 31, Year 7, Anderson sold its investment in Carter for $37 per share.

Required:

(a) Prepare the journal entry at December 31, Year 6, to reclassify the investment from significant influence to FVTPL.
(b) Prepare all journal entries for Year 7 related to Anderson's investment in Carter.

Problem 2-2
LO2, 3

Baskin purchased 20,000 common shares (20%) of Robbin on January 1, Year 5, for $275,000 and classified the investment as FVTPL. Robbin reported net income of $85,000 in Year 5 and $90,000 in Year 6, and paid dividends of $40,000 in each year. Robbin's shares were trading at $16 per share on December 31, Year 5, and January 1, Year 6. On January 1, Year 6, Baskin obtained significant influence over the operating, investing, and financing decisions of Robbin when the controlling shareholder sold some shares in the open market and lost control over Robbin. Accordingly, the investment in Robbin was reclassified to an investment in associate. On December 31, Year 6, Baskin sold its investment in Robbin for $17 per share.

Required:

Prepare all journal entries for Years 5 and 6 related to Baskin's investment in Robbin.

Problem 2-3
LO3, 5, 7

On January 1, Year 5, Blake Corporation purchased 30% of the outstanding common shares of Stergis Limited for $1,500,000.

The following relates to Stergis since the acquisition date:

Year	Net Income	Other Comprehensive Income	Dividends Paid
Year 5	$ 42,000	$10,000	$60,000
Year 6	120,000	25,000	60,000

Required:

(a) Assume that Blake is a public company and the number of shares held by Blake is enough to give it significant influence over Stergis. Prepare all the journal entries that Blake should make regarding this investment in Year 5 and Year 6. Also, state the disclosure requirements for Year 6 pertaining to Blake's investment in Stergis.
(b) Assume that Blake is a private company. Even though it has significant influence, it chose to use the cost method to account for its investment. Prepare all the journal entries that Blake should make regarding this investment in Year 5 and Year 6.
(c) If Blake wants to show the lowest debt-to-equity ratio at the end of Year 6, would it prefer to use the cost or equity method to report its investment in Stergis? Briefly explain.

Problem 2-4
LO3, 6
Pender Corp. paid $234,000 for a 30% interest in Saltspring Limited on January 1, Year 6. During Year 6, Saltspring paid dividends of $100,000 and reported profit as follows:

Profit before discontinued operations	$288,000
Discontinued operations loss (net of tax)	(30,000)
Profit	$258,000

Pender's profit for Year 6 consisted of $900,000 in sales, expenses of $400,000, income tax expense of $200,000, and its investment income from Saltspring. Both companies have an income tax rate of 40%.

Required:

(a) Assume that Pender reports its investment using the equity method.
   (i) Prepare all journal entries necessary to account for Pender's investment for Year 6.
   (ii) Determine the correct balance in Pender's investment account at December 31, Year 6.
   (iii) Prepare an income statement for Pender for Year 6.

(b) Assume that Pender uses the cost method.
   (i) Prepare all journal entries necessary to account for Pender's investment for Year 6.
   (ii) Determine the correct balance in Pender's investment account at December 31, Year 6.
   (iii) Prepare an income statement for Pender for Year 6.

(c) Which reporting method would Pender want to use if its bias is to report the highest possible return on investment to users of its financial statements? Briefly explain and show supporting calculations.

Problem 2-5
LO2, 3
Her Company purchased 20,000 common shares (20%) of Him Inc. on January 1, Year 4, for $340,000. Additional information on Him for the three years ending December 31, Year 6, is as follows:

Year	Net Income	Dividends Paid	Market Value per Share at December 31
Year 4	$200,000	$150,000	$18
Year 5	225,000	160,000	20
Year 6	240,000	175,000	23

On December 31, Year 6, Her sold its investment in Him for $460,000.

Required:

(a) Compute the balance in the investment account at the end of Year 5, assuming that the investment is classified as one of the following:
   (i) FVTPL
   (ii) Investment in associate
   (iii) FVTOCI

(b) Calculate how much income will be reported in net income and other comprehensive income in each of Years 4, 5, and 6, and in total for the three years assuming that the investment is classified as one of the following:

    (i) FVTPL

    (ii) Investment in associate

    (iii) FVTOCI

(c) What are the similarities and differences in your answers for the three parts of (b)?

Problem 2-6
LO2

COX Limited is a multinational telecommunication company owned by a Canadian businesswoman. It has numerous long-term investments in a wide variety of equity instruments.

Some investments have to be measured at fair value at each reporting date. In turn, the unrealized gains will be reported in either net income or other comprehensive income. Since COX has considerable external financing through a number of Canadian banks, it applies IFRSs for public companies in its general-purpose financial statements.

The CFO of COX has heard about the reporting standards for equity investments but has had limited time to study them in detail. He would like you to prepare a presentation on the reporting requirements. He wants to understand how equity investments should be reported. More specifically, he wants to know

- which investments must be measured at fair value and what the main rationale for this method of reporting is;
- how to determine whether the unrealized gains are to be reported in net income or other comprehensive income, and what the main rationale for the difference in reporting is; and
- which investments, if any, will still be reported using the cost method, using the equity method, or on a consolidated basis.

Required:

Prepare the slides for the presentation. Limit your presentation to six slides. Your presentation should cover the reporting of (1) FVTPL, (2) FVTOCI, (3) cost method, (4) investments in associates and (5) investment in subsidiaries.

(CGA-Canada adapted)

Problem 2-7
LO7

All facts are the same as in Problem 6 except that COX applies ASPE . Follow the same instructions as those given in the Required section of Problem 6.

WEB-BASED PROBLEMS

Web Problem 2-1
LO6

Access the 2011 financial statements of Rogers Communications Inc. by going to the investor's relations section of the company's website. Answer the questions below. Round percentages to one decimal point and other ratios to two decimal points. For each question, indicate where in the financial statements you found the answer, and/or provide a brief explanation.

(a) What percentage of total assets at the end of 2011 is represented by investments accounted for using the equity method?

(b) What was the before-tax rate of return for 2011 from the investments accounted for using the equity method?

(c) Calculate the three ratios listed below for 2011. Then, assume that each year the associates have generated a return similar to the return in part (b) and have paid dividends equal to 75% of the income earned. If the company had used the cost method rather than the equity method since the date of acquisition of the investments, how would this change affect the following ratios:

   (i) Current ratio

   (ii) Debt-to-equity ratio

   (iii) Return on average equity

(d) How much comprehensive income after tax was earned from available-for-sale investments during 2011?

(e) What percentage of shareholders' equity at the end of 2011 is represented by cumulative unrealized gains from available-for-sale investments?

(f) What accounts on the balance sheet would change and would they increase or decrease if the available-for-sale investments had always been classified as FVTPL investments?

Web Problem 2-2
LO6

Access the 2011 financial statements for Goldcorp Inc. by going to investor's relations section of the company's website. Answer the same questions as in Problem 1. For each question, indicate where in the financial statements you found the answer, and/or provide a brief explanation. (Some questions may not be applicable.)

Business Combinations

LEARNING OBJECTIVES

After studying this chapter, you should be able to do the following:

L01 Define a business combination and evaluate relevant factors to determine whether control exists in a business acquisition.

L02 Describe the basic forms for achieving a business combination.

L03 Prepare and compare consolidated balances sheets under the acquisition and new-entity methods.

L04 Apply the acquisition method to a purchase-of-net-assets business combination.

L05 Apply the acquisition method to a purchase-of-shares business combination.

L06 Analyze and interpret financial statements involving business combinations.

L07 Identify some of the differences between IFRSs and ASPE for business combinations.

L08 Explain a reverse takeover and its reporting implications.

INTRODUCTION

In Chapter 2, we illustrated the accounting for nonstrategic investments and significant influence investments. The next six chapters are largely devoted to situations where the investor has control of the investee. When one company obtains control of one or more businesses, a business combination has occurred.

Some of the reasons for business combinations are to[1]

- defend a competitive position within a market segment or at a particular customer;
- diversify into a new market and/or geographic region;
- gain access to new customers and/or partners;
- acquire new and/or complementary products or services;
- acquire new expertise or capabilities;
- accelerate time to market (for a product and/or service);
- improve the company's rate of innovation either by acquiring new technology and/or intellectual property;

- gain control over a supplier; and
- position the company to benefit from industry consolidation

Business combinations are frequent events in Canada, the United States, and throughout the world. Hardly a week passes without some reference in the press to actual or proposed takeovers and mergers. Many people think that the typical takeover involves an American multinational swallowing up a smaller Canadian firm. But that is not always the case. In 2011, the biggest deals involving Canadian companies were as follows:

Mergers and acquisitions occur regularly in Canada and throughout the world.

- Barrick Gold of Canada bought Equinox Minerals of Canada for $7.5 billion.
- Cliffs Natural Resources Inc. of the United States bought Consolidated Thompson Iron Mines Limited of Canada for $4.6 billion.
- Brookfield Renewable Energy Partners of Bermuda bought assets of Brookfield Renewable Power Inc. of Canada for $3.4 billion.
- Intact Financial Corporation of Canada bought AXA Canada from AXA SA of France for $2.8 billion.
- Sinopec of China bought Daylight Energy Ltd. of Canada for $2.8 billion.
- Berkshire Partners of the United States and OMERS of Canada bought Husky International of Canada for $2.5 billion.
- Newmont Mining of USA bought Fronteer Gold Inc of Canada for $2.0 billion

Business combinations can be described as either friendly or hostile. Often a merger is initiated by one company submitting a formal tender offer to the shareholders of another company. In a friendly combination, the top management and the board of directors of the companies involved negotiate the terms of the combination and then submit the proposal to the shareholders of both companies along with a recommendation for approval. An unfriendly combination occurs when the board of directors of the target company recommends that its shareholders reject the tender offer. The management of the target company will often employ defences to resist the takeover. They include the following:

Business acquisitions can be friendly or hostile.

- *Poison pill.* This occurs when a company issues rights to its existing shareholders, exercisable only in the event of a potential takeover, to purchase additional shares at prices below market.

There are many tactics to resist takeovers.

- *Pac-man defence.* This involves the target company making an unfriendly countervailing takeover offer to the shareholders of the company that is attempting to take it over.
- *White knight.* In this case, the target company searches out another company that will come to its rescue with a more appealing offer for its shares.
- *Selling the crown jewels.* This involves selling certain desirable assets to other companies so that the would-be acquirer loses interest.

In the next section of this chapter, we define a business combination. The discussion then proceeds to the accounting for business combinations in Canada.

L01 ## BUSINESS COMBINATIONS

A business combination occurs when an acquirer obtains control of a business.

A business combination is defined in International Financial Reporting Standard 3 (IFRS 3) as a transaction or other event in which an acquirer obtains control of one or more businesses. This definition has two key aspects: control and businesses. We will discuss each aspect in considerable depth, starting with businesses.

A business is defined as an integrated set of activities and assets that is capable of being conducted and managed for the purpose of providing a return in the form of dividends, lower costs, or other economic benefits directly to investors or other owners, members, or participants.

A business consists of inputs and processes applied to those inputs that have the ability to create outputs.

A business consists of inputs and processes applied to those inputs that have the ability to create outputs. An input is any economic resource that creates, or has the ability to create, outputs when one or more processes are applied to it. Examples of inputs would include raw materials for a manufacturing company, intellectual property of a hi-tech company, and employees.

A process is any system, standard, protocol, convention, or rule that, when applied to an input or inputs, creates or has the ability to create outputs. Examples include strategic management processes, operational processes, and resource management processes. A workforce with the necessary skills and experience following rules and conventions may provide the necessary processes capable, when applied to inputs, of creating outputs. An output is the result of inputs plus processes applied to those inputs, which then provide or have the ability to provide a return in the form of dividends, lower costs, or other economic benefits directly to investors or other owners, members, or participants. Any product or service that is sold is obviously an example of an output.

The two essential elements of a business are inputs and processes applied to those inputs. Although businesses usually have outputs, outputs are not required for an integrated set of inputs and processes to qualify as a business. As long as the inputs and processes have the ability to produce outputs, the inputs and processes would qualify as a business. A company in the development stage may have materials and processes developed sufficiently that a prospective buyer could buy the company, complete the development, and begin producing outputs for sale to prospective customers. Or the buyer could integrate the seller's materials and processes with its own inputs and processes.

Determining whether a particular set of assets and activities is a business should be based on whether a potential buyer will be able to manage the integrated set as a business. In this evaluation, it is not relevant whether a seller operated the set as a business or whether the acquirer intends to operate the set as a business.

Buying a group of assets that do not constitute a business is a basket purchase, not a business combination.

When a business combination does occur, the requirements of IFRS 3 must be applied. On the other hand, if an entity acquires all of the assets of another entity but they do not meet the definition of a business, IFRS 3 would not be applicable. Instead, the assets acquired would be treated as a basket purchase, and the total cost would be allocated to the individual assets in proportion to their fair market values. Basket purchases were studied in the property, plant, and equipment section of intermediate accounting.

Let us now turn our attention to the other key aspect of a business combination: control. Guidance for determining control is provided in IFRS 10.

IFRS 10 states that an investor controls an investee when it is exposed or has rights to variable returns from its involvement with the investee, and it has the ability to affect those returns through its power over the investee. This definition contains the following three elements:

(a) The investor has power over the investee.

(b) The investor has exposure, or rights, to variable returns from its involvement with the investee.

(c) The investor has the ability to use its power over the investee to affect the amount of the investor's returns.

All three elements must be met for the investor to have control. If the investor does have control over the investee, the investor is called the parent and the investee is called the *subsidiary*. Let us now discuss each element of control.

Power An investor has power over an investee when the investor has existing rights giving it the current ability to direct relevant activities, that is, the activities that significantly affect the investee's returns. Sometimes, assessing power is straightforward, such as when power over an investee is obtained directly and solely from the voting rights granted by equity instruments such as shares and can be assessed by considering the voting rights from those shareholdings. In other cases, the assessment will be more complex and require consideration of more than one factor, for example, when power results from one or more contractual arrangements. An investor with the current ability to direct the relevant activities has power, even if its rights to direct have yet to be exercised. Evidence that the investor has been directing relevant activities can help determine whether the investor has power, but such evidence is not, in itself, conclusive in determining whether the investor has power over an investee. If two or more investors each have existing rights giving them unilateral ability to direct different relevant activities, the investor with the current ability that *most significantly* affects the returns of the investee has power over the investee.

> Control is the power to direct the relevant activities of the investee.

Returns An investor is exposed or has rights to variable returns from its involvement with the investee when those returns from its involvement could vary as a result of the investee's performance; the investor's returns can be only positive, only negative, or both positive and negative. An investment in common shares is exposed to variable returns because the common shareholders receive the residual returns in the company. If the company is very profitable, the dividends to the shareholders or appreciation in the price of common shares will be positive and can be substantial. On the other hand, if the company is incurring losses, the prospects for dividends or appreciation in the share price is minimal or non-existent.

> The definition of control requires that the investor has exposure, or rights, to variable returns from its involvement with the investee.

Link between power and returns An investor controls an investee if the investor not only has power over the investee and exposure or rights to variable returns from its involvement with the investee, but the investor also has the ability to use its power to affect his or her returns from its involvement. A common shareholder usually has the power through voting rights and exposure to variable returns. A preferred shareholder may have exposure to a variable return. However, the preferred shareholder typically does not have voting rights and, therefore, does not have power over the relevant activities of the investee.

> The definition of control requires that the investor has the ability to use its power over the investee to affect the amount of the investor's returns.

Appendix B of IFRS 10 provides extensive guidance to determine whether an entity has control. It states that the following factors may assist in making the determination about control:

(a) The purpose and design of the investee
(b) What the relevant activities are and how decisions about those activities are made
(c) Whether the rights of the investor give it the current ability to direct the relevant activities
(d) Whether the investor is exposed, or has rights, to variable returns from its involvement with the investee
(e) Whether the investor has the ability to use its power over the investee to affect the amount of the investor's returns

A key aspect of control is the ability to direct the activities that most significantly affect the investor's returns.

The following example is taken from Appendix B of IFRS 10. Two investors form an investee to develop and market a medical product. One investor is responsible for developing and obtaining regulatory approval of the medical product, a responsibility that includes having the unilateral ability to make all decisions relating to the development of the product and obtaining regulatory approval. Once the regulator has approved the product, the other investor will manufacture and market it. This investor has the unilateral ability to make all decisions about the manufacture and marketing of the project. If all the activities—developing and obtaining regulatory approval, as well as manufacturing and marketing of the medical product—are relevant activities, each investor needs to determine whether it is able to direct the activities that most significantly affect the investee's returns. Accordingly, each investor needs to consider which of developing and obtaining regulatory approval or manufacture and marketing of the medical product is the activity that most significantly affects the investor's returns, and whether he or she is able to direct that activity. In determining which investor has power, the investors would consider the following:

(a) Purpose and design of the investee
(b) Factors that determine the profit margin, revenue, and value of the investee, as well as the value of the medical product
(c) Effect on the investee's returns resulting from each investor's decision-making authority, with respect to the factors in (b)
(d) Investors' exposure to variability of returns

In this particular example, the investors would also consider these:

(e) The uncertainty of and effort required in obtaining regulatory approval (considering the investor's record of successfully developing and obtaining regulatory approval of medical products)
(f) Which investor controls the medical product once the development phase is successful

Let us now apply the elements of control to other practical situations.

If the means of paying for the business is cash or a promise to pay cash in the future, the company making the payment is usually the one obtaining control. If shares were issued as a means of payment, relative holdings of voting shares of the combined company by shareholders of the combining companies is key. In a combination involving two companies, if one shareholder group holds more than 50% of the voting shares of the combined company, that company would usually have control. If more than two companies are involved, the shareholder group holding the largest number of voting shares would usually be identified as the company with control.

> Owning more than 50% of the voting shares usually, but not always, indicates control.

Since the board of directors establishes the strategic policies of a corporation, the ability to elect a majority of the members of the board would generally be evidence of control. Therefore, the first element of control is presumed to exist if the parent owns, directly or indirectly, enough voting shares to elect the majority of the board of directors of a subsidiary.

In most situations, more than 50% of the voting shares are required to elect the majority of the board, and so the first element of control is presumed to exist with 50% ownership. However, we have to look at all factors. For example, if D Company owns 60% of the voting shares of E Company and F Company owns the other 40%, then we can presume that D Company has power over the activities of E Company. But if F Company owns convertible bonds of E Company or options or warrants to purchase E Company shares, which, if converted or exercised, would give F Company 62% of the outstanding shares of E Company, then F Company, not D Company, would have power over the activities of E Company.

There is also a general presumption that a holding of less than 50% of the voting shares does not constitute control. This presumption can be overcome if other factors clearly indicate control. For example, an irrevocable agreement with other shareholders to convey voting rights to the parent would constitute control, even if the parent owned less than 50% of the voting shares. A parent may also have power despite owning less than 50% of the voting shares if its holdings of rights, warrants, convertible debt, or convertible preferred shares would give it enough voting power to control the board of directors of the subsidiary. Exercise or conversion would not be necessary, only the right to exercise or convert is.

It is also possible for a parent to have power without a majority share ownership if it also has agreements in writing allowing it to dictate the operating policies of the subsidiary, and resulting in it receiving fees, royalties, and profits from intercompany sales. In Chapter 9, we will discuss special-purpose entities where control exists through operating agreements. For these situations, the parent makes the key decisions, receives the majority of the benefits, and absorbs most of the risk, even though the parent may own very few, if any, of the shares in the controlled company.

> A company could have control with less than 50% of the voting shares when contractual agreements give it control.

In another example, X Company owns 40% of Y Company, which is the largest single block of Y Company's outstanding shares. The other 60% is very widely held and only a very small proportion of the holders appear at the annual meeting of Y Company. As a result, X Company has had no trouble electing the majority of the board of directors. Thus, X Company could be deemed to have control in this situation as long as the other shareholders do not actively cooperate when they exercise their votes so as to have more voting power than X Company.

Temporary control of an entity does not of itself change the fact that control exists. During the time that control is held and until such time as control ceases, the reporting requirements for controlled entities should be applied.

The seizure of the company's assets by a trustee in a receivership or bankruptcy situation would be evidence that control has probably ceased, as would the imposition of governmental restrictions over a foreign company's ability to pay

> Normal business restrictions do not preclude control by the parent.

dividends to its Canadian investor. However, when a receiver seizes a specific asset in satisfaction of a default under a loan agreement but permits the company to continue in business under the direction of the parent, this is not a loss of control.

A reporting entity can control another entity, even though other parties have protective rights relating to the activities of that other entity. Protective rights are designed to protect the interests of the party holding those rights, without giving that party control of the entity to which they relate. They include, for example, the following:

A parent can control a subsidiary, even though other parties have protective rights relating to the subsidiary.

(a) Approval or veto rights granted to other parties that do not affect the strategic operating and financing policies of the entity. Protective rights often apply to fundamental changes in the activities of an entity, or apply only in exceptional circumstances. For example,
  (i) a lender might have rights that protect the lender from the risk that the entity will change its activities to the detriment of the lender, such as selling important assets or undertaking activities that change the credit risk of the entity.
  (ii) non-controlling shareholders might have the right to approve capital expenditures greater than a particular amount, or the right to approve the issue of equity or debt instruments.

(b) The ability to remove the party that directs the activities of the entity in circumstances such as bankruptcy or on breach of contract by that party.

(c) Limitations on the operating activities of an entity. For example, a franchise agreement for which the entity is the franchisee might restrict the pricing, advertising, or other operating activities of the entity but would not give the franchisor control of the franchisee. Such rights usually protect the brand of the franchisor.

Let us now discuss the common forms of business combinations and the reporting requirements for business combinations.

FORMS OF BUSINESS COMBINATIONS

L02

Essentially, there are three main forms of business combinations. One company can obtain control over the net assets of another company by (a) purchasing its net assets, (b) acquiring enough of its voting shares to control the use of its net assets or (c) gaining control through a contractual arrangement.

When purchasing assets, the transaction is carried out with the selling company.

Purchase of Assets An obvious way to obtain control over a business is by outright purchase of the assets that constitute a business. The selling company is left only with the cash or other consideration received as payment from the purchaser, and the liabilities present before the sale. Often, the acquirer purchases all the assets of the acquiree and assumes all its liabilities, recording these assets and liabilities in its accounting records. The shareholders of the selling company have to approve the sale, as well as decide whether their company should be wound up or continue operations after the sale.

When purchasing shares, the transaction is usually consummated with the shareholders of the selling company.

Purchase of Shares As an alternative to the purchase of assets, the acquirer could purchase enough voting shares from the acquiree's shareholders to give it the power to determine the acquiree's strategic operating and financing policies. This is the most common form of combination, and it is often achieved through a tender offer made by the management of the acquirer to the shareholders of the acquiree. These shareholders are invited to exchange their shares for cash or for shares of the acquirer company.

The share-purchase form of combination is usually the least costly to the acquirer because control can be achieved by purchasing less than 100% of the outstanding voting shares. In addition, in Canada there can be important tax advantages to the vendor if shares rather than assets are sold. Because the transaction is between the acquirer and the acquiree's shareholders, the acquiree's accounting for its assets and liabilities is not affected,[2] and the company carries on as a subsidiary of the acquirer. The acquirer becomes a parent company and, therefore, must consolidate its subsidiary when it prepares its financial statements.

> The acquired company makes no journal entries when the acquiring company purchases shares.

Control through Contractual Arrangement

A company can get control of another company by signing an agreement with the acquiree's shareholders to give it control, without actually acquiring any shares of the other company. Nevertheless, the company with control will be deemed a parent and the controlled company will be a subsidiary. Since there were no actual transactions between the parent and the subsidiary for the transfer of control, there will be no entries made on the subsidiary's books to record this change in control. However, the parent would have to consolidate this subsidiary when it prepares its financial statements. We will discuss this type of arrangement in further detail in Chapter 9.

> Control can be obtained through a contractual arrangement that does not involve buying assets or shares.

All three forms of business combination result in the assets and liabilities of the two companies being combined. If control is achieved by purchasing net assets, the combining takes place in the accounting records of the acquirer. If control is achieved by purchasing shares or through contractual arrangement, the combining takes place when the consolidated financial statements are prepared.

> There are many different legal forms in which a business combination can be consummated.

Variations

One variation from the forms of business combinations described above occurs when the companies involved agree to create a new company, which either purchases the net assets of the combining companies or purchases enough shares from the shareholders of the combining companies to achieve control of these companies.

Another variation that can occur is a *statutory amalgamation,* whereby, under the provisions of federal or provincial law, two or more companies incorporated under the same Companies Act can combine and continue as a single entity. The shareholders of the combining companies become shareholders of the surviving company, and the non-surviving companies are wound up. The substance of a statutory amalgamation indicates that it is simply a variation of one of the basic forms. If only one of the companies survives, it is essentially a purchase of net assets, with the method of payment being shares of the surviving company.

> A statutory amalgamation occurs when two or more companies combine to form a single legal entity.

Exhibit 3.1 shows the intercompany shareholdings, both before and after a business combination, under a variety of forms. Intercompany shareholdings are often depicted in this manner. The arrow points from the investor to the investee company, with the number beside the arrow showing the number of shares owned by the investor. Mr. A and Mr. X were the sole shareholders in A Co. and X Co. prior to the business combination. We will be exposed to all of these different forms of business combinations as we proceed through the next few chapters.

EXHIBIT 3.1 **Different Forms of Business Combinations**

Stick diagrams can be an effective way to depict intercompany shareholdings.

Consolidated financial statements are not required when an acquirer directly purchases the net assets of a business.

Under a reverse takeover, the shareholders of the acquired company control the acquiring company.

Intercompany Shareholdings
before the Business Combination

Mr. A   Mr. X
100 ↓   10 ↓
A Co.   X Co.

Intercompany Shareholdings
after the Business Combination

Consolidated Statements Not Required

A Co. purchased net assets of X Co. with cash

Mr. A   Mr. X
100 ↓   10 ↓
A Co.   X Co.

A Co. purchased net assets of X Co. with 50 shares

Mr. A   Mr. X
100 ↓   10 ↓
A Co. ←50— X Co.

New company purchased net assets of both companies with cash

Mr. A   Mr. X
100 ↙ ↘500   250↙ ↘10
A Co.   New Co.   X Co.

A Co. purchased net assets of X Co. with shares & X Co. is wound up (Statutory amalgamation)

Mr. A   Mr. X
100 ↓   50
A Co.

Intercompany Shareholdings
after the Business Combination

Consolidated Statements Are Required

A Co. purchased shares of X Co. with cash

Mr. A   Mr. X
100 ↓
(A Co. —10→ X Co.)

A Co. purchased shares of X Co. with 50 shares

Mr. A   Mr. X
100 ↓   50
(A Co. —10→ X Co.)

A Co. purchased shares of X Co. with 150 shares (Reverse Takeover)

Mr. A   Mr. X
100 ↓   150
(A Co. —10→ X Co.)

New company purchased shares of both companies with shares

Mr. A   Mr. X
500 ↘   ↙250
New Co.
100 ↙   ↘10
A Co.   X Co.

A Co. obtained control of X Co. through contractual arrangement

Mr. A   Mr. X
100 ↓   10 ↓
A Co.   X Co.

LO3   METHODS OF ACCOUNTING FOR BUSINESS COMBINATIONS

There are three methods of accounting for business combinations that have either been recently used in practice or discussed in theory:

- Purchase method
- Acquisition method
- New-entity method

These methods differ in how identifiable net assets of the acquiring company and acquired company are measured at the date of a business combination. The following table indicates the measurement basis and the current status and effective usage dates for these three methods:

| Method | Measurement basis for net assets of | | Status |
	Acquiring company	Acquired company	
Purchase method	Carrying amount	Allocation of purchase price	Was required prior to adoption of acquisition method
Acquisition method	Carrying amount	Fair value	Was required starting in 2011
New-entity method	Fair value	Fair value	Never achieved status as an acceptable method, but worthy of future consideration

We will now briefly discuss the merits of these three methods.

Prior to 2011, the *purchase method* was used to account for the combination. Under this method, the acquiring company's net assets are measured at their carrying amount and the acquired company's net assets are measured at the price paid for the assets by the acquiring company. This price included any cash payment, the fair value of any shares issued, and the present value of any promises to pay cash in the future. Any excess of the price paid over the fair value of the acquired company's identifiable net assets was recorded as goodwill. This method of accounting was consistent with the historical cost principle of accounting for any assets acquired by a company. Such assets were initially recorded at the price paid for them, and subsequently their cost was charged against earnings over their useful lives.

> The net assets of the acquired company are reported at the amount paid by the acquiring company under the purchase method.

Starting in 2011, the *acquisition method* must be used to account for business combinations. Under this method, the acquiring company reports the *identifiable net assets being acquired at the fair value of these net assets, regardless of the amount paid for them. When the purchase price is greater than the fair value of identifiable net assets, the excess is reported as goodwill, similar to the purchase method. When the purchase price is less than the fair value of identifiable net assets, the identifiable net assets are still reported at fair value and the deficiency in purchase price is reported as a gain on purchase. This practice is not consistent with the historical cost principle, where assets are reported at the amount paid for the assets. However, it is consistent with the general trend in financial reporting to use fair value more and more often to report assets and liabilities. Fair value is viewed as a relevant benchmark to help investors and creditors assess the success or failure of business activity. Fair value of the investee is likely to be readily available since the investor likely determined fair value when deciding on the price to be paid in acquiring the investee. Therefore, the cost involved in determining the fair value of the investee's assets and liabilities is more than offset by the benefits of the more relevant information. We will illustrate the acquisition method in detail later in this chapter. Unless otherwise noted, all of the illustrations throughout this text and in the end-of-chapter material will use the acquisition method.

> The identifiable net assets of the acquired company are reported at their fair value under the acquisition method.

The third method, the *new-entity method,* has been proposed in the past by proponents of fair value accounting. It has been suggested that a new entity has been created when two companies combine by the joining together of two ownership groups. As a result, the assets and liabilities contributed by the two combining companies should be reported by this new entity at their fair values. This would make the relevant contributions by the combining companies more comparable because the net assets are measured on the same basis. However, this method has

> The net assets of both the acquiring company and acquired company are reported at their fair value under the new entity method.

received virtually no support in the accounting profession because of the additional revaluation difficulties and costs that would result. Furthermore, it has been argued that if the owners were simply combining their interests, there would be no new invested capital and, therefore, no new entity created.

See Self-Study Problem 1 for a simple example to compare the new entity and acquisition methods of reporting a business combination. It shows that the values are quite different.

L04 Accounting for Business Combinations under Acquisition Method—Main Principles

IFRS 3 outlines the accounting requirements for business combinations:

> The acquisition method is required for all business combinations in Canada as of 2011.

- All business combinations should be accounted for by applying the acquisition method.
- An acquirer should be identified for all business combinations.
- The acquisition date is the date the acquirer obtains control of the acquiree.
- The acquirer should attempt to measure the fair value of the acquiree, as a whole, as of the acquisition date. The fair value of the acquiree as a whole is usually determined by adding together the fair value of consideration transferred by the acquirer (i.e., the acquisition cost) plus the value assigned to the non-controlling shareholders. In this text, we will refer to the sum of the acquisition cost plus value assigned to the non-controlling shareholders as total consideration given. The value assigned to the non-controlling interest is measured as either the fair value of the shares owned by the non-controlling shareholders or as the non-controlling interest's proportionate share of the fair value of the acquiree's identifiable net assets. Business valuation techniques would be used to measure the fair value of the business acquired, especially if the parent acquired less than 100% of the shares, if control is obtained without transferring any consideration or if the consideration transferred does not represent the fair value of the business acquired. Certain business valuation techniques are referred to in IFRS 3 but are beyond the scope of this book.
- The acquirer should recognize and measure the identifiable assets acquired and the liabilities assumed at fair value and report them separately from goodwill.
- The acquirer should recognize goodwill, if any.

> An acquirer must be identified for all business combinations.

Identifying the Acquirer and Date of Acquisition The acquirer is the entity that obtains control of one or more businesses in a business combination. The concept of control and how to determine who has control was discussed earlier in this chapter. It is important to determine who has control because this determines whose net assets are reported at carrying amount and whose assets are reported at fair value at the date of acquisition. The date of acquisition is the date that one entity obtains control of one or more businesses.

> The acquisition cost is measured as the fair value of consideration given to acquire the business.

Acquisition Cost The acquisition cost is made up of the following:

- Any cash paid
- Fair value of assets transferred by the acquirer

- Present value of any promises by the acquirer to pay cash in the future
- Fair value of any shares issued—the value of shares is based on the market price of the shares on the acquisition date
- Fair value of contingent consideration

The acquisition cost does not include costs such as fees for consultants, accountants, and lawyers as these costs do not increase the fair value of the acquired company. These costs should be expensed in the period of acquisition. This treatment differs from the treatment under the purchase method (historical cost accounting) where these costs would be capitalized as a cost of the purchase.

The acquisition cost does not include costs such as professional fees or costs of issuing shares.

Costs incurred in issuing debt or shares are also not considered part of the acquisition cost. These costs should be deducted from the amount recorded for the proceeds received for the debt or share issue; for example, deducted from loan payable or common shares as applicable. The deduction from loan payable would be treated like a discount on notes payable and would be amortized into income over the life of the loan using the effective interest method.

Recognition and Measurement of Net Assets Acquired   The acquirer should recognize and measure the identifiable assets acquired and the liabilities assumed at fair value and report them separately from goodwill. An identifiable asset is not necessarily one that is presently recorded in the records of the acquiree company. For example, the acquiree company may have patent rights that have a fair value but are not shown on its balance sheet because the rights had been developed internally. Or the acquiree's balance sheet may show a pension asset, though an up-to-date actuarial valuation may indicate a net pension obligation.

Identifiable assets and liabilities should be recorded separately from goodwill.

IAS 38 defines an identifiable asset if it either

(a) is separable; that is, is capable of being separated or divided from the entity and sold, transferred, licensed, rented, or exchanged, either individually or together with a related contract, identifiable asset, or liability, regardless of whether the entity intends to do so; or

(b) arises from contractual or other legal rights, regardless of whether those rights are transferable or separable from the entity or from other rights and obligations.

To qualify for recognition, as part of applying the acquisition method, the identifiable assets acquired and liabilities assumed must meet the definitions of assets and liabilities in IASB's *The Conceptual Framework for Financial Reporting* at the acquisition date. For example, costs that the acquirer expects but is not obliged to incur in the future to effect its plan to exit an activity of an acquiree or to terminate the employment of or to relocate an acquiree's employees do not meet the definition of a liability at the acquisition date. Therefore, the acquirer does not recognize those costs as a liability at the date of acquisition. Instead, the acquirer recognizes those costs in its post-combination financial statements in accordance with other IFRSs.

Appendix B to IFRS 3 provides guidance in identifying assets to be recognized separately as part of a business combination.

There are some exceptions to the general principle in accounting for a business combination that all assets and liabilities of the acquired entity must be recognized and measured at fair value. One of the exceptions for recognition pertains to contingent liabilities. For the acquired company, the contingent liability would only be recognized in its separate entity financial statements if it were probable that an outflow of resources would be required to settle the obligation. The acquirer must recognize a contingent liability if it is a present obligation that arises from past events and its fair value can be measured reliably. Therefore, the acquirer recognizes the liability even if it is not probable that an outflow of resources embodying economic benefits will be required to settle the obligation.

Most, but not all, of the acquiree's assets and liabilities are recognized and measured at fair value at the date of acquisition.

Special requirements for recognition and measurement of financial statement items at the date of acquisition also apply to employee benefits, indemnification assets, reacquired rights, share-based payment awards, and assets held for sale. Deferred income tax assets and liabilities are not fair valued and carried forward. Instead, new amounts for deferred tax assets and liabilities are determined at the date of acquisition. Because of the added complexity that this brings, discussion and illustration of this topic is delayed until Chapter 9.

Goodwill is the excess of total consideration given over the fair value of identifiable assets and liabilities.

Recognition of Goodwill   If the total consideration given by the controlling and non-controlling shareholders is greater than the fair value of identifiable assets and liabilities acquired, the excess is recorded in the acquirer's financial statements as goodwill. Goodwill represents the amount paid for excess earning power plus the value of other benefits that did not meet the criteria for recognition as an identifiable asset.

Negative goodwill could result in the reporting of a gain on purchase by the acquiring company.

If the total consideration given is less than the fair value of the identifiable net assets acquired, we have what is sometimes described as a "negative goodwill" situation. This negative goodwill is recognized as a gain attributable to the acquirer on the acquisition date. We will illustrate the accounting for negative goodwill in Chapter 4.

ILLUSTRATIONS OF BUSINESS COMBINATION ACCOUNTING

To illustrate the accounting involved using the acquisition method, we will use the summarized balance sheets of two companies. Summarized statements are used here so that we can focus completely on the broad accounting concepts. In later examples, more detailed statements will be used. Exhibit 3.2 presents the December 31, Year 1, balance sheets of the two companies that are party to a business combination.

Because the identification of an acquirer requires the analysis of shareholdings after the combination, Notes 1 and 2 are presented in the exhibit to identify the shareholders of each company as belonging to two distinct groups.

Company A and Company B are separate legal entities.

A Company Ltd. will initiate the takeover of B Corporation. The first two illustrations will involve the purchase of net assets with cash and the issuance of shares as the means of payment. Later illustrations will have A Company purchasing enough shares of B Corporation to obtain control over that company's net assets and will introduce the preparation of consolidated statements.

EXHIBIT 3.2

A COMPANY LTD. BALANCE SHEET
December 31, Year 1

Assets	$300,000
Liabilities	$120,000
Shareholders' equity	
Common shares (Note 1)	100,000
Retained earnings	80,000
	$300,000

Note 1
The shareholders of the 5,000 common shares issued and outstanding are identified as
Group X.

B CORPORATION BALANCE SHEET
December 31, Year 1

Assets	$ 88,000
Liabilities	$ 30,000
Shareholders' equity	
Common shares (Note 2)	25,000
Retained earnings	33,000
	$ 88,000

The fair values of B Corporation's identifiable assets
and liabilities are as follows as at December 31, Year 1:

Fair value of assets	$109,000
Fair value of liabilities	29,000
Fair value of net assets	$ 80,000

Note 2
The shareholders of the common shares of B Corporation are identified as Group Y.
The actual number of shares issued and outstanding has been purposely omitted because
this number would have no bearing on the analysis required later.

Control through Purchase of Net Assets

In the following independent illustrations, A Company offers to buy all assets
and assume all liabilities of B Corporation. The management of B Corporation
accepts the offer.

Illustration 1   Assume that on January 1, Year 2, A Company pays $95,000 in _cash_
cash to B Corporation for all of the net assets of that company, and that no other
direct costs are involved. Because cash is the means of payment, A Company is the
acquirer. Goodwill is determined as follows:

Acquisition cost	= cash paid	$95,000
Fair value of net assets acquired		80,000
Goodwill		$15,000

A Company would make the following journal entry to record the acquisition
of B Corporation's net assets:

Assets (in detail)	109,000	
Goodwill	15,000	
Liabilities (in detail)		29,000
Cash		95,000

The acquiring company
records the net assets
purchased on its own books
at fair value.

A Company's balance sheet after the business combination would be as follows:

A COMPANY LTD. BALANCE SHEET
January 1, Year 2

The acquiring company's own assets and liabilities are not revalued when it purchases the net assets of the acquired company.

Assets (300,000 − 95,000* + 109,000)	$314,000
Goodwill	15,000
	$329,000
Liabilities (120,000 + 29,000)	$149,000
Shareholders' equity	
Common shares	100,000
Retained earnings	80,000
	$329,000

* Cash paid by A Company to B Corporation

The selling company records the sale of its net assets on its own books.

While this illustration focuses on the balance sheet of A Company immediately after the business combination, it is also useful to look at B Corporation in order to see the effect of this economic event on that company. B Corporation would make the following journal entry to record the sale of its assets and liabilities to A Company:

Cash	95,000	
Liabilities (in detail)	30,000	
Assets (in detail)		88,000
Gain on sale of assets & liabilities		37,000

The balance sheet of B Corporation immediately after the sale of all of its net assets follows:

B CORPORATION BALANCE SHEET
January 1, Year 2

After the sale of net assets, B Corporation's sole asset is cash.

Cash	$95,000
Shareholders' equity	
Common shares	$25,000
Retained earnings (33,000 + 37,000*)	70,000
	$95,000

* The gain on sale of the net assets amounts to $37,000 (95,000 − [88,000 − 30,000]).

The management of B Corporation must now decide the future of their company. They could decide to invest the company's cash in productive assets and carry on in some other line of business. Alternatively, they could decide to wind up the company and distribute the sole asset (cash) to the shareholders.

Illustration 2   Assume that on January 1, Year 2, A Company issues 4,000 common shares, with a market value of $23.75 per share, to B Corporation as payment for the company's net assets. B Corporation will be wound up after the sale of its net assets. Because the method of payment is shares, the following analysis is made to determine which company is the acquirer.

	Shares of A Company
Group X now holds	5,000
Group Y will hold (when B Corporation is wound up)	4,000
	9,000

The acquirer is determined based on which shareholder group controls Company A after B Corporation is wound up.

Group X will hold 5/9 (56%) of the total shares of A Company after the combination, and Group Y will hold 4/9 (44%) of this total after the dissolution of B Corporation. Because one shareholder group holds more than 50% of the voting shares, that group will have power to make the key decisions for A Company.

Accordingly, A Company is identified as the acquirer. Goodwill is determined as follows:

Acquisition cost (4,000 shares @ 23.75)	$95,000
Fair value of net assets acquired	80,000
Goodwill	$15,000

A Company would make the following journal entry to record the acquisition of B Corporation's net assets and the issuance of 4,000 common shares at fair value on January 1, Year 2:

Assets (in detail)	109,000	
Goodwill	15,000	
Liabilities (in detail)		29,000
. Common shares		95,000

A Company's balance sheet after the business combination would be as follows:

A COMPANY LTD. BALANCE SHEET
January 1, Year 2

Assets (300,000 + 109,000)	$409,000	
Goodwill	15,000	
	$424,000	
Liabilities (120,000 + 29,000)	$149,000	
Shareholders' equity		
Common shares (100,000 + 95,000)		195,000
Retained earnings		80,000
		$424,000

> The recently purchased assets are recorded at fair value and the old assets are retained at carrying amount.

This balance sheet was prepared by combining the carrying amounts of A Company's assets and liabilities with the fair values of those of B Corporation.

B Corporation would make the following journal entry to record the sale of its assets and liabilities to A Company:

Investment in shares of A Company	95,000	
Liabilities (in detail)	30,000	
Assets (in detail)		88,000
Gain on sale of assets and liabilities		37,000

> The selling company records the sale of its net assets in exchange for shares of the acquiring company.

B Corporation's balance sheet immediately following the sale of its net assets is given below:

B CORPORATION BALANCE SHEET
January 1, Year 2

Investment in shares of A Company	$95,000
Shareholders' equity	
Common shares	$25,000
Retained earnings (33,000 + 37,000)	70,000
	$95,000

> After the sale of net assets, B Corporation's sole asset is investment in shares of A Company.

B Corporation's sole asset is 4,000 of the issued shares of A Company. This single block represents a voting threat to A Company's shareholders (Group X). A Company will likely insist that B Corporation be wound up and distribute these 4,000 shares to its shareholders (Group Y), who presumably will not get together to determine how to vote them.

L05 # Consolidated Financial Statements

Distinguish between separate-entity financial statements and consolidated financial statements.

When an investor acquires sufficient voting shares to obtain control over the investee, a parent-subsidiary relationship is established. The investor is the parent, and the investee is the subsidiary. Usually, the two (or more) companies involved continue as separate legal entities, with each maintaining separate accounting records and producing separate financial statements. However, the two entities now operate as a family of companies. In effect, they operate or have the ability to operate as one economic entity. Users of the parent's financial statements would generally prefer to get one financial statement for the entire family rather than obtain separate statements for each company in the family. Therefore, it is not surprising that IFRSs require the preparation of consolidated financial statements to present the financial position and financial performance for the family as a whole. The accounting principles involved in the preparation of consolidated financial statements are found in IFRS 10. In the material that follows in this and later chapters, the preparation of consolidated statements will follow this standard's requirements. Consolidated statements consist of a balance sheet, a statement of comprehensive income, a statement of changes in equity, a cash flow statement, and the accompanying notes. In this chapter and in Chapter 4, we will illustrate the preparation of the consolidated balance sheet on the date that control is obtained by the parent company. Consolidation of other financial statements will be illustrated in later chapters.

The following definitions are provided in IFRS 10:

(a) *Consolidated financial statements:* The financial statements of a group in which the assets, liabilities, equity, income, expenses, and cash flows of the parent and its subsidiaries are presented as those of a single economic entity

(b) *Group:* A parent and its subsidiaries

(c) *Parent:* An entity that controls one or more entities

(d) *Subsidiary:* An entity that is controlled by another entity

(e) *Non-controlling interest:* Equity in a subsidiary not attributable, directly or indirectly, to a parent

Consolidated financial statements combine the financial statements of the parent and its subsidiaries as if they were one entity.

When a parent company has control over one or more subsidiaries, it has the right to benefit economically from the subsidiaries' resources and, at the same time, is exposed to the related risks involved. Consolidated financial statements reflect a group of economic resources that are under the common control of the parent company, even though these resources are owned separately by the parent and the subsidiary companies. Note that the key concept is common control. This concept is reinforced in *Conceptual Framework for Financial Reporting,* where the definition of an asset focuses on control rather than ownership.[3] When control over a subsidiary is present, the parent is required to consolidate its subsidiaries for external reporting purposes. In other words, the parent and subsidiary will each prepare their own financial statements (which we will refer to as separate-entity financial statements or financial statements for internal purposes). The consolidated financial statements are additional financial statements that combine the separate-entity financial statements of the parent and subsidiary under the hypothetical situation that these two legal entities were operating as one single entity. The consolidated financial statements are prepared by the parent company and are referred to in this text as the third set of financial statements.

The following diagram shows the interrelationship of the two companies and the number of financial statements involved:

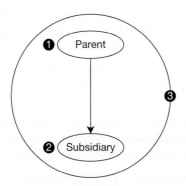

Consolidated financial statements are a separate set of financial statements supported by a working paper that combines the separate-entity financial statements of the parent and subsidiaries.

Financial statements 1 and 2 are the separate entity statements of the parent and subsidiary, respectively. Financial statements 3 are the consolidated financial statements. As we will soon see, consolidated financial statements are supported by working papers or worksheets that combine the accounts of the parent and subsidiaries. As we proceed through the next few chapters, it is important to understand in whose records or on which financial statements the journal entries or adjustments are being made. Consolidation adjustments are made to the consolidated financial statements (statements 3) and are not typically made to the separate entity records of the parent and subsidiary (statements 1 and 2).

Adjustments on consolidation are not typically recorded in the separate entity records for the parent or subsidiary.

All intercompany transactions are eliminated in the preparation of the consolidated statements. As a result, these statements reflect only transactions of this single entity with those outside the entity. (The process required to eliminate these intercompany transactions will be discussed thoroughly in later chapters.)

Consolidated statements are considered more useful to financial statement users than the separate financial statements of all of the companies that make up the group. Present and prospective shareholders of the parent company are interested in future profitability and cash flows. Creditors of the parent company want to be repaid and, accordingly, have information needs similar to those of the shareholders. The profitability and financial health of the parent are directly related to those of the companies it controls.

Consolidated financial statements are prepared primarily for the benefit of the shareholders and creditors of the parent company.

While consolidated statements are considered the best vehicle to satisfy the needs of stakeholders in the parent, they also have limitations. A poor performance by certain subsidiaries can be hidden as a result of the aggregation process. In addition, many parent companies have subsidiaries in different industries in various countries throughout the world, and this can be hidden in a single set of statements. Footnote disclosures that present details about the companies' operating segments help to alleviate this problem. Segment reporting will be discussed in Chapter 9. Finally, the information needs of non-controlling shareholders and creditors of the subsidiary companies are not served by consolidated statements. These users are better served with the separate entity statements of the subsidiary by itself. Therefore, separate entity financial statements for the subsidiary will have to be prepared to satisfy the information needs of the subsidiary's stakeholders.

The non-controlling shareholders and creditors of the subsidiary find the separate-entity statements of the subsidiary more useful than the consolidated statements.

A parent company does not have to issue consolidated financial statements if its parent issues consolidated financial statements.

IAS 27 states that a parent is not required to present consolidated financial statements for external reporting purposes if it meets all of the following conditions:

(a) It is a wholly-owned subsidiary, or is a partially-owned subsidiary, of another entity and its other owners, including those not otherwise entitled to vote, have been informed about, and do not object to, the parent not presenting consolidated financial statements.

(b) Its debt or equity instruments are not traded in a public market (a domestic or foreign stock exchange or an over-the-counter market, including local and regional markets).

(c) It did not file, nor is it in the process of filing, its financial statements with a securities commission or other regulatory organization for the purpose of issuing any class of instruments in a public market.

(d) Its ultimate or any intermediate parent produces consolidated financial statements available for public use and comply with IFRSs.

In the parent's *separate financial statements* for external users, the investment in subsidiary would be reported at cost or fair value.

If the parent meets these conditions, it *can* (but is not required to) present *separate financial statements* in accordance with IFRSs as its only financial statements to external users. When an entity prepares *separate financial statements*, it shall account for investments in subsidiaries

(a) at cost, or

(b) in accordance with IAS 39: Financial Instruments—Recognition and Measurement (or IFRS 9: Financial Instruments if it is early adopted).

If a parent does not issue either consolidated or separate financial statements in accordance with IFRSs to external users, it may still prepare financial statements for internal record-keeping purposes and/or for special external users with special needs. The accounting policies used for these special-purpose financial statements should be disclosed. Unless otherwise noted, our illustrations throughout the text will comply with IFRSs and will produce general-purpose financial statements for use by external users.

Now that we have a better understanding of the concept of consolidated financial statements, we will turn our attention to business combinations resulting from the purchase of shares. We will continue to use the financial statements of the two companies from Exhibit 3.2.

Control through Purchase of Shares

In the next two illustrations, A Company issues a tender offer to the shareholders of B Corporation (Group Y) for all of their shareholdings. Group Y accepts the offer.

Illustration 3   Assume that on January 1, Year 2, A Company pays $95,000 in cash to the shareholders of B Corporation for all of their shares and that no other direct costs are involved. Because cash was the means of payment, A Company is the acquirer.

A Company's journal entry to record the acquisition of 100% of B Corporation's shares on January 1, Year 2, is as follows:

Investment in B Corporation	95,000	
Cash		95,000

The financial statements of B Corporation have not been affected by this transaction because the shareholders of B Corporation, not B Corporation itself, sold their shares. A Company is now a parent company and must prepare consolidated financial statements for external reporting purposes. We will now illustrate the preparation of the consolidated balance sheet as at January 1, Year 2, using a working paper approach.

With a purchase of shares, the transaction is with the shareholders of the acquired company, not with the acquired company itself.

Before preparing the working paper, it is useful to calculate and allocate the acquisition differential. The acquisition differential is defined as the difference between the total consideration given and the carrying amount of the assets of the acquired company at the date of acquisition.

The required calculation and allocation is shown in Exhibit 3.3.

EXHIBIT 3.3

CALCULATION AND ALLOCATION OF THE ACQUISITION DIFFERENTIAL

Total consideration given	= cash paid by A Company		$ 95,000
Carrying amount of B Corporation's net assets			
Assets		$88,000	
Liabilities		30,000	
			58,000
Acquisition differential			37,000
Allocated as follows:			
Fair value excess	*Fair value* − *Carrying amount*		
Assets	109,000 − 88,000	= $21,000	
Liabilities	29,000 − 30,000	= 1,000	22,000
Balance—goodwill			$ 15,000

Since A Company purchased all of the shares in an arm's length transaction, it is reasonable to conclude that the $95,000 cost of the investment represents the total fair value of the subsidiary on the date of acquisition. The $95,000 value can be segregated into three components as indicated in the following bar chart:

Total Value of Subsidiary

Carrying amount of identifiable assets and liabilities $58,000
Excess of fair value over carrying amount of identifiable assets and liabilities $22,000
Goodwill $15,000

The total value of the subsidiary can be segregated into three components.

Since assets minus liabilities equals shareholders' equity, the top component of the bar chart could be described as either carrying amount of identifiable assets and liabilities or carrying amount of shareholders' equity. The carrying amount component is the amount reflected on the subsidiary's separate-entity balance sheet.

Goodwill is the difference between the total consideration given and the fair value of identifiable net assets.

The sum of the top two components is equal to the fair value of identifiable assets and liabilities. The bottom component, goodwill, represents the additional value of the acquiree over and above the fair value of the identifiable net assets. When the parent acquires 100% of the subsidiary, goodwill can be calculated as follows:

Cost of A Company's investment		$95,000
Fair value of B Corporation's identifiable net assets		
Assets	109,000	
Liabilities	29,000	
		80,000
Balance—goodwill		$15,000

The fair value excess is added to the carrying amount of the subsidiary's assets on the consolidated balance sheet; it is not added to the tax basis of the assets for income tax purposes. The fair value excess meets the definition of a temporary difference. Accordingly, deferred taxes should be set up for the tax effect on these temporary differences. We will ignore the deferred tax implications for this illustration and for most illustrations in the text because they overly complicate the allocation of the acquisition differential. We will revisit this issue in Chapter 9.

Because consolidated working papers use the financial statements of the parent and its subsidiary as the starting point, the calculation and allocation of the acquisition differential is necessary because it provides the amounts needed to make the working paper eliminations and adjustments. The working paper for the preparation of the consolidated balance sheet on the date of acquisition is shown in Exhibit 3.4.

The consolidation entries are made on the consolidated working papers and not in the accounting records of the combining companies.

EXHIBIT 3.4

A COMPANY LTD.
CONSOLIDATED BALANCE SHEET WORKING PAPER
January 1, Year 2

	A Company	B Corp.	Adjustments and Eliminations Dr.		Adjustments and Eliminations Cr.		Consolidated balance sheet
Assets	$205,000	$88,000	(2)	$ 21,000			$314,000
Investment in B Corporation	95,000				(1)	$ 95,000	
Acquisition Differential			(1)	37,000	(2)	37,000	
Goodwill			(2)	15,000			15,000
	$300,000	$88,000					$329,000
Liabilities	$120,000	$30,000	(2)	1,000			$149,000
Common shares	100,000						100,000
Retained earnings	80,000						80,000
Common shares		25,000	(1)	25,000			
Retained earnings		33,000	(1)	33,000			
	$300,000	$88,000		$132,000		$132,000	$329,000

The following points should be noted regarding the preparation of this working paper:

1. A Company's asset "Investment in B Corporation" and B Corporation's common shares and retained earnings do not appear on the consolidated balance sheet. These items are eliminated by a working paper elimination entry because they are reciprocal in nature. The entry labelled **(1)** eliminates the parent's ownership percentage of the shareholders' equity of the subsidiary against the parent's investment account. These shareholders' equity accounts are separately shown in the working paper to facilitate this. The acquisition differential that results is the portion of the investment account not yet eliminated.

2. The acquisition differential line does not appear as a separate account on the consolidated balance sheet. With reference to the calculations of Exhibit 3.3, the acquisition differential is allocated to revalue the net assets of B Corporation for consolidation purposes. This is accomplished by the entry labelled **(2).**

3. When we add the acquisition differential to the carrying amount of the net assets of B Corporation, the resulting amount used for the consolidation is the fair value of each individual asset and liability of B Corporation.

> The consolidated balance sheet reflects the acquiring company's net assets at carrying amount and the acquired company's net assets at fair value.

4. The elimination entries are made on the working paper only. They are not entered in the accounting records of the parent or the subsidiary.

5. The consolidated balance sheet is prepared from the amounts shown in the last column of the working paper.

6. Under the acquisition method of accounting, consolidated shareholders' equity on acquisition date is that of the parent.

It is worth noting that the consolidated balance sheet for illustration 3 is exactly the same as A Company's balance sheet in illustration 1. This is not a coincidence. In both illustrations, the net assets of the two companies were combined and the amount paid for B Corporation was $95,000 in cash. In illustration 1, A Company acquired the net assets directly; in illustration 3, A Company acquired a percentage of B Corporation's shares and thereby indirectly acquired B Corporation's net assets. As we proceed through more complicated examples of consolidation, it is important to remember that the consolidated financial statements should present the same results as if the parent had acquired the net assets directly.

> The consolidated balance sheet produces the same financial position as when A Company purchased the net assets directly.

Illustration 4   Assume that on January 1, Year 2, A Company issues 4,000 common shares, with a fair value of $23.75 per share, to the shareholders of B Corporation (Group Y) for all of their shares and that there are no direct costs involved. The analysis made in Illustration 2 indicates that A Company is the acquirer.

A Company's January 1, Year 2, journal entry to record the issuance of 4,000 shares at market value in payment for the acquisition of 100% of B Corporation's shares is as follows:

Investment in B Corporation (4,000 shares × 23.75)	95,000	
Common shares		95,000

Once again, B Corporation would not make any journal entry because the transaction was with the shareholders of B Corporation and not with B Corporation itself.

The calculation and allocation of the acquisition differential is identical to the one used in the last illustration (see Exhibit 3.3). The working paper for the preparation of the consolidated balance sheet as at January 1, Year 2, is shown in Exhibit 3.5.

Once again, it is worth noting that the consolidated balance sheet for illustration 4 is exactly the same as A Company's balance sheet in Illustration 2. This is not a coincidence. In both illustrations, the net assets of the two companies were combined and the amount paid for B Corporation was $95,000 in the form of A Company shares.

Goodwill appears on the consolidated balance sheet; that is, on the third set of statements

The Direct Approach   An alternative approach to the preparation of consolidated financial statements is to prepare the statements directly without the use of a working paper. We know from the working paper approach that the parent's investment account does not appear on the consolidated balance sheet because it is replaced with the underlying assets and liabilities of the subsidiary. The subsidiary's shareholders' equity accounts also do not appear on the consolidated balance sheet because they are not part of the consolidated entity's shareholders' equity. Therefore, we will never incorporate the investment account from the parent's balance sheet or the shareholders' equity accounts from the subsidiary's balance sheet when preparing the consolidated balance sheet at the date of acquisition.

We also know from the working paper approach that the allocation of the acquisition differential provides the amounts used to revalue the net assets of the subsidiary. By adding the acquisition differential to the carrying amount of the subsidiary's net assets on a line-by-line basis, we end up with the fair value of the subsidiary's assets and liabilities.

EXHIBIT 3.5							

A COMPANY LTD.
CONSOLIDATED BALANCE SHEET WORKING PAPER
January 1, Year 2

The allocation of the acquisition differential is made on the consolidated worksheet and is not recorded in the accounting records of either of the combining companies.

	A Company	B Corp.		Adjustments and Eliminations Dr.		Cr.	Consolidated balance Sheet
Assets	$300,000	$88,000	**(2)**	$ 21,000			$409,000
Investment in B Corporation	95,000				**(1)**	$ 95,000	
Acquisition Differential			**(1)**	37,000	**(2)**	37,000	
Goodwill			**(2)**	15,000			15,000
	$395,000	$88,000					$424,000
Liabilities	$120,000	$30,000	**(2)**	1,000			$149,000
Common shares	195,000						195,000
Retained earnings	80,000						80,000
Common shares		25,000	**(1)**	25,000			
Retained earnings		33,000	**(1)**	33,000			
	$395,000	$88,000		$132,000		$132,000	$424,000

The direct approach achieves the same results as the working paper approach but with a slightly different format. The basic process involved in the direct approach is as follows:

$$
\begin{array}{ccccccc}
\text{Carrying} & & \text{Carrying} & & & & \\
\text{amount} & + & \text{amount} & + (-) & \text{Acquisition} & = & \text{Consolidated} \\
\text{(parent)} & & \text{(subsidiary)} & & \text{differential} & & \text{amounts} \\
\end{array}
$$

The preparation of the consolidated balance sheet using the direct approach for illustration 4 is shown in Exhibit 3.6. The non-bolded amounts shown in brackets come from the separate-entity balance sheets of A Company and B Corporation. The bolded amounts in brackets are consolidation adjustments related to the allocation of the acquisition differential. Consolidated shareholders' equity on acquisition date is always that of the parent company.

> On the date of acquisition, consolidated shareholders' equity = parent's shareholders' equity.

EXHIBIT 3.6 | Illustration of the Direct Approach

A COMPANY LTD.
CONSOLIDATED BALANCE SHEET
January 1, Year 2

Assets (300,000 + 88,000 + **21,000**)	$409,000
Goodwill (0 + 0 + **15,000**)	15,000
	$424,000
Liabilities (120,000 + 30,000 − **1,000**)	$149,000
Common shares	195,000
Retained earning	80,000
	$424,000

> Under the direct approach, the acquisition differential and other consolidation adjustments are added or subtracted to the appropriate line on the consolidated financial statements.

The accounting for a business combination has been examined in four illustrations. The first two involved the acquisition of net assets directly, and the last two the acquisition of 100% of shareholdings. Because the amount paid was the same in each of these paired illustrations, the balance sheets prepared immediately after the combination are identical for each pair.

In the last two illustrations, it was quite clear that A Company was the acquirer. The former shareholders of A Company own 56% of the shares after the new 4,000 shares were issued to acquire B Corporation. If A Company had issued 6,000 rather than 4,000 new shares, the former shareholders of B Corporation would own 55% (6,000 / 11,000) of the outstanding shares of A Company and would control the combined company. This is an example of a reverse takeover where the shareholders of the company being acquired (in this case, B Corporation) own the majority of the shares of the acquirer (in this case, A Company). The legal parent, being A Company, is treated as the subsidiary and the legal subsidiary, being B Corporation, is treated as the parent for accounting purposes. Therefore, the consolidated balance sheet would incorporate B Corporation's net assets at carrying amounts and A Company's net assets at fair value. See Appendix 3A for a more detailed explanation and illustration of a reverse takeover situation.

> In a reverse takeover, the consolidated balance sheet incorporates the carrying amount of the net assets of the deemed parent (the legal subsidiary) and the fair value of the deemed subsidiary (the legal parent).

Push-down Accounting   Under push-down accounting, the acquisition differential is "pushed down" to the actual accounting records of the subsidiary on the date of acquisition. The subsidiary revalues its assets and liabilities, including goodwill, to

> Under push-down accounting, the subsidiary revalues its assets and liabilities, including goodwill, to the amounts included in the consolidated balance sheet.

the same amount that is being used on the consolidated balance sheet. This practice became permissible under Canadian generally accepted accounting principles (GAAP) in 1992 with the issuance of Section 1625, "Comprehensive Revaluation of Assets and Liabilities." Push-down accounting is not presently addressed and is, therefore, not allowed under IFRSs. However, it is still permissible under Accounting Standards for Private Enterprises (ASPE). Since it may be incorporated in IFRSs in the future, we will briefly describe how it works.

Push-down accounting is another instance where GAAP allow a departure from historical cost accounting and allows the use of fair values in financial reporting. Even though the subsidiary was not involved in the transaction with the parent (the transaction involved the parent and the shareholders of the subsidiary), the subsidiary is allowed to revalue its identifiable assets and liabilities to fair value and its goodwill to the amount reported on the consolidated balance sheet. Since the parent and subsidiary were not related prior to the acquisition, the amount paid by the parent was probably equal to or fairly close to the fair value of these net assets. So, it is appropriate to use these values to provide more relevant, yet very reliable, information to the users of the subsidiary's financial statements.

Section 1625 in Part II of the *Handbook* allows push-down accounting only when a subsidiary is at least 90% owned by a parent. Theoretically, a parent could demand a 95%-owned subsidiary to use it. Practically, it probably would not, because when a non-controlling interest is present, the consolidation becomes very complex and the benefits from its use disappear. We will not provide a detailed illustration of push-down accounting in this textbook; however, for those readers that wish to pursue this further, a full discussion and illustration of comprehensive revaluations can be found on Connect at www.mcgrawhillconnect.ca.

> When the parent establishes a new company as a subsidiary, there should be no acquisition differential.

Subsidiary Formed by Parent

In some situations, a subsidiary is not acquired through a share purchase from an outside party. Rather, it is quite common in Canada and the United States for the parent company to set up the subsidiary company. The parent company purchases all of the initial share issue after the subsidiary is incorporated.[4] At this time, the carrying amounts and fair values of the subsidiary's net assets are obviously equal, and there is no goodwill. It should also be obvious that the subsidiary has no retained earnings at this time. The preparation of the consolidated balance sheet on the date of formation of the subsidiary is simplified, requiring only the elimination of the parent's investment account against the subsidiary's share capital.

Reporting Depreciable Assets

In the previous illustrations, we did not show the details for the subsidiary's assets because we wanted to illustrate the concepts in a simple scenario. We will now consider the complications when the subsidiary has a depreciable asset.

Assume the following data pertaining to a building for the parent and subsidiary at the date of acquisition:

	Parent	Subsidiary
Cost	$500	$200
Accumulated depreciation	180	50
Carrying amount	320	150
Fair value	375	210

The consolidated balance sheet should incorporate the carrying amount of $320 for the parent's building and the fair value of $210 for the subsidiary's building for a total value of $530. But, how much should be reported for cost and accumulated depreciation?

IFRS 10 does not give any guidance on how to report these two components. However, IAS 16 does give some guidance when using the revaluation model to report property, plant, and equipment at fair value on an annual basis. IAS 16 states that when an item of property, plant, and equipment is revalued, any accumulated depreciation at the date of the revaluation is treated in one of the following ways:

(a) Restated proportionately with the change in the gross carrying amount of the asset so that the carrying amount of the asset after revaluation equals its revalued amount. This method is similar to a depreciated replacement cost method because it shows the fair value of the asset as if it was new and then deducts accumulated depreciation to derive the fair value of the used asset. This method shows that the asset is used because it reports accumulated depreciation. (We will refer to this approach as the *proportionate method*.)

(b) Eliminated against the gross carrying amount of the asset and the net amount restated to the revalued amount of the asset. Under this method, it will appear as if the asset is new because it does not report any accumulated depreciation. (We will refer to this approach as the *net method*.)

Cautionary Note: In this textbook, we will use the net method unless otherwise indicated.

Under the proportionate method, both the cost and accumulated depreciation of the subsidiary's building would be grossed up by a factor of $210/150 = 1.40$ to produce a grossed up cost of $280 ($200 \times 1.4$) and a grossed up accumulated depreciation of $70 ($50 \times 1.4$). Under the net method, the accumulated depreciation will be reported at zero and the cost reported at $210. In both cases, the difference between cost and accumulated depreciation will be $210, which is the fair value of the building at that point in time.

The net method seems more appropriate because the parent is, in effect, acquiring the asset from the shareholders of the subsidiary at the date of acquisition. There should be no accumulated depreciation for a recently purchased asset.

The following presents the consolidated balance sheet amounts under the two different methods:

	Parent	Subsidiary Proportionate Method	Consolidated Proportionate Method	Subsidiary Net Method	Consolidated Net Method
Cost	$500	$280	$780	$210	$710
Accumulated depreciation	180	70	250	0	180
Carrying amount	320	210	530	210	530

Both methods report the subsidiary's depreciable asset at fair value but report different amounts for cost and accumulated depreciation.

See Self-Study Problem 2 for a further illustration and comparison of a purchase of assets compared with a purchase of shares. This problem also incorporates the presentation of cost and accumulated depreciation on the consolidated balance sheet.

Other Consolidated Financial Statements in Year of Acquisition

Consolidated financial statements must be prepared once an entity obtains controls of the net assets of another entity. The assets and liabilities of the two entities are combined

Consolidated net income, retained earnings, and cash flows include the subsidiary's income and cash flows only subsequent to the date of acquisition.

for reporting purposes as of the date that control has been obtained. Similarly, the revenues and expenses are combined starting on the date of acquisition; they are not combined on a retroactive basis. If a business combination occurs half way through the year, the consolidated income statement for the year will incorporate only the income of the parent for the first half of the year and the income for both the parent and subsidiary for the second half of the year.[5] The column in the consolidated statements for last year (i.e., the comparative year) will only include the parent's income because the two companies were not one economic entity in the prior year. This treatment is consistent with what would be done if the parent had purchased the net assets directly from the subsidiary. That is, when a company acquires assets, it reports income from those assets starting on the date of purchase. It does not retroactively adjust to state what income would have been had these assets always belonged to the purchaser. Therefore, consolidated net income and retained earnings do not change on the date of acquisition. The consolidated statements will combine the results of the parent and subsidiary for transactions occurring on and subsequent to the date of acquisition.

To illustrate these financial reporting requirements, assume the following information for G Corporation and H Company for Years 1 and 2:

	Year 1	Year 2
G Corporation:		
Separate income (excluding any income from H)	$30,000	$30,000
Common shares outstanding, December 31	10,000	14,000
H Company:		
Net income	$14,800	$14,800

On January 1, Year 2, G Corporation issued 4,000 common shares to buy 100% of H Company's common shares. Assume that there was no acquisition differential on this business combination. The net income and earnings per share that G Corporation would present on its comparative consolidated financial statements at the end of Year 2 would be as follows:

	Year 1	Year 2
Net income (30,000 + 0; 30,000 + 14,800)	$30,000	$44,800
Earnings per share (30,000/10,000; 44,800/14,000)	$3.00	$3.20

The acquirer must disclose information that enables users of its financial statements to evaluate the nature of, and risks associated, with its interests in subsidiaries.

Disclosure Requirements   The acquirer must disclose information that enables users of its financial statements to do the following:

(a) Evaluate the nature of, and risks associated with, its interests in subsidiaries

(b) Evaluate the effects of those interests on its financial position, financial performance and cash flows

(c) Understand the significant judgments and assumptions it has made in determining that it has control of another entity

(d) Understand the composition of the group

(e) Evaluate the nature and extent of significant restrictions on its ability to access or use assets, and settle liabilities, of the group

RONA Inc. is a distributor and a retailer of hardware, home improvement, and gardening products in Canada. It reported business combinations in 2011 involving both the purchase of net assets and the acquisition of several subsidiaries. Excerpts from its 2011 financial statements are presented in Exhibit 3.7.

Rona acquired businesses through direct asset purchases and by way of share purchases.

EXHIBIT 3.7

EXTRACTS (IN PART) FROM RONA INC.'S 2011 FINANCIAL STATEMENTS
9. Business acquisitions (in 000s)

On December 20, 2011, the Corporation acquired the assets of Centre de Rénovations Mirabel Inc., a dealer located in Quebec operating in the retail and commercial segment.
On October 25, 2011, the Corporation acquired the assets of 9202-8950 Québec Inc., a dealer located in Quebec operating in the retail and commercial segment.
On August 2, 2011, the Corporation acquired the assets of Palliser Lumber Sales Ltd, a company located in Alberta operating in the distribution segment.
On June 29, 2011, the Corporation acquired all the shares of Gestion 2HL Inc., a dealer located in Quebec operating in the retail and commercial segment.
On April 11, 2011, the Corporation acquired the assets of Duncan Pacific, located in Vancouver, British Columbia. This dealer, operating in the retail and commercial segment, has four outlets with major lumberyards in Duncan, Nanaimo, Campbell River, and Cobble Hill.
On January 31, 2011, the Corporation acquired the assets of La Boutique Plomberie Décoration 25 Inc. in Quebec. The company is a retailer of basic and finishing plumbing products. The company operates in the retail and commercial segment.
On January 24, 2011, the Corporation acquired the minority interests in the assets of a store previously held by one of its 51%-owned subsidiaries. This transaction resulted in a $490 decrease in non-controlling interests with a corresponding change in contributed surplus.
During 2010, the Corporation acquired nine companies in the retail and commercial segment through asset purchases and one company in the distribution segment by way of a share purchase.
The financial performance of these companies is consolidated from their acquisition date. The consideration paid for these acquisitions amounted to $56,195 ($136,566 in 2010). Direct acquisition costs of $666 were recognized in selling, general, and administrative expenses for the year ended December 25, 2011 ($4,062 in 2010).
The Corporation financed these acquisitions from its available cash and existing credit facilities. The preliminary purchase price allocation of these acquisitions was established as follows:

	2011	2010
Trade and other receivables	$ 6,298	$ 50,567
Inventory	19,956	60,511
Other current assets	244	3,272
Other financial assets	–	1,959
Property, plant, and equipment	30,040	34,386
Goodwill on acquisition	16,777	74,040
Intangible assets	45	5,481
Deferred tax assets	–	849
Current liabilities	(15,251)	(62,924)
Long-term debt	(1,144)	(31,513)
Deferred tax liabilities	(770)	(62)
Cost of acquisitions	56,195	136,566
Less: Issuance of common shares	–	(35,722)
Balances of purchase prices	(8,488)	(20,569)
Cash consideration paid	$ 47,707	$ 80,275

(continued)

EXHIBIT 3.7   *(continued)*

The Corporation expects that an amount of $6,989 ($8,590 in 2010) of goodwill will be
deductible for tax purposes.
The excess of the purchase price over the value of net identifiable items of property, plant,
and equipment and intangible assets acquired, less liabilities assumed, is recognized as
goodwill and represents expected synergies in connection with the acquisitions.
The preliminary purchase price allocation of the 2011 acquisitions may be subject to adjustment pending completion of the final valuations.
During 2011, as a result of additional information obtained concerning the preliminary
purchase price allocation of fourth quarter 2010 acquisitions, the Corporation reduced
the goodwill on acquisition by $1,903 with a corresponding change in property, plant, and
equipment.

Source: Reproduced with permission from Rona Inc. http://www.rona.ca/corporate/financial-documents

The acquirer has up to
one year from the date of
acquisition to finalize the
determination of fair value
for the identifiable net
assets.

ANALYSIS AND INTERPRETATION OF FINANCIAL STATEMENTS

Consolidated financial statements combine the financial statements of the separate entity financial statements of the parent and subsidiary. The separate entity
financial statements of the parent present the investment in subsidiary as one line
on the balance sheet. When the consolidated balance sheet is prepared, the investment account is replaced by the underlying assets and liabilities of the subsidiary.
This gives the same result as if the investor had bought the subsidiary's assets and
liabilities directly.

Exhibit 3.8 presents the separate-entity balance sheet of the parent and the
parent's consolidated balance sheet. The values are taken directly from Exhibit 3.7.
It also indicates the debt-to-equity ratio for each situation.

The separate-entity balance presents the legal situation for Company A in that
Company A does, in fact, own an investment in shares of B Corporation. The consolidated balance sheet presents the combined financial position of the parent and
subsidiary as if they were one economic entity. The debt-to-equity ratio is substantially higher for the consolidated balance sheet. This may better present the risk
of insolvency to the parent's shareholders because it presents the total debt of the
combined entity.

EXHIBIT 3.8   **Impact of Presentation Method on Debt-to-Equity Ratio**

	Separate Entity	Consolidated
Assets	$300,000	$409,000
Investment in B Corporation	95,000	
Goodwill		15,000
	$395,000	$424,000
Liabilities	$120,000	$149,000
Shareholders' equity		
Common shares	195,000	195,000
Retained earnings	80,000	80,000
	$395,000	$424,000
Debt-to-equity ratio	0.44	0.54

The debt-to-equity ratio
is substantially higher for
the consolidated balance
sheet as compared with
the separate-entity balance
sheet.

ASPE DIFFERENCES

L07

The following paragraphs from Part II of the *CICA Handbook* outline the main accounting and reporting requirements for investments in subsidiaries:

- An enterprise shall make an accounting policy choice to either consolidate its subsidiaries or report its subsidiaries using either the equity method or the cost method. All subsidiaries should be reported using the same method. (Section 1590)

- When a subsidiary's equity securities are quoted in an active market and the parent would normally choose to use the cost method, the investment should not be reported at cost. Under such circumstances, the investment should be reported at fair value, with changes in fair value reported in net income. (Section 1590)

- Private companies can apply push-down accounting but must disclose the amount of the change in each major class of assets, liabilities, and shareholders' equity in the year that push-down accounting is first applied. (Section 1625)

A private entity can choose to report an investment in a subsidiary by preparing consolidation financial statements, by using the cost or equity methods or at fair value in limited situations.

U.S. GAAP DIFFERENCES

U.S. GAAP and IFRSs for business combination have many similarities. Some of the significant differences are summarized as follows:

1. Whereas IFRSs define control as the power to direct relevant activities of the investee, U.S. GAAP generally looks for majority voting rights, except for variable interest entities, where it looks for control and other factors.

2. Whereas IFRSs requires that potential voting rights be considered when assessing whether control exists, U.S. GAAP does not require that potential voting rights be considered.

3. Whereas IFRSs provide an exemption from the requirement to prepare consolidated financial statements if the reporting entity's parent prepares consolidated financial statements, U.S. GAAP does not provide an exemption.

4. Whereas IFRSs require that the accounting policies of the parent and subsidiary conform, the SEC staff does not require policies to conform provided that policies are in accordance with U.S. GAAP.

There are some significant differences between IFRSs and U.S. GAAP for the accounting for business combinations.

SUMMARY

A *business combination* takes place when one company gains control over the net assets of a business. An investor controls an investee when it is exposed, or has rights, to variable returns from its involvement with the investee, and has the ability to affect those returns through its power over the investee. Control can be achieved by purchasing the net assets directly, by purchasing enough voting shares to gain control over the use of the net assets, or through contractual arrangements. In the latter two situations, a parent–subsidiary relationship is created that requires the preparation of consolidated financial statements.

Under IFRS 3, the *acquisition method* must be used to report a business combination. Under the acquisition method, an acquirer must be identified based on the definition of control. The balance sheet for the combined entity at the date of acquisition includes the assets and liabilities of the acquirer at their carrying amounts and the identifiable assets and liabilities of the acquiree at their fair value. Any excess of the total consideration given over the fair value of the subsidiary's identifiable assets and liabilities is recorded as goodwill.

The preparation of consolidated financial statements is usually supported by a consolidation worksheet, or by a direct approach for calculating account balances for each line on the consolidated financial statements. Consolidation adjustments for the allocation of the acquisition differential are reflected on the worksheet and are not typically incorporated in the general ledger of the parent or subsidiary.

Significant Changes in GAAP in the Last Three Years

1. The definition of control has changed. It now focuses on whether the investor is exposed, or has rights, to variable returns from its involvement with the investee and has the ability to affect those returns through its power over the investee.

Changes Expected in GAAP in the Next Three Years

No major changes are expected in the next three years for topics covered in this chapter.

SELF-STUDY PROBLEM 1

LO3, 6   On December 31, Year 1, P Company obtains control over the net assets of S Company by purchasing 100% of the ordinary shares of S Company. P Company paid for the purchase by issuing ordinary shares with a fair value of $44,000. In addition, P Company paid $1,000 for professional fees to facilitate the transaction. The following information has been assembled:

	P Company		S Company	
	Carrying amount	Fair value	Carrying amount	Fair value
Goodwill	$ 0	$ 38,000	$ 0	$ 22,000
Plant assets (net)	80,000	90,000	20,000	26,000
Current assets	50,000	55,000	15,000	14,000
	$130,000	$ 183,000	$35,000	$ 62,000
Shareholders' equity	$ 75,000		$18,000	
Long-term debt	25,000	$ 29,000	7,000	$ 8,000
Current liabilities	30,000	30,000	10,000	10,000
	$130,000		$35,000	

Required:

(a) Prepare a consolidated statement of financial position for P Company and calculate the debt-to-equity ratio immediately after the combination under
   (i) the acquisition method, and
   (ii) the new entity method.

(b) Which method shows the better solvency position? Briefly explain.

(c) In your opinion, which method best reflects the true economic reality for the combined economic entity? Briefly explain.

SOLUTION TO SELF-STUDY PROBLEM 1

(a)

P COMPANY

Consolidated Statement of Financial Position at December 31, Year 1

(See notes)

	(i)	(ii)
Goodwill	$ 22,000	$ 60,000
Plant assets (net)	106,000	116,000
Current assets	63,000	68,000
	$191,000	$244,000
Shareholders' equity	$118,000	$167,000
Long-term debt	33,000	37,000
Current liabilities	40,000	40,000
	$191,000	$244,000
Debt-to-equity ratio	0.62:1	0.46:1

(b) The new entity method shows the better solvency position because its debt-to-equity ratio is lower than the acquisition method. Both the debt and equity are higher under the new entity method. However, the increase in equity is proportionately greater than the increase in debt.

(c) In the opinion of the author, fair values are better measures of the economic value of assets and liabilities than historical cost-based values. If so, the new entity method would best reflect the true economic value of the combined economic entity. This method is not generally accepted at the present time, primarily because the cost of measuring the fair value of all of the parent's assets and liabilities, including goodwill, could be quite expensive and may not be worth the effort. If users continue to ask for more fair value information, and if the cost of measuring fair values of assets and liabilities decreases, the new entity method could become generally accepted in the future.

Notes:

1. The statement of financial position values for assets and liabilities are calculated as follows:
   (i) Carrying amounts for P plus fair values for S.
   (ii) Fair values for P plus fair values for S.

2. The $1,000 paid for professional fees reduces cash (which is included in current assets) and increases expenses (which reduce retained earnings, a component of shareholders' equity).

3. Shareholders' equity is the amount required to balance the statement of financial position. Under the acquisition method, it is the parent's carrying amount for shareholders' equity plus the value of shares issued less the expense for the professional fees.

SELF-STUDY PROBLEM 2

LO4, 5 On December 31, Year 1, the condensed balance sheets for ONT Limited and NB Inc. were as follows:

	ONT	NB
Assets:		
Cash	$ 44,000	$ 80,000
Accounts receivable	480,000	420,000
Inventories	650,000	540,000
Property, plant & equipment	2,610,000	870,000
Accumulated depreciation	(1,270,000)	(130,000)
	$2,514,000	$1,780,000
Liabilities:		
Current liabilities	$ 660,000	$ 560,000
Bonds payable	820,000	490,000
	1,480,000	1,050,000
Shareholders' equity:		
Common shares	200,000	400,000
Retained earnings	834,000	330,000
	1,034,000	730,000
	$2,514,000	$1,780,000

The fair value of all of NB's assets and liabilities were equal to their carrying amounts except for the following:

Asset	Carrying amount	Fair value
Inventories	$540,000	$570,000
Property, plant & equipment	740,000	790,000
Bonds payable	490,000	550,000

Required:

(a) Assume that on January 1, Year 2, ONT acquired all of NB's net assets by issuing new common shares with a fair value of $1,000,000. This was the only transaction on this day.

   (i) Prepare the journal entry on ONT's book to record the purchase of NB's net assets.

   (ii) Prepare a balance sheet for ONT at January 1, Year 2, after recording the purchase of NB's net assets.

(b) Ignore part (a). Assume instead that on January 1, Year 2, ONT acquired all of NB's common shares by issuing new common shares with a fair value of $1,000,000. This was the only transaction on this day.

   (i) Prepare the journal entry on ONT's book to record the purchase of NB's common shares.

   (ii) Prepare a schedule to calculate and allocate the acquisition differential.

   (iii) Prepare a consolidated balance sheet for ONT and its subsidiary at January 1, Year 2, after recording the purchase of NB's common shares.

(c) What are the similarities and differences between the balance sheets in parts (a) and (b)?

SOLUTION TO SELF-STUDY PROBLEM 2

(a) (i)

Cash	80,000	
Accounts receivable	420,000	
Inventories	570,000	
Property, plant & equipment	790,000	
Goodwill (see [b] [ii])	250,000	
Current liabilities		560,000
Bonds payable		550,000
Common shares		1,000,000

(ii)

ONT LIMITED
Balance sheet
January 1, Year 2

Cash (44,000 + 80,000)	$ 124,000
Accounts receivable (480,000 + 420,000)	900,000
Inventories (650,000 + 570,000)	1,220,000
Property, plant & equipment (2,610,000 + 790,000)	3,400,000
Accumulated depreciation (1,270,000 + 0)	(1,270,000)
Goodwill	250,000
	$4,624,000
Liabilities:	
Current liabilities (660,000 + 560,000)	$1,220,000
Bonds payable (820,000 + 550,000)	1,370,000
	2,590,000
Shareholders' equity:	
Common shares (200,000 + 1,000,000)	1,200,000
Retained earnings	834,000
	2,034,000
	$4,624,000

(b) (i)

Investment in NB	1,000,000	
Common shares		1,000,000

(ii)

Cost of ONT's investment in NB		$1,000,000
Carrying amount of NB's net assets		
Assets	$1,780,000	
Liabilities	(1,050,000)	730,000
Acquisition differential		270,000
Allocated as follows:		
Inventories (570,000 − 540,000)	$ 30,000	
Property, plant & equipment (790,000 − 740,000)	50,000	
Bonds payable (550,000 − 490,000)	(60,000)	20,000
Balance—goodwill		$ 250,000

(iii)

ONT LIMITED
Consolidated Balance Sheet
January 1, Year 2

Cash (44,000 + 80,000)	$ 124,000
Accounts receivable (480,000 + 420,000)	900,000
Inventories (650,000 + 540,000 + 30,000)	1,220,000
Property, plant & equipment (2,610,000 + 870,000 − 130,000 + 50,000)	3,400,000
Accumulated depreciation (1,270,000 + 130,000 − 130,000)	(1,270,000)
Goodwill	250,000
	$ 4,624,000
Liabilities:	
Current liabilities (660,000 + 560,000)	$ 1,220,000
Bonds payable (820,000 + 490,000 + 60,000)	1,370,000
	2,590,000
Shareholders' equity:	
Common shares (200,000 + 1,000,000)	1,200,000
Retained earnings	834,000
	2,034,000
	$ 4,624,000

c. The balance sheets are exactly the same, except for the wording in the second line of the title. In part (a), it is ONT Limited's balance sheet for ONT by itself. In part (b), it is ONT Limited's consolidated balance sheet.

Appendix 3A

Reverse Takeovers

L08

For reporting purposes, the acquirer is identified based on which shareholder group has control over the combined entity.

A reverse takeover occurs when an enterprise obtains ownership of the shares of another enterprise but, as part of the transaction, issues enough voting shares as consideration that control of the combined enterprise passes to the shareholders of the acquired enterprise. Although, legally, the enterprise that issues the shares is regarded as the parent or continuing enterprise, the enterprise whose former shareholders now control the combined enterprise is treated as the acquirer for reporting purposes. As a result, the issuing enterprise (the legal parent) is deemed to be the acquiree and the company being acquired in appearance (the legal subsidiary) is deemed to have acquired control of the assets and business of the issuing enterprise.

While not a common event, this form of business combination is often used by active non-public companies as a means to obtain a stock exchange listing without having to go through the listing procedures established by the exchange. A takeover of a public company that has a stock exchange listing is arranged in such a way that the public company emerges as the legal parent, but the former shareholders of the non-public company have control of the public company.

EXHIBIT 3A.1

BALANCE SHEETS

	Reverse Ltd.		Takeover Co.
	Carrying amount	Fair value	Carrying amount
Current assets	$ 560	$ 700	$1,560
Plant assets	1,600	1,650	5,100
	$2,160		$6,660
Liabilities	$ 720	$ 720	$3,060
Common shares (160 shares)	500		
Retained earnings	940		
Common shares (96 shares)*			1,080
Retained earnings			2,520
	$2,160		$6,660

* The shares of Takeover Co. have a fair value of $30 per share.

Reverse Takeover Illustration

The balance sheets of Reverse Ltd. and Takeover Co. on the date of a reverse takeover business combination are shown in Exhibit 3A.1.

Reverse is a small public company engaged in business activity with a listing on a major stock exchange. Takeover is an active company not listed on any exchange. A business combination is initiated by Takeover whereby Reverse issues 240 shares to the shareholders of Takeover for 100% of their shareholdings. By structuring the combination in this manner, Reverse becomes the legal parent and Takeover the legal subsidiary.

An examination of the shares held by the two shareholder groups in the following manner clearly indicates that Takeover is identified as the acquirer:

	Shares of Reverse Ltd.	%
Shareholders of Reverse Ltd.	160	40%
Shareholders of Takeover Co.	240	60%
	400	100%

> In a reverse takeover, the legal parent is deemed to be the subsidiary for reporting purposes and the legal subsidiary is deemed to be the parent.

Under the acquisition method of accounting for a business combination, the fair value of the net assets of the acquiree is combined with the carrying amount of the net assets of the acquirer. Because Takeover is the acquirer, the acquisition cost is determined *as if* Takeover had issued shares to the shareholders of Reverse. A calculation has to be made to determine the number of shares that Takeover would have issued to achieve the same result (i.e., so that its shareholders would end up holding 60% of Takeover's outstanding shares). The number of shares can be determined as follows:

> The acquisition cost for the deemed parent is determined based on a hypothetical situation that could have achieved the same percentage ownership in the combined entity.

1. Before the combination, the shareholders of Takeover hold 96 shares in that company.
2. Takeover would have to issue X additional shares such that the 96 shares will represent 60% of the total shares outstanding.
3. After the share issue, the total shares outstanding will be $96 + X$ shares.
4. $96 = 0.6(96 + X)$. Therefore, $X = 64$ shares.

If Takeover had issued 64 shares, the holdings of the two groups of shareholders would have been as follows:

	Shares of Takeover Co.	%
Shareholders of Takeover	96	60%
Shareholders of Reverse	64	40%
	160	100%

Goodwill of the deemed subsidiary is based on the hypothetical acquisition cost.

The acquisition cost is the number of shares that Takeover would have issued, measured at their fair value, and is allocated in the following manner:

Acquisition cost—64 shares @ $30	$1,920
Fair value of identifiable net assets of Reverse Co.	1,630
Goodwill	$ 290

Shareholders' equity should reflect the shareholders' equity of the deemed parent.

The balance sheet of the consolidated company immediately after the business combination is prepared by combining the fair value of the net assets of Reverse, including the goodwill from the combination, with the carrying amount of the net assets of Takeover. It should be noted that Takeover's shareholders' equity becomes the shareholders' equity of the combined company. The dollar amount shown for common shares is determined by summing the dollar amount of the common shares of Takeover before the combination and the deemed issue of 64 shares at fair value. However, the number of shares shown as issued is the number of outstanding shares of the legal parent Reverse. The consolidated balance sheet of Reverse immediately after the reverse takeover takes place is shown in Exhibit 3A.2.

Note disclosure is required to explain that the reporting follows the substance (rather than the legal form) of who has control.

The financial statements of Reverse would contain the following footnote to describe this event: During the year, Reverse Ltd. entered into a share exchange agreement with the shareholders of Takeover Co. Under this agreement, Reverse exchanged 240 common shares for 100% of the issued and outstanding shares of Takeover. As a result of the share exchange, Reverse obtained control over Takeover.

Legally, Reverse is the parent of Takeover; however, as a result of the share exchange, control of the combined companies passed to the shareholders of Takeover, which for reporting purposes is deemed to be the acquirer. For financial reporting purposes, this share exchange is considered to be a reverse takeover and

---

EXHIBIT 3A.2

REVERSE LTD. CONSOLIDATED BALANCE SHEET

The legal parent/deemed subsidiary's assets are brought in at fair value while the legal subsidiary/deemed parent's assets are brought in at carrying amount.

Current assets (700 + 1,560)	$2,260
Plant assets (1,650 + 5,100)	6,750
Goodwill	290
	$9,300
Liabilities (720 + 3,060)	$3,780
Common shares* (1,080 + 1,920)	3,000
Retained earnings	2,520
	$9,300

The number of shares issued and outstanding would be shown as 400 shares (160 + 240).

Reverse is considered to be a continuation of Takeover. The net assets of Takeover are included in the balance sheet at carrying amounts, and the deemed acquisition of Reverse is accounted for by the acquisition method, with the net assets of Reverse recorded at fair values. The fair value of Reverse on the date of acquisition was as follows:

Current assets	$ 700
Plant assets	1,650
Goodwill	290
Liabilities	(720)
	$1,920

In this example, the acquisition cost was determined by multiplying the number of shares that the legal subsidiary would have had to issue by the fair value of that company's shares. However, because the legal subsidiary is often a private company, the fair value of its shares may have to be determined using business valuation concepts. If a fair value cannot be determined for the shares of the legal subsidiary, the fair value of the net assets of the legal parent are used to determine acquisition cost.

Comparative amounts presented in the consolidated financial statements of the legal parent are those of the deemed parent. In the year of the reverse takeover, consolidated net income is made up of the income of the deemed parent *before* the takeover and the income of the combined company *after* the takeover.

The comparative amounts are those of the legal subsidiary/deemed parent.

Because the outstanding shares shown on the consolidated balance sheet are those of the legal parent, the calculation of earnings per share is based on these shares; so is the calculation of the weighted average shares outstanding in the year of the takeover.

In the example of Reverse, assuming the combination date was July 31, the weighted average shares outstanding for the fiscal year December 31 is 307 shares, calculated as follows:

The consolidated financial statements use the name and shares outstanding of the legal parent.

- 240 shares deemed outstanding for 7 months, *and*
- 400 shares outstanding for 5 months.

This calculation is in contrast to the normal calculation of weighted average shares outstanding, and requires further clarification. Remember that the consolidated statements of Reverse (the legal parent) are considered to be a continuation of those of Takeover (the deemed parent) and that the accounting assumes that the deemed parent (the legal subsidiary) acquired the legal parent. But the shares outstanding are those of the legal parent.

The consolidated financial statements use values consistent with whoever, in substance, is the parent and who, in substance, is the subsidiary.

Consolidated net income for the year *does not* contain the income of Reverse prior to the takeover date because this income is considered to be pre-acquisition earnings. Reverse picked up the first seven months' income of Takeover with the issue of 240 shares. The last five months' income is that of Takeover and Reverse, during which time 400 shares (160 + 240) were outstanding.

The consolidated balance sheet of Reverse Ltd. (Exhibit 3A.2) was prepared using a non-working paper (or direct) approach. We will now illustrate the preparation of the consolidated balance sheet using a working paper (Exhibit 3A.3). On the date of the reverse takeover, Reverse (the legal parent)

EXHIBIT 3A.3

REVERSE LTD. CONSOLIDATED BALANCE SHEET WORKING PAPER
(at date of acquisition)

	Reverse Ltd.	Takeover Co.	Adjustments and Eliminations Dr.	Adjustments and Eliminations Cr.	Consolidated balance sheet
Current assets	$ 560	$1,560	(2) $ 140		$2,260
Plant assets	1,600	5,100	(2) 50		6,750
Investment in Takeover Co.	1,920			(1) $1,920	
Acquisition differential			(1) 480	(2) 480	
Goodwill			(2) 290		290
	$4,080	$6,660			$9,300
Liabilities	$ 720	$3,060			$3,780
Common shares (old)	500		(1) 500		
Retained earnings	940		(1) 940		
Common shares		1,080			3,000
Common shares (new)	1,920				
Retained earnings		2,520			2,520
	$4,080	$6,660	$2,400	$2,400	$9,300

The assets reflect the fair values of the deemed subsidiary and the carrying amounts of the deemed parent.

Retained earnings are the retained earnings of the deemed parent.

would make the following journal entry to record the acquisition of 100% of the outstanding shares of Takeover by the issuance of 240 common shares:

Investment in Takeover Co.	1,920	
Common shares (new)		1,920

These "new" shares are issued at the deemed acquisition cost and are shown separately on the working paper to simplify the consolidation process.

The calculation and allocation of the acquisition differential is as follows:

The calculation of the acquisition differential uses the acquisition cost under the hypothetical situation.

Acquisition cost of Takeover Co.			$1,920
Carrying amount of Reverse Ltd's net assets			
Assets		$2,160	
Liabilities		720	1,440
Acquisition differential			480
Allocated:			
Current assets (700 − 560)		$ 140	
Plant assets (1,650 − 1,600)		50	190
Goodwill			$ 290

Elimination entry **(1)** eliminates Reverse's investment in Takeover against Reverse's *precombination shareholders' equity,* with the acquisition differential the balancing amount.

Elimination **(2)** allocates the acquisition differential to revalue the net assets of Reverse.

The consolidated common shares are the common shares of Takeover (the deemed parent) before the takeover plus the new shares issued by Reverse, which are measured at Takeover's deemed acquisition cost of Reverse.

REVIEW QUESTIONS

Questions, cases, and problems that deal with the appendix material are denoted with an asterisk.

L01   1. What key element must be present in a business combination?

L02   2. Can a statutory amalgamation be considered a form of business combination? Explain.

L01   3. Explain how an acquirer is determined in a business combination for a 100%-owned subsidiary.

L03   4. Outline the accounting involved with the acquisition method for a 100%-owned subsidiary.

L03   5. Briefly describe the accounting involved with the new-entity method.

L02   6. If one company issued shares as payment for the net assets of another company, it would probably insist that the other company be wound up after the sale. Explain why this condition would be part of the purchase agreement.

L01   7. What criteria must be met for a subsidiary to be consolidated? Explain.

L01   8. What part do irrevocable agreements, convertible securities, and warrants play in determining whether control exists? Explain.

L05   9. What is an acquisition differential, and where does it appear on the consolidated balance sheet?

L04   10. What are some reasons for the purchase price being in excess of the carrying amount of the acquiree's assets and liabilities? What does this say about the accuracy of the values used in the financial statements of the acquiree?

L04   11. How is goodwill determined at the date of acquisition? Describe the nature of goodwill.

L04   12. When must an intangible asset be shown separately from goodwill? What are the criteria for reporting these intangible assets separately from goodwill?

L04   13. Does the historical cost principle or fair value reporting take precedence when preparing consolidated financial statements at the date of acquisition under the acquisition method? Explain.

L05   14. What are separate financial statements, and when can they be presented to external users in accordance with IFRSs?

L01   15. What are protective rights, and how do they affect the decision of whether one entity has control over another entity?

L05   16. In the preparation of a consolidated balance sheet, the differences between the fair value and the carrying amount of the subsidiary's net assets are used. Would these differences be used if the subsidiary applied push-down accounting? Explain.

L07   17. What are some of the main differences between IFRSs and ASPE for business combinations?

L08   *18. What is a reverse takeover, and why is such a transaction entered into?

L08   *19. Explain how the acquisition cost is determined for a reverse takeover.

CASES

Case 3-1
LO3, 7

On December 30, Year 7, Pepper Company agreed to form a business combination with Salt Limited. Pepper issued 2,320 of its common shares for all (2,900) of the outstanding common shares of Salt. This transaction increased the number of the outstanding Pepper shares from 3,800 to 6,120. The market value of the shares was $50 per share for Pepper and $40 for Salt. The balance sheets for the two companies just prior to the acquisition were as follows (in 000s):

	Pepper		Salt	
	Carrying amount	Fair value	Carrying amount	Fair value
Identifiable assets	$200	$250	$100	$130
Goodwill	0	100	0	70
	$200	$350	$100	$200
Liabilities	$150	$160	$ 80	$ 84
Shareholders' equity	50	190	20	116
	$200	$350	$100	$200

Consolidated financial statements will be prepared to combine the financial statements for the two companies. The management of Pepper is concerned about not exceeding a debt-to-equity ratio of 3:1 because of a covenant in a borrowing agreement with its bank. It wants to see how these consolidated statements would differ under two different methods of reporting: acquisition and new entity. Management also has the following questions when reporting this business combination:

- Why, under the acquisition method, is one set of assets and liabilities adjusted to fair value, whereas the other set is left at carrying amount?
- Given that under the acquisition method we can measure and report the net assets at fair values at the date of acquisition, why would we not report fair values at each subsequent reporting date?
- Which balance sheet best reflects the economic reality of the business combination?

Required:

Prepare a consolidated balance sheet at the date of acquisition under the two methods and respond to the questions asked by management.

Case 3-2
LO1

The directors of Atlas Inc. and Beta Corp. have reached an agreement in principle to merge the two companies and create a new company called AB Ltd. The basics of the agreement confirmed so far are outlined below:

The new company will purchase all of the assets and assume all of the liabilities of Atlas and Beta by issuing shares. After the sale the two companies will be wound up. Some but not all members of the top management of each company will be retained.

The number of AB shares that will be issued has not yet been determined.

The founding shareholders of Atlas Corp., who owned 60% of the voting shares of Atlas prior to the merger, have rights to veto any sale of patents, which they developed and registered. Some of the other shareholders of Atlas also owned non-voting preferred shares of Atlas. These preferred shares were convertible into common shares of Atlas on a one-for-one basis.

The chair of the merger committee has asked you to provide him with advice as to the accounting implications that will result from this merger, even though many of the details have not yet been ironed out. He has requested that you submit to him a preliminary report.

Required:

Prepare an outline of your report.

Case 3-3
LO2, 5, 8

Manitoba Peat Moss (MPM) was the first Canadian company to provide a reliable supply of high-quality peat moss to be used for greenhouse operations. Owned by Paul Parker, the company's founder and president, MPM began operations approximately 30 years ago when demand for peat moss was high. It has shown consistently high profits and stable growth for over 20 years. Parker holds all of the 50,000 outstanding common shares in MPM.

Prairie Greenhouses (PG), a publicly traded company that purchases over 70% of MPM's output, provides tree seedlings to various government agencies and logging companies for reforestation projects. In Year 5, PG approached MPM with an offer to buy all of the company's outstanding shares in exchange for a part ownership in PG, with a view to integrating vertically. Parker was very interested in the offer, since he hoped to retire soon. PG currently has 100,000 shares outstanding, and they are widely distributed. It would issue 100,000 new common shares to Paul Parker in a two-for-one exchange for all of MPM's shares. PG's shares are currently trading on the TSX at $65 per share.

The board of directors of PG is uncertain as to the accounting implications of the proposed share exchange. They believe that since they are purchasing all of the outstanding common shares of MPM, it is similar to buying the company outright. As a result, they want to report all of MPM's assets on PG's consolidated financial statements at fair value. This will be very advantageous to PG because the land carried on MPM's books was purchased 30 years ago and has appreciated substantially in value over the years.

The board has asked you, its accounting adviser, to prepare a report explaining how PG's purchase of shares should be reported. They are particularly interested in how the increase in the value of the land will be shown on the consolidated statements.

The condensed balance sheets of the two companies at the time of the offer are shown below:

	PG	MPM
Current assets	$ 870,000	$ 450,000
Property, plant & equipment	8,210,000	2,050,000
	$9,080,000	$2,500,000
Current liabilities	$ 525,000	$ 200,000
Long-term debt	2,325,000	1,300,000
Common shares	4,000,000	500,000
Retained earnings	2,230,000	500,000
	$9,080,000	$2,500,000

Note: Land held by MPM at a carrying amount of $1,000,000 has a fair value of $6,000,000. All other assets of both companies have carrying amounts approximately equal to their fair values.

Required:

Prepare the report to the board of directors.

(adapted from a case prepared by J.C. (Jan) Thatcher, Lakehead University, and Margaret Forbes, University of Saskatchewan)

Case 3-4
LO5

When Conoco Inc. of Houston, Texas, announced the CDN$7 billion acquisition of Gulf Canada Resources Limited of Calgary, Alberta, a large segment of the press release was devoted to outlining all of the expected benefits to be received from the assets acquired. The acquisition price represented a 35% premium over Gulf's closing share price on the announcement date. Included in the assets of Gulf were the following:

- Proven reserves of over 1 billion barrels of oil
- Probable reserves of approximately 1.2 billion barrels of oil
- Proven reserves of 1.4 trillion cubic feet of natural gas
- Probable reserves of 2.9 trillion cubic feet of natural gas
- Four million acres of undeveloped land in western Canada
- A 72% interest in Gulf Indonesia Resources Limited; included in this company's assets were reserves of 180 million barrels of oil and 1.5 trillion cubic feet of gas
- A 9% interest in joint venture, Syncrude Canada Ltd., which is developing the heavy oil tar sands in northern Alberta
- Long-term contracts to deliver 3 trillion cubic feet of natural gas to Southeast Asia
- Recent exploration successes in Sumatra and offshore Java

Required:

Many of the assets acquired in this business combination present particular valuation challenges. Provide guidance to the financial staff of Conoco as to how the price should be allocated among various tangible and intangible assets (including goodwill) and how liabilities included in the portfolio of Gulf Canada Resources Limited should be measured. Explain your answer in terms of the provisions of IFRSs.

(case prepared by Peter Secord, St. Mary's University)

Case 3-5
LO4, 7

Regina Communications Ltd. develops and manufactures equipment for technology and communications enterprises. Since its incorporation in Year 5, it has grown steadily through internal expansion. In the middle of Year 14, Arthur Lajord, the sole owner of Regina, met a couple of engineering students who were working on new technology to increase the efficiency of data transferred over cable lines. Arthur has provided moral support and some financial support to these students over the past few months. The company has developed some materials and processes sufficiently that a prospective buyer could buy the company, complete the development, and begin producing outputs for sale to prospective customers, or integrate the seller's materials and processes with its own inputs and processes.

At a lunch with the students last Friday, the students told Arthur that they had been able to register a patent to protect their technology. Furthermore, they were interested in selling their business, Davin Technologies Inc., which owns the patent and some other assets used in the development of this technology. After a week of negotiation, Arthur and the students agreed to the following:

- Rather than buying the shares of Davin, Regina would buy the assets and assume the liabilities of Davin effective January 1, Year 15.
- The purchase price would be payable as follows:

  - $200,000 on January 1, Year 15
  - $100,000 a year for three years commencing January 1, Year 16

- The students would commit to work for Regina as consultants over the next three years and would be paid $40 per hour for their services.

The condensed statement of financial position for Davin at January 1, Year 15, was as follows:

	Carrying amount	Fair value
Computer equipment	$ 30,000	$35,000
Patent registration costs	25,000	?
Current assets	50,000	50,000
	$105,000	
Shareholders' equity	$ 95,000	?
Liabilities	10,000	10,000
	$105,000	

Arthur was pleased and excited about the acquisition. He felt that it was a fair deal for both parties given that the business had not yet earned any revenue. He was particularly pleased that the students agreed to be paid over three years because he otherwise would have had to arrange a bank loan with an interest rate of 8%.

Arthur is now worried about the accounting for this acquisition because it is the first time that his company has purchased another business. Although Regina has always followed IFRSs, he is wondering whether now is the time to opt for a simpler approach. In particular, he is wondering whether IFRSs would allow the entire acquisition differential to be allocated to goodwill. This would keep it simple and would also avoid a charge to income over the first few years, since goodwill does not need to be amortized. If the acquisition differential is allocated to patent, then Arthur would like to write off the patent over the maximum period of 20 years.

Arthur has asked you, a CGA, to prepare a presentation on the accounting implications for the proposed acquisition. He wants to understand how to determine the acquisition cost, how to measure the individual assets and liabilities, and how this measurement would affect profit in the first year after the date of acquisition.

Required:

Prepare the presentation slides and related speaker's notes for the presentation. Limit your presentation to five slides. Your presentation should provide recommendations related to the issues raised by Arthur. Use financial statement concepts to support your recommendations. Provide a detailed calculation to show the impact on profit for Year 15. State your assumptions.

(CGA-Canada adapted)

*Case 3-6
LO1, 8

Uni-Invest Ltd. holds commercial and residential real estate interests in Nova Scotia, New Brunswick, Prince Edward Island, Alberta, and British Columbia. On October 23, Year 10, Basic Realty Investment Corporation acquired 100% of the outstanding common shares of Uni-Invest Ltd. in exchange for 32,584,051 common shares of Basic.

At October 31, Year 9, Basic had 3,333,320 common shares and 6,000,001 Class C preferred shares issued and outstanding. Prior to the acquisition, the 6,000,001 Class C preferred shares were converted to common shares on a share-for-share basis. Then, on October 23, Year 10, the 9,333,321 common shares were consolidated five for one to yield 1,866,664 common shares, with a carrying amount of $746 and a fair value of $2,024,845. Values for Basic's shareholders' equity are summarized as follows:

Capital shares issued	Number of shares	Amount
Balance prior to investment in Uni-Invest	1,866,664	$ 746
Issued to effect investment on October 23, Year 10, net of costs of $84,177	32,584,051	33,236,248
Balance December 31, Year 10	34,450,715	$33,236,994

Details of the fair value excess for the assets acquired and liabilities assumed on the transaction are as follows:

Assets acquired	
Property, plant & equipment	$4,632,398
Other assets	271,436
	4,903,834
Liabilities assumed	
Long-term debt	2,707,504
Other liabilities	143,000
	2,850,504
Fair value excess for net assets acquired	$2,053,330

Required:

Based on this information, how should this investment be reported? More specifically, which company is the parent? Which is the subsidiary? Why? What earnings, and for what period, are reported in the consolidated financial statements for the year ended December 31, Year 10? Why?

(adapted from a case prepared by Peter Second, St. Mary's University)

Case 3-7
LO1, 2, 5

Planet Publishing Limited (Planet) is a medium-sized, privately owned Canadian company that holds exclusive Canadian distribution rights for the publications of Typset Daily Corporation (TDC). Space Communications Ltd. (Space), an unrelated privately owned Canadian company, held similar distribution rights for the publications of Worldwide Affairs Limited (WAL).

TDC and WAL were unrelated US publishers of magazines and books. WAL went into receivership in early Year 3 and was then purchased by TDC. TDC did not want the exclusive rights for its publications split between two companies, and it did not believe that either Planet or Space, individually, could adequately distribute its products in Canada. In order to retain the distribution rights that otherwise would have been lost at the expiry of the contracts, Space merged with Planet on July 31, Year 3. Details regarding the merger and the restructuring that followed soon after the merger are provided in Exhibit I.

In September Year 3, the directors of Planet requested that your firm let its name be offered as auditor for the year ending February 28, Year 4. Your firm accepted the request. In prior years, two other firms audited Planet and Space. It is now October Year 3, and your firm was appointed as auditors at a shareholders' meeting. Subsequent to your appointment as auditors, the president requested a report on the following matters:

1. The accounting treatment that should be given to the merger and to the transactions that have arisen since February 28, Year 3, together with full reasons for all recommendations.
2. Any other issues (other than tax and assurance) that the president should be aware of, arising from the merger, or from recent events, together with recommendations.

The partner in charge of the engagement asked you, aCA, a manager in the firm, to prepare the draft report. You and your staff have gathered information on Planet. This information is contained in Exhibit II.

EXHIBIT I

INFORMATION REGARDING THE MERGER

1. The merger of Planet and Space took effect on July 31, Year 3, and involved these steps:
   a. Planet issued voting shares of the company to the shareholders of Space in exchange for all the outstanding shares of Space. Planet's original shareholders now own 75% of Planet's voting shares.
   b. Space was wound up.
   c. Space's offices were closed, and its operations were moved to Planet's offices. Space had a 10-year lease with four years remaining. All warehouses remained in operation.
   d. Several employees were terminated (and given two to six months' salary) or offered early retirement packages.
2. Planet retained the same year-end of February 28.
3. After the merger, Planet signed new exclusive distribution contracts with TDC and its wholly owned subsidiary, WAL. This gave Planet all the rights that had previously been assigned to Planet or to the former Space. The rights are for five years but are renewable for another five at the option of Planet. These rights include distribution of magazines, books, and videos that accompany books. TDC sells to Planet at a special discount that precludes Planet from returning any merchandise.
4. Before the merger Space had been in financial difficulty, incurring large losses over the past few years. During the merger negotiations Space and Planet approached Space's creditors with a plan to restructure Space's debt. In September Year 3, Planet had been able to finalize the restructuring of some of the debts of the former Space as follows:
   a. A trade account of US$320,000 due to TDC was converted into a two-year note payable, due in September Year 5. The note is non–interest bearing and is unsecured.

(continued)

EXHIBIT I   (*continued*)

b.   Loans of $500,000 due to shareholders and accrued interest of $125,000 were converted in September Year 3 into convertible, preferred shares bearing an 8% non-cumulative dividend.

c.   One of the major shareholders forgave a loan of $110,000 in September, Year 3.

d.   Creditors who were owed $200,000 agreed to accept $0.80 on the dollar provided that they were paid before November 17, Year 3. Approximately 10% had been paid by the end of September, Year 3.

5.   Under both the merger agreement and a separate contractual arrangement with Planet's banker, the shareholders of Planet were required to contribute $1.5 million of new equity into the company in August Year 3. After the funds had been deposited, the banker made the following loans:

a.   A $1 million demand loan to be secured by receivables, inventory, and a registered debenture on all unencumbered assets of Planet. In order to borrow the full $1 million, the company must maintain average balances of $1.2 million in receivables and $600,000 in inventory.

b.   A $2 million term loan on real property belonging to the original Planet, and chattels, for which the bank holds the first mortgage or a lien claim with priority over those of other creditors. The term loan is for up to two years and can be drawn upon as needed.

6.   As part of the distribution agreement with TDC, Planet must provide financial statements to TDC for fiscal Year 4, Year 5, and Year 6.

7.   The bank wants monthly listings of inventory, aged receivables, and cash flows. The bank loan agreement stipulates covenants that must be adhered to, including debt-to-equity ratios, no dividends on voting shares, maximum salary limits, and limits on bonuses.

EXHIBIT II

INFORMATION ON PLANET

1.   In August Year 3, Planet made the following transactions:

a.   To diversify, Planet invested $800,000 cash in a Canadian specialist magazine. This magazine has been successful for several years, and it is expected to generate over $150,000 per year in cash flows after taxes. Planet acquired customer and advertiser lists, title to the magazine, some files, and many back issues. Six staff members from the magazine joined Planet, forming the core management and providing continuity.

b.   Planet decided to invest about $350,000 in cash in an advertising program to attract new subscribers to the specialist magazine. The $350,000 is to be amortized over the expected subscription life of the group of new subscribers. The $350,000 was paid to an advertising agency in August Year 3. In addition, Planet and the agency have agreed that the agency will provide the equivalent of another $300,000 for a promotion campaign in exchange for free advertising space in Planet's specialist magazine. These free advertisements are expected to be published over the next six months.

In recent years, the cost of preparing or producing a magazine published in Canada has tended to be three to four times the average subscription price. Throughout Year 3, subscriptions were offered at half price if subscribers paid in advance for three years.

2.   The sales of magazines published by TDC and other publishers account for most of Planet's (and the former Space's) business. Retail sales dollars and margins have remained constant over the past few years in this market. Retailers are generally permitted to return each month's unsold magazines to the distributor for credit against future sales.

(*continued*)

| **EXHIBIT II** | *(continued)* |

3. Arrangements with book stores allow them to return half of the books that they pur-
    chase, as long as the returns occur within six months of purchase. Over the past five to
    eight years, returns have varied considerably. Most book stores pay about 120 days after
    purchase.
4. Several small book stores have gone bankrupt during the recent recession, and only
    some of the inventory was returned prior to bankruptcy. Minimal payments from trust-
    ees for these bankrupt stores are expected over the next three to five years.
5. Over $400,000 had been withdrawn from Planet by the major shareholders in the two
    years leading to the merger. There are rumours that some minority shareholders may
    file a lawsuit against Planet.
6. Before the merger, both Space and Planet engaged in various non-arm's length trans-
    actions that were materially different from fair values. Notes to the respective financial
    statements mentioned that non–arm's length transactions had occurred but did not
    provide any details.
7. Planet's Year 4 financial statements will be included in documents designed to attract
    capital through an initial public offering in the near future. Planet wants to apply
    accounting standards for public enterprises.
8. Considerable investment in subscription drives is expected over the next several
    months. Management wants to capitalize all expenditures and employ a 10-year amor-
    tization period.
9. In the fiscal year ended in Year 3, about one-third of both Planet's and Space's sales
    came from Canadian published products and two-thirds from TDC and WAL products.

Required:

Prepare the draft report.

(CICA adapted)

PROBLEMS

Problem 3-1
LO3, 6

G Company is considering the takeover of K Company whereby it will issue
6,000 common shares for all of the outstanding shares of K Company. K Company
will become a wholly owned subsidiary of G Company. Prior to the acquisition,
G Company had 20,000 shares outstanding, which were trading at $4.90 per share.
The following information has been assembled:

	G Company		**K Company**	
	Carrying amount	*Fair value*	*Carrying amount*	*Fair value*
Current assets	$ 40,000	$47,500	$ 10,000	$9,200
Plant assets (net)	60,000	70,000	20,000	25,000
	$100,000		$ 30,000	
Current liabilities	$ 20,000	20,000	$ 5,000	5,000
Long-term debt	15,000	19,000	2,500	3,200
Common shares	30,000		10,000	
Retained earnings	35,000		12,500	
	$100,000		$ 30,000	

Required:

(a) Prepare G Company's consolidated balance sheet immediately after the combination using
  (i) the new-entity method, and
  (ii) the acquisition method.

(b) Calculate the current ratio and debt-to-equity ratio for G Company under both methods. Explain which method shows the strongest liquidity and solvency position and which method best reflects the true financial condition of the company.

Problem 3-2
LO2, 4

Three companies, A, L, and M, whose December 31, Year 5, balance sheets below, have agreed to combine as at January 1, Year 6.

Each of the companies has a very small proportion of an intensely competitive market dominated by four much larger companies. In order to survive, they have decided to merge into one company. The merger agreement states that Company A will buy the assets and liabilities of each of the other two companies by issuing 27,000 common shares to Company L and 25,000 common shares to Company M, after which the two companies will be wound up.

Company A's shares are currently trading at $5 per share.

Company A will incur the following costs:

Costs of issuing shares	$ 8,000
Professional fees	20,000
	$28,000

The following information has been assembled regarding the three companies:

COMPANY A

	Carrying amount	Fair value
Current assets	$ 99,900	$102,000
Plant and equipment (net)	147,600	160,000
	$247,500	
Liabilities	$ 80,000	75,000
Common shares (50,000 shares)	75,000	
Retained earnings	92,500	
	$247,500	

COMPANY L

	Carrying amount	Fair value
Current assets	$ 60,000	$ 65,000
Plant and equipment (net)	93,000	98,000
	$153,000	
Liabilities	$ 35,000	36,000
Common shares (24,000 shares)	48,000	
Retained earnings	70,000	
	$153,000	

COMPANY M

	Carrying amount	Fair value
Current assets	$ 52,000	$ 68,000
Plant and equipment (net)	115,000	120,000
	$167,000	
Liabilities	$ 72,000	70,000
Common shares (33,000 shares)	60,000	
Retained earnings	35,000	
	$167,000	

Required:

Prepare the balance sheet of Company A on January 2, Year 6, after Company L and Company M have been wound up.

Problem 3-3
LO4

The statement of financial position of Bagley Incorporated as at July 31, Year 4, is as follows:

BAGLEY INCORPORATED STATEMENT OF FINANCIAL POSITION
at July 31, Year 4

	Carrying amount	Fair value
Plant and equipment — net	$ 910,000	$1,053,000
Patents	—	78,000
Current assets	455,000	507,000
	$1,365,000	
Ordinary shares	$ 182,000	
Retained earnings	520,000	
Long-term debt	390,000	416,000
Current liabilities	273,000	273,000
	$1,365,000	

On August 1, Year 4, the directors of Bagley considered a takeover offer from Davis Inc., whereby the corporation would sell all of its assets and liabilities. Davis's costs of investigation and drawing up the merger agreement would amount to $19,500.

Required:

(a) Assume that Davis made a $1,040,000 cash payment to Bagley for its net assets. Prepare the journal entries in the accounting records of Davis to record the business combination.

(b) Assume that Davis issued 130,000 ordinary shares, with a market value of $8 per share, to Bagley for its net assets. Legal fees associated with issuing these shares amounted to $6,500 and were paid in cash. Davis had 150,000 shares outstanding prior to the takeover.

   (i) Prepare the journal entries in the records of Davis to record the business combination.

   (ii) Prepare the statement of financial position of Bagley immediately after the sale.

Problem 3-4
LO2, 5

The shareholders of Prong Company and Horn Company agreed to a statutory amalgamation under which a share exchange took place. On September 1, Year 5, Prong Company issued 60,000 ordinary shares for all of the ordinary shares of Horn Company, after which Horn Company was dissolved. The ordinary shares of Prong Company traded at $7 per share on this date.

After the amalgamation, Prong Company changed its name to Pronghorn Corporation.

The statements of financial position of the two companies on August 31, Year 5, were as follows:

	Prong Company	Horn Company
Plant and equipment	$ 635,000	$ 489,000
Accumulated depreciation	(205,000)	(189,000)
Other assets	41,000	20,000
Current assets	135,000	170,000
	$ 606,000	$ 490,000
Ordinary shares (note 1)	$ 70,000	$ 100,000
Retained earnings	260,000	200,000
Long-term debt	180,000	160,000
Current liabilities	96,000	30,000
	$ 606,000	$ 490,000
Note 1		
Ordinary shares outstanding	70,000	25,000

The carrying amounts of the net assets of both companies were equal to fair values except for plant and equipment. The fair values of plant and equipment were as follows:

Prong Company	$500,000
Horn Company	280,000

Prong's other assets include patent registration costs with a carrying amount of $25,000. An independent appraiser placed a value of $100,000 on this patent.

Required:

Prepare the statement of financial position of Pronghorn Corporation immediately after the statutory amalgamation.

Problem 3-5
LO5, 6, 7

The balance sheet of Drake Enterprises as at December 31, Year 5, is as follows:

Assets

Cash	$ 99,000
Accounts receivable	143,000
Inventory	191,400
Property, plant, and equipment	1,692,000
Accumulated depreciation	(900,000)
	$1,225,400

Liabilities and Equity

Current liabilities	$ 242,000
Bonds payable	352,000
Common shares (100,000 shares)	220,000
Retained earnings	411,400
	$1,225,400

Effective January 1, Year 6, Drake proposes to issue 82,500 common shares (currently trading at $20 per share) for all of the common shares of Hanson Industries. In determining the acquisition price, the management of Drake noted that Hanson Industries has unrecorded customer service contracts and directed its accounting staff to reflect this when recording the acquisition. An independent appraiser placed a value of $150,000 on this unrecorded intangible asset. Direct costs associated with the acquisition were as follows:

Costs of issuing shares	$44,000
Professional fees	38,500
	$82,500

The balance sheet of Hanson Industries as at December 31, Year 5, is as follows:

	Carrying amount	Fair value
Cash	$ 55,000	$ 55,000
Accounts receivable	275,000	280,500
Inventory	187,000	178,200
Property, plant, and equipment	1,169,000	1,017,500
Accumulated depreciation	(300,000)	
	$1,386,000	
Current liabilities	$ 137,500	137,500
Liability for warranties	99,000	129,800
Common shares	660,000	
Retained earnings	489,500	
	$1,386,000	

Hanson Industries is to be wound up after the sale.

Required:

(a) Assume that the shareholders of Hanson accept Drake's offer on the proposed date. Prepare Drake's January 1, Year 6, consolidated balance sheet after the proposed transaction occurred.

(b) Assume that Drake is a private entity, uses ASPE, and chooses to use the equity method to account for its investment in Hanson. Prepare Drake's January 1, Year 6, balance sheet after the proposed transaction occurred.

(c) Compare the balance sheets in parts (a) and (b). Which balance sheet shows the highest debt-to-equity ratio? Which balance sheet better reflects Drake's solvency risk? Briefly explain.

Problem 3-6
LO4
D Ltd. and H Corporation are both engaged in the manufacture of computers. On July 1, Year 5, they agree to a merger, whereby D will issue 300,000 shares with current market value of $9 each for the net assets of H.

Summarized balance sheets of the two companies prior to the merger are presented below:

BALANCE SHEET
June 30, Year 5

	D Ltd.	H Corporation	
	Carrying amount	Carrying amount	Fair value
Current assets	$ 450,000	$ 500,000	$ 510,000
Non-current assets (net)	4,950,000	3,200,000	3,500,000
	$5,400,000	$3,700,000	

(continued)

BALANCE SHEET

June 30, Year 5

	D Ltd.	H Corporation	
	Carrying amount	Carrying amount	Fair value
Current liabilities	$ 600,000	$ 800,000	800,000
Long-term debt	1,100,000	900,000	920,000
Common shares	2,500,000	500,000	27000
Retained earnings	1,200,000	1,500,000	
	$5,400,000	$3,700,000	

In determining the purchase price, the management of D Ltd. noted that H Corporation leases a manufacturing facility under an operating lease that has terms that are favourable relative to market terms. However, the lease agreement explicitly prohibits transfer of the lease (through either sale or sublease). An independent appraiser placed a value of $60,000 on this favourable lease agreement.

Required:

Prepare the July 1, Year 5, balance sheet of D, after the merger.

Problem 3-7
LO5, 6, 7

The July 31, Year 3, balance sheets of two companies that are parties to a business combination are as follows:

	Red Corp.	Sax Inc.	
	Carrying amount	Carrying amount	Fair value
Current assets	$1,600,000	$ 420,000	$468,000
Property, plant, and equipment (net)	1,080,000	840,000	972,000
Patents	—	—	72,000
	$2,680,000	$1,260,000	
Current liabilities	$1,360,000	$ 252,000	252,000
Long-term debt	480,000	360,000	384,000
Common shares	720,000	168,000	
Retained earnings	120,000	480,000	
	$2,680,000	$1,260,000	

In addition to the property, plant, and equipment identified above, Red Corp. attributed a value of $100,000 to Sax's assembled workforce. They have the knowledge and skill to operate Sax's manufacturing facility and are critical to the success of the operation. Although the eight manufacturing employees are not under any employment contracts, management of Red was willing to pay $100,000 as part of the purchase price on the belief that most or all of these employees would continue to work for the company.

Effective on August 1, Year 3, the shareholders of Sax accepted an offer from Red Corporation to purchase all of their common shares. Red's costs for investigating and drawing up the share purchase agreement amounted to $18,000.

Required:

(a) Assume that Red made a $960,000 cash payment to the shareholders of Sax for 100% of their shares.

(i) Prepare the journal entry in the records of Red to record the share acquisition.

(ii) Prepare the consolidated balance sheet of Red Corp. as at August 1, Year 3. Explain the rationale for the accounting for the $100,000 value attributed to Sax's assembled workforce.

(b) Assume that Red issued 120,000 common shares, with market value of $8 per share to the shareholders of Sax for 100% of their shares. Legal fees associated with issuing these shares amounted to $6,000 and were paid in cash. Red is identified as the acquirer.

(i) Prepare the journal entries in the records of Red to record the share acquisition and related fees.

(ii) Prepare the consolidated balance sheet of Red as at August 1, Year 3.

(c) Assume the same facts as part (b) expect that Red is a private company, uses ASPE, and chooses to use the cost method to account for its investment in Sax.

(i) Prepare the journal entries in the records of Red to record the share acquisition and related fees.

(ii) Prepare the balance sheet of Red as at August 1, Year 3.

Problem 3-8
LO4

The following are summarized statements of financial position of three companies as at December 31, Year 3:

	Company X	Company Y	Company Z
Assets	$400,000	$300,000	$250,000
Ordinary shares (note 1)	$ 75,000	$ 48,000	$ 60,000
Retained earnings	92,500	70,000	35,000
Liabilities	232,500	182,000	155,000
	$400,000	$300,000	$250,000
Note 1			
Shares outstanding	50,000	12,000	16,500

The fair values of the identifiable assets and liabilities of the three companies as at December 31, Year 3, were as follows:

	Company X	Company Y	Company Z
Assets	$420,000	$350,000	$265,000
Liabilities	233,000	180,000	162,000

On January 2, Year 4, Company X will purchase the assets and assume the liabilities of Company Y and Company Z. It has been agreed that Company X will issue common shares to each of the two companies as payment for their net assets as follows:

To Company Y—13,500 shares
To Company Z—12,000 shares

The shares of Company X traded at $15 on December 31, Year 3.
Company X will incur the following costs associated with this acquisition:

Costs of registering and issuing shares	$12,000
Other professional fees associated with the takeover	30,000
	$42,000

Company Y and Company Z will be wound up after the sale.

Required:

(a) Prepare a summarized pro forma statement of financial position of Company X as at January 2, Year 4, after the purchase of net assets from Company Y and Company Z.

(b) Prepare the pro forma statements of financial position of Company Y and Company Z as at January 2, Year 4, after the sale of net assets to Company X and prior to being wound up.

Problem 3-9
LO4

Myers Company Ltd. was formed 10 years ago by the issuance of 22,000 common shares to three shareholders. Four years later, the company went public and issued an additional 30,000 common shares.

The management of Myers is considering a takeover in which Myers would purchase all of the assets and assume all of the liabilities of Norris Inc. Two alternative proposals are being considered:

PROPOSAL 1

Myers would offer to pay $400,000 cash for the Norris net assets, to be financed by a $400,000 bank loan due in five years. In addition, Myers would incur legal, appraisal, and finders' fees for a total cost of $5,000.

PROPOSAL 2

Myers would issue 50,000 shares currently trading at $8 each for the Norris net assets. Other costs associated with the takeover would be as follows:

Legal, appraisal, and finders' fees	$ 5,000
Costs of issuing shares	7,000
	$12,000

Norris shareholders would be offered five seats on the 10-member board of directors of Myers, and the management of Norris would be absorbed into the surviving company.

Balance sheet data for the two companies prior to the combination are as follows:

	Myers	Norris	
	Carrying amount	Carrying amount	Fair value
Cash	$ 140,000	$ 52,500	$ 52,500
Accounts receivable	167,200	61,450	56,200
Inventory	374,120	110,110	134,220
Land	425,000	75,000	210,000
Buildings (net)	250,505	21,020	24,020
Equipment (net)	78,945	17,705	15,945
	$1,435,770	$337,785	492,885
Current liabilities	$ 133,335	$ 41,115	41,115
Non-current liabilities	—	150,000	155,000
Common shares	500,000	100,000	196,115
Retained earnings	802,435	46,670	
	$1,435,770	$337,785	

Required:

(a) Prepare the journal entries of Myers for each of the two proposals being considered.

(b) Prepare the balance sheet of Myers after the takeover for each of the proposals being considered.

Problem 3-10
LO5

Refer to Problem 9. All of the facts and data are the same except that in the proposed takeover, Myers Company will purchase all of the outstanding common shares of Norris Inc.

Required:

(a) Prepare the journal entries of Myers for each of the two proposals being considered.
(b) Prepare the consolidated balance sheet of Myers after the takeover for each of the proposals being considered.

Problem 3-11
LO5

Baker Corporation has the following account balances at December 31, Year 4:

Receivables	$ 80,000
Inventory	200,000
Land	600,000
Building (net)	500,000
Liabilities	400,000
Common shares	200,000
Retained earnings, 1/1/Year 4	700,000
Revenues	300,000
Expenses	220,000

Several of Baker's accounts have fair values that differ from carrying amount: land, $400,000; building, $600,000; inventory, $280,000; and liabilities, $330,000. Home Inc. purchases all of the outstanding shares of Baker by issuing 20,000 common shares with a market value of $56 per share. Stock issuance costs amount to $10,000.

Required:

(a) What is the acquisition cost in this business combination?
(b) What is the carrying amount of Baker's net assets on the date of the takeover?
(c) How does the issuance of these shares affect the shareholders' equity accounts of Home, the parent?
(d) How are the stock issuance costs handled?
(e) What amounts are incorporated on the consolidated balance sheet for each of Baker's assets (including goodwill, if any) and liabilities at the date of acquisition?
(f) How do Baker's revenues and expenses affect consolidated totals? Why?
(g) How do Baker's common shares affect consolidated totals?
(h) If Home's shares had been worth only $40 per share rather than $56, how would the consolidation of Baker's assets and liabilities have been affected?

Problem 3-12
LO5

The financial statements for CAP Inc. and SAP Company for the year ended December 31, Year 5, follow:

	CAP	SAP
Revenues	$ 900,000	$ 300,000
Expenses	660,000	200,000
Profit	$ 240,000	$ 100,000

	CAP	SAP
Retained earnings, 1/1/Year 5	$ 800,000	$ 200,000
Profit	240,000	100,000
Dividends paid	90,000	0
Retained earnings, 12/31/Year 5	$ 950,000	$ 300,000
Equipment (net)	$ 700,000	$ 600,000
Patented technology (net)	900,000	300,000
Receivables and inventory	400,000	170,000
Cash	80,000	110,000
Total assets	$2,080,000	$1,180,000
Ordinary shares	$ 530,000	$ 470,000
Retained earnings	950,000	300,000
Liabilities	600,000	410,000
Total equities and liabilities	$2,080,000	$1,180,000

On December 31, Year 5, after the above figures were prepared, CAP issued $300,000 in debt and 15,000 new shares to the owners of SAP to purchase all of the outstanding shares of that company. CAP shares had a fair value of $40 per share.

CAP also paid $30,000 to a broker for arranging the transaction. In addition, CAP paid $40,000 in stock issuance costs. SAP's equipment was actually worth $710,000 but its patented technology was valued at only $270,000.

Required:

What are the balances for following accounts on the on the Year 5 consolidated financial statements?

(a) Profit
(b) Retained earnings, 12/31/Year 5
(c) Equipment
(d) Patented technology
(e) Goodwill
(f) Ordinary shares
(g) Liabilities

Problem 3-13
L01

Z Ltd. is a public company with factories and distribution centres located throughout Canada. It has 100,000 common shares outstanding. In past years, it has reported high earnings, but in Year 5, its earnings declined substantially in part due to a loss of markets as a result of the North American Free Trade Agreement. In Year 6, it closed a large number of its manufacturing and distribution facilities and reported a substantial loss for the year.

Prior to Year 6, 70,000 of Z Ltd.'s shares were held by C Ltd., with the remaining shares being widely distributed in the hands of individual investors in Canada and the United States. On January 1, Year 6, C Ltd. sold 40,000 of its shares in Z Ltd. to W Corporation.

Required:

(a) How should C Ltd. report its investment in Z Ltd., both before the sale of 40,000 shares and after the sale?
(b) How should W Corporation report its investment in Z Ltd.? Explain fully, and include in your answers a reference to Z Ltd.'s Year 6 loss.

*Problem 3-14
LO8

The balance sheets of X Ltd. and Y Ltd. on December 30, Year 7, are as follows:

	X Ltd.		Y Ltd.	
	Book value	Fair value	Book value	Fair value
Current assets	$ 300	$ 300	$1,000	$1,000
Non-current assets	1,500	1,700	2,700	2,800
	$1,800		$3,700	
Current liabilities	$ 400	400	$ 900	900
Long-term debt	300	300	800	800
Common shares—100 issued	400			
Common shares—60 issued			600	
Retained earnings	700		1,400	
	$1,800		$3,700	

On December 31, Year 7, X issued 150 common shares for all 60 outstanding common shares of Y. The fair value of each of Y's common shares was $40 on this date.

Required:

(a) Explain why this share issue most likely occurred.
(b) Prepare the consolidated balance sheet of X Ltd. on December 31, Year 7.

(CICA adapted)

WEB-BASED PROBLEMS

Web Problem 3-1
LO3, 6

Access the 2011 consolidated financial statements for Rogers Communications Inc. by going to the investor's relations section of the company's website. Answer the questions below. Round percentages to one decimal point and other ratios to two decimal points. For each question, indicate where in the financial statements you found the answer, and/or provide a brief explanation.

(a) What method was used to account for business combinations?
(b) Describe the most significant business acquisition during the year. Was it a purchase of net assets or shares?
(c) How much cash was paid for all business acquisitions during the year?
(d) In the allocation of the acquisition cost for the most significant business acquisition, what amounts were allocated to (i) intangible assets and (ii) goodwill?
(e) What percentage of total assets at the end of the year is represented by (i) intangible assets and (ii) goodwill?
(f) Assume that the company had paid 10% more for its acquisitions of 100%-owned subsidiaries, and that the extra amount was paid in cash. How would this have affected the (i) current ratio and (ii) debt-to-equity ratio at the date of acquisition?
(g) Assume that the market capitalization of the company's shares (i.e., number of shares outstanding times market value per share) was double the carrying amount of shareholders' equity on the date when the business acquisitions occurred, and that the company uses the new-entity method

to account for business combinations. How would this have affected the (i) debt-to-equity ratio at the date of acquisition and (ii) the return on equity for the first year after the date of acquisition?

Web Problem 3-2
LO3, 6

Access the 2011 consolidated financial statements for ATCO Ltd. by going to the investor's relations section of the company's website. Answer the same questions as in Web Problem 1. For each question, indicate where in the financial statements you found the answer, and/or provide a brief explanation. (Some questions may not be applicable.)

Consolidation of Non–Wholly Owned Subsidiaries

LEARNING OBJECTIVES

After studying this chapter, you should be able to do the following for non–wholly owned subsidiaries at the date of acquisition:

LO1 Explain the basic differences between the four theories of consolidation.

LO2 Prepare a consolidated balance sheet using the entity theory.

LO3 Prepare a consolidated balance sheet using the parent company extension theory.

LO4 Explain the concept of negative goodwill and describe how it should be treated when it arises in a business combination.

LO5 Account for contingent consideration based on its classification as a liability or equity.

LO6 Analyze and interpret financial statements involving consolidation of non–wholly owned subsidiaries.

LO7 Identify some of the differences between IFRSs and ASPE involving consolidation of non–wholly owned subsidiaries.

LO8 Prepare a consolidated balance sheet using the working paper approach.

INTRODUCTION

Financial statements published and distributed to owners, creditors, and other interested parties appear to report the operations and financial position of a single company. In reality, these statements frequently represent a number of separate organizations tied together through common control as a result of a business combination. Whenever financial statements represent more than one corporation, we refer to them as *consolidated financial statements*.

Consolidated financial statements are typical in today's business world. Most major organizations, and many smaller ones, have control over an array of organizations. For example, between 2006 and 2009, Cisco Systems Inc. acquired or established more than 60 subsidiaries that now are consolidated in its financial reports. PepsiCo Inc., as another example, consolidates data from a multitude of companies into a single set of financial statements. By gaining control over these companies, which include, among others, Pepsi-Cola Company, Quaker Foods, and Frito-Lay, a single reporting entity is formed by PepsiCo.

The consolidation of financial information as exemplified by Cisco Systems and PepsiCo is one of the most complex procedures in all of accounting. To comprehend this process completely, the theoretical logic that underlies the

> Consolidated financial statements report the combined results of the parent and all its subsidiaries.

creation of a business combination must be understood. Furthermore, a variety of procedural steps must be mastered to ensure that proper accounting is achieved for this single reporting entity. In Chapter 3, we introduced the preparation of a consolidated balance sheet at the date of acquisition using the acquisition method. Summarized financial statements were used to focus on the basic concepts involved. In this chapter, we elaborate on these concepts and use more detailed financial statements. We will now focus on the consolidation of non–wholly owned subsidiaries.

NON–WHOLLY OWNED SUBSIDIARIES

In the illustrations in Chapter 3, the parent acquired 100% of the subsidiary. The subsidiary's assets and liabilities were brought onto the consolidated balance at fair value.[1] We will now consider situations where the parent acquires less than 100% of the shares.

> These balance sheets present the financial position just prior to the business combination.

The following example will form the basis of many of the illustrations that will be used in this chapter. We will call the two companies to be consolidated P Ltd. and S Ltd. Both companies have a June 30 fiscal year-end. The balance sheets of the two companies on June 29, Year 1, are shown in Exhibit 4.1.

On June 30, Year 1, P Ltd. obtains control over S Ltd. by paying cash to the shareholders of S Ltd. for a portion of that company's outstanding common shares. No additional transactions take place on this date. Immediately after the share acquisition, P Ltd. prepares a consolidated balance sheet.

> The part of the subsidiary not owned by the parent is called non-controlling interest (NCI).

The shares not acquired by the parent are owned by other shareholders, who are referred to as the non-controlling shareholders. The value of the shares attributed to the non-controlling shareholders, when presented on the consolidated

EXHIBIT 4.1

BALANCE SHEET
At June 29, Year 1

	P Ltd.	S Ltd.	
	Carrying amount	Carrying amount	Fair value
Cash	$100,000	$ 12,000	$ 12,000
Accounts receivable	90,000	7,000	7,000
Inventory	130,000	20,000	22,000
Plant	280,000	50,000	59,000
Patent	—	11,000	10,000
Total Assets	$600,000	$100,000	$110,000
Current liabilities	$ 60,000	$ 8,000	$ 8,000
Long-term debt	180,000	22,000	25,000
Total liabilities	240,000	30,000	$ 33,000
Common shares	200,000	40,000	
Retained earnings	160,000	30,000	
Total Liabilities and Shareholders' Equity	$600,000	$100,000	

financial statements, is referred to as *non-controlling interests,* abbreviated as NCI. The non-controlling interests represent an additional set of owners who have legal claim to the subsidiary's net assets.

Three questions arise when preparing consolidated financial statements for less-than-100%-owned subsidiaries:

1. How should the portion of the subsidiary's assets and liabilities that was not acquired by the parent be measured on the consolidated financial statements?

2. How should NCI be measured on the consolidated financial statements?

3. How should NCI be presented on the consolidated financial statements?

There are many ways of measuring and presenting NCI on the consolidated financial statements.

The following theories have developed over time and have been proposed as solutions to preparing consolidated financial statements for non–wholly owned subsidiaries:

- Proprietary theory
- Parent company theory
- Parent company extension theory
- Entity theory

The entity theory is sometimes referred to as the fair value of subsidiary method. The parent company extension theory is sometimes referred to as the *net identifiable assets method.* In this text, we will refer to the different theories by the names introduced in the previous paragraph.

Each of the theories has been or is currently required by generally accepted accounting principles (GAAP). The following table indicates the current status and effective usage dates for these four theories:

All four theories have been or now are required under Canadian GAAP under specified situations.

Method	Status
Proprietary theory	Present GAAP for consolidating certain types of joint arrangements; was an option under GAAP prior to 2013 when consolidating joint ventures.
Parent company theory	Was GAAP for consolidating subsidiaries prior to January 1, 2011.
Parent company extension theory	An acceptable method for consolidating subsidiaries after January 1, 2011.
Entity theory	An acceptable method for consolidating subsidiaries after January 1, 2011.

The merits of these four theories are discussed in the following section.

INTRODUCTION TO CONSOLIDATION THEORIES

LO1

These four theories differ in the valuation of the NCI and in how much of the subsidiary's value pertaining to the NCI is brought onto the consolidated financial statements. The following chart highlights the differences between the four theories. The left side for each theory shows the portion of the subsidiary owned by the parent while the right side shows the portion owned by the NCI. The shaded area represents the values brought onto the consolidated financial statements.

	Proprietary		Parent Company		Parent Company Extension		Entity	
	Parent	NCI	Parent	NCI	Parent	NCI	Parent	NCI
Carrying amount of Subsidiary's net assets								
Fair value excess								
Goodwill								

The parent's portion of the subsidiary's value is fully represented under all theories. The NCI's share varies under the four theories.

We will illustrate the preparation of consolidated financial statements under these four theories using the following example. Assume that on June 30, Year 1, S Ltd. had 10,000 shares outstanding and P Ltd. purchases 8,000 shares (80%) of S Ltd. for a total cost of $72,000. P Ltd.'s journal entry to record this purchase is as follows:

| Investment in S Ltd. | 72,000 | |
| Cash | | 72,000 |

The balance sheets of P Ltd. and S Ltd. just prior to this purchase on June 30, Year 1, were shown in Exhibit 4.1.

Proprietary Theory

Proprietary theory focuses solely on the parent's percentage interest in the subsidiary.

Proprietary theory views the consolidated entity from the standpoint of the shareholders of the parent company. The consolidated statements do not acknowledge or show the equity of the non-controlling shareholders. The consolidated balance sheet on the date of acquisition reflects only the parent's share of the assets and liabilities of the subsidiary, based on their fair values, and the resultant goodwill from the combination.

The calculation and allocation of the acquisition differential is a useful first step in the preparation of the consolidated balance sheet. The information provided in this calculation forms the basis of the elimination and adjusting entries required. This calculation is shown in Exhibit 4.2. Goodwill is determined as part of this calculation.

Only the parent's share of the fair values of the subsidiary is brought onto the consolidated balance sheet.

Using the direct approach, the consolidated balance sheet is prepared by combining, on an item-by-item basis, the carrying amounts of the parent with the *parent's share* of the fair values of the subsidiary, which is derived by using the parent's share of the carrying amount of the subsidiary plus the acquisition differential. This consolidation process is shown in Exhibit 4.3.

The consolidation process becomes increasingly more complex as we proceed from one chapter to the next. To make it easier to follow the consolidation adjustments, a referencing system will be adopted for Exhibit 4.3 and subsequent illustrations in the book. The references will be placed either after the account name or before the dollar figure to which they relate. The references will look

EXHIBIT 4.2

CALCULATION OF ACQUISITION DIFFERENTIAL
(proprietary theory)

Cost of 80% investment in S Ltd.		$72,000	
Carrying amount of S Ltd.'s net assets			
Assets	100,000		
Liabilities	(30,000)		
	70,000		
P Ltd.'s ownership	80%	56,000	
Acquisition differential		16,000	
Allocated:	(FV − CA) × 80%		
Inventory	+ 2,000 × 80% = + 1,600		(a)
Plant	+ 9,000 × 80% = + 7,200		(b)
Patent	− 1,000 × 80% = − 800		(c)
	8,000		
Long-term debt	+ 3,000 × 80% = + 2,400	5,600	(d)
Balance—goodwill		$10,400	(e)

The acquisition differential consists of 80% of the fair value excess plus the parent's share of the goodwill.

something like this, (1b), which means that we are referring to item "b" in Exhibit 1 for this chapter.

Proprietary theory is not used in practice to consolidate a parent and its subsidiaries. However, it is used to report certain types of joint arrangements. This consolidation process is described as "proportionate consolidation" and will be illustrated in Chapter 9.

EXHIBIT 4.3

Illustration of the Direct Approach
(Proprietary Theory)
P LTD.
CONSOLIDATED BALANCE SHEET
At June 30, Year 1

Cash (100,000 − 72,000* + 80% × 12,000)		$ 37,600
Accounts receivable (90,000 + 80% × 7,000)		95,600
Inventory (130,000 + 80% × 20,000 + **[2a] 1,600**)		147,600
Plant (280,000 + 80% × 50,000 + **[2b] 7,200**)		327,200
Patent (0 + 80% × 11,000 − **[2c] 800**)		8,000
Goodwill (0 + 0 + **[2e] 10,400**)		10,400
		$626,400
Current liabilities (60,000 + 80% × 8,000)		$ 66,400
Long-term debt (180,000 + 80% × 22,000 + **[2d] 2,400**)		200,000
Total liabilities		266,400
Shareholders' equity		
Common shares	200,000	
Retained earnings	160,000	360,000
		$626,400

* Cash paid by P Ltd. to acquire S Ltd.

The consolidated amounts include 100% of the parent's carrying amount plus the parent's share of the fair value of the subsidiary's net assets.

NCI is not recognized under the proprietary theory.

Parent Company Theory

Parent company theory focuses on the parent company but gives some recognition to NCI.

Parent company theory is similar to proprietary theory in that the focus of the consolidated statements is directed toward the shareholders of the parent company. However, NCI is recognized and reflected as a liability in the consolidated balance sheet; its amount is based on the carrying amounts of the net assets of the subsidiary.

NCI is calculated as follows:

Carrying amount of S Ltd.'s net assets	
Assets	$100,000
Liabilities	(30,000)
	70,000
Non-controlling ownership percentage	20%
Non-controlling interest	$ 14,000

The consolidated balance sheet is prepared by combining, on an item-by-item basis, the carrying amount of the parent with 100% of the carrying amount of the subsidiary *plus* the parent's share of the acquisition differential.

The NCI's share of the subsidiary's net assets is measured at their carrying amount.

Under this theory, the parent's share of the subsidiary is measured at fair value, whereas the NCI's share is based on the subsidiary's carrying amount on the consolidated balance sheet. This process is consistent with the historical cost principle, because the parent's portion of the subsidiary's net asset is being acquired by the parent at the date of acquisition. Since the NCI's share of the subsidiary's net assets is not being purchased and is not changing hands, this portion is retained at carrying amount. Exhibit 4.4 shows the preparation of

---

EXHIBIT 4.4

Illustration of the Direct Approach
(Parent Company Theory)
P LTD.
CONSOLIDATED BALANCE SHEET
At June 30, Year 1

100% of the subsidiary's carrying amounts plus the parent's share of the fair value excess are brought onto the consolidated balance sheet.

Cash (100,000 − 72,000* + 12,000)		$ 40,000
Accounts receivable (90,000 + 7,000)		97,000
Inventory (130,000 + 20,000 + **[2a] 1,600**)		151,600
Plant (280,000 + 50,000 + **[2b] 7,200**)		337,200
Patent (0 + 11,000 − **[2c] 800**)		10,200
Goodwill (0 + 0 + **[2e] 10,400**)		10,400
		$646,400
Current liabilities (60,000 + 8,000)		$ 68,000
Long-term debt (180,000 + 22,000 + **[2d] 2,400**)		204,400
Non-controlling interest		14,000
Total liabilities		286,400
Shareholders' equity		
Common shares	200,000	
Retained earnings	160,000	360,000
		$646,400

NCI is presented as a liability.

Cash paid by P Ltd. to acquire S Ltd.

the consolidated balance sheet under parent company theory. This theory was required by GAAP prior to January 1, 2011.

Entity Theory

Entity theory views the consolidated entity as having two distinct groups of shareholders—the controlling shareholders and the non-controlling shareholders. NCI is presented as a separate component of shareholders' equity on the consolidated balance sheet.

In acquiring a controlling interest, a parent company becomes responsible for managing all the subsidiary's assets and liabilities, even though it may own only a partial interest. If a parent can control the business activities of its subsidiary, it directly follows that the parent is accountable to its investors and creditors for all of the subsidiary's assets, liabilities, and profits. To provide the users with a complete picture about the performance of the entity and the resources under its control, the consolidated statements should include 100% of the subsidiary's assets and liabilities. Furthermore, these assets and liabilities should be measured at full fair value at the date of acquisition, to enable users to better assess the cash-generating abilities of the identifiable net assets acquired in the business combination and the accountability of management for the resources entrusted to it.

The full fair value of the subsidiary is typically determined by combining the fair value of the controlling interest and the fair value of the NCI. Measurement of the controlling interest's fair value is straightforward in the vast majority of cases. The consideration paid by the parent typically provides the best evidence of fair value of the acquirer's interest. However, there is no parallel consideration transferred by the NCI to value the NCI. Therefore, the parent must employ other valuation techniques to estimate the fair value of the non-controlling interest at the acquisition date.

Usually, a parent can rely on readily available market trading activity to provide a fair valuation for its subsidiary's non-controlling interest. Market trading prices for the non-controlling interest's shares in the weeks before and after the acquisition provide an objective measure of their fair value. The fair value of these shares then becomes the initial basis for reporting the non-controlling interest in consolidated financial statements.

Acquirers frequently must pay a premium price per share to garner sufficient shares to ensure a controlling interest. A control premium, however, typically is needed only to acquire sufficient shares to obtain a controlling interest. The remaining (non-controlling interest) shares provide no added benefit of transferring control to the new owner, and, therefore, may sell at a price less than that paid by the parent to obtain shares that provided control. Such control premiums are properly included in the fair value of the controlling interest but usually do not affect the fair values of the remaining subsidiary shares. Therefore, separate independent valuations for the controlling and non-controlling interests are typically best for measuring the total fair value of the subsidiary.

In the absence of fair value evidence based on market trades, firms must turn to less objective measures for determining the fair value of the non-controlling interest. For example, comparable investments may be available to estimate fair value. Alternatively, valuation models based on subsidiary discounted cash flows

L02

Entity theory gives equal attention to the controlling and non-controlling shareholders.

The trading price of the subsidiary's shares or shares of a comparable company in an active market is probably the most accurate reflection of the value of the NCI.

An investor typically pays a premium over the trading price of a company's shares when acquiring sufficient shares to obtain control of the company.

Discounted cash flow analysis could be used to estimate the fair value of the subsidiary.

or residual income projections can be employed to estimate the acquisition-date fair value of the non-controlling interest. Finally, if a control premium is unlikely, the consideration paid by the parent can be used to imply a fair value for the entire subsidiary. The non-controlling interest's fair value is then simply measured as its percentage of this implied subsidiary fair value. The following illustrations explain how NCI is measured under different scenarios.

Illustration 1 Fair Value of Non-controlling Interest as Evidenced by Market Trades

In the majority of cases, direct evidence based on market activity in the outstanding subsidiary shares (not owned by the parent) will provide the best measure of acquisition-date fair value for the non-controlling interest. For example, assume that P Ltd. wished to acquire 8,000 of S Ltd.'s shares in order to obtain substantial synergies from the proposed acquisition. P Ltd. estimated that a 100% acquisition was not needed to extract these synergies. Also, P Ltd. projected that financing more than an 80% acquisition would be too costly.

P Ltd. then offered all of S Ltd.'s shareholders a premium price for up to 80% of the outstanding shares. To induce a sufficient number of shareholders to sell, P Ltd. needed to offer $9 per share, even though the shares had been trading in the $7.65 to $7.85 range. During the weeks following the acquisition, the 20% non-controlling interest shares in S Ltd. continued to trade in the $7.65 to $7.85 range.

In this case, the $9 per share paid by P Ltd. does not appear representative of the fair value of all the shares of S Ltd. The fact that the non-controlling interest shares continued to trade around $7.75 per share indicates a fair value for the 2,000 shares not owned by P Ltd of $15,500 (7.75 × 2,000 shares). Therefore, the valuation of the non-controlling interest is best evidenced by the trading price of S Ltd.'s shares, not the price paid by P Ltd.

The $9 share price paid by P Ltd. nonetheless represents a negotiated value for the 8,000 shares. In the absence of any evidence to the contrary, P Ltd.'s shares have a fair value of $72,000 incorporating the additional value P Ltd. expects to extract from synergies with S Ltd. Thus, the fair value of S Ltd. as a whole is measured as the sum of the respective fair values of the controlling and non-controlling interests as follows:

Fair value of controlling interest ($9 × 8,000 shares)	$72,000
Fair value of non-controlling interest ($7.75 × 2,000 shares)	15,500
Total acquisition-date fair value of S Ltd.	$87,500

At the acquisition date, P Ltd. assessed the total fair value of S Ltd.'s identifiable net assets at $77,000, as indicated in Exhibit 4.1. Therefore, we compute goodwill as the excess of the total fair value of the firm over the fair values of the identifiable net assets as follows:

Total acquisition-date fair value of S Ltd.	$87,500
Fair value of identifiable net assets acquired	77,000
Goodwill	$10,500

To provide a basis for potential future allocations of goodwill impairment charges, acquisition-date goodwill should be apportioned across the controlling and non-controlling interests. The parent first allocates goodwill to its controlling interest for the excess of the fair value of the parent's equity interest over its share of the fair value of the identifiable net assets. Any remaining goodwill is then attributed to the non-controlling interest. As a result, goodwill allocated to the controlling and non-controlling interests will not always be proportional to the percentages owned. Continuing with our example, the acquisition goodwill is allocated as follows:

	Controlling Interest	NCI	Total
Fair value at acquisition date	$72,000	$15,500	$87,500
Relative fair value of identifiable net assets acquired (80% and 20%) 77000 × 80%	61,600	15,400	77,000
Goodwill	$10,400	$ 100	$10,500

The goodwill component as a percentage of total value is much higher for the controlling interest as compared with the non-controlling interest when a parent pays a premium to obtain control.

Illustration 2 Fair Value of Non-controlling Interest Implied by Parent's Consideration Transferred

In some cases, the price paid by the parent on a per share basis may reflect what would have been paid on a per share basis for 100% of the subsidiary's shares. This is true in the following situations:

1. The parent acquired a large percentage of the acquiree's voting stock.
2. The parent's offer to buy shares was based on the value of the subsidiary as a whole.
3. The trading price of the acquiree's share just before and just after the business combination was similar to the price paid by the parent.
4. The non-controlling shareholders could use their minority shareholder rights to demand the same price per share that was paid to the other shareholders.

Sometimes, it is appropriate to measure NCI using the price per share paid by the parent to obtain control.

Therefore, if there was no compelling evidence that the $9 acquisition price was not representative of all of S Ltd.'s 10,000 shares, then it appears reasonable to estimate the fair value of the 20% non-controlling interest using the price paid by P Ltd. The total fair value of S Ltd. is then estimated at $90,000 and allocated as follows:

Fair value of controlling interest ($9 × 8,000 shares)	$72,000
Fair value of non-controlling interest ($9 × 2,000 shares)	18,000
Total acquisition-date fair value of S Ltd.	$90,000

Alternatively, the total fair value can be calculated using basic math by simply dividing the amount paid of $72,000 by the percentage ownership, 80% or 0.8, to get $90,000. Goodwill for the subsidiary as a whole would be valued at $13,000, as indicated in Exhibit 4.5.

The implied value assumes that the parent's purchase price can be extrapolated linearly to determine the total value of the subsidiary.

A third approach for valuing the NCI is to perform an independent business valuation. This involves many assessments and assumptions relating to future cash flows, inflation rates, growth rates, discount rates, synergies between the parent and subsidiary, valuation of identifiable assets and liabilities, etc. Not only is a business valuation a very costly exercise, it also involves a lot of judgment. In some cases, the cost of determining the implied value of the subsidiary as a whole

NCI could be valued using business valuation techniques, but this is a costly exercise.

EXHIBIT 4.5			

CALCULATION OF ACQUISITION DIFFERENTIAL
(Entity Theory)

Cost of 80% investment in S Ltd.			$72,000
Implied value of 100% investment in S Ltd. (72,000 ÷ 80%)			$90,000
Carrying amount of S Ltd.'s net assets			
Assets		$100,000	
Liabilities		(30,000)	
			70,000
Implied acquisition differential			20,000
Allocated:	(FV − CA) × 100%		
Inventory	+ 2,000 × 100% = +	2,000	(a)
Plant	+ 9,000 × 100% = +	9,000	(b)
Patent	− 1,000 × 100% = −	1,000	(c)
		10,000	
Long-term debt	+ 3,000 × 100% = +	3,000	7,000	(d)
Balance—goodwill			$13,000	(e)

CALCULATION OF NCI

Implied value of 100% investment in S Ltd.	$90,000
NCI ownership	20%
	$18,000	(f)

The acquisition differential consists of 100% of the fair value excess plus the implied value of total goodwill.

NCI can be easily measured, if we assume a linear relationship between percentage ownership and value of that ownership.

In this text, we will assume a linear relationship to calculate the value of NCI except when we are given the market price of the subsidiary's shares.

Cautionary Note: Unless otherwise noted, all of the illustrations throughout this text and in the end-of-chapter material will use the entity theory. It is one of the acceptable methods in IFRS 10. It was the only method proposed in the exposure draft leading up to IFRS 3 and is the only method allowed by the FASB. It will likely be used when the total value of goodwill of the subsidiary can be reasonably measured at the date of acquisition.

may not be worth the benefit of the information provided. If so, the reporting entity may be reluctant to use the entity theory.

We should note that the value assigned to the subsidiary as a whole will have a big impact on the value allocated to goodwill. The fair values of the identifiable assets and liabilities are usually readily available because these items (or similar items) are bought and sold quite often in the marketplace. However, goodwill is not traded in the marketplace by itself. Therefore, determining a value for goodwill is quite subjective and is directly tied to the overall value of the firm and the price paid by the parent.

Throughout this text, when the market price of the subsidiary's shares at the date of acquisition is not given, the implied value of the subsidiary as a whole will be calculated by dividing the price paid for the shares purchased by the percentage acquired. We recognize that this is an oversimplification; however, the material in this text is complex enough as is, and by keeping it simple in some cases, we may be able to see the forest rather than the multitude of trees. When the market price of the subsidiary's shares at the date of acquisition is given, we will use this price to value the NCI and then calculate the goodwill attributable to each of the controlling and non-controlling interests.

Using the direct approach and the implied value of $90,000, the consolidated balance sheet is prepared by combining, on an item-by-item basis, the carrying amounts of P Ltd. with the fair values of S Ltd. The calculated goodwill is

EXHIBIT 4.6	

Illustration of the Direct Approach
(Entity Theory)
P LTD.
CONSOLIDATED BALANCE SHEET
At June 30, Year 1

Cash (100,000 − 72,000* + 12,000)	$ 40,000	100% of the subsidiary's fair values are brought on to the consolidated balance sheet.
Accounts receivable (90,000 + 7,000)	97,000	
Inventory (130,000 + 20,000 + **[5a] 2,000**)	152,000	
Plant (280,000 + 50,000 + **[5b] 9,000**)	339,000	
Patent (0 + 11,000 − **[5c] 1,000**)	10,000	
Goodwill (0 + 0 + **[5e] 13,000**)	13,000	
	$651,000	
Current liabilities (60,000 + 8,000)	$ 68,000	
Long-term debt (180,000 + 22,000 + **[5d] 3,000**)	205,000	
Total liabilities	273,000	
Shareholders' equity		NCI is presented as a separate component in shareholders' equity.
Controlling interest		
Common shares	200,000	
Retained earnings	160,000	
	360,000	
Non-controlling interest **[5f]**	18,000	378,000
		$651,000

* Cash paid by P Ltd. to acquire S Ltd.

inserted as an asset, and the calculated NCI is shown in shareholders' equity. Exhibit 4.6 above illustrates the preparation of the consolidated balance sheet using the direct approach.

The working paper used to prepare the consolidated balance sheet under the entity theory is shown in Exhibit A4.1 in Appendix 4A.

Parent Company Extension Theory

L03

Parent company extension theory was invented to address the concerns about goodwill valuation under entity theory. Given that many people feel that goodwill for the subsidiary, as a whole, is very difficult to measure when the parent does not purchase 100% of the subsidiary, they did not support the use of entity theory. However, there is much support for valuing the subsidiary's identifiable assets and liabilities at their full fair value on the consolidated statements at the time of acquisition. Parent company extension theory does just that—it values both the parent's share and the NCI's share of identifiable net assets at fair value. Only the parent's share of the subsidiary's goodwill is brought onto the consolidated statements at the value paid by the parent. Since the total value of the subsidiary's goodwill is not reasonably measurable, the NCI's portion of the subsidiary's goodwill is not measured and not brought onto the consolidated statements.

Under parent company extension theory, NCI is recognized in shareholders' equity in the consolidated balance sheet, similar to entity theory. Its amount is

All of the subsidiary's value except for the NCI's share of goodwill is brought onto the consolidated balance sheet.

NCI is based on the fair value of identifiable assets and liabilities.

based on the fair values of the identifiable net assets of the subsidiary; it excludes any value pertaining to the subsidiary's goodwill. NCI is calculated as follows:

Carrying amount of S Ltd.'s net assets	
Assets	$100,000
Liabilities	(30,000)
	70,000
Excess of fair value over carrying amount for identifiable net assets (see Exhibit 4.5)	7,000
Fair value of identifiable net assets	77,000
Non-controlling ownership percentage	20%
Non-controlling interest	$ 15,400

The consolidated balance sheet is prepared by combining, on an item-by-item basis, the carrying amount of the parent with the fair value of the subsidiary's identifiable net assets plus the parent's share of the subsidiary's goodwill. Exhibit 4.7 shows the preparation of the consolidated balance sheet under parent company extension theory.

Either entity theory or parent company extension theory can be used under IFRSs.

Either entity theory or parent company extension theory can be used under IFRSs. It is an accounting policy choice. However, IFRS 3 does not use the term *parent company extension theory*. It simply states the following in paragraph 19:

> For each business combination, the acquirer shall measure any non-controlling interest in the acquiree either at fair value or at the non-controlling interest's proportionate share of the acquiree's identifiable net assets.

EXHIBIT 4.7

Illustration of the Direct Approach
(Parent Company Extension Theory)
P LTD.
CONSOLIDATED BALANCE SHEET
At June 30, Year 1

100% of the subsidiary's fair values of identifiable assets and liabilities plus the parent's share of the subsidiary's goodwill are brought onto the consolidated balance sheet.

Cash (100,000 − 72,000* + 12,000)		$40,000
Accounts receivable (90,000 + 7,000)		97,000
Inventory (130,000 + 20,000 + **[5a] 2,000**)		152,000
Plant (280,000 + 50,000 + **[5b] 9,000**)		339,000
Patent (0 + 11,000 − **[5c] 1,000**)		10,000
Goodwill (0 + 0 + **[2e] 10,400**)		10,400
		$648,400
Current liabilities (60,000 + 8,000)		$ 68,000
Long-term debt (180,000 + 22,000 + **[5d] 3,000**)		205,000
Total liabilities		273,000
Shareholders' equity		
Common shares	$200,000	
Retained earnings	160,000	
Non-controlling interest	15,400	375,400
		$648,400

NCI is presented in shareholders' equity.

* *Cash paid by P Ltd. to acquire S Ltd.*

See Self-Study Problem 1 for another example of preparing and comparing the consolidated balance sheet under these four theories. It shows that the values are quite different, and, in turn, the current ratio and debt-to-equity ratios are different. Also, see Self-Study Problem 2 for an illustration of the entity and parent company extension theories in a more complex situation. The problem also compares the consolidated balance sheet for a non–wholly owned subsidiary with the same data for a wholly owned subsidiary. There are a lot of similarities and only a few differences.

Cautionary Note: Unless otherwise noted, assume, in this text, that the parent has chosen to use entity theory.

Bargain Purchases

LO4

In all of the business combinations in Chapter 3 and to this point in Chapter 4, the total consideration given by the controlling and non-controlling shareholders always exceeded the fair value of the identifiable net assets. Accordingly, goodwill appeared under a direct purchase of net assets on the balance sheet of the acquirer, or on the consolidated balance sheet when the parent acquired shares of the subsidiary. We will now consider situations where the total consideration given is less than the fair value of the subsidiary's identifiable net assets.

Assume that on January, Year 1, P Ltd. purchased 100% of the outstanding shares of S Ltd. at a total cost of $72,000. The calculation and allocation of the acquisition differential on this date is shown in Exhibit 4.8.

A business combination that results in negative goodwill is often described as a "bargain purchase." This means that the parent gained control over the subsidiary's assets and liabilities at a price that was less than the fair values assigned to the identifiable assets and liabilities. This can occur when the subsidiary is an awkward situation and the shares are sold under conditions of a distressed sale. Or it could be that the fair value of the identifiable assets is overstated and/or the fair value of the liabilities is understated. Therefore, prior to recognizing a gain on bargain purchase, IFRS 3 requires that all components of the negative goodwill

Since negative goodwill is very rare, the parent should check the valuations of the identifiable net assets before recording a gain on bargain purchase.

EXHIBIT 4.8

CALCULATION AND ALLOCATION OF ACQUISITION DIFFERENTIAL
(Negative Goodwill, Wholly Owned Subsidiary)

Cost of investment in S Ltd.		$ 72,000
Carrying amount of S Ltd.'s net assets		
Assets	100,000	
Liabilities	(30,000)	70,000
Acquisition differential		2,000
Allocated:	(FV − CA)	
Inventory	+ 2,000	
Plant	+ 9,000	
Patent	− 1,000	
	10,000	
Long-term debt	+ 3,000	7,000
Balance—"negative goodwill" (gain on bargain purchase)		$ −5,000

Negative goodwill arises when the total consideration given is less than the fair value of identifiable net assets.

The negative goodwill is recognized as a gain on bargain purchase.

calculation be reassessed to ensure that they are correct. After reassessment, the gain can be recognized if it is determined that no errors were made in the various valuations involved with the calculation.

To record a gain on a purchase of any asset may seem very strange. It goes against the long-standing tradition of recording assets at cost and recording gains only when realized. However, under the acquisition method, the subsidiary's identifiable net assets are reported at fair value. If the acquirer pays less than the fair value of the identifiable net assets, it has realized a gain on a purchase. It does not have to wait to sell the assets to recognize the gain.

Since, for this example, there is no goodwill on the subsidiary's books, none of the negative goodwill can be used to reduce goodwill to zero. Therefore, the entire $5,000 of negative goodwill is recorded as a gain on the consolidated income state-ment and ends up in consolidated retained earnings at the date of acquisition. If the parent company uses the equity method to account for its investment in the subsidiary, the following entry should be made in the parent's separate-entity records to record the $5,000 gain resulting from the bargain purchase:

Investment in S Ltd.	5,000	
Gain on purchase of S Ltd.		5,000

This entry will result in the investment account being valued at the parent's share of the fair value of identifiable net assets of the subsidiary.

Let us now modify the situation by reducing the percentage of shares acquired in the business combination and changing the purchase price. Assume that on January, Year 1, P Ltd. purchased 80% of the outstanding shares of S Ltd. at a total cost of $60,000. If we used the implied value approach, the value of the subsidiary as a whole would be set at $75,000 (60,000/0.8). This is less than the fair value of identifiable net assets of $77,000 and would imply negative goodwill of $2,000. Normally, the $2,000 gain would be split between the parent and non-controlling interests. However, IFRS 3 states that a gain on a bargain purchase can only be recognized by the acquirer. This implies that only the parent's share of the nega-tive goodwill can be recognized. It also implies that non-controlling interest must be measured at its share of the fair value of the identifiable net assets. In effect, the parent company extension method must be used for valuing the NCI. The calculation and allocation of the acquisition differential on this date is shown in Exhibit 4.9.

> The parent company extension theory must be used in situations involving negative goodwill for a non–wholly owned subsidiary.

Exhibit 4.10 illustrates the preparation of the consolidated balance sheet using the direct approach.

The working paper to prepare the consolidated balance sheet is shown in Exhibit A4.2 in Appendix 4A.

> A negative acquisition differential is not the same as negative goodwill.

Negative Acquisition Differential   It is possible for an acquisition differential to be negative. In this situation, the total consideration given would be less than the carrying amount of the subsidiary's net assets. A negative acquisition differential is not the same as negative goodwill, nor does it necessarily imply that there will be negative goodwill. If the fair values of the subsidiary's net assets are less than their carrying amounts, and if the total consideration given is greater than the fair value of the subsidiary's identifiable net assets, there will be positive goodwill.

EXHIBIT 4.9

CALCULATION AND ALLOCATION OF ACQUISITION DIFFERENTIAL
(Negative Goodwill, Non–Wholly Owned Subsidiary)

	Parent 80%	NCI 20%	Total 100%
Cost of 80% investment in S Ltd.	$60,000		$60,000
Value of NCI (20% × 77,000)		$15,400	15,400
Total value of subsidiary			75,400
Carrying amount of S Ltd.'s net assets			
Assets	$100,000		
Liabilities	(30,000)		
	$ 70,000	56,000	14,000	70,000
Acquisition differential		4,000	1,400	5,400
Allocated:	(FV − CA)		
Inventory	+$2,000		
Plant	+ 9,000		
Patent	− 1,000		
	10,000		
Long-term debt	+ 3,000		
	$ 7,000	5,600	1,400	7,000
Balance—"negative goodwill" (gain on bargain purchase)		$ 1,600	0	$ 1,600

Only the parent can recognize a gain on bargain purchase.

EXHIBIT 4.10

Illustration of the Direct Approach
(Negative Goodwill, Non–Wholly Owned Subsidiary)
P LTD.
CONSOLIDATED BALANCE SHEET
At June 30, Year 1

Cash (100,000 − 60,000* + 12,000)		$ 52,000
Accounts receivable (90,000 + 7,000)		97,000
Inventory (130,000 + 20,000 + **[5a] 2,000**)		152,000
Plant (280,000 + 50,000 + **[5b] 9,000**)		339,000
Patent (0 + 11,000 − **[5c] 1,000**)		10,000
		$650,000
Current liabilities (60,000 + 8,000)		$ 68,000
Long-term debt (180,000 + 22,000 + **[5d] 3,000**)		205,000
Total liabilities		273,000
Shareholders' equity		
Common shares	$200,000	
Retained earnings (160,000 + **[9a] 1,600**)	161,600	
Non-controlling interest	15,400	377,000
		$650,000

Cash paid by P Ltd. to acquire S Ltd.

The negative goodwill is not recognized as a separate item on the balance sheet.

The gain on bargain purchase ends up in consolidated retained earnings.

The subsidiary's goodwill arose in a previous business combination.

Subsidiary with Goodwill   The goodwill appearing on the balance sheet of a subsidiary on the date of a business combination is not carried forward when the consolidated balance sheet is prepared. At some date in the past, the subsidiary was the acquirer in a business combination and recorded the goodwill as the difference between the acquisition cost and the fair value of the identifiable net assets acquired. Now this company has itself become an acquiree. From the perspective of its new parent, the goodwill is not considered to be an identifiable asset at the time of the business combination. The acquisition differential is calculated as if the goodwill had been written off by the subsidiary, even though in fact this is not the case. The acquisition differential is allocated first to the fair value excess for identifiable net assets, and then the remaining balance goes to goodwill. In effect, the old goodwill is ignored and the acquisition cost determines the value, if any, of new goodwill at the date of acquisition. The following illustration will examine the consolidation process when the subsidiary has existing goodwill.

Assume that on June 30, Year 1, P Ltd. purchased 80% of the outstanding shares of S Ltd. for a total cost of $62,000, paid in cash. Exhibit 4.11 shows the balance sheets of the two companies at this time.

Note that the goodwill (highlighted in boldface) of $11,000 was called a patent in Exhibit 4.1. Note also that the acquisition cost is the same as in the last example, where the result turned out to be negative goodwill. When we calculate and allocate the acquisition differential in this illustration, the result is positive goodwill of $10,500, as shown in Exhibit 4.12.

The preparation of the June 30, Year 1, consolidated balance sheet using the direct approach is presented in Exhibit 4.13, and the working paper approach is presented in Exhibit A4.3 in Appendix 4A.

EXHIBIT 4.11

BALANCE SHEET
At June 29, Year 1

	P Ltd.	S Ltd.	
	Carrying amount	Carrying amount	Fair value
Cash	$100,000	$ 12,000	$12,000
Accounts receivable	90,000	7,000	7,000
Inventory	130,000	20,000	22,000
Plant	280,000	50,000	59,000
Goodwill	—	11,000	
	$600,000	$100,000	
Current liabilities	$ 60,000	$ 8,000	8,000
Long-term debt	180,000	22,000	25,000
Common shares	200,000	40,000	
Retained earnings	160,000	30,000	
	$600,000	$100,000	

The goodwill on the subsidiary's books (it is old goodwill) will be remeasured on the date of acquisition.

EXHIBIT 4.12

CALCULATION AND ALLOCATION OF ACQUISITION DIFFERENTIAL
(Subsidiary with Goodwill)

Cost of 80% investment in S Ltd.		$62,000
Implied value of 100% investment in S Ltd. (62,000/0.80)		$77,500
Carrying amount of S Ltd.'s net assets		
Assets	$100,000	
Liabilities	(30,000)	
	70,000	
Deduct old goodwill of S Ltd.	11,000	
Adjusted net assets	59,000	
Acquisition differential	18,500	
Allocated:	(FV − CA)	
Inventory	+$2,000	(a)
Plant	+ 9,000	(b)
	11,000	
Long-term debt	+ 3,000 (c)	8,000
Balance—goodwill		$10,500 (d)

The subsidiary's goodwill is now worth $10,500, based on the recent price paid by the parent.

CALCULATION OF NCI

Implied value of 100% investment in S Ltd.		$77,500
NCI ownership		20%
		$15,500 (e)

The subsidiary's goodwill was revalued at the date of acquisition.

EXHIBIT 4.13

Illustration of the Direct Approach
(Subsidiary with Goodwill)

P LTD.
CONSOLIDATED BALANCE SHEET
At June 30, Year 1

Cash (100,000 − 62,000* + 12,000)	$ 50,000
Accounts receivable (90,000 + 7,000)	97,000
Inventory (130,000 + 20,000 + **[12a] 2,000**)	152,000
Plant (280,000 + 50,000 + **[12b] 9,000**)	339,000
Goodwill (0 + 11,000 − **11,000** + **[12d] 10,500**)	10,500
	$648,500
Current liabilities (60,000 + 8,000)	$ 68,000
Long-term debt (180,000 + 22,000 + **[12c] 3,000**)	205,000
Common shares	200,000
Retained earnings	160,000
Non-controlling interests **[12e]**	15,500
	$648,500

Cash paid by P Ltd. to acquire S Ltd.

The direct approach produces the same results as the working paper approach but appears to be easier to perform.

L05

CONTINGENT CONSIDERATION

Contingent consideration should be recorded at the date of acquisition at its expected value.

The terms of a business combination may require an additional cash payment, or an additional share issue contingent on some specified future event. The accounting for contingent consideration is contained in IFRS 3. The material that follows illustrates the concepts involved.

Contingent consideration should be measured at fair value at the date of acquisition. To do so, the parent should assess the amount expected to be paid in the future under different scenarios, assign probabilities as to the likelihood of the scenarios occurring, derive an expected value of the likely amount to be paid, and use a discount rate to derive the value of the expected payment in today's dollars. This is all very subjective and involves a lot of judgment.

The contingent consideration will be classified as either a liability or equity depending on its nature. If the contingent consideration will be paid in the form of cash or another asset, it will be classified as a liability. If issuing additional shares will satisfy the contingent consideration, it will be classified as equity. After the initial recognition, the contingent consideration classified as equity will not be remeasured.

After the acquisition date, the fair value of a contingent consideration classified as a liability may change due to changes in circumstances, such as meeting specified sales targets, fluctuations in share price, or subsequent events, such as receiving government approval on an in-process research and development project. Changes in the fair value of a contingent consideration classified as a liability due to changes in circumstances since the acquisition date should be recognized in earnings. Changes in the fair value of a contingent consideration due to gathering of new information about facts and circumstances that existed at the acquisition date and within a maximum of one year subsequent to the acquisition date would be considered as an adjustment of the acquisition cost.

The range of potential payment for contingent consideration should be disclosed.

Given the uncertainty involved, the following should be disclosed regarding contingent consideration:

- The amount of contingent consideration recognized on the acquisition date.
- A description of the arrangement and the basis for determining the amount of the payment.
- An estimate of the range of outcomes (undiscounted) or, if a range cannot be estimated, that fact and the reasons why a range cannot be estimated. If the maximum amount of the payment is unlimited, the acquirer shall disclose that fact.

The following discussions illustrate the two types of contingent consideration discussed above.

Changes in contingent consideration classified as a liability are reported in net income.

Contingent Consideration Classified as a Liability   If the contingency is classified as a liability, any consideration issued at some future date is recorded at fair value and the change in fair value is recognized in net income. The following example will illustrate this situation.

Able Corporation issues 500,000 common shares for all of the outstanding common shares of Baker Company on January 1, Year 1. The shares issued have a fair value of $10 at that time. The business combination agreement states that if the earnings of Baker Company exceed an average of $1.75 per share over the next two years, Able Corporation will make an additional cash payment of $600,000 to the former shareholders of Baker Company on January 1, Year 3. Able predicts that there is a 30% probability that Baker's earnings will be less than $1.75 per share and a 70% probability that it will be greater than $1.75 per share. The probability-adjusted expected payment is $420,000 (30% $\times$ 0 + 70% $\times$ 600,000). Using a discount rate of 7%, the fair value of the contingent consideration at January 1, Year 1, is $366,844 (420,000/1.07^2). Able's journal entry on January 1, Year 1, is as follows:

The expected value incorporates the probability of payments being made.

Investment in Baker Company	5,366,844	
Common shares		5,000,000
Liability for contingent consideration		366,844

The consolidated financial statements at January 1, Year 1 would be prepared using the $5,366,844 acquisition cost. This amount is allocated to the identifiable net assets of Baker Company in the usual manner and may result in goodwill, or "negative goodwill." If at the end of Year 1, the probability assessment has not changed, the undiscounted probability-adjusted expected payment remains at $420,000; but the present value is now $392,523 (420,000/1.07), an increase of $25,679 since the beginning of the year. Able's journal entry at December 31, Year 1, is as follows:

The likelihood of having to make an additional payment should be reassessed and the liability remeasured, if necessary, at the end of each reporting period.

Interest expense	25,679	
Liability for contingent consideration		25,679

If at the end of the two-year period it is determined that Baker's earnings exceeded the average of $1.75 per share, the change in contingent consideration will be recorded by Able on December 31, Year 2, as follows:

Liability for contingent consideration	392,523	
Interest expense (392,523 $\times$ 0.07)	27,477	
Loss from contingent consideration	180,000	
Liability for contingent consideration		600,000

If Baker did not exceed the earnings level and Able does not have to pay the contingent consideration, Able would make the following journal entry at December 31, Year 2:

Liability for contingent consideration	392,523	
Interest expense (392,523 $\times$ 0.07)	27,477	
Gain from contingent consideration		420,000

Each period, the liability is increased by the amount of interest accruing on the liability.

The following is an example of a Canadian company that had a business combination in 2011 involving contingent consideration. It indicates how the initial amount and change in contingent consideration were accounted for.

Intact Financial Corporation is the leading provider of property and casualty (P&C) insurance in Canada, with $6.7 billion in direct premiums written on an annual basis. It insures more than five million individuals and businesses through its insurance subsidiaries and is the largest private-sector provider of P&C insurance in British Columbia, Alberta, Ontario, Quebec, and Nova Scotia. It manages its own investment portfolio, totalling approximately $11.8 billion. One of its subsidiaries, Intact Insurance, was formerly known as ING Insurance.

On September 23, 2011, the Company acquired all of the issued and outstanding shares of AXA Canada for a cash consideration of $2,621 million and contingent consideration of up to $100 million based on the development of the consolidated reserves of AXA Canada. During the fourth quarter of 2011, the Company determined that based on development of AXA Canada's reserves prior to September 23, 2011, the fair value of the contingent consideration as at September 23, 2011, was $48 million. That contingent consideration was recorded as an increase in goodwill and a payable to AXA. As at December 31, 2011, the fair value of the contingent consideration was reassessed to be $89 million. The increase in value of $41 million was recorded as a non-operating expense. Any future amounts payable, up to an additional $11 million, will be recorded in a similar manner.

Contingent Consideration Classified as Equity   If the contingency is classified as equity, any consideration issued at some future date will be recorded at fair value, but will not be considered an additional cost of the purchase. Instead, the consideration issued will be recognized but offset by a reduction in the amount recorded for the original share issue. The following example illustrates this.

Alpha Corporation issues 500,000 common shares for all the outstanding common shares of Beta Company on July 1, Year 1. If the shares issued have a fair market value of $5.00 per share, Alpha's journal entry is as follows:

Investment in Beta Company	2,500,000	
Common shares		2,500,000

The purchase agreement states that if the market price of Alpha's shares is below $5.00 one year from the date of the agreement, Alpha will issue additional shares to the former shareholders of Beta in an amount that will compensate them for their loss in value. On July 1, Year 2, the market price of Alpha's shares is $4.50. In accordance with the agreement, Alpha Corporation issues an additional 55,555.55 shares ($2,500,000 ÷ 4.50 − 500,000 shares) and records the transaction as follows:

The additional shares compensates for the loss in value for shares originally issued as consideration for the purchase.

Common shares—old shares (55,555.55 shares × 4.50)	250,000	
Common shares—new shares		250,000

Alternatively, Alpha could simply make a memorandum entry to indicate that 55,555 additional shares were issued for no consideration. Footnote disclosure in the Year 2 statements will be made for the amount of and reasons for the consideration and the accounting treatment used.

Companies must disclose the value for NCI at the date of acquisition and how it was measured.

IFRS 3 requires that a reporting entity disclose the following for each business combination in which the acquirer holds less than 100% of the equity interests in the acquiree at the acquisition date:

(a) The amount of the NCI in the acquiree recognized at the acquisition date and the measurement basis for that amount.

(b) For each NCI in an acquiree measured at fair value, the valuation techniques and key model inputs used for determining that value.

Goldcorp Inc. is a gold producer engaged in the operation, exploration, development and acquisition of precious metal properties in Canada, the United States, Mexico, and Central and South America. The Company's current sources of operating cash flows are primarily from the sale of gold, silver, copper, lead and zinc. The extracts in Exhibit 4.14 are taken from Goldcorp's 2011 consolidated financial statements.

EXHIBIT 4.14	Extracts in Part from Goldcorp's 2011 Financial Statements

7. ACQUISITIONS OF MINING INTERESTS

c) Acquisition of 70% interest in Sociedad Contractual Minera El Morro

On February 16, 2010, the Company acquired Xstrata Copper Chile S.A.'s ("Xstrata Copper") 70% interest in Sociedad Contractual Minera El Morro ("SCM"), the owner of the El Morro project, and associated loan receivable balances held by Xstrata Copper from a subsidiary of New Gold Inc. ("New Gold") in exchange for total consideration of $513 million in cash. The New Gold subsidiary had completed its acquisition of Xstrata Copper's 70% interest in SCM and associated loan receivable balances on February 16, 2010, just prior to the acquisition by the Company, pursuant to the exercise of its right of first refusal on January 7, 2010. The right of first refusal came into effect on October 12, 2009 when Barrick Gold Corporation ("Barrick") entered into an agreement with Xstrata Copper to acquire Xstrata Copper's 70% interest in SCM. Goldcorp now holds a 70% interest in the El Morro project with the remaining 30% held by New Gold (note 34(a)). The El Morro project is an advanced gold/copper project in northern Chile and is expected to benefit the Company's already strong organic growth pipeline.

Goldcorp, as the project operator has agreed to fund, through interest bearing loans, New Gold's share of development and construction costs until intended operating levels are achieved. The amounts outstanding will be repaid to the Company during the production period of the El Morro project. The acquisition of the 70% interest in SCM and loan receivable balances held by Xstrata Copper has been accounted for as a business combination, with Goldcorp as the acquirer. The El Morro project has been classified as a separate reportable operating segment in these consolidated financial statements.

The final allocation of the purchase price was as follows:

Purchase price:	
Cash	$513
Net assets acquired:	
Cash and cash equivalents	1
Mining interests	1,146
Current liabilities	(1)
Deferred income tax liabilities	(419)
Other non-current liabilities	(1)
Non-controlling interest	(213)
	$513

The amount assigned to non-controlling interest represents New Gold's 30% interest in SCM which was measured as New Gold's proportionate share of the fair value of SCM's identifiable net assets at the date of acquisition.

Total transaction costs incurred relating to the acquisition and included in other expenses during the year ended December 31, 2010 amounted to $6 million.

The net loss of SCM for the period from February 16, 2010, the acquisition date, to December 31, 2010 included in these consolidated financial statements was negligible. The impact to net earnings of the Company for the year ended December 31, 2010, had the acquisition of the 70% interest in SCM and loan receivable balances held by Xstrata Copper occurred on January 1, 2010, would be negligible.

Source: Reproduced with permission from Goldcorp Inc. http://www.goldcorp.com/files/april-24-2012/_docs/Goldcorp_AR_2011_mda_financials.pdf

Goldcorp uses the parent company extension theory to account for its business combinations.

ANALYSIS AND INTERPRETATION OF FINANCIAL STATEMENTS

L06

When preparing consolidated financial statements for a parent and one or more non–wholly owned subsidiaries, the parent company can value non-controlling interest based on the fair value of the subsidiary as a whole (entity theory) or the

The key ratios are different under the different reporting methods.

The classification of non-controlling interest has a big impact on the debt-to-equity ratio.

fair value of identifiable net assets (parent company extension theory). Prior to 2011, parent company theory was required. Exhibit 4.15 presents consolidated balance sheets, the current ratio, and the debt-to-equity ratio for these three theories based on Exhibits 4.4, 4.6 and 4.7, respectively.

Note the following from Exhibit 4.15:

- The current ratio is highest and therefore the liquidity position looks the best under the entity theory.

- Non-controlling interest is classified as debt under the parent company theory and as equity under the other two theories. This has a significant impact on the debt-to-equity ratio.

- The debt-to-equity ratio is lowest, and therefore the solvency position looks the best under entity theory. This could affect whether or not the company is in compliance with covenants for lending agreements.

- Financial analysts need to be aware of accounting policy choices and may need to make adjustments to companies' financial statements to make the financial statements truly comparable from one company to another.

EXHIBIT 4.15	Impact of Consolidation Theories on Current and Debt-to-Equity Ratios

P LTD.
CONSOLIDATED BALANCE SHEET
At June 30, Year 1

	Parent Company (Exhibit 4.4)	Entity (Exhibit 4.6)	Parent Company Extension (Exhibit 4.7)
Cash	$ 40,000	$ 40,000	$ 40,000
Accounts receivable	97,000	97,000	97,000
Inventory	151,600	152,000	152,000
Current assets	288,600	289,000	289,000
Plant	337,200	339,000	339,000
Patent	10,200	10,000	10,000
Goodwill	10,400	13,000	10,400
	$646,400	$651,000	$648,400
Current liabilities	$ 68,000	$ 68,000	$ 68,000
Long-term debt	204,400	205,000	205,000
Non-controlling interest	14,000		
Total liabilities	286,400	273,000	273,000
Common shares	200,000	200,000	200,000
Retained earnings	160,000	160,000	160,000
Non-controlling interest		18,000	15,400
Shareholders' equity	360,000	378,000	375,400
	$646,400	$651,000	$648,400
Current ratio	4.24	4.25	4.25
Debt-to-equity ratio	0.80	0.72	0.73

The value and classification of NCI is significantly different under the three theories.

ASPE DIFFERENCES

L07

- As mentioned in Chapter 3, private companies can either consolidate their subsidiaries or report their investments in subsidiaries under the cost method or the equity method, or at fair value if they would otherwise have chosen the cost method and the equity securities of the investee are quoted in an active market.

U.S. GAAP DIFFERENCES

U.S. GAAP and IFRSs for consolidated statements have many similarities. The significant differences are summarized as follows:

1. Whereas IFRSs do not allow push-down accounting, it is required for SEC registrants in some cases.
2. Whereas IFRSs allow either the parent company extension theory or the entity theory, U.S. GAAP requires entity theory.
3. Whereas IFRSs require that contingent payments be recognized at fair value using best estimates at the date of acquisition, U.S. GAAP requires that contingent payments be recognized only if the obligation is probable and the amount is reasonably estimated.

There are some significant differences between U.S. GAAP and IFRSs with respect to consolidated financial statements.

SUMMARY

A consolidated balance sheet presents the financial position of a group of companies under common control as if they constitute a single entity. The preparation of the consolidated balance sheet at the date of acquisition involves eliminating the parent's investment account and the parent's share of the subsidiary's shareholders' equity accounts, revaluing the net assets of the subsidiary to fair value, and establishing the non-controlling interest (NCI). Either entity theory or parent company extension theory must be used when consolidating non–wholly owned subsidiaries.

When the total consideration given is less than the fair value of identifiable net assets, a gain on bargain purchase is reported on the consolidated income statement. When a subsidiary has goodwill on its separate-entity balance sheet, this goodwill is eliminated on consolidation and replaced by the goodwill inherent in the parent's purchase of the subsidiary at the date of acquisition.

When the terms of a business combination require an additional payment contingent on some specified future event, the fair value of the contingent consideration should be estimated and recorded as part of the acquisition cost at the date of acquisition.

A working paper can be used to prepare the consolidated statements, and is necessary if there are a large number of subsidiaries to consolidate. A computerized spreadsheet is particularly useful in this situation. When there are only one or two subsidiaries, the direct approach is a more efficient way to arrive at the desired results.

Significant Changes in GAAP in the Last Three Years

1. The definition of control has changed. Extensive guidance is given in IFRS 10 to evaluate whether one entity has control of another entity.

Changes Expected in GAAP in the Next Three Years

*   No major changes are expected related to the topics in this chapter.

SELF-STUDY PROBLEM 1

L01, 6 On December 31, Year 1, CAN Company (CAN) takes control over the net assets of UKS Company (UKS) by purchasing 80% of the ordinary shares of UKS. CAN paid for the purchase by issuing ordinary shares with a market value of $35,200. The following information has been assembled:

	CAN Company	UKS Company	
	Carrying amount	Carrying amount	Fair value
Plant assets	$ 80,000	$20,000	$26,000
Goodwill	0	0	22,000
Current assets	50,000	15,000	14,000
	$130,000	$35,000	$62,000
Shareholders' equity	$ 75,000	$18,000	
Long-term debt	25,000	7,000	$ 8,000
Current liabilities	30,000	10,000	10,000
	$130,000	$35,000	

Required:

(a) Prepare a consolidated statement of financial position for CAN and calculate the current and debt-to-equity ratios immediately after the combination under

  (i) proprietary theory,
  (ii) parent company theory,
  (iii) parent company extension theory, and
  (iv) entity theory.

(b) Which theory shows the better liquidity position, and which theory shows the best solvency position? Briefly explain.

(c) Which theory best portrays the economic value of the subsidiary? Briefly explain.

SOLUTION TO SELF-STUDY PROBLEM 1

CAN COMPANY
Balance Sheet
At December 31, Year 1
(See notes)

See notes below	Proprietary (a.i)	Parent Company (a.ii)	Parent Company Extension (a.iii)	Entity (a.iv)
Plant assets	$100,800	$104,800	$106,000	$106,000
Goodwill	17,600	17,600	17,600	22,000
Current assets	61,200	64,200	64,000	64,000
	$179,600	$186,600	$187,600	$192,000
Shareholders' equity				
CAN	$110,200	$110,200	$110,200	$110,200
Non-controlling interest			4,400	8,800
Non-controlling interest		3,600		
Long-term debt	31,400	32,800	33,000	33,000
Current liabilities	38,000	40,000	40,000	40,000
	$179,600	$186,600	$187,600	$192,000
Current ratio	1.611	1.605	1.600	1.600
Debt-to-equity ratio	0.63	0.69	0.64	0.61

(b) Proprietary theory shows the best liquidity position because its current ratio is higher than the other theories. Entity theory shows the best solvency position because its debt-to-equity ratio is lower than the other theories. Both the debt and equity are higher under entity theory. However, the increase in equity is proportionately greater than the increase in debt.

(c) In the opinion of the author of this text, fair values are better measures of the economic value of assets and liabilities than historical cost-based values. If so, entity theory best reflects the true economic value of the subsidiary. All of the subsidiaries' identifiable assets and liabilities are reported at fair value, and the full value of the subsidiary's goodwill is included in the consolidated financial statements.

Notes:

1.   The assets and liabilities are calculated as follows:
     - (a.i)   Carrying amounts for CAN and 80% of fair values for UKS
     - (a.ii)   Carrying amounts for CAN and carrying amounts for UKS plus 80% of fair value excess for UKS's identifiable assets and liabilities plus 80% of the value of UKS's goodwill
     - (a.iii)   Carrying amounts for CAN and carrying amounts for UKS plus 100% of fair value excess for UKS's identifiable assets and liabilities plus 80% of the value of UKS's goodwill
     - (a.iv)   Carrying amounts for CAN and carrying amounts for UKS plus 100% of fair value excess for UKS's identifiable assets and liabilities plus 100% of the value of UKS's goodwill

2. The non-controlling interest is calculated as follows:

(a.ii)   20% × carrying amount of UKS's identifiable assets and liabilities
(a.iii) 20% × fair value of UKS's identifiable assets and liabilities
(a.iv)   20% × fair value of UKS's identifiable assets, identifiable liabilities, and goodwill

SELF-STUDY PROBLEM 2

LO2, 3   On December 31, Year 1, the condensed balance sheets for ONT Limited and NB Inc. were as follows:

	ONT	NB
Assets:		
Cash	$ 44,000	$ 80,000
Accounts receivable	480,000	420,000
Inventories	650,000	540,000
Property, plant & equipment	2,610,000	870,000
Accumulated depreciation	(1,270,000)	(130,000)
	$2,514,000	$1,780,000
Liabilities:		
Current liabilities	$ 660,000	$ 560,000
Bonds payable	820,000	490,000
	1,480,000	1,050,000
Shareholders' equity:		
Ordinary shares	200,000	400,000
Retained earnings	834,000	330,000
	1,034,000	730,000
	$2,514,000	$1,780,000

The fair value of all of NB's assets and liabilities were equal to their carrying amounts except for the following:

Asset	Carrying amount	Fair value
Inventories	$540,000	$570,000
Property, plant & equipment	740,000	790,000
Bonds payable	490,000	550,000

Required:

(a) Assume that on January 1, Year 2, ONT acquired 70% of NB's ordinary shares by issuing new ordinary shares with a fair value of $700,000. This was the only transaction on this day.

  (i) Prepare the journal entry on ONT's book to record the purchase of NB's ordinary shares.
  (ii) Prepare a schedule to calculate and allocate the acquisition differential.
  (iii) Prepare a consolidated balance sheet for ONT and its subsidiary at January 1, Year 2, after recording the purchase of NB's ordinary shares.

(b) In Self-Study Problem 2 in Chapter 3, the same set of data was presented except that ONT acquired 100% of NB's ordinary shares for $1,000,000. What are the similarities and differences between the balance sheet above and the balance from part (b) in Self-Study Problem 2 in Chapter 3?

(c) Calculate goodwill and non-controlling interest on the consolidated balance sheet on January 1, Year 2, under the parent company extension theory.

SOLUTION TO SELF-STUDY PROBLEM 2

(a) (i)	Investment in NB	700,000	
	Common shares		700,000 (a)

(ii)	Cost of ONT's 70% investment in NB			$ 700,000	
	Implied value of 100% investment in NB (700,000/0.70)			$1,000,000	(b)
	Carrying amount of NB's net assets				
	Assets		$1,780,000		
	Liabilities		(1,050,000)	730,000	
	Acquisition differential			270,000	
	Allocated as follows:				
	Inventories (570,000 − 540,000)		$ 30,000		(c)
	Property, plant & equipment (790,000 − 740,000)		50,000		(d)
	Bonds payable (550,000 − 490,000)		(60,000) (e)	20,000	
	Balance—goodwill			$ 250,000	(f)
	Non-controlling interest (30% × [b] 1,000,000)			$ 300,000	(g)

(iii)

ONT LIMITED
Consolidated Balance Sheet
January 1, Year 2

Cash (44,000 + 80,000)	$ 124,000
Accounts receivable (480,000 + 420,000)	900,000
Inventories (650,000 + 540,000 + **[c] 30,000**)	1,220,000
Property, plant & equipment (2,610,000 + 870,000 − **130,000*** + **[d] 50,000**)	3,400,000
Accumulated depreciation (1,270,000 + 130,000 − **130,000***)	(1,270,000)
Goodwill **[f]**	250,000
	$4,624,000
Liabilities:	
Current liabilities (660,000 + 560,000)	$1,220,000
Bonds payable (820,000 + 490,000 + **[e] 60,000**)	1,370,000
	2,590,000
Shareholders' equity:	
Common shares (200,000 + **[a] 700,000**)	900,000
Retained earnings	834,000
Non-controlling interests **[g]**	300,000
	2,034,000
	$4,624,000

* *eliminates NB's accumulated depreciation*

(b) The balance sheets are exactly the same except for shareholders' equity. The assets and liabilities are exactly the same because the implied value of the subsidiary as a whole is $1,000,000 in both cases. In Chapter 3, the purchase price was $1,000,000 for 100% of the subsidiary. In Chapter 4, the parent paid $700,000 for 70%, which produces an implied value of $1,000,000 for the subsidiary as a whole. The difference between the total value of $1,000,000 and the purchase price of $700,000 for 70% is attributed to non-controlling interest. Therefore, consolidated common shares is $300,000 less and NCI is $300,000 more when the parent only acquired 70% of the subsidiary.

(c)

Goodwill under entity theory	$250,000
Less: NCI's share (30%)	75,000
Goodwill under parent company extension theory	$175,000
NCI under entity theory	$300,000
Less: NCI's share of goodwill (30%)	75,000
NCI under parent company extension theory	$225,000

Appendix 4A

Working Paper Approach for Consolidation of Non–Wholly Owned Subsidiaries

L08 In this chapter, we illustrated the direct approach for preparing a consolidated balance sheet for non–wholly owned subsidiaries at the date of acquisition. We considered four different theories of consolidations, bargain purchases, and subsidiaries with goodwill on their own balance sheet. We will now illustrate the working paper approach using the same examples.

A number of methods can be used to prepare consolidation working papers at the date of acquisition. All methods must result in identical consolidated amounts. Our approach is to prepare adjusting entries to eliminate the investment account, establish non-controlling interest, and allocate the acquisition differential to appropriate accounts. The entries are supported by the same calculations and schedules used under the direct approach.

Entity Theory

Exhibit 4A.1 shows the preparation of the consolidated balance sheet when P Ltd. acquires 80% of the common shares of S Ltd. for $72,000. P Ltd. uses the entity theory and thereby reports 100% of the fair value of the S Ltd.'s goodwill on the consolidated balance sheet. To compare it with the direct approach, see Exhibit 4.6.

EXHIBIT A4.1

P LTD.
CONSOLIDATED BALANCE SHEET WORKING PAPER
(Entity Theory)

	P Ltd.	S Ltd.	Adjustments and Eliminations Dr.		Adjustments and Eliminations Cr.		Consolidated balance sheet	
Cash	$ 28,000	$ 12,000					$ 40,000	The subsidiary's assets and
Accounts receivable	90,000	7,000					97,000	liabilities are brought onto
Inventory	130,000	20,000	(3)	$ 2,000			152,000	the consolidated balance
Plant	280,000	50,000	(3)	9,000			339,000	sheet at 100% of their fair
Patent		11,000			(3) $	1,000	10,000	values.
Investment in S Ltd.	72,000				(1)	72,000		
Acquisition differential			(1)	16,000	(3)	20,000		
			(2)	4,000				
Goodwill			(3)	13,000			13,000	
	$600,000	$100,000					$651,000	
Current liabilities	$ 60,000	$ 8,000					$ 68,000	
Long-term debt	180,000	22,000			(3)	3,000	205,000	
Common shares	200,000						200,000	
Retained earnings	160,000						160,000	
Common shares		40,000	(1)	32,000				
			(2)	8,000				
Retained earnings		30,000	(1)	24,000				
			(2)	6,000				
Non-controlling interest					(2)	18,000	18,000	NCI is presented as a component of shareholders' equity on the consolidated balance sheet.
	$600,000	$100,000		$114,000		$114,000	$651,000	

Three working paper entries are used. Entry **(1)** eliminates the parent's share of the subsidiary's shareholders' equity accounts and the parent's investment account, with the difference established as the acquisition differential. Entry **(2)** eliminates the NCI's share of the subsidiary's shareholders' equity accounts and establishes the NCI on the consolidated balance sheet, with the difference going to acquisition differential. Entry **(3)** allocates the acquisition differential to revalue the identifiable net assets of the subsidiary, and establishes the resulting goodwill.

The three working paper elimination entries are as follows:

(1)	Common shares—S Ltd.	32,000	
	Retained earnings—S Ltd.	24,000	
	Acquisition differential	16,000	
	Investment in S Ltd.		72,000
(2)	Acquisition differential	4,000	
	Common shares	8,000	
	Retained earnings—S Ltd.	6,000	
	Non-controlling interest		18,000

The first two entries record the acquisition differential and the NCI on the consolidated balance sheet.

The implied acquisition differential is allocated to identifiable assets and liabilities and goodwill.

(3)	Inventory—S Ltd.	2,000	
	Plant—S Ltd.	9,000	
	Goodwill	13,000	
	Patent—S Ltd.		1,000
	Long-term debt—S Ltd.		3,000
	Acquisition differential		20,000

It must be emphasized again that these worksheet entries are made only in the working paper; they are *not* entered in the accounting records of either P Ltd. or S Ltd.

BARGAIN PURCHASE

Exhibit 4A.2 shows the preparation of the consolidated balance sheet when P Ltd. acquires 80% of the common shares of S Ltd. for $60,000. This results in negative goodwill, which is reported as a gain on bargain purchase. To compare it with the direct approach, see Exhibit 4.10.

Three working paper entries are used. Entry **(1)** eliminates the parent's share of the subsidiary's shareholders' equity accounts and the parent's investment account, with the difference established as the acquisition differential. Entry **(2)**

EXHIBIT A4.2

P LTD.
CONSOLIDATED BALANCE SHEET WORKING PAPER
(Bargain Purchase, Parent Company Extension Theory)

The subsidiary's identifiable assets and liabilities are measured at fair value on the consolidated balance sheet.

The gain from the bargain purchase is recorded in income and ends up in consolidated retained earnings on the date of acquisition.

	P Ltd.	S Ltd.		Adjustments and Eliminations Dr.		Adjustments and Eliminations Cr.	Consolidated balance sheet
Cash	$ 40,000	$ 12,000					$ 52,000
Accounts receivable	90,000	7,000					97,000
Inventory	130,000	20,000	(3)	2,000			152,000
Plant	280,000	50,000	(3)	9,000			339,000
Patent		11,000			(3)	$ 1,000	10,000
Investment in S Ltd.	60,000				(1)	60,000	
Acquisition differential			(1)	4,000	(3)	5,400	
			(2)	1,400			
	$600,000	$100,000					$650,000
Current liabilities	$ 60,000	$ 8,000					$ 68,000
Long-term debt	180,000	22,000			(3)	3,000	205,000
Common shares	200,000						200,000
Retained earnings	160,000				(3)	1,600	161,600
Common shares		40,000	(1)	32,000			
			(2)	8,000			
Retained earnings		30,000	(1)	24,000			
			(2)	6,000			
Non-controlling interest					(2)	15,400	15,400
	$600,000	$100,000		$86,400		$86,400	$651,000

eliminates the NCI's share of the subsidiary's shareholders' equity accounts and establishes the NCI on the consolidated balance sheet, with the difference going to acquisition differential. Entry **(3)** allocates the acquisition differential to revalue the identifiable net assets of the subsidiary, and establishes the resulting gain on purchase.

The three working paper elimination entries are as follows:

(1)	Common shares—S Ltd.	32,000	
	Retained earnings—S Ltd.	24,000	
	Acquisition differential	4,000	
	Investment in S Ltd.		60,000
(2)	Acquisition differential	1,400	
	Common shares	8,000	
	Retained earnings—S Ltd.	6,000	
	Non-controlling interest		15,400
(3)	Inventory—S Ltd.	2,000	
	Plant—S Ltd.	9,000	
	Patent—S Ltd.		1,000
	Long-term debt—S Ltd.		3,000
	Retained earnings (gain on bargain purchase)		1,600
	Acquisition differential		5,400

Subsidiary with Goodwill

Exhibit 4A.3 shows the preparation of the consolidated balance sheet when S Ltd. had goodwill on its own balance sheet. P Ltd. pays $62,000 for 80% of the common shares of S Ltd. This results in goodwill of $10,500 on the consolidated balance sheet. To compare it with the direct approach, see Exhibit 4.13.

Three working paper entries are required. Entry **(1)** writes off the previous goodwill (labelled "old" goodwill in the working paper) to S Ltd.'s retained earnings for purposes of consolidation. Entry **(2)** eliminates the parent's share of the subsidiary's common shares and adjusted retained earnings and the parent's investment account, and establishes the difference as the acquisition differential. Entry **(3)** eliminates the NCI's share of the subsidiary's shareholders' equity accounts and establishes the NCI on the consolidated balance sheet, with the difference going to acquisition differential. Entry **(4)** allocates the acquisition differential to revalue the net assets of the subsidiary, and establishes the new goodwill from the business combination.

The three working paper elimination entries are shown below:

(1)	Retained earnings—S Ltd.	11,000	
	Goodwill—old: S Ltd.		11,000
(2)	Common shares—S Ltd.	32,000	
	Retained earnings—S Ltd. ([30,000 − 11,000] × 80%)	15,200	
	Acquisition differential	14,800	
	Investment in S Ltd.		62,000
(3)	Common shares—S Ltd.	8,000	
	Retained earnings—S Ltd. ([30,000 − 11,000] × 20%)	3,800	
	Acquisition differential	3,700	
	NCI		15,500

These worksheet entries establish the appropriate account balances for the consolidated balance sheet.

EXHIBIT A4.3

P LTD.
CONSOLIDATED BALANCE SHEET WORKING PAPER
At June 30, Year 1

	P Ltd.	S Ltd.	Adjustments and Eliminations Dr.	Adjustments and Eliminations Cr.	Consolidated balance sheet
Cash	$ 38,000	$ 12,000			$ 50,000
Accounts receivable	90,000	7,000			97,000
Inventory	130,000	20,000	**(4)** $ 2,000		152,000
Plant	280,000	50,000	**(4)** 9,000		339,000
Goodwill—old		11,000		**(1)** $ 11,000	
Investment in S Ltd.	62,000			**(2)** 62,000	
Acquisition differential			**(2)** 14,800	**(4)** 18,500	
			(3) 3,700		
Goodwill			**(4)** 10,500		10,500
	$600,000	$100,000			$648,500
Current liabilities	$ 60,000	$ 8,000			$ 68,000
Long-term debt	180,000	22,000		**(4)** 3,000	205,000
Common shares	200,000				200,000
Retained earnings	160,000				160,000
Common shares		40,000	**(2)** 32,000		
			(3) 8,000		
Retained earnings		30,000	**(1)** 11,000		
			(2) 15,200		
			(3) 3,800		
NCI				**(3)** 15,500	15,500
	$600,000	$100,000	$110,000	$ 110,000	$648,500

The revalued goodwill appears on the consolidated balance sheet.

The working paper approach produces the same results as the direct approach.

(4) Inventory—S Ltd.	2,000	
Plant—S Ltd.	9,000	
Goodwill	10,500	
Long-term debt—S Ltd.		3,000
Acquisition differential		18,500

All entries were working paper entries and were not recorded in the records of
S Ltd. Since S Ltd. does not write off its goodwill in its separate-entity records, the
preparation of consolidated statements in Year 2 and all future years will require
working paper entries to write off any goodwill that still exists in S Ltd.'s records,
and to reverse goodwill impairment that has been recorded.

REVIEW QUESTIONS

L02   1.   Is a negative acquisition differential the same as negative goodwill? Explain.

L01   2.   With respect to the valuation of non-controlling interest, what are the major
differences among proprietary, parent company, and entity theories?

LO1   3. How does the presentation of non-controlling interest on the consolidated balance sheet differ under the four theories of consolidating a non–wholly owned subsidiary?

LO2   4. How is the goodwill appearing on the statement of financial position of a subsidiary prior to a business combination treated in the subsequent preparation of consolidated statements? Explain.

LO2   5. Under the entity theory, consolidated goodwill is determined by inference. Describe how this is achieved, and comment on its shortcomings.

LO2   6. What is non-controlling interest, and how is it reported in the consolidated balance sheet under entity theory?

LO3   7. What accounts on the consolidated balance sheet differ in value between entity theory and parent company extension theory? Briefly explain why they differ.

LO5   8. What is contingent consideration, and how is it measured at the date of acquisition?

LO5   9. Explain how changes in the fair value of contingent consideration should be reported, assuming that the contingent consideration will be paid in the form of cash.

LO7   10. What reporting options related to business combinations are available to private companies?

LO4   11. What is negative goodwill, and how is it accounted for?

LO4   12. Explain whether or not the historical cost principle is applied when accounting for negative goodwill.

LO2   13. How is the net income earned by a subsidiary in the year of acquisition incorporated in the consolidated income statement?

LO8   14. In whose accounting records are the consolidation elimination entries recorded? Explain.

LO2   15. Don Ltd. purchased 80% of the outstanding shares of Gunn Ltd. Before the purchase, Gunn had a deferred charge of $10.5 million on its balance sheet. This item consisted of organization costs that were being amortized over a 20-year period. What amount should be reported in Don's consolidated statements with respect to this deferred charge? Explain briefly.

LO2   16. How would the consolidation of a parent-founded subsidiary differ from the consolidation of a purchased subsidiary?

CASES

Case 4-1
LO1
On December 31, Year 7, Maple Company issued preferred shares with a fair value of $600,000 to acquire 12,000 (60%) of the common shares of Leafs Limited. The Leafs shares were trading in the market at around $40 per share just days prior to and just after the purchase by Maple. Maple had to and was willing to pay a premium of $10 per share, or $120,000, in total in order to gain control over Leafs.

The balance sheets for the two companies just prior to acquisition were as follows (in 000s):

	Maple		Leafs	
	Carrying amount	Fair value	Carrying amount	Fair value
Identifiable assets	$2,000	$2,500	$1,000	$1,400
Goodwill	0	??	0	??
	$2,000		$1,000	
Liabilities	$1,500	1,600	$ 800	840
Shareholders' equity	500	??	200	??
	$2,000		$1,000	

Consolidated financial statements will be prepared to combine the financial statements for the two companies. The management of Maple is concerned about the valuation of goodwill on the consolidated financial statements. It was willing to pay a premium of $120,000 to gain control of Leafs. It maintains that it would have paid the same premium in total whether it acquired 60% or 100% of the shares of Leafs.

Given that the return on assets is a closely monitored ratio by the shareholders, the management of Maple would like to minimize the value assigned to goodwill on consolidation. Management wants to see how the consolidated balance sheet would differ under four different theories of reporting: proprietary, parent company, parent company extension, and entity. Management also has the following questions when reporting this business combination:

- How will we determine the value of the goodwill for the subsidiary?
- How will this affect the valuation of NCI?
- Will we have to revalue the subsidiary's assets and liabilities every year when we prepare the consolidated financial statements?
- Which consolidation theory best reflects the economic reality of the business combination?

Required:

Prepare a consolidated balance sheet at the date of acquisition under the four theories, and respond to the questions asked by management.

Case 4-2
LO2   Eternal Rest Limited (ERL) is a public company; its shares are traded on a stock exchange in Canada. ERL operates both funeral homes and cemeteries in Canada. Funeral services (casket, flowers, cemetery stone, prayer service) are sold on an "as needed" basis and also "in advance" (prepaid). ERL recognizes revenue only as the funeral services are performed.

Cemetery land is purchased years in advance, and carrying costs (e.g., interest and property taxes) are capitalized. The company sells burial plots or gravesites in advance, or on an "as needed" basis. Revenues from plots sold in advance are recognized upon signing a contract, regardless of the timing of receipt of cash. The cost of maintenance for 100 years is recognized as an expense of earning revenue.

By law, funds for maintenance are sent to a trustee, for investment. Funds are allowed to be withdrawn annually for current maintenance costs. The cost of the cemetery land and land improvements (including trees, fencing, and pathways) is allocated to cost of sales.

As a result of acquisitions, ERL tripled its assets in fiscal Year 5. Effective September 1, Year 4, ERL acquired the assets and liabilities of Tranquil Cemeteries Limited (Tranquil) by issuing common shares and debt. ERL also acquired, effective November 1, Year 4, 70% of the voting common shares of Peaceful Cemeteries Limited (Peaceful) in exchange for $1 million cash (borrowed from ERL's banker) plus common shares of ERL. Peaceful was privately owned by a single shareholder before the purchase of its shares by ERL. The common shares of ERL that were issued with respect to the acquisitions have been escrowed and may not be sold for one year from their issuance date.

You, a CA, are a new manager with a CA firm. Your firm was appointed as the auditor of ERL in September Year 4, for the year ending June 30, Year 5. Your firm was also appointed as the auditor of Peaceful.

It is now September Year 5. Your firm has experienced severe staffing shortages. The partner has advised you that because of the recent departure of another manager, you have been assigned to the ERL and Peaceful engagements. The audit fieldwork has been completed, but the file review has not taken place. The partner has asked you to review the audit files and notes prepared by the senior in charge of the engagements and to prepare a memo that provides your analysis and disposition of the accounting issues.

The following information was assembled from your review of the working papers of ERL and Peaceful.

1. The acquisition of Tranquil's net assets resulted in the following additions to ERL's balance sheet as at September 1, Year 4 (in thousands of dollars):

Working capital	$ 850
Land	1,400
Buildings and equipment, net	3,700
Non-competition agreements	3,000
Goodwill	11,250
Total net assets of Tranquil	$20,200
The $20.2 million was paid as follows:	
5-year non-interest-bearing first mortgage bonds of ERL	$18,150
Common shares of ERL, escrowed for one year	2,050
	$20,200

The auditors read the purchase and sale agreement and noted that $820,000 of the working capital represented funds that were being held in trust for future maintenance of the cemetery lands. The new common shares issued by ERL were measured at the market price on the day prior to the signing of the agreement.

The $3 million paid for non-competition agreements represents a payment to the sellers of Tranquil in exchange for their commitment not to engage in the same type of business for five years. The $3 million represents the otherwise expected earnings of the sellers, discounted at the 9% market rate of interest that prevailed at the time. The $1.4 million and $3.7 million assigned to land, buildings, and equipment represent management's estimates of the fair values of these assets and coincide with carrying amounts on Tranquil's books.

2. The shares of Peaceful were acquired primarily because the company had non–capital loss carry-forwards for income tax purposes. The purchase price for the acquisition was a $1 million cash payment by ERL plus the issuance of $24 million of ERL shares for the 70% ownership. The acquisition cost was allocated to assets and liabilities in a manner similar to the allocation for the Tranquil acquisition. The auditors did not request that the estimated value of the loss carry-forward be recorded. ERL attributed $4 million to non-competition agreements (to be amortized over five years) and $14 million to goodwill.

3. After the acquisition of Peaceful by ERL, sufficient business was directed to Peaceful to commence the process of utilizing the tax loss carry-forwards. During fiscal Year 5, the benefit realized from the utilization of the loss carry-forwards amounted to $2.36 million and was recognized as a gain on the income statement.

4. Excess cemetery land (acquired in the purchase of Tranquil) was sold in December Year 4 at a gain of $1.2 million. The proceeds were reported as "other revenue."

5. One working paper entitled "Land" contains the following note: "Land recorded on the books at $2,305,600 and called 'Sunset Hill' is undeveloped and is not scheduled for use until Year 8 or Year 9. It is subject to a Year 5 government order requiring that ERL clear up environmental concerns on the site. I asked one employee what the cost would be and was told 'half a million dollars.' No amount was accrued because of uncertainty."

6. A working paper entitled "Management Compensation" shows that senior management shares in what is called a "Bonus Pool." The bonus is 15% of income before income taxes.

Required:

Prepare the memo.

(CICA adapted)

Case 4-3
LO2   Factory Optical Distributors (FOD) is a publicly held manufacturer and distributor of high-quality eyeglass lenses located in Burnaby, British Columbia. For the past 10 years, the company has sold its lenses on a wholesale basis to optical shops across Canada. Beginning in Year 3, the company began to offer franchise opportunities to opticians wanting to sell only FOD lenses.

The franchise agreements contain the following stipulations:

- Each franchise must be a corporation. FOD (Burnaby) will purchase 35% of the corporation's outstanding common shares and the franchisee will hold the remaining 65%. No other equity instruments can be issued.
- Franchises can be established in new locations or in existing locations under the name Factory Optical Distributors. If a new building is required, FOD (Burnaby) will guarantee the mortgage to ensure that the best interest rates can be obtained. If an existing location is used, it must be renovated to meet company specifications, and again FOD (Burnaby) will guarantee any required financing.

- To qualify as a franchisee, an individual must be a licensed optician and must commit to 40 hours a week in the franchise location, managing the day-to-day activities.
- Franchisees are to be paid a salary that does not exceed 1.5 times the industry average for opticians with equivalent experience.
- The franchise agreement specifies that only FOD lenses can be sold in franchise locations. FOD lenses can be purchased by franchisees at 20% below normal selling price for the first $500,000 of purchases and at 25% below normal selling price if purchases exceed $500,000 on an annual basis.
- The agreement also requires that frames sold by the franchisee be purchased from designated suppliers, to ensure the best quality and fit to FOD lenses.
- All franchise advertising must be approved by FOD (Burnaby). Franchisees must allocate 1% of revenue to advertising each month.
- The franchisee is required to participate in special promotions and seasonal sales as determined by FOD (Burnaby).
- A franchise fee of 2% of sales is payable monthly to FOD (Burnaby).
- Other products and services can be sold from the franchise location provided that they do not negatively impact the sale of FOD lenses.

During Year 5, eight franchise agreements were signed in locations across Canada. At December 31, Year 5, the company's year-end, five of these locations were open for business.

It is now January Year 6. You are the senior auditor on the FOD (Burnaby) account. The company's corporate controller has come to you with the franchise agreement to discuss how FOD must report its share ownership in the five operating franchises. She has heard that the definition of control in IFRS 10 encompasses some situations where 50% share ownership does not exist.

Required:

Examine the details of the franchise agreement. Do you think FOD controls the franchise operations? Would consolidation be required? Explain.

(adapted from a case prepared by J.C. Thatcher, Lakehead University, and Margaret Forbes, University of Saskatchewan)

Case 4-4   The following are a number of scenarios that show variations in the nature of long-
LO2   term intercorporate investments. Assume that all companies are public companies.

1. A Ltd. owns 45% of B Co. Typically, only about 70% of the outstanding shares are voted at the annual meetings of B Company. Because of this, A Ltd. always casts a majority of the votes on every ballot when it votes the shares it holds.

2. A Ltd. holds no shares of B Co.; however, it holds convertible bonds issued by B Co. that, if A Ltd. converted them, would result in the ownership of 51% of the outstanding shares of B Co.

3. A Ltd. owns 75% of B Co. Recently a receiver, acting on behalf of a bank, seized a portion of B Co.'s inventory when B Co. defaulted on a loan.

4. Last year B Co. was a wholly owned subsidiary of C Inc. At the beginning of this year, B Co. was put up for sale and A Ltd. purchased all of its 100,000

voting shares from C Inc. by making a cash payment of 40% of the purchase price and issuing a promissory note for the balance owing, due in equal installments over the next two years.

B Co. has a bond issue outstanding that can be converted at the option of the holder into 150,000 voting common shares of that company. At the time of the sale, C Inc. held 100% of these bonds; it has agreed to sell these bonds proportionately to A Ltd. as it receives the proceeds from the promissory note.

5. A Ltd. owns 100% of B Co., which is insolvent. A licensed trustee has seized all of its assets in bankruptcy.

6. B Co. is located in a foreign country. This country requires that its citizens hold a majority of the ownership of all businesses. A Ltd. has the expertise and technical knowledge required to successfully operate B Co. In order to satisfy the country's foreign ownership requirements, B Co. has been structured as a partnership, with 50 partners each having a 2% equity interest. Forty-nine of the partners, who are all citizens of the foreign country, have signed an irrevocable agreement that establishes A Ltd. as the managing partner, with complete authority to determine the operating, financing, and investing policies of B Co.

Required:

For each scenario, discuss how A Ltd. should report its investment in B Co.

Case 4-5
LO2

Smith & Stewart (Stewart) is a partnership of lawyers. It was recently formed from a merger of two predecessor partnerships: Becker and Brackman (Becker) and Copp and Copp (Copp). The merged firm has 38 partners, six from Becker and 32 from Copp, and a total of 75 employees. At the date of the merger, Stewart purchased land and an office building for $1.25 million and fully computerized the new offices. The partners have decided that the financial statements will be audited annually, although neither of the predecessor firms was audited.

The partnership agreement requires an annual valuation of the assets and liabilities of the firm. This valuation is to be used to determine the payment to be made by the partnership to a withdrawing partner, and the contribution to be made to the partnership by a newly admitted partner. The partners are unsure of the accounting implications of this requirement.

The partners have been actively engaged in establishing and managing the practice and have paid little attention to the accounting policies.

Before the merger, Becker recorded revenue when it invoiced the client. Time reports were used to keep track of the number of hours worked for each client, although this information was not recorded in the accounting system. In general, its accounting records were not well maintained.

In contrast, work in progress was recorded for employees of Copp at their regular billing rate, on a client-by-client basis, based on the hours worked, even though the full amount was not always recoverable. At year-end, an adjustment was made to reduce work in progress to reflect the actual costs incurred by Copp. Copp recorded revenue for partner hours at the time that clients were invoiced.

The new partnership agreement requires a valuation of the work in progress at the merger date, with this amount to be recorded as goodwill. This amount has not yet been determined.

Stewart has arranged a line of credit with a bank that allows the partnership to borrow up to 75% of the carrying amount of receivables and 40% of the carrying amount of work in progress, as recorded in the monthly financial statements. The bank has also provided mortgage financing of $750,000 on the recently acquired land and building. As well as annually audited financial statements, the bank requires unaudited financial statements monthly.

As of the date of the merger, property, plant, and equipment owned by the predecessor firms were transferred to the new partnership.

Each partner receives a monthly "draw" payment, which represents an advance on the partner's share of annual profit.

Although the individual partners cannot incorporate, the partnership is considering incorporating a company to provide management services to the partnership. If it proceeds with this idea, the land and building and related mortgage, and the equipment would be transferred to this company.

Your firm has been engaged by Stewart to prepare a report advising the partnership on financial accounting issues. The manager in charge of the Stewart engagement has asked you, a CA, to prepare a draft report to the client addressing its concerns.

Required:

Prepare the draft report.

(CICA adapted)

Case 4-6
LO2

Lauder Adventures Limited (LAL) was incorporated over 40 years ago as an amusement park and golf course. Over time, a nearby city has grown to the point where it borders on LAL's properties. In recent years LAL's owners, who are all members of one family, have seen LAL's land values increase significantly. LAL's majority shareholder, Hassan Poosti, owns 55% of the outstanding shares and is not active in LAL's day-to-day activities.

Last year, Hassan hired a new chief executive officer, Leo Titan. Leo has a reputation for being an aggressive risk taker. Hassan is committed, and has the personal financial resources required, to support Leo's plans.

Eight months ago, LAL became the successful bidder for a new sports franchise, in conjunction with a minority partner. Under the terms of the franchise agreement, LAL is required to build a sports arena, which is currently being constructed. The arena is being built on a section of the amusement park. Another section of the amusement park is being relocated to ensure that the entrances to the arena are close to public transportation and parking. Consequently, some of the rides will be relocated. LAL is the sole owner of the arena at present.

The sports franchise is separately incorporated as Northern Sports Limited (NSL); LAL holds 75% of the shares in the company. Another bid is being prepared by NSL to obtain a second sports franchise so that the arena can be used more often. NSL will be required to lease space from LAL when the arena is completed, in about 22 months.

For the first two sports seasons, NSL will have to lease arena space from Aggressive Limited (AL). During this time, NSL does not expect to be profitable because

- it may take time to build a competitive team;
- AL is charging a high rent, and it is not giving NSL a share of concession (hot dogs, drinks) revenue;
- AL cannot make the better dates (e.g., Saturday night) available to NSL to attract sports fans; and
- as a newcomer to the league, NSL is restricted with regard to the players who are available to it and the days of the week it can play in its home city.

Consequently, NSL has arranged to borrow funds from LAL and from others to finance costs and losses.

Your employer, Fabio & Fox, Chartered Accountants, has conducted the audit of LAL for several years. LAL has tended to be marginally profitable one year and then have losses the next year. The company has continued to operate because the directors know that the real estate holdings were becoming increasingly valuable.

Leo is expected to oversee the expanded accounting and finance functions in the company. He has met with you and the partner in charge of the LAL audit and discussed various issues related to the year ending September 30, Year 8. His comments are provided in Exhibit I.

It is September 5, Year 8. You have been asked by the partner to prepare a report for him, which will be used for the next meeting with Leo. He would like

---

EXHIBIT I

NOTES FROM DISCUSSION WITH LEO TITAN

1. In order to build a road to the arena's parking lot, two holes of the 18-hole golf course will be relocated next spring. Costs of $140,000 are expected to be incurred this year in design, tree planting, ground preparation, and grass seeding in order to ready the area for next spring. These costs are to be capitalized as part of the golf course lands, along with related property taxes of $13,000 and interest of $15,000.

2. In May Year 8, LAL acquired, for $4.25 million, all of the shares of an amusement park in a different city when its land lease expired. The amusement park company was wound up and the equipment, rides, concessions, and other assets are being transported to LAL at a cost of $350,000. The estimated fair value of the assets and liabilities (according to Leo) is as follows:

Concession prizes (e.g., stuffed animals)	$ 22,500
Rides and games	4,200,000
Equipment and parts	1,650,000
Electrical supplies	75,000
Lighting and signs	100,000
Estimated present value of tax loss carry-forward	700,000
	6,747,500
Liabilities	1,200,000
Net assets	$ 5,547,500

LAL expects to spend approximately $400,000 in getting the assets in operating order and $500,000 on foundations and site preparations for the rides. Leo wants to "capitalize as much as possible."

(continued)

EXHIBIT I **(*continued*)**

3. Approximately $600,000 will be required to relocate the rides that are currently on land that is needed for the arena. This amount is to be capitalized, net of scrap recovery of $60,000 on dismantled and redundant equipment. Virtually all the rides were fully depreciated years ago.

4. To assist in financing the new ventures, LAL sold excess land to developers who intend to construct a shopping centre, office buildings, and expensive homes adjacent to the golf course and away from the amusement park.

The developers and LAL agreed to these terms:	
Paid to LAL on May 1, Year 8	$ 6,000,000
To be paid to LAL on March 1, Year 9	10,000,000
To be paid to LAL on March 1, Year 10	8,000,000
	$24,000,000

The land is to be turned over to the developers on or about February 1, Year 9, but the sale is to be reported in fiscal Year 8.

5. An additional "contingent profit" will accrue to LAL if the developers earn a return on investment of more than 25% when they re-sell the newly constructed buildings. Leo wants a note to the Year 8 financial statements that describes the probability of a contingent gain.

6. The excess land that was sold to developers was carried on LAL's books at $1.35 million, on a pro rata cost basis. Leo would like to revalue the remaining land from $5.4 million to about $100 million in the Year 8 financial statements.

7. The golf course has been unprofitable in recent years. However, green fees are to be raised and specific tee-off times will be allotted to a private club, which is currently being organized. Members of the private club will pay a non-refundable entrance fee of $2,000 per member plus $100 per month for five years. The $2,000 is to be recorded as revenue on receipt. Approximately $350,000 is to be spent to upgrade the club facilities.

8. Leo wants to capitalize all costs of NSL on NSL's books until it has completed its first year of operations. In addition to the franchise fee, $20 million will have to be spent on the following:

Acquisition of player contracts	$12,000,000
Advertising and promotion	1,500,000
Equipment	3,200,000
Wages, benefits, and bonuses	6,800,000
Other operating costs	3,300,000
	26,800,000
Less	
Revenue - ticket sales	(6,000,000)
- other	(800,000)
	$20,000,000

The value of players can change quickly, depending upon their performance, injuries, and other factors.

9. The new sports arena will have private boxes in which a company can entertain groups of clients. The boxes are leased on a five-year contract basis, and they must be occupied for a fixed number of nights at a minimum price per night. To date, 12 boxes have been leased for $15,000 per box for a five-year period, exclusive of nightly charges. A down payment of $3,000 was required; the payments have been recorded as revenue.

(continued)

EXHIBIT I   *(continued)*

10. Three senior officers of LAL, including Leo, receive bonuses based on income before income taxes. The three have agreed to have their fiscal Year 8 bonuses accrued in fiscal Year 9 along with their fiscal Year 9 bonuses. Actual payments to them are scheduled for January Year 10.
11. Insurance premiums on the construction activity that is taking place total $1.4 million in fiscal Year 8, and to date they have been capitalized.
12. A $500,000 fee was paid to a mortgage broker to arrange financing for LAL. This amount has been recorded as "Other assets." No financing has been arranged to date.

you to discuss the accounting issues related to your discussion with Leo. The partner wants a thorough analysis of all important issues as well as support for your position. LAL has been and wishes to continue using IFRSs.

In your review of documents, and as a result of various conversations, you have learned the following:

1. The arena will be mortgaged, but only for about 50% of its expected cost. Lenders are concerned about the special-use nature of the arena and whether it will be successfully rented for other events such as concerts.

2. The mortgage lenders to LAL and the non-controlling shareholders in NSL are both expected to want to see appraisals and financial statements before deciding whether to invest. Covenants will be required by the lenders to ensure that excessive expenditures are not undertaken and that cash is preserved.

3. Leo does not intend to consolidate NSL until it is profitable. The investment in NSL will be reported on LAL's financial statements at cost. Thus, LAL's financial statements will also be used for income tax purposes.

4. LAL's non-controlling shareholders are not active in the business and want quarterly financial statements in order to monitor progress and assess Leo's performance. The non-controlling shareholders have all expressed concern over Leo's growth strategy over the past year. Most are relying on LAL to supplement their income.

Required:

Prepare the report.

(CICA adapted)

PROBLEMS

Problem 4-1
LO2, 3
The statements of financial position of Pork Co. and Barrel Ltd. on December 31, Year 2, are shown next:

	Pork Co.	Barrel Ltd.
Plant and equipment (net)	$400,000	$270,000
Investment in Barrel Ltd.	329,000	—
Inventory	120,000	102,000
Accounts receivable	45,000	48,000
Cash	22,000	60,000
	$916,000	$480,000

(continued)

	Pork Co.	Barrel Ltd.
Ordinary shares	$260,000	$120,000
Retained earnings	200,000	180,000
Long-term debt	240,000	108,000
Current liabilities	216,000	72,000
	$916,000	$480,000

Pork acquired 70% of the outstanding shares of Barrel on December 30, Year 2, for $329,000. Direct costs of the acquisition amounted to $12,000. The carrying amounts of the net assets of Barrel approximated fair values except for plant and equipment, which had a fair value of $320,000.

Required:

(a) Prepare a consolidated statement of financial position at December 31, Year 2, under entity theory.
(b) Calculate goodwill and non-controlling interest on the consolidated statement of financial position at December 31, Year 2, under parent company extension theory.

Problem 4-2
LO2, 4

The balance sheets of Par Ltd. and Sub Ltd. on December 31, Year 1, are as follows:

	Par Ltd.	Sub Ltd.
Cash	$100,000	$ 2,000
Accounts receivable	25,000	7,000
Inventory	30,000	21,000
Plant	175,000	51,000
Trademarks	—	7,000
	$330,000	$88,000
Current liabilities	$ 50,000	$10,000
Long-term debt	80,000	20,000
Common shares	110,000	30,000
Retained earnings	90,000	28,000
	$330,000	$88,000

The fair values of the identifiable net assets of Sub on December 31, Year 1, are as follows:

Cash		$ 2,000
Accounts receivable		7,000
Inventory		26,000
Plant		60,000
Trademarks		14,000
		109,000
Current liabilities	$10,000	
Long-term debt	19,000	29,000
Net assets		$ 80,000

Assume that the following took place on January 1, Year 2. (Par acquired the shares with a cash payment to the shareholders of Sub.)

Case 1. Par paid $95,000 to acquire all of the common shares of Sub.
Case 2. Par paid $76,000 to acquire 80% of the common shares of Sub.

Case 3. Par paid $80,000 to acquire all of the common shares of Sub.

Case 4. Par paid $70,000 to acquire all of the common shares of Sub.

Case 5. Par paid $63,000 to acquire 90% of the common shares of Sub.

Required:

For each of the five cases, prepare a consolidated balance sheet as at January 1, Year 2.

Problem 4-3
LO2, 4, 7

The balance sheets of Petron Co. and Seeview Co. on June 29, Year 2, were as follows:

	Petron	*Seeview*
Cash and receivables	$ 80,000	$16,250
Inventory	47,500	7,500
Plant assets (net)	190,000	58,750
Intangible assets	20,000	5,000
	$337,500	$87,500
Current liabilities	$ 52,500	$25,000
Long-term debt	81,250	37,500
Common shares	127,500	38,750
Retained earnings (deficit)	76,250	(13,750)
	$337,500	$87,500

On June 30, Year 2, Petron Co. purchased 90% of the outstanding shares of Seeview Co. for $40,500 cash. Legal fees involved with the acquisition were an additional $1,000. These two transactions were the only transaction on this date. The carrying amounts of Seeview's net assets were equal to fair value except for the following:

	Fair value
Inventory	$8,750
Plant assets	67,500
Intangible assets	7,500
Long-term debt	32,500

Seeview has a five-year agreement to supply goods to Bardier. Both Petron and Seeview believe that Bardier will renew the agreement at the end of the current contract. The agreement is between Seeview and Bardier; it cannot be transferred to another company without Seeview's consent. Seeview does not report any value with respect to this contract on its balance sheet. However, an independent appraiser feels that this contract is worth $10,000.

Required:

(a) Assume that Petron Co. is a public entity. Prepare the consolidated balance sheet of Petron Co. on June 30, Year 2. (Round all calculations to the nearest dollar.)

(b) Assume that Petron is a private entity, uses ASPE, and chooses to use the equity method to account for its investment in Seeview. Prepare Petron's June 30, Year 2, separate-entity balance sheet after the business combination.

Problem 4-4
LO2, 5

The balance sheets of Hill Corp. and McGraw Ltd. on December 31, Year 4, were as follows:

	Hill Corp.	McGraw Ltd.
Cash	$ 13,000	$ 6,500
Accounts receivable	181,300	45,500
Inventory	117,000	208,000
Land	91,000	52,000
Plant and equipment	468,000	377,000
Investment in McGraw Ltd.	288,000	—
Goodwill	117,000	39,000
	$1,275,300	$728,000
Current liabilities	$ 156,000	$104,000
Long-term debt	416,000	286,000
Common shares	520,000	390,000
Retained earnings	183,300	(52,000)
	$1,275,300	$728,000

On December 31, Year 4, Hill purchased 80% of the common shares of McGraw for $288,000 plus a commitment to pay an additional $100,000 in 2 years if sales grow by more than 30% over the next two years. An independent business valuator stated that Hill could have paid an extra $40,000 at the date of acquisition instead of agreeing to a potential payment of $100,000 in 2 years. On this date, the inventory of McGraw had a fair value of $214,500, its land had a fair value of $91,000, and its plant and equipment had a fair value of $364,000.

Required:

Prepare a consolidated balance sheet as at December 31, Year 4.

Problem 4-5
LO2

On December 31, Year 2, Blue purchased a percentage of the outstanding ordinary shares of Joy. On this date all but two categories of Joy's identifiable assets and liabilities had fair values equal to carrying amounts.

Following are the statements of financial position of Blue Ltd. and Joy Corp. on December 31, Year 2 subsequent to the acquisition.

	Blue Ltd.	Joy Corp.
Plant and equipment	$ 640,000	$430,000
Accumulated amortization	(200,000)	(110,000)
Investment in Joy Corp.	424,000	—
Inventory	105,000	220,000
Accounts receivable	78,000	35,000
Cash	17,000	5,000
	$1,064,000	$580,000
Ordinary shares	$ 422,000	$300,000
Retained earnings	224,000	(40,000)
Long-term debt	250,000	240,000
Current liabilities	168,000	80,000
	$1,064,000	$580,000

Below is the consolidated statement of financial position for Blue at December 31, Year 2.

BLUE LTD.
CONSOLIDATED STATEMENT OF FINANCIAL POSITION
December 31, Year 2

Plant and equipment	$1,060,000
Accumulated amortization	(200,000)
Goodwill	150,000
Inventory	345,000
Accounts receivable	113,000
Cash	22,000
	$1,490,000
Ordinary shares	$ 422,000
Retained earnings	224,000
Non-controlling interest	106,000
Long-term debt	490,000
Current liabilities	248,000
	$1,490,000

Required:

(a) From the information provided, determine the percentage of Joy's ordinary shares purchased by Blue on December 31, Year 2.

(b) Which of Joy's assets or liabilities had fair values that were not equal to their carrying amounts at acquisition? Calculate the fair value of each of these assets at December 31, Year 2.

Problem 4-6
L01, 2, 3, 4, 6

The balance sheets of E Ltd. and J Ltd. on December 30, Year 6, were as follows:

	E Ltd.	J Ltd.
Cash and receivables	$ 96,000	$ 19,500
Inventory	57,000	9,000
Plant assets (net)	228,000	70,500
Intangible assets	24,000	6,000
	$405,000	$105,000
Current liabilities	$ 63,000	$ 30,000
Long-term debt	97,500	45,000
Common shares	153,000	46,500
Retained earnings (deficit)	91,500	(16,500)
	$405,000	$105,000

On December 31, Year 6, E Ltd. issued 350 shares, with a fair value of $40 each, for 70% of the outstanding shares of J Ltd. Costs involved in the acquisition, paid in cash, were as follows:

Costs of arranging the acquisition	$2,500
Costs of issuing shares	1,600
	$4,100

The carrying amounts of J Ltd.'s net assets were equal to fair values on this date except for the following:

	Fair value
Plant assets	$65,000
Long-term debt	40,000

E Ltd. was identified as the acquirer in the combination.

Required:

(a) Prepare the consolidated balance sheet of E Ltd. on December 31, Year 6, under each of the following:

    (i) Proprietary theory
    (ii) Parent company theory
    (iii) Parent company extension theory
    (iv) Entity theory

(b) Calculate the current ratio and debt-to-equity ratio for E Ltd. under the four different theories. Explain which theory shows the strongest liquidity and solvency position and which method best reflects the true financial condition of the company.

Problem 4-7
LO1, 2, 3, 6

On December 31, Year 1, P Company purchased 80% of the outstanding shares of S Company for $6,960 cash.

The statements of financial position of the two companies immediately after the acquisition transaction appear below.

	P Company	S Company	
	Book value	Book value	Fair value
Plant and equipment (net)	$ 8,100	$ 6,900	$6,000
Investment in S Company	6,960	—	
Inventory	5,160	3,750	3,900
Accounts receivable	3,150	1,800	1,800
Cash	1,500	1,050	1,050
	$24,870	$13,500	
Ordinary shares	$10,500	$ 3,000	
Retained earnings	8,370	6,000	
Long-term liabilities	4,200	2,000	2,000
Other current liabilities	1,200	1,800	1,800
Accounts payable	600	700	700
	$24,870	$13,500	

Required:

(a) Prepare a consolidated statement of financial position at the date of acquisition under each of the following:

    (i) Proprietary theory
    (ii) Parent company theory
    (iii) Parent company extension theory
    (iv) Entity theory

(b) Calculate the current ratio and debt-to-equity ratio for P Company under the four different theories. Explain which theory shows the strongest liquidity and solvency position and which method best reflects the true financial condition of the company.

Problem 4-8
LO2

On January 1, Year 5, Black Corp. purchased 90% of the common shares of Whyte Inc. On this date, the following differences were observed with regard to specific net assets of Whyte:

	Fair value – carrying amount differences
Land	+ 50,000
Buildings (net)	+ 20,000
Equipment (net)	− 10,000
Notes payable	+ 5,000

The non-consolidated and consolidated balance sheets of Black Corp. on January 1, Year 5, are presented below. Whyte's retained earnings were $140,000 on this date.

	Non-consolidated	Consolidated
Cash	$ 36,000	$ 52,000
Accounts receivable	116,000	168,000
Inventory	144,000	234,000
Investment in Whyte	292,500	—
Land	210,000	280,000
Buildings (net)	640,000	720,000
Equipment (net)	308,000	338,000
Goodwill	—	50,000
	$1,746,500	$1,842,000
Accounts payable	$ 88,000	$ 96,000
Notes payable	507,500	562,500
Common shares	380,000	380,000
Retained earnings	771,000	771,000
Non-controlling interest	—	32,500
	$1,746,500	$1,842,000

Required:

Prepare the January 1, Year 5, balance sheet of Whyte Inc.

Problem 4-9
LO2

The balance sheets of Percy Corp. and Saltz Ltd. on December 31, Year 10, are shown below:

	Percy	Saltz
Cash	$200,000	$ 4,000
Accounts receivable	50,000	14,000
Inventory	60,000	42,000
Plant	475,000	192,000
Accumulated amortization	(125,000)	(90,000)
Trademarks—net	—	14,000
	$660,000	$176,000
Current liabilities	$100,000	$ 20,000
Long-term debt	160,000	40,000
Common shares	220,000	60,000
Retained earnings	180,000	56,000
	$660,000	$176,000

The fair values of the identifiable net assets of Saltz Ltd. on December 31, Year 10, were as follows:

Cash		$ 4,000
Accounts receivable		14,000
Inventory		52,000
Plant		120,000
Trademarks		28,000
		218,000
Current liabilities	$20,000	
Long-term debt	38,000	58,000
Net assets		$160,000

In addition to the assets identified above, Saltz owned a taxi licence in the City of Moose Jaw. This licence expires in 9 years. These licenses are selling in the open market at approximately $40,000.

On January 1, Year 11, Percy Corp paid $175,000 in cash to acquire 7,000 (70%) of the common shares of Saltz Ltd. Saltz's shares were trading for $20 per share just after the acquisition by Percy.

Required:

Prepare the consolidated balance sheet on January 1, Year 11.

Problem 4-10
LO2, 3
The balance sheets of Prima Ltd. and Donna Corp. on December 31, Year 5, are shown below:

	Prima	Donna
Cash	$ 370,000	$ 6,400
Accounts receivable	80,000	22,400
Inventory	96,000	67,200
Plant	510,000	163,200
Patents	100,000	22,400
	$1,156,000	$281,600
Current liabilities	$ 160,000	$ 32,000
Long-term debt	256,000	64,000
Common shares	352,000	96,000
Retained earnings	388,000	89,600
	$1,156,000	$281,600

The fair values of the identifiable net assets of Donna Corp. on this date are as follows:

Cash	$ 6,400
Accounts receivable	20,000
Inventory	85,000
Plant	192,000
Trademarks	30,000
Patents	60,000
Current liabilities	32,000
Long-term debt	70,000

In addition to the assets identified above, Donna owned a significant number of Internet domain names, which are unique alphanumeric names that are used to identify a particular numeric Internet address. These domain names can be sold separately and are estimated to be worth $50,000.

On January 1, Year 6, Prima Ltd. paid $351,000 in cash to acquire 90% of the common shares of Donna Corp.

Required:

(a) Prepare the consolidated balance sheet on January 1, Year 6, under entity theory.
(b) Now assume that an independent business valuator valued the NCI at $35,000 at the date of acquisition. What accounts on the consolidated balance would change, and at what amount would they be reported?
(c) Assume that Prima is a private entity, uses ASPE, and chooses to use the cost method to account for its investment in Donna. Prepare Prima's January 1, Year 6, separate-entity balance sheet after the business combination.

Problem 4-11
L01, 2, 3

On January 1, Year 5, FLA Company issued 6,300 ordinary shares to purchase 9,000 ordinary shares of MES Company. Prior to the acquisition, FLA had 180,000 and MES had 10,000 ordinary shares outstanding, which were trading at $5 and $3 per share, respectively. The following information has been assembled for these two companies just prior to the acquisition:

	acquirer		acquiree	
	FLA Company		**MES Company**	
	Carrying amount	Fair value	Carrying amount	Fair value
Plant assets	$ 60,000	$70,000	$20,000	$25,000
Current assets	40,000	47,500	10,000	11,200
	$100,000		$30,000	
Ordinary shares	$ 30,000		$10,000	
Retained earnings	35,000		12,500	
Long-term debt	15,000	19,000	2,500	3,200
Current liabilities	20,000	20,000	5,000	5,000
	$100,000		$30,000	

Required:

(a) Prepare a consolidated statement of financial position for FLA Company and its non–wholly owned subsidiary at January 1, Year 5, under each of the following:
   (i) Proprietary theory
   (ii) Parent company theory
   (iii) Parent company extension theory
   (iv) Entity theory
(b) Which of the above theories is required under IFRS 3?

Problem 4-12
L02

The condensed financial statements for OIL Inc. and ERS Company for the year ended December 31, Year 5, follow:

	OIL	ERS
Revenues	$ 900,000	$ 300,000
Expenses	660,000	200,000
Net income	$ 240,000	$ 100,000

(continued)

	OIL	ERS
Retained earnings, 1/1/Year 5	$ 800,000	$ 200,000
Net income	240,000	100,000
Dividends paid	90,000	0
Retained earnings, 12/31/Year 5	$ 950,000	$ 300,000
Cash	$ 80,000	$ 110,000
Receivables and inventory	400,000	170,000
Patented technology (net)	900,000	300,000
Equipment (net)	700,000	600,000
Total assets	$2,080,000	$1,180,000
Liabilities	$ 600,000	$ 410,000
Common shares	530,000	470,000
Retained earnings	950,000	300,000
Total liabilities and equities	$2,080,000	$1,180,000

On December 31, Year 5, after the above figures were prepared, OIL issued $240,000 in debt and 12,000 new shares to the owners of ERS for 80% of the outstanding shares of that company. OIL shares had a fair value of $40 per share.

OIL also paid $30,000 to a broker for arranging the transaction. In addition, OIL paid $32,000 in stock issuance costs. ERS's equipment was actually worth $690,000, but its patented technology was appraised at only $280,000.

Required:

What are the consolidated balances for the year ended/at December 31, Year 5, for the following accounts?

(a) Net income
(b) Retained earnings, 1/1/Year 5
(c) Equipment
(d) Patented technology
(e) Goodwill
(f) Liabilities
(g) Common shares
(h) Non-controlling interests

Problem 4-13
L02

The July 31, Year 3, balance sheets of two companies that are parties to a business combination are as follows:

	Ravinder Corp.	Robin Inc.	
	Carrying amount	Carrying amount	Fair value
Current assets	$1,600,000	$ 420,000	$468,000
Plant and equipment	1,330,000	1,340,000	972,000
Accumulated depreciation	(250,000)	(500,000)	
Patents—net	—	—	72,000
	$2,680,000	$1,260,000	
Current liabilities	$1,360,000	$ 252,000	252,000
Long-term debt	480,000	360,000	384,000
Common shares	720,000	168,000	
Retained earnings	120,000	480,000	
	$2,680,000	$1,260,000	

In addition to the assets identified above, Ravinder Corp. attributed a value of $100,000 to a major research project that Robin Inc. was working on. Robin Inc. feels that it is within a year of developing a prototype for a state-of-the-art bio-medical device. If this device can ever be patented, it could be worth hundreds of thousands of dollars.

Effective on August 1, Year 3, the shareholders of Robin Inc. accepted an offer from Ravinder Corp. to purchase 80% of their common shares for $1,040,000 in cash. Ravinder Corp.'s legal fees for investigating and drawing up the share pur-chase agreement amounted to $25,000.

Required:

(a) Prepare the journal entries in the records of Ravinder Corp. to record the share acquisition and cost of legal fees.
(b) Prepare a schedule to calculate and allocate the acquisition differential. Explain the rationale for the accounting treatment of the $100,000 attributed to the research project.
(c) Prepare Ravinder Corp.'s consolidated balance sheet as at August 1, Year 3. Assume there were no transactions on this date other than the transactions described above.

WEB-BASED PROBLEMS

Web Problem 4-1
LO2, 3, 6

When accounting for the acquisition of a non–wholly owned subsidiary, the par-ent can use entity theory or parent company extension theory to account for the business combination. Access the 2011 consolidated financial statements for BCE Inc. by going to investor's relations section of the company's website. Answer the questions below for 2011. Round percentages to one decimal point and other ratios to two decimal points. For each question, indicate where in the financial statements you found the answer, and/or provide a brief explanation.

(a) Which theory of consolidation is used to value non-controlling interest at the date of acquisition?
(b) What portion of the additions to property, plant, and equipment during the year came from business combinations, and what portion came from direct purchases?
(c) What percentage of shareholders' equity at the end of the year pertains to non-controlling interests?
(d) How were costs directly attributable to the business combination accounted for?
(e) Were any of the subsidiaries controlled, even though the percentage own-ership was equal to or less than 50%? If so, what explanation was provided to explain how control was achieved with ownership of 50% or less?
(f) Assume that the company used the other acceptable theory of consolida-tion for valuing non-controlling interest and that the fair value of the sub-sidiary as a whole was greater than the fair value of the identifiable net assets at the date of acquisition. How would this change in theory affect the debt-to-equity ratio at the date of acquisition?

Web Problem 4-2
LO2, 3, 6

Access the 2011 consolidated financial statements for Barrick Gold Corporation by going to investor's relations section of the company's website. Answer the same questions as in Problem 1. For each question, indicate where in the financial statements you found the answer, and/or provide a brief explanation. (Some questions may not be applicable.)

 Practise and learn online with Connect

Consolidation Subsequent to Acquisition Date

LEARNING OBJECTIVES

After studying this chapter, you should be able to do the following for consolidations subsequent to the date of acquisition:

LO1 Perform impairment tests on property, plant, equipment, intangible assets, and goodwill.

LO2 Prepare schedules to allocate and amortize the acquisition differential on both an annual and a cumulative basis.

LO3 Prepare consolidated financial statements using the entity theory subsequent to the date of acquisition.

LO4 Prepare consolidated financial statements using parent company extension theory subsequent to the date of acquisition.

LO5 Prepare journal entries and calculate balance in the investment account under the equity method.

LO6 Analyze and interpret financial statements involving consolidations subsequent to the date of acquisition.

LO7 Identify some of the differences between IFRSs and ASPE involving consolidations subsequent to the date of acquisition.

INTRODUCTION

In Chapters 3 and 4, we discussed and illustrated the preparation of a consolidated balance sheet immediately after a parent company gained control over a subsidiary. We saw that the acquisition differential was allocated to identifiable assets and liabilities when the fair values were different than carrying amounts, and the excess was recognized as goodwill. In this chapter, we will see that the acquisition differential must be amortized and tested for impairment when preparing consolidated financial statements subsequent to the date of acquisition. The impairment testing can result in huge impairment losses. Some of the more significant losses in recent years were as follows:

- Manulife Financial Corporation, one of Canada's largest life insurance companies, reported a goodwill impairment loss of $2.3 billion in 2010 attributable to the U.S. Life Insurance, U.S. Variable Annuity and Fixed Products, and Canadian Individual Life cash-generating units.

- Bell Aliant Regional Communications Inc. is one of Canada's largest telecommunications providers. It provides telephone services primarily in Ontario, Quebec, and Atlantic Canada. In 2010, it reported a $1.7 billion loss attributable to a decline in value of customer relationships, a finite life intangible asset.

- The biggest impairment loss in Canadian history was the goodwill impairment loss of $12.1 billion reported by Nortel Networks in 2001. Nortel was Canada's largest public company in terms of market capitalization at the time.

> Some Canadian companies have reported substantial impairment losses on goodwill and other intangible assets.

In this chapter, we will prepare the consolidated income statement, retained earnings statement, and balance sheet at fiscal year-ends after the date of acquisition. The consolidated cash flow statement will be discussed in a later chapter. We will start by looking at how the parent accounts for its investment in its own internal records.

METHODS OF ACCOUNTING FOR AN INVESTMENT IN A SUBSIDIARY

For a parent company, there are two methods available to account for an investment in a subsidiary in its own internal accounting records in periods subsequent to the date of acquisition: the *cost method* and the *equity method*. The cost and equity methods of accounting for various types of equity investments were discussed in Chapter 2. While this chapter is concerned with control investments (requiring consolidation), the accounting concepts involved with the cost and equity methods are identical to those presented in Chapter 2. These concepts will be applied in this chapter and in the ones that follow. The key difference is that here they are discussed in relation to the preparation of consolidated financial statements, whereas earlier the emphasis was on the presentation in an investor's unconsolidated financial statements for external users.

> The cost and equity methods are used in the parent's own internal records for accounting for investments in subsidiaries.

The cost method is a method of accounting for investments whereby the investment is initially recorded at cost; income from the subsidiary is recognized in net income when the investor's right to receive a dividend is established. This usually occurs when the dividend is declared.

> The cost method records income when the investor's right to receive a dividend is established.

IAS 28 defines the equity method as a method of accounting whereby the investment is initially recognized at cost and adjusted thereafter for the post-acquisition change in the investor's share of net assets of the investee. The profit or loss of the investor includes the investor's share of the profit or loss of the investee. Distributions received from an investee reduce the carrying amount of the investment. Adjustments to the carrying amount may also be necessary for changes in the investor's proportionate interest in the investee's other comprehensive income. Such changes include those arising from the revaluation of property, plant, and equipment and from foreign-exchange translation differences. The investor's share of those changes is recognized in other comprehensive income.

> The equity method captures the investor's share of any changes to the investee's shareholders' equity.

The cost method is the simpler of the two methods because, typically, the only entry made by the parent each year is to record, as income, its pro rata share of dividends declared by the subsidiary. Occasionally, there may be an entry to record an impairment loss on the investment.

IAS 28 states that the concepts underlying the procedures used in accounting for the acquisition of a subsidiary are also adopted in accounting for the acquisition of an investment in an associate, which is reported using the equity method. This means that the types of adjustments made for consolidation purposes will also be made under the equity method. For this reason, the equity method is often referred to as the "one-line consolidation." If used fully and correctly for an investment in a subsidiary, the net income, other comprehensive income, and retained earnings under the equity method on the internal records of the parent will be equal to net income, other comprehensive income, and retained earnings

The equity method captures the net effect of any adjustments that would be made on the consolidated financial statements.

attributable to the parent's shareholders on the parent's consolidated financial statements. The only difference is that the consolidated financial statements incorporate the subsidiary's values on a line-by-line basis, whereas the equity method incorporates the net amount of the subsidiary's values on one line (investment in the subsidiary) on the balance sheet and, typically, on one line (investment income from the subsidiary) on the income statement.

As we will see later in this chapter, the acquisition differential must be amortized or written off over the useful lives of the related assets. The consolidated financial statements must be adjusted to reflect the amortization and/or impairment. In Chapters 6 and 7, we will make consolidation adjustments to eliminate unrealized profits from intercompany transactions. When the parent uses the equity method to account for its investment in the subsidiary, the net effect of the aforementioned consolidation adjustments must be processed through the investment and investment income accounts on the parent's internal records.

We must differentiate between accounting in the internal records and reporting in the external financial statements.

It is very important that we differentiate between the internal accounting records and the financial statements for external users. Each entity maintains its own internal accounting records; that is, a general ledger supported by various subledgers. In the internal records for the parent, there will be an investment in subsidiary account, which will be accounted for using the cost, equity, or fair value method. Since the parent controls the subsidiary, it will prepare consolidated financial statements for distribution to its external users. The consolidated financial statements will be supported by a worksheet or set of working papers.

An entity could issue nonconsolidated financial statements to external users in addition to consolidated financial statements.

In addition to the consolidated financial statements, the parent could also prepare nonconsolidated financial statements for its external users. In this text, we will refer to these nonconsolidated financial statements as separate-entity financial statements, which may or may not be prepared in accordance with IFRSs. Since income tax is assessed in Canada at a separate-entity level, a Canadian company must prepare nonconsolidated statements for the Canada Revenue Agency.[1] Since dividends received and investment income pertaining to a subsidiary are not usually taxable for income tax purposes, this income will have to be reversed when calculating taxable income. Accordingly, the income tax authorities are indifferent as to whether the parent uses the cost method or the equity method on its separate-entity financial statements. In fact, the statements given to the tax authorities may be prepared using tax laws rather than IFRSs.

When a bank or other external user wants to receive nonconsolidated statements, it may insist that they be prepared in accordance with IFRSs. If so, IAS 27 requires that the investment in subsidiary on the separate-entity financial statements be reported at cost or in accordance with IFRS 9.

The following diagram shows the interrelationships between the various records and financial statements:

Each circle represents a different set of records/financial statements. The triangle indicates the number given to the set of records/financial statements—the parent's set is number 1, the subsidiary's set is number 2, and the consolidated set is number 3. In the first part of this chapter, the parent will be using the cost method on set number 1.

At the end of this chapter, we will show the entries if the parent had used the equity method in its internal records. The adjustments on consolidation will be different, depending on whether the parent uses the cost method or the equity method on set 1. However, the consolidated financial statements will look exactly the same regardless of whether the parent used the cost method or the equity method in its internal records.

Consolidated net income will be the same regardless of whether the parent used the cost method or the equity method for its internal accounting records.

The parent can choose any method to account for its investment for internal purposes. In most cases, it will use the cost method because it is simple and involves little effort. However, if the entity wants to capture its share of the income earned by the subsidiary without having to prepare consolidated financial statements, the equity method should be used. Since comprehensive income under the equity method should be equal to consolidated comprehensive income attributable to the parent's shareholders, the results from the equity method should be compared with the consolidated financial statements to ensure that no errors have been made. In the end, it is a cost-benefit decision. The equity method should be used for internal purposes only if the benefits derived from the information provided exceed the extra cost involved in using this method.

CONSOLIDATED INCOME AND RETAINED EARNINGS STATEMENTS

Before examining the details for preparing consolidated income and retained earnings statements,[2] it is useful to outline the overall consolidation process. Just as a consolidated balance sheet is prepared basically by combining, on an item-by-item basis, the assets and liabilities of the parent and the subsidiary, the consolidated statement of comprehensive income is prepared by combining, on an item-by-item basis, the revenues, expenses, and other comprehensive income of the two companies. The parent's investment does not appear on the consolidated balance sheet, and some of the subsidiary's assets and liabilities are remeasured to reflect the fair values used in the consolidation process. In a similar manner, the parent's investment income from its subsidiary does not appear on the consolidated statement of comprehensive income, and some of the revenues and expenses of the subsidiary are remeasured to reflect the amortizations and impairments of the fair values being used in the consolidated balance sheet. Except for the eliminations and adjustments that are required, the whole consolidation process is basically one of combining the components of financial statements. No preparation is required for the consolidated retained earnings statement when the parent has used the equity method because, as previously mentioned, the parent's retained earnings reported in its internal records under the equity method should be equal to consolidated retained earnings.

The investment income from subsidiary is replaced by the subsidiary's revenues and expenses on a line-by-line basis.

We commence our discussion of the preparation of the consolidated income statement by describing the make-up of the bottom line, consolidated net income. Consolidated net income for any fiscal period is made up of the following:

The amortization of the acquisition differential is reflected on the consolidated financial statements—not on the subsidiary's financial statements.

The net income of the parent from its own operations
	(i.e., excluding any income resulting from its investment in the subsidiary)	$ XXX
plus:	**the net income of the subsidiary**	XXX
less:	**the amortization and impairment of the acquisition differential**	(XXX)
equals:	**consolidated net income**	$ XXX
Attributable to		
	Shareholders of parent company	$ XXX
	Non-controlling interest	XXX

It is important to note the distinction between consolidated net income and consolidated net income attributable to the shareholders of the parent company. Consolidated net income includes the combined income of the parent and subsidiary, plus or minus consolidation adjustments. Consolidated net income attributable to the shareholders of the parent company is the parent's shareholders' share of consolidated net income. It is the latter amount that is recorded by the parent when the parent uses the equity method for its own internal records.

Assume that a 100%-owned subsidiary was purchased at carrying amount (i.e., no acquisition differential and no fair value–carrying amount differences). Consolidated net income will be made up of the sum of the parent's and the subsidiary's net incomes. If the subsidiary was purchased at a price greater than carrying amount, the subsidiary's net income from its separate-entity financial statements will not be correct from a consolidated point of view because the subsidiary's expenses have not been measured using amortizations of the fair values being used in the consolidated balance sheet. Therefore, the third component—the amortization and impairment of the acquisition differential—must be deducted in determining consolidated net income.

The acquisition differential is amortized or written off on consolidation as if the parent had purchased these net assets directly.

The acquisition differential is allocated to remeasure the assets and liabilities of the subsidiary at fair value for consolidation purposes. It must be amortized or written off for consolidation purposes to reflect the use, impairment, or sale of the underlying net assets. The amount amortized or written off is calculated in the same way as if these items were owned directly by the parent. The acquisition differential related to long-term assets with definite useful lives (such as buildings, equipment, and patents) is amortized over the useful lives of these assets. Inventory is not amortized but is reflected on the income statement as cost of goods sold expense when it is sold. The amount allocated to land is not amortized; it is incorporated in the calculation of the gain or loss and recognized on the income statement only when it is sold or impaired. Goodwill and certain other intangible assets are also not amortized, but, instead, a loss is reflected on the income statement when a test indicates that they are impaired. Testing for impairment is explained in more detail in the following section.

The parent's separate-entity retained earnings accounted for under the equity method should always be equal to consolidated retained earnings.

Consolidated retained earnings on the date of acquisition are the parent's retained earnings only. Subsequent to acquisition, consolidated retained earnings reflect the parent's shareholders' share of the combined operations. The NCI's share of the combined operations is reflected in the NCI account, which is a separate account within the shareholders' equity section of the consolidated balance sheet. The changes in consolidated retained earnings subsequent to acquisition consist of the yearly consolidated net incomes attributable to the parent, less the yearly dividends declared by the parent. The changes in NCI subsequent to acquisition consist of the yearly consolidated net incomes attributable to the NCI, less the dividends paid by the subsidiary to the NCI. Dividends paid or declared by a subsidiary company to the parent do not appear on the consolidated statements because they do not change the financial position of the combined entity. This is an example of an intercompany transaction that must be eliminated when preparing consolidated financial statements. Intercompany transactions are discussed and illustrated in much more detail in Chapter 6.

TESTING GOODWILL AND OTHER ASSETS FOR IMPAIRMENT

Prior to July 1, 2001, pre-change-over GAAP required that all long-term tangible and intangible assets, except for land, had to be amortized over their estimated useful life, which could not exceed 40 years. This resulted in substantial reductions to reported earnings due to yearly amortization of goodwill and other intangible assets, even though these assets may have been increasing in value and/or had indefinite useful lives. On July 1, 2001, new rules were introduced. They provided more practical guidelines for the recognition and measurement of intangibles other than goodwill, and, in addition, replaced the annual amortization of goodwill and other assets with indefinite lives with periodic reviews for impairment. In addition, extensive guidelines were provided for the impairment testing of all long-lived assets, including intangibles.

In 2011, the impairment test for long-term tangible and intangible assets changed with the adoption of IFRSs. Now, IAS 36: Impairment of Assets applies to all assets, unless they are specifically excluded because of a requirement in another standard. IAS 36 prescribes the procedures that an entity applies to ensure that its assets are carried at no more than their recoverable amount. It indicates that an asset, a group of assets, or a cash-generating unit should be written down if its carrying amount exceeds the amount to be recovered through use or sale of the asset. The write-down is called an *impairment loss* and is reported in net income, unless the asset is carried at a revalued amount in accordance with another standard such as the revaluation model in IAS 16. In certain cases, the revaluation loss would be reported in other comprehensive income.

Recoverable amount is defined as the higher of fair value less costs of disposal and value in use. *Fair value* is defined as the price that would be received to sell an asset or paid to transfer a liability in an orderly transaction between market participants at the measurement date (i.e., an exit price). It would reflect the highest and best use for nonfinancial assets. It can be determined by using quoted market prices, if available, or by making comparisons with the prices of other similar assets. *Value in use* is the present value of the future cash flows expected to be derived from the asset or group of assets.

It may not be necessary to measure both fair value less costs of disposal and value in use when testing for impairment. If it is determined that one of these values is higher than the carrying amount, then the asset is not impaired and the other value need not be determined. Sometimes, it will not be possible to determine fair value less costs of disposal because there is no basis for making a reliable estimate of the amount obtainable from the sale of the asset in an orderly transaction. In this case, the entity may use the asset's value in use as its

LO1

Starting in 2001, goodwill and certain intangible assets were no longer amortized but tested for impairment on an annual basis.

An asset is impaired if its carrying amount exceeds its recoverable amount.

Recoverable amount is the higher of fair value less costs of disposal and value in use.

recoverable amount. When an asset is being held for disposal, most of its value in use will consist of the net disposal proceeds to be received in the near term, and future cash flows from continuing use of the asset until its disposal are likely to be negligible. In this situation, the fair value less costs of disposal would be very similar to value in use, and it would be unnecessary to explicitly determine a value in use.

Impairment testing requires the estimation of future net cash flows (cash inflows less cash outflows) associated with an individual asset. In many instances, it is impossible to associate cash flows with a single asset, and so the standard suggests that it should be accomplished with a cash-generating unit, which is defined as the smallest identifiable group of assets that generates cash inflows that are largely independent of the cash inflows from other assets or groups of assets. In the ensuing discussion on impairment testing, any reference to an individual asset is equally applicable to an individual asset or a cash-generating unit.

It is possible for an asset not to be impaired at the subsidiary level but to be impaired at the consolidated level.

In this chapter, we will discuss impairment at the level of the consolidated financial statements. Although the principles of impairment testing are the same, whether it is applied at the consolidated level or at the separate-entity level, the results could be different. For example, a subsidiary could determine that there is no impairment of its assets based on the carrying amounts used in its separate-entity statements. Since the values used on the consolidated statements are often reported at a higher amount than the separate-entity statements because of the acquisition differential, there could be impairment at the consolidated level.

IAS 36 has different requirements for impairment testing for the following types of assets:

- Property, plant, equipment, and intangible assets with definite useful lives
- Intangible assets with indefinite useful lives or not yet available for use
- Cash-generating units and goodwill

We will discuss these three different groups separately in the following sections.

Property, Plant, Equipment, and Intangible Assets with Definite Useful Lives

The recoverable amount needs to be determined only if indicators exist that the asset may be impaired.

Property (except for land with an unlimited useful life), plant, equipment, and intangible assets with definite useful lives should be amortized over their useful lives. At the end of each reporting period, there is a two-step approach to determining whether an impairment loss should be reported. In step 1, the entity assesses whether indicators exist that an asset may be impaired. If, in the preparer's judgment, any such indicators exist, then step 2 must be performed and the recoverable amount must be determined. If no indicators exist, then it is not necessary to perform step 2.

In step 2, the recoverable amount is determined and compared with the asset's carrying amount. If the recoverable amount is greater than the carrying amount, no impairment exists and the asset is reported at the carrying amount. If the recoverable amount is less than the carrying amount, impairment exists and the asset is written down to its recoverable amount.

The following factors should be considered at a minimum when assessing whether there is an indication of impairment:

External Factors	Internal Factors
An asset's market value has declined significantly.	There is evidence of obsolescence or physical damage of an asset.
Significant adverse changes in the technological, market, economic, or legal environment of the entity have occurred.	There have been significant adverse changes in how an asset is used or expected to be used.
A significant increase in market rates of return has occurred that will cause a reduction to value in use.	Evidence has arisen that the economic performance of an asset is, or will be, worse than expected.
The carrying amount of the net assets of the entity is more than its market capitalization.	The carrying amount of the investment in subsidiary in the separate-entity financial statements exceeds the carrying amounts in the consolidated financial statements of the investee's net assets, including associated goodwill.
	The dividend from the subsidiary exceeds the total comprehensive income of the subsidiary.

Internal and external factors are considered when assessing if there is an indication that the asset may be impaired.

Intangible Assets with Indefinite Useful Lives

Intangible assets with indefinite[3] useful lives are not amortized but must be assessed for impairment on an annual basis, regardless of whether there is any indication that it may be impaired. In other words, step 1 as mentioned in the previous section is ignored and step 2 must be performed. This same requirement is applied to an intangible asset that is not yet available for use.

An intangible asset that is not subject to amortization is tested for impairment annually (step 2).

This impairment test may be performed at any time during an annual period, provided it is performed at the same time every year. Different intangible assets may be tested for impairment at different times. However, if such an intangible asset was initially recognized during the current annual period, that intangible asset must be tested for impairment before the end of the current annual period.

In exceptional circumstances, the entity can use the recoverable amount from a preceding period rather than determine a new recoverable amount this period. This cost-saving measure may be used, provided all of the following criteria are met:

When certain criteria are met, the recoverable amount from a preceding period can be used rather than determining a new recoverable amount for the current year.

(a) If the intangible asset does not generate cash inflows from continuing use that are largely independent of those from other assets or groups of assets, and is therefore tested for impairment as part of the cash-generating unit to which it belongs, the assets and liabilities making up that unit have not changed significantly since the most recent recoverable amount calculation.

(b) The most recent recoverable amount calculation resulted in an amount that exceeded the asset's carrying amount by a substantial margin.

(c) Based on an analysis of events that have occurred and circumstances that have changed since the most recent recoverable amount calculation, the likelihood that a current recoverable amount determination would be less than the asset's carrying amount is remote.

Cash-Generating Units and Goodwill

Cash-generating units that have goodwill assigned to them must be assessed for impairment on an annual basis, and more frequently if there is an indication that the unit may be impaired. In identifying individual cash-generating units, the entity must consider whether the cash inflows from an asset (or group of assets) are largely independent of the cash inflows from other assets (or groups of assets). Various factors should be considered, such as how management monitors the entity's operations—that is, by product lines, businesses, individual locations, districts, or regional areas—or by how management makes decisions about continuing or disposing of the entity's assets and operations. Each unit or group of units to which the goodwill is so allocated shall

(a) represent the lowest level within the entity at which the goodwill is monitored for internal management purposes; and

(b) not be larger than an operating segment determined in accordance with IFRS 8: Operating Segments.[4] The following example from IAS 36 illustrates the application of this requirement:

> A bus company provides services under contract with a municipality that requires minimum service on each of five separate routes. Assets devoted to each route and the cash flows from each route can be identified separately. One of the routes operates at a significant loss. Because the entity does not have the option to curtail any one bus route, the lowest level of identifiable cash inflows that are largely independent of the cash inflows from other assets or groups of assets is the cash inflows generated by the five routes together. Therefore, the individual bus routes cannot be identified as cash generating units. The company as a whole is identified as the cash-generating unit.

To test goodwill for impairment, the recoverable amount for the subsidiary as a whole is compared with the carrying amount of the subsidiary's assets and liabilities, including goodwill. If the recoverable amount exceeds the carrying amount, goodwill is not impaired. If the recoverable amount is less than the carrying amount, an impairment loss should be recognized and should be allocated to reduce the carrying amount of the assets in the following order:

(a) First, to reduce the carrying amount of any goodwill

(b) Then, to the other assets of the unit pro rata on the basis of the carrying amount of each asset

The following example illustrates the goodwill impairment test when the subsidiary as a whole is identified as the cash-generating unit: On January 1, Year 1, P Co. acquired 100% of S Co. for $1,000. At the date of acquisition, $900 was assigned to identifiable net assets and $100 was recognized as goodwill. At the end of Year 1, the carrying amount of S Co.'s net assets was $950, including the goodwill of $100. Since S Co is now wholly owned by P Co., the shares of S are not being traded and a market value is not readily available. Therefore, the recoverable amount for S Co. at the end of Year 1 is based on the present value of future cash flows.

The following table shows the goodwill impairment test under three different scenarios:

	#1	#2	#3
Recoverable amount	995	945	840
Carrying amount	950	950	950
Total impairment	n/a	5	110
Goodwill impairment loss	n/a	5	100
Impairment of other assets	n/a	n/a	10
Goodwill before impairment	100	100	100
Goodwill after impairment	100	95	0

Appendix 5A provides further details of the tests for goodwill impairment and illustrations of goodwill impairment in more complex situations.

Reversing an Impairment Loss

An impairment loss recognized in a prior period for an asset or cash-generating unit can be reversed under certain conditions. However, an impairment loss recognized for goodwill cannot be reversed in a subsequent period. A two-step process for reversing an impairment loss is followed, similar to the process followed for the initial recognition of impairment losses. In step 1, an entity assesses whether there is any indication that an impairment loss may no longer exist or may have decreased. If any such indication exists, then step 2 must be performed and the recoverable amount determined. If no such indication exists, it is not necessary to perform step 2.

> Impairment losses on assets other than goodwill can be reversed.

Indications of a potential decrease in an impairment loss are basically the same as those of a potential impairment loss, which were described earlier. If there is an indication that an impairment loss may no longer exist or may have decreased, this may signal that the remaining useful life, the depreciation method, or the residual value may need to be reviewed and adjusted in accordance with the IFRS applicable to the asset, even if no impairment loss is reversed for the asset.

An impairment loss shall be reversed if, and only if, there has been a change in the estimates used to determine the asset's recoverable amount. An impairment loss is not reversed when the recoverable amount increases strictly due to the passage of time; that is, the present value of future cash inflows increases as they become closer to occurring.

The reversal of an impairment loss is reported in net income unless the asset is carried at a revalued amount in accordance with another standard (e.g., in accordance with the revaluation model in IAS 16). The assets should not be written up to an amount exceeding the carrying amount that would have been determined had no impairment loss been recognized for the asset in prior years.

> The asset cannot be written up to an amount higher than it would have been if impairment losses had not been recognized.

A reversal of an impairment loss for a cash-generating unit must be allocated to the assets of the unit pro rata with the carrying amount of those assets. However, an asset should never be reduced to less than its recoverable amount. An impairment loss relating to goodwill must not be reversed. Any increase in the recoverable amount of goodwill is likely to be an increase in internally generated goodwill, rather than a reversal of the impairment loss recognized for the acquired goodwill. IAS 38 prohibits the recognition of internally generated goodwill.

Disclosure Requirements

The disclosure requirements related to impairment of assets are quite extensive. The following summarizes the main requirements:

Substantial information relating to impairment losses and reversals of impairment losses must be disclosed.

- For each class of assets—the amount of impairment losses and reversals of impairment losses segregated by what amounts are recognized in net income versus other comprehensive income
- For each major impairment loss recognized or reversed related to individual assets—the events and circumstances that led to the recognition or reversal, whether the recoverable amount is its fair value less costs of disposal or value in use; the basis used to determine fair value less costs of disposal; and the discount rate(s) used in determining value in use
- For cash-generating units or intangible assets with indefinite lives—the carrying amount of goodwill and of intangible assets with indefinite useful lives allocated to the unit, the basis used in determining recoverable amount, a description of key assumptions on which management has based its cash flow projections, and the methodology used to determine fair value less costs of disposal

RONA inc. is a distributor and a retailer of hardware, home improvement and gardening products in Canada. It reported goodwill impairment losses of $117 million in its 2011 financial statements. Excerpts from these statements are presented in Exhibit 5.1.

EXHIBIT 5.1

EXTRACTS (IN PART) FROM RONA'S 2011 FINANCIAL STATEMENTS

3. Significant accounting policies

(j) Goodwill
Goodwill represents the future economic benefits arising from a business combination that are not individually identifiable and recorded separately. Goodwill is not amortized and is tested for impairment annually or more frequently if events or changes in circumstances indicate that it is impaired. Goodwill is measured at cost less accumulated impairment losses.

(k) Impairment of non-current assets
At the end of each reporting period, the carrying amounts of property, plant and equipment and intangible assets with finite useful lives are assessed to determine if there is any evidence that an asset is impaired. If there is such evidence, the recoverable amount of the asset is estimated. The recoverable amount of intangible assets with indefinite useful lives or that are not ready for use is estimated on the same date each year.

The recoverable amount of an asset or a cash generating unit is the higher of value-in-use and fair value less costs to sell. To determine value-in-use, expected future cash flows are discounted using a before-tax rate that reflects current market assessments of the time value of money and the risks specific to the asset. In the process of measuring expected future cash flows, the Corporation makes assumptions about future operating profit. These assumptions relate to future events and circumstances. Although the assumptions are based on market information available at the time of the assessment, actual results may vary.

Assets that cannot be tested individually for the impairment test are grouped into the smallest group of assets that generates cash inflows through continued use that are largely independent of the cash inflows from other assets or groups of assets ("cash-generating unit" or "CGU"). For the impairment test of goodwill, CGUs to which goodwill has been

(continued)

Value-in-use incorporates expected future cash flows discounted using a before-tax rate that reflects current market assessments of the time value of money and the risks specific to the asset.

EXHIBIT 5.1   *(continued)*

allocated are grouped so that the level at which the impairment is tested represents the lowest level at which management monitors goodwill for internal management purposes. CGU groupings are limited to the operating sector. Goodwill acquired in a business combination is allocated to CGU groups that are expected to benefit from synergies of the related business combination.

The Corporation's corporate assets do not generate separate cash flows. If there is evidence that a corporate asset is impaired, the recoverable amount is determined for the CGU to which the corporate asset belongs. Impairments are recorded when the carrying amount of an asset or its CGU is higher than its recoverable amount. Impairment charges are recognized in income or loss.

Impairment losses recognized for a CGU (or group of CGU) first reduce the carrying amount of any goodwill allocated to that CGU and then reduce the carrying amounts of the other assets of the CGU (or group of CGU) pro rata on the basis of the carrying amount of each asset in the CGU (or group of CGU).

An impairment loss recognized for goodwill may not be reversed. On each reporting date, the Corporation assesses if there is an indication that impairment losses recognized in previous periods for other assets have decreased or no longer exist. An impairment loss is reversed if there has been a change in the estimates used to determine the recoverable amount. The increased carrying amount of an asset attributable to a reversal of an impairment loss shall not exceed the carrying amount that would have been determined (net of amortization or depreciation) had no impairment loss been recognized.

> Goodwill acquired in a business combination is allocated to CGU groups that are expected to benefit from synergies of the related business combination.

14. Goodwill

	2011 As at December 25
Balance at beginning	$ 529,094
Acquisition through business combinations (Note 9)	16,777
Impairment	(117,000)
Adjustment related to the purchase price allocation of a 2010 acquisition (Note 9)	(1,903)
Balance at end	$ 426,968

For the purpose of the annual impairment testing, goodwill is allocated to the following CGU groups, which are the groups of units expected to benefit from the synergies of the business combinations:

	2011 As at December 25	2010 As at December 26	2009 As at December 28
Corporate and franchised stores	$187,056	$299,993	$254,856
Commercial and professional stores	130,416	126,726	116,167
Distribution	109,496	102,375	84,549
Goodwill allocation	$426,968	$529,094	$455,572

The Corporation performed its annual test for goodwill impairment as at December 25, 2011. The carrying amount of the CGU groups has been determined using the value in use. To determine value in use, five-year cash flow forecasts were prepared using the budget and strategic plan approved by the Board of Directors. Cash flow forecasts for periods beyond that of the budget and strategic plan were prepared using a stable growth rate for future periods, not exceeding the rate of long term average growth of the Corporation's sectors of activity. These forecasts were based on historical data and future trends expected by the Corporation.

> RONA primarily uses value in use to determine if goodwill is impaired.

(continued)

EXHIBIT 5.1	*(continued)*

A key assumption in determining value is use is the projected growth in same-store sales.

For the impairment test carried out as at December 25, 2011, management's key assumptions were average annual increases in same-store sales of 2.25% (average of 3.0% as at December 26, 2010) for the first five years and hereafter (2.5% as at December 26, 2010).

The Corporation's valuation model also takes account of working capital and capital investments to maintain the condition of the assets of each group of CGU.

Forecasted cash flows are discounted using pre-tax rates ranging from 11.8% to 11.9% (11.9% to 13.0% as at December 26, 2010) which reflect current market assessments of the time value of money and the risks specific to the asset.

As the Corporation's strategic plan evolves, the Corporation regularly reviews the allocation of net assets and corporate assets between CGU groups. In 2011, the Corporation changed the classification of part of goodwill and some corporate assets. Comparable amounts reflect this reclassification.

RONA reported a goodwill impairment loss of $117.0 million in 2011. This resulted in a loss before income taxes of $60.9 million.

Based on its impairment test, the fair value of the corporate and franchise store CGU group was less than its carrying amount. As a result, and considering the difficult market conditions, the Corporation recognized a goodwill impairment loss of $117,000 in respect of this CGU group.

In addition to its various programs already in effect to enhance sales in the corporate and franchise store sector, as part of its business plan 2012, the Corporation has prepared a new strategy focusing on improving efficiency, optimizing the capital structure and increasing the return on capital. This is a critical sector for the Corporation and in 2012 sustained efforts has been and will be deployed to improve this sector's profitability.

The fair value of the other groups of CGUs was higher than their carrying amount. The sensitivity analysis indicated that no reasonably possible changes in the assumptions would cause the carrying amount of each group of CGU to exceed its recoverable amount.

Source: Reproduced with permission from Rona Inc. http://www.rona.ca/corporate/financial-documents

Now that we have seen how to test for impairment, we will illustrate the preparation of consolidated financial statements subsequent to the date of acquisition. The first illustrations assume that the subsidiary is 100% owned. Later illustrations will assume a less than 100%-owned subsidiary.

L02 CONSOLIDATION OF A 100%-OWNED SUBSIDIARY

Company P purchased 100% of the outstanding common shares of Company S on January 1, Year 1, for $19,000. On that date, Company S's common shares had a carrying amount of $10,000 and its retained earnings balance was $6,000. The inventory of Company S had a fair value that was $2,000 greater than carrying amount, and the carrying amounts of all other assets and liabilities of Company S were equal to fair values. Any goodwill will be tested yearly for impairment. Both companies have a December 31 year-end. The journal entry made by Company P to record the acquisition of 100% of Company S was as follows:

Investment in S	19,000	
Cash		19,000

There is no compelling reason for Company P to prepare a consolidated balance sheet on acquisition date; however, it is useful to illustrate its preparation as the starting point for the preparation of consolidated statements in subsequent years. The calculation and allocation of the acquisition differential is shown in Exhibit 5.2.

EXHIBIT 5.2

CALCULATION OF ACQUISITION DIFFERENTIAL
January 1, Year 1

Cost of 100% of Company S		$19,000	
Carrying amount of Company S's net assets			
Assets	$ 27,000		
Liabilities	(11,000)		
		16,000	
Acquisition differential		3,000	
Allocated:	FV − CA		
Inventory	2,000	2,000	**(a)**
Balance—goodwill		$ 1,000	**(b)**

Below are the individual balance sheets of Company P and Company S on January 1, Year 1, along with Company P's consolidated balance sheet prepared using the *direct approach*:

BALANCE SHEETS—January 1, Year 1

	Company P	Company S	Consolidated	
Assets (miscellaneous)	$139,000	$17,000	$156,000	The investment account is
Inventory	22,000	10,000	34,000	replaced by the carrying
Investment in S	19,000	—	—	amount of the subsidiary's
Goodwill	—	—	1,000	assets and liabilities plus the
	$180,000	$27,000	$191,000	acquisition differential.
Liabilities	$ 45,000	$11,000	$ 56,000	
Common shares	50,000	10,000	50,000	
Retained earnings	85,000	6,000	85,000	
	$180,000	$27,000	$191,000	

The consolidated balance sheet was prepared by eliminating the shareholders' equity of Company S ($16,000) against Company P's investment account ($19,000) and then by allocating the resultant acquisition differential ($3,000) to the inventory of Company S ($2,000), with the unallocated balance recognized as goodwill ($1,000).

Consolidated Statements, End of Year 1

L03

In Year 1, Company S reported net income of $7,300 and paid a cash dividend of $2,500. Company P's net income for the year was $18,300 (not including income from its investment in Company S). Using the cost method to account for its investment, Company P makes a single entry to record the dividend received from Company S on December 31, Year 1, as follows:

The cost method records income when dividends are received or receivable.

Cash	2,500	
Dividend income		2,500
Dividend received from Company S		

Company P adds the dividend income ($2,500) to its earnings from its own operations ($18,300) and reports a final net income for Year 1 of $20,800. An impairment test on goodwill conducted on December 31, Year 1, indicated that a $50 loss had occurred.

The financial statements of Company P and Company S as at December 31, Year 1, are presented in Exhibit 5.3.

EXHIBIT 5.3

YEAR 1 INCOME STATEMENTS

	Company P	Company S
Sales	$ 50,000	$30,000
Dividend income	2,500	—
Total revenue	52,500	30,000
Cost of sales	26,500	14,700
Expenses (miscellaneous)	5,200	8,000
Total expenses	31,700	22,700
Net income	$ 20,800	$ 7,300

The parent's income from its own operations is $20,800 − $2,500 = $18,300.

YEAR 1 RETAINED EARNINGS STATEMENTS

	Company P	Company S
Balance, January 1	$ 85,000	$ 6,000
Net income	20,800	7,300
	105,800	13,300
Dividends	6,000	2,500
Balance, December 31	$ 99,800	$10,800

BALANCE SHEETS—December 31, Year 1

	Company P	Company S
Assets (misc.)	$147,800	$18,300
Inventory	30,000	14,000
Investment in S (cost method)	19,000	—
	$196,800	$32,300
Liabilities	$ 47,000	$11,500
Common shares	50,000	10,000
Retained earnings	99,800	10,800
	$196,800	$32,300

The investment account remains at the original cost in the parent's separate-entity balance sheet.

Before beginning to prepare the consolidated financial statements, Company P prepares Exhibit 5.4, which shows the amortization of the acquisition differential for Year 1. This schedule and the financial statements of the two companies shown in Exhibit 5.3 form the basis for the preparation of Company P's Year 1 consolidated statements, shown in Exhibit 5.5.

The details of the Year 1 amortizations are explained as follows:

The acquisition differential related to inventory is expensed when the inventory is sold.

1. The inventory of Company S was remeasured for consolidated purposes on January 1, Year 1, to reflect its fair value. If we assume that Company S uses a FIFO cost flow,[5] it would be safe to assume that this inventory was sold during Year 1. Since the cost of sales of Company S does not reflect the $2,000 additional cost, cost of sales on the Year 1 consolidated income statement will be increased by $2,000 to reflect the additional cost of Company S.

2. An impairment test on goodwill conducted on December 31, Year 1, indicated that a $50 loss had occurred.

3. The $1,000 goodwill is not reflected in the financial statements of Company S, nor is the impairment loss. The consolidated income statement will have to reflect this loss, and at December 31, Year 1, the consolidated balance sheet will have to show the goodwill at cost less accumulated impairment losses.

EXHIBIT 5.4

ACQUISITION DIFFERENTIAL AMORTIZATION AND IMPAIRMENT SCHEDULE

	Balance Jan. 1, Year 1	Amortization and Impairment Year 1	Balance Dec. 31, Year 1	
Inventory **(2a)**	$2,000	$2,000	$ —	**(a)**
Goodwill **(2b)**	1,000	50	950	**(b)**
	$3,000	$2,050	$ 950	**(c)**

The amortization and impairment of the acquisition differential will be reflected on the consolidated financial statements.

Using the schedule we introduced in the Consolidated Income and Retained Earnings Statements section earlier in this chapter, we make the following calculation:

CALCULATION OF CONSOLIDATED NET INCOME—Year 1

Company P net income—cost method		$20,800
Less dividend income from Company S		2,500
Company P net income, own operations		18,300
Company S net income	7,300	
Acquisition differential amortization and impairment **(4c)**	(2,050)	5,250
Consolidated net income		$23,550

This calculation starts with income under the cost method and converts it to consolidated net income.

Since Company P owns 100% of Company S, all of the consolidated net income is attributable to the shareholders of Company P.

Note that dividend income from Company S is not included in consolidated net income. The consolidated income statement is prepared by excluding the dividend income and adding the revenues and expenses of the two companies.

EXHIBIT 5.5

Year 1 Consolidated Financial Statements
(Direct Approach)
COMPANY P
CONSOLIDATED INCOME STATEMENT
for the Year Ended December 31, Year 1

Sales (50,000 + 30,000)	$ 80,000
Cost of sales (26,500 + 14,700 + **[4a]** 2,000)	43,200
Goodwill impairment loss (0 + 0 + **[4b]** 50)	50
Expenses (misc.) (5,200 + 8,000)	13,200
	56,450
Net income	$ 23,550

Consolidated net income is the same regardless of whether the parent used the cost method or the equity method in its internal records.

COMPANY P
CONSOLIDATED STATEMENT OF RETAINED EARNINGS
for the Year Ended December 31, Year 1

Balance, January 1	$ 85,000
Net income	23,550
	108,550
Dividends	6,000
Balance, December 31	$102,550

Dividends on the consolidated statement of retained earnings are the dividends of the parent.

(continued)

EXHIBIT 5.5 **(continued)**

COMPANY P
CONSOLIDATED BALANCE SHEET
December 31, Year 1

Assets (misc.) (147,800 + 18,300)	$166,100
Inventory (30,000 + 14,000 + **[4a]** 0)	44,000
Goodwill (0 + 0 + **[4b]** 950)	950
	$211,050
Liabilities (47,000 + 11,500)	$ 58,500
Common shares	50,000
Retained earnings	102,550
	$211,050

The amortization/impairment of the various components of the acquisition differential is reflected on the consolidated financial statements.

The preparation of the Year 1 consolidated financial statements is shown in Exhibit 5.5. The consolidated amounts were determined by adding the amounts shown in brackets. These amounts came from the financial statements of Company P and Company S and from the acquisition differential amortization and impairment schedule. Note the bracketed amounts shown for goodwill impairment loss and for goodwill on the balance sheet. The two zero amounts indicate that these items do not appear in the separate-entity financial statements of Company P and Company S.

The Year 1 consolidated retained earnings statement is prepared using the January 1 retained earnings of Company P, consolidated net income attributable to Company P, and Company P's dividends. Only Company P's retained earnings are included on January 1 because, as we learned in Chapter 3, consolidated retained earnings at the date of acquisition consist only of the parent's retained earnings. Only the parent's dividends are included on the consolidated statement of retained earnings, because only the parent's dividends were paid to shareholders outside of the consolidated entity. The subsidiary's dividends were received by the parent and were not paid to anyone outside of the consolidated entity, and they are therefore eliminated when preparing the consolidated financial statements.

The underlying assets and liabilities of the subsidiary plus the unamortized acquisition differential replace the investment account.

The parent's investment account does not appear on the consolidated balance sheet. Consolidated shareholders' equity contains the common shares of the parent and retained earnings from the consolidated retained earnings statement. The net assets of the parent are combined with the net assets of the subsidiary after they have been remeasured with the unamortized acquisition differential.

If the parent had used the equity method in its internal records, the entries made during the year would have been different than under the cost method. When preparing the consolidated net income at the end of the year, the subsidiary's assets, liabilities, revenues, and expenses replace the investment account and investment income account. After making the adjustments for the amortization of the acquisition differential, the consolidated financial statements will look exactly the same as the statements above. Further explanation and illustration of the consolidation process when the parent used the equity method is provided later in this chapter in the Parent Company Extension Theory section.

Consolidated Statements, End of Year 2

In Year 2, Company S reported net income of $10,000 and paid a cash dividend of $3,000. Company P's net income for the year was $19,000 (not including income from its investment in Company S). An impairment test conducted on December 31, Year 2, indicated that the goodwill had a recoverable amount of $870. As a result, a loss of $80 has occurred.

On December 31, Year 2, Company P makes the following cost-method journal entry:

Cash	3,000	
Dividend income		3,000
Dividend received by Company S		

The dividend income ($3,000) combined with the previous operating earnings ($19,000) gives Company P a final net income for Year 2 of $22,000.

The financial statements of the two companies as at December 31, Year 2, are presented in Exhibit 5.6, and the acquisition differential amortization and impairment schedule at the end of Year 2 follow, in Exhibit 5.7.

Because Company P has used the cost method, it is necessary to make two preliminary calculations before preparing the consolidated income statement and retained earnings statement. We first calculate consolidated net income for Year 2, as follows:

Company P net income—cost method		$22,000	Only the Year 2 amortization
Less: dividend income from Company S		3,000	of the acquisition differential
Company P net income, own operations		19,000	is deducted when calculating
Company S net income	10,000		consolidated net income for
Acquisition differential amortization and impairment **(7c)**	(80)	9,920	Year 2.
Consolidated net income		$28,920	

EXHIBIT 5.6

YEAR 2 INCOME STATEMENTS

	Company P	Company S	
Sales	$ 60,000	$40,000	The parent's income includes
Dividend income	3,000	—	dividend income from the
Total revenue	63,000	40,000	subsidiary, which can be
Cost of sales	32,000	18,000	reconciled to dividends paid
Expenses (misc.)	9,000	12,000	by the subsidiary.
Total expenses	41,000	30,000	
Net income	$ 22,000	$10,000	

YEAR 2 RETAINED EARNINGS STATEMENTS

	Company P	Company S
Balance, January 1	$ 99,800	$10,800
Net income	22,000	10,000
	121,800	20,800
Dividends	8,000	3,000
Balance, December 31	$113,800	$17,800

(continued)

EXHIBIT 5.6	(continued)

BALANCE SHEETS—December 31, Year 2

	Company P	Company S
Assets (misc.)	$131,800	$21,000
Inventory	35,000	16,000
Investment in S (cost method)	19,000	—
	$185,800	$37,000
Liabilities	$ 22,000	$ 9,200
Common shares	50,000	10,000
Retained earnings	113,800	17,800
	$185,800	$37,000

The investment account still remains at the original cost.

EXHIBIT 5.7	

ACQUISITION DIFFERENTIAL AMORTIZATION AND IMPAIRMENT SCHEDULE

The amortization of the acquisition differential is not reflected in the investment account when the parent uses the cost method.

	Balance Jan. 1, Year 1	Amort. & Impair. to end of Year 1	Balance Dec. 31, Year 1	Amort. & Impair. Year 2	Balance Dec. 31, Year 2	
Inventory (2a)	$2,000	$2,000	$ —	$—	$ —	(a)
Goodwill (2b)	1,000	50	950	80	870	(b)
	$3,000	$2,050	$950	$80	$870	(c)

Because we are consolidating more than one year after the date of acquisition, an additional calculation is required. Company P's separate-entity retained earnings on January 1, Year 2, are not equal to consolidated retained earnings. The calculation of consolidated retained earnings as at January 1, Year 2, is as follows:

This calculation converts retained earnings from the cost method to the equity method at a point in time.

Company P retained earnings, Jan. 1, Year 2 (cost method)		$ 99,800
Company S retained earnings, Jan. 1, Year 2	10,800	
Company S retained earnings, acquisition date	6,000	
Increase since acquisition	4,800	
Acquisition differential amortization and impairment to end of Year 1 (7c)	(2,050)	
	2,750	
Company P ownership	100%	2,750
Consolidated retained earnings, Jan. 1, Year 2		$102,550

Retained earnings reflect the cumulative effect of all adjustments to a point in time.

The points that follow are presented as further explanation of why a calculation of this nature adjusts a parent's retained earnings under the cost method to retained earnings under the equity method. These points require careful reading because it is very important that you understand fully why this particular process actually works.

1. Consolidated retained earnings at the acquisition date consist only of the retained earnings of the parent company. Consolidated retained earnings subsequent to the date of acquisition represent only the parent's portion of retained earnings of the combined entities. The non-controlling interest's

portion of retained earnings is incorporated in non-controlling interest, which is reported in a separate line in shareholders' equity.

2. Consolidated net income attributable to the parent company in any single year since the acquisition date consists of the net income of the parent company (from its own operations), plus the parent's share of the net income of the subsidiary, less the parent's share of the acquisition-differential amortization for that year.

3. It should logically follow that the consolidated retained earnings balance at any time subsequent to the acquisition date must contain the parent's share of the subsidiary's net incomes earned since the acquisition date, less the total of the amortization of the acquisition differential to that date.

4. Since the parent has used the cost method for internal record keeping, the parent's retained earnings contain only the parent's share of the dividends that the subsidiary has declared since the acquisition date.

> The parent's retained earnings under the cost method include dividend income from the subsidiary since the date of acquisition.

5. The sum of net incomes less the sum of dividends, both measured from the acquisition date, equals the change (increase or decrease) in retained earnings measured from the same date.

6. When we add the parent's share of the change in the retained earnings of the subsidiary to the retained earnings of the parent (which contain the parent's share of the subsidiary's dividends under the cost method), the resulting calculated amount now contains the parent's share of the subsidiary's net income earned since the date of acquisition. By deducting the parent's share of the total amortization of the acquisition differential to date from this amount, we arrive at a retained earnings number that represents the retained earnings of the parent under the equity method, which of course is equal to consolidated retained earnings.

> The change in retained earnings plus cumulative dividends paid is equal to cumulative net income.

The consolidated income statement is prepared—using the income statements of the two companies (see Exhibit 5.6), the Year 2 acquisition differential amortization and impairment schedule, and the calculation of consolidated net income for Year 2—by adding the revenues and expenses of the two companies, adjusting the expenses for the Year 2 amortization, excluding the dividend income, and verifying that the net income on the statement equals the calculated net income.

The consolidated retained earnings statement for Year 2 is prepared using the calculated amount for consolidated retained earnings for January 1, adding consolidated net income, and deducting the dividends of Company P.

The consolidated balance sheet is prepared in the usual manner, except that the amount for retained earnings is taken from the consolidated retained earnings statement.

> The consolidated financial statements present the combined position of the parent and the subsidiary as if the parent had acquired the subsidiary's assets and liabilities directly.

Exhibit 5.8 shows the preparation of the Year 2 consolidated financial statements using the direct approach.

CONSOLIDATION OF AN 80%-OWNED SUBSIDIARY— DIRECT APPROACH

We now illustrate the consolidation of Company P and its 80%-owned subsidiary, Company S, over a two-year period when the cost method has been used to account for the investment.

EXHIBIT 5.8

YEAR 2 CONSOLIDATED FINANCIAL STATEMENTS
(Direct Approach)
COMPANY P
CONSOLIDATED INCOME STATEMENT
for the Year Ended December 31, Year 2

Sales (60,000 + 40,000)	$100,000
Cost of sales (32,000 + 18,000)	50,000
Goodwill impairment loss (0 + 0 + **(7b) 80**)	80
Expenses (misc.) (9,000 + 12,000)	21,000
	71,080
Net income	$ 28,920

COMPANY P
CONSOLIDATED STATEMENT OF RETAINED EARNINGS
for the Year Ended December 31, Year 2

Consolidated retained earnings are the same regardless of whether the parent used the cost method or the equity method in its internal records.

Balance, January 1	$102,550
Net income	28,920
	131,470
Dividends	8,000
Balance, December 31	$123,470

COMPANY P
CONSOLIDATED BALANCE SHEET
December 31, Year 2

The unamortized acquisition differential related to goodwill is reported on the consolidated balance sheet and is the same amount regardless of whether the parent used the cost method or the equity method in its internal records.

Assets (misc.) (131,800 + 21,000)	$152,800
Inventory (35,000 + 16,000)	51,000
Goodwill (0 + 0 + **(7b) 870**)	870
	$204,670
Liabilities (22,000 + 9,200)	$ 31,200
Common shares	50,000
Retained earnings	123,470
	$204,670

Assume that on January 1, Year 1, instead of purchasing 100% of Company S for $19,000, Company P purchased 80% for $15,200. Non-controlling interest is measured using the fair value enterprise approach; that is, entity theory. All other facts about the two companies are the same as in the previous example. The journal entry of Company P on January 1, Year 1, is as follows:

Investment in S	15,200	
Cash		15,200

The calculation and allocation of the acquisition differential and the calculation of the non-controlling interest on January 1, Year 1, are shown in Exhibit 5.9. The following are the individual balance sheets of Company P and Company S, as well as Company P's consolidated balance sheet on January 1, Year 1, prepared using the direct approach:

BALANCE SHEETS—January 1, Year 1

	Company P	Company S	Consolidated	
Assets (misc.)	$142,800	$17,000	$159,800	The subsidiary's assets and
Inventory	22,000	10,000	34,000	liabilities are brought onto
Investment in S	15,200	—	—	the consolidated financial
Goodwill	—	—	1,000	statements at 100 percent of
	$180,000	$27,000	$194,800	their fair values.
Liabilities	$ 45,000	$11,000	$ 56,000	
Common shares	50,000	10,000	50,000	
Retained earnings	85,000	6,000	85,000	
Non-controlling interest	—	—	3,800	
	$180,000	$27,000	$194,800	

The consolidated balance sheet was prepared as follows:

1. Eliminate the investment account and Company S's shareholders' equity.

2. Add the implied acquisition differential to Company S's assets and liabilities in order to use 100% of the fair values for Company S's assets and liabilities.

3. Report non-controlling interest as a component of shareholders' equity at a value representing the non-controlling interest's share of Company S's implied value.

Consolidated Statements, End of Year 1

In Year 1, Company S reported net income of $7,300 and paid a cash dividend of $2,500. Company P's net income for the year was $18,300 (not including income from its investment in Company S).

EXHIBIT 5.9

COMPANY P
CALCULATION AND ALLOCATION OF ACQUISITION DIFFERENTIAL
January 1, Year 1

Cost of 80% of Company S		$15,200		The implied value of the
Implied value of 100% of Company S		$19,000		subsidiary is derived
Carrying amount of Company S's net assets				by taking the purchase
Assets	$27,000			price and dividing by the
Liabilities	(11,000)			percentage ownership
		16,000		acquired by the parent.
Acquisition differential		3,000		
Allocated:	(FV − CA)			
Inventory	2,000	2,000	(a)	
Balance—goodwill		$ 1,000	(b)	

CALCULATION OF NON-CONTROLLING INTEREST—January 1, Year 1

Implied fair value, Company S (above)	$19,000		NCI is based on the implied
Non-controlling interest's percentage ownership	20%		value of the subsidiary as a
Non-controlling interest	$ 3,800	(c)	whole.

Company P's dividend income is 80% of dividends paid by the subsidiary.

The cost method journal entry of Company P on December 31, Year 1, is as follows:

| Cash | 2,000 | |
| Dividend income | | 2,000 |

80% of the dividend received from Company S

Company P's net income for Year 1 is reported as $20,300 after the receipt of the dividend from Company S. An impairment test on goodwill conducted on December 31, Year 1, indicated that a $50 loss had occurred. The financial statements of Company P and Company S as at December 31, Year 1, are shown in Exhibit 5.10.

The Year 1 amortizations of the acquisition differential and consolidated net income must be calculated before the consolidated financial statements can be prepared. These calculations are as shown in Exhibit 5.11.

These calculations form the basis for preparing the Year 1 consolidated financial statements for both the direct and the working paper approaches (see Appendix 5B for the latter).

EXHIBIT 5.10

YEAR 1 INCOME STATEMENTS

	Company P	Company S	
Sales	$ 50,000	$30,000	
Dividend income	2,000	—	(a)
Total revenue	52,000	30,000	
Cost of sales	26,500	14,700	
Expenses (miscellaneous)	5,200	8,000	
Total expenses	31,700	22,700	
Net income	$ 20,300	$ 7,300	(b)

The parent's income includes dividend income from the subsidiary, which can be reconciled to dividends paid by the subsidiary.

YEAR 1 RETAINED EARNINGS STATEMENTS

	Company P	Company S	
Balance, January 1	$ 85,000	$ 6,000	(c)
Net income	20,300	7,300	
	105,300	13,300	
Dividends	6,000	2,500	
Balance, December 31	$ 99,300	$10,800	

The parent's retained earnings include the parent's income under the cost method, which includes dividend income from the subsidiary.

BALANCE SHEETS—December 31, Year 1

	Company P	Company S	
Assets (misc.)	$151,100	$18,300	
Inventory	30,000	14,000	
Investment in S (cost method)	15,200	—	
	$196,300	$32,300	
Liabilities	$ 47,000	$11,500	
Common shares	50,000	10,000	(d)
Retained earnings	99,300	10,800	(e)
	$196,300	$32,300	

These are the separate-entity balance sheets of the two legal entities.

EXHIBIT 5.11

ACQUISITION DIFFERENTIAL AMORTIZATION AND IMPAIRMENT SCHEDULE

	Balance Jan. 1, Year 1	Amortization and Impairment Year 1	Balance Dec. 31, Year 1	
Inventory (9a)	$2,000	$2,000	$ —	(a)
Goodwill (9b)	1,000	50	950	(b)
	$3,000	$2,050	$950	(c)

This schedule reflects 100% of the acquisition differential, which will be attributed to the shareholders of the parent and the non-controlling interest.

CALCULATION OF CONSOLIDATED NET INCOME—Year 1

Company P net income—cost method (10b)		$20,300
Less: dividend income from Company S (10a)		2,000
Company P net income, own operations		18,300
Company S net income (10b)	$7,300	
Less: Acquisition differential amortization and impairment	(2,050)	
		5,250 (d)
Consolidated net income		$23,550 (e)
Attributable to		
Shareholders of Company P		$22,500 (f)
Non-controlling interest (20% × [d] 5,250)		1,050 (g)

Exhibit 5.12 shows the preparation of the consolidated financial statements when the direct approach is used. The consolidated income statement is prepared by combining the revenues and expenses of the two companies, adjusted for the Year 1 amortization of the acquisition differential. Company P's dividend income is excluded. The bottom portion of the consolidated income statement attributes the consolidated net income between the shareholders of the parent company and the non-controlling interest. First, the portion attributable to the non-controlling interest is calculated by multiplying the non-controlling interest's percentage ownership times the subsidiary's net income less the amortization of the acquisition differential. The portion attributable to the parent is equal to consolidated net income less the portion attributable to the non-controlling interest.

The consolidated income statement combines the income statements of the separate legal entities and incorporates consolidation adjustments for the amortization of the acquisition differential.

Alternatively, consolidated net income attributable to the parent's shareholders could be calculated directly as follows:

Company P net income, own operations	$18,300
Share of Company S net income after consolidation adjustments (80% × [d] 5,250)	4,200
	$22,500

The consolidated retained earnings statement contains the retained earnings of Company P at the beginning of the year, consolidated net income attributable to Company P, and the dividends of Company P.

The consolidated balance sheet is prepared by combining the assets and liabilities of the two companies, adjusted for the unamortized acquisition differential. The parent's investment account is excluded, and the non-controlling interest in the net assets of the subsidiary is shown as a component of shareholders' equity. The non-controlling interest is 20% of the December 31 shareholders' equity of Company S plus 20% of the unamortized acquisition differential.

EXHIBIT 5.12

Year 1 Consolidated Financial Statements
(Direct Approach)

COMPANY P
CONSOLIDATED INCOME STATEMENTS
for the Year Ended December 31, Year 1

Consolidated net income is attributed to the controlling shareholders and non-controlling interest.

Sales (50,000 + 30,000)	$ 80,000
Cost of sales (26,500 + 14,700 + **[11a]** 2,000)	43,200
Goodwill impairment loss (0 + 0 + **[11b]** 50)	50
Expenses (miscellaneous) (5,200 + 8,000)	13,200
	56,450
Net income	$ 23,550
Attributable to	
Shareholders of Company P **(11f)**	$ 22,500
Non-controlling interest **(11g)**	1,050

COMPANY P
CONSOLIDATED STATEMENT OF RETAINED EARNINGS
for the Year Ended December 31, Year 1

Balance, January 1	$ 85,000
Net income	22,500
	107,500
Dividends	6,000
Balance, December 31	$101,500

COMPANY P
CONSOLIDATED BALANCE SHEET
December 31, Year 1

Assets (misc.) (151,100 + 18,300)	$169,400
Inventory (30,000 + 14,000)	44,000
Goodwill (0 + 0 + **(11b) 950**)	950
	$214,350

Non-controlling interest is shown as a component of shareholders' equity.

Liabilities (47,000 + 11,500)	$ 58,500
Common shares	50,000
Retained earnings	101,500
Non-controlling interest (20% × [**(10d) 10,000** + **(10e)** **10,800** + **(11c) 950**])	4,350
	$214,350

The changes in non-controlling interest would be presented in the column for non-controlling interest in the statement of changes in equity as follows:

CHANGES IN NON-CONTROLLING INTEREST

Non-controlling interest on the balance sheet increases when the subsidiary earns income and decreases when the subsidiary pays a dividend.

Balance, January 1 **(9c)**	$3,800
Allocated income of entity **(11g)**	1,050
	4,850
Dividends to non-controlling shareholders	500*
Balance, December 31	$4,350

* $2,500 × 20% = $500

It is often useful to prepare this reconciliation when preparing a solution to consolidation problems because it helps show where the allocated income of this single entity and the dividends of the subsidiary end up in the consolidated financial statements. The consolidated retained earnings statement does not contain the dividends of the subsidiary. In this example, Company S paid $2,500 in dividends. Eighty percent of this amount ($2,000) was paid to Company P and therefore did not leave the consolidated entity. The other 20% ($500) was paid to the non-controlling shareholders and reduced the equity of that group, as shown in the statement.

The consolidation of the 80%-owned subsidiary for Year 1 financial statements using the working paper approach is illustrated in Appendix 5B.

Consolidated Statements, End of Year 2

In Year 2, Company S reported earnings of $10,000 and paid a cash dividend of $3,000. Company P's earnings for the year were $19,000 (excluding any income from its investment in Company S). Company P's journal entry to record the dividend received from Company S is as follows:

Cash	2,400	
Dividend income (80% × 3,000)		2,400
80% of the dividend paid by Company S		

Under the cost method, investment income is reported when dividends are received or receivable from the investee company.

Company P reports earnings of $21,400 in Year 2. That amount includes this dividend income. An impairment test conducted on December 31, Year 2, indicated that the goodwill had a recoverable amount of $870, and therefore an $80 impairment loss had occurred. The financial statements of the two companies as at December 31, Year 2, are shown in Exhibit 5.13.

Regardless of the approach to be used (direct or working paper), the four calculations shown in Exhibit 5.14 must be made before the consolidated financial

---

EXHIBIT 5.13

YEAR 2 INCOME STATEMENTS

	Company P	Company S	
Sales	$ 60,000	$40,000	
Dividend income	2,400	—	**(a)**
Total revenue	62,400	40,000	
Cost of sales	32,000	18,000	
Expenses (misc.)	9,000	12,000	
Total expenses	41,000	30,000	
Net income	$ 21,400	$10,000	**(b)**

These statements are the separate-entity statements of the parent and the subsidiary.

YEAR 2 RETAINED EARNINGS STATEMENTS

	Company P	Company S	
Balance, Jan. 1	$ 99,300	$10,800	**(c)**
Net income	21,400	10,000	
	120,700	20,800	
Dividends	8,000	3,000	
Balance, Dec. 31	$112,700	$17,800	**(d)**

The parent's retained earnings include dividend income received from the subsidiary since the date of acquisition.

(continued)

EXHIBIT 5.13 (*continued*)

BALANCE SHEETS—December 31, Year 2

	Company P	Company S	

The parent has used the cost method on its separate-entity financial statements.

	Company P	Company S	
Assets (misc.)	$134,500	$21,000	
Inventory	35,000	16,000	
Investment in S (cost method)	15,200	—	
	$184,700	$37,000	
Liabilities	$ 22,000	$ 9,200	
Common shares	50,000	10,000	**(e)**
Retained earnings	112,700	17,800	**(f)**
	$184,700	$37,000	

EXHIBIT 5.14

ACQUISITION DIFFERENTIAL IMPAIRMENT SCHEDULE

This schedule is used to support adjustments made when preparing consolidated financial statements.

	Balance Jan. 1, Year 2	Impairment Year 2	Balance Dec. 31, Year 2	
Inventory **(11a)**	$ —	$ —	$ —	
Goodwill **(11b)**	950	80	870	
	$950	$80	$870	**(a)**

CALCULATION OF CONSOLIDATED NET INCOME—Year 2

This schedule calculates the bottom line for the consolidated income statement.

Company P net income—cost method **(13b)**		$21,400
Less: Dividend income from Company S **(13a)**		2,400
Company P net income, own operations		19,000
Company S net income **(13b)**	10,000	
Less: Acquisition differential impairment **(14a)**	(80)	
		9,920 **(b)**
Consolidated net income		$28,920 **(c)**
Attributable to		
Shareholders of Company P		$26,936 **(d)**
Non-controlling interest (20% × **[14b]** 9,920)		1,984 **(e)**

CALCULATION OF CONSOLIDATED RETAINED EARNINGS
as at January 1, Year 2

This schedule incorporates cumulative adjustments to a point in time.

Company P retained earnings, Jan. 1, Year 2 (cost method) **(13c)**		$ 99,300
Company S retained earnings, Jan. 1, Year 2 **(13c)**	10,800	
Company S retained earnings, acquisition date **(10c)**	6,000	
Increase since acquisition	4,800	
Less: Acquisition differential amortization and impairment to end of Year 1 **(11c)**	(2,050)	
	2,750	**(f)**
Company P's ownership percentage	80%	
	2,200	
Consolidated retained earnings (which is equal to Company P's retained earnings—equity method)		$101,500 **(g)**

(*continued*)

EXHIBIT 5.14	*(continued)*

CALCULATION OF NON-CONTROLLING INTEREST
December 31, Year 2

Shareholders' equity—Company S	
Common shares **(13e)**	$10,000
Retained earnings **(13f)**	17,800
	27,800
Unamortized acquisition differential **(14a)**	870
	28,670
Non-controlling interest's ownership	20%
	$ 5,734 **(h)**

This schedule calculates non-controlling interest on the balance sheet at a point in time.

statements are prepared. These four calculations are the starting point for the preparation of the consolidated financial statements whether the direct or the working paper approach is used.

Exhibit 5.15 shows the consolidated financial statements prepared using the direct approach. The concepts involved are the same as were outlined earlier for a 100%-owned subsidiary. The only difference here is that the non-controlling interest is reflected in the consolidated income statement and balance sheet.

EXHIBIT 5.15	

Year 2 Consolidated Financial Statements
(Direct Approach)

COMPANY P
CONSOLIDATED INCOME STATEMENT
for the Year Ended December 31, Year 2

Sales (60,000 + 40,000)	$100,000
Cost of sales (32,000 + 18,000)	50,000
Goodwill impairment loss (0 + 0 + **[14a] 80**)	80
Expenses (misc.) (9,000 + 12,000)	21,000
	71,080
Net income	$ 28,920
Attributable to	
Shareholders of Company P **(14d)**	$ 26,936
Non-controlling interest **(14e)**	1,984

The income statement includes adjustments for only one year and non-controlling interest's share of income for only one year.

COMPANY P
CONSOLIDATED STATEMENT OF RETAINED EARNINGS
for the Year Ended December 31, Year 2

Balance, January 1 **(14g)**	$101,500
Net income	26,936
	128,436
Dividends	8,000
Balance, December 31	$120,436

(continued)

EXHIBIT 5.15   *(continued)*

COMPANY P
CONSOLIDATED BALANCE SHEET
December 31, Year 2

The balance sheet reflects adjustments at the end of the year and non-controlling interest's share of net assets at the end of the year.

Assets (misc.) (134,500 + 21,000)	$155,500
Inventory (35,000 + 16,000)	51,000
Goodwill (0 + 0 + **[14a]** 870)	870
	$207,370
Liabilities (22,000 + 9,200)	$ 31,200
Common shares	50,000
Retained earnings	120,436
Non-controlling interest **(14h)**	5,734
	$207,370

The consolidation of the 80%-owned subsidiary for Year 2 financial statements using the working paper approach is illustrated in Appendix 5B.

Additional Calculations   The preparation of the consolidated financial statements of companies P and S for Year 2 has been illustrated. Because the parent, Company P, used the cost method, additional calculations had to be made to determine certain consolidated amounts. An additional calculation can be made to verify the consolidated retained earnings shown on the balance sheet. This calculation is shown below:

CALCULATION OF CONSOLIDATED RETAINED EARNINGS
at December 31, Year 2

This schedule incorporates cumulative adjustments to the end of Year 2 and is used to verify retained earnings at the end of Year 2.

Company P retained earnings, Dec. 31, Year 2—cost method **(13d)**		$112,700	
Company S retained earnings, Dec. 31, Year 2 **(13d)**	17,800		
Company S retained earnings, acquisition date **(10c)**	6,000		
Increase since acquisition	11,800		
Less acquisition differential amortization and impairment to the end of Year 2 (**[11c]** 2,050 + **[14a]** 80)	(2,130)		
	9,670		**(a)**
Company P's ownership	80%	7,736	
Consolidated retained earnings		$120,436	

An alternative way to calculate NCI at the end of year 2 under the entity theory is as follows:

NCI at date of acquisition **(9c)**		$3,800
Increase is Company S retained earnings, since acquisition net of consolidation adjustments (as per **a**) above)	9,670	
Non-controlling interest's ownership	20%	1,934
NCI, end of year 2		$5,734

Parent Company Extension Theory

If the non-controlling interest was measured based on the fair value of identifiable net assets approach—that is, parent company extension theory—only the parent's share of the subsidiary's goodwill would be included on the consolidated financial statements. The NCI's share of the subsidiary's goodwill would be excluded. Once goodwill and NCI have been calculated under the entity theory, we can simply back out the NCI's share of goodwill to determine these two accounts under parent company extension theory. The following shows these calculations at the end of Year 2:

Goodwill under entity theory **(14a)**	$ 870
Less: NCI's share of goodwill (× 20%)	174
Goodwill under parent company extension theory	$ 696
NCI under entity theory **(14h)**	$5,734
Less: NCI's share of goodwill	174
NCI under parent company extension theory	$5,560

Goodwill and NCI are the only two accounts on the consolidated balance sheet that would be different under parent company extension theory compared with entity theory.

Self-Study Problem 2 involves the parent company extension theory throughout the problem and solutions. All of the schedules and financial statements are prepared using this theory. The problem also involves amortization and impairment of the acquisition differential pertaining to depreciable assets.

Acquisition Differential Assigned to Liabilities

With the considerable swings in interest rates over the past decade, companies often find that liabilities assumed in a business combination have fair values different from their carrying amounts. As with assets acquired, liabilities assumed in a business combination must be measured at their fair values. The difference between fair value and carrying amount for these liabilities is similar to a bond premium or discount that must be amortized over its remaining life.

Prior to 2006, the *CICA Handbook* was silent on the amortization method to be used in amortizing any premium or discount on a bond payable or investment in bonds. Companies could use either the straight-line method or the effective interest method. Most companies used the straight-line method because it is simpler to use. IFRS 9 requires the use of the effective interest method. Some companies may continue to use the straight-line method where the difference between the two methods is not material. In this text, we will use both the straight-line and the effective interest methods.

The effective interest method should be used to account for financial assets and liabilities.

For situation A, assume that Pubco acquires 100% of the common shares of Subco on December 31, Year 2. On that date, Pubco had no bonds payable outstanding and Subco had bonds payable with a carrying amount of $100,000 and a fair value of $105,154. These bonds were issued on January 1, Year 1, at their par value of $100,000, and mature on December 31, Year 5. The bonds pay interest on December 31 each year at a stated rate of 10%. The market rate of interest was 8% on December 31, Year 2. Given that the stated rate of interest was higher than the market rate, the bonds were trading at a premium. The fair value of the bonds can be determined by taking the present value of future cash flows using a discount rate of 8% as follows:

Bonds trade at a premium when the stated rate is greater than the market rate of interest.

Principal $100,000 × (P/F, 8%, 3 years) (0.79383)	$ 79,383
Interest $10,000 × (P/A, 8%, 3 years) (2.57710)	25,771
	$105,154

The acquisition differential of $5,154 is considered a premium on the bonds from a consolidated viewpoint. On the date of acquisition, the entire $5,154 is assigned to the bonds payable, and bonds payable will be reported at $105,154 on the consolidated balance sheet. The following schedule shows the amortization of this premium using the effective interest method as if Pubco had actually issued these bonds at $105,154 on December 31, Year 2:

Period	Interest paid	Interest expense	Amortization of bond premium	Amortized cost of bonds
Year 2				$105,154
Year 3	$10,000[1]	$8,412[2]	$1,588[3]	103,566[4]
Year 4	10,000	8,285	1,715	101,851
Year 5	10,000	8,149	1,851	100,000

[1] $100,000 × 10% = $10,000   [2] $105,154 × 8% = $8,412
[3] $10,000 − $8,412 = $1,588   [4] $105,154 − $1,588 = $103,566

In preparing consolidated financial statements subsequent to the date of acquisition, interest expense and bonds payable must be adjusted as follows to obtain the same results as if the parent had issued the bonds itself:

Period	Subco's interest expense	Adjustment on consolidation	Consolidated interest expense	Subco's Bond Payable	Adjustment on consolidation	Consolidated bond payable
Year 2				$100,000	$5,154	$105,154
Year 3	$10,000	$1,588	$8,412	100,000	3,566	103,566
Year 4	10,000	1,715	8,285	100,000	1,851	101,851
Year 5	10,000	1,851	8,149	100,000	0	100,000

The acquisition differential related to bonds payable should, theoretically, be amortized using the effective interest method.

Subco's interest expense is equal to the interest paid because the bonds were issued at par; that is, there is no premium or discount on the bonds.

For situation B, assume that Subco had issued the bonds on January 1, Year 1, at $92,791 when the market rate of interest was 12% and everything else was the same as in situation A. Given that the stated rate of interest was lower than the market rate, the bonds were issued at a discount. The following schedule shows how Subco would amortize this discount on its separate-entity financial statements:

Period	Interest paid	Interest expense	Amortization of bond discount	Amortized cost of bonds
Year 0				$ 92,791
Year 1	$10,000[1]	$11,135[2]	$1,135[3]	93,926[4]
Year 2	10,000	11,271	1,271	95,197
Year 3	10,000	11,424	1,424	96,621
Year 4	10,000	11,594	1,594	98,215
Year 5	10,000	11,785	1,785	100,000

The subsidiary amortizes the bond discount for its separate-entity financial statements.

[1] $100,000 × 10% = $10,000   [2] $92,791 × 12% = $11,135
[3] $10,000 − $11,135 = − $1,135   [4] $92,791 + $1,135 = $93,926

The acquisition differential on December 31, Year 2, the date of acquisition, would now be $9,957 (105,154 − 95,197) and is considered a premium on the bonds from a consolidated viewpoint. The entire $9,957 is assigned to the bonds payable, and bonds payable will be reported at $105,154 (same amount as in situation A) on the consolidated balance sheet. In preparing consolidated financial statements subsequent to the date of acquisition, interest expense and bonds payable must be adjusted as follows to obtain the same results as in situation A:

Period	Subco's interest expense	Adjustment on consolidation	Consolidated interest expense	Subco's bond payable	Adjustment on consolidation	Consolidated bond payable
Year 2				$95,197	$9,957	$105,154
Year 3	$11,424	$3,012	$8,412	96,621	6,945	103,566
Year 4	11,594	3,309	8,285	98,215	3,636	101,851
Year 5	11,785	3,636	8,149	100,000	0	100,000

In both situations, the acquisition differential was amortized over the three-year term to maturity of the bonds. Under the effective interest method, the annual amortization changes over time. If the straight-line method were used, the annual amortization would be the same each year. The following schedule summarizes the amortization of the acquisition differential under the effective interest and straight-line methods:

The straight-line and effective interest methods produce the same results in total over the life of the bond.

	Acquisition differential at acquisition	Amortization of acquisition differential Effective interest method			St-line per year
		Year 3	Year 4	Year 5	
A	$5,154	$1,588	$1,715	$1,851	$1,718
B	9,957	3,012	3,309	3,636	3,319

If Pubco acquired less than 100% of Subco, the non-controlling interest would absorb their share of the acquisition differential and amortization of the acquisition differential.

See Self-Study Problem 1 for a comprehensive example of consolidating a non–wholly owned subsidiary subsequent to the date of acquisition. It includes most of the issues we have covered in this chapter and includes a bond amortization schedule using the effective interest method.

Intercompany Receivables and Payables

Consolidated financial statements are designed to reflect the results of transactions between the single consolidated entity and those outside the entity. All transactions between the parent and its subsidiaries, or between the subsidiaries of a parent, must be eliminated in the consolidation process to reflect this single-entity concept. While many of these intercompany eliminations are discussed in later chapters, we will introduce the topic now by discussing the elimination of intercompany receivables and payables. If the parent's accounts receivable contain a receivable of $5,000 from its subsidiary, then the accounts payable of the subsidiary must contain a $5,000 payable to the parent. If these intercompany receivables and payables were not eliminated in the consolidation process, both the accounts receivable and the accounts payable on the consolidated balance sheet would be overstated from a single-entity point of view. The entry to eliminate these intercompany balances on the consolidated worksheet or working papers is as follows:

The consolidated financial statements should reflect only the result of transactions with outsiders.

Accounts payable—subsidiary	5,000	
Accounts receivable—parent		5,000

Because the net assets (assets less liabilities) are unchanged after this elimination, the equities of the non-controlling and controlling interests are not affected.

Subsidiary Acquired during the Year

In all of our examples to date, we have assumed that the parent acquired the subsidiary on the first day of the fiscal year. As a result, when we prepared the first consolidated income statement at the end of the first fiscal year, it contained all of the subsidiary's revenue and expenses for that year. We will now describe the consolidation process if the acquisition took place *during* the year.

Assume that Parent Inc. (which has a December 31 year-end) acquired 80% of Subsidiary Ltd. on September 30, Year 2. The Year 2 operations of Subsidiary would impact the December 31, Year 2, consolidated income statement in the following manner:

Revenues: Subsidiary's revenues October 1 to December 31

Expenses: Subsidiary's expenses plus amortization and impairment of acquisition differential October 1 to December 31

Net impact on consolidated net income attributable to shareholders of Parent Inc.: Increased by 80% of Subsidiary's net income adjusted for amortization and impairment of acquisition differential for last three months

Net impact on consolidated net income attributable to non-controlling interest: 20% × Subsidiary's net income adjusted for amortization and impairment of acquisition differential for period October 1 to December 31

> The consolidated financial statements should include the subsidiary's income only from the date of acquisition.

This form of presentation makes subsequent-year comparisons difficult for readers. To assist users, IFRS 3 requires disclosure of what the revenue and profit or loss of the combined entity for the current reporting period would have been if the acquisition date for all business combinations that occurred during the year had been as of the beginning of the annual reporting period. Alternatively, a pro forma consolidated income statement could be prepared as if the subsidiary had been acquired at the beginning of the fiscal year. This pro forma consolidated income statement could be presented in summary form in the notes to the financial statements.

L05 | EQUITY METHOD OF RECORDING

> The parent can use the cost method or equity method in its general ledger to account for an investment in a subsidiary.

The illustrations throughout this chapter have assumed that the parent used the cost method of recording its investment for its internal records. We will use the same example for an 80%-owned subsidiary to illustrate the use of the equity method. The key events of the example are repeated here for ease of use.

On January 1, Year 1, Company P purchased 80% of Company S for $15,200. In Year 1, Company S reported net income of $7,300 and paid a cash dividend of $2,500. Company P's net income for the year was $18,300 (not including income from its investment in Company S).

Company P would make the following journal entries in Year 1 under the equity method:

January 1, Year 1

Investment in S	15,200	
Cash		15,200
Purchased 80% of Company S		

December 31, Year 1

Investment in S (7,300 × 80%)	5,840	
Investment income		5,840
80% of Company S Year 1 net income		
Cash (2,500 × 80%)	2,000	
Investment in S		2,000
80% of the dividend received from Company S		
Investment income (2,050 × 80%)	1,640	
Investment in S		1,640
80% of acquisition differential amortization and impairment for Year 1		

Only the investor's share of the investee's income, dividends, and amortization of acquisition differential are recorded in the investor's records.

After these journal entries are posted, the two related accounts in the records of Company P will show the following changes and balances under the equity method:

	Investment in S	Investment income
January 1, Year 1	$15,200	
Changes during Year 1		
Income from S	5,840	$5,840
Dividends from S	(2,000)	—
Acquisition differential amortization and impairment	(1,640)	(1,640)
Balance, December 31, Year 1	$17,400	$4,200

Company P's net income for Year 1 would now be $22,500 (18,300 + 4,200). It is not a coincidence that P's net income is now equal to P's share of consolidated net income. In fact, it should be equal to the consolidated net income attributable to the shareholders of Company P, as reported on the consolidated income statement. That is why the equity method is sometimes referred to as *one-line consolidation*. The one line on Company P's non-consolidated income statement, being investment income, captures the net effect of all entries related to the subsidiary such that net income from the separate-entity books for Company P equals the consolidated net income attributable to the shareholders of Company P.

The parent's separate-entity net income should be equal to consolidated net income attributable to shareholders of the parent.

Even though Company P has used the equity method for its internal record keeping, the amounts reported on the consolidated financial statements would be exactly the same as in our previous illustration when P used the cost method. What differs is what is recorded in Company P's general ledger. This does not change what is reported on the consolidated financial statements.

At this point, it is useful to discuss a further relationship that results from the use of the equity method of accounting. The balance in the investment account at any point in time can be broken down into two components—the carrying amount of the subsidiary's shareholders' equity and the unamortized acquisition differential. The following illustrates this point at December 31, Year 1:

The investment account can be reconciled to the carrying amount of the subsidiary's shareholders' equity and the unamortized acquisition differential.

	Total 100%	P's share 80%	NCI's share 20%
Shareholders' equity, Company S			
Common shares	$10,000		
Retained earnings	10,800		
	20,800	$16,640	$4,160
Unamortized acquisition differential	950	760	190
	$21,750		
Balance in the investment account		$17,400	
Non-controlling interest			$4,350

Let us now look at what happens in Year 2.

In Year 2, Company S reported earnings of $10,000 and paid a cash dividend of $3,000. Company P's earnings for the year were $19,000 (excluding any income from its investment in Company S).

On December 31, Year 2, Company P would make the following journal entries under the equity method:

Investment in S (10,000 × 80%)	8,000	
Investment income		8,000
80% of Company S, Year 2, net income		
Cash (3,000 × 80%)	2,400	
Investment in S		2,400
Dividends received from Company S		
Investment income (80 × 80%)	64	
Investment in S		64
80% of acquisition differential amortization and impairment for Year 2		

The investment account captures all adjustments since the date of acquisition, whereas investment income captures adjustments for the current period.

After these journal entries are posted, the investment in S account and the investment income account in the records of P Company will show the following changes and balances:

	Investment in S	Investment income
December 31, Year 1	$17,400	
Changes during Year 2		
Income from S	8,000	$8,000
Dividends from S	(2,400)	
Acquisition differential amortization and impairment	(64)	(64)
Balance, December 31, Year 2	$22,936	$7,936

Company P combines its Year 2 investment income ($7,936) with the earnings from its own operations ($19,000) and reports a final net income of $26,936. Once again, it is not a coincidence that P's net income is now equal to P's share of consolidated net income.

The parent's use of the equity method should always produce the following results:

The parent's retained earnings under the equity method should be equal to consolidated retained earnings.

- Consolidated net income attributable to the shareholders of the parent in any one year will always be equal to the parent's net income reported in its internal records for that year.

- Consolidated retained earnings are always equal to the parent's retained earnings in its internal records.

The equity method captures the parent's share of the net effect of any adjustments made on consolidation. When the cost method is used, the consolidated net income attributable to the parent and consolidated retained earnings *do not* equal the parent's net income and retained earnings recorded in its internal records. However, one of the consolidation procedures involved when using the working paper approach is to adjust the parent's accounts from the cost method to the balances that would have resulted if the equity method had been used instead.

The following schedule converts the investment account from the cost equity to the equity method:

Investment in Company S, Dec. 31, Year 2—cost method		$15,200
Company S retained earnings, Dec. 31, Year 2 **(13d)**	17,800	
Company S retained earnings, acquisition date **(10c)**	6,000	
Increase since acquisition	11,800	
Less acquisition differential amortization and impairment to the end of Year 2 (**[11c]** 2,050 + **[14a]** 80)	(2,130)	
	9,670 (a)	
Company P's ownership	80%	7,736
Investment in Company S, Dec. 31, Year 2—equity method		$22,936

Compare the calculation above to the calculation of consolidated retained earnings found after Exhibit 5.15. The adjustments are exactly the same. When you adjust the investment account, something else must change on the balance sheet. The other change is to retained earnings.

A thorough understanding of the equity method and the financial statement numbers that it produces will help you to understand the consolidation process. See Self-Study Problem 2 for a comprehensive example of consolidating a non–wholly owned subsidiary when the parent uses the equity method for its internal records.

Investment in subsidiary and retained earnings are the only two accounts on the separate-entity balance sheet that would be different under the equity method as compared with the cost method.

ANALYSIS AND INTERPRETATION OF FINANCIAL STATEMENTS

L06

The parent company can use the cost or equity method to account for the investment in subsidiary for its internal records. The separate-entity financial statements of the parent present the investment in subsidiary as one line on the balance sheet and investment income from the subsidiary as one line on the income statement. When the consolidated financial statements are prepared, the one line on the balance sheet and the one line on the income statement are replaced by the underlying assets, liabilities, revenues, and expenses of the subsidiary, plus or minus the acquisition differential. The consolidated financial statements are not affected by the method used by the parent to account for its investment in the subsidiary. The adjustments to get from the separate-entity statements to the consolidated statements may be different, depending on the method used by the parent. But the end result is the exact same set of consolidated financial statements.

Exhibit 5.16 presents the income statements and balance sheets for the parent's separate-entity statements under two scenarios: first, when the parent uses the cost method and, second, when the parent uses the equity method. The last column presents the consolidated financial statements. The values for the cost method are taken directly from Exhibit 5.13. The values for the equity method are the same as the cost method, except for the investment account and investment income (which are taken from the previous section) and retained earnings (which is taken from the consolidated balance sheet in Exhibit 5.15). The consolidated statements are taken from Exhibit 5.15. The exhibit also indicates the debt-to-equity ratio and return-on-equity ratio for each set of financial statements. The return on equity for all shareholders uses consolidated net income and total shareholders' equity, including the non-controlling interest. The return on equity for shareholders of Company P uses consolidated net income attributable to the shareholders of Company P and total shareholders' equity, excluding the non-controlling interest.

Consolidated financial statements are exactly the same and do not depend on whether the parent uses the cost method or equity method for internal record keeping.

EXHIBIT 5.16   Impact of Presentation Method on Debt-to-Equity and Return-on-Equity Ratios

INCOME STATEMENTS
for the Year Ended December 31, Year 2

	Company P-Separate Entity		Consolidated
	Cost	Equity	
Sales	$ 60,000	$60,000	$100,000
Income from Company S	2,400	7,936	—
Total revenue	62,400	67,936	100,000
Cost of sales	32,000	32,000	50,000
Goodwill impairment loss			80
Expenses (misc.)	9,000	9,000	21,000
Total expenses	41,000	41,000	71,080
Net income	$ 21,400	$ 26,936	$ 28,920
Attributable to			
Shareholders of Company P			$ 26,936
Non-controlling interest			1,984

Net income on the parent's separate-entity income statement should always be equal to net income attributable to the shareholders of the parent on the consolidated income statement.

BALANCE SHEETS
at December 31, Year 2

	Company P- Separate Entity		Consolidated
	Cost	Equity	
Assets (misc.)	$134,500	$134,500	$155,500
Inventory	35,000	35,000	51,000
Goodwill			870
Investment in S	15,200	22,936	
	$184,700	$192,436	$207,370
Liabilities	$ 22,000	$ 22,000	$ 31,200
Common shares	50,000	50,000	50,000
Retained earnings	112,700	120,436	120,436
Non-controlling interest			5,734
	$184,700	$192,436	$207,370
Debt-to-equity	0.14	0.13	0.18
Return-on-equity			
- for all shareholders (28,920 / (50,000 + 120,436 + 5,734)	n/a	n/a	16.4%
- for shareholders of Company P	13.2%	15.8%	15.8%

Retained earnings on the parent's separate-entity balance under the equity method should always be equal to consolidated retained earnings sheet.

Note the following from Exhibit 5.16:

- The separate-entity net income and return-on-equity ratio under the cost and equity methods are different.

- The separate-entity net income and retained earnings under the equity method are equal to consolidated net income attributable to the shareholders of Company P and consolidated retained earnings, respectively.

- The separate-entity return on equity under the equity method is equal to the consolidated return on equity for the shareholders of Company P.

- The solvency position looks worst on the consolidated financial statements because the subsidiary's debt is included on the consolidated financial statements. This increases the debt-to-equity ratio.

Return on equity for the parent's separate-entity financial statements under the equity method should always to equal to the return on equity for the shareholders of Company P on the consolidated financial statements.

ASPE DIFFERENCES

L07

- As mentioned in Chapter 3, private companies could either consolidate their subsidiaries or report their investments in subsidiaries under the cost method, equity method, or at fair value if the market value is quoted in an active market.

- The investments in and income from non-consolidated subsidiaries should be presented separately from other investments.

- All intangible assets and goodwill should be tested for impairment whenever events or changes in circumstances indicate that the carrying amount may exceed the fair value.

- The impairment test for property, plant, and equipment and for intangible assets with definite useful lives has three steps. In step 1, consider whether there are any indicators; that is, events or circumstances that indicate that the asset may be impaired. If not, no further testing is required. In step 2, determine if the carrying amount exceeds its recoverable amount (i.e., the sum of the undiscounted cash flows expected to result from its use and eventual disposition). If not, no further testing is required. In step 3, determine if the carrying amount exceeds its fair value. If so, an impairment loss should be recognized. If not, there is no impairment.

Undiscounted cash flows are considered in step 3.

- For intangible assets with indefinite useful lives and goodwill, an impairment loss should be recognized when the carrying amount exceeds its fair value.

- In all cases, the impairment loss is equal to the excess of carrying amount over the fair value, and impairment losses cannot be reversed.

The impairment loss is equal to the excess of carrying amount over the fair value.

U.S. GAAP DIFFERENCES

U.S. GAAP and IFRSs for consolidated statements subsequent to the date of acquisition have many similarities. The significant differences are summarized as follows:

1. Whereas goodwill is allocated to cash-generating units under IFRSs, it is allocated to reporting units under U.S. GAAP. A reporting unit is defined as an operating segment or one level below an operating segment.

The impairment test for goodwill is quite different under U.S. GAAP as compared to IFRSs.

2. Impairment testing is a two-step approach. In step 1, the fair value and the carrying amount of the reporting unit, including goodwill, are compared. If the fair value is less than the carrying amount, step 2 is performed. In step 2, goodwill impairment is measured as the excess of the carrying amount of goodwill over its implied fair value, which is calculated in the same manner that goodwill is determined at the date of acquisition; that is, the difference between fair value of the reporting unit as a whole and the fair value of the identifiable net assets.

3. The goodwill impairment loss is not permitted to exceed the carrying amount of the goodwill.

SUMMARY

While a parent company can account for its investment by either the equity method or the cost method in its internal records, the consolidated statements are the same regardless of the method used. The method of presentation is quite different between the separate-entity financial statements and the consolidated financial statements.

When the parent uses the equity method on its separate-entity financial statements, the parent's share of the subsidiary's income and net assets is typically shown on one line on the income statement (investment income) and one line on the balance sheet (investment in subsidiary). Accordingly, the equity method is sometimes referred to as *one-line consolidation*. The income and retained earnings reported by the parent on its separate-entity financial statements will be equal to the consolidated net income attributable to shareholders of the parent and consolidated retained earnings, respectively.

This chapter has illustrated the preparation of consolidated financial statements covering a two-year period after the date of acquisition when the parent has used the cost method to account for its investment. Additional calculations were performed to convert the income and retained earnings from the amounts shown on the separate-entity financial statements to the consolidated financial statements.

The basic steps in the consolidation process when the parent has used the equity and cost methods are outlined in Exhibit 5.17. It is important to have a good grasp of the procedures under both methods, because these procedures are the foundation for the consolidation issues we will introduce in the chapters that follow.

Significant Changes in GAAP in the Last Three Years

No significant changes for the topics discussed in this chapter.

Changes Expected in GAAP in the Next Three Years

No major changes are expected in the next three years for the topics discussed in this chapter.

EXHIBIT 5.17

PREPARATION OF CONSOLIDATED FINANCIAL STATEMENTS
Basic Steps

	Parent company uses	
	Cost method	Equity method
1. Calculate and allocate the acquisition differential at the date of acquisition.	Yes	Yes
2. Prepare an acquisition differential amortization and impairment schedule (date of acquisition to present date).	Yes	Yes
3. Calculate consolidated net income—current year.	Yes	No*
4. Prepare the consolidated income statement.	Yes	Yes
5. Calculate the start-of-year balance of consolidated retained earnings.**	Yes	No*
6. Prepare the consolidated retained earnings statement.***	Yes	Yes
7. Calculate the end-of-year balance of consolidated retained earnings.	Yes	No*
8. Calculate non-controlling interest at the end of the year (for the consolidated balance sheet).	Yes	Yes
9. Prepare a statement of changes in non-controlling interest (optional).	Yes	Yes
10. Prepare a consolidated balance sheet.	Yes	Yes

If the parent company uses the equity method of accounting, the parent's net income equals consolidated net income attributable to the shareholders of the parent, and the parent's retained earnings always equal consolidated retained earnings. Therefore, the calculations in steps 3, 5, and 7 are not necessary.
**Only do so if preparing a statement of retained earnings.*
***Not required in all problems.*

SELF-STUDY PROBLEM 1

L01, 2, 3   On January 1, Year 1, Allen Company acquired 7,000 (70%) of the outstanding common shares of Bell Company for $87,500 in cash. On that date, Bell had common shares of $50,000 and retained earnings of $45,000. The Bell shares were trading for $11 per share just after the date of acquisition. At acquisition, the identifiable assets and liabilities of Bell had fair values that were equal to carrying amounts, except for equipment, which had a fair value of $150,000, a cost of $200,000, and accumulated depreciation of $80,000; inventory, which had a fair value $8,000 less than carrying amount; and bonds payable, which had a fair value $12,420 greater than carrying amount. The equipment had a remaining useful life of eight years on January 1, Year 1, and is amortized on a straight-line basis. The bonds payable mature on December 31, Year 8; pay interest annually; and are amortized using the effective interest method. The market rate of interest for similar bonds is 6%.

Financial statements for the Year 6 fiscal year are as follows:

	Allen	Bell
Income statements		
Sales	$ 400,000	$250,000
Rent revenue	15,000	—
Dividend revenue	3,500	—
	418,500	250,000
Cost of sales	200,000	160,000
Depreciation	55,000	20,000
Interest expense	32,000	8,000
Other expenses	28,000	42,000
	315,000	230,000
Profit	$ 103,500	$ 20,000
Retained earnings statements		
Balance, January 1	$ 400,000	$ 65,000
Profit	103,500	20,000
	503,500	85,000
Dividends	30,000	5,000
Balance, December 31	$ 473,500	$ 80,000
Statement of financial position		
Property, plant, and equipment	$1,200,000	$400,000
Accumulated depreciation	(300,000)	(210,000)
Investment in Bell—cost method	87,500	—
Inventory	200,000	40,000
Accounts receivable	60,000	25,000
Cash	12,500	10,000
	$1,260,000	$265,000
Ordinary shares	$ 300,000	$ 50,000
Retained earnings	473,500	80,000
Bonds payable, 8%	400,000	100,000
Accounts payable	86,500	35,000
	$1,260,000	$265,000

Additional Information

In Year 2, a goodwill impairment loss of $7,000 was recorded ($6,300 pertained to Allen's 70% interest). Subsequent goodwill testing yielded no further evidence of impairment until Year 6, when a decline in the recoverable amount of Bell Company occurred and management decided to reflect an impairment loss of $6,000 in the year's consolidated statements ($5,400 pertained to Allen's 70% interest).

On December 31, Year 6, Bell Company owes Allen Company $9,000.

Required:

(a) Using the direct approach, prepare the following Year 6 consolidated financial statements:

  (i)   Income statement
  (ii) Retained earnings statement
  (iii) Statement of financial position

(b) Prepare a schedule of the Year 6 changes in non-controlling interest.

SOLUTION TO SELF-STUDY PROBLEM 1

CALCULATION OF ACQUISITION DIFFERENTIAL

	Parent's 70%	Non-controlling interest's 30%	Total 100%
Cost of 70% of Bell	$87,500		
Value of 30% of Bell		$33,000	
(3,000 shares × 11)			
Implied value of 100% of Bell			$120,500
Carrying amount of Bell's net assets = Carrying amount of shareholders' equity			
Ordinary shares	50,000		
Retained earnings	45,000		
	95,000	66,500	28,500	95,000
Acquisition differential		21,000	4,500	25,500
Allocated:	FV − CA			
Equipment	30,000 (a)			
(150,000 − [200,000 − 80,000])				
Inventory	− 8,000 (b)			
Bonds payable	−12,420 (c)			
	9,580	6,706	2,874	9,580
Goodwill (approximately 90% of total)	$14,294 (d)			
Goodwill (approximately 10% of total)		$ 1,626 (e)		
Total goodwill				$ 15,920

BOND AMORTIZATION SCHEDULE

Date	Cash paid	Interest expense	Bond premium amortization	Amortized cost of bonds
Jan 1/ Year 1				$112,420
Dec 31/ Year 1	$ 8,000	$ 6,745	$ 1,255	111,165
Dec 31/ Year 2	8,000	6,670	1,330	109,835
Dec 31/ Year 3	8,000	6,590	1,410	108,425
Dec 31/ Year 4	8,000	6,506	1,494	106,931
Dec 31/ Year 5	8,000	6,416	1,584	105,347
	40,000	32,927	7,073	
Dec 31/ Year 6	8,000	6,321	1,679	103,668 (f)
Dec 31/ Year 7	8,000	6,220	1,780	101,888
Dec 31/ Year 8	8,000	6,112	1,888	100,000
	$64,000	$51,580	$12,420	

ACQUISITION DIFFERENTIAL AMORTIZATION AND IMPAIRMENT

	Balance Jan. 1/Year 1	Amortization and Impairment To end of Year 5	Year 6	Balance Dec. 31/Year 6	
Equipment (a)	$ 30,000	$18,750	$ 3,750	$ 7,500	(g)
Inventory (b)	− 8,000	− 8,000	—	—	(h)
Bonds payable (c)	−12,420	−7,073	−1,679	−3,668	(i)

(continued)

	Balance Jan. 1/Year 1	Amortization and Impairment To end of Year 5	Year 6	Balance Dec. 31/Year 6	
	9,580	3,677	2,071	3,832	(j)
Goodwill—parent **(d)**	14,294	6,300	5,400	2,594	**(k)**
Goodwill—NCI **(e)**	1,626	700	600	326	**(l)**
Goodwill—total	15,920	7,000	6,000	2,920	**(m)**
	$25,500	$10,677	$ 8,071	$ 6,752	

CALCULATION OF CONSOLIDATED NET INCOME ATTRIBUTABLE TO PARENT
Year 6

Profit—Allen		$103,500	
Less dividend from Bell		3,500	**(n)**
		100,000	
Profit—Bell	20,000		**(o)**
Allen's ownership	70%	14,000	
Parent's share of acquisition differential amortization and impairment			
(70% × **[j]** 2,071 + **[k]** 5,400)		−6,850	**(p)**
		$107,150	**(q)**

CALCULATION OF CONSOLIDATED NET INCOME ATTRIBUTABLE TO NCI

Net income—Bell	$ 20,000	
NCI's ownership	30%	
	6,000	
NCI's share of acquisition differential amortization and impairment		
(30% × **[j]** 2,071 + **[l]** 600)	−1,221	
	$ 4,779	**(r)**

CALCULATION OF CONSOLIDATED RETAINED EARNINGS
January 1, Year 6

Retained earnings—Allen		$400,000	
Retained earnings—Bell	65,000		
Retained earnings—Bell, acquisition date	45,000		
Increase since acquisition	20,000		
Allen's ownership	70%		
		14,000	
Parent's share of acquisition differential amortization and impairment			
(70% × **[j]** 3,677 + **[k]** 6,300)		−8,874	**(s)**
		$405,126	**(t)**

CALCULATION OF CONSOLIDATED RETAINED EARNINGS
December 31, Year 6

Retained earnings—Allen		$473,500	
Retained earnings—Bell	80,000		
Retained earnings—Bell, acquisition date	45,000		
Increase since acquisition	35,000		
Allen's ownership	70%	24,500	
Parent's share of acquisition differential amortization and impairment			
(**[p]** 6,850 + **[s]** 8,874)		−15,724	**(u)**
		$482,276	**(v)**

CALCULATION OF NON-CONTROLLING INTEREST (Method 1)
at December 31, Year 6

Ordinary shares—Bell	$ 50,000
Retained earnings—Bell	80,000
	130,000
NCI's ownership	30%
	39,000
NCI's share of unamortized acquisition differential	
(30% × **[j]** 3,832 + **[l]** 326)	1,476
	$ 40,476 **(w)**

CALCULATION OF NON-CONTROLLING INTEREST (Method 2)

Non-controlling interest at acquisition	33,000
(3,000 shares × 11)	
Increase in Bell's retained earnings since acquisition	35,000
NCI's share @ 30%	10,500
NCI's share of amortization of acquisition differential	
([**(j)** 3,677 + **(j)** 2,071] × 30% + **[l]** 700 + **[l]** 600)	(3,024)
	40,476 **(w)**

Accumulated depreciation and equipment need to be reduced by $80,000 so that equipment held by subsidiary is reported at a cost of $150,000 with no accumulated depreciation at date of acquisition	$ 80,000 **(x)**

(a) (i)

ALLEN COMPANY
CONSOLIDATED INCOME STATEMENT
for the Year Ended December 31, Year 6

Sales (400,000 + 250,000)	$650,000
Rent revenue	15,000
Dividend revenue (3,500 + 0 − **[n]** 3,500)	—
	665,000
Cost of sales (200,000 + 160,000)	360,000
Depreciation (55,000 + 20,000 + **[g]** 3,750)	78,750
Interest expense (32,000 + 8,000 − **[i]** 1,679)	38,321
Other expenses (28,000 + 42,000)	70,000
Goodwill impairment loss **(m)**	6,000
	553,071
Profit	$111,929
Add: Attributable to	
Shareholders of Allen **(q)**	$107,150
Non-controlling interest **(r)**	4,779

(ii)

ALLEN COMPANY
CONSOLIDATED RETAINED EARNINGS STATEMENT
for the Year Ended December 31, Year 6

Balance, January 1 **(t)**	$405,126
Profit	107,150
	512,276
Dividends	30,000
Balance, December 31 **(v)**	$482,276

& dividends

(iii)

ALLEN COMPANY
CONSOLIDATED STATEMENT OF FINANCIAL POSITION
December 31, Year 6

Plant and equipment (1,200,000 + 400,000 + **[a]** 30,000 − **[x]** 80,000)	$1,550,000
Accumulated depreciation	
(300,000 + 210,000 + **[g]** 18,750 + **[g]** 3,750 − **[x]**) 80,000)	(452,500)
Goodwill **(m)**	2,920
Inventory (200,000 + 40,000)	240,000
Accounts receivable (60,000 + 25,000 − *__9,000__)	76,000
Cash (12,500 + 10,000)	22,500
	$1,438,920
Ordinary shares	$ 300,000
Retained earnings **(v)**	482,276
Non-controlling interest **(w)**	40,476
	822,752
Bonds payable (400,000 + 100,000 + **[i]** 3,668)	503,668
Accounts payable (86,500 + 35,000 − *__9,000__)	112,500
	$1,438,920

Intercompany receivable/payable

(b)   **YEAR 6 CHANGES IN NON-CONTROLLING INTEREST**

Balance, January 1*	$37,197
Allocation of entity net income **(r)**	4,779
	41,976
Dividends (30% × 5,000)	1,500
Balance, December 31 **(v)**	$40,476
*Ordinary shares	$50,000
Retained earnings, January 1	65,000
	115,000
NCI's ownership	30%
	34,500
NCI's share of unamortized acquisition differential	
(30% × **[j]** [9,580 − 3,677] + **[l]** [1,626 − 700])	2,697
	$37,197

SELF-STUDY PROBLEM 2

L01, 2, 4, 5   On December 31, Year 2, Pat Inc. purchased 80% of the outstanding common shares of Sam Company for $620,000. At that date, Sam had common shares of $400,000 and retained earnings of $125,000. In negotiating the purchase price, it was agreed that the assets on Sam's balance sheet were fairly valued, except for plant assets, which had an $80,000 excess of fair value over carrying amount. It was also agreed that Sam had unrecognized intangible assets consisting of trademarks that had an estimated value of $50,000. The plant assets had a remaining useful life of 8 years at the acquisition date, and the trademarks would be

amortized over a 10-year period. Any goodwill arising from this business combination would be tested periodically for impairment. Pat accounts for its investment using the equity method and prepares consolidated statements using the
parent company extension theory.

Additional Information

- Impairment tests performed at the end of Year 6 indicated that Pat's portion of
  the goodwill had a recoverable amount of $85,000 and the trademarks had a
  recoverable amount of $29,000. The impairment loss on these assets occurred
  entirely in Year 6.
- On December 26, Year 6, Pat declared dividends of $72,000 while Sam declared
  dividends of $40,000.
- Amortization expense is reported in selling expenses, while impairment losses
  are reported in other expenses.

Condensed financial statements for Pat and Sam for the year ended December 31, Year 6, were as follows:

STATEMENTS OF FINANCIAL POSITION
December 31, Year 6

	Pat	Sam
Assets		
Plant assets—net	$ 460,000	$ 320,000
Investment in Sam Company	700,200	—
Other assets	580,000	804,000
	$1,740,200	$1,124,000
Shareholders' Equity and Liabilities		
Common shares	$1,000,000	$400,000
Retained earnings	300,200	300,000
Liabilities	440,000	424,000
	$1,740,200	$1,124,000

INCOME STATEMENTS
Year ended December 31, Year 6

	Pat	Sam
Sales	$1,740,000	$1,030,000
Cost of goods sold	(1,276,000)	(720,000)
Gross profit	464,000	310,000
Selling expenses	(44,000)	(70,000)
Other expenses	(296,000)	(144,000)
Interest and investment income	92,200	4,000
Profit	$ 216,200	$ 100,000

Required:

(a) Prepare a schedule to allocate the acquisition differential at the date of acquisition and a schedule to amortize the acquisition differential from the date of
acquisition to the end of Year 6

(b) Prepare the journal entries for Pat's separate-entity books to account for the investment in Sam for Year 6, and determine the investment income from Sam for Year 6 under the

    i) equity method, and

    ii) cost method.

(c) Prepare consolidated financial statements for Year 6.

SOLUTION TO SELF-STUDY PROBLEM 2

(a)

CALCULATION OF ACQUISITION DIFFERENTIAL

Cost of 80% of Sam	$620,000	
Implied value of 100% (620,000/0.8)	$775,000	
Carrying amount of Sam's net assets = Carrying amount of Sam's shareholders' equity		
Common shares	400,000	
Retained earnings	125,000 525,000	**(a)**
Acquisition differential	250,000	
Allocated:	FV − CA	
Plant assets	80,000	
Trademarks	50,000 130,000	**(b)**
Goodwill for 100%	120,000	
Less: NCI's share at 20%	24,000	
Goodwill for Sam's 80%	96,000	
NCI at date of acquisition (20% × [**(a)** 525,000 + **(b)** 130,000])	131,000	**(c)**

	Bal Dec. 31/Yr2	Amortization to Dec.31/Yr5	Yr6	Loss Yr6	Bal Dec. 31/Yr6	
Plant assets (8 years)	80,000	30,000	10,000		40,000	**(d)**
Trademarks (10 years)	50,000	15,000	5,000	1,000	29,000	**(e)**
Subtotal	130,000	45,000	15,000	1,000	69,000	**(f)**
Goodwill for Sam's 80%	96,000	--------	--------	11,000	85,000	**(g)**
Total	226,000	45,000	15,000	12,000	154,000	**(h)**
NCI's share [20% × **(f)**]	26,000	9,000	3,000	200	13,800	**(i)**
Pat's share	200,000	36,000	12,000	11,800	140,200	**(j)**

(b)

	(i) Equity Method	(ii) Cost Method
Investment in Sam (80% × 100,000)	80,000	
Investment income	80,000	
To record Pat's share of Sam's income		
Cash (80% × 40,000)	32,000	32,000
Investment in Sam	32,000	
Investment income		32,000
To record Pat's share of Sam's dividend		
Investment income [**(j)** (12,000 + **(j)** 11,800)]	23,800	
Investment in Sam	23,800	
To record Pat's share of amortization and impairment of acquisition differential		

Investment income for Year 6 under the equity method is $56,200   **(k)**
(80,000 − 23,800) and $32,000 under the cost method.

(c)

Calculation of consolidated profit attributable to NCI

Sam's profit	100,000	
NCI's share @ 20%	20,000	
Acquisition differential amortization [**(i)** (3,000 + **(i)** 200)]	(3,200)	
	16,800	**(l)**

Pat Inc.
Consolidated Income Statement
Year ended December 31, Year 6

Sales (1,740,000 + 1,030,000)	$2,770,000
Interest & investment income (92,200 + 4,000 − **[k]** 56,200)	40,000
	2,810,000
Cost of sales (1,276,000 + 720,000)	1,996,000
Selling expenses (44,000 + 70,000 + **[h]** 15,000)	129,000
Other expenses (296,000 + 144,000 + **[h]** 12,000)	452,000
	2,577,000
Profit	$ 233,000
Attributable to:	
Pat's shareholders (= income under equity method)	$ 216,200
Non-controlling interest **(l)**	16,800
	$ 233,000

Calculation of NCI at December 31, Year 6

NCI at acquisition **(c)**		131,000
Sam retained earnings Dec. 31, Year 6	300,000	
Acquisition retained earnings	125,000	
Increase	175,000	
NCI's share	× 20%	35,000
Less: Acquisition differential amortization ((i) 9,000 + 3,000 + 200)		(12,200)
		153,800

Pat Inc.
Consolidated Balance sheet
December 31, Year 6

Plant assets (460,000 + 320,000 + **[d]** 40,000)	$ 820,000
Trademarks (0 + 0 + **[e]** 29,000)	29,000
Goodwill (0 + 0 + **[f]** 85,000)	85,000
Other assets (580,000 + 804,000)	1,384,000
	$2,318,000
Common shares	$1,000,000
Retained earnings (= retained earnings under equity method)	300,200
Non-controlling interest **(m)**	153,800
Liabilities (440,000 + 424,000)	864,000
	$2,318,000

APPENDIX 5A

GOODWILL IMPAIRMENT

L01 Goodwill is recorded only when it is purchased as part of a business combination. When the subsidiary is made up of more than one cash-generating unit (CGU), these CGUs must be identified at the date of acquisition. The assets and liabilities (including goodwill) acquired in a business combination are then assigned to these identified CGUs. The assignment should consider where the acquired assets and liabilities will be employed. The goodwill should be assigned to those units that are expected to benefit from the synergies of the combination. Overall, the objective of the assignment of acquired assets and liabilities to CGUs is to facilitate the required fair value/carrying amount comparisons for periodic impairment testing.

At the date of acquisition, the total value of the subsidiary is segregated by cash-generating units.

Each year, starting with the year of acquisition, goodwill in each cash-generating unit is tested for impairment. At the time of impairment testing of a cash-generating unit to which goodwill has been allocated, there may be an indication of an impairment of an asset within the unit containing the goodwill. In such circumstances, the entity tests the individual asset for impairment first and recognizes any impairment loss for that asset before testing for impairment of the CGU containing the goodwill. In other words, the impairment procedures are applied at the single asset level first and the CGU levels last.

Individual assets should be tested for impairment before each cash-generating unit is tested for impairment.

The recoverable amount is compared with the carrying amount of net assets for each cash-generating unit.

To test goodwill for impairment, the recoverable amount of each CGU is compared with its carrying amount, including goodwill. If the recoverable amount exceeds the carrying amount, goodwill is not impaired. If the recoverable amount is less than the carrying amount, an impairment loss should be recognized and allocated to reduce the carrying amount of the assets of the unit (group of units) in the following order:

Any impairment loss is applied first to goodwill and then to other assets.

(a) First, to reduce the carrying amount of any goodwill allocated to the cash-generating unit

(b) Then, to the other assets of the unit, pro rata on the basis of the carrying amount of each asset in the unit

However, an entity shall not reduce the carrying amount of an individual asset below the higher of its recoverable amount and zero. The amount of the impairment loss that could not be allocated to an individual asset because of this limitation must be allocated pro rata to the other assets of the unit (group of units).

Several alternative methods exist for determining the recoverable amount of the cash generating units that compose a consolidated entity. First, any quoted market prices that exist can provide a basis for assessing fair value, especially for subsidiaries with actively traded non-controlling interests. Second, comparable businesses may exist that can help indicate market values. Third, present value of future cash flow streams or profit projections can be calculated to determine the value in use. The discount rate used in the present value calculations should consider the riskiness of the future flows.

The following example[6] illustrates impairment testing for a subsidiary with more than one CGU. At the end of year 1, T Company acquires 100% of the common shares of M Limited for $10,000. M has manufacturing plants in three countries. Each country is deemed to be a separate cash-generating unit because activities in each country represent the lowest level at which the goodwill is monitored for internal management purposes. The acquisition cost was allocated to the CGUs as follows at the date of acquisition:

CGUs are identified based on the lowest level at which the goodwill is monitored for internal management purposes.

CGU	Allocation of acquisition cost	Fair value of identifiable assets	Goodwill
Activities in Country A	$ 3,000	$2,000	$1,000
Activities in Country B	2,000	1,500	500
Activities in Country C	5,000	3,500	1,500
Total	$10,000	$7,000	$3,000

Because goodwill has been allocated to the activities in each country, each of those activities must be tested for impairment annually, or more frequently if there is any indication that it may be impaired. The recoverable amounts of the cash-generating units are determined on the basis of value in use calculations. At the end of Year 1 and Year 2, the value in use of each cash-generating unit exceeds its carrying amount. Therefore, the activities in each country and the goodwill allocated to those activities are regarded as not impaired.

At the beginning of Year 3, a new government is elected in Country A. It passes legislation significantly restricting exports of T's main product. As a result, and for the foreseeable future, T's production in Country A will be cut by 40%. The significant export restriction and the resulting production decrease require T also to estimate the recoverable amount of the Country A operations at the beginning of Year 3.

The new legislation in Country A is an example of an indicator that goodwill may be impaired.

To determine the value in use for the Country A cash-generating unit, T does the following:

(a) Prepares cash flow forecasts derived from the most recent financial budgets/ forecasts for the next five years (Years 3–7) approved by management

(b) Estimates subsequent cash flows (Years 8–13) based on declining growth rates. The growth rate for Year 8 is estimated to be 3%. This rate is lower than the average long-term growth rate for the market in Country A

The value in use is determined by calculating the present value of future cash flows.

(c) Selects a 15% discount rate, which represents a pre-tax rate that reflects current market assessments of the time value of money and the risks specific to the Country A cash-generating unit

Exhibit 5A.1 shows the calculation of the value in use of the Country A cash-generating unit at the beginning of Year 3.

Based on the calculation in Exhibit 5A.1, the recoverable amount of the Country A cash-generating unit is $1,360. Assuming that the carrying amount of Country A's identifiable net assets is $1,833 at the beginning of Year 3, there would be an impairment loss of $1,473 calculated as follows:

Carrying amount of Country A's:	
Identifiable net assets	$1,833
Goodwill	1,000
Total carrying amount	2,833
Recoverable amount	1,360
Total impairment loss	$1,473

EXHIBIT 5A.1

VALUE IN USE OF COUNTRY A CASH-GENERATING UNIT

Year	Long-term growth rates	Future cash flows	Present value at 15% discount rate	Discounted future factor cash flows
Year 3 (n = 1)		$230	0.86957	$ 200
Year 4		253	0.75614	191
Year 5		273	0.65752	180
Year 6		290	0.57175	166
Year 7		304	0.49718	151
Year 8	3%	313	0.43233	135
Year 9	- 2%	307	0.37594	115
Year 10	- 6%	289	0.32690	94
Year 11	- 15%	245	0.28426	70
Year 12	- 25%	184	0.24719	45
Year 13	- 67%	61	0.21494	13
Value in use				$1,360

Future cash flows are discounted using a pre-tax rate that reflects current market assessments of the time value of money and the risks specific to the cash-generating unit.

The impairment loss is applied first to goodwill to reduce it to zero and then to identifiable assets as indicated by the following:

The impairment loss is allocated to goodwill first and then to other identifiable net assets.

	Goodwill	Identifiable assets	Total
Carrying amount	1,000	1,833	2,833
Impairment loss	(1,000)	(473)	(1,473)
Carrying amount after impairment loss	0	1,360	1,360

In the example above, the subsidiary is wholly owned by the parent. The value in use was calculated for the CGU as a whole and compared to the carrying amount of goodwill and identifiable net assets for the unit as a whole. When the subsidiary is non–wholly owned, certain adjustments may be required when making this comparison. This is especially important when parent company extension theory is used to account for NCI. In this situation, the carrying amount of goodwill allocated to the unit will have to be grossed up to include the goodwill attributable to the non-controlling interest. This adjusted carrying amount is then compared with the recoverable amount of the unit to determine whether the cash-generating unit is impaired. The following example[7] illustrates impairment testing for a non-wholly subsidiary accounted for using parent company extension theory.

Parent acquired an 80% ownership interest in Subsidiary for $2,200 on January 1, Year 3. At that date, Subsidiary's net identifiable assets had a fair value of $1,500. Parent chooses to measure the non-controlling interests as the proportionate interest of Subsidiary's net identifiable assets of $300 (20% × 1,500). Goodwill of $1,000 is the difference between the total consideration given, $2,500 (2,200 + 300) and the fair value of the identifiable net assets, $1,500.

Goodwill at the date of acquisition is allocated to the CGUs that benefit from the synergies of the business combination.

The assets of Subsidiary together are the smallest group of assets that generate cash inflows that are largely independent of the cash inflows from other assets or groups of assets. Therefore, Subsidiary is a cash-generating unit. Because other cash-generating units of Parent are expected to benefit from the synergies of the combination, goodwill of $600 related to those synergies has been allocated to other cash-generating units within Parent. Therefore, only $400 of goodwill is allocated to Subsidiary. Because the cash-generating unit Subsidiary is made up of includes goodwill within its carrying amount, it must be tested for impairment annually, or more frequently if there is an indication that it may be impaired.

At the end of Year 3, Parent determines that the recoverable amount of cash-generating unit Subsidiary is $1,200. The carrying amount of the net assets of Subsidiary, excluding goodwill, is $1,350.

Goodwill attributable to non-controlling interests is included in Subsidiary's recoverable amount of $1,200 but has not been recognized in Parent's consolidated financial statements. Therefore, the carrying amount of Subsidiary is grossed up to include goodwill attributable to the non-controlling interests, before being compared with the recoverable amount of $1,200. Goodwill attributable to Parent's 80% interest in Subsidiary at the acquisition date is $400 after allocating $600 to other cash-generating units within Parent. The goodwill attributable to the 20% non-controlling interests in Subsidiary at the acquisition date is $100 (400 × 20/80). The adjusted carrying amount of goodwill is $500 ($400 pertaining to parent's 80% interest plus $100 pertaining to the NCI's unrecognized interest). The impairment loss is $650 calculated as follows:

> The carrying amount of the subsidiary must be grossed up for the unrecognized portion of its goodwill (i.e., the NCI's portion) to make it comparable to the recoverable amount for the subsidiary as a whole.

Carrying amount of Subsidiary's:	
Identifiable net assets	$1,350
Goodwill	500
Total carrying amount	1,850
Recoverable amount	1,200
Total impairment loss	$ 650

The impairment loss is applied first to goodwill to reduce it to zero and then to identifiable assets. Since the calculation of impairment loss included a value for the NCI's unrecognized share of goodwill, part of the impairment loss should be allocated to the NCI as follows:

	Parent's Goodwill	NCI's Goodwill	Identifiable assets	Total
Carrying amount	$400	$100	$1,350	$1,850
Impairment loss	(400)	(100)	(150)	(650)
Carrying amount after impairment loss	0	0	$1,200	$1,200

The previous examples have shown that the impairment testing for goodwill has added a new and complex valuation exercise to the consolidation process. The determination of recoverable amounts will be a costly one for many companies and will likely require the yearly services of business valuation specialists.

> The impairment tests are complex and often require considerable professional judgment.

Although impairment testing for goodwill and intangible assets with indefinite lives is required on an annual basis, a detailed evaluation of the recoverable amount may not be required annually. The most recent detailed calculation made in a preceding period of the recoverable amount of a CGU to which goodwill has been allocated may be used in the impairment test of that unit in the current period given the following:

(a) There is very little change in the make-up of the assets and liabilities of the CGU since the most recent recoverable amount determination.

(b) The most recent recoverable amount determination yielded an amount that substantially exceeded the carrying amount of the unit

(c) Based on analyzing events since the most recent recoverable amount determination, the likelihood that a current recoverable amount determination would be less than the carrying amount of the unit is remote.

Appendix 5B

Working Paper Approach for Consolidations Subsequent to Acquisition

L03

In this chapter, we illustrated the direct approach for preparing consolidated financial statements when the parent used the cost method to account for its investment. In the examples used, we first examined the situation where the subsidiary was 100% owned, and then the situation where the parent's ownership was 80%. We will now illustrate the working paper approach using the same examples.

Year 1 Consolidated Financial Statement Working Paper

There are many different ways of using a working paper to support the preparation of consolidated financial statements.

A number of methods can be used to prepare consolidated financial statement working papers when the parent has used the cost method. All methods used must result in identical consolidated amounts. The approach that we will illustrate adjusts the parent's retained earnings account on the working paper to what they would have been if the equity method had been used to account for the investment. Since retained earnings under the equity method are equal to consolidated retained earnings, we are, in effect, adjusting the parent's cost-method retained earnings to consolidated retained earnings. The adjustment is made as of the earliest date that retained earnings are needed for the current year's financial statements. If a statement of retained earnings or a statement of changes in shareholders' equity is prepared, the balance for retained earnings is needed as of the beginning of the reporting period.

The working paper approach requires the same additional calculations used in the direct approach. Then, we make "adjustments and eliminations" similar to Chapters 3 and 4. In this chapter, we have shortened the description to "eliminations." Exhibit 5B.1 shows the preparation of the consolidated financial statements for Year 1 using a working paper, assuming Company S is a 100%-owned subsidiary of Company P. To compare it with the direct approach, see Exhibit 5.5. Before explaining the various entries, a few comments about the overall format would be useful.[8]

1. In observing the effect of the elimination entries, the reader must take into account the debit and credit balances of the financial statement items. Revenues, net income, retained earnings, liabilities, and share capital accounts have credit balances, while expenses, dividends, and assets have debit balances. The debit and credit elimination entries are either increasing or decreasing these financial statement items, depending on their nature.

2. Some elimination entries affect two or more of the financial statements, but the total debits and credits for each entry are equal.

Total debits must equal total credits on the consolidated worksheet.

3. The totals from the net income line from the income statement, including the totals of the elimination entries made there, are carried down to the net income line in the retained earnings statement. In a similar manner, the end-of-year retained earnings totals are carried down to the retained earnings on the balance sheet. Because the cumulative effect of the elimination entries from each statement has been carried down to the balance sheet, the total elimination debits and credits on that statement are equal.

EXHIBIT 5B.1

CONSOLIDATED FINANCIAL STATEMENT WORKING PAPER
December 31, Year 1 (Cost Method)

	P	S	Eliminations Dr.	Eliminations Cr.	Consolidated	
Sales	$ 50,000	$30,000			$80,000	The consolidated balances
Dividend income	2,500		(1) $ 2,500			are derived by combining
	52,500	30,000			80,000	the carrying amount from
Cost of sales	26,500	14,700	(3) 2,000		43,200	the parent's and subsidiary's
Goodwill impairment loss			(3) 50		50	separate-entity financial
Misc. expenses	5,200	8,000			13,200	statements, plus or minus
	31,700	22,700			56,450	consolidation adjustments.
Net income	$ 20,800	$ 7,300	$ 4,550	$ 0	$ 23,550*	
Retained earnings, Jan. 1	$ 85,000	$ 6,000	(2) $ 6,000		$ 85,000	
Net income	20,800	7,300	4,550	$ 0	23,550	
	105,800	13,300			108,550	
Dividends	6,000	2,500		(1) 2,500	6,000	
Retained earnings,						
Dec. 31	$ 99,800	$10,800	$10,550	$ 2,500	$102,550	
Assets, misc.	$147,800	$18,300			$166,100	
Inventory	30,000	14,000			44,000	
Investment in S	19,000			(2) 19,000		The investment account is
Acquisition differential			(2) 3,000	(3) 3,000		replaced by the carrying
Goodwill			(3) 950		950	amount of the subsidiary's
	$196,800	$32,300			$211,050	assets and liabilities plus
						the unamortized acquisition
Liabilities	$ 47,000	$11,500			$ 58,500	differential.
Common shares	50,000	10,000	(2) 10,000		50,000	
Retained earnings	99,800	10,800	10,550	2,500	102,550	
	$196,800	$32,300	$24,500	$24,500	$211,050	

* Attributable to shareholders of Company P.

Since Year 1 is the first period since the date of acquisition, the retained earnings at the beginning of Year 1 would be the same amount under both the cost and equity methods. Therefore, no adjustment is necessary to convert retained earnings at the beginning of this reporting period to the equity method.

The working paper elimination entries are reproduced below, with an explanation of each.

(1) Dividend income—Company P		2,500	
Dividends—Company S			2,500

Dividend income is eliminated against the dividends paid by the subsidiary.

The parent's dividend income does not appear in the consolidated income statement, and the subsidiary's dividends do not appear in the consolidated retained earnings statement. Therefore, these accounts need to be eliminated. Now, the revenue and expenses of the parent and subsidiary can be combined, plus or minus adjustments for amortization of the acquisition differential, to determine consolidated revenues and expenses.

The investment account is eliminated since it will be replaced by the carrying amount of the subsidiary's assets and liabilities plus the unamortized acquisition differential.

(2)

Retained earnings Jan. 1—Company S	6,000	
Common shares—Company S	10,000	
Acquisition differential	3,000	
Investment in S—Company P		19,000

This entry eliminates the parent's share of the start-of-year retained earnings and common shares of Company S, and the investment in S account of Company P, and establishes the acquisition differential at the beginning of the year. (In Year 1, this is the acquisition differential on the date of acquisition.)

(3)

Cost of sales—Company S	2,000	
Goodwill impairment loss	50	
Goodwill	950	
Acquisition differential		3,000

This entry eliminates the acquisition differential established by entry **(2)**, and allocates it in accordance with the acquisition differential amortization schedule by (a) adjusting the expenses of Company S and (b) reflecting the unamortized balance at the end of the year on the consolidated balance sheet.

Year 2 Consolidated Financial Statement Working Paper

The working papers for the preparation of the Year 2 consolidated financial statements are presented in Exhibit 5B.2. See Exhibit 5.8 to compare with the direct approach.

Elimination entry **(a)** adjusts Company P's retained earnings to the balance under the equity method as at the beginning of Year 2, which is the same balance as at the end of Year 1. Retained earnings under the equity method is equal to consolidated retained earnings. Therefore, retained earnings at the beginning of Year 2 has to be adjusted from $99,800 under the cost method to $102,550 under the equity method.

(a)

Investment in S—Company P	2,750	
Retained earnings, Jan. 1—Company P (102,550 − 99,800)		2,750

First, convert the parent's beginning retained earnings from the cost method to the equity method.

This entry adjusts the investment in S account and the January 1 retained earnings of Company P to the equity method balances at the beginning of the year. The calculation of consolidated retained earnings as at January 1, Year 2, following Exhibit 5.7 provides the amounts for this entry.

The working paper elimination entries are reproduced below, with an explanation of each.

(1)

Dividend income—Company P	3,000	
Dividends—Company S		3,000

This entry eliminates Company P's dividend income account and the dividend account of Company S. Now, the revenue and expenses of the parent and subsidiary can be combined, plus or minus adjustments for amortization of the acquisition differential, to determine consolidated revenues and expenses.

(2)

Retained earnings Jan. 1—Company S	10,800	
Common shares—Company S	10,000	
Acquisition differential	950	
Investment in S		21,750

EXHIBIT 5B.2

CONSOLIDATED FINANCIAL STATEMENT WORKING PAPER
December 31, Year 2 (Cost Method)

	P	S	Eliminations Dr.	Eliminations Cr.	Consolidated	
Sales	$ 60,000	$40,000			$100,000	The entries on the income statement are adjustments for one period to bring the accounts to the desired balance for one period of time, that is, for one year.
Dividend income	3,000		(1) $ 3,000			
	63,000	40,000			100,000	
Cost of sales	32,000	18,000			50,000	
Goodwill impairment loss			(3) 80		80	
Expenses, misc.	9,000	12,000			21,000	
	41,000	30,000			71,080	
Net income	$ 22,000	$10,000	$ 3,080	$ 0	$ 28,920*	
Retained earnings, Jan. 1	$ 99,800	$10,800	(2) $10,800	(a) $ 2,750	$102,550	
Net income	22,000	10,000	3,080	0	28,920	
	121,800	20,800			131,470	
Dividends	8,000	3,000		(1) 3,000	8,000	
Retained earnings, Dec. 31	$113,800	$17,800	$13,880	$ 5,750	$123,470	
Assets, misc.	$131,800	$21,000			$152,800	
Inventory	35,000	16,000			51,000	
Investment in S	19,000		(a) $ 2,750	(2) 21,750		
Acquisition differential			(2) 950	(3) 950		The entries on the balance sheet are cumulative adjustments to bring the accounts to the desired balance at the end of the period, that is, at a point in time.
Goodwill			(3) 870		870	
	$185,800	$37,000			$204,670	
Liabilities	$ 22,000	$ 9,200			$ 31,200	
Common shares	50,000	10,000	(2) 10,000		50,000	
Retained earnings	113,800	17,800	13,880	5,750	123,470	
	$185,800	$37,000	$28,450	$28,450	$204,670	

Attributable to shareholders of Company P.

This entry eliminates the common shares and retained earnings of Company S on December 31, Year 1, against the December 31, Year 1, balance of Company P's investment account; it also establishes the difference as the *unamortized* acquisition differential on that date.

(3)	Goodwill impairment loss	80	
	Goodwill	870	
	Acquisition differential		950

These entries bring the consolidated account balances to the desired amounts.

This entry eliminates the unamortized acquisition differential at the end of Year 1 and allocates it in accordance with the Year 2 acquisition differential amortization schedule.

80%-Owned Subsidiary—Year 1

Exhibit 5B.3 shows the preparation of the consolidated financial statements as at December 31, Year 1, using a working paper. See Exhibit 5.12 to compare with the direct approach.

The working paper entries are produced and explained below. The only new items here are the entries required to establish the non-controlling interest.

(1) Dividend income—Company P   2,000
          Dividends—Company S   2,000

This entry eliminates the dividend income against Company P's share of the dividends of Company S.

EXHIBIT 5B.3

CONSOLIDATED FINANCIAL STATEMENT WORKING PAPER
December 31, Year 1 (Cost Method)

	P	S	Eliminations Dr.	Eliminations Cr.	Consolidated
Sales	$ 50,000	$30,000			$ 80,000
Dividend income	2,000		**(1)** $ 2,000		
	52,000	30,000			80,000
Cost of sales	26,500	14,700	**(3)** 2,000		43,200
Goodwill impairment loss			**(3)** 50		50
Misc. expenses	5,200	8,000			13,200
	31,700	22,700			56,450
Net income	$ 20,300	$ 7,300			$ 23,550
Attributable to:					
Non-controlling interest			**(4)** 1,050		$ 1,050
Company P's					
shareholders					22,500
			$ 5,100	$ 0	23,550
Retained earnings,					
Jan. 1	$ 85,000	$ 6,000	**(2)** $ 6,000		$ 85,000
Net income	20,300	7,300	5,100	$ 0	22,500
	105,300	13,300			107,500
Dividends	6,000	2,500		**(1)** 2,000	6,000
				(5) 500	
Retained earnings,					
Dec. 31	$ 99,300	$10,800	$11,100	$ 2,500	$101,500
Assets, misc.	$151,100	$18,300			$169,400
Equipment (net)	30,000	14,000			44,000
Investment in S	15,200			**(2)** 15,200	
Acquisition differential			**(2)** 3,000	**(3)** 3,000	
Goodwill			**(3)** 950		950
	$196,300	$32,300			$214,350
Liabilities	$ 47,000	$11,500			$ 58,500
Common shares	50,000	10,000	**(2)** 10,000		50,000
Retained earnings	99,300	10,800	11,100	2,500	101,500
Non-controlling					
interest				**(2)** 3,800	
			(5) 500	**(4)** 1,050	4,350
	$196,300	$32,300	$25,550	$25,550	$214,350

**Side notes (left margin):**

The entries on the worksheet are recorded only on the worksheet and not in the separate-entity books of the parent or the subsidiary.

Non-controlling interest appears both on the income statement (for a period of time) and on the balance sheet (at a point in time).

(2)	Retained earnings, Jan. 1—Company S	6,000	
	Common shares—Company S	10,000	
	Acquisition differential	3,000	
	Investment in S—Company P		15,200
	Non-controlling interest		3,800

> The investment account is eliminated, since it will be replaced by the carrying value of the subsidiary's assets and liabilities, the unamortized acquisition differential, and non-controlling interest.

This entry eliminates 100% of the start-of-year shareholders' equity of Company S and the investment account, and establishes the acquisition differential and the non-controlling interest as at the beginning of the year. Note that there is no separate section of the working paper for changes in non-controlling interest. Instead, the establishment of non-controlling interest at the beginning of the year is recorded directly to non-controlling interest in the balance sheet section of the working paper. Entries (4) and (5), below, record the changes to non-controlling interest during the year. They are also recorded directly to non-controlling interest in the balance sheet section of the working paper. These entries to non-controlling interest will be needed to prepare the non-controlling interest column in the statement of changes in equity during the year.

(3)	Cost of sales—Company S	2,000	
	Goodwill impairment loss	50	
	Goodwill	950	
	Acquisition differential		3,000

In accordance with the Year 1 amortization schedule, this entry reflects the acquisition differential amortization on the consolidated income statement and the unamortized balance of the acquisition differential on the consolidated balance sheet.

| (4) | Non-controlling interest (income statement) | 1,050 | |
| | Non-controlling interest (balance sheet) | | 1,050 |

This entry allocates the net income attributable to the non-controlling interest to the non-controlling interest on the consolidated balance sheet.

| (5) | Non-controlling interest (balance sheet) | 500 | |
| | Dividends—Company S | | 500 |

This final entry eliminates 20% of the dividends of Company S that were paid to the non-controlling interest shareholders and reduces the equity of that group on the consolidated balance sheet.

80%-Owned Subsidiary—Year 2

Exhibit 5B.4 shows the working paper approach to the preparation of the Year 2 consolidated financial statements. See Exhibit 5.15 to compare with the direct approach.

Elimination entry (a) adjusts the accounts of Company P to equity method balances at the beginning of Year 2, which is the same balance as at the end of Year 1. Retained earnings under the equity method is equal to consolidated retained earnings. Therefore, retained earnings at the beginning of Year 2 has to be adjusted from $99,300 under the cost method to $101,500 under the equity method.

> Adjust the investment in subsidiary at the beginning of the current period from the balance under the cost method to the balance under the equity method.

| (a) | Investment in S—Company P | 2,200 | |
| | Retained earnings, Jan. 1—Company P (101,500 − 99,300) | | 2,200 |

EXHIBIT 5B.4

CONSOLIDATED FINANCIAL STATEMENT WORKING PAPER
December 31, Year 2 (Cost Method)

	P	S	Eliminations Dr.	Eliminations Cr.	Consolidated
Sales	$ 60,000	$40,000			$100,000
Dividend income	2,400		**(1)** $ 2,400		
	62,400	40,000			100,000
Cost of sales	32,000	18,000			50,000
Goodwill impairment loss			**(3)** 80		80
Expenses, misc.	9,000	12,000			21,000
	41,000	30,000			71,080
Net income	$ 21,400	$10,000			$ 28,920
Attributable to					
Non-controlling interest			**(4)** 1,984		$ 1,984
Company P's shareholders					
			$ 4,464	$ 0	26,936
					$ 28,920
Retained earnings,					
Jan. 1	$ 99,300	$10,800	**(2)** $10,800	**(a)** $ 2,200	$101,500
Net income	21,400	10,000	4,464	0	26,936
	120,700	20,800			128,436
Dividends	8,000	3,000		**(1)** 2,400	8,000
				(5) 600	
Retained earnings,					
Dec. 31	$112,700	$17,800	$15,264	$ 5,200	$120,436
Assets, misc.	$134,500	$21,000			$155,500
Inventory	35,000	16,000			51,000
Investment in S	15,200		**(a)** $ 2,200	**(2)** 17,400	
Acquisition differential			**(2)** 950	**(3)** 950	
Goodwill			**(3)** 870		870
	$184,700	$37,000			$207,370
Liabilities	$ 22,000	$ 9,200			$ 31,200
Common shares	50,000	10,000	**(2)** 10,000		50,000
Retained earnings	112,700	17,800	15,264	5,200	120,436
Non-controlling interest				**(2)** 4,350	5,734
			(5) 600	**(4)** 1,984	
	$184,700	$37,000	$29,884	$29,884	$207,370

Consolidated net income attributable to parent's shareholders is equal to the parent's separate-entity income under the equity method.

Consolidated retained earnings are equal to the parent's separate-entity retained earnings under the equity method.

The remaining elimination entries are produced and explained below.

(1)   Dividend income—Company P   2,400
          Dividends—Company S   2,400

This entry eliminates Company P's dividend income account against 80% of the dividends of Company S. The remaining 20% of the dividends of Company S are eliminated in entry **(5)**.

(2) Retained earnings, January 1—Company S   10,800
     Common shares—Company S   10,000
     Acquisition differential   950
       Investment in S—Company P   17,400
       Non-controlling interest   4,350

This entry eliminates 100% of the start-of-year retained earnings and common share accounts of Company S against the start-of-year balance in Company P's investment account, and it establishes both the unamortized acquisition differential and the non-controlling interest at the beginning of Year 2. The amount for non-controlling interest ($4,350) is 20% of the start-of-year common shares and retained earnings accounts of Company S, plus 20% of the unamortized acquisition differential.

(3) Goodwill impairment loss   80
     Goodwill   870
       Acquisition differential   950

Entry **(3)** allocates the unamortized acquisition differential in accordance with the Year 2 amortization schedule.

(4) Non-controlling interest (income statement)   1,984
       Non-controlling interest (balance sheet)   1,984

These journal entries appear only on the consolidated worksheet and are not posted to the separate-entity accounting records.

Entry **(4)** allocates the net income attributable to the non-controlling interest for Year 2 to the equity of the non-controlling interest on the balance sheet.

(5) Non-controlling interest (balance sheet)   600
       Dividends—Company S   600

The final entry eliminates the remaining 20% of the dividends of Company S and reduces the equity of the non-controlling interest on the balance sheet by this amount.

In this appendix, we have illustrated the working paper approach, which allows the reader to see where all of the eliminations end up. However, as we proceed with some of the more difficult aspects of consolidated statement preparation, the number of elimination entries used becomes overwhelming. Additionally, there is no set standard working paper approach. This appendix presented elimination entries associated with a financial statement working paper. Other approaches could use a different set of entries and still arrive at the same consolidated amounts. If a trial balance working paper approach had been used instead, the entries would have been different. In practice, a computerized spreadsheet or a specialized software program would probably be used in the majority of cases. The working paper entries required by these programs would no doubt be different from those illustrated here.

As you will see, working papers are not used in the chapters that follow because the major focus of this text is the direct approach, which stresses understanding of relationships rather than memorization of working paper entries. If a thorough understanding of the consolidation process is present, it can then be applied to any computerized working paper program that may be seen in practice. When consolidation questions appear on professional accounting examinations in Canada, a direct approach is invariably expected to be used when formulating an answer.

The direct approach will be used exclusively in subsequent chapters of this text.

REVIEW QUESTIONS

Questions, cases, and problems that deal with the appendix material are denoted with an asterisk.

LO1   1.   Briefly outline the process for determining if goodwill is impaired.

LO1   2.   Is the impairment test for intangibles other than goodwill the same as the one used for goodwill? Briefly explain.

LO3, 4   3.   When the parent has used the equity method, its net income equals consolidated net income attributable to its shareholders, and its retained earnings equal consolidated retained earnings. However, the parent's financial statements are not the same as consolidated statements. On consolidated statements, which assets and income are replaced from the parent's statements, and what are they replaced with?

LO5   4.   A parent company's 75%-owned subsidiary declared and paid a dividend totalling $10,000. How would the parent company record this dividend under the equity method? under the cost method?

LO5   5.   By which method , cost or equity, do IFRSs require a parent company to record its investment in a subsidiary? Why?

LO3, 4   6.   The retained earnings column in the statement of changes in equity shows dividends declared during the year. Do these dividends consist of the parent's, the subsidiary's, or both? Explain.

LO2   7.   "An acquisition differential allocated to revalue the land of a subsidiary on acquisition date will always appear on subsequent consolidated balance sheets." Do you agree? Explain.

LO5   8.   "Under the equity method, the investment account is adjusted for the investor's share of post-acquisition earnings computed by the consolidation method." Explain this statement.

LO5   9.   At the end of the year, the parent's investment account had an equity method balance of $120,000. At this time, its 75%-owned subsidiary had shareholders' equity totalling $125,000. How much was the unamortized acquisition differential at the end of the year?

LO3, 4   10.   On the consolidated balance sheet, what effect does the elimination of intercompany receivables and payables have on shareholders' equity and non-controlling interest?

LO2   11.   Explain how the matching principle is applied when amortizing the acquisition differential.

LO5   12.   What accounts in the financial statements of the parent company have balances that differ depending on whether the cost or the equity method has been used?

LO3, 4   13.   Why does adding the parent's share of the increase in retained earnings of the subsidiary and the parent's retained earnings under the cost method result in consolidated retained earnings? Assume that there is no acquisition differential.

LO3, 4   14.   A subsidiary was acquired in the middle of the fiscal year of the parent. Describe the preparation of the consolidated income statement for the year.

LO2 *15. What are the initial entries on the working paper when the parent has used the cost method to account for its investment?

LO3, 4, 5 *16. When the parent company uses the cost method, an adjustment must be made to its retained earnings on consolidation in every year after the year of acquisition. Why is this entry necessary? Why is a similar entry not required when the parent utilized the equity method?

CASES

Case 5-1
LO1

BIO Company is a private company. It employs 30 engineers and scientists who are involved with research and development of various biomedical devices. All of the engineers and scientists are highly regarded and highly paid in the field of biomedical research. BIO is 50% owned by Rod Smart, who started the company in Year 3, and 50% owned by a group of venture capitalists who contributed $10 million of equity capital in Year 4 to fund the R & D activity of the group.

On January 1, Year 6, REX Ltd., a public company listed on the TSX Venture Exchange, acquired 100% of the shares of BIO by issuing 5 million of its own shares. Its shares were trading at $4 per share on the date of this transaction.

The balance sheet for BIO on January 1, Year 6, was as follows:

Cash and marketable securities	$2,500,000
Property, plant, and equipment—net	800,000
Development costs	3,000,000
	$6,300,000
Liabilities	$ 900,000
Common shares	10,100,000
Deficit	(4,700,000)
	$6,300,000

The cash, marketable securities, property, plant and equipment, and liabilities have fair values equal to carrying amounts. Prior to Year 5, all of the research and development costs were expensed. Starting in Year 5, the developments costs were capitalized because the management of BIO felt that they were getting close to patenting some of their products.

The management of REX is aware that BIO will need to be included in REX's consolidated financial statements. Management has the following questions related to these consolidated financial statements:

Required:

(a) Will any part of the acquisition cost be allocated to BIO's skilled workers? If so, how will this asset be measured, and how will it be amortized or checked for impairment on an annual basis?

(b) Will any part of the acquisition cost be allocated to identifiable intangible assets? If so, how will this asset be measured, and how will it be amortized or checked for impairment on an annual basis?

(c) How much of the purchase price will be recognized as goodwill, and how will goodwill be evaluated for impairment on an annual basis?

Case 5-2
LO2

E

When Valero Energy Corp. acquired Ultramar Diamond Shamrock Corp. (UDS) for US$6 billion, it created the second-largest refiner of petroleum products in North America, with over 23,000 employees in the United States and Canada, total assets of $10 billion, and combined revenues of $32 billion. Combined, it had 13 refineries with a total throughput capacity of just under 2 million barrels per day (BPD); it also became one of the continent's largest retailers, with more than 5,000 retail outlets in the United States and Canada. The Canadian operations of UDS continued to operate under the Ultramar brand.

It was announced that the combination of Valero's complex refining system and an extensive UDS refining, logistics, and retail network created synergies and strategic benefits that would result in cost savings of approximately $200 million per year and the enhanced ability to compete effectively in a rapidly consolidating industry.

The retail assets included in the acquisition were the brands Ultramar, Diamond Shamrock, Beacon, and Total. UDS had more than 2,500 company-owned sites in the United States and Canada, and also supplied 2,500 dealer, truck stop, and cardlock sites. The company-owned stores had extensive brand support programs such as proprietary consumer and fleet credit cards, radio and television brand support, and strong in-store marketing programs, to which Valero was able to add its 350-store retail network in California. In addition, UDS operated one of the largest home heating oil businesses in North America, selling heating oil to approximately 250,000 households.

The acquisition clearly included more than the physical assets of Ultramar Diamond Shamrock. A variety of unrecorded intangible assets were represented in the portfolio of assets held by UDS, and these are the matters that require your attention at this time.

Required:

With reference to IFRS 3, prepare a memorandum including the following items to the chief financial officer of Valero:

- Discuss the valuation of the various intangible assets included in this acquisition.
- Indicate which items should be included in the amount assigned to goodwill in the acquisition.
- Indicate which items should be separately identified as intangible assets.
- Discuss how you would measure the various items identified and what amortization policy (if any) is appropriate.

(case prepared by Peter Secord, St. Mary's University)

Case 5-3
LO3

It is now mid-September Year 3. Growth Investments Limited (GIL) has been owned by Sam and Ida Growth since its incorporation under the Canada Business Corporations Act many years ago. The owners, who are both 55 years of age, have decided to effect a corporate reorganization of capital in the form of an estate freeze. Sam and Ida will maintain control by holding voting preferred shares that carry a fixed dividend. New common shares will be issued to the three Growth children and to Mario Thibeault, a GIL manager who has been with the company since its inception.

GIL operates primarily in the real estate industry. It holds raw land, which will be subdivided and sold in the future, and it owns a variety of revenue-producing properties. The land and the properties are either directly or through wholly owned subsidiaries. A valuation of GIL's net assets will be done as of November 30, Year 3, the date of the proposed corporate reorganization.

Innes & Panners has audited GIL's financial statements for the past several years. The financial statements are used by the owners and the company's banker as well as for tax purposes. One of the rights of the preferred shareholders (Sam and Ida) will be to have audited financial statements for GIL's year-end, which has always been November 30.

You, the CA, have been hired as a consultant to GIL for the year ending November 30, Year 3. The board of directors of GIL has engaged your firm, at the request of Mario Thibeault, to advise on alternatives available with respect to accounting and reporting policies for the company for Year 3 and subsequent years. This engagement is separate from the audit engagement.

You will prepare a report that should be addressed to the board of directors of GIL. It should outline the feasible accounting and reporting alternatives that exist in preparing audited, comparative financial statements for Year 3 and subsequent years.

You and your staff have learned the following about GIL's activities during the current fiscal year:

1. Under the plan for reorganizing capital, Sam and Ida are to be issued preferred shares on November 30, Year 3 in exchange for all their common shares. The preferred shares will be redeemable at the fair value of the company as determined at November 30, Year 3. Each of the four new shareholders will pay $100 for 25% of the new voting common shares of GIL. The valuation of GIL's net assets is nearly complete.

2. Except for one parcel of raw land, all of GIL's real estate assets have an appraisal value that exceeds cost, or cost less capital cost allowance to date. (GIL has always used income tax methods and rates for depreciation purposes.) Each asset's fair value is based on an estimated net selling price as at November 30, Year 3. For the one parcel of raw land, fair value is expected to be approximately 70% of cost.

3. Current five-year mortgage interest rates on properties similar to GIL's range between 10% and 10 ½% per annum. GIL's debt, as of November 30, Year 3, will consist of:

$2,200,000;	14% rate; due in 3 years
1,600,000;	8% rate; due in 4 years
1,300,000;	10 ½% rate; due to bank on demand

4. In December Year 2, GIL sold an apartment building for $2,500,000 in a province that is subject to rent controls and took back a non–interest bearing note. Payments of $500,000 per year are due on December 15 for each of the next five years, commencing in Year 3. GIL's financial statements at August 31, Year 3, show the $2,500,000 as a current asset.

5. In all years to November 30, Year 2, GIL had expensed real estate taxes and interest on debt incurred to finance raw land purchases. The new shareholders have asked whether these sums ought to be capitalized retroactively for all raw land held at November 29, Year 3.

6. An application is pending to have one of GIL's apartment buildings converted to condominium status. Several levels of government have to approve the conversion, but ultimate approval is expected in Year 4 because other buildings in the vicinity have already been accepted as condominiums.

When approval is received, the fair value of this building will increase from $4,300,000 to about $5,700,000. Each condominium apartment unit will be offered for sale to its occupants, or to others.

7. GIL leases its head office building space on a 20-year lease; 14 years are left in the lease. GIL pays $100,000 per year plus all occupancy costs such as light, heat, insurance, and cleaning. Current leasing costs have increased, and GIL would have to pay $220,000 per year for equivalent space in the same building if it were to sign a lease in Year 3. The financial statements at November 30, Year 2 treat the head office situation as an operating lease. They contain a short note on lease obligations.

8. Construction of a shopping centre is in progress for GIL. A fixed-price contract for $8 million has been signed with a construction company, which has undertaken to complete the centre by August Year 4. Financing for 10 years at 12% interest per annum on a $6 million mortgage has been approved. GIL purchased the land on which the centre is being located several years ago. It paid $750,000 for the land and sold one-half interest to the 50% partner for $1,800,000 in December Year 2. Approximately one-half of the shopping centre space has been leased for 5 or 10 years commencing August Year 4. Several of the leases contain escalation-of-rent clauses tied to store sales. GIL paid a demolition company $120,000 in December Year 2 to clear old farm buildings and fences and ready the site for construction. It also paid $110,000 in July Year 3 to the agent who arranged the leases.

9. In December Year 2, GIL sold a small office building for $4,200,000 cash, and paid off the $2 million mortgage on the property plus a penalty of $82,000. The purchase/sale agreement contains a clause that enables GIL to receive sums additional to the $4,200,000 if rental receipts for the next four years exceed an average of $700,000 per year. On the basis of new leases signed by the purchaser in Year 3, GIL ought to be receiving some additional compensation each year.

10. Traditionally, the senior management of GIL has received a bonus based on audited net income.

Required:

Prepare the report to the Board of Directors.

(CICA adapted)

Case 5-4
LO2, 7

Total Protection Limited (TPL) was incorporated on January 1, Year 1, by five homebuilders in central Canada to provide warranty protection for new-home buyers. Each shareholder owns a 20% interest in TPL. While most homebuilders provide one-year warranties, TPL offers ten-year warranties and includes protection for a number of items not usually covered. For example, if a problem arose as a result of faulty construction or construction materials, TPL would protect its customers against any resulting decline in the market value of their property and would provide for the costs of restoring the property. TPL does not, however, cover general declines in market value.

The five shareholders believe TPL will increase their home sales and at the same time minimize their individual risks. The idea for TPL originated with Safe-Way Builders and, therefore, this shareholder will receive a royalty payment of 5% of income before income taxes. The shareholders have engaged your firm to prepare a report that will assist them in managing TPL in order to maximize its long-term profitability.

In particular, they are wondering whether TPL is pricing its services appropriately and adequately controlling its costs. In addition, as a separate report, the shareholders would like your firm to recommend appropriate financial accounting policies for TPL.

It is mid-December Year 1. You, the CA, and the partner on the engagement, meet with Gina Filmore, president of Safe-Way Builders. Filmore is currently operating TPL from the offices of Safe-Way Builders, for which TPL will be charged rent. Filmore provides you with the following information on TPL's operations.

"TPL's revenues consist of an initial fee paid at the time of purchase of the warranty and an annual maintenance fee paid over the term of the warranty. Currently, the initial fee and annual maintenance fee depend on a number of factors, including the cost of the home, reputation of the builder, construction design of the home (e.g., brick versus aluminum siding), and the home's location. The warranties are sold through each builder, who can adjust the initial fee and the annual maintenance fee if it is considered necessary to make the sale. The builder receives a commission of 10% of the total warranty revenue, which should ensure that the builder would try to maximize the initial fee and the annual maintenance fee. Typically, a buyer of a brick house worth $250,000 that was constructed by a good-quality builder should expect to pay an initial fee of $2,000 plus an annual maintenance fee of $250.

"To date, TPL has been doing very well, primarily as a result of two factors: central Canada has been experiencing a boom in the residential construction industry, and TPL has expanded to offer coverage for homes built by builders other than the shareholders. Quite frankly, an increasing share of our business is from these outside builders, many of which have entered the industry just to try to capitalize on the demand. We don't think that permitting these homebuilders to sell coverage will hurt our home sales, since most of them are in the low-price segment of the market, keeping costs down by employing new, less expensive construction methods and materials. We require that their initial fee be at least $1,500 per home to ensure that they don't lower the price just to make a sale.

"Our real problem is keeping up with the paperwork. I have my own business to run and cannot devote much time to TPL. We haven't even had time to get organized or set up any system for TPL. Lately, I must admit that I've lost track of what's going on. All I know is that we're making money. In just 11 months, TPL has collected about $1.6 million while paying out only $224,000 in repair costs. Keep in mind, however, that I've been able to keep these repair costs down by having Safe-Way Builders do the repairs. Business will only get better when we expand within the next month to offer coverage in western Canada and the southwestern United States.

"Since we have accumulated a lot of cash, we recently decided, in a 3-to-2 vote among the shareholders, to buy 100% of the shares of Gainery Construction Ltd., a local construction company. Mr. Gainery, the owner of the company, had a heart attack about six months ago and wanted to get out of the business. Details of the purchase agreement are provided in Exhibit I."

Just before you leave the client's premises, you manage to collect some additional information on the operations of TPL (see Exhibit II).

When you return to the office, the partner reminds you that he will be meeting with TPL shareholders in one week and asks you to prepare the reports requested by the shareholders.

Required:

Prepare the reports requested by the partner.

(CICA adapted)

EXHIBIT I

INFORMATION GATHERED FROM PURCHASE AGREEMENT

1. Closing date will be December 31, Year 1.
2. TPL will purchase 100% of the shares of Gainery Construction Ltd. for $500,000 in cash on closing, plus $500,000 per year for the next two years.
3. Mr. Gainery will provide, without additional consideration, a minimum of 300 hours of consulting services in the first year and a minimum of 150 hours in the second year, to ensure a smooth transition of the business.
4. The carrying amount and estimated fair value of identifiable assets and liabilities were as follows on the date of acquisition:

	Carrying value	Fair value
Cash	$ 100,000	$ 100,000
Accounts receivable	200,000	200,000
Homes under construction	1,300,000	1,500,000
Undeveloped land	1,000,000	1,600,000
Equipment, net	700,000	650,000
Other assets	70,000	70,000
	$3,370,000	$4,120,000
Liabilities	$2,470,000	$2,470,000
Common shares	100,000	
Retained earnings	800,000	
	$3,370,000	

EXHIBIT II

INFORMATION GATHERED FROM CLIENT'S RECORDS
TPL Shareholders

	Larkview Estates	Towne Homes	Granite Homes	Kings Road	Safe-Way Builders	Other Builders	Total
Number of warranties sold	50	85	190	250	175	465	1,215
Warranty revenue ($000s)	$120	$165	$395	$90	$160	$705	$1,635
Repair costs incurred ($000s)	$ 6	$ 9	$ 21	$42	$ 39	$107	$ 224

Case 5-5
LO3, 6, 7
Beaver Ridge Oilers' Players Association and Mr. Slim, the CEO of the Beaver Ridge Oilers Hockey Club (Club), ask for your help in resolving a salary dispute. Mr. Slim presents the following income statement to the player representatives:

BEAVER RIDGE OILERS HOCKEY CLUB INCOME STATEMENT

Ticket revenues		$3,000,000
Player salaries	$ 600,000	
Stadium rent	2,100,000	
Staff salaries	500,000	
Advertising	200,000	3,400,000
Net income (loss)		$ (400,000)

Mr. Slim argues that the Club loses money and cannot afford a salary increase. After further investigation, you determine that the Club owns 90% of the voting shares of Oilers Stadium Inc. (Stadium), which is used primarily by the Oilers. The Club accounts for its investment in the Stadium under the cost method. The Stadium has not declared any dividends since its inception three years ago. As such, the Club has never reported any income on its investment in the Stadium.

Mr. Slim insists that the income for the Stadium should not be a factor in the negotiation of the players' salaries since the Stadium is a separate legal entity and is taxed as a separate legal entity. The income statement for the Stadium is as follows:

OILERS STADIUM INC. INCOME STATEMENT

Stadium rent revenue	$2,100,000	
Concession revenue	1,200,000	
Parking revenue	100,000	$3,400,000
Cost of concessions	400,000	
Depreciation of stadium	500,000	
Staff salaries	700,000	1,600,000
Net income		$1,800,000

Required:

(a) What advice would you give the negotiating parties regarding the issue of whether to consider the Stadium's income in the salary negotiations? Give supporting arguments. Indicate what other pertinent information you would need to provide specific recommendations.

(b) How would your advice change if the Stadium were 90% owned by Mr. Slim directly rather than by the Club? Explain.

Case 5-6
LO1, 5, 6, 7

Gerry's Fabrics Ltd. (GFL), a private company, manufactures a variety of clothing for women and children and sells it to retailers across Canada. Until recently, the company has operated from the same plant since its incorporation under federal legislation 40 years ago. Over the years, the profits of the company have varied widely, and there have been periods of losses.

In the year ended March 31, Year 1, the company entered into an arrangement whereby it issued common shares from treasury to a group of new shareholders. At the same time, the existing shareholders were given the option of exchanging their common shares for preferred shares, which are redeemable at the option of the company and retractable at the option of the shareholder. One shareholder, who had held 25 percent of the common shares, elected to accept the preferred shares, while the other shareholders elected to retain their common shares.

A "Preferred Share Agreement" (the Agreement), was signed by the shareholder who had accepted the preferred shares (the "preferred shareholder"). Under the Agreement, the preferred shareholder can require GFL to redeem all of his shares in any year, after giving at least 90 days' notice prior to the fiscal year-end. The Agreement does not provide for partial redemptions. The total redemption price for all shares is 1.25 times "income before taxes" for that year. The term *income before taxes* is defined in the Agreement as follows:

1. Income before taxes for the year of redemption must be calculated
   - in accordance with the accounting policies set forth in this Agreement, or
   - where no accounting policy has been clearly specified, in accordance with policies consistent in intent with the policies contained in this Agreement.
2. Income before taxes for the year of redemption need not, for the purposes of the Agreement, be the same as that which is reported to shareholders or that which is used for calculating income taxes payable.

The Agreement specifies the applicable accounting policies as follows:

A. Revenue recognition:

1. In cases where a deposit of 10 percent or more of the sales price has been received from the customer, revenue shall be recognized on completion of the manufacturing of the goods ordered.

2. In all other cases, revenue shall be recognized upon shipment to the customer, and no allowance shall be made for returned merchandise or adjustments.

B. Cost of goods sold and inventory:

1. All inventory on hand at the end of a fiscal year (excluding raw materials) shall be costed at actual production costs, including its full share of all overhead expenditures.

2. Raw materials inventory shall include all expenditures that were needed to make the inventory available for use, including unpacking and storing costs.

C. Amortization:

1. All applicable amortization shall be computed on a straight-line basis using realistic residual values.

2. Amortization shall be recorded over the physical life of the assets, regardless of their useful life to the company.

3. No amortization shall be recorded on assets that are increasing in value.

D. Capitalization:

1. All expenditures shall be capitalized as assets unless their life is limited to the current financial period. All maintenance and repair costs that extend an asset's useful life shall be capitalized.

2. Assets shall be recorded at cost and amortized in accordance with C above.

E. Liabilities:

1. Each liability shall be recorded at the amount required to settle the obligation. A debt-to-equity ratio of 1:1 is assumed to exist. Interest incurred on debt in excess of this ratio will not be deductible in computing income before taxes.

F. Errors and adjustments:

1. All errors, adjustments, and changes in value shall be attributed to the year to which the error or adjustment or change relates.

G. Compensation and related transactions:

1. Average compensation per employee shall be in accordance with levels used in fiscal Year 1 adjusted by the Consumer Price Index.

2. All related-party transactions must be measured at fair value or values established in the marketplace for transactions between GFL and unrelated third parties.

The Agreement also contains a separate clause that deals with "arbitration procedures." These procedures allow an independent arbitrator to calculate the share redemption price after having obtained full access to the books and records of GFL.

The preferred shareholder has advised GFL of his intention to have GFL redeem his preferred shares and has provided GFL with the required 90 days' notice. The redemption price, calculated by GFL, was based on the March 31, Year 5, financial statements. However, the preferred shareholder disagrees with GFL's figure for income before taxes.

Since the price is being disputed, the matter is to be resolved by an independent arbitrator. Both parties have agreed to engage Cook & Co., Chartered Accountants, to make a binding decision. You, CA, are employed by Cook & Co. The engagement partner has asked you to prepare a memo providing complete analyses required for and recommendations to be considered in the calculation of the share-redemption price. Your notes from your investigations are contained in Exhibit III.

Required:

Prepare the memo to the partner.

(CICA adapted)

EXHIBIT III

NOTES FROM INVESTIGATION OF GFL

1. The disputed share-redemption price calculation was prepared by the vice-president of finance of GFL and is 1.25 times the company's unaudited income before taxes of $895,420 for the year ended March 31, Year 5.

2. The unaudited financial statements for the year ended March 31, Year 5, reflect the following transactions and accounting policies:

   - During fiscal Year 4, GFL acquired all the shares of a competing company (J Ltd.) for $8 million. Most of the amount by which the purchase price exceeded the book value of the assets and liabilities acquired was recorded as goodwill and is being amortized over 10 years. The purchase was financed almost entirely by debt at 10 percent interest for five years.
   - On January 1, Year 5, a volume discount policy was introduced. At March 31, Year 5, an estimated liability of $95,500 was provided for volume discounts that may become due.
   - In fiscal Year 4, the manufacturing processes were altered to introduce more mechanization, and standard costing was adopted. All variances from standard costs are being expensed.
   - In order to reduce taxable income and save cash, all employee incentives are being accrued at year-end and paid five months later.
   - In Year 3, GFL decided to account for one of its successful investments on the equity basis. During fiscal Year 5, the directors of GFL chose to revert to the cost basis for the investment.
   - In fiscal Year 5, GFL commenced construction of another manufacturing facility at a cost of $1.8 million, including equipment. Some manufacturing occurred in a part of the new facility before the whole facility was ready for use. To be conservative, any costs that were incurred after manufacturing had commenced were expensed, except for new equipment installations.
   - Land that has been held for several years for future expansion of the company was recorded at cost plus carrying costs (property taxes, maintenance, and similar) until fiscal Year 5. The land was reclassified in late fiscal Year 5 as inventory and was written down to the lower of cost and net realizable value.
   - In March Year 5, GFL sold some of its capital assets under a deferred payment arrangement. Gains on disposal will be recorded as payment is received, on a proportional basis.
   - In April Year 5, an enhanced executive pension plan was introduced. The March 31, Year 5, financial statements include pension expenses that reflect the additional costs resulting from the new pension plan enhancements.

3. Notes to the financial statements for fiscal Year 5 disclose the following:

   - During the year, GFL sold $4 million worth of goods to DGR Ltd. DGR is owned by several of the common shareholders of GFL. DGR paid a special price for goods that was about $380,000 lower than the price paid by other retailers.
   - A $200,000 liability has been recorded for legal costs pertaining to a patent infringement case that is before the courts.

PROBLEMS

Problem 5-1
L02, 3, 5

When Pill Ltd. acquired 85% of Sill Corporation on January 1, Year 1, for $238,000, the imputed acquisition differential of $60,000 was allocated entirely to goodwill. On December 31, Year 1, a goodwill impairment loss of $1,500 was recognized. Pill uses the cost method for internal purposes to account for its investment. Pill reported a separate-entity Year 1 net income of $25,000 and declared no dividends. Sill reported a separate-entity net income of $40,000 and paid dividends of $9,000 in Year 1.

Required:

Compute the following:

(a) Consolidated net income attributable to Pill's shareholders for Year 1.
(b) Consolidated net income attributable to non-controlling interest that would appear on the Year 1 consolidated income statement.
(c) Investment in Sill at December 31, Year 1 (equity method).

Problem 5-2
L02, 3, 5

Large Ltd. purchased 75% of Small Company on January 1, Year 1, for $600,000, when the statement of financial position for Small showed common shares of $400,000 and retained earnings of $100,000. On that date, the inventory of Small was undervalued by $40,000, and a patent with an estimated remaining life of 5 years was overvalued by $70,000.

Small reported the following subsequent to January 1, Year 1:

	Profit	Dividends
Year 1	$ 80,000	$25,000
Year 2 (loss)	(35,000)	10,000
Year 3	90,000	40,000

A test for goodwill impairment on December 31, Year 3, indicated a loss of $19,300 being recorded for Year 3 on the consolidated income statement. Large uses the cost method to account for its investment in Small and reported the following for Year 3 for its separate-entity statement of changes in equity:

Retained earnings, beginning	$500,000
Profit	200,000
Dividends	(70,000)
Retained earnings, end	$630,000

Required:

(a) Prepare the cost method journal entries of Large for each year.
(b) Compute the following on the consolidated financial statements for the year ended December 31, Year 3:

    (i) Goodwill
    (ii) Non-controlling interest on the statement of financial position
    (iii) Retained earnings, beginning of year
    (iv) Profit attributable to Large's shareholders
    (v) Profit attributable to non-controlling interest

(c) Now assume that Large is a private entity, uses ASPE, and chooses to use the equity method to report its investment in Small.

  (i) Prepare Large's journal entries for each year related to its investment in Small.

  (ii) Determine the investment in Small at December 31, Year 3.

Problem 5-3
LO2, 3

On January 1, Year 2, Gros Corporation acquired 70% of the outstanding common shares of Petite Company for a total cost of $84,000. On that date, Petite had $35,000 of common shares and $25,000 of retained earnings. The carrying amounts of each of Petite's identifiable assets and liabilities were equal to their fair values except for the following:

	Carrying amount	Fair value
Inventory	$45,000	$55,000
Equipment	70,000	90,000

The equipment had an estimated useful life of 10 years as at January 1, Year 2, and the entire inventory was sold during Year 2.

Selected account balances from the records of Gros and Petite for the year ended December 31, Year 6, were as follows:

	Gros	Petite
Inventory	$150,000	$ 80,000
Equipment, net	326,000	160,000
Goodwill		
Retained earnings, end of year	270,000	50,000
Non-controlling interest on balance sheet		
Cost of goods purchased	500,000	450,000
Change in inventory	20,000	12,000
Amortization expense	35,000	20,000
Non-controlling interest on income statement		
Net income	90,000	48,000
Dividends paid	30,000	10,000

Additional Information

- Gros uses the cost method to account for its investment in Petite.
- An independent valuator has estimated that the goodwill associated with Gros's acquisition of Petite had a recoverable amount of $28,000 as of December 31, Year 6. (Note: No impairment losses have been recognized in all years prior to Year 6.)

Required:

(a) Determine the amounts on the Year 6 consolidated financial statements for the above-noted accounts.

(b) If the independent appraisal of the recoverable amount for goodwill as at December 31, Year 6, showed an amount of $8,000 instead of the $28,000 indicated above, what would be the impact on the following?

  (i) Consolidated net income attributable to Gros's shareholders

  (ii) Consolidated retained earnings

  (iii) Consolidated net income attributable to non-controlling interest

Problem 5-4
LO3, 5

Summarized balance sheets of Corner Company and its subsidiary Brook Corpo-ration on December 31, Year 4, were as follows:

	Corner	Brook	Consolidated
Current assets	$ 160,000	$ 700,000	$ 860,000
Investment in Brook (cost)	640,000		
Other assets	600,000	900,000	1,500,000
	$1,400,000	$1,600,000	$2,360,000
Liabilities	$ 800,000	$ 200,000	$1,000,000
Common shares	900,000	600,000	900,000
Retained earnings	(300,000)	800,000	180,000
Non-controlling interest	—	—	280,000
	$1,400,000	$1,600,000	$2,360,000

On the date that Corner acquired its interest in Brook, there was no acquisi-tion differential and the carrying amounts of Brook's net assets were equal to fair values. During Year 4, Corner reported a net loss of $60,000, while Brook reported a net income of $140,000. No dividends were declared by either company during Year 4. Corner uses the cost method to account for its investment.

Required:

Compute the following:

(a) The percentage of Brook's shares owned by Corner
(b) Consolidated net income attributable to Corner's shareholders for Year 4
(c) Corner's December 31, Year 3, retained earnings if it had used the equity method to account for its investment
(d) The retained earnings of Brook on the date that Corner acquired its interest in Brook

Problem 5-5
LO2, 3, 5

Pen Ltd. acquired an 85% interest in Silk Corp. on December 31, Year 1, for $646,000. On that date, Silk had common shares of $500,000 and retained earn-ings of $100,000. The imputed acquisition differential was allocated $70,000 to inventory, with the balance to patents being amortized over 10 years. Silk reported profit of $30,000 in Year 2 and $52,000 in Year 3. While no dividends were declared in Year 2, Silk declared a dividend of $15,000 in Year 3.

Pen, which uses the cost method, reported a profit of $28,000 in Year 2 and a *loss* of $45,000 in Year 3. Pen's retained earnings on December 31, Year 3, were $91,000.

Required:

Compute the following:

(a) Non-controlling interest in profit for Year 2 and Year 3
(b) Consolidated profit attributable to Pen's shareholders for Year 2 and Year 3
(c) Consolidated retained earnings at December 31, Year 3
(d) Non-controlling interest at December 31, Year 3
(e) Investment in Silk at December 31, Year 3, if Pen had used the equity method
(f) Consolidated patents at December 31, Year 3

Problem 5-6
LO2, 3, 5

Peach Ltd. acquired 70% of the common shares of Cherry Company on January 1, Year 4. On that date, Cherry had common shares of $600,000 and retained earnings of $300,000.

The following is a summary of the changes in Peach's investment account from January 1, Year 4, to December 31, Year 6:

INVESTMENT IN CHERRY

January 1, Year 4	Cost	$651,000
December 31, Year 4	Investment income	51,800
	Dividends	(28,000)
December 31, Year 5	Investment income	63,700
	Dividends	(35,000)
December 31, Year 6	Investment income	78,400
	Dividends	(42,000)
	Balance	$739,900

Additional Information

- Dividends declared by Cherry each year were equal to 50% of Cherry's reported profit each year.
- On January 1, Year 4, the carrying amounts of the identifiable net assets of Cherry were equal to fair values.

Required:

Calculate the following:

(a) The amount of dividends declared by Cherry in Year 4
(b) The reported profit of Cherry for Year 5
(c) The amount for non-controlling interest that would appear in the Year 6 consolidated income statement and statement of financial position
(d) The amount of goodwill that would appear on the December 31, Year 6, consolidated statement of financial position

Problem 5-7
LO2, 3

not use linear for NCI

On January 1, Year 4, Grant Corporation bought 8,000 (80%) of the outstanding common shares of Lee Company for $70,000 cash. Lee's shares were trading for $7 per share on the date of acquisition. On that date, Lee had $25,000 of common shares outstanding and $30,000 retained earnings. Also on that date, the carrying amount of each of Lee's identifiable assets and liabilities was equal to its fair value except for the following:

	Carrying amount	Fair value
Inventory	$50,000	$55,000
Patent	10,000	20,000

The patent had an estimated useful life of 5 years at January 1, Year 4, and the entire inventory was sold during Year 4. Grant uses the cost method to account for its investment.

Additional Information

- The recoverable amount for goodwill was determined to be $10,000 on December 31, Year 6. The goodwill impairment loss occurred in Year 6.
- Grant's accounts receivable contains $30,000 owing from Lee.
- Amortization expense is grouped with distribution expenses and impairment losses are grouped with other expenses.

The following are the separate-entity financial statements of Grant and Lee as at December 31, Year 6.

BALANCE SHEETS
December 31, Year 6

	Grant	Lee
Assets		
Cash	$ 5,000	$ 18,000
Accounts receivable	185,000	82,000
Inventory	310,000	100,000
Investment in Lee	70,000	—
Equipment, net	230,000	205,000
Patent, net	—	2,000
	$800,000	$407,000
Liabilities and Shareholders' Equity		
Accounts payable	$190,000	$195,000
Other accrued liabilities	60,000	50,000
Income taxes payable	80,000	72,000
Common shares	170,000	25,000
Retained earnings	300,000	65,000
	$800,000	$407,000

INCOME STATEMENT
Year ended December 31, Year 6

	Grant	Lee
Sales	$900,000	$360,000
Cost of goods sold	(340,000)	(240,000)
Gross margin	560,000	120,000
Distribution expense	(30,000)	(25,000)
Other expenses	(180,000)	(56,000)
Income tax expense	(120,000)	(16,000)
Net income	$230,000	$ 23,000

Required:

(a) Calculate consolidated retained earnings at December 31, Year 6.

(b) Prepare consolidated financial statements for Year 6.

Problem 5-8
LO2, 3   Paris Corporation and Slater Company prepared the following statements of income and retained earnings on December 31 of the current year:

	Paris	Slater
Sales	$900,000	$500,000
Dividend income	60,000	—
	960,000	500,000
Cost of sales	600,000	300,000
Operating expenses	200,000	80,000
	800,000	380,000
Net income	160,000	120,000
Retained earnings, January 1	301,000	584,000
	461,000	704,000
Dividends	150,000	75,000
Retained earnings, December 31	$311,000	$629,000

Paris obtained its 80% interest in Slater 8 years ago when Slater had retained earnings of $53,000. The $100,000 acquisition differential on acquisition date was allocated entirely to intangible assets with an estimated remaining useful life of 10 years. Paris uses the cost method to account for its investment.

Required:

Prepare the following statements for the current year:

(a) Consolidated income statement
(b) Consolidated retained earnings statement

Problem 5-9
LO2, 3

On July 1, Year 5, Big purchased 80% of the outstanding common shares of Little for $122,080. On that date, Little's equipment had a fair value that was $21,600 less than carrying amount. The equipment had accumulated depreciation of $20,000 and an estimated remaining useful life of 8 years. Also, at the date of acquisition, Little had an exclusive contract with the provincial government to perform periodic environmental audits of selected mining companies for the next five years. An independent business valuator indicated that a third party might pay up to $50,000 to take over this contract. All other assets and liabilities had carrying amounts equal to fair values. On June 30, Year 6, goodwill had a recoverable amount of $20,000.

On June 30, Year 6, the following financial statements were prepared. Big uses the cost method to account for its investment.

INCOME STATEMENTS

	Big	Little
Sales	$ 270,000	$162,000
Investment income	10,800	—
	280,800	162,000
Cost of sales	140,100	94,380
Expenses (misc.)	31,080	28,200
	171,180	122,580
Net income	$ 109,620	$ 39,420

RETAINED EARNINGS STATEMENTS

	Big	Little
Balance, July 1	$ 459,000	$ 32,400
Net income	109,620	39,420
	568,620	71,820
Dividends	32,400	13,500
Balance, June 30	$ 536,220	$ 58,320

BALANCE SHEETS—June 30, Year 6

	Big	Little
Miscellaneous assets	$ 835,940	$128,820
Equipment	162,000	95,600
Accumulated depreciation	(60,000)	(50,000)
Investment in Little	122,080	—
	$1,060,020	$174,420
Liabilities	$ 253,800	$ 62,100
Common shares	270,000	54,000
Retained earnings	536,220	58,320
	$1,060,020	$174,420

Required:

(a) Prepare a schedule to calculate and allocate the acquisition differential. Explain the rationale for the accounting treatment of the $50,000 attributed to the government contract.

(b) Prepare the consolidated financial statements of Big as at June 30, Year 6.

(c) Prepare a schedule showing the changes in non-controlling interest during the year.

Problem 5-10
LO2, 3, 6

On December 31, Year 2, Palm Inc. purchased 80% of the outstanding ordinary shares of Storm Company for $310,000. At that date, Storm had ordinary shares of $200,000 and retained earnings of $60,000. In negotiating the purchase price, it was agreed that the assets on Storm's statement of financial position were fairly valued except for plant assets, which had a $40,000 excess of fair value over carrying amount. It was also agreed that Storm had unrecognized intangible assets consisting of trademarks that had an estimated value of $24,000. The plant assets had a remaining useful life of 8 years at the acquisition date and the trademarks would be amortized over a 12-year period. Any goodwill arising from this business combination would be tested periodically for impairment. Palm accounts for its investment using the cost method.

Additional Information

• At December 31, Year 5, an impairment test of Storm's goodwill revealed the following:

Fair value less disposal costs based on recent offer from prospective purchaser	$46,000
Value in use based on undiscounted future net cash flows	65,000
Value in use based on discounted future net cash flows using a discount rate of	
6%, which is Storm's incremental borrowing rate	50,000
3%, which is the risk-free rate on government bonds	55,000

• An impairment test indicated that the trademarks had a recoverable amount of $13,750. The impairment loss on these assets occurred entirely in Year 6.

• On December 26, Year 6, Palm declared dividends of $36,000, while Storm declared dividends of $20,000.

• Amortization expense is reported in selling expenses, while impairment losses are reported in other expenses.

Financial statements for Palm and Storm for the year ended December 31, Year 6, were as follows:

STATEMENTS OF FINANCIAL POSITION
December 31, Year 6

	Palm	Storm
Assets		
Plant assets—net	$230,000	$160,000
Investment in Storm	310,000	—
Other investments	82,000	22,000
Notes receivable	—	10,000
Inventory	100,000	180,000
Accounts receivable	88,000	160,000
Cash	20,000	30,000
	$830,000	$562,000

(continued)

	Palm	Storm
Shareholders' Equity and Liabilities		
Ordinary shares	$500,000	$200,000
Retained earnings	110,000	150,000
Notes payable	130,000	100,000
Other current liabilities	10,000	50,000
Accounts payable	80,000	62,000
	$830,000	$562,000

INCOME STATEMENTS
Year ended December 31, Year 6

	Palm	Storm
Sales	$870,000	$515,000
Cost of goods sold	(638,000)	(360,000)
Gross profit	232,000	155,000
Selling expenses	(22,000)	(35,000)
Other expenses	(148,000)	(72,000)
Interest and dividend income	34,000	2,000
Profit	$ 96,000	$ 50,000

Required:

(a) Prepare consolidated financial statements.

(b) If none of the acquisition differential had been allocated to trademarks at the date of acquisition, how would this affect

   (i) the return on total shareholders' equity for Year 6?

   (ii) the debt-to-equity ratio at the end of Year 6?

Problem 5-11
LO2, 3, 4

On July 1, Year 4, Aaron Co. purchased 80% of the voting shares of Bondi Ltd. for $543,840. The statement of financial position of Bondi on that date follows. The accounts receivable of Bondi were collected in October Year 4, and the inventory was completely sold by May Year 5. Bondi's fixed assets had a remaining life of 15 years on July 1, Year 4, and the bonds payable mature on June 30, Year 8. The bonds were issued on July 1, Year 1. The stated rate of interest on the bonds is 6% payable semi-annually. The market rate of interest was 8% on July 1, Year 4. Tests for impairment of goodwill indicated a loss of $8,329 in Year 5 and $5,553 in Year 6.

BONDI LTD.
STATEMENT OF FINANCIAL POSITION
as at July 1, Year 4

	Carrying amount	Fair value
Plant assets (net)	$540,000	$450,000
Inventory	180,000	228,000
Accounts receivable	120,000	144,004
Cash	96,000	96,000
	$936,000	
Ordinary shares	$120,000	
Retained earnings	508,800	
Bonds payable	200,000	186,534
Current liabilities	107,200	107,200
	$936,000	

The financial statements for Aaron and Bondi at December 31, Year 6, are presented below. Aaron has used the equity method to account for its investment in Bondi.

STATEMENTS OF FINANCIAL POSITION

	Aaron	Bondi
Plant assets (net)	$ 720,000	$ 540,000
Investment in Bondi	520,319	—
Other investments	250,666	—
Inventory	300,000	276,000
Accounts receivable	180,000	114,000
Cash	120,000	84,000
	$2,090,985	$1,014,000
Ordinary shares	$ 300,600	$ 120,000
Retained earnings	1,295,185	558,200
Bonds payable	315,000	200,000
Current liabilities	180,200	135,800
	$2,090,985	$1,014,000

INCOME STATEMENTS

	Aaron	Bondi
Sales	$1,261,000	$1,200,000
Investment income from Bondi	4,394	—
Income from other investments	25,000	—
	1,290,394	1,200,000
Raw materials used	880,000	1,005,000
Change in inventory	(40,000)	15,000
Depreciation	60,000	54,000
Interest expense	37,000	26,400
Other expenses	227,000	91,200
	1,164,000	1,191,600
Profit	$ 126,394	$ 8,400

Required:

(a) Prepare the consolidated financial statements for the year ended December 31, Year 6.

(b) Calculate goodwill impairment loss and non-controlling interest on the consolidated income statement for the year ended December 31, Year 6, under parent company extension theory.

(c) Calculate goodwill and non-controlling interest on the consolidated statement of financial position at December 31, Year 6, under the parent company extension theory.

Problem 5-12
LO2, 3, 4

Foxx Corp. purchased 75% of the outstanding shares of Rabb Ltd. on January 1, Year 3, at a cost of $117,000. Non-controlling interest was valued at $35,000 by an independent business valuator at the date of acquisition. On that date, Rabb had common shares of $50,000 and retained earnings of $30,000. Fair values were equal to carrying amounts for all the net assets except the following:

	Carrying amount	Fair value
Inventory	$30,000	$19,000
Equipment	45,000	69,000
Software	—	15,000

The equipment had an estimated remaining useful life of 6 years on January 1, Year 3, and the software was to be amortized over 10 years. Foxx uses the cost method to account for its investment. The testing for impairment at December 31, Year 6, yielded the following fair values:

Software	$ 8,000
Goodwill	20,000

The impairment loss on these assets occurred entirely in Year 6. Amortization expense is grouped with administrative expenses, and impairment losses are grouped with miscellaneous expenses. The parent's share of the goodwill noted above is $15,000.

The following are the financial statements of Foxx Corp. and its subsidiary Rabb Ltd. as at December 31, Year 6:

BALANCE SHEETS
December 31, Year 6

	Foxx Corp.	Rabb Ltd.
Cash	$ —	$ 10,000
Accounts receivable	40,000	30,000
Note receivable	—	40,000
Inventory	66,000	44,000
Equipment, net	220,000	76,000
Land	150,000	30,000
Investment in Rabb	117,000	—
	$593,000	$230,000
Bank indebtedness	$ 90,000	$ —
Accounts payable	70,000	60,000
Notes payable	40,000	—
Common shares	150,000	50,000
Retained earnings	243,000	120,000
	$593,000	$230,000

STATEMENTS OF RETAINED EARNINGS
Year ended December 31, Year 6

	Foxx Corp.	Rabb Ltd.
Retained earnings, January 1, Year 6	$153,000	$ 92,000
Net income	120,000	48,000
Dividends	(30,000)	(20,000)
Retained earnings, December 31, Year 6	$243,000	$120,000

INCOME STATEMENTS
Year ended December 31, Year 6

	Foxx Corp.	Rabb Ltd.
Sales	$821,000	$320,000
Investment income	15,000	3,600
	836,000	323,600
Cost of sales	480,000	200,000
Administrative expenses	40,000	12,000
Miscellaneous expenses	116,000	31,600
Income taxes	80,000	32,000
	716,000	275,600
Net income	$120,000	$ 48,000

Additional Information

The notes payable are intercompany.

Required:

(a) Prepare the Year 6 consolidated financial statements.

(b) Calculate goodwill impairment loss and non-controlling interest on the consolidated income statement for the year ended December 31, Year 6, under parent company extension theory.

(c) If Foxx used parent company extension theory rather than entity theory, how would this affect the debt-to-equity ratio at the end of Year 6?

Problem 5-13
LO2, 3, 4

The following financial statements were prepared on December 31, Year 6.

BALANCE SHEET

	Pearl	Silver
Cash	$ 300,000	$ 100,000
Accounts receivable	200,000	—
Inventory	2,000,000	420,000
Plant and equipment	3,000,000	2,690,000
Accumulated depreciation	(750,000)	(310,000)
Investment in Silver Company—at cost	2,400,000	—
	$7,150,000	$2,900,000
Liabilities	$ 900,000	$ 300,000
Common shares	2,850,000	1,600,000
Retained earnings	3,400,000	1,000,000
	$7,150,000	$2,900,000

INCOME STATEMENT

	Pearl	Silver
Sales	$4,000,000	$1,000,000
Dividend income	150,000	—
	4,150,000	1,000,000
Cost of sales	2,500,000	400,000
Miscellaneous expenses	320,000	70,000
Administrative expense	80,000	10,000
Income tax expense	250,000	120,000
	3,150,000	600,000
Net income	$1,000,000	$ 400,000

RETAINED EARNINGS STATEMENT

	Pearl	Silver
Balance, January 1	$2,900,000	$ 800,000
Net income	1,000,000	400,000
	3,900,000	1,200,000
Dividends	500,000	200,000
Balance, December 31	$3,400,000	$1,000,000

Additional Information

Pearl purchased 75% of the outstanding voting shares of Silver for $2,400,000 on July 1, Year 2, at which time Silver's retained earnings were $400,000, and accumulated depreciation was $60,000. The acquisition differential on this date was allocated as follows:

- 30% to undervalued inventory
- 40% to equipment—remaining useful life 8 years
- Balance to goodwill

During Year 3, a goodwill impairment loss of $70,000 was recognized, and an impairment test conducted as at December 31, Year 6, indicated that a further loss of $20,000 had occurred.

Amortization expense is grouped with cost of goods sold and impairment losses are grouped with administrative expenses.

Silver owes Pearl $75,000 on December 31, Year 6.

Required:

(a) Prepare consolidated financial statements on December 31, Year 6.
(b) Calculate goodwill impairment loss and non-controlling interest on the consolidated income statement for the year ended December 31, Year 6, under parent company extension theory.
(c) Calculate goodwill and non-controlling interest on the consolidated balance sheet at December 31, Year 6, under parent company extension theory.

Problem 5-14
LO2, 3

Balance sheet and income statement data for two affiliated companies for the current year appear below.

Additional Information

- Albeniz acquired an 80% interest in Bach on January 1, Year 1, for $272,000. On that date the following information was noted about specific net assets of Bach:

	Carrying amount	Fair value
Inventory	$20,000	$50,000
Land	25,000	45,000
Equipment (estimated useful life 15 years)	60,000	78,000
Misc. intangibles (estimated useful life 20 years)	—	42,000

Amortization expense is grouped with distribution expenses. Albeniz's accumulated depreciation was $240,000 at the date of acquisition.

- On January 1, Year 1, Bach had a retained earnings balance of $30,000.
- Albeniz carries its investment at cost.

BALANCE SHEET
as at December 31, Year 4

	Albeniz	Bach
Cash	$ 40,000	$ 21,000
Receivables	92,000	84,000
Inventories	56,000	45,000
Land	20,000	60,000
Plant and equipment	200,000	700,000
Accumulated depreciation	(80,000)	(350,000)
Investment in Bach Company (cost)	272,000	—
Advances to Bach Company	100,000	—
Total assets	$700,000	$560,000

(continued)

	Albeniz	Bach
Accounts payable	$130,000	$ 96,500
Advances payable	—	100,000
Common shares	400,000	200,000
Retained earnings	170,000	163,500
Total liabilities and shareholders' equity	$700,000	$560,000

INCOME STATEMENT
Year Ended December 31, Year 4

	Albeniz	Bach
Sales revenues	$600,000	$400,000
Interest income	6,700	—
Dividend income from Bach	6,400	—
Total revenues	613,100	400,000
Cost of goods sold	334,000	225,000
Distribution expense	20,000	70,000
Selling and administrative expense	207,000	74,000
Financing expense	1,700	6,000
Income taxes expense	20,700	7,500
Total expenses	583,400	382,500
Net income	$ 29,700	$ 17,500

Required:

Prepare the following:

(a) Consolidated income statement
(b) Consolidated balance sheet

Problem 5-15
LO2, 3, 5, 6, 7

On January 2, Year 1, Brady Ltd. purchased 80% of the outstanding shares of Partridge Ltd. for $4,120,000. Partridge's statement of financial position and the fair values of its identifiable assets and liabilities for that date appear later in this section.

The patents had a remaining useful life of 10 years on the acquisition date. The bonds were issued on January 1, Year 1, and mature on December 31, Year 10. Goodwill impairment losses were recorded as follows:

- Year 1: $25,000
- Year 3: $12,500

Partridge declared and paid dividends of $100,000 in Year 3.

	Carrying amount	Fair value
Plant and equipment (net)	$4,500,000	$4,500,000
Patents (net)	1,000,000	1,500,000
Inventory	2,000,000	2,200,000
Accounts receivable	1,500,000	1,500,000
Cash	500,000	500,000
	$9,500,000	
Ordinary shares	$2,000,000	
Retained earnings	2,500,000	
10% bonds payable	3,000,000	3,300,000
Accounts payable	2,000,000	2,000,000
	$9,500,000	

On December 31, Year 3, the financial statements of the two companies were as follows:

STATEMENT OF FINANCIAL POSITION

	Brady	Partridge
Plant and equipment (net)	$ 8,000,000	$5,000,000
Patents (net)	—	700,000
Investment in Partridge Ltd. (equity method)	4,362,000	—
Inventory	4,600,000	1,900,000
Accounts receivable	1,000,000	1,300,000
Cash	400,000	600,000
	$18,362,000	$9,500,000
Ordinary shares	$ 5,000,000	$2,000,000
Retained earnings	6,362,000	3,100,000
Bonds payable	4,000,000	3,000,000
Accounts payable	3,000,000	1,400,000
	$18,362,000	$9,500,000

INCOME STATEMENTS

	Brady	Partridge
Sales	$10,000,000	$5,000,000
Investment revenue from Partridge	134,000	—
	10,134,000	5,000,000
Cost of goods purchased	6,930,000	2,890,000
Change in inventory	70,000	110,000
Depreciation expense	900,000	400,000
Patent amortization expense	—	100,000
Interest expense	480,000	300,000
Other expenses	680,000	850,000
Income taxes	600,000	150,000
	9,660,000	4,800,000
Profit	$ 474,000	$ 200,000

Required:

(a) Prepare consolidated financial statements on December 31, Year 3.
(b) Assume that Brady is a private entity, uses ASPE, and chooses to use the cost method to account for its investment in Partridge. Which items on Brady's separate-entity financial statements would have amounts different from those shown? Compute the equity method balances of these items.
(c) Calculate the current ratio, debt-to-equity ratio, and return on total shareholders' equity for Brady's Year 3 financial statements assuming that the

   i) equity method was used to report its investment in Partridge;
   ii) cost method was used to report its investment in Partridge; and
   iii) consolidated statements were used to the business combination with Partridge.

   Round percentages to one decimal point and other ratios to two decimal points.

(d) Briefly explain which of the different reporting methods in (c) report the highest

   i) liquidity.
   ii) risk of insolvency.
   iii) profitability.

WEB-BASED PROBLEMS

Web Problem 5-1
LO3, 4, 6

When accounting for the acquisition of a non–wholly owned subsidiary, the parent can use entity theory or parent company extension theory to account for the business combination. Access the 2011 consolidated financial statements for Thomson Reuters Corporation by going to the investor relations section of the company's website. Answer the questions below for 2011. Round percentages to one decimal pint and other ratios to two decimal points. For each question, indicate where in the financial statements you found the answer, and/or provide a brief explanation.

(a) Which theory of consolidation is used to value non-controlling interest at the date of acquisition?

(b) What percentage of net income for the year is represented by non-controlling interest (sometimes referred to as *minority interest*)?

(c) What portion of the additions to other intangible assets during the year came from business combinations, and what portion came from direct purchases?

(d) What was the goodwill impairment loss for the year, or what were total impairment losses? Describe the two main factors contributing to the goodwill impairment.

(e) Assume that performance bonuses for the company's top executives are based, in part, on net income. How will the goodwill impairment loss for the year affect the bonuses for the executives in the current year? in future years?

(f) Explain why different discount rates are used for different geographical areas, and explain how a change in discount rate can negatively affect the value of goodwill.

(g) Assume that the company used the other acceptable theory of consolidation for valuing non-controlling interest accounting. How would this change in theory affect the return on total shareholders' equity for the first year after the date of acquisition?

Web Problem 5-2
LO3, 4, 6

Access the 2011 consolidated financial statements for BCE Inc. by going to the investor relations section of the company's website. Answer the same questions as in Web Problem 1, for 2011. For each question, indicate where in the financial statements you found the answer, and/or provide a brief explanation. (Some questions may not be applicable.)

Mc Graw Hill **connect**™ | Practise and learn online with Connect

Intercompany Inventory and Land Profits

LEARNING OBJECTIVES

After studying this chapter, you should be able to do the following:

LO1 Describe the effect on consolidated profit of the elimination of both intercompany revenues (and expenses) and intercompany asset profits.

LO2 Prepare consolidated financial statements that reflect the elimination of upstream and downstream intercompany profits in inventory and land.

LO3 Explain how the cost, revenue recognition, and matching principles are used to support adjustments for intercompany transactions when preparing consolidated financial statements.

LO4 Prepare consolidated financial statements that reflect the realization of upstream and downstream intercompany profits in inventory and land that were held back in previous periods.

LO5 Prepare the journal entries under the equity method to reflect the elimination and subsequent realization of intercompany profits in inventory and land.

LO6 Analyze and interpret financial statements involving intercompany transactions.

LO7 Identify some of the differences between IFRSs and ASPE involving intercompany transactions.

INTRODUCTION

In previous discussions, we stressed that consolidated financial statements report the activities of a group of affiliated companies as if they constitute a single company. While these companies may transact business with one another as well as with non-affiliated companies, all intercompany transactions are eliminated so that the final consolidated statements reflect only the result of transactions with entities outside the group. The elimination of intercompany transactions and unrealized profit is one of the most complex topics encountered in the consolidation process. The volume of transfers within most large enterprises can be quite large. For example, Vodaphone Group, a world leader in wireless communication, reported intersegment revenue of €359 million in 2011. Such transactions are especially common in companies that have been constructed as a vertically integrated chain of organizations. These entities reduce their costs and risks by developing affiliations in which one operation furnishes products to another.

Intercompany transactions are also used to shift income from one jurisdiction to another to minimize or avoid paying income taxes. As a result, Canadian

Consolidated financial statements should reflect only transactions with entities outside of the consolidated entity.

legislation prevents Canadian companies from trying to avoid paying income tax by using offshore tax havens such as non-resident trusts and foreign investment entities. The legislation was enacted because the government felt that multinational companies operating in Canada had avoided "hundreds of millions" of dollars in taxes over the previous decade through the use of tax havens.

Chapter 5 illustrated the elimination of intercompany receivables and payables. The next two chapters focus on the elimination of other transactions that occur between a parent and its subsidiaries or between two or more subsidiaries that have a common parent.

LO1 INTERCOMPANY REVENUE AND EXPENSES

Intercompany Sales and Purchases

The following simple example will be used to illustrate the basic idea behind the elimination of intercompany sales and purchases in the preparation of a consolidated income statement.

The transaction with the dealer is an arm's-length transaction (i.e., with an outsider).

Let your imagination stray a bit, and suppose that when you went shopping for groceries, the change you received from the cashier included some dollar coins. When you got home you noticed that the loon on one of these coins was upside down. You took the coin to a dealer and learned that some coins with this flaw had been accidentally released into circulation by the Royal Canadian Mint and as a result were worth substantially more than their face value. The dealer offered you $41 for this dollar coin, which you accepted. It is obvious that you made a profit of $40 on this transaction. An income statement showing only this transaction would appear as follows:

Revenue is recognized when it is earned in a transaction with an outsider in accordance with the revenue recognition principle.

INCOME STATEMENT—COIN TRANSACTION

Sales	$41
Cost of goods sold	1
Net income	$40

Now let your imagination stray even further, and assume that the following events took place between the time you received the coin from the supermarket and the time you sold it to the coin dealer. Your pants have four pockets. Let us call them pocket 1, pocket 2, pocket 3, and pocket 4. Pocket 1 received the coin from the supermarket and sold it to pocket 2 for $10. Pocket 2 sold the coin to pocket 3 for $15. Pocket 3 sold the coin to pocket 4 for $25, and then pocket 4 sold the coin to the dealer for $41. Has any part of the transaction changed as far as you (as an entity) are concerned? The answer is, of course, no. You still had sales of $41, cost of goods sold of $1, and a net income of $40. But assume that each of your pockets recorded its part in the transaction and prepared an income statement:

INCOME STATEMENTS OF FOUR POCKETS

	Pocket 1	Pocket 2	Pocket 3	Pocket 4
Sales	$10	$15	$25	$41
Cost of goods sold	1	10	15	25
Net income	$ 9	$ 5	$10	$16

Income was recorded when the coin was moved from one pocket to another.

The arrows indicate the interpocket transactions that took place. Also, the sum of the net incomes of your four pockets is equal to your net income of $40. We should therefore be able to prepare an income statement for you (as an entity) by combining the components of the income statements of your four pockets as follows:

COMBINED INCOME STATEMENT

Sales (10 + 15 + 25 + 41)	$91
Cost of goods sold (1 + 10 + 15 + 25)	51
Net income	$40

However, sales and cost of goods sold are not the correct amounts because they contain the interpocket sales and purchases. Both items should reflect only sales to and purchases from *outside* the entity. If we eliminate the interpocket sales and purchases, we will have an income statement that reflects only transactions that you as an entity incurred with others outside the entity. This statement can be prepared as follows:

COMBINED INCOME STATEMENT—ENTITY

	Total of four pockets	Interpocket sales & purchases	Total	
Sales	$91	$50	$41	The cost of the coin is
Cost of goods sold	51	50	1	expensed in the same period
Net income	$40	$ 0	$40	as the revenue in accordance
				with the matching principle.

Note that if we eliminate an equal amount of revenue and expense from an income statement, the resultant net income remains unchanged.

Your four pockets in this example are similar in all respects to a parent company and its subsidiary companies. Let us assume that a parent company (P) has holdings in three subsidiaries as follows: P owns 80% of S1, 90% of S2, and 75% of S3. The coin transactions previously illustrated were carried out by P and its three subsidiaries. These were the only transactions that took place during the current year. At year-end, the parent and its subsidiaries prepared the following income statements:

INCOME STATEMENTS—PARENT AND SUBSIDIARIES

	P	S1	S2	S3	
Sales	$10	$15	$25	$41	Only S3 had a transaction
Cost of goods sold	1	10	15	25	with an outsider.
Net income	$ 9	$ 5	$10	$16	

We are assuming that P uses the equity method but has made no entries during the current year and that all acquisition differentials have been fully amortized in prior years.

Before preparing a consolidated income statement, we can calculate consolidated net income attributable to P as follows:

	S1	S2	S3	Total	
P's net income					$ 9
Subsidiary net income	$ 5	$ 10	$ 16	$31	
P's ownership	80%	90%	75%		
Share of subsidiary's net income	$ 4	$ 9	$ 12		25
Consolidated net income attributable to P					$34

Suppose we prepare a consolidated income statement without eliminating intercompany sales and purchases, in the following manner:

P AND SUBSIDIARIES
CONSOLIDATED INCOME STATEMENT
for Current Year

Sales (10 + 15 + 25 + 41)	$91
Cost of goods sold (1 + 10 + 15 + 25)	51
Net income	$40
Attributable to	
Shareholders of parent	$34
Non-controlling interest	6

Sales and cost of sales are overstated because intercompany sales and purchases have not yet been eliminated.

CALCULATION OF NET INCOME
ATTRIBUTABLE TO NON-CONTROLLING INTEREST

S1 (20% × 5)	$ 1
S2 (10% × 10)	1
S3 (25% × 16)	4
	$ 6

Note that the net income of the consolidated entity is made up of the net incomes of the parent and its three subsidiaries. But we have not eliminated the intercompany sales and purchases that took place during the year. If we eliminate these intercompany transactions, the bottom-line net income earned by the consolidated entity will not change. Non-controlling interest and consolidated net income are only *allocations* of the entity's net income, so they also will not be affected by the elimination of these intercompany sales and purchases. The consolidated income statement after the elimination of intercompany sales and purchases is as follows:

CONSOLIDATED INCOME STATEMENT
(after Elimination of Intercompany Items)

Sales (91 − 50)	$41
Cost of goods sold (51 − 50)	1
Net income	$40
Attributable to	
Shareholders of parent	$34
Non-controlling interest	6

The consolidated income statement now reflects only the transactions with outsiders.

Other Examples of Intercompany Revenue and Expenses

Suppose the parent company lends $100,000 to the subsidiary company and receives a note payable on demand with interest at 10% paid annually. The transactions would be recorded as follows:

These transactions are recorded on the separate-entity books of the parent and the subsidiary.

Parent Company			*Subsidiary Company*		
Note receivable	100,000		Cash	100,000	
Cash		100,000	Note payable		100,000

To record intercompany borrowings on January 1 of the current year

Cash	10,000		Interest expense	10,000	
Interest revenue		10,000	Cash		10,000

To record the intercompany payment of interest on December 31 of the current year.

From the consolidated entity's point of view, all that has happened is that cash has been transferred from one bank account to another. No revenue has been earned, no expense has been incurred, and there are no receivables or payables with parties outside the consolidated entity. The elimination of $10,000 interest revenue and interest expense on the consolidated income statement does not change the net income of the consolidated entity. If total net income is not affected, then the amount allocated to the non-controlling and controlling interest is also not affected. On the consolidated balance sheet, we eliminate $100,000 from notes receivable and notes payable. An equal elimination of assets and liabilities on the balance sheet leaves the amounts of the two equities (non-controlling interest and controlling interest) unchanged.

> Consolidated net income does not change when we eliminate an equal amount of revenue and expense.

Note also that if the roles are reversed and the *subsidiary* lends $100,000 to the *parent*, the eliminations on the consolidated income statement and balance sheet are the same and have no effect on the amount of the non-controlling interest appearing on each statement.

Intercompany Management Fees   Often the parent will charge its subsidiary companies a yearly management fee as a means of allocating head office costs to all the companies within the group. (We will not discuss the pros and cons of this procedure here. Readers who are interested in the reasons for, and effectiveness of, allocations of this nature are advised to consult a management accounting textbook.) From an external reporting point of view, we have intercompany revenues and expenses that must be eliminated on the consolidated income statement.

Intercompany Rentals   Occasionally, buildings or equipment owned by one company are used by another company within the group. Rather than transfer legal title, the companies agree on a yearly rental to be charged. In such cases, intercompany rental revenues and expenses must be eliminated from the consolidated income statement.

The four examples mentioned above and any other intercompany revenues and expenses are eliminated to ensure that revenue is recognized only when it is earned with a party outside of the consolidated entity and to stop the double-counting of revenues and expenses. This has no effect on the calculation of the non-controlling interest in the net income of the subsidiary companies, since there is no change to consolidated net income.

> The elimination entries are recorded on the consolidated working papers and not in the separate-entity books of the parent and the subsidiary.

Intercompany Profits in Assets

When one affiliated company sells assets to another affiliated company, it is possible that the profit or loss recorded on the transaction has not been realized from the point of view of the consolidated entity. If the purchasing affiliate has sold these assets outside the group, all profits (losses) recorded are realized. If, however, all or a portion of these assets have not been sold outside the group, we must eliminate the remaining intercompany profit and may need to eliminate the intercompany loss[1] from the consolidated statements. The intercompany profit (loss) will be realized for consolidation purposes during the accounting period in which the particular asset is sold to outsiders. The sale to outsiders may also result in an additional profit (loss) that is not adjusted in the consolidation process. Three types of unrealized intercompany profits (losses) are eliminated:

- Profits in inventory
- Profits in nondepreciable assets
- Profits in depreciable assets

The first two of these will be discussed in this chapter; the last one will be discussed in Chapter 7.

The examples that follow illustrate the holdback of unrealized intercompany profits in one accounting period and the realization of the profit in a subsequent period.

In a downstream transaction, the parent sells to a subsidiary. In an upstream transaction, the subsidiary sells to the parent or another subsidiary of the parent.

Upstream versus Downstream Transactions   When we talk about intercompany transactions, it is important to distinguish between downstream and upstream transactions. When the parent sells to the subsidiary, the transaction is referred to as a downstream transaction. When the subsidiary sells to the parent, it is referred to as an upstream transaction. The name of the method is consistent with the common perception that the parent is the head of the family and the subsidiary is the child of the parent. The parent looks down to the child, while the child looks up to the parent.

The company doing the selling is the company recognizing the profit on the sale. When we eliminate the profit from intercompany transactions, we should take it away from the selling company, that is, from the company that recognized the profit in the first place. On downstream transactions, we will eliminate the profit that the parent had recognized. On upstream transactions, we will eliminate the profit that the subsidiary had recognized.

Downstream and upstream transactions are defined by who the seller is.

The name of the method is also based on which company was the selling company. When one subsidiary sells to another subsidiary, the profit must also be eliminated because it is not realized with an outside party. Since a subsidiary was the selling company, this lateral type of transaction is also referred to as an upstream transaction.

To illustrate the concepts involved in the elimination of intercompany profits, we will use as a simple example the financial statements of a parent and its 90%-owned subsidiary one year after the acquisition date.

On January 1, Year 1, Parent Company acquired 90% of the common shares of Sub Incorporated for $11,250. On that date, Sub had common shares of $8,000 and retained earnings of $4,500, and there were no differences between the fair values and the carrying amounts of its identifiable net assets. The acquisition differential was calculated as follows:

Cost of 90% of Sub		$11,250
Implied value of 100% of Sub		$12,500
Carrying amount of Sub's net assets (equals Sub's shareholders' equity)		
Common shares	8,000	
Retained earnings	4,500	
		12,500
Acquisition differential		$ 0

The financial statements of Parent and Sub as at December 31, Year 1, are presented in Exhibit 6.1. Parent accounts for its investment using the cost method, and because there were no dividends declared by Sub, no entry was made on December 31, Year 1.

EXHIBIT 6.1

YEAR 1 INCOME STATEMENTS

	Parent	Sub
Sales	$20,000	$ 8,000
Cost of sales	13,000	4,300
Miscellaneous expenses	1,400	900
Income tax expense	2,200	1,100
	16,600	6,300
Net income	$ 3,400	$ 1,700

These are the separate-entity statements of the parent and the subsidiary.

BALANCE SHEETS—December 31, Year 1

	Parent	Sub
Inventory	$ 7,500	$ 4,000
Assets (miscellaneous)	21,650	19,200
Investment in Sub Inc.	11,250	—
	$40,400	$23,200
Liabilities	$12,000	$ 9,000
Common shares	15,000	8,000
Retained earnings	13,400	6,200
	$40,400	$23,200

The parent uses the cost method in its separate-entity records.

Intercompany Inventory Profits: Subsidiary Selling (Upstream Transactions)

The following intercompany transactions occurred during Year 1:

1. During Year 1, Sub made sales to Parent amounting to $5,000 at a gross profit rate of 30%.

2. At the end of Year 1, Parent's inventory contained items purchased from Sub for $1,000.

3. Sub paid (or accrued) income tax on its taxable income at a rate of 40%.

From Sub's separate-entity perspective, it earned the income on the sale to the Parent.

Holdback of Inventory Profits—Year 1   It should be noted that the subsidiary recorded a gross profit of $1,500 (30% × 5,000) on its sales to the parent during the year and paid income tax of $600 (40% × 1,500) on this profit. If the parent had sold all of its intercompany purchases to customers outside the entity, this $1,500 gross profit would be considered realized from the point of view of this consolidated single entity. But the parent's inventory contains items purchased from the subsidiary for $1,000. There is an unrealized intercompany profit of $300 (30% × 1,000) in this inventory, which must be held back from consolidated income in Year 1 and realized in the period in which it is sold to outsiders. In addition, the $120 tax expense relating to this profit must also be held back from the Year 1 consolidated income statement. When this $300 gross profit is realized on a future consolidated income statement, the income tax expense will be matched on that statement with the profit realized.

From the consolidated perspective, some of Sub's income was not realized with an outsider.

Not only do we have to hold back an unrealized profit for consolidation purposes, but also we must make an adjustment for the income taxes relating to that profit. Since income taxes are computed at the individual company level rather than at the consolidated-entity level, the company that recorded the profit also paid (or accrued) income taxes on that profit, and the income tax expense on its

Income tax should be expensed in the same period as profit.

income statement reflects this. The matching of expenses with revenues is a basic accounting concept; the adjustment made for income taxes on intercompany profits is a perfect example of this matching process.

The difference between the buyer's tax basis and the cost of transferred assets as reported in the consolidated financial statements meets the definition of a temporary difference and will give rise to deferred income taxes. While IAS 27 explicitly states that profits and losses resulting from intragroup transactions should be eliminated in full, it does not explicitly state how the eliminated amount should be allocated between the controlling and non-controlling interests. Because the amount attributed to non-controlling interest will affect the amount attributed to the shareholders of the parent, the handling of this issue can affect the reported profitability of a business combination.

From a consolidated perspective, some of the tax paid by the subsidiary was prepaid, since the income was not yet earned.

Non-controlling interest is not affected by intercompany profits made on downstream transactions.

To determine an appropriate allocation, the relationship between an intercompany transaction and the non-controlling shareholders must be analyzed. If a transfer were downstream, a logical view would be that the unrealized gross profit belongs to the parent company. The parent made the original sale; therefore, the gross profit is included in its financial records. Since the non-controlling shareholders do not have any interest in the parent company, it seems appropriate that they should not be affected by the elimination of the profit on downstream transactions.

Non-controlling interest is affected and will share in intercompany profits made on upstream transactions.

In contrast, if the subsidiary sells inventory to the parent, the subsidiary's financial records recognize the gross profit. If this profit is eliminated when preparing the consolidated financial statements, the parties having an interest in the subsidiary's profit are affected by the elimination of the profit. Since the non-controlling shareholders do have an interest in the subsidiary, it seems appropriate that they should be affected by the elimination of the profit on upstream transactions. Throughout this textbook, the non-controlling interest's share of profit and retained earnings will be computed based on the reported profit and retained earnings of the subsidiary after they have been adjusted for any unrealized profits on upstream transactions.

LO2

Using the direct approach, we will now prepare the Year 1 consolidated statements after making the consolidation adjustments shown in Exhibit 6.2.

EXHIBIT 6.2

INTERCOMPANY TRANSACTIONS

Intercompany sales and purchases	$ 5,000	**(a)**
Intercompany inventory profits:		
Ending inventory—Sub Inc. selling	$ 300	**(b)**
Income tax (40%)	120	**(c)**
After-tax profit	$ 180	**(d)**

CALCULATION OF CONSOLIDATED NET INCOME — Year 1

The unrealized profit is always deducted from the selling company's income.

Net income—Parent Co.		$ 3,400
Net income—Sub Inc.	1,700	
Less after-tax profit in ending inventory **(2d)**	180	
Adjusted net income—Sub Inc.		1,520
Net income		$ 4,920
Attributable to		
Shareholders of parent		$ 4,768 **(e)**
Non-controlling interest (10% × 1,520)		152 **(f)**

(continued)

EXHIBIT 6.2 **(continued)**

CALCULATION OF CONSOLIDATED RETAINED EARNINGS
at December 31, Year 1

Retained earnings—Parent Co.		$13,400
Retained earnings—Sub Inc.	6,200	
Acquisition retained earnings	4,500	
Increase since acquisition	1,700	
Less profit in ending inventory **(2d)**	180	
Adjusted increase since acquisition	1,520	**(g)**
Parent Co.'s share	90%	1,368
Consolidated retained earnings		$14,768 **(h)**

The unrealized profit at the end of Year 1 must be eliminated when calculating consolidated retained earnings at the end of Year 1.

CALCULATION OF NON-CONTROLLING INTEREST (METHOD 1)
at December 31, Year 1

Shareholders' equity—Sub Inc.	
Common shares	$ 8,000
Retained earnings	6,200
	14,200
Less after-tax profit in ending inventory	180
Adjusted shareholders' equity	14,020
Non-controlling interest's share	10%
	$ 1,402 **(i)**

Non-controlling interest is affected when there are unrealized profits on upstream transactions.

CALCULATION OF NON-CONTROLLING INTEREST (METHOD 2)

Non-controlling interest at date of acquisition (10% × [11,250 / .9])		$ 1,250
Sub's adjusted increase in retained earnings **(g)**	1,520	
NCI's share @ 10%		152
Non-controlling interest, December 31, Year 3		$ 1,402 **(i)**

Remember that the purpose of the calculation of consolidated net income is to adjust the parent's cost method net income to what it would have been under the equity method. Note that the after-tax profit is deducted from the net income of Sub because the subsidiary was the selling company and its net income contains this profit being held back for consolidation purposes. Note also that the non-controlling interest's share of the Year 1 income is based on the *adjusted income* of Sub.

Exhibit 6.3 illustrates the preparation of the Year 1 consolidated financial statements.

The first two numbers in brackets are from the statements of Parent and Sub. Any additional numbers, which are in boldface and labelled, are adjustments made to eliminate the intercompany transactions. The eliminations made on the income statement require further elaboration:

1. The eliminations of intercompany sales and purchases are equal reductions of revenues and expenses that do not change the net income of the consolidated entity or the amount allocated to the non-controlling and controlling equities.

EXHIBIT 6.3

YEAR 1 CONSOLIDATED STATEMENTS
Elimination of Intercompany Profits in Inventory
(Direct Approach)

PARENT COMPANY
CONSOLIDATED INCOME STATEMENT
for the Year Ended December 31, Year 1

The unrealized profits are eliminated on the consolidated financial statements.

Sales (20,000 + 8,000 − **[2a] 5,000**)	$23,000
Cost of sales (13,000 + 4,300 − **[2a] 5,000** + **[2b] 300**)	12,600
Miscellaneous expenses (1,400 + 900)	2,300
Income tax expense (2,200 + 1,100 − **[2c] 120**)	3,180
	18,080
Net income	$ 4,920
Attributable to	
Shareholders of parent **(2e)**	$ 4,768
Non-controlling interest **(2f)**	152

PARENT COMPANY
CONSOLIDATED BALANCE SHEET
at December 31, Year 1

By eliminating the unrealized profit, inventory is now stated at cost to the consolidated entity.

Inventory (7,500 + 4,000 − **[2b] 300**)	$11,200
Assets—miscellaneous (21,650 + 19,200)	40,850
Deferred income taxes (0 + 0 + **[2c] 120**)	120
	$52,170
Liabilities (12,000 + 9,000)	$21,000
Common shares	15,000
Retained earnings **(2h)**	14,768
Non-controlling interest **(2i)**	1,402
	$52,170

2. To hold back the gross profit of $300 from the consolidated entity's net income, we increase cost of goods sold by $300. The reasoning is as follows:
   (a) Cost of goods sold is made up of opening inventory, plus purchases, less ending inventory.

When ending inventory is overstated, cost of sales is understated.

   (b) The ending inventory contains the $300 gross profit.
   (c) If we subtract the $300 profit from the ending inventory on the balance sheet, the ending inventory is now stated at cost to the consolidated entity.
   (d) A reduction of $300 from ending inventory in the cost of goods sold calculation increases cost of goods sold by $300.
   (e) This increase to cost of goods sold reduces the before-tax net income earned by the entity by $300.

When cost of sales is increased, income decreases and income tax expense should decrease.

3. Because the entity's before-tax net income has been reduced by $300, it is necessary to reduce the income tax expense (the tax paid on the profit held back) by $120.

4. A reduction of income tax expense increases the net income of the consolidated entity.

5. A $300 increase in cost of goods sold, together with a $120 reduction in income tax expense, results in the after-tax profit of $180 being removed from consolidated net income.

The $300 adjustment to inventory and cost of goods sold is similar to the adjustment we studied in intermediate accounting to correct errors in inventory. If you have difficulty understanding the adjustments for unrealized profits in inventory, you may want to go back to your intermediate accounting text to review the adjustment for errors in inventory.

As a result of the adjustments above, the following accounting principles have been properly applied:

L03

The adjustments to eliminate the unrealized profits are needed in order to properly apply the cost, revenue recognition, and matching principles.

Cost principle—inventory is reported at $11,200, which is the original cost to the consolidated entity when the inventory was purchased from outsiders.

Revenue recognition principle—sales are reported at $23,000, which is the amount earned on sales to outsiders.

Matching principle—cost of goods sold is recognized as an expense in the same period as the related revenue, and therefore is matched to the revenue. The amount of $12,600 is the inventory actually sold to outsiders at the amount paid when the goods were originally purchased from outsiders. Similarly, income tax is expensed in the same period as the related income and in proportion to the income earned.

It is important to realize that all of the above adjustments are being made on the consolidated working papers and not on the separate-entity financial statements. What was recorded on the subsidiary's own books was legitimate from its own perspective. But from the consolidated perspective, some of the profit was not yet realized. It must be held back from the consolidated financial statements.

The unrealized profits are not eliminated on the separate-entity financial statements.

Again it is important to note the following components of the entity's net income:

Net Income—Parent Co.	$3,400
Adjusted net income—Sub Inc.	1,520
Consolidated net income	$4,920

The only new concepts relating to the preparation of the consolidated balance sheet involve the adjustments made on the asset side (a) to eliminate the unrealized profit in inventory and (b) to set up the deferred income taxes on this profit. These adjustments are shown in boldface in Exhibit 6.3 and are labelled to correspond with the calculations in Exhibit 6.2. The reasons for these adjustments can be further explained as follows:

1. The holdback of the $300 gross profit on the consolidated income statement was accomplished by reducing the amount of ending inventory in calculating the cost of goods sold. (A reduction in ending inventory increases cost of goods sold.) The ending inventory in the cost of goods sold calculation is the inventory balance on the consolidated balance sheet. Removing the $300 gross profit from the asset will result in the consolidated inventory being reflected at cost to the entity.

The unrealized profit is deducted from the inventory to bring inventory back to its original cost in accordance with the historical cost principle.

2. On the consolidated income statement, we reduced income tax expense by $120, representing the tax paid on the gross profit. As far as the consolidated entity is concerned, this tax of $120 was paid prematurely because the income was not yet earned. The tax will become an expense when the inventory is sold

Income tax will be expensed when the profit is realized in accordance with the matching principle.

to outsiders. This results in a temporary difference for the consolidated entity. The resultant deferred income taxes are "added into" the assets on the consolidated balance sheet. (The illustration assumes that neither the parent nor the subsidiary had deferred income taxes on their individual balance sheets.)

3. A reduction of $300 from inventory and a $120 increase in deferred income taxes results in a net reduction to consolidated assets of $180, which equals the $180 reduction that has been made on the equity side.

Equity Method Journal Entries   While our example has assumed that Parent uses the cost method to account for its investment, it is useful to see where the differences would lie if the equity method was used. If Parent was using the equity method, the following journal entries would be made on December 31, Year 1:

> The equity method captures the net effect of all consolidation entries.

Investment in Sub Inc.	1,530	
Investment income		1,530
90% of the net income of Sub Inc.		
(90% × 1,700 = 1,530)		
Investment income	162	
Investment in Sub Inc.		162
To hold back 90% of the after-tax inventory profit recorded by Sub Inc. (90% × 180 = 162)		

After these entries were posted, the two related equity method accounts of Parent would show the following changes and balances:

	Investment in Sub Inc.	Investment income
January 1, Year 1	$11,250	$ —
December 31, Year 1		
Income from Sub Inc.	1,530	1,530
After-tax inventory profit (held back)	(162)	(162)
Balance, December 31, Year 1	$12,618	$1,368

> The parent's income under the equity method should be equal to consolidated net income attributable to Parent's shareholders.

Parent's total income under the equity method would be $4,768, consisting of $3,400 from its own operations as reported in Exhibit 6.1, plus investment income of $1,368, as reported above. This income of $4,768 should be and is equal to consolidated net income attributable to Parent's shareholders.

LO4 **Realization of Inventory Profits—Year 2**   The previous example illustrated the holdback of an unrealized intercompany inventory profit in Year 1. We will continue our example of Parent Company and Sub Inc. by looking at the events of Year 2. On December 31, Year 2, Parent reported earnings from its own operations of $4,050 and declared dividends of $2,500. Sub reported a net income of $3,100 and, again, did not declare a dividend. Using the cost method, Parent made no journal entries with respect to the operations of Sub. During Year 2, there were no intercompany transactions, and at year-end, the inventory of Parent contained no items purchased from Sub. In other words, the December 31, Year 1, inventory of Parent

> In Year 2, the parent sold its Year 1 inventory to outsiders.

was sold during Year 2, and the unrealized profit that was held back for consolidated purposes in Year 1 will have to be released into income in Year 2.

The financial statements of Parent and Sub are presented in Exhibit 6.4. Before we prepare the Year 2 consolidated income statement, we must carry out the calculations shown in Exhibit 6.5.

EXHIBIT 6.4

YEAR 2 INCOME STATEMENTS

	Parent	Sub
Sales	$25,000	$12,000
Cost of sales	16,000	5,500
Miscellaneous expenses	2,350	1,400
Income tax expense	2,600	2,000
	20,950	8,900
Net income	$ 4,050	$ 3,100

Cost of sales for the parent includes the inflated inventory value at the beginning of the year.

BALANCE SHEETS—December 31, Year 2

	Parent	Sub
Inventory	$ 9,900	$ 7,500
Assets (miscellaneous)	22,800	20,800
Investment in Sub Inc.	11,250	—
	$43,950	$28,300
Liabilities	$14,000	$11,000
Common shares	15,000	8,000
Retained earnings	14,950	9,300
	$43,950	$28,300

Inventory at the end of Year 2 does not include any unrealized profit.

EXHIBIT 6.5

INTERCOMPANY INVENTORY PROFITS—Year 2

Intercompany inventory profits:		
Opening inventory—Sub Inc. selling	$ 300	(a)
Income tax (40%)	120	(b)
After-tax profit	$ 180	(c)

CALCULATION OF CONSOLIDATED NET INCOME—Year 2

Net income—Parent Co.		$ 4,050
Net income—Sub Inc.	3,100	
Add after-tax profit in opening inventory (5c)	180	
Adjusted net income—Sub Inc.		3,280
Net income		$ 7,330
Attributable to		
Shareholders of parent		$ 7,002 (d)
Non-controlling interest (10% × 3,280)		328 (e)

When the profits are realized, they are credited to the income of the original seller.

CALCULATION OF CONSOLIDATED RETAINED EARNINGS
December 31, Year 2

Retained earnings—Parent Co.		$14,950
Retained earnings—Sub Inc.	9,300	
Acquisition retained earnings	4,500	
Increase since acquisition	4,800	(f)
Parent Co.'s share	90%	4,320
Consolidated retained earnings		$19,270 (g)

(continued)

EXHIBIT 6.5 **(continued)**

CALCULATION OF NON-CONTROLLING INTEREST (METHOD 1)
December 31, Year 2

All of subsidiary's shareholders' equity is legitimate from a consolidated perspective at the end of Year 2.

Common shares—Sub Inc.	$ 8,000
Retained earnings—Sub Inc.	9,300
	17,300
	10%
	$ 1,730 **(h)**

CALCULATION OF NON-CONTROLLING INTEREST (METHOD 2)

Non-controlling interest at date of acquisition (10% × [11,250/.9])		$ 1,250
Sub's adjusted increase in retained earnings **(g)**	4,800	
Non-controlling interest's share @ 10%		480
Non-controlling interest, December 31, Year 2		$ 1,730 **(i)**

L04

The after-tax inventory profit of $180 that was held back in Year 1 is being realized in Year 2 and is added to the net income of Sub, because the subsidiary was the company that originally recorded the profit. Note that the non-controlling interest's share of the Year 2 net income of Sub is based on the *adjusted net income* of that company.

The calculation of consolidated retained earnings at December 31, Year 2, does not require any adjustments for unrealized profits because there are no unrealized profits at the end of Year 2. The subsidiary had reported profits in Year 1 on an intercompany sale to the parent. The unrealized profits were eliminated when calculating consolidated retained earnings at the end of Year 1. When the parent sold the inventory to outsiders, the previous unrealized profit was realized from a consolidated perspective. Since neither the parent nor the subsidiary had any inventory at the end of Year 2 that had been purchased through an intercompany sale, there was no unrealized profit in ending inventory. Consequently, there is no unrealized profit in retained earnings at the end of Year 2.

Exhibit 6.6 illustrates the preparation of the Year 2 consolidated financial statements using the *direct* approach.

EXHIBIT 6.6

Year 2 Consolidated Statements
(Direct Approach)
PARENT COMPANY
CONSOLIDATED INCOME STATEMENT
for the Year Ended December 31, Year 2

The unrealized profits from the end of Year 1 are released into consolidated income in Year 2.

Sales (25,000 + 12,000)	$37,000
Cost of sales (16,000 + 5,500 − **[5a] 300**)	21,200
Miscellaneous expenses (2,350 + 1,400)	3,750
Income tax expense (2,600 + 2,000 + **[5b] 120**)	4,720
	29,670
Net income	$ 7,330
Attributable to	
Shareholders of parent **(5d)**	$ 7,002
Non-controlling interest **(5e)**	328

(continued)

EXHIBIT 6.6	*(continued)*

PARENT COMPANY
CONSOLIDATED BALANCE SHEET
December 31, Year 2

Inventory (9,900 + 7,500)	$17,400
Assets—miscellaneous (22,800 + 20,800)	43,600
	$61,000
Liabilities (14,000 + 11,000)	$25,000
Common shares	15,000
Retained earnings **(5g)**	19,270
Non-controlling interest **(5h)**	1,730
	$61,000

There are no unrealized profits at the end of Year 2.

In preparing the Year 2 consolidated income statement, we make consolidation adjustments that bring the original before-tax profit into the income statement and increase income tax expense for the tax on this profit. The eliminations (i.e., adjustments) made are shown in boldface and are labelled. The elimination entries are explained as follows:

1. There were no intercompany sales or purchases in Year 2, and therefore no elimination is required on the income statement.

2. To realize the gross profit of $300 in Year 2, we decrease cost of goods sold by $300. The reasoning behind this is as follows:
   (a) Cost of goods sold is made up of opening inventory, plus purchases, less ending inventory.
   (b) Parent's opening inventory contains the $300 gross profit. After we reduce it by $300, the opening inventory is at cost to the entity.
   (c) A reduction of $300 from opening inventory decreases cost of goods sold by $300.
   (d) This decrease in cost of goods sold increases the before-tax net income earned by the entity by $300.

   Since beginning inventory was inflated, cost of sales for Year 2 was inflated.

3. Using the concepts of matching, we increase income tax expense by $120 in order to match it with the $300 gross profit being realized. Note that the deferred income tax on the December 31, Year 1, consolidated balance sheet (see Exhibit 6.3) becomes an expense on the Year 2 consolidated income statement, because the December 31, Year 1, inventory was sold in Year 2.

   When cost of sales is decreased, income increases, and tax expense should increase.

4. A $300 decrease in cost of goods sold, together with a $120 increase in income tax expense, results in the after-tax intercompany Year 1 profit of $180 being realized for consolidation purposes in Year 2.

Before the consolidated balance sheet is prepared, we must calculate non-controlling interest at December 31, Year 2. This calculation was shown in Exhibit 6.5.

The preparation of the consolidated balance sheet on December 31, Year 2, is straightforward because no inventory profit eliminations are required. The inventory of Parent does not contain any unrealized profit, and there are no related deferred income taxes on the balance sheet. All previous unrealized inventory profits have now been realized for consolidation purposes.

When you view the adjustments that were made to prepare the Year 2 consolidated statements (see Exhibit 6.6), it may strike you that the adjustments made on the income statement have not been reflected in the rest of the consolidated statements, and that, as a result, the statements should not balance. But they *do* balance, so the $180 increase in the after-tax net income of the entity must have been offset by a $180 change in the retained earnings statement and balance sheet. To see where this $180 difference ended up, it is useful to prepare a calculation that shows the changes in non-controlling interest during Year 2. This calculation is shown below.

CHANGES IN NON-CONTROLLING INTEREST—Year 2

Sub Inc.		
Common shares	$8,000	
Retained earnings—January 1	6,200	
	14,200	
Less unrealized inventory profit	180	
Adjusted	14,020	
	10%	
Non-controlling interest, January 1		$1,402
Allocation of Year 2 consolidated net income **(5e)**		328
Non-controlling interest, December 31		$1,730

Non-controlling interest is based on Sub's shareholders' equity after it has been adjusted for unrealized profit on upstream transactions.

In examining this calculation and the calculation of consolidated retained earnings on December 31, Year 1, in Exhibit 6.2, we see that the $180 increase in the entity's Year 2 consolidated net income was offset by a $180 *decrease* in the December 31, Year 1, balances of non-controlling interest and retained earnings, allocated as follows:

To non-controlling interest (10% × 180)	$ 18
To controlling interest (90% × 180)	162
	$180

The intercompany profit of $180 was recorded in Sub's separate-entity income in Year 1 but reported in consolidated income in Year 2.

L05 **Equity Method Journal Entries**   If Parent had used the equity method, the following journal entries would have been made on December 31, Year 2:

Investment in Sub Inc.	2,790	
Investment income		2,790
To record 90% of the reported income of Sub Inc. (90% × 3,100)		
Investment in Sub Inc.	162	
Investment income		162
To release in Year 2 the after-tax inventory profit held back in Year 1 (90% × 180)		

The equity method captures the net effect of all consolidation entries, including the adjustment for realized profits.

After these entries are posted, the two related equity method accounts of Parent show the following changes and balances:

	Investment in Sub Inc.	Investment income
January 1, Year 2	$12,618	$ —
Changes during Year 2		
Income from Sub Inc.	2,790	2,790
After-tax inventory profit (realized)	162	162
Balance, Dec. 31, Year 2	$15,570	$2,952

Note that the January 1 balance ($12,618) included the $162 holdback and that this amount was realized during the year with a journal entry. It should be obvious that the December 31 balance ($15,570) does not contain any holdback.

Intercompany Inventory Profits: Parent Selling (Downstream Transactions)

In our previous example, the subsidiary was the selling company in the intercompany profit transaction (an upstream transaction). This resulted in the $180 after-tax profit elimination being allocated to the controlling and non-controlling equities.

Suppose we had assumed that it was the parent company that sold the inventory to the subsidiary (a downstream transaction). The calculation of consolidated net income for each of the two years should indicate where the differences lie.

CALCULATION OF CONSOLIDATED NET INCOME—YEAR 1

Net income—Parent Co.	$3,400	Unrealized profits on
Less after-tax profit in ending inventory	180	downstream transactions are
Adjusted net income—Parent Co.	3,220	deducted from the parent's
Net income—Sub Inc.	1,700	separate-entity income.
Consolidated net income	$4,920	
Attributable to		
Shareholders of parent	$4,750	
Non-controlling interest (10% × 1,700)	170	

Note that the after-tax profit is deducted from the net income of Parent because it was the selling company, and that Parent's net income contains this profit being held back for consolidation purposes.

The eliminations on the consolidated income statement for intercompany sales and purchases and for unrealized profit in inventory, and the related adjustment to income tax expense would not change. But the split of the consolidated net income between the shareholders of the parent and the non-controlling interest is different, as indicated in the previous calculation. Because Parent was the selling company, all of the $180 holdback was allocated to the parent and none was allocated to the non-controlling interest.

Non-controlling interest is not affected by the elimination of unrealized profits on downstream transactions.

On the December 31, Year 1, consolidated balance sheet, the elimination entries to adjust inventory and deferred income taxes would be the same as before. However, the non-controlling interest on the consolidated balance sheet is based on the December 31, Year 1, balances of the common shares and retained earnings of Sub. The after-tax inventory holdback is *not* allocated to non-controlling interest; because Parent was the selling company, it has been allocated entirely to consolidated retained earnings.

Year 2 consolidated net income is calculated as follows:

Net income—Parent Co.	$4,050	When unrealized profits on
Add: After-tax profit in opening inventory	180	downstream transactions are
Adjusted net income—Parent Co.	4,230	realized, they are added to
Net income—Sub Inc.	3,100	the parent's separate-entity
Consolidated net income	$7,330	income.
Attributable to		
Shareholders of parent	$7,020	
Non-controlling interest (10% × 3,100)	310	

The elimination entries on the Year 2 consolidated income statement would be the same as in the previous illustration (see Exhibit 6.6), but because the amount for non-controlling interest is $310, the consolidated net income attributable to Parent's shareholders is a higher amount, as indicated in the previous calculations.

To summarize, the holdback and subsequent realization of intercompany profits in assets is allocated to the non-controlling and controlling equities *only if* the subsidiary was the original seller in the intercompany transaction. If the parent was the original seller, the allocation is entirely to the controlling equity.

Equity Method Journal Entries

If Parent used the equity method to account for its investment, it would make the following entries as at December 31, Year 1:

Investment in Sub Inc.	1,530	
Investment income		1,530

To record 90% of the reported Year 1, net income of Sub Inc. (90% × 1,700)

Investment income	180	
Investment in Sub Inc.		180

To hold back the after-tax inventory profit recorded by Parent Co. in Year 1

> The parent absorbs the full charge for unrealized profits on downstream transactions in Year 1.

> The equity method is referred to as the one-line consolidation.

An astute reader will notice that because the parent was the selling company, the second entry is removing the profit from accounts that did not contain it in the first place. This is, of course, quite true. However, it is the investment income account that establishes the equality between Parent's net income (under the equity method) and consolidated net income attributable to Parent's shareholders. In the same manner, the investment in Sub on the balance sheet of Parent establishes the equality between Parent's retained earnings (under the equity method) and consolidated retained earnings. This means that all adjustments that affect consolidated net income are reflected in these two accounts.

Rather than preparing two separate entries, the following entry could be made to capture the overall impact of the two separate entries:

Investment in Sub Inc.	1,350	
Investment income		1,350

To record investment income from Sub Inc. net of adjustment for unrealized profit in ending inventory (90% × 1,700 − 100% × 180)

On December 31, Year 2, Parent would make the following journal entries if it used the equity method:

Investment in Sub Inc.	2,790	
Investment income		2,790

To record 90% of the reported net income of Sub Inc. (90% × 3,100)

Investment in Sub Inc.	180	
Investment income		180

To release in Year 2 the after-tax inventory profit held back in Year 1

> The parent receives the full benefit when unrealized profits on downstream transactions are realized in Year 2.

Alternatively, the following entry could be made to capture the overall impact of the two separate entries:

Investment in Sub Inc.	2,970	
Investment income		2,970

To record investment income from Sub Inc. net of adjustment for unrealized profit in ending inventory (90% × 3,100 + 100% × 180)

Unrealized Profits with Associates   When the investor only has significant influence in an associate, it cannot control the decisions made by the associate. As such, transactions with the associate are similar to transactions with outsiders. Therefore, the accounting for unrealized profits on downstream transactions is a bit different for an investment in an associate. Rather than eliminating all of the profit, only the investor's percentage ownership of the associate, times the profit earned on the transaction with the associate is eliminated. For example, if X Co. had a 40% interest in Y Co. and made a profit of $100 on a transaction with Y Co., only $40 (40% × 100) of the profit would be eliminated as part of the entries under the equity method. The $100 of profit would be recorded in the sales and cost of sales account, and the $40 would be eliminated through the investment account. That leaves $60 of profit remaining in income. This $60 is deemed to be a transaction with outsiders.

> Only the investor's share of profit on intercompany transactions with associates is eliminated.

Self-Study Problem 6-1 illustrates the preparation of consolidated financial statements when there are intercompany sales of inventory. It also shows the accounting for unrealized profits with an associate.

Income Statement with Expenses Classified by Nature   The previous illustrations in this chapter presented cost of goods sold as a separate line on the income statement. This would typically occur under two scenarios:

1. When expenses are classified according to their function and cost of goods sold represents the expenses of the production function.

2. When expenses are classified by nature and the reporting entity is a merchandising company; that is, it buys and sells finished goods.

When a manufacturing company presents its expenses according to their nature, a cost-of-goods-sold line typically does not exist. Instead, raw materials consumed, labour costs, depreciation of factory equipment, and other conversion costs are shown separately. In addition, there is a separate line for changes in inventories of work in progress and finished goods.

The adjustments on consolidation to eliminate the intercompany transactions and any unrealized profits are slightly different when expenses are classified according to their nature. If the intercompany transaction involves raw materials, all consolidation adjustments are put through the raw materials account on the balance sheet and the raw materials consumed account on the income statement. If the intercompany transaction involves work in progress or finished goods, the intercompany purchase is eliminated from the purchases of work in progress and finished goods account on the income statement; the unrealized profits are eliminated from work in progress and finished goods inventory on the balance sheet, and from the changes in inventories of work in progress and finished goods account on the income statement.

> Consolidation adjustments for unrealized profits in inventory will likely be made to the changes in inventory account rather than cost of goods sold.

Losses on Intercompany Transactions

When one affiliated company sells inventory to another affiliated company at a loss, the intercompany transaction and any unrealized losses should be eliminated on consolidation in a similar fashion to the previous discussion for unrealized profits. However, selling inventory at a loss raises a red flag that it may be impaired. If the inventory is impaired, it should be written down to its net realizable value. Ideally, the impairment should be reported on the separate-entity statements. If not, the impairment will have to be reported on the consolidated statements. The following example illustrates these issues.

Sub has inventory with an original cost of $5,500 and a net realizable value of $4,800. If Sub were to value its inventory at net realizable value at this point, it would recognize a loss of $700.

Impairment tests for inventory are usually performed at the end of the fiscal period.

In Year 1, Sub sells this inventory to Parent for $5,000. It had not written down the inventory to its net realizable value prior to the sale to Parent. Before the end of Year 1, Parent sells 80% of these goods to outsiders for $3,840, which equals their net realizable value. It has the remaining inventory purchased from Sub on its books at $1,000 at the end of Year 1. The net realizable value of this inventory is $960, which is the same net realizable value prior to the sale by Sub.

Based solely on the above information, selected accounts from the financial statements for Parent and Sub for Year 1 are as follows:

	Parent	Sub
Inventory on balance sheet	$1,000	
Sales	3,840	$5,000
Cost of sales	4,000	5,500
Gross profit	$−160	$−500

The following adjustments would normally be made on consolidation:

When intercompany losses are eliminated, the inventory is brought back to the original cost to the selling entity.

(a) Sales and cost of goods sold should be reduced by $5,000, being the amount of the intercompany sale.

(b) Unrealized loss in ending inventory of $100 (500/5,000 × 1,000) should be eliminated.

The consolidated financial statements show the following amounts for the selected accounts:

Inventory on balance sheet (1,000 + 0 + **[b] 100**)	$1,100
Sales (3,840 + 5,000 − **[a] 5,000**)	3,840
Cost of sales (4,000 + 5,500 − **[a] 5,000** − **[b] 100**)	4,400
Gross profit	$−560

By eliminating the unrealized loss and not making any adjustment for impairment of the inventory, the inventory is measured at $1,100, which is 20% of the original cost to Sub. This is consistent with the historical cost principle. However, this inventory is stated above its net realizable value of $960. It should be written down from $1,100 to $960, a write-down of $140. If the write-down were made as adjustment (c) on consolidation, the consolidated financial statements would show the following amounts for the selected accounts:

Inventory on the consolidated balance sheet should be reported at the lower of cost and net realizable value.

Inventory on balance sheet (1,000 + 0 + **[b] 100** − **[c] 140**)	$ 960
Sales (3,840 + 5,000 − **[a] 5,000**)	3,840
Cost of sales (4,000 + 5,500 − **[a] 5,000** − **[b] 100**)	4,400
Gross profit	$−560
Loss in value of inventory (0 + 0 + **[c] 140**)	−140
Profit before tax on the above items	$−700

Now the consolidated balance sheet reports inventory at the lower of cost and net realizable value, and the consolidated income statement reports a loss of $700, being the total impairment loss on the inventory. This more faithfully represents the situation for the consolidated entity.

It may appear strange to adjust the inventory upward by $100 in (b), and then to adjust it downward by $140 in (c). The same result could have been achieved by not eliminating the unrealized loss in (b) and then writing down the inventory from $1,000 to $960 for a $40 adjustment in (c). For this reason, some people believe that unrealized losses should not be eliminated on consolidation, but the losses should be a warning sign for potential impairment.

If the subsidiary had not sold any of the inventory to the parent or to outsiders, it should have tested the inventory for impairment at the end of Year 1. In so doing, it would have determined that inventory was impaired and that an impairment loss of $700 would need to be reported.

In some cases, the exchange price on intercompany transactions between the parent and the subsidiary does not reflect the true value of the inventory. Even though the net realizable value of the inventory in the above example was $4,800, the subsidiary could have sold the inventory to the parent for $4,000. If so, the inventory would be reported by the parent at less than net realizable value on its separate-entity balance sheet. If the unrealized loss is not eliminated, the inventory and net income of the consolidated entity will be understated. For this reason, IFRSs suggest that the intercompany loss be eliminated on consolidation. Then, the reporting entity should perform an impairment test to determine if the inventory is impaired from the perspective of the consolidated entity.

> Intercompany transactions are not always consummated at market value.

Intercompany Land Profit Holdback

The holdback and realization of an intercompany profit in land is accomplished in a more straightforward manner on the consolidated income statement. Suppose that in Year 1 there was an intercompany sale of land for $2,300 on which a before-tax profit of $300 was recorded, that $120 tax was accrued, and that on December 31, Year 1, the land was still held by the purchasing company. (Throughout the text and end-of-chapter material, we assume that these gains are not capital gains.) The selling company would make the following entry to record the intercompany transaction:

Cash	2,300	
Land		2,000
Gain on sale of land		300

> The purchasing company's cost is $300 higher than the selling company's cost.

The purchasing company would record the intercompany transaction as follows:

Land	2,300	
Cash		2,300

When consolidated financial statements are prepared, the profit elimination and the related income tax adjustment will take place as follows:

PARENT COMPANY
CONSOLIDATED INCOME STATEMENT
Year 1

Gain on sale of land (300 − **300**)	$ 0
Income tax expense (**P** + **S** − **120**)	XXX
Net income	$XXX
Attributable to	
Shareholders of parent	$XXX
Non-controlling interest	XXX

It should be obvious that the holdback of the gain, along with the reduction of the income tax expense, has reduced the consolidated entity's net income by $180.

The after-tax profit is deducted from the selling company's separate-entity income.

If the subsidiary is the selling company, the $180 after-tax profit held back will be used to calculate non-controlling interest in the consolidated income statement; in this manner, it will be allocated to the two equities. If the parent is the selling company, non-controlling interest will not be affected and the entire after-tax holdback will be allocated to the controlling entity.

The following shows the eliminations required in the preparation of the assets section of the Year 1 balance sheet:

PARENT COMPANY
CONSOLIDATED BALANCE SHEET
December 31, Year 1

After eliminating the profit, the land is stated at the original cost to the consolidated entity.

Land (2,300 − **300**)	$2,000
Deferred income taxes (P + S + **120**)	120
Total assets	$ XXX

The balance sheet eliminations for a land profit are very similar to those for an inventory profit. The before-tax profit is deducted from land rather than from inventory. The tax asset is added into the consolidated balance sheet. We will refer to this tax asset as deferred income taxes.

The equity side of the balance sheet is not presented. If the subsidiary is the selling company, the calculation of non-controlling interest on December 31, Year 1, will have to reflect this fact. If the parent is the selling company, the entire $180 after-tax profit holdback is attributed to the parent company's shareholders and is reflected in the retained earnings shown on the balance sheet.

Realization of Intercompany Land Profits

An unrealized intercompany inventory profit held back for consolidation purposes in Year 1 is considered realized in Year 2 because any inventory on hand at the beginning of a year has usually been sold by the end of that year.

The unrealized profits will be eliminated from retained earnings of the selling company on the consolidated working papers each year until the land is sold to outsiders.

When are intercompany land profits considered realized for consolidation purposes? The answer is this: when the land is sold to outsiders, which may be many years later. At the end of each successive year prior to the sale to outsiders, the preparation of the consolidated balance sheet requires the same adjustments as those of Year 1. Consolidated income statements require no adjustment until the year of the sale to outsiders because in each year prior to that event, the income statements of both affiliates will not contain any transactions with regard to the land.

However, assuming that Parent Company uses the cost method, the calculation of beginning consolidated retained earnings each year will have to include an adjustment to hold back the $180 unrealized land profit. The calculation would be identical to that shown in Exhibit 6.5, except that it would be described as land profit rather than profit in opening inventory. (This particular calculation is based on the assumption that Sub Inc. was the selling company.) Each successive year would require the same adjustment, until the land is sold to outsiders.

In this case, let us assume that the land was sold to outsiders during Year 8 at a profit of $1,300. The company making the sale in Year 8 would record the following journal entry:

The gain on the separate-entity income statement is $1,300.

Cash	3,600	
Land		2,300
Gain on sale of land		1,300

While the selling company recorded a gain of $1,300, the gain to the entity is $1,600 (1,300 + 300). On the Year 8 consolidated income statement, the gain held back in Year 1 is realized and the income tax expense is adjusted as follows:

**PARENT COMPANY
CONSOLIDATED INCOME STATEMENT**
Year 8

Gain on sale of land (1,300 + **300**)	$1,600	The gain on the consolidated
Income tax expense (P + S + **120**)	XXX	income statement is $1,600
Net income	$ XXX	(1,300 + 300 previously held
		back).
Attributable to		
Shareholders of parent	$ XXX	
Non-controlling interest	XXX	

The entity's consolidated net income is increased by $180 (300 − 120). If the subsidiary was the original selling company, the net income of the non-controlling interest is affected in Year 8; the entire $180 is attributed to the controlling interest if the parent was the original seller.

Appendix 6A of this chapter illustrates the consolidation adjustments relating to an intercompany sale of land when the parent company uses the revaluation model under IAS 16 and periodically revalues its land to fair value.

Equity Method Journal Entries   Parent Co.'s equity journal entries for the land gain in Years 1 and 8 would be identical to the entries illustrated previously for inventory in Years 1 and 2, depending of course on which company was the original seller in the intercompany profit transaction.

> The equity method reports only the investor's share of the subsidiary's profit that has been realized from a consolidated viewpoint.

The examples in this chapter regarding the elimination of unrealized intercompany profits follow the dictates of entity theory, which requires the same accounting treatment for measuring the controlling and non-controlling shareholders' interest in the subsidiary. Entity theory is also required when measuring the subsidiary's assets and liabilities at fair value at the date of acquisition, as we learned in Chapter 4. Therefore, the standard-setters are consistent in requiring the use of entity theory in many different aspects of preparing consolidated financial statements.

See Self-Study Problem 6-2 for a comprehensive problem that includes acquisition differential and intercompany sales of inventory and land.

Intercompany Transfer Pricing

In our coin example at the beginning of this chapter, we saw a loonie sold for a gross profit of $40, which was allocated to the four related companies as follows:

> Intercompany transactions are sometimes undertaken to transfer profit from high-tax to low-tax jurisdictions.

Parent	$ 9
Sub 1	5
Sub 2	10
Sub 3	16
Total	$40

From a financial reporting point of view, we are not concerned with the amount of profit earned by each company, but only with eliminating intercompany transactions and profits that are unrealized because they have not been sold outside the consolidated "single entity." From a Canadian taxation point of view, the consolidated entity is not subject to tax; rather each company pays tax on its taxable income. It should seem obvious that the management of the parent company would be interested in maximizing the after-tax profit of this single entity, if possible. If all of the companies are in one taxation jurisdiction, there is nothing that management can do to increase the after-tax profit. However, if some of the companies are in jurisdictions with low rates of corporate income tax while others are in high-tax-rate jurisdictions, management may try to structure each company's transfer price so that the majority (or all) of the $40 profit is earned in low-tax-rate jurisdictions. This will often bring companies into conflict with the governments of the high-tax-rate jurisdictions.

> Companies always disclose that all significant intercompany transactions and balances have been eliminated.

Disclosure Requirements The disclosure requirements for consolidated financial statements were summarized in Chapters 3 and 4. In addition to those requirements, the entity would normally indicate that intercompany transactions have been eliminated. The excerpt in Exhibit 6.7 above is taken from the 2011 financial statements of Eastern Platinum Limited, Canada's leading platinum group metals producer.

ANALYSIS AND INTERPRETATION OF FINANCIAL STATEMENTS

L06

> The parent's separate-entity income statement reports the parent's revenues and expenses, whereas the consolidated income statement reports the combined revenues and expenses of the parent and its subsidiaries.

In this chapter, we prepared consolidated financial statements under two scenarios: first, for upstream transactions and, second, for downstream transactions. In both cases, the unrealized profits from the intercompany transactions had to be eliminated. The elimination entries were made on the consolidated financial statements. The net effect of the consolidation adjustments was captured in the parent's internal records when the parent used the equity method.

Exhibit 6.8 presents the Year 1 separate entity and consolidated financial statements that were developed for the intercompany transactions involving inventory. The first three columns present the statements when the intercompany transactions were upstream. In the last three columns, the intercompany transactions were downstream.

> The parent's separate-entity balance sheet reports the parent's assets and liabilities, whereas the consolidated balance sheet reports the combined assets and liabilities of the parent and its subsidiaries.

The exhibit also indicates the debt-to-equity and return-on-equity ratios for each set of financial statements. The return on equity for all shareholders uses consolidated net income and total shareholders' equity including the non-controlling interests. The return on equity for shareholders of Parent uses consolidated net income attributable to the shareholders of Parent and total shareholders' equity excluding the non-controlling interests.

EXHIBIT 6.7

Extracts from Eastern Platinum's 2011 Financial Statements

(a) Basis of consolidation

These consolidated financial statements incorporate the financial statements of the Company and the entities controlled by the Company (its subsidiaries, including special purpose entities). Control exists when the Company has the power, directly or indirectly, to govern the financial and operating policies of an entity so as to obtain benefits from its activities. The financial statements of subsidiaries are included in the consolidated financial statements from the date that control commences until the date that control ceases. All significant intercompany transactions and balances have been eliminated.

Source: Reproduced with permission from Eastern Platinum Limited http://eastplats.com/

EXHIBIT 6.8	Impact of Presentation Method on Debt-to-Equity and Return-on-Equity Ratios

INCOME STATEMENTS—December 31, Year 1

	Upstream Transaction			Downstream Transaction		
	Parent Cost	*Parent Equity*	*Consol.*	*Parent Cost*	*Parent Equity*	*Consol.*
Sales	$20,000	$20,000	$23,000	$20,000	$20,000	$23,000
Investment income	0	1,368	0	0	1,350	0
Total income	20,000	21,368	23,000	20,000	21,350	23,000
Cost of sales	13,000	13,000	12,600	13,000	13,000	12,600
Miscellaneous expenses	1,400	1,400	2,300	1,400	1,400	2,300
Income tax expense	2,200	2,200	3,180	2,200	2,200	3,180
	16,600	16,600	18,080	16,600	16,600	18,080
Net income	$ 3,400	$ 4,768	$ 4,920	$ 3,400	$ 4,750	$ 4,920
Attributable to						
Shareholders of Parent			$ 4,768			$ 4,750
Non-controlling interests			152			170

BALANCE SHEETS—December 31, Year 1

Inventory	$ 7,500	$ 7,500	$11,200	$ 7,500	$ 7,500	$11,200
Assets (miscellaneous)	21,650	21,650	40,850	21,650	21,650	40,850
Deferred income tax			120			120
Investment in Sub Inc.	11,250	12,618	0	11,250	12,600	0
	$40,400	$41,768	$52,170	$40,400	$41,750	$52,170
Liabilities	$12,000	$12,000	$21,000	$12,000	$12,000	$21,000
Common shares	15,000	15,000	15,000	15,000	15,000	15,000
Retained earnings	13,400	14,768	14,768	13,400	14,750	14,750
Non-controlling interests	0	0	1,402	0	0	1,420
	$40,400	$41,768	$52,170	$40,400	$41,750	$52,170
Debt-to-equity	0.42	0.40	0.67	0.42	0.40	0.67
Return on equity						
– for all shareholders	n/a	n/a	15.78%	n/a	n/a	15.78%
– for shareholders of Parent	11.97%	16.02%	16.02%	11.97%	15.97%	15.97%

Note the following from Exhibit 6.8:

- The separate-entity statements under the cost method are the same for upstream and downstream transactions because the cost method does not record anything pertaining to the subsidiary's income or unrealized profits from intercompany transactions.
- The separate-entity statements under the cost method are the same as the statements under the equity method except for the investment account, retained earnings, and investment income.
- Consolidated net income is the same regardless of whether the transactions were upstream or downstream. However, the split of the consolidated net income between the shareholders of the parent and the non-controlling interest is different. In turn, consolidated retained earnings and non-controlling interests are different, depending on whether the transactions were upstream or downstream. The separate-entity net income and retained earnings under

The return on equity for the separate-entity statements under the equity method is equal to the consolidated return on equity for the shareholders of Parent.

the equity method are equal to consolidated net income attributable to the shareholders of Parent and consolidated retained earnings, respectively.

- The return on equity for the separate-entity statements under the equity method is equal to the consolidated return on equity for the shareholders of Parent.

- The return on equity for the downstream scenario is lower than the upstream scenario because the shareholders of Parent absorb the full charge when the unrealized profits are eliminated.

- The solvency position looks worst on the consolidated financial statements, because the subsidiary's debt is included on the consolidated financial statements. This increases the debt-to-equity ratio.

> The return on equity for shareholders of Parent for the downstream scenario is lower than the upstream scenario because the shareholders of Parent absorb the full charge when the unrealized profits are eliminated.

ASPE DIFFERENCES

L07

1. As mentioned in Chapter 3, private companies can either consolidate their subsidiaries or report their investments in subsidiaries under the cost method, under the equity method, or at fair value.

2. When eliminating unrealized profits on downstream transactions between an investor and its associate, the entire profit is eliminated under ASPE, whereas only the investor's proportionate interest is eliminated under IFRSs.

U.S. GAAP DIFFERENCES

U.S. GAAP and IFRSs for intercompany transactions have many similarities. The significant differences are summarized as follows:

1. Whereas IFRSs do not allow the use of LIFO for reporting inventory, LIFO is allowed under U.S. GAAP.

2. Whereas IFRSs require the use of net realizable value to determine whether inventory is impaired, U.S. GAAP uses either net realizable value, replacement cost, or net realizable value less normal gross margin.

SUMMARY

To ensure that consolidated financial statements reflect only transactions between the single entity and those outside the entity, all intercompany transactions are eliminated. The elimination of intercompany revenues and expenses does not affect the net income of this entity; therefore, it cannot affect the amounts allocated to the two equities in the balance sheet.

Intercompany profits in assets are not recognized in the consolidated financial statements until the assets have been sold outside the group or consumed. (The concept of realization as a result of consumption is discussed in the next chapter.)

The elimination of unrealized intercompany profits in assets reduces the net income of the consolidated entity. It will affect the amount allocated to non-controlling interest only if the subsidiary was the selling company. The income tax recorded on the unrealized profit is also removed from the consolidated income statement and is shown as a deferred income tax asset or liability until a sale to outsiders takes place.

When the assets that contain the intercompany profit are sold outside (or consumed), the profit is considered realized and is reflected in the consolidated income statement. The appropriate income tax is removed from the consolidated balance sheet and reflected as an expense in the income statement. The adjustments for income tax ensure that income tax expense is properly matched to income recognized on the consolidated income statement.

Significant Changes in GAAP in the Last Three Years

No major changes occurred in the last three years for the topics presented in this chapter.

Changes Expected in GAAP in the Next Three Years

No major changes are expected in the next three years for the topics presented in this chapter.

SELF-STUDY PROBLEM 1

LO2,3,5 On December 31, Year 5, the EL Company purchased 70% of the outstanding common shares of the BOW Company for $5.6 million in cash when BOW's shareholders' equity consisted of $2,000,000 of common shares and $6,000,000 of retained earnings. There was no acquisition differential. For the year ending December 31, Year 10, the income statements for EL and BOW were as follows:

	EL	BOW
Sales and other income	$28,800,000	$13,000,000
Cost of goods sold	18,000,000	8,200,000
Depreciation expense	3,400,000	1,800,000
Income tax and other expenses	4,200,000	1,600,000
Total expenses	25,600,000	11,600,000
Net income	$ 3,200,000	$ 1,400,000

At December 31, Year 10, the condensed balance sheets for the two companies were as follows:

	EL	BOW
Current assets	$15,000,000	$8,800,000
Investment in BOW	5,600,000	
Other noncurrent assets	23,000,000	17,400,000
Total assets	$43,600,000	$26,200,000
Liabilities	$26,400,000	$13,800,000
Common shares	4,000,000	2,000,000
Retained earnings	13,200,000	10,400,000
Total	$43,600,000	$26,200,000

OTHER INFORMATION:

1. During Year 10, EL sold merchandise to BOW for $600,000. Seventy-five percent of this merchandise remains in BOW's inventory at December 31, Year 10. On December 31, Year 9, the inventory of BOW contained $100,000 of merchandise purchased from EL. EL earns a gross margin of 30% on its intercompany sales.

2. On January 2, Year 8, BOW sold land to EL for $1,200,000. BOW purchased the land on January 1, Year 6, for $1,100,000. EL still owns this land at December 31, Year 10.

3. During Year 10, EL declared and paid dividends of $2,600,000, while BOW declared and paid dividends of $800,000.

4. EL accounts for its investment in BOW using the cost method.

5. Both companies pay income tax at the rate of 40%.

Required:

(a) Prepare a consolidated income statement for the year ended December 31, Year 10. Show supporting calculations.

(b) Calculate consolidated retained earnings at December 31, Year 10. Show supporting calculations.

(c) Assume that BOW is a subsidiary and EL is a private entity. EL uses ASPE and chooses to use the equity method to account for its investment in BOW. Prepare EL's separate entity balance sheet at December 31, Year 10.

(d) Assume that BOW is an associate rather than a subsidiary and that EL uses IFRSs. Calculate the balance in the investment in BOW account under the equity method at December 31, Year 10.

SOLUTION TO SELF-STUDY PROBLEM 1

(a) **Supporting Schedules**

Intercompany transactions

Intercompany sales and cost of goods sold		$600,000 **(a)**
Intercompany dividend (800,000 × 70%)		560,000 **(b)**
Intercompany inventory profits—EL selling		

gross margin

	Before tax	40% tax	After tax	
Beginning inventory (100,000 × 30%)	$30,000	$12,000	$18,000	**(c)**
Ending inventory (600,000 × 75% × 30%)	135,000	54,000	81,000	**(d)**
Gain on sale of land in Year 6 (1,200,000 − 1,100,000)	100,000	40,000	60,000	**(e)**

EL COMPANY
Consolidated Statement of Income
for Year Ended December 31, Year 10

Sales and other income	
[28,800,000 + 13,000,000 − **(a) 600,000** − **(b) 560,000**] *BT BT*	$40,640,000
Cost of goods sold	
[18,000,000 + 8,200,000 − **(a) 600,000** − **(c) 30,000** + **(d) 135,000**]	25,705,000
Depreciation expense [3,400,000 + 1,800,000]	5,200,000
Income tax and other expenses *BT* *BT*	
[4,200,000 + 1,600,000 + **(c) 12,000** − **(d) 54,000**]	5,758,000
Total expenses	36,663,000
Net income	$ 3,977,000
Attributable to	
Shareholders of EL	
(3,200,000 − **(b) 560,000** + **(c) 18,000** − **(d) 81,000** + 70% × 1,400,000)	$ 3,557,000
Non-controlling interests (30% × 1,400,000)	420,000

(b)

EL's retained earnings, Dec. 31, Year 10		$ 13,200,000
Unrealized profit in ending inventory—net of tax **(d)**		(81,000)
BOW's retained earnings, Dec. 31, Year 10	10,400,000	
BOW's retained earnings, at acquisition	6,000,000	
Change in retained earnings since acquisition	4,400,000	
Gain on sale of land **(e)**	(60,000)	
	4,340,000	
EL's share @ 70%		3,038,000
Consolidated retained earnings, Dec. 31, Year 10		$ 16,157,000

(c) **Supporting Schedules**

Investment in BOW, cost method		$ 5,600,000
Unrealized profit in ending inventory—net of tax (d)		(81,000)
BOW's retained earnings, Dec. 31, Year 10	$ 10,400,000	
BOW's retained earnings, at acquisition	6,000,000	
Change in retained earnings since acquisition	4,400,000	
Gain on sale of land	(60,000)	
	4,340,000	
EL's share @ 70%		3,038,000
Investment in BOW, equity method		$ 8,557,000

OR

Consolidated retained earnings, Dec. 31, Year 10	$ 16,157,000
EL's retained earnings, cost method, Dec. 31, Year 10	13,200,000
Change from cost to consolidation	2,957,000
Investment in BOW, cost method	5,600,000
Investment in BOW, equity method	$ 8,557,000

EL COMPANY
Balance Sheet
December 31, Year 10

Current assets	$ 15,000,000
Investment in BOW	8,557,000
Other noncurrent assets	23,000,000
Total assets	$ 46,557,000
Liabilities	$ 26,400,000
Common shares	4,000,000
Retained earnings (same as consolidation)	16,157,000
Total	$ 46,557,000

(d) For a downstream transaction with an associate, only the investor's share of the profit in ending inventory is considered unrealized.

Investment in BOW, cost method		$ 5,600,000
Unrealized profit in ending inventory—net of tax (81,000 × 70%)		(56,700)
BOW's retained earnings, Dec. 31, Year 10	10,400,000	
BOW's retained earnings, at acquisition	6,000,000	
Change in retained earnings since acquisition	4,400,000	
Gain on sale of land **(e)**	(60,000)	
	4,340,000	
EL's share @ 70%		3,038,000
Investment in BOW, equity method		$ 8,581,300

SELF-STUDY PROBLEM 2

L01, 2, 4, 5   The following are the Year 5 financial statements of Peter Corporation and its subsidiary, Salt Company:

	Peter	Salt
Year 5 Income Statements		
Sales	$900,000	$250,000
Management fees	25,000	—
Interest	—	3,600
Gain on land sale	—	20,000
Dividends	12,000	—
	937,000	273,600
Cost of sales	540,000	162,000
Interest expense	3,600	—
Other expenses	196,400	71,600
Income tax expense	80,000	16,000
	820,000	249,600
Profit	$117,000	$ 24,000
Year 5 Statements of Retained Earnings		
Balance, January 1	$153,000	$ 72,000
Profit	117,000	24,000
	270,000	96,000
Dividends	50,000	15,000
Balance, December 31	$220,000	$ 81,000
Statements of Financial Position—December 31, Year 5		
Land	$175,000	$ 19,000
Plant and equipment, net	238,000	47,000
Investment in Salt Co.	65,000	—
Inventory	32,000	27,000
Notes receivable	—	60,000
Accounts receivable	70,000	10,000
Cash	12,000	8,000
	$592,000	$171,000
Ordinary shares	$100,000	$ 50,000
Retained earnings	220,000	81,000
Notes payable	60,000	—
Other liabilities	212,000	40,000
	$592,000	$171,000

Additional Information

- On January 1, Year 3, Peter purchased 80% of the ordinary shares of Salt for $65,000. On that date, Salt had retained earnings of $10,000, and the carrying amounts of its identifiable net assets were equal to fair values.
- The companies sell merchandise to each other. Peter sells to Salt at a gross profit rate of 35%; Salt earns a gross profit of 40% from its sales to Peter.
- The December 31, Year 4, inventory of Peter contained purchases made from Salt amounting to $7,000. There were no intercompany purchases in the inventory of Salt on this date.

- During Year 5, the following intercompany transactions took place:
  - (a) Salt made a $25,000 payment to Peter for management fees, which was recorded as "other expense."
  - (b) Salt made sales of $75,000 to Peter. The December 31, Year 5, inventory of Peter contained merchandise purchased from Salt amounting to $16,500.
  - (c) Peter made sales of $100,000 to Salt. The December 31, Year 5, inventory of Salt contained merchandise purchased from Peter amounting to $15,000.
  - (d) On July 1, Year 5, Peter borrowed $60,000 from Salt and signed a note bearing interest at 12% per annum. Interest on this note was paid on December 31, Year 5.
  - (e) In Year 5, Salt sold land to Peter, recording a gain of $20,000. This land is being held by Peter on December 31, Year 5.
- Goodwill impairment tests have been conducted yearly since the date of acquisition. Losses due to impairment were as follows: Year 3, $2,600; Year 4, $800; Year 5, $1,700.
- Peter accounts for its investment using the cost method.
- Both companies pay income tax at a rate of 40%.

Required:

(a) Prepare the Year 5 consolidated financial statements.
(b) Prepare the following:
  - (i) A calculation of consolidated retained earnings as at December 31, Year 5
  - (ii) A calculation of non-controlling interest at December 31, Year 5
  - (iii) A statement of changes in deferred income taxes for Year 5
(c) Assume that Peter changes from the cost method to the equity method for its internal records.
  - (i) Calculate the balance in the investment account under the equity method as at December 31, Year 4.
  - (ii) Prepare Peter's equity method journal entries for Year 5.

SOLUTION TO SELF-STUDY PROBLEM 2

(a) **Supporting Schedules**

① **CALCULATION AND IMPAIRMENT OF THE ACQUISITION DIFFERENTIAL**

Cost of 80% of Salt, Jan. 1, Year 3			$65,000
Implied value of 100% of Salt			$81,250
Carrying amount of Salt, Jan. 1, Year 3			
Ordinary shares		50,000	
Retained earnings		10,000	
			60,000
Acquisition differential			21,250
Allocated to revalue the net assets of Salt			0
Goodwill, Jan. 1, Year 3			21,250
Impairment losses			
Year 3–Year 4	3,400	**(a)**	
Year 5	1,700	**(b)**	5,100
Goodwill, Dec. 31, Year 5			$16,150 **(c)**
Non-controlling interest at date of acquisition (20% × 81,250)			$16,250 **(d)**

INTERCOMPANY ITEMS

Notes receivable and payable	$ 60,000	**(e)**
Management fee revenue and expense	$ 25,000	**(f)**
Sales and purchases (100,000 + 75,000)	$175,000	**(g)**
Interest revenue and expense (12% × 60,000 × ½ year)	$ 3,600	**(h)**
Dividend from Salt (80% × 15,000)	$ 12,000	**(i)**

UNREALIZED PROFITS

	Before tax	40% tax	After tax	
Inventory				
Opening (7,000 × 40%)—Salt selling	$ 2,800	$1,120	$ 1,680	**(j)**
Ending				
Salt selling (16,500 × 40%)	$ 6,600	$2,640	$ 3,960	**(k)**
Peter selling (15,000 × 35%)	5,250	2,100	3,150	**(l)**
	$11,850	$4,740	$ 7,110	**(m)**
Land—Salt selling	$20,000	$8,000	$ 12,000	**(n)**

CALCULATION OF CONSOLIDATED PROFIT—Year 5

Profit of Peter			$117,000
Less: Dividends from Salt **(i)**		12,000	
Ending inventory profit **(l)**		3,150	15,150
Adjusted profit			101,850
Profit of Salt		24,000	
Less: Ending inventory profit **(k)**	3,960		
Land gain **(n)**	12,000		
Impairment of acquisition differential **(b)**	1,700	17,660	
		6,340	
Add: Opening inventory profit **(j)**		1,680	
Adjusted profit			8,020
Profit			$109,870
Attributable to			
Shareholders of parent			$108,266 **(o)**
Non-controlling interest (20% × 8,020)			1,604 **(p)**

CALCULATION OF CONSOLIDATED RETAINED EARNINGS
January 1, Year 5

Retained earnings—Peter		$153,000	
Retained earnings—Salt	72,000		
Acquisition retained earnings	10,000		
Increase	62,000		
Less: Opening inventory profit **(j)**	1,680		
Less: Acquisition-differential impairment Year 3—Year 4 **(a)**	3,400		
Adjusted increase	56,920		
Peter's share	80%	45,536	**(q)**
Consolidated retained earnings, Jan. 1, Year 5		$198,536	**(r)**

CALCULATION OF DEFERRED INCOME TAXES—December 31, Year 5

Ending inventory **(m)**	$ 4,740	
Land **(n)**	8,000	
	$12,740	**(s)**

CALCULATION OF NON-CONTROLLING INTEREST—December 31, Year 5

Ordinary shares—Salt		$50,000
Retained earnings—Salt		81,000
		131,000
Add: Unamortized acquisition differential **(c)**		16,150
Less: Ending inventory profit **(k)**	3,960	
Land gain **(n)**	12,000	(15,960)
Adjusted		131,190
Non-controlling interest's share		20%
		$26,238 **(t)**

PETER CORPORATION
CONSOLIDATED INCOME STATEMENT—Year 5

Sales (900,000 + 250,000 − **[g] 175,000**)	$975,000
Management fees (25,000 + 0 − **[f] 25,000**)	0
Interest (0 + 3,600 − **[h] 3,600**)	0
Gain on land sale (0 + 20,000 − **[n] 20,000**)	0
Dividends (12,000 + 0 − **[i] 12,000**)	0
Cost of sales (540,000 + 162,000 − **[g] 175,000** − **[j] 2,800** + **[m] 11,850**)	536,050
Interest expense (3,600 + 0 − **[h] 3,600**)	0
Other expenses (196,400 + 71,600 + **[b] 1,700** − **[f] 25,000**)	244,700
Income tax (80,000 + 16,000 − **[n] 8,000** + **[j] 1,120** − **[m] 4,740**)	84,380
Total expense	865,130
Net income	$109,870
Attributable to	
Shareholders of parent **(o)**	$108,266
Non-controlling interest **(p)**	1,604

cy end *sub selling*

PETER CORPORATION
CONSOLIDATED RETAINED EARNINGS STATEMENT—Year 5

Balance, January 1 **(r)**	$198,536
Profit	108,266
	306,802
Dividends	50,000
Balance, Dec. 31	$256,802

PETER CORPORATION
CONSOLIDATED STATEMENT OF FINANCIAL POSITION
—December 31, Year 5

Land (175,000 + 19,000 − **[n] 20,000**)	$174,000
Plant and equipment, net (238,000 + 47,000)	285,000
Goodwill **(c)**	16,150
Deferred income taxes **(s)**	12,740
Inventory (32,000 + 27,000 − **[m] 11,850**)	47,150
Accounts receivable (70,000 + 10,000)	80,000
Cash (12,000 + 8,000)	20,000
	$635,040
Ordinary shares	$100,000
Retained earnings	256,802
Non-controlling interest **(t)**	26,238
Other liabilities (212,000 + 40,000)	252,000
	$635,040

before tax

(b) (i)   **CALCULATION OF CONSOLIDATED RETAINED EARNINGS**
—December 31, Year 5

Retained earnings, Dec. 31, Year 5—Peter		$220,000
Less: Ending inventory profit **(l)** only ending		3,150
Adjusted		216,850
Retained earnings, Dec. 31, Year 5—Salt	81,000	
Acquisition retained earnings	10,000	
Increase	71,000	
Less: Acquisition-differential impairment **(a) + (b)** to date	5,100	
Ending inventory profit **(k)**	3,960	
Land gain **(n)**	12,000	21,060
Adjusted increase	49,940	**(u)**
Peter's share	80%	39,952
Consolidated retained earnings, December 31, Year 5		$256,802

(ii)   **CALCULATION OF NON-CONTROLLING INTEREST**—Dec. 31 Year 5

Non-controlling interest at date of acquisition **(d)**		$16,250
Increase is Company S retained earnings, since acquisition net of consolidation adjustments **(u)**	49,940	
Non-controlling interest's ownership	20%	9,988
NCI, end of Year 2		$26,238

(iii)   **CHANGES IN DEFERRED INCOME TAXES**—Year 5

Balance, Jan. 1, Year 5 (inventory) **(j)**		$ 1,120
Taxes paid in Year 5 but deferred		
Inventory **(m)**	4,740	
Land **(n)**	8,000	12,740
		13,860
Expensed Year 5 **(j)**		1,120
Balance, Dec. 31, Year 5		$12,740

(c) (i)

Investment in Salt, Dec. 31, Year 4 (cost method)		$ 65,000
Retained earnings, Dec. 31, Year 4—Salt	72,000	
Acquisition retained earnings	10,000	
Increase	62,000	
Less: Inventory profit **(j)**	1,680	
Amort. of acquisition differential **(a)**	3,400	5,080
Adjusted increase	56,920	
Peter's share	80%	45,536
Investment in Salt, Dec. 31, Year 4 (equity method)		$110,536

(ii)   **EQUITY METHOD JOURNAL ENTRIES**—Year 5
(See Calculation of Consolidated Profit)

Investment in Salt Co.	6,416	
Investment income		6,416
80% of adjusted profit of Salt Co. (80% × 8,020)		
Cash	12,000	
Investment in Salt Co.		12,000
Dividends from Salt Co. **(i)**		
Investment income	3,150	
Investment in Salt Co.		3,150
Ending inventory profit—Peter selling **(l)**		

APPENDIX 6A

REPORTING LAND UNDER REVALUATION MODEL

IAS 16: Property, Plant and Equipment allows a reporting entity the option to periodically revalue its property, plant, and equipment to fair value. Any increase in the fair value of the asset over the carrying amount without the revaluation is reported in other comprehensive income. Any decrease in the fair value below the carrying amount without the revaluation is an impairment loss and is reported in net income. The reversal of an impairment loss is also reported in net income. Any balance in accumulated other comprehensive income relating to the revaluation surplus is transferred directly to retained earnings, either when the asset is sold or as the asset is being depreciated over its useful life.

In the example found in the sections "Intercompany Land Profit Holdback" and "Realization of Intercompany Land Profits" earlier in this chapter, the companies used the cost model to account for land. We will use the same figures from that example to illustrate the accounting when the companies periodically revalue land to fair value under the revaluation model. At the end of Year 0, selected account balances from the separate-entity balance sheet for the company holding the land were as follows:

Land at cost	$2,000
Fair value excess for land	250
Deferred income tax liability (40% × 250)	100
Accumulated revaluation surplus, net of tax (250 − 100)	150

An entity can report its property, plant, and equipment at fair value on an annual basis.

The fair value excess for land is a contra account[2] to the land account. When added to the land account, land will be reported at fair value. The accumulated revaluation surplus account is reported separately as a component of shareholders' equity. It is also referred to as accumulated other comprehensive income.

The selling company would make the following entries pertaining to the sale of the land in Year 1:

Cash	2,300	
Land		2,000
Fair value excess for land		250
Gain on sale of land		50
To record sale of land		
Accumulated revaluation surplus	150	
Retained earnings		150
To transfer revaluation surplus to retained earnings on sale of land		
Income tax expense	20	
Deferred income tax liability	100	
Income tax payable		120
To record tax on sale and transfer deferred income tax liability to current income taxes payable		

The revaluation surplus is transferred to retained earnings when the property is sold.

Assuming that the fair value of the land is $2,325 at the end of Year 1, the purchasing company would make the following entries pertaining to the land in Year 1:

Land	2,300	
Cash		2,300
To record purchase of land		

The revaluation surplus is reported through other comprehensive income on an after-tax basis.

Fair value excess for land	25	
Other comprehensive income—revaluation surplus for land		25
To revalue land to fair value		

Other comprehensive income—income tax on revaluation surplus for land	10	
Deferred income tax liability		10
To record income tax on revaluation surplus		

The following summarizes what would be reported on the separate-entity statements and what should be reported on the consolidated statements for Year 1:

	Selling Co.	Buying Co.	Consolidated
Land		$2,300	$2,000
Fair value excess for land		25	325
Income tax payable	$120		
Deferred income tax liability		10	130
Accumulated revaluation surplus		15	195
Gain on sale of land	50		
Income tax expense	20		
Other comprehensive income—revaluation surplus for land, net of tax		15	
(2,325 − 2,250) × (1 − 40%)			45

The consolidated statements should report amounts that would have existed had the intercompany transaction not occurred.

The consolidated statements present what would have been reported on the selling company's statements had the intercompany transaction not taken place.

REVIEW QUESTIONS

LO1   1. In what way are an individual's pants with four pockets similar to a parent company with three subsidiaries? Explain, with reference to intercompany revenues and expenses.

LO1, 2   2. List the types of intercompany revenue and expenses that are eliminated in the preparation of a consolidated income statement, and indicate the effect that each elimination has on the amount of net income attributable to non-controlling interest.

LO1   3. "From a consolidated-entity point of view, intercompany revenue and expenses and intercompany borrowings do nothing more than transfer cash from one bank account to another." Explain.

LO4   4. If an intercompany profit is recorded on the sale of an asset to an affiliate within the consolidated entity in Period 1, when should this profit be considered realized? Explain.

LO3   5. Explain how the revenue recognition principle supports the elimination of intercompany transactions when preparing consolidated financial statements.

LO2   6. "The reduction of a $1,000 intercompany gross profit from ending inventory should be accompanied by a $400 increase to deferred income taxes in consolidated assets." Do you agree? Explain.

LO3   7. Explain how the matching principle supports adjustments to income tax expense when eliminating intercompany profits from consolidated financial statements.

LO1   8. A parent company rents a sales office to its wholly owned subsidiary under an operating lease requiring rent of $2,000 a month. What adjustments to income tax expense should accompany the elimination of the parent's $24,000 rent revenue and the subsidiary's $24,000 rent expense when a consolidated income statement is being prepared? Explain.

LO2   9. "Intercompany losses recorded on the sale of assets to an affiliate within the consolidated entity should always be eliminated when consolidated financial statements are prepared." Do you agree with this statement? Explain.

LO1, 2   10. Describe the effects that the elimination of intercompany sales and intercompany profits in ending inventory will have on the various elements of the consolidated financial statements.

LO2   11. What difference does it make on the consolidated financial statements if there are unrealized profits in land resulting from a downstream transaction as compared with an upstream transaction?

LO2, 4   12. When there are unrealized profits in inventory at the end of Year 1, consolidated profit would normally be affected for Years 1 and 2. Explain.

LO2, 4   13. An intercompany gain on the sale of land is eliminated in the preparation of the consolidated statements in the year that the gain was recorded. Will this gain be eliminated in the preparation of subsequent consolidated statements? Explain.

LO1, 2   14. A subsidiary periodically revalues its land to fair value under the revaluation option for property, plant, and equipment. Explain the adjustments required to the consolidated financial statements if the subsidiary sells this land to the parent at an amount in excess of its carrying amount.

LO5   15. Describe the journal entry on the parent's books under the equity method to adjust for unrealized profits in ending inventory for upstream transactions.

LO7   16. Describe the difference in accounting under ASPE versus IFRSs for the elimination of unrealized profits in ending inventory on a downstream transaction between an investor and an associate.

CASES

Case 6-1
LO1, 2, 3, 4

You, the controller, recently had the following discussion with the president:

President: I just don't understand why we can't recognize the revenue from the intercompany sale of inventory on the consolidated financial statements. The subsidiary company sold the goods to the parent at fair value and received the cash for the sale. We need to record the profit on this sale in order to maintain a steady earnings growth for our company. Otherwise, the bank will be concerned about our ability to repay the loan.

Controller: You are right that the subsidiary has received the cash, but that is not the main criterion for determining when to recognize the revenue. Furthermore, you need to understand that the consolidated financial statements are different from the individual financial statements for the parent and the subsidiary.

President: I have never understood why we need to prepare consolidated financial statements. It is just extra work. Who uses these statements? Furthermore, the profit on the intercompany transaction should be reported on the income statement because tax had to be paid on this profit. Surely, if tax is paid, the profit is legitimate.

Controller: Once again, cash payments do not determine when we report income tax expense on the income statement. How about we get together for lunch tomorrow? I will prepare a brief presentation to illustrate the difference between the income for the parent and subsidiary and the income for the consolidated entity and will explain how all of these statements properly apply generally accepted accounting principles for revenue and expense recognition.

As part of the presentation, you decided to prepare monthly income statements for the parent, subsidiary, and consolidated entity for the following situation:

- Parent owns 100% of the subsidiary.
- Subsidiary buys goods from outsiders for $200 in July and sells them to Parent in August at a markup of 20% of cost.
- In September, Parent sells these goods to an outsider at a markup of 20% of selling price.
- Both companies pay income tax at the rate of 40%.

Required:

Prepare notes for your presentation to the president.

Case 6-2
LO1, 2

In the course of the audit of King Limited (King), you, the CA, while reviewing the draft financial statements for the year ended August 31, Year 17, noticed that King's investment in Queen Limited (Queen) was measured on the cost basis. In Year 16, it had been measured on the equity basis. Representing a 22% interest in Queen, this investment had been made 10 years ago to infuse fresh equity, with a view to protecting King's source of supply for drugs.

King's controller informed you that Queen had suffered a large loss in Year 17, as shown by the May interim financial statements. King's representative on Queen's board of directors had resigned because King's purchases from Queen now constitute less than 5% of its total purchases. In addition, Queen had been uncooperative in providing profit data in time to make the year-end equity adjustment. Consequently, King's controller had revised the method of accounting for the investment in Queen.

You then found out that King's managers are planning a share issue in Year 18 and do not want their earnings impaired by Queen's poor performance. However, they are reluctant to divest themselves of Queen in case the rumoured development by Queen of a vaccine for a serious viral disease materializes.

When you approached Queen's managers, they refused to disclose any information on Queen's operations. You then learned from a stockbroker friend that Queen's poor results were due to its market being undercut by generic drug manufacturers. The loss had been increased when Queen's management wrote off most of Queen's intangible assets. You summarized the relevant information on the treatment of the investment for your audit file (Exhibit I).

Required:

Discuss how King should report its investment in Queen, and describe what should be disclosed in the notes to the Year 17 financial statements. Assume that King and Queen are public companies.

(CICA adapted)

EXHIBIT I

YOUR (THE CA'S) NOTES ON KING'S INVESTMENT IN QUEEN'S SHARES

Extracts from King's draft financial statements for the year ended August 31, Year 17, in thousands of dollars, follow:

	Year 17	Year 16
Investment in Queen (Note 1)	$25,000	$27,400
Retained Earnings:		
Opening balance	$ 6,500	$ 2,350
Plus: Net earnings	4,500	7,300
	11,000	9,650
Less: Prior-period adjustment (Note 2)	2,400	—
dividends	2,250	3,150
Closing balance	$ 6,350	$ 6,500

Note 1:

The investment in Queen originally cost $25 million. The carrying value under the equity method at the end of Year 16 was $27.4 million. The equity adjustment for Year 16 involved the elimination of King's share of the $5 million unrealized profit included in ending inventory, on sales from Queen to King.

Note 2:

In the nine months ended May 31, Year 17, Queen reported a net loss of $140 million after writing off development and patent costs as unusual items. At the end of Year 17, King changed its method of accounting for the investment from the equity method to the cost method and reduced the investment account from $27.4 million back to its original cost of $25 million. The unrealized profit in King's ending inventory for Year 17 amounts to $1 million. King has not made any adjustment for its share of this unrealized profit in the investment account.

Stock market trading in Queen's common shares has been heavy in the last year. Prices were as follows:

August 31, Year 16	$20
February 28, Year 17	5
August 31, Year 17	13

King owns 2,000,000 common shares of Queen. Queen did not pay any dividends in Year 16 or Year 17.

Case 6-3
L01, 2, 3, 7

Metal Caissons Limited (MCL) was incorporated on December 15, Year 8, to build metal caissons, which are large containers used for transporting military equipment. John Ladd (president) and Paul Finch (vice-president) each own 50% of MCL's shares. Until September 30, Year 9, MCL's first fiscal year-end, they applied their energy to planning and organizing the business. John and Paul developed the product, sought government assistance, designed the plant, and negotiated a sales contract.

In October Year 9, MCL signed a $7.5 million contract with the Canadian Department of National Defence (DND). The contract stipulates that MCL must deliver one caisson to DND on the first business day of each month over a period of five years, commencing on April 1, Year 10. Any delay in delivery entails a $2,000 penalty per day, per caisson delivered late, up to a maximum of $50,000 per caisson. DND has the right to cancel its contract with MCL at any time if the company is unable to meet its commitments. The caissons must be manufactured according to DND's detailed plans and specifications. Any caisson not meeting the specifications will be rejected, thereby causing a delay in delivery.

During November Year 9, MCL obtained two government grants. Details of the grant agreements are as follows:

1. *A $1 million grant for the construction of a manufacturing plant.* The plant must be located in a designated area of the country and must be constructed primarily of Canadian-made components, failing which MCL must repay the grant in full.

2. *A $500,000 grant for job creation.* As a condition of the grant, MCL must employ at least 85% of its total workforce in the plant for a period of three years. If employment at the plant falls below this minimum level, MCL will have to repay the grant in full.

On December 1, Year 9, MCL borrowed $1 million from the bank to construct the plant in northern Quebec, one of the designated areas. Construction was scheduled to start immediately and to be completed by the end of February Year 10. Unfortunately, construction was delayed, and the manufacturing section of the plant was not fully operational until the beginning of May. As a result, the April, May, and June caissons were delivered 25, 18, and 12 days late, respectively. The inexperienced employees had to work quickly but met the delivery deadlines for the July and August caissons. The administrative section of the plant (supervisors' office, etc., representing 5% of the total area) is still under construction.

As a condition of a bank loan and the DND contract, the company must issue audited financial statements commencing with the year ending September 30, Year 10.

It is now mid-September, Year 10. Linda Presner, a partner with Presner & Wolf, Chartered Accountants, and you, the CA in charge of the audit, have just met with MCL's senior management to discuss MCL's accounting policies. During the meeting, you obtained the condensed internal financial statements of MCL for the eleven months ended August 31, Year 10 (Exhibit II) and other information on MCL (Exhibit III in Case 6-3). After the meeting, Linda asks you to prepare a memo for her dealing with the accounting issues connected with this engagement.

EXHIBIT II

METAL CAISSONS LIMITED CONDENSED BALANCE SHEET
(in Thousands of Dollars, Unaudited)

	Aug. 31 Year 10	Sept. 30 Year 9
Current assets	$2,388	$242
Property, plant, and equipment, net of amortization (Note 1)	2,154	
Capitalized expenditures, net of amortization (Note 1)	109	120
Investment in MSL, at cost	240	
	$4,891	$362
Current liabilities	$2,489	$120
Long-term liabilities	1,000	
Shareholders' equity	1,402	242
	$4,891	$362

METAL CAISSONS LIMITED CONDENSED INCOME STATEMENT
for the 11 Months Ended August 31, Year 10
(in Thousands of Dollars)

Revenues	$2,125
Cost of sales	375
Gross margin	1,750
Administrative expenses	590
Net income	$1,160

METAL CAISSONS LIMITED
EXTRACTS FROM NOTES TO CONDENSED FINANCIAL STATEMENTS
for the 11 Months Ended August 31, Year 10

1. Accounting policies

Inventories. Inventories are valued at the lower of cost and net realizable value. Cost is determined on a first-in, first-out basis.

Property, plant, and equipment. Property, plant, and equipment are recorded at cost. Depreciation is calculated on a straight-line basis over the following periods:

Plant	50 years
Production equipment	15 years
Office equipment	20 years
Computer equipment	10 years

Capitalized expenditures. Capitalized expenditures consist of costs incurred during the start-up of the company. Amortization is calculated on a straight-line basis over a 10-year period.

Capitalized interest. The company is capitalizing 100% of the interest on the long-term debt until construction of the plant is complete. This interest is included in the cost of the plant.

EXHIBIT III

INFORMATION GATHERED BY CA

The bank loan bears interest at 8% and is secured by a mortgage on the plant. The loan is repayable over 10 years, with monthly payments of interest and principal of $12,133.

The head office of MCL, located in Montreal, is strictly an administrative unit. Twenty-four people, including the president and the vice-president, work at head office. A bookkeeper who joined MCL in February Year 10 supervises the preparation of the various financial and administrative reports. The plant employs 90 people.

As at September 30, Year 9, capitalized expenditures included the following items:

Incorporation costs	$ 5,000
Office equipment	24,000
Travel costs related to search for plant site	16,000
Costs of calls for tenders for manufacturing plant	12,000
Product development costs	22,000
Grant negotiation costs	13,000
Costs related to contract negotiations with DND	10,000
Miscellaneous administrative costs	11,000
Miscellaneous legal fees	7,000
	$120,000

The capitalized legal fees of $7,000 as at September 30, Year 9, include $2,000 in fees related to a $2.5 million lawsuit filed by Deutsch Production (a German company) against MCL for patent infringements. As at September 15, Year 10, John Ladd is unable to determine the outcome of the suit. In fiscal Year 10, $12,000 in legal fees has been incurred and expensed.

MCL reported no income or expenses in its Year 9 fiscal year.
DND did not take any action following the delays in delivery.

On October 1, Year 9, MCL purchased 60% of the shares of Metal Supply Inc. (MSI) for $240,000. There was no acquisition differential on this acquisition. During fiscal Year 10, MSI sold parts to MCL for $300,000 and earned a gross margin of 30%. At August 31, Year 10, there was $100,000 of these intercompany purchases in MCL's inventory. MSI reported a profit of $40,000 but paid no dividends for the 11 months ended August 31, Year 10.

Required:

Prepare the memo requested by the partner.

(CICA adapted)

Case 6-4
LO1, 2

In early September Year 1, your firm's audit client, D Ltd. (D) acquired in separate transactions an 80% interest in N Ltd. (N) and a 40% interest in K Ltd. (K). All three companies are federally incorporated Canadian companies and have August 31 year ends. They all manufacture small appliances, but they do not compete with each other.

You are the senior on the audit of D. The partner has just received the preliminary consolidated financial statements from the controller of D along with unconsolidated statements for the three separate companies. Extracts from these statements are summarized in Exhibit IV. The partner has requested that you provide him with a memorandum discussing the important financial accounting issues of D. Account balances for the consolidated financial statements should be recalculated to the extent that information is available.

EXHIBIT IV

EXTRACTS FROM FINANCIAL STATEMENTS
At August 31, Year 2
(in Thousands)

	Unconsolidated			Consolidated
	D	N	K	D
Investment in N Ltd., at cost	$4,000			
Investment in K Ltd., at cost	2,100			$2,100
Deferred development costs		$ 90		
Goodwill		60		
Non-controlling interest				590
Common shares	6,000	1,000	$2,000	6,000
Retained earnings, beginning	618	1,850	1,760	618
Profit	600	300	100	660
Dividends	(400)	(200)	(150)	(400)
Retained earnings, end of year	$ 818	$1,950	$1,710	$ 878

D acquired the 80% interest in N for $4,000,000 paid as follows:

(1) $2,000,000 in cash, and

(2) 160,000 common shares of D recorded in the books of D at $2,000,000.

D acquired its 40% interest in K at a cost of $2,100,000 paid as follows:

(1) $100,000 in cash, and

(2) 160,000 common shares of D recorded in the books of D at $2,000,000.

During the course of the audit, the following information was obtained:

1. The carrying amount of 80% of N's net assets at the date of acquisition was $2,280,000. The acquisition differential consisted of the following:

The excess of fair value of land over carrying amount	$ 800,000
The excess of fair value of plant and equipment over carrying amount	700,000
20% non-controlling interest's share of excess of fair value over carrying amount	(300,000)
Goodwill of N written off	(48,000)
Deferred research and development expenditures written off	(72,000)
Unallocated excess	640,000
	$1,720,000

The plant and equipment had a remaining useful life of 10 years when D acquired N.

2. The price paid by D for its investment in K was 10% lower than 40% of the fair value of K's identifiable net assets.

3. During August Year 2, K sold goods to D as follows:

Cost to K	$1,000,000
Normal selling price	1,250,000
Price paid by D	1,200,000

D had not sold these goods as of August 31, Year 2.

N also sold goods to D in August Year 2 and D had not sold them by August 31, Year 2.

Cost to N	$630,000
Normal selling price	750,000
Price paid by D	850,000

4. For the year ended August 31, Year 2, D's sales were $8,423,300 and N's sales were $6,144,500.

5. The companies pay income tax at the rate of 40%.

Required:

Prepare the memorandum requested by the partner.

(CICA adapted)

Case 6-5
LO1, 2, 6

Good Quality Auto Parts Limited (GQ) is a medium-sized, privately owned producer of auto parts, which are sold to car manufacturers, repair shops, and retail outlets. In March Year 10, the union negotiated a new three-year contract with the company for the 200 shop-floor employees. At the time, GQ was in financial difficulty and management felt unable to meet the contract demands of the union. Management also believed that a strike of any length would force the company into bankruptcy.

The company proposed that in exchange for wage concessions, the company would implement a profit-sharing plan whereby the shop floor employees would receive 10% of the company's annual after-tax profit as a bonus in each year of the contract. Although the union generally finds this type of contract undesirable, it believed that insisting on the prevailing industry settlement would jeopardize GQ's survival. As a result, the contract terms were accepted.

The contract specifies that no major changes in accounting policies may be made without the change being approved by GQ's auditor. Another clause in the contract allows the union to engage a chartered accountant to examine the books of the company and meet with GQ's management and auditor to discuss any issues. Under the terms of the contract, any controversial accounting issues are to be negotiated by the union and management to arrive at a mutual agreement. If the parties cannot agree, the positions of the parties are to be presented to an independent arbitrator for resolution.

GQ presented to the union its annual financial statements and the unqualified audit report, for the year ended February 28, Year 11, the first year during which the profit-sharing plan was in effect. The union engaged you, the CA, to analyze these financial statements and determine whether there are any controversial accounting issues. As a result of your examination, you identified a number of issues that are of concern to you. You met with the controller of the company and obtained the following information:

1. GQ wrote off $250,000 of inventory manufactured between Year 4 and Year 7. There have been no sales from this inventory in over two years. The controller explained that up until this year she had some hope that the inventory could be sold as replacement parts. However, she now believes that the parts cannot be sold.

2. The contracts GQ has with the large auto manufacturers allow the purchaser to return items for any reason. The company has increased the allowance

for returned items by 10% in the year just ended. The controller contends that because of the weak economy and stiff competition faced by the auto manufacturers with whom GQ does business, there will likely be a significant increase in the parts returned.

3. In April Year 10, GQ purchased $500,000 of new manufacturing equipment. To reduce the financial strain of the acquisition, the company negotiated a six-year payment schedule. Management believed that the company would be at a serious competitive disadvantage if it did not emerge from the current downturn with updated equipment. GQ decided to use accelerated depreciation at a rate of 40% for the new equipment. The controller argued that because of the rapid technological changes occurring in the industry, equipment purchased now is more likely to become technologically, rather than operationally, obsolete. The straight-line depreciation method applied to the existing equipment has not been changed.

4. In Year 5, GQ purchased 100% of the shares of Brake Inc., a manufacturer of car brakes. At the time of acquisition, $35,000 of goodwill was reported on CG's consolidated financial statements and was being amortized over 35 years. The company has written off the goodwill in the year just ended. The controller explained that the poor performance of the auto parts industry, and of GQ in particular, has made the goodwill worthless.

5. During Year 11, Brake Inc. sold brakes to GQ for $800,000. Ten percent of this merchandise remains in CQ's inventory at February 28, Year 11. On February 28, Year 10, the inventory of CQ contained $200,000 of merchandise purchased from Brake. Brake earns a gross margin of 35% on its intercompany sales. GQ has not made any adjustments for the intercompany transactions for Year 11.

6. In February Year 11, the president and the chairman of the board, who between them own 75% of the voting shares of the company, received bonuses of $250,000 each. GQ did not pay any dividends during the current year. In the prior year, dividends amounting to $650,000 were paid. The controller said that the board of directors justified the bonuses as a reward for keeping the company afloat despite extremely difficult economic times.

7. Until this year, GQ used the taxes-payable method for accounting purposes. This year, the company has used the liability method of accounting for income taxes. The change has been made retroactively. The effect of the change has been to reduce net income for fiscal Year 11. The controller argued that, because the company is likely to need significant external financing from new sources in the upcoming year, the company should adopt policies under ASPE that are the same as IFRSs.

The union has asked you to prepare a report on the position it should take on the issues identified when discussing them with management. The union also wants to know what additional information you require in order to support this position.

Required:

Prepare the report.

(CICA adapted)

Case 6-6

LO1, 2, 7

You, the CA, an audit senior at Grey & Co., Chartered Accountants, are in charge of this year's audit of Plex-Fame Corporation (PFC). PFC is a rapidly expanding, diversified, and publicly owned entertainment company with operations throughout Canada and the United States. PFC's operations include movie theatres, live theatre production, and television production. It is June 22, Year 7, the week before PFC's year-end. You meet with the chief financial officer of PFC to get an update on current developments and learn the following.

PFC acquires real estate in prime locations where an existing theatre chain does not adequately serve the market. After acquiring a theatre site, the company engages a contractor to construct the theatre complex. During the year, the company received a $2 million payment from one such contractor who had built a 10-theatre complex for PFC in Montreal. This payment represents a penalty for not completing the theatre complex on time. Construction began in June Year 6 and was to have been completed by December Year 6. Instead, the complex was not completed until the end of May Year 7.

The company is staging a Canadian version of "Rue St. Jacques," which is to open in November Year 7. The smash-hit musical has been running in Paris for three years and is still playing to sold-out audiences. PFC started receiving advance bookings in November Year 6, and the first 40 weeks of the show's run are completely sold out. As at June 22, Year 7, PFC has already collected $22 million from the advance bookings and invested the cash in interest-bearing securities. It included in revenue $1.7 million of interest collected on the funds received from advance ticket sales. In addition to the substantial investment in advertising for this production ($4 million), the company will have invested $15 million in pre-production costs by November Year 7 and will incur weekly production costs of $250,000 once the show opens.

PFC has retained Media Inc. (Media), a company that specializes in entertainment-related advertising and promotion, to promote PFC's activities. Media bills PFC's corporate office for all advertising and promotion related to PFC's activities. Advertising and promotions have significantly increased this year, in part due to large costs associated with the forthcoming opening of "Rue St. Jacques." Media has billed PFC $12 million this year for advertising and promotion, an increase of $7 million over the preceding year.

PFC has $43 million invested in Government of Canada treasury bills. During the past year, $30 million of these treasury bills were set aside to cover interest and principal obligations on the company's syndicated loan of US$25 million. At the time the loan agreement was signed, PFC entered into a forward contract to buy U.S. dollars for the same amounts as the obligations under the syndicated loan and for the same dates as the obligations came due. PFC considers that in substance the debt has been settled, and as a result, both the treasury bills and the syndicated loan have been removed from the company's balance sheet.

PFC started selling movie theatres a couple of years ago. Each theatre's contribution to long-run operating cash flow is assessed and, if the value of the real estate is greater than the present value of future theatre operating profits, the theatre is sold. In the past, revenue from these sales has been relatively minor, but this year 25% of net income (i.e., $6 million) came from the sale of theatres. Since these sales are considered an ongoing part of the company's operations, proceeds from the sale of theatres are recorded as revenue in the income statement.

On May 31, Year 7, PFC and an unrelated company, Odyssey Inc. (Odyssey), formed a partnership, Phantom. Odyssey contributed $40 million in cash.

PFC contributed the assets of its TV production company, which had a carrying amount of $65 million. The $90 million value assigned to PFC's contribution may be adjusted if the net income of Phantom earned between July 1, Year 7, and June 30, Year 8, does not meet expectations. PFC has recorded a gain of $25 million. The partnership agreement states that PFC is permitted to withdraw the $40 million for its own use, and it has done so. As a result, Odyssey has a 45% interest in the partnership and PFC has the remaining 55% interest.

PFC's bank operating loan in the amount of $200 million is well within its maximum of $240 million. The loan agreement calls for a maximum debt-to-equity ratio of 2:1, where debt is defined as monetary liabilities. Failure to meet the loan covenant would cause the operating loan to become payable within 30 days. On the May 31, Year 7, interim financial statements, PFC meets the restriction because its debt is $1,490 million while its shareholders' equity is $780 million.

PFC's consolidated income before tax was $147 million for the 11 months ended May 31, Year 7. PFC hopes to maintain its recent trend of reporting a minimum before-tax return on shareholders' equity of 20%.

When you return to the office, you discuss the aforementioned issues with the partner in charge of the PFC audit. She asks you to prepare a report on the accounting implications of the issues you have identified as a result of your meeting. When the accounting for an individual transaction has not been specified, you should indicate how it should be accounted for and the impact that the accounting would have had on the key metric(s).

Required:

Prepare the report to the partner. Ignore income taxes.

(CICA adapted)

PROBLEMS

Problem 6-1
LO1, 2, 4

On January 1, Year 2, PAT Ltd. acquired 90% of SAT Inc. when SAT's retained earnings were $900,000. There was no acquisition differential. PAT accounts for its investment under the cost method. SAT sells inventory to PAT on a regular basis at a markup of 30% of selling price. The intercompany sales were $150,000 in Year 2 and $180,000 in Year 3. The total amount owing by PAT related to these intercompany sales was $50,000 at the end of Year 2 and $40,000 at the end of Year 3. On January 1, Year 3, the inventory of PAT contained goods purchased from SAT amounting to $60,000, while the December 31, Year 3, inventory contained goods purchased from SAT amounting to $70,000. Both companies pay income tax at the rate of 40%.

Selected account balances from the records of PAT and SAT for the year ended December 31, Year 3, were as follows:

Inventory	$ 500,000	$ 300,000
Accounts payable	600,000	320,000
Retained earnings, beginning of year	2,400,000	1,100,000
Sales	4,000,000	2,500,000
Cost of sales	3,100,000	1,700,000
Income tax expense	80,000	50,000

Required:

(a) Determine the amount to report on the Year 3 consolidated financial statements for the above noted accounts.

(b) Indicate how non-controlling interest on the Year 3 consolidated income statement and Year 3 consolidated balance sheet will be affected by the intercompany transactions noted above.

Problem 6-2
LO2, 3, 4

The consolidated income statement of a parent and its 90%-owned subsidiary appears below. It was prepared by an accounting student before reading this chapter.

CONSOLIDATED INCOME STATEMENT

Sales	$500,000
Rental revenue	24,000
Interest revenue	50,000
Total revenue	574,000
Cost of goods sold	350,000
Rent expense	24,000
Interest expense	35,000
Administration expenses	45,000
Income tax expense	42,000
Non-controlling interest in profit	9,000
Total costs and expenses	505,000
Profit	$ 69,000

The following items were overlooked when the statement was prepared:

- The opening inventory of the parent contained an intercompany profit of $5,000. This inventory was sold by the parent during the current year.
- During the year, intercompany sales (at a 30% gross profit rate) were made as follows:

By the parent to the subsidiary	$100,000
By the subsidiary to the parent	80,000

- At the end of the year, half of the items purchased from the parent remained in the inventory of the subsidiary and none of the inventory purchased from the subsidiary remained in the parent's inventory.
- All of the rental revenue and 70% of the interest revenue were intercompany and appeared on the income statement of the parent.
- Assume a 40% rate for income tax.

Required:

(a) Prepare a correct consolidated income statement.

(b) Use the matching principle to explain the adjustments for unrealized profits on intercompany sales when preparing consolidated financial statements.

Problem 6-3
LO2, 4

On January 1, Year 1, Spike Ltd. purchased land from outsiders for $100,000. On December 31, Year 1, Pike Co. acquired all of the common shares of Spike. The fair value of Spike's land on this date was $115,000.

On December 31, Year 2, Spike sold its land to Pike for $128,000. On December 31, Year 3, Pike sold the land to an arm's-length party for $140,000.

Both companies use the cost model for valuing their land and pay income tax at the rate of 40%. Assume that any gain on sale of land is fully taxable. The only land owned by these two companies is the land purchased by Spike in Year 1.

Required:

Determine the account balances for land, gain on sale of land, and income tax on gain for Years 1, 2, and 3 for three sets of financial statements (i.e., separate-entity statements for Pike and Spike and consolidated statements) by completing the following table:

	Pike	Spike	Consolidated
December 31, Year 1			
Land			
Gain on sale			
Income tax on gain			
December 31, Year 2			
Land			
Gain on sale			
Income tax on gain			
December 31, Year 3			
Land			
Gain on sale			
Income tax on gain			

Problem 6-4
LO1, 2, 3, 4, 5, 6

The income statements for Paste Company and its subsidiaries, Waste Company, and Baste Company were prepared for the year ended December 31, Year 6, and are shown below:

	Paste	Waste	Baste
Income			
Sales	$450,000	$270,000	$190,000
Dividend	43,750	—	—
Rent	—	130,000	—
Interest	10,000	—	—
Total income	503,750	400,000	190,000
Expenses			
Cost of sales	300,000	163,000	145,000
General and administrative	93,000	48,000	29,000
Interest	—	10,000	—
Income tax	27,000	75,000	7,000
Total expenses	420,000	296,000	181,000
Profit	$ 83,750	$104,000	$ 9,000

Additional Information

- Paste purchased its 80% interest in Waste on January 1, Year 1. On this date, Waste had a retained earnings balance of $40,000, and the acquisition differential amounting to $15,000 was allocated entirely to plant, with an estimated remaining life of eight years. The plant is used exclusively for manufacturing goods for resale.

- Paste purchased its 75% interest in Baste on December 31, Year 3. On this date, Baste had a retained earnings balance of $80,000. The acquisition differential amounting to $19,000 was allocated to goodwill; however, because Baste had failed to report adequate profits, the goodwill was entirely written off for consolidated purposes by the end of Year 5.
- Paste has established a policy that any intercompany sales will be made at a gross profit rate of 30%.
- On January 1, Year 6, the inventory of Paste contained goods purchased from Waste for $15,000.
- During Year 6, the following intercompany sales took place:

Paste to Waste	$ 90,000
Waste to Baste	170,000
Baste to Paste	150,000

- On December 31, Year 6, the inventories of each of the three companies contained items purchased on an intercompany basis in the following amounts:

Inventory of	
Paste from Baste	$ 60,000
Waste from Paste	22,000
Baste from Waste	60,000

- In addition to its merchandising activities, Waste is in the office equipment rental business. Both Paste and Baste rent office equipment from Waste. General and administrative expenses for Paste and Baste include rent expense of $25,000 and $14,000, respectively.
- During Year 6, Waste paid $10,000 interest to Paste for intercompany advances.
- All of Paste's dividend revenue pertains to its investments in Waste and Baste.
- Retained earnings at December 31, Year 6, for Paste, Waste, and Baste were $703,750, $146,000, and $79,000, respectively.
- Paste Company uses the cost method to account for its investments, and uses tax allocation at a rate of 40% when it prepares consolidated financial statements.

Required:

(a) Prepare a consolidated income statement for Year 6.

(b) Calculate consolidated retained earnings at December 31, Year 6.

(c) Now assume that Paste is a private company, uses ASPE, and chooses to use the equity method. Calculate its income from investments for Year 6.

(d) Use the criteria for revenue recognition to explain the adjustments for unrealized profits on intercompany sales when preparing consolidated financial statements.

Problem 6-5
LO2, 4, 5, 6

X Co. acquired 75% of Y Co. on January 1, Year 1, when Y Co. had common shares worth $100,000 and retained earnings of $70,000. The acquisition differential was allocated as follows on this date:

Inventory	$ 60,000
Equipment (15-year life)	45,000
Total acquisition differential	$105,000

Since this date the following events have occurred:

Year 1

- Y Co. reported a net income of $130,000 and paid dividends of $25,000.
- On July 1, X Co. sold land to Y Co. for $112,000. This land was carried in the records of X Co. at $75,000.
- On December 31, Year 1, the inventory of X Co. contained an intercompany profit of $30,000.
- X Co. reported a net income of $400,000 from its own operations.

Year 2

- Y Co. reported a net loss of $16,000 and paid dividends of $5,000.
- Y Co. sold the land that it purchased from X Co. to an unrelated company for $130,000.
- On December 31, Year 2, the inventory of Y Co. contained an intercompany profit of $12,000.
- X Co. reported a net income from its own operations of $72,000.

Required:

Assume a 40% tax rate.

(a) Prepare X Co.'s equity method journal entries for each of Years 1 and 2.
(b) Calculate consolidated net income attributable to X Co.'s shareholders for each of Years 1 and 2.
(c) Prepare a statement showing the changes in non-controlling interest in each of Years 1 and 2.
(d) Now assume that X Co. is a private company, uses ASPE, and chooses to use the equity method. Calculate the balance in the Investment in Y Co. account as at December 31, Year 2.

Problem 6-6
LO2, 4

L Co. owns a controlling interest in M Co. and Q Co. L Co. purchased an 80% interest in M Co. at a time when M Co. reported retained earnings of $500,000. L Co. purchased a 70% interest in Q Co. at a time when Q Co. reported retained earnings of $50,000. There was no acquisition differential for either of these acquisitions.

An analysis of the changes in retained earnings of the three companies during the current year appears below:

	L Co.	M Co.	Q Co.
Retained earnings balance, beginning of current year	$ 976,000	$ 843,000	$682,000
Profit	580,000	360,000	240,000
Dividends paid or declared	(250,000)	(200,000)	(150,000)
Retained earnings balance, end of current year	$1,306,000	$1,003,000	$772,000

Q Co. sells parts to L Co., which after further processing and assembly are sold by L Co. to M Co., where they become a part of the finished product sold by M Co. Intercompany profits included in raw materials inventories at the beginning and end of the current year are estimated as follows:

	Beginning inventory	Ending inventory
Intercompany profit in raw materials inventory		
On sales from Q to L	$80,000	$ 35,000
On sales from L to M	52,000	118,000

L Co. uses the cost method to account for its investments and income tax allocation at a 40% rate when it prepares consolidated financial statements.

Required:

(a) Calculate consolidated profit attributable to M Co's shareholders for the current year.
(b) Calculate consolidated retained earnings at the beginning of the current year.

Problem 6-7
LO1, 2, 3, 4, 7

On January 1, Year 3, the Most Company purchased 80% of the outstanding voting shares of the Least Company for $1.6 million in cash. On that date, Least's balance sheet and the fair values of its identifiable assets and liabilities were as follows:

	Carrying value	Fair value
Cash	$ 25,000	$ 25,000
Accounts receivable	310,000	290,000
Inventories	650,000	600,000
Plant and equipment (net)	2,015,000	2,050,000
Total assets	$3,000,000	
Current liabilities	$ 300,000	300,000
Long-term liabilities	1,200,000	1,100,000
Common shares	500,000	
Retained earnings	1,000,000	
Total liabilities and shareholders' equity	$3,000,000	

On January 1, Year 3, Least's plant and equipment had a remaining useful life of 8 years. Its long-term liabilities matured on January 1, Year 7. Goodwill, if any, is to be tested yearly for impairment.

The balance sheets as at December 31, Year 9, for the two companies were as follows:

BALANCE SHEETS
December 31, Year 9

	Most	Least
Cash	$ 500,000	$ 40,000
Accounts receivable	1,700,000	500,000
Inventories	2,300,000	1,200,000
Plant and equipment, net	8,200,000	4,000,000
Investment in Least, at cost	1,600,000	—
Land	700,000	260,000
Total assets	$15,000,000	$6,000,000
Current liabilities	$ 600,000	$ 200,000
Long-term liabilities	3,000,000	3,000,000
Common shares	1,000,000	500,000
Retained earnings	10,400,000	2,300,000
Total liabilities and shareholders' equity	$15,000,000	$6,000,000

Additional Information

• The inventories of both companies have a maximum turnover period of one year. Receivables have a maximum turnover period of 62 days.

- On July 1, Year 7, Most sold a parcel of land to Least for $100,000. Most had purchased this land in Year 4 for $150,000. On September 30, Year 9, Least sold the property to another company for $190,000.
- During Year 9, $2 million of Most's sales were to Least. Of these sales, $500,000 remain in the December 31, Year 9, inventories of Least. The December 31, Year 8, inventories of Least contained $312,500 of merchandise purchased from Most. Most's sales to Least are priced to provide it with a gross profit of 20%.
- Most and Least reported net income of $1,000,000 and $400,000, respectively, for Year 9.
- During Year 9, $1.5 million of Least's sales were to Most. Of these sales, $714,280 remains in the December 31, Year 9, inventories of Most. The December 31, Year 8, inventories of Most contained $857,140 of merchandise purchased from Least. Least's sales to Most are priced to provide it with a gross profit of 30%.
- Dividends declared on December 31, Year 9, were as follows:

| Most | $350,000 |
| Least | 100,000 |

- Goodwill impairment tests resulted in losses of $52,200 in Year 4 and $8,700 in Year 9.
- Assume a 40% tax rate for both companies and that dividends have not yet been paid.

Required:

(a) Prepare the consolidated statement of changes in equity for Year 9.
(b) Prepare the consolidated balance sheet.
(c) Explain how the cost principle supports the adjustments to inventory when eliminating unrealized profits from intercompany sales from the consolidated financial statements.
(d) If Most had used the parent company extension theory rather than the entity theory, how would this affect the debt-to-equity ratio at the end of Year 9?

Problem 6-8
LO2, 4, 5

H Co. has controlling interests in three subsidiaries, as shown in the data below:

		Subsidiaries		
	H Co.	*L Co.*	*J Co.*	*K Co.*
Retained earnings at acquisition		$30,000	$40,000	$25,000
Percentage ownership		95%	90%	85%
Retained earnings, Jan. 1, Year 5	$12,000	50,000	43,000	30,000
Profit (loss), Year 5		20,000	(5,000)	30,000
Dividends paid, Year 5	10,000	5,000	3,000	15,000
Intercompany sales		50,000	70,000	

K Co. had items in its inventory on January 1, Year 5, on which L Co. had made a profit of $5,000. J Co. had items in its inventory on December 31, Year 5, on which K Co. had made a profit of $8,000. J Co. rents premises from L Co. at an annual rental of $8,500. The parent company has no income (other than from its investments) and no expenses. It uses the equity method of recording its investments but has made no entries during Year 5. Assume a 40% tax rate.

Required:

Prepare the following related to its investments:

(a) Entries that H Co. would make in Year 5.
(b) A calculation of consolidated retained earnings, January 1, Year 5.
(c) A calculation of consolidated profit attributable to shareholders of H Co. for Year 5.

Problem 6-9
L02, 4

Purple Company purchased a 70% interest in Sand Company several years ago in order to obtain retail outlets for its major products. Since that time, Purple has sold to Sand a substantial portion of its merchandise requirements. At the beginning of the current year, Sand's inventory of $690,000 was composed of 60% of goods purchased from Purple at markups averaging 30% on Purple's cost. Sales from Purple to Sand during the current year were $5,600,000. The estimated intercompany profit in Sand's ending inventory was $194,000.

Purple owns buildings and land used in Sand's retail operations and rented to Sand. Rentals paid by Sand to Purple during the current year amounted to $743,000. At the end of the current year, Purple sold to Sand for $260,000 land to be used in the development of a shopping centre that had cost Purple $203,500. The gain was included in Purple's net income for the current year. Purple also holds a one-year, 6% note of Sand on which it has accrued interest revenues of $22,500 during the current year.

During the current year, Purple reported net income of $568,100 and Sand reported net income of $248,670. Purple uses the cost method to account for its investment.

Required:

Calculate the current year's consolidated net income attributable to Purple's shareholders. Assume a 40% tax rate.

Problem 6-10
L02, 4

The income statements of Evans Company and Falcon Company for the current year are shown below:

	Evans	Falcon
Sales revenues	$450,000	$600,000
Dividend revenues	32,000	—
Rental revenues	33,600	—
Interest revenues	—	18,000
	515,600	618,000
Raw materials and finished goods purchased	268,000	328,000
Changes in inventory	20,000	25,000
Other expenses	104,000	146,000
Interest expense	30,000	—
Income taxes	31,700	43,500
	453,700	542,500
Profit	$ 61,900	$ 75,500

The following amounts were taken from the statement of changes in equity for the two companies:

	Evans	Falcon
Retained earnings, beginning of year	$632,000	$348,000
Dividends declared	30,000	40,000

Evans owns 80% of the outstanding common shares of Falcon, purchased at the time the latter company was organized.

Evans sells parts to Falcon at a price that is 25% above cost. Total sales from Evans to Falcon during the year were $90,000. Included in Falcon's inventories were parts purchased from Evans amounting to $21,250 in beginning inventories and $28,750 in the ending inventory.

Falcon sells back to Evans certain finished goods, at a price that gives Falcon an average gross profit of 30% on these intercompany sales. Total sales from Falcon to Evans during the year were $177,000. Included in the inventories of Evans were finished goods acquired from Falcon amounting to $11,000 in beginning inventories and $3,000 in ending inventories.

Falcon rents an office building from Evans and pays $2,800 per month in rent. Evans has borrowed $600,000 through a series of 5% notes, of which Falcon holds $360,000 as notes receivable. Use income tax allocation at a 40% rate.

Required:

(a) Prepare a consolidated income statement with expenses classified by nature.
(b) Calculate retained earnings, beginning of year, and dividends declared for the consolidated statement of changes in equity for the current year.

Problem 6-11
LO2, 4

The partial trial balances of P Co. and S Co. at December 31, Year 5, were as follows:

	P Co.		S Co.	
	Dr.	Cr.	Dr.	Cr.
Investment in S. Co.	90,000			
Common shares		150,000		60,000
Retained earnings (charged with dividends, no other changes during the year)		101,000		34,000

Additional Information

- The investment in the shares of S Co. (a 90% interest) was acquired January 2, Year 1, for $90,000. At that time, the shareholders' equity of S Co. was common shares of $60,000 and retained earnings of $20,000 and the common shares for P Co. of $150,000.
- Net incomes of the two companies for the year were as follows:

P Co.	$60,000
S Co.	48,000

- During Year 5, sales of P Co. to S Co. were $10,000, and sales of S Co. to P Co. were $50,000. Rates of gross profit on intercompany sales in Years 4 and 5 were 40% of sales.
- On December 31, Year 4, the inventory of P Co. included $7,000 of merchandise purchased from S Co., and the inventory of S Co. included $3,000 of merchandise purchased from P Co. On December 31, Year 5, the inventory of P Co. included $20,000 of merchandise purchased from S Co. and the inventory of S Co. included $5,000 of merchandise purchased from P Co.
- During the year ended December 31, Year 5, P Co. paid dividends of $12,000 and S Co. paid dividends of $10,000.
- At the time that P Co. purchased the shares of S Co., the acquisition differential was allocated to patents of S Co. These patents are being amortized for consolidation purposes over a period of five years.

- In Year 3, land that originally cost $40,000 was sold by S Co. to P Co. for $50,000. The land is still owned by P Co.
- Assume a corporate tax rate of 40%.

Required:

Prepare a consolidated statement of changes in equity for the year ended December 31, Year 5.

Problem 6-12
LO1, 2, 4, 7

On January 2, Year 1, Road Ltd. acquired 70% of the outstanding voting shares of Runner Ltd. The acquisition differential of $280,000 on that date was allocated in the following manner:

Inventory	$100,000	
Land	50,000	
Plant and equipment	60,000	estimated life, 5 years
Patent	40,000	estimated life, 8 years
Goodwill	30,000	
	$280,000	

The Year 5 income statements for the two companies were as follows:

	Road	Runner
Sales	$4,000,000	$2,100,000
Intercompany investment income	210,700	—
Rental revenue	—	70,000
Total income	4,210,700	2,170,000
Materials used in manufacturing	2,000,000	800,000
Changes in work-in-progress and finished goods inventory	45,000	(20,000)
Employee benefits	550,000	480,000
Interest expense	250,000	140,000
Depreciation	405,000	245,000
Patent amortization	—	25,000
Rental expense	35,000	—
Income tax	300,000	200,000
Total expenses	3,585,000	1,870,000
Profit	$ 625,700	$ 300,000

Additional Information

- Runner regularly sells raw materials to Road. Intercompany sales in Year 5 totalled $420,000.
- Intercompany profits in the inventories of Road were as follows:

January 1, Year 5	$75,000
December 31, Year 5	40,000

- Road's entire rental expense relates to equipment rented from Runner.
- A goodwill impairment loss of $3,000 occurred in Year 5.
- Retained earnings at December 31, Year 5, for Road and Runner were $2,525,700 and $1,150,000, respectively.
- Road uses the equity method to account for its investment, and uses income tax allocation at the rate of 40% when it prepares consolidated statements.

Required:

(a) Prepare a consolidated income statement for Year 5 with expenses classified by nature.

(b) Calculate consolidated retained earnings at December 31, Year 5.

(c) If Road had used parent company extension theory rather than entity theory, how would this affect the return on equity attributable to shareholders of Road for Year 5?

Problem 6-13
L01, 2, 4

The following are the financial statements of Post Corporation and its subsidiary, Sage Company, as at December 31, Year 3:

STATEMENTS OF FINANCIAL POSITION
December 31, Year 3

	Post	Sage
Land	$175,000	$ 19,000
Plant and equipment	520,000	65,000
Accumulated depreciation	(229,400)	(17,000)
Investment in Sage	103,707	—
Inventory	34,000	27,000
Notes receivable	—	55,000
Accounts receivable	17,200	9,100
Cash	12,200	12,900
	$632,707	$171,000
Ordinary shares	$100,000	$ 50,000
Retained earnings	265,707	81,000
Notes payable	55,000	—
Accounts payable	212,000	40,000
	$632,707	$171,000

STATEMENTS OF PROFIT—Year 3

	Post	Sage
Sales	$900,000	$240,000
Management fee revenue	26,500	—
Interest revenue	—	6,800
Investment income from Sage	1,479	—
Gain on sale of land	—	30,000
	927,979	276,800
Cost of goods sold	540,000	162,000
Interest expense	20,000	—
Other expenses	180,000	74,800
Income tax expense	80,000	16,000
	820,000	252,800
Profit	$107,979	$ 24,000

Additional Information

- Post purchased 70% of the outstanding shares of Sage on January 1, Year 1, at a cost of $63,000, and has used the cost method to account for its investment. On that date, Sage had accumulated depreciation of $10,000, retained earnings of $15,000, and fair values were equal to carrying amounts for all its net assets, except inventory (overvalued by $12,000).

① Acg diff
③ Impairment

- In determining the purchase price, the management of Post noted that Sage, as lessee, leases a warehouse under an operating lease that has terms that are unfavourable relative to market terms. However, the lease agreement explicitly prohibits transfer of the lease (through either sale or sublease). An independent appraiser indicated that the fair value of this unfavourable lease agreement is $18,000. There were five years remaining on this lease on the date of acquisition.
- The companies sell merchandise to each other at a gross profit rate of 25%.
- The December 31, Year 2, inventory of Post contained purchases made from Sage amounting to $14,000. There were no intercompany purchases in the inventory of Sage on this date.
- During Year 3 the following intercompany transactions took place:

  - Sage made a payment of $26,500 to Post for management fees, which was recorded under the category "other expenses."
  - Sage made sales of $90,000 to Post. The December 31, Year 3, inventory of Post contained goods purchased from Sage amounting to $28,000.
  - Post made sales of $125,000 to Sage. The December 31, Year 3, inventory of Sage contained goods purchased from Post amounting to $18,000.
  - On July 1, Year 3, Post borrowed $55,000 from Sage and signed a note bearing interest at 12% per annum. The interest on this note was paid on December 31, Year 3.
  - During the year, Sage sold land to Post and recorded a gain of $30,000 on the transaction. This land is being held by Post on December 31, Year 3.

- Goodwill impairment losses occurred as follows: Year 1, $2,600; Year 2, $460; Year 3, $1,530.
- Post uses the equity method to account for its investment in Sage.
- Both companies pay income tax at 40% on their taxable incomes.

Required:

(a) Prepare the following consolidated financial statements for Year 3:

  (i) Income statement
  (ii) Statement of financial position

(b) Calculate goodwill impairment loss and profit attributable to non-controlling interest for the year ended December 31, Year 3, under parent company extension theory.

(c) Calculate goodwill and non-controlling interest on the consolidated statement of financial position at December 31, Year 3, under parent company extension theory.

Problem 6-14
LO2, 4, 5

75%

non-level

On January 1, Year 1, the Vine Company purchased 60,000 of the 80,000 ordinary shares of the Devine Company for $80 per share. On that date, Devine had ordinary shares of $3,500,000, and retained earnings of $2,100,000. When acquired, Devine had inventories with fair values $100,000 less than carrying amount, a parcel of land with a fair value $200,000 greater than the carrying amount, and equipment with a fair value $200,000 less than carrying amount. There were also internally generated patents with an estimated market value of $400,000 and a five-year remaining life. A long-term liability had a market value $100,000 greater than carrying amount; this liability was paid off December 31, Year 4. All other identifiable assets and liabilities of Devine had fair values equal to their carrying amounts. Devine's accumulated depreciation on the plant and equipment was $500,000 at the date of acquisition.

At the acquisition date, the equipment had an expected remaining useful life of 10 years. The equipment and patents are used in manufacturing. Both companies use the straight-line method for all depreciation and amortization calculations and the FIFO inventory cost flow assumption. Assume a 40% income tax rate on all applicable items and that there were no impairment losses for goodwill.

On September 1, Year 5, Devine sold a parcel of land to Vine and recorded a total non-operating gain of $400,000.

Sales of finished goods from Vine to Devine totalled $1,000,000 in Year 4 and $2,000,000 in Year 5. These sales were priced to provide a gross profit margin on selling price of 33 ⅓% to the Vine Company. Devine's December 31, Year 4, inventory contained $300,000 of these sales; December 31, Year 5, inventory contained $600,000.

Sales of finished goods from Devine to Vine were $800,000 in Year 4 and $1,200,000 in Year 5. These sales were priced to provide a gross profit margin on selling price of 40% to the Devine Company. Vine's December 31, Year 4, inventory contained $100,000 of these sales; the December 31, Year 5, inventory contained $500,000.

Vine's investment in Devine's account is carried in accordance with the cost method and includes advances to Devine of $200,000.

There are no intercompany amounts other than those noted, except for the dividends of $500,000 (total amount) declared and paid by Devine.

INCOME STATEMENTS
for Year Ending December 31, Year 5
(in Thousands of Dollars)

	Vine	Devine
Sales	$11,600	$3,000
Dividends, investment income, and gains	400	1,000
Total income	12,000	4,000
Cost of goods sold	8,000	1,500
Other expenses	500	300
Income taxes	500	200
Total expenses	9,000	2,000
Profit	$ 3,000	$2,000

STATEMENTS OF FINANCIAL POSITION
December 31, Year 5
(in Thousands of Dollars)

	Vine	Devine
Land	$ 6,000	$ 2,500
Plant and equipment	18,800	11,800
Accumulated depreciation	(5,800)	(5,000)
Investment in Devine, cost	5,000	
Inventories	4,600	2,400
Cash and current receivables	900	300
Total assets	$29,500	$12,000

(continued)

	Vine	Devine
Ordinary shares	$10,000	$ 3,500
Retained earnings	12,000	7,000
Long-term liabilities	6,600	1,100
Deferred income taxes	200	100
Current liabilities	700	300
Total equity and liabilities	$29,500	$12,000

Required:

(a) Show the allocation of the acquisition cost at acquisition and the related amortization schedule. Show and label all calculations.
(b) Prepare a consolidated income statement with expenses classified by function.
(c) Calculate consolidated retained earnings at December 31, Year 5.
(d) Prepare a consolidated statement of financial position for Vine Company at December 31, Year 5.
(e) Assume that Devine's shares were trading at $75 per share shortly before and after the date of acquisition, and that this data was used to value non-controlling interest at the date of acquisition. Calculate goodwill and non-controlling interest at December 31, Year 5.

(adapted from a problem prepared by Peter Secord, St. Mary's University)

Problem 6-15
LO2, 4, 5, 6

Paper Corp. purchased 70% of the outstanding shares of Sand Ltd. on January 1, Year 2, at a cost of $84,000. Paper has always used the equity method to account for its investments. On January 1, Year 2, Sand had common shares of $50,000 and retained earnings of $30,000, and fair values were equal to carrying amounts for all its net assets, except inventory (fair value was $9,000 less than carrying amount) and equipment (fair value was $24,000 greater than carrying amount). The equipment, which is used for research, had an estimated remaining life of 6 years on January 1, Year 2.

The following are the financial statements of Paper Corp. and its subsidiary Sand Ltd. as at December 31, Year 5:

BALANCE SHEETS
at December 31, Year 5

	Paper	Sand
Cash	$ —	$ 10,000
Accounts receivable	36,000	30,000
Note receivable	—	40,000
Inventory	66,000	44,000
Equipment, net	220,000	76,000
Land	150,000	30,000
Investment in Sand	112,350	—
	$584,350	$230,000
Bank indebtedness	$ 90,000	$ —
Accounts payable	50,000	60,000
Notes payable	40,000	—
Common shares	150,000	50,000
Retained earnings	254,350	120,000
	$584,350	$230,000

INCOME STATEMENTS
for the Year Ended December 31, Year 5

	Paper	Sand
Sales	$798,000	$300,000
Management fee revenue	24,000	—
Investment income from Sand	1,500	—
Interest income	—	3,600
Gain on sale of land	—	20,000
	823,500	323,600
Cost of sales	480,000	200,000
Research and development expenses	40,000	12,000
Interest expense	10,000	—
Miscellaneous expenses	106,000	31,600
Income taxes	80,000	32,000
	716,000	275,600
Net income	$107,500	$ 48,000

Additional Information

- During Year 5, Sand made a cash payment of $2,000 per month to Paper for management fees, which is included in Sand's "Miscellaneous expenses."
- During Year 5, Paper made intercompany sales of $100,000 to Sand. The December 31, Year 5, inventory of Sand contained goods purchased from Paper amounting to $30,000. These sales had a gross profit of 35%.
- On April 1, Year 5, Paper acquired land from Sand for $40,000. This land had been recorded on Sand's books at a carrying amount of $20,000. Paper paid for the land by signing a $40,000 note payable to Sand, bearing yearly interest at 8%. Interest for Year 5 was paid by Paper in cash on December 31, Year 5. This land was still being held by Paper on December 31, Year 5.
- The fair value of consolidated goodwill remained unchanged from January 1, Year 5 to July Year 5. On July 1, Year 5, a valuation was performed, indicating that the recoverable amount of consolidated goodwill was $3,500.
- During the year ended December 31, Year 5, Paper paid dividends of $80,000 and Sand paid dividends of $20,000.
- Sand and Paper pay taxes at a 40% rate. Assume that none of the gains or losses were capital gains or losses.

Required:

(a) Prepare, in good form, a calculation of goodwill and any unamortized acquisition differential as of December 31, Year 5.

(b) Prepare Paper's consolidated income statement for the year ended December 31, Year 5, with expenses classified by function.

(c) Calculate the following balances that would appear on Paper's consolidated balance sheet as at December 31, Year 5:

  (i)   Inventory
  (ii) Land
  (iii) Notes payable
  (iv) Non-controlling interest
  (v)   Common shares

(d) Assume that an independent business valuator valued the non-controlling interest at $30,000 at the date of acquisition. Calculate goodwill impairment loss and profit attributable to non-controlling interest for the year ended December 31, Year 5.

(CGA–Canada adapted)

WEB-BASED PROBLEMS

Web Problem 6-1
LO6

Access the 2011 consolidated financial statements for RONA Inc. by going to investor relations section of the company's website. Answer the questions below. Round percentages to one decimal point and other ratios to two decimal points. For each question, indicate where in the financial statements you found the answer, and/or provide a brief explanation.

(a) What inventory costing method does the company use?

(b) What portion of the company's assets is inventory? Has the portion increased or decreased from last year?

(c) Does the company eliminate intercompany transactions and unrealized profits when preparing consolidated financial statements?

(d) Ignore your answer to part (c), and assume the following: (1) 25% of the inventory at December 31, 2011, had been sold by the parent to a wholly owned subsidiary during the year and that this inventory was the only intercompany sale during the year; (2) the gross margin on the sale was the same as the average gross margin for the consolidated entity as a whole; and (3) the intercompany sale and unrealized profit were not eliminated when preparing the consolidated financial statements. What is the impact of these errors on inventory turnover and earnings per share for the year?

(e) Does the company value its land at cost or fair value?

(f) Now assume that the company changes its policy to report its land at fair value under the revaluation option in IAS 16 (or to cost if it was using fair value). Also, assume that the fair value of land has increased steadily since it was acquired. What impact would this change in policy have on the debt-to-equity ratio at the end of the year and on return on average equity for the year?

Web Problem 6-2
LO6

Access the 2011 financial statements for Cenovus Energy Inc. by going to investor relations section of the company's website. Answer the same questions as in Web Problem 1. For each question, indicate where in the financial statements you found the answer, and/or provide a brief explanation. (Some questions may not be applicable.)

 | Practise and learn online with Connect

(A) Intercompany Profits in Depreciable Assets
(B) Intercompany Bondholdings

INTRODUCTION

The elimination of intercompany transactions and unrealized profit is one of the most significant problems encountered in the consolidation process. The volume of transfers within most large enterprises can be quite large. For example, Suncor Energy Inc., Canada's largest integrated energy company, reported intersegment revenue of $3,967 million in 2011,[1] which represented 9.5% of total revenues.

In this chapter, we complete our examination of intercompany profits in assets. We also examine the consolidation issues that arise from intercompany bondholdings. Because these transactions are so distinctly different in their impact on the consolidated statements, this chapter is divided into two parts.

Part (A) looks at the elimination and realization of intercompany profits (losses) in depreciable assets. The concepts involved in the holdback of profits (losses) are similar to those examined previously with regard to intercompany

349

land profits (losses), but the realization concepts are different because they are based on consumption rather than a sale.

Part (B) examines the gains (losses) that are created in the consolidated financial statements when intercompany bondholdings are eliminated.

L01

(A) Intercompany Profits in Depreciable Assets
Holdback and Realization—Year 1

Profit is recognized when the goods are sold to outsiders.

In Chapter 6, we illustrated the holdback of an intercompany profit in inventory and land. In both cases, the before-tax profit of $300 and the corresponding income tax of $120 were held back in the year of the intercompany transaction and realized in the year that the asset was sold to outsiders. In both cases, the profit was eventually recognized in both the financial statements of the individual companies and the consolidated financial statements. Only the timing of the recognition was different. We will now examine the holdback and the realization in the consolidated statements of an intercompany profit in a depreciable asset.

We return to the Chapter 6 example of Parent Company and its 90%-owned subsidiary, Sub Inc. The Year 1 financial statements of the two companies are shown in Exhibit 7.1. Parent has used the cost method to account for its investment.

Note that although the net incomes and total assets of the two companies are unchanged, the details on each statement have been changed so that we can focus on the following intercompany transaction involving equipment that occurred during the year. On July 1, Year 1, Sub sold highly specialized equipment with a very short useful life to Parent and recorded a profit of $300 on the transaction. We are assuming that Sub purchased this equipment for $1,500 on this date with the intention of using it, but instead immediately sold it to Parent for $1,800. The two companies recorded this intercompany transaction in the following manner:

Parent Company			*Sub Inc.*		
Equipment	1,800		Cash	1,800	
Cash		1,800	Equipment		1,500
			Gain on sale		
			of equipment		300

It is also assumed that this transaction was not a capital gain for tax purposes, and that Sub's tax rate is 40%. This means that Sub paid $120 (40% × 300) income tax on this profit. We further assume that this is the only depreciable asset held by either company and that the equipment is expected to be obsolete in one-and-a-half years. On December 31, Year 1, Parent recorded depreciation expense on this equipment in the following manner:

The parent's depreciation expense is based on the parent's cost.

Depreciation expense	600	
Accumulated depreciation		600

To record depreciation for half a year (1,800 ÷ 1½ = 1,200; 1,200 × ½ = 600)

L02

The cost of the equipment to the combined economic entity was $1,500.

It should be noted that if Sub had sold the equipment at its cost, Parent's Year 1 depreciation expense would have been $500 (1,500 ÷ 1½ × ½). This is the amount of depreciation expense that should appear in the income statement of the entity (i.e., in the consolidated income statement) for Year 1 in that it represents depreciation based on the historical cost of the equipment to the entity.

EXHIBIT 7.1

INCOME STATEMENTS—for Year 1

	Parent	Sub
Sales	$20,000	$ 7,700
Gain on sale of equipment	—	300
	20,000	8,000
Depreciation expense	600	—
Miscellaneous expenses	13,800	5,200
Income tax expense	2,200	1,100
	16,600	6,300
Net income	$ 3,400	$ 1,700

> The gain on sale is recorded on the separate-entity books of Sub.

RETAINED EARNINGS STATEMENTS—for Year 1

	Parent	Sub
Balance, January 1	$12,000	$ 4,500
Net income	3,400	1,700
	15,400	6,200
Dividends	2,000	—
Balance, December 31	$13,400	$ 6,200

BALANCE SHEETS—at December 31, Year 1

	Parent	Sub
Assets (miscellaneous)	$27,950	$ 23,200
Equipment	1,800	—
Accumulated depreciation	(600)	—
Investment in Sub Inc.	11,250	—
	$40,400	$ 23,200
Liabilities	$12,000	$ 9,000
Common shares	15,000	8,000
Retained earnings	13,400	6,200
	$40,400	$ 23,200

> The equipment is recorded at the parent's cost on the separate-entity books of Parent.

When we examine the separate income statements of the two companies (see Exhibit 7.1), it should be obvious that the $300 gain is not a gain from a combined entity point of view and that the $600 depreciation expense does not represent historical cost depreciation to the entity. Two adjustments need to be made when the Year 1 consolidated income statement is prepared; these have opposite effects on the before-tax income of the entity. The first adjustment eliminates the gain on sale of equipment recorded on July 1, Year 1, because as of that date the gain is unrealized from the combined entity point of view. This adjustment reduces before-tax income by $300 and holds back this profit for consolidation purposes. A corresponding reduction of $120 should be made to income tax expense so that a net after-tax gain of $180 is held back. This concept is similar in all respects to the holdback of the land gain that was illustrated in Chapter 6.

The second adjustment reduces depreciation expense by $100 (300 ÷ 1½ × ½). The amount of the reduction represents the depreciation taken in Year 1 on this $300 gain and results in a consolidated depreciation expense of $500 based on historical cost, as required. This reduction of depreciation expense increases the before-tax income of the entity by $100. In other words, the parent uses the equipment to

> The depreciation expense for the combined economic entity was $500.

carry out its business of selling goods or providing services to its customers. Even though the equipment is not sold to outsiders, the products or services are sold to outsiders. Therefore, the gain from the intercompany sale of the equipment is realized over the life of the equipment as the parent uses it to produce goods or provide services for outsiders. This concept bases the realization of the gain on the consumption (by depreciation) of the asset containing the unrealized gain. A corresponding increase of $40 should be made to income tax expense, to match the tax with the portion of the gain realized. The result will be a net after-tax realization of $60 for consolidation purposes.

The net effect of the two after-tax adjustments results in the entity's Year 1 net income being reduced by $120 (180 − 60). Because Sub was the selling company, this $120 reduction is allocated to the non-controlling and controlling interests in the same manner as was illustrated in Chapter 6.

The preceding paragraphs have briefly outlined the concepts involved in the holdback and realization of an intercompany gain in a depreciable fixed asset. We will now apply these concepts by preparing the Year 1 consolidated financial statements of Parent using the direct approach. It is useful to start by preparing the three calculations shown in Exhibit 7.2.

EXHIBIT 7.2

EQUIPMENT GAIN—SUB INC. SELLING

	Before tax	40% tax	After tax
Gain, July 1, Year 1	$300	$120	$ 180 **(a)**
Less realized by depreciation for Year 1	100	40	60 **(b)**
Balance, unrealized at Dec. 31, Year 1	$200	$ 80	$ 120 **(c)**

This is an upstream transaction, since Sub sold to Parent.

CALCULATION OF CONSOLIDATED NET INCOME—for Year 1

Net income—Parent Co.		$ 3,400
Net income—Sub Inc.	1,700	
Less after-tax gain on sale of equipment **(2a)**	180	
	1,520	
Add after-tax gain realized by depreciation **(2b)**	60	
Adjusted net income—Sub Inc.		1,580
Consolidated net income		$ 4,980
Attributable to		
Shareholders of Parent		$ 4,822 **(d)**
Non-controlling interest (10% × 1,580)		158 **(e)**

Sub's income is adjusted for both the unrealized gain and the realization of the gain through depreciation by Parent.

CALCULATION OF NON-CONTROLLING INTEREST
at December 31, Year 1

Shareholders' equity—Sub Inc.	
Common shares	$ 8,000
Retained earnings	6,200
	14,200
Less net unrealized equipment gain after tax **(2c)**	120
Adjusted shareholders' equity	14,080
Non-controlling interest's share	10%
	$ 1,408 **(f)**

Non-controlling interest is affected by unrealized profits on upstream transactions.

It should be noted that the calculation of consolidated net income attributable to the parent is made to adjust the net income of the parent from the cost method to the equity method. If the parent had used the equity method, we would still have to adjust for unrealized profits from intercompany transactions.

Exhibit 7.3 illustrates the preparation of the consolidated financial statements using the direct approach. The consolidated income statement was prepared by combining, line by line, the revenues and expenses of the two companies. The amount

---

EXHIBIT 7.3

Year 1 Consolidated Statements
Adjusted for Intercompany Equipment Profit
(Direct Approach)

PARENT COMPANY
CONSOLIDATED INCOME STATEMENT
for the Year Ended December 31, Year 1

Sales (20,000 + 7,700)	$27,700
Gain on sale of equipment (0 + 300 − **[2a] 300**)	–0–
	27,700
Depreciation expense (600 + 0 − **[2b] 100**)	500
Miscellaneous expenses (13,800 + 5,200)	19,000
Income tax expense (2,200 + 1,100 − **[2a] 120** + **[2b] 40**)	3,220
	22,720
Net income	$ 4,980
Attributable to	
Shareholders of Parent **(2d)**	$ 4,822
Non-controlling interest **(2e)**	158

Income tax expense is matched to the income of the consolidated entity.

PARENT COMPANY
CONSOLIDATED RETAINED EARNINGS STATEMENT
for the Year Ended December 31, Year 1

Balance, January 1	$12,000
Net income	4,822
	16,822
Dividends	2,000
Balance, December 31	$14,822

PARENT COMPANY
CONSOLIDATED BALANCE SHEET
at December 31, Year 1

Assets—miscellaneous (27,950 + 23,200)	$51,150
Equipment (1,800 + 0 − **[2a] 300**)	1,500
Accumulated depreciation (600 + 0 − **[2b] 100**)	(500)
Deferred income taxes (0 + 0 + **[2a] 120** − **[2b] 40**)	80
	$52,230
Liabilities (12,000 + 9,000)	$21,000
Common shares	15,000
Retained earnings	14,822
Non-controlling interest	1,408
	$52,230

The equipment is reported at the cost when it was purchased from outsiders.

for non-controlling interest is based on the *adjusted income* of Sub. The intercompany eliminations are shown in the exhibit in boldface and are summarized as follows:

(i) The $300 gain on sale of the equipment and the income tax expense for the tax on this gain are eliminated. The net effect is to reduce the after-tax income of the entity by $180.

(ii) The excess depreciation to the consolidated entity in Year 1 is eliminated. Consolidated depreciation is now based on historical cost. Because this elimination results in a realization of $100 of the original gain, income tax expense is increased by $40 to match the tax with the gain realized. The net result is an after-tax realization of $60.

The two eliminations decreased the entity's net income by $120, which was allocated to the two equities as follows:

To non-controlling interest (10% × 120)	$ 12
To controlling interest (90% × 120)	108
	$120

The consolidated retained earnings statement has been prepared in the normal manner. Because we are consolidating one year after acquisition, the parent's retained earnings at the beginning of the year are equal to consolidated retained earnings on that date.

The consolidated balance sheet was prepared by combining the assets and liabilities of the two companies and by making the following adjustments (shown in Exhibit 7.3 in boldface) for the equipment gain:

The tax paid on the unrealized profits represents a prepayment from a consolidated viewpoint.

(i) When the before-tax gain of $300 is removed from the equipment, the resulting balance of $1,500 represents the original cost to the entity. The $120 increase to deferred income taxes represents the tax on this gain and corresponds to the reduction of tax expense in the income statement.

Accumulated depreciation is based on the original cost to the consolidated entity.

(ii) The amount of the gain contained in accumulated depreciation is removed. The resulting amount ($500) is the accumulated depreciation on the original cost. The $40 decrease to deferred income taxes corresponds to the increase in income tax expense made in the income statement.

Note that the $200 reduction of the carrying amount of the equipment ($300 − $100), together with an increase in deferred income taxes of $80 (40% × $200), results in total consolidated assets being reduced by $120, which corresponds to the reduction made to the entity's net income in the consolidated income statement. The fact that this reduction was allocated to the two equities was noted above.

L03   Equity Method Journal Entries

Our example has assumed that Parent uses the cost method to account for its investment. If Parent were using the equity method, the following journal entries would be made on December 31, Year 1:

The equity method captures the net effect of all consolidation entries.

Investment in Sub Inc.	1,530	
Investment income		1,530
90% of the net income of Sub Inc. (90% × 1,700 = 1,530)		

Investment income	162	
Investment in Sub Inc.		162

To hold back 90% of the after-tax equipment profit recorded by Sub
(90% × 180 = 162)

Investment in Sub Inc.	54	
Investment income		54

To realize 90% of the after-tax profit realized by depreciation (90% × 60 = 54)

After these entries are posted, the two related equity method accounts of Parent would show the following changes and balances:

	Investment in Sub Inc.	Investment Income
Balance, January 1, Year 1	$11,250	
Income from Sub Inc.	1,530	$1,530
Equipment profit (held back)	(162)	(162)
Equipment profit realized	54	54
Balance, December 31, Year 1	$12,672	$1,422

The investment account is a balance sheet account at the end of the year, whereas investment income is an income statement account for one period of time.

Parent's total income under the equity method would be $4,822, consisting of $3,400 from its own operations as reported in Exhibit 7.1 plus investment income of $1,422 as reported above. This income of $4,822 should be and is equal to consolidated net income attributable to the parent.

The parent's income under the equity method should be equal to consolidated net income attributable to the parent.

Downstream Transaction If the sale of equipment had been from the parent to the subsidiary—a downstream transaction—the consolidated net income would be the same as before. The elimination of after-tax unrealized profits of $180 and subsequent realization of after-tax profit of $60 would be charged and credited, respectively, entirely to the parent. The non-controlling interest would not have been charged anything for the consolidation adjustments. Therefore, consolidated net income attributable to non-controlling interest would increase by $12 from $158 to $170. The consolidated net income attributable to the parent's shareholders and the parent's net income under the equity method would decrease by $12 (from $4,822 to $4,810) to offset the increase to the non-controlling interest.

ANALYSIS AND INTERPRETATION OF FINANCIAL STATEMENTS

LO4

In this chapter, we prepared consolidated financial statements where there were unrealized profits from the intercompany sale of depreciable assets. The elimination entries were made on the consolidated financial statements. The net effect of the consolidation adjustments was captured in the parent's internal records when the parent used the equity method.

Exhibit 7.4 presents selected accounts from the Year 1 separate entity and consolidated financial statements that were developed for the intercompany transactions involving equipment. The first three columns present the statements when the intercompany transactions were upstream. In the last three columns, the intercompany transactions were downstream.

The exhibit also indicates the debt-to-equity and return-on-equity ratios for each set of financial statements. The return on equity for all shareholders uses consolidated net income and total shareholders' equity, including the non-controlling interests. The return on equity for shareholders of Parent uses consolidated net

The net income for the parent's separate-entity income statement under the equity method is equal to consolidated net income attributable to the shareholders of the parent.

EXHIBIT 7.4	Impact of Presentation Method on Debt-to-Equity and Return-on-Equity Ratios

INCOME STATEMENTS—December 31, Year 1

	Upstream Transaction			Downstream Transaction		
	Parent Cost	Parent Equity	Consol.	Parent Cost	Parent Equity	Consol.
Investment income	$ 0	$ 1,422	$ 0	$ 0	$ 1,410	$ 0
Net income	3,400	4,822	4,980	3,400	4,810	4,980
Attributable to						
Shareholders of Parent			$ 4,822			$ 4,810
Non-controlling interests			158			170

BALANCE SHEETS—December 31, Year 1

	Parent Cost	Parent Equity	Consol.	Parent Cost	Parent Equity	Consol.
Equipment	$ 1,800	$ 1,800	$ 1,500	$ 1,800	$ 1,800	$ 1,500
Accumulated depreciation	(600)	(600)	(500)	(600)	(600)	(500)
Investment in Sub Inc.	11,250	12,672	0	11,250	12,660	0
Liabilities	$12,000	$12,000	$21,000	$12,000	$12,000	$21,000
Common shares	15,000	15,000	15,000	15,000	15,000	15,000
Retained earnings	13,400	14,822	14,822	13,400	14,810	14,810
Non-controlling interests	0	0	1,408	0	0	1,420
Debt-to-equity	0.42	0.40	0.67	0.42	0.40	0.67
Return on equity						
- for all shareholders	n/a	n/a	15.94%	n/a	n/a	15.94%
- for shareholders of Parent	12.0%	16.2%	16.2%	12.0%	16.14%	16.14%

income attributable to the shareholders of Parent, and total shareholders' equity excluding the non-controlling interests.

Note the following from Exhibit 7.4:

Retained earnings for the parent's separate-entity balance sheet under the equity method are equal to consolidated retained earnings.

- The separate-entity statements under the cost method are the same for upstream and downstream transactions because the cost method does not record any adjustments pertaining to the subsidiary's income or unrealized profits from intercompany transactions.

- The separate-entity statements under the cost method are the same as the statements under the equity method except for the investment account, investment income, and retained earnings.

- Consolidated net income is the same regardless of whether the transactions where upstream or downstream. However, the split of the consolidated net income between the shareholders of the parent and the non-controlling interest is different. In turn, consolidated retained earnings and non-controlling interests are different, depending on whether the transactions were upstream or downstream. The separate-entity net income and retained earnings under the equity method are equal to consolidated net income attributable to the shareholders of Parent and consolidated retained earnings, respectively.

The return on equity for the separate-entity statements under the equity method is equal to the consolidated return on equity for the shareholders of Parent.

- The return on equity for the separate-entity statements under the equity method is equal to the consolidated return on equity for the shareholders of Parent.

- The return on equity for the downstream scenario is lower than the upstream scenario because the shareholders of Parent absorb the full charge when the unrealized profits are eliminated.

- The solvency position looks worst on the consolidated financial statements because the subsidiary's debt is included on the consolidated financial statements. This increases the debt-to-equity ratio.

The return on equity for the downstream scenario is lower than the upstream scenario because the shareholders of Parent absorb the full charge when the unrealized profits are eliminated.

Realization of Remaining Gain—Year 2

The equipment sold to the parent on July 1, Year 1, had a remaining life of 1½ years on that date. When the Year 1 consolidated income statement was prepared, both the holdback of the total gain and the realization of one-third of the gain took place. When the Year 2 consolidated income statement is prepared, adjustments will be made to realize the remaining two-thirds of the gain. This intercompany gain will be fully realized for consolidation purposes at the end of Year 2, only because the equipment had an unusually short remaining life of 1½ years on the date of the intercompany sale. The Year 2 financial statements for the two companies are shown in Exhibit 7.5.

Before the consolidated financial statements are prepared, we must make the four calculations shown in Exhibit 7.6. In the first table in Exhibit 7.6, you should

EXHIBIT 7.5

INCOME STATEMENTS—for Year 2

	Parent	Sub
Sales	$ 25,000	$ 12,000
Depreciation expense	1,200	–
Miscellaneous expenses	17,150	6,900
Income tax expense	2,600	2,000
	20,950	8,900
Net income	$ 4,050	$ 3,100

The parent reports depreciation expense for one full year on its separate-entity income statement.

RETAINED EARNINGS STATEMENTS—for Year 2

	Parent	Sub
Balance, January 1	$ 13,400	$ 6,200
Net income	4,050	3,100
	17,450	9,300
Dividends	2,500	–
Balance, December 31	$ 14,950	$ 9,300

BALANCE SHEETS—at December 31, Year 2

	Parent	Sub
Assets (miscellaneous)	$ 32,700	$ 28,300
Equipment	1,800	–
Accumulated depreciation	(1,800)	–
Investment in Sub Inc.	11,250	–
	$ 43,950	$ 28,300
Liabilities	$ 14,000	$ 11,000
Common shares	15,000	8,000
Retained earnings	14,950	9,300
	$ 43,950	$ 28,300

The parent reports accumulated depreciation for 1½ years on its separate-entity balance sheet.

EXHIBIT 7.6

EQUIPMENT GAIN—SUB INC. SELLING

	Before tax	40% tax	After tax
Gain, July 1, Year 1	$300	$120	$180 **(a)**
Less realized by depreciation for Year 1	100	40	60 **(b)**
Balance unrealized at Dec. 31, Year 1	200	80	120 **(c)**
Less realized by depreciation for Year 2	200	80	120 **(d)**
Balance unrealized at Dec. 31, Year 2	$–0–	$–0–	$–0–

CALCULATION OF CONSOLIDATED NET INCOME—for Year 2

Net income—Parent Co.		$ 4,050
Net Income—Sub Inc.	3,100	
Add after-tax equipment gain realized by depreciation **(d)**	120	
Adjusted net income—Sub Inc.		3,220
Consolidated net income		$ 7,270
Attributable to		
Shareholders of Parent		$ 6,948 **(e)**
Non-controlling interest (10% × 3,220)		322 **(f)**

CALCULATION OF CONSOLIDATED RETAINED EARNINGS
at January 1, Year 2

Retained earnings—Parent Co.		$13,400
Retained earnings—Sub Inc.	6,200	
Acquisition retained earnings	4,500	
Increase since acquisition	1,700	
Less unrealized after-tax equipment gain, Jan. 1 **(c)**	120	
Adjusted increase since acquisition	1,580	
Parent Co.'s share	90%	1,422
Consolidated retained earnings		$14,822 **(g)**

CALCULATION OF NON-CONTROLLING INTEREST
at December 31, Year 2

Common shares—Sub Inc.	$ 8,000
Retained earnings—Sub Inc.	9,300
	17,300
Non-controlling interest's share	10%
	$ 1,730 **(h)**

Differentiate between adjustments for *a period* of time (i.e., for Year 2) versus *a point* in time (i.e., at the end of Year 2).

This schedule shows the calculation for a period of time, that is, for Year 2.

This schedule shows the calculation at a point in time, that is, at the beginning of Year 2, which is the same as the end of Year 1.

At the end of Year 2, the intercompany gain has been fully realized and no adjustment is necessary from a consolidated viewpoint.

note that the $300 gain on sale in Year 1 is fully realized from a consolidated perspective by the end of Year 2. From a consolidated perspective, the $300 gain was eliminated in Year 1 but was realized by adjusting depreciation expense over the remaining life of the equipment. Since the remaining life of the equipment was only 1½ years at the date of the intercompany sale, the $300 gain was brought into consolidated income over 1½ years. If the remaining useful life were five years, the $300 gain would be brought into consolidated income over five years.

The Year 2 consolidated financial statements prepared using the direct approach are shown in Exhibit 7.7. (Eliminations required for the intercompany equipment gain are shown in boldface.)

EXHIBIT 7.7

Year 2 Consolidated Statements
Adjusted for Intercompany Equipment Profit
(Direct Approach)
PARENT COMPANY
CONSOLIDATED INCOME STATEMENT
for the Year Ended December 31, Year 2

Sales (25,000 + 12,000)	$37,000	Depreciation expense for one
Depreciation expense (1,200 + 0 − **[6d] 200**)	1,000	year is based on the original
Miscellaneous expenses (17,150 + 6,900)	24,050	cost to the consolidated
Income tax expense (2,600 + 2,000 + **[6d] 80**)	4,680	entity.
	29,730	
Net income	$ 7,270	
Attributable to		
Shareholders of Parent **(6e)**	$ 6,948	
Non-controlling interest **(6f)**	322	

PARENT COMPANY
CONSOLIDATED RETAINED EARNINGS STATEMENT
for the Year Ended December 31, Year 2

Balance, January 1	$14,822
Net income	6,948
	21,770
Dividends	2,500
Balance, December 31	$19,270

PARENT COMPANY
CONSOLIDATED BALANCE SHEET
at December 31, Year 2

Assets—miscellaneous (32,700 + 28,300)	$61,000	Accumulated depreciation
Equipment (1,800 + 0 − **[6a] 300**)	1,500	is total depreciation taken
Accumulated depreciation (1,800 + 0 − **[6b + 6d] 300**)	(1,500)	to the end of Year 2, based
	$61,000	on the original cost to the
		consolidated entity.
Liabilities (14,000 + 11,000)	$25,000	
Common shares	15,000	
Retained earnings	19,270	
Non-controlling interest **(6h)**	1,730	
	$61,000	

When the consolidated income statement is prepared, the depreciation expense is reduced by $200. The result is a consolidated depreciation expense of $1,000 based on the consolidated entity's cost. This adjustment realizes $200 of the equipment gain for consolidation purposes. Income tax expense is increased by $80 to match expense with the gain realized. The net effect of the two adjustments in the income statement is to increase the consolidated entity's net income by an after-tax realization amounting to $120.

The Year 2 consolidated retained earnings statement is prepared using the calculated January 1 balance, consolidated net income attributable to the parent, and the dividends of Parent Company.

At the end of Year 2, the equipment's carrying amount is zero on Parent's separate-entity balance sheet and on the consolidated balance sheet.

Two adjustments are required in the preparation of the consolidated balance sheet. A reduction of $300 in equipment removes the gain and restates the equipment to the $1,500 historical cost to the entity. This equipment is fully depreciated on December 31, Year 2; therefore, accumulated depreciation should be equal to the historical cost of $1,500. When the accumulated depreciation is reduced by $300, the resulting balance ($1,500) is equal to the entity's historical cost.

Note that when both the equipment and the accumulated depreciation are reduced by $300, total consolidated assets are not changed. The net gain held back on the Year 1 consolidated balance sheet has been realized as at the end of Year 2. If no unrealized gains are being held back, there will be no deferred income tax adjustments made in the consolidated balance sheet. The deferred charge of $80 that appeared in the December 31, Year 1, consolidated balance sheet became an expense in the Year 2 consolidated income statement.

The unrealized profit at the end of Year 1 was realized in income for Year 2.

As discussed above, the adjustments made in the consolidated income statement increased the entity's net income by $120, while the adjustments made in the asset side of the consolidated balance sheet did not change total assets. In order for this to balance out, there must have been both an increase and a decrease of $120 on the liability side of the consolidated balance sheet. The $120 increase occurred in the income statement and was allocated to the two equities in the balance sheet. The $120 decrease occurred in Sub's retained earnings at the beginning of the year and was allocated to the two equities. In the calculation of consolidated retained earnings in Exhibit 7.6, Parent absorbs $108 (90% × 120). In the schedule below, which shows the changes in non-controlling interest for the year, we see that the remaining $12 (10% × 120) decreases non-controlling interest.

CHANGES IN NON-CONTROLLING INTEREST—for Year 2

Sub Inc.:	
Common shares	$8,000
Retained earnings, Jan. 1	6,200
	14,200
Less after-tax equipment profit **(6c)**	120
Adjusted	14,080
	10%
Non-controlling interest Jan. 1	1,408
Year 2 entity net income allocated **(6f)**	322
Non-controlling interest, Dec. 31 **(6h)**	$1,730

NCI is affected by the realization of the gain in Year 2, even though Parent recorded the excess depreciation.

Equity Method Journal Entries If Parent had been using the equity method, the following journal entries would have been made on December 31, Year 2:

Investment in Sub Inc.	2,790	
Investment income		2,790
90% of Sub Inc.'s Year 2 net income (90% × 3,100 = 2,790)		
Investment in Sub Inc.	108	
Investment income		108
90% of the portion of the after-tax equipment gain realized by depreciation in Year 2 (90% × 120 = 108)		

After these entries are posted, the two related equity method accounts of Parent show the following changes and balances:

	Investment in Sub Inc.	Investment income
Balance, January 1, Year 2	$12,672	
Income from Sub Inc.	2,790	$2,790
Equipment gain realized	108	108
Balance, December 31, Year 2	$15,570	$2,898

The investment account contains all adjustments to the end of the period, whereas the investment income account contains adjustments for only one period.

Intercompany Sale of a Used Depreciable Asset   In the preceding illustration, the equipment sold by Sub was a new asset. As such, Sub had not yet recorded any accumulated depreciation, and the cost to Sub was the same as the carrying amount on the date of the intercompany sale. Let us now consider the sale of a used depreciable asset, that is, an asset with accumulated depreciation.

Assume that Sub had acquired the equipment for $5,000 three-and-one-half years prior to the intercompany sale, and had been depreciating it over an estimated useful life of five years. The accumulated depreciation on July 1, Year 1, would have been $3,500 and the carrying amount would have been $1,500. Sub would have made the following entry when it sold the equipment to Parent for $1,800:

Cash	1,800	
Accumulated depreciation	3,500	
Equipment		5,000
Gain on sale of equipment		300

All of the previous calculations of unrealized gains and excess depreciation would be the same for this situation. However, the consolidated balance sheet at the end of Year 1 should reflect the equipment at $5,000, the original cost to the consolidated entity, and accumulated depreciation at $4,000, the amount that would have appeared on Sub's books had the intercompany transaction not occurred. Therefore, the following journal entry should be made in the consolidation working papers at the end of Year 1 to gross up the equipment and accumulated depreciation:

Equipment	3,500	
Accumulated depreciation		3,500

Equipment and accumulated depreciation need to be grossed up to the original cost to the consolidated entity.

This entry does not change the carrying amount of the equipment but does change the cost and accumulated depreciation on the consolidated balance sheet. This entry should be made on the consolidation working papers year after year as long as Parent has this equipment on its separate-entity books.

Appendix 7A of this chapter illustrates the consolidation adjustments relating to an intercompany sale of a depreciable asset when the parent company periodically revalues its equipment to fair value under IAS 16.

Comparison of Realization of Inventory and Equipment Profits over a Two-Year Period

In Chapter 6, the holdback and realization of an intercompany profit in inventory was illustrated. In this chapter, we have illustrated the holdback and realization of an intercompany gain in equipment. In both cases, the after-tax profit (gain) was \$180 (60% × 300), and the subsidiary was the selling company. The following summarizes the effect on the entity's net income over a two-year period:

INTERCOMPANY INVENTORY PROFIT

	Year 1	Year 2	Total
Parent Co., net income	\$3,400	\$4,050	\$7,450
Sub Inc., net income	1,700	3,100	4,800
	5,100	7,150	12,250
After-tax profit (held back) realized	(180)	180	–0–
Net income—consolidated entity	\$4,920	\$7,330	\$12,250
Allocated to the two equities:			
Non-controlling interest	\$ 152	\$ 328	\$ 480
Shareholders of parent	4,768	7,002	11,770
	\$4,920	\$7,330	\$12,250

The intercompany profits are eventually realized from a consolidated viewpoint.

INTERCOMPANY EQUIPMENT GAIN

	Year 1	Year 2	Total
Parent Co., net income	\$3,400	\$4,050	\$ 7,450
Sub Inc., net income	1,700	3,100	4,800
	5,100	7,150	12,250
After-tax gain (held back)	(180)	–0–	(180)
After-tax gain realized	60	120	180
Net income—consolidated entity	\$4,980	\$7,270	\$12,250
Allocated as follows:			
Non-controlling interest	\$ 158	\$ 322	\$ 480
Shareholders of parent	4,822	6,948	11,770
	\$4,980	\$7,270	\$12,250

Intercompany profits on depreciable assets are realized as the assets are used over their useful lives.

The two-year summaries just shown help illustrate a number of significant points in relation to consolidated financial statements:

Differentiate between point-in-time (balance sheet) and period-of-time (income statement) adjustments.

1. The consolidated entity's net income is measured for periods of time that are usually one year in length.

2. During this measurement process, the holdback and subsequent realization of profits (losses) resulting from intercompany transactions takes place.

3. The realization of previously held back profits (losses) occurs during the period in which the acquiring company either sells the asset containing the profit (loss) to outsiders or depreciates the asset, thereby consuming the asset while it produces other products or services for outsiders.

4. If we examine a time period longer than one year, and if, at the end of that period, the assets of the constituent companies do not contain intercompany profits, the following becomes evident:

   The consolidated entity's net income for this longer period consists of

   (a) the reported net income of the parent company, exclusive of intercompany investment or dividend income,

   (b) *plus* the reported net income of the subsidiary company (or companies),

   (c) *minus* the acquisition-differential amortization.

   In the illustration above, we assumed that the acquisition differential was zero.

5. The entity's net income measurement for this longer time period is not affected by the fact that assets were sold at intercompany profits (losses) during the period. (See the two-year total column.) The same is true of the allocation to the two equities.

6. When consolidated statements are prepared at the end of an intervening time period (e.g., Year 1, Year 2) we have to determine whether there were profits (losses) recorded by any of the constituent companies that were not realized by the end of the period.

7. The profit holdbacks and realizations are used in the measurement of the consolidated entity's net income and are adjustments to the reported net income of the selling constituent in the allocation of that net income.

> Adjustments for unrealized and realized profits from intercompany transactions are always charged or credited to the original seller.

In Chapter 6, we also illustrated the holdback and realization of a $180 after-tax intercompany gain in land. In that case, the realization process took place in Year 8; however, the overall concepts discussed above remain the same.

See Self-Study Problem 1 for a comprehensive consolidation problem involving intercompany profits in depreciable assets. It includes most of the issues we have covered so far in this chapter.

(B) Intercompany Bondholdings

L05

Our discussions so far have focused on gains (losses) resulting from the intercompany sale of inventory, land, and depreciable assets. The treatment of these gains (losses) in the preparation of consolidated financial statements can be summarized as follows: Gains (losses) resulting from the intercompany sale of assets are realized subsequent to the recording of the intercompany transaction by the selling affiliate.

Occasionally, one affiliate will purchase all or a portion of the bonds issued by another affiliate. When consolidated financial statements are being prepared, the elimination of the intercompany accounts (investment in bonds and bonds payable, interest revenue and interest expense) may result in a gain (loss) being reflected in those statements. The treatment of this type of gain (loss) can be summarized in the following manner: Gains (losses) arising because of the elimination of intercompany bondholding accounts are realized prior to the recording of these gains (losses) by the affiliates on their separate-entity statements. Before we examine how these gains and losses occur in the elimination of the intercompany accounts, let us look at intercompany bondholding situations that do not result in gains or losses.

> Gains or losses on intercompany bondholdings are reported on consolidated statements prior to recording them on the separate-entity statements.

Intercompany Bondholdings—No Gain or Loss

Not all intercompany bondholdings result in gains or losses being reflected in the consolidated statements. For example, let us assume that one affiliate issued $10,000 in bonds and that another affiliate acquired the whole issue. (The amounts used are unrealistically low for a bond issue but are realistic in relation to the size of Parent Company and Sub Inc., the two companies that we have been using in our illustrations. In any case, the concepts are the same regardless of the amounts used.) Immediately after the issue, the records of the two companies would show the following accounts:

> The asset and liability appear on the separate-entity financial statements.

Acquiring Affiliate's Records		*Issuing Affiliate's Records*	
Investment in bonds	10,000	Bonds payable	10,000

From the entity's point of view, the two accounts are similar to intercompany receivables and payables and would be eliminated by the following working paper entry when the consolidated balance sheet is being prepared:

This entry is made on the consolidation working papers.

| Bonds payable | 10,000 | |
| Investment in bonds | | 10,000 |

It is important to note that the eliminations are equal, and because of this, there is no gain or loss resulting from the working paper elimination of these two intercompany accounts. At the end of each succeeding year, this working paper elimination is repeated until the bonds mature. After that date, the two accounts no longer exist in the affiliates' records and further working paper eliminations are not required.

The consolidated balance sheet is not the only statement requiring working paper eliminations. If we assume that the bonds pay interest at the rate of 10%, the income statement of the issuing affiliate will show interest expense of $1,000, while the income statement of the acquiring affiliate will show interest revenue of $1,000. These intercompany revenue and expense accounts are eliminated by the following working paper entry when the consolidated income statement is being prepared:

This entry does not change the net income of the consolidated entity.

| Interest revenue | 1,000 | |
| Interest expense | | 1,000 |

Again, it is important to note that the amounts are equal and that because of this, there is no gain or loss resulting from this working paper elimination. The consolidated income statement working paper elimination is repeated each year until the bonds mature.

Our example has assumed that the bonds were issued at par. Suppose, now, that the bonds were issued to the purchasing affiliate at a premium or a discount. Provided that both affiliates use the same methods to amortize the issue premium or discount and the purchase premium or discount, the amounts in the intercompany accounts on all successive balance sheets and income statements will be equal. The important concept of equal eliminations on both statements would still be true.

Intercompany Bondholdings—with Gain or Loss

The market price of bonds moves inversely with changes in interest rates.

When the market rate is different from the coupon rate on the date of a bond issue, the bonds will be issued at a price that is different from the par or face value. If the interest rates are higher (lower) than the coupon rate, the bonds will be issued at a discount (premium). Subsequent to the issue, bond market prices will rise (fall) if the market interest rate falls (rises). It is the market price differential on the date of an intercompany purchase, combined with any unamortized issue discount or premium, that causes the consolidated gains or losses that result from the elimination of intercompany bondholdings. Let us change our example slightly to illustrate this.

Parent Co. has a $10,000 bond issue outstanding that pays 10% interest annually on December 31. The bonds were originally issued at a premium, which is being amortized by the company on a straight-line basis at the rate of $25 per year.[2] On December 31, Year 1, the unamortized issue premium amounts to $100. The bonds mature on December 31, Year 5.

On December 31, Year 1, Sub purchases all of the outstanding bonds of Parent on the open market at a cost of $9,800. Immediately after Sub acquires these bonds, the records of the two companies would show the following accounts:

Sub Inc.'s Records		*Parent Co.'s Records*	
Investment in bonds of		Bonds payable	$10,000
Parent Co.	$10,000	Add unamortized issue	
Less discount on purchase	200	premium	100
Net	$ 9,800	Net	$10,100

Sub purchased the bonds in the market for $9,800, which is $300 less than the carrying amount of these bonds on Parent's books.

The net amounts reflect how the asset and the liability would be presented on the respective balance sheets of the two companies on December 31, Year 1. The preparation of the consolidated balance sheet on this date would require the elimination of the two intercompany amounts by the following working paper entry:

Bonds Payable—Parent Co.	10,100	
Investment in bonds of Parent Co.—Sub. Inc.		9,800
Gain on bond retirement		300
To eliminate the intercompany bond accounts and recognize the resulting		
gain on the retirement of bonds		

A gain of $300 is recorded on the consolidation working papers.

The eliminations of the asset and the liability would appear in the consolidated balance sheet working paper. The balancing amount of the elimination entry "Gain on bond retirement" appears in the consolidated income statement working paper. From the consolidated entity's point of view, the bonds of the entity have been purchased on the open market and retired. The retirement gain can be calculated in the following manner:

LO6

From the consolidated perspective, Parent's bonds have been retired; Parent no longer has a bond payable to outsiders.

Carrying amount of the bond liability	$10,100
Cost of purchasing bonds in the open market	9,800
Gain on bond retirement	$ 300

The gain should be recognized because the benefits and risks of the consolidated entity have substantially changed in a transaction with outsiders. From a consolidated perspective, the entity has retired a liability of $10,100 by paying $9,800. Its financial position has improved; the gain has been realized and should be recognized.

The gain on bond retirement was realized on a transaction with outsiders.

Note that if Parent had acquired and retired its own bonds in the same manner, it would have recorded a gain on bond retirement of the same amount. This gain would appear on Parent's income statement and would also appear on the consolidated income statement. The actual event was different (Sub purchased the bonds), but because the two companies are a single economic entity, the gain will still appear on the consolidated income statement. The only difference is that the gain on the consolidated income statement does not appear on the income statement of the parent. Instead, it appears on the consolidated income statement as a result of the unequal elimination of the intercompany asset and liability accounts in the preparation of the consolidated balance sheet.

The gain is reported on the consolidated statements, not on the single-entity statements.

An examination of the makeup of the asset and liability accounts will indicate why there is a gain of $300. If the bonds had originally been issued at par (face value), and if they had been acquired on the open market at a price equal to par, there would be no gain on retirement. It is the unamortized issue premium and the discount on the bond purchase that cause the gain. This premium and discount will be amortized by the two companies in Years 2 to 5, and thus will be reflected in the individual income statements of the two companies in those future periods. This will become clearer when we examine the consolidation procedures in Year 2. The important point to note at this stage is that the constituent companies will pay tax on this gain in future periods when the actual recording of the gain takes place. The consolidated entity is realizing the gain in Year 1; therefore, this requires income tax allocation if a proper matching is to take place. Assuming a 40% tax rate, the following additional working paper elimination entry is required:

Income tax expense is reported on the consolidated statements in accordance with the matching principle.

Income tax expense	120	
Deferred income tax liability		120

To record the deferred income tax liability and expense on the Year 1
  intercompany bond gain (40% × 300 = 120)

The effect of the two eliminating entries on the Year 1 consolidated income is to increase the net income of the entity by $180 (300 − 120). The entity's net income consists of the net income of the parent plus the net income of the subsidiary; therefore, the after-tax increase must affect one or the other, or perhaps both.

Four possible approaches could be taken:

There are various approaches to allocate the gain between the two companies.

1. Allocate the gain to the issuing company because the company purchasing the bonds is acting as an agent for the issuing company. (This approach is commonly referred to as the *agency approach*.)

2. Allocate the gain to the purchasing company because its investment led to the retirement of the bonds for consolidation purposes.

3. Allocate the gain to the parent company because its management controls the actions of all the affiliated companies in the group. This would only be a separate alternative if both parties to the transaction were subsidiaries of that parent.

4. Allocate the gain between the issuing and purchasing companies because each will record its portion of the gain in future periods.

We will use approach 4 because it is consistent with the income measurement by the separate entities in future years.

An allocation of the gain would not be required in the case of 100%-owned subsidiaries because there would be no non-controlling interest in the consolidated financial statements. The approach adopted is very important when the subsidiaries are less than 100% owned because approaches 1, 2, and 4 could result in all or a portion of the gain being allocated to the subsidiary company, and this would affect non-controlling interest. IFRSs are silent regarding the approach to be taken. In the illustrations that follow, any gains (losses) from the elimination of intercompany bondholding will be allocated to the purchasing and issuing affiliates (approach 4) because it reflects how each company will actually record the transaction in future years. The agency approach is briefly discussed in the section "Gains (Losses) Not Allocated to the Two Equities" later in this chapter.

L07 Calculation of the Portion of the Gain Allocated to the Affiliates

From the point of view of the purchasing affiliate, the cost of the acquisition is compared with the par value of the bonds acquired, the difference being a gain or loss. From the point of view of the issuing affiliate, the cost to retire the bonds is compared with the par value of the bonds; the difference between the par value and the carrying amount is the gain or loss. The gain and its allocation can be calculated in the following manner:

Par (face) value of bond liability	$10,000
Cost of investment in bonds	9,800
Gain allocated to purchasing affiliate—before tax	$ 200
Carrying amount of bond liability	$10,100
Par (face) value of bond liability	10,000
Gain allocated to issuing affiliate—before tax	$ 100

Note that the gain to the consolidated entity of $300 is made up of the two gains allocated to the affiliates (200 + 100). The gain allocated to the purchasing affiliate is equal to the discount on the purchase affiliate's books, and the gain allocated to the issuing affiliate is equal to the premium on the issuing affiliate's books. Both the entity's gain and the amounts allocated are expressed in before-tax dollars. The chart in Exhibit 7.8 is useful in calculating the after-tax amounts required when the entity's after-tax net income is being allocated to the two equities.

The Year 1 financial statements of the two companies are shown in Exhibit 7.9. Parent Co. has used the cost method to account for its investment.

> The $300 gain is allocated to the affiliates based on the premium or discount on their separate-entity books.

EXHIBIT 7.8

ALLOCATION OF GAIN ON BOND

	Entity			Parent Co.			Sub Inc.		
	Before tax	40% tax	After tax	Before tax	40% tax	After tax	Before tax	40% tax	After Tax
Gain on bond retirement— Dec. 31, Year 1	$300	$120	$180	$100	$40	$60	$200	$80	$120
	(a)	(b)	(c)	(d)	(e)	(f)	(g)	(h)	(i)

> This chart shows how the after-tax gains are allocated for consolidation purposes.

EXHIBIT 7.9

INCOME STATEMENTS—for Year 1

	Parent	Sub
Sales	$ 20,000	$ 8,000
Interest expense	975	—
Miscellaneous expenses	13,425	5,200
Income tax expense	2,200	1,100
	16,600	6,300
Net income	$ 3,400	$ 1,700

> Sub has no interest revenue because it purchased the bonds on the last day of the year.

RETAINED EARNINGS STATEMENTS—for Year 1

	Parent	Sub
Balance, January 1	$ 12,000	$ 4,500
Net income	3,400	1,700
	15,400	6,200
Dividends	2,000	—
Balance, December 31	$ 13,400	$ 6,200

BALANCE SHEETS—at December 31, Year 1

	Parent	Sub
Assets (miscellaneous)	$ 29,150	$ 13,400
Investment in Parent Co. bonds	—	9,800
Investment in Sub Inc.	11,250	—
	$ 40,400	$ 23,200
Miscellaneous liabilities	$ 1,900	$ 9,000
Bonds payable	10,100	—
Common shares	15,000	8,000
Retained earnings	13,400	6,200
	$ 40,400	$ 23,200

> The investment in bonds and bonds payable are reported on the separate-entity balance sheets.

The net incomes and total assets of the two companies are unchanged from previous examples. However, the details on each statement have been changed to reflect the intercompany bond transaction that occurred on December 31, Year 1. Remember that the intercompany bond purchase occurred on that date and that the interest expense of Parent for Year 1 relates to bonds held by bondholders outside the consolidated entity. The amount of expense ($975) is made up of the $1,000 interest paid, less the $25 amortization of the issue premium.

Before the Year 1 consolidated financial statements are prepared, the three calculations in Exhibit 7.10 are made. Exhibit 7.11 illustrates the direct approach to the preparation of the Year 1 consolidated financial statements.

Exhibit 7.8, which was prepared to allocate the gain in both before-tax and after-tax dollars, was used in preparing the consolidated income

Parent has interest expense of $975 on its separate-entity books.

EXHIBIT 7.10

CALCULATION OF CONSOLIDATED NET INCOME—for Year 1

The gain on bond retirement is allocated to the two affiliates as a consolidation adjustment.

Net income—Parent Co.		$ 3,400
Add after-tax bond gain allocated **(8f)**		60
Adjusted		3,460
Net income—Sub Inc.	1,700	
Add after-tax bond gain allocated **(8i)**	120	
Adjusted		1,820
Consolidated net income		$ 5,280
Attributable to		
Shareholders of Parent		$ 5,098 **(a)**
Non-controlling interest (10% × 1,820)		182 **(b)**

CALCULATION OF NON-CONTROLLING INTEREST
at December 31, Year 1

The gain allocated to Sub affects non-controlling interest at the end of the year.

Sub Inc.	
Common shares	$ 8,000
Retained earnings	6,200
	14,200
Add after-tax bond gain allocated **(8i)**	120
Adjusted	14,320
Non-controlling interest's ownership	10%
	$ 1,432 **(c)**

CALCULATION OF CONSOLIDATED RETAINED EARNINGS
at December 31, Year 1

This schedule shows the calculation at a point in time; that is, at the end of Year 1.

Retained earnings—Parent Co.		$13,400
Add after-tax bond gain allocated **(8f)**		60
Adjusted		13,460
Retained earnings—Sub Inc.	6,200	
Acquisition retained earnings	4,500	
Increase since acquisition	1,700	
Add after-tax bond gain allocated **(8i)**	120	
Adjusted	1,820	
Parent's ownership	90%	1,638
		$15,098 **(d)**

EXHIBIT 7.11

Year 1 Consolidated Statements
Adjusted for Intercompany Bondholdings
(Direct Approach)

PARENT COMPANY
CONSOLIDATED INCOME STATEMENT
for the Year Ended December 31, Year 1

Sales (20,000 + 8,000)	$28,000
Gain on bond retirement (0 + 0 + **[8a] 300**)	300
	28,300
Interest expense (975 + 0)	975
Miscellaneous expenses (13,425 + 5,200)	18,625
Income tax expense (2,200 + 1,100 + **[8b] 120**)	3,420
	23,020
Net income	$ 5,280
Attributable to	
Shareholders of Parent **(10a)**	$ 5,098
Non-controlling interest **(10b)**	182

The gain on bond retirement appears on the consolidated income statement because the gain was realized with a transaction with outsiders.

PARENT COMPANY
CONSOLIDATED RETAINED EARNINGS STATEMENT
for the Year Ended December 31, Year 1

Balance, January 1	$12,000
Net income	5,098
	17,098
Dividends	2,000
Balance, December 31	$15,098

PARENT COMPANY
CONSOLIDATED BALANCE SHEET
at December 31, Year 1

Assets—miscellaneous (29,150 + 13,400)	$42,550
Investment in Parent Co. bonds (0 + 9,800 − **9,800**)	–0–
	$42,550
Miscellaneous liabilities (1,900 + 9,000)	$10,900
Bonds payable (10,100 + 0 − **10,100**)	–0–
Deferred income tax liability (0 + 0 + **[8b] 120**)	120
Total liabilities	11,020
Common shares	15,000
Retained earnings	15,098
Non-controlling interest **(10c)**	1,432
	$42,550

The bonds payable are zero on the consolidated balance sheet because outsiders no longer hold them.

statement and in calculating consolidated net income and retained earnings, as follows:

1. The entity column reflects the amounts used in preparing the consolidated income statement. Note that the after-tax column is not used because the before tax amount and the tax amount are adjusted separately.

2. Both of the allocation columns (Parent Co. and Sub Inc.) were used to calculate consolidated net income attributable to the parent and non-controlling interest for the year, and to calculate non-controlling interest and consolidated retained earnings at the end of the year, but only using after-tax amounts. This is because they are used to adjust the after-tax net incomes and equities of the two companies. The before-tax and tax columns are presented only to show that the columns cross-add.

In summary, the eliminations made for the intercompany bondholdings had the following effect on the consolidated statements:

1. The elimination of $9,800 in assets and $10,100 in liabilities resulted in a $300 before-tax gain, which was reflected in the income statement.

Income tax is accrued on the consolidated financial statements to match the gain on bond retirement.

2. An increase of $120 (40% × 300) to income tax expense and to a deferred tax liability reflected the tax effects of the gain.

3. The two adjustments in the income statement increased the net income of the entity by $180; this was allocated to the two equities in the balance sheet, as follows:

	Total	Non-controlling interest	Controlling interest
Gain allocated to Parent Co.	$ 60	$ —	$ 60
Gain allocated to Sub Inc.	120	12	108
	$180	$12	$168

The after-tax gain is allocated to non-controlling and controlling interests.

4. The adjustments made in preparing the consolidated balance sheet can be summarized conceptually as follows:

Debit side:

Investment in bonds		− 9,800

Credit side:

Bonds payable	−10,100
Deferred income tax liability	+ 120
Non-controlling interest	+ 12
Retained earnings	+ 168
	− 9,800

Equity Method Journal Entries

If Parent used the equity method, the following entries would be made on December 31, Year 1:

These entries capture the net effect of all consolidation adjustments.

Investment in Sub Inc.	1,530	
Investment income		1,530

90% of the Year 1 net income of Sub Inc. (90% × 1,700 = 1,530)

Investment in Sub Inc.	60	
Investment income		60

Bond gain allocated to Parent Co.

Investment in Sub Inc.	108	
Investment income		108

90% of bond gain allocated to Sub Inc. (90% × 120 = 108)

The related equity method accounts of Parent will show the following changes and balances in Year 1:

	Investment in Sub Inc.	Investment Income
January 1, Year 1	$11,250	
Changes during Year 1		
Income from Sub Inc.	1,530	$1,530
Bond gain to parent	60	60
90% of bond gain to subsidiary	108	108
Balance, December 31, Year 1	$12,948	$1,698

The investment account contains cumulative adjustments to the end of the period, whereas the investment income account contains adjustments for only one period.

Accounting for Gain in Subsequent Years

We will now focus on Year 2 so that we can illustrate the consolidation eliminations that must be made in years subsequent to the original intercompany bond purchase.

At the end of Year 2, the two companies prepared the financial statements shown in Exhibit 7.12.

Focus initially on the items "interest revenue"[3] and "interest expense," which each company recorded in the following manner:

Parent Company

Interest expense	1,000	
Cash		1,000
To record payment of Year 2 interest		

Bonds payable	25	
Interest expense		25
To amortize issue premium		
(100 ÷ 4 = 25)		

Sub Inc.

Cash	1,000	
Interest revenue		1,000
To record receipt of Year 2 interest		

Investment in bonds of		
Parent Co.	50	
Interest revenue		50
To amortize discount on		
the purchase of bonds		
(200 ÷ 4 = 50)		

These entries are made on the separate-entity books of Parent and Sub.

Note that the entries recording the amortization of the issue premium and the purchase discount increased the respective net incomes of the two companies. The $25 of income reported by Parent is equal to one-quarter of the gain that was attributed to Parent from a consolidated point of view on December 31, Year 1, from the deemed retirement of the bonds. In the same manner, the $50 of income reported by Sub is equal to one-quarter of the gain that was attributed to Sub from a consolidated point of view on December 31, Year 1, from the deemed retirement of the bonds. Because the bonds mature four years after the date of the intercompany purchase and because the original gain on bond retirement was created due to the existence of the unamortized issue premium and the discount on the intercompany purchase of bonds (100 + 200 = 300), the concept that the gain is realized on the consolidated financial statements before it is recorded by the constituent companies becomes evident.

The income resulting from the premium and discount amortization, which is being reported by the separate entities, has already been reported on the consolidated financial statements.

Both Sub's interest revenue of $1,050 (1,000 + 50) and Parent's interest expense of $975 (1,000 − 25) represent intercompany revenues and expenses that

EXHIBIT 7.12

INCOME STATEMENTS—for Year 2

	Parent	Sub
Sales	$25,000	$10,950
Interest revenue	—	1,050
	25,000	12,000
Interest expense	975	—
Miscellaneous expenses	17,375	6,900
Income tax expense	2,600	2,000
	20,950	8,900
Net income	$ 4,050	$ 3,100

The separate-entity income statements show interest revenue and expense for bonds that were retired from a consolidated viewpoint.

RETAINED EARNINGS STATEMENTS—for Year 2

	Parent	Sub
Balance, January 1	$13,400	$ 6,200
Net income	4,050	3,100
	17,450	9,300
Dividends	2,500	—
Balance, December 31	$14,950	$ 9,300

BALANCE SHEETS—at December 31, Year 2

	Parent	Sub
Assets (miscellaneous)	$32,700	$18,450
Investment in Parent Co. bonds	—	9,850
Investment in Sub Inc.	11,250	—
	$43,950	$28,300
Miscellaneous liabilities	$ 3,925	$11,000
Bonds payable	10,075	—
Common shares	15,000	8,000
Retained earnings	14,950	9,300
	$43,950	$28,300

The separate-entity balance sheets show investment and bonds payable for bonds that were retired from a consolidated viewpoint.

are eliminated on the Year 2 consolidated income statement with the following *incomplete* working paper entry:

The difference between interest revenue and interest expense is due to the difference in amortization of the bond premium and discount.

Interest revenue	1,050	
Interest expense		975

To eliminate Year 2 intercompany interest revenue and expense

In past examples, the elimination of intercompany revenues and expenses (sales and purchases, rental revenue and expense, etc.) had no effect on the net income of the entity because the amounts eliminated were always equal. Referring back to the journal entries made by both companies, you will see that this equal component is still present. We are still eliminating $1,000 in interest revenue and expense in the working paper elimination. However, we are also eliminating the portions of the gain on bond retirement that were recorded by both companies as a result of the amortization of the premium and discount in Year 2. Failure to do this would result in the gain on bond retirement being recorded twice over the life of the bonds. It is because we do not allow this portion of the gain to be reflected in the Year 2 consolidated income statement that we have an unequal elimination of intercompany revenue and expense on the working paper elimination entry. The elimination of $1,050 intercompany interest revenue and $975 intercompany interest expense decreases the before-tax net income of the entity by $75. We will describe this reduction of the entity's before-tax net income as the "interest elimination loss."

> The intercompany interest must be eliminated on consolidation to avoid double counting of income pertaining to the bonds.

The realization of a gain on bond retirement on the consolidated income statement in the year of acquisition of intercompany bonds will always result in an interest elimination loss affecting the entity's before-tax net income in all subsequent consolidated income statements until the bonds mature. This interest elimination loss does not appear as such in the consolidated income statement because it results from eliminating an amount of intercompany interest revenue that is larger than the amount of intercompany interest expense eliminated. Conversely, the realization of a loss on bond retirement in the year of acquisition of intercompany bonds will always result in an "interest elimination gain" in all subsequent consolidated income statements because the amount of interest expense eliminated will always be larger than the amount of interest revenue eliminated.

As stated previously, the entity's Year 2, before-tax net income has been decreased by $75. This results from eliminating the portion of the gain on bond retirement recorded by the constituent companies in Year 2. Recall that the entire before-tax gain was realized for consolidated purposes in Year 1; also recall that to satisfy the matching principle an income tax expense was recorded and a deferred tax liability was set up on the consolidated balance sheet. Both companies paid (or accrued) income tax on a portion of this gain in Year 2—a total of $30 (75 × 40%). These companies also recorded the income tax paid (or accrued) as an expense, but from a consolidated point of view, the payment was a reduction of the deferred tax liability previously set up. We must therefore decrease income tax expense when preparing the consolidated income statement because it is not a consolidated expense.[4] The *incomplete* income statement working paper elimination entry is as follows:

> Income tax expense must be eliminated on consolidation to match with the elimination of the interest revenue and interest expense.

Interest revenue	1,050	
Interest expense		975
Income tax expense		30
To eliminate Year 2 intercompany interest revenue and expense and to		
adjust for the income tax effect of the elimination		

The addition of the income tax expense entry still leaves us with an unequal elimination on the consolidated income statement. However, this interest elimination loss is now in after-tax dollars and amounts to $45 (1,050 − 975 − 30). A reconstruction of the intercompany bond chart for the life of the bonds as shown in Exhibit 7.13 will illustrate how this loss is allocated to the two constituents each year.

To further illustrate this, examine the interest accounts of the two companies from the date of the intercompany purchase to the date of maturity of the bonds.

EXHIBIT 7.13

ALLOCATION OF GAIN ON BOND

	Entity			Parent Co.			Sub Inc.		
	Before tax	40% tax	After tax	Before tax	40% tax	After tax	Before tax	40% tax	After tax
Gain on bond, Dec. 31, Year 1	$300	$120	$180	$100	$ 40	$ 60	$200	$ 80	$120 **(a)**
Interest elimination loss—Year 2	75	30	45	25	10	15	50	20	30 **(b)**
Balance—gain— Dec. 31, Year 2	225	90	135	75	30	45	150	60	90 **(c)**
Interest elimination loss—Year 3	75	30	45	25	10	15	50	20	30
Balance—gain— Dec. 31, Year 3	150	60	90	50	20	30	100	40	60
Interest elimination loss—Year 4	75	30	45	25	10	15	50	20	30
Balance—gain— Dec. 31, Year 4	75	30	45	25	10	15	50	20	30
Interest elimination loss—Year 5	75	30	45	25	10	15	50	20	30
Balance, Dec. 31, Year 5	$-0-	$-0-	$-0-	$-0-	$-0-	$-0-	$-0-	$-0-	$-0-

The interest elimination loss for each year is equal to the amortization of the bond premium and bond discount on the separate-entity books.

By the end of Year 5, the cumulative income recorded on the separate-entity books of Parent and Sub is equal to the $300 gain on bond retirement that was reported in the Year 1 consolidated income statement.

Year ended Dec. 31	Parent's interest expense	Sub's interest revenue	Difference
Year 2	$ 975	$1,050	$ 75
Year 3	975	1,050	75
Year 4	975	1,050	75
Year 5	975	1,050	75
	$3,900	$4,200	$300

The preparation of a bond chart would be the first step in the preparation of the Year 2 consolidated statements. This chart would have the same format as the one shown above but would comprise only the first three lines from that particular chart. Before the Year 2 consolidated financial statements are prepared, the three calculations in Exhibit 7.14 are made. The Year 2 consolidated financial statements prepared using the direct approach are shown in Exhibit 7.15.

The unequal elimination of the intercompany interest revenue and expense and the income tax adjustment made in the preparation of the consolidated income statement were explained earlier. This created the "hidden" after-tax interest elimination loss of $45 in this statement. This loss is depicted and allocated in the chart above.

The eliminations made in the preparation of the Year 2 consolidated balance sheet require elaboration. The item "Investment in Parent Co. bonds" in the balance sheet of Sub has a balance of $9,850 after the Year 2 amortization of the discount on purchase (9,800 + 50). Bonds payable in the balance sheet of Parent Co. has a balance of $10,075 after the Year 2 amortization on

EXHIBIT 7.14

CALCULATION OF CONSOLIDATED NET INCOME—Year 2

Net income—Parent Co.		$ 4,050	The interest elimination loss
Less after-tax interest elimination loss allocated **(13b)**		15	is allocated to Parent and
Adjusted		4,035	Sub based on Exhibit 7.13.
Net income—Sub Inc.	3,100		
Less after-tax interest elimination loss allocated **(13b)**	30		
Adjusted		3,070	
Consolidated net income		$ 7,105	
Attributable to			
Shareholders of Parent		$ 6,798 **(a)**	
Non-controlling interest (10% × 3,070)		307 **(b)**	

CALCULATION OF CONSOLIDATED RETAINED EARNINGS
at January 1, Year 2

Retained earnings—Parent Co.		$13,400	This schedule shows the
Add after-tax bond gain allocated (Dec. 31, Year 1) **(13a)**		60	calculation at a point in time;
Adjusted		13,460	that is, at the beginning of
Retained earnings—Sub Inc.	6,200		Year 2, which is the same as
Acquisition retained earnings	4,500		at the end of Year 1.
Increase since acquisition	1,700		
Add after-tax bond gain allocated (Dec. 31, Year 1) **(13a)**	120		
Adjusted	1,820		
Parent Co. ownership	90%	1,638	
Consolidated retained earnings		$15,098 **(c)**	

CALCULATION OF NON-CONTROLLING INTEREST
at December 31, Year 2

Sub Inc.		Only the portion of the
Common shares	$ 8,000	gain on bond retirement
Retained earnings	9,300	allocated to Sub affects non-
	17,300	controlling interest.
Add after-tax bond gain allocated as at Dec. 31, Year 2 **(13c)**	90	
Adjusted shareholders' equity	17,390	
Non-controlling interest's ownership	10%	
	$ 1,739 **(d)**	

When the consolidated balance sheet is being prepared, these two intercompany accounts are eliminated by the following *incomplete* entry:

Bonds payable	10,075	
Investment in Parent Co. bonds		9,850
To eliminate the intercompany bonds on December 31, Year 2		

This entry eliminates the bonds payable and investment in bonds but is not yet complete.

This entry is somewhat similar to the entry made on December 31, Year 1 (see under the section "Intercompany Bondholdings—with Gain or Loss") except that the before-tax amount needed to balance at this time is a gain of $225 instead of the $300 gain that was required a year ago. Furthermore, the $225 gain does not appear as such in the consolidated income statement in Year 2. Recall that the $300 gain appeared on the Year 1 consolidated income statement. A gain on bond retirement appears as such only once in the year of the intercompany purchase. Recall also that

EXHIBIT 7.15

Year 2 Consolidated Statements
Adjusted for Intercompany Bondholdings
(Direct Approach)

PARENT COMPANY
CONSOLIDATED INCOME STATEMENT
for the Year Ended December 31, Year 2

Sales (25,000 + 10,950)	$35,950
Interest revenue (0 + 1,050 − **1,050**)	–0–
	35,950
Interest expense (975 + 0 − **975**)	–0–
Miscellaneous expenses (17,375 + 6,900)	24,275
Income tax expense (2,600 + 2,000 − **[13b] 30**)	4,570
	28,845
Net income	$ 7,105
Attributable to	
Shareholders of Parent **(14a)**	$ 6,798
Non-controlling interest **(14b)**	307

PARENT COMPANY
CONSOLIDATED RETAINED EARNINGS STATEMENT
for the Year Ended December 31, Year 2

Balance, January 1 **(14c)**	$15,098
Net income	6,798
	21,896
Dividends	2,500
Balance, December 31	$19,396

PARENT COMPANY
CONSOLIDATED BALANCE SHEET
at December 31, Year 2

Assets—miscellaneous (32,700 + 18,450)	$51,150
Investment in Parent Co. bonds (0 + 9,850 − **9,850**)	–0–
	$51,150
Miscellaneous liabilities (3,925 + 11,000)	$14,925
Bonds payable (10,075 + 0 − **10,075**)	–0–
Deferred income tax liability (0 + 0 + **[13c] 90**)	90
Total liabilities	15,015
Shareholders' equity	
Common shares	15,000
Retained earnings	19,396
Non-controlling interest **(14d)**	1,739
	$51,150

There was no interest revenue earned from outsiders and no interest expense paid to outsiders *during the year.*

There is no bond payable to outsiders and no investment in bonds by outsiders *at the end of the year.*

At the end of Year 2, the deferred tax liability is the 40% tax on the difference between income recognized for consolidation purposes ($300) and income recognized by the separate entities ($75).

Recall also that a portion of the gain was recorded in Year 2 by Parent and Sub, was eliminated in preparing the Year 2 consolidated income statement and is not reflected again. The $225 needed to balance this journal entry is, therefore, a credit of $300 to retained earnings at the beginning of Year 2 and the combined effect of $75 from eliminating the intercompany interest revenue and interest expense pertaining to the bonds. The bond chart (see Exhibit 7.13) indicates that the entity's deferred with respect to this gain is $90 as at this date. We can now extend the working paper entry by including the deferred tax component as follows:

Bonds payable	10,075	
Investment in Parent Co. bonds		9,850
Deferred income tax liability		90

To eliminate the intercompany bond accounts and set up the deferred tax
  liability as at December 31, Year 2

The after-tax gain needed to balance is now $135. The bond chart (see Exhibit 7.13) shows this gain as allocated $45 to Parent and $90 to Sub.

To summarize, the Year 2 elimination entries made for the intercompany bondholdings had the following effect on the consolidated statements:

1. The adjustments made in the income statement created an after-tax interest elimination loss of $45, which decreased the entity's net income and was allocated to the two equities as follows:

	Total	Non-controlling interest	Controlling interest
Loss allocated to Parent Co.	$15	$—	$15
Loss allocated to Sub Inc.	30	3	27
	$45	$ 3	$42

The interest elimination loss for the year is first allocated to Parent and Sub and then to non-controlling and controlling interests for the year.

2. The elimination of $9,850 in assets and $10,075 in bond liabilities, together with the adjustment to reflect the $90 deferred tax liability, resulted in an after-tax increase of $135 in the equity side of the balance sheet. This was allocated to the two equities, at December 31, Year 2, as follows:

	Total	Non-controlling interest	Controlling interest
Gain allocated to Parent Co.	$ 45	$—	$ 45
Gain allocated to Sub Inc.	90	9	81
	$135	$ 9	$126

The difference between gain on bond retirement and interest elimination loss for all years to date is first allocated to Parent and Sub and then to non-controlling and controlling interests at the end of the year.

Remember that the original $300 gain in Year 1 was allocated to the two equities in the consolidated balance sheet as at December 31, Year 1 (see Exhibit 7.8).

3. The adjustments made in the preparation of both the December 31, Year 2, balance sheet and the Year 2 income statement can be summarized conceptually with respect to their effect on the consolidated balance sheet as follows:

Asset side: Investment in bonds		− $ 9,850	
Liability side:			
Bonds payable		− $10,075	
Deferred income tax liability		+ 90	
Non-controlling interest			
Balance, Dec. 31, Year 1	+ 12		
Year 2 entity net income	− 3	+ 9	
Consolidated retained earnings			
Balance, Dec. 31, Year 1	+168		
Year 2 entity net income	− 42	+ 126	
		$ 9,850	

This chart shows the adjustments to the consolidated balance sheet at the end of Year 2.

The $126 increase in consolidated retained earnings is automatically reflected when the consolidated income and retained earnings statements are prepared.

The $9 increase in non-controlling interest is captured in the calculation of the amount of this equity (preceding item 2).

Equity Method Journal Entries   If Parent has used the equity method, the following entries will be made on December 31, Year 2:

Investment in Sub Inc.	2,790	
Investment income		2,790

90% of the Year 2 net income of Sub Inc. (90% × 3,100 = 2,790)

These entries should cause Parent's separate-entity income under the equity method to be equal to consolidated net income attributable to Parent's shareholders.

Investment income	15	
Investment in Sub Inc.		15

Interest elimination loss allocated to Parent Co.

Investment income	27	
Investment in Sub Inc.		27

90% of interest elimination loss allocated to Sub Inc. (90% × 30 = 27)

The related equity method accounts of Parent will show the following changes and balances in Year 2:

	Investment in Sub Inc.	Investment income
December 31, Year 1	$12,948	
Change during Year 2		
Income from Sub Inc.	2,790	$2,790
Interest loss to parent	(15)	(15)
90% of interest loss to subsidiary	(27)	(27)
Balance, December 31, Year 2	$15,696	$2,748

The investment account under the equity method ($15,696) is different than the investment account under the cost method ($11,250 as per page 372).

Less Than 100% Purchase of Affiliate's Bonds

Our example assumed that Sub purchased 100% of Parent's bonds for $9,800 on December 31, Year 1. Suppose we changed the assumption so that only 40% of Parent's bonds were purchased, for $3,920. The elimination needed to prepare the Year 1 consolidated statements would be as follows:

A gain on bond retirement is recognized only on the portion of the bonds being retired from a consolidated perspective.

Bonds payable (40% × 10,100)	4,040	
Investment in bonds of Parent Co.		3,920
Gain on bond retirement		120

If only 40% of the bond liability has been eliminated, the consolidated balance sheet will show bonds payable amounting to $6,060, representing the 60% that is not intercompany and is payable to bondholders outside the entity. When consolidated income statements are later prepared, only 40% of the interest expense will be eliminated; the remaining 60% will be left as consolidated interest expense.

Intercompany Purchases during the Fiscal Year

Our previous example also assumed that the intercompany purchase of bonds took place on the last day of the fiscal year. If the purchase took place *during* the fiscal year, the Year 1 consolidated income statement contains both the gain on bond retirement and the hidden loss resulting from the elimination of intercompany interest revenue earned and expense incurred for the period subsequent to the acquisition.

Gains (Losses) Not Allocated to the Two Equities

The four approaches that can be taken to allocate bond gains (losses) were outlined in the section "Intercompany Bondholdings—with Gain or Loss." The illustrations used approach 4 because it is the most logical. It allocates the gain or loss on consolidation based on how the separate entities will eventually report the income or loss on their separate-entity financial statements. The calculations for this approach may be a bit more cumbersome, but they do have a lot of merit. Because IFRSs are silent on this matter, any of these approaches may be used. Under approaches 1 to 3, the gain or loss is allocated to only one of the companies, and the bond chart (see Exhibit 7.13) is much simpler, as it needs only the entity columns.

The "agency" method (approach 1) also has a lot of merit because only a company that has issued bonds can logically retire them; allocating the gain or loss to the issuing company puts the emphasis on the economic substance of the transaction rather than on its actual form. In the example used, the entire $300 gain would be allocated to Parent Co. If the example used was changed so that the bonds were originally issued by Sub Inc., and the agency method was followed, the $300 gain would at first be allocated to the subsidiary; however, because Parent owns 90% of Sub, non-controlling interest would reflect 10% of this gain.

> The other approaches would allocate the gain on bond retirement differently to Parent and Sub, which changes the amounts allocated to non-controlling interest.

Gains (Losses) Allocated to Two Equities—Loss to One, Gain to the Other

Suppose that the issuing affiliate had $10,000 in bonds outstanding with a carrying amount of $10,350, and the purchasing affiliate paid $10,050 to acquire all of the issue on the open market. From the entity point of view, there is a before-tax gain on bond retirement of $300, calculated as follows:

Carrying amount of bonds	$10,350
Cost to purchase bonds	10,050
Gain on bond retirement	$ 300

> The gain is equal to the difference between the cost to retire the bonds and the carrying amount of the bonds when they are retired.

If we allocate the gain to the two affiliates (approach 4), we see that the issuing affiliate is allocated a gain of $350, while the purchasing affiliate is allocated a loss of $50. This can be verified by the following calculation:

Carrying amount of bond liability	$10,350
Par value of bond liability	10,000
Gain to issuing affiliate	$ 350
Cost of investment in bonds	$10,050
Par value of bond liability	10,000
Loss to purchasing affiliate	$ 50

> The $300 gain is allocated to the affiliates based on the premium or discount on their separate-entity books.

In subsequent years, the entity's interest elimination loss will be allocated as a loss to the issuing affiliate and a gain to the purchasing affiliate.

See Self-Study Problem 2 for a comprehensive consolidation problem involving intercompany bondholdings. It includes most of the issues we have covered in Part B of this chapter.

Effective-Yield Method of Amortization

Our previous examples have assumed that both companies use the straight-line method to amortize the premiums and discounts. All of the end-of-chapter problems assume the straight-line method, unless stated otherwise. This method leads to fairly easy calculations because the yearly amortizations are equal. If one or both companies use the effective-interest method of amortization, the calculations become more complex, but the concepts remain the same. The following examples illustrate the effective-interest method.

On December 31, Year 0, Subco issued $100,000 face value bonds for a price of $92,791. The bonds pay interest on December 31 each year at a stated rate of 10%, and mature on December 31, Year 5. The market rate of interest was 12% on December 31, Year 0. Given that the stated rate of interest was lower than the market rate, the bonds were issued at a discount. The issue price of the bonds can be determined by taking the present value of future cash flows using a discount rate of 12% as follows:

The effective rate used in the present value calculations and bond amortization tables is the market rate of 12%.

Principal $100,000 × (P/F, 12%, 5 years) (0.56743)	$56,743
Interest 10,000 × (P/A, 12%, 5 years) (3.60478)	36,048
	$92,791

The following schedule shows how Subco would amortize the discount for its separate-entity financial statements and that the amortization of the bond discount increases interest expense (decreases income) each year over the term of the bonds:

The bond discount is amortized on Subco's separate-entity books over the remaining term of the bonds using the effective rate of 12%.

Period	Interest paid	Interest expense	Amortization of bond discount	Amortized cost of bonds
Year 0				$ 92,791
Year 1	$10,000[1]	$11,135[2]	$1,135[3]	93,926[4]
Year 2	10,000	11,271	1,271	95,197
Year 3	10,000	11,424	1,424	96,621
Year 4	10,000	11,594	1,594	98,215
Year 5	10,000	11,785	1,785	100,000

[1] $100,000 × 10% = $10,000   [2] $92,791 × 12% = $11,135
[3] $10,000 − $11,135 = − $1,135   [4] $92,791 + $1,135 = $93,926

The market value of the bonds will increase when the market rate decreases.

The market rate of interest for these bonds decreased to 8%, and these bonds were trading at a price of $105,154 on December 31, Year 2. If Subco redeems the bonds on this date, it will prepare the following journal entry:

Loss on bond redemption	9,957	
Bonds payable	95,197	
Cash		105,154

Now assume that Subco did not redeem its own bonds but Pubco purchased them in the open market on December 31, Year 2, for $105,154. The following schedule shows the amortization of this premium by Pubco using the effective-interest method and shows that the amortization of the bond premium decreases interest revenue (decreases income) each year over the remaining term of the bonds:

Pubco amortizes its bond premium on its separate-entity books using its effective rate of 8%.

Period	Interest received	Interest revenue	Amortization of bond premium	Amortized cost of bonds
Year 2				$105,154
Year 3	$10,000[1]	$8,412[2]	$1,588[3]	103,566[4]
Year 4	10,000	8,285	1,715	101,851
Year 5	10,000	8,149	1,851	100,000

[1] $100,000 × 10% = $10,000   [2] $105,154 × 8% = $8,412
[3] $10,000 − $8,412 = $1,588   [4] $105,154 − $1,588 = $103,566

From a separate legal entity perspective, Subco has bonds payable on its balance sheet, while Pubco has an investment in bonds on its balance sheet. From a consolidated perspective, these bonds were redeemed when Pubco purchased them on the open market. A loss on redemption of $9,957 (105,154 − 95,197) should be recorded on the consolidated income statement. In subsequent years, Subco and Pubco will amortize the bond discount and premium on their separate-entity books. From a consolidated perspective, the amortization of the bond discount and premium should be eliminated because the bonds no longer exist. The following bond chart shows how the loss on bond redemption and the elimination of bond amortization is allocated to Pubco and Subco each year over the remaining life of the bonds:

From a consolidated perspective, the bonds were redeemed at a loss of $9,957.

	Entity	Pubco	Subco
Loss on bond, Dec. 31, Yr 2	$9,957	$5,154	$4,803
Interest elimination gain—Yr 3	3,012	1,588	1,424
Balance—loss, Dec. 31, Yr 3	6,945	3,566	3,379
Interest elimination gain—Yr 4	3,309	1,715	1,594
Balance—loss, Dec. 31, Yr 4	3,636	1,851	1,785
Interest elimination gain—Yr 5	3,636	1,851	1,785
Balance—loss, Dec. 31, Yr 5	$ –0–	$ –0–	$ –0–

To further illustrate, examine the interest accounts of the two companies from the date of the intercompany purchase to the date of maturity of the bonds:

Year ended Dec. 31	Pubco's interest revenue	Subco's interest expense	Difference
Year 3	$ 8,412	$11,424	$3,012
Year 4	8,285	11,594	3,309
Year 5	8,149	11,785	3,636
	$24,846	$34,803	$9,957

From the separate-entity perspective, Pubco and Subco continue to amortize the bond discount or premium using their effective rates.

Under the effective-interest method, the difference between interest revenue and interest expense changes over time. Under the straight-line method, the difference would be $3,319 ($9,957/3) each year for three years. Under both methods, a loss on bond redemption of $9,957 is recorded on the consolidated income statement in Year 2. In turn, consolidated income is increased by a total of $9,957 over the three-year remaining term of the bonds as the amortization of the bond premium and discount is eliminated.

The loss on redemption was recognized in Year 2 from a consolidated perspective and over the three-year period ending in Year 5 from a single-entity perspective.

Disclosure Requirements The disclosure requirements for consolidated financial statements were summarized in Chapters 3 and 4. In addition to those requirements, the entity would normally indicate that intercompany transactions have been eliminated. The excerpt below is taken from the 2011 financial statements of Bell Canada Enterprises Inc., Canada's largest telecommunications company.

> **Basis of Consolidation** We consolidate the financial statements of all our subsidiaries. Subsidiaries are entities we control, where control is the power to govern the financial and operating policies of an entity so as to obtain benefits from its activities.
>
> The results of subsidiaries acquired or sold during the year are consolidated from the date of acquisition and up to the date of disposal. Where necessary, adjustments are made to the financial statements of subsidiaries to conform their accounting policies with ours. All intercompany transactions, balances, income and expenses are eliminated on consolidation.[5]

ASPE DIFFERENCES

- As mentioned in Chapter 3, private companies can either consolidate their subsidiaries or report their investments in subsidiaries under the cost method, equity method, or fair value method.
- Whereas public companies can adopt the revaluation model or the cost model to value property, plant, and equipment, private companies using ASPE, must use the cost model.
- Whereas impairment losses for property, plant, and equipment and intangible assets other than goodwill can be reversed under IFRSs, they cannot be reversed under ASPE.

U.S. GAAP DIFFERENCES

U.S. GAAP and IFRSs for intercompany transactions have many similarities. The significant differences are summarized as follows:

1. Whereas IFRSs require that property, plant, and equipment and intangible assets be accounted for using the cost method or the revaluation method, these assets must be reported at cost less accumulated amortization and accumulated impairment losses under U.S. GAAP.
2. Whereas impairment losses on property, plant, and equipment and intangible assets other than goodwill can be reversed under IFRSs in certain circumstances, they cannot be reversed under U.S. GAAP.

SUMMARY

This chapter completed the illustrations of the holdback and realization of intercompany profits and gains in assets by examining the consolidation procedures involved when the profit relates to an asset subject to depreciation. The gain is held back in order to state the depreciable asset at its historical cost less accumulated depreciation from a consolidated perspective. The intercompany profit is subsequently realized as the assets are used or consumed in generating revenues over its remaining life. Because there are differences between the periods in which the tax is paid and those in which the gains are realized in the consolidated statements, income tax must be allocated.

The second part of the chapter examined the gains and losses that are created in the consolidated statements by the elimination of intercompany bondholdings. When the investing company purchases the bonds from outsiders, the bonds are effectively retired from a consolidated perspective. The difference between the price paid to retire the bonds and the carrying amount of the bonds is a gain or a loss. These gains and losses can occur only if there were premiums or discounts involved in the issue or purchase of these bonds. In the case of intercompany bondholdings, the gains or losses are recognized in the consolidated statements before they are recorded by the affiliated companies, whereas intercompany asset gains are recorded by the affiliated companies before they are recognized in the consolidated statements.

When the parent company uses the revaluation model to revalue its property, plant, and equipment under IAS 16, the consolidated financial statements should reflect the fair value of these assets at the revaluation date, less accumulated depreciation since the revaluation date. When intercompany transactions occur, the gain or loss on the intercompany transaction must be eliminated and the values reinstated as if the intercompany transaction had not occurred.

Significant Changes in GAAP in the Last Three Years

No major changes occurred in the last three years for the topics presented in this chapter

Changes Expected in GAAP in the Next Three Years

No major changes are expected in the next three years.

SELF-STUDY PROBLEM 1

LO1, 3 The following are the Year 15 financial statements of Penn Company and its subsidiary Sill Corp.

	Penn	Sill
Year 15 income statements		
Miscellaneous revenues	$500,000	$300,000
Investment income	9,194	—
Gain on sale of equipment	14,000	—
Gain on sale of patent	—	7,500
	523,194	307,500
Miscellaneous expenses	309,600	186,500
Depreciation expense	120,000	80,000
Patent amortization expense	800	—
Income tax expense	33,000	16,000
	463,400	282,500
Profit	$ 59,794	$ 25,000
Year 15 retained earnings statements		
Balance, January 1	$162,000	$154,000
Profit	59,794	25,000
	221,794	179,000
Dividends	25,000	8,000
Balance, December 31	$196,794	$171,000
Statement of financial position, December 31, Year 15		
Miscellaneous assets	$271,600	$131,000
Land and buildings	200,000	656,000
Equipment	—	44,000*
Accumulated depreciation	(80,000)	(250,000)
Patent (net)	19,200	—
Investment in Sill Corp.	285,994	—
	$696,794	$581,000
Ordinary shares	$400,000	$200,000
Retained earnings	196,794	171,000
Miscellaneous liabilities	100,000	210,000
	$696,794	$581,000

For illustrative purposes, we are assuming that this is the only equipment owned by either company.

Additional Information

Penn owns 80% of Sill and has used the equity method to account for its invest-ment. The acquisition differential on acquisition date has been fully amortized for consolidation purposes prior to Year 15, and there were no unrealized intercom-pany profits or losses in the assets of the companies on December 31, Year 14. Dur-ing Year 15, the following intercompany transactions took place:

- On January 1, Year 15, Penn sold used equipment to Sill and recorded a $14,000 gain on the transaction as follows:

Selling price of equipment		$44,000
Carrying amount of equipment sold		
Cost	70,000	
Accumulated depreciation—Dec. 31, Year 14	40,000	30,000
Gain on sale of equipment		$14,000

This equipment had an estimated remaining life of 8 years on this date.

- On January 1, Year 5, Sill developed a patent at a cost of $34,000. It has been amortizing this patent over 17 years. On October 1, Year 15, Sill sold the patent to Penn and recorded a $7,500 gain, calculated as follows:

Selling price of patent			$20,000
Carrying amount of patent sold			
Cost		34,000	
Amortization:			
To December 31, Year 14 (10 × 2,000)	20,000		
Year 15 (¾ × 2,000)	1,500	21,500	12,500
Gain on sale of patent			$ 7,500

Penn is amortizing this patent over its remaining legal life of 6¼ years.

- Both gains were assessed income tax at a rate of 40%.

Required:

(a) Using the reported profits of both companies, prepare a calculation which shows that Penn's separate-entity profit is equal to consolidated profit attrib-utable to Penn's shareholders.

(b) Using Penn's investment account, prepare a calculation which shows that the acquisition differential is fully amortized.

(c) Prepare the following Year 15 consolidated financial statements:

  (i) Income statement
  (ii) Retained earnings statement
  (iii) Statement of financial position

SOLUTION TO SELF-STUDY PROBLEM 1

UNREALIZED PROFITS

	Before tax	40% tax	After tax
Equipment (Penn selling):			
Gain recorded, Jan. 1, Year 15	$14,000	$5,600	$ 8,400 **(a)**
Depreciation, Year 15 (14,000 ÷ 8)	1,750	700	1,050 **(b)**
Balance unrealized, Dec. 31, Year 15	$12,250	$4,900	$ 7,350 **(c)**

	Before tax	40% tax	After tax
Patent (Sill selling):			
Gain recorded, Oct. 1, Year 15	$ 7,500	$3,000	$ 4,500 **(d)**
Amortization, Year 15 (7,500 ÷ 6¼ × ¼)	300	120	180 **(e)**
Balance unrealized Dec. 31, Year 15	$ 7,200	$2,880	$ 4,320 **(f)**
Deferred income tax asset—December 31, Year 15:			
Equipment profit			$ 4,900 **(g)**
Patent profit			2,880 **(h)**
			$ 7,780 **(i)**

(a)
Profit Penn Co.	$ 59,794
Less: Investment income	9,194
Profit Penn—own operations	50,600
Less: January 1 equipment gain **(a)**	8,400
	42,200
Add: After-tax equipment gain realized in Year 15 **(b)**	1,050
Adjusted profit	43,250

Profit Sill Corp.	25,000	
Less: October 1 patent gain **(d)**	4,500	
	20,500	
Add: After-tax patent gain realized in Year 15 **(e)**	180	
Adjusted profit		20,680
Consolidated profit		$ 63,930

Attributable to	
Shareholders of Penn	$ 59,794 **(j)**
Non-controlling interest (20% × 20,680)	4,136 **(k)**

(b)
Investment in Sill Corp. (equity method):	
Balance, Dec. 31, Year 15	$285,994
Add: Unrealized after-tax equipment gain, Dec. 31, Year 15 **(c)**	7,350
	293,344

Sill Corp., Dec. 31, Year 15:		
Ordinary shares	200,000	
Retained earnings	171,000	
	371,000	
Less: Unrealized after-tax patent gain, Dec. 31, Year 15 **(f)**	4,320	
Adjusted shareholders' equity	366,680	
Penn's ownership	80%	293,344
Unamortized acquisition differential		$ –0–

(c) (i)
CONSOLIDATED INCOME STATEMENT—for Year 15

Miscellaneous revenues (500,000 + 300,000)	$ 800,000
Gain on sale of equipment (14,000 + 0 − **[a] 14,000**)	–0–
Gain on sale of patents (0 + 7,500 − **[d] 7,500**)	–0–
Miscellaneous expenses (309,600 + 186,500)	496,100
Depreciation expense (120,000 + 80,000 − **[b] 1,750**)	198,250
Patent amortization expense (800 − **[e] 300**)	500
Income tax expense (33,000 + 16,000 − **[c] 4,900** − **[f] 2,880**)	41,220
	736,070
Profit	$ 63,930
Attributable to	
Shareholders of Parent **(j)**	$ 59,794
Non-controlling interest **(k)**	4,136

(ii)   **CONSOLIDATED RETAINED EARNINGS STATEMENT**—for Year 15

Balance, January 1	$ 162,000
Profit	59,794
	221,794
Dividends	25,000
Balance, December 31	$ 196,794

(iii)   **CONSOLIDATED STATEMENT OF FINANCIAL POSITION**—
at December 31, Year 15

Miscellaneous assets (271,600 + 131,000)	$ 402,600
Land and buildings (200,000 + 656,000)	856,000
Equipment (0 + 44,000 − **[a] 14,000** + **40,000***)	70,000
Accumulated depreciation (80,000 + 250,000 − **[b] 1,750** + **40,000***)	(368,250)
Patent (19,200 + 0 − **[f] 7,200**)	12,000
Deferred income taxes (0 + 0 + **[i] 7,780**)	7,780
	$ 980,130
Ordinary shares	$400,000
Retained earnings	196,794
Non-controlling interest**	73,336
Miscellaneous liabilities (100,000 + 210,000)	310,000
	$ 980,130

* *It is necessary to increase equipment and accumulated depreciation by $40,000
in order to re-establish the original historical cost of the equipment and the accumulated
depreciation as at the date of the intercompany sale.*

** *Sill Corp.—Adjusted shareholders' equity (see part [b])*	$366,680
	20%
Non-controlling interest	$ 73,336

SELF-STUDY PROBLEM 2

L05, 7   The financial statements of Parson Corp. and Sloan Inc. for the year ended
December 31, Year 5, are as follows:

INCOME STATEMENTS—for Year 5

	Parson	Sloan
Miscellaneous revenues	$650,000	$200,000
Interest revenue	5,662	—
Dividend revenue	7,500	—
	663,162	200,000
Miscellaneous expenses	432,000	129,600
Interest expense	—	9,723
Income tax expense	92,000	24,000
	524,000	163,323
Profit	$139,162	$ 36,677

RETAINED EARNINGS STATEMENTS—for Year 5

Balance, January 1	$245,000	$ 90,000
Profit	139,162	36,677
	384,162	126,677
Dividends	70,000	10,000
Balance, December 31	$314,162	$116,677

STATEMENTS OF FINANCIAL POSITION—at December 31, Year 5

Investment in Sloan shares	$ 96,000	$ —
Investment in Sloan bonds	61,210	—
Miscellaneous assets	607,000	372,600
	$764,210	$372,600
Ordinary shares	$150,000	$ 80,000
Retained earnings	314,162	116,677
Bonds payable	—	101,002
Miscellaneous liabilities	300,048	74,921
	$764,210	$372,600

Additional Information

- Parson acquired 75% of Sloan on January 1, Year 1, at a cost of $96,000. On this date, Sloan's retained earnings amounted to $40,000, and the acquisition differential was allocated entirely to goodwill. Impairment tests conducted yearly since acquisition yielded a loss of $3,200 in Year 2 and a further loss of $800 in Year 5. Parson uses the cost method to account for the investment.
- Sloan has a 10%, $100,000 bond issue outstanding. These bonds were originally issued at a premium to reduce the effective interest cost to 9.6%, and mature on December 31, Year 8. On January 1, Year 5, the unamortized issue premium amounted to $1,279. Sloan uses the effective interest method to amortize the premium.
- On January 1, Year 5, Parson acquired $60,000 face value of Sloan's bonds at a cost of $61,548, which generates an effective rate of return of 9.2%. The purchase premium is being amortized by Parson using the effective interest method.
- Both companies pay income tax at a rate of 40%.
- Gains and losses from intercompany bondholdings are to be allocated to the two companies when consolidated statements are prepared.

Required:

(a) Prepare the following Year 5 consolidated financial statements:
  - (i) Income statement
  - (ii) Retained earnings statement
  - (iii) Statement of financial position
(b) Prepare a calculation of consolidated retained earnings at December 31, Year 5.
(c) Prepare the Year 5 journal entries that would be made by Parson if the equity method was used to account for the investment in Sloan's shares.
(d) Calculate the balance in the "Investment in Sloan shares" account as at December 31, Year 5, if Parson had used the equity method.

SOLUTION TO SELF-STUDY PROBLEM 2

Cost of 75% of Sloan		$ 96,000
Implied value of 100% of Sloan		$128,000
Carrying amount of Sloan, January 1, Year 1		
Ordinary shares	80,000	
Retained earnings	40,000	
		120,000

(continued)

Acquisition differential—January 1, Year 1	8,000
Allocated to revalue Sloan's identifiable net assets	–0–
Balance—goodwill	8,000
Impairment losses	
Year 1 to Year 4	3,200 **(a)**
Year 5	800 **(b)**
Balance—goodwill, December 31, Year 5	$ 4,000 **(c)**
Non-controlling interest, January 1, Year 1 (25% × 128,000))	$ 32,000 **(d)**

INTERCOMPANY TRANSACTIONS
YEAR 5 BEFORE-TAX BOND LOSS

Cost of 60% of Sloan's bonds acquired Jan. 1, Year 5		$ 61,548
Carrying amount of liability		
Bonds payable	100,000	
Bond premium	1,279	
	101,279	
Amount acquired by Parson	60%	60,767
Bond loss to be reflected in the Year 5 consolidated income statement		$ 781 **(e)**
Allocated as follows:		
Cost of bonds		$ 61,548
Face value of bonds (intercompany portion)		60,000
Before-tax loss—Parson		$ 1,548 **(f)**
Face value of bonds		$ 60,000
Carrying amount of bonds (intercompany portion)		60,767
Before-tax gain—Sloan		$ 767 **(g)**

BOND AMORTIZATION SCHEDULE—SLOAN

Period	Interest paid	Interest expense	Amortization of bond Premium	Amortized cost of bonds
Jan. 1, Year 5				$101,279
Year 5	$10,000[1]	$9,723[2]	$277[3]	101,002[4]

[1] $100,000 × 10% = $10,000   [2] $101,279 × 9.6% = $9,723
[3] $10,000 − $9,723 = $277   [4] $101,279 − $277 = $101,002

BOND AMORTIZATION SCHEDULE—PARSON

Period	Interest received	Interest revenue	Amortization of bond premium	Amortized cost of bonds
Jan. 1, Year 5				$61,548
Year 5	$6,000[1]	$5,662[2]	$338[3]	61,210[4]

[1] $60,000 × 10% = $6,000   [3] $6,000 − $5,662 = $338
[2] $61,548 × 9.2% = $5,662   [4] $61,548 − $338 = $61,210

INTERCOMPANY INTEREST REVENUE AND EXPENSE

Interest paid by Sloan		
10% × 100,000	10,000	
Premium amortization	277	
Total expense	9,723	
Intercompany portion	60%	$5,834 **(h)**

(continued)

Interest received by Parson		
10% × 60,000	6,000	
Premium amortization	338	5,662 **(i)**
Before-tax interest elimination gain to entity		$ 172 **(j)**
Allocated:		
Before-tax loss to Sloan (277 × 60%)		$ 166 **(k)**
Before-tax gain to Parson		338 **(l)**
Total gain allocated (before-tax dollars)		$ 172 **(m)**

SUMMARY

	Entity			Parson Co.			Sloan Inc.		
	Before tax	40% tax	After tax	Before tax	40% tax	After tax	Before tax	40% tax	After tax
Jan. 1/Year 5 bond loss (gain)	$781	$312	$469	$1,548	$619	$929	$(767)	$(307)	$(460) **(n)**
Int. elim. gain (loss) Year 5	172	69	103	338	135	203	(166)	(66)	(100) **(o)**
Dec. 31, Year 5 Balance, loss (gain)	$609	$243	$366	$1,210	$484	$726	$(601)	$(241)	$(360) **(p)**

(a) (i) **CALCULATION OF CONSOLIDATED NET INCOME**—for Year 5

Profit—Parson		$139,162
Less: Dividend from Sloan	7,500	
January 1 after-tax bond loss allocated **(n)**	929	8,429
		130,733
Add: Year 5 after-tax interest elimination gain allocated **(o)**		203
Adjusted profit—Parson		130,936
Profit—Sloan	36,677	
Add: January 1 after-tax bond gain allocated **(n)**	460	
Less: Year 5 after-tax interest elimination loss allocated **(o)**	(100)	
Acquisition-differential amortization **(b)**	(800)	
Adjusted profit—Sloan		36,237
Consolidated profit		$167,173
Attributable to		
Shareholders of Parson		$158,114 **(q)**
Non-controlling interest (25% × 36,267)		9,059 **(r)**

CONSOLIDATED INCOME STATEMENT—for Year 5

Miscellaneous revenues (650,000 + 200,000)	$850,000
Interest revenue (5,662 + 0 − **[i] 5,662**)	—
Dividend revenue (7,500 + 0 − **7,500**)	—
Miscellaneous expenses (432,000 + 129,600)	561,600
Loss on bond retirement **(n)**	781
Interest expense (9,723 − **[h] 5,834**)	3,889
Goodwill impairment loss **(b)**	800
Income tax expense (92,000 + 24,000 − **[p] 243**)	115,757
	682,827
Profit	$167,173
Attributable to	
Shareholders of Parson **(q)**	$158,114
Non-controlling interest **(r)**	9,059

(ii)

CALCULATION OF CONSOLIDATED RETAINED EARNINGS
at January 1, Year 5

Retained earnings—Parson		$245,000
Retained earnings—Sloan	90,000	
Acquisition retained earnings	40,000	
Increase since acquisition	50,000	
Less: Goodwill impairment loss **(a)**	3,200	
	46,800 **(s)**	
Parson's ownership	75%	35,100
Consolidated retained earnings, Jan. 1, Year 5		$280,100 **(t)**

CONSOLIDATED RETAINED EARNINGS STATEMENT—for Year 5

Balance, January 1 **(t)**	$280,100
Profit	158,114
	438,214
Dividends	70,000
Balance, December 31	$368,214

(iii)

CALCULATION OF NON-CONTROLLING INTEREST
at December 31, Year 5

Shareholders' equity—Sloan	
Ordinary shares	$80,000
Retained earnings	116,677
	196,677
Add: Net Year 5 after-tax bond gain allocated **(p)**	360
Add: Unimpaired goodwill **(c)**	4,000
Adjusted shareholders' equity	201,037
	25%
	$50,259 **(u)**

ALTERNATIVE FORMAT

Non-controlling interest, date of acquisition **(d)**	$32,000
Adjusted increase in Sloan's retained earnings since	
acquisition (25% × **[v]** 73,037)	18,259
	$50,259

CONSOLIDATED STATEMENT OF FINANCIAL POSITION—
at December 31, Year 5

Goodwill **(c)**	$ 4,000
Deferred income tax asset **(p)**	243
Investment in Sloan bonds (61,210 + 0 − 61,210)	—
Miscellaneous assets (607,000 + 372,600)	979,600
	$983,843
Ordinary shares	$150,000
Retained earnings	368,214
Non-controlling interest **(u)**	50,259
Bonds payable (101,002 − 60,000 − **[p] 601**)	40,401
Miscellaneous liabilities (300,048 + 74,921)	374,969
	$983,843

(b)
PROOF—CONSOLIDATED RETAINED EARNINGS
at December 31, Year 5

Retained earnings—Parson		$314,162
Less: Net Year 5 after-tax bond loss allocated (p)		726
Adjusted retained earnings		313,436
Retained earnings—Sloan	116,677	
Acquisition retained earnings	40,000	
Increase since acquisition	76,677	
Less: Goodwill impairment losses		
([a] 3,200 + [b] 800)	(4,000)	
Add: Net Year 5 after-tax bond gain allocated (p)	360	
Adjusted increase	73,037	(v)
Parsons' ownership	75%	54,778
Consolidated retained earnings		$368,214

(c)
EQUITY METHOD JOURNAL ENTRIES

Investment in Sloan	27,508	
Investment income		27,508
75% of Sloan's Year 5 profit (75% × 36,677)		
Investment in Sloan	270	
Investment income		270
75% of the net Year 5 bond gain allocated to Sloan (75% × 360)		
Cash	7,500	
Investment in Sloan		7,500
Dividends received from Sloan		
Investment income	600	
Investment in Sloan		600
Year 5 goodwill impairment loss (75% × 800)		
Investment income	726	
Investment in Sloan		726
Year 5 net bond loss allocated to Parson		

(d)

	Investment in Sloan shares
Balance, December 31, Year 4—cost method	$ 96,000
Increase in retained earnings to Jan. 1, Year 5 ([s] 46,800 × 75%)	35,100
Balance, December 31, Year 4—equity method	131,100
Investment income, Year 5 (see equity method journal entries)	26,452
Dividends from Sloan	(7,500)
Balance, December 31, Year 5—equity method	$150,052

APPENDIX 7A

DEPRECIABLE ASSETS UNDER REVALUATION MODEL

L09

An entity can report its property, plant, and equipment at fair value on an annual basis.

IAS 16: Property, Plant and Equipment allows a reporting entity to use either the revaluation method or the amortized cost method to measure its property, plant, and equipment. The same method must be used for each class of property, plant, and equipment. The revaluation adjustment is reported in other comprehensive income unless it indicates an impairment loss, in which case it is reported in net income. The reversal of an impairment loss is also reported in net income to the extent of any previous impairment loss. Depreciation expense is based on the revalued amount. The revaluation surplus is transferred directly to retained earnings, either as the asset is depreciated or when the asset is sold.

We will illustrate the preparation of consolidated financial statements when there has been an intercompany sale of equipment, which had been remeasured under the revaluation model allowed in IAS 16.

Sub acquired the equipment for $5,000 and was depreciating the equipment over an estimated useful life of five years. After three years, the accumulated depreciation was $3,000 and the carrying amount was $2,000. Let us now assume that Sub remeasured its equipment to $2,300, the fair value of the equipment, and that both the original cost and the accumulated depreciation were to be grossed up using the proportional method for the increase in value. Sub had not revalued the equipment since it was acquired. Sub would make the following entry on its separate-entity books:

The revaluation surplus is reported through other comprehensive income.

Equipment [(2,300/2,000 × 5,000) − 5,000]	750	
Accumulated depreciation [(2,300/2,000 × 3,000) − 3,000]		450
Other comprehensive income—revaluation surplus		300

Depreciation expense for the first six months of Year 1 would have been $575 (2,300/2 years × 6/12). When Sub sold the equipment to Parent for $2,100 on July 1, Year 1, it would make the following entries on its separate-entity books:

Cash	2,100	
Accumulated depreciation (3,000 + 450 + 575)	4,025	
Equipment (5,000 + 750)		5,750
Gain on sale of equipment[6]		375
To record sale of equipment		

The revaluation surplus is transferred to retained earnings when the property is sold.

Accumulated other comprehensive income—revaluation surplus	300	
Retained earnings		300
To transfer revaluation surplus to retained earnings		

Given that the parent controls the subsidiary, the parent could have imposed the sale price for the equipment. It does not necessarily reflect the fair value of the equipment. The parent would make the following entries related to the equipment in Year 1:

Equipment	2,100	
Cash		2,100
To purchase equipment		

Depreciation expense (2,100/1½ × ½)	700	
Accumulated depreciation		700
Depreciation expense for six months		

When preparing the consolidated financial statements at the end of Year 1, the following entries would have to be made in the consolidated working papers to report the amounts that would have appeared had the intercompany transaction not occurred:

Gain on sale of equipment	375	
Equipment		375
To reverse gain on sale		
Equipment	4,025	
Accumulated depreciation		4,025
To reinstate accumulated depreciation at date of intercompany sale		
Accumulated depreciation	125	
Depreciation expense		125
To recognize gain through usage of equipment by reversing excess depreciation		
Retained earnings	300	
Accumulated other comprehensive income—revaluation surplus		300
To reinstate revaluation surplus		

The following table summarizes what would have appeared on the three sets of financial statements for Year 1 after processing the journal entries indicated above:

	Parent	Sub	Consolidated	
Equipment	2,100		5,750	The consolidated statements
Accumulated depreciation	700		4,600	should report amounts that
Equipment—net	1,400		1,150	would have existed had the
Accumulated other comprehensive income			300	intercompany transaction
Gain on sale		375		not occurred.
Depreciation expense	700	575	1,150	

The consolidated amounts reflect what would have been on Sub's separate-entity financial statements and on the consolidated financial statements had the intercompany transaction not occurred.

REVIEW QUESTIONS

Questions, cases, and problems that deal with the appendix material are denoted with an asterisk.

L01, 2   1. Explain how an intercompany gain of $2,700 on the sale of a depreciable asset is held back on the consolidated income statement in the year of sale and realized on subsequent consolidated income statements. What income tax adjustments should be made in each instance?

L01, 2   2. "The realization of intercompany inventory and depreciable asset profits is really an adjustment made in the preparation of consolidated income statements to arrive at historical cost numbers." Explain.

L02   3. An intercompany inventory profit is realized when the inventory is sold outside the entity. Is this also the case with respect to an intercompany profit in a depreciable asset? Explain.

LO1, 2   4.   An intercompany gain on a depreciable asset resulting from a sale by the parent company is subsequently realized by an adjustment to the subsidiary's depreciation expense in the preparation of consolidated income statements. Should this adjustment be taken into account in the calculation of net income attributable to non-controlling interest? Explain.

LO1, 2   5.   Why does an intercompany sale of a depreciable asset (such as equipment or a building) require subsequent adjustments to depreciation expense within the consolidation process?

LO1, 2   6.   If an intercompany sale of a depreciable asset has been made at a price above carrying amount, the beginning retained earnings of the seller are reduced when preparing each subsequent consolidation. Why does the amount of the adjustment change from year to year?

LO1, 2   7.   When there has been an intercompany sale of a used depreciable asset (i.e., accumulated depreciation has been recorded for this asset), it is necessary to gross up the asset and accumulated depreciation when preparing the consolidated financial statement. Explain what is meant by grossing up the asset and accumulated depreciation and why this action is necessary.

LO9   *8.   When a company sells equipment that had previously been remeasured to fair value under the revaluation model of IAS 16, it transfers the revaluation surplus from accumulated other comprehensive income directly to retained earnings. What adjustments must be made to accumulated other comprehensive income when preparing consolidated financial statements if the sale is from the parent to the subsidiary?

LO9   *9.   "There should never be a gain on an intercompany sale of equipment when the selling company uses the revaluation model under IAS 16 and the equipment is sold at fair value." Is this statement true or false? Explain.

LO5   10.   Four approaches could be used to allocate gains (losses) on the elimination of intercompany bondholdings in the preparation of consolidated financial statements. Outline these four approaches. Which approach is conceptually superior? Explain.

LO5   11.   An interest elimination gain (loss) does not appear as a distinguishable item on a consolidated income statement. Explain.

LO1, 5   12.   The adjustment for the holdback of an intercompany gain in assets requires a corresponding adjustment to a consolidated deferred tax asset. The adjustment for a gain from intercompany bondholdings requires a corresponding adjustment to a consolidated deferred tax liability. In both cases, the tax adjustment is made because of a gain. Why is the tax adjustment different? Explain.

LO1, 5   13.   "Some intercompany gains (losses) are realized for consolidation purposes subsequent to their actual recording by the affiliates, while others are recorded by the affiliates subsequent to their realization for consolidation purposes." Explain, referring to the type of gains (losses) that apply in each case.

LO6   14.   Explain how the recognition of gains on the elimination of intercompany bondholdings is consistent with the principle of recording gains only when they are realized.

LO6   15.   Explain how the matching principle supports the recognition of deferred income tax expense when a gain is recognized on the elimination of intercompany bondholdings.

CASES

Case 7-1
LO1, 3

Enron Corporation's 2000 financial statements disclosed the following transaction with LIM2, a nonconsolidated special purpose entity (SPE) that was formed by Enron:

> In June 2000, LIM2 purchased dark fibre optic cable from Enron for a purchase price of $100 million. LIM2 paid Enron $30 million in cash and the balance in an interest-bearing note for $70 million. Enron recognized $67 million in pre-tax earnings in 2000 related to the asset sale.

Investigators later discovered that LIM2 was in many ways controlled by Enron. In the wake of the bankruptcy of Enron, both American and Canadian standard-setters introduced accounting standards that require the consolidation of SPEs that are essentially controlled by their sponsor firm.

By selling goods to SPEs that it controlled but did not consolidate, did Enron overstate its earnings?

Required:

Determine how this transaction should have been accounted for assuming that

(a) Enron controlled LIM2 and used consolidated financial statements to report its investment in LIM2;

(b) Enron had significant influence over LIM2 and used the equity method to report its investment; and

(c) Enron did not have control or significant influence over LIM2 but LIM2 was considered a related party and Enron had to apply IAS 24: Related Party Disclosures.

Case 7-2
LO5

Several years ago, the Penston Company purchased 90% of the outstanding shares of Swansan Corporation. The acquisition was made because Swansan produced a vital component used in Penston's manufacturing process. Penston wanted to ensure an adequate supply of this item at a reasonable price. The former owner, James Swansan, who agreed to continue managing this organization, retained the remaining 10% of Swansan's shares. He was given responsibility over the subsidiary's daily manufacturing operations but not for any of the financial decisions.

At a recent meeting, the president of Penston and the company's chief financial officer began discussing Swansan's debt position. The subsidiary had a debt-to-equity ratio that seemed unreasonably high considering the significant amount of cash flows being generated by both companies. Payment of the interest expense, especially on the subsidiary's outstanding bonds, was a major cost, one that the corporate officials hoped to reduce. However, the bond indenture specified that Swansan could retire this debt prior to maturity only by paying 107% of face value.

This premium was considered prohibitive. Thus, to avoid contractual problems, Penston acquired a large portion of Swansan's liability on the open market for 101% of face value. Penston's purchase created an effective loss on the debt of $300,000: the excess of the price over the carrying amount of the debt as reported on Swansan's books.

Company accountants are currently computing the non-controlling interest's share of consolidated net income to be reported for the current year. They are unsure about the impact of this $300,000 loss. The subsidiary's debt was retired, but officials of the parent company made the decision.

Required:

(a) Determine who lost the $300,000.

(b) Explain how the loss should be allocated on the consolidated financial statements.

Case 7-3
LO1, 2

On January 1, Year 1, Plum purchased 100% of the common shares of Slum. On December 31, Year 2, Slum purchased a machine for $84,000 from an external supplier. The machine had an estimated useful life of six years with no residual value. On December 31, Year 4, Plum purchased the machine from Slum for $100,000. The estimated remaining life at the time of the intercompany sale was four years. Plum pays income tax at the rate of 40%, whereas Slum is taxed at a rate of 30%.

When preparing the consolidated statements for Year 5, the controller and manager of accounting at Plum got into a heated debate as to the proper tax rate to use when eliminating the tax on the excess depreciation being taken by Plum. The controller thought that Slum's tax rate should be used since Slum was the owner of this machine before the intercompany sale. The manager of accounting thought that Plum's tax rate should be used since Plum was the actual company saving the tax at the rate of 40%.

In Year 6, the Canada Revenue Agency (CRA) audited Plum. It questioned the legitimacy of the intercompany transaction for the following reasons:

1. Was the selling price of $100,000 a fair reflection of market value?

2. Was Plum trying to gain a tax advantage by saving tax at a rate of 40% rather than the 30% saving that Slum used to realize?

Plum argued that, under the terms of the sale, CRA was better off because CRA received tax in Year 4 from the gain on the intercompany sale. Had the intercompany sale not occurred, CRA would not have received this tax.

Required:

(a) Determine the economic benefits, if any, to the consolidated entity from tax savings as a result of this intercompany transaction. Was it a good financial decision to undertake this transaction? Explain.

(b) Would your answer to (a) be any different if Plum owned only 60% of the common shares of Slum? Explain.

(c) Indicate what amount of tax savings related to depreciation expense would be reflected on the consolidated income statement under the alternatives suggested by the controller and manager, or other options you could suggest. Which method would you recommend? Explain your answer using basic accounting principles.

Case 7-4
LO1, 2

Stephanie Baker is an audit senior with the public accounting firm of Wilson & Lang. It is February Year 9, and the audit of Canadian Development Limited (CDL) for the year ended December 31, Year 8, is proceeding. Stephanie has identified several transactions that occurred in the Year 8 fiscal year that have major accounting implications. The engagement partner has asked Stephanie to draft a memo addressing the accounting implications, financial statement disclosure issues, and any other important matters regarding these transactions.

CDL is an important player in many sectors of the economy. The company has both debt and equity securities that trade on a Canadian stock exchange. Except for a controlling interest (53%) owned by the Robichaud family, CDL's shares are widely held. The company has interests in the natural resources, commercial and residential real estate, construction, transportation, and technology development sectors, among others.

Changes in Capital Structure

During Year 8, CDL's underwriters recommended some changes to the company's capital structure. As a result, the company raised $250 million by issuing one million convertible, redeemable debentures at $250 each. Each debenture is convertible into one common share at any time. CDL's controlling shareholders acquired a sizeable block of the one million debentures issued; a few large institutional investors took up the remainder.

The company proposes to partition the balance sheet in a manner that will include a section titled "Shareholders' Equity and Convertible Debentures." The company views this classification as appropriate because the convertible debt, being much more akin to equity than debt, represents a part of the company's permanent capital. Maurice Richard, the controller of CDL, has emphasized that the interest rate on the debentures is considerably lower than on normal convertible issues and that it is expected that the majority of investors will exercise their conversion privilege. The company has the option of repaying the debt at maturity in 20 years' time, through the issuance of common shares. The option will be lost if the company is unable to meet certain solvency tests at the maturity date. The company's intention was to raise additional permanent capital, and convertible debt was chosen because of the attractive tax savings. The debentures are redeemable at $250 from January 1, Year 15, to January 1, Year 18.

At the same time as the company issued the convertible debentures, two million common shares were converted into two million preferred, redeemable shares. The carrying amount of the two million common shares was $20 million. The preferred shares do not bear dividends and are mandatorily redeemable in five years at $20 per share. They have been recorded at their redemption value of $40 million, and the difference between this redemption value and the carrying amount of the common shares ($20 million) has been charged against retained earnings.

Disposal of Residential Real Estate Segment

Intercity Real Estate Corporation (IRE) is a wholly owned subsidiary of CDL and has two operating divisions: a money-losing residential real estate division and a highly profitable commercial real estate division. The two divisions had been combined into one legal entity for tax purposes as the losses arising from the residential real estate division have more than offset the profits from the commercial real estate division.

During Year 8, CDL decided to dispose of its shares of IRE. However, CDL wished to retain the commercial real estate division and decided to transfer the division's assets to another corporation prior to selling the shares of IRE. As part of the sale agreement, just before the closing, the commercial real estate assets were transferred out of IRC to CDL, which then transferred the assets to a newly created subsidiary, Real Property Inc. (RPI). In order to maximize the asset base of RPI, the commercial real estate assets were transferred at fair values, which greatly increased their tax base and created considerable income for tax purposes.

Maurice has explained to Stephanie that since the transfer would create income for tax purposes, it was necessary for both CDL and the purchaser to agree on the fair value of the commercial real estate assets, even though they were not part of the IRC sale. IRC's purchaser agreed to the values used because the loss carry-forwards, which would otherwise have expired, offset the income for tax purposes.

CDL is planning to take RPI public sometime this year. The commercial real estate assets of RPI have been recorded at the values established in the sale of IRC, because management believes that this amount represents the cost of acquiring the business from IRC. Maurice has stressed that the transfer between IRC and RPI is very different from the majority of transactions between companies under common control. He argues that the transfer of the commercial real estate assets to RPI represents a bona fide business combination, since there is a change of substance and not just of form. CDL maintains a policy of granting subsidiaries a high degree of autonomy and, in substance, they do not function "under common control." Maurice indicated that the real estate assets are worth more to CDL as a result of this transaction because of the increase in the tax values of the assets. Finally, an unrelated party was involved in the transaction and in the determination of the fair value of the assets.

Stephanie noted that after the transfer the real estate business changed. RPI has undertaken a major refurbishing program and has just bought a large chain of shopping centres that has doubled the company's asset base.

Required:

Assume the role of Stephanie Baker, and prepare the memo for the partner.

(CICA adapted)

Case 7-5
LO1, 8

Bakersfield Ball Boys Limited (BBB) operates a Canadian professional baseball club, the Bakersfield Ball Boys, that won the Canadian Baseball League title in October Year 10. BBB is 30% owned by Mr. Bill Griffin, Bakersfield's wealthiest citizen; 19% by Excavating Inc., a real estate development company; and 51% by Tall Bottle Ltd. (Tall Bottle), a national brewery and a public company.

Your employer, Mayer & Partners, has audited BBB's financial statements for the past several years. It is now May 3, Year 11, and you, the CA, are responsible for the audit of BBB for the year ending June 30, Year 11. The club's year-end was chosen to correspond with the year-end of Tall Bottle, even though the baseball season runs from April to October.

In addition to marking BBB's first-ever Canadian championship, the year ending June 30, Year 11, will be noteworthy from an operational standpoint. You and your staff have become aware of the following:

1. BBB moved into Big Top, a newly built stadium with a retractable roof, on August 1, Year 10. Seating capacity is 70,000. The new stadium is a great improvement over the 30,000-seat NoWay Park stadium used for the preceding seven years. On July 20, Year 10, BBB signed a 10-year lease with the new stadium's owners. However, BBB's lease on the old premises was not due to expire until January 1, Year 14. BBB therefore paid $3.6 million to terminate its lease.

2. Commencing with the Year 10 baseball season (April Year 10 to October Year 10), the league started a new revenue equalization program. In October, each baseball club in the league is required to remit to the league 50% of the revenues from the ticket sales for the season. The league then distributes these revenues, after deducting league costs, in equal amounts to each club. For the Year 10 baseball season, BBB contributed $11.6 million to the league and received $9.2 million, its share of net league revenues. The new equalization program was not accounted for in the June 30, Year 10, financial statements.

3. Immediately before the start of the Year 11 baseball season in April, three of the club's top players were signed to long-term contracts. As a result of these commitments, the club decided to purchase annuities on behalf of these players that would fund the amount required to cover each salary. The annuities for each player were purchased on April 2, Year 11. Amounts of the contracts and annuities are as follows:

Player	Term	Salary	Annuity purchased
Frank Ferter	3 years	$1,500,000 per year	$4,166,000
Hugh G. Blast	5 years	$ 900,000 per year	$3,950,000
Bill Board	4 years	$1,200,000 per year	$4,370,000

The contracts of Ferter and Blast specify that if they suffer a career-ending injury, their contracts will become null and void. Board's contract is guaranteed for the full term.

On April 15, Year 11, Board was injured, forcing him to retire from playing baseball. As required by his contract, he has since been moved to the front office and is performing public relations and administrative services for both BBB and Tall Bottle. Tall Bottle pays BBB $5,000 for each of Board's appearances at a Tall Bottle function. Board has made two appearances at Tall Bottle since his injury.

Ferter has a bonus clause in his contract under which he will be paid $50,000 if he is selected to play for the All Star Team. Although he is favoured to capture this honour, the selections will not be announced until after the financial statements have been issued.

Because of Ferter's exceptional ability and the fact that he is considered a "player who will increase the popularity of the sport in this city for many years to come," management proposes to amortize the cost of his contract over a 10-year period.

4. On April 2, Year 11, the club renewed its contract with Sportsplus, a local television station, for three years. Sportsplus will pay BBB $30,000 per game for the right to televise 25 regular season games and $75,000 for each play-off game. In addition, BBB received a $250,000 bonus for re-signing, and $315,000 for its high ratings over the previous contract term. Tall Bottle enjoys an exclusive advertising contract with Sportsplus as BBB's official sponsor. The contract provides Tall Bottle with three one-minute ads for each game televised by Sportsplus. The advertising was granted to Tall Bottle by Sportsplus free of charge in exchange for BBB's local television rights.

5. BBB's contract with its management includes a bonus clause, to take effect in the year ended June 30, Year 11. Bill Griffin and Excavating Inc. had opposed the scheme, as the bonus is based on annual pre-tax income. However, they agreed to it after much pressure from management and Tall Bottle.

6. On October 3, Year 10, the day before the last playoff game, a windstorm caused the roof at Big Top to collapse, resulting in structural damage of $4,500,000 to the stadium. This unforeseen event forced BBB's last playoff game to be played at NoWay Park. Hence, the club announced that some of the 70,000 seats sold for Big Top could be used at NoWay Park and that the $35 cost of the remaining tickets could be either refunded or applied toward the cost of tickets for any of BBB's Year 11 games. Also, the 40,000 fans who could not attend the game at NoWay were given $12 gift certificates that could be used toward purchasing tickets for any future BBB game.

As a result of the roof collapse at Big Top, BBB incurred the following costs for its final playoff game at NoWay:

Groundskeepers	$ 9,000
Cleaning crew	15,250
Food vendors	19,200
Stadium rental	132,500

A separate cleaning crew had to be hired for the NoWay Park game, as the club's regular cleaning crew was required to assist in the cleanup at Big Top. BBB's lease costs of $50,000 were not waived during the reconstruction of Big Top.

Had the playoff game been played at Big Top, the following costs would have been incurred:

Groundskeepers	$16,500
Cleaning crew	25,750
Food vendors	32,900

Actual food sales at NoWay were $191,750, with food costs averaging 50% of sales. BBB was required to pay the stadium owners a 10% share of sales, whereas, at Big Top, BBB would have been required to pay a 15% share of sales.

BBB's management has asked your firm to prepare a statement of loss to support its claim for damages in accordance with its business-interruption insurance policy. The insurance policy covers the loss of income as well as the additional expenses that result from a disaster.

The partner in charge of the engagement has asked you, the CA, to prepare the information requested by the client. In addition, the partner would like you to present a memo with your analysis of the accounting issues that you and your staff have become aware of, as well as your recommendations.

Required:

Prepare the information requested by the client and the memo to the partner.

(CICA adapted)

Case 7-6
LO1, 8

Enviro Facilities Inc. (EFI) is a large, diversified Canadian-controlled private company with several Canadian and U.S. subsidiaries, operating mainly in the waste management and disposal industry. EFI was incorporated more than 50 years ago, and has grown to become one of the top four waste management firms in Canada. The Glass family started the business, but currently no family members are actively involved in the management. The shares are owned by family members, family trusts, and a limited number of friends. In Year 4, the Glass family decided to sell the company to a third party within the next two or three years, to realize the value of their shareholdings. EFI has an August 31 year-end. The company has elected to report using International Financial Reporting Standards ("IFRSs").

Up until the Year 4 fiscal year-end, a national firm of chartered accountants had audited EFI. In early Year 5, the company put the audit up for tender and replaced the incumbent firm with Bevan & Bevan (BB), Chartered Accountants, a regional firm.

It is now October 18, Year 6. Three days ago, BB resigned from the engagement because of a conflict of interest, although the audit was reportedly 60% complete. Chu and Partners (Chu), Chartered Accountants, was the runner-up firm in the Year 5 audit tender. EFI offered the engagement to Chu. After speaking with the BB partner in charge of the audit, Chu accepted the audit engagement on condition that BB provides all the audit documentation prepared to date. Chu was formally appointed auditors, and an engagement letter has been signed. Materiality has been set by Chu at $6.5 million, based on income and balance sheet trends.

You, the CA, work for Chu. BB's audit files have now arrived, and you and your staff have prepared the following notes:

1. A team of provincial sales tax auditors has been auditing EFI for nearly six months, but the audit is still not complete. The auditors are disputing the exemption claimed by EFI from the 8% tax on purchases of certain waste processing supplies and equipment. About 20% of total purchases of $451 million fell into this category during the four-year audit period, according to EFI.

2. On June 23, Year 6, EFI received a wire transfer of 10 million Hong Kong dollars to its general Canadian dollar bank account, in payment of an outstanding customer invoice. EFI's bank converted the funds to $7.5 million Canadian, incorrectly assuming that the transfer was for Singapore dollars. On that day, 7.290 Hong Kong dollars would buy a Canadian dollar. EFI has not informed the bank of the error and has taken the difference into income.

3. During Year 6, EFI lost a decision in the Federal Court of Appeal in a lawsuit brought by Waste Systems Integrated Limited for patent infringement. In an unusual award, the court ordered EFI to pay $18 million for shares of Waste Systems Integrated Limited, a private company, which had been in some financial difficulty. EFI has decided not to appeal the decision to the Supreme Court, and the shares were purchased before year-end.

4. EFI issues debt for long-term financing purposes through three major investment dealers. In July Year 6, Moody's, the credit rating agency, put EFI's credit rating on alert for downgrade due to the potential negative effects of progressive toughening of environmental legislation applying to waste disposal sites.

5. EFI bids on various municipal waste pick-up and disposal contracts. EFI buys waste-disposal sites to dump the waste collected and defers and amortizes the cost of the sites over the expected useful lives, stated in tonnes of capacity, years of remaining usage, or cubic metres of waste capacity. Amortization of the cost of these sites represents 41% of EFI's operating expenses. Of EFI's assets, 64% are waste disposal sites. Provisions for cleanup and site sealing costs are accrued on the same basis as the amortization of the sites.

6. EFI defers and amortizes over five years the costs of locating new waste disposal sites and negotiating agreements with municipalities.

7. During Year 6, EFI was awarded a contract to collect and dispose of all the waste for the Regional Municipality of Onkon-Lakerton for five years, commencing in Year 7. The contract requires the municipality to pay EFI $9.50 per metric tonne of waste collected. Because of aggressive recycling, composting, and waste reduction programs being carried out by the municipality, EFI negotiated a clause in the agreement that states that the company will be paid a minimum of $3.2 million per annum, regardless of the collection volume. EFI has recorded $16 million ($3.2 million × 5 years) as revenue in Year 6.

8. In July Year 6, two U.S. subsidiaries of the company were notified that they are potentially responsible for violations of U.S. law. The legal proceedings have commenced, based on allegations that prior to being acquired by EFI, these subsidiaries improperly disposed of hazardous waste. The sale-purchase agreement under which the subsidiaries were acquired contains price-adjustment clauses to protect EFI against pre-purchase liabilities.

9. In October Year 6, EFI sold trucks and other garbage collection equipment to a U.S. subsidiary for $20 million, and reported a gain of $9 million. The terms of the sale required a cash payment of $12 million on delivery, with the balance due in annual installments of $4 million, plus interest over a 2-year period.

10. Every year, EFI updates the estimates of the remaining useful lives of waste disposal sites, using the services of a consulting engineering firm. In the past, EFI used Folk & Co., Environmental Engineers, for these reviews. Folk & Co. did no other work for EFI. Starting in Year 6, EFI used Cajanza Consulting Engineers for the reviews. Based on the new consultants' report, the useful lives of all waste-disposal sites have been increased between 4% and 26%, and the sealing/cleanup provision reduced by $13.6 million.

11. In light of the planned sale of EFI, the board of directors has decided to stop buying waste-disposal sites and to sell two sites where the cleanup provisions exceed the sites' carrying amounts. EFI plans to sell the two sites to Enviro (Bermuda) Inc. for a dollar. The controlling shareholders of Enviro (Bermuda) Inc. are the same as the controlling shareholders of EFI. EFI plans to dump waste in these sites. Chu's audit personnel heard a rumour that Enviro (Bermuda) Inc. does not plan to comply with environmental legislation.

12. During the year, EFI implemented a new cost accounting system for the production of composting material. Organic material is extracted from residential garbage collected, and then processed, composted, bagged, and sold for use by gardeners. In the past, no cost has been assigned to the raw material inputs. The new system allocates a portion of total collection costs to these raw material inputs at standard cost.

Required:

The partner has requested a memo that deals with the significant accounting issues.

(CICA adapted)

PROBLEMS

Problem 7-1
LO3

X Company owns 80% of Y Company and uses the equity method to account for its investment. On January 1, Year 2, the investment in Y Company account had a balance of $86,900, and Y Company's common shares and retained earnings totalled $100,000. The unamortized acquisition differential had an estimated remaining life of six years at this time. The following intercompany asset transfers took place in Years 2 and 3: January 1, Year 2, sale of asset to X at a profit of $45,000; and April 30, Year 3, sale of asset to Y at a profit of $60,000. Both assets purchased are being depreciated over five years. In Year 2, Y reported a net income of $125,000 and dividends paid of $70,000, while in Year 3 its net income and dividends were $104,000 and $70,000, respectively.

Required:

Calculate the December 31, Year 3, balance in the account "Investment in Y." (Assume a 40% tax rate.)

Problem 7-2
LO1

Peggy Company owns 75% of Sally Inc. and uses the cost method to account for its investment. The following data were taken from the Year 4 income statements of the two companies:

	Peggy	Sally
Revenues	$580,000	$270,000
Miscellaneous expenses	110,000	85,000
Depreciation expense	162,000	97,000
Income tax expense	123,000	35,000
Total expenses	395,000	217,000
Profit	$185,000	$ 53,000

In Year 2, Sally sold equipment to Peggy at a gain of $15,000. Peggy has been depreciating this equipment over a five-year period. Sally did not pay any dividends in Year 4. Use income tax allocation at a rate of 40%.

Required:

(a) Calculate consolidated profit attributable to Peggy's shareholders for Year 4.
(b) Prepare a consolidated income statement for Year 4.
(c) Calculate the deferred income tax asset that would appear on the Year 4 consolidated statement of financial position.

Problem 7-3
LO1

The comparative consolidated income statements of a parent and its 75%-owned subsidiary were prepared incorrectly as at December 31 and are shown in the following table. The following items were overlooked when the statements were prepared:

- The Year 5 gain on sale of assets resulted from the subsidiary selling equipment to the parent on September 30. The parent immediately leased the equipment back to the subsidiary at an annual rental of $12,000. This was the only intercompany rent transaction that occurred each year. The equipment had a remaining life of five years on the date of the intercompany sale.

- The Year 6 gain on sale of assets resulted from the January 1 sale of a building, with a remaining life of seven years, by the subsidiary to the parent.
- Both gains were taxed at a rate of 40%.

CONSOLIDATED INCOME STATEMENTS

	Year 5	Year 6
Miscellaneous revenues	$750,000	$825,000
Gain on sale of assets	8,000	42,000
Rental revenue	3,000	12,000
	761,000	879,000
Miscellaneous expenses	399,800	492,340
Rental expense	52,700	64,300
Depreciation expense	75,000	80,700
Income tax expense	81,000	94,500
Non-controlling interest	32,500	5,160
	641,000	737,000
Net income	$120,000	$142,000

Required:

Prepare correct consolidated income statements for Years 5 and 6.

Problem 7-4
LO1, 3, 4

On December 31, Year 2, HABS Inc. sold equipment to NORD at its fair value of $2,000,000 and recorded a gain of $500,000. This was HABS's only income (other than any investment income from NORD) during the year. NORD reported income (other than any investment income from HABS) of $200,000 for Year 2. Both companies paid dividends of $100,000 during Year 2.

Required:

(a) Calculate NORD's income before taxes for Year 2 assuming that

  (i) HABS and NORD are not related;
  (ii) NORD owns 75% of HABS and reports its investment in HABS on a consolidated basis;
  (iii) NORD owns 75% of HABS and reports its investment in HABS using the equity method; and
  (iv) NORD owns 75% of HABS and reports its investment in HABS using the cost method.

(b) Calculate HABS's income before taxes for Year 2 assuming that

  (i) NORD and HABS are not related;
  (ii) HABS owns 75% of NORD and reports its investment in NORD on a consolidated basis;
  (iii) HABS owns 75% of NORD and reports its investment in NORD using the equity method; and
  (iv) HABS owns 75% of NORD and reports its investment in NORD using the cost method.

(c) Compare and contrast the income reported under the reporting methods (ii), (iii), and (iv) above. Which method best reflects the economic reality of the business transaction?

Problem 7-5
LO4, 5, 7

The balance sheets of Forest Company and Garden Company are presented below as at December 31, Year 8.

BALANCE SHEETS—at December 31, Year 8

	Forest	Garden
Cash	$ 13,000	$ 48,800
Receivables	25,000	86,674
Inventories	80,000	62,000
Investment in shares of Garden	207,900	—
Plant and equipment	740,000	460,000
Accumulated depreciation	(625,900)	(348,400)
Patents	—	4,500
Investment in bonds of Forest	—	58,426
	$440,000	$372,000
Current liabilities	$ 59,154	$ 53,000
Dividends payable	6,000	30,000
Bonds payable 6%	94,846	—
Common shares	200,000	150,000
Retained earnings	80,000	139,000
	$440,000	$372,000

Additional Information

- Forest acquired 90% of Garden for $207,900 on July 1, Year 1, and accounts for its investment under the cost method. At that time, the shareholders' equity of Garden amounted to $175,000, the accumulated amortization was $95,000, and the assets of Garden were undervalued by the following amounts:

Inventory	$12,000	
Buildings	$10,000	remaining life, 10 years
Patents	$16,000	remaining life, 8 years

- During Year 8, Forest reported net income of $41,000 and declared dividends of $25,000, whereas Garden reported net income of $63,000 and declared dividends of $50,000.
- During Years 2 to 7, goodwill impairment losses totalled $1,950. An impairment test conducted in Year 8 indicated a further loss of $7,150.
- Forest sells goods to Garden on a regular basis at a gross profit of 30%. During Year 8, these sales totalled $150,000. On January 1, Year 8, the inventory of Garden contained goods purchased from Forest amounting to $18,000, while the December 31, Year 8, inventory contained goods purchased from Forest amounting to $22,000.
- On August 1, Year 6, Garden sold land to Forest at a profit of $18,000. During Year 8, Forest sold one-quarter of the land to an unrelated company.
- Forest's bonds have a par value of $100,000, pay interest annually on December 31 at a stated rate of 6%, and mature on December 31, Year 11. Forest incurs an effective interest cost of 8% on these bonds. They had a carrying amount of $93,376 on January 1, Year 8. On that date, Garden acquired $60,000 of these bonds on the open market at a cost of $57,968. Garden will earn an effective rate of return of 7% on them. Both companies use the effective-interest method to account for their bonds.

The Year 8 income statements of the two companies show the following with respect to bond interest.

	Forest	Garden
Interest expense	$7,470	
Interest revenue		$4,058

- Garden owes Forest $22,000 on open account on December 31, Year 8.
- Assume a 40% corporate tax rate and allocate bond gains (losses) between the two companies.

Required:

(a) Prepare the following statements:

   (i) Consolidated balance sheet

   (ii) Consolidated retained earnings statement

(b) Prepare the Year 8 journal entries that would be made on the books of Forest if the equity method was used to account for the investment.

(c) Explain how a loss on the elimination of intercompany bondholdings is viewed as a temporary difference and gives rise to a deferred income tax asset.

(d) If Forest had used parent company extension theory rather than entity theory, how would this affect the debt-to-equity ratio at the end of Year 9?

Problem 7-6
LO1, 3, 8

Income statements of M Cop. and K Co. for the year ended December 31, Year 6, are presented below:

	M Co.	K Co.
Sales	$600,000	$350,000
Rent revenue	—	50,000
Interest revenue	6,700	—
Income from subsidiary	30,320	—
Gain on land sale	—	8,000
	637,020	408,000
Cost of goods sold	334,000	225,000
Distribution expense	80,000	70,000
Administrative expense	147,000	74,000
Interest expense	1,700	6,000
Income tax expense	20,700	7,500
	583,400	382,500
Profit	$ 53,620	$ 25,500

Additional Information

- M Co. uses the equity method to account for its investment in K Co.
- M Co. acquired its 80% interest in K Co. on January 1, Year 1. On that date, the acquisition differential of $25,000 was allocated entirely to buildings; it is being amortized over a 20-year period.
- Amortization expense is grouped with distribution expenses, and impairment losses, if any, are grouped with other expenses.
- M Co. made an advance of $100,000 to K Co. on July 1, Year 6. This loan is due on demand and requires the payment of interest at 12% per year.
- M Co. rents marine equipment from K Co. During Year 6, $50,000 rent was paid and was charged to administrative expense.

- In Year 4, M Co. sold land to K Co. and recorded a profit of $10,000 on the sale. K Co. held the land until October, Year 6, when it was sold to an unrelated company.
- During Year 6, K Co. made sales to M Co. totalling $90,000. The December 31, Year 6, inventories of M Co. contain an unrealized profit of $5,000. The January 1, Year 6, inventories of M Co. contained an unrealized profit of $12,000.
- On January 1, Year 4, M Co. sold machinery to K Co. and recorded a profit of $13,000. The remaining useful life on that date was five years. Assume straight-line depreciation.
- K Co. paid dividends of $20,000 during Year 6.
- Tax allocation is to be used, assuming a 40% average corporate tax rate for this purpose.

Required:

(a) Prepare a consolidated income statement for Year 6.
(b) Now assume that M Co. is a private company, uses ASPE, and chooses to use the cost method to report its investment in K Co. Prepare M Co.'s income statement for Year 6 under the cost method.

Problem 7-7
LO1, 5

Pure Company purchased 70% of the ordinary shares of Gold Company on January 1, Year 6, for $483,000 when the latter company's accumulated depreciation, ordinary shares and retained earnings were $75,000, $500,000 and $40,000, respectively. Non-controlling interest was valued at $195,000 by an independent business valuator at the date of acquisition. On this date, an appraisal of the assets of Gold disclosed the following differences:

	Carrying amount	Fair value
Land	$150,000	$200,000
Plant and equipment	700,000	770,000
Inventory	120,000	108,000

The plant and equipment had an estimated life of 20 years on this date.
The statements of financial position of Pure and Gold, prepared on December 31, Year 11, follow:

	Pure	Gold
Land	$ 100,000	$ 150,000
Plant and equipment	625,000	940,000
Less accumulated depreciation	(183,000)	(220,000)
Patent (net of amortization)	31,500	—
Investment in Gold Co. shares (equity method)	546,670	—
Investment in Gold Co. bonds	227,000	—
Inventory	225,000	180,000
Accounts receivable	212,150	170,000
Cash	41,670	57,500
	$1,825,990	$1,277,500
Ordinary shares	$ 750,000	$ 500,000
Retained earnings	1,019,960	200,000
Bonds payable (due Year 20)	—	477,500
Accounts payable	56,030	100,000
	$1,825,990	$1,277,500

Additional Information

- Goodwill impairment tests have resulted in impairment losses totalling $18,000.
- On January 1, Year 1, Gold issued $500,000 of 8½% bonds at 90, maturing in 20 years (on December 31, Year 20).
- On January 1, Year 11, Pure acquired $200,000 of Gold's bonds on the open market at a cost of $230,000.
- On July 1, Year 8, Gold sold a patent to Pure for $63,000. The patent had a carrying amount on Gold's books of $42,000 on this date and an estimated remaining life of seven years.
- Pure uses tax allocation (40% rate) and allocates bond gains between affiliates when it consolidates Gold.
- Pure uses the equity method to account for its investment.

Required:

Prepare a consolidated statement of financial position as at December 31, Year 11.

Problem 7-8
LO1, 3, 5, 6, 7

On January 2, Year 1, Poplar Ltd. purchased 80% of the outstanding shares of Spruce Ltd. for $2,000,000. At that date, Spruce had common shares of $500,000 and retained earnings of $1,250,000 and accumulate depreciation of $600,000. Poplar acquired the Spruce shares to obtain control of mineral rights owned by Spruce. At the date of acquisition, these mineral rights were valued at $750,000, were not recognized on Spruce's separate-entity balance sheet, and had an indefinite useful life. Except for the mineral rights, the carrying amount of the recorded assets and liabilities of Spruce were equal to their fair values. On December 31, Year 4, the trial balances of the two companies were as follows:

	Poplar	Spruce
Cash	$ 1,000,000	$ 500,000
Accounts receivable	2,000,000	356,000
Inventory	3,000,000	2,250,000
Plant and equipment	14,000,000	2,900,000
Investment in Spruce (cost)	2,000,000	—
Investment in Poplar bonds	—	244,000
Cost of goods sold	2,400,000	850,000
Other expenses	962,000	300,000
Interest expense	38,000	—
Income tax expense	600,000	350,000
Dividends	600,000	250,000
	$26,600,000	$8,000,000
Accounts payable	$ 2,492,000	$2,478,500
Accumulated depreciation: plant and equipment	4,000,000	1,000,000
Bonds payable	500,000	—
Premium on bonds payable	8,000	—
Common shares	4,500,000	500,000
Retained earnings, January 1	10,000,000	2,000,000
Sales	4,900,000	2,000,000
Dividend revenue	200,000	—
Interest revenue	—	21,500
	$26,600,000	$8,000,000

Additional Information

- The Year 4 net incomes of the two companies are as follows:

Poplar Ltd.	$1,100,000
Spruce Ltd.	521,500

- The mineral rights owned by Spruce have increased in value since the date of acquisition and were worth $925,000 at December 31, Year 4.
- On January 2, Year 2, Spruce sold equipment to Poplar for $500,000. The equipment had a carrying amount of $400,000 at the time of the sale. The remaining useful life of the equipment was five years.
- The Year 4 opening inventories of Poplar contained $500,000 of merchandise purchased from Spruce during Year 3. Spruce had recorded a gross profit of $200,000 on this merchandise.
- During Year 4, Spruce's sales to Poplar totalled $1,000,000. These sales were made at a gross profit rate of 40%.
- Poplar's ending inventory contains $300,000 of merchandise purchased from Spruce.
- Other expenses include depreciation expense and copyright amortization expense.
- On January 2, Year 2, Poplar issued 8%, 7-year bonds with a face value of $500,000 for $514,000. Interest is paid annually on December 31. On January 2, Year 4, Spruce purchased one-half of this issue on the open market at a cost of $242,500. Intercompany bond gains (losses) are to be allocated between the two affiliates.
- Tax allocation will be at a rate of 40%.

Required:

(a) Prepare the following consolidated financial statements:
- (i) Income statement
- (ii) Retained earnings statement
- (iii) Balance sheet

(b) Calculate the December 31, Year 4, balance in the account "Investment in Spruce" if Poplar had used the equity method to account for its investment.

(c) Explain how the recognition of gains on the elimination of intercompany bondholdings is consistent with the principle of recording gains only when they are realized.

Problem 7-9
LO1, 3, 8
On January 1, Year 1, Porter Inc. purchased 85% of the voting shares of Sloan Ltd. for $3,026,000 in cash. On this date, Sloan had common shares outstanding in the amount of $2,200,000 and retained earnings of $1,100,000. The identifiable assets and liabilities of Sloan had fair values that were equal to their carrying amount, except for the following:

- Plant and equipment (net) had a fair value $200,000 greater than its carrying amount. The remaining useful life on January 1, Year 1, was 20 years with no anticipated salvage value.
- Accounts receivable had a fair value $75,000 less than carrying amount.
- Long-term liabilities had a fair value $52,680 less than carrying amount. These liabilities were issued at par and mature on December 31, Year 10.

Additional Information

- Between January 1, Year 1, and December 31, Year 3, Sloan earned $345,000 and paid dividends of $115,000.
- Goodwill impairment tests yielded losses as follows: Year 1, $30,300; Year 2, $6,075; Year 4, $12,125.
- On January 1, Year 2, Sloan sold a patent to Porter for $160,000. On this date, the patent had a carrying amount on the books of Sloan of $185,000 and a remaining useful life of five years.
- On September 1, Year 3, Porter sold land to Sloan for $93,000. The land had a carrying amount on the books of Porter of $72,000. Sloan still owned this land on December 31, Year 4.
- For the year ending December 31, Year 4, the income statements revealed the following:

	Porter	Sloan
Total revenues	$2,576,000	$973,000
Cost of goods sold	1,373,000	467,000
Amortization expense	483,000	176,000
Interest expense	115,000	44,700
Other expenses (including income tax)	237,000	108,300
Total expenses	2,208,000	796,000
Net income	$ 368,000	$177,000

Porter records its investment in Sloan using the cost method and includes dividend income from Sloan in its total revenues.

- Porter and Sloan paid dividends of $125,000 and $98,000, respectively, in Year 4.
- Sloan issued no common shares subsequent to January 1, Year 1. Selected balance sheet accounts for the two companies as at December 31, Year 4, were as follows:

	Porter	Sloan
Accounts receivable (net)	$ 987,000	$ 133,000
Inventories	1,436,000	787,000
Plant and equipment (net)	3,467,000	1,234,000
Patent (net)	263,000	–0–
Land	872,000	342,000
Long-term liabilities	1,876,000	750,000
Retained earnings	4,833,000	1,409,000

- During Year 4, Porter's merchandise sales to Sloan were $150,000. The unrealized profits in Sloan's inventory on January 1 and December 31, Year 4, were $14,000 and $10,000, respectively. At December 31, Year 4, Sloan still owed Porter $5,000 for merchandise purchases.
- During Year 4, Sloan's merchandise sales to Porter were $55,000. The unrealized profits in Porter's inventory on January 1 and December 31, Year 4, were $1,500 and $2,500, respectively. At December 31, Year 4, Porter still owed Sloan $2,000 for merchandise purchases.
- Use income tax allocation at a rate of 40% and straight-line amortization of property, plant, and equipment and long-term liabilities.

Required:

(a) Compute the balances that would appear in the consolidated balance sheet of Porter and Sloan as at December 31, Year 4, for the following:

(i) Patent (net)
(ii) Goodwill
(vi) Retained earnings
(iv) Non-controlling interest
(v) Long-term liabilities

(b) Now assume that Porter is a private company, uses ASPE, and chooses to use the equity method to report its investment in K Co. Calculate the total revenues, including investment income, that would be presented in the income statement drawn up by Porter for the year ended December 31, Year 4.

(c) Assume that Sloan pays interest annually at the rate of 6% on its long-term liabilities. When Porter acquired Sloan on January 1, Year 1, the fair value of Sloan's long-term liabilities would have produced an effective yield of 7%. Calculate long-term liabilities on the consolidated financial statements, assuming that Porter and Sloan use the effective-interest method to account for their long-term liabilities.

(SMA adapted)

Problem 7-10
L05, 7

Alpha Corporation owns 90% of the ordinary shares of Beta Corporation and uses the equity method to account for its investment.

On January 1, Year 4, Alpha purchased $160,000 of Beta's 10% bonds for $150,064. Beta's bond liability on this date consisted of $800,000 par 10% bonds due January 1, Year 8, and unamortized discount of $73,065. Interest payment dates are June 30 and December 31. The effective rate of interest is 6% every six months on Alpha's bond investment and 6.5% every six months for Beta's bond liability.

Both companies have a December 31 year-end and use the effective-interest method to account for bonds. Alpha uses income tax allocation at a 40% tax rate when it prepares its consolidated financial statements.

Beta reported a profit of $114,000 in Year 4 and declared a dividend of $30,000 on December 31.

Required:

(a) Calculate the amount of the gain or the loss that will appear as a separate item on the Year 4 consolidated income statement as a result of the bond transaction that occurred during the year.

(b) Prepare the equity method journal entries that Alpha would make on December 31, Year 4.

(c) Calculate the amount of the bond liability that will appear on the December 31, Year 4, consolidated statement of financial position.

Problem 7-11
L05, 7

Parent Co. owns 75% of Sub Co. and uses the cost method to account for its investment. The following are summarized income statements for the year ended December 31, Year 7. (Sub Co. did not declare or pay dividends in Year 7.)

INCOME STATEMENTS—for Year 7

	Parent	Sub
Interest revenue	$ 8,750	$ —
Other misc. revenues	900,000	500,000
	908,750	500,000
Interest expense	—	44,000
Other misc. expenses	600,000	350,000
Income tax expense	124,000	42,000
	724,000	436,000
Net income	$184,750	$ 64,000

Additional Information

On July 1, Year 7, Parent purchased 40% of the outstanding bonds of Sub for $152,500. On that date, Sub had $400,000 of 10% bonds payable outstanding, which mature in five years. The bond discount on the books of Sub on July 1, Year 7, amounted to $20,000. Interest is payable January 1 and July 1. Any gains (losses) are to be allocated to each company. Both companies use the straight-line method to account for bonds.

Required:

Prepare a consolidated income statement for Year 7 using a 40% tax rate.

Problem 7-12
L05, 7

Palmer Corporation owns 70% of the ordinary shares of Scott Corporation and uses the equity method to account for its investment.

Scott purchased $80,000 par of Palmer's 10% bonds on October 1, Year 5, for $76,000. Palmer's bond liability on October 1, Year 5, consisted of $400,000 par of 10% bonds due on October 1, Year 9, with unamortized discount of $8,000. Interest payment dates are April 1 and October 1 of each year, and straight-line amortization is used. Intercompany bond gains (losses) are to be allocated to each affiliate.

Both companies have a December 31 year-end. Scott's financial statements for Year 5 indicate that it earned profit of $70,000 and that on December 31, Year 5, it declared a dividend of $15,000.

Required:

(a) Prepare the journal entries under the equity method that Palmer would make in Year 5. (Assume a 40% tax rate.)
(b) Compute the amount of the bond liability that will appear on the December 31, Year 5, consolidated statement of financial position.

Problem 7-13
L01, 4

On December 31, Year 1, RAV Company purchased 60% of the outstanding common shares of ENS Company for $780,000. On that date, ENS had common shares of $500,000 and retained earnings of $120,000. In negotiating the purchase price, it was agreed that recorded assets and liabilities were fairly valued except for equipment, which had a $30,000 excess of carrying amount over fair value, and land, which had a $120,000 excess of fair value over carrying amount. The equipment had a remaining useful life of six years at the acquisition date and no salvage value. ENS did not record the fair value deficiency on the equipment because ENS felt that it would recover the carrying amount of this equipment through future cash flows. In addition, ENS registered and owns a number of Internet domain names, which are estimated to be worth $100,000. The right to the names expires in 12 years but the registration can be renewed for 20 years every 20 years, for a nominal fee.

The adjusted trial balances for RAV and ENS for the year ended December 31, Year 5, were as follows:

	RAV	ENS
Cash	$ 150,000	$ 75,000
Accounts receivable	275,000	226,000
Inventory	594,000	257,000
Land	600,000	170,000
Building—net	710,000	585,000
Equipment—net	690,000	349,000
Investment in ENS	516,000	
Cost of goods purchased	2,340,000	2,137,000
Change in inventory	60,000	(30,000)
Amortization expense	240,000	120,000
Income taxes and other expenses	960,000	432,000
Dividends paid	540,000	304,000
Total debits	$7,675,000	$4,625,000
Accounts payable	$ 465,000	$ 296,000
Long-term debt	900,000	540,000
Common shares	1,200,000	500,000
Retained earnings, beginning	600,000	279,000
Sales	4,220,000	3,010,000
Other revenues	80,000	
Investment income from ENS	210,000	
Total credits	$7,675,000	$4,625,000

Additional Information

- Each year, goodwill is evaluated to determine if there has been a loss. The recoverable impairment amount for ENS's goodwill was valued at $100,000 at the end of Year 4 and $75,000 at the end of Year 5.
- RAV's inventories contained $200,000 of merchandise purchased from ENS at December 31, Year 5, and $250,000 at December 31, Year 4. During Year 5, sales from ENS to RAV were $600,000. Merchandise was priced at the same profit margin as applicable to other customers. RAV owed $150,000 to ENS at December 31, Year 5, and $157,000 at December 31, Year 4.
- On July 1, Year 2, ENS purchased a building from RAV for $750,000. The building had an original cost of $800,000 and a carrying amount of $600,000 on RAV's books on July 1, Year 2. ENS estimated the remaining life of the building was 15 years at the time of the purchase from RAV.
- ENS rented another building from RAV throughout the year for $5,000 per month.
- RAV uses the equity method of accounting for its long-term investments.
- Both companies pay tax at the rate of 40%. Ignore deferred income taxes when allocating and amortizing the acquisition differential.

Required:

(a) Prepare a consolidated income statement for the year ended December 31, Year 5.

(b) Prepare the current assets, property, plant, and equipment and intangible assets sections of the consolidated balance sheet at December 31, Year 5.

(c) Calculate non-controlling interest on the consolidated balance sheet at December 31, Year 4.

(d) If RAV had used the cost method instead of the equity method of accounting for its investment in ENS, would RAV's net income for Year 5 increase, decrease, or remain the same on

    (i) its separate-entity income statement?

    (ii) the consolidated income statement?

Briefly explain.

(CGA-Canada adapted)

Problem 7-14
LO5, 7

Shown below are selected ledger accounts from the trial balance of a parent and its subsidiary as of December 31, Year 9.

	P Co.	S Co.
Investment in bonds of P	$ —	$ 39,000
Investment in shares of S (equity method)	139,899	—
Sales	630,000	340,000
Interest income	—	1,850
Investment income	15,339	—
Gain on sale of land	7,000	—
Common shares	300,000	100,000
Retained earnings	85,000	50,000
Bonds payable 8%	198,000	—
Cost of sales	485,000	300,000
Interest expense	17,000	—
Selling and administrative expense	50,000	20,000
Income tax expense	34,000	8,740
Dividends	10,000	8,000

Additional Information

- P Company purchased its 90% interest in S Company in Year 1, on the date that S Company was incorporated, and has followed the equity method to account for its investment since that date.

- On April 1, Year 5, land that had originally cost $15,000 was sold by S Company to P Company for $21,000. P purchased the land with the intention of developing it, but in Year 9 it decided that the location was not suitable and the land was sold to a chain of drug stores.

- On January 1, Year 2, P Company issued $200,000 face value bonds due in 10 years. The proceeds from the bond issue amounted to $190,000.

- On July 1, Year 9, S Company purchased $40,000 of these bonds on the open market at a cost of $38,750. Intercompany bondholding gains (losses) are allocated between the two affiliates.

- S Company had $75,000 in sales to P Company during Year 9.

- Use income tax allocation at a 40% tax rate.

Required:

(a) Prepare a consolidated income statement for Year 9.

(b) Prepare a consolidated statement of retained earnings for Year 9.

Problem 7-15
LO1, 2, 4

Financial statements of Champlain Ltd. and its 80%-owned subsidiary Samuel Ltd. as at December 31, Year 5, are presented below.

STATEMENTS OF FINANCIAL POSITION—at December 31, Year 5

	Champlain	Samuel
Property, plant, and equipment	$198,000	$104,000
Accumulated depreciation	(86,000)	(30,000)
Investment in Samuel—at cost	129,200	—
Inventories	35,000	46,000
Accounts receivable	60,000	55,000
Cash	18,100	20,600
	$354,300	$195,600
Ordinary shares	$225,000	$50,000
Retained earnings	68,300	70,000
Dividends payable	5,000	5,500
Accounts payable	56,000	70,100
	$354,300	$195,600

STATEMENTS OF INCOME AND RETAINED EARNINGS
for the Year Ended December 31, Year 5

	Champlain	Samuel
Sales	$535,400	$270,000
Dividend and miscellaneous income	9,900	—
	545,300	270,000
Cost of sales	364,000	206,000
Selling expense	78,400	24,100
Administrative expense (including depreciation and goodwill impairment)	46,300	20,700
Income taxes	13,800	6,200
	502,500	257,000
Profit	42,800	13,000
Retained earnings, January 1	45,500	68,000
Dividends paid	(20,000)	(11,000)
Retained earnings, December 31	$ 68,300	$ 70,000

Additional Information

- Champlain acquired 8,000 ordinary shares of Samuel on January 1, Year 1, for $129,200. Samuel's shares were trading for $14 per share on the date of acquisition. The retained earnings and accumulated depreciation of Samuel were $12,000 and $17,000, respectively, on that date, and there have been no subsequent changes in the ordinary shares account. On January 1, Year 1, fair values were equal to carrying amounts except for the following:

	Carrying value	Fair value
Inventory	$50,000	$32,000
Patent	–0–	14,000

- The patent of Samuel had a remaining legal life of eight years on January 1, Year 1, and any goodwill was to be tested annually for impairment. As a result, impairment losses occurred as follows:

Pertaining to	Year 2	Year 4	Year 5
Champlain's purchase	$21,000	$13,800	$19,200
Non-controlling interest's share	4,000	2,600	3,600
	$25,000	$16,400	$22,800

- On January 1, Year 5, the inventories of Champlain contained items purchased from Samuel on which Samuel had made a profit of $1,900. During Year 5, Samuel sold goods to Champlain for $92,000, of which $21,000 remained unpaid at the end of the year. Samuel made a profit of $3,300 on goods remaining in Champlain's inventory at December 31, Year 5.
- On January 1, Year 3, Samuel sold equipment to Champlain at a price that was $21,000 in excess of its carrying amount. The equipment had an estimated remaining life of six years on that date.
- Champlain sold a tract of land to Samuel in Year 2 at a profit of $7,000. This land is still held by Samuel at the end of Year 5.
- Assume a corporate tax rate of 40%.

Required:

(a) Prepare the following consolidated financial statements:

    (i) Income statement
    (ii) Retained earnings statement
    (iii) Statement of financial position

(b) Explain how the historical cost principle supports the elimination of the profit on the sale of the equipment from Samuel to Champlain when preparing Samuel's consolidated financial statements.

(c) If Champlain had used the parent company extension theory rather than the entity theory, how would this affect the return on equity attributable to shareholders of Champlain for Year 5?

(d) Calculate goodwill and non-controlling interest on the consolidated statement of financial position at December 31, Year 5, under the parent company extension theory.

Problem 7-16
LO1, 2

On December 31, Year 1, the Peach Company purchased 80% of the outstanding voting shares of the Orange Company for $964,000 in cash. The balance sheet of Orange on that date and the fair values of its tangible assets and liabilities were as follows:

	Carrying amount	Fair value
Cash and accounts receivable	$ 200,000	$175,000
Inventories	300,000	300,000
Plant and equipment	600,000	800,000
Accumulated depreciation	(100,000)	
	$1,000,000	
Current liabilities	$ 100,000	100,000
Long-term liabilities	200,000	216,850
Common shares	500,000	
Retained earnings	200,000	
	$1,000,000	

The difference between the fair value and the carrying amount of cash and accounts receivable of the subsidiary at December 31, Year 1, was adjusted by Orange in Year 2. At the acquisition date, the plant and equipment had an estimated remaining useful life of 10 years with no residual value. The long-term liabilities mature on December 31, Year 6. Any goodwill arising from the business combination will be tested for impairment. Peach uses the cost method to account for its investment in Orange. Both Peach and Orange use the straight-line method to calculate all depreciation for depreciable assets and amortization of premiums or discounts on long-term liabilities.

The statements of income and changes in retained earnings of the two companies for the year ending December 31, Year 5, were as follows:

	Peach	Orange
Sales of merchandise	$6,000,000	$1,000,000
Other revenues	200,000	20,000
Total revenues	6,200,000	1,020,000
Cost of goods purchased	2,525,000	390,000
Change in inventory	(25,000)	10,000
Depreciation expense	500,000	80,000
Interest expense	400,000	16,000
Other expenses (including income tax)	1,300,000	194,000
Total expenses	4,700,000	690,000
Net income	1,500,000	330,000
Retained earnings, 1/1/Year 5	4,200,000	300,000
Dividends	(200,000)	(50,000)
Retained earnings, 31/12/Year 5	$5,500,000	$ 580,000

Additional Information

- Goodwill impairment losses were recorded as follows: Year 2, $3,600; Year 4, $30,000; Year 5, $11,200.
- On December 31, Year 4, Orange sold a warehouse to Peach for $54,000. It had been purchased on January 1, Year 3, for $100,000 and had an estimated 20-year life on that date with no salvage value.
- During Year 4, Orange sold merchandise that it had purchased for $120,000 to Peach for $250,000. None of this merchandise had been resold by Peach by December 31, Year 4. Both companies account for inventories on the first-in, first-out basis.
- Peach had sales of $200,000 to Orange during Year 4, which gave rise to a gross profit of $125,000. This inventory was resold by Orange during Year 4 for $225,000.
- During Year 5, Orange sold merchandise that had been purchased for $160,000 to Peach for $300,000. Since the sales occurred in December of Year 5, all of this merchandise remained in the December 31, Year 5, inventories of Peach and had not been paid for.
- During September Year 5, Peach had sales of $280,000 to Orange, which increased Peach's gross profit by $160,000. By December 31, Year 5, one-half of this merchandise had been sold to the public by Orange.
- On January 1, Year 5, Peach sold to Orange for $28,000 a machine that had cost $32,000. On January 1, Year 5, it had been depreciated for six years of its estimated eight-year life.
- During Year 5, Peach charged Orange $25,000 for management fees.
- Assume a 40% corporate tax rate.

Required:

(a) Prepare a consolidated income statement for Peach and its subsidiary, Orange, for the year ending December 31, Year 5. Assume that the loss from sale of the warehouse will be eliminated.

(b) Prepare a consolidated statement of retained earnings for Peach and its subsidiary, Orange, for the year ending December 31, Year 5.

(c) Explain the rationale for not always eliminating losses on intercompany sales of depreciable assets when preparing consolidated financial statements.

(d) Assume that Orange pays interest annually at the rate of 8% on its long-term liabilities. When Peach acquired Orange on December 31, Year 1, the fair value of Sloan's long-term liabilities would have produced an effective yield of 6%. Calculate interest expense and non-controlling interest on the consolidated income statement assuming that Peach and Orange use the effective-interest method to account for their long-term liabilities.

(SMA adapted)

Problem 7-17
LO1, 2, 4

On January 1, Year 1, Handy Company (Handy) purchased 70% of the outstanding common shares of Dandy Limited (Dandy) for $7,000. On that date, Dandy's shareholders' equity consisted of common shares of $250 and retained earnings of $4,500. The financial statements for Handy and Dandy for Year 6 were as follows:

BALANCE SHEETS
at December 31, Year 6

	Handy	*Dandy*
Cash	$ 1,340	$ 780
Accounts receivable	2,800	1,050
Inventory	3,400	2,580
Property, plant, and equipment—net	4,340	3,010
Investment in Dandy	7,000	—
Total	$18,880	$7,420
Current liabilities	$ 4,200	$ 540
Long-term liabilities	3,100	1,230
Common shares	1,000	250
Retained earnings	10,580	5,400
Total	$18,880	$7,420

STATEMENTS OF INCOME AND RETAINED EARNINGS
for Year Ended December 31, Year 6

	Handy	*Dandy*
Sales	$21,900	$7,440
Cost of sales	14,800	3,280
Gross profit	7,100	4,160
Other revenue	1,620	—
Selling and administrative expense	(840)	(420)
Other expenses	(5,320)	(2,040)
Income before income taxes	2,560	1,700
Income tax expense	800	680
Net income	1,760	1,020
Retained earnings, beginning of year	10,420	5,180
Dividends paid	(1,600)	(800)
Retained earnings, end of year	$10,580	$5,400

Additional Information

- In negotiating the purchase price at the date of acquisition, it was agreed that the fair values of all of Dandy's assets and liabilities were equal to their carrying amounts, except for the following:

	Carrying amount	Fair value
Inventory	$2,100	$2,200
Equipment	2,500	3,000

- Both companies use FIFO to account for their inventory and the straight-line method for amortizing their property, plant, and equipment. Dandy's equipment had a remaining useful life of 10 years at the acquisition date.
- Goodwill is not amortized on a systematic basis. However, each year, goodwill is evaluated to determine if there has been a permanent impairment. It was determined that goodwill on the consolidated balance sheet should be reported at its recoverable amount of $1,100 on December 31, Year 5, and $1,030 on December 31, Year 6.
- During Year 6, inventory sales from Dandy to Handy were $5,000. Handy's inventories contained merchandise purchased from Dandy for $2,000 at December 31, Year 5, and $2,500 at December 31, Year 6. Dandy earns a gross margin of 40% on its intercompany sales.
- On January 1, Year 2, Handy sold some equipment to Dandy for $1,000 and recorded a gain of $200 before taxes. This equipment had a remaining useful life of eight years at the time of the purchase by Dandy.
- Handy charges $50 per month to Dandy for consulting services and has been doing so throughout Years 5 and 6.
- Handy uses the cost method of accounting for its long-term investment.
- Both companies pay taxes at the rate of 40%.
- Amortization expense is grouped with production expenses, and impairment losses are grouped with other expenses.

Required:

(a) Prepare a consolidated statement of income for the year ended December 31, Year 6. Show supporting calculations.

(b) Calculate consolidated retained earnings at January 1, Year 6, and then prepare a consolidated statement of retained earnings for the year ended December 31, Year 6. Show supporting calculations.

(c) Explain how the historical cost principle supports the adjustments made on consolidation when there has been an intercompany sale of equipment.

(d) Calculate goodwill impairment loss and non-controlling interest on the consolidated income statement for the year ended December 31, Year 6, under the parent company extension theory.

(CGA-Canada adapted)

*Problem 7-18
LO9

SENS Ltd. acquired equipment on January 1, Year 1, for $500,000. The equipment was depreciated on a straight-line basis over an estimated useful life of 10 years.

On January 1, Year 3, SENS sold this equipment to MEL Corp., its parent company, for $420,000. MEL is depreciating this equipment on a straight-line basis over an estimated useful life of 8 years.

MEL and SENS revalue their property, plant, and equipment to fair value each year under IAS 16 and transfer the revaluation surplus to retained earnings over the useful life of the asset or upon sale of the asset. The fair value of this equipment was $460,000 at the end of Year 1, $416,000 at the end of Year 2, and $370,000 at the end of Year 3. When the equipment is remeasured to fair value, both the original cost and accumulated depreciation are grossed up for the increase in value.

Required:

Assume that this is the only equipment owned by the two companies and ignore income tax. Compute the balances that would appear in MEL's separate-entity statements, SENS's separate-entity statements, and MEL's consolidated statements for Years 1, 2, and 3 for each of the following:

(a) Equipment
(b) Accumulated depreciation
(c) Accumulated other comprehensive income—revaluation surplus
(d) Gain on sale of equipment
(e) Depreciation expense

WEB-BASED PROBLEMS

Web Problem 7-1
LO1, 4, 9

Access the 2011 consolidated financial statements for Barrick Gold Corporation by going to investor relations section of the company's website. Answer the questions below. Round percentages to one decimal point and other ratios to two decimal points. For each question, indicate where in the financial statements you found the answer, and/or provide a brief explanation.

(a) Are the expenses on the income statement presented by function or nature? Briefly explain.
(b) What is amortization on the other intangible assets during the year, and why does amortization expense not appear as a separate component on the income statement?
(c) Review the useful lives of the company's intangible and tangible assets. If you had to pick one instance where you felt that the useful life was either understated or overstated, which asset would it be, and why?
(d) What portion of the company's assets is property, plant, and equipment? Has the portion increased or decreased from last year?
(e) How does the company value its plant and equipment?
(f) Assume that one of the subsidiaries sold equipment to the parent two years ago and reported a substantial gain. The parent still owns and uses this equipment. Due to an oversight, the intercompany gain has never been eliminated when preparing the consolidated statements. What is the impact of this error on total asset turnover and return on assets for the current year?
(g) Now assume that the company changes its policy to report its plant and equipment at fair value. Also, assume that the fair value of plant and equipment is greater than its carrying amount. What impact would this change in policy have on return on equity for the year and the share price for the company?

Web Problem 7-2
LO1, 4, 9
Access the 2011 financial statements for RONA Inc. by going to investor relations section of the company's website. Answer the same questions as in Web Problem 7-1. For each question, indicate where in the financial statements you found the answer, and/or provide a brief explanation. (Some questions may not be applicable.)

Practise and learn online with Connect

8
CHAPTER

Consolidated Cash Flows and Ownership Issues

INTRODUCTION

While it is still the norm in Canada for the capital structure of a company to consist of common and/or preferred shares, some companies no longer use the terms *common shares* and *preferred shares* to describe their shares. Instead, they may use terms such as *Class A* and *Class B* shares and then describe the essential features of them. In other parts of the world, common shares are often referred to as *ordinary shares*.

Celestica Inc., a world leader in the delivery of innovative electronics manufacturing services, refers to its two classes of shares as *subordinate voting shares* and *multiple voting shares*. The subordinate shares entitle the holder to one vote per share, whereas the multiple voting shares entitle the holder to 25 votes per share. The holders of the subordinate voting shares and multiple voting shares are entitled to share ratably in any dividends of the company. Onex Corporation, one of Canada's largest corporations, with global operations in the services, manufacturing, and technology industries, owns the multiple voting shares of Celestica, while the non-controlling shareholders own most of the subordinated voting shares. This share distribution gives Onex Corporation 71% of the votes but only 8% of the dividends. The non-controlling interests get 29% of the votes but 92% of the dividends.

Different classes of shares typically have different voting and/or different dividend rights.

422

Up to now in this text, the companies involved in the business combination had only common shares outstanding, and the parent obtained control over the subsidiary in one purchase. In this chapter, we will consider situations where the subsidiary also has preferred shares outstanding and those where the parent's ownership interest changes. We commence the chapter with a discussion of certain factors that are unique to the overall consolidation process and that must be considered when the consolidated cash flow statement is prepared.

CONSOLIDATED CASH FLOW STATEMENT

LO1

In the previous chapters, we illustrated the direct approach to preparing the consolidated balance sheet and the consolidated income and retained earnings statements. In this approach, the individual statements of the parent and its subsidiaries are combined. We will now focus on the preparation of the final consolidated statement—the cash flow statement. While this statement could be prepared by combining the separate cash flow statements of the parent and its subsidiaries, this would involve eliminating all intercompany transactions, including intercompany transfers of cash. It is much easier to prepare the cash flow statement using comparative consolidated balance sheets and the consolidated income statement because these statements do not contain any intercompany transactions. In all of the illustrations in this chapter, we will assume that cash flows from operations are presented using the indirect method, whereby net income is adjusted for the effects of non-cash items such as depreciation, amortization, and changes in working capital items and for gains and losses associated with investing and financing cash flows. If the direct method were used, only the items affecting cash would be presented in the first place. Therefore, we would not need to adjust for non-cash items.

> Under the indirect method, we start with net income and show the adjustments to convert it to a cash basis.

The preparation of the cash flow statement for a single unconsolidated company is well covered in introductory and intermediate accounting texts. The basic process used to determine the reasons for the change in cash or cash equivalents is one of analyzing the changes that have occurred in all non-cash items on the balance sheet. The procedures used to carry out this analysis (a working paper or a series of T-accounts) will not be repeated here. Instead, we will describe items that are unique to consolidated statements and that must be taken into account in the analysis. The major items that require special attention are summarized below:

> The change in cash can be determined by analyzing the change in non-cash items during the period.

1. Acquisition-date fair value differences are depreciated in the consolidated income statement. While some of the amortizations may be obvious from their descriptions in the income statement, others may be buried in expense accounts. Because amortizations have no effect on cash flows, we must adjust the year's net income for them in order to arrive at cash flow from operations.

2. Dividends paid by subsidiaries to the parent company do not change the consolidated entity's cash. Dividends paid by the parent to its shareholders, and dividends paid by the subsidiaries to non-controlling shareholders, reduce the cash of the consolidated entity. These dividends can be presented as either operating or financing activities. The dividends paid to non-controlling shareholders should be disclosed or presented separately.

> The consolidated cash flow statement contains adjustments for items that are unique to consolidated financial statements, such as amortization of acquisition differential.

3. A change in the parent's ownership percentage during the year requires a careful analysis to determine its effect on consolidated assets, liabilities, and equities. This will be illustrated in a later section of this chapter (on ownership changes).

4. In the year that a subsidiary is acquired, special disclosures are required in the cash flow statement. The following example illustrates this.

The consolidated balance sheet of Parent Company and its five subsidiaries as at September 30, Year 1, is shown below:

PARENT COMPANY
CONSOLIDATED BALANCE SHEET
at September 30, Year 1

Cash	$ 500,000
Other assets	900,000
Goodwill	120,000
	$1,520,000
Liabilities	$ 500,000
Common shares	200,000
Retained earnings	720,000
Non-controlling interest	100,000
	$1,520,000

On October 1, Year 1, Parent acquired 80% of the outstanding common shares of its sixth subsidiary, Sable Ltd., for a total cost of $140,000. The shareholders of Sable received cash of $90,000 and common shares of Parent with a market value of $50,000 in this transaction. The management of Parent determined that the other assets of Sable had a fair value of $205,000 on this date. The balance sheet of Sable on September 30, Year 1, is shown below:

SABLE LTD.
BALANCE SHEET
at September 30, Year 1

This is the separate-entity balance sheet of Sable.

Cash	$ 30,000
Other assets	200,000
	$230,000
Liabilities	$ 70,000
Common shares	100,000
Retained earnings	60,000
	$230,000

Parent's journal entry to record the acquisition of 80% of the common shares of Sable would be as follows on October 1, Year 1:

This entry is recorded on the separate-entity records for Parent.

Investment in Sable Ltd.	140,000	
Common shares		50,000
Cash		90,000

We will now prepare the consolidated balance sheet of Parent on October 1, Year 1, incorporating the latest acquisition and assuming that this acquisition was the only transaction that occurred on October 1, Year 1, for the parent and all of its subsidiaries.

The calculation and allocation of the acquisition differential for the Sable investment is shown:

Cost of 80% investment in Sable	$140,000	The components of the
		acquisition differential are
Implied value of 100% of Sable	$175,000	reported on the consolidated
Carrying amount of Sable	160,000	balance sheet.
Acquisition differential	15,000	
Allocated:		
Other assets	5,000	
Goodwill	$ 10,000	
Non-controlling interest (175,000 × 20%)	$ 35,000	

The consolidated balance sheet appears below:

PARENT COMPANY
CONSOLIDATED BALANCE SHEET
at October 1, Year 1

Cash (500,000 + 30,000 − **90,000**)	$ 440,000	The assets and liabilities of
Other assets (900,000 + 200,000 + **5,000**)	1,105,000	the subsidiary are added to
Goodwill (120,000 + **10,000**)	130,000	the consolidated balance
	$1,675,000	sheet.
Liabilities (500,000 + 70,000)	$ 570,000	
Common shares (200,000 + **50,000**)	250,000	
Retained earnings	720,000	
Non-controlling interest (100,000 + **35,000**)	135,000	
	$1,675,000	

Preparing the Consolidated Cash Flow Statement

We can now prepare the consolidated cash flow statement for the day that has elapsed by analyzing the changes in the two consolidated balance sheets. We know that the only transaction that has taken place is Parent's acquisition of 80% of Sable. The journal entry of Parent to record the acquisition was illustrated earlier. If we were preparing the cash flow statement of the parent company, we would use our knowledge of this entry in our analysis. But we are preparing the consolidated cash flow statement, and the account "Investment in Sable" does not appear in the consolidated balance sheet. In order to do the proper analysis we need to visualize the effect of this new acquisition on the consolidated balance sheet. We can depict this effect in the form of a "consolidating entry" in the following manner:

Cash	30,000		This entry shows the
Other assets (200,000 + 5,000)	205,000		incremental effect of
Goodwill	10,000		purchasing the subsidiary.
Liabilities		70,000	
Non-controlling interest		35,000	
Cash		90,000	
Common shares		50,000	

Note that the portion of the entry shown in boldface is the amount of the account "Investment in Sable" that made up the parent's acquisition journal entry.

The investment account is replaced by the underlying assets and liabilities in the consolidation process.

Using this analysis, we would normally show the purchase of other assets and goodwill as cash outflows from investing activities and the increase in liabilities, non-controlling interest, and common shares as cash inflows from financing activities. However, IAS 7 requires that only the net cash outflow from a business combination be presented on the cash flow statement, and the details of the changes in non-cash accounts arising from the business combination be disclosed in the notes to financial statements.[1] Therefore, the consolidated cash flow statement for Parent Company would be presented as follows:

PARENT COMPANY
CONSOLIDATED CASH FLOW STATEMENT
for the Day Ended October 1, Year 1

Only the net change in cash is presented on the consolidated cash flow statement.

Operating cash flow	$ nil
Investing cash flow:	
Acquisition of Sable, less cash acquired in acquisition $30,000 (note 1)	(60,000)
Financing cash flow:	nil
Net change in cash for the two-day period	(60,000)
Cash, September 30, Year 1	500,000
Cash, October 1, Year 1	$440,000

Note 1: Effective October 1, Year 1, the company acquired 80% of the common shares of Sable for a total consideration of $140,000. The acquisition, which was accounted for by the acquisition method, is summarized as follows:

The details of the changes in non-cash items are disclosed in the notes to the consolidated cash flow statement.

Net assets acquired:	
Other assets	$205,000
Goodwill	10,000
Liabilities	(70,000)
Non-controlling interest	(35,000)
	$110,000
Consideration given:	
Common shares	$ 50,000
Cash	90,000
	140,000
Less cash acquired on acquisition	30,000
	$110,000

Note that the only item appearing on the cash flow statement is a $60,000 cash outflow under investing activities. The $60,000 is the difference between the cash paid for the shares of the subsidiary ($90,000) and the cash held by the subsidiary on the date of acquisition ($30,000). The other assets acquired and liabilities assumed in the business acquisition are not shown on the face of the cash flow statement as investing and financing activities but are disclosed in the notes to the financial statements. Therefore, when we prepare a cash flow statement, we must differentiate between those changes in non-cash items arising from a business combination and those arising from other activities. Those changes arising from the business combination are netted and given one line on the cash flow statement, with the details disclosed in the notes to the financial statements. The other changes are presented on the face of the cash flow statement, according to normal practices.

In our discussion of the consolidated cash flow statement, we have focused entirely on items unique to consolidated statements, on the assumption that the overall process for preparing such statements has been covered in earlier financial accounting courses. The next major topic in this chapter, *ownership changes,* also presents items that require analysis as to their effects on consolidated cash flows. The cash flow effects for these ownership changes will be discussed in the appropriate sections.

CHANGES IN PARENT'S OWNERSHIP INTEREST

A parent's ownership interest will change for any of the following:

(a) The parent purchases additional holdings in its subsidiary (block acquisitions).

(b) The parent sells some of its holdings in its subsidiary.

(c) The subsidiary issues additional common shares to the public, and the parent does not maintain its previous ownership percentage.

(d) The subsidiary repurchases some of its common shares from the non-controlling interest.

> The parent's percentage of ownership can change when the parent buys or sells shares of the subsidiary or when the subsidiary issues or repurchases shares.

When the parent's ownership changes, the percentage of subsidiary common shares held by the non-controlling interest also changes. The major consolidation problem involved with ownership change is the effect such changes have on the valuation of subsidiary net assets and non-controlling interest in the consolidated statements. When the parent's ownership percentage *increases,* a portion of the unamortized acquisition differential will be transferred from the non-controlling interest to the parent. When the parent's ownership *decreases,* a portion of the unamortized acquisition differential will be transferred from the parent to the non-controlling interest. We will use a comprehensive example to illustrate various changes in a parent's ownership interest. We will begin with step-by-step acquisitions.

> Any time the parent's percentage of ownership increases, we will account for the transaction as a purchase. Any time the parent's percentage decreases, we will account for the transaction as a sale.

Block Acquisitions of Subsidiary (Step Purchases)

L02

The consolidation illustrations that we have used in previous chapters have assumed that the parent company achieved its control in a subsidiary by making a single purchase of the subsidiary's common shares. On the date of acquisition, the fair values of the subsidiary's assets (including goodwill) and liabilities were determined and then brought onto the consolidated balance sheet along with the carrying amounts of the parent's assets and liabilities. The non-controlling interest at the date of acquisition was also measured at fair value. In periods subsequent to the date of acquisition, the subsidiary's net assets were accounted for based on the values determined at the date of acquisition. They were not remeasured to fair value at each reporting date.

> The subsidiary is measured at fair value on the consolidated balance sheet on the date the parent obtains control.

We will now consider a situation where the parent achieves its control position through a series of block acquisitions (sometimes described as "step purchases").

Purchase of First Block of Shares   On January 1, Year 1, Par Company acquires 1,000 common shares (10% of the outstanding shares) of Star Company for $20,000. The 10% voting interest does not give Par control or significant influence. The investment is classified as fair value through profit or loss. On this date, the shareholders' equity of Star consists of common shares of $100,000 and retained earnings of $70,000. During Year 1, Star reported net income of $10,000 and did not declare any dividends. At the end of Year 1, the fair value of Star's shares was $22 per share. Par's journal entries for Year 1 for the FVTPL investment follow:

Investment in Star	20,000	
Cash		20,000
To record purchase of 1,000 shares of Star for $20 per share		

Investment in Star	2,000	
Gain on Star		2,000
To record unrealized gain on FVTPL investment in Star		

FVTPL investments are reported at fair value at each reporting date.

The acquisition differential at the date of acquisition is ignored. Par's share of Star's income for the year is also ignored because the investment is reported at its fair value of $22,000 at the end of Year 1.

Purchase of Second Block of Shares   On January 1, Year 2, Par acquires another 2,000 common shares of Star for $44,000. The carrying amounts of Star's net assets are equal to fair values except for specialized equipment, which is undervalued by $10,000. The equipment has an estimated remaining useful life of five years. During Year 2, Star reported a net income of $30,000 and paid dividends of $20,000. At December 31, Year 2, the fair value of Star's shares was $25 per share.

The equity method is used once the investor obtains significant influence.

Par now owns 30% of Star and, presuming no other factors to the contrary, has obtained significant influence in the key decisions for Star. As a result, Star is now an associate and Par will now adopt the equity method of accounting for its 30% interest. The change in reporting method will be accounted for prospectively as a change in estimate because the circumstances changed from not having significant influence to having significant influence.[2] In our current example, the investment in Star will reflect the fair value of Star's share at January 1, Year 2. Par paid fair value for the 2,000 shares it just purchased. The carrying amount of the previous investment also reflects its fair value because as a FVTPL investment it must be reported at fair value.

The investment account is adjusted to fair value when the investor obtains significant influence over the investee.

If the previous investment had been reported at cost, it would be revalued to fair value when the equity method was first adopted, and a gain or loss on revaluation would be reported in net income. The carrying amount of the investment in Star after the new investment would be equal to the fair value of the shares in Star at this date. Support for revaluing to fair value can be found in paragraph 26 of IAS 28, which states that the concepts underlying the procedures used in accounting for the acquisition of a subsidiary are also adopted in accounting for the acquisition of an investment in an associate. As we will see later, the revaluation of a previous investment to fair value is consistent with the requirements when an investor first obtains control of a subsidiary. Revaluing to fair value can also be supported by the use of the equity method, which requires that an investment in an associate must initially be recorded at cost. The cost of the asset 30% interest in Star is the fair value of the 10% investment in Star plus the $44,000 in cash.

Under the equity method, an acquisition differential is calculated and subsequently amortized, similar to the process used for consolidation. The acquisition differential is first calculated when the equity method first becomes applicable and is calculated as if the entire 30% were purchased on this date. The acquisition cost incorporates the cost of the current purchase plus the fair value of the prior investments.

The calculation and allocation of the acquisition differential as at January 1, Year 2, is as follows:

Acquisition cost for 30% of Star (44,000 + 20,000 + 2,000)		$66,000	The acquisition differential
Carrying amount of Star's net assets:			must be identified and
Common shares	100,000		amortized under the equity
Retained earnings (70,000 + 10,000)	80,000		method.
Total shareholders' equity	180,000		
Par's ownership interest	30%	54,000	
Acquisition differential		12,000	
Allocated:			
Equipment (10,000 × 30%)		3,000	
Goodwill		$ 9,000	

The investment in Star is reported as a separate line on Par's balance sheet and is accounted for using the equity method. Consolidated financial statements are not appropriate, since Par only has significant influence and does not have control over Star. The acquisition differential, which includes the fair value excess pertaining to the equipment and the goodwill, is retained as a component of the investment account and not reported separately on Par's balance sheet. Since the fair value of Star's shares went up during Year 2, there appears to be no impairment in the investment in Star or the underlying goodwill. The fair value excess component pertaining to the equipment must be depreciated over its useful life of five years. Par's journal entries for Year 2 for the significant-influence investment would be as follows:

Investment in Star	44,000	
Cash		44,000
To record purchase of 2,000 shares of Star for $22 per share		
Investment in Star	9,000	
Investment income		9,000
To record 30% of reported income for the year (30% × 30,000)		
Investment income	600	
Investment in Star		600
To record amortization of acquisition differential related to		
equipment (3,000/5 years)		
Cash	6,000	
Investment in Star		6,000
To record dividends received during the year (30% × 20,000)		

The balance in the investment account at the end of Year 2 is $68,400 (22,000 + 44,000 + 9,000 − 600 − 6,000). The fair value of the investment is $75,000 (3,000 shares × $25 per share) but is ignored under the equity method, since it exceeds the carrying amount of the investment.

The investment is not reported at fair value under the equity method.

Purchase of Third Block of Shares   On January 1, Year 3, Par acquires another 1,000 common shares of Star for $25,000. The carrying amounts of Star's net assets are equal to fair values except for specialized equipment, which is undervalued by $10,000. The equipment has an estimated remaining useful life of four years. During Year 3, Star reported a net income of $40,000 and paid dividends of $20,000. At December 31, Year 3, the fair value of Star's shares was $29 per share.

Par now owns 40% of Star, still has significant influence in the key decisions for Star, and will continue using the equity method. An acquisition differential for this 10% step is calculated and allocated as follows:

<table>
<tr><td>Cost of 10% of Star</td><td></td><td>$25,000</td></tr>
<tr><td>Carrying amount of Star's net assets:</td><td></td><td></td></tr>
<tr><td>Common shares</td><td>100,000</td><td></td></tr>
<tr><td>Retained earnings (80,000 + 30,000 − 20,000)</td><td>90,000</td><td></td></tr>
<tr><td>Total shareholders' equity</td><td>190,000</td><td></td></tr>
<tr><td>Par's ownership interest</td><td>10%</td><td>19,000</td></tr>
<tr><td>Acquisition differential</td><td></td><td>6,000</td></tr>
<tr><td>Allocated:</td><td></td><td></td></tr>
<tr><td>Equipment (10,000 × 10%)</td><td></td><td>1,000</td></tr>
<tr><td>Goodwill</td><td></td><td>$ 5,000</td></tr>
</table>

A separate allocation of the acquisition differential should be prepared for each incremental investment.

There are now two separate and incremental calculations and allocations of acquisition differential based on the purchase price for each step. The allocation for the 30% step is carried forward with its previous values and is not revalued to fair value on the date of the third step. The following acquisition-differential amortization schedule is prepared to keep track of the allocation and amortization of the acquisition differentials for each step:

ACQUISITION-DIFFERENTIAL AMORTIZATION SCHEDULE					
	Second Step		**Third Step**		
	Equip.	*Goodwill*	*Equip.*	*Goodwill*	*Total*
Jan 1, Year 2, purchase	$3,000	$9,000			$12,000
Amortization for Year 2	(600)				(600)
Balance, December 31, Year 2	2,400	9,000			11,400
Jan 1, Year 3, purchase			$1,000	$5,000	6,000
Amortization for Year 3	(600)		(250)		(850)
Balance, December 31, Year 3	$1,800	$9,000	$ 750	$5,000	$16,550

The previous block acquisitions are not normally revalued when there is a new acquisition.

Since the fair value of Star's shares went up during Year 3, there appears to be no impairment in the investment in Star or the underlying goodwill. The fair value excess component of the investment account is being depreciated over its useful life.

Par's journal entries for Year 3 for the investment in Star, an associate, would be as follows:

Investment in Star	25,000	
Cash		25,000
To record purchase of 1,000 shares of Star for $25 per share		

Investment in Star	16,000	
Investment income		16,000
To record 40% of reported income for the year (40% × 40,000)		

The amortization of the acquisition differential is recorded in the investment account under the equity method.

Investment income	850	
Investment in Star		850
To record amortization of acquisition differential related to equipment		

Cash	8,000	
Investment in Star		8,000
To record dividends received during the year (40% × 20,000)		

The balance in the investment account at the end of Year 3 is $100,550 (68,400 + 25,000 + 16,000 − 850 − 8,000). The fair value of the investment is $116,000 (4,000 shares × $29 per share) but is ignored under the equity method, since it exceeds the carrying amount of the investment.

Purchase of Fourth Block of Shares   On January 1, Year 4, Par acquires another 3,000 common shares of Star for $87,000. The carrying amounts of Star's net assets are equal to fair values except for specialized equipment, which is undervalued by $7,500. The equipment has an estimated remaining useful life of three years. During Year 4, Star reported a net income of $50,000 and paid dividends of $20,000. At December 31, Year 4, the fair value of Star's shares was $34 per share.

Par now owns 70% and has control over Star. The business combination should be reported on a consolidated basis. The change in reporting method will be accounted for prospectively as a change in estimate because the circumstances changed from not having control to having control. IFRS 3 states that the previously held equity interest should be revalued at fair value with the revaluation adjustment reported in net income. If, before the business combination, the acquirer recognized changes in the value of its non-controlling equity investment in other comprehensive income, the amount that was recognized in other comprehensive income is reclassified and included in the calculation of any gain or loss as of the acquisition date. Therefore, Par will make the following entries on January 1, Year 4:

> *The investment account is adjusted to fair value when the investor first obtains control of the investee.*

Investment in Star	15,450	
Unrealized gain on investment		15,450
To adjust investment in Star to fair value (116,000 − 100,550)		

Investment in Star	87,000	
Cash		87,000
To record purchase of 3,000 shares at $29 per share		

The investment in Star now contains a balance of $203,000 (100,550 + 15,450 + 87,000), which is equal to the fair value of the 7,000 shares. When the parent first obtains control of the subsidiary, we must prepare a new calculation and allocation of the acquisition differential for the percentage ownership at the time of the purchase, to reflect the revaluation of the entire subsidiary to fair value. In so doing, we will ignore the acquisition differentials and amortizations from the previous steps. The acquisition-differential calculation and amortization for the 70% interest as at January 1, Year 4 is as follows:

> *Any previous acquisition cost allocations are replaced by a new acquisition cost allocation on the date of a business combination.*

Value of 70% of Star		$203,000
Implied value of 100% of Star		$290,000
Carrying amount of Star's net assets:		
Common shares	100,000	
Retained earnings (90,000 + 40,000 − 20,000)	110,000	
Total shareholders' equity		210,000
Acquisition differential		80,000
Allocated:		
Equipment		7,500
Goodwill		$72,500

> *The acquisition differential is calculated and allocated to value the subsidiary at 100% of its fair value.*

Since the fair value of Star's shares went up during Year 4, there appears to be no impairment in Star's goodwill. The fair value excess attributed to the equipment must be depreciated over its useful life of three years. The following acquisition-differential amortization schedule is prepared to keep track of the allocation and amortization of the acquisition differential.

ACQUISITION-DIFFERENTIAL AMORTIZATION SCHEDULE

	Balance Jan. 1, Year 4	Amortization Year 4	Balance Dec. 31, Year 4
Equipment	$ 7,500	$2,500	$ 5,000
Goodwill	72,500		72,500
	$80,000	$2,500	$77,500

Assuming that Par continues to use the equity method on its separate-entity books, the journal entries for Year 4 would be as follows:

Investment in Star	35,000	
Investment income		35,000

To record 70% of reported income for the year (70% × 50,000)

Investment income	1,750	
Investment in Star		1,750

To record Par's share of amortization of acquisition differential related
to equipment (70% × 2,500)

Cash	14,000	
Investment in Star		14,000

To record dividends received during the year (70% × 20,000)

Only the parent's share of the amortization of the acquisition differential is recorded in the parent's books.

The investment account is not adjusted to fair value subsequent to the date of acquisition.

The balance in the investment account at the end of Year 4 is $222,250 (203,000 + 35,000 − 1,750 − 14,000). The fair value of the investment is $238,000 (7,000 shares × $34 per share) but is ignored under the equity method and under consolidation, since it exceeds the carrying amount of the investment.

Purchase of Fifth Block of Shares

On January 1, Year 5, Par acquires another 2,000 common shares of Star for $68,000. The carrying amounts of Star's net assets are equal to fair values except for specialized equipment, which is undervalued by $6,000. The equipment has an estimated remaining useful life of two years. During Year 5, Star reported a net income of $60,000 and paid dividends of $20,000. At December 31, Year 5, the fair value of Star's shares was $38 per share.

Par now owns 90% of Star, continues to have control over Star, and continues to report its investment on a consolidated basis. However, it does not treat this additional purchase like the other step purchases because there is no change in control; that is, it does not calculate an acquisition differential for this purchase and does not revalue the existing acquisition differential. The transaction is treated as an equity transaction; that is, a transaction with owners in their capacity as owners. Simply put, the parent is acquiring an additional 20% of Star from the non-controlling interests. In such circumstances, the carrying amount of the portion of the non-controlling interests sold to the parent will be allocated to the parent. Any difference between the amounts by which the non-controlling interests are adjusted and the fair value of the consideration paid or received by the parent must be recognized as a direct charge or credit to owners' equity, and attributed to the owners of the parent.

The subsidiary's net assets are not revalued on the consolidated financial statements when the parent's percentage ownership increases.

The carrying amount of the non-controlling interests sold to the parent was $63,500, calculated as follows:

Star's common shares	$100,000
Star's retained earnings (110,000 + 50,000 − 20,000)	140,000
	240,000
Unamortized acquisition differential	77,500
	317,500
Non-controlling interests' percentage ownership	30%
Non-controlling interests at December 31, Year 4	$ 95,250
Portion sold to controlling interest (2,000/3,000)	$ 63,500

Any difference between the amount paid and the carrying amount of net assets being purchased from the non-controlling interest is recognized as a direct charge or credit to owner's equity.

Since Par paid $68,000 for the shares, it paid $4,500 more than the carrying amount previously attributed to these shares on the consolidated balance sheet. This $4,500 would be recognized as a direct charge to Par's retained earnings on the date of the purchase.

Since the fair value of Star's shares went up during the year, there appears to be no impairment in Star's goodwill. The acquisition-differential amortization schedule for Year 5 is as follows:

	Balance Jan. 1, Year 5	Amortization Year 5	Balance Dec. 31, Year 5
Equipment	$ 5,000	$2,500	$ 2,500
Goodwill	72,500		72,500
	$77,500	$2,500	$75,000

Assuming that Par continues to use the equity method on its separate-entity books, the journal entries for Year 5 would be as follows:

Investment in Star	63,500	
Retained earnings	4,500	
Cash		68,000
To record purchase of 2,000 shares at $34 per share		

These entries are recorded on the separate-entity books of the parent.

Investment in Star	54,000	
Investment income		54,000
To record 90% of reported income for the year (90% × 60,000)		

Investment income	2,250	
Investment in Star		2,250
To record Par's share of amortization of acquisition differential related to equipment (90% × 2,500)		

Cash	18,000	
Investment in Star		18,000
To record dividends received during the year (90% × 20,000)		

The balance in the investment account at the end of Year 5 is $319,500 (222,250 + 63,500 + 54,000 − 2,250 − 18,000). The investment account can be segregated as follows:

The investment account can be reconciled to the subsidiary's equity at any point in time when the parent uses the equity method.

Carrying amount of Star's net assets:		
Common shares	$100,000	
Retained earnings (140,000 + 60,000 − 20,000)	180,000	
Total shareholders' equity	280,000	
Unamortized acquisition differential	75,000	
	355,000	
Par's ownership interest	90%	
Total	$319,500	

Non-controlling interest on the balance sheet comprises the non-controlling interest's share of the subsidiary's equity and the unamortized acquisition differential at the balance sheet date.

Similarly, the non-controlling interest can be calculated using these same components as follows:

Carrying amount of Star's net assets:	$280,000
Unamortized acquisition differential	75,000
	355,000
Non-controlling interest's ownership interest	10%
	$ 35,500

We will now illustrate the consolidation process by using the following condensed balance sheets for Par and Star at the end of Year 5:

The parent's retained earnings under the equity method are equal to consolidated retained earnings.

	Par	Star
Investment in Star (equity method)	$ 319,500	
Equipment—net	500,000	$140,000
Other assets	700,000	490,000
	$1,519,500	$630,000
Liabilities	$ 450,000	$350,000
Common shares	500,000	100,000
Retained earnings	569,500	180,000
	$1,519,500	$630,000

The consolidated balance sheet at December 31, Year 5, is as follows:

PAR COMPANY
CONSOLIDATED BALANCE SHEET
at December 31, Year 5

Both the parent's and the non-controlling interest's shares of the unamortized acquisition differential appear on the consolidated balance sheet.

Equipment—net (500,000 + 140,000 + **2,500**)	$ 642,500
Other assets (700,000 + 490,000)	1,190,000
Goodwill (0 + 0 + **72,500**)	72,500
	$1,905,000
Liabilities (450,000 + 350,000)	$ 800,000
Common shares	500,000
Retained earnings	569,500
Non-controlling interest	35,500
	$1,905,000

Numerous small purchases can be grouped into one block purchase when calculating and allocating the acquisition differential.

Numerous Small Purchases Assume that Par attempts to purchase the remaining outstanding shares of Star by making daily open-market purchases of the subsidiary's shares. At the end of two months, it abandons the idea. During this period, it has made 35 separate share purchases, which, in total, represent 4% of the subsidiary's outstanding shares. Since it would be impractical to calculate 35 acquisition differentials, these purchases can be combined and treated as a single block purchase of 4%.

Repurchase of Shares by Subsidiary When the subsidiary repurchases and cancels some or all of the common shares being held by the non-controlling shareholders, the parent's percentage ownership in the common shares will increase. The increase in ownership will be accounted for as an equity transaction similar to the purchase of the fifth block of shares.

Consolidated Retained Earnings—Cost Method The examples used to illustrate block purchases have assumed that the parent company uses the equity method to account for its investment. If the parent had used the cost method, schedules would have to be prepared to derive account balances such as retained earning for the consolidated financial statements. These schedules have been extensively illustrated in earlier chapters and require only slight modification when block acquisitions have been made.

In our comprehensive example, Par used the equity method during the period it had control of Star. If Par had used the cost method for internal record keeping, it likely would have adopted the cost method when it first obtained control of Star on January 1, Year 4. It would simply have added the $87,000 cost of the fourth purchase to the carrying amount of the investment at that point, which was $100,550 as per our earlier discussion. It would not likely have made any adjustment to value the investment at fair value as required for consolidation purposes. If so, the balance in the investment account at January 1, Year 4 would have been $187,550 (100,550 + 87,000). The $68,000 cost of the fifth purchase would be added on January 1, Year 5 to bring the investment account to $255,550 (187,550 + 68,000) at that date and at December 31, Year 5. This compares to a balance of $319,500 under the equity method at the end of Year 5. The difference of $63,950 (319,500 − 255,550) for the investment account would be offset by a $63,950 reduction in retained earnings. Therefore, retained earnings for Par under the cost method would have been $505,550 (569,500 under equity method minus 63,950) at December 31, Year 5. Consolidated retained earnings would be calculated as follows:

CALCULATION OF CONSOLIDATED RETAINED EARNINGS
at December 31, Year 5

Retained earnings of parent—cost method		$505,550	Consolidated retained
Adjust investment account to fair value at date of business combination		15,450	earnings should recognize
Less: Parent's share of acquisition-differential amortizations			the parent's percentage
Year 4 purchase	1,750		ownership for each
Year 5 purchase	2,250	(4,000)	step of the step-by-step
Retained earnings of subsidiary at the time of			acquisitions.
Year 5 purchase	140,000		
Retained earnings of subsidiary at the time of			
Year 4 purchase	110,000		
Increase since Year 4 purchase	30,000		
Parent's ownership percentage	70%	21,000	
Retained earnings of subsidiary—Dec. 31, Year 5	180,000		
Retained earnings of subsidiary at the time of Year 5 purchase	140,000		
Increase since Year 5 purchase	40,000		
Parent's ownership percentage	90%	36,000	
Loss on purchase of shares from non-controlling interest,			
Jan. 1, Year 5		(4,500)	
Consolidated retained earnings		$569,500	

Consolidated Cash Flow Analysis Par Company's fifth block purchase of shares (on January 1, Year 5, for $68,000) requires further analysis to determine the effect on the Year 5 consolidated balance sheet. This cash has left the consolidated entity, so the effect of the transaction must appear on the Year 5 consolidated cash flow statement. We can depict the effect of the fifth purchase on the consolidated balance sheet with the following entry:

The cost of purchasing additional shares in the subsidiary should be reported in financing activities on the consolidated cash flow statement.

Retained earnings	4,500	
Non-controlling interest	63,500	
Cash		68,000

This transaction simply moved cash and reallocated shareholders' equity between the controlling and non-controlling interests. No new assets were acquired. The $68,000 cash outflow should appear in the financing activities section of the cash flow statement, since it is similar to purchasing shares from a shareholder. It would be described as "Purchase of additional shares in subsidiary from non-controlling interests."

L03 Parent Sells Some of Its Holdings in Subsidiary

Let us continue with the previous illustration involving Par and Star. Assume that on January 1, Year 6, Par sold 900 shares in Star Company on the open market for $34,200. Note that after the sale, Par's ownership percentage is 81% (8,100 ÷ 10,000). Note also that Par has disposed of 10% of its investment in Star (900 ÷ 9,000). Another way of calculating the percentage of investment disposed is as follows:

Ownership before sale	90%
Ownership after sale	81%
Change	9%
Percentage of investment sold: 9 ÷ 90 = 10%	

Gains (losses) on transactions with shareholders are credited (charged) directly to shareholders' equity.

Since Par still has control of Star, consolidated financial statements will continue to be prepared. This transaction is, once again, treated as an equity transaction; that is, a transaction between shareholders of the consolidated entity. The parent is selling part of its interest in Star to the non-controlling interest. The carrying amount of the portion sold is $31,950 (10% × 319,500); it will be allocated from the parent to the non-controlling interest. Since the amount received was $34,200, the owners of the parent are better off by $2,250 as a result of this transaction. This benefit is not reported in net income since this transaction between owners has not resulted in a change in control. The gain will be recognized as a direct increase to consolidated contributed surplus.

Since the equity method should produce the same results as the consolidated financial statements, Par would make the following entry to record the sale of 900 shares:

Cash	34,200	
Investment in Star (10% × $319,500)		31,950
Contributed surplus		2,250

Non-controlling interest is increased by the carrying amount of the shares sold by the parent.

The total unamortized acquisition differential to be reported on the consolidated financial statements would remain the same in total. However, the portion belonging to the non-controlling interest would increase because the non-controlling interest now owns 19% of the subsidiary. The portion belonging to the controlling interest would decrease because the parent has sold 10% of its interest.

The following schedule shows the change in values for the controlling and noncontrolling interests as a result of Par's sale of 900 shares:

	Controlling Interest			*Non-controlling Interest*		
	Before	*Sold*	*After*	*Before*	*Bought*	*After*
Percentage ownership	90%	9%	81%	10%	9%	19%
Share of Star's shareholders' equity	$252,000	$25,200	$226,800	$28,000	$25,200	$53,200
Unamortized acquisition differential						
Equipment	2,250	225	2,025	250	225	475
Goodwill	65,250	6,525	58,725	7,250	6,525	13,775
Total	$319,500	$31,950	$287,550	$35,500	$31,950	$67,450

We will now illustrate the consolidation process by using the following condensed balance sheets for Par and Star at January 1, Year 6. The previous balance sheets have been updated for the entry to record the sale of 900 shares by Par.

	Par	*Star*
Investment in Star (319,500 − 31,950)	$ 287,550	
Equipment—net	500,000	$140,000
Other assets (700,000 + 34,200)	734,200	490,000
	$1,521,750	$630,000
Liabilities	$ 450,000	$350,000
Common shares	500,000	100,000
Retained earnings	569,500	180,000
Contributed surplus	2,250	
	$1,521,750	$630,000

The consolidated balance sheet at January 1, Year 6, is as follows:

PAR COMPANY
CONSOLIDATED BALANCE SHEET
at January 1, Year 6

Equipment—net (500,000 + 140,000 + **2,025 + 475**)	$ 642,500	The subsidiary's net assets
Other assets (734,200 + 490,000)	1,224,200	are not revalued when the
Goodwill (**58,725 + 13,775**)	72,500	parent sells a portion of its
	$1,939,200	investment in the subsidiary.
Liabilities (450,000 + 350,000)	$ 800,000	
Common shares	500,000	
Retained earnings	569,500	
Contributed surplus	2,250	
Non-controlling interest	67,450	
	$1,939,200	

The sale of the shares to the non-controlling interest increased the entity's cash by $34,200. This cash inflow must appear on the consolidated cash flow statement. We can depict the effect of the sale on the consolidated balance sheet with the following entry:

Cash	34,200	
Non-controlling interest		31,950
Contributed surplus		2,250

This transaction simply reallocated shareholders' equity between the controlling and non-controlling interests. The $34,200 cash inflow should appear in the financing activities section of the cash flow statement and would be described as "Sale of shares in subsidiary to non-controlling interest."

Income Statement Analysis

On December 31, Year 6, Star reported a net income of $40,000 and paid dividends amounting to $15,000. A goodwill impairment test conducted on December 31, Year 6, indicated that an impairment loss of $6,000 had occurred. The following acquisition-differential amortization schedule would be made on December 31, Year 6:

ACQUISITION-DIFFERENTIAL AMORTIZATION AND IMPAIRMENT SCHEDULE

	Balance Jan. 1, Year 6	Amortization/Impairment Year 6	Balance Dec. 31, Year 6
Equipment	$ 2,500	$2,500	$ 0
Goodwill	72,500	6,000	66,500
	$75,000	$8,500	$66,500

Note that the Year 6 amortization completely eliminates the acquisition differential related to the equipment because this is the last year of the equipment's useful life.

Par's equity method journal entries for Year 6 would be as follows:

Investment in Star	32,400	
Investment income		32,400
To record 81% of Star's net income for Year 6 (40,000 × 81%)		

Cash	12,150	
Investment in Star		12,150
To record dividends received from Star in Year 6 (15,000 × 81%)		

Investment income	6,885	
Investment in Star		6,885
To record Par's share of amortization of the acquisition differential for Year 6 (8,500 81%)		

The following are the Year 6 income statements of Par and Star:

	Par	Star
Miscellaneous revenue	$200,000	$150,000
Investment income	25,515	—
	225,515	150,000
Miscellaneous expenses	130,000	90,000
Equipment depreciation expense	—	20,000
	130,000	110,000
Net income	$ 95,515	$ 40,000

Investment income is replaced with the revenues and expenses of Star, the amortization of the acquisition differentials, and the non-controlling interest. The Year 6 consolidated income statement prepared using the direct approach appears below:

PAR COMPANY
CONSOLIDATED INCOME STATEMENT
for the Year Ended December 31, Year 6

Miscellaneous revenues (200,000 + 150,000)	$350,000
Miscellaneous expenses (130,000 + 90,000)	220,000
Equipment depreciation (0 + 20,000 + **2,500**)	22,500
Goodwill impairment loss (0 + 0 + **6,000**)	6,000
	248,500
Net income	$101,500
Attributable to	
Shareholders of Par Company	$ 95,515
Non-controlling interest [19% × (40,000 − 8,500)]	5,985

> The non-controlling interest is charged with its share of the amortization of the acquisition differential.

Over the past few pages, we have accounted for a series of acquisitions and dispositions of shares in an investee. Exhibit 8.1 summarizes the key decisions made in each step of the process.

See Self-Study Problem 1 for a comprehensive problem involving changes in ownership. It includes most of the issues we have covered so far this chapter.

SUBSIDIARY ISSUES ADDITIONAL SHARES TO PUBLIC

Let us assume that Par did not sell 900 shares on January 1, Year 6, and that, instead, Star Company issued an additional 2,500 shares for $95,000 on January 1, Year 6. Star would record this transaction as follows:

Cash	95,000	
Common shares		95,000
To record the issuance of 2,500 shares		

> The parent's percentage interest decreases when the subsidiary issues additional shares and the parent does not purchase any of the additional shares.

Star now has 12,500 common shares issued. Because Par did not buy any of the new issue, its holdings have remained constant (9,000 shares) but its ownership interest has declined to 72% (9,000 ÷ 12,500). This represents a 20% reduction in its investment, calculated as follows:

Ownership before share issue	90%
Ownership after share issue	72%
Change	18%

Percentage of investment reduced: 18 ÷ 90 = 20%

EXHIBIT 8.1 | **Overview of Step-by-Step Acquisitions**

	Step Number					
	1	2	3	4	5	6
Percentage acquired	10	20	10	30	20	(9)
Percentage owned	10	30	40	70	90	81
Reporting method	FVTPL	Equity	Equity	Cons	Cons	Cons
Previous investment revalued to fair value	N.A.	Yes	No	Yes	No	No
New allocation of acquisition differential required	No	Yes	Yes	Yes	No	No
Acquisition differential for what percentage	N.A.	30	10	100	N.A.	N.A.

The effect of this reduction on the unamortized acquisition differential is the same as if the parent had sold a portion of its holding in the subsidiary to the non-controlling interest. In this case, 20% of the parent's share of the unamortized acquisition differential has been "disposed of" as a result of the share issue. However, at this point, the only entry to record the transaction is made by Star. Parent must also adjust its investment account to record the effect of this transaction on its investment. The following analysis indicates the amount of the adjustment:

The parent gave up 20% of its old investment and received 72% of the increase in the subsidiary's equity.

Loss due to reduction of investment account—20% × 319,500	$63,900
Gain due to ownership of new assets resulting from subsidiary share issue—72% × 95,000	68,400
Net benefit to parent due to share issue	$ 4,500

In our previous example, we explained the reasoning for removing 20% from the investment account. The unamortized acquisition differential is included in the $319,500 amount, and if this differential has been reduced by 20%, a logical extension is to remove 20% from the total investment balance. If the subsidiary had issued the 2,500 shares for no consideration, the investment account would have to be reduced by $63,900 (20% × 319,500), and a loss equal to that amount would be recorded by Par as a direct charge to owner's equity. But Star received $95,000 for its new share issue, and Par now owns 72% of the net assets of its subsidiary, including the additional cash received as a result of the new share issue. Par has gained by the 72% ownership interest in the assets received by Star. It should be obvious that the net charge or credit to owners' equity resulting from the transaction depends on the amount that the subsidiary received from its new share issue. This gain is not reported in net income, since this transaction between owners has not resulted in a change in control. The gain will be recognized as a direct increase to consolidated contributed surplus and to the parent's separate-entity contributed surplus under the equity method. Given the facts of this particular example, Par would make the following journal entry under the equity method on January 1, Year 6:

Gains (losses) on transactions with shareholders are not reported in net income.

Investment in Star	4,500	
Contributed surplus		4,500
To record the effect of subsidiary's issue of 2,500 shares on parent's investment		

As in our previous example, we assume that in Year 6, Star reported a net income of $40,000 and paid $15,000 in dividends. Par's equity method journal entries for Year 6 would be as follows:

Investment in Star	28,800	
Investment income		28,800
To record 72% of Star's net income for Year 6 (40,000 × 72%)		

Cash	10,800	
Investment in Star		10,800
To record dividends received from Star in Year 6 (15,000 × 72%)		

The parent absorbs 72% of the amortization of the acquisition differential.

Investment income	6,120	
Investment in Star		6,120
To record Par's share of the amortization of the acquisition differential for Year 6 (8,500 × 72%)		

The elimination of the parent's interest in the subsidiary's shareholders' equity against the parent's investment account leaves a balance equal to the unamortized acquisition differential. This will now be illustrated.

Investment in Star		
Balance, December 31, Year 5		$319,500
Increase due to subsidiary share issue		4,500
Star net income (40,000 × 72%)		28,800
Star dividends (15,000 × 72%)		(10,800)
Acquisition-differential amortization		(6,120)
Balance, December 31, Year 6		335,880
Shareholders' equity of Star		
Common shares—December 31, Year 5	100,000	
Share issue—Year 6	95,000	
Common shares, December 31, Year 6	195,000	
Retained earnings, December 31, Year 6		
(180,000 + 40,000 − 15,000)	205,000	
Total, December 31, Year 6	400,000	
Par's ownership interest	72%	288,000
Balance—unamortized acquisition differential		$ 47,880

> The investment account comprises the parent's share of the subsidiary's equity plus the unamortized acquisition differential.

The $47,880 represents Par's 72% of the total acquisition differential of $66,500, as per the earlier discussion under "Income Statement Analysis". Non-controlling interest at December 31, Year 6, is $130,620 (28% × [400,000 + 66,500]).

The Year 6 income statements of Par and Star are shown below, followed by the consolidated income statement.

> The unamortized acquisition differential is not revalued when the parent's percentage ownership changes as long as the parent still has control.

	Par	Star
Miscellaneous revenue	$200,000	$150,000
Investment income	22,680	—
	222,680	150,000
Miscellaneous expenses	130,000	90,000
Equipment depreciation expense	—	20,000
	130,000	110,000
Net income	$ 92,680	$ 40,000

PAR COMPANY
CONSOLIDATED INCOME STATEMENT
for the Year Ended December 31, Year 6

Miscellaneous revenues (200,000 + 150,000)	$350,000
Miscellaneous expenses (130,000 + 90,000)	220,000
Equipment depreciation (0 + 20,000 + **2,500**)	22,500
Goodwill impairment loss (0 + 0 + **6,000**)	6,000
	248,500
Net income	$101,500
Attributable to	
Shareholders of Par Company	$ 92,680
Non-controlling interest [28% × (40,000 − 8,500)]	8,820

Consolidated Cash Flow Analysis   To recap, the issue of 2,500 shares on January 1, Year 6, was recorded by Star Company with the following journal entry:

Cash	95,000	
Common shares		95,000

Also, in order to record the effect of the reduction on its investment, Par made the following journal entry on this date:

| Investment in Star | 4,500 | |
| Contributed surplus | | 4,500 |

As a result of this share issue, the non-controlling interests increased by $90,500 calculated as follows:

Non-controlling interest can be reconciled to the subsidiary's shareholders' equity and the unamortized acquisition differential at any point in time.

NCI after subsidiary share issue:

Shareholders' equity before issue	$280,000
New share issue	95,000
Shareholders' equity after issue	375,000
Unamortized acquisition differential	75,000
	450,000
NCI's share	28%
	126,000
NCI before subsidiary share issue	35,500
Increase in non-controlling interest	$ 90,500

The effect of this transaction on the consolidated financial statements can be depicted as follows:

The consolidated entity received cash from the non-controlling interest.

Cash	95,000	
Non-controlling interest		90,500
Contributed surplus		4,500

This transaction increased the equity of both the controlling and the non-controlling interests. The $95,000 cash inflow should appear in the financing activities section of the cash flow statement and would be described as "Issuance of shares by subsidiary to non-controlling interest."

The excess of proceeds over the value of the transfer of equity to the non-controlling interests was recorded directly to retained earnings.

Disclosure Requirements   The disclosure requirements for a business combination were listed near the end of Chapter 3. Exhibit 8.2 is an extract from Goldcorp Inc.'s 2011 consolidated financial statements. It provides an example of disclosure when a parent sells a partial interest in a subsidiary. Goldcorp is a gold producer engaged in the operation, exploration, development, and acquisition of precious metal

| EXHIBIT 8.2 | Extracts in Part from Goldcorp's 2011 Financial Statements |

30. NON-CONTROLLING INTERESTS

	El Morro	Terrane	Total
At January 1, 2010	$ –	$ 51	$ 51
Acquisition of El Morro project	213	–	213
Share of net earnings (loss)	–	(8)	(8)
Impact of change in ownership interest			
Prior to disposition of remaining interest in Terrane (a)	–	53	53
Disposition of remaining interest in Terrane (b)	–	(96)	(96)
	–	(43)	(43)
At December 31, 2010	$213	$ –	$213
Share of net earnings (loss)	–	–	–
At December 31, 2011	$213	$ –	$213

EXHIBIT 8.2   *(continued)*

(a) On April 16, 2010, Terrane completed a bought-deal financing agreement with a syndicate of underwriters for the sale of 63,637,000 Units which were sold to the public at a price of C$1.10 per Unit for gross proceeds of C$70 million ($70 million). Each Unit consists of one common share and one-half common share purchase warrant. Each whole warrant entitles the holder to purchase one additional common share of Terrane at a price of C$1.50 per share for a period of 12 months from closing. Concurrent with the issuance of Units to the underwriters, 27,273,000 Units were issued at the same price on a non-brokered private placement basis to Goldcorp for C$30 million ($30 million). These issuances resulted in a decrease to Goldcorp's interest in Terrane and gave rise to an increase in non-controlling interests of $50 million. An adjustment was made to increase retained earnings directly by $15 million to reflect the difference between the increase in non-controlling interests and the Company's share of proceeds received. Issuances of common shares resulting from exercises of stock options outstanding during the period from January 1, 2010 to October 20, 2010 also gave rise to an increase in non-controlling interests of $3 million and a decrease of $1 million to retained earnings.

(b) On October 20, 2010, the Company disposed of its remaining 58.1% interest in Terrane and derecognized the carrying amount of non-controlling interests on the date of disposition (note 11(b)).

Source: Reproduced with permission from http://www.goldcorp.com/files/Goldcorp_AR%202011_L.pdf

---

properties in Canada, the United States, Mexico, and Central and South America. In 2010, it reported a direct credit of $14 million to retained earnings pertaining to partial sales of operating companies under continuing control. In our previous examples, we recorded the gain from these transfers of equity in contributed surplus. In both cases, the gain went directly to shareholders' equity without being recognized in net income. Both methods are acceptable under IFRSs.

> The difference between Goldcorp's share of proceeds from issuance of new shares and the increase in non-controlling interests was recorded directly to retained earnings.

Subsidiary with Preferred Shares Outstanding

L04

All of the consolidation examples that we have used up to this point have assumed that the subsidiary companies have only one class of shares, common shares, in their capital structures. We now examine situations where the subsidiary also has preferred shares. The basic concepts of consolidation do not change, but when there is more than one class of shares outstanding, there is an additional problem involved in determining the amount of non-controlling interest in the net assets and net income of the subsidiary. The following example will illustrate the approach that is used.

Illustration—Preferred Shareholdings

On December 31, Year 1, the shareholders' equity of Sonco Inc. was as follows:

Preferred shares, $10 dividend, cumulative, redeemable at $105 per share	
Issued and outstanding 1,000 shares	$100,000
Common shares	
Issued and outstanding 30,000 shares	360,000
Total share capital	460,000
Retained earnings (Note 1)	140,000
	$600,000

> If the subsidiary were wound up today, how much of its equity would go to the preferred shareholders?

Note 1: On December 31, Year 1, dividends on preferred shares were one year in arrears.

On January 1, Year 2, Parco Ltd. purchased 27,000 common shares of Sonco for $450,000. The acquisition differential was allocated entirely to franchise agreements, to be amortized over a 10-year period.

Because the parent company acquired control by purchasing 90% of the voting common shares, the non-controlling interest consists of the shareholdings represented by 10% of the common shares and 100% of the preferred shares. In order to calculate any acquisition differential associated with the common share purchase, and the amount of the non-controlling interest in both classes of shares, it is necessary to split the shareholders' equity of Sonco into its preferred and common share capital components in the following manner:

<table>
<tr><td></td><td>Total</td><td>Preferred</td><td>Common</td></tr>
<tr><td>Preferred shares</td><td>$100,000</td><td>$100,000</td><td>$ —</td></tr>
<tr><td>Redemption premium on preferred</td><td>—</td><td>5,000</td><td>(5,000)</td></tr>
<tr><td>Common shares</td><td>360,000</td><td>—</td><td>360,000</td></tr>
<tr><td>Total share capital</td><td>460,000</td><td>105,000</td><td>355,000</td></tr>
<tr><td>Retained earnings</td><td>140,000</td><td>10,000</td><td>130,000</td></tr>
<tr><td></td><td>$600,000</td><td>$115,000</td><td>$485,000</td></tr>
</table>

The preferred shareholders would get the first $115,000, and the common shareholders would get the rest.

The $115,000 allocated to preferred share capital represents the total amount that the company would have to pay to the preferred shareholders if the preferred shares were redeemed on this date. It is made up of the redemption price on 1,000 shares ($105,000) and the one year's dividends in arrears ($10,000) on these shares.

By using the two components of shareholders' equity, both the acquisition differential and the non-controlling interest on the date of acquisition can be calculated, as follows:

The acquisition differential on the common shares is calculated in the same way as before.

Cost of 90% of common shares	$450,000
Implied value of 100% of Sonco's common shares	$500,000
Carrying amount of common shares of Sonco	485,000
Acquisition differential	15,000
Allocated: Franchise agreement	15,000
Balance	$ —0—
Non-controlling interest, January 1, Year 2	
Preferred shares (115,000 × 100%)	$115,000
Common shares (500,000 × 10%)	50,000
	$165,000

The preparation of the consolidated balance sheet on January 1, Year 2, will not be illustrated, but it should be obvious that the only difference from previous examples lies in how the non-controlling interest is calculated on this date.

The financial statements of Parco and Sonco on December 31, Year 2, are shown in Exhibit 8.3. Parco uses the cost method to account for its investment.

In order to prepare the Year 2 consolidated financial statements, it is again necessary to split the shareholders' equity of Sonco into its preferred and common share components. Because there has been no change in total share capital, the allocation of this component is identical to the one made as at January 1 (see above).

EXHIBIT 8.3

YEAR 2 INCOME STATEMENTS

	Parco	Sonco	
Revenues—miscellaneous	$750,000	$420,000	The parent received 90%
Dividends from Sonco	27,000	—	of the dividends paid to
	777,000	420,000	common shareholders.
Expenses—miscellaneous	688,000	360,000	
Net income	$ 89,000	$ 60,000	

YEAR 2 RETAINED EARNINGS STATEMENTS

	Parco	Sonco
Balance, January 1	$381,000	$140,000
Net income	89,000	60,000
	470,000	200,000
Dividends	90,000	50,000
Balance, December 31	$380,000	$150,000

BALANCE SHEETS—December 31, Year 2

	Parco	Sonco	
Assets—miscellaneous	$ 510,000	$810,000	The parent has an
Investment in Sonco—at cost	450,000	—	investment in the common
	$ 960,000	$810,000	shares of the subsidiary
			but no investment in the
Liabilities	$ 180,000	$200,000	preferred shares.
Preferred shares	—	100,000	
Common shares	400,000	360,000	
Retained earnings	380,000	150,000	
	$ 960,000	$810,000	

But retained earnings *has* changed, so we will allocate the retained earnings statement in the following manner:

	Total	Preferred	Common	
Balance, January 1, Year 2	$140,000	$ 10,000	$130,000	Any calculations involving
Net income (see point 2)	60,000	10,000	50,000	the subsidiary's equity must
	200,000	20,000	180,000	be split between common
Dividends (see point 1)	50,000	20,000	30,000	and preferred shareholders.
Balance, December 31, Year 2	$150,000	$ —0—	$150,000	

It is important to note the following regarding the allocation process:

1. All dividends in arrears plus the current year's dividends must be paid to preferred shareholders before any dividends are paid to common shareholders. In this situation the dividends paid by Sonco were as follows:

Preferred ($10 × 1,000 × 2 years)	$20,000
Common	30,000
	$50,000

For cumulative shares, the preferred shareholders' claim on income is one year's worth of dividends in any given year, whether or not dividends are declared in that year.

2. When preferred shares are cumulative, the preferred shareholders are entitled to income equal to the yearly dividend, even when the company has no income or has suffered a loss for the year. This means that the net income (or loss) for a particular year must be allocated to its preferred and common shareholders. In the situation we are examining, the Year 2 net income is allocated as follows:

To preferred shareholders	$ 10,000
To common shareholders	50,000
Total net income	$ 60,000

The allocation of total shareholders' equity as at December 31, Year 2, can now be prepared as shown below:

	Total	Preferred	Common
Share capital	$460,000	$105,000	$355,000
Retained earnings	150,000	–0–	150,000
	$610,000	$105,000	$505,000

Because Parco has used the cost method to account for its investment, we must make the two calculations shown in Exhibit 8.4 before preparing the Year 2 consolidated financial statements:

The Year 2 consolidated financial statements are shown in Exhibit 8.5.

EXHIBIT 8.4

CALCULATION OF CONSOLIDATED NET INCOME, YEAR 2

The preferred shareholders' claim on income is one year's worth of dividends.

Net income, Parco		$ 89,000
Less: Common dividends from Sonco (90% × 30,000)		27,000
		62,000
Net income, Sonco	60,000	
Less: Allocated to preferred shares	10,000	
Net income, common shares	50,000	
Less: Acquisition-differential amortization (15,000 ÷ 10)	1,500 (a)	
Adjusted income for common shares		48,500
Income for preferred shares		10,000
Consolidated net income		$120,500
Attributable to		
Shareholders of Parent (62,000 + 90% × 48,500)		$105,650 (b)
Non-controlling interest		
Preferred net income (100% × 10,000)	10,000	
Common net income (10% × 48,500)	4,850	
		14,850 (c)

CALCULATION OF NON-CONTROLLING INTEREST
at December 31, Year 2

The non-controlling interest owns all of the preferred shares and 10% of the common shares of the subsidiary.

Non-controlling interest	
Date of acquisition (see text just prior to Exhibit 8.3)	$165,000
Share of income from subsidiary (c)	14,850
Share of dividends (100% × 20,000 + 10% × 30,000)	(23,000)
At December 31, Year 2	$156,850 (d)

EXHIBIT 8.5

YEAR 2 CONSOLIDATED STATEMENTS
(When Subsidiary Has Preferred Shares)
PARCO LTD.
CONSOLIDATED INCOME STATEMENT
for the Year Ended December 31, Year 2

Revenues (750,000 + 420,000)	$1,170,000
Expenses (688,000 + 360,000 + **[4a] 1,500**)	1,049,500
Net income	$ 120,500
Attributable to	
Shareholders of Parent **(4b)**	$ 105,650
Non-controlling interest **(4c)**	14,850

The non-controlling interest includes all of the income pertaining to the preferred shares and 10% of the income pertaining to the common shares.

PARCO LTD.
CONSOLIDATED RETAINED EARNINGS STATEMENT
for the Year Ended December 31, Year 2

Balance, January 1	$ 381,000
Net income	105,650
	486,650
Dividends	90,000
Balance, December 31	$ 396,650

PARCO LTD.
CONSOLIDATED BALANCE SHEET
at December 31, Year 2

Assets—miscellaneous (510,000 + 810,000)	$1,320,000
Franchise agreements (15,000 − **[4a] 1,500**)	13,500
	$1,333,500
Liabilities (180,000 + 200,000)	$ 380,000
Common shares	400,000
Retained earnings	396,650
Non-controlling interest **(4d)**	156,850
	$1,333,500

The subsidiary's common and preferred shares do not appear on the consolidated balance sheet.

Other Types of Preferred Shares

In the example above, the preferred shares are cumulative. If the shares were non-cumulative, net income would be allocated to the preferred shares only if preferred dividends were declared during the year, since dividends are never in arrears with this type of preferred share. If dividends are not declared in a particular year, no income would be allocated to the preferred shares because the preferred shareholders would never get a dividend for that year. If the preferred shares are participating, the allocation of net income will follow the participation provisions.

The amount of income, dividends, and equity belonging to the preferred shareholders depends on the rights of the preferred shareholders.

Subsidiary Preferred Shares Owned by Parent

A parent company may own all or a portion of its subsidiary's preferred shares in addition to its common share investment. When the cost of the investment in preferred shares is different from the carrying amount of the shares acquired, a problem arises as to how to treat the preferred share acquisition differential in the consolidated financial statements. Since preferred shares do not typically share in earnings beyond the amount of the specified dividend rate (the exception is fully participating shares), the value of the preferred shares is usually based on the present value of future dividends and not any goodwill or fair value excess for identifiable net assets. Therefore, it would not be appropriate to allocate any acquisition differential to identifiable net assets or goodwill.

> Any acquisition differential related to the preferred shares should be treated similarly to a retirement of the preferred shares by the subsidiary itself.

Since the dividend rate is usually specified when the preferred shares are issued, there is a fair amount of certainty as to the amount of future dividends. Interest rates have the biggest impact on the value of preferred shares because they affect the discount rate used in determining the present value of future dividends; the higher the discount rate, the lower the value of the preferred shares, and vice versa. The acquisition of the subsidiary's preferred shares by the parent is viewed as a retirement of the preferred shares. Any acquisition differential should be charged to consolidated retained earnings or credited to contributed surplus. This practice is consistent with the accounting treatment when a company repurchases its own shares from the market.

Let us now assume that in addition to Parco's 90% investment in Sonco's common shares, it also purchased 30% of Sonco's cumulative preferred shares for $40,000. The purchase price would be allocated as follows:

Cost of 30% of preferred shares		$40,000
Carrying amount of Sonco's preferred shares	115,000	
Portion acquired by Parco (30%)		34,500
Acquisition differential		5,500
Allocated to consolidated retained earnings		5,500
Balance		$ —0—

The non-controlling interest's share of the preferred shares at January 1, Year 2 would be $80,500 (115,000 × 70%).

If Parco used the equity method to account for both investments, the journal entry to record its investment in Sonco's preferred shares would be as follows:

Investment in Sonco's preferred shares	34,500	
Retained earnings	5,500	
Cash		40,000

Consolidated retained earnings at the date of acquisition would be $375,500 (Parco's separate-entity retained earnings of 381,000 − premium paid to retire Sonco's preferred shares of 5,500).

See Self-Study Problem 2 for a comprehensive consolidation problem where the parent has an investment in both the common shares and preferred shares of its subsidiary.

L05 INDIRECT SHAREHOLDINGS

When one company has control over another company, financial reporting by means of consolidated financial statements is required. In all the examples that we have used up to this point, the parent has had a direct ownership of over 50%

of the common shares of the subsidiary. We continue to assume that over 50% ownership of the voting shares is necessary for control, but we now modify the assumption to allow this percentage to be achieved by both direct and indirect ownership. The following diagrams illustrate both direct and indirect holdings. In this first diagram, B and C are subsidiaries of A through direct control:

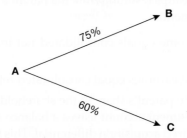

The second example, below, illustrates indirect control. G is a subsidiary of F, but F, in turn, is a subsidiary of E. Because E can control the voting shares of G through its control of F, G is also a subsidiary of E.

Both F and G are considered to be subsidiaries of E and therefore should be consolidated with E.

In the third example, K is a subsidiary of J through direct control. L is also a subsidiary of J through indirect control, because 55% of its voting shares are controlled directly or indirectly by J, even though only 43% [25% + (60% × 30%)] of L's net income will flow to J under the equity method of accounting.

J can control L because it has control of 55% of the votes at L's shareholders' meetings.

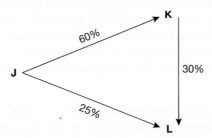

While many Canadian companies have intercorporate structures that are far more complex than those illustrated, the consolidation procedures for indirect holdings are not as complicated as the diagrams might indicate. Remember that if a parent company has 50 subsidiaries, the amount of cash appearing on the consolidated balance sheet is the sum of the cash from 51 separate balance sheets. This basic concept applies to most items appearing in the consolidated statements. In addition, we emphasized in past chapters the following statements that describe the fundamental relationships resulting from the parent's use of the equity method to account for its investment:

The parent's separate-entity net income under the equity method should be equal to consolidated net income attributable to the parent's shareholders.

1. The parent's net income equals consolidated net income attributable to the parent.

2. The parent's retained earnings equal consolidated retained earnings.

3. The elimination of the parent's share of the shareholders' equity of the subsidiary against the investment account leaves a balance consisting of the parent's share of the unamortized acquisition differential. This balance is used to revalue the net assets of the subsidiary when the consolidated balance sheet is prepared.

4. The portion of the shareholders' equity of the subsidiary that is not eliminated, and the non-controlling interest's share of the unamortized acquisition differential appear on the consolidated balance sheet as non-controlling interest.

The principles applied when consolidating directly controlled subsidiaries apply equally well when consolidating indirectly controlled subsidiaries.

Since these fundamental relationships also apply when we have indirect holdings, the key to the preparation of consolidated statements when control is achieved by a mixture of direct and indirect investments is the use of the equity method of accounting for each investment for internal record-keeping purposes. (If the cost method has been used, adjustments to the equity method must be made.) The following example will illustrate these concepts.

Parent Inc. owns 80% of the common shares of Subone Ltd. (which is sufficient for control) and 45% of the common shares of Subtwo Ltd. (which we assume is not sufficient for control). However, Subone owns 25% of the common shares of Subtwo. This investment combined with the parent's 45% investment gives the parent control of 70% of the voting shares; therefore, Subtwo is considered a subsidiary of Parent.

Each investment is accounted for using the equity method for internal record-keeping purposes. In order to simplify the illustration, we assume that on acquisition date the fair values of the identifiable net assets of the investee corporations were equal to their carrying amounts, with the acquisition differentials from each investment being allocated to unrecorded computer databases.

We will illustrate the preparation of consolidated financial statements for Year 6, during which Parent had a net income from its own operations amounting to $135,000. Subone had a net income from its own operations amounting to $75,000, while the net income of Subtwo was $40,000. Exhibit 8.6, which shows the calculation of the Year 6 consolidated net income, is useful because it illustrates the use of the equity method of accounting by both Subone and Parent.

Regarding the preparation and interpretation of Exhibit 8.6, the following should be noted:

The amortization of the acquisition differential is allocated to the subsidiary to which it pertains.

1. Acquisition-differential amortizations are recorded by each company owned by another company in the group. This is the first adjustment shown. The amounts have been assumed. Any adjustments required for intercompany gains and losses are also made here (as would the deduction for intercompany dividends if the cost method had been used by Parent and Subone).

EXHIBIT 8.6

CALCULATION OF CONSOLIDATED NET INCOME—Year 6

	Parent	Subone	Subtwo	Total
Net income before				
investment income	$135,000	$75,000	$40,000	$250,000
Less: Database amortization—Subtwo			(300)	(300) **(a)**
			39,700	
Allocate Subtwo				
25% to Subone		9,925	(9,925)	
45% to Parent	17,865		(17,865)	
Less: Database amortization—Subone		(200)		(200) **(b)**
Consolidated net income	152,865	84,725	11,910	249,500
Allocate Subone				
80% to Parent	67,780	(67,780)		
Non-controlling interest		$16,945	$11,910	28,855 **(c)**
Parent net income—equity method	$220,645			
Consolidated net income				
attributable to parent				$220,645 **(d)**

Subone accrues its share of Subtwo's income before Parent accrues its share of Subone's income.

2. Because Parent cannot record its 80% share of Subone's net income until Subone has recorded its 25% share of Subtwo's net income, Subtwo's net income is allocated first.

3. Subone's net income using the equity method can now be determined.

4. After Subone's net income has been allocated, Parent's net income using the equity method is determined. This amount, of course, equals consolidated net income attributable to Parent.

The allocation of income to investors must start at the lowest level of the corporate hierarchy and work its way up.

5. The portion of the net income of Subtwo and Subone that was not allocated is the non-controlling interest in that net income.

6. The "Total" column shows amounts that appear in the consolidated income statement. Consolidated net income attributable to the parent is $220,645, while non-controlling interest is $28,855.

Exhibit 8.7 shows the Year 6 financial statements of the three companies.

EXHIBIT 8.7

INCOME STATEMENTS—Year 6

	Parent	Subone	Subtwo
Miscellaneous revenues	$475,000	$285,000	$90,000
Investment income—Subone	67,780	—	—
Investment income—Subtwo	17,865	9,925	—
	560,645	294,925	90,000
Miscellaneous expenses	340,000	210,000	50,000
Net income	$220,645	$ 84,925	$40,000

For these separate-entity statements, the investor has used the equity method to account for its investment.

(continued)

EXHIBIT 8.7 (*continued*)

RETAINED EARNINGS STATEMENTS—Year 6

	Parent	Subone	Subtwo
Balance, January 1	$279,120	$116,400	$ 80,000
Net income	220,645	84,925	40,000
	499,765	201,325	120,000
Dividends	45,000	30,000	10,000
Balance, December 31	$454,765	$171,325	$110,000

BALANCE SHEETS—December 31, Year 6

	Parent	Subone	Subtwo
Other assets	$608,500	$402,925	$460,000
Investment in Subone	281,900	—	—
Investment in Subtwo	104,365	53,400	—
	$994,765	$456,325	$460,000
Liabilities	$300,000	$110,000	$250,000
Common shares	240,000	175,000	100,000
Retained earnings	454,765	171,325	110,000
	$994,765	$456,325	$460,000

In preparing the Year 6 consolidated income statement, we eliminate the three investment income accounts and replace them with the revenues and expenses of the two subsidiaries, the database amortization expense, and the non-controlling interest in the net incomes of the subsidiaries. The consolidated retained earnings statement is identical to that of Parent and requires no preparation.

In preparing the consolidated balance sheet, we eliminate the investors' portion of the shareholders' equity of the investee companies against the investment accounts; this leaves a balance consisting of the unamortized acquisition differentials. The amount of shareholders' equity not eliminated represents non-controlling interest. The following calculations illustrate this:

The unamortized acquisition differential can be derived by backing out the parent's share of the subsidiary's equity from the investment account.

Parent:

Investment in Subone		$281,900
Shareholders' equity, Subone		
Common shares	175,000	
Retained earnings	171,325	
	346,325	
Parent ownership	80%	277,060
Balance—Parent's share of unamortized databases		4,840
Non-controlling interest's share of unamortized databases (assumed)		1,210
Total unamortized databases from Subone		$ 6,050
Investment in Subtwo		$104,365
Shareholders' equity, Subtwo		
Common shares	100,000	
Retained earnings	110,000	
	210,000	
Parent's ownership	45%	94,500
Balance—Parent's share of unamortized databases		9,865

Subone:

Investment in Subtwo		53,400
Shareholders' equity, Subtwo (above)	210,000	
Subone ownership	25%	52,500
Balance—Investor's share of unamortized databases		900
Parent's total share of unamortized databases		10,765
Non-controlling interest's share of unamortized databases (assumed)		4,615
Total unamortized databases from Subtwo		$ 15,380

The unamortized acquisition differential relating to the non-controlling interest is an assumed figure, which must be incorporated in the consolidated financial statements.

CALCULATION OF NON-CONTROLLING INTEREST
at December 31, Year 6

Shareholders' equity, Subone (346,325 × 20% + 1,210)	$ 70,475
Shareholders' equity, Subtwo (210,000 × 30% + 4,615)	67,615
	$138,090

Exhibit 8.8 shows the preparation of the Year 6 consolidated financial statements using the direct approach.

EXHIBIT 8.8

PARENT INC.
CONSOLIDATED FINANCIAL STATEMENTS
at December 31, Year 6
CONSOLIDATED INCOME STATEMENT

Miscellaneous revenues (475,000 + 285,000 + 90,000)	$ 850,000
Miscellaneous expense (340,000 + 210,000 + 50,000)	600,000
Database amortization (**[6a] 300 + [6b] 200**)	500
	600,500
Net income	$ 249,500
Attributable to	
Shareholders of Parent **(6d)**	$ 220,645
Non-controlling interest **(6c)**	28,855

The consolidated income statement includes the amortization of the acquisition differential for a period of time for the directly controlled and indirectly controlled subsidiaries.

CONSOLIDATED RETAINED EARNINGS STATEMENT

Balance, January 1	$ 279,120
Net income	220,645
	499,765
Dividends	45,000
Balance, December 31	$ 454,765

CONSOLIDATED BALANCE SHEET

Other assets (608,500 + 402,925 + 460,000)	$1,471,425
Databases (**6,050 + 15,380**)	21,430
	$1,492,855
Liabilities (300,000 + 110,000 + 250,000)	$ 660,000
Common shares	240,000
Retained earnings	454,765
Non-controlling interest	138,090
	$1,492,855

The consolidated balance sheet includes the unamortized acquisition differential at a point in time for the directly controlled and indirectly controlled subsidiaries.

[L06] ANALYSIS AND INTERPRETATION OF FINANCIAL STATEMENTS

Under ASPE, the parent company can report its investment in a subsidiary using the cost method or the equity method or on a consolidated basis. In this chapter, we prepared consolidated financial statements where the subsidiary had preferred shares in its capital structure. We will now compare how the financial statements would look if the parent had used the cost method or equity method.

Exhibit 8.9 presents the Year 2 income statements and balance sheets for Parco's separate-entity statements under two scenarios: (1) when Parco uses the cost method and (2) when Parco uses the equity method. The last column presents the consolidated financial statements taken from Exhibit 8.5. The values for the cost method are taken directly from Exhibit 8.3. The values for the equity method are the same as the cost method except for the investment income, retained earnings, and investment in Sonco. The investment income replaces the dividend income and is the amount required to make net income under the equity method equal to

EXHIBIT 8.9	Impact of Presentation Method on Debt-to-Equity and Return-on-Equity Ratios

INCOME STATEMENTS
for the Year Ended December 31, Year 2

	Parco-Separate Entity		Cons.
	Cost	Equity	
Revenues—miscellaneous	$750,000	$750,000	$1,170,000
Dividends from Sonco	27,000		
Investment income from Sonco		43,650	
	777,000	793,650	1,170,000
Expenses—miscellaneous	688,000	688,000	1,049,500
Net income	$ 89,000	$105,650	$ 120,500
Attributable to			
Shareholders of Parco			$ 105,650
Non-controlling interest			14,850

The net income for the parent's separate-entity income statement under the equity method is equal to consolidated net income attributable to the shareholders of the parent.

BALANCE SHEETS
at December 31, Year 2

	Cost	Equity	Cons.
Assets—miscellaneous	$510,000	$510,000	$1,320,000
Investment in Sonco	450,000	466,650	
Franchise agreements			13,500
	$960,000	$976,650	$1,333,500
Liabilities	$180,000	$180,000	$380,000
Common shares	400,000	400,000	400,000
Retained earnings	380,000	396,650	396,650
Non-controlling interest			156,850
	$960,000	$976,650	$1,333,500
Debt to equity	0.23	0.23	0.40
Return on equity			
– for all shareholders	n/a	n/a	12.6%
– for shareholders of Parco	11.4%	13.3%	13.3%

consolidated net income attributable to the shareholders of Parco. Retained earnings under the equity method are equal to consolidated retained earnings. The investment account under the equity method changes by the same amount as the change in retained earnings. The exhibit also indicates the debt-to-equity ratio and return-on-equity ratio for each set of financial statements.

Note the following from Exhibit 8.9:

- The separate-entity net income and return-on-equity ratio under the cost and equity methods are different.

- The separate-entity net income and retained earnings under the equity method are equal to consolidated net income attributable to the shareholders of Parco and consolidated retained earnings, respectively.

- The separate-entity return on equity under the equity method is equal to the consolidated return on equity for the shareholders of Parco.

- The solvency position looks worst on the consolidated financial statements because the subsidiary's debt is included on the consolidated financial statements. This increases the debt-to-equity ratio.

> Retained earnings for the parent's separate-entity balance sheet under the equity method are equal to consolidated retained earnings.
>
> The return on equity for the separate-entity statements under the equity method is equal to the consolidated return on equity for the shareholders of Parent.

ASPE DIFFERENCES

L07

- As mentioned in Chapter 3, private companies can either consolidate their subsidiaries or report their investments in subsidiaries under the cost or equity method.

- When consolidated statements are not prepared, any investment in preferred shares that are quoted in an active market should be reported at fair value, with any adjustments to fair value reported in net income. These are the requirements normally applied to equity instruments traded in an active market. Investments in preferred shares that are not quoted in an active market should be reported at cost less accumulated impairment losses and the impairment losses reported in net income, unless the entity has made an irrevocable election to measure at fair value.

U.S. GAAP DIFFERENCES

U.S. GAAP and IFRSs for topics in this chapter are virtually the same.

SUMMARY

In this chapter, we examined four topics that present special problems in consolidated financial statement preparation. While the consolidated balance sheet and income statement are prepared by combining the statements of the parent and its subsidiaries, the consolidated cash flow statement is best prepared by analyzing the changes in successive consolidated balance sheets.

The next topic addressed changes in the parent's percentage ownership and the effect that such changes have on the non-controlling interest, and particularly on unamortized acquisition differentials. These ownership changes also require special attention when the consolidated cash flow statement is prepared.

Preferred shares in the capital structure of subsidiary companies present unique problems in calculating non-controlling interest if the parent's ownership of the preferred shares is not the same as its ownership of the common shares. The problem is solved by allocating shareholders' equity and any changes therein to preferred and common share components.

Control by a parent company can be achieved through direct ownership of the subsidiary's voting shares or through indirect ownership by other subsidiaries or investees. If the equity method is used for all of the investment accounts, the consolidation process is fairly easy because the major problem involved with indirect holdings is how to determine the amount for non-controlling interest. If the cost method is used to account for the investments, we apply the basic procedure of adjusting from cost to equity, and then continue preparing the consolidated statements in the normal manner. This adjustment from cost to equity can be very involved when the affiliation structure is complex.

Significant Changes in GAAP in the Last Three Years

When the investor first obtains significant influence over an investee, any previous investments in the investee, which were reported under the cost method, are revalued to fair value and the revaluation gain or loss is reported in net income.

Changes Expected in GAAP in the Next Three Years

The direct method may be required for the cash flow statement. The notes to the financial statements would require a reconciliation of cash flows (starting point) to net income (ending point).

SELF-STUDY PROBLEM 1

LO2, 3   On January 1, Year 1, Mio Company acquired 1,000 ordinary shares of Aaron Company for $12,000 when the shareholders' equity of Aaron was as follows:

Ordinary shares (10,000 no par value shares issued and outstanding)	$50,000
Retained earnings	40,000
	$90,000

In addition, Mio had the following investments and divestments in Aaron:

Date	Action	# of shares	Price
Jan. 1, Year 2	Bought	2,000	26,000
Jan. 1, Year 3	Bought	2,500	35,000
Jan. 1, Year 4	Bought	3,000	45,000
Jan. 1, Year 5	Sold	1,500	24,000

The following are the statements of retained earnings for Mio from Year 1 to Year 5:

	Year 1	Year 2	Year 3	Year 4	Year 5
Retained earnings, beginning of year	$70,000	$78,000	$87,000	$ 96,000	$105,000
Profit	17,000	18,000	19,000	20,000	21,000
Dividends	(9,000)	(9,000)	(10,000)	(11,000)	(12,000)
Retained earnings, end of year	$78,000	$87,000	$96,000	$105,000	$114,000

The following are the statements of retained earnings for Aaron from Year 1 to Year 5:

	Year 1	Year 2	Year 3	Year 4	Year 5
Retained earnings, beginning of year	$40,000	$44,000	$48,000	$52,000	$57,000
Profit	10,000	11,000	12,000	13,000	14,000
Dividends	(6,000)	(7,000)	(8,000)	(8,000)	(10,000)
Retained earnings, end of year	$44,000	$48,000	$52,000	$57,000	$61,000

Additional Information

- For internal record-keeping purposes, Mio uses the cost method to account for its investment in Aaron.
- Aaron's ordinary shares are publicly traded. The market value of the shares at the close on December 31 of one year was the same as the market value on January 1 of the next year.
- Any acquisition differential is allocated to patents with a life expectancy until December 31, Year 8. Neither company has any patents recorded on their separate-entity records.
- There were no unrealized profits from intercompany transactions since the date of acquisition.

Required:

A. For each of Years 1 to 5, determine and prepare the following items for Mio's general-purpose financial statements prepared in accordance with IFRSs:

    (a) Method to be used to report the investment in Aaron and the balance in the investment account under the relevant reporting method

    (b) Net income attributable to the shareholders of Mio

    (c) Patents

    (d) Non-controlling interests on the balance sheet

    (e) Statement of retained earnings

B. Prepare a schedule to show that the difference in the investment account between the cost and equity methods is equal to the difference in the sum of retained earnings (RE) and contributed surplus between the cost and equity methods for each of Years 1 through 5.

SOLUTION TO SELF-STUDY PROBLEM 1

	Jan. 1, Year 2		Jan. 1, Year 3	
Cost of purchase		26,000		35,000
Previous equity interest remeasured at fair value				
1,000 shares @ $13 per share		13,000		
3,000 shares @ $14 per share				42,000
Acquisition cost of 30%		39,000		
Acquisition cost of 55%				77,000
Implied value of 100%				140,000
Carrying amount of Aaron's net assets				
Common shares	50,000		50,000	
Retained earnings	44,000		48,000	
	94,000		98,000	
	30%	28,200	100%	98,000
Acquisition differential		10,800		42,000
Allocated to:				
Patents		10,800		42,000[1]
Patent amortization, Year 2				
(over 7 years)		1,543		(a)

Allocation and amortization of acquisition differential allocated to patents

	Total	Parent	NCI	
Purchase on Jan. 1, Year 3	42,000	23,100	18,900	
Amortization for Year 3 (over 6 years)	(7,000)	(3,850)	(3,150)	(b)
Dec. 31, Year 3	35,000	19,250	15,750	(c)
NCI sold 3,000/4,500 × 15,750		10,500	(10,500)	
	35,000	29,750	5,250	
Amortization for Year 4 (over 5 years)	(7,000)	(5,950)	(1,050)	(d)
Dec. 31, Year 4	28,000	23,800	4,200	(e)
Mio sold 1,500/8,500 × 23,800		(4,200)	4,200	
		19,600	8,400	
Amortization for Year 5 (over 4 years)	(7,000)	(4,900)	(2,100)	(f)
Dec. 31, Year 5	21,000	14,700	6,300	(g)

(a) Investment in Aaron:

	Year 1	Year 2	Year 3	Year 4	Year 5
Percentage owned, end of year	10	30	55	85	70
Reporting method	FVTPL	Equity	Consol[1]	Consol[1]	Consol[1]
Balance, beginning of year	0	13,000	38,657	75,350	114,750
Cost of purchase	12,000	26,000	35,000	45,000	
Adjustment to fair value on Jan 1			3,343[5]		
Loss on equity transaction				(3,900)[8]	
Average cost of investment sold					(20,250)[11]
Equity income		3,300[3]	6,600[6]	11,050[9]	9,800[13]
Dividends received		(2,100)[4]	(4,400)[7]	(6,800)[10]	(7,000)[14]
Amortization of patent		(1,543)[a]	(3,850)[b]	(5,950)[d]	(4,900)[f]
Adjustment to fair value on Dec 31	1,000[2]				
Balance, end of year	13,000	38,657	75,350	114,750	92,400

Notes

1. Consolidated statements are required. Investment account does not appear on consolidated statements. However, equity method will provide all relevant information required for consolidated statements.
2. $26,000/2,000$ shares $\times 1,000$ shares $- 12,000 = 1,000$ through net income
3. $30\% \times 11,000 = 3,300$
4. $30\% \times 7,000 = 2,100$
5. $35,000/2,500 \times 3,000 - 38,657 = 3,343$
6. $55\% \times 12,000 = 6,600$
7. $55\% \times 8,000 = 4,400$
8. $45,000 - 61,650$ (from d below) $\times 3,000/4,500 = 3,900$
9. $85\% \times 13,000 = 11,050$
10. $85\% \times 8,000 = 6,800$
11. $114,750 \times 1,500/8,500 = 20,250$
12. $24,000 - 20,250 = 3,750$ through contributed surplus
13. $70\% \times 14,000 = 9,800$
14. $70\% \times 10,000 = 7,000$
15. $24,000 - (12,000 + 26,000 + 35,000 + 45,000) \times 1,500/8,500 = 3,176$

(b)   Net income attributable to shareholders of Mio:

	Year 1	Year 2	Year 3	Year 4	Year 5
Mio's net income under cost method	17,000	18,000	19,000	20,000	21,000
Dividends from Aaron		$(2,100)^4$	$(4,400)^7$	$(6,800)^{10}$	$(7,000)^{14}$
Reverse gain on sale under cost method					$(3,176)^{15}$
Equity income		$3,300^3$	$6,600^6$	$11,050^9$	$9,800^{13}$
Amortization of patent		$(1,543)^a$	$(3,850)^b$	$(5,950)^d$	$(4,900)^f$
Adjustment to fair value	$1,000^2$		$3,343^5$		
Mio's net income under FVTPL	18,000				
Mio's net income under equity method		17,657	20,693	18,300	15,724

(c)   Patents on consolidated balance sheet:

	Year 1	Year 2	Year 3	Year 4	Year 5
	n/a	n/a	35,000	28,000	21,000

(d)   NCI on balance sheet:

			Year 3	Year 4	Year 5
Aaron's ordinary shares			50,000	50,000	50,000
Aaron's retained earnings			52,000	57,000	61,000
			102,000	107,000	111,000
NCI's share			45%	15%	30%
			45,900	16,050	33,300
NCI's share of patent			$15,750^c$	$4,200^e$	$6,300^g$
Total NCI			61,650	20,250	39,600

(e)   Statement of Retained Earnings:

	Year 1	Year 2	Year 3	Year 4	Year 5
Retained earnings, beginning of year	$70,000	$79,000	$87,657	$ 98,350	$101,750
Profit	18,000	17,657	20,693	18,300	15,724
Loss on equity transaction				$(3,900)^8$	
Dividends	(9,000)	(9,000)	(10,000)	(11,000)	(12,000)
Retained earnings, end of year	$79,000	$87,657	$98,350	$101,750	$105,474

(f)

	Year 1	Year 2	Year 3	Year 4	Year 5
Retained earnings—cost method	$78,000	$87,000	$96,000	$105,000	$114,000
RE & contributed surplus—equity method	79,000	87,657	98,350	101,750	109,224
Difference	$ (1,000)	$ (657)	$ (2,350)	$ 3,250	$ 4,776
Investment—cost method	$12,000	$38,000	$73,000	$118,000	$ 97,176
Investment—equity method	13,000	38,657	75,350	114,750	92,400
Difference	$ (1,000)	$ (657)	$ (2,350)	$ 3,250	$ 4,776

SELF-STUDY PROBLEM 2

LO4   On January 1, Year 1, X Company acquired 800 common shares of Y Company for $24,000 and 180 $5 cumulative, nonparticipating preferred shares for $19,800. On this date, the shareholders' equity accounts of Y Company were as follows:

Common shares (1,000 no par value shares issued)	$10,000
Preferred shares (200 no par value shares issued)	20,000
Retained earnings (note 1)	12,000

Note 1: Preferred dividends were two years in arrears on January 1, Year 1.

The income statements for the two companies for the year ended December 31, Year 5, are presented below.

Additional Information

- Any acquisition differential is allocated to patents, to be amortized over 10 years.
- In Year 5, Y paid dividends totalling $9,000. Preferred dividends were two years in arrears on December 31, Year 4.
- X uses the cost method to account for its investment in Y.
- Y purchases merchandise for resale from X. In Year 5, Y purchased $33,000 in merchandise from X and had items in inventory on December 31, Year 5, on which X had made a profit of $2,500. The January 1, Year 5, inventory contained an intercompany profit of $1,400.
- X rents equipment from Y, and in Year 5 paid a rental charge of $3,000 and recorded an account payable to Y of $2,000 for the balance of the rentals.
- On July 1, Year 3, Y sold a building to X at a profit of $13,000. X is depreciating this building on a straight-line basis over a 10-year useful life.
- Depreciation and rent of tangible capital assets are included in distribution expense, whereas amortization of intangible assets is included in selling and administrative expense.
- Y paid $20,000 to X for management fees in Year 5.
- Assume a corporate tax rate of 40%.

INCOME STATEMENTS
for year ended December 31, Year 5

	X Company	Y Company
Sales	$600,000	$400,000
Dividend and management fees	27,500	—
Rental revenue	—	11,200
	627,500	411,200
Cost of sales	343,900	234,700
Distribution expense	25,000	70,000
Selling and administrative expense	207,000	74,000
Interest expense	1,700	6,000
Income tax expense	20,000	9,000
	597,600	393,700
Profit	$ 29,900	$ 17,500

Required:

Prepare a consolidated income statement for Year 5.

SOLUTION TO SELF-STUDY PROBLEM 2

Calculation of acquisition differential

Cost of 90% of preferred shares (180/200)		$19,800
Carrying amount of preferred:		
Preferred shares	$20,000	
Dividends in arrears (200 × 5 × 2)	2,000	
	22,000	
	90%	19,800
Acquisition differential		$ –0–
Cost of 80% of common shares (800/1,000)		$24,000
Implied value of 100% of common shares		$30,000
Carrying amount of common:		
Common shares	10,000	
Retained earnings	12,000	
Less: Preferred dividend arrears	(2,000)	
		20,000
Acquisition differential—patents		$10,000

Intercompany revenues and expenses

Dividends—preferred (90% × 1,000 × 3)		$ 2,700
—common (80% × [9,000 − 3,000])		4,800
		$ 7,500 **(a)**
Management fees		$20,000 **(b)**
Rent (3,000 + 2,000)		$ 5,000 **(c)**
Sales		$33,000 **(d)**

Intercompany profits	Before Tax	Tax 40%	After Tax	
Opening inventory—X selling	$1,400	$ 560	$ 840	**(e)**
Closing inventory—X selling	$2,500	$1,000	$1,500	**(f)**
Building realized—Y selling	$1,300	$ 520	$ 780	**(g)**

Calculation of consolidated net income—Year 5

X net income		$29,900
Less: Dividends from Y **(a)**	7,500	
Closing inventory profit **(f)**	1,500	9,000
		20,900
Add: Opening inventory profit **(e)**		840
		21,740

	Total	Preferred	Common	
Y net income	17,500	1,000	16,500	
Less: Patent amortization (10,000 ÷ 10)			(1,000) **(h)**	
Add: Building profit **(g)**			780	
		1,000	16,280 **(i)**	17,280
Consolidated net income				$39,020

Attributable to
Shareholders of Parent
(21,740 + 90% × 1,000 + 80% × 16,280) $35,664 **(j)**
Non-controlling interest   3,356 **(k)**
(10% × 1,000 + 20% × 16,280)

CONSOLIDATED INCOME STATEMENT—Year 5

Sales (600,000 + 400,000 − **[d] 33,000**)	$967,000
Dividend and management fees (27,500 + 0 − **[a] 7,500** − **[b] 20,000**)	0
Rental revenue (0 + 11,200 − **[c] 5,000**)	6,200
	973,200
Cost of sales (343,900 + 234,700 − **[d] 33,000** − **[e] 1,400** + **[f] 2,500**)	546,700
Distribution (25,000 + 70,000 − **[c] 5,000** − **[g] 1,300**)	88,700
Selling and administrative (207,000 + 74,000 − **[b] 20,000**) + **[h] 1,000**)	262,000
Interest (1,700 + 6,000)	7,700
Income tax (20,000 + 9,000 + **[e] 560** + **[g] 520** − **[f] 1,000**)	29,080
	934,180
Net income	$ 39,020

Attributable to
Shareholders of Parent **(j)** $ 35,664
Non-controlling interest **(k)**   3,356

REVIEW QUESTIONS

LO1   1. Is the consolidated cash flow statement prepared in the same manner as the consolidated balance sheet and income statement? Explain.

LO1   2. A parent company acquired a 75% interest in a subsidiary company in Year 4. The acquisition price was $1,000,000, made up of cash of $700,000 and the parent's common shares with a current market value of $300,000. Explain how this acquisition should be reflected in the Year 4 consolidated cash flow statement.

LO1   3. Why is the amortization of the acquisition differential added back to consolidated net income to compute net cash flow from operating activities in the consolidated cash flow statement?

LO1   4. Why are dividend payments to non-controlling shareholders treated as an outflow of cash in the consolidated cash flow statement but not included as dividends paid in the consolidated retained earnings statement?

LO2   5. When should the change in accounting for a long-term investment from the cost method to the equity method be accounted for retroactively, and when should it be accounted for prospectively?

LO2   6. When a parent increases its investment in a subsidiary from 60 to 75%, should the acquisition differential from the 60% purchase be remeasured at fair value? Explain.

LO3 7. When a parent decreases its investment in a subsidiary from 76 to 60%, should the non-controlling interest be remeasured at fair value? Explain.

LO3 8. A parent company will realize a loss or a gain when its subsidiary issues common shares at a price per share that differs from the carrying amount per share of the parent's investment, and the parent's ownership percentage declines. Explain why this is so. Also explain how the gain or loss is recognized in the financial statements.

LO3 9. If a gain or a loss is realized by a parent company as a result of the sale of a portion of the investment in a subsidiary, should the gain or loss be eliminated in the preparation of the consolidated income statement? Explain.

LO4 10. The shareholders' equity of a subsidiary company contains preferred and common shares. The parent company owns 100% of the subsidiary's common shares. Will the consolidated financial statements show non-controlling interest? Explain.

LO4 11. A company's net income for the year was $17,000. During the year, the company paid dividends on its non-cumulative preferred shares amounting to $12,000. Calculate the amount of the year's net income that "belongs to" the common shares.

LO4 12. Explain how an acquisition differential from an investment in preferred shares should be reflected in the consolidated financial statements.

LO4 13. Explain how the non-controlling interest in the net assets and net income of a subsidiary is reported when the parent owns 90% of the subsidiary's common shares and 30% of the subsidiary's cumulative preferred shares.

LO4 14. Explain the difference in the calculation of consolidated net income attributable to shareholders of parent and consolidated retained earnings depending on whether the preferred shares of a subsidiary are cumulative or non-cumulative.

LO5 15. What is the major consolidation problem associated with indirect shareholdings?

CASES

Case 8-1
LO3
On December 31, Year 7, Pepper Company, a public company, agreed to a business combination with Salt Limited, an unrelated private company. Pepper issued 72 of its common shares for all (50) of the outstanding common shares of Salt. This transaction increased the number of outstanding Pepper shares from 100 to 172. Pepper's shares were trading at around $10 per share in days leading up to the business combination. The condensed balance sheets for the two companies on this date were as follows:

	Pepper		Salt	
	Book value	Fair value	Book value	Fair value
Tangible assets	$500	$600	$100	$120
Intangible assets (excluding goodwill)	200	500	250	350
	$700		$350	
Liabilities	$400	410	$170	200
Shareholders' equity	300		180	
	$700		$350	

On January 1, Year 8, Pepper sold 40% of its investment in Salt to an unrelated third party for $450 in cash. The CFO at Pepper stated that Salt must have been worth $1,125 if the unrelated third party was willing to pay $450 for a 40% interest in Salt. If so, Pepper saved $405 by buying Salt for only $720. Accordingly, the CFO wants to recognize a gain of $405 in the Year 7 income statement to reflect the true value of the Salt shares.

You have been asked by the CFO to prepare a presentation to senior management on the accounting implications for the business combination and subsequent sale of 40% of the investment. She would like you to consider two alternative methods of valuing Salt on the consolidated balance at the date of acquisition— one based on cost of purchase and one based on the implied value of the subsidiary based on the sales price on January 1, Year 8.

Required:

Prepare this presentation, answering the following questions:

(a) How would Pepper's consolidated balance sheet differ at the date of acquisition under the two different valuation alternatives? Which method best reflects economic reality? Which method is required by GAAP?

(b) How would Pepper's consolidated balance sheet look after the sale of the 40% interest in Salt to the unrelated third party under the two alternatives?

Case 8-2
LO2

For the past 10 years, Prince Company (Prince) has owned 75,000 or 75% of the common shares of Stiff Inc. (Stiff). Elizabeth Winer owns another 20% and the other 5% are widely held. Although Prince has the controlling interest, you would never know it during the annual shareholders' meetings. Winer keeps the board of directors on its toes by asking a lot of tough questions and continually threatening legal action if her rights as a minority shareholder are not protected.

Rick Impatient owns 100% of the shares of Prince. After Prince's latest shareholders' meeting, he decided that Prince would offer to purchase Winer's shares in Stiff or Prince would sell its interest in Stiff as Impatient was tired of all of the heckling from Winer. The shares of Stiff were recently trading for $100 per share.

On November 13, Year 13, Prince offered to pay $108 per share to Winer for her 20% interest in Stiff. To Impatient's surprise, Winer accepted the offer and the transaction was consummated on December 31, Year 13. At December 31, Year 13, the unamortized acquisition differential relating to prior purchases by Prince was $500,000, which pertained solely to goodwill. On the closing date, the shares of Stiff had a carrying amount of $70 per share and all identifiable net assets had a fair value equal to carrying amount except for unrecognized patents, which had a fair value of $1.3 million and an estimated useful life of four years.

The CFO of Prince wants to recognize the entire acquisition differential related to the new purchase from Winer as goodwill in order to minimize the impact on earnings for Years 13 and 14. The controller, on the other hand, believes that some of the acquisition differential should be charged to income in Year 13 as a loss because of the excessive price paid for the shares.

Required:

How would you resolve the dispute? Provide the arguments to support your position, and indicate the impact of your decision on consolidated profit attributable to Prince's shareholders for Years 13 and 14. State your assumptions.

Case 8-3
LO3
Traveller Bus Lines Inc. (TBL) is a wholly owned subsidiary of Canada Transport Enterprises Inc. (CTE), a publicly traded transportation and communications conglomerate. TBL is primarily in the business of operating buses over short- and long-distance routes in central and western Canada and the United States. TBL also has a school bus division operating in eastern Canada. CTE and its subsidiaries are audited by DeBoy Shoot, which issued an unqualified audit opinion on CTE's June 30, year-end consolidated financial statements. This was the only audit opinion issued on the CTE group of companies. TBL has a July 31 year-end. It is now September 8, Year 7. CTE has been reporting operating losses for several years and has put TBL up for sale as part of a strategy to change its focus. This is the first of several planned divestitures, designed to restore CTE's lacklustre share price.

Currently, the only interested party is an employee group led by TBL's president, Dan Williams. Williams's management buyout team consists of the vice-president of operations and the CFO. Handling the negotiations at CTE's corporate office is Eva Joel, vice-president of strategic divestitures.

The buyout team has submitted the first draft agreement of purchase and sale for review. Exhibit I, below, contains extracts from the draft agreement; notes made by CTE's lawyer are shown in italics. You, a CA at Heatley Dan LLP, have gathered some additional background information (Exhibit II).

Andrew wants to maximize the total selling price. He asked the partner in charge of the advisory services at Heatley Dan LLP to review the information given and provide recommendations on how CTE can maximize the total selling price and how the agreement should be changed to minimize possible disputes in the future. In addition, he would like a summary of the accounting issues of significance to CTE that will arise on the sale of TBL. The partner has asked you to prepare the draft report to Joel.

Required:

Prepare the draft report.

(CICA adapted)

EXHIBIT I

EXTRACTS OF DRAFT PURCHASE AND SALE AGREEMENT

Agreement of purchase and sale between the employee group (hereinafter the Purchaser) and Canada Transport Enterprises Inc. (hereinafter CTE) for the assets and liabilities of the business known as Traveller Bus Lines Inc. (TBL).

1. The assets and liabilities of TBL are those included in its draft July 31, Year 7, financial statements.
2. Excluded from the liabilities to be assumed by the purchaser are all environmental liabilities, including, but not limited to, gasoline and diesel fuel spills and tank leakage, pesticide residues, and all other chemical contamination.
3. The purchase price is determined by the sum of (A) the carrying amount of the net assets at July 31, Year 7, which is twelve million dollars ($12 million), plus (B) 55% of the net reported income after taxes, for the 12-month period ending July 31, Year 8 (the contingent consideration). *Lawyer's Note: The contingent consideration should be worth at least $3.6 million, since the division's earnings computed on this basis have averaged more than $6.6 million for the last four years before deducting head office charges.*
4. This agreement is conditional on the Purchaser obtaining adequate financing and, after inspection, finding TBL's records satisfactory.

(continued)

EXHIBIT I   *(continued)*

5. CTE agrees not to compete with the Purchaser for 10 years.
6. CTE will provide a loan guarantee for up to 25% of the purchase price for the Purchaser.
7. The Purchaser agrees to provide full maintenance services to the truck and trailer fleet of one of CTE's other subsidiaries for five years. Charges will be based on cost plus 10%.
8. The central bus station will be restored by CTE to its original condition by December 31, Year 7.
9. CTE will provide free advertising to the Purchaser, on request, for one year following the closing date. The Purchaser will create all the advertising material, including TV commercials.
10. All bus route rights will be assigned to the Purchaser.
11. The purchase price will be allocated based on carrying amounts.
12. The sale will close on October 1, Year 7, at 12:01 A.M., and the entire consideration with the exception of the contingent consideration will be due and payable one (1) month after closing. The contingent consideration is due one (1) month after the July 31, Year 8, financial statements are finalized.
13. Overdue amounts will be charged interest at a rate of 11% per annum.
14. CTE will act in a consulting capacity to advise the Purchaser for a fee of $25,000 per annum.

EXHIBIT II

INFORMATION GATHERED

1. Exclusive rights to most bus routes were obtained almost 40 years ago when the provincial governments were handing out the routes at no cost to the local bus lines. They had no competition at that time. Other similar bus routes were subsequently purchased for significant amounts.
2. TBL's summary draft financial statements for July 31, Year 7, are as follows (in thousands of dollars):

Revenue	$48,123
Expenses (including $2,403 of head office charges)	40,239
Income before income taxes	7,884
Current taxes	2,995
Deferred taxes	567
Net income	$ 4,322
Current assets	$14,133
Long-term assets	25,131
Liabilities	(21,264)
Deferred taxes	(6,000)
Equity	$12,000

3. The TBL maintenance department has recently completed a study that demonstrated that the school buses would last 15 years, rather than the 10 years on which the straight-line depreciation rates have always been based.
4. All school boards pay a non-refundable deposit, three months before the beginning of the school year in September, to guarantee bus service for the coming school year.
5. TBL ran a "Travel the Country" promotion in June Year 7. Sales of the three-month passes for unlimited travel, costing $400, were brisk. The driver punches the pass

(continued)

EXHIBIT II   *(continued)*

each time the holder takes a trip. To compensate travellers who use their passes fewer than 10 times in the three-month period, TBL permits them to trade in their passes for either a pair of skis or a pair of in-line skates or the cash value of these items ($150).

6. CTE's consolidation entries for Year 7 related to TBL are a fair value increment of $432,300 for property, plant, and equipment and $2,332,000 for goodwill, which is checked for impairment on an annual basis.

7. Included in TBL's long-term assets is a note receivable for $3.1 million, secured by the real property of a chain of four gas stations. Because of fierce competition from stations owned by the large oil companies, the value of the properties has declined from $4.2 million, the amount stated in the May Year 6 appraisal, to $2.4 million, according to the May Year 7 appraisal released on July 22, Year 7. The payments on the note are being made on schedule.

8. On August 18, Year 7, the Panamee School District announced the cancellation of all school bus services previously contracted for Year 7/8 in the school district.

9. The management buyout team plans to spend $500,000 on TV advertisements that promote bus travel in a national advertising campaign starting in early Year 8. The team also plans to retrofit all long-distance buses at substantial cost.

10. TBL moved all maintenance operations to a new facility in June Year 7. The building was purchased for $3.4 million, and the company had to vacate a leased facility 18 months before the end of the lease. The prospects of subletting the facility do not look good.

Case 8-4
LO3, 7
Capilano Forest Company Ltd. (CFCL) has been owned and managed by an experienced forester, Don Strom, for 20 years. The company has performed well in the last few years, but the industry is cyclical. In the interior of British Columbia, CFCL manufactures lumber of all grades from raw logs. A small lumberyard and sales office are located in Vancouver.

Your firm has been re-appointed auditor for CFCL, and you, a CA, the senior on this engagement, have been going over some issues with the recently hired controller of the company, Everett Green. CFCL had been searching for a controller for several months. Green agreed to accept the position with the condition that his compensation package include a bonus based on net income. Strom finally agreed to this form of remuneration, despite initial resistance.

A large Japanese lumber importer has recently expressed an interest in purchasing CFCL. Therefore, Green proposes to make changes to CFCL's accounting policies, which he believes will maximize the value of the company.

During the year, CFCL was granted, by the Ministry of Forests, the right to log a large area of standing timber on Crown land. Although CFCL does not own the land, it does have the right to log all the timber on it, subject to an allowable annual limit. This right was granted to the company at no initial cost. However, a fee is paid to the Ministry based on the number of logs removed from the forest. Shortly after CFCL received this right, the Ministry announced that all holders of logging rights over Crown land are responsible for reforesting the lands at their own cost; the ruling applies to all rights granted in the last five years. After eight months of logging, CFCL has still not carried out any reforestation. The controller is proposing that CFCL record receipt of this right at fair value. In addition, he would like to include in the financial statements the fair value of rights received from the Ministry two years ago. These rights do not currently appear on the company's balance sheet.

CFCL recently purchased the right to log the standing timber on a mine site. As part of the purchase contract, CFCL agreed that it would cease logging in five years when mining commenced. Although CFCL would probably be unable to log all the timber in this period, the five-year rights were considered to be worth considerably more than the purchase price. Since logging operations began, however, it has become apparent that many of the trees are infested by insects and are therefore worthless. Green does not think that this presents a valuation problem for financial reporting. "These rotten trees are part of the cost of the good ones and will be expensed as the good trees are sold. The purchase price will be allocated to all the good trees on the mine site."

With respect to the costing of trees on land that CFCL owns, Green contends that these trees really have no cost. "We paid for the land, which produces the trees. The trees themselves do not have any cost. If anything, replanting and pesticide expenses are the only costs we have. The situation is similar to owning land on which we have a building and machinery producing widgets. When we sell the widgets, we don't expense the land, do we?"

Last year, the company acquired 100% of the common shares of NAN Limited, a forestry company operating out of Nanaimo, British Columbia, for $3 million. The acquisition differential of $500,000 was assigned to the timber. NAN owned a large tract of land and timber along the Pacific Coast. This year, 20% of this tract, along the shoreline, was sold to a resort developer. CFCL has assigned a cost of $25,000 to this parcel. At the date of original purchase, CFCL considered this parcel to be worthless from a logging standpoint. The rest of this land is abundant in timber. CFCL paid a premium for NAN because its land had rich soil and a moist, coastal climate ideal for tree growth. Lately, however, the company has been having problems logging the area. Environmentalists have vowed that no one will be allowed to destroy its natural beauty. Roadways have been blocked on several occasions by these protesters. In addition, they have campaigned aggressively against the company and its products. In response, CFCL has spent large amounts on public relations advertising and on legal costs in order to obtain injunctions. These amounts, as well as the estimated costs of idle time related to the protests, will be capitalized as goodwill.

On December 1, CFCL signed an agreement to sell 25% of its interest in NAN for $800,000. It wants to report a gain of $50,000 on the sale.

Green intends to include in goodwill costs relating to forest fires burning in areas surrounding CFCL's land. Although none of CFCL's timber has been damaged by the fires, the company did pay for resources to help control the disaster. As the controller explained, "It was in our best interests to help combat fires because they were headed toward our timber." The fires continue to burn, and CFCL has promised an additional $300,000 in aid.

CFCL has gained a reputation among Japanese companies as a good source of clear pine. CFCL can sell the Japanese as much pine as it can cut. Orders currently outstanding will take the company at least six months to fill. Under the terms of the contracts, the purchase price, denominated in yen, may be increased or decreased by a maximum of 5%, depending on the grade, as determined by inspection at a Japanese harbour. The company would like to record the revenue on these contracts as soon as the lumber is cut.

The company sells wood chips as a by-product of its sawmill operations. It entered into a three-year contract with a large pulp mill, Remul Ltd., under which

Remul can purchase all the chips produced by CFCL. CFCL would have plenty of willing customers, given the current market demand, for any chips that Remul did not take. CFCL transports the chips by truck and rail car. The truck drivers have been on strike for the last two weeks. Green does not see this strike lasting much longer, and he would, therefore, like to recognize the revenue on the chips as they are produced.

The partner on this engagement has asked you to prepare a memo discussing the accounting alternatives and to make recommendations for the issues raised with the controller.

Required:

Prepare the requested memo.

Case 8-5
LO2

You, a CA, have recently accepted a job at the accounting firm of Cat, Scan, & Partners, as a manager, and have been assigned the audit of Vision Clothing Inc. (VCI). The partner in charge had been at VCI the previous week and had met with the controller to discuss the year-end audit. The partner has requested that you review his notes and prepare a detailed report for the client regarding accounting and other issues (excluding tax and assurance).

He handed you his notes and extracts from the current year's preliminary financial statements (Exhibit III), from which you learn the following about the company.

EXHIBIT III

VISION CLOTHING COMPANY
EXTRACTS FROM CONSOLIDATED INCOME STATEMENT
for the years ended January 31
(in Thousands of Dollars)

	Year 3 (Preliminary)	Year 2 (Audited)
Sales	$1,305,125	$1,244,102
Cost of goods sold	848,332	721,579
Gross margin	456,793	522,523
Selling expenses	272,453	315,333
Head office expenses	138,938	150,186
Earnings before the following:	45,402	57,004
Amortization	52,600	42,380
Interest	37,484	31,381
Earnings before taxes	(44,682)	(16,757)
Income taxes	17,873	6,660
	(26,809)	(10,097)
Earnings (loss) from investment in affiliated companies	4,700	(850)
Net earnings	$ (22,109)	$ (10,947)
Attributable to:		
Shareholders of VCI	$ (19,684)	$ (7,523)
Non-controlling interest	(2,425)	(3,424)
	$ (22,109)	$ (10,947)

(continued)

EXHIBIT III   *(continued)*

VISION CLOTHING COMPANY
EXTRACTS FROM CONSOLIDATED BALANCE SHEET
as at January 31
(in Thousands of Dollars)

	Year 3 (Preliminary)	Year 2 (Audited)
Assets		
Current		
Cash and short-term investment	$ 42,420	$145,400
Inventory	250,713	250,209
Other current assets	61,962	57,432
Income taxes recoverable	0	2,660
Deferred taxes	17,873	0
	372,968	455,701
Investment in affiliated companies	27,825	23,125
Property, plant, and equipment—net	353,420	312,800
Goodwill	127,472	123,842
	$881,685	$915,468
Liabilities and Shareholders' Equity		
Accounts payable	$212,790	$257,135
Current portion of long-term debt and financing lease		
obligations	55,412	22,160
Other current liabilities	34,800	4,200
	303,002	283,495
Long term		
Long-term debt	93,000	133,000
Finance lease obligations	58,208	48,889
Debentures payable	100,000	150,000
	251,208	331,889
Shareholders' equity		
Ordinary shares	195,500	146,000
Retained earnings	75,566	95,250
Non-controlling interest	56,409	58,834
	327,475	300,084
	$881,685	$915,468

General background:

VCI was incorporated 15 years ago under the *Canada Business Corporations Act* and operates stores across Canada and the United States. Its principal business is the operation of women's and men's clothing stores. These chains operate through different divisions and subsidiaries. The retail clothing industry has been hit hard by the recession in recent years, and many large companies and familiar names have been forced out of business.

Each VCI chain functions as an autonomous unit to which VCI provides capital and central services. This decentralized organization permits the chains to remain sensitive to the needs of their markets.

The corporation's year-end is January 31. It is now February Year 3.

Notes from the meeting with the client:

1. In February Year 2, VCI successfully completed a public share offering of 6 million Class A non-voting shares at an offering price of $8.25 per share. Underwriter's fees amounted to $5 million. In November Year 2, VCI considered another public offering; however, the price per share had fallen to $4.00 and the directors decided to defer the issue to a later date. To date, fees of $1 million related to this deferred offering have been incurred and capitalized to current assets.

   The share issue was used to redeem debentures of $50 million in March Year 2. Under the provisions of the debenture agreement, one third of the original $150 million debenture can be redeemed each March at the discretion of the debenture holders. At any time, debenture holders have the option to convert the debentures at their face value for voting shares at their market value.

2. The company recorded a gain of $3.7 million from an increase in its ownership interest of an affiliated company, XYZ Ltd. The increase occurred as a result of a share redemption by XYZ Ltd. Following the redemption, VCI's ownership rose from 25% to 29%. The gain represents 4% of the fair market value of XYZ Ltd.

3. Two years ago, VCI decided to diversify and purchased the assets of a chain of children's shoe stores, Tiny Tot Togs (TTT). They have operated TTT as a division of VCI. The assets of TTT will be sold in the near future for an estimated $5 million. TTT has lost $18 million to date. VCI believes that $5 million is the fair market value for the company, even though it has invested over $30 million in TTT.

4. During the year, VCR invested in a new management reporting and consolidation software package, which the finance department has just implemented and tested. VCI's management information systems department produced the package internally. Total costs to develop, implement, and test the software package have been estimated at about $2 million. This amount has been allocated to property, plant, and equipment. It includes about $800,000 to $1 million in salaries and benefits for those employees who devoted most of their time to this project. The amount also includes $700,000 to $1 million spent on new hardware, including monitors, enhanced keyboards, computer chips, and extended memory upgrades necessary to run the new software package.

5. On October 31, Year 2, VCI amalgamated with a subsidiary, Style Co. The amalgamation occurred because VCI had large loss carry-forwards due to expire soon, and future losses were anticipated. Style Co. had been profitable for several years and was forecasting further profits of $9 million for the year ending January Year 3.

   Because of Style Co.'s size, inventory was counted at year-end only. The quarterly inventory valuations were estimated using prior-year gross margins less a provision for shrinkage. During Year 2, Style Co. began installing a state-of-the-art inventory system that was far superior to its old system. The new system was installed prior to the year-end inventory count at January 31, Year 3.

   When the count was taken, inventory was found to be overstated by $20 million, turning Style Co.'s original $9 million profit for the year into an $11 million loss. The problem was explained as being possibly a combination of a shrinkage problem, gross margin miscalculations (on which original budgets were based), and/or system conversion problems (e.g., incorrectly inputted data). Inventory averages approximately $100 million at cost and $150 million at retail.

VCI's controller suggested that the inventory shortage must have occurred throughout the year and that Style Co.'s third-quarter profit should be restated.

6. VCI has strong representation in many shopping malls, so it has been able to negotiate favorable leases. In many cases, landlords have provided funds to cover all, or a significant portion of, the leasehold improvements as a result of the economic pressures to attract and keep good tenants. VCI received approximately $20 million in September Year 2, to remodel new and existing locations. Leases are generally signed for seven years, at the end of which time the stores are usually remodeled. VCI has recorded these transactions as a credit against divisional expenses on the preliminary January 31, Year 3 statements.

Required:

Prepare the report to the client and the memo to partner.

PROBLEMS

Problem 8-1
L01

The following Year 1 consolidated cash flow statement was prepared for Standard Manufacturing Corp. and its 60%-owned subsidiary, Pritchard Windows Inc.:

STANDARD MANUFACTURING CORP.
CONSOLIDATED CASH FLOW STATEMENT
for the Year Ended December 31, Year 1

Cash flows from operating activities:		
Consolidated net income*	$129,800	
Non-cash items included in income		
Depreciation	45,200	
Goodwill impairment loss	1,000	
Bond premium amortization	(2,000)	
Loss on sale of equipment	23,000	
Decrease in inventory	20,000	
Increase in accounts receivable	(12,000)	
Net cash provided by operating activities		$205,000
Cash flows from investing activities		
Purchase of buildings	(150,000)	
Sale of equipment	60,000	
Net cash used in investing activities		(90,000)
Cash flows from financing activities		
Dividends paid		
To Standard's shareholders	(50,000)	
To non-controlling shareholders	(6,000)	
Bond issue	100,000	
Preferred share redemption	(120,000)	
Net cash used in financing activities		(76,000)
Net increase in cash		39,000
Cash balance, January 1		50,000
Cash balance, December 31		$ 89,000

* Consolidated net income was $120,000 attributable to Standard's shareholders and $9,800 attributable to non-controlling interests.

Required:

(a) Did the loss on the sale of equipment shown above result from a sale to an affiliate or a non-affiliate? Explain.

(b) Explain why the amortization of bond premium is treated as a deduction from net income in arriving at net cash flow from operations.

(c) Determine the net income of Pritchard Windows for Year 1. (Assume no inter-company transactions or unrealized profits and that the only change in the unamortized acquisition differential during the year was the goodwill impairment loss.)

(d) Explain why dividends to non-controlling shareholders are not shown as a dividend in the consolidated retained earnings statement but are shown as a distribution of cash in the consolidated cash flow statement.

(e) Determine the amount of dividends paid by Pritchard Windows in Year 1.

Problem 8-2
LO3, 4, 6

Financial statements of Par Corp. and its subsidiary Star Inc. on December 31, Year 12, are shown below:

BALANCE SHEETS
at December 31, Year 12

	Par	Star
Cash	$ 40,000	$ 1,000
Accounts receivable	100,000	85,000
Inventories	55,000	48,000
Land	30,000	70,000
Plant and equipment	400,000	700,000
Accumulated depreciation	(180,000)	(300,000)
Investment in Star common shares	280,000	—
	$725,000	$604,000
Accounts payable	$ 92,000	$180,000
Accrued liabilities	8,000	10,000
Preferred shares	—	50,000
Common shares	450,000	200,000
Retained earnings	175,000	164,000
	$725,000	$604,000

RETAINED EARNINGS STATEMENTS
for the Year Ended December 31, Year 12

	Par	Star
Balance, January 1	$180,000	$208,000
Net income (loss)	30,000	(24,000)
	210,000	184,000
Dividends	35,000	20,000
Balance, December 31	$175,000	$164,000

Other Information

- On January 1, Year 5, the balance sheet of Star showed the following shareholders' equity:

$8 cumulative preferred shares, 500 shares issued	$ 50,000
Common shares, 2,000 shares issued	200,000
Deficit (Note 1)	(80,000)
	$170,000

Note 1: Dividends on preferred shares are two years in arrears.

On this date, Par acquired 1,400 common shares of Star for a cash payment of $280,000.

The fair values of Star's identifiable net assets differed from carrying amounts only with respect to the following:

	Carrying amount	*Fair value*
Accounts receivable	$42,000	$40,000
Inventory	65,000	72,000
Plant	600,000	650,000
Long-term liabilities	400,000	420,000

The plant had an estimated remaining useful life of five years on this date, and the long-term liabilities had a maturity date of December 30, Year 12. Any goodwill is to be tested annually for impairment.

- Both Par and Star make substantial sales to each other at an intercompany selling price that yields the same gross profit as the sales they make to unrelated customers. Intercompany sales in Year 12 were as follows:

Par to Star	$400,000
Star to Par	330,000

- During Year 12, Par billed Star $2,000 per month in management fees. At year-end, Star had paid for all months except for December.
- The January 1, Year 12, inventories of the two companies contained unrealized intercompany profits as follows:

Inventory of Par	$30,000
Inventory of Star	21,000

- The December 31, Year 12, inventories of the two companies contained unrealized intercompany profits as follows:

Inventory of Par	$35,000
Inventory of Star	37,000

- On July 1, Year 7, Star sold equipment to Par for $82,000. The equipment had a carrying amount in the records of Star of $60,000 on this date and an estimated remaining useful life of five years.
- Goodwill impairment losses were recorded as follows: Year 7, $92,500; Year 9, $46,470; and Year 12, $19,710.
- Assume a 40% corporate tax rate.
- Par has accounted for its investment in Star by the cost method.
- All dividends in arrears were paid by December 31, Year 11.

Required:

(a) Prepare, with all necessary calculations, the following:

(i) Year 12 consolidated retained earnings statement

(ii) Consolidated balance sheet as at December 31, Year 12

(b) How would the return on equity attributable to Par's shareholders for Year 12 change if Star's preferred shares were non-cumulative instead of cumulative?

(c) On January 1, Year 13, Star issued common shares for $100,000 in cash. Because Par did not purchase any of these shares, Par's ownership percentage declined from 70 to 56%.

Calculate the gain or loss that would be charged or credited to consolidated shareholders' equity as a result of this transaction.

Problem 8-3
LO2, 3, 7

On December 31, Year 5, the accountant of Regent Corporation prepared a reconciliation (see below), which was used in the preparation of the consolidated financial statements on that date.

Investment in Argyle Ltd.—equity method balance		$315,000
Shareholders' equity of Argyle		
8,000 common shares	50,000	
Retained earnings	175,000	
	225,000	
Regent's ownership	90%	202,500
Regent's share of unamortized acquisition differential		112,500
Non-controlling interest's share of unamortized acquisition differential		12,500
Total unamortized acquisition differential		$125,000
Allocated: Land		$ 28,333
Equipment—remaining useful life, 8 years		44,444
Trademarks—remaining useful life, 10 years		52,223
		$125,000

Additional Information

- On December 31, Year 6, Argyle reported a net income of $50,000 (earned evenly throughout the year) and declared dividends of $20,000.
- On April 1, Year 6, Argyle issued an additional 2,000 common shares at a price of $75 each. Regent did not acquire any of these shares.
- On October 1, Year 6, because the market price of Argyle's common shares had fallen, Regent purchased 1,300 shares of Argyle on the open market at $60 per share. The decline in value is not believed to be permanent. Any acquisition differential was allocated 20% to land, 35% to equipment, and 45% to trademark.

Required:

(a) Prepare an acquisition-differential amortization schedule for Year 6 while showing the controlling and non-controlling interests' share of the changes occurring throughout the year.

(b) Now assume that Regent is a private company, uses ASPE, and chooses to use the equity method to report its investment in Argyle. Calculate the equity method balance in the investment in Argyle account as at December 31, Year 6, and reconcile this balance to Argyle's shareholders' equity and to the unamortized acquisition differential.

Problem 8-4
LO1, 3   The comparative consolidated statement of financial position at December 31, Year 2, and the consolidated income statement for Year 2, of Parent Ltd. and its 70%-owned subsidiary are shown below.

	Year 2	Year 1
Plant and equipment	$5,350,000	$5,100,000
Accumulated depreciation	(2,350,000)	(1,980,000)
Goodwill	530,000	565,000
Inventory	989,500	490,000
Accounts receivable	600,000	710,000
Cash	810,000	335,000
	$5,929,500	$5,220,000
Ordinary shares	$ 800,000	$ 800,000
Retained earnings	916,000	520,000
Non-controlling interest	515,000	—
Long-term liabilities	3,100,000	2,600,000
Current liabilities	598,500	1,300,000
	$5,929,500	$5,220,000
Revenues	$8,500,000	
Cost of purchases and other expenses	8,179,600	
Change in inventory	(499,500)	
Depreciation	370,000	
Goodwill impairment loss	35,000	
	8,085,100	
Profit	$ 414,900	
Attributable to		
Shareholders of Parent	$ 376,500	
Non-controlling interest	38,400	

Additional Information

- On December 31, Year 1, Parent owned 100% of Sub. On this date, the shareholders' equity of Sub amounted to $1,120,000, and the parent's unamortized acquisition differential of $565,000 was allocated entirely to the goodwill of Sub.
- On January 1, Year 2, Parent sold 30% of its shares of Sub for $629,000 cash and recorded an increase to retained earnings of $123,500 on the transaction. Parent uses the equity method to account for its investment.
- Parent paid $104,000 in dividends during Year 2.

Required:

Prepare, in good form, a consolidated cash flow statement for Year 2 in accordance with the requirements of IAS 7.

Problem 8-5
LO5, 7   On April 1, Year 7, Princeton Corp. purchased 70% of the ordinary shares of Simon Ltd. for $910,000. On this same date, Simon purchased 60% of the ordinary shares of Fraser Inc. for $600,000. On April 1, Year 7, the acquisition differentials from the two investments were allocated entirely to broadcast rights to be amortized over 10 years. The cost method is being used to account for both investments.

During Year 7, the three companies sold merchandise to each other. On December 31, Year 7, the inventory of Princeton contained merchandise on which Simon recorded a gross margin of $32,000. On the same date, the inventory of Fraser contained merchandise on which Princeton recorded a gross margin of $18,000. Assume a 40% tax rate.

The following information is available:

	Princeton	Simon	Fraser
Ordinary shares	$600,000	$550,000	$300,000
Retained earnings—Jan. 1, Year 7	650,000	400,000	300,000
Profit—Year 7*	100,000	200,000	150,000
Dividends declared—Dec. 31	25,000	30,000	70,000

* Earned evenly throughout the year.

Required:

Calculate the following:

(a) Consolidated profit attributable to Princeton's shareholders for Year 7.
(b) Non-controlling interest as at December 31, Year 7.
(c) Consolidated broadcast rights as at December 31, Year 7.
(d) Profit on Princeton's separate-entity income statement, assuming that Princeton was a private company, uses ASPE, and uses the equity method to report its investments in subsidiaries.

Problem 8-6
LO4

On January 1, Year 5, PET Company acquired 900 ordinary shares of SET Company for $63,000. On this date, the shareholders' equity accounts of SET Company were as follows:

Ordinary shares (1,000 no par value shares issued)	$20,000
Preferred shares (4,000 no par value shares issued) (Note 1)	40,000
Retained earnings	30,000
	$90,000

Note 1: The preferred shares are $1, cumulative, nonparticipating with a liquidation value of 1.05. They were two years in arrears on January 1, Year 5.

The following are the statements of retained earnings for the two companies for Year 5:

	PET	SET
Retained earnings, beginning of year	$50,000	$30,000
Profit	30,000	22,000
Dividends	(25,000)	(15,000)
Retained earnings, end of year	$55,000	$37,000

Additional Information

- PET uses the cost method to account for its investment in SET.
- Any acquisition differential is allocated to patents with an estimated useful life of six years as at January 1, Year 5. Neither company has any patents recorded on their separate-entity records.

Required:

(a) Prepare a consolidated statement of retained earnings for Year 5.
(b) Prepare an independent calculation of consolidated retained earnings at the end of Year 5.
(c) Calculate non-controlling interest for the consolidated income statement for Year 5 and non-controlling interest for the consolidated statement of financial position at the end of Year 5.

Problem 8-7
LO3

On January 1, Year 8, Summer Company's shareholders' equity was as follows:

Common shares	$20,000
Retained earnings	70,000
	$90,000

Plumber Company held 90% of the 4,000 outstanding shares of Summer on January 1, Year 8, and its investment in Summer Company account had a balance of $126,000 on that date. Plumber accounts for its investment by the equity method. Any acquisition differential was allocated to unrecorded trademarks with a remaining useful life on January 1, Year 8, of 10 years.

The following events took place subsequent to January 1, Year 8:

- On July 1, Year 8, Plumber sold 720 of the Summer Company shares it held at a price of $30 per share.
- During Year 8, Summer reported a net income of $20,000 (earned equally throughout the year) and declared dividends of $5,000 on December 31.
- During Year 9, Summer reported a net income of $28,000 and paid dividends of $8,000 on November 15.
- On December 29, Year 9, Summer issued an additional 500 shares to third parties at a price of $46 per share.

Required:

(a) Calculate the gain or loss in Year 8 and Year 9 as a result of the ownership change that took place each year.
(b) Would the gain or loss appear on the consolidated income statement each year? Explain.
(c) Calculate the consolidated trademarks as at December 31, Year 9.
(d) Does the value for the trademarks on the consolidated balance sheet as calculated in part (c) comply with the historical cost principle? Explain.

Problem 8-8
LO1

The accountant of Kara Enterprises has just finished preparing the consolidated balance sheet, income statement, and retained earnings statement for Year 2, and has asked you for assistance in preparing the consolidated cash flow statement. Kara has only one subsidiary, which is 80% owned, and in addition has a long-term investment of 45% in the outstanding shares of Pacific Finance Co.

The following items have been prepared from the analysis of the Year 2 consolidated statements:

Decrease in accounts receivable	$25,000
Increase in accounts payable	3,000
Increase in inventory	15,000
Equity earnings from Pacific Finance	90,000

Increase in bonds payable	120,000
Building purchased for cash	580,000
Depreciation reported for current period	73,000
Gain recorded on sale of equipment	8,000
Carrying amount of equipment sold	37,000
Goodwill impairment loss	3,000
Dividends received from Pacific Finance	25,000
Net income attributable to Kara's shareholders	450,000
Net income attributable to non-controlling interest	14,000
Dividends paid by parent company	60,000
Dividends paid by subsidiary company	30,000
Cash balance, January 1, Year 2	42,000

Required:

Prepare the consolidated cash flow statement.

Problem 8-9
LO1, 3 Parent Co. owns 9,500 shares of Sub Co. and accounts for its investment by the equity method. On December 31, Year 5, the shareholders' equity of Sub was as follows:

Common shares (10,000 shares issued)	$100,000
Retained earnings	170,000

On January 1, Year 6, Parent sold 1,900 shares from its holdings in Sub for $66,500. On this date and prior to the sale, the balance in the investment in Sub account was $320,000, and the unamortized acquisition differential was allocated in the following manner:

45% to land

30% to equipment (remaining useful life, 4 years)

25% to patents (remaining useful life, 10 years)

During Year 6, Sub reported a net income of $150,000 and paid dividends totalling $70,000.

Required:

(a) (i) Prepare the journal entry that Parent would make on January 1, Year 6, to record the sale of the 1,900 shares.

(ii) Calculate the amount of the unamortized acquisition differential that would be allocated to land, equipment, and patents on December 31, Year 6.

(iii) Prepare an independent proof of the unamortized acquisition differential on December 31, Year 6.

(b) The accountant of Parent must prepare a consolidated cash flow statement for Year 6 by analyzing the changes in the consolidated balance sheets from December 31, Year 5, to December 31, Year 6. She needs some assistance in determining what effect Parent's sale of 1,900 shares had on the consolidated financial statements.

Prepare a journal entry to record the effect that the January 1, Year 6, sale of shares had on the consolidated entity.

Problem 8-10
LO2

On January 1, Year 5, Pic Company acquired 7,500 ordinary shares of Sic Company for $600,000. On January 1, Year 6, Pic Company acquired an additional 2,000 ordinary shares of Sic Company for $166,000. On January 1, Year 5, the shareholders' equity of Sic was as follows:

Ordinary shares (10,000 no par value shares issued)	$200,000
Retained earnings	300,000
	$500,000

The following are the statements of retained earnings for the two companies for Years 5 and 6:

	Pic		Sic	
	Year 5	Year 6	Year 5	Year 6
Retained earnings, beginning of year	$500,000	$530,000	$300,000	$310,000
Profit	130,000	140,000	100,000	110,000
Dividends	(100,000)	(120,000)	(90,000)	(90,000)
Retained earnings, end of year	$530,000	$550,000	$310,000	$330,000

Additional Information

- Pic uses the cost method to account for its investment in Sic.
- Any acquisition differential is allocated to customer contracts, which are expected to provide future benefits until December 31, Year 7. Neither company has any customer contracts recorded on their separate-entity records.
- There were no unrealized profits from intercompany transactions since the date of acquisition.

Required:

(a) Calculate consolidated profit attributable to Pic's shareholders for Year 6.
(b) Calculate the following account balances for the consolidated statement of financial position at December 31, Year 6:

   (i) Customer contracts
  (ii) Non-controlling interest
 (iii) Retained earnings

Problem 8-11
LO5

Intercompany shareholdings of an affiliated group during the year ended December 31, Year 2, were as follows:

York Ltd.	Queen's Company	McGill Company
90% of Queen's Company	70% of Carleton Ltd.	60% of Trent Ltd.
80% of McGill Company	10% of McGill Company	

The equity method is being used for intercompany investments, but no entries have been made in Year 2. The profits before equity method earnings for Year 2 were as follows:

	Profit
York Ltd.	$54,000
Queen's Company	22,000
McGill Company	26,700
Carleton Ltd.	15,400
Trent Ltd.	11,600

Intercompany profits before taxes in the December 31, Year 2, inventories and the selling companies were as follows:

Selling corporation	Profit made by selling corporation
York Ltd.	$10,000
McGill Company	1,000
Carleton Ltd.	2,400

Use income tax allocation at a 40% rate. Assume that there is no acquisition differential for any of the intercompany shareholdings.

Required:

(a) Calculate consolidated profit attributable to York's shareholders for Year 2.
(b) Calculate the amount of consolidated profit attributable to non-controlling interest that would appear on the Year 2 consolidated income statement.
(c) Will the consolidation adjustment for unrealized profits be any different if McGill Company sells inventory to Carleton Ltd. or York Ltd.? Use the revenue recognition principle to explain your answer.

✳Problem 8-12
LO3, 6

Craft Ltd. held 80% of the outstanding ordinary shares of Delta Corp. as at December 31, Year 12. In order to establish a closer relationship with Nonaffiliated Corporation, a major supplier to both Craft and Delta, all three companies agreed that Nonaffiliated would take an equity position in Delta. Accordingly, for a cash payment of $15 per share, Delta issued 12,250 additional ordinary shares to Nonaffiliated on December 31, Year 12. This was the last transaction that occurred on this date. Statements of financial position for the two companies just prior to this transaction were as follows:

CRAFT LTD.
STATEMENT OF FINANCIAL POSITION
at December 31, Year 12

Buildings and equipment (net)	$ 600,000
Investment in Delta	490,000
Inventory	180,000
Accounts receivable	90,000
Cash	50,000
	$1,410,000
Ordinary shares	$ 480,000
Retained earnings	610,000
Mortgage payable	250,000
Accounts payable	70,000
	$1,410,000

DELTA CORP.
STATEMENT OF FINANCIAL POSITION
at December 31, Year 12

Buildings and equipment (net)	$400,000
Inventory	200,000
Accounts receivable	120,000
Cash	65,000
	$785,000

Ordinary shares (Note)	$250,000
Retained earnings	350,000
Accrued liabilities	85,000
Accounts payable	100,000
	$785,000

Note: 49,000 ordinary shares outstanding on December 31, Year 12.

Additional Information

- Craft has used the equity method of accounting for its investment in Delta since it acquired its 80% interest in Delta in Year 2. At that time, the acquisition differential was entirely allocated to inventory and patent, which still exists but is not recorded on Delta's separate-entity books.
- There were no unrealized intercompany asset profits as at December 31, Year 12.

Required:

(a) Prepare a consolidated statement of financial position as at December 31, Year 12 (show calculations for all items on the balance sheet).
(b) If Craft had used parent company extension theory rather than entity theory, how would this affect the return-on-equity ratio for Year 12?

Problem 8-13
LO5

A Company owns 75% of B Company and 40% of C Company. B Company owns 40% of C Company. The following information was assembled at December 31, Year 7.

	A Company	B Company	C Company
Cash	$ 117,800	$ 49,300	$ 20,000
Accounts receivable	200,000	100,000	44,000
Inventory	277,000	206,000	58,000
Investment in C	85,000	92,000	—
Investment in B	409,250	—	—
Property, plant, and equipment	2,800,000	1,500,000	220,000
Accumulated depreciation	(1,120,000)	(593,000)	(90,000)
	$2,769,050	$1,354,300	$252,000
Accounts payable	$ 206,000	$ 88,000	$ 2,000
Bonds payable	1,000,000	700,000	—
Preferred shares	—	50,000	—
Common shares	1,200,000	400,000	200,000
Retained earnings, January 1	314,250	61,000	30,000
Net income	118,800	55,300	20,000
Dividends	(70,000)	—	—
	$2,769,050	$1,354,300	$252,000

Additional Information

- A Company purchased its 40% interest in C Company on January 1, Year 4. On that date, the negative acquisition differential of $10,000 on the 40% investment was allocated to equipment with an estimated useful life of 10 years.
- A Company purchased its 75% of B Company's common shares on January 1, Year 6. On that date, the 100% implied acquisition differential was allocated $40,000 to buildings with an estimated useful life of 20 years, and $53,333 to patents to be amortized over 8 years. The preferred shares of B Company are non-cumulative.

- On January 1, Year 7, B Company purchased its 40% interest in C Company for $92,000. The carrying amount of C Company's identifiable net assets approximated fair value on this date.
- The inventory of B Company contains a profit of $2,400 on merchandise purchased from A Company. The inventory of A Company contains a profit of $3,000 on merchandise purchased from C Company.
- On December 31, Year 7, A Company owes $20,000 to C Company and B Company owes $2,000 to A Company.
- Both A Company and B Company use the equity method to account for their investments but have made no equity method adjustments in Year 7.
- An income tax rate of 40% is used for consolidation purposes.

Required:

(a) Calculate non-controlling interest's share of consolidated net income for Year 7.
(b) Prepare a consolidated statement of retained earnings for Year 7.
(c) Prepare a consolidated balance sheet as at December 31, Year 7. Show all calculations.

Problem 8-14
L01

Parento Inc. owns 80% of Santana Corp. The consolidated financial statements of Parento follow:

PARENTO INC.
CONSOLIDATED BALANCE SHEET
at December 31, Year 4

	Year 4	Year 3
Cash	$118,600	$ 49,800
Accounts receivable	115,000	126,000
Inventory	232,000	192,000
Land	86,000	114,000
Buildings and equipment	598,000	510,000
Accumulated depreciation	(205,000)	(168,000)
Databases	16,800	19,200
	$961,400	$843,000
Accounts payable	$ 54,400	$ 31,200
Accrued liabilities	7,200	27,000
Bonds payable	320,000	240,000
Bond premium	9,600	10,800
Common shares	180,000	180,000
Retained earnings	363,480	330,000
Non-controlling interest	26,720	24,000
	$961,400	$843,000

PARENTO INC.
CONSOLIDATED INCOME STATEMENT
for the Year Ended December 31, Year 4

Sales		$960,000
Cost of sales	535,000	
Selling expense	144,600	
Administrative expense	159,800	
Interest expense	31,400	
Income tax	37,000	907,800
Net income		$ 52,200
Attributable to		
Parento's shareholders		$ 47,880
Non-controlling interest		4,320

Parento Inc. purchased its 80% interest in Santana Corp. on January 1, Year 2, for $114,000 when Santana had net assets of $90,000. The acquisition differential was allocated $24,000 to databases (10-year life), with the balance allocated to equipment (20-year life). Parento issued $80,000 in bonds on December 31, Year 4. Santana reported a net income of $24,000 for Year 4 and paid dividends of $8,000.

Selling and administrative expense includes the following:

Depreciation of buildings and equipment	$37,000
Database amortization	2,400
Loss on land sale	2,000

Parento reported a Year 4 equity method income of $47,880 and paid dividends of $14,400.

Required:

(a) Prepare a consolidated cash flow statement for Year 4.
(b) Why are 100% of the dividends paid by Santana not shown as a cash outflow on the cash flow statement?

Problem 8-15
LO3, 7

On January 1, Year 5, Wellington Inc. owned 90% of the outstanding common shares of Sussex Corp. Wellington accounts for its investment using the equity method. The balance in the investment account on January 1, Year 5, amounted to $235,800. The unamortized acquisition differential on this date was allocated entirely to vacant land held by Sussex.

The shareholders' equity of Sussex on January 1, Year 5, was as follows:

Common shares (7,200 shares outstanding)	$ 28,000
Retained earnings	134,000
	$162,000

The following events occurred in Year 5:

- The net income of Sussex for Year 5 amounted to $36,000, earned equally throughout the year.
- On April 1, Year 5, Sussex issued 1,800 shares at a price of $25 per share. Wellington did not acquire any of these shares.
- On June 30, Year 5, Sussex paid dividends amounting to $12,000.
- On September 15, Year 5, Sussex sold 30% of its vacant land at its carrying amount.
- On December 31, Year 5, Wellington sold 648 shares of its investment in Sussex for $22,000.

Required:

Calculate the following as at December 31, Year 5:

(a) The acquisition differential allocated to vacant land and the split in value between the parent and the non-controlling interest.
(b) The balance in the investment account, assuming that Wellington is a private company, uses ASPE, and chooses to use the equity method to report its investment in Sussex.
(c) The amount of non-controlling interest on the consolidated balance sheet.

Problem 8-16
LO2, 4, 6

On January 1, Year 8, Panet Company acquired 40,000 common shares of Saffer Corporation, a public company, for $500,000. This purchase represented 8% of the outstanding shares of Saffer. It was the intention of Panet to acquire more shares in the future in order to eventually gain control of Saffer.

On January 1, Year 10, Panet purchased an additional 135,000 common shares of Saffer for $1,890,000. Saffer's shareholders' equity section was as follows:

10% non-cumulative preferred shares	$ 500,000
Common shares, no par value, 500,000 shares outstanding	3,000,000
Retained earnings	2,700,000

On this date, the fair values of Saffer's assets were equal to carrying amounts, except for inventory, which was undervalued by $120,000, and land, which was undervalued by $1,000,000.

On January 1, Year 11, Panet purchased an additional 225,000 common shares of Saffer for $3,600,000. Saffer's shares were trading on the open market for $15 per share on the date of acquisition. The shareholders' equity section for Saffer was as follows:

10% non-cumulative preferred shares	$ 500,000
Common shares, no par value, 500,000 shares outstanding	3,000,000
Retained earnings	3,200,000

On January 1, Year 11, the fair values of Saffer's assets were equal to carrying amounts except for the following:

	Carrying amount	Fair value
Accounts receivable	$ 200,000	$ 140,000
Plant and equipment (net)	10,000,000	10,900,000
Long-term liabilities	2,000,000	2,200,000

The plant and equipment had a remaining useful life of 20 years. The long-term liabilities mature on December 31, Year 20.

The balance sheets as at December 31, Year 12, and the income statements for the year ending December 31, Year 12, for the two companies are as follows:

BALANCE SHEET

	Panet	Saffer
Assets:		
Cash	$ 500,000	$ 200,000
Accounts receivable	2,400,000	300,000
Inventories	500,000	400,000
Plant and equipment (net)	10,610,000	9,000,000
Investment in Saffer	7,417,300	—
Land	5,500,000	1,000,000
Total assets	$26,927,300	$10,900,000
Liabilities:		
Current liabilities	$ 3,000,000	$ 500,000
Long-term liabilities	4,000,000	2,000,000
	7,000,000	2,500,000
Shareholders' equity:		
10% non-cumulative preferred shares	—	500,000
Common shares	9,000,000	3,000,000
Retained earnings	10,927,300	4,900,000
	19,927,300	8,400,000
Total liabilities and shareholders' equity	$26,927,300	$10,900,000

INCOME STATEMENT

	Panet	Saffer
Sales	$15,000,000	$9,000,000
Investment income from Saffer	697,700	—
	15,697,700	9,000,000
Cost of goods sold	9,500,000	6,200,000
Selling and administrative expense	2,500,000	530,000
Income tax	1,032,000	730,000
Other expenses	468,000	440,000
	13,500,000	7,900,000
Net Income	$ 2,197,700	$1,100,000

Additional Information

- Dividends declared and paid during Year 12:

Panet	$500,000
Saffer	200,000

- On January 1, Year 12, the inventory of Panet contained an $85,000 intercompany profit, and the inventory of Saffer contained an intercompany profit amounting to $190,000.
- During Year 12, Saffer sold inventory to Panet for $2,600,000 at a gross profit margin of 35%. Sales of $400,000 remained in Panet's inventory at December 31, Year 12.
- During Year 12, Panet sold inventory to Saffer for $3,900,000 at a gross profit margin of 45%. Sales of $250,000 remained in Saffer's inventory at December 31, Year 12.
- Saffer sold a piece of equipment to Panet on July 1, Year 12, for $450,000. At that time, the carrying amount of the equipment in Saffer's books was $240,000, and it had a remaining useful life of 10.5 years. Panet still owes Saffer for 30% of the purchase price of the equipment. The gain on sale has been netted against other expenses in Saffer's Year 12 income statement.
- Panet uses the equity method to account for its investment in Saffer. Both companies follow the straight-line method for depreciating plant and equipment, and for premiums or discounts on long-term liabilities.
- A goodwill impairment loss of $92,000 was recorded in Year 11, and a further loss of $58,000 occurred in Year 12. The impairment losses are to be applied at 80% to Panet's shareholders and 20% to non-controlling interest.
- Depreciation expense is included with selling and administrative expenses, whereas goodwill impairment losses are included in other expenses.
- Assume a 40% tax rate.

Required:

(a) Prepare the following Year 12 consolidated financial statements:
  - (i) Income statement
  - (ii) Balance sheet
(b) Calculate goodwill impairment loss and non-controlling interest on the consolidated income statement for the year ended December 31, Year 12, under parent company extension theory.

(c) If Panet had used parent company extension theory rather than entity theory, how would this affect the debt-to-equity ratio at the end of Year 12?

Problem 8-17
LO3, 4

On December 31, Year 6, Ultra Software Limited purchased 70,000 common shares (70%) of a major competitor, Personal Program Corporation (PPC), at $30 per share. Several shareholders who were unwilling to sell at that time owned the remaining common shares and the preferred shares.

The preferred shares, which are non-cumulative, are entitled to a $12 dividend. Each is convertible into two common shares. Immediate conversion of these preferred shares has been, and will continue to be, highly unlikely due to the current market conditions for the shares. Management is concerned, however, about the effect that any future conversion would have.

At December 31, Year 6, PPC's net assets had a carrying amount of $1,525,000. The identifiable assets and liabilities had carrying amounts equal to fair values, with the following exceptions:

- Software patents and copyrights had a total market value estimated as $300,000 above carrying amount. These were expected to have a five-year useful life.
- Inventories of packaged software had a cost to PPC of $20,000 and an estimated selling price of $140,000. Estimated future selling expenses for these items were $15,000.
- An unrecorded brand name had an estimated fair value of $2,375,000. This will be amortized over 40 years.
- In determining the purchase price, the management of Ultra noted that PPC has two years remaining on a long-term contract to supply seats to a major car manufacturer. Given the rapid rise in input costs, PPC earns a negative gross margin on this contract. An independent appraiser indicated that the fair value of this unfavourable supply contract is a negative $500,000.

The trial balances at December 31, Year 8, for these two companies are provided as Exhibit IV.

EXHIBIT IV		
TRIAL BALANCES		
at December 31, Year 8 in Thousands of Dollars		
	Ultra	*PPC*
Cash	$ 320	$ 150
Accounts receivable	300	280
Inventory	350	380
Patents and copyrights	350	450
Furniture and equipment (net)	540	675
Building (net)	800	925
Land	450	200
Investment in PPC	2,100	
Accounts payable	$ 340	$ 138
Mortgage payable	350	
Bank loan payable		320

(continued)

EXHIBIT IV **(continued)**

	Ultra		PPC	
Preferred shares (12,500 outstanding)				1,400
Common shares (300,000 outstanding)		3,000		
Common shares (100,000 outstanding)				100
Retained earnings		1,300		117
Sales		6,200		4,530
Other income		120		7
Gain on sale of patent				50
Loss on sale of computer	1,080			
Cost of purchases	4,035		2,590	
Change in inventory	15		10	
Other expenses (incl. tax)	850		675	
Depreciation	75		142	
Interest	45		35	
Dividends			150	
	$11,310	$11,310	$6,662	$6,662

In Year 7, PPC sold packaged software costing $30,000 to Ultra at a price of $45,000. Of this software, 60% was still in Ultra's inventory at December 31, Year 7. During Year 8, packaged software costing $42,000 was sold by PPC to Ultra for $60,000. Ultra's inventory at December 31, Year 8, included $22,000 of goods purchased in this sale. Neither of these packaged software inventories sold to Ultra had a fair value difference at acquisition.

Goodwill is tested for impairment on an annual basis. Each year, it was determined that goodwill was not impaired.

Included in the Year 8 income of PPC was a gain of $50,000 on the sale of patents to another company. This sale took place on June 30, Year 8. These patents had a fair value difference of $20,000 at acquisition.

On September 30, Year 8, Ultra sold surplus computer hardware to PPC. This equipment had a cost of $6,000,000, was one-half depreciated, and was sold for its fair value of $2,000,000. Disassembly and shipping costs of $80,000 were paid by Ultra. There was estimated to be a nine-year remaining useful life in its new use.

Preferred dividends were paid in all years, and no new shares have been issued since the acquisition date.

Assume a 40% tax rate.

Required:

(a) In accordance with GAAP, prepare the following:

(i) Consolidated income statement for the year ended December 31, Year 8.

(ii) Consolidated statement of retained earnings for the year ended December 31, Year 8.

(iii) Schedule showing the values of the following consolidated balance sheet accounts as at December 31, Year 8:

(1) Software patents and copyrights

(2) Packaged software inventory

(3) Non-controlling interest

(b) Write a brief note to the management of Ultra outlining the financial reporting implications in the event that the preferred shareholders of PPC exercise their conversion privilege.

(problem prepared by Peter Secord, St. Mary's University)

Problem 8-18
LO2

The summarized trial balances of Phase Limited and Step Limited as of December 31, Year 5, are as follows (amounts in thousands):

	Phase	Step
Property, plant, and equipment	$ 540	$298
Investment in Step	257	—
Current assets	173	89
Dividends declared	80	40
Cost of goods sold	610	260
Other expenses	190	55
	$1,850	$742
Ordinary shares	$ 400	$200
Retained earnings, beginning	360	104
Liabilities	88	38
Sales, gains, and other revenue	1,002	400
	$1,850	$742

Phase had acquired the investment in Step in three stages:

Date	Shares	Cost	Step's retained earnings
Jan. 1/Year 2	4,000	$ 50,700	$ 28,000
Jan. 1/Year 4	6,000	98,300	69,000
Jan. 1/Year 5	6,000	108,000	104,000

The January 1, Year 2, acquisition enabled Phase to elect 3 members to the 10-member board of directors of Step. The January 1, Year 4, acquisition did not give Phase control over Step. Any difference between cost and the underlying carrying amount for each acquisition is attributable equally to land and to patents, which are expected to produce benefits until December 31, Year 11. Step had issued 20,000 shares on July 1, Year 1, the date of incorporation, and has neither issued nor retired shares since that date. Other information follows:

- Sale of depreciable assets (six-year remaining useful life), from Phase to Step, on June 30, Year 5, at a gain of $60,000.
- Intercompany sales:

Year 4	Phase to Step	$50,000
	Step to Phase	20,000
Year 5	Phase to Step	80,000
	Step to Phase	10,000

- Opening inventory of Phase contained merchandise purchased from Step for $10,000. Company policy was for a 20% gross margin on intercompany sales. Ending inventory of Phase contained merchandise purchased from Step for $5,000. One-half of the goods sold intercompany during Year 5 had not been paid for by year-end.
- Assume a 40% tax rate.

Required:

Compute the following consolidated amounts as of December 31, Year 5:

(a) Patents
(b) Property, plant, and equipment
(c) Current assets (ignore deferred income taxes)
(d) Non-controlling interest on statement of financial position
(e) Retained earnings, beginning
(f) Cost of goods sold
(g) Profit attributable to Phase's shareholder's (statement not required)

(adapted from a problem prepared by Peter Secord, St. Mary's University)

WEB-BASED PROBLEMS

Web Problem 8-1
L01, 2, 3, 6
Access the 2011 consolidated financial statements for Thomson Reuters Corporation by going to investor relations section of the company's website. Answer the questions below. For each question, indicate where in the financial statements you found the answer, and/or provide a brief explanation.

(a) Does the company employ the direct or indirect method of accounting for operating cash flows?
(b) What was the biggest cash outflow during the year?
(c) Describe how the cash paid for business acquisitions was reported in the statement of cash flows.
(d) State the company's accounting policy for reporting share transactions between the company and non-controlling shareholders that do not result in a loss of control of a subsidiary.
(e) Were there any share transactions between the company and non-controlling shareholders in 2010 and/or 2011 that did not result in gaining or losing control? If so, describe how the transactions were reported and the impact, if any, on consolidated net income.
(f) Assume that the company sold a subsidiary during the year and realized a substantial gain. If the company had reported the income from discontinued operations rather than in income from continuing operations, what impact would this have had on the company's share price? Briefly explain.

Web Problem 8-2
L01, 2, 3, 6
Access the 2011 financial statements for BCE Inc. by going to investor relations section of the company's website. Answer the same questions as in Problem 1. Round percentages to one decimal point and other ratios to two decimal points. For each question, indicate where in the financial statements you found the answer, and/or provide a brief explanation. (Some questions may not be applicable.)

Mc Graw Hill connect™ | Practise and learn online with Connect

Other Consolidation Reporting Issues

LEARNING OBJECTIVES

After studying this chapter, you should be able to do the following:

LO1 Identify when a special-purpose entity should be consolidated and prepare consolidated statements for a sponsor and its controlled special-purpose entities.

LO2 Describe and apply the current accounting standards that govern the reporting of interests in joint arrangements.

LO3 Understand the deferred tax implications of the accounting for a business combination.

LO4 Describe the requirements for segment disclosures and apply the quantitative thresholds to determine reportable segments.

LO5 Analyze and interpret financial statements involving other consolidation reporting issues.

LO6 Identify some of the differences between IFRSs and ASPE involving other consolidation reporting issues.

INTRODUCTION

In the previous chapters, the parent controlled the subsidiary through voting rights. However, there are other means of controlling the operating and financial policies of the subsidiary. Shoppers Drug Mart, the leading player in Canada's retail drugstore marketplace and the number-one provider of pharmacy products and services, controls associate-owned stores through franchise and operating agreements. As we will see in this chapter, the entities that are controlled by contracts and operating agreements must be consolidated in a fashion similar to that used in previous chapters.

An entity can be controlled without holding the majority of the voting shares.

Many Canadian companies participate in arrangements whereby they jointly control the operations of another entity. For example, West Fraser Timber Co. Ltd., a British Columbia-based integrated wood products company, has significant investments in a newsprint company and a pulp and paper company, which are jointly controlled with other entities. West Fraser's sales and income before taxes in 2011 in these joint ventures represented 8% and 89% of the company's total sales and income before taxes, respectively. Later in this chapter, we will consider various types of joint arrangements. After that, we look at how deferred income taxes affect the accounting for a business combination. This chapter concludes with the disclosure requirements associated with a company's operating segments.

L01 SPECIAL-PURPOSE ENTITIES

Special-purpose entities (SPEs) have long been used by businesses as a vehicle to carry out specific activities. Until recently, the only financial reporting involvement for a company establishing an SPE was the disclosure requirements regarding related-party transactions. Now GAAP require that some types of SPEs be subject to consolidation in the same manner as is a subsidiary.

An SPE is a proprietorship, partnership, corporation, or trust set up to accomplish a very specific and limited business activity. Over the past decade, SPEs have been used to lease manufacturing assets, hedge financial instruments, borrow against high-quality receivables, conduct research and development activities, and carry out a variety of other specified functions.

Low-cost financing of asset purchases is often a major benefit of establishing an SPE. Rather than engaging in the business transaction directly, the sponsoring business sets up an SPE to purchase and finance the asset acquisition. The SPE then leases the asset to the sponsor. This strategy saves the business money because the SPE is often eligible for a lower interest rate. This advantage is achieved for several reasons. First, the SPE typically operates with a very limited set of assets—in many cases, just one. By isolating an asset in an SPE, the risk of the asset is isolated from the overall risk of the sponsoring firm. Thus, the SPE's creditors remain protected by the specific collateral in the asset. Second, the business activities of an SPE can be strictly limited by its governing documents. These limits further protect lenders by preventing the SPE from engaging in any activities not specified in its agreements.

Another apparent reason for establishing an SPE was to avoid the consolidation of the SPE with the sponsoring enterprise and to thereby avoid having to show additional debt on the consolidated balance sheet. Because governing agreements limited the activities and decision making in most SPEs, the sponsoring enterprise was able to control the activities of the SPEs through the governing agreements. They did not have to own a majority of the voting shares to maintain control. In fact, a sponsoring enterprise usually owned very little, if any, of the voting shares of the SPE. Therefore, the sponsoring enterprise did not control the SPE through a voting interest and did not, until the late 1990s, have to consolidate the SPE. Like all business entities, SPEs generally have assets, liabilities, and investors with equity interests. Unlike most businesses, the role of the equity investors can be fairly minor. They may serve simply as a technical requirement to allow the SPE to function as a legal entity. Because they bear relatively low economic risk, equity investors are typically provided only a small rate of return.

Small equity investments are normally insufficient to induce lenders to provide a low-risk interest rate for an SPE. As a result, another party (often the sponsoring firm that benefits from the SPE's activities) must be prepared to contribute substantial resources to enable the SPE to secure the additional financing needed to accomplish its purpose. For example, the sponsoring firm may guarantee the debt of the SPE. Other contractual arrangements may limit returns to equity holders, while participation rights provide increased profit potential and risks to the sponsoring firm. Risks and rewards such as these cause the sponsor's economic interest to vary depending on the success of the created entity—hence the term *variable-interest entity* (VIE). In contrast to a traditional entity, an SPE's risks and rewards may not be distributed according to share ownership but according to other variable interests. Exhibit 9.1 provides several examples of variable interests in SPEs.

An SPE is an entity created to accomplish a very specific business activity.

SPEs are often able to obtain debt financing at very favourable interest rates.

Before GAAP were changed, many companies used SPEs as a vehicle for "off-balance-sheet financing."

The risks and rewards may not be distributed in accordance with equity ownership but rather with some other variable interest attaching to a sponsoring firm as a result of contractual arrangements.

EXHIBIT 9.1

VARIABLE INTERESTS IN SPEs

The following are some examples of variable interests in SPEs and the related potential for losses or returns accruing to the sponsor:

Variable interests	*Potential losses or returns*
• Guarantees of debt	• If an SPE cannot repay liabilities, sponsor will pay and incur a loss.
• Subordinated debt instruments	• If an SPE cannot repay its senior debt, the sponsor as subordinated debt holder may be required to absorb the loss.
• Variable-rate liability	• Sponsor as holder of debt may participate in returns of SPE.
• Lease residual guarantee	• If leased asset declines below the residual value, sponsor, as lessee, will make up the shortfall.
• Non-voting equity instruments	• Sponsor as holder of debt or equity may participate in residual profits.
• Services	• Sponsor as service provider receives portion of residual profits.

A firm with variable interests in an SPE increases its risk with the level (or potential level in the case of a guarantee) of resources provided. With increased risks come increased incentives to exert greater influence over the decision making of the SPE. In fact, the primary sponsor of the SPE will regularly limit the decision-making power of the equity investors through the governance documents that establish the SPE. Although, technically, the equity investors are the owners of the SPE, in reality they may retain little of the traditional responsibilities, risks, and benefits of ownership. In fact, the equity investors often cede financial control of the SPE to the primary sponsor in exchange for a guaranteed rate of return.

> The equity investors of an SPE typically receive a guaranteed rate of return as a reward for ceding control to the SPE's sponsor.

Consolidation of SPEs   In 1998, the IASB issued SIC 12 Consolidation—Special-Purpose Entities. It required that an SPE should be consolidated when the substance of the relationship between an entity and the SPE indicates that the SPE is controlled by that entity. Canada and the United States did not adopt any special requirements related to an SPE until 2003, after the collapse of Enron, a large American public company.

Enron Corp. provided what was undoubtedly the most famous example in recent memory of the improper use of SPEs. In the investigation of its bankruptcy, in which its creditors and employees lost an estimated $60 billion, the following questionable accounting practices came to light:

- Not consolidating SPEs and thereby keeping billions of dollars of debt off its balance sheet
- Recognizing inflated profits on sales to the nonconsolidated SPEs
- Recognizing revenue from sales of forward contracts that were, in effect, disguised loans
- Inflating the fair value of investments
- Not adequately disclosing related-party transactions

In the wake of the Enron collapse, the American and Canadian accounting standards boards adopted accounting standards for the consolidation of SPEs that were controlled by means other than voting interests. These standards have been commonly referred to as the "Enron standards."

Although Canada did not have any special requirements for consolidating SPEs at the time of Enron's collapse, Canadian GAAP did require a Canadian company to prepare consolidated statements when one company controlled another entity regardless of the form of control, that is, voting control or control through other means. In the United States, consolidation was required when one entity owned the majority of the voting shares. Therefore, SPEs would typically not have been consolidated in the United States prior to 2004.

> In order to determine if consolidation is required, it is first necessary to determine if there is a primary beneficiary of the VIE.

In 2003, the CICA issued Accounting Guideline 15 (AcG-15): Consolidation of Variable Interest Entities. Each enterprise involved with a variable interest entity (VIE) must determine whether the financial support provided by that enterprise makes it the primary beneficiary of the VIE's activities. The primary beneficiary of the VIE is then required to include the assets, liabilities, and results of the VIE in its consolidated financial statements.

In May 2011, the IASB issued IFRS 10, Consolidated Financial Statements. It replaced IAS 27 and SIC 12. It provides a broader and more encompassing definition of control, as outlined in Chapter 3. IFRS 10 does not use the terms *primary beneficiary* or *variable interest entity*. It uses the more generic terms of *parent* and *subsidiary*. In this chapter, we will continue to use the terms *primary beneficiary* and *variable interest entity*, to distinguish between control achieved through contractual agreements, versus *parent and subsidiary*, for control achieved through voting shares.

As we learned in Chapter 3, when assessing control, it is necessary to identify how returns from the entity's activities are shared and how decisions, if any, are made about the activities that affect those returns. A reporting entity must consider all relevant facts and circumstances, including the items discussed below, in making the judgment as to whether it has control.

> Many SPEs are created to conduct activities that are part of the primary beneficiary's ongoing activities.

Understanding the purpose and design of a structured entity helps us assess how the activities of that entity are directed and how returns are shared among its participants. For example, a reporting entity is likely to control a structured entity that has been created to undertake activities that are part of the reporting entity's ongoing activities (e.g., the entity might have been created to hold legal title to an asset that the reporting entity uses in its own activities, providing a source of financing for the reporting entity).

> The more risks taken on by the sponsor, the greater the returns received by the sponsor.

Generally, the more a reporting entity is exposed to the variability of returns from its involvement with an entity, the more power the reporting entity likely has to direct the activities of that entity which cause the returns to vary. A reporting entity likely has the power to direct the activities of a structured entity if it is exposed to a variability of returns that is potentially significant to the structured entity, and if the reporting entity's exposure is more than that of any other party.

Control of an entity that has a limited range of activities, such as an entity that manages an asset securitization, is determined on the basis of how that limited range of activities is directed and how the returns it receives from its involvement with the entity are shared. A reporting entity identifies what activities cause the returns to vary and assesses whether it has the power to direct those activities. A reporting entity's ability to act when circumstances arise constitutes power if that ability relates to the activities that cause the reporting entity's returns to vary. A reporting entity does not have to exercise its power in order to have power to direct the activities of a structured entity.

For example, if the only assets of an entity are receivables, then managing any defaulting receivables is the only activity that causes the returns to vary and, thus, affects the returns of the structured entity's participants. In this example, the party with the power to direct how defaulting receivables are managed and can affect its returns from its involvement through this power, controls that entity.

Control of an SPE is usually based on who directs the key activities of the SPE.

A reporting entity can control a structured entity by means of related arrangements. For example, a reporting entity could establish a structured entity whose founding documents restrict its activities to purchasing fixed-rate receivables of the reporting entity for cash, collecting payments from those receivables, and passing those payments to the investors in the structured entity. Receivables that are overdue by more than a specified period are put back to the reporting entity.

A reporting entity can have the power to direct the activities of a structured entity if it can change the restrictions or predetermined strategic operating and financing policies by which the structured entity operates. For example, a reporting entity can have the power to direct the activities of a structured entity by having the right to dissolve the entity or to change (or veto any changes to) the entity's charter or by-laws. Or it can have the right to dissolve an entity by holding liquidation, redemption, or other rights.

Since the primary beneficiary controls the resources of the VIE and will obtain the future returns from these resources, these resources meet the definition of an asset and should be included on the consolidated balance sheet of the primary beneficiary. Similarly, since the primary beneficiary usually bears the risk of absorbing the bulk of any expected loss of the VIE, it is effectively assuming responsibility for the liabilities of the VIE. Accordingly, these liabilities should be included on the consolidated balance sheet of the primary beneficiary. The fact that the primary beneficiary may own no voting shares whatsoever becomes inconsequential because such shares do not effectively allow the equity investors to exercise control. Thus, in assessing control, a careful examination of the VIE's governing documents and the contractual arrangements among the parties involved is necessary, to determine who bears the majority of the risks and has the greatest participation in the potential upside in the value of the net assets of the VIE. The following scenario provides an example of a structured entity and its primary beneficiary.

The definitions of assets and liabilities can be used to support the inclusion of the SPE's assets and liabilities on the consolidated balance sheet.

Example   Fleur Co. is a Quebec-based utility company. It is negotiating to acquire a power-generating plant from Rouyn Inc. for $105 million. If Fleur purchased the plant directly, it would finance the acquisition with a 5% bank loan for $100 million and $5 million in cash. Alternatively, it could set up a separate legal entity whose sole purpose would be to own the power-generating plant and lease it back to Fleur. Because the separate entity would isolate the plant from Fleur's other risky assets and liabilities and provide specific collateral, the interest rate of the financing would be 4%, which would save the company $1 million per year. To obtain the lower interest rate, Fleur must guarantee the separate entity's debt and must also maintain certain predefined debt-to-equity ratios on its own balance sheet.

To take advantage of the lower interest rate, on January 1, Year 1, Fleur establishes Energy Co. for the sole purpose of owning and leasing the power plant to Fleur. An outside investor will provide $5 million in cash in exchange for 100% of the common shares of Energy Co. Fleur and Energy sign an agreement with the following terms:

- Energy's sole purpose is to purchase and own a power-generating plant. The purchase price will be financed by a $100 million loan and a $5 million equity investment.

- Fleur has veto power on all key operating, investing, and financing decisions.

- Fleur will lease the power plant for five years for annual payments of $4.5 million to cover the cost of the interest and provide a 10% return on the $5 million investment by the outside investor.

- At the end of five years (or any extension), Fleur can renew the lease for a further five years, purchase the power plant for $105 million, or pay $5 million to buy the common shares from the outside investor.

It appears that Energy is a structured entity controlled by Fleur for the following three reasons:

1. Energy was established to provide power solely to Fleur, and the power is essential to Fleur's ongoing activities.

2. The outside investor will earn a 10% return and has very little risk. Fleur bears most of the risk of a change in utility rates and will receive any profit from the sale of power or the sale of the plant at the end of the lease term after the investor has received the guaranteed return.

3. The activities of Energy are restricted to owning and operating a power-generating plant. Fleur has the power to direct these activities through its veto power on all key operating, investing, and financing decisions.

Fleur is the primary beneficiary. It has control over Energy, receives most of the benefits, and is exposed to the major risks, even though it has invested no assets in Energy. Accordingly, Energy should be consolidated with Fleur.

An implied value of the VIE has to be determined in order to perform the initial consolidation.

Initial Measurement Issues   The financial reporting principles for consolidating VIEs are basically the same as for consolidating a parent and its subsidiary. The total consideration given is identified, and this determines the total implied value of the VIE. When the primary beneficiary gets control of the net assets of an existing business by purchasing these net assets from the existing owners, the total consideration given is the sum of the following:

- Fair value of consideration paid by the primary beneficiary to the owners of the business (plus the fair value of any previously held interests)

- Fair value of the NCI of the VIE

When the primary beneficiary contributes its own assets to an existing business and gets control of the net assets of this business, these assets are measured at the carrying amount of these assets prior to the transfer. Since the primary beneficiary had control of these assets both before and after this transfer, there is no change in the benefits and risks associated with them. Accordingly, these assets are measured at carrying amount rather than fair value. Any profit recognized by the

The equity investors will earn a 10% return and bear very little risk.

The primary beneficiary bears most of the risks and receives the residual returns.

primary beneficiary will be eliminated when determining the carrying amount for the SPE. This treatment is consistent with the entries made in Chapters 6 and 7 to eliminate unrealized profits from intercompany transactions.

Once the total implied value is determined, this value is allocated first to the identifiable assets received and the liabilities assumed in this business combination. In general, the identifiable assets and liabilities are measured at fair value. However, the assets contributed by the primary beneficiary are measured at carrying amount. In addition, IFRS 3 identifies some instances where the VIE's assets and liabilities are not reported at fair value at the date of acquisition.

If the implied value of consideration given is greater than the value attributed to the identifiable net assets, the difference is reported as goodwill when the VIE is a business or as a loss on purchase when the SPE is not a business. The definition of a business was discussed in Chapter 3. If the implied value of consideration given is less than the value attributed to the identifiable net assets received, then there is negative goodwill. All fair values used for NCI and assets and liabilities of the structured entity must be carefully reviewed to ensure that they are accurate. Once the values are confirmed, the excess of the value attributed to the net assets received over the implied value of the consideration given is reported as a gain on purchase if the VIE is a business. If the VIE is not a business, then the total consideration given is allocated to the identifiable assets on a proportionate basis such that there is no negative goodwill.

> With a few exceptions, the initial consolidation records the assets and liabilities of a VIE at fair values.

> The amounts of the implied value and the consideration received are compared to determine the amount of any goodwill or negative goodwill.

The following example will illustrate the consolidation process for a VIE.

Example XYZ Co. contributes a patent to VAR Inc. on January 1, Year 3. VAR is a business and is deemed to be a VIE. XYZ is the primary beneficiary. The patent had a carrying amount of $1 million on XYZ's separate-entity balance sheet and a fair value of $5 million. Var owned property, plant, and equipment with a carrying amount of $60 million and a fair value of $80 million. The balance sheet of VAR at the date of acquisition after XYZ's investment is as follows (in millions):

	Carrying amount	Fair value
Patent	$ 5	$15
Property, plant, and equipment	60	80
Total assets	$65	
Liabilities	40	40
Owners' equity		
XYZ	5	5
NCI	20	??
Total liabilities and equity	$65	

The allocations to be used in the consolidation of XYZ and VAR depend on the value assigned to NCI. We will demonstrate these valuation principles using the following fair values for NCI:

Situation	Fair value of NCI
A	$40
B	37
C	44

> In this example, the fair value of NCI is varied for illustrative purposes.

	A	B	C
Implied value of consideration given			
Carrying amount of amount contributed by XYZ	5	5	5
Fair value of NCI in VAR	40	37	44
Total implied value	45	42	49
Value of VAR's identifiable net assets received			
Carrying amount of amount invested by XYZ	5	5	5
Fair value of VAR's own assets	80	80	80
Less: Fair value of VAR's liabilities	(40)	(40)	(40)
Total value allocated to net assets received	45	45	45
Difference between consideration given and received	0	(3)	4
Assigned on consolidation to			
Goodwill			4
Gain on purchase		(3)	
Balance to assign	0	0	0

Note that the fair value assigned to the NCI is used to determine the total value of consideration given for VAR Inc. as a whole. This amount becomes the equivalent of the acquisition cost. In situation A, the total consideration given equals the sum of the values attributed to VAR's identifiable assets and liabilities. In situation B, the consideration given is less than the sum of VAR's net assets, resulting in a "negative goodwill" situation, which is accounted for as prescribed in IFRS 3. In situation C, the consideration given is greater than the sum of the values attributed to VAR's identifiable net assets and the difference is reflected as goodwill. The following journal entries summarize the values for VAR to be consolidated with XYZ under the three different scenarios:

	A	B	C
Goodwill			4
Patent	5	5	5
Property, plant, and equipment	80	80	80
Liabilities	(40)	(40)	(40)
NCI	(40)	(37)	(44)
Owners' equity re: XYZ	(5)	(5)	(5)
Gain on purchase		(3)	

If VAR meets the definition of a business, positive goodwill can be reported on the consolidated balance sheet.

The credit to owners' equity of $5 million will be eliminated against the debit balance for the investment in VAR on XYZ's books when preparing the consolidated balance sheet.

In subsequent years, the normal consolidation procedures are followed.

Consolidation Issues Subsequent to Initial Measurement   After the initial measurement, consolidations of VIEs with their primary beneficiary should follow the same process as if the entity were consolidated based on voting interests. The implied acquisition differential must be amortized. All intercompany transactions must be eliminated. The income of the VIE must be allocated among the parties involved (i.e., equity holders and the primary beneficiary). For a VIE, contractual arrangements, as opposed to ownership percentages, typically specify the distribution of its income.

Disclosure Requirements   IFRS 12 requires an entity to disclose information that enables users of its consolidated financial statements to understand the nature of, and changes in, the risks associated with its interests in consolidated structured entities. In particular, an entity shall disclose the terms of any contractual arrangements that could require the parent or its subsidiaries to provide financial support to a consolidated structured entity, including events or circumstances that could expose the reporting entity to a loss.

The primary beneficiary must disclose its basis of control and the nature and extent of risks resulting from its involvement with the SPE.

Canadian Tire Corporation is a leading Canadian retailer with a Canadian Tire outlet within 15 minutes for 90% of Canadians. Canadian Tire consolidates a number of SPEs, which it controls. Relevant excerpts from Canadian Tire's 2011 financial statements are presented in Exhibit 9.2.[1]

EXHIBIT 9.2

EXTRACTS (IN PART) FROM CANADIAN TIRE'S 2011 FINANCIAL STATEMENTS

3. Significant Accounting Policies

The accounting policies set out below have been applied consistently to all periods presented in these consolidated financial statements, and have been applied consistently throughout the Company.

Basis of consolidation

These consolidated financial statements include the accounts of Canadian Tire Corporation, Limited and entities it controls. Control exists when Canadian Tire Corporation, Limited has the power, directly or indirectly, to govern the financial and operating policies of an entity/arrangement so as to obtain benefit from its activities.

Special-purpose entities

The Company has established a number of SPEs. The Company does not have direct or indirect shareholdings in these entities. An SPE is consolidated, if, based on the evaluation of the substance of its relationship with the Company, including consideration of the Company's exposure to the SPE's risks and rewards, the Company concludes that it controls the SPE. SPEs were established under terms that impose strict limitations on the decision-making powers of the SPEs' management. As a result, in such instances, since the Company either receives the majority of the benefits related to the SPEs' operations and net assets, the Company is exposed to risks related to the SPEs' activities, and/or the Company obtains the majority of the residual or ownership risk related to the SPEs, these SPEs are controlled by the Company. See Note 44 for further discussion on the consolidation of SPEs.

Canadian Tire controls a number of SPEs even though it does not own any shares of these SPEs.

41. Guarantees and Commitments

The Company has provided the following significant guarantees to third parties:

Standby letters of credit and performance guarantees

Franchise Trust, a legal entity sponsored by a third party bank, originates loans to Dealers for their purchase of inventory and fixed assets. While Franchise Trust is consolidated as part of these financial statements, the Company has arranged for the third party bank to provide standby letters of credit to Franchise Trust to support the credit quality of the Dealer loan portfolio. The third party bank may also draw against the standby letters of credit to cover any shortfalls in certain related fees owing to it. In any case where a draw is made against the standby letters of credit, the Company has agreed to reimburse the third party bank issuing the standby letters of credit for the amount so drawn. In the unlikely event that all the standby letters of credit had been fully drawn simultaneously, the maximum payment by the Company under this reimbursement obligation would have been $137.2 million at December 31, 2011 (2010 – $179.4 million). The Company has not recorded any liability for these amounts, due to the credit quality of the Dealer loans and to the nature of the underlying collateral, represented by the inventory and fixed assets of the borrowing Dealers.

(continued)

> **EXHIBIT 9.2** *(continued)*
>
> *44. Transition to International Financial Reporting Standards*
>
> **D. Reconciliation of shareholders' equity from previous GAAP to IFRS**
>
> *(viii) Consolidation*
>
> **Dealer loan program**
>
> Franchise Trust, a legal entity sponsored by a third party bank, originates loans to Dealers for their purchase of inventory and fixed assets. The Company has arranged for several major Canadian banks to provide standby letters of credit to Franchise Trust to support the credit quality of the loan portfolio. The Company was not required to consolidate any part of Franchise Trust under previous GAAP. Under IFRS,[1] the Company is required to consolidate an entity/arrangement (or a portion thereof) it is considered to control based on the criteria set forth in IAS 27 and SIC 12. The Company has determined that it controls the portion (silo) of Franchise Trust that issues loans to Dealers under the Dealer loan program and accordingly, is required to consolidate the silo of Franchise Trust containing the Dealer loan program.
>
> *Source: Reproduced with permission from Canadian Tire Corporation. http://corp.canadiantire.ca/EN/ Investors/FinancialReports/Annual%20Reports%20Library/CTC_AR_2011.pdf*

Some examples of VIEs in Canada are described below.

Air Canada uses SPEs for leasing aircraft and engines and for the fueling of aircraft.

1. Air Canada has aircraft and engine leasing transactions with a number of SPEs that are VIEs. As at December 31, 2011, Air Canada controlled leasing entities covering 35 aircraft. The company also participates in fuel facilities arrangements operated through fuel facility corporations along with other airlines to contract for fuel services at various major Canadian airports. The fuel facility corporations are entities incorporated under federal or provincial statutes in order to acquire, finance, and lease assets used in connection with the fuelling of aircraft and ground support equipment. As at December 31, 2011, Air Canada controlled three of the fuel facility corporations in Canada. Air Canada's involvement with five other fuel facility corporations was not consolidated because the company felt that its risk of loss was remote.

Empire consolidates many of its franchise affiliate stores, even though it does not own a majority interest in these stores.

2. Empire Company Limited, which owns 100% of Sobeys, consolidates many of its franchise affiliate stores because franchise agreements result in the company being deemed the primary beneficiary of the stores. The company also consolidates an independent entity that provides warehouse and distribution services for one of its distribution centres.

LO2 JOINT ARRANGEMENTS

In a joint arrangement, participants contribute resources to carry out a specific undertaking.

A joint arrangement is a contractual arrangement whereby two or more parties undertake an activity together and jointly control that activity. Joint arrangements are established for a variety of purposes (e.g., as a way for parties to share costs and risks, or as a way to provide the parties with access to new technology or new markets) and can be established using different structures and legal forms. IFRS 11, Joint Arrangements, requires that parties to a joint arrangement assess their rights and obligations to determine the type of joint arrangement in which they are involved. A common example of a joint arrangement is where one venturer provides the technical expertise, and the other provides marketing and/or financial expertise. Joint arrangements are often formed for expensive and risky projects. They are fairly common in the oil-and-gas exploration sector and in large real estate developments. Also, a Canadian company will often form a joint arrangement with a foreign company or the government of a foreign country as a means of expanding into international markets. For example, Bombardier produces trains for China by operating under a joint agreement with a Chinese car manufacturer.

Joint arrangements are classified into two types: joint operations and joint ventures. The type of joint arrangement an entity is a party to depends on the rights and obligations that arise from the arrangement. An entity assesses its rights and obligations by considering the structure and legal form of the arrangement, the contractual terms agreed to by the parties to the arrangement, and, when relevant, other facts and circumstances. A joint arrangement that is not structured through a separate vehicle is a joint operation. A joint arrangement in which the assets and liabilities relating to the arrangement are held in a separate vehicle can be either a joint venture or a joint operation.

> In many joint operations, the venturers contribute the use of assets but retain title to the assets.

A joint operation is a joint arrangement whereby the parties that have joint control of the arrangement (i.e., joint operators) have rights to the assets, and obligations for the liabilities, relating to the arrangement. Each operator contributes the use of assets or resources to the activity. An example would be a case in which one venturer manufactures part of a product, a second venturer completes the manufacturing process, and a third venturer handles the marketing of the product. Revenue and expenses are shared in accordance with the joint arrangement agreement. Some joint operations involve the establishment of a corporation, partnership, or other entity, or a financial structure that is separate from the venturers themselves. An example of this type of arrangement is an oil pipeline. The venturers may contribute assets to a separate legal entity for the construction of the pipeline. Once the pipeline is completed, it is jointly owned and used by the venturers, who share the costs in accordance with an agreement.

A joint venture is a arrangement whereby the parties that have joint control of the arrangement (i.e., joint venturers) have rights to the net assets of the arrangement. An entity is a party to a joint venture if it has rights only to a share of the outcome generated by a separate entity, which has its own assets and liabilities.

We will illustrate the accounting for both types of joint arrangements.

> In joint ventures, the venturers contribute assets to a separate legal entity, which has title to the assets.

The accounting principles involved with reporting a joint arrangement are contained in IFRS 11. It deals with the financial reporting of an interest in a joint arrangement. IFRS 11 presents the following definitions relevant to our discussions:

> **Joint control** is the contractually agreed sharing of control of an arrangement, which exists only when decisions about the relevant activities require the unanimous consent of the parties sharing control.
>
> **Joint operator** is a party to a joint operation that has joint control of that joint operation.
>
> **Joint venturer** is a party to a joint venture that has joint control of that joint venture.

A distinctive feature of these descriptions is the concept of *joint control*, which must be present for a joint arrangement to exist. Joint control is established by an agreement between the parties (usually in writing) whereby no one party can

Joint control is the key feature in a joint arrangement. This means that no one venturer can unilaterally control the venture regardless of the size of its equity contribution.

unilaterally control the joint arrangement regardless of the number of assets it contributes. For example, a single entity (Company L) could own more than 50% of the voting shares of Company M. This would normally indicate that Company M is a subsidiary; however, if there was an agreement establishing joint control, Company M would be a joint arrangement and not a subsidiary, and Company L would be a joint operator or venturer and not a parent.

Accounting for Joint Operations

An operator's interest in a joint operation is reported in a fashion similar to activities carried out by any entity. It applies relevant IFRSs as it recognizes the following:

(a) The assets it controls and the liabilities it incurs

(b) The expenses it incurs

(c) Its share of the revenue and expenses from the sale of goods or services by the joint arrangement

Example 1 APP Inc., BIB Ltd., and COT Inc. sign an agreement to produce fridges for sale to wholesalers. APP will produce the motors and condensers for use in the fridges. BIB will receive the motors and condensers from APP, purchase all other parts, and assemble the fridges. COT will market, sell, and distribute the fridges to wholesalers. The three companies must agree to all major operating and financing decisions. The proceeds from sale of the fridges will be distributed 25% to APP, 45% to BIB, and 30% to COT.

APP reports the assets contributed to the joint operations on its own books until the final product is sold to the end customer.

APP will account for the assets, liabilities, and expenses involved with producing the motors and condensers for the joint operations in the same manner as it would if it were producing these items for its own operations. The cost of the motors and condensers would be included in inventory. When the inventory is shipped to BIB, it is similar to inventory on consignment. No revenue is recognized until the inventory is eventually sold by COT. At that time, APP would recognize its 25% share of the sales revenue related to the sale of the fridges. In this example, each of the three companies used their own assets to fulfill their contribution to the joint arrangement. They shared in the revenues only from the sale of the fridges.

When the venturers jointly own certain assets, the accounting becomes a bit more complicated. In addition to accounting for their own assets and liabilities used in the joint operation, they would have to account for their share of the costs and expenses involved with the jointly owned assets. This is a form of proportionate consolidation but on a very limited basis.

Example 2 DOC Inc., EGG Ltd., and FRY Inc. sign an agreement to collectively purchase an oil pipeline and to hire a company to manage and operate the pipeline on their behalf. The costs involved in running the pipeline and the revenue earned from the pipeline are shared by the three parties based on their ownership percentage. All major operating and financing decisions related to the pipeline must be agreed to by the three companies. The cost of purchasing the pipeline was $10,000,000. The pipeline has an estimated 20-year useful life with no residual value. The management fee for operating the pipeline for Year 1 was $2,000,000. Revenue earned from the pipeline in Year 1 was $3,300,000. DOC invested $3,000,000 for a 30% interest.

DOC would prepare the following entries for Year 1 to capture its share of the activities related to the pipeline:

DOC reports its proportionate share of the assets, liabilities, revenues, and expenses of the joint operation.

Pipeline	3,000,000	
Cash		3,000,000
Pipeline operating expenses (30% × 2,000,000)	600,000	
Cash		600,000
Cash (30% × 3,300,000)	990,000	
Revenue from pipeline		990,000
Amortization expense—pipeline (3,000,000/20 years)	150,000	
Accumulated amortization—pipeline		150,000

Example 3   Instead of contributing cash for a 30% interest in the pipeline, DOC contributed steel pipes to be used by the company constructing the pipeline. DOC had manufactured the pipes at a cost of $2,200,000. All parties to the contract agreed that the fair value of these pipes was $3,000,000 and the fair value of the pipeline once it was completed was $10,000,000. All other facts are the same as in Example 2.
IFRS 11 indicates the following:

> When an entity enters into a transaction with a joint operation in which it is a joint operator, such as a sale or contribution of assets, it is conducting the transaction with the other parties to the joint operation and, as such, the joint operator shall recognize gains and losses resulting from such a transaction only to the extent of the other parties' interests in the joint operation. When such transactions provide evidence of a reduction in the net realizable value of the assets to be sold or contributed to the joint operation, or of an impairment loss of those assets, those losses shall be recognized fully by the joint operator.

A portion of the gain can be recognized on the contribution of assets to a joint operation.

In our illustration, the other venturers have a 70% interest in the joint operation. DOC should recognize a gain of $560,000 (70% × [3,000,000 − 2,200,000]). The following journal entries would be recorded:

A gain can be recognized when the significant risks and rewards have been transferred.

Pipeline	3,000,000	
Steel pipes		2,200,000
Gain on steel pipes (70% of gain)		560,000
Unrealized gain — contra account (30% of gain)		240,000
Amortization expense (3,000,000/20)	150,000	
Accumulated amortization		150,000
Unrealized gain — contra account (240,000/20)	12,000	
Amortization expense		12,000

The unrealized gain is a contra account to the pipeline account; it should not be reported as a deferred gain on the liability side of the balance sheet. When DOC prepares a balance sheet, the unrealized gain will be offset against the pipeline such that the pipeline's net cost is $2,760,000 ($3,000,000 − $240,000). As the net cost of the pipeline is being amortized, the unrealized gain account is also being amortized. In effect, the unrealized gain is being brought into income over the life of the pipeline. As the pipeline is being used to generate revenue on transactions with outsiders, the venturer's own share of the unrealized gain is being recognized in income. This is similar to what happened in Chapter 7, when the unrealized profits from an intercompany sale of a depreciable asset were realized over the life of the depreciable asset.

The joint operator's own interest in the gain is recognized over the life of the asset.

Accounting for an Interest in a Joint Venture

When parties to an agreement to establish or purchase a corporation, partnership, or other entity, or a financial structure that is separate from the venturers themselves, and this entity is jointly controlled by two or more venturers, this entity is called a joint venture. The reporting of investments in joint ventures has undergone considerable change in Canada in recent years. The following table indicates the current status and effective usage dates for different reporting methods:

Proportionate consolidation was required for reporting joint ventures in Canada prior to 2011.

Method	Status
Proportionate consolidation	GAAP in Canada prior to adoption of IFRSs in 2011
Proportionate consolidation or equity method	GAAP under IFRSs prior to adoption of IFRS 11 in 2013
Equity method	GAAP under IFRSs upon adoption of IFRS 11 in 2013
Equity method	U.S. GAAP both in the past and going forward

Proportionate consolidation is a method of accounting whereby a venturer's share of each of the assets, liabilities, income, and expenses of a jointly controlled entity is combined line by line with similar items in the venturer's financial statements or reported as separate line items in the venturer's financial statements. Proportionate consolidation is an application of the proprietary theory, which was illustrated in Chapter 4.

The equity method is required for reporting joint ventures under IFRS 11.

Under IFRS 11, the venturer must use the equity method to report its investment in a joint venture. The equity method is described in IAS 28. Under this method, the venturer recognizes its share of the income earned by the joint venture through one line on the income statement, income from joint venture, and through one line on the balance sheet, investment account. In addition, the venturer needs to make adjustments through these same accounts for its share of the following items, which are illustrated below:

- Allocation and amortization of acquisition differentials
- Unrealized profits from intercompany transactions
- Contributions to the joint venture

Acquisition Differentials   The formation of a joint venture by its venturers cannot result in acquisition differentials in the investment accounts of the venturers. However, if a venturer purchased an interest in an existing entity, it could pay an amount different from its interest in the carrying amount of the joint venture's net assets, resulting in an acquisition differential. This acquisition differential would be allocated and amortized in the same manner illustrated previously for parent–subsidiary affiliations.

Intercompany Transactions   You will recall from our discussions in past chapters that intercompany profits in assets are fully eliminated from the consolidated statements of a parent and its subsidiaries. If the subsidiary was the selling company, 100% of the profit, net of income tax, is eliminated and allocated to both the

NCI and the controlling interest. If the parent was the selling company, the entire net-of-tax profit is eliminated and allocated to the shareholders of the parent.

For intercompany transactions between a venturer and the joint venture, only the venturer's share of the unrealized profit is eliminated. The other venturers' share of the profit from the intercompany transaction is considered realized if the other venturers are not related to each other. Since none of the venturers can individually control the entity, any transaction carried out by the joint venture should be viewed as an arm's-length transaction to the extent of the other venturers' interest in the joint venture. The venturer's own interest in the profit from the intercompany transaction is not realized because the venturer cannot make a profit by selling to or buying from itself.

> For a joint venture, the venturer's share of any intercompany asset profits is eliminated regardless of whether the sale was upstream or downstream.

The same treatment is prescribed for the sale of assets at a loss except in situations where the transaction provides evidence of a reduction in the net realizable value of the asset, in which case the full amount of the loss is immediately recognized.

Example 4 below illustrates the use of the equity method to report an interest in a joint venture. Appendix 9A repeats Example 4 using proportionate consolidation rather than the equity method. The method of presentation is quite different. However, the net income attributable to and the retained earnings of the investor in the joint venture are the same under both methods.

Example 4   Explor Ltd., a Calgary-based oil exploration company, is a joint venture in which A Company has a 45% ownership interest. A Company, an original founder of Explor, uses the equity method to account for its investment but has made no entries to its investment account for Year 4. The following are the financial statements of the two companies on December 31, Year 4:

INCOME STATEMENTS—Year 4

	A Company	Explor
Sales	$900,000	$370,000
Cost of sales	500,000	180,000
Miscellaneous expenses	100,000	40,000
	600,000	220,000
Income before taxes	300,000	150,000
Income tax expense	120,000	60,000
Net income	$180,000	$ 90,000

BALANCE SHEETS—December 31, Year 4

	A Company	Explor
Miscellaneous assets	$654,500	$277,000
Inventory	110,000	90,000
Investment in Explor	85,500	—
	$850,000	$367,000
Liabilities	$130,000	$ 87,000
Common shares	300,000	100,000
Retained earnings	420,000	180,000
	$850,000	$367,000

> These statements are the financial statements of a venturer and a joint venture.

During Year 4, A Company sold merchandise totalling $110,000 to Explor and recorded a gross profit of 30% on these sales. On December 31, Year 4, the inventory of Explor contained items purchased from A Company for $22,000, and Explor had a payable of $5,000 to A Company on this date.

The unrealized after-tax profit to be eliminated at the end of Year 4 is $1,782, calculated as follows:

Only the venturer's own 45% interest of the gain is considered to be unrealized.

Intercompany profits in inventory:

Total at end of year (22,000 × 30%)	$6,600
Before-tax profit considered realized — 55%	3,630
Unrealized before-tax profit — 45%	2,970
Tax on profit (40%)	1,188
After-tax unrealized profit	$1,782

The following entries would be made by Company A in Year 4 under the equity method:

Only the venturer's share of profits is eliminated.

Invest in Explor (45% × 90,000)	40,500	
Income from joint venture (45% × 90,000)		40,500
Income from joint venture	1,782	
Invest in Explor		1,782
To eliminate unrealized profits		

These entries will increase Company A's net income to $218,718, calculated as follows:

Income of A Company		$180,000
Less after-tax unrealized inventory profit		1,782
Adjusted net income		178,218
Income of Explor	$90,000	
A's ownership interest	45%	40,500
Net income		$218,718

Since A Company used the equity method prior to this year, no adjustments are necessary for its retained earnings at the beginning of the year.

Contributions to the Joint Venture

Suppose that on the date of formation of a joint venture, instead of contributing cash, a venturer contributes non-monetary assets and receives an interest in the joint venture and that the assets contributed have a fair value that is greater than their carrying amount in the records of the venturer. Would it be appropriate for the venturer to record a gain from investing these non-monetary assets in the joint venture? If so, how much, and when should it be recognized? The requirements set out in IFRS 11 regarding this matter are as follows:

1. The investment should be recorded at the fair value of the non-monetary assets transferred to the joint venture.

2. Only the gain represented by interests of the other nonrelated venturers should be recognized on the date of the contribution and only if the transaction has commercial substance as per IAS 16. This same principle was applied in Example 3 on a transfer of an asset to a joint operation. If the transaction does not have commercial substance, then the entire gain is considered to be unrealized. It shall be accounted for in the same manner as the venturer's share of the gain, which is described in the next paragraph.

3. The portion of the gain represented by the venturer's own interest should be unrealized until the asset has been sold to unrelated outsiders by the joint

venture. Alternatively, the unrealized gain can be recognized over the life of the asset if the asset is being used to generate a positive gross profit for the joint venture. In effect, the product or service being sold by the joint venture to an outsider is allowing the venturer to recognize a portion of the unrealized gain. It is similar to selling a portion of the asset to outsiders. The unrealized gains are contra accounts to the investment in joint venture account. They will be offset in the investment account on the balance sheet.

The unrealized gain is recognized as the asset is used to generate a profit on transactions with outsiders.

4. If a loss results from the recording of the investment, the portion of the loss represented by the interest of the other unrelated venturers is recognized immediately into income. When it is evident that the asset contributed to the joint venture is impaired, the entire loss is immediately recognized.

5. When the venturer transfers assets to the joint venture and receives assets in addition to an interest in the joint venture, the assets received can be considered the proceeds from the partial sale of the assets to the other unrelated venturers, provided that the assets came from the investment of the other venturers or from the other venturers' share of joint venture borrowings.

When assets are indirectly received from the other venturers, the assets are considered to be proceeds of a partial sale to the other venturers.

The following examples will illustrate these concepts.

Example 5   A Co. and B Inc. formed JV Ltd. on January 1, Year 1. A Co. invested equipment with a carrying amount of $200,000 and a fair value of $700,000 for a 40% interest in JV Ltd., while B Inc. contributed equipment, which was similar to the equipment contributed by A Co., with a total fair value of $1,050,000, for a 60% interest in JV Ltd. We will concern ourselves only with the recording by A Co. of its 40% interest in JV Ltd., and we will assume that the equipment has an estimated useful life of 10 years. On December 31, Year 1, JV Ltd. reported a net income of $204,000. We will assume that the transaction does not have commercial substance in this situation because A Co. owned a similar portion of the same type of equipment both before and after the contribution to the joint venture. The gains are calculated as follows:

Fair value of equipment transferred to JV Ltd.	$700,000
Carrying amount of equipment on A Co.'s books	200,000
Unrealized gain on transfer to JV Ltd.	$500,000

A Co.'s journal entry to record the initial investment on January 1, Year 1, is as follows:

Investment in JV Ltd.	700,000	
Equipment		200,000
Unrealized gain—contra account		500,000

A Co.'s $500,000 gain from investing equipment is unrealized.

Using the equity method of accounting, A Co. will record its 40% share of the yearly net incomes or losses reported by JV Ltd.; in addition, it will recognize the unrealized gains in income over the life of the equipment.

The December 31, Year 1, entries are as follows:

Investment in JV Ltd.	81,600	
Equity earnings from JV Ltd. (40% × 204,000)		81,600
Unrealized gain—contra account (500,000 / 10)	50,000	
Gain on transfer of equipment to JV Ltd.		50,000

This method of recognizing the gain from investing will be repeated over the next nine years, unless JV Ltd. sells this equipment before that period expires. If it does, A Co. will immediately take the balance in the unrealized gains account into income.

Example 6 The facts from this example are identical in all respects to those from Example 5, except that we assume that B Co. contributes technology (rather than equipment) with a fair value of $1,050,000. We will assume that the transaction does have commercial substance in this situation because A Co. owned equipment before its contribution to the joint venture but indirectly owned a portion of equipment and technology after the contribution. Of the $500,000 difference between the fair value and carrying amount of the equipment, the percentage ownership of the other venturers, 60%, can be recognized as a gain. A Co.'s 40% portion is an unrealized gain and is presented as a contra account to the investment account.

A Co.'s journal entry to record the initial investment on January 1, Year 1, is as follows:

A Co. recognizes a gain of $300,000, which is the portion of the gain deemed sold to outsiders.	Investment in JV Ltd.	700,000	
	Equipment		200,000
	Gain on sale of equipment		300,000
	Unrealized gain—contra account		200,000

The December 31, Year 1, entries are as follows:

Investment in JV Ltd.	81,600	
Equity earnings from JV Ltd. (40% × 204,000)		81,600

A portion of the unrealized gain is taken into income each year.

Unrealized gain—contra account (200,000/10)	20,000	
Gain on transfer of equipment to JV Ltd.		20,000

This method of recognizing the gain from investing will be repeated over the next nine years, unless JV Ltd. sells this equipment before that period expires. If it does, A Co. will immediately take the balance in the unrealized gains account into income.

Example 7 The facts from this example are identical in all respects to those from Example 5, except that we assume that A Co. receives a 40% interest in JV Ltd., plus $130,000 in cash in return for investing equipment with a fair value of $700,000, while B Inc. contributed equipment with a fair value of $725,000 plus cash of $130,000, for a total contribution of $855,000.

The original gain on the transfer ($500,000) is the same as in Example 5. However, because the $130,000 in cash received by A Co. came entirely from the cash invested by B Inc., it is considered to be the sale proceeds of the portion of the equipment deemed to have been sold. In other words, A Co. is considered to have sold a portion of the equipment to B Inc. (through the joint venture) and will immediately record a gain from selling, computed as follows:

A gain is recognized for the portion (130 ÷ 700) of the equipment deemed to be sold.

Sale proceeds	$130,000
Carrying amount of equipment sold (130 ÷ 700 × 200,000)	37,143
Immediate gain from selling equipment to B Inc.	$ 92,857

A Co.'s January 1, Year 1, journal entry to record the investment of equipment and the receipt of cash would be as follows:

Cash	130,000	
Investment in JV Ltd.	570,000	
Equipment		200,000
Gain on transfer of equipment to JV Ltd.		92,857
Unrealized gain—contra account		407,143

The December 31, Year 1, entries are as follows:

Investment in JV Ltd.	81,600	
Equity earnings from JV Ltd. (40% × 204,000)		81,600
Unrealized gain—contra account (407,143/10)	40,714	
Gain on transfer of equipment to JV Ltd.		40,714

Assuming a December 31 year-end, the $133,571 (92,857 + 40,714) gain on transfer of equipment to JV Ltd. will appear in A Co's Year 1 income statement. The unamortized balance of the A's share of the unrealized gain of $366,429 (407,143 − 40,714) will be offset against the investment account.

Example 8   In this last example, we will increase the amount of cash that A Co. received when it invested equipment for a 40% interest in JV Ltd. Let us assume that the cash received was $150,000 instead of the $130,000 that we used in Example 7. Because B Inc. invested only $130,000 cash in the joint venture, the additional $20,000 was borrowed by JV Ltd. In this situation, the $150,000 cash received is considered to be partly sale proceeds and partly a return of equity to A Co. The allocation of the cash between sale proceeds and return of equity is made as follows:

Sale proceeds:			
From B Inc.'s investment in JV Ltd.			$130,000
From borrowings of JV Ltd.	20,000		
B Inc.'s proportion	60%	12,000	
		142,000	
Return of equity to A Co.:			
A Co.'s proportion of JV borrowings	40%	8,000	
Total cash received		$150,000	

When some of the cash received by A Co. comes from joint venture borrowings, only B Co.'s share of the cash borrowed is considered proceeds from the sale of equipment.

The gain from selling is computed as follows:

Sale proceeds	$142,000
Carrying amount of assets sold (142/700 × 200,000)	40,571
Immediate gain from selling equipment to B Inc.	$101,429

A Co.'s January 1, Year 1, journal entry would be as follows:

Cash	150,000	
Investment in JV Ltd.	550,000	
Equipment		200,000
Gain from transfer of equipment to JV Ltd.		101,429
Unrealized gain—contra account		398,571

The realized gain is based on the portion of the equipment deemed to be sold to the other venturers.

On December 31, Year 1, A Co.'s journal entries would be as follows:

Investment in JV Ltd.	81,600	
Equity earnings from JV Ltd. (40% × 204,000)		81,600
Unrealized gain—contra account	39,857	
Gain from transfer of equipment to JV Ltd. (398,571 ÷ 10 years)		39,857

In the preceding examples, A Co. used the equity method to report its interest in the joint venture. If A Co. had used proportionate consolidation, the "unrealized gain—contra account" becomes a contra account to the assets originally contributed to the joint venture. It will be deducted from the venturer's share of the related assets. These assets on the proportionately consolidated balance sheet will be reported at an amount equal to the venturer's share of what would remain of the carrying amount of the assets had they not been contributed to the joint venture. In effect, the contra account brings these assets back to the historical cost amounts on the consolidated balance sheet.

Disclosure Requirements   IFRS 12 requires an entity to disclose information that enables users of its financial statements to evaluate the following:

(a) The nature, extent, and financial effects of its interests in joint arrangements, including the nature and effects of its contractual relationship with the other investors with joint control of joint arrangements

(b) The nature of, and changes in, the risks associated with its interests in joint ventures. To meet these objectives, the more substantial items required to be disclosed are as follows:

An entity must disclose the nature and extent of its operations conducted through joint arrangements.

• The nature of the entity's relationship with the joint arrangement and and the proportion of ownership interest held.

• The venturer's interest in each of current assets, non-current assets, current liabilities, non-current liabilities, revenues, and profit or loss from joint ventures.

• The nature and extent of any significant restrictions on the ability of the joint ventures to transfer funds to the venture.

Exhibit 9.3 is an extract from TransAlta Corporation's 2011 consolidated financial statements. It provides an example of disclosure for joint arrangements. Since IFRS 12 was not effective until 2013, TransAlta was not yet using IFRS 12 in 2011. As such, the note disclosure in Exhibit 9.3 did not comply with all of the requirements of IFRS 12. In particular, the note did not disclose the nature of the entity's relationship with the joint arrangement, the proportion of ownership interest held, or the interests in each of the joint ventures. TransAlta is Canada's largest publicly traded power generator and marketer of electricity and renewable energy.

Differentiate between venturers who have joint control and investors who do not have joint control.

Investor in Joint Arrangement   An investor in a joint arrangement is a party to a joint arrangement and does not have joint control over that joint arrangement. For example, a joint venture could have some owners who have joint control over the key decisions and other investors who are passive investors and do not participate in the key decisions for the joint venture. The investor receives a return on investment without being actively involved in the operating and financing decisions of the joint arrangement. The investor must account for the investment in accordance with IAS 39, or by using the equity method if it has significant influence in the joint arrangement.

EXHIBIT 9.3

EXTRACTS IN PART FROM TRANSALTA'S 2011 FINANCIAL STATEMENTS

2. Accounting Policies

W. Joint Ventures

A joint venture is a contractual arrangement that establishes the terms by which two or more parties agree to undertake and jointly control an economic activity. TransAlta's joint ventures are generally classified as two types: jointly controlled assets and jointly controlled entities.

A jointly controlled asset arises when the joint venturers have joint control or joint ownership of one or more assets contributed to, or acquired for and dedicated to, the purpose of the joint venture. Generally, each party takes a share of the output from the asset and each bears an agreed upon share of the costs incurred in respect of the joint venture. The Corporation reports its interests in jointly controlled assets in its consolidated financial statements using the proportionate consolidation method by recognizing its share of the assets, liabilities, revenues, and expenses in respect of its interest in the joint venture.

> TransAlta uses the proportionate consolidation method to account for its investments in jointly controlled assets.

In jointly controlled entities, the venturers do not have rights to individual assets or obligations of the venture. Rather, each venturer is entitled to a share of the net earnings of the jointly controlled entity. The Corporation reports its interests in jointly controlled entities using the equity method. Under the equity method, the investment in the jointly controlled entity is initially recognized at cost and the carrying amount is increased or decreased to recognize the Corporation's share of the jointly controlled entity's net earnings after the date of acquisition. The Corporation's share of net earnings resulting from transactions between the Corporation and the jointly controlled entities are eliminated based on the Corporation's ownership interest. Distributions received from the jointly controlled entities reduce the carrying amount of the investment. Any excess of the cost of an acquisition less the fair value of the recognized identifiable assets, liabilities, and contingent liabilities of an acquired jointly controlled entity is recognized as goodwill and is included in the carrying amount of the investment and is assessed for impairment as part of the investment.

> TransAlta uses the equity method to account for its investments in jointly controlled entities.

Investments in jointly controlled entities are evaluated for impairment at each statement of financial position date by first assessing whether there is objective evidence that the investment is impaired. Objective evidence could include, for example, such factors as significant financial difficulty of the investee, or information about significant changes with an adverse effect that have taken place in the technological, market, economic, or legal environment in which the investee operates, which may indicate that the cost of the investment may not be recovered. If such objective evidence is present, an impairment loss is recognized if the investment's recoverable amount is less than its carrying amount. The investment's recoverable amount is determined as the higher of value in use and fair value less costs to sell.

7. Investments

The Corporation's investment in jointly controlled entities, accounted for using the equity method, consists of its investments in CE Gen and Wailuku. The change in investments is as follows:

Balance, Jan. 1, 2010	202
Equity income	7
Distributions received	(9)
Change in foreign exchange rates	(10)
Balance, Dec. 31, 2010	190
Equity income	14
Distributions received	(15)
Change in foreign exchange rates	4
Balance, Dec. 31, 2011	193

(continued)

TransAlta disclosed the amount of revenues, expenses, assets and liabilities relating to its interests in jointly controlled entities.

EXHIBIT 9.3   *(continued)*

Summarized information on the results of operations and financial position relating to the Corporation's pro-rata interests in its jointly controlled entities is as follows:

Year ended Dec. 31		2011	2010
Results of operations:			
Revenues		133	136
Expenses		(119)	(129)
Proportionate share of net earnings		14	7

As at	Dec. 31, 2011	Dec. 31, 2010	Jan. 1, 2010
Financial position:			
Current assets	42	42	48
Long-term assets	423	437	486
Current liabilities	(29)	(28)	(36)
Long-term liabilities	(229)	(246)	(280)
Non-controlling interests	(14)	(15)	(16)
Proportionate share of net assets	193	190	202

Source: Reproduced with permission from TransAlta. http://www.transalta.com/investor-centre

See Self-Study Problem 1 for a comprehensive problem involving joint ventures. It includes most of the issues we have covered in this chapter pertaining to joint ventures.

L03   DEFERRED INCOME TAXES AND BUSINESS COMBINATIONS

Up to this point, we have ignored the income tax implications associated with business combinations. Corporate tax law in this area is quite complex and can be fully understood only by readers who have been exposed to the topic through in-depth tax courses. There is always the danger that essential accounting concepts associated with business combinations and consolidated financial statements could be overshadowed if an attempt is made to combine basic accounting issues with complex tax allocation procedures. Attentive readers will now have achieved a reasonable understanding of the broad accounting concepts behind consolidated statements. To complete our coverage of this financial reporting process, we now turn our attention to the additional effects that income tax allocation can have on the accounting for a business combination. But before we do this, we provide the following useful background material.

Deferred Income Tax Concepts

A temporary difference occurs when the carrying amount of an asset or a liability does not equal its tax base.

IAS 12: Income Taxes uses the balance sheet (or liability) approach. This approach requires that the differences between the carrying amount of an asset or a liability in the balance sheet and its tax base be accounted for. These differences are called *temporary differences.* The tax base of an asset is the amount that will be deductible for tax purposes against any taxable economic benefits that will flow to an entity when it recovers the carrying amount of the asset. If those economic benefits will not be taxable, the tax base of the asset is equal to its carrying amount. The tax base of a liability is its carrying amount, less any amount that will be deductible for tax purposes in respect of that liability in future periods. In the case of revenue received in advance, the tax base of the resulting liability is its carrying amount, less any amount of the revenue that will not be taxable in future periods.

Under IAS 12, there are two basic types of temporary differences: deductible and taxable. A *deductible temporary difference* is one that can be deducted in determining taxable income in the future when the asset or liability is recovered or settled for its carrying amount. These differences exist when (a) the carrying amount of an asset is less than its tax base, or (b) an amount related to a liability can be deducted for tax purposes. Accounting for these differences results in *deferred income tax assets*.

A *taxable temporary difference* is one that will result in future taxable amounts when the carrying amount of the asset or the liability is recovered or settled. Such differences, which result in *deferred income tax liabilities*, occur mainly when the carrying amount of an asset is greater than its tax base.

> When the carrying amount of an asset is greater than its tax base, the result is a deferred tax liability.

A few examples will illustrate some of these concepts. We assume a 40% tax rate in each case.

Example 1   A company has an account payable of $3,000 on its balance sheet at the end of Year 1 for unpaid expenses that were deducted for tax purposes during Year 1. The carrying amount is $3,000. The tax base of the liability is as follows:

Carrying amount	$3,000
Less: Amount deductible for tax in future periods	–0–
Tax base	$3,000

Because the carrying amount and the tax base are equal, a temporary difference does not exist.

Example 2   At the end of Year 1, a company has an account receivable of $1,000 from sales made during the year. This receivable is expected to be collected through a series of instalments during Years 2 and 3. For tax purposes, the revenue is taxable in the year of collection. The carrying amount at the end of Year 1 is $1,000, while the tax base is zero. This creates a taxable temporary difference of $1,000, requiring a deferred tax liability of $400.

Example 3   At the end of Year 1, a company has a warranty liability of $1,500. Warranty costs are deductible for tax purposes only when they have been paid. The carrying amount is $1,500, while the tax base is zero. We have a deductible temporary difference of $1,500, requiring a deferred tax asset of $600.

> A deductible temporary difference gives rise to a deferred tax asset.

Example 4   An asset is purchased at a cost of $2,000. For financial statement purposes, it will be depreciated using the straight-line method over a five-year life, with no estimated residual value. For tax purposes, capital cost allowance (CCA) will be taken at a 30% rate, subject to the half-year rule in the first year. The following illustrates the yearly depreciation and CCA over the first three years:

		Carrying amount	Tax base
Year 1 cost		$2,000	$2,000
Year 1:	Depreciation	400	—
	CCA	—	300

(continued)

	Carrying amount	Tax base
Balance, end of Year 1	1,600	1,700
Year 2: Depreciation	400	—
CCA	—	510
Balance, end of Year 2	1,200	1,190
Year 3: Depreciation	400	—
CCA	—	357
Balance, end of Year 3	$ 800	$ 833

When the cumulative amount of CCA taken exceeds cumulative book depreciation, the result is a deferred tax liability.

Note that at the end of Year 1, there is a deductible temporary difference of $100, requiring a deferred tax asset of $40. At the end of Year 2, we have a taxable temporary difference of $10, requiring a deferred tax liability of $4. By the end of Year 3, we are back to a deductible temporary difference of $33, requiring a deferred tax asset of approximately $13. Note also that while the carrying amount of this asset becomes zero at the end of Year 5, it will have a positive tax base for an infinite number of future years. In other words, the reversing that inevitably must occur is often a very long time happening.

These examples have focused on some of the basics behind the liabilility method and will be useful in understanding some of the business combination illustrations that follow. However, before we examine the deferred income tax effects associated with a business combination, there is one other interesting provision of IAS 12 that needs to be examined.

The Acquisition of an Asset at a Price Different from the Tax Base (other than in a business combination)

Because the liability method requires the recording of a deferred tax asset or liability whenever the carrying amount of an asset or liability differs from its tax base, a unique situation exists when a single asset is purchased and its tax base is different from its cost on the date that it was acquired. IAS 12 states that when an asset is acquired other than in a business combination, and the transaction does not affect accounting profit or taxable profit, the entity does not recognize any deferred tax liability or asset either on initial recognition or subsequently. For example, an entity purchases an asset for $1,000 with an estimated useful life of five years and an estimated residual value of zero. However, the tax base is zero because depreciation of the asset is not deductible for tax purposes. On disposal, any capital gain would not be taxable and any capital loss would not be deductible. Although there is a taxable temporary difference on the date the asset was acquired, IAS 12 states that a deferred tax liability should not be recognized in this situation. If the liability were recorded, the carrying amount of the asset would have to be increased by this amount. Then, the reported amount would be different than the amount paid, which may be confusing or less transparent to the users of the financial statements.

Deferred taxes are not recorded when acquiring a single asset for which there is a temporary difference.

Business Combination Illustrations

IAS 12 not only requires application of the liabilility method, but it also requires that deferred income taxes associated with the acquisition differential be accounted for. We use the following simple illustrations to convey the basic concepts involved and the reasoning behind them.

Example   Sub Co. has a single productive asset. The balance sheet of this company is shown below:

SUB CO.—BALANCE SHEET
at December 31, Year 3

Asset		$800
Deferred tax asset		12
		$812
Liabilities		$300
Shareholders' equity		512
		$812

There is a deferred tax asset on the separate-entity books of the subsidiary.

The tax base of the single asset and the liabilities is as follows:

Asset	$830
Liabilities	300
Net	$530

Using a 40% tax rate, Sub Co. has correctly applied the provisions of IAS 12 by setting up in its separate-entity statements a deferred tax asset of $12 for the deductible temporary difference of $30.

On January 1, Year 4, Parent Inc. purchased 100% of Sub Co. for $1,000 cash. Parent determines that the fair value of Sub's single asset is $950 and that the fair value of its liabilities is $300. The calculation of the acquisition differential is made in the following manner:

Cost of 100% of Sub Co.			$1,000
Book value of net assets of Sub Co.			512
Acquisition differential			488
Allocated:			
Asset (950 − 800)		150	
Deferred income tax asset (liability) (see calculation below)		(60)	90
Balance, goodwill			$ 398

When a business combination occurs, the acquirer records the net assets acquired at fair values, and when the tax base of these net assets are a different amount, a deferred tax asset or liability becomes part of the allocation of the acquisition cost.

The calculation of the deferred tax liability to be used for consolidation purposes is as follows:

Asset fair value used in consolidation	$950
Tax base of the asset	830
Taxable temporary difference	120
Tax rate of Sub Co.	40%
Deferred tax liability—as recalculated for consolidation	48
Deferred tax asset—as previously stated by Sub	12
Adjustment required on consolidation	$ 60

A subsidiary's deferred tax asset is replaced by a deferred tax liability upon consolidation.

Because the fair value and the tax base of Sub's liabilities are both $300, no deferred income tax implications are associated with these liabilities. Note that in applying these concepts, we are replacing a $12 deferred tax asset on the balance sheet of Sub Co. with a deferred tax liability of $48 on the consolidated balance sheet, with respect to the same asset. Note also that no deferred taxes are recorded

No deferred taxes are recognized for the difference between the tax base and carrying amount for goodwill.

in relation to the goodwill of $398. Goodwill is measured as a residual. Therefore, it would be inappropriate to recognize a deferred tax liability on the temporary difference related to the goodwill because it would increase the carrying amount of goodwill and it would no longer be a residual amount. Also, goodwill is usually not deductible for tax purposes. Any difference between the carrying amount for goodwill and the tax base would be a permanent difference.

Let us assume that Parent Inc. was formed on December 31, Year 3, by the issuance of common shares for $1,000 in cash. The nonconsolidated balance sheet of Parent is shown below, followed by the consolidated balance sheet (with bracketed amounts indicating its preparation using the direct approach):

PARENT INC.—BALANCE SHEET
at January 1, Year 4

Investment in Sub Co.	$1,000
Common shares	$1,000

PARENT INC.—CONSOLIDATED BALANCE SHEET
at January 1, Year 4

Assets (800 + 150)	$ 950
Goodwill	398
	$1,348
Liabilities	$ 300
Deferred tax liability	48
Common shares	1,000
	$1,348

The deferred tax liability that appears on the consolidated balance sheet can be verified as follows:

Carrying amount of assets above (excluding goodwill)	$ 950
Tax base of assets	830
Taxable temporary difference	120
Tax rate	40%
Deferred tax liability	$ 48

In preparing consolidated financial statements in subsequent periods, the values used for each subsidiary's net assets have to be compared with their tax base in order to determine new values for deferred tax assets and liabilities.

The treatment of the acquisition differential at the date of acquisition is fairly complicated in situations involving deferred income taxes. In subsequent periods, we must compare the carrying amount of an asset or liability with its tax base on each date that a balance sheet is prepared, and make an adjustment to previously recorded deferred tax balances. When we prepare a consolidated balance sheet subsequent to acquisition, we will amortize the acquisition differential for all items, including deferred income taxes. See Self-Study Problem 2 for a comprehensive problem involving deferred income taxes pertaining to the acquisition differential. It illustrates the calculation of deferred income taxes at the date of acquisition and the amortization of the acquisition differential pertaining to deferred income taxes subsequent to the date of acquisition.

Operating Loss Carry-Forwards

Under IAS 12, accounting recognition can be given to the carry-forward of unused tax losses, to the extent it is probable that there will be a taxable profit which the deductible temporary difference can be utilized against. If the acquired company has already recognized a deferred tax asset due to the potential carry-forward of unused tax losses, this deferred tax asset will be allowed to stand on the date of the business combination. The combining of the two companies does not ordinarily change this status. However, if the acquired company was not able to recognize unused tax losses, the fact that it is combining with the acquiring company may provide the additional impetus to satisfy the "probability" criterion. This could be the result of the combined companies doing business with each other or because they will be able to reduce future costs, both of which could result in greater possibilities of having future taxable incomes lower than they were before the combination. The deferred income tax asset would be identified as part of the acquisition differential and recognized on the consolidated financial statements. Note that recognizing such a deferred tax asset as part of the acquisition differential reduces the amount that otherwise would have been allocated to goodwill. This concept must also be taken into account in situations where a deferred tax asset was *not* recognized as an asset on the acquisition date, but subsequently becomes recognizable. An entity shall recognize acquired deferred tax benefits that it realizes after the business combination as follows:

> The tax benefits of operating loss carry-forwards, which were not previously recognizable by either party to the business combination, may be recognized as an asset.

(a) Acquired deferred tax benefits recognized within the measurement period (maximum of one year from acquisition date) that result from new information about facts and circumstances that existed at the acquisition date must be applied to reduce the carrying amount of any goodwill related to that acquisition. If the carrying amount of that goodwill is zero, any remaining deferred tax benefits must be recognized in profit or loss.

(b) All other acquired deferred tax benefits realized must be recognized in profit or loss.

The acquiring company could also benefit from a business combination in that the probability of realizing a pre-acquisition deferred tax asset of the acquirer could change. An acquirer may consider it probable that it will recover its own deferred tax asset that was not recognized before the business combination. For example, the acquirer may be able to utilize the benefit of its unused tax losses against the future taxable profit of the acquiree. In such cases, the acquirer recognizes a change in the deferred tax asset in the period of the business combination but does not include it as part of the accounting for the business combination. Therefore, the acquirer does not take it into account in measuring the goodwill or bargain purchase gain it recognizes in the business combination.

Disclosure Requirements The following summarizes the more substantial items required to be disclosed pertaining to deferred income tax arising from a business combination:

- The amount of the change, if it is a business combination in which the acquirer causes a change in the amount recognized for its pre-acquisition deferred tax asset.

> The entity must disclose the amount and reason for changes in deferred tax assets pertaining to a business combination.

- A description of the event or change in circumstances that caused the deferred tax benefits to be recognized, if the deferred tax benefits acquired in a business combination are not recognized at the acquisition date but then are recognized after.

L04

SEGMENT DISCLOSURES

For simplicity, most of the examples used in previous chapters were unrealistic, in that they consisted of a parent company and a single subsidiary. When you consider all companies that trade on the Toronto Stock Exchange, very few are made up of only two companies, and many of the larger ones consist of the parent and a substantial number of subsidiaries. The consolidation process treats these separate legal entities as a single economic entity by aggregating the components of their financial statements. In past years, all companies comprising a given consolidated group were often in a single line of business and located in Canada, so this aggregation of statements provided useful information to the users of the consolidated statements. However, the tremendous corporate expansion that started in the 1970s created companies engaged in diversified activities in many parts of the world, and it became obvious that the basic consolidated financial statements were not providing adequate information. Financial statement users needed information about a company that would allow them to assess all of its different components, which have different growth potentials, profitability characteristics, and inherent risks, which all vary with the products and services being provided and the markets being entered. Consolidated financial statements do not provide this information.

Corporate expansion has created multinational companies engaged in diversified activities.

IFRS 8: Operating Segments

Public companies are required to disclose information about their lines of business, products and services, countries where they operate, and major customers.

IFRS 8: Operating Segments must be applied for the separate and consolidated financial statements of an entity whose debt or equity instruments are traded in a public market, or of an entity that files, or is in the process of filing, the financial statements with a securities commission or other regulatory organization for the purpose of issuing any class of instruments in a public market. The entity must disclose information about its operating segments in addition to information about its products and services, the countries in which it operates, and its major customers. It is expected that such information will provide users with a better understanding of a company's performance and its prospects for future cash flows.

Operating segments are identified based on how a company's management organizes its components internally for assessing performance and making strategic decisions. This identification focuses on the financial information that the company's decision makers use for that purpose. Each component is called an operating segment and is defined as follows:

(a) Engages in business activities from which it may earn revenues[2] and incur expenses (including those relating to transactions with other components of the same enterprise)

(b) Operating results are regularly reviewed by the entity's chief operating decision maker to allocate resources the segment and assess its performance

(c) Discrete financial information is available for it

Identification of Reportable Operating Segments

IFRS 8 requires information to be disclosed about all operating segments that meet certain *quantitative thresholds.* The requirement description follows.

An enterprise should disclose separately information about an operating segment that meets *any* of the following quantitative thresholds:

(a) Its reported revenue, including both sales to external customers and inter-segment sales or transfers, is 10% or more of the combined revenue, internal and external, of all operating segments.

(b) The absolute amount of its reported profit or loss is 10% or more of the greater, in absolute amount, of the

   (i) combined reported profit of all operating segments that did not report a loss and

   (ii) combined reported loss of all operating segments that did report a loss.

(c) Its assets are 10% or more of the combined assets of all operating segments.

These quantitative thresholds establish which reportable operating segments require separate disclosures. Any segments falling outside these guidelines may be combined under the category "Other," provided that at least 75% of a company's total external revenue is included in reportable segments. If it is not, additional operating segments must be disclosed. IFRS 8 also suggests that from a practical point of view, the total number of operating segments reported will probably not exceed ten.

Example   The following illustrates an application of quantitative thresholds. For internal evaluation purposes, JK Enterprises Inc. generates information from its six divisions. In terms of IFRS 8, these divisions are operating segments. The following amounts (stated in millions) have been assembled to determine which of these operating segments are reportable in accordance with the standard's quantitative thresholds.

Operating segments	Revenues	Operating profit (loss)	Assets
Auto parts	$53.9	$18.1	$10.9
Office furnishings	8.6	1.3	1.2
Publishing	6.5	(2.1)	1.4
Retail	5.0	(2.8)	3.2
Finance	11.8	3.7	14.0
Software	7.9	3.9	0.9
	$93.7	$22.1	$31.6

Revenue Test

10% × $93.7 = $9.37

From this test, auto parts and finance are identified as reportable segments.

Operating Profit (Loss) Test

To apply this test, first compute separate totals for all profits and all losses. Then choose the largest of the absolute amount of the two totals, as follows:

Total of all operating profits	$27.0
Total of all operating losses	4.9
10% × $27.0 = $2.7	

Auto parts, retail, finance, and software are identified as reportable segments.

Asset Test

$$10\% \times \$31.6 = \$3.16$$

Auto parts, retail, and finance are identified as reportable segments.

Following is a summary of all three quantitative tests for JK Enterprises:

Operating segments	Revenues	Operating profit (loss)	Assets
Auto parts	X	X	X
Office furnishings			
Publishing			
Retail		X	X
Finance	X	X	X
Software		X	

Separate disclosure is required if a segment satisfies any one test.

Thus, separate disclosures are required for auto parts, retail, finance, and software, as each satisfies at least one of the tests. The cumulative revenue for these four segments is 83.9%, which satisfies the requirement of having at least 75% of total revenue being reported in segments other than the "Other" segment. Office furnishings and publishing can be combined and reported as "Other."

IFRS 8 outlines extensive disclosures required for each reportable segment.

Disclosure Requirements   The following disclosures are required for each reportable segment that has been identified by the quantitative thresholds:

1. Factors used by management to identify segments

2. The types of products and services that generate revenues

3. A measure of profit (loss)

4. Total assets

5. Liabilities for each reportable segment if such amounts are regularly provided to the chief operating decision maker

6. Each of the following, *if* the specific amounts are included in the measure of profit (loss) regularly reviewed by the chief operating decision maker:
   (a) Revenues from external customers
   (b) Intersegment revenues
   (c) Interest revenue and expense (This may be netted for a particular segment only if that segment receives a majority of its revenues from interest *and* if the chief operating decision maker uses the net number to assess performance.)
   (d) Depreciation and amortization
   (e) Material income and expense items
   (f) Equity income from associates and joint ventures
   (g) Income taxes
   (h) Significant non-cash items other than depreciation and amortization

7. The amount of investment in associates and joint ventures accounted for by the equity method

8. The amounts of additions to non-current assets other than financial instruments, deferred tax assets, and post-employment benefits assets

9. Explanations of how a segment's profit (loss) and assets have been measured, how common costs and jointly used assets have been allocated, and of the accounting policies that have been used

10. Reconciliations of the following:
    (a) The total of the reportable segments' revenues to the entity's revenue
    (b) The total of the reportable segments' measures of profit or loss to the entity's profit or loss
    (c) The total of the reportable segments' assets to the entity's assets
    (d) The total of the reportable segments' liabilities to the entity's liabilities if segment liabilities are reported separately
    (e) The total of the reportable segments' amounts for every other material item of information disclosed to the corresponding amount for the entity

> Reconciliations of the segments' total revenues, profits, assets, and liabilities to the entity's overall revenues, profits, assets, and liabilities must be provided.

The following information must also be disclosed, unless such information has already been clearly provided as part of the segment disclosures. This additional information is also required in situations where the company has only a single reportable segment:

1. The revenue from external customers for each product or service, or for each group of similar products and services, whenever practical.

> Revenue must be segregated by product or service and by geographical area.

2. The revenue from external customers broken down between those from the company's country of domicile (i.e., Canada) and those from all foreign countries. Where revenue from an individual country is material, it must be separately disclosed.

3. Goodwill; property, plant, and equipment; and intangible assets broken down between those located in Canada and those in foreign countries. Where assets located in an individual country are material, they must be separately disclosed.

4. When a company's sales to a single external customer are 10% or more of total revenues, the company must disclose this fact, as well as the total amount of revenues from each customer and which operating segment reported such revenues. The identity of the customer does not have to be disclosed.

As with all financial reporting, comparative amounts for at least the last fiscal year must also be presented.

The disclosures required by IFRS 8 provide external users with the information that top management uses to assess performance. The presentation of a measure of profit, revenue, and assets for each reportable segment allows a statement user to calculate a measure of return on assets, margin, and turnover and the risks associated with each segment, so that the relative contribution of each segment to the overall profitability of the company can be assessed and compared with that of the previous year.

> The entity must disclose a measure of profit, revenue, and assets for each reportable segment.

BCE is Canada's largest telecommunication company. Relevant excerpts from its 2011 financial statements pertaining to its different operating segments are presented in Exhibit 9.4.

EXHIBIT 9.4

EXTRACTS (IN PART) FROM BCE'S 2011 FINANCIAL STATEMENTS

Note 3 | Segmented Information

The accounting policies used in our segment reporting are the same as those we describe in Note 2, *Significant Accounting Policies.* Our net earnings are reported in four segments: *Bell Wireline, Bell Wireless, Bell Media* and *Bell Aliant.* Our segments reflect how we

(continued)

> BCE breaks down its operations into four different segments, based on how it manages its business.

EXHIBIT 9.4   *(continued)*

manage our business and how we classify our operations for planning and measuring performance. Accordingly, we operate and manage our segments as strategic business units organized by products and services. Segments negotiate sales with each other as if they were unrelated parties.

Certain costs are managed on a total company basis and are not segregated by segment.

We measure the performance of each segment based on segment profit, which is equal to operating revenues less operating costs for the segment. We also allocate severance, acquisition and other costs and depreciation and amortization to the segments. Substantially all of our finance costs, expected return on pension plan assets and other income are managed on a total company basis and, accordingly, are not reflected in segment results. The inter-segment eliminations eliminate any intercompany transactions included in each segment's results.

Our operations and most of our assets are located in Canada. The Bell Wireline segment provides local telephone, long distance, Internet, data, video and other services and products to Bell Canada's residential, small and medium-sized business and large enterprise customers, primarily in the urban areas of Ontario and Québec. Satellite video services are provided nationwide. Also included in this segment is our wholesale business, which buys and sells local telephone, long distance, data and other services from or to resellers and other carriers.

On January 1, 2011, Bell acquired xwave, a division of Bell Aliant, specializing in IT professional services and advanced technology solutions. As a result, 2010 results for Bell Wireline and Bell Aliant reflect the change in ownership of xwave.

The Bell Wireless segment provides wireless voice and data communication products and services to Bell Canada's residential, small and medium-sized business and large enterprise customers across Canada.

The Bell Media segment was reported as a separate segment for the first time in 2011 due to BCE's purchase of CTV.

On April 1, 2011, BCE acquired the remaining 85% of CTV Inc. (CTV) common shares that it did not already own. CTV is reported as a new segment, Bell Media, which also includes certain assets that we transferred to it from our wireline business. The Bell Media segment provides specialty TV, digital media, conventional TV and radio broadcasting entertainment services to customers across Canada.

Intersegment transactions are eliminated.

The Bell Aliant segment provides voice, data, Internet, video, wireless and value-added business solutions to residential and business customers in the Atlantic provinces and in rural and regional areas of Ontario and Québec.

SEGMENTED INFORMATION

For the Year Ended December 31, 2011	Note	Bell Wireline	Bell Wireless	Bell Media	Inter-Segment Eliminations	Bell	Bell Aliant	Inter-Segment Eliminations	BCE
Operating revenues									
External customers		10,308	5,191	1,455	–	16,954	2,543	–	19,497
Inter-segment		313	40	87	(261)	179	232	(411)	–
Total operating revenues		10,621	5,231	1,542	(261)	17,133	2,775	(411)	19,497
Operating costs	5	(6,466)	(3,408)	(1,208)	261	(10,821)	(1,458)	411	(11,868)
Segment profit[1]		4,155	1,823	334	–	6,312	1,317	–	7,629
Severance, acquisition and other costs	6	(189)	(13)	(165)	–	(367)	(42)	–	(409)
Depreciation and amortization		(2,195)	(433)	(81)	–	(2,709)	(552)	–	(3,261)

(continued)

EXHIBIT 9.4 **(continued)**

For the Year Ended December 31, 2011	Note	Bell Wireline	Bell Wireless	Bell Media	Inter-Segment Eliminations	Bell	Bell Aliant	Inter-Segment Eliminations	BCE
Finance costs									
Interest expense									(842)
Interest on employee benefit obligations									(984)
Expected return on pension plan assets									1,032
Other income									129
Earnings before income taxes									3,294
Goodwill allocated by groups of CGUs	16	2,521	2,302	1,393	–	6,216	969	–	7,185
Indefinite-life intangible assets allocated by groups of CGUs	14	1,314	2,058	1,511	–	4,883	339	–	5,222
Capital expenditures		1,973	619	91	–	2,683	573	–	3,256

(1) The chief operating decision maker uses only one measure of profit to make decisions and assess performance, being operating revenues less operating costs for the segment.

REVENUES BY PRODUCT

For the Year Ended December 31	2011	2010
Revenues		
Local and access	2,852	3,012
Long distance	903	923
Data	3,811	3,985
Wireless	4,769	4,469
Video	1,831	1,749
Media	1,455	–
Equipment and other	1,333	1,369
Total external revenues	16,954	15,507
Inter-segment revenues	179	162
Bell	17,133	15,669
Bell Aliant	2,775	2,808
Inter-segment eliminations	(411)	(408)
BCE	19,497	18,069

Wireless is the largest product line in terms of sales.

Source: Reproduced with permission from BCE. http://www.bce.ca/investors/investoroverview

ANALYSIS AND INTERPRETATION OF FINANCIAL STATEMENTS L05

Under IFRSs, the equity method must be used to report an investment in a joint venture. Under ASPE, investors can report their interest in joint ventures using proportionate consolidation, the cost method, or the equity method. Exhibit 9.5 presents the income statements and balance sheets for Example 4

EXHIBIT 9.5	Impact of Presentation Method on Return-on-Equity and Debt-to-Equity Ratios

INCOME STATEMENTS—Year 4

	Equity method	Proportionate consolidation
Sales	$900,000	$1,017,000
Income from joint venture	64,530	
	964,530	1,017,000
Cost of sales	500,000	534,470
Miscellaneous expenses	100,000	118,000
	600,000	652,470
Income before taxes	364,530	364,530
Income tax expense	145,812	145,812
Net income	$218,718	$ 218,718

The equity method reports income from the joint venture on one line, whereas proportionate consolidation reports the income on a line-by-line basis.

BALANCE SHEETS—December 31, Year 4

	Equity method	Proportionate consolidation
Miscellaneous assets	$654,500	$776,900
Inventory	110,000	147,530
Deferred charge—income taxes		1,188
Investment in Explor (85,500 + 40,500 − 1,782)	124,218	—
	$888,718	$925,618
Liabilities	$130,000	$166,900
Common shares	300,000	300,000
Retained earnings	458,718	458,718
	$888,718	$925,618
Return on equity (net income/shareholders' equity)	28.8%	28.8%
Debt to equity (liabilities/shareholders' equity)	17.1	22.0

Net income and retained earnings under the equity method are equal to consolidated net income and retained earnings using proportionate consolidation.

under two scenarios: equity method and proportionate consolidation. The exhibit also indicates the return-on-equity ratio and debt-to-equity ratio for each reporting method.

Note the following from Exhibit 9.5:

- The net income and retained earnings under the equity method are equal to consolidated net income and consolidated retained earnings, respectively.

- The return on equity under the equity method is equal to the consolidated return on equity.

The debt-to-equity ratio is higher under proportionate consolidation.

- The debt-to-equity ratio is higher on the consolidated statements because the venturer's share of the joint venture's debt is included on the consolidated financial statements but not included on the investor's balance sheet under the equity method.

- The solvency position looks worst on the consolidated financial statements due to the higher debt-to-equity ratio.

ASPE DIFFERENCES

An entity is a variable interest entity and subject to consolidation under ASPE when, by design, one or more of the following conditions exist: `L06`

(a) The total equity investment at risk is not sufficient to permit the entity to finance its activities without additional subordinated financial support provided by any parties, including equity holders. In most cases, if equity at risk is less than 10% of total assets, the risk is deemed insufficient.

(b) As a group, the holders of the equity investment at risk lack any one of the following three characteristics of a controlling financial interest:

　(i) The direct or indirect ability to make decisions about an entity's activities that have a significant effect on the success of the entity.
　(ii) The obligation to absorb the expected losses of the entity.
　(iii) The right to receive the expected residual returns of the entity.

The following pertain to private enterprises:

- May report association with VIEs using full consolidation, the cost method, or the equity method but must be consistent with the method used for reporting subsidiaries.
- May report interest in joint ventures using proportionate consolidation, the cost method, or the equity method.
- May use the taxes payable method or the future income tax payable method, which is similar to the liability method under IFRSs, to account for income tax.
- Not required to disclose any information about operating segments.

For the third point above, deferred income taxes need not be recognized; however, the entity must prepare and disclose reconciliation between the statutory rate and the effective tax rate.

> Private enterprises can use proportionate consolidation to report their investments in joint ventures.

U.S. GAAP DIFFERENCES

U.S. GAAP and IFRSs have many similarities for the topics presented in this chapter. The significant differences are summarized as follows:

1. IFRSs require that an interest in an SPE be consolidated when the parent controls the SPE. The same definition of control is used for assessing control based on voting interest versus contractual arrangements. U.S. GAAP assess control of an SPE by determining whether the reporting entity receives the majority of benefits from and is exposed to the majority of the risks of loss for the SPE.

2. Under IFRSs, there is an exemption from recognizing a deferred tax liability (asset) for the initial recognition of an asset or liability in a transaction that is not a business combination, and at the time of the transaction, which affects neither accounting profit nor taxable profit. Under U.S. GAAP, there is no such exemption.

> U.S. GAAP considers benefits and risks rather than control when determining whether or not an SPE should be consolidated.

3. Whereas IFRSs require the disclosure of liabilities of operating segments when this information is provided to the chief operating decision maker, U.S. GAAP does not require this disclosure even if this information is provided to the chief operating decision maker.

SUMMARY

In this chapter, we have examined four different topics, which almost wind up our study of business combinations and the preparation of consolidated financial statements. Consolidation is required for a VIE, which is controlled by a primary beneficiary on a basis of control other than through ownership of a voting interest. For an interest in a joint operation, the venturer should recognize the assets it controls and the liabilities it incurs, the expenses it incurs, and its share of the revenue and expenses from the sale of goods or services by the joint arrangement. The equity method should be used to report an investment in a joint venture.

Deferred tax assets and liabilities should be recognized on the consolidated financial statements for the differences between the carrying amounts and the tax bases of subsidiary's net assets.

Consolidation hides information about the lines of business conducted by multinational conglomerates. Required segment disclosures are designed to provide financial statement users with relevant information that will aid them in assessing company results.

Significant Changes in GAAP in the Last Three Years

1. Definition of control has broadened to include control through voting rights, contracts, or operating agreements.

2. Interests in joint ventures are reported using the equity method rather than having a choice between proportional consolidation and the equity method.

3. A venturer can recognize the portion of a gain that is attributable to the interests of the other venturers on contribution of a non-monetary asset to a joint venture if the transaction has commercial substance.

Changes Expected in GAAP in the Next Three Years

No major changes are expected for topics in this chapter.

SELF-STUDY PROBLEM 1

The following are the Year 5 financial statements of MAR Corporation and OTT Company, a joint venture in which MAR has a 35% ownership interest:

	MAR	OTT
Year 5 income statements		
Sales	$906,750	$250,000
Management fees	25,000	—
Interest	—	3,600

Gain on land sale	—	20,000
Dividends	5,250	—
	937,000	273,600
Cost of sales	540,000	162,000
Interest expense	3,600	—
Other expenses	196,400	71,600
Income tax expense	80,000	16,000
	820,000	249,600
Profit	$117,000	$ 24,000

Year 5 retained earnings statements

Balance, January 1	$153,000	$ 72,000
Profit	117,000	24,000
	270,000	96,000
Dividends	50,000	15,000
Balance, December 31	$220,000	$ 81,000

Balance Sheets—at December 31, Year 5

Cash	$ 12,000	$ 15,000
Accounts and notes receivable	70,000	63,000
Inventory	32,000	27,000
Property, plant, and equipment (net)	448,000	66,000
Investment in OTT Company	30,000	—
	$592,000	$171,000
Notes payable	$ 60,000	$ —
Other liabilities	212,000	40,000
Common shares	100,000	50,000
Retained earnings	220,000	81,000
	$592,000	$171,000

Additional Information

- On January 1, Year 3, MAR purchased 35% of the common shares of OTT for $30,000 and signed a joint venture agreement with the other two parties in the joint venture. On that date, OTT had retained earnings of $10,000, and the carrying amounts of its identifiable net assets were equal to fair values.
- The companies sell merchandise to each other. MAR sells to OTT at a gross profit rate of 38%; OTT earns a gross profit of 40% from its sales to MAR.
- The December 31, Year 4, inventory of MAR contained purchases made from OTT amounting to $7,000. There were no intercompany purchases in the inventory of OTT on this date.
- During Year 5 the following intercompany transactions took place:

  (a) OTT made a $25,000 payment to MAR for management fees, which was recorded as "other expense."
  (b) OTT made sales of $75,000 to MAR. The December 31, Year 5, inventory of MAR contained merchandise purchased from OTT amounting to $16,500.
  (c) MAR made sales of $100,000 to OTT. The December 31, Year 5, inventory of OTT contained merchandise purchased from MAR amounting to $15,000.
  (d) On July 1, Year 5, MAR borrowed $60,000 from OTT and signed a note bearing interest at 12% per annum. Interest on this note was paid on December 31, Year 5.
  (e) In Year 5, OTT sold land to MAR, recording a gain of $20,000. This land is being held by MAR on December 31, Year 5.

- Goodwill impairment tests have been conducted yearly by MAR since the date of acquisition. MAR's 35% share of the losses due to impairment was as follows: Year 3, $1,040; Year 4, $320; Year 5, $680.
- MAR has accounted for its investment using the cost method for internal record keeping.
- Both companies pay income tax at a rate of 40%. Ignore income tax on the acquisition differential.

Required:

(a) Calculate the following account balances to be reported by MAR under the equity method:

    (i)   Retained earnings as at January 1, Year 5.
    (ii) Net income for Year 5.
    (iii) Investment in OTT as at December 31, Year 5.

(b) Prepare MAR's journal entries under the equity method for Year 5.
*(c) Prepare consolidated financial statements for MAR for Year 5.

SOLUTION TO SELF-STUDY PROBLEM 1

CALCULATION AND AMORTIZATION OF THE ACQUISITION DIFFERENTIAL

Cost of 35% of OTT, Jan. 1, Year 3		$30,000
Carrying amount of OTT, Jan. 1, Year 3		
Common shares	50,000	
Retained earnings	10,000	
	60,000	
MAR's share (35%)		21,000
Acquisition differential		9,000
Allocated to revalue the net assets of OTT		–0–
Goodwill, Jan. 1, Year 3		9,000
Amortized (impairment losses):		
Year 3–Year 4	1,360 **(a)**	
Year 5	680 **(b)**	2,040
Goodwill, Dec. 31, Year 5		$ 6,960 **(c)**

INTERCOMPANY ITEMS

Notes receivable and payable (35% × 60,000)	$21,000 **(d)**
Management fee revenue and expense (35% × 25,000)	8,750 **(e)**
Sales and purchases (35% × [75,000 + 100,000])	61,250 **(f)**
Interest revenue and expense (35% × [12% × 60,000 × 1/2 yr])	1,260 **(g)**
Dividend from OTT (35% × 15,000)	5,250 **(h)**

UNREALIZED PROFITS

	Before tax	40% tax	After tax
Inventory			
Opening (7,000 × 40% × 35%)—OTT selling	$ 980	$ 392	$ 588 **(i)**
Ending			
OTT selling (16,500 × 40% × 35%)	$2,310	$ 924	$1,386 **(j)**
MAR selling (15,000 × 38% × 35%)	1,995	798	1,197 **(k)**
	$4,305	$1,722	$2,583 **(l)**
Land—OTT selling (20,000 × 35%)	$7,000	$2,800	$4,200 **(m)**

(a) (i)

CALCULATION OF RETAINED EARNINGS
at January 1, Year 5

Retained earnings, Jan. 1, Year 5—MAR		$153,000
Less: Amortization of acquisition differential **(a)**		1,360
		151,640
Retained earnings, Jan. 1, Year 5—OTT	72,000	
Acquisition retained earnings	10,000	
Increase	62,000	
MAR's interest (35%)	21,700	
Less: Opening inventory profit **(i)**	588	
Adjusted increase		21,112 **(n)**
Consolidated retained earnings, Jan. 1, Year 5		$172,752 **(o)**

(ii)

CALCULATION OF NET INCOME—Year 5

Income of MAR			$117,000
Less: Dividends from OTT **(h)**		5,250	
Ending inventory profit **(k)**		1,197	
Amortization of acquisition differential **(b)**		680	7,127
Adjusted net income			109,873
Income of OTT		24,000	
MAR's interest (35%)		8,400	
Less: Ending inventory profit **(j)**	1,386		
Land gain **(m)**	4,200	5,586	
		2,814	
Add: Opening inventory profit **(i)**		588	
Adjusted net income			3,402 **(p)**
Net income under equity method			$113,275 **(q)**

(iii)

BALANCE IN INVESTMENT ACCOUNT
at December 31, Year 5

Balance in investment account under cost method			$30,000
Less: Ending inventory profit **(k)**		1,197	
Amortization of acquisition differential **(a & b)** *full* *parent amount*		2,040	3,237
Adjusted			26,763
Retained earnings, Dec. 31, Year 5—OTT		81,000	
Acquisition retained earnings		10,000	
Increase		71,000	
MAR's interest (35%)		24,850	
Less: Ending inventory profit **(j)**	1,386		
Land gain **(m)**	4,200	5,586	
Adjusted increase			19,264
Balance in investment account under equity method			$46,027

(b)

YEAR 5 EQUITY METHOD JOURNAL ENTRIES
(See Calculation of Net Income)

Investment in OTT **(p)**	3,402	
Investment income **(p)**		3,402
Adjusted net income of OTT.		
Cash	5,250	
Investment in OTT **(h)**		5,250
Dividends from OTT		

Investment income	1,197	
Investment in OTT **(k)**		1,197
Ending inventory profit—MAR selling		
Investment income **(b)**	680	
Investment in OTT		680
Amortization of acquisition differential		

(c)

MAR CORPORATION
CONSOLIDATED INCOME STATEMENT

Sales (906,750 + 35% × 250,000 − **[f] 61,250**)	$933,000
Management fees (25,000 + 35% × 0 − **[e] 8,750**)	16,250
Interest (0 + 35% × 3,600 − **[g] 1,260**)	0
Gain on land sale (0 + 35% × 20,000 − **[m] 7,000**)	0
Dividends (5,250 + 35% × 0 − **[h] 5,250**)	0
	949,250
Cost of sales (540,000 + 35% × 162,000	
− **[f] 61,250** − **[i] 980** + **[j] 2,310** + **[k] 1,995**)	538,775
Interest expense (3,600 + 35% × 0 − **[g] 1,260**)	2,340
Other expenses (196,400 + 35% × 71,600 − **[e] 8,750**)	212,710
Goodwill impairment loss (0 + 35% × 0 + **[b] 680**)	680
Income tax expense (80,000 + 35% × 16,000	
+ **[i] 392** − **[j] 924** − **[k] 798** − **[m] 2,800**)	81,470
	835,975
Profit	$113,275

RETAINED EARNINGS STATEMENT

Balance, January 1	$172,752
Profit	113,275
	286,027
Dividends	50,000
Balance, December 31	$236,027

no UCI

BALANCE SHEET

Cash (12,000 + 35% × 15,000)	$ 17,250
Accounts and notes receivable (70,000 + 35% × 63,000 − **[d] 21,000**)	71,050
Inventory (32,000 + 35% × 27,000 − **[j] 2,310** − **[k] 1,995**)	37,145
Property, plant, and equipment (net) (448,000 + 35% × 66,000 − **[m] 7,000**)	464,100
Deferred income taxes (0 + 35% × 0 + **[j] 924** + **[k] 798** + **[m] 2,800**)	4,522
Goodwill **(c)**	6,960
	$601,027
Notes payable (60,000 + 35% × 0 − **[d] 21,000**)	$ 39,000
Other liabilities (212,000 + 35% × 40,000)	226,000
Common shares	100,000
Retained earnings	236,027
	$601,027

SELF-STUDY PROBLEM 2

L03   On December 31, Year 2, Pat Inc. purchased 80% of the outstanding ordinary shares of Sam Company for $620,000. At that date, Sam had ordinary shares of $400,000 and retained earnings of $125,000. In negotiating the purchase price, it was agreed that the assets on Sam's balance sheet were fairly valued except for plant assets, which had an $80,000 excess of fair value over carrying amount. It was also agreed that Sam had unrecognized intangible assets consisting of trademarks that had an estimated value of $50,000. The plant assets had a remaining useful life of 8 years at the acquisition date, and the trademarks would be amortized over a 10-year period. Any goodwill arising from this business combination would be tested periodically for impairment. Pat accounts for its investment using the cost method and prepares consolidated statements using the parent company extension theory.

Additional Information

- Impairment tests performed at the end of Year 6 indicated that Sam's portion of the goodwill had a recoverable amount of $85,000 and the trademarks had a recoverable amount of $29,000. The impairment loss on these assets occurred entirely in Year 6.
- On December 26, Year 6, Pat declared dividends of $72,000, while Sam declared dividends of $40,000.
- Depreciation and amortization expense is reported in selling expenses, while impairment losses are reported in other expenses.
- Both companies pay income tax at the rate of 40%.

Condensed financial statements for Pat and Sam for the year ended December 31, Year 6, were as follows:

STATEMENTS OF FINANCIAL POSITION
at December 31, Year 6

Assets	Pat	Sam
Plant assets—net	$ 460,000	$ 320,000
Investment in Sam Company	620,000	—
Other assets	580,000	804,000
	$1,660,000	$1,124,000
Shareholders' Equity and Liabilities		
Ordinary shares	$1,000,000	$ 400,000
Retained earnings	220,000	300,000
Deferred tax liability	40,000	30,000
Other liabilities	400,000	394,000
	$1,660,000	$1,124,000

INCOME STATEMENTS
for the Year Ended December 31, Year 6

	Pat	Sam
Sales	$1,740,000	$1,030,000
Interest and dividend income	68,000	4,000
	1,808,000	1,034,000
Cost of goods sold	1,276,000	720,000
Selling expenses	44,000	70,000
Other expenses	166,000	74,000
Income tax expense	130,000	70,000
	1,616,000	934,000
Profit	$ 192,000	$ 100,000

Required:

(a) Prepare a schedule to allocate the acquisition differential at the date of acquisition and a schedule to amortize the acquisition differential from the date of acquisition to the end of Year 6. Deferred income taxes should be recognized on the acquisition differential at the date of acquisition.

(b) Prepare the journal entries for Pat's separate-entity books to account for the investment in Sam for Year 6 and determine the investment income from Sam for Year 6 under:

  i) the equity method, and
  ii) the cost method.

(c) Prepare consolidated financial statements for Year 6.

SOLUTION TO SELF-STUDY PROBLEM 2

(a)

Cost of 80% of Sam			620,000	
Implied value of 100%			775,000	
Carrying amount of Sam's net assets				
= Carrying amount of Sam's shareholders' equity				
Ordinary shares		400,000		
Retained earnings		125,000	525,000	**(a)**
Acquisition differential			250,000	
Allocated:		FV – CA		
Plant assets		80,000		
Trademarks		50,000		
		130,000		
Deferred income tax liability (130,000 × 40%)		(52,000)		
Subtotal			78,000	**(b)**
Goodwill for 100%			172,000	
Less: NCI's share at 20% (not recognized on consolidated SFP)			34,400	
Goodwill for Pat's 80% (recognized on consolidated SFP)			137,600	
NCI at date of acquisition (20% × [**(a)** 525,000 + **(b)** 78,000])			120,600	**(c)**

	Bal	Amortization		Loss	Bal	
	Dec. 31/Yr2	to Dec. 31/Yr5	Yr6	Yr6	Dec. 31/Yr6	
Plant assets (8 years)	80,000	30,000	10,000		40,000	**(d)**
Trademarks (10 years)	50,000	15,000	5,000	1,000	29,000	**(e)**
	130,000	45,000	15,000	1,000	69,000	**(f)**
Deferred tax liability (@ 40%)	52,000	18,000	6,000	400	27,600	**(g)**
Subtotal	78,000	27,000	9,000	600	41,400	**(h)**
Goodwill for Pat's 80%	137,600	—	—	52,600	85,000	**(i)**
Total	215,600	27,000	9,000	53,200	126,400	**(j)**
NCI's share [20% × **(h)**]	15,600	5,400	1,800	120	8,280	**(k)**
Pat's share [**(j)** – **(k)**]	200,000	21,600	7,200	53,080	118,120	**(l)**

(b)

	Equity Method	Cost Method
Investment in Sam (80% × 100,000)	80,000	
Investment income		80,000
To record Pat's share of Sam's income		

(continued)

	Equity Method	Cost Method
Cash (80% × 40,000)	32,000	32,000
Investment in Sam	32,000	
Dividend income		32,000
To record Pat's share of Sam's dividend		
Investment income [**(l)** (7,200 + **(l)** 53,080)	60,280	
Investment in Sam	60,280	
To record Pat's share of amortization & impairment of acquisition differential		

Investment income for Year 6 under the equity method is $19,720 (80,000 − 60,280) and $32,000 under the cost method. Total income under equity method is $179,720 (192,000 − 32,000 + 19,720).   **(m)**

(c)   **Calculation of consolidated profit attributable to NCI**

Sam's profit	100,000
NCI's share @ 20%	20,000
Acquisition differential amortization [**(k)** 1,800 + **(k)** 120]	(1,920)
	18,080 **(n)**

Calculation of consolidated retained earnings at December 31, Year 6

Pat's retained earnings, Dec. 31, Year 6 (under cost method)		220,000
Sam's retained earnings Dec. 31, Year 6	300,000	
Acquisition retained earnings	125,000	
Increase	175,000	
Pat's share	× 80%	140,000
Less: Acquisition differential amortization		
[**(l)** 21,600 + **(l)** 7,200 + **(l)** 53,080]		(81,880)
		278,120 **(o)**

Calculation of NCI at December 31, Year 6

NCI at acquisition **(c)**		120,600
Sam's retained earnings Dec. 31, Year 6	300,000	
Acquisition retained earnings	125,000	
Increase	175,000	
NCI's share	× 20%	35,000
Less: Acquisition differential amortization		
[**(k)** 5,400 + **(k)** 1,800 + **(k)** 120]		(7,320)
		148,280 **(p)**

PAT INC.
CONSOLIDATED INCOME STATEMENT
for the Year Ended December 31, Year 6

Sales (1,740,000 + 1,030,000)	2,770,000
Interest & investment income (68,000 + 4,000 − **[m] 32,000**)	40,000
	2,810,000
Cost of sales (1,276,000 + 720,000)	1,996,000
Selling expenses (44,000 + 70,000 + **[f] 15,000**)	129,000
Other expenses (166,000 + 74,000 + **[f] 1,000** + **[i] 52,600**)	293,600
Income tax expense (130,000 + 70,000 − **[g] 6,000** − **[g] 400**)	193,600
	2,612,200

(continued)

Profit	197,800
Attributable to:	
Pat's shareholders (= income under equity method)	179,720
Non-controlling interest (n)	18,080
	197,800

PAT INC.
CONSOLIDATED BALANCE SHEET
at December 31, Year 6

Plant assets (460,000 + 320,000 + **[d] 40,000**)	820,000
Trademarks (0 + 0 + **[e] 29,000**)	29,000
Goodwill (0 + 0 + **[i] 85,000**)	85,000
Other assets (580,000 + 804,000)	1,384,000
	2,318,000
Ordinary shares	1,000,000
Retained earnings (o)	278,120
Non-controlling interest (p)	148,280
Deferred income tax liability (40,000 + 30,000 + **[g] 27,600**)	97,600
Other liabilities (400,000 + 394,000)	794,000
	2,318,000

APPENDIX 9A

REPORTING AN INTEREST IN A JOINT VENTURE USING PROPORTIONATE CONSOLIDATION

L02 **Example**   Explor Ltd., a Calgary-based oil exploration company, is a joint venture in which A Company has a 45% ownership interest. A Company, an original founder of Explor, uses the equity method to account for its investment but has made no entries to its investment account for Year 4. The following are the financial statements of the two companies on December 31, Year 4:

INCOME STATEMENTS—Year 4

	A Company	Explor
Sales	$900,000	$370,000
Cost of sales	500,000	180,000
Miscellaneous expenses	100,000	40,000
	600,000	220,000
Income before taxes	300,000	150,000
Income tax expense	120,000	60,000
Net income	$180,000	$ 90,000

BALANCE SHEETS—December 31, Year 4

	A Company	Explor	
Miscellaneous assets	$654,500	$277,000	These statements are the
Inventory	110,000	90,000	financial statements of a
Investment in Explor	85,500	—	venturer and a joint venture.
	$850,000	$367,000	
Liabilities	$130,000	$ 87,000	
Common shares	300,000	100,000	
Retained earnings	420,000	180,000	
	$850,000	$367,000	

During Year 4, A Company sold merchandise totalling $110,000 to Explor and recorded a gross profit of 30% on these sales. On December 31, Year 4, the inventory of Explor contained items purchased from A Company for $22,000, and Explor had a payable of $5,000 to A Company on this date. A Company will use the proportionate consolidation method when it reports its investment in Explor for Year 4. Following are the calculations of the amounts that are used in the elimination of intercompany transactions in the preparation of the consolidated financial statements:

Intercompany sales and purchases:		
Total for the year	$110,000	The other venturer's
A Company's ownership interest	45%	share of the intercompany
Amount eliminated	$ 49,500 **(a)**	transactions is considered
Intercompany receivables and payables:		realized from a consolidated
Total at end of year	$ 5,000	viewpoint.
A Company's ownership interest	45%	
Amount eliminated	$ 2,250 **(b)**	
Intercompany profits in inventory:		
Total at end of year (22,000 × 30%)	$ 6,600	
Profit considered realized—55%	3,630	
Unrealized—45%	$ 2,970 **(c)**	

The following explanations will clarify the calculations made:

1. Because the proportionate consolidation method will use 45% of Explor's financial statement items, we eliminate only 45% of the intercompany revenues, expenses, receivables, and payables. If we eliminated 100% of these items, we would be eliminating more than we are using in the consolidation process.

   Only the venturer's share of intercompany transactions is eliminated when consolidation takes place.

2. The inventory of Explor contains an intercompany profit of $6,600 recorded by A Company. Because there is joint control, A Company has realized $3,630 of this profit by selling to the other unaffiliated venturers, and therefore only A Company's 45% ownership interest is considered unrealized.

3. Income tax allocation is required when timing differences occur. Assuming that A Company pays income tax at a rate of 40%, the income tax effects of the inventory profit elimination can be calculated as follows:

   Unrealized profit is always eliminated from the selling company's income.

	Before tax	40% tax	After tax	
Inventory—A selling	$2,970	$1,188	$1,782 **(d)**	

Because A Company has not recorded this year's equity method journal entries, we must calculate consolidated net income for Year 4 as follows:

Income of A Company		$180,000
Less after-tax unrealized inventory profit **(d)**		1,782
Adjusted net income		178,218
Income of Explor	$90,000	
A's ownership interest	45%	40,500
Consolidated net income		$218,718

The preparation of the Year 4 consolidated statements without the use of a working paper is illustrated next.

A COMPANY
CONSOLIDATED INCOME STATEMENT
for the Year Ended December 31, Year 4

<table>
<tr><td>Sales (900,000 + [45% × 370,000] − [a] 49,500)</td><td style="text-align:right">$1,017,000</td></tr>
<tr><td>Cost of sales</td><td></td></tr>
<tr><td>(500,000 + [45% × 180,000] − [a] 49,500 + [c] 2,970)</td><td style="text-align:right">534,470</td></tr>
<tr><td>Miscellaneous expenses</td><td></td></tr>
<tr><td>(100,000 + [45% × 40,000])</td><td style="text-align:right">118,000</td></tr>
<tr><td></td><td style="text-align:right">652,470</td></tr>
<tr><td>Income before taxes</td><td style="text-align:right">364,530</td></tr>
<tr><td>Income taxes (120,000 + 45% × 60,000 − [d] 1,188)</td><td style="text-align:right">145,812</td></tr>
<tr><td>Net income</td><td style="text-align:right">$ 218,718</td></tr>
</table>

Intercompany revenues and expenses, receivables and payables, and unrealized profits in assets are eliminated in the preparation of the consolidated financial statements.

A COMPANY
CONSOLIDATED BALANCE SHEET
at December 31, Year 4

<table>
<tr><td>Miscellaneous assets</td><td></td><td></td></tr>
<tr><td>(654,500 + [45% × 277,000] − [b] 2,250)</td><td></td><td style="text-align:right">$776,900</td></tr>
<tr><td>Inventory (110,000 + [45% × 90,000] − [c] 2,970)</td><td></td><td style="text-align:right">147,530</td></tr>
<tr><td>Deferred income taxes (d)</td><td></td><td style="text-align:right">1,188</td></tr>
<tr><td>Total assets</td><td></td><td style="text-align:right">$925,618</td></tr>
<tr><td>Liabilities</td><td></td><td></td></tr>
<tr><td>(130,000 + [45% × 87,000] − [b] 2,250)</td><td></td><td style="text-align:right">$166,900</td></tr>
<tr><td>Shareholders' equity</td><td></td><td></td></tr>
<tr><td>Common shares</td><td style="text-align:right">300,000</td><td></td></tr>
<tr><td>Retained earnings</td><td style="text-align:right">458,718</td><td style="text-align:right">758,718</td></tr>
<tr><td>Total liabilities and shareholders' equity</td><td></td><td style="text-align:right">$925,618</td></tr>
</table>

The amounts used in the preparation are explained as follows:

Under the proportionate consolidation process, only the venturer's share of the joint venture's financial statement items is used.

1. With the exception of shareholders' equity and deferred income tax, the first two amounts used come from the individual financial statements and consist of 100% of A Company plus 45% of Explor.

2. The adjustments labelled **(a)** through **(d)** eliminate the intercompany revenues and expenses, receivables and payables, unrealized inventory profit, and income tax on the unrealized inventory profit. It is assumed that miscellaneous expenses include income tax expense.

3. Consolidated shareholders' equity consists of the common shares of A Company plus consolidated retained earnings.

REVIEW QUESTIONS

Questions, cases, and problems that deal with the appendix material are denoted with an asterisk.

L01 1. Explain the similarities and differences between a subsidiary and a variable interest entity and between a majority shareholder for a subsidiary and a primary beneficiary for a variable interest entity.

L01 2. Explain how the definitions of assets and liabilities can be used to support the consolidation of variable interest entities.

L02 3. Explain how to account for an interest in a joint operation.

L02 4. Y Company has a 62% interest in Z Company. Are there circumstances where this would not result in Z Company being a subsidiary of Y Company? Explain.

L02 5. The treatment of an unrealized intercompany inventory profit differs between a parent–subsidiary affiliation and a venturer–joint venture affiliation. Explain where the differences lie.

L02 6. A venturer invested non-monetary assets in the formation of a new joint venture and did not receive any monetary consideration. The fair value of the assets invested was greater than the carrying amount in the accounting records of the venturer. Explain how the venturer should account for the investment.

L02 7. Explain how the revenue recognition principle supports the recognition of a portion of gains occurring on transactions between the venturer and the joint venture.

L03 8. X Company recently acquired control over Y Company. On the date of acquisition, the fair values of Y Company's assets exceeded their tax bases. How does this difference affect the consolidated balance sheet?

L03 9. A parent company has recently acquired a subsidiary. On the date of acquisition, both the parent and the subsidiary had unused income tax losses that were unrecognized in their financial statements. How would this affect the consolidation figures on the date of acquisition?

L03 10. What is the difference between a *deductible* temporary difference and a *taxable* temporary difference?

L03 11. Explain how it is possible to have a deferred tax liability with regard to the presentation of a subsidiary's assets in a consolidated balance sheet, whereas on the subsidiary's balance sheet the same assets produce a deferred tax asset.

L03 12. Explain how the definition of a liability supports the recognition of a deferred income tax liability when the fair value of an asset acquired in a business combination is greater than the tax base of this asset.

L04 13. Describe the three tests for identifying reportable operating segments.

L04 14. For each of its operating segments that require separate disclosure, what information must an enterprise disclose?

L04 15. In accordance with IFRS 8, Operating Segments, answer the following:

(a) What information must be disclosed about business carried out in other countries?

(b) What information must be disclosed about a company's products or services?

(c) What information must be provided about a company's customers?

LO4   16. What sort of reconciliations is required for segmented reporting?

LO4   17. Explain how the use of the information provided in segment disclosures can aid in the assessment of the overall profitability of a company.

CASES

Case 9-1
LO1, 2, 6

Mr. Landman has spent the last 10 years developing small commercial strip malls and has been very successful. He buys a residential property in a high-traffic area, rezones the property, and then sells it to a contractor who builds the plaza and sells it to investors. Mr. Landman has often been hired to manage the commercial plazas for a fee. Now Mr. Landman wants to become a real estate baron. Rather than just developing the plazas for resale, he wants to form partnerships with builders and/or investors to build commercial properties and keep them as long-term investments.

He has found two properties suitable for development and made offers to the current owners to purchase these properties on January 1, Year 2. The offers are conditional upon arranging suitable financing for the acquisition.

Mr. Landman intends to set up two separate companies to buy, develop, and hold the properties. Elgin Company will purchase the property on Elgin Street for $1,200,000 and build a small office building at an expected cost of $2,800,000. Mr. Landman's holding company, Holdco, will invest $1,200,000 in Elgin for 30% of its common shares. Ms. Richer, a private investor, will invest $2,800,000 for a 70% interest in Elgin. According to the terms of the shareholders' agreement, Mr. Landman and Ms. Richer must agree on all major operating and financing decisions. Otherwise, the property will be sold in the open market and the company will be wound up.

The second company, Metcalfe Inc., will buy a recently developed strip mall on Metcalfe Street for $2,000,000. The purchase will be financed with a first mortgage of $1,500,000 and $500,000 of equity. Mr. Landman's holding company will invest $200,000 in Metcalfe for 40% of its common shares and will manage the property. Ms. Richer will invest $300,000 for a 60% interest in Metcalfe. The shareholders' agreement contains the following terms:

- Ms. Richer is guaranteed a return of her investment of $300,000 plus cumulative dividends of $24,000 a year.
- Mr. Landman is responsible for making all key operating, investing, and financing decisions.
- Mr. Landman's holding company guarantees the payment of dividends to Ms. Richer on an annual basis. After both shareholders have received cumulative dividends equal to 8% of their initial investments, Ms. Richer will receive 10% and Mr. Landman's holding company will receive 90% of the undistributed profits.

Holdco typically finances its acquisitions with 75% debt and 25% equity. The debt financing has a maximum debt-to-equity ratio of 3:1.

Required:

How should these two investments be reported on the financial statements of Holdco? Provide arguments to support your recommendations.

Case 9-2
LO1, 6

P Co. is looking for some additional financing in order to renovate one of the company's manufacturing plants. It is having difficulty getting new debt financing because its debt-to-equity ratio is higher than the 3:1 limit stated in its bank covenant. It is unable to attract an equity partner because the sole owner of P Co. has set equity partner conditions that make it practically impossible to find a new equity investor.

Part of the problem results from the use of historical cost accounting. If the company's assets were recorded at fair value, the debt-to-equity ratio would be much lower. In order to get around the requirements for historical cost accounting, the CFO for P Co. came up with the following plan.

On September 2, Year 5, P Co. will sell its manufacturing facility to SPE for $900,000 in the form of a non-interest-bearing note receivable. SPE will be set up for the sole purpose of renovating the manufacturing facility. No other activities may be carried out by SPE without the approval of P Co. Mr. Renovator, an unrelated party, will invest $600,000 in cash to cover the estimated cost of the renovation and will be the sole owner of SPE. On January 1, Year 6, after the renovation is complete and one day after P Co.'s year-end, SPE will sell the manufacturing facility back to P Co. at $1,560,000 and will be wound up. P will finance the repurchase with a $660,000 bank loan and by offsetting the remaining $900,000 against the note receivable from SPE from the original sale of the manufacturing facility to SPE. By selling the unrenovated facility and repurchasing the renovated facility, P Co. hopes to reflect the facility at its fair value, borrow the money to finance the renovation, and improve its debt-to-equity position.

The existing and pro forma balance sheets (in 000s) and debt-to-equity ratios for P Co. and SPE are presented below in condensed form:

	P Co. Sep. 1/5	P Co. Dec. 31/5	P Co. Jan. 1/6	SPE Dec. 31/5
Note receivable from SPE		$ 900		
Manufacturing facility	$ 150		$1,560	$1,500
Other assets	1,350	1,350	1,350	0
	$ 1,500	$ 2,250	$2,910	$1,500
Note payable to P Co.				$900
Other liabilities	$ 1,200	$ 1,200	$1,860	
Common shares	15	15	15	600
Retained earnings	285	1,035	1,035	0
	$ 1,500	$ 2,250	$2,910	$1,500
Debt-to-equity ratio	4:1	1.14:1	1.77:1	1.5:1

The CFO would like you to prepare a memo in which you discuss the accounting issues related to these proposed transactions.

Required:

Prepare the memo requested by the CFO. Ignore income taxes.

Case 9-3
LO1

IFRS 10 affects many Canadian business enterprises that are involved with variable-interest entities (VIEs) and special purpose entities (SPEs). Retrieve the annual reports (for the year specified) of any two of the following companies:

- Tim Hortons Inc. (2012)
- Air Canada (2011)
- Empire Company Limited (2011)

Required:

Write a brief report on each company that describes

1. the extent of its involvement with VIEs and SPEs, and
2. the effect of the requirements of IFRS 10 on the reporting of its interests in VIEs and SPEs.

Case 9-4
LO2, 6

Tropical Juices Limited (Tropical) was incorporated under Canadian federal legislation two years ago as a 50:50 joint venture of Citrus Growers Cooperative (Citrus) of the United States and Bottle Juices Corporation (Bottle) of Canada to sell Citrus's juices in Canada. Excerpts from the joint venture agreement are provided in Exhibit I. Both Citrus and Bottle produce and sell juices separately as well as through Tropical.

One year ago the owners of Bottle sold all their shares in Bottle to Douglas Investments Limited (DIL). The contract of sale between DIL and the former shareholders of Bottle included representations and warranties with respect to Tropical. Excerpts from the sale contract are provided in Exhibit II.

DIL required that representations and warranties about Tropical be written into the sale contract because Citrus and Bottle were still negotiating the accounting

---

EXHIBIT I

TROPICAL JUICES LIMITED
EXCERPTS FROM THE JOINT VENTURE AGREEMENT

Citrus shall provide the following to Tropical:

- Blending formula and drink recipes
- Brand names
- Ongoing supply of juice concentrates
- Advertising in Canada

Bottle shall provide the following to Tropical on an ongoing basis:

- Capital equipment and personnel needed to process the juice at their existing premises
- Returnable bottles supply
- Processing and distribution of the juice

Citrus and Bottle shall share equally in the net income of Tropical, after specific charges are made to Tropical for services provided by Citrus and Bottle. The specific charges are as follows:

1. Bottle is allowed to charge Tropical 1% per year on the capital investment in assets needed to process, bottle, and distribute the juices.
2. Both Bottle and Citrus are permitted to charge Tropical for

   a. Disbursements they make on behalf of Tropical, and
   b. Reasonable charges for administrative and other allocations of joint costs incurred on behalf of Tropical juices and their own juices.

3. Citrus is permitted to charge fair value for all juice concentrates provided to Tropical.

Citrus and Bottle shall help market Tropical juices, although Tropical shall have primary responsibility for selling its own juices. Citrus and Bottle shall allocate to Tropical its proportionate share of any revenue from sales that consist of both Tropical juices and their own juices.

EXHIBIT II

BOTTLE JUICES CORPORATION EXCERPTS FROM THE SALE CONTRACT

The following terms, representations, and warranties are made with respect to Tropical:

1. DIL is entitled to one-half of the net income of Tropical commencing with the second year of operations, which ends on June 30, Year 2. One-half of the net income of Tropical for the first year of operations shall be paid to the former shareholders of Bottle.
2. Bottle warrants that the total revenue will not be less than $3.3 million for each of the years ended June 30, Years 2 and 3.
3. Bottle warrants that operating expenses excluding depreciation, interest, and imputed charges shall not exceed $1.76 million for each of the years ended June 30, Years 2 and 3.
4. Bottle warrants that depreciation, interest, and imputed charges shall not exceed, for each of the years ended June 30, the following amounts:

Year 2	$605,000
Year 3	550,000

5. All computations are to be in accordance with generally accepted accounting principles for private enterprises.
6. If the representations and warranties are not fulfilled, then DIL shall be fully compensated for its portion of the amount of the deficiency.

policies to be used by Tropical. The selection of accounting policies is still not resolved, and the two parties cannot come to an agreement.

Draft financial statements for Tropical for the years ended June 30, Year 1, and June 30, Year 2, were prepared, based on the accounting policies selected by Bottle's controller. For the second year, the results were as follows:

Revenue	$2,959,000
Operating expenses, excluding depreciation, interest, and imputed charges	2,128,500
Depreciation, interest, and imputed charges	643,500

The joint venture agreement between Citrus and Bottle permits the appointment of an arbitrator to resolve disputes over accounting policies. Your firm has been appointed arbitrator and has been asked by all three parties (owners of Citrus and present and previous owners of Bottle) to submit a report containing binding decisions on all matters of contention. Each decision in this arbitration report must be supported by sound reasoning so that each party can fully understand the decisions.

You, the CA, have been asked to prepare the arbitration report. You interview each of the parties and are told the following:

Comments of Citrus

1. "We disagree with Bottle's charge for the cost of returnable bottles. It charged the entire cost of the bottles (which it owns) to the first year in Tropical even though the bottles have a life of 20 to 25 months."
2. "Bottle had to purchase new machinery for bottling Tropical juices because a different shape of bottle is used. It borrowed the necessary funds and charged the interest to Tropical. We reject this charge."

3. "Bottle spent $360,800 training its employees to manufacture and sell Tropical juices. We disagree with this sum being expensed and charged to Tropical in the first year."

4. "Bottle charged Tropical 16% on the capital investment being used to produce Tropical juices. We agree with the 16%, but we do not agree with the 16% being applied from the date that the first Tropical juices were produced."

5. "Bottle charged Tropical fair value for the computer services it provided. We believe that Bottle should have charged Tropical for these services at cost."

6. "Bottle had a three-week strike. When the strike was over, Bottle produced its own juices to replenish its own inventory, and did not produce Tropical juices for almost one month. We believe that Tropical should be credited in the first year for imputed gross profits during the months after the strike."

Comments of Previous Owners of Bottle

7. "Tropical has benefited from Citrus's advertising of the Citrus brand names in the United States. Citrus has charged Tropical for this advertising using the ratio of the Canadian population reached by the U.S. television-advertising signal to the combined Canadian and U.S. populations reached by the signal. In our opinion, this does not make sense."

8. "We understand that Citrus is complaining that we were charging proportionate repair costs for the machinery and equipment being used to produce Tropical juices and our own juices. We consider this to be an appropriate charge."

9. "We charged Tropical on the basis of our costs of producing Tropical juices. Citrus objects to our use of full absorption costing even though this was the method we used for our financial statements."

Comments of DIL

10. "After completing the purchase of Bottle, we discovered that Bottle's management had been manipulating the profits between years."

11. "Tropical sells large quantities of juices to distributors who pay Tropical only when the juices are resold. However, Tropical has recorded revenue when the juices are shipped to the distributors. We disagree with this practice."

12. "Citrus bought a new refrigerated tanker truck in the second year to deliver bulk concentrates to Tropical. It is charging the cost to Tropical at one-third per year, commencing in the second year. We disagree with this approach."

13. "Citrus charges interest to Tropical on the account receivable from Tropical. We disagree."

Required:
Prepare the report.

(CICA adapted)

Case 9-5
L04
Segment reporting can provide useful information for investors and competitors. Segment disclosures can result in competitive harm for the company making the disclosures. By analyzing segment information, potential competitors can identify and concentrate on the more successful areas of a disclosing company's business.

Indeed, the IASB recognizes that competitive harm is an issue of concern for companies disclosing segment information. In developing IFRS 8, the IASB considered giving, but ultimately decided not to give, companies an exemption from providing segment information if they believed that doing so would result in competitive harm. The IASB believed that such an exemption would be inappropriate because it would provide a means for broad non-compliance with the new standard.

IFRS 8 requires disclosures to be provided by country when revenues or long-lived assets in an individual country are material. However, IFRS 8 does not specify what is material for this purpose but leaves this to management judgment. Some commentators have expressed a concern that firms might use high materiality thresholds to avoid making individual country disclosures, perhaps to avoid potential competitive harm.

Required:

What factors might a company consider in determining whether an individual foreign country is material to its operations? Should the IASB establish a percentage test to determine when an individual country is material?

Case 9-6
LO2, 6

Pluto Technology Venture (PTV) is an unincorporated joint venture with three current owners. A few other prospective owners are awaiting an opportunity to invest in PTV. PTV was organized three months ago to combine the knowledge, assets, and finances of a group of organizations that specialize in computer graphics and animation. One of the venturers, Flash Limited (FL), required a considerable infusion of cash to survive. FL transferred the assets and liabilities of one of its major operating divisions to PTV in exchange for PTV ownership units and cash. The second venturer, Bulge Capital Corporation (BCC), invested in PTV mainly by way of a cash contribution. The third venturer, Everest Properties Limited (EPL), contributed a building to house PTV's main operations and also provided some office and administrative personnel. The three current owners have agreed that an unincorporated joint venture is the appropriate form of organization for the next several years.

The directors of PTV would like your firm to prepare a report that discusses all of the important accounting issues. They would like specific recommendations as to how PTV should account for its transactions, and explanations as to why the recommended accounting is appropriate.

In your meetings with various interested parties, you have learned the following:

1. Profits of PTV are to be divided in proportion to the number of ownership units that are held by each venturer. According to the Agreement Among Venturers:

   "Profits" are to be "all inclusive" for all activities of PTV. All inclusive is defined as profits from operations and from all changes in the valuation of assets and liabilities. In arriving at the profit, deductions are allowed for individual payments to the venturers for various services that they provide over and above the initial contribution to PTV.

2. Financial statements have to be provided each quarter to PTV's banker. The banker and PTV have arranged a lending formula that is closely linked to two PTV measurements: quarterly and annual cash flow, and the fair market value of PTV's assets less liabilities.

3. The financial statements are to be used in part to set the prices that are to be paid to PTV for any new joint venture units.

4. PTV develops software for specific clients and develops software products that it sells to the general educational market. Software that is developed for specific clients tends to be on a cost-plus basis, whereby PTV is paid 60–120 days after successful completion of each phase of the software. Different clients specify different definitions of cost. PTV carries the costs on its books as work in progress until clients are invoiced.

   FL has been granted non-exclusive marketing rights to some of PTV's educational products. FL may sell the products in specified regions at prices that it deems appropriate. FL is entitled to a 20% discount from the price that other distributors have to pay.

5. The identifiable assets and liabilities of FL initially contributed to PTV were (in thousands of dollars):

	Book Value	Fair Market Value
Receivables	$ 340	$ 310
Inventory	915	735
Prepaid expenses	60	60
Equipment	6,410	6,100
Accumulated amortization	(3,830)	
Software under development	100	1,500
Liabilities	(605)	(605)
	$3,390	$8,100

   The assets and liabilities were assigned a value of $8.8 million. In exchange, FL was given a 30% interest in PTV and $2.2 million in cash.

6. BCC invested $8.8 million in cash, in exchange for a 40% interest in PTV. In addition, BCC loaned $2 million to PTV at 5% interest. The market rate of interest is currently 8%.

7. EPL received a 30% interest in PTV in exchange for a building that was recorded on its books at $4.9 million (cost $6 million and accumulated depreciation of $1.1 million). EPL also rents space in another building to PTV at an amount below fair market value.

8. EPL has signed a "management agreement" with PTV to perform management services until PTV grows to the point where it needs its own management team. EPL is allowed under the agreement to charge for its services at cost plus 25%. The agreement also covers the use of equipment by PTV. PTV can either rent the equipment or rent with an option to purchase, at specified rates and amounts.

9. One prospective joint venturer has loaned PTV $1 million at the market rate of interest for a period of one year. After one year, the prospective venturer is permitted to acquire a 10% interest in PTV at its fair market value. At that time, the prospective venturer must pay the balance of the purchase price or forgo the $1 million.

10. PTV is in the process of renovating the building. The value of the building is expected to rise because of the renovations and because of general economic conditions.

11. PTV leases computers and equipment under a three-year contract. Since PTV signed the lease, prices have dropped by 30%, and a further drop is possible.

12. Competition in the industry has been very aggressive in recent months and is expected to persist. Costs of inputs can fluctuate significantly. The selling prices of finished goods can also fluctuate significantly.

13. PTV has invested some of the cash that was received from the current and prospective joint venturers in short-term, high-yielding bonds.

14. PTV has begun to conduct joint projects with other organizations and has contributed about $320,000 to date to developing specialized computer graphics packages.

15. Last week PTV signed a two-year contract with a film company to develop animation materials. The contract should generate revenue of $10 million to $14 million.

Required:

Prepare the draft report.

PROBLEMS

Problem 9-1
LO1

Pharma Company (Pharma) is a pharmaceutical company operating in Winnipeg. It is developing a new drug for treating multiple sclerosis (MS). On January 1, Year 3, Benefit Ltd. (Benefit) signed an agreement to guarantee the debt of Pharma and guarantee a specified rate of return to the common shareholders. In return, Benefit will obtain the residual profits of Pharma. After extensive analysis, it has been determined that Pharma is a variable interest entity and Benefit is its primary beneficiary.

The balance sheets (in millions) of Benefit and Pharma on January 1, Year 3, were as follows:

	Benefit	Pharma	
	Carrying amount	Carrying amount	Fair value
Current assets	$250	$ 50	$ 50
Property, plant, and equipment	400	80	90
Intangible assets	50	20	70
	$700	$150	$210
Current liabilities	$145	$ 60	$ 60
Long-term debt	325	120	125
Common shares	10	1	
Retained earnings	220	(31)	
	$700	$150	

An independent appraiser determined the fair values of Pharma's non-current assets. The appraiser was quite confident with the appraised value for the property, plant, and equipment but had some reservations in putting a specific value on the intangible assets.

Required:

Prepare a consolidated balance sheet at January 1, Year 3, assuming that the agreement between Benefit and Pharma established the following fair values for the common shares of Pharma:

(a) $25

(b) $20

(c) $35

Problem 9-2
LO3

Leighton Corp. has just acquired 100% of the voting shares of Knightbridge Inc. and is now preparing the financial data needed to consolidate this new subsidiary. Leighton paid $700,000 for its investment. Details of all of Knightbridge's assets and liabilities on acquisition date were as follows:

	Fair value	Tax base
Land	$100,000	$100,000
Buildings	180,000	110,000
Equipment	200,000	130,000
Inventory	150,000	150,000
Instalment accounts receivable	120,000	–0–
Trade liabilities	240,000	240,000

Required:

Determine the amounts that will be used to prepare a consolidated statement of financial position on the date of acquisition, assuming that Knightbridge's tax rate is 45%. Knightbridge has not set up deferred tax amounts for any of its assets or liabilities.

Problem 9-3
LO1

On December 31, Year 4, Russell Inc. invested $20,000 in Charger Corp. Prior to this Russell had no interest in Charger. Upon review of the documentation related to Russell's investment, the controller of Russell determined that Charger is a variable interest entity and Russell is its primary beneficiary. Immediately after Russell's investment, Charger Corp. prepared the following balance sheet:

Cash	$ 20,000	Long-term debt	$120,000
Marketing software	140,000	Russell equity interest	20,000
Computer equipment	40,000	Non-controlling interest	60,000
	$200,000		$200,000

Each of the above amounts represents the fair value at December 31, Year 4, except for marketing software. Charger Corp. is carrying on a business.

Required:

(a) If the marketing software was undervalued by $20,000, what reported amounts for Charger's financial statement items would appear in Russell's December 31, Year 4, consolidated balance sheet?

(b) If the marketing software was overvalued by $20,000, what reported amounts for Charger's financial statement items would appear in Russell's December 31, Year 4, consolidated balance sheet?

(c) Calculate goodwill and non-controlling interest for part (b) under parent company extension theory.

Problem 9-4
L03

On January 1, Year 5, AB Company (AB) purchased 80% of the outstanding common shares of Dandy Limited (Dandy) for $8,000. On that date, Dandy's shareholders' equity consisted of common shares of $1,000 and retained earnings of $6,000.

In negotiating the purchase price at the date of acquisition, it was agreed that the fair values of all of Dandy's assets and liabilities were equal to their carrying amounts and tax base except for the following:

	Fair value	Carrying value	Tax base
Equipment	$950	$700	$600

Dandy has recorded deferred income taxes on its separate-entity balance sheet on all temporary differences. Dandy had a loss carry-forward of $800 as at December 31, Year 4. This carry-forward can be applied against taxable income in the future. Dandy did not previously recognize the benefit of the carry-forward because it was not sure whether it would earn $800 in taxable income in the future. Now that AB controls Dandy, AB is sure that Dandy will be able to utilize the loss carry-forwards because AB will transfer income-earning assets to Dandy if necessary to generate taxable income in Dandy. AB plans to utilize these loss carry-forwards as soon as possible.

Both companies use the straight-line method for amortizing their property, plant, and equipment and pay taxes at a rate of 40%. Dandy's equipment had a remaining useful life of 10 years at the date of acquisition.

Dandy reported income before application of any loss carry-forwards as follows for the first three years after being acquired by AB:

Year	Net income
Year 5	$ 0
Year 6	100
Year 7	200

Required:

(a) Calculate goodwill at the date of acquisition. Be sure to consider the deferred tax implications on the acquisition differential.
(b) Calculate non-controlling interest at the date of acquisition.
(c) Prepare a schedule to show the amortization of the acquisition differential for the three-year period ending December 31, Year 7. Assume that the goodwill impairment loss was $300 in Year 6, the deferred income tax liability is amortized at the same rate as the equipment, and the loss carry-forwards are applied against income as the income is earned.
(d) Explain why the acquisition differential related to the equipment gives rise to a deferred income tax liability.

Problem 9-5
L03

On January 1, Year 1, Green Inc. purchased 100% of the common shares of Mansford Corp. for $335,000. Green's balance sheet data on this date just prior to this acquisition were as follows:

	Book value	Tax base
Cash	$ 340,000	$ 340,000
Accounts receivable	167,200	–0–
Inventory	274,120	274,120

(continued)

	Book value	Tax base
Land	325,000	325,000
Buildings (net)	250,000	150,000
Equipment (net)	79,000	46,200
	$1,435,320	$1,135,320
Current liabilities	$ 133,000	$ 133,000
Deferred tax liability	120,000	—
Non-current liabilities	—	
Common shares	380,000	
Retained earnings	802,320	
	$1,435,320	

The balance sheet and other related data for Mansford are as follows:

MANSFORD CORP.—BALANCE SHEET
at January 1, Year 1

	Book value	Fair value	Tax base
Cash	$ 52,500	$ 52,500	$ 52,500
Accounts receivable	61,450	61,450	61,450
Inventory	110,000	134,000	110,000
Land	75,000	210,000	75,000
Buildings (net)	21,000	24,000	15,000
Equipment (net)	17,000	16,000	12,000
	$336,950	$497,950	$325,950
Current liabilities	$ 41,115	$ 41,115	$ 41,115
Non-current liabilities	150,000	155,000	150,000
Deferred tax liability	4,400		—
Common shares	100,000		
Retained earnings	41,435		
	$336,950		

Additional Information

- As at January 1, Year 1, the estimated useful lives of the building and equipment were 15 years and 4 years, respectively, and the term to maturity was 10 years for the non-current liabilities.
- There has been no goodwill impairment since the date of acquisition.
- For both companies, the income tax rate is 40%. Deferred income taxes are recognized on the consolidated financial statement pertaining to the temporary differences arising from the acquisition differential.

Required:

(a) Prepare a consolidated balance sheet at January 1, Year 1.
(b) Prepare a schedule of amortization/impairment of the acquisition differential for the period from January 1, Year 1, to December 31, Year 4.

Problem 9-6
L03

Assume that all of the facts in Problem 5 remain unchanged except that Green paid $201,000 for 60% of the voting shares of Mansford.

Required:

(a) Prepare a consolidated balance sheet at January 1, Year 1.

(b) Calculate goodwill and non-controlling interest under parent company extension theory.

(c) Explain how the definition of a liability supports the recognition of a deferred income tax liability when a parent purchases shares in a subsidiary and the fair values of the subsidiary's identifiable net assets are greater than their carrying amounts.

Problem 9-7
LO1

The statements of financial position of Prime Inc. and Variable Ltd. on December 31, Year 11, were as follows:

	Prime	Variable Ltd.	
	Carrying amount	Carrying amount	Fair value
Land	$ 400,000	$ 80,000	$200,000
Manufacturing facility	1,050,000	520,000	300,000
Accumulated depreciation	(300,000)	(200,000)	
Accounts receivable	250,000	50,000	50,000
Cash	200,000		
	$1,600,000	$450,000	$550,000
Ordinary shares	$ 50,000	$ 10,000	
Retained earnings	750,000	90,000	
Long-term debt	525,000	290,000	$280,000
Current liabilities	275,000	60,000	60,000
	$1,600,000	$450,000	

Variable's manufacturing facility is old and very costly to operate. For the year ended December 31, Year 11, the company lost money for the first time in its history. Variable does not have the financial ability to refurbish the plant. It must either cease operations or find a partner to carry on operations.

On January 1, Year 12, Prime agreed to provide an interest-free loan of $200,000 to Variable on the following terms and conditions:

- Prime Inc. would be hired by Variable to refurbish the manufacturing facility at a fixed cost of $200,000 and would be retained to manage the business.
- Prime Inc. would have full authority to make all major operating, investing, and financing decisions related to Variable.
- The ordinary shares of Variable were valued at $208,000 as at January 1, Year 12. Prime has the option to buy the shares of Variable at any time after January 1, Year 17, at $208,000 plus any dividends in arrears.
- The existing shareholders of Variable would be guaranteed a cumulative dividend of 8% a year on the value of their shares. Prime would receive the residual profits after the dividends were paid to the ordinary shareholders.

Variable earned income of $200,000 and paid dividends of $50,000 over the five-year period ended December 31, Year 16. The statements of financial position of Prime Inc. and Variable Ltd. on December 31, Year 16 were as follows:

	Prime	Variable
Land	$ 400,000	$ 80,000
Manufacturing facility	650,000	260,000
Accounts receivable	275,000	70,000
Cash	20,000	180,000
	$1,345,000	$590,000
Ordinary shares	$ 50,000	$ 10,000
Retained earnings	660,000	240,000
Long-term debt	450,000	290,000
Current liabilities	185,000	50,000
	$1,345,000	$590,000

Assume that Variable is a variable interest entity and Prime is the primary beneficiary. The manufacturing facility had an estimated remaining useful life of 10 years as at January 1, Year 12. The long-term debt matures on December 31, Year 21. Prior to Year 12, Prime had no business relations with Variable.

Required:

(a) Calculate consolidated retained earnings at December 31, Year 16.
(b) Prepare a consolidated statement of financial position for Prime at December 31, Year 16.
(c) Use the definition of a liability to explain the rationale for including the liabilities of the variable interest entity on the consolidated statement of financial position for the primary beneficiary.

Problem 9-8
LO4

The following information has been assembled about Casbar Corp. as at December 31, Year 5 (amounts are in thousands):

Operating segment	Revenues	Profit	Assets
A	$12,000	$3,100	$24,000
B	9,600	2,680	21,000
C	7,200	(1,440)	15,000
D	3,600	660	9,000
E	5,100	810	8,400
F	1,800	(270)	3,600

Required:
Determine which operating segments require separate disclosures.

Problem 9-9
LO2, 6

The following are the December 31, Year 9, balance sheets of three related companies:

	Pro Ltd.	Forma Corp.	Apex Inc.
Cash	$ 70,000	$ 1,500	$200,000
Accounts receivable	210,000	90,000	110,000
Inventory	100,000	62,500	70,000
Investment in Forma Corp.—at cost	416,000	—	—
Investment in Apex Inc.—at cost	150,000	—	—

(continued)

	Pro Ltd.	Forma Corp.	Apex Inc.
Land	100,000	110,000	60,000
Plant and equipment	636,000	550,000	290,000
Accumulated depreciation	(185,000)	(329,000)	(60,000)
	$1,497,000	$485,000	$670,000
Accounts payable	$ 175,000	$ 90,000	$130,000
Bonds payable	312,000	—	—
Common shares	800,000	100,000	500,000
$12 preferred shares	—	200,000	—
Retained earnings	210,000	95,000	40,000
	$1,497,000	$485,000	$670,000

Additional Information

- On January 1, Year 5, Pro purchased 40% of Forma for $116,000. On that date, Forma's shareholders' equity was as follows:

Common shares	$100,000
Retained earnings	80,000
	$180,000

All of the identifiable net assets of Forma had fair values equal to carrying amounts except for the following, for which fair values exceeded carrying amounts as follows:

Inventory	$20,000
Plant and equipment	50,000

- One of Forma's products, the Epod, was unique in the market place and was a hot seller. Forma could not produce this product fast enough to meet the customer demand. The order backlog would take more than 6 months to complete. An independent appraiser valued the order backlog at $40,000 at the date of acquisition.
  - On September 30, Year 7, Pro purchased the remaining 60% of Forma for $300,000. On that date, Forma's shareholders' equity was as follows:

Common shares	$100,000
Retained earnings	110,000
	$210,000

On this date, the following net assets of Forma were undervalued by the amounts shown:

Inventory	$10,000
Land	60,000
Plant and equipment	70,000

- For consolidation purposes, any acquisition differential allocated to plant and equipment is amortized over 20 years from each date of acquisition. A goodwill impairment loss amounting to $2,025 was recorded in Year 8.
- During Year 8, Forma issued 2,000 cumulative, $12, no-par-value preferred shares. Pro did not acquire any of these shares.

- The inventories of Pro contained intercompany profits from items purchased from Forma in the following amounts:

December 31, Year 8	$40,000
December 31, Year 9	45,000

- During Year 9, Pro and two other unrelated companies formed Apex, which is a joint venture. Pro invested $150,000 cash for its 30% interest in Apex.
- The year-end inventories of Apex contained a $12,000 intercompany profit from items purchased from Pro since its formation in Year 9.
- Forma paid dividends in all years prior to Year 9.
- On December 31, Year 9, the accounts receivable of Pro contained the following:

Receivable from Forma	$13,000
Receivable from Apex	40,000

- Use income tax allocation at a 40% rate as it applies to unrealized profits only. Ignore deferred income taxes on the acquisition differential.

Required:

(a) Prepare the Year 9 consolidated balance sheet assuming that

    (i) Pro is a public company and reports its investment in Apex using the equity method; and

    *(ii) Pro is a private company and reports its investment in Apex using pro-portionate consolidation.

*(b) Calculate the current ratio for each of the balance sheets in Part (a). Which reporting method presents the strongest liquidity position? Briefly explain.

Problem 9-10
LO2, 6

The following are the Year 9 income statements of Kent Corp. and Laurier Ltd.

INCOME STATEMENTS
for the Year Ended December 31, Year 9

	Kent	Laurier
Sales	$3,000,000	$1,200,000
Other income	200,000	70,000
Gain on sale of land	—	100,000
	3,200,000	1,370,000
Cost of sales	1,400,000	560,000
Selling and administrative expenses	500,000	300,000
Other expenses	100,000	130,000
Income tax	400,000	150,000
	2,400,000	1,140,000
Net income	$ 800,000	$ 230,000

Additional Information

- Kent acquired its 40% interest in the common shares of Laurier in Year 3 at a cost of $825,000 and uses the cost method to account for its investment for internal record keeping.

- The acquisition-differential amortization schedule pertaining to Kent's 40% interest showed the following write-off for Year 9:

Buildings	$9,000
Goodwill impairment loss	13,000
	22,000
Long-term liabilities	12,500
Acquisition-differential amortization—Year 9	$9,500

- Depreciation expense and goodwill impairment loss are included with selling and administrative expenses.
- In Year 9, rent amounting to $125,000 was paid by Laurier to Kent. Kent has recorded this as other income.
- In Year 6, Kent sold land to Laurier and recorded a profit of $75,000 on the transaction. During Year 9, Laurier sold 30% of the land to an unrelated land development company.
- During Year 9, Laurier paid dividends totalling $80,000.
- It has been established that Kent's 40% interest would *not* be considered control in accordance with IFRSs.
- Assume a 40% tax rate.

Required:

(a) Assume that Kent is a public company and Laurier is a joint venture that is owned by Kent and two other unrelated venturers. Also assume that Kent acquired its interest after Laurier's initial formation, and that the acquisition differentials are therefore valid. Prepare the income statement of Kent for Year 9 using the equity method (show all calculations).

*(b) Assume that Kent is a private company and Laurier is a joint venture. Prepare Kent's consolidated income statement for Year 9 using proportionate consolidation. (Show all calculations.)

Problem 9-11
LO2

Albert Company has an investment in the voting shares of Prince Ltd. On December 31, Year 5, Prince reported a net income of $860,000 and declared dividends of $200,000.

During Year 5, Albert had sales to Prince of $915,000, and Prince had sales to Albert of $500,000. On December 31, Year 5, the inventory of Albert contained an after-tax intercompany profit of $40,000, and the inventory of Prince contained an after-tax intercompany profit of $72,000.

On January 1, Year 4, Albert sold equipment to Prince and recorded an after-tax profit of $120,000 on the transaction. The equipment had a remaining useful life of five years on this date. Albert uses the equity method to account for its investment in Prince.

Required:

Prepare Albert's Year 5 equity method journal entries under each of the following two assumptions:

(a) Albert owns 64% of Prince, and Prince is a subsidiary.
(b) Albert owns 30% of Prince, and Prince is a joint venture.

Problem 9-12
LO2

On January 1, Year 1, Amco Ltd. and Newstar Inc. formed Bearcat Resources, a joint venture. Newstar contributed miscellaneous assets with a fair value of $825,000 for a 60% interest in the venture. Amco contributed plant and equipment with a carrying amount of $300,000 and a fair value of $1,000,000 and received a 40% interest in the venture plus $450,000 in cash. On December 31, Year 1, Bearcat reported a profit of $180,000 and declared a dividend of $75,000. Amco has a December 31 year-end and will account for its 40% interest using the equity method. (Assume a 20-year useful life for the plant and equipment.)

Required:

(a) Assume that the miscellaneous assets contributed by Newstar included cash of $450,000. Also, assume that the transaction had commercial substance when Amco transferred the plant and equipment to the joint venture. Prepare Amco's Year 1 journal entries.

(b) Assume that there was no cash in the assets contributed by Newstar and that the cash received by Amco had been borrowed by Bearcat. Also, assume that the transaction did not have commercial substance when Amco transferred the plant and equipment to the joint venture. Prepare Amco's Year 1 journal entries.

Problem 9-13
LO2

The following are the Year 9 income statements of Poker Inc. and Joker Company:

INCOME STATEMENTS
for the Year Ended December 31, Year 9

	Poker	Joker
Sales	$1,000,000	$800,000
Other income	200,000	110,000
Gain on sale of trademark	—	40,000
	1,200,000	950,000
Cost of goods sold	600,000	550,000
Selling and administrative expenses	200,000	150,000
Other expenses	50,000	40,000
	850,000	740,000
Income before income taxes	350,000	210,000
Income taxes	105,000	63,000
Profit	$ 245,000	$147,000

Additional Information

- Poker acquired a 60% interest in the common shares of Joker on January 1, Year 4, at a cost of $420,000 and uses the cost method to account for its investment. At that time, Joker's carrying amount of shareholders' equity was $600,000 and the fair value of each of its assets and liabilities equalled carrying amount except for equipment, which had a fair value of $100,000 in excess of carrying amount and an estimated remaining useful life of 10 years.
- In Year 9, Joker paid a management fee of $50,000 to Poker. Poker recorded this as other income.
- In Year 5, Poker sold two trademarks with an indefinite life to Joker and recorded a total gain on sale of $60,000 ($30,000 for each trademark). During Year 9, Joker sold one of these trademarks to an unrelated company for a gain of $40,000.

- Depreciation expense is included with selling and administrative expenses.
- During Year 9, Joker declared and paid dividends totalling $200,000.
- The income tax rate is 30% for both companies.

Required:

(a) Assume that Joker is a joint venture that is jointly owned by Poker and several unrelated venturers, and that Poker uses the equity method to report its investment. Prepare Poker's income statement for the year ended December 31, Year 9.

(b) Assume that Joker is not a joint venture and, furthermore, that Poker's long-term investment provides it with control over Joker. Prepare Poker's consolidated income statement for the year ended December 31, Year 9.

Problem 9-14
LO2

Jager Ltd., a joint venture, was formed on January 1, Year 3. Clifford Corp., one of the three founding venturers, invested equipment for a 40% interest in the joint venture. The other two venturers invested land and cash for their 60% equity. All of the venturers agreed that the equipment had a fair value of $2,000,000, and a remaining useful life of approximately eight years. Clifford had acquired this equipment two years ago, and the carrying amount on Clifford's records on January 1 Year 3 was $1,800,000. Clifford recorded its investment in the joint venture at $2,000,000. On December 31, Year 3, Jager recorded a net income of $200,000. Clifford uses the equity method to record its investment.

Required:

(a) Assume that the transaction did not have commercial substance when Clifford transferred the equipment to the joint venture. Prepare Clifford's Year 3 journal entries.

(b) Assume Clifford had received a 40% interest and $1,000,000 in cash in return for investing this equipment in the venture. Also assume that the other venturers contributed cash in excess of $1,000,000 for their ownership interests, and that the transaction did not have commercial substance when Clifford transferred the equipment to the joint venture. Prepare Clifford's Year 3 journal entries.

Problem 9-15
LO2, 5

The following balance sheets have been prepared as at December 31, Year 5, for Kay Corp. and Adams Co. Ltd.:

	Kay	Adams
Cash	$ 60,000	$ 30,000
Accounts receivable	80,000	170,000
Inventory	600,000	400,000
Property and plant	1,400,000	900,000
Investment in Adams	360,000	—
	$2,500,000	$1,500,000
Current liabilities	$ 400,000	$ 150,000
Bonds payable	500,000	600,000
Common shares	900,000	450,000
Retained earnings	700,000	300,000
	$2,500,000	$1,500,000

Additional Information

- Kay acquired its 40% interest in Adams for $360,000 in Year 1, when Adams's retained earnings amounted to $170,000. The acquisition differential on that date was fully amortized by the end of Year 5.
- In Year 4, Kay sold land to Adams and recorded a gain of $60,000 on the transaction. Adams is still using this land.
- The December 31, Year 5, inventory of Kay contained a profit recorded by Adams amounting to $35,000.
- On December 31, Year 5, Adams owes Kay $29,000.
- Kay has used the cost method to account for its investment in Adams.
- Use income tax allocation at a rate of 40%, but ignore income tax on the acquisition differential.

Required:

(a) Prepare *three* separate balance sheets for Kay as at December 31, Year 5, assuming that the investment in Adams is a

   (i)   control investment;

   *(ii) joint venture investment, and is reported using proportionate consolidation; and

   (iii) significant influence investment.

(b) Calculate the debt-to-equity ratio for each of the balance sheets in Part (a). Which reporting method presents the strongest position from a solvency point of view? Briefly explain.

WEB-BASED PROBLEMS

Web Problem 9-1   Access the 2012 consolidated financial statements for Empire Company Limited
LO1, 2, 3, 5   by going to the investor relations section of the company's website. Answer the questions below. For each question, indicate where in the financial statements you found the answer, and/or provide a brief explanation.

(a) How does the company report its interest in companies it controls through means other than majority share ownership?

(b) What impact does the consolidation of special-purpose entities or variable interest entities have on the company's debt-to-equity ratio?

(c) What percentage of the company's net income is derived from investments in jointly controlled entities?

(d) What percentage of the company's assets is through investments in jointly controlled entities?

(e) Until 2013, jointly controlled entities could be reported using proportionate consolidation or the equity method. What method of reporting did the company use in the current year? If it had used the other method, what would have been the impact on its debt-to-equity ratio and return-on-equity ratio? Briefly explain.

(f) How would a bank change its assessment of the risk and solvency of the company based on the change in the debt-to-equity ratio?

(g) What were the statutory and effective tax rates on income from continuing operations? Identify the two biggest factors that caused these two rates to be different.

(h) What amount of deferred income tax was recorded as part of the accounting for the main business acquisition during the year, and how did this affect the amount allocated to goodwill?

Web Problem 9-2
LO1, 2, 3, 5

Access the 2012 consolidated financial statements for CAE Inc. by going to the investor relations section of the company's website. Answer the same questions as in Problem 1. For each question, indicate where in the financial statements you found the answer, and/or provide a brief explanation. (Some questions may not be applicable.)

Web Problem 9-3
LO4, 5

Access the 2011 consolidated financial statements for Rogers Communications Inc. by going to the investor relations section of the company's website. Answer the questions below. For each question, indicate where in the financial statements you found the answer, and/or provide a brief explanation.

(a) Are the company's operating segments based on product lines, geographical areas, or some other factor?

(b) Does the company provide disclosures about major customers? If so, what is the nature of the disclosure?

(c) Which of the operating segments is the biggest in terms of revenues?

(d) Which of the operating segments reported the highest percentage of growth in revenues from the previous year and what was that percentage? Based on this growth rate, approximately how many years will it take for the sales of this segment to double?

(e) Which of the operating segments is the biggest in terms of profit?

(f) Which of the operating segments reported the highest percentage of growth in profit margin from the previous year?

(g) Which of the operating segments is the biggest in terms of assets?

(h) Which of the operating segments reported the highest percentage of growth in return on assets from the previous year?

Web Problem 9-4
LO4, 5

Access the 2011 consolidated financial statements for Barrick Gold Corporation by going to the investor relations section of the company's website. Answer the same questions as in Problem 3. For each question, indicate where in the financial statements you found the answer, and/or provide a brief explanation. (Some questions may not be applicable.)

Practise and learn online with Connect

10
CHAPTER

Foreign Currency Transactions

INTRODUCTION

Many Canadian companies enter into foreign currency–denominated transactions.

Many Canadian companies conduct business in foreign countries as well as in Canada. For some companies, foreign business simply means purchasing products and services from foreign suppliers or selling products and services to foreign customers. Other companies go far beyond importing and exporting; they borrow and lend money in foreign markets and conduct business in foreign countries through sales offices, branches, subsidiaries, and joint ventures. Bombardier Inc., a Canadian transportation company, in its 2011 annual report, reported export revenues of $17.1 billion, representing 93% of total revenues.[1]

No specific accounting issues arise when the parties involved in an import or export transaction agree that the settlement will be in Canadian dollars. Because it is a *Canadian-dollar–denominated transaction*, the company will record the foreign purchase or sale in exactly the same manner as any domestic purchase or sale.

In many situations, however, the agreement calls for the transaction to be settled in a foreign currency. This means one of two things: (a) the Canadian company will have to acquire foreign currency in order to discharge the obligations resulting from its imports, or (b) the Canadian company will receive foreign currency as a result of its exports and will have to sell it in order to receive Canadian dollars. Transactions such as these are called *foreign currency–denominated transactions.*

As the foreign currency exchange rate fluctuates, so does the Canadian-dollar value of these foreign transactions. Companies often find it necessary to engage in some form of hedging activity to reduce losses arising from fluctuating exchange rates. The Bank of Nova Scotia uses derivative financial instruments to accommodate the risk management needs of its customers, for proprietary trading and asset/liability management purposes. Derivative instruments designated as "asset/liability management" are those used to manage the bank's interest rate, foreign currency, and other exposures, which include instruments designated as hedges. At the end of fiscal year 2011, the Bank of Nova Scotia, Canada's third-largest bank, had derivative financial instruments with a notional value of $2,542 billion.[2]

Aside from foreign currency risk, there are many other types of risk a company is exposed to and many different ways of hedging this risk. Bombardier used an innovative contract to increase sales by 38% in a past year. It offered buyers a $1,000 rebate on its snowmobiles if a pre-set amount of snow did not fall that season. The company was able to make such a guarantee by buying a weather derivative based on a snowfall index. When the season ended, the level of snowfall resulted in no payment received on the weather derivative. However, Bombardier did not have to pay any rebates to its customers either. Furthermore, the buyers purchased the snowmobiles earlier in the season because they did not wait for the snow to fall before making their purchase. This change led to a reduction in working-capital requirements (due to lower inventory-holding costs) and less strain on production capabilities. The company therefore benefited from lower costs as well as increased earnings.

> Many tools and techniques are available to hedge against different kinds of risks.

This chapter covers accounting issues related to foreign currency transactions and foreign currency hedging activities. Chapter 11 deals with the translation of the financial statements of a foreign operation. To provide background for subsequent discussions, this chapter begins with a brief look at exchange rates.

CURRENCY EXCHANGE RATES

Both the recording of foreign currency–denominated transactions and the translation of foreign currency financial statements require the use of currency exchange rates. An exchange rate is simply the price of one currency in terms of another currency. Exchange rates fluctuate on a continuous basis. Historically, governments have tried to stabilize rates between their currencies. Shortly after World War II, a group of the world's major trading nations agreed to "peg" the rates at which their currencies would be exchanged in terms of U.S. dollars. Since these pegged rates stayed reasonably steady, the accounting for foreign transactions was fairly simple. Differences in inflation rates and major changes in the balance of payments among the participating nations were contributing factors to the eventual demise of this agreement in the early 1970s.

> An exchange rate is the price to change one currency into another currency.

The end of pegged rates led to the present system, in which market forces determine exchange rates. This system of floating exchange rates is not totally market driven in the short term because governments often intervene in the market place to lessen the swings in the value of their currencies. It is not uncommon to hear that the Canadian dollar has weakened in relation to the U.S. dollar and the Bank of Canada has made massive purchases of Canadian dollars in order to soften the decline or that the U.S. Federal Reserve Bank and the central banks of other countries have intervened in the foreign currency markets by purchasing U.S. dollars because the U.S. dollar was declining in relation to other major currencies. Sometimes, interventions of this nature are fruitless, as was the case in 1994, when Mexico's central bank abandoned its attempt to prop up the peso and allowed a substantial devaluation to take place.

Reasons for Fluctuating Exchange Rates   Currencies trade in markets in such major cities as New York, London, Paris, and Tokyo, and transfers of enormous amounts of currency between countries can take place in a matter of seconds. The price of a currency will fluctuate in much the same manner as the price of any other commodity. There are many reasons why a country's currency price changes, of which the major ones are the following:

Exchange rates fluctuate over time due primarily to differences in inflation rates, interest rates, and trading practices between the two countries.	• *Inflation rates.* As a general rule, if country A has a higher rate of inflation than country B, the price of A's currency will weaken relative to B's. In a period of inflation, the purchasing power of a country's currency declines. If this currency will not buy as much in goods as it did before, then neither will it buy as much currency of another country as it did before. • *Interest rates.* Higher interest rates attract foreign investment and in so doing drive up the price of the currency of the country with the higher interest rates. • *Trade surpluses and deficits.* As a country exports more than it imports, its currency strengthens and becomes worth more.

Exchange rates can be quoted directly or indirectly.

Exchange Rate Quotations   Exchange rates showing the value of the Canadian dollar in terms of other foreign currencies are quoted daily on the Internet and in many Canadian business newspapers. The amounts that usually appear are called *direct quotations*, which mean that the amounts represent the cost in Canadian dollars to purchase one unit of foreign currency. For example, a quotation of EUR1.00 = CDN1.2883 means that it costs 1.2883 Canadian dollars to purchase one euro. An *indirect quotation* would state the cost in a foreign currency to purchase one Canadian dollar. For example, a quotation of CDN1.00 = EUR0.7762 indicates that it costs 0.7762 euros to purchase one Canadian dollar. An indirect quotation can be obtained by computing the reciprocal of the *direct* quotation. Conversely, a direct quotation can be obtained by computing the reciprocal of the *indirect* quotation (1 ÷ 1.2883 = 0.7762, and 1 ÷ 0.7762 = 1.2883).

The direct method is the reciprocal of the indirect method.

Direct quotations are the most useful ones for recording transactions denominated in foreign currencies. Using the exchange rates quoted above, a Canadian company would record the purchase of €10,000 of inventory from a European supplier as $12,883.

The spot rate is the rate to exchange currency today, whereas the forward rate is the rate agreed to today for exchanging currency at a future date.

Examples of foreign exchange quotations on particular days in 2009 and 2012 for three countries' currencies are shown in Exhibit 10.1. These rates represent the amount in Canadian dollars that a commercial bank would charge if it sold one unit of foreign currency to a major customer. The first rate quoted is called the *spot rate*. If a customer wanted to purchase 5,000 euros on the date in 2012 that

EXHIBIT 10.1

FOREIGN EXCHANGE DIRECT QUOTATIONS

Country	Currency	2009 CDN$ per unit	2012 CDN$ per unit
United States–spot rate	U.S. Dollar	1.0296	1.0334
1 month forward		1.0296	1.0340
2 months forward		1.0297	1.0347
3 months forward		1.0297	1.0354
6 months forward		1.0298	1.0376
12 months forward		1.0315	1.0420
European Union–spot rate	Euro	1.4805	1.2883
1 month forward		1.4803	1.2894
3 months forward		1.4802	1.2921
6 months forward		1.4799	1.2960
12 months forward		1.4802	1.3040
Japan–spot rate	Yen	0.011335	0.012999
1 month forward		0.011337	0.012999
3 months forward		0.011341	0.013000
6 months forward		0.011351	0.013002
12 months forward		0.011405	0.013007

> Notice that the Canadian dollar increased relative to the euro from 2009 to 2012.

these rates were quoted, the cost would be $6,442 (5,000 × 1.2883). Note that if the bank were to purchase euros from the customer, the amount that it would pay the customer would be slightly less than the amount quoted per euro. The bank's selling rate has to be greater than its purchasing rate if it is to make a profit dealing in foreign currencies. The forward rates quoted (one month forward, two months forward, etc.) are the rates for forward exchange contracts. A *forward exchange contract* is an agreement between a bank and a customer to exchange currencies on a specified future date at a specified rate. For example, when a bank enters into a forward exchange contract in 2012 with a customer to purchase 5,000 euros six months forward, the bank is committing itself to take delivery of this quantity of euros six months from this date, and to pay the customer $6,480 (5,000 × 1.2960) at that time. Of course, there is also a commitment on the part of the customer to sell 5,000 euros to the bank in six months' time. The use of forward exchange contracts in hedging transactions will be illustrated later in this chapter.

ACCOUNTING FOR FOREIGN CURRENCY TRANSACTIONS

LO1

Before we deal with the detailed accounting requirements for foreign currency transactions, it is important to note that currency issues can be discussed and analyzed from many different perspectives. For Chapters 10 and 11, we need to differentiate among the following perspectives:

- Currency in which the transaction is denominated (denominated currency)
- Currency in which the transaction is recorded in the internal accounting records (recording currency or internal record-keeping currency)

> We need to differentiate among the denominated, recording, functional, and presentation currencies.

- Currency of the primary economic environment in which the entity operates (functional currency)
- Currency in which the financial statements are presented by the reporting entity (presentation currency, which is commonly referred to as reporting currency)

Exhibit 10.2 shows examples of how these different currency perspectives could exist for individual companies. The last line indicates the method used to translate from one currency to another in the order in which the currencies are translated. Company E will need to translate three different times.

Up until now in this book, we have been dealing with Company A, where the Canadian dollar was the currency used for the four perspectives listed above. The transactions were denominated in Canadian dollars—that is, the invoices, agreements, cheques, and so on were written in Canadian dollars; the general ledger was maintained in Canadian dollars; the company operated in Canada; and the financial statements were presented in Canadian dollars. In this chapter, we deal with Company B-type situations where transactions are denominated in different currencies. We are then faced with deciding which currency should be used to record the transaction and which currency should be used when presenting the financial statements to external users. In Chapter 11, we will deal with Companies C, D, and E, where the recording currency is different from the functional and/or presentation currency.

IAS 21 requires that individual transactions be *translated into* the *functional currency* of the reporting entity. In turn, IAS 21 states that an entity can *present* or *report* its financial statements in any currency it wants to use. Presumably, the entity will present its financial statements in the currency most useful to its users. Most Canadian companies will present their financial statements in Canadian dollars. However, some Canadian companies may present their financial statements in U.S. dollars, because many of the users of the financial statements will be American investors or creditors, or will be international investors or creditors who understand and monitor the U.S. dollar more easily and readily than the Canadian dollar.

> A Canadian company would typically use the Canadian dollar as its recording and presentation currency.

> All transactions must be translated to the functional currency of the reporting entity.

> Company E must translate from one currency to another currency three different times.

EXHIBIT 10.2

EXAMPLES OF CURRENCY PERSPECTIVES

	Chapters 1–9	Chapter 10	Chapter 11		
Company type	Company A	Company B	Company C	Company D	Company E
Incorporated in	Canada	Canada	Germany	Japan	Argentina
Transactions denominated in	Canadian $	Various currencies	Various currencies	Various currencies	Various currencies
Transactions recorded in	Canadian $	Canadian $ (1)	Euro (1)	Yen (1)	Peso (1)
Functional currency	Canadian $	Canadian $	Canadian $ (2)	Yen	Canadian $ (2)
Presentation currency	Canadian $	Canadian $	Canadian $	Canadian $ (2)	US $ (3)
Method used for translation	N/A N/A	(1) Temporal N/A	(1) Temporal (2) Temporal	(1) Temporal (2) Current rate	(1) Temporal (2) Temporal (3) Current rate

IAS 21 defines *functional currency* as the currency of the primary economic environment in which the entity operates and *foreign currency* as any currency other than the functional currency of the entity. The primary economic environment is normally the one in which the entity primarily generates and expends cash. Exhibit 10.3 lists the indicators that should be considered when determining the functional currency and gives an example of a condition that would indicate that the Canadian dollar is or is not the functional currency.

When the above indicators are mixed and the functional currency is not obvious, management uses its judgment to determine the functional currency that most faithfully represents the economic effects of the underlying transactions, events, and conditions. As part of this approach, management gives priority to indicators 1 and 2 before considering the others, which are designed to provide additional supporting evidence to determine an entity's functional currency.

Professional judgment must be exercised in identifying the functional currency. In this chapter, we will assume, unless otherwise noted, that we are dealing with Company B, where the Canadian dollar is the recording currency, the functional currency, and the presentation currency.

> In this chapter, the Canadian dollar is the recording, functional, and presentation currency.

We will now focus on the issues associated with import/export transactions and foreign currency–denominated debt. Accounting problems arise when there are exchange rate changes between the date of a transaction and the eventual settlement in foreign currency. During this period, the company holds foreign currency–denominated monetary assets and liabilities, and questions arise as to how to measure these items if financial statements need to be prepared in the intervening period and what to do with any gains or losses that may result from such measurements. Monetary items are units of currency held and assets and liabilities to be received or paid in a fixed or determinable number of units of currency. Accounts receivable and investments in bonds are some obvious examples of monetary assets; accounts payable and bond liabilities are monetary liabilities. A foreign currency–denominated monetary position is a net asset position if monetary assets exceed monetary liabilities or a net liability position if monetary liabilities exceed monetary assets.

> A monetary item is converted into cash at a fixed and predetermined amount of currency.

EXHIBIT 10.3

INDICATORS FOR CHOOSING FUNCTIONAL CURRENCY

Functional currency

Indicator	Canadian dollar	Not Canadian dollar
1. Sales prices	Sales occur in Canada and are denominated in Canadian dollars.	Sales occur in foreign countries and are not denominated in Canadian dollars.
2. Operating costs	Labour and materials are obtained in Canada and denominated in Canadian dollars.	Labour and materials are obtained from foreign countries and are not denominated in Canadian dollars.
3. Competition and regulation	Competitors are Canadian, or company is listed on a Canadian exchange.	Competition comes from foreign entities or companies listed on a foreign exchange.
4. Financing	Debt and equity instruments are issued in Canadian dollars.	Debt and equity instruments are not issued in Canadian dollars.
5. Operating surpluses	Excess cash is retained in Canadian dollars.	Excess cash is not retained in Canadian dollars.

> The functional currency is the currency of the primary economic environment in which the entity operates.

Some not so obvious examples of monetary items are pensions and other employee benefits to be paid in cash, provisions that are to be settled in cash, and cash dividends that are recognized as a liability. Similarly, a contract to receive (or deliver) a variable number of the entity's own equity instruments, or a variable amount of assets in which the fair value to be received (or delivered) equals a fixed or determinable number of units of currency, is a monetary item. Conversely, the essential feature of a non-monetary item is the absence of a right to receive (or an obligation to deliver) a fixed or determinable number of units of currency. Examples are amounts prepaid for goods and services (e.g., prepaid rent); goodwill; intangible assets; inventories; property, plant, and equipment; deferred income taxes; and provisions that are to be settled by the delivery of a non-monetary asset.[3]

The historical rate is the rate on the date of the transaction, and the closing rate is the rate at the end of the reporting period.

For accounting purposes, there are basically three rates used in translating foreign currency into the reporting currency: the closing rate, the historical rate, and the forward rate. The spot rate at the end of the reporting period of the financial statements is called the *closing rate*. The spot rate on the date of a transaction is called the *historical rate* for that transaction. The agreed rate for exchange of currencies at a future date is called the *forward rate*. To illustrate the use of these terms, consider the following example.

Example ABC Co. has a year-end of December 31. On November 13, Year 1, ABC purchased inventory from a French supplier when the spot rate for one euro (€) was €1 = $1.50. On November 14, Year 1, ABC entered into a contract with a bank to purchase euros in 60 days at a rate of €1 = $1.48. The spot rate on December 31, Year 1, was €1 = $1.49. The financial statements for Year 1 were finalized on March 14, Year 2, and released to users on March 15, Year 2. In this example, the closing rate is $1.49, the historical rate for the purchase of the inventory is $1.50, and the forward rate for the planned purchase of euros is $1.48.

The average rate is the weighted average of the historical rates for the period.

If inventory was purchased every day throughout the year, the historical rate for each purchase should technically be used to translate the purchase for each day. This procedure is very costly and usually not worth the cost–benefit trade-off. From a practical point of view, it is usually sufficient to use an average rate to approximate the actual rates for the period. The average rate represents the average of the historical rates throughout the period. However, if exchange rates fluctuate significantly, the use of the average rate for a period is inappropriate.

Individual transactions must be translated into the functional currency at the historical rate.

According to IAS 21, a foreign currency transaction must be recorded, on initial recognition, in the functional currency by applying to the foreign currency amount the spot exchange rate between the functional currency and the foreign currency at the date of the transaction. At the end of each reporting period,

(a) foreign currency monetary items must be translated using the closing rate,

(b) non-monetary items that are measured in terms of historical cost in a foreign currency must be translated using the historical rate, and

(c) non-monetary items that are measured at fair value in a foreign currency must be translated using the exchange rates at the date when the fair value was determined.

For ease of identification, we will refer to this method of translation as the *temporal method*.

Any exchange adjustments arising on the settlement of monetary items or on the translation of them at rates different from those at which they were translated on initial recognition, during the period, or in previous financial statements must be recognized in profit or loss in the period in which they arise, with two exceptions. First, when a gain or loss on a non-monetary item is recognized in other comprehensive income, any exchange adjustment pertaining to that item must also be recognized in other comprehensive income. For example, IAS 16 requires some gains and losses arising on a revaluation of property, plant, and equipment to be recognized in other comprehensive income. When such an asset is measured in a foreign currency, any exchange difference resulting from the translation of the remeasured amount into the functional currency should also be recognized in other comprehensive income. Second, an available-for-sale financial asset (such as an investment in bonds) is treated as if it were carried at amortized cost in the foreign currency. Exchange differences resulting from changes in the amortized cost of this asset are recognized in profit or loss, and other changes in carrying amount are recognized in other comprehensive income.

This translation process should produce results consistent with the valuation practices for domestic operations. For a financial statement item to be reported at historical cost, the historical cost of the item in foreign currency multiplied by the historical rate will derive the historical cost in Canadian dollars. For a financial statement item to be reported at fair value at the end of the year, the fair value of the item in foreign currency multiplied by the spot rate on the date when fair value was determined will derive the fair value in Canadian dollars. If historical cost in foreign currency is multiplied by the closing rate or if the fair value in foreign currency is multiplied by the historical rate, the Canadian dollar figure is neither historical cost nor fair value.

> The translation method should, ideally, produce either historical cost in dollars or fair value in dollars consistent with normal measurement requirements for the financial statement items.

When an item is reported at fair value, the fair value is usually determined at the end of the reporting period. If so, the exchange rate at the end of the period (i.e., the closing rate) is used to translate this item into Canadian dollars. Unless otherwise specified, the examples in the text always assume that fair values were determined at the end of the reporting period.

According to Canadian GAAP, monetary assets and monetary liabilities are typically measured at fair value, non-monetary assets are usually measured at the lower of historical cost and market value, and non-monetary liabilities and shareholders' equity are usually measured at historical amounts. Revenues and expenses are usually measured at historical amounts. As we study the different translation methods in this and the next chapter, we should evaluate whether the translation methods preserve the normal measurement requirements under Canadian GAAP.

Import/Export Transactions Denominated in Foreign Currency

When a Canadian company purchases goods from a foreign supplier, it is usually billed in the currency of the foreign country. However, the transaction is recorded in the company's accounting records in the functional currency, which is assumed to be the Canadian dollar. The following example illustrates the accounting for an import transaction.

> Unless otherwise noted, all examples in this chapter assume that the Canadian dollar is the functional currency.

An Import Example On June 1, Year 1, Maritime Importers Inc. purchased merchandise from a supplier in Australia at a cost of 10,000 Australian dollars (A$), with payment in full to be made in 60 days. The exchange rate on the date of purchase was A$1 = CDN$0.941 and A$1 = CDN$0.949 on June 30, Year 1, the company's year-end. Maritime paid its supplier on July 30, Year 1, when the exchange rate was A$1 = CDN$0.953. The following journal entries, recorded in Canadian dollars, illustrate the company's purchase of merchandise, year-end adjustments, and subsequent payment.

June 1, Year 1

Inventory	9,410	
Accounts payable (10,000 × 0.941)		9,410

The cost of the purchase is finalized when the item is purchased.

The purchase of the inventory at a cost of A$10,000 and the related liability are translated at the spot rate on the date of purchase. The value of the inventory has been fixed at its historical cost and is not exposed to exchange fluctuations except in the situation where the selling price declines and the lower of cost and net realizable value requirement is applied. In such a case, the lower of cost and net realizable value requirement would be applied by comparing the Canadian dollar historical cost of the inventory with the net realizable value in Canadian dollars.[4]

On the other hand, Maritime now has a monetary position that is exposed to exchange fluctuations. The Canadian dollar amount required to pay A$10,000 will change as the exchange rate changes. To better reflect the cost of settling this obligation, this monetary liability should be remeasured to current value at each reporting date.

On the company's year-end, the account payable of A$10,000 must be translated at the closing rate. The previously recorded amount ($9,410) is increased by $80 to reflect a translated liability of $9,490 (10,000 × 0.949).

June 30, Year 1

Exchange loss	80	
Accounts payable		80
To adjust the account payable to the closing rate		

The resulting foreign exchange loss would be reported in net income for the year ended June 30, Year 1.

Foreign exchange adjustments are included in profit in the period in which they occur.

On the settlement date, the exchange rate has increased from CDN$0.949 to CDN$0.953. The A$10,000 account payable is increased by $40 to reflect its translation at the spot rate at this date (10,000 × 0.953 = 9,530). The company purchases 10,000 Australian dollars from its bank at a cost of $9,530 and remits Australian dollars to its Australian supplier. The foreign exchange loss of $40 will appear on the income statement for the year ended June 30, Year 2. The following journal entries record the transactions:

July 30, Year 1

Exchange loss	40	
Accounts payable		40
To adjust the account payable to the spot rate		

Accounts payable	9,530	
Cash (10,000 × 0.953)		9,530
Payment to supplier		

An Export Example   We will now consider an example of the export of goods by a Canadian company.

On November 15, Year 1, Regina Malt Producers Ltd. shipped a carload of malt to a brewery in the United States, with full payment to be received on January 31, Year 2. The selling price of the malt was US$26,000. Regina Malt has a December 31 year-end. The following exchange rates existed on the dates significant for accounting purposes:

Transaction date—Nov. 15, Year 1
    Selling price US$26,000
    Exchange rate US$1 = CDN$1.125
Year-end—Dec. 31, Year 1
    Exchange rate US$1 = CDN$1.129
Settlement date—Jan. 31, Year 2
    Exchange rate US$1 = CDN$1.119

The journal entries required on the dates noted above are as follows:

Nov. 15, Year 1

Accounts receivable	29,250	
Sales		29,250

> The sale is translated at the historical rate to produce a historical price in Canadian dollars. This is consistent with normal measurement requirements to record sales at historical values.

The accounts receivable and the sales are recorded at the November 15 spot rate (US$26,000 × 1.125 = CDN$29,250). The sales amount has been established at historical value and is unaffected by future exchange rate fluctuations. The accounts receivable (a monetary item) is at risk to exchange rate fluctuations. Note that while accounts receivable has been recorded at CDN$29,250, it is, in fact, a receivable of US$26,000.

At the company's year-end, the exchange rate has changed to US$1 = CDN$1.129, and the receivable must appear in the financial statements at $29,354 (US$26,000 × 1.129). The following journal entry adjusts the accounts receivable to the closing rate:

Dec. 31, Year 1

Accounts receivable	104	
Exchange gain		104

> The accounts receivable is translated at the closing rate to produce a current value in Canadian dollars. This is consistent with normal measurement requirements to record monetary items at current values.

This exchange gain will appear in the company's Year 1 income statement.

By January 31, Year 2, which is the settlement date, the value of the U.S. dollar has declined relative to the Canadian dollar. When Regina Malt collects US$26,000 from its customer and delivers the U.S. dollars to its bank, it receives only CDN$29,094 (26,000 × 1.119). The journal entry to record the receipt of US$26,000, its conversion to Canadian dollars and the resultant loss is as follows:

Jan. 31, Year 2

Cash	29,094	
Exchange loss	260	
Accounts receivable		29,354
Received from U.S. customer		

The exchange loss of $260 will appear in the Year 2 income statement. Note that the actual exchange loss between the transaction date and the settlement date was $156 (29,250 − 29,094). Because the company's year-end occurred between these two dates, the exchange loss will appear in the two income statements in the following manner:

Year 1 income statement	
Exchange gain	$104
Year 2 income statement	
Exchange loss	260
Total exchange loss on the transaction	$156

Exchange gains/losses are reported in profit, even though they may be unrealized.

The previous examples have illustrated the concept that exchange gains and losses resulting from the translation of a *monetary position* (i.e., a receivable or payable) are reflected in income in the year in which they occur. Note that these exchange gains and losses are actually unrealized in the sense that they result from the translation of a liability or a receivable. The exchange gain or loss is realized when the liability is paid or the receivable is collected.

Transaction Gains and Losses from Non-current Monetary Items

Many Canadian companies borrow money in foreign markets, mainly because the capital markets in Canada are relatively small. The following example illustrates the accounting for foreign currency–denominated debt.

Example   Sable Company has a calendar year-end. On January 1, Year 1, the company borrowed 2,000,000 Swiss francs from a Swiss bank. The loan is to be repaid on December 31, Year 4, and requires interest at 8% to be paid each December 31. Both the annual interest payments and the loan repayment are to be made in Swiss francs (SF).

During the term of the loan, the following exchange rates necessary for our analysis were in effect:

Jan. 1, Year 1	SF1 = $1.076
Average, Year 1	SF1 = $1.073
Dec. 31, Year 1	SF1 = $1.069
Dec. 31, Year 2	SF1 = $1.070
Dec. 31, Year 3	SF1 = $1.071
Dec. 31, Year 4	SF1 = $1.067

Sable Company would record the transactions as follows:

Jan. 1, Year 1

Cash	2,152,000	
Loan payable (2,000,000 × 1.076)		2,152,000

Interest expense is translated at the average of the historical rates to produce a historical price in Canadian dollars. This is consistent with normal measurement requirements to record interest expense at historical values.

This entry records the incurrence of a four-year loan of SF2,000,000 translated at the spot rate. On December 31, the company purchases 160,000 Swiss francs (2,000,000 × 8%) from its bank to make the interest payment, at a cost of $171,040 (160,000 × 1.069). A question arises as to whether the amount paid should be reflected as the interest expense for the past year. Remember that interest expense was SF160,000, which accrued throughout the year. It seems logical, therefore, to translate the interest expense using the average of the Year 1 exchange rates, or better still, to translate the monthly interest at the average rate for each month. In either case, when the interest is actually paid at the end of the year, an exchange gain or loss will have to be recorded. Using the average exchange rate for Year 1, the journal entry to record the interest expense and payment is as follows:

Dec. 31, Year 1

Interest expense	171,680	
Exchange gain		640
Cash		171,040

To record interest expense at the average Year 1 rate of SF1 = $1.073, and
  the payment of interest at the year-end rate of SF1 = $1.069

On December 31, the loan is translated for financial statement purposes at $2,138,000 (2,000,000 × 1.069). The next entry adjusts the loan payable to the amount required on that date:

Dec. 31, Year 1

Loan payable	14,000	
Exchange gain		14,000

> The loan payable is translated at the closing rate to produce a current value in Canadian dollars. This is consistent with normal measurement requirements to record monetary items at current values.

The $14,640 total exchange gain resulting from the interest payment and the translation of the loan will appear in the Year 1 income statement.

Journal entries for Years 2 through 4 will not be illustrated; however, the following summarizes the yearly exchange gains and losses from translating the principle amount of the loan liability. The exchange gains and losses on the interest are not included.

> Exchange gains and losses occur on items translated at the closing rate but not on items translated at historical rates.

	Total	Year 1	Year 2	Year 3	Year 4
Exchange gain (loss)	$18,000	$14,000	$(2,000)	$(2,000)	$8,000

SPECULATIVE FORWARD EXCHANGE CONTRACTS

> **L02**
>
> In a forward exchange contract, two parties agree today to exchange currencies at a future date at a specified exchange rate.

A forward exchange contract is one in which an exchange broker (usually a bank) and its customer agree to exchange currencies at a set price on a future date. Forward contracts can be either fixed dated or option dated. A fixed-dated contract specifies a fixed date such as June 18. An option-dated contract specifies a certain period, such as the month of June. A company may enter into a forward exchange contract purely to speculate on future exchange movements. For example, a company might enter into a contract to purchase foreign currency at a 60-day forward rate in anticipation that the spot rate in 60 days' time will be greater than the original forward rate. If its projection turns out to be accurate, it will purchase the foreign currency from the bank at the contracted price and immediately sell the currency to the bank at the higher spot rate. The following example deals with a speculative forward exchange contract.

Example   On December 1, Year 1, Raven Company enters into a forward contract to sell one million Philippines pesos (PP) to its bank in exchange for Canadian dollars on March 1, Year 2, at the market rate for a 90-day forward contract of PP1 = $0.0227. On December 31, Year 1, Raven's year-end, the 60-day forward rate to sell Philippines pesos on March 1 is quoted at PP1 = $0.0222. On March 1, Year 2, the currencies are exchanged when the spot rate is PP1 = $0.0220.

According to IAS 39 and IFRS 9, this forward contract is considered a financial instrument. It must be recorded at fair value on the date the contract is entered into and be remeasured at fair value throughout its life, with any gains or losses reflected in net income as they occur. There are two methods of recording this forward contract: the gross method and the net method. Under the gross method, the receivable from the bank and the payable to the bank are recorded separately at fair value. Under the net method, the receivable and payable are netted against each other and only the net receivable or net payable is recorded. The entries for this contract under the gross and net methods are shown in Exhibit 10.4. Either method is acceptable for internal recording-keeping purposes. However, when the financial statements are prepared, the receivable from the bank and the payable to the bank will be netted against each other and only the net amount shown as either an asset or a liability on the balance sheet. We will use the gross method for all subsequent illustrations in this chapter.

The "$" symbol behind receivable from bank in the first entry indicates that the account receivable is denominated in Canadian dollars, whereas the "PP" behind the payable to bank indicates that the accounts payable is denominated in

> Under the gross method, the receivable and payable under the forward contract will be offset against each other, and only the net amount will be reported on the balance sheet at each reporting date.

> A forward contract is a financial instrument that must be measured at fair value throughout its life.

> When the forward rate changes, the fair value of the forward contract changes.

EXHIBIT 10.4

JOURNAL ENTRIES FOR SPECULATIVE FORWARD CONTRACT

	Gross method		Net method
December 1, Year 1			
Receivable from bank ($)	22,700		
Payable to bank (PP)		22,700	
Record forward contract at forward rate			
(PP1,000,000 × 0.0227 = $22,700)			
December 31, Year 1			
Forward contract			500
Payable to bank (PP)	500		
Exchange gain		500	500
Revalue forward contract at fair value			
(PP1,000,000 × (0.0227 − 0.0222) = $500)			
March 1, Year 2			
Forward contract			200
Payable to bank (PP)	200		
Exchange gain		200	200
Revalue forward contract at fair value			
(PP1,000,000 × (0.0222 − 0.0220) = $200)			
Payable to bank (PP)	22,000		
Cash (PP)		22,000	
Deliver PP1,000,000 to bank to pay off liability			
(PP1,000,000 × 0.0220 = $22,000)			
Cash ($)	22,700		
Receivable from bank ($)		22,700	
Receive $22,700 from bank			
Cash ($)			700
Forward contract			700
Settle forward contract on net basis by receiving			
$700 (22,700 − 22,000)			

Philippines pesos. In other words, Raven will receive Canadian dollars and will pay Philippines pesos to settle this forward contract.

The fair value of the forward contract on December 1, Year 1, is zero because the two parties have just entered into a contract at the market rate for forward contracts. Under the gross method, the receivable and payable are both recorded at the future rate. Since the receivable and payable are equal and offsetting, there is no entry under the net method.

Some accountants may object to using the gross method for recording the forward contract on December 1 because forward exchange contracts are "executory" in nature. An *executory contract* is one in which neither party has performed its obligation to the other. Most contracts trigger accounting recognition only when one of the parties fulfills the obligation as agreed. For example, when a company places an order with a manufacturer for the purchase of machinery, neither party makes an accounting entry. The delivery of the machinery, or a down payment prior to delivery, results in accounting recognition by both parties because of the performance by one.

While forward exchange contracts are certainly executory, they are also firm commitments and once entered cannot be cancelled. For this reason, IFRSs require that the forward contract be recorded.

> Forward contracts must be recorded according to IFRSs.

On December 31, the forward contract is remeasured at fair value. We use the market rate for forward contracts maturing on March 1 to determine the fair value of Raven's contract. On this date, the 60-day forward rate to sell Philippines pesos on March 1 is PP1 = $0.0222, whereas Raven's contract is locked in at PP1 = $0.0227. Raven's contract will generate $22,700 on March 1, whereas contracts executed on December 31 would generate only $22,200 on March 1 for 1 million Philippines pesos. Therefore, Raven's contract is worth an extra $500 as of March 1. Theoretically, we should discount this $500 for two months. Practically speaking, the amount would usually not be discounted because the difference between the nominal amount of $500 and the present value of $500 for two months is not material and is not worth the effort to calculate.

> The forward contract is worth more when the Philippines peso declines in value; that is, the Canadian dollar increases in value.

In the appendix to this chapter, we illustrate how this forward contract would be accounted for with discounting. Unless otherwise noted, no examples in the text will use discounting. The forward contract will simply be measured at the forward rate for the term to maturity.

Note that the gain of $500 is recorded under both the gross and net methods. When financial statements are prepared at December 31 under the gross method, the "due from bank" of $22,700 and the "due to bank" of $22,200 will be offset against each other and only the net receivable of $500 will be presented on the balance sheet, and will likely be called forward contract. Therefore, the financial statement presentation will be the same under both the gross and net methods, even though the underlying accounts have different balances.

On March 1, Year 2, the forward contract is once again remeasured to fair value. Since the contract is being settled on this date, the market value of this forward contract is based on the spot rate for this date; that is, PP1 = $0.0220. The contract is worth $700 because Raven will get $22,700 from the bank, whereas PP1,000,000 is worth only $22,000 in the market on March 1. Therefore, Raven has gained $700 on this contract in total, and $200 since December 31. The first entry on March 1 records this $200 gain. The other entries record the exchange of pesos for dollars.

If we combine all of the journal entries under both the gross and net methods, we end up with the following entry:

Cash ($)	700	
Exchange gain—Year 1		500
Exchange gain—Year 2		200

In the end, Raven gained $700 by speculating on rate changes. If the exchange rates had changed in the other direction—that is, if the Canadian dollar had decreased rather than increased in value—Raven would have lost money on this speculative contract.

In the next few sections, we will illustrate how forward contracts can be used to hedge existing and anticipated exposure to foreign currency risk. Throughout the remainder of this chapter and in the end-of-chapter material, we will use the gross method of accounting for forward contracts. This makes it easier to see how the forward contract is effective in hedging against the currency risk under different situations.

L03 HEDGES

The previous examples illustrated the accounting for the foreign exchange gains and losses that result from holding a foreign currency–denominated monetary position during a period of exchange rate changes. There are many possible ways for an enterprise to protect itself from the economic (and accounting) effects that result from such a position. This type of protection is generally referred to as "hedging," which can be defined as a means of transferring risk arising from foreign exchange (or interest rate, or price) fluctuations from those who wish to avoid it to those who are willing to assume it.[5] In order to hedge the risk of exchange rate fluctuations, a company takes a foreign currency position opposite to the position that it wishes to protect. The item with the risk exposure that the entity wishes to hedge and has taken steps to hedge is called the *hedged item*. The item used to offset the risk is called the *hedging instrument*. In the ideal case, the hedged item is perfectly hedged by the hedging instrument and there is no longer any overall exposure to currency fluctuations. The entity has eliminated the overall risk of further exchange losses but also loses any possibility of gains from currency fluctuations.

When accounting for the hedge, we want to properly reflect whether the hedge has been effective. If the hedge is truly effective, there should be no overall exchange gain or loss reported on the income statement, other than the cost of establishing the hedge. The exchange gains or losses on the hedged item will be offset by exchange losses or gains on the hedging instrument. But what happens when the hedging instrument is purchased in advance of the hedged item? For example, a forward contract may be purchased in Year 1 to hedge a transaction expected to occur in Year 2. How can the Year 1 gains or losses on the forward contract be offset against the Year 2 losses or gains on the anticipated transaction when the anticipated transaction has not yet occurred?

The solution is hedge accounting as defined and described in IFRS 9. Under hedge accounting, the exchange gains or losses on the hedging instrument will be recognized in profit in the same period as the exchange gains or losses on the hedged item when they would otherwise be recognized in different periods.

It is important at this stage to differentiate between the terms "hedge" and "hedge accounting". While they may sound similar, they are very dissimilar. A hedge is an item that attempts to minimize or eliminate the risk of suffering a loss. The forward contract can be used to minimize the loss from changes in exchange rates. Hedge accounting, on the other hand, is a means of accounting for the hedging instrument—that is, the forward contract and the hedging item—in order to properly show that the two items acting together are effective in minimizing or eliminating the potential loss. Hedge accounting involves special accounting requirements that allow the entity to defer or accelerate income recognition in order to show that a gain or loss on the hedging item is being offset by a loss or gain on the hedging item.

> Under hedge accounting, the exchange gains or losses on the hedging instrument will be reported in income in the same period as the exchange gains or losses on the hedged item.

It is also important to note that hedge accounting is optional. The entity can choose to apply hedge accounting and thereby ensure that gains and losses on the hedged item are reported in the same period as the gains and losses on the hedging instrument. Alternatively, it could choose to not apply hedge accounting and account for the hedged item and the hedging instrument in isolation of each other.

Prior to 2013, the requirements for hedge accounting were contained in IAS 39. These requirements were developed when hedging activities were relatively new and not as widely understood as they are today. In general, the hedging item had to be a derivative; for example, a forward contract or an option. A derivative is a financial instrument or other contract with all three of the following characteristics:

(a) Its value changes in response to the change in a specified interest rate, financial instrument price, commodity price, foreign exchange rate, index of prices or rates, credit rating or credit index, or other variable (sometimes called the "underlying" variable).

(b) It requires either no initial net investment or an initial net investment that is smaller than would be required for other types of contracts with a similar expected response to changes in market factors.

(c) It is settled at a future date.

> A derivative is a financial instrument or other contract whose value changes in response to the change in some underlying variable, which requires no initial investment, and which will be settled at a future date.

Over the years, managers have developed a better understanding of risks and ways to mitigate risk. Many new financial instruments and other management strategies have been invented to deal with risk. As such, the requirements in IAS 39 now appear to be too restrictive and may make it impossible to apply hedge accounting to faithfully represent the effectiveness of the companies hedging activities. With these restrictions, investors may not be able to understand the risks an entity faces, what management is doing to manage those risks, and how effective those risk management strategies are.

In 2013, new requirements for hedge accounting were adopted by the IASB and are now contained in IFRS 9. These requirements are effective January 1, 2015, but can be adopted earlier. Some of the major changes and how they differ from IAS 39 are as follows:

1. The requirements for hedge accounting are less restrictive and are more closely aligned with risk management activities undertaken by companies when hedging their financial and nonfinancial risk exposures. IFRS 9 allows any financial asset or most financial liabilities measured at fair value through profit or loss to be designated as a hedging instrument. However, only contracts with a party external to the reporting entity can be designated as hedging instruments.

> The new hedge accounting requirements in IFRS 9 are less restrictive and more closely aligned with the entity's risk management activities.

Cautionary Note: At the time of writing this textbook, the requirements pertaining to hedge accounting were contained in IAS 39. However, there was an exposure draft to change certain requirements for hedging. The textbook has been written under the assumption that the requirements in the exposure draft will be adopted. Any changes from what is finally adopted in IFRS 9 and what is written in the textbook will be communicated through the OLC in future years.

2. An entity may view in combination, and jointly designate as the hedging instrument, any combination of the following: (a) derivatives or a proportion of them and (b) non-derivatives or a proportion of them.

3. Under IAS 39, components (parts) of financial items can be hedged, but not components of nonfinancial items. IFRS 9 allows any item that has a risk component that can be identified and measured to be a hedged item. This would include nonfinancial items. These new requirements would enable entities to apply hedge accounting that reflect their risk management activities.

4. IAS 39 does not allow net positions to be hedged. However, companies often hedge net positions; for example, they may hedge a net foreign exchange position of 20 that is made up of an asset of 100 and a liability of 80. This creates an inconsistency between hedge accounting and risk management activity. IFRS 9 extends the use of hedge accounting to net positions for a group of items and to components of a group and, thereby, improves the link to risk management.

5. IAS 39 sets a high hurdle before hedge accounting is available. It also sets a high hurdle for hedge accounting to continue. These hurdles result from a strict quantitative test. The accounting consequences of failing this test are drastic. This is widely criticized as being arbitrary and for causing hedge accounting not to be available or to stop when a hedge is a good one economically. IFRS 9 bases the qualification for hedge accounting on how entities design hedges for risk management purposes. It allows hedging relationships to be adjusted without necessarily stopping and potentially restarting hedge accounting. This enables hedge accounting to better reflect risk management activity, which often requires adjustments to hedges to accommodate changes in market conditions.

The new hedge accounting requirements in IFRS 9 will help investors to better understand the extent and effect of an entity's hedging activities and to assist them in forecasting future cash flows.

6. Disclosure requirements are more comprehensive and focus on the risks that entities are managing, how they are managing those risks, and the outcomes of that risk management activity, including the effect on the financial statements. This is to help investors to understand better the extent and effect of companies' hedging activities and to assist them in forecasting future cash flows.

We will now discuss and illustrate the requirements for hedge accounting as per IFRS 9 in more detail.

A hedged item can be a recognized asset or liability, an unrecognized firm commitment, a highly probable forecast transaction, or a net investment in a foreign operation. The hedged item can be a single item, a group of items, or a component of these items. The hedged item must be reliably measurable. If a hedged item is a forecast transaction (or a component thereof), that transaction must be highly probable.

To qualify for hedge accounting, the following three conditions must be met:

To qualify for hedge accounting, the entity must expect that the hedge will be effective and must document how the hedging relationship will meet the hedge effectiveness requirements.

(a) The hedging relationship consists only of eligible hedging instruments and eligible hedged items.

(b) At the inception of the hedge, there is formal designation and documentation of the hedging relationship and the entity's risk management objective and strategy for undertaking the hedge. That documentation includes identification of the hedging instrument, the hedged item, and the nature of the risk being hedged and how the entity will assess whether the hedging relationship meets the hedge effectiveness requirements.

(c) The hedging relationship meets the hedge effectiveness requirements.

Hedge effectiveness is the extent to which changes in the fair value or cash flows of the hedging instrument offset changes in the fair value or cash flows of the hedged item. Hedge ineffectiveness is the extent to which there is no such offset or the changes in the fair value or cash flows of the hedging instrument more than offset those on the hedged item. An entity considers the relationship between the weightings of the hedging instrument and the hedged item (the hedge ratio) when assessing whether the hedging relationship will minimize the expected ineffectiveness. For example, an entity wants to hedge a forecast purchase of 100 tonnes of a commodity of a particular grade in Location A, and that commodity usually trades at about 90% of the price for the exchange-traded benchmark grade of the same commodity in Location B. If the entity wants to hedge the forecast purchase of 100 tonnes with exchange-traded forward contracts, then a forward contract volume to purchase 90 tonnes of the benchmark grade of the commodity in Location B would be expected to offset best the entity's exposure to changes in the cash flows for the hedged purchase. Hence, a hedge ratio of 1.11:1 would minimize expected hedge ineffectiveness.

At the inception of the hedging relationship and on an ongoing basis, an entity must assess whether a hedging relationship meets the hedge effectiveness requirements. At a minimum, an entity must perform the ongoing assessment at each reporting date or at a significant change in the circumstances affecting the hedge effectiveness requirements, whichever comes first. The assessment relates to expectations about hedge ineffectiveness and offsetting and therefore is only forward looking.

> Hedge effectiveness must be assessed at the inception of the hedging relationship and on an ongoing basis.

Hedges can be designated for accounting purposes as fair value hedges, cash flow hedges, or hedges of a net investment in a foreign operation.[6] In a fair value hedge, the entity uses a hedging instrument to hedge against the fluctuation in the fair value of the hedged item. This method will be used when the hedged item (such as long-term debt) will be measured at fair value. The gain or loss in the fair values of the hedging instrument and hedged items are both recognized in profit or loss in the period of the change in values, with one exception. If the hedging instrument hedges an equity instrument for which an entity has elected to present changes in fair value in other comprehensive income, then the gain or loss on the hedging instrument is also presented in other comprehensive income.

> A hedge is designated as a fair value hedge or a cash flow hedge based on the exposure hedged.

In a cash flow hedge, the entity uses a hedging instrument (such as a derivative) to hedge against the fluctuation in the Canadian-dollar value of future cash flows (such as future sales). The gain or loss on the hedging instrument is initially reported in other comprehensive income and subsequently reclassified to profit when the hedged item affects profit.

There are many different types of hedging instruments such as forward exchange contracts, futures contracts, and options. We will use forward exchange contracts to illustrate hedge accounting.

Hedging a Recognized Monetary Item

Vulcan Corporation of Toronto, Ontario, has a December 31 year-end. On November 1, Year 1, when the Bulgarian lev (BL) was worth $0.870, Vulcan sold merchandise to a Bulgarian customer for BL200,000. The terms of the sale required payment in full on February 15, Year 2. On November 15, Year 1, the spot rate was BL1 = $0.865 and the three-month forward rate was BL1 = $0.842. In order to protect the account receivable from further exchange losses, Vulcan entered into a contract with its bank on this date, to deliver BL200,000 in three months' time.

At year-end, the spot rate was BL1 = $0.869 and the 45-day forward rate was $0.852. On February 15, Year 2, Vulcan received BL200,000 from the customer and settled the forward contract with the bank when the spot and forward rates were $0.860.

Before preparing the journal entries, try to understand the rationale for entering into the hedge and the expected results. From November 1 to November 15, the Canadian-dollar value of the receivable declined from $174,000 (200,000 × 0.870) to $173,000 (200,000 × 0.865) because of the strengthening of the Canadian dollar relative to the Bulgarian lev. Vulcan was concerned about a further slide in the value of the lev and further erosion in the value of the receivable. To minimize the loss from a further decline, Vulcan was entered into a forward exchange contract to fix the amount it will receive in Canadian dollars when the receivable is collected, and that is $168,400 (200,000 × 0.842). In effect, Vulcan was prepared to pay $4,600 ($173,000 − $168,400) in order to avoid bigger losses. This differential of $4,600 is called a *discount on the forward contract*. It will be expensed as a foreign exchange loss over the term of the forward exchange contract.

> The forward contract is used to offset the risk of decline in value of the accounts receivable from the customer.

Although the forward contract is a hedge of the accounts receivable, we will not apply hedge accounting in this situation. Both the accounts receivable and the forward contract are measured at fair value at each reporting date, with the exchange adjustments reported in profit. Since the exchange adjustments on both items are already being reported in profit in the same period, it is not necessary to use hedge accounting. We will account for each item separately as we did for the previous examples in this chapter. If the company wanted to use hedge accounting and designated the forward contract as a fair value hedge, the accounting would look exactly the same as accounting for each item separately. So there is no point in using hedge accounting in this particular situation. Hedge accounting is necessary only when the exchange adjustments would otherwise be reported in profit in different periods.

> Hedge accounting is optional and will not be applied in this situation.

A timeline for the transactions follows:

Nov 1	Nov 15	Dec 31	Feb 15
Sell goods on account	Hedge receivable	Year-end	Collect receivable and settle forward exchange contract

Vulcan will record the sale and the receivable at the spot rate on the transaction date with the following journal entry:

> The "BL" indicates that the accounts receivable is denominated in Bulgarian levs. The "$" indicates that the sale is being measured in dollars and will not be adjusted for exchange rate changes.

Nov. 1, Year 1

Accounts receivable (BL)	174,000	
Sales ($)		174,000

BL200,000 × 0.870 = 174,000

On November 15, the receivable is hedged when the spot rate is BL1 = $0.865. The exchange loss that occurred during the period when the account receivable was *not* hedged is recorded next, followed by the entry to record the forward contract.

Nov. 15, Year 1

Exchange gains and losses	1,000	
Accounts receivable (BL)		1,000

Exchange loss prior to the date of hedge, BL200,000 × (0.870 − 0.865)

Receivable from bank ($)	168,400	
Payable to bank (BL)		168,400
To record forward contract at forward rate—BL 200,000 × 0.842		

The receivable from the bank represents the amount of Canadian dollars that Vulcan will receive when it delivers BL200,000 to the bank in three months. As this is denominated in Canadian dollars, it will not be affected by subsequent changes in the spot rate or forward rate. The payable to bank represents an obligation of Vulcan to deliver BL200,000 to the bank in three months' time and is denominated in Bulgarian levs. It should be reported at fair value throughout the term of the contract. The fair value is determined by multiplying BL200,000 by the forward rate for the remaining term of the contract. At year-end, the accounts receivable and payable to the bank are adjusted to fair value as follows:

Dec. 31, Year 1

Accounts receivable (BL)	800	
Exchange gains and losses		800
To adjust the account receivable to the December 31 spot rate		
—BL200,000 × (0.869 − 0.865)		

Exchange gains and losses	2,000	
Payable to bank (BL)		2,000
To adjust the forward contract to the December 31 forward rate		
—BL200,000 × (0.852 − 0.842)		

> The closing rate is used when the item can be settled at any time, whereas the forward rate is used when the item must be settled at a future date.

The $2,000 adjustment can be broken down as follows:

> The discount on the forward contract is, in effect, expensed over the term of the forward contract.

- An $800 loss on forward contract, the hedging instrument offsets the $800 gain on the accounts receivable, the hedged item.

- The other $1,200 is the portion of the $4,600 discount on the forward contract being expensed in this period.

Financial statements are prepared as at December 31. The following partial trial balance is presented to show only the accounts used to record these particular transactions.

PARTIAL TRIAL BALANCE
at December 31, Year 1

	Dr.	Cr.
Accounts receivable	$173,800	
Exchange gains and losses	2,200	
Sales		$174,000
Receivable from bank ($)	168,400	
Payable to bank (BL)		170,400
	$344,400	$344,400

The accounts associated with the hedge have been segregated in the trial balance to emphasize their nature. These executory contract items should be shown at their net amount in the balance sheet because they will be settled simultaneously and on a net basis. The presentation of how the items shown on the trial balance will be presented in the year-end financial statements is shown next.

VULCAN CORP.
PARTIAL BALANCE SHEET
at December 31, Year 1

Assets

Accounts receivable	$173,800
Other items	XXX
	$ XXX

Liabilities and Shareholders' Equity

Forward contract (170,400 − 168,400)	$ 2,000
Other items	XXX
	$ XXX

> The receivable from and payable to the bank are offset against each other and only the net difference of a $2,000 liability is reported.

VULCAN CORP.
PARTIAL INCOME STATEMENT
for the Year Ended December 31, Year 1

Sales		$174,000
Expenses:		
Foreign exchange loss	$2,200	
Other	XXX	XXX
Profit		$ XXX

The $2,200 foreign exchange loss consists of the $1,000 loss before the hedge was put in place and $1,200 expense pertaining to the $4,600 discount on the forward contract.

On the February 15 settlement date, the receivable from the Bulgarian customer and the payable to bank are adjusted to current value as follows:

> Only the foreign-denominated receivables and payables must be remeasured. The receivable from the bank is denominated in Canadian dollars and is not affected by changes in exchange rates.

Feb. 15, Year 2		
Exchange gains and losses	1,800	
Accounts receivable (BL)		1,800
To adjust the account receivable to the spot rate—		
BL200,000 × (0.869 − 0.860)		
Exchange gains and losses	1,600	
Payable to bank (BL)		1,600
To adjust the forward contract to the forward rate—		
BL200,000 × (0.860 − 0.852)		

The total of the exchange losses recognized in Year 2 is $3,400, which is the remaining amount of the discount on the forward contract. This brings the total exchange loss on the forward contract to $4,600 ($1,200 from Year 1 and $3,400 for Year 2), which is equal to the discount on the forward contract.

The Bulgarian customer sends BL200,000 to Vulcan, which is deposited in a Bulgarian lev cash account. Vulcan delivers the BL200,000 to the bank to discharge its forward contract obligation and receives $168,400 as agreed. The following journal entries record these events:

Feb. 15, Year 2		
Cash (BL)	172,000	
Accounts receivable (BL)		172,000
Collection from Bulgarian customer		

Payable to bank (BL)	172,000	
Cash (BL)		172,000
Delivery of levs to bank		
Cash	168,400	
Receivable from bank		168,400
Receipt of Canadian dollars from bank		

You may be overwhelmed with the number of entries above and may not appreciate the overall effect. To see the big picture, all of the above entries for Year 1 and Year 2 can be condensed into one entry as follows:

Cash ($)	168,400	
Foreign exchange loss before hedge	1,000	
Foreign exchange loss (= discount on forward contract)	4,600	
Sales		174,000

The net impact on profit is equal to the amount of cash received. This is a typical result in accounting. Sales were recorded at the historical rate, which is consistent with our measurement model. The exchange losses occurred for two reasons. First, the company lost $1,000 in the value of the accounts receivable due to the increase in value of the Canadian dollar relative to the Bulgarian lev before the hedge was put into place. Then, the company incurred a loss of $4,600 to put the hedge into place. In the end, the accounting for the hedge reflects the objective of the hedge in the first place.

See Self-Study Problem 1 for an illustration of a hedge of accounts payable arising from a purchase of merchandise.

> Accrual accounting is more complicated than cash accounting, but in total and over time, it presents the same overall effect on profit as cash accounting.

Hedging an Unrecognized Firm Commitment

L05

> The forward contract is used to offset the risk of an increase in the cost of the inventory.

On June 2, Year 2, when the spot rate was US$1 = CDN$1.26, Manning Inc. of Vancouver ordered merchandise from an American supplier for US$350,000. Delivery was scheduled for August 1 with payment to be made in full on delivery. Upon placing the order, Manning immediately entered into a 60-day forward contract with its bank to purchase US$350,000 on August 1 at the forward rate of US$1 = CDN$1.28. Manning's year-end is June 30. On August 1, the merchandise was received, and Manning purchased the U.S. dollars from the bank and paid its supplier.

In this example, the purpose of the forward contract is to fix the amount to be paid for the inventory. The hedged item is the commitment and the hedging instrument is the forward contract. The commitment to purchase the inventory is normally not recognized for accounting purposes because there is no asset or liability at the time of the commitment. The inventory and related accounts payable will be recorded only when the inventory is actually received. Since we must report the forward contract when the contract is signed, we will have a mismatch in the current year because the hedging instrument is recognized but the hedged item is not. Without hedge accounting, the exchange gains or losses on the forward contract would be reported in the current year, whereas no exchange gain or losses would be reported on the accounts payable because it does not legally exist in the current year. Therefore, hedge accounting is necessary to report the exchange gains or losses on the hedged item and the hedging instrument in the same period.

We can designate the forward contract as a cash flow hedge and defer the recognition in net income by recognizing the exchange gains or losses on the forward contract in other comprehensive income (OCI) and not recording anything with respect to commitment to purchase goods. Alternatively, we could designate the forward contract as a fair value hedge and advance the recognition in profit of the exchange gains or losses on the commitment to purchase goods so that they match against the exchange gains or losses being recorded in profit on the forward contract.

The premium on the forward contract is a cost of fixing the purchase price of the inventory.

The premium on the forward contract is $7,000 [US$350,000 × (1.28 − 1.26)]. It is the amount that Manning is prepared to pay to fix the amount of the cash flows required to purchase the inventory. Since the forward contract was intended to fix the cost of the inventory, the $7,000 will be reported as a cost of the inventory and will be reflected in income when the inventory is sold.

The relevant exchange rates for this example are as follows:

Date	Spot Rate	Forward Rate
June 2	US$1 = CDN$1.260	US$1 = CDN$1.280
June 30	US$1 = CDN$1.268	US$1 = CDN$1.275
August 1	US$1 = CDN$1.272	US$1 = CDN$1.272

A timeline for the transactions follows:

June 2	June 30	August 1
Order goods and hedge order	Year-end	Receive goods, settle forward contract, and pay supplier

Manning's journal entries to record the forward contract and the purchase of inventory are presented in Exhibit 10.5 under three different accounting methods: (1) the forward contract is designated as a cash flow hedge, (2) the forward contract is designated as a fair value hedge, and (3) hedge accounting is not applied. The rationale for each entry is explained below.

The gross method is used to account for the forward contract.

The first journal entry would be made if Manning uses the gross method of accounting for the forward contract. *Payable to bank* represents the amount in Canadian dollars that Manning will pay the bank in August when it receives US$350,000. The amount recorded will not be affected by future exchange rate fluctuations. *Receivable from bank* is the hedge of the expected future liability. It is denominated in U.S. dollars and represents Manning's right to receive U.S. dollars from the bank in August. It should be reported at fair value and is accordingly translated at the forward exchange rate. Note that the net balance of this executory contract is zero, and if a balance sheet were prepared at this time, the receivable from bank and payable to bank would be offset, and no amount would appear on the balance sheet.

At year-end, the second journal entry is made to adjust the receivable from the bank to its fair value.

The exchange gains or losses on the hedging instrument for the cash flow hedge are reported in other comprehensive income for now and will be reported in profit when the exchange gains or losses on the hedged items are reported in profit.

Note that the exchange adjustment on the forward contract is reported in other comprehensive income for the cash flow hedge and in net income for the fair value hedge. However, if hedge accounting is not applied the exchange adjustment is reported in net income, which is the same treatment we used when accounting for a speculative forward contract. On the June 30, Year 2, balance sheet, the $1,750 difference between the receivable from the bank ($446,250) and the payable to the bank ($448,000) would be reported as forward contract under current liabilities. The OCI is reported in comprehensive income. In turn, the balance at the end of the year for accumulated OCI for cash flow hedges is reported as a separate component of shareholders' equity.

EXHIBIT 10.5

JOURNAL ENTRIES FOR HEDGING A FIRM COMMITMENT

Transaction No.	Cash flow hedge		Fair value hedge		No hedge accounting	
June 2, Year 2						
1. Receivable from bank (US$)	448,000		448,000		448,000	
Payable to bank (CDN$)		448,000		448,000		448,000
To record forward contract at forward rate—350,000 × 1.280						
June 30, Year 2						
2. OCI–Exchange gains and losses	1,750					
Exchange gains and losses			1,750		1,750	
Receivable from bank (US$)		1,750		1,750		1,750
To adjust forward contract to June 30 forward rate—350,000 × (1.280 − 1.275)						
3. Commitment asset			1,750			
Exchange gains and losses				1,750		
To adjust value of upcoming accounts receivable to June 30 forward rate —350,000 × (1.280 − 1.275)						
August 1, Year 2						
4. OCI–Exchange gains and losses	1,050					
Exchange gains and losses			1,050		1,050	
Receivable from bank (US$)		1,050		1,050		1,050
To adjust forward contract to August 1 forward rate—350,000 × (1.275 − 1.272)						
5. Commitment asset			1,050			
Exchange gains and losses				1,050		
To adjust value of upcoming accounts receivable to August 1 forward rate—350,000 × (1.275 − 1.272)						
6. Payable to bank (CDN$)	448,000		448,000		448,000	
Cash (CDN$)		448,000		448,000		448,000
Payment to bank						
7. Cash (US$)	445,200		445,200		445,200	
Receivable from bank (US$)		445,200		445,200		445,200
Receipt of US$350,000 from bank at August 1 spot rate—350,000 × 1.272						
8. Inventory	445,200		445,200		445,200	
Cash (US$)		445,200		445,200		445,200
To record the inventory purchase and pay cash at the August 1 spot rate—350,000 × 1.272						
9. Inventory	2,800		2,800			
OCI—reclassification of exchange gains and losses		2,800				
Commitment asset				2,800		
To reclassify OCI and commitment asset to cost of inventory						

*Side notes:*

The forward rate is used to revalue the forward contract and commitment asset at each reporting date.

The exchange loss on the forward contract is reported in profit for the fair value hedge to match against the exchange gain on the commitment asset.

The exchange loss on the forward contract is reported in OCI for the cash flow hedge and will be removed from OCI when the hedged item is recognized; that is, when the inventory is received.

If Manning designated the forward contract as a fair value hedge, the third entry would be made. It records a gain on the firm commitment through profit to match the loss on the forward contract. Both the forward contract and the firm commitment are measured at fair value using the forward rate. As such, the

The change in value of the commitment is recognized in profit to match the change in value of the forward contract.

exchange loss on the forward contract will be offset by the exchange gain on the firm commitment. The commitment asset would be reported as a current asset.

On August 1, the receivable from the bank is adjusted to its fair value in the fourth journal entry. Once again, the exchange adjustment is recorded in OCI for the cash flow hedge and in net income for the fair value hedge and when hedge accounting is not applied. In turn, journal entry number five adjusts the commitment asset to fair value to offset the loss from revaluing the forward contract to fair value. Journal entries six and seven record the exchange of currencies with the bank under the terms of the forward contract. Manning settled its obligation to the bank by giving the bank $448,000 in Canadian dollars. The bank gives Manning $350,000 in U.S. dollars. Then, journal entry eight records the payment of $350,000 in U.S. dollars to the supplier upon delivery of the inventory.

The exchange losses incurred on the hedging instrument increase the cost of the inventory and will be reported in net income when the inventory is sold.

There are two options for removing the accumulated exchange adjustment of $2,800 from other comprehensive income for the cash flow hedge and from the commitment asset for the fair value hedge. Option one is to remove the $2,800 when the inventory is delivered and report it as an adjustment of the inventory. In turn, this amount will affect the amount reported as cost of goods sold when the inventory is sold. The second option is to remove the $2,800 when the inventory is sold and show it as other income or net against cost of goods sold on the income statement. In both cases, the $2,800 will be reflected in the income statement when the inventory is sold. Since the objective of the hedge was to fix the price of the inventory, the first option will be used and is accounted for in journal entry nine.

The summarized entries for the combined effect of all of entries in Exhibit 10.5 are as follows

	Cash Flow Hedge	Fair Value Hedge	No Hedge Accounting
Inventory	448,000	448,000	445,200
Exchange gains and losses			2,800
Cash (CDN$)	448,000	448,000	448,000

Under hedge accounting, the forward contract fixed the purchase price of the inventory at the forward rate on the date of the hedge.

Under all three methods, the net cash outflow is $448,000. This amount was fixed when the forward contract was signed. Under hedge accounting, the inventory is recorded at $448,000, the amount fixed by the forward contract. When hedge accounting is not used, the inventory and forward contract are reported separately as if they were not related. The inventory is reported at $445,200, which is the value of US$350,000 paid to the supplier using the spot rate on the date of the payment. The $2,800 exchange loss on the forward contract is reported in net income in the same manner as a speculative forward contract.

Under all three reporting methods, $448,000 will eventually be expensed. However, the timing and line description on the income statement are different. Under hedge accounting, the $448,000 will be expensed as cost of goods sold when the inventory is sold. When hedge accounting is not applied, the $448,000 is expensed through a combination of $2,800 in exchange losses over a two-year period, and $445,200 as cost of goods sold when the inventory is sold. This is a typical result in accounting. The amount expensed on a cumulative basis is equal to the cash paid on a cumulative basis.

At the beginning of this problem, we determined that the company was willing to pay a premium of $7,000 to fix the amount of the inventory. When hedge accounting was applied, the inventory was recorded at $448,000. Furthermore, no exchange gains or losses were reported in profit because the commitment to pur-chase inventory was effectively hedged by the forward contract. When hedge accounting was not applied, there was no relationship between the forward con-tract and the amount recorded for the cost of the inventory.

When hedge accounting is not applied, the forward contract is accounted for as if it were a speculative contract.

In the above example, the inventory was paid for on delivery. If Manning had purchased the inventory on credit, it would have been exposed to foreign cur-rency risk on the accounts payable. It could have entered into a forward contract to hedge both the commitment to buy inventory and the amount required to set-tle the account payable. In this case, the $7,000 premium would have to be split between the two objectives. Part of the $7,000 would be reported as a cost of the inventory and reflected in net income when the inventory is sold. The other part would be recognized in net income over the period of time between the origina-tion and settlement of the accounts payable.

For further analysis and discussion of the impact of the three reporting meth-ods on key financial ratios, see the Analysis and Interpretation of Financial State-ments section. Also, see Self-Study Problem 2 for another illustration of a cash flow hedge of a firm commitment to sell equipment.

Hedging a Highly Probable Forecasted Transaction

L06

The following example illustrates the accounting when long-term debt is used as a hedge of a future revenue stream. The hedge will be accounted for as a cash flow hedge because it is hedging the variability of future cash flows.

Alana Enterprises, a Canadian company that has carried out business activi-ties in Singapore for a number of years, has decided to protect itself against foreign currency fluctuations over the next three years, during which it expects a revenue stream of at least 200,000 Singapore dollars (SD) per year. On January 1, Year 1, the company borrows SD600,000, payable in full at the end of three years, and desig-nates the loan as a hedge against the future three-year revenue stream. In order to simplify the illustration, we will omit the payment of yearly interest and assume that there is no difference between the exchange rate at the end of each year and the average exchange rate for that year. Furthermore, we will assume that the cash received in Singapore dollars will be immediately used to pay operating expenses.

The loan payable is the hedging instrument, and the future revenue stream is the hedged item.

Relevant exchange rates for the Singapore dollar are as follows:

Jan. 1, Year 1	SD1 = $0.852
Dec. 31, Year 1	SD1 = $0.849
Dec. 31, Year 2	SD1 = $0.835
Dec. 31, Year 3	SD1 = $0.840

Applying the concepts of hedge accounting, Alana will make the following journal entries:

Jan. 1, Year 1

Cash	511,200	
Loan payable (SD) (600,000 × 0.852)		511,200

During Year 1, the revenue stream is recorded at the average exchange rate for the year. Thus, the following entry is recorded:

Cash	169,800	
Sales revenue (200,000 × 0.849)		169,800

In Year 1, the entire loan is needed to hedge three years of forecasted revenues, and the entire exchange gain on the loan should be reported in other comprehensive income to be eventually offset against the future revenue stream.

On December 31, Year 1, the loan payable has to be reflected in the financial statements at fair value using the closing rate. The entry to record the exchange gain on the loan payable resulting from a decrease in the exchange rate from $0.852 to $0.849 is as follows:

Dec. 31, Year 1

Loan payable (SD)	1,800	
OCI—cash flow hedge (Year 1) (600,000 × [0.852 − 0.849])		1,800

One-third of the hedged revenue stream has been received, and so the following adjusting entry is made to match one-third of the gain from the hedge against the revenue received:

Since one-third of the revenue stream has been realized, one-third of the other comprehensive income should be brought into income.

Dec. 31, Year 1

OCI—cash flow hedge (Year 1)	600	
Sales revenue (200/600 × 1,800)		600

Two-thirds of the exchange gain is deferred in other comprehensive income to be matched against the foreign currency revenues when they are received in the following two years. The company has *lost* because it has received less revenue in Canadian dollars than would be the case if the exchange rate had not changed, but it has also *gained* due to the fact that its liability (measured in Canadian dollars) has decreased. The liability hedges the revenue stream; consequently, the gain in one offsets the loss in the other. The total revenue for the year is $170,400, which is made up of the translated revenue of $169,800 plus the recognized exchange gain on the hedge of $600. Note that this is the same amount as would have been received in translated revenue if the exchange rates had not changed since January 1, Year 1 (200,000 × 0.852). If the exchange rates do not change over the next two years, the total translated revenue *plus* the recognized revenue from the hedge will be $170,400 each year.

Note also that while the loan is still SD600,000, one-third of the foreign revenue stream has been received; therefore, one-third of this loan balance no longer qualifies as a hedge and is exposed to foreign currency risk. Because of this, any future exchange gains and losses on this portion must be reflected immediately in income.

During Year 2, revenue in Singapore dollars is received and translated at the average rate. This results in the following entry:

Cash	167,000	
Sales revenue (200,000 × 0.835)		167,000

In Year 2, only two-thirds of the loan is a hedging instrument. The other one-third of the loan is exposed to foreign currency risk; the related exchange gain is reported in profit.

On December 31, Year 2, the loan payable is reduced by $8,400 (600,000 × [0.849 − 0.835]) to reflect its translation at the closing rate; also, the gain on the one-third portion that no longer qualifies as a hedge is immediately reflected in profit, and the balance of the gain from the hedge portion is initially deferred with the following entry:

Dec. 31, Year 2

Loan payable (SD)	8,400	
Exchange gain (⅓ × 8,400)		2,800
OCI—cash flow hedge (Year 2)		5,600

The other comprehensive income hedges the foreign currency revenues of Years 2 and 3. Year 2 revenue has been received and translated at the average exchange rate for the year. Therefore, the Year 2 portion (one-half) of the deferred gain is matched against this revenue with the following entry:

Dec. 31, Year 2

OCI—cash flow hedge (Year 2)	2,800	
Sales revenue (½ × 5,600)		2,800

In addition, the portion of the deferred Year 1 exchange gain must be matched against Year 2 revenues with the following entry:

Dec. 31, Year 2

OCI—cash flow hedge (Year 1)	600	
Sales revenue		600

Remember that the purpose of the hedge was to ensure that the foreign currency revenue in Year 2 was at least $170,400 (200,000 × 0.852). The actual foreign revenue adjusted for the hedge gains was equal to this amount, as the following calculation indicates:

The final revenue figure of $170,400 is the equivalent Canadian dollar value of the anticipated sale when the hedge was first put into place.

Foreign currency revenue (200,000 × 0.835)	$167,000
Exchange gain on Year 1 hedge	600
Exchange gain on Year 2 hedge	2,800
	$170,400

In addition, the Year 2 income statement will reflect the additional exchange gain ($2,800) that came from the portion of the loan that no longer qualifies as a hedge.

The balance of the accumulated other comprehensive income (AOCI) that will appear on the December 31, Year 2, balance sheet is calculated as follows:

OCI, Year 1		1,800	
Less reflected in income:			
Year 1	600		
Year 2	600	1,200	$ 600
OCI, Year 2		5,600	
Less reflected in income Year 2		2,800	2,800
AOCI, December 31, Year 2			$3,400

Because SD400,000 from the total revenue of SD600,000 has been received at the end of Year 2, the loan balance that still qualifies as a hedge is only SD200,000.

The Year 3 entries to record the foreign currency revenues and to adjust the loan to the current rate are as follows:

Cash	168,000	
Sales revenue (200,000 × 0.840)		168,000

In Year 3, only one-third of the loan is a hedging instrument. The other two-thirds of the loan is exposed to foreign currency risk; the related exchange gain is reported in profit.

Dec. 31, Year 3

OCI—cash flow hedge (Year 3) (⅓ × 3,000)	1,000	
Exchange loss (⅔ × 3,000)	2,000	
Loan payable (SD) (600,000 × 0.005)		3,000

The foreign currency revenue has all been received, so none of the Year 3 loss pertaining to the hedge ($1,000) needs to be deferred. The remaining loss from the portion of the loan that is not a hedge ($2,000) is also expensed in the year.

A final entry is made to match the balance of the other comprehensive income from prior years against the Year 3 foreign currency revenue:

> By the end of Year 3, all of the other comprehensive income has been transferred to profit to match the timing of the income recognition on the hedged item, being the revenue stream.

OCI—cash flow hedge (Year 1)	600	
OCI—cash flow hedge (Year 2)	2,800	
OCI—cash flow hedge (Year 3)		1,000
Sales revenue		2,400

An entry would also be made to pay off the loan that is due on this date. The following calculation summarizes the amount reflected in profit in Year 3 from the foreign currency revenue, the hedge gains and losses, and the exchange loss from the non-hedge portion of the loan:

> The hedging instrument was used to fix the final revenue figure at $170,400, the equivalent Canadian dollar value of the anticipated sale when the hedge was first put into place.

Foreign currency revenue (200,000 × 0.840)		$168,000
Year 1 and 2 exchange gains on hedge	3,400	
Year 3 exchange loss on hedge	1,000	2,400
Hedged foreign currency revenue		170,400
Remainder of Year 3 loan exchange loss		2,000
Effect on Year 3 profit		$168,400

This simplified example has illustrated a possible use of hedge accounting. In a more realistic situation, differences would occur because the average rates used to translate the revenue stream are different from the year-end rates used to translate the foreign currency loan, and the actual revenues would probably turn out to be different from those expected when the hedge was designated. However, the broad concepts illustrated would still apply, and because an increasing portion of the foreign currency–denominated debt ceases to be eligible for a hedge each year, the resultant income recognition pattern is similar to the defer-and-amortize pattern that used to occur for foreign currency debt.

Disclosure Requirements   The following summarize the main disclosures required in IAS 21 for the effects of changes in foreign exchange rates:

(a) The amount of exchange differences recognized in profit or loss

(b) Net exchange differences recognized in other comprehensive income

The following summarize the main disclosures required in IFRS 9 related to hedges:

> The entity must disclose the type of hedge and the risks being hedged.

(a) An entity's risk management strategy and how it is applied to manage risk

(b) How the entity's hedging activities may affect the amount, timing, and uncertainty of its future cash flows

(c) The effect that hedge accounting has had on the entity's primary financial statements

Some of the specific disclosure requirements are as follows:

(a) The carrying amount of the hedging instruments (financial assets separately from financial liabilities)

(b) The notional amounts or other quantity (e.g., tonnes or cubic metres) related to the hedging instruments

For fair value hedges:

(i) The carrying amount of the accumulated gains or losses on the hedged item presented in a separate line item in the statement of financial position, separating assets from liabilities

For cash flow hedges:

(i) The balance in the cash flow hedge reserve for continuing hedges that will be reclassified when the hedged item affects profit or loss

(ii) For hedges of net positions, the hedging gains or losses recognized in a separate line item in the income statement

(iii) The amount reclassified from the cash flow hedge reserve into profit or loss as a reclassification adjustment

For fair value and cash flow hedges

(i) Changes in the value of the hedging instrument recognized in other comprehensive income

(ii) Hedge ineffectiveness recognized in profit or loss

> The disclosure requirements pertaining to hedges and hedge accounting are quite extensive.

Bombardier Inc., a Canadian company, is a manufacturer of transportation equipment, including business and commercial aircraft and rail transportation equipment and systems. It is the world's only manufacturer of both planes and trains. Exhibit 10.6 contains excerpts from Bombardier's 2011 financial statements pertaining to foreign currency transactions and hedges. In 2011, Bombardier had not yet adopted IFRS 9 and, therefore, did not provide the extensive disclosure required by this IFRS.

EXHIBIT 10.6

EXTRACTS (IN PART) FROM BOMBARDIER'S 2011 FINANCIAL STATEMENTS

Summary of significant accounting policies

Foreign currency transactions—Transactions denominated in foreign currencies are initially recorded in the functional currency of the related entity using the exchange rates in effect at the date of the transaction. Monetary assets and liabilities denominated in foreign currencies are translated using the closing exchange rates. Any resulting exchange difference is recognized in income except for exchange differences related to retirement benefits asset and liability, as well as financial liabilities designated as hedges of the Corporation's net investments in foreign operations, which are recognized in OCI. Non-monetary assets and liabilities denominated in foreign currencies and measured at historical cost are translated using historical exchange rates, and those measured at fair value are translated using the exchange rate in effect at the date the fair value is determined. Revenues and expenses are translated using the average exchange rates for the period or the exchange rate at the date of the transaction for significant items.

> Some revenues and expenses are translated at the exchange rate at the date of the transaction rather than the average rate for the period.

Financial instruments

(a) Financial instruments classified as HFT

Derivative financial instruments—Derivative financial instruments are mainly used to manage the Corporation's exposure to foreign exchange and interest-rate market risks, generally

(continued)

EXHIBIT 10.6 *(continued)*

through forward foreign exchange contracts, interest rate swap agreements, cross currency interest-rate swap agreements and interest-rate cap agreements. Derivative financial instruments include derivatives that are embedded in financial or nonfinancial contracts that are not closely related to the host contracts.

Derivative financial instruments are classified as HFT, unless they are designated as hedging instruments for which hedge accounting is applied (see below). Changes in the fair value of derivative financial instruments not designated in a hedging relationship, excluding embedded derivatives, are recognized in cost of sales or financing expense or financing income, based on the nature of the exposure.

Embedded derivatives of the Corporation include financing rate commitments, call options on long-term debt and foreign exchange instruments. Upon initial recognition, the fair value of financing rate commitments linked to the sale of products is recognized as deferred charge in other assets. The deferred charge is recorded as an adjustment of the sale price of the related products. Call options on long-term debt that are not closely related to the host contract are measured at fair value, with the initial value recognized as an increase of the related long-term debt and amortized to net income using the effective interest method. Upon initial recognition, the fair value of the foreign exchange instruments not designated in a hedge relationship is recognized in cost of sales. Subsequent changes in fair value of embedded derivatives are recorded in cost of sales, other expense (income) or financing expense or financing income, based on the nature of the exposure.

Hedge accounting

The company formally documents and assesses whether the hedging instruments are highly effective.

Designation as a hedge is only allowed if, both at the inception of the hedge and throughout the hedge period, the changes in the fair value of the derivative and non-derivative hedging financial instruments are expected to substantially offset the changes in the fair value of the hedged item attributable to the underlying risk exposure. The Corporation formally documents all relationships between the hedging instruments and hedged items, as well as its risk management objectives and strategy for undertaking various hedge transactions. This process includes linking all derivatives to forecasted cash flows or to a specific asset or liability. The Corporation also formally documents and assesses, both at the hedge's inception and on an ongoing basis, whether the hedging instruments are highly effective in offsetting the changes in the fair value or cash flows of the hedged items. There are three permitted hedging strategies.

The company applies both fair value and cash flow hedge accounting.

Fair value hedges – The Corporation generally applies fair value hedge accounting to certain interest-rate derivatives and forward foreign exchange contracts hedging the exposures to changes in the fair value of recognized financial assets and financial liabilities. In a fair value hedge relationship, gains or losses from the measurement of derivative hedging instruments at fair value are recorded in net income, while gains or losses on hedged items attributable to the hedged risks are accounted for as an adjustment to the carrying amount of hedged items and are recorded in net income.

Cash flow hedges – The Corporation generally applies cash flow hedge accounting to forward foreign exchange contracts and interest-rate derivatives entered into to hedge foreign exchange risks on forecasted transactions and recognized assets and liabilities. In a cash flow hedge relationship, the portion of gains or losses on the hedging item that is determined to be an effective hedge is recognized in OCI, while the ineffective portion is recorded in net income. The amounts recognized in OCI are reclassified in net income as a reclassification adjustment when the hedged item affects net income. However, when an anticipated transaction is subsequently recorded as a nonfinancial asset, the amounts recognized in OCI are reclassified in the initial carrying amount of the related asset.

(continued)

12. FINANCIAL INSTRUMENTS

Derivatives and hedging activities

The carrying amounts of all derivative and non-derivative financial instruments in a hedge relationship were as follows as at:

	December 31, 2011		January 31, 2011	
	Assets	Liabilities	Assets	Liabilities
Derivative financial instruments designated as fair value hedges				
Cross-currency interest-rate swap	$ 12	$ 39	$ 22	$ 68
Interest-rate swap	297	—	80	—
	309	39	102	68
Derivative financial instruments designated as cash flow hedges[1]				
Forward foreign exchange contracts	195	284	390	509
Derivative financial instruments designated as hedges of net investment				
Cross-currency interest-rate swap	—	—	—	36
Derivative financial instruments classified as HFT[2]				
Forward foreign exchange contracts	19	14	9	48
Interest-rate swap	—	4	—	6
Cross-currency interest-rate swap	—	—	—	—
Embedded derivative financial instruments:				
Foreign exchange	4	3	16	8
Call options on long-term debt	21	—	40	—
Financing rate commitments	—	—	—	2
	44	21	65	64
Total derivative financial instruments	$548	$344	$557	$677
Non-derivative financial instruments designated as hedges of net investment				
Long-term debt	$ —	$1,029	$ —	$715

[1] The maximum length of time of the derivative financial instruments hedging the Corporation's exposure to the variability in future cash flows for anticipated transactions is 22 months as of December 31, 2011.
[2] Held as economic hedges, except for embedded derivative financial instruments.

The net gains on the hedging instruments designated in fair value hedge relationships and the net losses on the related hedged items attributable to the hedged risk recognized in financing expense, amounted to $311 million and $304 million respectively for the fiscal year ended December 31, 2011 ($123 million and $119 million respectively for the fiscal year ended January 31, 2011).

The methods and assumptions used to measure the fair value of financial instruments are described in note 32-Fair value of financial instruments.

31 FINANCIAL RISK MANAGEMENT

Market risk

Foreign exchange risk

The Corporation is exposed to significant foreign exchange risks in the ordinary course of business through its international operations, in particular to the Canadian dollar, pound sterling and euro. The Corporation employs various strategies, including the use of derivative financial instruments and by matching asset and liability positions, to mitigate these exposures.

(continued)

Forward foreign exchange contracts were designated as cash flow hedges.

Long-term debt was designated as hedges of net investment.

The net gains on the hedging instruments designated in fair value hedge relationships were reported in financing expense.

EXHIBIT 10.6   *(continued)*

The Corporation's main exposures to foreign currencies are managed by the segments and covered by a central treasury function. Foreign currency exposures are managed in accordance with the Corporation's Foreign Exchange Risk Management Policy (the "FX Policy"). The objective of the FX Policy is to mitigate the impact of foreign exchange movements on the Corporation's consolidated financial statements. Under the FX Policy, potential losses from adverse movements in foreign exchange rates should not exceed pre-set limits. Potential loss is defined as the maximum expected loss that could occur if an unhedged foreign currency exposure was exposed to an adverse change of foreign exchange rates over a one-quarter period. The FX Policy also strictly prohibits any speculative foreign exchange transactions that would result in the creation of an exposure in excess of the maximum potential loss approved by the Board of Directors of the Corporation.

Under the FX Policy, it is the responsibility of the segments' management to identify all actual and potential foreign exchange exposures arising from their operations. This information is communicated to the central treasury group, which has the responsibility to execute the hedge transactions in accordance with the FX Policy. In order to properly manage their exposures, each segment maintains long-term cash flow forecasts in each currency. BA has adopted a progressive hedging strategy while BT hedges all its identified foreign currency exposures to limit the effect of currency movements on their results. The segments also mitigate foreign currency risks by maximizing transactions in their functional currency for their operations such as material procurement, sale contracts and financing activities.

The company tries to mitigate foreign currency risk by matching asset and liability positions.

In addition, the central treasury function manages balance sheet exposures to foreign currency movements by matching asset and liability positions. This program consists mainly in matching the long-term debt in foreign currency with long-term assets denominated in the same currency.

The Corporation mainly uses forward foreign exchange contracts to manage the Corporation's exposure from transactions in foreign currencies and to synthetically modify the currency of exposure of certain balance sheet items. The Corporation applies hedge accounting for a significant portion of anticipated transactions and firm commitments denominated in foreign currencies, designated as cash flow hedges. Notably, the Corporation enters into forward foreign exchange contracts to reduce the risk of variability of future cash flows resulting from forecasted sales and purchases and firm commitments.

The Corporation's foreign currency hedging programs are typically unaffected by changes in market conditions, as related derivative financial instruments are generally held to maturity, consistent with the objective to lock in currency rates on the hedged item.

Sensitivity analysis

Foreign exchange risk arises on financial instruments that are denominated in foreign currencies. The foreign exchange rate sensitivity is calculated by aggregation of the net foreign exchange rate exposure of the Corporation's financial instruments recorded in its statement of financial position. The following impact on EBT for the fiscal year ended December 31, 2011, is before giving effect to cash flow hedge relationships.

		Effect on EBT				
		CAD/USD	*GBP/USD*	*EUR/USD*	*EUR/SEK*	*Other*
Gain (loss)	+10%	$21	$(3)	$14	$25	$19

A 10% change in the U.S. dollar/Canadian dollar exchange rate would change earnings before taxes by $21, which is equal to 2% of earnings before taxes.

The following impact on OCI for the fiscal year ended December 31, 2011 is for derivatives designated in a cash flow hedge relationship. For derivatives that qualify for hedge accounting, any change in fair value is mostly offset by the re-measurement of the underlying exposure.

(continued)

	Effect on OCI before income taxes				
	Variation	*CAD/USD*	*GBP/USD*	*EUR/USD*	*EUR/SEK*	*Other*
Gain (loss)	+10%	$190	$4	$49	$29	$74

Source: Reproduced with permission from Bombardier, Inc. http://ir.bombardier.com/modules/misc/documents/99/28/87/48/13/Bombardier_AR2011_en.pdf

ANALYSIS AND INTERPRETATION OF FINANCIAL STATEMENTS

L07

Earlier in this chapter, we prepared journal entries to account for the hedge of a firm commitment by Manning Inc. to purchase inventory from a foreign supplier under three reporting methods. Exhibit 10.7 shows the net impact of the aforementioned journal entries on selected items on Manning's Year 2 income statement and balance sheet and on three key financial ratios. The first column shows assumed amounts for the numerator and denominator for three key ratios before Manning signed the purchase order and entered into the forward contract. The last three columns show the cumulative effect of the journal entries on the Year 2 financial statements and on the key ratios. We assume that there were no transactions other than the purchase order and the forward contract.

EXHIBIT 10.7   Impact of Hedge Accounting Method on Key Ratios

	Before transactions	Cash flow hedge	Fair value hedge	No hedge accounting
Impact on income statement				
Net income				(1,750)
OCI		(1,750)		
Comprehensive income		(1,750)		(1,750)
Impact on balance sheet				
Current assets			1,750	
Current liabilities		1,750	1,750	1,750
Shareholders' equity		(1,750)		(1,750)
Impact on key ratios:				
Current ratio				
Current assets	2,000,000	2,000,000	2,001,750	2,000,000
Current liabilities	1,000,000	1,001,750	1,001,750	1,001,750
	=2.000	=1.997	=1.998	=1.997
Debt-to-equity ratio				
Total debt	3,300,000	3,301,750	3,301,750	3,301,750
Shareholders' equity	1,100,000	1,098,250	1,100,000	1,098,250
	=3.000	=3.006	=3.002	=3.006
Return on equity				
Net income	165,000	165,000	165,000	163,250
Shareholders' equity	1,100,000	1,098,250	1,100,000	1,098,250
	=15.00%	=15.02%	=15.00%	=14.86%

The fair value hedge method shows the best liquidity position (i.e., highest current ratio) because the commitment asset is included in current assets.

The cash flow hedge method shows the best performance (i.e., highest return on equity) because exchange losses are reported in OCI and do not negatively affect net income.

Note the following from Exhibit 10.7:

- There is no impact on net income or comprehensive income under the fair value hedge, because the exchange loss on the forward contract is offset by an exchange gain on the commitment asset.

Total shareholders' equity is the same for all three methods but the components of shareholders' equity will have different values.

- There is a negative impact of $1,750 on comprehensive income for the other two methods, but the cash flow hedge shows the loss in OCI, whereas the loss is reported in net income when hedge accounting is not used. The loss through OCI ends up in accumulated OCI, which is a separate component of shareholders' equity, whereas the negative net income ended up in retained earnings.

- All methods report a current liability of $1,750 but only the fair value hedge shows a current asset, which is the commitment asset of $1,750.

- Manning's liquidity looks the best under the fair value hedge because the current ratio is highest. The commitment asset was included in current assets under this method but not in the other methods.

The fair value hedge method shows the best solvency position (i.e., lowest debt-to-equity ratio) because shareholders' equity is not negatively affected by exchange losses.

- Manning's solvency looked the best under the fair value hedge because the debt-to-equity ratio was lowest. Shareholders' equity was not negatively affected by any exchange losses under the fair value hedge, whereas it was negatively affected for the other two methods.

- The return on equity uses net income rather than comprehensive income as the numerator. The cash flow method shows the best return on equity because of the higher net income and lower shareholders' equity. The no hedge accounting method shows the worst return on equity because the exchange loss is reported in net income.

L08 ## ASPE DIFFERENCES

- Hedge accounting is permitted only when the critical terms of the hedging instrument match those of the hedged item. Enterprises are not required to assess hedge effectiveness. An enterprise is required to determine only that the critical terms of the two components of the hedging arrangement continue to match.

- An entity may designate only the following hedging relationships pertaining to foreign currency exposure:

  — An anticipated purchase or sale of a commodity hedged with a forward contract to mitigate the effect of future price changes of the commodity.

  — An anticipated transaction denominated in a foreign currency hedged with a forward contract to mitigate the effect of changes in future foreign currency exchange rates.

  — a foreign currency–denominated interest-bearing asset or liability hedged with a cross–currency interest rate swap to mitigate the effect of changes in interest rates and foreign currency exchange rates.

  — The net investment in a self-sustaining foreign operation hedged with a derivative or a non-derivative financial instrument to mitigate the effect of changes in foreign currency exchange rates.

- Hedge accounting for private companies follows an accrual-based model and is much simpler than hedge accounting for public companies. For example, an entity accounts for a qualifying hedge of an anticipated transaction as follows:

  — When the anticipated transaction occurs, it is recognized initially at the amount of consideration paid or received.

  — When the hedging item matures before the hedged item is recognized, the gain or loss on the hedging item is recognized as a separate component of equity until the hedged item is recognized. When the hedged item is recognized, the gain or loss on the hedging item is transferred from the separate component of equity to the carrying amount of the hedged item or to net income.

  — When the forward contract matures, the gain or loss on the contract is recorded as an adjustment of the carrying amount of the hedged item. When the hedged item is recognized directly in net income, the gain or loss on the forward contract is included in the same category of net income.

- Disclosure is minimal compared to the disclosure required for public companies.

> Hedge accounting is more restrictive and much simpler for private enterprises.

U.S. GAAP DIFFERENCES

U.S. GAAP and IFRSs for foreign currency transactions have many similarities. The significant differences are summarized as follows:

1. Whereas IFRSs give priority to certain indicators when determining the functional currency, U.S. GAAP do not give priority to any of the indicators.

2. Whereas IFRSs report foreign currency gains or losses on available-for-sale debt securities in net income, U.S. GAAP report these exchange gains or losses in other comprehensive income.

SUMMARY

Transactions denominated in foreign currency are recorded in Canadian dollars at the spot rate in effect on the date of the transaction. At the date of the balance sheet, foreign currency assets and liabilities are translated into Canadian dollars to preserve the normal measurement at either historical cost or current value. Any gains or losses arising from changes in exchange rates on the exposed items are reflected in profit for the period.

The use of hedging instruments such as forward exchange contracts minimizes or completely eliminates the risks associated with exchange rate changes. If all risks are removed, the hedge is "perfect." It also is possible to have a situation in which only a portion of a position is hedged and the balance is at risk or in which, as was illustrated, a portion of the hedging instrument ceases to act as a hedge and becomes exposed to foreign currency risk.

In a speculative forward exchange contract and for a fair value hedge, exchange gains and losses are recognized in profit in the period of the change in exchange rates. In a cash flow hedge, the exchange gains and losses on the hedging instrument are initially reported in other comprehensive income and subsequently reclassified to profit when the hedged item affects profit.

Significant Changes in GAAP in the Last Three Years

1. The requirements for hedge accounting have changed and are now contained in IFRS 9 rather than IAS 39. IFRS 9 is effective for 2015, with the option for early adoption. IAS 39 is effective until IFRS 9 is adopted.

2. The requirements for hedge accounting in IFRS 9 are less restrictive and are more closely aligned with risk management activities undertaken by companies when hedging their financial and nonfinancial risk exposures.

3. In a fair value hedge, if the hedging instrument hedges an equity instruments for which an entity has elected to present changes in fair value in OCI, then the gain or loss on the hedging instrument is also presented in OCI.

4. Disclosure requirements are more comprehensive and focus on the risks that entities are managing, how they are managing those risks, and the outcomes of that risk management activity, including the effect on the financial statements.

Changes Expected in GAAP in the Next Three Years

1. The new requirements for hedge accounting as per IFRS 9 must be adopted for fiscal years beginning on or after January 1, 2015, or earlier, with early adoption allowed.

2. No other major changes are expected in the area of foreign currency transactions or hedge accounting for foreign currency risk.

SELF-STUDY PROBLEM 1

LO1, 4   **Hedging an Existing Monetary Position**

On November 15, Year 1, Domco Ltd. of Montreal bought merchandise from a supplier located in Brunei for 100,000 Brunei dollars (BD). The Brunei dollar was trading at $0.81 on that date, and the terms of the purchase required Domco to pay the account on January 30, Year 2. On December 1, when the spot rate was BD1 = $0.813, Domco entered into a forward contract with its bank to receive BD100,000 at the 60-day forward rate of BD1 = $0.82. On December 31, Year 1, Domco's year-end, the spot rate was BD1 = $0.825 and the 30-day forward rate was BD1 = $0.831. On January 30, Year 2, when the spot rate was BD1 = $0.838, Domco settled the forward contract with its bank and paid BD100,000 to the Swiss supplier.

Required:

(a) Prepare the journal entries required in Year 1 and Year 2, assuming that hedge accounting is not applied.

(b) Prepare a partial statement of financial position as at December 31, Year 1, which shows accounts payable and the forward contract.

(c) Prepare one journal entry to summarize the combined effect of all entries in Part (a).

SOLUTION TO SELF-STUDY PROBLEM 1

(a)   *Nov. 15, Year 1*

Inventory ($)	81,000	
Accounts payable (BD) (BD100,000 × 0.81)		81,000

Dec. 1, Year 1

Exchange gains/losses	300	
Accounts payable (BD)		300
To adjust the accounts payable to the Dec. 1 spot rate		
(BD100,000 × [0.813 − 0.810])		

Receivable from bank (BD)	82,000	
Payable to bank ($)		82,000
To record the forward contract (BD100,000 × 0.82)		

Dec. 31, Year 1

Exchange gains/losses	1,200	
Accounts payable (BD)		1,200
To adjust the accounts payable to the Dec. 31 spot rate		
(BD100,000 × [0.825 − 0.813])		

Receivable from bank (BD)	1,100	
Exchange gains/losses		1,100
To adjust the forward contract to the Dec. 31 forward rate		
(BD100,000 × [0.831 − 0.820])		

Jan. 30, Year 2

Exchange gains/losses	1,300	
Accounts payable (BD)		1,300
To adjust the accounts payable to the Jan. 30 spot rate		
(BD100,000 × [0.838 − 0.825])		

Receivable from bank (BD)	700	
Exchange gains/losses		700
To adjust the forward contract to the Jan. 30 forward rate		
(BD100,000 × [0.838 − 0.831])		

Payable to bank ($)	82,000	
Cash ($)		82,000
Deliver Canadian dollars to bank		

Cash (BD)	83,800	
Receivable from bank (BD)		83,800
Receive BD100,000 from bank (BD100,000 × 0.838)		

Accounts payable (BD)	83,800	
Cash (BD)		83,800
Pay BD100,000 to supplier (BD100,000 × 0.838)		

(b)

DOMCO LTD.
STATEMENT OF FINANCIAL POSITION
at December 31, Year 1

Assets	
Forward contract (Note 1)	$ 1,100
Liabilities	
Accounts payable	$82,500

Note 1:

Receivable from bank	$83,100
Payable to bank	(82,000)
Net amount of forward contract	$ 1,100

(c)

Inventory	81,000	
Exchange loss (before hedge)	300	
Exchange loss (= premium on contract)	700	
Cash		82,000

SELF-STUDY PROBLEM 2

LO1, 5 **Hedging an Unrecognized Firm Commitment**

On October 15, Year 2, Sellcompany Ltd., located in Canada, signed a contract to sell equipment to Buycompany, which is located in a country whose currency is the foreign currency unit (FC). The selling price of the equipment was FC200,000 and the terms of the sale called for delivery to be made on January 30, Year 3, with payment in full due on delivery.

Having signed the sales order, Sellcompany immediately entered into a forward contract with its bank to sell FC200,000 on January 30, Year 3, at the forward rate of FC1 = $1.22. The spot rate on October 15 was FC1 = $1.20. On December 31, the year-end of Sellcompany, the spot rate was FC1 = $1.222 and the 30-day forward rate was FC1 = $1.231. On January 30, Year 3, when the spot rate was FC1 = $1.24, Sellcompany delivered the equipment, received FC200,000 from Buycompany, and settled the forward contract with the bank.

Required:

(a) Prepare the journal entries required in Year 2 and Year 3 for Sellcompany, assuming that the forward contract is designated as a cash flow hedge.
(b) Prepare a partial statement of financial position as at December 31, Year 2, which shows the presentation of the hedge accounts.
(c) Prepare one journal entry to summarize the combined effect of all entries in Part (a).

SOLUTION TO SELF-STUDY PROBLEM 2

(a)

Oct. 15, Year 2

Receivable from bank ($)	244,000	
Payable to bank (FC)		244,000
To record the forward contract (FC200,000 × 1.22)		

Dec. 31, Year 2

OCI—cash flow hedge	2,200	
Payable to bank (FC)		2,200
To adjust the forward contract to the forward rate		
FC200,000 × (1.231 − 1.220)		

Jan. 30, Year 3

OCI—cash flow hedge	1,800	
Payable to bank (FC)		1,800
To adjust the forward contract to the Jan. 30 forward rate		
FC200,000 × (1.240 − 1.231)		

Cash (FC)	248,000	
Sales		248,000
To record equipment sale at FC200,000 × 1.24		
Payable to bank (FC)	248,000	
Cash (FC)		248,000
Deliver FC to bank		
Cash ($)	244,000	
Receivable from bank ($)		244,000
Receive Canadian dollars from bank		
Sales	4,000	
OCI—cash flow hedge		4,000
To reclassify other comprehensive income as an adjustment of sales		

(b)

SELLCOMPANY LTD.
STATEMENT OF FINANCIAL POSITION
at December 31, Year 2

Liabilities	
Forward contract (Note 1)	$ 2,200
Note 1:	
Payable to bank	$246,200
Receivable from bank	(244,000)
Net amount of forward contract	$ 2,200

(c)

Cash	244,000	
Sales		244,000

In the end, the sales were recorded at $244,000, the amount fixed by the forward contract. Furthermore, no exchange gains or losses were reported in income because the commitment to sell the equipment was effectively hedged by the forward contract.

APPENDIX 10A

DETERMINING THE FAIR VALUE OF FORWARD EXCHANGE CONTRACTS

The fair value of a forward exchange contract is based on the relative merits of the contract compared with other contracts in the market and the time value of money. If the contract states that the company must sell foreign currency at a rate that is better than what is currently available in the market, the contract has a positive value. On the other hand, if the contract states that the company must sell foreign currency at a rate that is worse than what is currently offered in the market, the contract has a negative value. Therefore, the following factors

The fair value of a forward contract is based on its relative merits compared with other contracts in the market and the time value of money.

are usually considered to determine the fair value of a forward contract at any point in time:

1. The forward rate when the forward contract was entered into
2. The current forward rate for a contract that matures on the same date as the forward contract entered into
3. A discount rate, typically the company's incremental borrowing rate

In Exhibit 10.4, we considered the first two factors above when we measured the forward contract at $500 at December 31, Year 1. Since the $500 value will be realized only on March 1, Year 2, it should be discounted to derive its present value at December 31, Year 1. Assuming that Raven's incremental borrowing rate is 12% per annum or 1% per month, the fair value of the forward contract at December 31 is $490.15 ($500 × 0.9803).[7]

The journal entries to record the fair value of the forward contract in Exhibit 10.4 under the gross and net methods when discounting is applied are shown in Exhibit 10A.1. Only the first three entries are shown here because the remaining entries would be the same as in Exhibit 10.4.

EXHIBIT 10A.1

JOURNAL ENTRIES FOR SPECULATIVE FORWARD CONTRACT

	Gross method		Net method	
December 1, Year 1				
Receivable from bank ($)	22,700			
Payable to bank (PP)		22,700		
Record forward contract at forward rate				
(PP1,000,000 × 0.0227 = $22,700)				
December 31, Year 1				
Forward contract			490	
Payable to bank (PP)	490			
Exchange gain		490		490
Revalue forward contract at fair value				
(PP1,000,000 × (0.0227 − 0.0222) × 0.9803 = $490)				
March 1, Year 2				
Forward contract			210	
Payable to bank (PP)	210			
Exchange gain		210		210
Revalue forward contract at fair value				
([22,700 − 490] − PP1,000,000 × 0.0220 = $210)				

The value of a forward contract should be recorded in present value terms.

REVIEW QUESTIONS

L01   1. Briefly summarize the accounting issues arising from foreign currency–denominated transactions.

L01   2. What is the difference between pegged and floating exchange rates?

LO1   3. You read in the newspaper, "One U.S. dollar can be exchanged for 1.15 Canadian dollars." Is this a direct or an indirect quotation? If your answer is *indirect*, what is the direct quotation? If your answer is *direct*, what is the indirect quotation?

LO1   4. Differentiate between a spot rate and a forward rate.

LO1   5. How are foreign currency–denominated assets and liabilities measured on the transaction date? How are they measured on a subsequent balance sheet date?

LO1   6. Describe when to use the closing rate and when to use the historical rate when translating assets and liabilities denominated in a foreign currency. Explain whether or not this practice is consistent with the way we normally measure assets and liabilities.

LO1   7. Differentiate between a spot rate and a closing rate.

LO3, 5   8. Differentiate between the accounting for a fair value hedge and a cash flow hedge.

LO3   9. List some ways that a Canadian company could hedge against foreign currency exchange rate fluctuations.

LO3   10. What are some typical reasons for acquiring a forward exchange contract?

LO4   11. If a foreign currency–denominated payable has been hedged, why is it necessary to adjust the liability for balance sheet purposes?

LO1   12. Explain the application of lower of cost and net realizable value to inventory that was purchased from a foreign supplier.

LO5   13. How does the accounting for a fair value hedge differ from the accounting for a cash flow hedge of an unrecognized firm commitment?

LO2   14. What is the suggested financial statement presentation of hedge accounts recorded under the gross method? Why?

LO5   15. What is meant by *hedge accounting*?

LO2, 3   16. Would hedge accounting be used in a situation where the hedged item and the hedging instrument were both monetary items on a company's statement of financial position? Explain.

LO6   17. When long-term debt hedges a revenue stream, a portion of the long-term debt becomes exposed to the risk of changes in exchange rates. Why is this?

LO5   18. When will the premium paid on a forward contract to hedge a firm commitment to purchase inventory be reported in income under a cash flow hedge? Explain.

CASES

Case 10-1
LO3, 4   Interfast Corporation, a fastener manufacturer, has recently been expanding its sales through exports to foreign markets. Earlier this year, the company negotiated the sale of several thousand cases of fasteners to a wholesaler in the country of Loznia. The customer is unwilling to assume the risk of having to make payment in Canadian dollars. Desperate to enter the Loznian market, the vice-president for international sales agrees to denominate the sale in lrubles (LR), the national currency of Loznia. The current exchange rate for the lruble is $2. In addition, the customer indicates that he cannot make payment until all of the fasteners have been sold. Payment of LR200,000 is scheduled for six months from the date of sale.

Fearful that the lruble might depreciate in value over the next six months, the head of the risk management department at Interfast enters into a forward contract to sell lrubles in six months at a forward rate of $1.80. The forward contract is designated as a fair value hedge of the lruble receivable. Six months later, when payment is received from the Loznian customer, the exchange rate for the lruble is $1.70. The corporate treasurer calls the head of the risk management department into her office.

Treasurer: I see that your decision to hedge our foreign currency position on that sale to Loznia was a bad one.

Department Head: What do you mean? We have a gain on that forward contract. We're $20,000 better off from having entered into that hedge.

Treasurer: That's not what the books say. The accountants have recorded a net loss of $40,000 on that particular deal. I'm afraid I'm not going to be able to pay you a bonus this year. Another bad deal like this one and I'm going to have to demote you back to the interest rate swap department.

Department Head: Those bean counters have messed up again. I told those guys in international sales that selling to customers in Loznia was risky, but at least by hedging our exposure, we managed to receive a reasonable amount of cash on that deal. In fact, we ended up with a gain of $20,000 on the hedge. Tell the accountants to check their debits and credits again. I'm sure they just put a debit in the wrong place or some accounting thing like that.

Required:

Have the accountants made a mistake? Does the company have a loss, a gain, or both from this forward contract? Explain.

Case 10-2
LO3

Long Life Enterprises was a well-established Toronto-based company engaged in the importation and wholesale marketing of specialty grocery items originating in various countries of the western Pacific Rim. They had recently also entered the high-risk business of exportation, to several of these same countries, of fresh Atlantic lobster and crab.

Although Canada has extensive trading relationships with several countries in the Pacific Rim, these transactions were not normally priced or settled in terms of the Canadian dollar. Both the U.S. dollar and the Japanese yen were somewhat more common in these transactions. Further, various local currencies were involved, especially for small transactions involving specialty items, and a wide variety of credit terms were in use for both imports and exports. The entire situation was complicated by the perishable nature of some of the imports and the high mortality risk for both lobster and crab. Both situations led to uncertainty as to the face amount of the associated receivable or payable and hindered the ability of the firm to adopt the policy of specific hedging of each of the receivable or payable contracts.

Most recently, the Canadian dollar had risen against other major currencies, leading to major losses on the large receivables outstanding because of the seasonal lobster harvest. More generally, management was concerned about losses that might arise from both export and import transactions. For the most recent fiscal year, foreign currency losses had exceeded gains by some $40,000—an amount the company could not afford during the present stage of rapid growth.

Required:

What steps would you propose to the management of Long Life Enterprises to reduce the foreign exchange costs associated with their receivables and payables? As a part of this process, suggest a way of structuring transactions or affairs that would reduce the impact of fluctuations in the relative values of currencies.

(case prepared by Peter Secord, St. Mary's University)

Case 10-3
LO1

Canada Cola Inc. (CCI) is a public company engaged in the manufacture and distribution of soft drinks across Canada. Its primary product is Canada Cola ("Fresh as a Canadian stream"), which is a top seller in Canada and generates large export sales.

You met with Jane MacNamara, the partner in charge of the CCI audit engagement, to commence planning for the upcoming audit of CCI. During this meeting, MacNamara informed you that early this year CCI entered into an agreement with the government of Russia and has commenced the manufacture and sale of Canada Cola in Russia. A short summary of this agreement is contained in Exhibit I. MacNamara would like you to prepare a detailed report that discusses the accounting implications of this new division of CCI for this engagement.

Required:

Prepare the report.

(CICA adapted)

EXHIBIT I

SUMMARY OF AGREEMENT

1. The Russian government will provide the land and the building for the plant. It will make no further investment.
2. CCI will install bottling machinery costing $5 million in the Russian plant. Once installed, this machinery may not be removed from Russia. No other plants may be established in Russia without the consent of the Russian government.
3. CCI will be required to provide the funds for the initial working capital. CCI will sell U.S. dollars to the Russian government in exchange for local currency (rubles).
4. CCI will be wholly responsible for the management and daily operations of the plant. Canadian managers will be transferred to Russia.
5. CCI will be permitted to export its cola syrup to Russia at CCI's Canadian cost.
6. Only Canada Cola may be bottled at the Russian plant and the entire output from the plant can only be sold in Russia. CCI and the Russian government will share equally in the profits from the sale of Canada Cola in Russia.
7. Although foreign currency can be converted into rubles, rubles cannot be converted back into any foreign currency. Therefore, the Russian government will sell vodka to CCI (at the prevailing export market price in Russia) in exchange for the rubles CCI earns in profits. CCI will be permitted to export this vodka to Canada, where it may be sold in the Canadian domestic market only.

Case 10-4
LO3, 4, 6

International Manufacturing Company (IMC) is a large, Canadian-based corporation with worldwide operations. IMC has issued debt instruments in Swiss francs, euros, and U.S. dollars to take advantage of low interest rates. All these financing arrangements were completed on a fixed-interest-rate basis.

The Canadian dollar has weakened considerably in the past few years, and as a result, IMC has accrued substantial foreign exchange losses on the debt instruments. These losses have seriously impaired IMC's ability to report increased earnings during the last few years, in spite of its successful operations.

IMC's investment banker has recommended the following alternatives to management:

1. IMC considers using the currency-swap market to minimize losses on its debt. IMC would enter into an agreement with a third party, whereby IMC agreed to pay the obligation of the third party's debt in Canadian dollars in exchange for the third party agreeing to pay the obligation of IMC's foreign debt. Pursuing this option would entail an additional cost if the investment banker were required to guarantee the payment of the foreign debt.

2. IMC considers buying back the Swiss franc, euro, and U.S.-dollar bonds on the bond market and refinancing them now. Interest rates for all currencies are much higher at present than at the time that these bonds were issued.

Management has asked you, the CA, to prepare a report that discusses the accounting and financial reporting implications of each of the investment banker's recommendations. Management is considering a third option as well: using the existing debt to hedge forecasted sales of IMC products in these foreign countries. Management also wants to know the accounting and financial reporting implications of this option.

Required:

Prepare the report.

(CICA adapted)

Case 10-5
LO1, 2, 3

ZIM Inc. (ZIM) is a high-technology company that develops, designs, and manufactures telecommunications equipment. ZIM was founded in Year 5 by Dr. Alex Zimmer, the former assistant head of research and development at a major telephone company. He and the director of marketing left the company to found ZIM. ZIM has been very successful. Sales reached $8.3 million in its first year and have grown by 80% annually since then. The key to ZIM's success has been the sophisticated software contained in the equipment it sells.

ZIM's board of directors recently decided to issue shares to raise funds for strategic objectives through an initial public offering of common shares. The shares will be listed on a major Canadian stock exchange. ZIM's underwriter, Mitchell Securities, believes that an offering price of 18 to 20 times the most recent fiscal year's earnings per share can be achieved. This opinion is based on selected industry comparisons.

ZIM has announced its intention to go public, and work has begun on the preparation of a preliminary prospectus. It should be filed with the relevant securities commissions in 40 days. The offering is expected to close in about 75 days. The company has a July 31 year-end. It is now September 8, Year 8.

You, a CA, work for Chesther Chathan, Chartered Accountants, the auditors of ZIM since its inception. You have just been put in charge of ZIM's audit, due to the sudden illness of the senior. ZIM's year-end audit has just commenced. At the same time, ZIM's staff and the underwriters are working 15-hour days trying to write the prospectus, complete the required legal work, and prepare for the public offering. The client says that the audit must be completed so that the financial statements can go to the printer in 22 days. ZIM plans to hire a qualified chief financial officer as soon as possible.

An extract from ZIM's accounting records is found in Exhibit II. You have gathered the information in Exhibit III from the client. You have been asked by the audit partner to prepare a memo dealing with the key accounting issues.

EXHIBIT II

EXTRACT FROM ACCOUNTING RECORDS
(in Thousands of Dollars)

| | Revenue | | Deferred |
	Month of July	Total fiscal Year 8	development costs[1]
Product			
Zibor	$ 815	$ 8,802	$ 9,463
Resale components	540	4,715	—
Webstar	700	4,241	359
IDSL 600	—	2,104	1,431
Transact training	2,077	2,077	—
Firewall Plus	402	1,640	1,500
Transact	670	1,350	2,159
700J	—	400	725
ATM 4000	—	394	1,825
Photon phasing project	—	—	691
	$5,204	$25,723	$18,153

[1] Cumulative costs for each product that have been deferred and recorded on the balance sheet.

EXHIBIT III

INFORMATION GATHERED FROM THE CLIENT

1. The job market for top software and hardware engineering talent is very tight. As a result, ZIM has turned to information technology "head hunters" to attract key personnel from other high-technology companies. During the year, ZIM paid $178,000 in placement fees, and the company is amortizing the payments over five years. The search firm offers a one-year money-back guarantee if any of the people hired leaves the company or proves to be unsatisfactory.
2. On July 29, Year 8, the company made a payment of $100,000 to a computer hacker. The hacker had given the company ten days to pay her the funds. Otherwise, she said she would post on the Internet a security flaw she had detected in the ZIM's Firewall Plus software.
3. Ale Zimmer had been working on a photon-phasing project when he left the telephone company. He has moved this technology ahead significantly at ZIM, and a prototype has been built at a cost of $691,000. The project has been delayed pending a decision on the direction that the project will take.
4. ZIM defers and amortizes software and other development costs according to the following formula:

Annual amortization rate = $\dfrac{\text{Sales in units for the year}}{\text{Total expected sales in units during product life}}$

(continued)

EXHIBIT III **(continued)**

5. In line with normal software company practice, ZIM releases, via the Internet, software upgrades that correct certain bugs in previously released software.

6. During a routine visit to the AC&C Advanced Telecommunications laboratory in southern California, a ZIM engineer discovered that nearly 600 lines of code in an AC&C program were identical to those of some ZIM software written in Year 6—right down to two spelling mistakes and a programming error.

7. The ATM 4000 has been the company's only product flop. High rates of field failures and customer dissatisfaction led ZIM to issue an offer, dated July 30, Year 8, to buy back all units currently in service for a total of $467,500. Southwestern Utah Telephone is suing ZIM for $4 million for damages related to two ATM 4000 devices that it had purchased through a distributor. The devices broke down, affecting telephone traffic for two weeks before they were replaced.

8. ZIM also resells components manufactured by a Japanese telecommunications company. The effort required to make these sales to existing customers is minimal, but the gross margin is only 12% versus an average of 60% for the company's other products, excluding the Transact and 700J lines.

9. During the first two years of operation, ZIM expensed all desktop computers (PCs) when purchased, on the grounds that they become obsolete so fast that their value after one year is almost negligible. In the current year, ZIM bought $429,000 worth of PCs and plans to write them off over two years.

10. Revenue is recognized on shipment for all equipment sold. Terms are FOB ZIM's shipping location.

11. ZIM's director of marketing, Albert Buzzer, has come up with a novel method of maximizing profits on the Transact product line. Transact is one of the few ZIM products that has direct competition. Transact routes telephone calls 20% faster than competing products but sells for 30% less. ZIM actually sells the product at a loss. However, without a special training course offered by ZIM, field efficiency cannot be maximized. Customers usually realize that they need the special training a couple of months after purchase. Buzzer estimates that the average telephone company will spend three dollars on training for every dollar spent on the product. Because of the way telephone companies budget and account for capital and training expenditures, most will not realize that they are spending three times as much on training as on the product.

12. In May Year 2, ZIM paid back a U.S. denominated, $25 million long-term debt prematurely to take advantage of a favourable interest rate. The US$25 million loan was subject to a cross-currency swap. The agreement with the third party was to pay CAN$33 million and receive US$25 million from the third party in May Year 4. This represented the exchange rate at the time the transactions were entered into. Although the swap was used to hedge the currency risk on the long-term debt, it was not formally designated as a hedge for reporting purposes. The U.S. dollars exchange rate at the time of the payout was CAN$1.20. ZIM recognized the $3 million gain on the repayment of the U.S. loan. ZIM negotiated a CAN$30 million one-year loan with Beemow Bank to repay the US$25 million loan. The spot exchange rate as at January 31, Year 3, was CAN$1.27, whereas the forward exchange rate for contracts expiring in May Year 4 was CAN$1.25.

13. The IDSL equipment was sold to customers in May Year 8. In September Year, ZIM provided the custom software required to operate the IDSL 600 equipment. The software was "shipped" via the Internet.

Required:

Prepare the memo.

(CICA adapted)

PROBLEMS

Note: Some problems use direct exchange rate quotations; others use indirect quotations.

Problem 10-1
L01, 2, 4, 9

Manitoba Exporters Inc. (MEI) sells Inuit carvings to countries throughout the world. On December 1, Year 5, MEI sold 10,000 carvings to a wholesaler in a foreign country at a total cost of 600,000 foreign currency units (FCs) when the spot rate was FC1 = $0.741. The invoice required the foreign wholesaler to remit by April 1, Year 6. On December 3, Year 5, MEI entered into a forward contract with the Royal Bank at the 120-day forward rate of FC1 = $0.781. Hedge accounting is not applied.

The fiscal year-end of MEI is December 31, and on this date the spot rate was FC1 = $0.757 and the forward rate was FC1 = $0.791. The payment from the foreign customer was received on April 1, Year 6, when the spot rate was FC1 = $0.802.

Required:

(a) Prepare the journal entries to record

   (i)   the sale and the forward contract,
   (ii) any adjustments required on December 31, and
   (iii) the cash received in Year 6.

(b) Prepare a partial balance sheet of MEI on December 31, Year 5, that shows the presentation of the receivable and the accounts associated with the forward contract.

*(c) Now assume that a discount rate of 6% per annum, or 0.5% per month, is applied when determining the fair value of the forward contract at December 31, Year 5. Prepare the journal entries to record

   (i)   the sale and the forward contract,
   (ii) any adjustments required on December 31, and
   (iii) the cash received in Year 6.

Problem 10-2
L01

Moose Utilities Ltd. (MUL) borrowed $40,000,000 in U.S. funds on January 1, Year 1, at an annual interest rate of 12%. The loan is due on December 31, Year 4, and interest is paid annually on December 31. The Canadian exchange rates for U.S. dollars over the life of the loan were as follows:

January 1, Year 1	CDN$1.159
December 31, Year 1	CDN$1.168
December 31, Year 2	CDN$1.160
December 31, Year 3	CDN$1.152
December 31, Year 4	CDN$1.155

Exchange rates changed evenly throughout the year.

Required:

(a) Prepare journal entries for MUL for Year 1.
(b) Calculate the exchange gains or losses that would be reported in the profit of the company each year over the life of the loan.

Problem 10-3
LO1

Grammy Ltd., a Canadian company, is dealing with a supplier in a foreign country. On May 1, Year 4, the company made purchases totalling FF3,270,000; this amount is payable in six months. Grammy did not hedge the transaction in any way.

On the due date, Grammy found itself in financial difficulty. The supplier agreed to accept a non-interest-bearing note payable for FF3,000,000 and FF270,000 in cash. The note payable is due July 1, Year 6. Grammy did not hedge the note.

Grammy has a December 31 fiscal year-end.

May 1, Year 4	$1 = FF2
November 1, Year 4	$1 = FF2.6
December 31, Year 4	$1 = FF3.8

Required:

Prepare the journal entries for Year 4 for the accounts payable and the note payable.

(*CGA-Canada adapted*)

Problem 10-4
LO1

On January 1, Year 5, Ornate Company Ltd. purchased US$2,000,000 of the bonds of the Gem Corporation. The bonds were trading at par on this date, pay interest at 9% each December 31, and mature on December 31, Year 7. The following Canadian exchange rates were quoted during Year 5:

January 1, Year 5	US$1 = CDN$1.372
December 31, Year 5	US$1 = CDN$1.321

Exchange rates changed evenly throughout the year. These bonds were trading at 102 at December 31, Year 5.

Required:

Prepare the journal entries for Year 5 assuming that the investment in bonds is

(a) held to maturity,
(b) held for trading, and
(c) available for sale.

Problem 10-5
LO1, 2, 5, 7

On October 1, Year 6, Versatile Company contracted to sell merchandise to a customer in Switzerland at a selling price of SF400,000. The contract called for the merchandise to be delivered to the customer on January 31, Year 7, with payment due on delivery. On October 1, Year 6, Versatile arranged a forward contract to deliver SF400,000 on January 31, Year 7, at a rate of SF1 = $1.20. Versatile's year-end is December 31.

The merchandise was delivered on January 31, Year 7, and SF400,000 were received and delivered to the bank.

Exchange rates were as follows:

	Spot rates	Forward rates
October 1, Year 6	SF1 = $1.18	SF1 = $1.20
December 31, Year 6	SF1 = $1.21	SF1 = $1.22
January 31, Year 7	SF1 = $1.19	SF1 = $1.19

Required:

(a) Prepare the journal entries that Versatile should make to record the events described assuming that the forward contract is designated as a cash flow hedge.

(b) Prepare a partial trial balance of the accounts used as at December 31, Year 6, and indicate how each would appear on the company's financial statements.

(c) Prepare the journal entries that Versatile should make to record the events described, assuming that the forward contract is designated as a fair value hedge.

(d) Prepare a partial trial balance of the accounts used as at December 31, Year 6, and indicate how each would appear on the company's financial statements.

(e) Describe how the accounting for the hedge affects the current ratio, and indicate which accounting treatment for the hedge would show the strongest liquidity position.

Problem 10-6
L01, 2, 4, 9

Hamilton Importing Corp. (HIC) imports goods from countries around the world for sale in Canada. On December 1, Year 3, HIC purchased 10,000 watches from a foreign wholesaler for DM600,000 when the spot rate was DM1 = $0.741. The invoice called for payment to be made on April 1, Year 4. On December 3, Year 3, HIC entered into a forward contract with the Royal Bank at the 120-day forward rate of DM1 = $0.781. Hedge accounting is not applied.

The fiscal year-end of HIC is December 31. On this date, the spot rate was DM1 = $0.757 and the 90-day forward rate was DM1 = $0.786. The payment to the foreign supplier was made on April 1, Year 4, when the spot rate was DM1 = $0.802.

Required:

(a) Prepare the journal entries to record

(i) the purchase and the forward contract,

(ii) any adjustments required on December 31, and

(iii) the payment in Year 4.

(b) Prepare a partial statement of financial position for HIC on December 31, Year 3, that presents the liability to the foreign supplier and the accounts associated with the forward contract.

*(c) Now assume that a discount rate of 6% per annum or 0.5% per month is applied when determining the fair value of the forward contract at December 31, Year 3. Prepare the journal entries to record

(i) the purchase and the forward contract,

(ii) any adjustments required on December 31, and

(iii) the payment in Year 4.

Problem 10-7
L01, 5, 7, 8

On August 1, Year 3, Carleton Ltd. ordered machinery from a supplier in Hong Kong for HK$500,000. The machinery was delivered on October 1, Year 3, with terms requiring payment in full by December 31, Year 3. On August 2, Year 3, Carleton entered a forward contract to purchase HK$500,000 on December 31, Year 3, at a rate of $0.165. On December 31, Year 3, Carleton settled the forward contract and paid the supplier.

Exchange rates were as follows:

	Spot rates	Forward rates
August 1 and 2, Year 3	HK$1 = C$0.160	HK$1 = C$0.165
October 1, Year 3	HK$1 = C$0.164	HK$1 = C$0.168
December 31, Year 3	HK$1 = C$0.169	HK$1 = C$0.169

Required:

(a) Assume that the forward contract was designated as a cash flow hedge of the anticipated transaction to purchase the machinery and that the entire balance in accumulated other comprehensive income on October 1 was transferred to the machinery account when the machinery was delivered. Calculate the following amounts for the financial statements for the year ended December 31, Year 3:

   (i)   Machinery
   (ii) Exchange gains/losses
   (iii) Cash flows for the period

(b) Assume that the forward contract was designated as a cash flow hedge of both the purchase of the machinery and the payment of the accounts payable. Of the balance in accumulated other comprehensive income on October 1, 50% was transferred to the machinery account when the machinery was delivered and the other 50% was reclassified into net income when the supplier was paid. Calculate the following amounts for the financial statements for the year ended December 31, Year 3:

   (i)   Machinery
   (ii) Exchange gains/losses
   (iii) Cash flows for the period

(c) Assume that Carleton is a private company and uses ASPE for reporting purposes. Calculate the following amounts for the financial statements for the year ended December 31, Year 3:

   (i)   Machinery
   (ii) Exchange gains/losses
   (iii) Cash flows for the period

(d) Explain the similarities and differences between the account balances under the three scenarios above. Which scenario would present the higher return on equity for Carleton for Year 3?

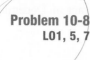

Problem 10-8
LO1, 5, 7

EnDur Corp (EDC) is a Canadian company that exports computer software. On February 1, Year 2, EDC contracted to sell software to a customer in Denmark at a selling price of 600,000 Danish krona (DK) with payment due 60 days after installation was complete. On February 2, Year 2, EDC entered into a forward contract with the Royal Bank at the five-month forward rate of CDN$1 = DK5.20. The installation was completed on April 30, Year 2. On June 30, Year 2, the payment from the Danish customer was received and the forward contract was settled.

Exchange rates were as follows:

	Spot rates	Forward rates
February 1 and 2, Year 2	$1 = DK5.06	$1 = DK5.20
April 30, Year 2	$1 = DK5.09	$1 = DK5.18
June 30, Year 2	$1 = DK5.14	$1 = DK5.14

Required:

(a) Assume that the forward contract was designated as a cash flow hedge of the anticipated sale and that the entire balance in accumulated other comprehensive income (AOCI) on April 30 was transferred to sales when the installation was completed. Calculate the following amounts for the financial statements for the year ended June 30, Year 2:

   (i)   Sales
   (ii) Exchange gains/losses
   (iii) Cash flows for the period

(b) Assume that EDC could have entered into a three-month forward contract on February 2, Year 2, to hedge the sale of the software with a forward rate of $1 = DK5.15. If so, this forward contract would have fixed the sales price for the software. Also, assume that the amount transferred from AOCI to the sales account on April 30 is the amount required to fix the sales price at the three-month forward rate and the balance of the AOCI is reclassified into net income when EDC received payment from the customer. Calculate the following amounts for the financial statements for the year ended June 30, Year 2:

   (i)   Sales
   (ii) Exchange gains/losses
   (iii) Cash flows for the period

(c) Explain the similarities and differences between the account balances under the two scenarios above.

Problem 10-9
LO1

Winn Ltd. conducted two foreign currency transactions on September 1, Year 4. In the first transaction, it sold DM750,000 in merchandise to a foreign company. Since this sale was so special, Winn agreed to collect the note receivable on September 1, Year 8. There is no risk of default on the receivable, since the customer is a very large and prosperous company. The note has an interest rate of 10% per year, payable at the end of December each year. Both the interest and the note will be paid in DMs. This receivable was not hedged in any way.

In the second transaction, Winn purchased FF1,200,000 worth of inventory from a company in another foreign country. This amount will be payable on November 1, Year 5. There is no interest on this liability, and it is not hedged.

EXCHANGE RATES

September 1, Year 4	Spot rate	$1 = DM2.5	$1 = FF3.9
December 31, Year 4	Spot rate	$1 = DM2.8	$1 = FF3.4
Year 4	Average rate	$1 = DM2.3	$1 = FF4.1
Sept.–Dec., Year 4	Average rate	$1 = DM2.6	$1 = FF3.6
November 1, Year 5	Spot rate		$1 = FF3.1
December 31, Year 5	Spot rate	$1 = DM3.6	
Year 5	Average rate	$1 = DM3.0	

Required:

Prepare all the journal entries for Years 4 and 5 for the two transactions. Assume a December 31 year-end.

(CGA-Canada adapted)

Problem 10-10
LO1, 2, 4

On August 1, Year 1, Zip Ltd. purchased some merchandise from a foreign company for DM450,000. The liability was not due until March 1, Year 2. Zip was quite confident that the exchange rate fluctuations were not a problem and took no action to hedge the liability. On November 1, Year 1, Zip looked at the exchange rates and decided that they had better hedge the liability with a 120-day forward contract. Assume a December 31 year-end, assume all months have 30 days, and assume hedge accounting is not adopted.

EXCHANGE RATES

August 1, Year 1	Spot rate	$1 = DM2.5
November 1, Year 1	Spot rate	$1 = DM2.1
November 1, Year 1	120-day forward rate	$1 = DM1.9
December 31, Year 1	Spot rate	$1 = DM1.7
December 31, Year 1	60-day forward rate	$1 = DM1.8
March 1, Year 2	Spot rate	$1 = DM2.7
December 31, Year 2	Spot rate	$1 = DM2.9
March 1, Year 3	Spot rate	$1 = DM2.4

Required:

(a) Prepare all the journal entries for Years 1 and 2 for Zip for these transactions.
(b) Assume that the liability was a note due on March 1, Year 3 (instead of Year 2, as given above), and that Zip does not hedge in any way. Prepare all the journal entries for Year 1.
(c) Explain why some of the financial statement items in this problem are translated at historical rates whereas other items are translated at closing rates.

(CGA-Canada adapted)

Problem 10-11
LO1, 2, 4

On February 1, Year 3, Harrier Ltd., a Canadian company, sold goods to a company in a foreign country and took a note receivable for FF6,200,000. The note matures on February 1, Year 5, and bears interest at the market rate of 6%, payable annually. There was no danger of default on the note, but Harrier decided to hedge the cash receivable from the note with a forward contract. The contract was for one year and matured on February 1, Year 4. On that date, Harrier settled the forward contract and decided to leave the note in an unhedged position for the remainder of its life. Hedge accounting is not applied.

Harrier has a December 31 year-end.

	Spot rates	Forward rates
February 1, Year 3	$1 = FF3.9	$1 = FF3.3
December 31, Year 3	$1 = FF3.1	$1 = FF3.0
February 1, Year 4	$1 = FF4.2	$1 = FF4.2
December 31, Year 4	$1 = FF3.4	
February 1, Year 5	$1 = FF3.3	

Required:

Prepare all the journal entries related to the note receivable for Years 3 and 4.

(CGA-Canada adapted)

Problem 10-12
LO1, 5, 7, 8

On June 1, Year 3, Forever Young Corp. (FYC) ordered merchandise from a supplier in Turkey for Turkish lira (TL) 200,000. The goods were delivered on September 30, with terms requiring cash on delivery. On June 2, Year 3, FYC entered a forward contract as a cash flow hedge to purchase TL200,000 on September 30, Year 3, at a rate of $0.73. FYC's year-end is June 30.

On September 30, Year 3, FYC paid the foreign supplier in full and settled the forward contract.

Exchange rates were as follows:

	Spot rates	Forward rates
June 1 and 2, Year 3	TL1 = $0.70	TL1 = $0.730
June 30, Year 3	TL1 = $0.69	TL1 = $0.725 145 000
September 30, Year 3	TL1 = $0.74	TL1 = $0.740

Required:

(a) (i) Prepare all journal entries required to record the transactions described above.

   (ii) Prepare a June 30, Year 3, partial trial balance of the accounts used in Part (i), and indicate how each account would appear in the year-end financial statements.

(b) Prepare all necessary journal entries under the assumption that no forward contract was entered.

(c) Prepare all necessary journal entries to record the transactions described above, assuming that the forward contract was designated as a fair value hedge.

(d) Assume that Carleton is a private company and uses ASPE for reporting purposes. Prepare all necessary journal entries to record the transactions described in the body of the question above.

(e) Which of the above reporting methods would present the highest current ratio at September 30, Year 3? Briefly explain.

Problem 10-13
LO1, 2, 4

Hull Manufacturing Corp. (HMC), a Canadian company, manufactures instruments used to measure the moisture content of barley and wheat. The company sells primarily to the domestic market, but in Year 3, it developed a small market in Argentina. In Year 4, HMC began purchasing semi-finished components from a supplier in Romania. The management of HMC is concerned about the possible adverse effects of foreign exchange fluctuations. To deal with this matter, all of HMC's foreign currency–denominated receivables and payables are hedged with contracts with the company's bank. The year-end of HMC is December 31.

The following transactions occurred late in Year 4:

- On October 15, Year 4, HMC purchased components from its Romanian supplier for 800,000 Romanian leus (RL). On the same day, HMC entered into a forward contract for RL800,000 at the 60-day forward rate of RL1 = $0.408. The Romanian supplier was paid in full on December 15, Year 4.
- On December 1, Year 4, HMC made a shipment to a customer in Argentina. The selling price was 2,500,000 Argentinean pesos (AP), with payment to be received on January 31, Year 5. HMC immediately entered into a forward contract for AP2,500,000 at the two-month forward rate of AP1 = $0.226.

During this period, the exchange rates were as follows:

	Spot rates	Forward rates
October 15, Year 4	RL1 = $0.395	
December 1, Year 4	AP1 = $0.249	
December 15, Year 4	RL1 = $0.387	
December 31, Year 4	AP1 = $0.233	AP1 = $0.222

Hedge accounting is not adopted.

Required:

(a) Prepare the Year 4 journal entries to record the transactions described above and any adjusting entries necessary.
(b) Prepare the December 31, Year 4, balance sheet presentation of the receivable from the Argentinean customer, and the accounts associated with the forward contract.

Problem 10-14
LO1, 6, 8   As a result of its export sales to customers in Switzerland, the Lenox Company has had Swiss franc denominated revenues over the past number of years. In order to gain protection from future exchange rate fluctuations, the company decides to borrow its current financing requirements in Swiss francs. Accordingly, on January 1, Year 1, it borrows SF1,400,000 at 12% interest, to be repaid in full on December 31, Year 3. Interest is paid annually on December 31. The management designates this loan as a cash flow hedge of future SF revenues, which are expected to be received as follows:

Year 1	SF 560,000
Year 2	490,000
Year 3	350,000
	SF1,400,000

Actual revenues turned out to be exactly as expected each year and were received in cash. Exchange rates for the Swiss franc during the period were as follows:

January 1, Year 1	$1.05
Average, Year 1	$1.10
December 31, Year 1	$1.15
Average, Year 2	$1.20
December 31, Year 2	$1.25
Average, Year 3	$1.27
December 31, Year 3	$1.30

Required:

Prepare the journal entries required each year.

Problem 10-15
LO1   On January 1, Year 4, a Canadian firm, Canuck Enterprises Ltd., borrowed US$200,000 from a bank in Seattle, Washington. Interest of 7% per annum is to be paid on December 31 of each year during the four-year term of the loan. Principal

is to be repaid on the maturity date of December 31, Year 7. The foreign exchange rates for the first two years were as follows:

January 1, Year 4	US$1.00 = CDN$1.38
December 31, Year 4	US$1.00 = CDN$1.41
December 31, Year 5	US$1.00 = CDN$1.35

Exchange rates changed evenly throughout the year.

Required:

Determine the exchange gain (loss) on the loan to be reported in the financial statements of Canuck Enterprises for the years ended December 31, Year 4 and Year 5.

(CGA-Canada adapted)

WEB-BASED PROBLEMS

Web Problem 10-1
LO3, 5, 7

Access the 2011 consolidated financial statements for Barrick Gold Corporation by going to investor relations section of the company's website. Answer the questions below. For each question, indicate where in the financial statements you found the answer, and/or provide a brief explanation.

(a) What currency is used in presenting the financial statements?

(b) What percentage of net income is represented by foreign exchange gains or losses?

(c) Identify the location(s) in the annual report where the company provides disclosures related to its management of foreign exchange risk.

(d) Indicate if and how the company describes the significance of foreign currency issues to the overall success/profitability of the company and sensitivity of its income to a change in foreign exchange rates.

(e) Describe the types of hedging instruments the company uses to hedge foreign exchange risk.

(f) Describe the manner in which the company discloses the fact that its hedges are effective in offsetting gains and losses on the underlying items being hedged.

(g) Does the company apply hedge accounting to accounting for its hedging instruments? If so, what portion of its hedging instruments are fair value hedges, and what portion are cash flow hedges?

(h) What was the amount of foreign exchange gains or losses for the year on cash flow hedges? Describe how these gains or losses are reported.

Web Problem 10-2
LO3, 5, 7

Access the 2011 financial statements for Atco Ltd. by going to investor relations section of the company's website. Answer the same questions as in Problem 1. For each question, indicate where in the financial statements you found the answer, and/or provide a brief explanation. (Some questions may not be applicable.)

Practise and learn online with Connect

Translation and Consolidation of Foreign Operations

INTRODUCTION

Consolidated financial statements are required when one entity has control over another entity. With the ever-expanding global economy, it is now very common for a subsidiary to be in a foreign country, as is indicated by the following:

Most Canadian public companies have subsidiaries in foreign countries.

- Manulife Financial Corporation, a leading Canadian-based financial services company, operating worldwide, offering a diverse range of financial protection products and services, directly or indirectly owned 58 or more foreign subsidiaries in 14 countries at December 31, 2011.

- Potash Corporation of Saskatchewan, the world's largest producer of potash, directly or indirectly owned 55 or more foreign subsidiaries in nine countries at December 31, 2011.

- Royal Bank of Canada, Canada's largest bank and one of the world's most highly rated financial institutions, directly or indirectly owned 58 foreign subsidiaries in 14 countries at October 31, 2011.

Companies establish operations in foreign countries for a variety of reasons, including developing new markets for their products, taking advantage of lower production costs, or gaining access to raw materials. Some multinational companies have reached a stage in their development in which domestic operations are no longer considered to be of higher priority than international operations.

Prior to preparing consolidated financial statements or accounting for an investment under the equity method, the financial statements of the foreign subsidiary or investee company must be translated into the investor company's presentation currency. IAS 27 requires that consolidated financial statements be prepared using uniform accounting policies for like transactions and other events in similar circumstances. This means that the financial statements of the foreign operations should be adjusted to reflect the accounting policies of the parent company. Unless otherwise noted, we will assume the reporting entity is a Canadian company and its functional currency is the Canadian dollar. This chapter deals with the issue of translating the foreign entity's financial statements into the parent's presentation currency prior to consolidation.

> Foreign-currency–denominated financial statements must be translated to the presentation currency of the reporting entity.

Three major issues are related to the translation process: (1) what the functional currency of the foreign operation is, (2) what the presentation currency (also known as the reporting currency) of the parent company is, and (3) where the resulting translation adjustment should be reported in the consolidated financial statements. These issues are examined first from a conceptual perspective and second by the manner in which they have been resolved by the IASB. We will start by discussing the difference between accounting exposure and economic exposure.

LO1 ACCOUNTING EXPOSURE VERSUS ECONOMIC EXPOSURE

Exposure is the risk that something could go wrong. Foreign currency exposure is the risk that a loss could occur if foreign exchange rates changed. Foreign currency risk can be viewed from three different perspectives: translation exposure (accounting exposure), transaction exposure, and economic exposure. Readers must keep these in mind as they interpret financial statements that contain foreign currency gains and losses.

Translation (Accounting) Exposure   This exposure results from the translation of foreign-currency–denominated financial statements into Canadian dollars. Only those financial statement items translated at the closing rate or the forward rate create an accounting exposure. If an item is translated at the historical rate, the Canadian-dollar amount is fixed at historical cost and will not be affected by rate changes. However, if an item is translated at the closing rate or the forward rate, the Canadian-dollar amount will change every time the exchange rate changes. Each item translated at the closing rate is exposed to translation adjustment. A separate translation adjustment exists for each of the exposed items. Positive translation adjustments increase shareholders' equity, whereas negative translation adjustments decrease shareholders' equity. Positive translation adjustments on assets can be offset by negative translation adjustments on liabilities. If total exposed assets are equal to total exposed liabilities throughout the year, the translation adjustments (although perhaps significant on an individual basis) net to a zero balance. The *net* translation adjustment needed to keep the consolidated balance sheet in balance is based solely on the *net asset* or *net liability* exposure.

> Accounting exposure exists when financial statement items are translated at the closing rate or the forward rate.

Net asset exposure means that more assets than liabilities are exposed.

A foreign operation has a net asset exposure when assets translated at the closing or forward exchange rate are larger in amount than liabilities translated at the closing or forward exchange rate. A net liability exposure exists when liabilities translated at the closing or forward exchange rate are larger than assets translated at the closing or forward exchange rate. The relationship among exposure, exchange rate fluctuations, and effect on shareholders' equity (S/E) is summarized as follows:

	Foreign currency	
Balance sheet exposure	*Appreciates*	*Depreciates*
Net asset	Increases S/E	Decreases S/E
Net liability	Decreases S/E	Increases S/E

The gains and losses that result from the translation are usually unrealized in the sense that they do not represent actual cash flows. Because these accounting gains and losses are reflected in the financial statements, they may have an impact on the enterprise's dividend policies, share prices, and so on. It is important to assess the extent to which they represent transaction and/or economic exposure.

Transaction exposure exists when there is a lapse in time between the origination of a receivable or payable and the settlement of the receivable or payable.

Transaction Exposure   This exposure exists between the time of entering a transaction involving a receivable or payable and the time of settling the receivable or payable with cash. It affects the current cash flows of the enterprise. The resulting cash gains and losses are realized and affect the enterprise's working capital and earnings. The concept of transaction exposure was discussed in Chapter 10.

Economic exposure exists when the present value of future cash flows would change as a result of changes in exchange rates.

Economic Exposure   Economic exposure is the risk that the economic value of the entity could decrease due to the occurrence of a future event such as a change in foreign exchange rates. Economic value, theoretically speaking, is the present value of future cash flows. Practically speaking, it is difficult to measure the impact on economic value because it is affected by so many variables. When exchange rates change, it could affect the cost of purchases, the selling price of sales, the volume of sales, interest rates, inflation rates, and so on. The economic impact could vary from company to company or from year to year depending on the nature of operations of the company.

Economic exposure is not easy to measure.

For example, a Canadian assembly plant that purchases components from a company in Japan will suffer economically if the dollar weakens in relation to the Japanese yen. It will cost the Canadian importer more dollars to purchase the product, and the Canadian competition may be such that the cost increase cannot be passed on to the customers. On the other hand, a Canadian company selling to customers in Japan may be economically better off when the dollar weakens relative to the Japanese yen. The Japanese customer's cost to buy the goods would go down and that could increase the volume of purchases.

What is the impact for a Canadian parent when it has a subsidiary in Japan and the Canadian dollar weakens relative to the yen? It depends on the nature of operations of the subsidiary and whether it is highly integrated with the Canadian parent or fairly independent. If the subsidiary manufactures locally and sells locally, its own income in yen may not be affected. However, the Canadian-dollar equivalent will increase because each yen of income translates in to more dollars. If it buys from and sells to the Canadian market, its income may go down because the volume of sales may decrease with the higher cost to Canadian customers.

But, the Canadian-dollar equivalent of the reduced net income may be similar to before. Therefore, the economic exposure is dependent on whether the foreign subsidiary is closely linked to the activities of the parent or operating independently of the parent. IAS 21 tries to capture the economic effects by establishing a situational approach to determining the translation method to be used for certain foreign operations.

Even though it is difficult to measure the net impact of exchange rate changes on the present value of future cash flows, it is desirable to capture as much of the impact as possible in the financial statements. We do report assets and liabilities at fair values for certain situations. In so doing, we are capturing the economic value of these assets and liabilities.

To illustrate the difference between accounting exposure and economic exposure, let us consider a basic example with simplified assumptions. Distant Ltd. is a wholly owned subsidiary of Parent Co. Distant was incorporated on January 1, Year 1, with Parent Co. being its sole shareholder. It is located in ForeignLand, whose currency is foreign currency (FC). Throughout Year 1, the exchange rate was FC1 = $2, and there was no inflation in ForeignLand. Its condensed balance sheet as at December 31, Year 1, is presented below both in FC and Canadian dollars:

Monetary assets	FC 300	$ 600
Inventory	800	1,600
Property, plant, and equipment	1,900	3,800
	FC3,000	$6,000
Monetary liabilities	FC2,100	$4,200
Shareholders' equity	900	1,800
	FC3,000	$6,000

The fair value was equal to carrying amount for all assets and liabilities at December 31, Year 1. General price levels increased by 10% and the exchange rate changed to FC1 = $1.81818 on January 1, Year 2.

Distant's balance sheet as at January 1, Year 2, is presented below under two different scenarios: (1) using traditional GAAP, and (2) where all assets and liabilities are revalued to their true economic value, which is represented by fair value. The 10% general price level increase will cause the non-monetary assets to increase in value. Initially, we assume that they will also increase by 10%. However, the monetary items remain at their previous values because these values were set by contract and the values do not change when economic conditions change. Under traditional GAAP, the balance sheet does not change to reflect the change in purchasing power of the foreign currency units and the non-monetary assets are retained at their historical cost. Under the second scenario, the non-monetary assets are revalued to fair value to reflect their true economic value on that date.

> Generally, there is an inverse relationship between inflation rates and exchanges rates; that is, when inflation goes up, the value of the currency goes down.

	GAAP	Economic value
Monetary assets	FC 300	FC 300
Inventory	800	880
Property, plant, and equipment	1,900	2,090
	FC3,000	FC3,270
Monetary liabilities	FC2,100	FC2,100
Shareholders' equity	900	1,170
	FC3,000	FC3,270

> Fair values may be a good proxy for economic values.

There are two methods for translating financial statements of foreign operations: the temporal method and the current rate method. We will discuss these methods in detail throughout this chapter. These methods would be applied to the GAAP-based balance sheet above. To present the true economic value of Distant to the Canadian shareholders, the economic value balance sheet should be translated into Canadian dollars. The three balances sheets would appear as follows:

The temporal and current rate methods use the GAAP-based balance sheet where some items are measured at current value and some items are measured at historical cost.

	Temporal	Current rate	Economic value
Monetary assets	$ 545	$ 545	$ 545
Inventory	1,600	1,455	1,600
Property, plant, and equipment	3,800	3,455	3,800
	$5,945	$5,455	$5,945
Monetary liabilities	$3,818	$3,818	$3,818
Shareholders' equity, as previously reported	1,800	1,800	1,800
Gain (loss) due to change in value of assets in FC			540
Gain (loss) due to change in exchange rate	327	(163)	(213)
	$5,945	$5,455	$5,945

As we will see later in this chapter, the temporal method translates certain items at the historic rate and certain items at the closing rate, whereas the current rate method translates all assets and liabilities at the closing rate. For the economic value column, all assets and liabilities are translated at the closing rate. It is a coincidence that the temporal method and economic values are equal. This occurred because the non-monetary assets increased in value by 10%, which is offset by a 10% change in the exchange rate. If the non-monetary assets had increased in value by 12% (i.e., fair value of inventory increased to FC896 and fair value of property, plant, and equipment increased to FC2,128) and the exchange rate changed to FC1 = $1.81818, then the three balance sheets would be as follows:

The economic value column measures all assets and liabilities at fair value.

	Temporal	Current rate	Economic value
Monetary assets	$ 545	$ 545	$ 545
Inventory	1,600	1,455	1,629
Property, plant, and equipment	3,800	3,455	3,869
	$5,945	$5,455	$6,043
Monetary liabilities	$3,818	$3,818	$3,818
Shareholders' equity, as previously reported	1,800	1,800	1,800
Gain (loss) due to change in value of assets in FC			648
Gain (loss) due to change in exchange rate	327	(163)	(223)
	$5,945	$5,455	$6,043

Note the following from the above balance sheets:

- Neither the temporal method nor the current rate method truly reflects economic reality. In order to accurately reflect economic reality, all assets and liabilities should be reported at fair value. At present, GAAP requires some, but not all, assets and liabilities to be reported at fair value.

Neither translation method captures the true economic value of the reporting entity.

- The temporal method shows a gain from translating at the new exchange rate, whereas the current rate method reports a loss. Which one is right? We will now direct our attention to the two translation methods.

TRANSLATION UNDER IAS 21

L02

Until the adoption of IFRSs in 2011, two major methods for translating foreign operations were used under Canadian GAAP: (1) the temporal method and (2) the current rate method. IAS 21 uses a similar approach for translating foreign operations but does not refer to the approaches by a particular name. For ease of identification, we will continue to refer to these methods using the same names; that is, temporal and current rate methods. Where differences exist between the IFRS requirements and the old Canadian requirements, the IFRS requirements will be used.

The objective of translation is to express financial statements of the foreign operation in Canadian dollars (or other presentation currency) in the manner that best reflects the reporting enterprise's exposure to exchange rate changes, as determined by the economic facts and circumstances. We will discuss these methods from the perspective of a Canadian-based multinational company translating foreign currency financial statements into Canadian dollars. The same principles could be applied if the Canadian company decided to use a reporting currency other than the Canadian dollar. For example, the Canadian company may choose to use the U.S. dollar as its reporting currency in order to satisfy the external users of the financial statements. We will discuss this option later in this chapter.

The translated statements should reflect the reporting enterprise's exposure to exchange rate changes.

IAS 21 establishes accounting standards for the translation of the financial statements of a foreign operation (a subsidiary, joint venture, associate, or branch) for use by a reporting enterprise (a Canadian investor). A foreign operation is viewed as either *integrated* or *self-sustaining* for translation purposes, depending on whether the functional currency of the foreign entity is the same as or different from the functional currency of the Canadian reporting entity.

To determine whether a specific foreign operation is integrated with its parent or self-sustaining, IAS 21 created the concept of the functional currency. As discussed in Chapter 10, the functional currency is the primary currency of the entity's operating environment. The foreign entity's functional currency can be either the parent's functional currency (usually the Canadian dollar) or a foreign currency (usually the local currency of the foreign entity). The interrelationship of the functional currency, the classification of the foreign entity, and the translation method can be depicted as follows:

The functional currency is the primary currency of the entity's operating environment.

Functional currency of foreign entity	Classification of foreign entity	Translation method	Translation adjustment reported in
Same as parent's	Integrated	Temporal method	Net income
Currency of country where its resides	Self-sustaining	Current rate method	Other comprehensive income
Currency of a country other than parent's country and other than country where it resides	Self-sustaining	Current rate method	Other comprehensive income

The foreign operation is integrated with the parent if it has the same functional currency as the parent.

In addition to introducing the concept of functional currency, IAS 21 introduced some new terminology. The *presentation currency* is the currency in which the entity presents its financial statements. For Canadian-based corporations, this is typically the Canadian dollar. The presentation currency of a foreign operation is typically the currency of the country in which its main operations are located.

The financial statements of the foreign operation must be translated in order to prepare consolidated financial statements. If the foreign operation's presentation

The foreign operation is self-sustaining if it has a different functional currency than the parent.

currency is a foreign currency, but its functional currency is the same as the parent's functional currency (i.e., the Canadian dollar), the foreign entity's financial statements must be translated to Canadian dollars using the temporal method; any translation adjustments must be reported as exchange gains or losses in net income. (This is the example of Company C from Exhibit 10.2 in Chapter 10.) If the foreign operation's functional currency is the not the same as the parent's functional currency, the foreign entity's financial statements must be translated to Canadian dollars using the current rate method; any translation adjustments must be reported as exchange gains or losses in other comprehensive income. (This is the example of Company D from Exhibit 10.2.)

Foreign exchange adjustments are reported in other comprehensive income for self-sustaining foreign operations.

The exchange adjustments for the self-sustaining subsidiary are not recognized in net income because the changes in exchange rates have little or no direct effect on the present and future cash flows from operations. They merely serve to keep the balance sheet in equilibrium and are a mechanical by-product of the translation process. The cumulative amount of the exchange differences is presented in a separate component of equity until disposal of the foreign operation. When the exchange differences relate to a foreign operation that is consolidated but not wholly owned, they must be allocated to the shareholders of the parent company and the non-controlling interest in the consolidated statement of comprehensive income and, in turn, in the consolidated statement of changes in equity.

When the parent sells all or part of its self-sustaining foreign operations, or receives a liquidating dividend, a proportionate amount of the accumulated exchange gains and losses is taken out of equity through other comprehensive income, and the realized exchange gains or losses are reported in net income. We will illustrate the presentation of other comprehensive income and a separate component of equity for accumulated other comprehensive income later in this chapter. If the parent hedges its investment in a self-sustaining foreign operation with a forward exchange contract, the exchange gains or losses on the forward contract are also reported in other comprehensive income to offset the unrealized losses or gains on the investment.

Exhibit 11.1 lists the indicators that should be considered when determining the functional currency for a foreign operation and gives an example of a condition

In effect, the indicators determine whether the foreign operation is integrated or self-sustaining.

EXHIBIT 11.1

INDICATORS FOR EVALUATING A FOREIGN OPERATION

Indicator	Functional Currency	
	Canadian dollar	Not Canadian dollar
1. to 5.	See Exhibit 10.3.	See Exhibit 10.3.
6. Extension of parent	Only goods imported from the parent are sold.	The foreign operation generates income, incurs expenses, and accumulates cash in its local currency.
7. Autonomy	The parent dictates the operating procedures.	The foreign entity has a significant degree of autonomy.
8. Intercompany transactions	Intercompany transactions are a high proportion of overall activities.	Intercompany transactions are a low proportion of overall activities.
9. Cash flows	Cash flows of the foreign operation directly affect cash flows of the parent.	Cash flows of the foreign operation have little effect on cash flows of the parent.
10. Financing cash flows	The parent provides cash to pay obligations.	Cash from local operations is sufficient to pay obligations.

that would indicate whether the Canadian dollar is the functional currency. The first five indicators were explained in Chapter 10; they apply to domestic and foreign operations.

When the above indicators are mixed and the functional currency is not obvious, management uses its professional judgment to determine the functional currency that most faithfully represents the economic effects of the underlying transactions, events, and conditions. As part of this approach, management gives priority to the first three indicators before considering the others, which are designed to provide additional supporting evidence in determining an entity's functional currency.

TRANSLATION METHODS
The Temporal Method

The *temporal method* of translation is used for integrated operations. The basic objective underlying the temporal method is to produce a set of translated financial statements as if the transactions had occurred in Canada in the first place; in other words, use the same process we used in Chapter 10 to translate individual transactions and account balances into Canadian dollars. For example, assume a subsidiary in Germany had sales of €100,000 when the exchange rate was €1 = $1.25. These sales would be reported on its income statement in euros. When the subsidiary's income statement is translated to Canadian dollars under the temporal method, the Canadian-dollar amount would be $125,000. Similarly, if a Canadian company had sales to a customer in Germany on the same date, it would report this sale at $125,000 in its Canadian-dollar general ledger. In both cases, the temporal method was used to report sales at $125,000 being the Canadian-dollar equivalent on the date of the sale. In effect, the temporal method preserves the Canadian dollar as the unit of measure and measures financial statement items according to the normal measurement practices for Canadian domestic transactions and operations. It is entirely consistent with our traditional accounting model. Under normal measurement practices, certain financial statement items are reported at historical cost, whereas other items are reported at fair value. The temporal method is designed to maintain this reporting practice when translating the foreign currency statements into Canadian dollars.

If the financial statement item is supposed to be reported at fair value, when translating the item into Canadian dollars we need to take the fair value of the item in foreign currency and apply the rate of the date that the fair value was determined.

To obtain historical values, revenues and expenses should be translated in a manner that produces substantially the same reporting currency amounts that would have resulted had the underlying transactions been translated on the dates they occurred. To translate revenues of a foreign subsidiary, use the exchange rate on the date that the transaction giving rise to the revenue occurred. The following examples illustrate this concept. In all of these examples, assume the following exchange rates:

January 1	FC1 = $1.50
January 31	FC1 = $1.60
Average for January	FC1 = $1.56

Example A On January 1, Subco sold goods for cash of FC100. The revenue is earned and determined on this date. The revenue of FC100 would be translated into $150, its historical value.

The temporal method gives the same results, as if the transactions had occurred in Canada.

Use historical exchange rates to translate revenues and expenses.

Example B On January 1, Subco sold goods for FC100 with payment due within 30 days. On January 31, FC100 was received from the customer. The revenue is earned and determined on January 1. The revenue of FC100 would be translated into $150. Receiving the cash on January 31 does not change the historical value of the sale. It does result in an exchange gain on the accounts receivable of $10 [FC100 × ($1.60 − $1.50)].

Example C On January 1, Subco received FC100 as a prepayment for goods to be delivered within 30 days. On January 31, Subco delivered the goods and earned the sale. Although the revenue was earned on January 31, the amount of the revenue in Canadian dollars was determined on January 1 when the cash was received. The revenue of FC100 would be translated into $150.

Example D On each day in January, Subco sold goods for cash of FC100. Rather than using 31 different exchange rates for the 31 days of the month, the average rate for the month, $1.56, can be applied to the total revenue for the month, FC100 × 31 × $1.56 = $4,836.

The same concept can be applied in translating expenses. Use the exchange rate on the date that the transaction giving rise to the expense occurred. Since depreciation expense is directly related to the purchase of a depreciable asset, depreciation expense should be translated using the exchange rate on the date that the depreciable asset was purchased. Similarly, cost of goods sold is based on the cost of the inventory. Therefore, use the exchange rate on the date when the inventory was purchased when translating the cost of goods sold.

The Current Rate Method

The *current rate method* is used for translating self-sustaining operations except when the foreign operation operates in a highly inflationary economy. For a foreign operation to be classified as self-sustaining, its functional currency must be different from the functional currency of the parent. The foreign operation must be financially and operationally independent of the reporting enterprise such that the exposure to exchange rate changes is limited to the reporting enterprise's net investment in the foreign operation. For example, the subsidiary may arrange its own financing to buy property, plant, and equipment in its own country. The foreign cash it gets from selling its products in the local environment is used to pay off its foreign debt. The Canadian parent is not concerned only with the exchange risk on monetary items as it would for transactions in Canada. It is concerned with the overall risk of its net investment in the foreign subsidiary. Therefore, all assets and liabilities should be translated at the closing rate in order to present its exposure to currency risk on its net investment in the foreign operation. This method is also much simpler than the temporal method because it uses the same rate for all assets and liabilities, which maintains the relationship between assets and liabilities when switching from the foreign currency to the reporting currency.

Under the current rate method, share capital is translated at historical rates. All revenues and expenses are translated using the exchange rate in effect on the dates on which such items are recognized in income during the period. If the revenues or expenses were recognized in income evenly throughout the period, the average rate for the period is used to translate these items.

Use average rates to approximate historical exchange rates throughout the period.

Use historical rates to measure expenses based on the historical cost of the related balance sheet items.

The current rate method should be used to translate a self-sustaining foreign operation.

The current rate method preserves the relationship of balance sheet items.

A peculiarity resulting from the current rate method is that a property carried at historical cost in the foreign entity's statements will be translated into differing Canadian dollar values if exchange rates fluctuate over some time frame. The following example will illustrate this.

Example   A German entity has land on its balance sheet with a historical cost of €100,000 euros. On five successive balance sheets, denominated in euros, the land appears as €100,000. If the value of the euro changes with respect to the Canadian dollar each year during the five-year period and the current rate method of translation is used, the translated amount will be different each year. A reader of the German financial statements would observe the same amount reflected each year, while a reader of the translated financial statements would see a different amount each year and may improperly conclude that land sales or purchases have taken place. Despite this particular shortcoming, this method is one of the two currently sanctioned under IFRSs. The IASB recognizes that the exchange adjustments under the current rate method have little or no direct effect on the present and future cash flows from operations. Accordingly, the exchange adjustments are not recognized in profit or loss; they are included in other comprehensive income.

> Using historical cost in foreign currency and the current rate does not provide historical cost or fair value in Canadian dollars.

Both of the translation methods that have been discussed will produce different amounts for balance sheet and income statement items and different amounts for the translation gain or loss because the total amount of the balance sheet items at risk to exchange rate changes is different under each. It is not inconceivable to have an exchange gain from the use of one method and an exchange loss from the use of the other method. In fact, we saw this result in the Distant company example at the beginning of this chapter.

The current rate method is used to translate the foreign currency financial statements of a self-sustaining operation, with *one* exception, discussed next.

Highly Inflationary Economies   While Canada has had fairly low rates of inflation in the past 25 years, this has not been the case in other parts of the world. Argentina, Brazil, Chile, Mexico, Turkey, and Israel have all had inflation rates higher than Canada's during this period. Between 1985 and 1993, Argentina experienced yearly rates of between 120% and 3,000%.

If the self-sustaining foreign operation operates in a highly inflationary environment relative to that of the reporting enterprise, translation using the current rate method could produce distorted and meaningless results. IAS 29 does not establish an absolute rate at which hyper-inflation is deemed to arise. Hyper-inflation is indicated by characteristics of the economic environment of a country that include, but are not limited to, the following:

(a) The general population prefers to keep its wealth in non-monetary assets or in a relatively stable foreign currency.

> Hyper-inflation causes the population to measure wealth and value using a currency of a more stable country.

(b) The general population regards monetary amounts not in terms of the local currency but in terms of a relatively stable foreign currency. Prices may be quoted in that currency.

(c) Sales and purchases on credit take place at prices that compensate for the expected loss of purchasing power during the credit period, even if the period is short.

(d) Interest rates, wages, and prices are linked to a price index.

(e) The cumulative inflation rate over three years is approaching, or exceeds, 100%.

The following example illustrates the kind of distortion that can occur when the current rate method is used during a period of very high inflation.

Example   In Year 1, a Canadian company purchases a self-sustaining foreign subsidiary located in Chile. The exchange rate at this time is 1 peso (Ps) = $1.00, and it remains constant during the year. The subsidiary has land carried at a historical cost of Ps1,000,000. On December 31, Year 1, the land is translated into dollars for consolidation purposes as follows:

$$Ps1,000,000 \times 1.00 = \$1,000,000$$

There is usually an inverse relationship between the strength of a country's currency and the level of inflation in that country.

During Year 2, Chile experiences an inflation rate of 500%. Because the inflation rate in Canada is minuscule during this period, this large inflation differential is fully reflected in the foreign exchange market. The result is a weakening of the peso relative to the Canadian dollar. On December 31, Year 2, the exchange rate is Ps1 = $0.20. If the land were translated at the closing rate on this date, the result would be as follows:

$$Ps1,000,000 \times 0.20 = \$200,000$$

While it is easy to see in this example that the $800,000 difference is due to the exchange rate change, large differences such as this are difficult to interpret without all the facts.

If the Chilean subsidiary prepared price-level-adjusted historical cost statements, the land would appear on the subsidiary's balance sheet at Ps5,000,000. Translation using the current rate method on December 31, Year 2, would *not* produce distorted results, as the following illustrates:

$$Ps5,000,000 \times 0.20 = \$1,000,000$$

When a self-sustaining foreign operation operates in a hyper-inflationary economy, its financial statements must be translated into Canadian dollars using the following procedures:

(a) All amounts (i.e., assets, liabilities, equity items, income, and expenses for the current year) must be translated at the closing rate.

(b) Comparative amounts must be those that were presented as current-year amounts in the relevant prior-year financial statements (i.e., they are not adjusted for subsequent changes in exchange rates).

The foreign entity must restate its financial statements in accordance with IAS 29 before applying the translation method set out above. When the economy ceases to be hyper-inflationary and the entity no longer restates its financial statements in accordance with IAS 29, it must use as the historical costs for translation the amounts restated to the price level at the date the entity ceased restating its financial statements.

Price-level-adjusted financial statements are useful for countries experiencing high inflation.

Under IAS 29, both the current year's figures and last year's comparatives must be stated in terms of the measuring unit current at the end of the reporting period. Using the example of the Chilean subsidiary above, the measuring unit is the peso, which experienced 500% inflation during the year. Non-monetary items that were carried at historical costs are restated by applying a general price index. Monetary and non-monetary items that were carried at fair value or recoverable amount are not restated because they are already expressed in terms of the monetary unit current at the end of the reporting period. After the restatement, all assets and liabilities are stated at fair value or at a price-level-adjusted value, which may approximate fair value. When these items are translated to the Canadian dollar at the closing rate, the translated values will approximate the fair value in terms of Canadian dollars.

ILLUSTRATION OF TRANSLATION AND CONSOLIDATION

L03

The translation and preparation of consolidated financial statements will now be illustrated under the two translation methods required by IAS 21.

Example On December 31, Year 1, Starmont Inc., a Canadian company, acquired 100% of the common shares of Controlada S.A., located in Estonia, at a cost of 2,000,000 kroons (K). The exchange rate was K1 = $0.128 on this date. Starmont's journal entry (in Canadian dollars) to record the share acquisition is as follows:

Dec. 31, Year 1
Investment in Controlada	256,000	
Cash		256,000

(K2,000,000 × 0.128)

This example assumes that the carrying amounts of the subsidiary's net assets were equal to fair values and that there is no goodwill on consolidation. Because this is an "acquisition" business combination, the exchange rate on the date of acquisition is used to translate all accounts of the subsidiary on acquisition date and becomes the historical rate to be used in subsequent years, where appropriate.

The translation of the balance sheet of Controlada from kroons into Canadian dollars at December 31, Year 1, is shown in Exhibit 11.2. Note that the translation of a subsidiary on the date of acquisition is the same regardless of whether the entity is integrated or self-sustaining.

The preparation of the acquisition-date consolidated balance sheet appears in Exhibit 11.3. The figures in the Starmont column come from Starmont's separate-entity financial statements. Note that the translated shareholders' equity of the

> When the parent acquires the subsidiary, the parent indirectly buys all of the net assets of the subsidiary.

EXHIBIT 11.2

CONTROLADA S.A.
TRANSLATION OF BALANCE SHEET TO CANADIAN DOLLARS
at December 31, Year 1

	Estonian Kroons	Exchange rate	Canadian dollars	
Cash	K 40,000	0.128	$ 5,120	
Accounts receivable	360,000	0.128	46,080	
Inventories	1,200,000	0.128	153,600	(a)
Plant and equipment (net)	900,000	0.128	115,200	
	K2,500,000		$320,000	(b)
Current liabilities	K 50,000	0.128	$ 6,400	
Bonds payable	450,000	0.128	57,600	
	500,000		64,000	(c)
Common shares	1,500,000	0.128	192,000	
Retained earnings	500,000	0.128	64,000	
	K2,500,000		$320,000	

> Controlada has to be translated into dollars in order to consolidate with Starmont's Canadian-dollar financial statements.
>
> For consolidation purposes, we never use an exchange rate older than the rate at the date of acquisition.

EXHIBIT 11.3

PREPARATION OF CONSOLIDATED BALANCE SHEET

at December 31, Year 1

	Starmont	Controlada (From Ex. 11.2)	Starmont Consolidated
Cash	$ 70,000	$ 5,120	$ 75,120
Accounts receivable	90,000	46,080	136,080
Inventories	200,000	153,600	353,600
Plant and equipment	300,000	115,200	415,200
Investment in Controlada	256,000	—	—
	$916,000	$320,000	$980,000
Current liabilities	$ 80,000	$ 6,400	$ 86,400
Bonds payable	300,000	57,600	357,600
Common shares	200,000	192,000	200,000
Retained earnings	336,000	64,000	336,000
	$916,000	$320,000	$980,000

With no acquisition differential and the subsidiary wholly owned, the investment account is equal to the subsidiary's shareholders' equity.

subsidiary is equal to the parent's investment account, so the consolidating procedure is simply to eliminate one against the other.

Translation and Consolidation Subsequent to Acquisition

On December 31, Year 2, Controlada forwarded the financial statements shown in Exhibit 11.4 to the Canadian parent. Sales, purchases, bond interest, and other

EXHIBIT 11.4

CONTROLADA S.A.
FINANCIAL STATEMENTS

at December 31, Year 2 (in kroons)

INCOME STATEMENT

The subsidiary uses its local currency, kroon, in its own financial records and for reporting in its own country.

Sales	K9,000,000	(a)
Cost of goods purchased	7,400,000	(b)
Change in inventory	(400,000)	
Depreciation expense	100,000	
Bond interest expense	45,000	(c)
Other expenses	1,555,000	(d)
	8,700,000	
Net income	K 300,000	

STATEMENT OF RETAINED EARNINGS

Balance, beginning of year	K 500,000	
Net income	300,000	
	800,000	
Dividends	100,000	(e)
Balance, end of year	K 700,000	

(continued)

EXHIBIT 11.4	(*continued*)

BALANCE SHEET

Cash	K 100,000	
Accounts receivable	400,000	
Inventory	1,600,000	**(f)**
Plant and equipment (net)	800,000	
	K2,900,000	
Current liabilities	K 250,000	
Bonds payable	450,000	
Common shares	1,500,000	
Retained earnings	700,000	
	K2,900,000	

expenses occurred evenly throughout the year. The translation process will now be illustrated under these two assumptions:

(a) The subsidiary is integrated because its functional currency is the Canadian dollar.

(b) The subsidiary is self-sustaining because its functional currency is not the Canadian dollar.

The exchange rates for the year were as follows:

Dec. 31, Year 1	K1 = $0.128	The Canadian dollar
Dec. 31, Year 2	K1 = $0.104	strengthened during Year 2.
Average for Year 2	K1 = $0.115	
Date of purchase for inventory on hand at end of Year 2	K1 = $0.110	
Date dividends declared and paid	K1 = $0.1064	

Exhibit 11.5 illustrates the rates to be used for self-sustaining operations (the current rate method) and integrated operations (the temporal method). Translation of the numerous revenues, expenses, gains, and losses at the historical rates is generally impractical. A weighted-average exchange rate for the period would normally be used to translate such items.

When goodwill is impaired, it is not measured at fair value as it is at the date of acquisition. It is written down by an amount equal to the excess of the carrying amount of the net assets over the recoverable amount for the cash generating unit. The impairment loss is more like amortization than it is a revaluation to fair value. Therefore, the value of goodwill after the write-down is similar to an amortized cost amount. Accordingly, goodwill should be translated at the historical rate under the temporal method.

The temporal method uses translation rates to produce either historical cost or fair values for all assets and liabilities.

Integrated Foreign Operation Assuming that Controlada is an integrated foreign operation, the statements would be translated using the temporal method. Exhibit 11.6 illustrates this process. The following discussion regarding the exchange rates used and the disposition of the translation gain should be noted:

L04

- Monetary items are translated at the current rate, while non-monetary items are translated at appropriate historical rates, unless the non-monetary item is to be reported at fair value.

EXHIBIT 11.5

Exchange Rates

Financial statement items	Temporal method	Current rate method
	Integrated operations	Self-sustaining operations
Monetary	Closing	Closing
Non-monetary—at cost or amortized cost	Historical	Closing
Non-monetary—at fair values	(Note 1)	(Note 1)
Goodwill	Historical	Closing
Deferred revenues	Historical	Closing
Common shares	Historical	Historical
Dividends	Historical	Historical
Revenues	Historical	Historical
Depreciation and amortization	Historical	Historical
Cost of sales		Historical
Opening inventory	Historical	—
Purchases	Historical	—
Ending inventory	Historical	—

For depreciation, historical rate for temporal method is the rate when the asset was acquired whereas it is the rate when expense was incurred for current rate method.

Note 1: The rate of the date that fair value was determined should be used. If fair value was determined on the last day of the period, then the closing rate should be used.

EXHIBIT 11.6

CONTROLADA S.A.
TRANSLATION OF FINANCIAL STATEMENTS TO CANADIAN DOLLARS
at December 31, Year 2
(Integrated Foreign Operation)

INCOME STATEMENT

	Kroons (From Ex. 11.4)	Exchange rate	Canadian dollars
Sales	K9,000,000	0.115	$1,035,000
Cost of goods purchased	7,400,000	0.115	851,000
Change in inventory	(400,000)	Calculated	(22,400)
Depreciation expense	100,000	0.128	12,800
Bond interest expense	45,000	0.115	5,175
Other expenses	1,555,000	0.115	178,825
Foreign exchange gain **(7a)**			(2,600)
Total expenses	8,700,000		1,022,800
Net income	K 300,000		$ 12,200 **(a)**

Cost of goods sold and depreciation expense are translated using the historical rates of the related balance sheet accounts.

RETAINED EARNINGS

	Kroons	Exchange rate	Canadian dollars
Balance—beginning	K 500,000	0.128	$ 64,000
Net income **(a)**	300,000		12,200
	800,000		76,200
Dividends	100,000	0.106	10,600 **(b)**
Balance—end	K 700,000		$ 65,600

(continued)

EXHIBIT 11.6	(continued)

BALANCE SHEET

	Kroons	Exchange rate	Canadian dollars
Cash	K 100,000	0.104 *end*	$ 10,400
Accounts receivable	400,000	0.104 *end*	41,600
Inventory	1,600,000	0.110	176,000
Plant and equipment (net)	800,000	0.128 *h*	102,400
	K2,900,000		$330,400
Current liabilities	K 250,000	0.104 *end*	$ 26,000
Bonds payable	450,000	0.104	46,800
Common shares	1,500,000	0.128	192,000
Retained earnings	700,000		65,600
	K2,900,000		$330,400

Assets to be reported at fair value are translated at the closing rate and assets to be reported at cost are translated at the historical rates.

- Common shares and beginning-of-year retained earnings are translated at the historical rate on the date of acquisition. In future years, the translated amount for retained earnings will have to be calculated.

Shareholders' equity accounts are translated at historical rates.

- Revenue and expenses, with the exception of depreciation and cost of goods sold, are translated at the average rate for the year. Depreciation is translated at the historical rates used to translate the related assets. The three components of cost of goods sold are translated at the historical rates when these goods were purchased.

Because the components of cost of goods sold are translated using different rates, the translated amount for this items is calculated as follows:

	Kroons		rate	Canadian dollars
Beginning inventory **(2a)**	K1,200,000	×	0.128	$153,600
Less: Ending inventory **(4f)**	1,600,000	×	0.110	176,000
Change in inventory	(400,000)			(22,400)
Purchases **(4b)**	7,400,000	×	0.115	851,000
Cost of goods sold	K7,000,000			$828,600

The three components of cost of goods sold are each translated at the rate when these goods were purchased.

Purchases are translated at the average rate for the year. Inventories are translated at historical rates.

The foreign exchange gain is calculated in Exhibit 11.7. It represents the change in values due to accounting exposure, which was defined at the outset of this chapter. Accounting exposure exists only on items translated at the closing rate. In most cases, under the temporal method, the exposed items are the monetary items. However, when non-monetary items are measured at fair value, these non-monetary items will be translated at the closing rate and will be included in the exposed position. When the rate changes, items translated at the closing rate will be measured at a different amount in Canadian dollars. At the start of Year 2, the net exposed position was a net liability position of K100,000. These items were translated at the closing rate of 0.128 at the end of Year 1. If there were no new transactions during Year 2, there would still be a net exposed liability position of K100,000 at the end of year. These exposed items would be translated at 0.104 to equal $(10,400). The translated amounts would have changed from $(12,800) to $(10,400) for an exchange gain of $2,400. However, there were new transactions

Exchange gains or losses only occur on items translated at the closing rate.

EXHIBIT 11.7

CALCULATION OF YEAR 2 TRANSLATION ADJUSTMENT
(Integrated Foreign Operation)

This schedule reconciles the change in accounting exposure during the year and calculates the gains or losses due to the change in exchange rates.

	Kroons	Exchange rates	Canadian dollars
Net monetary position		*Dec 31*	
Dec. 31, Year 1* **below**	K (100,000)	0.128	$ (12,800)
Changes during Year 2			
Sales	9,000,000	0.115	1,035,000
Purchases	(7,400,000)	0.115	(851,000)
Bond interest expense	(45,000)	0.115 *AV*	(5,175)
Other expenses	(1,555,000)	0.115	(178,825)
Dividends	(100,000)	0.106	(10,600)
Net changes	(100,000)		(10,600)
Calculated net monetary position			
Dec. 31, Year 2			(23,400)
Actual net monetary position			
Dec. 31, Year 2* **below**	K (200,000)	0.104	(20,800)
Exchange gain, Year 2			$ 2,600 **(a)**

*NET MONETARY POSITION, KROONS

	December 31	
	Year 2 (From Ex. 11.4)	Year 1 (From Ex. 11.2)
Cash	K 100,000	K 40,000
Accounts receivable	400,000	360,000
Current liabilities	(250,000)	(50,000)
Bonds payable	(450,000)	(450,000)
Net monetary position	K(200,000)	K(100,000)

Only monetary items are exposed to exchange rate changes in this illustration.

that changed the net monetary position during the year. These new transactions were initially translated at the rate on the date of the transaction. These new transactions changed the net exposed position to a net liability position of K200,000 at the end of Year 2. The items comprising the exposed position at the end of Year 2 are translated at the closing rate at the end of that year. This results in an overall exchange gain of $2,600 for the year for all items.

To determine the items that changed the exposed position during the year, we need to follow a process similar to that used when we prepare a cash flow statement, looking at all non-cash items on the balance sheet and determining whether cash was involved. For the exposed position, we look at all non-exposed items on the balance sheet and determine whether an exposed item was involved. For example, when sales occurred during the year, cash or accounts receivable would have increased. However, when depreciation was recorded, the other side of the entry was accumulated depreciation, which is not part of the exposed items. Therefore, sales do change the exposed position but depreciation does not.

The exchange gain or loss is reported in net income under the temporal method.

The exchange gain is reported in net income under the temporal method. This is consistent with the reporting of exchange gains or loss on individual foreign currency transactions, which were covered in Chapter 10.

After the translation adjustment is reflected in Controlada's income statement, the translated statements are ready for the consolidation process. They also become the basis for the following equity method journal entries by Starmont on December 31, Year 2:

Investment in Controlada	12,200	
Equity earnings **(6a)**		12,200
To record 100% of the Year 2 net income of Controlada Company		

Cash **(6b)**	10,600	
Investment in Controlada		10,600
Dividend received from Controlada Company		

Exhibit 11.8 shows the Year 2 financial statements of Starmont (which would be taken from Starmont's separate-entity financial statements), the translated statements of Controlada using the temporal method, and the consolidated financial statements. Note that the investment account equals the shareholders' equity of the subsidiary, and that there is no non-controlling interest or acquisition differential. The investment account is replaced with the assets and the liabilities of Controlada, and equity earnings are replaced with revenues and expenses.

The exchange gains or losses are based on the accounting exposure, which is based on the translation method.

EXHIBIT 11.8

PREPARATION OF CONSOLIDATED FINANCIAL STATEMENTS YEAR 2
(Integrated Foreign Operation)

INCOME STATEMENT

	Starmont	Controlada (From Ex. 11.6)	Starmont Consolidated
Sales	$3,000,000	$1,035,000	$4,035,000
Equity earnings	12,200	—	—
	3,012,200	1,035,000	4,035,000
Cost of goods purchased	2,520,000	851,000	3,371,000
Change in inventory	(20,000)	(22,400)	(42,400)
Depreciation	20,000	12,800	32,800
Bond interest	30,000	5,175	35,175
Other expenses	200,000	178,825	378,825
Foreign exchange gain **(7a)**	—	(2,600)	(2,600)
	2,750,000	1,022,800	3,772,800
Net income	$ 262,200	$ 12,200	$ 262,200

The exchange gain is reported in net income.

RETAINED EARNINGS

	Starmont	Controlada	Starmont Consolidated
Balance—beginning	$ 336,000	$ 64,000	$ 336,000
Net income	262,200	12,200	262,200
	598,200	76,200	598,200
Dividends	50,000	10,600	50,000
Balance—end	$ 548,200	$ 65,600	$ 548,200

The parent's income under the equity method is equal to consolidated net income attributable to the parent's shareholders.

(continued)

EXHIBIT 11.8   (continued)

BALANCE SHEETS

	Starmont	Controlada	Starmont Consolidated
Cash	$ 100,200	$ 10,400	$ 110,600
Accounts receivable	290,400	41,600	332,000
Inventories	220,000	176,000	396,000
Plant and equipment (net)	280,000	102,400	382,400
Investment in Controlada (equity)	257,600	—	—
	$1,148,200	$ 330,400	$1,221,000
Current liabilities	$ 100,000	$ 26,000	$ 126,000
Bonds payable	300,000	46,800	346,800
Common shares	200,000	192,000	200,000
Retained earnings	548,200	65,600	548,200
	$1,148,200	$ 330,400	$1,221,000

The subsidiary's assets and liabilities replace the investment account when preparing the consolidated balance sheet.

See Self-Study Problem 1, Part (a), for another example of the translation of an integrated foreign operation.

Self-sustaining Foreign Operation   If the subsidiary is considered self-sustaining, the translation of its Year 2 financial statements will be as shown in Exhibit 11.9.

EXHIBIT 11.9

CONTROLADA S.A.
TRANSLATION OF FINANCIAL STATEMENTS TO CANADIAN DOLLARS
at December 31, Year 2
(Self-Sustaining Foreign Operation)

INCOME STATEMENT

	Kroons (From Ex. 11.4)	Exchange rate	Canadian dollars
Sales	K9,000,000	0.115	$1,035,000
Cost of goods purchased	7,400,000	0.115	851,000
Change in inventory	(400,000)	0.115	(46,000)
Depreciation expense	100,000	0.115	11,500
Bond interest expense	45,000	0.115	5,175
Other expenses	1,555,000	0.115	178,825
	8,700,000		1,000,500
Net income	K 300,000	0.115	$ 34,500 **(a)**

All revenues and expenses are assumed to have occurred evenly throughout the year.

STATEMENT OF COMPREHENSIVE INCOME

	Kroons	Exchange rate	Canadian dollars
Net income	K 300,000	0.115	$ 34,500
Other comprehensive income Currency translation adjustments **(10a)**			(51,100) **(b)**
Comprehensive income	K 300,000		$ (16,600)

(continued)

EXHIBIT 11.9 *(continued)*

STATEMENT OF RETAINED EARNINGS

	Kroons	Exchange rate	Canadian dollars	
Balance, beginning of year	K 500,000	0.128	$ 64,000	
Net income	300,000	0.115	34,500	
	800,000		98,500	
Dividends	100,000	0.106	10,600	**(c)**
Balance, end of year	K 700,000		$ 87,900	

Only the net income from the regular income statement is carried forward to the statement of retained earnings.

BALANCE SHEET

	Kroons	Exchange rate *Closing*	Canadian dollars	
Cash	K 100,000	0.104	$ 10,400	
Accounts receivable	400,000	0.104	41,600	
Inventory	1,600,000	0.104	166,400	
Plant and equipment (net)	800,000	0.104	83,200	
	K2,900,000		$ 301,600	
Current liabilities	K 250,000	0.104	$ 26,000	
Bonds payable	450,000	0.104	46,800	
Common shares	1,500,000	0.128	192,000	**(d)**
Retained earnings	700,000		87,900	**(e)**
Accumulated translation adjustments **(b)**			(51,100)	**(f)**
	K2,900,000		$ 301,600	

All assets and liabilities are translated at the current rate.

Other comprehensive income is carried forward to accumulated other comprehensive income.

The procedure used in Exhibit 11.9 was to translate the income statement first, then the retained earnings statement, and then the balance sheet. The following features of the current rate translation process are emphasized:

- The average rate for Year 2 is used for all revenues and expenses in the income statement.

  The average rate is used when the revenues and expenses occur evenly throughout the year.

- All assets and liabilities are translated at the closing rate.

- Common shares and beginning retained earnings are translated at the acquisition date historical rate, thus establishing the translated amount on that date. In future periods, the amount for the translated beginning retained earnings will have to be calculated. In practice, the accountant will look at last year's translated financial statements for this amount. Dividends are translated at the historical rate on the date of declaration. In situations where the dividends were not paid by year-end, the dividends payable will be translated at the closing rate, and a hidden exchange gain or loss will result from the translation of these items. (In this example, the dividends were declared and paid on December 31.)

  All items within shareholders' equity are translated using the historical rate applicable for each item.

- The amount required to balance the balance sheet is the unrealized exchange loss from the translation of the subsidiary's financial statements using the current rate method. The unrealized exchange losses for the year must be presented in other comprehensive income on the statement of comprehensive income. The accumulated exchange gains and losses for all years to date are presented as a separate component of shareholders' equity. Since Year 2 is

  Differentiate between other comprehensive income for the year that is reported in comprehensive income and accumulated other comprehensive income that is reported in shareholders' equity.

the first year in which Controlada is reporting unrealized exchange losses, the cumulative losses on the balance sheet are equal to the loss reported in comprehensive income for the year. In this example, comprehensive income is presented as a separate statement. It includes net income from the income statement and other comprehensive income.

In this illustration, the financial statements were translated sequentially, with the foreign exchange loss being the last item needed to balance the balance sheet. In reality, the gain or loss can be calculated before attempting the translation process. Exhibit 11.10 illustrates this process. In a self-sustaining operation such as this one, it is the net assets (assets less liabilities) that are at risk and exposed to currency fluctuations. Net assets equal shareholders' equity, and if the common shares remain unchanged, the only changes that usually occur are changes to retained earnings, which are net income and dividends. The process involves translating the opening position, using the closing rates at that time, and translating the changes to the exposed items at the rates at which they occurred. The result is a calculated position. The actual end-of-year net asset position is translated at closing rates, with the difference between the two numbers representing the exchange gain or loss from translation. Notice that if the exchange rate had remained constant throughout Year 2, all items in Exhibit 11.10 would have been translated at $0.128 with no exchange gain or loss occurring.

Starmont uses the equity method for internal record keeping purposes. It would make the following journal entries on December 31, Year 2:

> *Exchange gains and losses occur only on those items translated at the closing rate and only if the rates change during the period.*

> *Starmont's journal entries are recorded in Canadian dollars.*

Investment in Controlada **(9a)**	34,500	
Equity earnings		34,500
100% of translated net income		
Cash **(9c)**	10,600	
Investment in Controlada		10,600
Dividend received		
Other comprehensive income **(9b)**	51,100	
Investment in Controlada		51,100
To record 100% of the change in the unrealized exchange loss from translation for Year 2		

EXHIBIT 11.10

**INDEPENDENT CALCULATION OF YEAR 2
TRANSLATION LOSS**
(Self-Sustaining Foreign Operation)

> *Assets minus liabilities are called net assets and are equal in amount to shareholders' equity.*

	Kroons	Exchange rate	Canadian dollars
Net assets, Dec. 31, Year 1	K2,000,000	0.128	$256,000
Changes in net assets, Year 2			
Net income	300,000	0.115	34,500
Dividends	(100,000)	0.106	(10,600)
Calculated net assets			279,900
Actual net assets	K2,200,000	0.104	228,800
Exchange loss from translation			$ 51,100 **(a)**

Exhibit 11.11 illustrates the preparation of the consolidated financial statements. Starmont uses the equity method for internal record keeping. Note that equity earnings are equal to the subsidiary's net income ($34,500) and are therefore eliminated and replaced with the subsidiary's revenue and expenses.

Net equity earnings should be equal to the subsidiary's net income when there is no acquisition differential or non-controlling interest.

EXHIBIT 11.11

PREPARATION OF CONSOLIDATED FINANCIAL STATEMENTS YEAR 2
(Self-Sustaining Foreign Operation)

STATEMENT OF NET INCOME AND COMPREHENSIVE INCOME

	Starmont	Controlada (From Ex. 11.9)	Starmont Consolidated	
Sales	$3,000,000	$1,035,000	$4,035,000	
Equity earnings	34,500	—	—	
	3,034,500	1,035,000	4,035,000	
Cost of goods purchased	2,520,000	851,000	3,371,000	
Change in inventory	(20,000)	(46,000)	(66,000)	
Depreciation	20,000	11,500	31,500	
Bond interest	30,000	5,175	35,175	
Other expenses	200,000	178,825	378,825	
	2,750,000	1,000,500	3,750,500	
Net income	284,500	34,500	284,500	(a)
Other comprehensive income				
Foreign currency translation adjustments (10a)	(51,100)	(51,100)	(51,100)	(b)
Comprehensive income	$ 233,400	$ (16,600)	$ 233,400	

Other comprehensive income is reported separately from net income.

RETAINED EARNINGS

	Starmont	Controlada	Starmont Consolidated	
Balance—beginning	$ 336,000	$ 64,000	$ 336,000	
Net income	284,500	34,500	284,500	
	620,500	98,500	620,500	
Dividends	50,000	10,600	50,000	(c)
Balance—end	$ 570,500	$ 87,900	$ 570,500	

Consolidated retained earnings are the same as the parent's retained earnings under the equity method.

BALANCE SHEETS

	Starmont	Controlada	Starmont Consolidated	
Cash	$ 100,200	$ 10,400	$ 110,600	
Accounts receivable	290,400	41,600	332,000	
Inventories	220,000	166,400	386,400	
Plant and equipment (net)	280,000	83,200	363,200	
Investment in Controlada (equity method)	228,800	—	—	(d)
	$1,119,400	$ 301,600	$1,192,200	
Current liabilities	$ 100,000	$ 26,000	$ 126,000	
Bonds payable	300,000	46,800	346,800	
Common shares	200,000	192,000	200,000	(e)
Retained earnings	570,500	87,900	570,500	(f)
Accumulated translation adjustments	(51,100)	(51,100)	(51,100)	(g)
	$1,119,400	$ 301,600	$1,192,200	

Accumulated translation adjustments are reported separately from retained earnings.

The parent's investment account is eliminated against the shareholders' equity of the subsidiary in the following manner:

The investment account under the equity method should be equal to the subsidiary's shareholders' equity when there is no acquisition differential or non-controlling interest.

Investment in Controlada **(11d)**		$228,800
Shareholders' equity—Controlada		
Common shares **(11e)**	192,000	
Retained earnings **(11f)**	88,100	
Accumulated translation adjustments **(11g)**	(51,300)	228,800
Acquisition differential		$ –0–

With no acquisition differential or non-controlling interest, the investment account is replaced with the assets and the liabilities of the subsidiary. Note that the parent's share (in this case, 100%) of the subsidiary's accumulated translation adjustments appears as a separate component of consolidated shareholders' equity. The parent's equity method journal entries made the consolidation process straightforward.

The consolidated statement of changes in equity for the year ended December 31, Year 2, is presented in Exhibit 11.12. Note that net income is added to retained earnings, whereas other comprehensive income is added to accumulated translation adjustments.

Comparative Observations of the Two Translation Methods

Integrated subsidiaries usually have a net liability exposure, whereas self-sustaining subsidiaries usually have a net asset exposure.

Under the current rate method, the net assets position of the foreign entity is at risk from currency fluctuations, while under the temporal method it is typically the net monetary position that is at risk. For most companies, monetary liabilities are greater than monetary assets, so they are usually in a net monetary liability position. This is the case with Controlada S.A. If the foreign currency weakens with respect to the Canadian dollar, a self-sustaining operation will show a foreign exchange loss while an integrated foreign operation will show a foreign exchange gain. This can be seen in Exhibit 11.7, where an integrated operation produced a gain of $2,600 and in Exhibit 11.10, where a self-sustaining operation produced a loss of $51,100. If the Canadian dollar weakens with respect to the foreign currency (i.e., the foreign currency strengthens) a self-sustaining operation will reflect an exchange gain and an integrated operation will reflect an exchange loss. These observations are only true when monetary liabilities are greater than monetary assets and when there is not a major change in exposed position from beginning to the end of the period.

EXHIBIT 11.12

CONSOLIDATED STATEMENT OF CHANGES IN EQUITY
(Self-Sustaining Foreign Operation)

	Common shares	Retained earnings	ATA*	Total
Balance—beginning	$200,000	$336,000	$ 0	$536,000
Net income **(11a)**		284,500		284,500
Other comprehensive income **(11b)**			(51,100)	(51,100)
Dividends **(11c)**		(50,000)		(50,000)
Balance—end	$200,000	$570,500	$(51,100)	$719,400

* ATA = Accumulated translation adjustments

See Self-Study Problem 1, Part (b), for another example of the translation of a self-sustaining foreign operation.

Complications with an Acquisition Differential   L05

The previous example assumed a 100% controlled subsidiary and no acquisition differential. The existence of an acquisition differential presents complications in the consolidation process when the current rate method is used and the subsidiary is less than 100% owned. We will change some of the facts from the previous example in order to illustrate this.

Example   Assume that Starmont purchased 90% of Controlada on December 31, Year 1, at a cost of K2,340,000. The carrying amounts of Controlada's net assets were equal to fair values on this date except for a patent, which had a fair value of K600,000 in excess of carrying amount. The patent had a remaining useful life of 10 years and no residual value at the date of acquisition. The same exchange rates are assumed; thus, the financial statements of Controlada and their translation will not change from the previous example. However, the change in the acquisition cost and the percentage purchased creates an acquisition differential and a non-controlling interest. Starmont's journal entry to record the acquisition on December 31, Year 1, is as follows:

Investment in Controlada	299,520	
Cash		299,520

To record the acquisition of 90% of Controlada for $299,520
(2,340,000 × 0.128)

The calculation in Exhibit 11.13 of the acquisition differential in kroons and Canadian dollars on December 31, Year 1, is made to prepare the acquisition-date consolidated balance sheet.

Exhibit 11.14 shows the balance sheets of the parent and the subsidiary and the consolidated balance sheet at December 31, Year 1, the date of acquisition.

The subsidiary's separate-entity financial statements are the same regardless of the parent's percentage ownership in the subsidiary.

Consolidation Integrated   We assume that 90%-owned Controlada is an integrated foreign operation. In this case, the existence of an acquisition differential

EXHIBIT 11.13

CALCULATION OF ACQUISITION DIFFERENTIAL

Cost of 90% investment	K2,340,000	×	0.128	=	$299,520	
Implied value of 100%	K2,600,000	×	0.128	=	$332,800	**(a)**
Book value of subsidiary's net assets						
Assets	2,500,000	×	0.128	=	320,000	
Liabilities	(500,000)	×	0.128	=	(64,000)	
Net assets	2,000,000				256,000	
Acquisition differential	600,000	×	0.128	=	76,800	
Patent	600,000	×	0.128	=	76,800	**(b)**
Balance—goodwill	K —0—				$ —0—	
Non-controlling interests (10% × **[a]** 332,800)					33,280	**(c)**

The acquisition differential is translated at the exchange rate on the date of acquisition.

EXHIBIT 11.14

PREPARATION OF CONSOLIDATED BALANCE SHEET
at December 31, Year 1

	Starmont	Controlada (From Ex. 11.3)	Starmont Consolidated
Cash	$ 26,480	$ 5,120	$ 31,600
Accounts receivable	90,000	46,080	136,080
Inventories	200,000	153,600	353,600
Plant and equipment	300,000	115,200	415,200
Investment in Controlada	299,520	—	—
Patent **(13b)**	—	—	76,800
	$916,000	$320,000	$1,013,280
Current liabilities	$80,000	$ 6,400	$ 86,400
Bonds payable	300,000	57,600	357,600
Common shares	200,000	192,000	200,000
Retained earnings	336,000	64,000	336,000
Non-controlling interest **(13c)**	—	—	33,280
	$916,000	$320,000	$1,013,280

Patent and non-controlling interest appear on the consolidated balance sheet.

and a non-controlling interest pose no particular consolidation problems. The acquisition differential amortization schedule for Year 2 is shown in Exhibit 11.15.

Using the Year 2 acquisition differential amortization schedule and Controlada's translated financial statements (Exhibit 11.16), Starmont would make the following equity method journal entries on December 31, Year 2:

Cash (90% × **[6b]** 10,600)	9,540	
Investment in Controlada	1,440	
Equity earnings (90% × **[6a]**12,200)		10,980
To record parent's share of dividends and net income		
Equity earnings (90% × **[15a]** 7,680)	6,912	
Investment in Controlada		6,912
Amortization of acquisition differential		

Exhibit 11.16 shows the preparation of the Year 2 consolidated financial statements.

EXHIBIT 11.15

ACQUISITION DIFFERENTIAL AMORTIZATION SCHEDULE

Patent—Dec. 31, Year 1 **(13b)**	K600,000	×	0.128	=	$76,800	
Amortization—Year 2	60,000	×	0.128	=	7,680	**(a)**
Patent—Dec. 31, Year 2	K540,000	×	0.128	=	$69,120	**(b)**

There is no exchange adjustment because patent is translated at the historical rate under the temporal method.

EXHIBIT 11.16

PREPARATION OF CONSOLIDATED FINANCIAL STATEMENTS—YEAR 2
(Integrated Foreign Operation)

INCOME STATEMENT

	Starmont	Controlada (From Ex. 11.6)	Starmont Consolidated
Sales	$3,000,000	$1,035,000	$4,035,000
Equity earnings	4,068	—	—
	3,004,068	1,035,000	4,035,000
Cost of goods purchased	2,520,000	851,000	3,371,000
Change in inventory	(20,000)	(22,400)	(42,400)
Depreciation	20,000	12,800	32,800
Bond interest	30,000	5,175	35,175
Other expenses	200,000	178,825	378,825
Patent amortization **(15a)**	—	—	7,680
Foreign exchange gain **(7a)**	—	(2,600)	(2,600)
	2,750,000	1,022,800	3,780,480
Net income	$ 254,068	$ 12,200	$ 254,520 **(a)**
Attributable to			
Shareholders of Starmont (**[a]** 254,520 – **[b]** 452)			$ 254,068
Non-controlling interest			452 **(b)**

RETAINED EARNINGS

	Starmont	Controlada	Starmont Consolidated	
Balance—beginning	$ 336,000	$ 64,000	$ 336,000	The parent's retained
Net income	254,068	12,200	254,068	earnings under the equity
	590,068	76,200	590,068	method are equal to
Dividends	50,000	10,600	50,000	consolidated retained
Balance—end	$ 540,068	$ 65,600	$ 540,068	earnings.

BALANCE SHEETS

	Starmont	Controlada	Starmont Consolidated	
Cash	$ 55,620	$ 10,400	$ 66,020	
Accounts receivable	290,400	41,600	332,000	
Inventories	220,000	176,000	396,000	
Plant and equipment (net)	280,000	102,400	382,400	
Investment in Controlada (equity)	294,048	—	— **(c)**	
Patent **(15b)**	—	—	69,120 **(d)**	
	$ 1,140,068	$ 330,400	$ 1,245,540	
Current liabilities	$ 100,000	$ 26,000	$ 126,000	There is no accumulated
Bonds payable	300,000	46,800	346,800	translation adjustment for
Common shares	200,000	192,000	200,000 **(e)**	exchange gains or losses
Retained earnings	540,068	65,600	540,068 **(f)**	under the temporal method.
Non-controlling interest	—	—	32,672	
	$ 1,140,068	$ 330,400	$ 1,245,540	

The following points are worth noting in regard to the preparation of the consolidated statements:

1. Consolidated income statement:

Patent amortization and
non-controlling interest are
consolidation adjustments.

(a) Equity earnings are eliminated and replaced with the revenues and the expenses of the subsidiary, patent amortization, and the non-controlling interest as follows:

Net income, Controlada **(6a)**	$12,200
Patent amortization **(15a)**	(7,680)
	4,520
Non-controlling interest @ 10%	(452)
Equity earnings	$ 4,068

(b) Non-controlling interest is 10% of the subsidiary's net income less 10% of the patent amortization.

2. Consolidated retained earnings:
Because the parent has used the equity method, all items are identical to the parent's retained earnings.

3. Consolidated balance sheet:

(a) The investment account is eliminated and replaced with the assets and the liabilities of the subsidiary, the unamortized acquisition differential, and the non-controlling interest.

(b) The non-controlling interest is calculated as follows:

Non-controlling interest
on the balance sheet is
based on the subsidiary's
shareholders' equity plus the
unamortized patent at the
end of the year.

Common shares **(16e)**	$192,000
Retained earnings **(16f)**	65,600
Patent **(16d)**	69,120
	326,720
	10%
	$ 32,672

The unamortized acquisition differential can be verified by the following calculation:

Investment in Controlada **(16c)**		$294,048
Shareholders' equity of Controlada (**[16e]** 192,000 + **[16f]** 65,600)	257,600	
	90%	231,840
Unamortized acquisition differential (patent)—parent's share		62,208
—non-controlling interest's share (10% × **[16d]** 69,120)		6,912
Total unamortized acquisition differential (patent)		$ 69,120

Consolidation—Self-Sustaining   Assuming that Controlada is a self-sustaining operation, we will now illustrate the preparation of the Year 2 consolidated financial statements. The translated financial statements are the same as were shown in the previous example, and are reproduced again as part of Exhibit 11.18. Included in the subsidiary's shareholders' equity is the accumulated unrealized loss of $51,100. The non-controlling interest in the consolidated balance sheet includes 10% of the subsidiary's shareholders' equity, and therefore includes 10% of this accumulated loss. Consolidated shareholders' equity attributable to the parent will show the other 90% of this translation adjustment. A further exchange loss arises in the consolidation process because of the manner in which the acquisition differential amortization schedule is translated. Assume that the amortization expense related to the patent occurred evenly throughout the year. The acquisition differential amortization schedule is translated as shown in Exhibit 11.17.

EXHIBIT 11.17

TRANSLATION OF ACQUISITION-DIFFERENTIAL AMORTIZATION SCHEDULE

Patent—Dec. 31, Year 1 **(13b)**	K600,000	×	0.128	=	$76,800	
Patent amortization—Year 2	60,000	×	0.115	=	6,900 **(a)**	
Calculated patent—Dec. 31, Year 2					69,900	
Actual patent—Dec. 31, Year 2	K540,000	×	0.104	=	56,160 **(b)**	
Exchange loss—unrealized					$13,740 **(c)**	

A patent for a self-sustaining subsidiary is translated at the closing rate.

DISPOSITION OF ACCUMULATED UNREALIZED LOSSES

	Total	90% control	10% non-control	
Accumulated unrealized loss—subsidiary statements **(9b)**	$51,100	$45,990	$5,110 **(d)**	
Accumulated unrealized loss—acquisition differential **(c)**	13,740	12,366	1,374 **(e)**	
	$64,840	$58,356	$ 6,484	

EXHIBIT 11.18

PREPARATION OF CONSOLIDATED FINANCIAL STATEMENTS—YEAR 2
(Self-Sustaining)

STATEMENT OF NET INCOME AND COMPREHENSIVE INCOME

	Starmont	Controlada (From Ex. 11.9)	Starmont Consolidated	
Sales	$3,000,000	$1,035,000	$4,035,000	
Equity earnings	24,840	—	—	
	3,024,840	1,035,000	4,035,000	
Cost of goods purchased	2,520,000	851,000	3,371,000	
Change in inventory	(20,000)	(46,000)	(66,000)	
Depreciation	20,000	11,500	31,500	
Bond interest	30,000	5,175	35,175	
Other	200,000	178,825	378,825	
Patent amortization **(17a)**	—	—	6,900	
	2,750,000	1,000,500	3,757,400	
Individual net incomes	274,840	34,500		**(a)**
Net income			277,600	**(b)**
Other comprehensive income				
Foreign currency translation adjustments	(58,356)	(51,100)	(64,840)	
Comprehensive income	$ 216,484	$ (16,600)	$ 212,760	**(c)**
			(continued)	

The parent accrues its share of the subsidiary's income after it has been translated into Canadian dollars.

Consolidated other comprehensive income includes $51,100 from translating the subsidiary's separate-entity statements plus $13,740 from translating the acquisition differential on consolidation.

EXHIBIT 11.18 **(continued)**

	Starmont	Controlada (From Ex. 11.9)	Starmont Consolidated	
Net income attributable to Shareholders of Starmont ([b] 277,600 − [d] 2,760)			$ 274,840	
Non-controlling interest (10% × [(a) 34,500 − (17a) 6,900])			2,760	**(d)**
			$ 277,600	
Comprehensive income attributable to Shareholders of Starmont ([c] 212,760 − [e] (3,724))			$ 216,484	
Non-controlling interest (10% × [(c) (16,600) − (17a) 6,900 − (17e) 13,740])			(3,724)	**(e)**
			$ 212,760	

RETAINED EARNINGS

	Starmont	Controlada	Starmont Consolidated
Balance—beginning	$ 336,000	$ 64,000	$ 336,000
Net income	274,840	34,500	274,840
	610,840	98,500	610,840
Dividends	50,000	10,600	50,000
Balance—end	$ 560,840	$ 87,900	$ 560,840

BALANCE SHEETS

	Starmont	Controlada	Starmont Consolidated	
Cash	$ 55,620	$ 10,400	$ 66,020	
Accounts receivable	290,400	41,600	332,000	
Inventories	220,000	166,400	386,400	
Plant and equipment	280,000	83,200	363,200	
Investment in Controlada (equity)	256,464	—	—	**(f)**
Patent **(17b)**	—	—	56,160	**(g)**
	$1,102,484	$ 301,600	$1,203,780	
Current liabilities	$ 100,000	$26,000	$ 126,000	
Bonds payable	300,000	46,800	346,800	
Common shares	200,000	192,000	200,000	**(h)**
Retained earnings	560,840	87,900	560,840	**(i)**
Accumulated translation adjustments	(58,356)	(51,100)	(58,356)	**(j)**
Non-controlling interest	—	—	28,496	
	$1,102,484	$ 301,600	$1,203,780	

Accumulated translation adjustments are only the parent's share. The non-controlling interest's share of accumulated translation adjustments is included in the $28,496 for non-controlling interest.

The following points should be noted:

Amortization expense is translated at the average rate.

- The acquisition differential (in this case, patent) on December 31, Year 1, is translated at the historical rate on that date.
- The Year 2 amortization expense is translated at the average rate for Year 2 because the expense was incurred evenly throughout the year.
- The unamortized balance on December 31, Year 2, is translated at the closing rate.

An exchange adjustment occurs because the patent is restated when it is translated at the closing rate at the end of the year.

When different exchange rates are used to translate the schedule, an exchange gain or loss will always result. In this case, there is a loss of $13,740, which appears as part of the accumulated translation adjustments in the shareholders' equity of the parent company. The allocation of the two exchange losses resulting from the translation of the financial statements and the acquisition differential to controlling and non-controlling interest was illustrated above.

Using the translated financial statements of Controlada (see Exhibit 11.18) and the translated acquisition differential amortization schedule, Starmont would make the following equity method journal entries on December 31, Year 2:

Cash (90% × **[9c]** 10,600)	9,540	
Other comprehensive income (90% × **[9b] 51,100**)	45,990	
Equity earnings (90% × **[9a] 34,500**)		31,050
Investment in Controlada		24,480

To record the parent's share of dividends, net income, and loss on translation of statement

Equity earnings (90% × **[17a] 6,900**)	6,210	
Other comprehensive income (90% × **[17c] 13,740**)	12,366	
Investment in Controlada		18,576

To record the amortization and exchange adjustment on the acquisition differential

Note that Year 2 equity earnings are $24,840 (31,050 – 6,210) above when the subsidiary is classified as self-sustaining. In the previous example, when the subsidiary was classified as integrated, the equity earnings were $4,068. The difference is due to (a) the use of different exchange rates in the translation, and (b) the fact that there is no exchange loss on the translation of the acquisition differential amortization schedule under the temporal method.

The equity earnings are quite different under the temporal method than under the current rate method.

The preparation of the Year 2 consolidated financial statements is illustrated in Exhibit 11.18. The following explanations regarding the preparation of the consolidated statements should be noted:

1. Consolidated statement of comprehensive income:
   (a) Equity earnings are eliminated and replaced with the revenues and expenses of the subsidiary, the patent amortization expense, and the non-controlling interest.
   (b) Non-controlling interest in net income is 10% of subsidiary net income less 10% of the patent amortization expense.
   (c) This statement takes the net income and deducts the unrealized foreign exchange loss to determine comprehensive income.
   (d) Non-controlling interest absorbs 10% of the unrealized exchange loss reported in other comprehensive income.

Non-controlling interest on the consolidated statement of comprehensive income is based on the income recorded by the subsidiary, plus the consolidation adjustments for patent amortization loss and exchange loss.

2. Consolidated retained earnings:
   Because the parent has used the equity method, all items are identical to the parent's retained earnings.

3. Consolidated balance sheet:
   (a) The investment account is eliminated and replaced with the assets and the liabilities of the subsidiary, the unamortized acquisition differential, and the non-controlling interest.
   (b) The non-controlling interest is calculated as follows:

Common shares **(18h)**	$192,000
Retained earnings **(18i)**	87,900
Accumulated translation adjustments **(18j)**	(51,100)
Patent **(18g)**	56,160
	284,960
	10%
	$ 28,496

Non-controlling interest on the balance sheet is based on the subsidiary's shareholders' equity, plus the consolidation adjustment for unamortized patent at the end of the year.

4. Consolidated accumulated translation adjustments:

This account shows the parent's share of the accumulated translation adjustments at the end of the year. Since Year 2 is the first year after acquisition, the accumulated losses are equal to the losses reported in other comprehensive income for the year.

The unamortized acquisition differential can be verified by the following calculation:

Investment in Controlada **(18f)**		$256,464
Shareholders' equity of Controlada **(18h + 18i + 18j)**	228,800	
	90%	205,920
Unamortized acquisition differential (patent)—parent's share		50,544
Non-controlling interest's share (10% × **[18g] 56,160**)		5,616
Total unamortized acquisition differential (patent)		$ 56,160

Other Considerations

The previous examples have illustrated the translation of a foreign operation's financial statements and the consolidation of these statements with those of the reporting enterprise. We will now look at some other items that must be considered when a foreign subsidiary is being consolidated.

Inventory is translated at the closing rate for a self-sustaining operation and the LCNRV principle need not be applied.

For an integrated operation, the LCNRV principle must be applied using historical cost in Canadian dollars and net realizable value in Canadian dollars.

Lower of Cost and Net Realizable Value (LCNRV)   Certain items, such as inventory, will be measured at the LCNRV. If the subsidiary is self-sustaining, the method of valuation used is of no consequence in the translation because all of the assets are translated at the closing rate, regardless of whether they are carried at cost or net realizable value.

If the foreign operation is integrated, assets carried at cost are translated at historical rates, while assets carried at net realizable value are translated at the closing rate. Remember that the temporal method remeasures, in Canadian dollars, transactions that have been incurred by the foreign operation. Therefore, the translated financial statements should reflect the LCNRV in Canadian dollars as if the parent itself had carried out the inventory acquisitions of its foreign subsidiary. When assets are measured at the LCNRV, a write-down to net realizable value may be required in the translated financial statements, even though no write-down is required in the foreign currency financial statements. For example, if the net realizable value (denominated in foreign currency) is greater than historical cost (denominated in foreign currency), no write-down will have occurred in the foreign operation's statements. But if the foreign currency weakens, it is quite possible that the net realizable value translated at the closing rate will be less than historical cost translated at the historical rate. In this situation, translated net realizable value will be used in the translated financial statements.

On the other hand, it may be necessary to reverse a write-down in the foreign currency financial statements prior to translation, if the net realizable value amount translated at the closing rate exceeds historical cost translated at the historical rates. For example, if the net realizable value (denominated in foreign currency) is less than historical cost (denominated in foreign currency), a write-down would have taken place in the foreign operation's statements. If the foreign currency has strengthened so that the net realizable value translated at the closing rate is greater than historical cost translated at the historical rate, this write-down will have to be reversed prior to translation. The inventory (now carried at cost) will be translated at the historical rate.

Intercompany Profits   In the preparation of consolidated financial statements, intercompany profits in assets are eliminated. If the profits are contained in the assets of the Canadian parent, there is no particular problem eliminating them. The asset acquired was recorded by the parent at the foreign-currency–denominated price, translated at the exchange rate on the date of the transaction. The profit rate can be applied for the items still on hand to determine the amount of profit to be eliminated. If the profits are contained in the assets of an integrated subsidiary, the amount of unrealized profit can still be determined in foreign currency. Because the asset itself is translated at the historical rate, using the historical rate to translate and eliminate the profit will result in a translated asset at historical cost to the consolidated entity.

> The historical rate should be used in determining the intercompany profit to be eliminated. This eliminates the same profit that was recorded in the first place.

When the profit is contained in the assets of a translated self-sustaining subsidiary, the asset has been translated at the closing rate. The historical exchange rate should be used to calculate the amount of the profit. This eliminates the same profit that was recorded in the first place. However, the translated assets will not be reported at historical cost to the consolidated entity. This is one of the anomalies of the current rate method.

Cash Flow Statement   To prepare a cash flow statement for a foreign subsidiary, we ignore the cash flow statement of the foreign subsidiary; that is, we do not translate each item on the foreign currency cash flow statement into Canadian dollars by applying a translation rate to each item. Rather, we use the translated balance sheet and translated income statement to determine the cash flows during the year. We analyze the changes in the translated balance sheet accounts from last year to this year using either a worksheet approach or T-account approach and then prepare the cash flow statement based on this analysis. This is a similar approach to what we used in Chapter 8 when we prepared a consolidated cash flow statement by analyzing the changes in the consolidated balance sheet from last year to this year.

> A cash flow statement is prepared by analyzing the change in a non-cash item on the balance sheet after it has been translated into Canadian dollars.

Tax Effects of Exchange Adjustments   Exchange differences arising from translating the financial statements of a foreign operation into Canadian dollars are usually not taxable or deductible until the gains or losses are realized. Since these differences were recognized for accounting purposes but not for tax purposes, a temporary difference occurs, and deferred income taxes should be recognized in the financial statements of the reporting entity.

Also, as we learned in Chapter 9, a temporary difference arises on the consolidated financial statements when an acquisition differential is allocated to an asset other than goodwill. We ignored the tax impact on the acquisition differential and for the foreign exchange adjustments in the illustrations in this chapter to avoid complicating the illustrations.

Disclosure Requirements   The following summarizes the main disclosures required in IAS 21 for the effects of changes in foreign exchange rates related to foreign operations:

(a) The amount of exchange differences recognized in profit or loss.

(b) Net exchange differences recognized in other comprehensive income.

> An entity must disclose the exchange adjustments reported in profit and other comprehensive income.

(c) When the presentation currency is different from the functional currency, that fact must be stated with disclosure of the functional currency and the reason for using a different presentation currency.

(d) When there is a change in the functional currency, that fact and the reason for the change in functional currency must be disclosed.

TransAlta Corporation is Canada's largest publicly traded power generator and marketer of electricity and renewable energy. Exhibit 11.19 contains excerpts from TransAlta's 2011 financial statements pertaining to foreign currency operations.

EXHIBIT 11.19

EXTRACTS (IN PART) FROM TRANSALTA'S 2011 FINANCIAL STATEMENTS

2. Accounting Policies

D. Foreign Currency Translation

The Corporation, its subsidiary companies, and joint ventures each determine their functional currency based on the currency of the primary economic environment in which they operate. The Corporation's functional currency is the Canadian dollar, while the functional currencies of the subsidiary companies and joint ventures' are either the Canadian, U.S., or Australian dollar. Transactions denominated in a currency other than the functional currency of an entity are translated at the exchange rate in effect on the transaction date. The resulting exchange gains and losses are included in each entity's net earnings in the period in which they arise.

> The Canadian dollar is both the functional currency and the presentation currency.

The Corporation's foreign operations are translated to the Corporation's presentation currency, which is the Canadian dollar, for inclusion in the consolidated financial statements. Foreign-denominated monetary and non-monetary assets and liabilities of foreign operations are translated at exchange rates in effect at the end of the reporting period, and revenue and expenses are translated at exchange rates in effect on the transaction date. The resulting translation gains and losses are included in Other Comprehensive Income ("OCI") with the cumulative gain or loss reported in Accumulated Other Comprehensive (Loss) Income ("AOCI"). Amounts previously recognized in AOCI are recognized in net earnings when there is a reduction in the net investment as a result of a disposal, partial disposal, or loss of control.

E. Financial Instruments and Hedges

> The current rate method is used when the functional currency differs from the presentation currency.

II. Hedges

c. Hedges of Foreign Currency Exposures of a Net Investment in a Foreign Operation

In hedging a foreign currency exposure of a net investment in a foreign operation, the effective portion of foreign exchange gains and losses on the hedging instrument is recognized in OCI, and the ineffective portion is recognized in net earnings. The amounts previously recognized in AOCI are recognized in net earnings when there is a reduction in the hedged net investment as a result of a disposal, partial disposal, or loss of control.

The Corporation primarily uses foreign currency forward contracts, and foreign-denominated debt to hedge exposure to changes in the carrying amounts of the Corporation's net investments in foreign operations that result from changes in foreign exchange rates. Gains and losses on these instruments that qualify for hedge accounting are reported in OCI with fair values recorded in risk management assets or liabilities, as appropriate.

(continued)

EXHIBIT 11.19   **(continued)**

14. Risk Management Activities

I. Hedges

a. Net Investment Hedges

i. Hedges of Foreign Operations Long-Term Debt

U.S. dollar denominated long-term debt with a face value of US$820 million (Dec. 31, 2010 – US$820 million), and borrowings under a U.S. dollar denominated credit facility with a face value of US$300 million (Dec. 31, 2010 – US$300 million) have been designated as a part of the hedge of TransAlta's net investment in foreign operations.

U.S.-dollar–denominated long-term debt has been designated as a part hedge of the net investment in foreign operations.

   The Corporation hedges its net investment in foreign operations with U.S. denominated borrowings, cross-currency interest rate swaps, and foreign currency forward sale contracts.

ii. Effect on the Consolidated Statement of Comprehensive Income

For the year ended Dec. 31, 2011, a net after-tax loss of $1 million (Dec. 31, 2010 – loss of $24 million), relating to the translation of the Corporation's net investment in foreign operations, net of hedging, was recognized in OCI. All net investment hedges currently have no ineffective portion.

B. Nature and Extent of Risks Arising from Financial Instruments

The following discussion is limited to the nature and extent of risks arising from financial instruments.

I. Market Risk

c. Currency Rate Risk

The Corporation has exposure to various currencies, such as the euro, the U.S. dollar, and the Australian dollar, as a result of investments and operations in foreign jurisdictions, the net earnings from those operations, and the acquisition of equipment and services from foreign suppliers.

   The foreign currency risk sensitivities outlined below are limited to the risks that arise on financial instruments denominated in currencies other than the functional currency.

   The possible effect on net earnings and OCI, for the years ended Dec. 31, 2011 and 2010, due to changes in foreign exchange rates associated with financial instruments outstanding as at the date of the Statements of Financial Position, is outlined below. The sensitivity analysis has been prepared using management's assessment that a six-cent (2010 – six-cent) increase or decrease in these currencies relative to the Canadian dollar is a reasonable potential change over the next quarter.

Year ended Dec. 31	2011		2010	
	Net earnings (decrease)		Net earnings (decrease)	
Currency	increase[2]	OCI gain[2,3]	increase[2]	OCI gain[2,3]
USD	(4)	11	(4)	9
AUD	–	–	1	–
EUR	–	3	–	–
Total	(4)	14	(3)	9

TransAlta discloses the effect on net earnings of a six-cent increase in the exchange rate.

2 *These calculations assume an increase in the value of these currencies relative to the Canadian dollar. A decrease would have the opposite effect.*
3 *The foreign exchange impacts related to financial instruments used as hedging instruments in net investment hedges have been excluded.*

Source: Reproduced with permission from TransAlta Corporation. http://www.transalta.com/sites/default/files/TA_Statements_2011_Final_SEDAR_0.pdf

L06 ANALYSIS AND INTERPRETATION OF FINANCIAL STATEMENTS

A company must use the temporal method when translating an integrated foreign operation and the current rate method when translating self-sustaining foreign operation. Exhibit 11.20 presents the statements of comprehensive income and balance sheets for Controlada under these two translation methods. The exhibit also indicates the return on equity, debt-to-equity ratio, and current ratio for each translation method.

Note the following from Exhibit 11.20:

- The temporal method reports a gain from foreign currency, whereas the current rate method shows a loss; the gain is reported in net income under

Exhibit 11.20	Impact of Translation Methods on Key Ratios

CONTROLADA'S STATEMENTS OF COMPREHENSIVE INCOME

	Temporal method (From Ex. 11.6)	Current rate method (From Ex. 11.9)
Sales	$1,035,000	$1,035,000
Foreign exchange gain	2,400	
	1,037,400	1,035,000
Cost of goods purchased	851,000	851,000
Change in inventory	(22,400)	(46,000)
Depreciation	12,800	11,500
Bond interest	5,175	5,175
Other expenses	178,825	178,825
	1,025,400	1,000,500
Net income	12,000	34,500
OCI—translation adjustment		(51,300)
Comprehensive income	$ 12,000	$ (16,800)

Exchange gains and losses are reported in net income under the temporal method and in other comprehensive income under the current rate method.

The temporal method reports an exchange gain, whereas the current rate method reports an exchange loss.

CONTROLADA'S BALANCE SHEETS

Cash	$ 10,400	$ 10,400
Accounts receivable	41,600	41,600
Inventories	176,000	166,400
Current assets	228,000	218,400
Plant and equipment (net)	102,400	83,200
	$ 330,400	$ 301,600
Current liabilities	$ 26,000	$ 26,000
Bonds payable	46,800	46,800
Common shares	192,000	192,000
Retained earnings	65,600	88,100
Accumulated translation adjustment		(51,300)
	$ 330,400	$ 301,600
Return on equity (net income / shareholders' equity)	4.7%	15.1%
Debt to equity (liabilities / shareholders' equity)	0.28	0.32
Current ratio (current assets / current liabilities)	8.8	8.4

Exchange gains and losses end up in retained earnings under the temporal method and in accumulated other comprehensive income under the current rate method.

the temporal method, and the loss is reported in OCI under the current rate method.

- The temporal method reports a positive comprehensive income, whereas the current rate method reports a negative comprehensive income.

- The main profitability ratio, being return on equity, is better under the current rate method because it uses net income rather than comprehensive income as the numerator.

- The debt-to-equity ratio is lower under the temporal method because shareholders' equity is higher due to the foreign exchange gain as compared with a negative translation adjustment under the current rate method.

- The solvency position looks worse under the current rate method due to the higher debt-to-equity ratio because of the lower equity.

- The current ratio is higher under the temporal method due to the higher amount for inventory.

- The liquidity position looks better under the temporal method due to the higher current ratio.

> Profitability ratios look better under the current rate method, whereas liquidity and solvency ratios look better under the temporal method.

These ratios refer to one company for the same year. Which set of ratios more faithfully represents the true economic position of the company? That question needs to be answered to determine which accounting method should be used to better reflect the true financial position of the company.

ASPE DIFFERENCES

L07

- As mentioned in Chapter 3, private companies can either consolidate their subsidiaries or report their investments in subsidiaries under the cost method or the equity method or at fair value if the securities are traded in an active market. Under the cost method or the fair value method, the financial statements of a foreign subsidiary do not have to be translated.

- The exchange rate at the end of the reporting period is called the current rate, not the closing rate.

- The functional currency is not used to classify foreign operations. Instead, the foreign operation is classified as either integrated or self-sustaining using similar, but not exactly the same, factors to those used under IFRSs to determine the functional currency.

- The translation gains and losses from translating self-sustaining foreign subsidiaries do not go through OCI but are reported as a separate component of shareholders' equity because OCI does not exist under ASPE.

> OCI does not exist under ASPE.

- When the foreign operations are located in a highly inflationary environment, the temporal method is used regardless of whether the operation is integrated or self-sustaining. No adjustments are made for inflation prior to translation.

U.S. GAAP Differences

U.S. GAAP and IFRSs for foreign operations have many similarities. The only significant difference is summarized as follows: Under IFRSs, the financial statements of a foreign operation whose functional currency is highly inflationary are adjusted for inflation prior to being translated to the presentation currency. Under U.S. GAAP, no adjustments are made for inflation. Instead, the financial statements are translated as if the parent's reporting currency were the functional currency.

SUMMARY

Before the equity method or consolidation reporting can be used, the financial statements of foreign entities must be translated into the parent company's presentation currency. If the entity is considered to be an integrated foreign operation, the temporal method of translation is used. This method produces results that are consistent with the normal measurement and valuation of assets and liabilities for domestic transactions and operations. Exchange gains or losses are included in net income.

The current rate method is used when the foreign operation is self-sustaining. This method translates all assets and liabilities at the current rate to reflect that all assets and liabilities are exposed as part of the net investment in the foreign subsidiary. This results in some assets being reported in the presentation currency at values other than historical cost or current value. Exchange gains and losses from the translation are not reflected in net income but rather are shown in other comprehensive income, which ends up being reported on a cumulative basis as a separate component of shareholders' equity. The consolidation of the translated financial statements of a self-sustaining subsidiary creates additional exchange gains and losses from the translation of the acquisition differential.

Significant Changes in GAAP in the Last Three Years

No major changes have occurred in the translation and reporting of foreign operations.

Changes Expected in GAAP in the Next Three Years

No major changes are expected for the translation and reporting of foreign operations.

SELF-STUDY PROBLEM 1

LO3, 4   Barros Corp. is located in Brazil. The company was incorporated on January 1, Year 1, and issued its no-par common shares for 3.0 million Brazilian reals (R). The Canadian parent acquired 90% of these shares on January 1, Year 4. The financial statements for Barros on December 31, Year 5, are shown below:

STATEMENT OF FINANCIAL POSITION
at December 31, Year 5

	Year 5	Year 4
Property, plant, and equipment	R5,000,000	R 5,000,000
Accumulated depreciation	(2,500,000)	(2,000,000)
Inventory	1,050,000	1,155,000
Accounts receivable	2,710,000	2,550,000
Cash	1,000,000	500,000
	R7,260,000	R 7,205,000
Ordinary shares	R3,000,000	R 3,000,000
Retained earnings	1,660,000	1,505,000
Bonds payable—due Jan. 3, Year 11	2,500,000	2,500,000
Accounts payable	100,000	200,000
	R7,260,000	R 7,205,000

INCOME STATEMENT
for the Year Ended December 31, Year 5

Sales	R35,000,000
Cost of sales	28,150,000
Selling and administrative	2,440,000
Miscellaneous expenses	2,000,000
Income tax	1,045,000
	33,635,000
Profit	R 1,365,000

STATEMENT OF RETAINED EARNINGS
for the Year Ended December 31, Year 5

Balance, January 1	R 1,505,000
Profit	1,365,000
	2,870,000
Dividends	1,210,000
Balance, December 31	R 1,660,000

Additional Information

- On January 1, Year 1, Barros issued bonds at par for R2.5 million.
- Barros acquired the plant assets on January 1, Year 1, for R5.0 million. The plant assets are being depreciated on a straight-line basis over a 10-year life.
- Barros uses the FIFO basis to value inventory. The December 31, Year 4, inventory was acquired on October 1, Year 4. The inventory on hand on December 31, Year 5, was acquired on December 15, Year 5.
- Selling and administrative expense includes depreciation expense of R500,000.
- Barros declared and paid dividends on December 31, Year 5.
- Under the temporal method, Barros's December 31, Year 4, retained earnings were translated as $778,607. Under the current rate method, Barros's December 31, Year 4, retained earnings were translated as $684,091 and accumulated other comprehensive income were translated as $174,547.

- Exchange rate information:

Jan. 1, Year 1	CDN$1 = R2.50
Jan. 1, Year 4	CDN$1 = R2.00
Oct. 1, Year 4	CDN$1 = R1.94
Average, Year 4	CDN$1 = R1.95
Dec. 31, Year 4	CDN$1 = R1.91
Dec. 15, Year 5	CDN$1 = R1.80
Average, Year 5	CDN$1 = R1.86
Dec. 31, Year 5	CDN$1 = R1.82

Required:

(a) Translate Barros's Year 5 financial statements into dollars, assuming that Barros's functional currency is the Canadian dollar.

(b) Assume that Barros's functional currency is the Brazilian real:

   (i) Translate the Year 5 financial statements.

   (ii) Prepare the Year 5 equity method journal entries that would be made by the Canadian parent.

SOLUTION TO SELF-STUDY PROBLEM 1

(a) Canadian dollar is functional currency

	Reals	Rate	Dollars
Year 5			*when acquired*
Inventory Jan. 1	1,155,000	/ 1.94	595,361
Purchases	28,045,000	/ 1.86	15,077,956
	29,200,000		15,673,317
Inventory Dec. 31	1,050,000	/ 1.80	583,333
Cost of sales	28,150,000		15,089,984
Depreciation expense	500,000	/ 2.00	250,000
Other selling and administrative	1,940,000	/ 1.86	1,043,011
Total selling and administrative	2,440,000		1,293,011
Net monetary position			
Dec. 31, Year 4*	350,000	/ 1.91	183,246
Changes Year 5			
Sales	35,000,000	/ 1.86	18,817,204
Purchases	(28,045,000)	/ 1.86	(15,077,956)
Selling and administrative	(1,940,000)**	/ 1.86	(1,043,011)
Miscellaneous expenses	(2,000,000)	/ 1.86	(1,075,269)
Income tax	(1,045,000)	/ 1.86	(561,828)
Dividends	(1,210,000)	/ 1.82	(664,835)
	760,000		394,305
Calculated Dec. 31, Year 5			577,551
Actual Dec. 31, Year 5***	1,110,000	/ 1.82	609,890
Exchange gain Year 5			32,339

* 2,550 + 500 − 2,500 − 200 = 350
** Excluding R500,000 of depreciation expense
*** 2,710 + 1,000 − 2,500 − 100 = 1,110

Translation of Year 5 income statement

Sales	35,000,000	/ 1.86	18,817,204
Cost of sales	28,150,000	Calc.	15,089,984
Selling and administrative	2,440,000	Calc.	1,293,011
Miscellaneous expenses	2,000,000	/ 1.86	1,075,269
Income tax	1,045,000	/ 1.86	561,828
	33,635,000		18,020,092
Net income before exchange gain	1,365,000		797,112
Exchange gain		Calc.	32,339
Profit	1,365,000		829,451

Translation of Year 5 retained earnings

Balance Jan. 1	1,505,000	Given	778,607
Profit	1,365,000	Above	829,451
	2,870,000		1,608,058
Dividends	1,210,000	/ 1.82	664,835
Balance Dec. 31	1,660,000		943,223

Translation of Year 5 balance sheet

Property, plant, and equipment	5,000,000	/ 2.00	2,500,000
Accumulated depreciation	(2,500,000)	/ 2.00	(1,250,000)
Inventory	1,050,000	/ 1.80	583,333
Accounts receivable	2,710,000	/ 1.82	1,489,011
Cash	1,000,000	/ 1.82	549,451
	7,260,000		3,871,795
Ordinary shares	3,000,000	/ 2.00	1,500,000
Retained earnings	1,660,000	Above	943,223
Bonds payable	2,500,000	/ 1.82	1,373,627
Accounts payable	100,000	/ 1.82	54,945
	7,260,000		3,871,795

(b) (i) Brazilian real is functional currency

Year 5

Net assets Jan. 1, Year 5	4,505,000	/ 1.91	2,358,639
Profit—Year 5	1,365,000	/ 1.86	733,871
	5,870,000		3,092,510
Dividends	1,210,000	/ 1.82	664,835
Calculated Dec. 31, Year 5			2,427,675
Actual net assets Dec. 31, Year 5	4,660,000	/ 1.82	2,560,440
Exchange gain Year 5 (to be reported in other comprehensive income)			132,765

Cumulative translation adjustment

Balance Dec. 31, Year 4	174,547
Exchange gain—Year 5	132,765
Balance Dec. 31, Year 5	307,312

Translation of Year 5 income statement

Sales	35,000,000	/ 1.86	18,817,204
Cost of sales	28,150,000	/ 1.86	15,134,408
Selling and administrative	2,440,000	/ 1.86	1,311,828
Miscellaneous expenses	2,000,000	/ 1.86	1,075,269
Income tax	1,045,000	/ 1.86	561,828

(continued)

	33,635,000		18,083,333
Profit	1,365,000		733,871
Other comprehensive income—unrealized exchange gains			132,765
Comprehensive income			866,636

Translation of Year 5 retained earnings

Balance Jan. 1	1,505,000	Given	684,091
Profit	1,365,000	/ 1.86	733,871
	2,870,000		1,417,962
Dividends	1,210,000	/ 1.82	664,835
Balance Dec. 31	1,660,000		753,127

Translation of Year 5 balance sheet

Property, plant, and equipment	5,000,000	/ 1.82	2,747,252
Accumulated depreciation	(2,500,000)	/ 1.82	(1,373,626)
Inventory	1,050,000	/ 1.82	576,923
Accounts receivable	2,710,000	/ 1.82	1,489,011
Cash	1,000,000	/ 1.82	549,451
	7,260,000		3,989,011
Ordinary shares	3,000,000	/ 2.00	1,500,000
Retained earnings	1,660,000		753,127
Accumulated translation adjustment			307,312
Bonds payable	2,500,000	/ 1.82	1,373,627
Accounts payable	100,000	/ 1.82	54,945
	7,260,000		3,989,011

(ii) Equity method journal entries of Canadian parent—Year 5

Investment in Barros Corp.	660,484	
Investment income		660,484
90% of Year 5 translated net income (90% × 733,871)		

Cash	598,352	
Investment in Barros Corp.		598,352
90% of Year 5 dividends (90% × 664,835)		

Investment in Barros Corp.	119,489	
Other comprehensive income		119,489
90% of Year 5 exchange gain (90% × 132,765)		

SELF-STUDY PROBLEM 2

L05   On January 1, Year 4, Parento Ltd. purchased 90% of the shares of Barros Limited for 5.4 million Brazilian reals (R). The exchange rate at that time was CDN$1 = R2. Financial statements of Parento are presented below. Financial statements of Barros were presented and translated in Self-Study Problem 1.

PARENTO LTD
STATEMENT OF FINANCIAL POSITION
at December 31, Year 5

Property, plant, and equipment	$ 8,000,000
Accumulated depreciation	(3,000,000)
Investment in Barros—at cost	2,700,000
Inventory	1,400,000
Accounts receivable	1,960,000
Cash	800,000
	$11,860,000
Ordinary shares	$ 5,000,000
Retained earnings	1,500,000
Bonds payable	2,000,000
Accounts payable	3,360,000
	$11,860,000

STATEMENT OF PROFIT AND RETAINED EARNINGS
for the Year Ended December 31, Year 5

Sales	$15,000,000
Dividend income	598,352
	15,598,352
Cost of sales	11,509,352
Selling and administrative expense	2,100,000
(including depreciation and impairment losses)	
Miscellaneous expense	889,000
Income taxes	440,000
	14,938,352
Profit	660,000
Retained earnings, Jan. 1	1,240,000
Dividends paid	(400,000)
Retained earnings, Dec. 31	$ 1,500,000

Additional Information

- On January 1, Year 4, Barros's shareholders' equity consisted of common shares of R3,000,000 and retained earnings of R1,350,000. The fair values of all identifiable net assets were equal to carrying amounts except for the following:

	Carrying amount	Fair value
Inventory	R850,000	R970,000
Patent	–0–	400,000

- The patent of Barros had a remaining legal life of eight years on January 1, Year 4. Any goodwill was tested annually for impairment. There was a goodwill impairment loss of R100,000 in Year 5 and no impairment loss in Year 4.
- On January 1, Year 5, the inventories of Parento contained items purchased from Barros on October 1, Year 4, on which Barros had made a profit of R90,000. During Year 5, Barros sold goods to Parento for R920,000, of which R210,000 remained unpaid at the end of the year. Barros made a profit of R330,000 on goods remaining in Parento's inventory at December 31, Year 5. These goods had been purchased from Barros on December 15, Year 2.

- Assume a corporate tax rate of 40%. Ignore income taxes on the acquisition differential.
- Parento's functional currency and presentation currency are the Canadian dollar.
- Exchange rates were provided in Self-Study Problem 1

Required:

(a) Prepare Parento's consolidated statement of financial position and consolidated statement of profit for Year 5, assuming that Barros' functional currency is the Canadian dollar. *Hint:* Use Barros' translated financial statements from Part (a) of Self-Study Problem 1.

(b) Prepare Parento's consolidated statement of financial position and consolidated statement of comprehensive income for Year 5, assuming that Barros's functional currency is the Brazilian real. *Hint:* Use Barros' translated financial statements from Part (b) of Self-Study Problem 1.

SOLUTION TO SELF-STUDY PROBLEM 2

Calculation, allocation, and amortization of acquisition differential

Cost of 90% investment in Barros		R5,400,000
Implied value of 100% investment in Barros (5,400,000 / 0.9)		R6,000,000
Carrying amounts of Barros's net assets:		
Ordinary shares	R3,000,000	
Retained earnings	1,350,000	
Total shareholders' equity		4,350,000
Acquisition differential, Jan. 1, Year 4		1,650,000
Allocation:	FV – BV	
Inventory	R 120,000	
Patent	400,000	520,000
Balance—Goodwill		R1,130,000
NCI at date of acquisition (10% × 6,000,000)		R 600,000

	Balance Jan. 1/4	Amortization Year 4	Balance Year 4	Amortization Year 5	Balance Dec. 31/5
Inventory	R 120,000	R120,000	–	–	–
Patent	400,000	50,000	R 350,000	R 50,000	R 300,000
Goodwill	1,130,000	–	1,130,000	100,000	1,030,000
	R1,650,000	R170,000	R1,480,000	R150,000	R1,330,000

Intercompany profits and transactions

	Reals	Rate	CDN$	Tax	After tax	
Opening inventory—Barros selling	90,000	1.94	46,392	18,557	27,835	**(a)**
Closing inventory—Barros selling	330,000	1.80	183,333	73,333	110,000	**(b)**
Sales and purchases	920,000	1.86	494,624			**(c)**
Receivables and payables	210,000	1.82	115,385			**(d)**
Dividend income (1,210,000 × 90%)	1,089,000	1.82	598,352			**(e)**
Deferred income taxes (Dec. 31, Year 5)						
Closing inventory **(b)**			73,333			**(f)**

(a) Temporal method:

Use rate of CDN$1 = R2.00 for all items in acquisition differential because all items are measured at historical cost.

	Balance Jan. 1/4	Amortization Year 4	Balance Year 4	Amortization Year 5	Balance Dec. 31/5	
Inventory	60,000	60,000	–	–	–	(g)
Patent	200,000	25,000	175,000	25,000	150,000	(h)
Goodwill	565,000	–	565,000	50,000	515,000	(i)
	825,000	85,000	740,000	75,000	665,000	(j)

Calculation of consolidated profit—Year 5

Profit of Parento		660,000
Less: Dividends from Barros **(e)**		598,352
Adjusted profit		61,648 **(k)**
Profit of Barros	829,451	
Add: Opening inventory profit **(a)**	27,835	
Less: Closing inventory profit **(b)**	(110,000)	
Less: Amortization of acquisition differential **(j)**	(75,000)	672,286 **(l)**
Profit		733,934

Attributable to
Shareholders of Parento (61,648 + 90% × **[l] 672,286**)		666,705 **(m)**
NCI (10% × **[l] 672,286**)		67,229 **(n)**
		733,934

Calculation of consolidated retained earnings—End of Year 5

Parento's retained earnings, end of Year 5		1,500,000
Barros' retained earnings, end of Year 5	943,223	
Barros' retained earnings, date of acquisition (1,350,000 / 2.00)	675,000	
Change since acquisition	268,223	
Closing inventory profit **(b)**	(110,000)	
Amortization of acquisition differential **(j) (85,000 + 75,000)**	(160,000)	
Adjusted change since acquisition	(1,777)	**(o)**
Parento's share @ 90%		(1,599)
Consolidated retained earnings, end of Year 5		1,498,401 **(p)**

Calculation of non-controlling interests—End of Year 5

NCI, date of acquisition (R600,000 / 2.00)		300,000
Change in Barros' retained earnings since acquisition **(o)**	(1,777)	
NCI's share @10%		(178)
		299,822 **(q)**

CONSOLIDATED STATEMENT OF FINANCIAL POSITION—at December 31, Year 5
(Temporal Method)

Property, plant, and equipment (8,000,000 + 2,500,000)	10,500,000
Accumulated depreciation (3,000,000 + 1,250,000)	(4,250,000)
Patents (0 + 0 + **[h] 150,000**)	150,000
Goodwill (0 + 0 + **[i] 515,000**)	515,000
Deferred income tax (0 + 0 + **[f] 73,333**)	73,333
Inventories (1,400,000 + 583,333 − **[b] 183,333**)	1,800,000
Accounts receivable (1,960,000 + 1,489,011 − **[d] 115,385**)	3,333,626
Cash (800,000 + 549,451)	1,349,451
	$13,471,410

(continued)

Ordinary shares	$ 5,000,000
Retained earnings **(p)**	1,498,401
Non-controlling interests **(q)**	299,822
Bonds payable (2,000,000 + 1,373,627)	3,373,627
Accounts payable (3,360,000 + 54,945 − **[d] 115,385**)	3,299,560
	$13,471,410

CONSOLIDATED STATEMENT OF PROFIT
for the Year Ended December 31, Year 5
(Temporal Method)

Sales (15,000,000 + 18,817,204 − **[c] 494,624**)	$33,322,580
Dividend income (598,352 − **[e] 598,352**)	0
	33,322,580
Cost of sales (11,509,352 + 15,089,984 − **[c] 494,624** + **[b] 183,333** − **[a] 46,392**)	26,241,653
Selling & administrative expense (2,100,000 + 1,293,011 + **[h] 25,000** + **[i] 50,000**)	3,468,011
Miscellaneous expense (889,000 + 1,075,269)	1,964,269
Exchange gain (0 + 32,339)	(32,339)
Income taxes (440,000 + 561,828 − **[b] 73,333** + **[a] 18,557**)	947,052
	32,588,646
Profit	$ 733,934
Attributable to	
Shareholders of Parento **(m)**	$ 666,705
NCI **(n)**	67,229

(b) Current rate method

Translate to Canadian dollars. Use average rate for amortization. Then, adjust to amount using closing rate at end of year.

	Balance Jan. 1/4	Amort Year 4	Adjust Year 4	Balance Dec. 31/4	Amort Year 5	Adjust Year 5	Balance Dec. 31/5	
Inventory	60,000[1]	61,538[2]	1,538[3]	–	–	–		**(ba)**
Patent	200,000[4]	25,641[5]	8,887[3]	183,246[6]	26,882[7]	8,471[8]	164,835[9]	**(bb)**
Goodwill	565,000[10]	–	26,623[3]	591,623[11]	53,763[12]	28,074[8]	565,934[13]	**(bc)**
	825,000	87,179	37,048	774,869	80,645	36,545	730,769	**(bd)**

Notes:

1. 120,000 / 2.00
2. 120,000 / 1.95
3. Exchange adjustment to get to desired amount at end of Year 4 as per next column
4. 400,000 / 2.00
5. 50,000 / 1.95
6. 350,000 / 1.91
7. 50,000 / 1.86
8. Exchange adjustment to get to desired amount at end of Year 5 as per next column
9. 300,000 / 1.82
10. 1,130,000 / 2.00
11. 1,130,000 / 1.91
12. 100,000 / 1.86
13. 1,030,000 / 1.82

Calculation of consolidated profit—Year 5

Profit of Parento		660,000
Less: Dividends from Barros **(e)**		598,352
Adjusted profit		61,648 **(be)**
Profit of Barros	733,871	
Add: Opening inventory profit **(a)**	27,835	
Less: Closing inventory profit **(b)**	(110,000)	
Less: Amortization of acquisition differential **(bd)**	(80,645)	571,061 **(bf)**
Profit		632,709
Attributable to		
Shareholders of Parento (61,648 + 90% × **[bf] 571,061**)		575,603 **(bg)**
NCI (10% × **[bf] 571,061**)		57,106 **(bh)**
		632,709

Calculation of consolidated retained earnings—End of Year 5

Parento's retained earnings, end of Year 5		1,500,000
Barros' retained earnings, end of Year 5	753,127	
Barros' retained earnings, date of acquisition (1,350,000/2.00)	675,000	
Change since acquisition	78,127	
Closing inventory profit **(b)**	(110,000)	
Amortization of acquisition differential **(bd)**	(167,824)	
	(199,697)	**(bi)**
Parento's share @ 90%		(179,727)
Consolidated retained earnings, end of Year 5		1,320,273 **(bj)**

Calculation of accumulated translation adjustment—End of Year 5

On Barros' separate-entity statement of financial position		307,312
Adjustments on consolidation (**[bd] 37,048** + **[bd] 36,545**)		73,593
		380,905
Attributable to		
Shareholders of Parento (90%)		342,814 **(bk)**
NCI (10%)		38,091
		380,905

Calculation of non-controlling interests—End of Year 5

NCI, date of acquisition (R600,000/2.00)		300,000
Change in Barros' retained earnings since acquisition **(bi)**	(199,697)	
NCI's share @10%		(19,970)
Share of accumulated translation adjustment **(bl)**		38,091
		318,121 **(bm)**

CONSOLIDATED STATEMENT OF FINANCIAL POSITION—at December 31, Year 5
(current rate method)

Property, plant, and equipment (8,000,000 + 2,747,252)	10,747,252
Accumulated depreciation (3,000,000 + 1,373,626)	(4,373,626)
Patents (0 + 0 + **[bb] 164,835**)	164,835
Goodwill (0 + 0 + **[bc] 565,934**)	565,934
Deferred income tax (0 + 0 + **[f] 73,333**)	73,333
Inventories (1,400,000 + 576,923 − **[b] 183,333**)	1,793,590
Accounts receivable (1,960,000 + 1,489,011 − **[d] 115,385**)	3,333,626
Cash (800,000 + 549,451)	1,349,451
	$13,654,395

(continued)

Ordinary shares	$ 5,000,000
Retained earnings **(bj)**	1,320,273
Accumulated translation adjustment **(bk)**	342,814
Non-controlling interests **(bm)**	318,121
Bonds payable (2,000,000 + 1,373,627)	3,373,627
Accounts payable (3,360,000 + 54,945 − **[d] 115,385**)	3,299,560
	$13,654,395

CONSOLIDATED STATEMENT OF COMPREHENSIVE INCOME
for the Year Ended December 31, Year 5

Sales (15,000,000 + 18,817,204 − **[c] 494,624**)	$33,322,580	
Dividend income (598,352 − **[e] 598,352**)	0	
	33,322,580	
Cost of sales (11,509,352 + 15,134,408 − **[c] 494,624**		
+ **[b] 183,333** − **[a] 46,392**)	26,286,077	
Selling & administrative expense (2,100,000 + 1,311,828		
+ **[bb] 26,882** + **[bc] 53,763**)	3,492,473	
Miscellaneous expense (889,000 + 1,075,269)	1,964,269	
Income taxes (440,000 + 561,828 − **[b] 73,333** + **[a] 18,557**)	947,052	
	32,689,871	
Profit	632,709	
Other comprehensive income		
Exchange adjustments (0 + 132,765 + **[bd] 36,545**)	169,310	**(bo)**
Comprehensive income	$ 802,019	
Profit attributable to		
Shareholders of Parento **(bg)**	$ 575,603	
NCI **(bh)**	57,106	
	$ 632,709	
Comprehensive income attributable to		
Shareholders of Parento (**[bg] 575,603** + 90% × **[bo] 169,310**)	$ 727,982	
NCI (**[bh] 57,106** + 10% × **[bo] 169,310**)	74,037	
	$ 802,019	

REVIEW QUESTIONS

L01   1. The temporal and current rate methods each produce different amounts for translation gains and losses due to the items at risk. Explain.

L01   2. What are the three major issues related to the translation of foreign currency financial statements?

L01   3. Why might a company want to hedge its balance sheet exposure? What is the paradox associated with hedging balance sheet exposure?

L03   4. How are gains and losses on financial instruments used to hedge the net investment in a self-sustaining foreign operation reported in the consolidated financial statements?

L02   5. What is the major objective to be achieved in the translation of foreign-currency–denominated financial statements?

L02   6. What should happen if a foreign subsidiary's financial statements have been prepared using accounting principles different from those used in Canada?

LO2   7. What is the difference between a self-sustaining and an integrated foreign operation? What method of translation should be used for each?

LO3   8. What translation method should be used for a self-sustaining subsidiary that operates in a highly inflationary environment? Why?

LO2   9. How are translation exchange gains and losses reflected in financial statements if the foreign operation's functional currency is the Canadian dollar? Would the treatment be different if the foreign operation's functional currency were not the Canadian dollar? Explain.

LO3, 4   10. Does the temporal method use the same unit of measure as the current rate method? Explain.

LO5   11. The amount of the accumulated foreign exchange adjustments appearing in the translated financial statements of a subsidiary could be different from the amount appearing in the consolidated financial statements. Explain how.

LO5   12. The application of the lower of cost and net realizable value requirement to the translated financial statements requires different treatment with regard to the two classifications of foreign operations described in IAS 21. Explain fully.

LO3, 4   13. "If the translation of an integrated foreign operation produced a gain, the translation of the same company could produce a loss if the operation were instead considered to be self-sustaining." Do you agree with this statement? Explain.

LO1   14. Explain how the temporal method produces results that are consistent with the normal measurement and valuation of assets and liabilities for domestic transactions and operations.

LO5   15. When translating the financial statements of the subsidiary at the date of acquisition by the parent, the exchange rate on the date of acquisition is used to translate plant assets rather than the exchange rate on the date when the subsidiary acquired the plant assets. Explain the rationale for this practice.

LO3, 4   16. If the sales of a foreign subsidiary all occurred on one day during the year, would the sales be translated at the average rate for the year or the rate on the date of the sales? Explain.

CASES

Case 11-1
LO1, 3, 4   The Rider Corporation operates throughout Canada buying and selling widgets. In hopes of expanding into more profitable markets, the company recently decided to open a small subsidiary in California. On October 1, Year 2, Rider invested CDN$928,000 in Riderville USA Ltd. Its investment was immediately converted into US$940,000. One-half of this money was used to purchase land to be held for the possible construction of a plant, and one-half was invested in held-for-trading equity securities. Nothing further happened at Riderville throughout the remainder of Year 2. However, the U.S. dollar weakened relative to the Canadian dollar and the exchange rate at December 31, Year 2, was US$1 = CDN$0.95. Fortunately, the value of the land purchased by Riderville increased to US$500,000 and the securities were worth US$490,000 at the end of the year.

The accountant for Rider realized that the investments of the U.S. subsidiary had increased in value but did not plan to report this unrealized gain in the consolidated financial statements. However, the CEO wants to report the true economic value of these investments.

Required:

(a) What is the true economic value of the assets owned by Riderville USA at the end of Year 2?

(b) Can Rider report the economic value of these assets in the consolidated balance sheet under IFRSs? If not, how should Rider report each of these assets on its consolidated balance sheet and how should the related gains be reported? Assume that the securities are classified as fair value through profit or loss.

Case 11-2
LO4

Summarized below are the balances in the accumulated unrealized exchange accounts in the consolidated balance sheets of four companies at the end of two successive years. Each company reported in footnote disclosures that its foreign subsidiaries were self-sustaining and that the financial statements of the subsidiaries had been translated into Canadian dollars using the current rate method. Assume that the balance sheets of each of the companies' foreign subsidiaries have not changed significantly during Year 6.

	Accumulated unrealized exchange gains (losses) ($millions)	
	Year 6	Year 5
A Company	201	30
B Company	52	(75)
C Company	(170)	(190)
D Company	(180)	(164)

Required:

For each company, give a logical explanation for the change that has occurred in the accumulated unrealized exchange accounts during the year. For each company, indicate whether the Canadian dollar is stronger or weaker in Year 6, compared with Year 5.

Case 11-3
LO2, 4

Nova Mine Engineering is a junior Canadian company with a variety of operating subsidiaries and other undertakings that provide mine engineering and management services in Canada and in several less-developed countries. One of these subsidiaries is active in Zimbabwe, which is rich in mineral resources and has an active mining industry. This company, Zimbabwe Platinum Management (ZPM), is under review prior to year-end translation and consolidation. The staff of ZPM consists primarily of junior and intermediate Nova staff who have been seconded to the operation on one- to three-year terms. Between the companies there is information flow but no product movement. Capital investment in Zimbabwe is restricted to movable equipment and working capital with a value of about CDN$3,000,000.

Management of Nova has long been concerned about its inability to hedge against fluctuations in the Zimbabwean dollar. All payments to ZPM from the state Mineral Marketing Corporation have recently been made in this currency, rather than in U.S. dollars as specified in earlier contracts. It is this inability to hedge that has increased Nova's concern about the long-run fit of ZPM within the portfolio of Nova companies, as well as the current financial statement presentation. The currency has declined in value by 65% during the year. Other concerns include Zimbabwe's persistent high inflation, recently about 35%, which is expected to increase even further. Political uncertainty is also a concern, as a result of recent nationalizations in the agricultural sector and growing unrest among the poor.

Required:

In a briefing note, advise senior management of Nova how the investment in the subsidiary ZPM should be measured and reported, and what disclosures should be made with respect to this investment in the annual report of the parent company.

(case prepared by Peter Secord, St. Mary's University)

Case 11-4
LO2, 3, 4

Vulcan Manufacturing Limited (VML) is a Canadian-based multinational plastics firm, with subsidiaries in several foreign countries and worldwide consolidated total assets of $500 million. VML's shares are listed on a Canadian stock exchange. VML is attracted to developing countries by their growing demand for its products. In recognition of trade barriers designed to encourage domestic production in those countries, and in order to service local demand, VML incorporated a foreign subsidiary in a South American country on September 1, Year 4. The subsidiary, South American Plastics Inc. (SAPI), manufactures patented sheet plastic and sells virtually all of its output locally. Also, almost all labour and raw materials are provided locally. SAPI finances its day-to-day activities from its own operations and local borrowing.

During Year 4 and Year 5, the South American country suffered an inflation rate of more than 100%, accompanied by substantial devaluation of the local currency and a drastic increase in interest rates. The government is expected to impose wage and price controls in Year 6. The inflation rate is expected to stabilize at more moderate levels sometime in Year 6 or Year 7.

The CFO of VML has recently received SAPI's draft balance sheet as at August 31, Year 5 (Exhibit I), together with some comments prepared by SAPI's controller (Exhibit II). He is somewhat surprised by the return on investment of nearly 12%. This figure is well above the target rate agreed upon for bonus purposes, which was set at 3% in recognition of start-up costs associated with the first year of operations. The apparently favourable performance will result in large bonuses for SAPI's management.

Increases in SAPI's domestic selling price have kept pace with the general rate of inflation and increases in input prices and borrowing costs in the South American country. The CFO is satisfied that the inflation and devaluation the country has experienced has not seriously affected SAPI's cash flows from operations.

In the annual report to Canadian shareholders for the year ended August 31, Year 5, the CFO wants to communicate to shareholders the economic impact that inflation and devaluation in the South American country have had on VML's investment in SAPI. He is concerned that gains or losses arising from translation of the statements in accordance with IAS 21 will mislead shareholders.

EXHIBIT I

SOUTH AMERICAN PLASTICS INC.
Extracts from Draft Balance Sheet as at August 31, Year 5 (in Thousands)

Assets

Cash	FC* 10,020
Held-to-maturity investments	3,120
Accounts receivable	93,000
Inventory (at cost)	67,200
Prepaid expenses	8,040
	181,380
Plant assets	143,111
Less accumulated depreciation	14,311
	128,800
	FC 310,180

Liabilities and Shareholders' Equity

Current monetary liabilities	FC 65,140
Long-term debt	157,200
	222,340
Common shares	51,000
Retained earnings	36,840
	87,840
	FC 310,180

An FC is a unit of the currency used in the South American country in which SAPI is located.

EXHIBIT II

SOUTH AMERICAN PLASTICS INC.
Controller's Comments on Financial Statements

1. Opening Balances:
   SAPI's balance sheet on September 1, Year 4, consisted of cash of FC208,200,000; long-term debt of FC157,200,000; and common shares of FC51,000,000.
2. Held-to-maturity Investments:
   The held-to-maturity investments were purchased when 1FC = $0.31. The aggregate market value for the investments at August 31, Year 5, was FC3,000,000 due to an increase in interest rates in the market.
3. Inventories:
   Inventories were purchased when 1FC = $0.30. VML values inventory at the lower of cost and net realizable value. The aggregate net realizable value of the inventory was FC100,000,000 at August 31, Year 5.
4. Prepaid Expenses:
   The amounts, representing prepaid rent and property taxes, were paid when 1FC = $0.26.
5. Plant Assets:
   Plant assets were purchased shortly after the date of SAPI's formation at a time when 1FC = $0.40. The recoverable amount of the fixed assets (in their current condition) was FC200,000,000 at August 31, Year 5.
6. Current Liabilities:
   All current liabilities were incurred at a time when 1FC = $0.25.

(continued)

EXHIBIT II **(continued)**

7. Long-Term Debt:
   The debt represents a floating interest rate loan, which will be repaid in foreign currency units on August 31, Year 8.
8. Retained Earnings:
   No dividends were paid during the Year 5 fiscal year.
9. Exchange Rates:

Sep. 1, Year 4	1 FCU = $0.40
Aug. 31, Year 5	1 FCU = $0.20
Average rate for year	1 FCU = $0.30

The CFO believes that the exchange gains and losses will obscure the true impact of foreign inflation and devaluation on SAPI's economic value in Canadian-dollar terms. He has called the audit partner and you, the Senior, into his office. The following conversation ensues:

CFO: We have to issue our financial statements soon, and we have to apply IAS 21 to our South American subsidiary. I must confess that I don't know IAS 21 as well as you two do. My staff tells me that we must use a special method this year, due to the local hyper-inflation, although I confess that I don't see why. Apparently we will have a choice between the temporal method and the current rate method once the inflation rate stabilizes, which I expect to happen in Year 6 or Year 7. I am very reluctant to use a special method on this year's statements. It forces me to include fictitious gains and losses in our consolidated income statement.

Partner: Your staff is correct in stating that IAS 21 requires the use of a special method for the year just ended. However, shareholders should not be misled by exchange gains or losses in comprehensive income provided that they are fully disclosed as such.

CFO: I guess I just do not understand IAS 21. For example, how might the adoption of the current rate method in Year 6 or Year 7 improve matters? It seems to me that an overall exchange loss will arise if the rate keeps on going down. What does the loss mean? As long as our subsidiary's cash flows keep pace with local inflation, it will be able to maintain its expected rate of profitability and therefore its ability to pay dividends to us. Yet shareholders will see an exchange loss!

Partner: I will have Senior prepare a report that explains to you how the exchange gains or losses under either translation method tie in with the notion of risk underlying IAS 21. We will also explain how this notion alleviates your concern about communicating the true economic risk to shareholders. Senior will recommend ways to tell the whole story to shareholders.

CFO: Sounds great. I would also like Senior to provide advice on any other important issues related to SAPI. For starters, I have some concerns about the way our bonus plan for SAPI's management is working. One possibility I am considering is to evaluate SAPI's performance in Canadian-dollar terms.

Required:

Prepare the report to the CFO.

(CICA adapted)

Case 11-5
LO5

RAD Communications Ltd. (RAD), a Canadian public company, recently purchased the shares of TOP Systems Inc. (TOP), a Canadian-controlled private corporation. Both companies are in the communications industry and own television, radio, and magazine and newspaper businesses. Both companies have subsidiaries operating worldwide.

After it purchased TOP, RAD decided to divest itself of some of the TOP subsidiaries (the Group). BritCo is a private British company that is in the process of acquiring the shares of the Group from TOP. The purchase price for the Group being sold has been determined, in general terms, to be a fixed price adjusted for the working capital balance of the Group at RAD's year-end date of March 31, Year 9. March 31, Year 9, was also the closing date of the purchase-and-sale transaction. The parties have 90 days after the closing date of the transaction to agree on the calculation of the working capital balance.

Janis Marczynski, the chief negotiator for BritCo, has approached Paul Bouchard, a partner at Bouchard and Beatrix, Chartered Accountants (B&B), to provide her with advice on the purchase transaction. Specifically, Marczynski wants B&B to review the agreement and relevant facts to determine whether RAD has appropriately determined the amount of the closing working capital. Furthermore, if any matters come to B&B's attention that suggest the financial statements of the Group may have misled BritCo, then B&B should bring these items to her attention.

Marczynski has stated that BritCo now thinks that the purchase price for the Group may be too high and is looking for ways to reduce the price. Thus, she wants to be made aware of any possible points that she can use in her final negotiations.

BritCo has provided B&B with a copy of the purchase-and-sale agreement, excerpts of which are presented in Exhibit III.

EXHIBIT III

TOP SYSTEMS INC. (VENDOR) AND BRITCO (PURCHASER) EXCERPTS FROM PURCHASE-AND-SALE AGREEMENT

5.1. The share purchase price shall be adjusted by an amount equal to the "consolidated working capital." This amount is hereafter referred to as the "price adjustment," as defined in clause 5.2.

5.2. The price adjustment shall be determined as follows:
   a. Combine the working capital of the Group (aggregated current assets of the Group less aggregated current liabilities of the Group), less the non-controlling interest as at March 31, Year 9, adjusted for any sums payable to or receivable from other members of the Group.
   b. Include accounts for each of the companies of the Group and, in the case of those companies with subsidiaries, on a consolidated basis, in accordance with International Financial Reporting Standards ("IFRSs").

5.3. The vendor shall prepare a draft consolidated working capital statement as soon as practicable after the agreement date.

5.4. For the purpose of review, the vendor agrees to instruct JR to permit the purchaser to examine all final working papers, schedules, and other documents used or prepared by JR.

5.5. If the purchaser objects to the calculation of the price adjustment, the purchaser shall give notice in writing to the vendor. The purchaser shall set out in reasonable detail the nature of any such objections and the amount by which the purchase price will be reduced if the purchaser's objections are accepted. The vendor shall have the right to recover from the purchaser any costs associated with reviewing and analyzing objections of the purchaser that are of a frivolous and unsupportable nature.

It is now May 15, Year 9, and BritCo has received the unaudited consolidated working capital statement of the Group prepared by RAD (Exhibit IV). Marczynski is concerned about the dramatic increase in the working capital compared with that reflected in previous financial statements.

RAD has arranged for Jeanette Riley, Chartered Accountant (JR), the auditor of TOP's financial statements for the year in question, to supply the necessary working papers to assist B&B in its review. JR will provide B&B with her working papers once they have completed their audit for Year 9. RAD has already provided B&B with excerpts of JR's working papers for Year 8, reproduced in Exhibit V, copies of which TOP had obtained informally from the audit staff during the course of the audit.

EXHIBIT IV

CONSOLIDATED WORKING CAPITAL STATEMENT OF THE GROUP (NOTE 1)
at March 31, Year 9
(in Millions of Canadian Dollars)

Current assets	
Cash	$ 215
Receivables	19,763
Inventory	4,225
Prepaids	7,655
Other	2,917
	34,775
Current liabilities	
Bank indebtedness	7,000
Accounts payable	1,191
Deferred revenue	6,332
Other	1,345
	15,868
Consolidated working capital (price adjustment)	$18,907

Note 1: Comprises the accounts of the companies being sold; i.e., GermanyCo., FranceCo., U.K.Co., SwitzerlandCo., and a Canadian subsidiary, CanadaCo.

EXHIBIT V

EXCERPTS FROM THE WORKING PAPERS OF JR
RELATING TO THE AUDIT OF TOP SYSTEMS INC. AND ITS SUBSIDIARIES
FOR THE YEAR 8 FISCAL PERIOD

1. Only selected subsidiaries of TOP were audited. Those companies were audited on a limited basis only, owing to the consolidated materiality level.
2. Included in the "Receivables" balance of FranceCo. is an intercompany note receivable from a Canadian company that is not part of the Group. The note bears interest at the prime rate in Canada plus 3%. The rate charged on the note was generally about 4% below interest rates on French notes of similar terms and risks at the time that the note was issued. The Canadian company has recorded the note as a long-term obligation.
3. "Other current assets" include an amount reflecting the refundable dividend tax on hand (RDTOH). The amount of the RDTOH was immaterial; thus, no audit work in this area was warranted.

(continued)

EXHIBIT V   **(continued)**

4. Included in the "Receivables" balance are certain income tax refunds that GermanyCo. will receive when dividends are paid to its shareholders. No accruals are made for foreign withholding taxes that may be payable when dividends are paid by GermanyCo.

5. "Other current assets" include an amount for goodwill. This goodwill relates to the acquisition of a subsidiary by CanadaCo.

6. "Deferred revenues" include payments made by advertisers for long-term contracts. Some of these contracts can be for up to five years. Some advertisers pay up-front signing fees, which are taken into income when received. Some advertisers who sign up for long-term contracts may receive one additional year of free advertising. Advertisers can elect to take this free year at the beginning or at the end of the contract term.

7. "Prepaids" include costs for various broadcasting licences. The accounts include the initial costs of obtaining the licences, such as various regulatory fees, legal and accounting fees, other consulting fees, etc., and various fees for limited-term licences, ranging from one- to ten-year periods.

8. Certain printing presses of SwitzerlandCo. were leased instead of being purchased. The future lease payments were not disclosed in the consolidated financial statements. The lease was immaterial and thus did not warrant any further audit work.

9. A Belgian company that is not being acquired effectively hedged certain current debts payable by CanadaCo. The financial statements did not record any gain or loss because of the fluctuations in the value of the Canadian dollar.

10. Foreign exchange losses on transactions were included as part of "Deferred revenue," while gains were taken into income in the current period.

You, a CA, work for B&B. Bouchard asks you to draft a memo addressing the concerns and requirements of Marczynski.

Required:

Prepare the memo.

(CICA adapted)

Case 11-6
LO4

Mega Communications Inc. (MCI) is a Canadian-owned public company operating throughout North America. Its core business is communications media, including newspapers, radio, television and cable. The company's year-end is December 31.

You, a CA, have recently joined MCI's corporate office as a finance director, reporting to the chief financial officer, Robert Allen. It is October Year 3. Mr. Allen has asked you to prepare a report that discusses the accounting issues that might arise with the auditors during their visit in November.

MCI's growth in Year 3 was achieved through expansion into the United States by acquiring a controlling interest in a number of newspapers, television, and cable companies. Since the U.S. side of MCI's operations is now significant, management has decided to change the reporting currency from the Canadian dollar to the U.S. dollar for MCI's consolidated financial statements.

MCI uses the Canadian dollar for its internal record keeping and to account for its Canadian operations. All of MCI's foreign subsidiaries, which are all wholly owned, use the local currency for internal record keeping and for reporting purposes. MCI's shareholders' equity at the beginning of the period was $220 million, including a separately disclosed cumulative foreign exchange gain of $45 million primarily relating to its U.S. subsidiaries. Management merged this balance with retained earnings because "the operations it relates to are no longer considered foreign for accounting purposes, and as a result, no foreign currency exposure will arise."

With recent trends to international free trade, MCI decided to position itself for future expansion into the South American market. Therefore, in Year 3, MCI bought a company that owns a radio network in a country in South America, which has high inflation. MCI was willing to incur losses in the start-up, since it was confident that in the long run it would be profitable. The South American country has had a democratic government for the last two years. Its government's objectives are to open the country's borders to trade and lower its inflation rate. The government was rather reluctant to let a foreign company purchase such a powerful communication tool. In exchange for the right to buy the network, MCI agreed, among other conditions, not to promote any political party, to broadcast only pre-approved public messages, and to let the government examine its books at the government's convenience. Management has recorded this investment on the books using the cost method.

In Year 3, MCI acquired a conglomerate, Cyril's Holdings (CH), which held substantial assets in the communications business. Over the past three months, MCI has sold off 80% of CH's non-communications related businesses. In the current month, MCI sold CH's hotel and recreational property business for $175 million, realizing a gain of $22 million ($14.5 million after tax). The assets related to the non-communications businesses were scattered throughout the U.S. and MCI lacked the industry expertise to value them accurately. Management therefore found it difficult to determine the net realizable value of each of these assets at the time CH was acquired.

Newspaper readership has peaked leaving no room for expansion. In Year 2, to increase its share of the market, MCI bought all the assets of a competing newspaper for $10 million. In Year 3, MCI ceased publication of the competing newspaper and liquidated the assets for $4.5 million.

In Year 3, MCI decided to rationalize its television operations. Many of CH's acquisitions in the television business included stations in areas already being served by other stations operated by MCI. MCI systematically identified stations that are duplicating services and do not fit with MCI's long-range objectives. These assets have been segregated on the balance sheet and classified as current. The company anticipates generating a gain on the disposal of the entire pool of assets, although losses are expected on some of the individual stations. Operating results are capitalized in the pool. Once a particular station is sold, the resulting gain or loss is reflected in income.

Nine stations are in the pool at the present time. In Year 3, three were sold, resulting in gains of $6.5 million after tax. Losses are expected to occur on several of the remaining stations. Although serious negotiations with prospective buyers are not underway at present, the company hopes to have disposed of them in early Year 4. In order to facilitate the sale of these assets, MCI is considering taking back mortgages.

In Year 3, MCI estimated the fair market value of its intangible assets at $250 million. Included, as intangibles, are newspaper and magazine circulation lists, cable subscriber lists, and broadcast licences. Some of these assets have been acquired through the purchase of existing businesses; others have been generated internally by operations that have been part of MCI for decades.

Amounts paid for acquired intangibles are not difficult to determine; however, it has taken MCI staff some time to determine the costs of internally generated intangibles. In order to increase subscriptions for print and electronic media, MCI spends heavily on subscription drives by way of advertisements, cold calls, and free products. For the non-acquired intangibles, MCI staff has examined the accounting records for the past 10 years and have identified expenditures totalling $35 million that were expensed in prior years. These costs relate to efforts to expand customer bases. In addition, independent appraisers have determined the fair market value of these internally generated intangibles to be in the range of $60 million to $80 million. In order to be conservative, management has decided to reflect these intangibles on the December 31, Year 3, balance sheet at $60 million.

The market value of companies in the communications industry has been escalating in the past few years, indicating that the value of the underlying assets (largely intangibles) is increasing over time. MCI management would prefer not to amortize broadcasting licences, arguing that these licences do not lose any value and, in this industry, actually increase in value over time.

One of the items included in the intangible category is MCI's patented converter, which was an unplanned by-product of work being done on satellite communications devices a few years ago.

MCI has sold $25 million of its accounts receivables to a medium-sized financial intermediary, PayLater Corp. The receivables are being re-sold to a numbered company whose common shares are owned by PayLater Corp. MCI receives one half of the consideration in cash and one half in subordinate non-voting, redeemable shares of the numbered company, bearing a dividend rate of 9%. The dividend payments and share redemption are based on the collectibility of the receivables. The purchase price is net of a 4% provision for doubtful accounts. MCI has recorded a loss of $1 million on this transaction. PayLater has an option to return the receivables to MCI at any time for 94% of their face value.

The arrival of direct broadcast satellite that transmits multiple TV signals to digital boxes will revolutionize the television industry. The technology is expected to provide the choice of over 150 channels. In response to this new development, which is seen as a threat, the communication industry is developing its own interactive communication services at a cost of over $6 billion. This service will allow viewers to interact with banks, shops, and other viewers through the television. MCI hopes this will allow it to maintain its market share of viewers.

MCI has invested in the installation of fibre optic cable, which can transmit far more, far faster than conventional cable. The cost of the cable itself is negligible. MCI will be using it for transmission between its stations in two major Canadian cities. MCI needed only six cables to link all its television and radio stations between the two cities, but decided that it might as well put in 36 cables, since it was doing the digging anyway. To date, MCI has sold six cables and charges a monthly fee to new owners to cover their share of all maintenance expenses. MCI is leasing 10 other cables for 15-year periods.

Required:

Prepare the report.

PROBLEMS

Note: Some problems use direct exchange rate quotations, while others use indirect quotations. For direct quotations, the foreign currency is multiplied by the exchange rate to arrive at Canadian dollars; for indirect quotations, division is used.

Problem 11-1
LO3, 4, 6

On December 31, Year 1, Precision Manufacturing Inc. (PMI) of Edmonton purchased 100% of the outstanding ordinary shares of Sandora Corp. of Flint, Michigan.

Sandora's comparative statement of financial position and Year 2 income statement are as follows:

STATEMENT OF FINANCIAL POSITION
at December 31

	Year 2	Year 1
Plant and equipment (net)	US$ 6,600,000	US$ 7,300,000
Inventory	5,700,000	6,300,000
Accounts receivable	6,100,000	4,700,000
Cash	780,000	900,000
	US$19,180,000	US$19,200,000
Ordinary shares	US$ 5,000,000	US$ 5,000,000
Retained earnings	7,480,000	7,000,000
Bonds payable—due Dec. 31, Year 6	4,800,000	4,800,000
Current liabilities	1,900,000	2,400,000
	US$19,180,000	US$19,200,000

INCOME STATEMENT
for the Year Ended December 31, Year 2

Sales	US$30,000,000
Cost of purchases	23,400,000
Change in inventory	600,000
Depreciation expense	700,000
Other expenses	3,800,000
	28,500,000
Profit	US$ 1,500,000

Additional Information

- Exchange rates

Dec. 31, Year 1	US$1 = CDN$1.10
Sep. 30, Year 2	US$1 = CDN$1.07
Dec. 31, Year 2	US$1 = CDN$1.05
Average for Year 2	US$1 = CDN$1.08

- Sandora declared and paid dividends on September 30, Year 2.
- The inventories on hand on December 31, Year 2, were purchased when the exchange rate was US$1 = CDN$1.06.

Required:

(a) Assume that Sandora's functional currency is the Canadian dollar:

  (i) Calculate the Year 2 exchange gain (loss) that would result from the translation of Sandora's financial statements.

  (ii) Translate the Year 2 financial statements into Canadian dollars.

(b) Assume that Sandora's functional currency is the U.S. dollar:

  (i) Calculate the Year 2 exchange gain (loss) that would result from the translation of Sandora's financial statements and would be reported in other comprehensive income.

  (ii) Translate the Year 2 financial statements into Canadian dollars.

(c) Which functional currency would Sandora prefer to use if it wants to show the following:

  (i) The strongest solvency position for the company

  (ii) The best return on shareholders' equity

  Briefly explain your answers.

Problem 11-2
LO3, 4, 6
On December 31, Year 1, Kelly Corporation of Toronto paid 13 million Libyan dinars (LD) for 100% of the outstanding common shares of Arkenu Company of Libya. On this date, the fair values of Arkenu's identifiable assets and liabilities were equal to their carrying amounts. Arkenu's comparative balance sheets and Year 2 income statement are as follows:

BALANCE SHEET
at December 31

	Year 2	Year 1
Current monetary assets	LD10,780,000	LD 9,600,000
Inventory	1,800,000	2,400,000
Plant and equipment (net)	6,600,000	7,200,000
	LD19,180,000	LD19,200,000
Current monetary liabilities	LD 1,900,000	LD 2,400,000
Bonds payable, due Dec. 31, Year 6	4,800,000	4,800,000
Common shares	5,000,000	5,000,000
Retained earnings	7,480,000	7,000,000
	LD19,180,000	LD19,200,000

INCOME STATEMENT
for the Year Ended December 31, Year 2

Sales	LD16,000,000
Inventory, Jan. 1	2,400,000
Purchases	10,840,000
Inventory, Dec. 31	(1,800,000)
Depreciation expense	600,000
Other expenses	2,360,000
	14,400,000
Net income	LD 1,600,000

Additional Information

- Exchange rates

Dec. 31, Year 1	LD1 = $0.52
Sep. 30, Year 2	LD1 = $0.62
Dec. 31, Year 2	LD1 = $0.65
Average for Year 2	LD1 = $0.58

- Arkenu Company declared and paid dividends on September 30, Year 2.
- The inventories on hand on December 31, Year 2, were purchased when the exchange rate was LD1 = $0.63.

Required:

(a) Assume that Arkenu's functional currency is the Canadian dollar: *temporal*

    (i) Calculate the Year 2 exchange gain or loss that would result from the translation of Arkenu's financial statements.

    (ii) Prepare translated financial statements for Year 2.

(b) Assume that Arkenu's functional currency is the Libyan dinar:

    (i) Calculate the Year 2 exchange gain or loss that would result from the translation of Arkenu's financial statements.

    (ii) Prepare translated financial statements for Year 2.

    (iii) Calculate the amount of goodwill that would appear on the December 31, Year 2, consolidated balance sheet if there was an impairment loss of LD50,000 during the year.

    (iv) Calculate the amount, description, and location of the exchange gain or loss that would appear in Kelly's Year 2 consolidated financial statements.

(c) Which functional currency would Arkenu prefer to use if it wants to show the following:

    (i) The strongest solvency position for the company

    (ii) The best return on shareholders' equity

    Briefly explain your answers.

Problem 11-3
LO3, 7   On January 1, Year 3, Jets Ltd., a Winnipeg-based private company, purchased 80% of the shares of Buenos Inc. for 1,900,000 Argentine pesos (AP)—an amount which, at that date, translated to $655,172.

The Year 3 financial statements for Buenos are as follows:

BALANCE SHEET
at December 31, Year 3

Cash	AP	820,000
Accounts receivable		317,500
Inventory		730,000
Plant assets, net		1,722,500
		AP3,590,000
Current monetary liabilities	AP	380,000
Notes payable		700,000
Common shares		900,000
Retained earnings		1,610,000
		AP3,590,000

INCOME STATEMENT
for the Year Ended December 31, Year 3

Sales	AP10,350,000
Cost of sales	6,400,000
Gross profit	3,950,000
Other expenses	3,590,000
Net income	AP 360,000

Additional Information

- The FIFO inventory method is used. The opening inventory, which was purchased before December 31, Year 2, cost AP600,000. The exchange rate at the time of inventory purchase was $1 = AP2.71.
  The purchases during the year were

	AP	Exchange rate
Purchase Number 1	2,000,000	$1 = AP3.0
Purchase Number 2	4,530,000	$1 = AP3.12

- The plant assets were purchased when the company was formed (January 1, Year 1). The common shares were issued at the same time. The exchange rate at that date was $1 = AP1.5. The cost of the plant assets is AP2,450,000, and the accumulated depreciation is AP727,500 at December 31, Year 3. Depreciation expense of AP122,500 is included with other expenses.
- The notes payable are due on January 1, Year 7, and were issued on December 31, Year 2.
- The "sales" and "other expenses" on the income statement were incurred evenly throughout the year.
- The dividends of AP200,000 were paid on December 31, Year 3.
- The balances in pesos at December 31, Year 2, were as follows:

Cash	AP 450,000
Accounts receivable	AP 405,000
Current monetary liabilities	AP(250,000)
Notes payable	AP(700,000)

- Exchange rates:

Dec. 31, Year 2	$1 = AP2.9
Jan. 1, Year 3	$1 = AP2.9
Year 3 average	$1 = AP3.25
Dec. 31, Year 3	$1 = AP3.6

Required:

(a) There will be a foreign exchange gain or loss on the translated income statement prepared in Part (b). Prepare a schedule to calculate the foreign exchange gain or loss under the temporal method.

(b) Prepare the Canadian-dollar income statement for Buenos for Year 3, using the temporal method and assuming that the income statement will be used to consolidate with Jets Ltd.

(CGA-Canada adapted)

Problem 11-4
LO3, 4, 5, 7

On January 1, Year 1, P Company (a Canadian company) purchased 90% of S Company (located in a foreign country) at a cost of 14,400 foreign currency units (FC).

The carrying amounts of S Company's net assets were equal to fair values on this date except for plant and equipment, which had a fair value of FC22,000, with a remaining useful life of 10 years. A goodwill impairment loss of FC100 occurred evenly throughout Year 1.

The following exchange rates were in effect during Year 1:

Jan. 1	FC1 = $1.10
Average for year	FC1 = $1.16
When ending inventory purchased	FC1 = $1.19
Dec. 31	FC1 = $1.22

The statement of financial position of S Company on January 1, Year 1, is as follows:

	S Company (FC)
Plant and equipment (net)	20,000
Inventory	8,000
Monetary assets (current)	10,000
	38,000
Ordinary shares	10,000
Retained earnings	3,000
Bonds payable (mature in eight years)	16,000
Current liabilities	9,000
	38,000

The December 31, Year 1, financial statements of P Company (in $) and S Company (in FC) are shown below:

STATEMENT OF FINANCIAL POSITION

	P Company $	S Company FC
Plant and equipment (net)	60,000	18,000
Investment in S Company (at cost)	15,840	—
Inventory	30,000	11,000
Monetary assets (current)	31,552	17,000
	137,392	46,000
Ordinary shares	30,000	10,000
Retained earnings	41,392	8,000
Bonds payable	40,000	16,000
Current monetary liabilities	26,000	12,000
	137,392	46,000

INCOME STATEMENT

	P Company $	S Company FC
Sales	360,000	100,000
Dividend income	4,392	—
Cost of sales	(180,000)	(59,000)
Other expenses (including depreciation)	(155,000)	(32,000)
Profit	29,392	9,000

Dividends were declared on December 31, Year 1, in the amount of $22,000 by P Company and FC4,000 by S Company.

Required:

(a) Prepare the December 31, Year 1, consolidated financial statements, assuming that S Company's functional currency is each of the following:

  (i) The Canadian dollar
  (ii) The foreign currency unit

(b) Now assume that P Company is a private company. It uses ASPE and has chosen to use the equity method to report its investment in S Company. Calculate the balance in the investment account at December 31, Year 1, assuming that S Company's functional currency is the Canadian dollar.

Problem 11-5
LO3

Mex Ltd. is an integrated foreign subsidiary. At the end of the current year, the inventory of the company was as follows:

Cost	14,862,000 pesos
Net realizable value	12,100,000 pesos

Applying the lower of cost and net realizable value, the company wrote the inventory down by Ps2,762,000 for presentation in its financial statements. When these financial statements were received by the parent company in Canada for translation, it was determined that the year-end spot rate was $1 = Ps382. The closing inventory at cost is composed of the following:

Purchase	Amount in pesos	Historical exchange rate
1	3,200,000	$1 = Ps341
2	6,132,000	$1 = Ps360
3	5,530,000	$1 = Ps375

Required:

(a) At what amount would the inventory be shown on the translated balance sheet of Mex? And what amount of loss from write-down would appear on the translated income statement?

(b) If the year-end spot rate was $1 = Ps281, at what amount would the inventory be shown on the translated balance sheet? And what amount of loss from write-down would appear on the translated income statement?

(CGA-Canada adapted)

Problem 11-6
LO3, 4

Maple Limited (Maple) was incorporated on January 2, Year 1, and commenced active operations immediately in Greece. Common shares were issued on the date of incorporation for 100,000 euros (€), and no more common shares have been issued since then.

On December 31, Year 4, the Oak Company (Oak) purchased 100% of the outstanding common shares of Maple. The balance sheet for Maple at December 31, Year 10, was as follows:

Cash	€ 100,000
Accounts receivable (Note 1)	200,000
Inventory (Note 2)	300,000
Equipment—net (Note 3)	1,100,000
	€1,700,000
Accounts payable	€ 250,000
Bonds payable (Note 4)	700,000
Common shares	100,000
Retained earnings	650,000
	€1,700,000

Additional Information

- The accounts receivable relate to sales occurring evenly throughout the month of December, Year 10.
- Maple uses the FIFO method to account for its inventory. The inventory available for sale during the year was purchased as follows:

Date of purchase	Cost of purchase	Exchange rate
December 31, Year 9	€100,000	€1 = $1.56
March 1, Year 10	1,000,000	€1 = $1.60
November 1, Year 10	180,000	€1 = $1.63

- The equipment was purchased on May 26, Year 4.
- The bonds were issued on May 26, Year 4, to finance the purchase of the equipment.
- Maple reported net income of €200,000, which was earned evenly throughout the year, and paid dividends of €160,000 on July 1, Year 10.
- Foreign exchange rates were as follows:

January 2, Year 1	€1 = $1.30
May 26, Year 4	€1 = $1.40
December 31, Year 4	€1 = $1.42
December 31, Year 9	€1 = $1.56
July 1, Year 10	€1 = $1.61
Average for Year 10	€1 = $1.59
Average for December Year 10	€1 = $1.64
December 31, Year 10	€1 = $1.66

Required:

(a) Translate the balance sheet of Maple at December 31, Year 10, into Canadian dollars assuming that Maple's functional currency is the Canadian dollar. Assume that the translated balance sheet will be consolidated with Oak's balance sheet. For retained earnings, simply use the amount required to balance your balance sheet.

(b) Calculate the foreign exchange gain or loss on the bonds payable for the year ended December 31, Year 10, and state how it would be reported on the year-end financial statements.

(c) Prepare an independent calculation of the unrealized exchange gains or losses that would be reported in other comprehensive income for Year 10, assuming that Maple's functional currency is the euro.

(d) Since the current rate method uses the closing rate to translate equipment, the translated amount should represent the fair value of the equipment in Canadian dollars. Do you agree or disagree? Briefly explain.

(CGA-Canada adapted)

Problem 11-7
LO1, 3, 4

In preparation for translating the financial statements of a foreign subsidiary that is highly integrated with its Canadian parent, you have the following information:

	FC
Inventory (FIFO cost, net realizable value of FC1,300,000)	1,150,000

An examination of the working papers of the foreign subsidiary's auditor shows the following information:

Opening inventory	FC 350,000
Purchases	
February 15, Year 3	205,000
April 15, Year 3	588,000
August 1, Year 3	410,000
October 12, Year 3	362,000
November 15, Year 3	547,000
Cost of goods sold for the year	1,312,000

Exchange rates:

January 1, Year 3 (opening inventory)	$1 = FC2.5
February 15, Year 3	$1 = FC3.1
April 15, Year 3	$1 = FC3.4
August 1, Year 3	$1 = FC4.3
October 12, Year 3	$1 = FC4.8
November 15, Year 3	$1 = FC5.5
December 31, Year 3	$1 = FC6.1
Year 3 average	$1 = FC4.0

Note: This is not considered excessive or high inflation in terms of the temporal method.

Required:

(a) Calculate the Canadian-dollar amount of the inventory at the fiscal year-end (December 31), and the Canadian-dollar amount of any item(s) that would appear on the income statement.
(b) If the foreign subsidiary were self-sustaining, what would your answer to Part (a) be?
(c) Define accounting exposure and describe its impact on the translation of financial statement items in this problem.

(CGA-Canada adapted)

Problem 11-8
LO1, 3, 4

On December 31, Year 2, PAT Inc. of Halifax, Nova Scotia, acquired 90% of the voting shares of Gioco Limited of Italy, for 690,000 euros (€). On the acquisition date, the fair values equalled the carrying amounts for all of Gioco's identifiable assets and liabilities. Selected account balances from Gioco's general ledger on December 31, Year 2, were as follows:

Equipment	€ 150,000
Building	1,350,000
Accumulated amortization	195,000
Common shares	600,000
Retained earnings	96,000

Gioco purchased the building and equipment on January 1, Year 1.

The condensed trial balance of Gioco for the year ending December 31, Year 5, was as follows:

Accounts receivable	€ 197,000
Inventory	255,000
Building	1,350,000
Equipment	350,000
Cost of goods purchased	1,080,000
Change in inventory	120,000
Amortization expense	130,000
Other expenses	470,000
Dividends paid	300,000
Total debits	€4,252,000
Current monetary liabilities	€ 682,000
Common shares	600,000
Retained earnings, beginning	300,000
Sales	2,250,000
Accumulated amortization	420,000
Total credits	€4,252,000

Additional Information

- Gioco's sales, inventory purchases, and other expenses occurred uniformly over the year.
- Gioco's inventory on hand at the end of each year was purchased uniformly over the last quarter. On December 31, Year 4, the inventories totalled €375,000, and on December 31, Year 5, they totalled €255,000.
- On January 1, Year 5, Gioco purchased equipment for €200,000. The equipment has an estimated useful life of eight years and a residual value of €5,000. Gioco uses the double-declining-balance method to calculate amortization expense. There were no other purchases of property, plant, and equipment between Year 2 and Year 5.
- The dividends were declared and paid on January 1, Year 5.
- The exchange rates for the euro and the Canadian dollar were as follows:

Jan. 1, Year 1	$1 = €0.50
Dec. 31, Year 2	$1 = €0.60
Average for the Year 4 fourth quarter	$1 = €0.68
Dec. 31, Year 4/Jan. 1, Year 5	$1 = €0.70
Dec. 31, Year 5	$1 = €0.80
Average for Year 5	$1 = €0.76
Average for the Year 5 fourth quarter	$1 = €0.79

Required:

(a) Translate into Canadian dollars the following items on Gioco's financial statements for the year ended December 31, Year 5, assuming that Gioco's functional currency is the Canadian dollar:

   (i) Accounts receivable

   (ii) Inventory

   (iii) Equipment

   (iv) Accumulated amortization

   (v) Common shares

(b) Translate into Canadian dollars the following items on Gioco's financial statements for the year ended December 31, Year 5, assuming that Gioco's functional currency is the euro:

   (i) Cost of goods purchased

   (ii) Amortization expense

   (iii) Inventory

   (iv) Common shares

(c) For Gioco, which functional currency would show the strongest current ratio for the company's translated financial statements? Briefly explain.

(d) Prepare an independent calculation of the unrealized exchange gains or losses to be included in other comprehensive income for Year 5, assuming that Gioco's functional currency is the euro.

(CGA-Canada adapted)

Problem 11-9
LO3, 7

Dom Ltd., a private Canadian company, has a subsidiary, Tarzan Inc., in a country that uses the tar (Tz) as its currency. Before this 100%-owned subsidiary can be consolidated, the financial statements must be translated from tars to Canadian dollars. However, the person responsible for the translation has quit suddenly and left you with a half-finished job. Certain information is available but you must determine the rest.

TARZAN INC. FINANCIAL STATEMENTS (IN Tz)
at December 31, Year 4

Land	Tz 500,000
Buildings (Note 1)	800,000
Accumulated depreciation	(300,000)
Inventory (Note 2)	400,000
Accounts receivable	200,000
Cash	100,000
	Tz1,700,000
Ordinary shares	Tz 300,000
Retained earnings	750,000
Note payable (Note 3)	400,000
Accounts payable	250,000
	Tz1,700,000
Sales	Tz5,200,000
Cost of goods sold	3,100,000
	2,100,000
Other expenses (including depreciation of 80,000)	(1,950,000)
Profit	Tz 150,000

Additional Information

1. There were two buildings and one piece of land. The land and building 1 (Tz300,000) were acquired when Dom formed Tarzan. The exchange rate at that time was $1 = Tz2. Building 2 was acquired when the exchange rate was $1 = Tz3.2. The depreciation expense is proportional to the purchase prices. The accumulated depreciation relating to Building 2 is Tz200,000.

2. The opening inventory was Tz500,000, and the purchases during the period were Tz3,000,000. Tarzan uses a periodic FIFO inventory system. The opening inventory had an exchange rate of $1 = Tz3.5, and the purchases were made 30% from the parent and 70% from the local area. The local area purchases were made evenly throughout the year; the purchases from the parent were recorded by the parent at $232,558. The ending inventory was purchased when the exchange rate was $1 = Tz4.

3. The note payable, which is due on January 1, Year 8, was created on July 1, Year 4.

4. The retained earnings at January 1, Year 4, translated into $181,818.

5. The other expenses were incurred evenly throughout the year.

6. No dividends were declared during the year.

7. Exchange rates:

Jan. 1, Year 4	$1 = Tz3.7
2004 average, July 1, Year 4	$1 = Tz3.9
Dec. 31, Year 4	$1 = Tz4.1

Required:

(a) Assume that Tarzan is an integrated foreign operation. Prepare the financial statements of Tarzan in Canadian dollars. Show your calculations *in good form.*

(b) If the net realizable value of the ending inventory was Tz350,000, what would the Canadian-dollar value of the inventory be? Assume all the other information given in the question remains constant.

(CGA-Canada adapted)

Problem 11-10
LO3, 4

In Year 1, Victoria Textiles Limited decided that its Asian operations had expanded such that an Asian office should be established. The office would be involved in selling Victoria's current product lines; it was also expected to establish supplier contacts. In the Asian market, there were a number of small manufacturers of top-quality fabrics, particularly silk and lace, but from Victoria's home office in Ontario it was difficult to find and maintain these suppliers. To assist in doing so, a wholly owned company, Victoria Textiles (India) Limited, was created, and a facility was established in India in January Year 2. The new company, VTIL, was given the mandate from head office to buy and sell with other Victoria divisions and offices across Canada, as if it were an autonomous, independent unit. To establish the company, an investment of 10,000,000 Indian rupees (IR) was made on January 1, Year 2.

VTIL proved to be quite successful, as shown in the following financial statements at December 31, Year 4. After one year of operations, VTIL had borrowed funds and expanded facilities substantially, as the initial market estimates had turned out to be quite conservative. However, during this time the rupee had fallen in value relative to the Canadian dollar. As a result, Victoria's management was somewhat confused about how to evaluate VTIL's success, given the changing currency values.

FINANCIAL STATEMENTS
(in Thousands of Indian Rupees)
BALANCE SHEETS

	Year 4	Year 3
Cash	4,100	3,900
Accounts receivable	2,900	2,100
Inventories	4,800	3,500
Prepaid expenses	1,900	1,700
Plant assets (net)	7,900	8,900
	21,600	20,100
Current monetary liabilities	2,400	900
Unearned revenue	800	500
Long-term debt	6,000	6,000
	9,200	7,400
Common shares	10,000	10,000
Retained earnings	2,400	2,700
	21,600	20,100

INCOME STATEMENTS

	Year 4	Year 3
Sales	20,200	12,000
Cost of sales	11,300	6,300
Gross profit	8,900	5,700
Operating expenses	4,400	2,800
Interest	700	400
Taxes	600	400
Net income	3,200	2,100

Additional Information

- The exchange rate at January 1, Year 2, when VTIL was originally established, was $0.075 per rupee.
- Of the original investment of IR10 million, IR4 million was used to acquire plant and equipment, which is being depreciated on a straight-line basis over 10 years.
- At June 30, Year 3, an expansion was completed at a cost of IR6 million, which was financed entirely by a six-year note obtained from an Indian bank. Interest is to be paid semiannually. The exchange rate at July 1, Year 3, was $0.062 per rupee. The new expansion is also to be depreciated on a straight-line basis over 10 years. (A half-year's depreciation was recorded in Year 3.) Depreciation expense of IR1,000 in Year 4 and IR700 in Year 3 is included in operating expenses.
- Inventory is accounted for on the FIFO basis. The inventory at the end of Year 3 and Year 4 was acquired when the exchange rates were $0.045 and $0.027 per rupee, respectively.
- Sales, purchases, and operating expenses were incurred evenly throughout the year, and the average exchange rate for the year was $0.031.
- The prepaid expenses and unearned revenue at December 31, Year 4, arose when the exchange rates were $0.03 and $0.028 per rupee, respectively.

- Income taxes were paid in equal monthly instalments throughout the year.
- Dividends of 3,500 in Year 4 and 500 in Year 3 were declared and paid each year on December 31.
- The foreign exchange rates per rupee at each of the following dates were as follows:

Dec. 31, Year 3	$0.041
June 30, Year 4	$0.036
Dec. 31, Year 4	$0.025

Required:

(a) Prepare a Canadian-dollar balance sheet at December 31, Year 4, and an income statement for the year then ended, assuming that VTIL's functional currency is as follows:

   (i) The Canadian dollar

   (ii) The Indian rupee

(*Note:* There is insufficient information to translate retained earnings and accumulated foreign exchange adjustments. Plug these two items with the amount required to balance the balance sheet.)

(b) Which method should Victoria Textiles Limited apply to its investment in this subsidiary? Explain.

(*adapted from a problem prepared by Peter Secord, St. Mary's University*)

Problem 11-11
LO1, 3, 4

The financial statements of Malkin Inc., of Russia, as at December 31, Year 11, follow the Additional Information section.

Additional Information

- On January 1, Year 11, Crichton Corporation of Toronto acquired a controlling interest in Malkin.
- Relevant exchange rates for the Russian ruble (RR) were as follows:

Jan. 1, Year 11	$1 = RR28.00
Dec. 31, Year 11	$1 = RR28.20
Average for Year 11	$1 = RR28.09

- The land and buildings were purchased in Year 5 when the exchange rate was RR26.50.
- During Year 11, equipment costing RR125,000 was purchased for cash. Depreciation totalling RR25,000 has been recorded on this equipment. The exchange rate on the date of the equipment purchase was RR28.18.

  The remaining equipment was purchased on the date the subsidiary was acquired, and no other changes have taken place since that date. Depreciation on the buildings of RR105,00 and depreciation of RR63,000 on all the equipment are included in other expenses.
- The December 31, Year 11, inventory was acquired during the last quarter of the year, when the average exchange rate was RR28.04.
- On January 1, Year 11, the inventory was RR525,000 and was acquired when the average exchange rate was RR28.27.

- The bonds mature on December 31, Year 16.
- Other operating expenses were incurred equally throughout the year.
- Dividends were declared and paid on December 31, Year 11.
- On January 1, Year 11, liabilities were greater than monetary assets by the amount of RR1,033,000.
- The common shares were issued in Year 1 when the exchange rate was RR25.00.

FINANCIAL STATEMENTS
at December 31, Year 11

BALANCE SHEET

Cash		RR 105,000
Accounts receivable		168,000
Inventories—at cost		357,000
Land		430,000
Buildings	1,460,000	
Accumulated depreciation	420,000	1,040,000
Equipment	483,000	
Accumulated depreciation	168,000	315,000
		RR2,415,000
Accounts payable		RR 210,000
Miscellaneous payables		105,000
Bonds payable LT		600,000
Common shares		850,000
Retained earnings		650,000
		RR2,415,000

RETAINED EARNINGS STATEMENT

Balance, January 1	RR 470,000
Net income	630,000
	1,100,000
Dividends	450,000
Balance, December 31	RR 650,000

INCOME STATEMENT

Sales	RR3,150,000
Cost of sales	1,680,000
Other expenses	840,000
	2,520,000
Net Income	RR 630,000

Required:

(a) Assume that Malkin's functional currency is the Canadian dollar. Translate the financial statements into Canadian dollars for consolidation purposes.

(b) Assume that Malkin's functional currency is the Russian ruble. Translate the balance sheet only into Canadian dollars for consolidation purposes.

(c) Explain whether the current rate method produces results that are consistent with the normal measurement and valuation of assets and liabilities for domestic transactions and operations.

Problem 11-12
LO2, 3, 4

SPEC Co. is a Canadian investment company. It acquires real estate properties in foreign countries for speculative purposes. On January 1, Year 5, SPEC incorporated a wholly owned subsidiary, CHIN Limited. CHIN immediately purchased a property in Shanghai, China, for 70 million Chinese yuan (Y). At that time, the land and building were valued at Y30 million and Y40 million, respectively. The previous owner had purchased the property in Year 1 for Y36 million when the exchange rate was $1 = Y5.13. The building had an estimated useful life of 20 years with no residual value on January 1, Year 5.

The draft financial statements for CHIN as at and for the year ended December 31, Year 5, follow:

CHIN LIMITED
STATEMENT OF FINANCIAL POSITION
at December 31, Year 5

Land	Y30,000,000
Building	40,000,000
Accumulated amortization	(2,000,000)
	Y68,000,000
Common shares	Y20,000,000
Retained earnings (deficit)	(2,000,000)
Mortgage payable	50,000,000
	Y68,000,000

CHIN LIMITED
INCOME STATEMENT
for the Year Ended December 31, Year 5

Rent revenue	Y 6,000,000
Interest expense	(5,000,000)
Amortization expense	(2,000,000)
Other expenses	(1,000,000)
Profit (loss)	Y (2,000,000)

Additional Information

- The purchase of the property was financed with Y20 million of equity provided by SPEC and a Y50 million mortgage from a Chinese investor. The mortgage payable has a term of 10 years and requires interest-only payments of Y5 million on December 31 each year, and a final payment of Y50 million on December 31, Year 14. The market rate of interest on the mortgage was equal to the stated rate throughout Year 5.
- The property is rented for Y0.5 million per month, which is consistent with rent being charged by other property owners in the area. The rent is due on the last day of each month. CHIN hires local workers and buys all of its materials and supplies from local suppliers. CHIN incurred the other expenses evenly throughout the year.
- The exchange rates were as follows:

Jan. 1, Year 5	$1 = Y6.92
Average for Year 5	$1 = Y7.20
Average for 12 days when rent payments were received	$1 = Y7.25
Dec. 31, Year 5	$1 = Y7.50

Required:

(a) Should CHIN be classified as a self-sustaining or an integrated subsidiary? Explain.

(b) Ignore your answer to Part (a). Calculate the foreign exchange adjustment for Year 5, assuming that CHIN's functional currency is the Chinese yuan, and indicate how this adjustment will be reported in CHIN's Canadian-dollar financial statements. Show supporting calculations.

(c) Ignore your answers to Parts (a) and (b). Translate CHIN's Year 5 income statement into Canadian dollars, assuming that CHIN's functional currency is the Canadian dollar. Ignore foreign exchange gains and losses.

(d) Assume that SPEC does not own any shares of CHIN. Instead, SPEC acquired the property in Shanghai directly. SPEC financed the acquisition with Y20 million of its own funds and a Y50 million mortgage. If SPEC argued that the mortgage payable is a hedge of the anticipated sale of the land, what difference would it make for reporting purposes whether or not the mortgage payable is deemed to be an effective hedge of the anticipated sale of the land? Briefly explain.

(CGA-Canada adapted)

Problem 11-13
LO3, 4

White Company was incorporated on January 2, Year 1, and commenced active operations immediately. Common shares were issued on the date of incorporation and no new common shares have been issued since then. On December 31, Year 5, Black Company purchased 70% of the outstanding common shares of White for 1.4 million foreign pesos (FP). On this date, the fair values of White's identifiable net assets were equal to their carrying amounts except for a building, which had a fair value of FP100,000 in excess of carrying amount. The remaining useful life of the building was 10 years at the date of acquisition.

The following information was extracted from the financial records of the two companies for the year ended December 31, Year 6:

	Black	White
Building—net	$3,000,000	FP2,700,000
Common shares	100,000	200,000
Retained earnings, beginning of year	800,000	900,000
Depreciation expense—buildings	200,000	300,000
Income before foreign exchange	150,000	160,000
Dividends paid	80,000	100,000

Additional Information

- Black uses the cost method to account for its investment in White.
- White purchased its building on December 31, Year 3.
- The recoverable amount for goodwill at the end of Year 6 was FP720,000.
- Dividends were declared and paid on July 1.
- Foreign exchange rates were as follows:

Jan. 2, Year 1	FP1 = $0.30
Dec. 31, Year 3	FP1 = $0.24
Dec. 31, Year 5	FP1 = $0.20
Average for Year 6	FP1 = $0.18
July 1, Year 6	FP1 = $0.17
Dec. 31, Year 6	FP1 = $0.15

Required:

(a) Compute the balances that would appear in the Year 6 consolidated financial statements for the following items, assuming that White's functional currency is the Canadian dollar. White's income before foreign exchange gains is $30,000, and the exchange gains from translating White's separate-entity financial statements to Canadian dollars is $50,000.

  (i) Building—net
  (ii) Goodwill
  (iii) Depreciation expense—building
  (iv) Net income (excluding other comprehensive income)
  (v) Other comprehensive income
  (vi) Non-controlling interest on the income statement
  (vii) Non-controlling interest on the balance sheet

(b) Compute the balances that would appear in the Year 6 consolidated financial statements for the same accounts as in Part (a), assuming that White's functional currency is the foreign peso.

Problem 11-14
LO5

On January 1, Year 1, Par Company purchased all the outstanding common shares of Bayshore Company, located in California, USA, for US$120,000. The carrying amount of Bayshore's shareholders' equity on January 1, Year 1, was US$90,000. The fair value of Bayshore's plant and equipment was US$10,000 more than carrying amount, and the plant and equipment are being depreciated over 10 years, with no salvage value. The remainder of the acquisition differential is attributable to a trademark, which will be amortized over 10 years.

During Year 1, Bayshore earned US$20,000 in income and declared and paid US$8,000 in dividends on December 1, Year 1. Par uses the equity method to account for its investment in Bayshore. Management has determined that the Canadian dollar is the recording functional and presentation currency for Par Company.

The exchange rates were as follows throughout the year:

Jan. 1, Year 1	US$1 = CDN$0.99
Dec. 1, Year 1	US$1 = CDN$0.96
Dec. 1, Year 1	US$1 = CDN$0.95
Average for year	US$1 = CDN$0.97

Required:

(a) Assume that the Canadian dollar is the function currency for Bayshore Company.

  (i) Prepare a schedule showing the differential allocation and amortization for Year 1. The schedule should present both Canadian dollars and U.S. dollars.
  (ii) Prepare Par Company's journal entry for adjustments pertaining to the amortization of the acquisition differential for Year 1.

(b) Assume that the U.S. dollar is the functional currency for Bayshore Company.

  (i) Prepare a schedule showing the differential allocation and amortization for Year 1. The schedule should present both Canadian dollars and U.S. dollars.
  (ii) Prepare Par Company's journal entry for adjustments pertaining to the amortization of the acquisition differential for Year 1.

WEB-BASED PROBLEMS

Web Problem 11-1
LO6

Access the 2011 annual report for Manulife Financial Corporation by going to investor relations section of the company's website. Answer the questions below. For each question, indicate where in the financial statements you found the answer, and/or provide a brief explanation.

(a) What is the functional currency of the parent company, and what currency is used in presenting the financial statements?

(b) What is the predominant currency of the company's foreign operations, and what other currencies are functional currencies of entities within the consolidated group?

(c) What were the foreign exchange gains or losses reported in net income during the year? Are the foreign exchange gains or losses segregated between foreign transactions and foreign operations?

(d) Explain if and how the company hedges its net investments in foreign operations and how it reports exchange gains or losses on these hedges.

(e) If the reporting currency appreciates by 10% relative to the U.S. dollar in the next year, will the company likely report foreign exchange gains or foreign exchange losses in operating income?

(f) If the company had used the U.S. dollar as its presentation currency this past year, would it likely have reported exchange gains or exchange losses? Briefly explain.

Web Problem 11-2
LO6

Access the 2011 annual report for Bombardier Inc. by going to investor relations section of the company's website. Answer the same questions as in Problem 1. For each question, indicate where in the financial statements you found the answer, and/or provide a brief explanation. (Some questions may not be applicable.)

 | Practise and learn online with Connect

Accounting for Not-for-Profit and Public Sector Organizations

INTRODUCTION

A substantial portion of Canada's economic activity is conducted by organizations whose purpose is to provide services (or products) on a non-profit basis. The size of the portion becomes clear when one considers that included in this *non-business area* is the *government sector,* encompassing the federal, provincial, and local governments, as well as the *not-for-profit sector.* This latter sector encompasses a wide variety of organizations such as charities, hospitals, universities, professional and fraternal organizations, and community clubs. A charity is a type of NFPO that is established and operated for charitable purposes and must devote its resources to charitable activities. It cannot use its income for the personal benefit of its members or governing officials.

While our major concern in this chapter is the accounting and financial reporting for Canadian not-for-profit organizations (NFPOs), the reporting requirements for governments are summarized in Appendix 12B. The NFPO sector is a very large one in our economy and consists of over 90,000 registered charities and an additional 70,000 voluntary organizations. It has been estimated that the

Over 160,000 NFPOs in Canada receive more than $112 billion each year from government grants and private donations.

charity sector alone receives over $112 billion a year from governments, private individuals, and corporations.

L01

Not-for-profit organizations are defined in Part III of the *CICA Handbook* as

> . . . entities, normally without transferable ownership interests, organized and operated exclusively for social, educational, professional, religious, health, charitable or any other not-for-profit purpose. A not-for-profit organization's members, contributors and other resource providers do not, in such capacity, receive any financial return directly from the organization. [4400.02]

NFPOs differ from profit-oriented organizations in the following ways:

There are a number of ways in which NFPOs differ from profit-oriented organizations.

- They typically provide services or goods to identifiable segments of society without the expectation of profit. They accomplish this by raising resources and subsequently spending or distributing these resources in a manner that fulfills the organization's objectives.

- The resources are provided by contributors without the expectation of gain or repayment. Most of these resources consist of donations from the general public and grants from governments and other NFPOs. Often, a portion of the resources received has restrictions attached that govern the manner in which they can be spent.

- As the definition cited above indicates, there is no readily defined ownership interest that can be sold, transferred, or redeemed in any way by the organization.

- While many NFPOs have paid employees, they are governed by volunteers who receive little or no remuneration or gain for the time and effort they provide. In some small organizations there are no paid employees and all effort is provided entirely by volunteers.

Well-defined GAAP for NFPOs have existed in Canada only since 1997.

While financial reporting for NFPOs in Canada is well defined today, this has been the case only since April 1997, when seven very detailed *Handbook* sections became operational. Prior to this date, accounting in this area was in a state of flux, moving from a situation where there were no real authoritative pronouncements at all, to one where there was just a single *Handbook* section that gave only broad guidance for some issues and left many other important ones unresolved. A few large organizations, such as hospitals and universities, published detailed manuals in an attempt to establish consistent reporting practices for all members of a given association. Unfortunately, the practices set out for hospitals were different from those recommended for universities, and in both situations members did not have to follow their organization's recommendations. Smaller NFPOs followed a wide range of diverse practices, such as using the cash basis only, or a mixture of cash and accrual accounting. Many did not capitalize capital asset acquisitions, and of the few that did capitalize, many did not provide for subsequent periodic amortization. A wide range of practices was also followed for donated materials, services, and capital assets, ranging from no recording to a full recording of all items. A large number of NFPOs used fund accounting in their end-of-year financial statement presentations, and many organizations still do. Later in this chapter we fully explore the concepts involved in fund accounting and fund presentations in accordance with current *Handbook* requirements. First, though, it is useful to examine the main accounting and reporting requirements for NFPOs today.

NOT-FOR-PROFIT REPORTING TODAY

L02

In 1997, seven new sections specifically dedicated to NFPOs were added to the *CICA Handbook.* In 2008, the NFPO *Handbook* sections underwent a major review. As a result, one new NFPO section was added and many changes were made to other NFPO sections.

In December 2010, the *Handbook* was restructured into five parts to implement the strategy of the Accounting Standards Board (AcSB) of adopting different sets of standards for different categories of entities. As part of this restructuring, the not-for-profit (NFP) sector was classified into two sectors: the public NFP sector and the private NFP sector. The public NFP sector includes NFPOs (such as hospitals) that are controlled by the government. These NFPOs have a choice to follow the *CICA Public Sector Accounting (PSA) Handbook* including the 4200 series or the *PSA Handbook* without the 4200 series. Appendix B of this chapter discusses accounting standards applicable to the public sector.

The private NFP sector includes NFPOs that are not controlled by the government. They have a choice to follow either Part I (International Financial Reporting Standards) or Part III (Accounting Standards for Not-for-Profit Organizations) of the *CICA Handbook.* In choosing between the two options, the organization would consider the needs of the users of their financial statements and the comparability of their financial reporting with counterparts in industry. It is expected that most private sector NFPOs will adopt Part III of the *CICA Handbook.* The remainder of this chapter will describe accounting standards for the private sector NFPOs, and will refer to the private NFPOs simply as NFPOs. Furthermore, any references to Part II or Part III will be references to these parts of the *CICA Handbook.*

> Private sector NFPOs can either follow IFRSs or Part III of the *CICA Handbook* combined with relevant sections from ASPE.

An NFPO applying Part III of the *Handbook* also applies Part II (Accounting Standards for Private Enterprises) to the extent that the Part II standards address topics not addressed in Part III. Some of the standards in Part II are of limited or no applicability to NFPOs either, because the topics are specifically addressed in Part III or the standards in Part II relate to transactions or circumstances that do not pertain to NFPOs.

> Many sections of the *Handbook* that previously applied only to profit-oriented organizations now apply to NFPOs as well.

The standards in Part III are based closely on standards in the *Handbook* prior to the restructuring into the different parts. Part III carries forward the 4400 series of sections from the old *Handbook,* largely without change, except for the split of Section 4230 into Sections 4231 and 4232. Five new sections were added, containing relevant material from Part II that were customized for the private NFP sector. The new standards became effective for fiscal periods beginning on or after January 1, 2012.

> Part III of the *Handbook* now contains the accounting standards that deal with issues that are unique to NFPOs.

In the material that follows, the pronouncements of each section of Part III will be discussed and in some instances illustrated. For the first five sections presented below, the standards in Part III are very similar to the standards in Part II. The main differences between the two sections will be described.[1]

> **Cautionary Note:** Unless otherwise noted, all of the illustrations in the body of the chapter and end-of-chapter material will use Part III of the *CICA Handbook* in combination with Part II.

Section 1001: Financial Statement Concepts for Not-for-Profit Organizations

This section describes the objectives of financial statements, qualitative characteristics of financial information, elements of financial statements, and recognition and measurement in financial statements. The mains users of the NFPOs' financial statements are the members, contributors, and creditors. They are interested, for the purpose of making resource allocation decisions, in the entity's cost of service

The cost of service and how that cost was funded are key information needs for the users of an NFPO.

and how that cost was funded and in predicting the ability of the entity to meet its obligations and achieve its service delivery objectives. The excess or deficiency of revenues and gains over expenses and losses can be an important indicator of the entity's ability to obtain resources to cover the cost of its services.

Members and contributors also require information about how the management of an entity has discharged its stewardship responsibility to those that have provided resources to the entity. Information regarding discharge of stewardship responsibilities is especially important as resources are often contributed for specific purposes, and management is accountable for the appropriate utilization of such resources.

Part II of the *Handbook* provides a substantial portion of GAAP for NFPOs.

Section 1101: Generally Accepted Accounting Principles for Not-for-Profit Organizations

This section describes the primary and other sources of GAAP for NFPOs. The primary sources of GAAP, in descending order of authority, follow:

(i) Sections 1470–4470 of Part III of the *Handbook*, including appendices

(ii) Sections 1505–3870 in Part II, to the extent that the topics in those sections are not specifically discussed in Part III, including appendices

(iii) "Accounting Guidelines" in Part II, including appendices

An NFPO should present only one set of general-purpose financial statements prepared under Part III of the *Handbook* in any particular period. If it prepares additional sets of financial statements under Part III for different purposes, these are special-purpose financial statements and should refer to the general-purpose financial statements.

The financial statements for an NFPO are similar to the financial statements required under ASPE.

Section 1401: General Standards of Financial Statement Presentation for Not-for-Profit Organizations

This section describes fair presentation in accordance with GAAP, going concern, financial statements required for NFPOs, and comparative information. The standards in this section are similar to the standards in Section 1400 in Part II. The general-purpose financial statements consist of the statement of financial position, statement of operations, statement of changes in net assets, and statement of cash flows. Notes to financial statements, and supporting schedules to which the financial statements are cross-referenced, are an integral part of such statements. When financial statements are not prepared on a going-concern basis, that fact shall be disclosed, together with the basis on which the financial statements are prepared and the reason why the organization is not regarded as a going concern. Financial statements shall be prepared on a comparative basis, unless the comparative information is not meaningful or the standards set out in Part III permit otherwise.

Section 1501: First Time Adoption by Not-for-Profit Organizations

This section applies when an NFPO is adopting Part III for the first time. Most NFPOs will have used this section when they converted from the old *Handbook* to Part III of the *Handbook* in 2012. For the NFPOs that adopted Part I rather than Part III in 2012 or earlier and later decide to change to Part III, they would follow Section 1501 of Part III at that time.

Changes in policies would normally be applied retrospectively when first adopting Part III of the *Handbook*.

When converting to Part III for the first time, changes in accounting policies must be applied retrospectively, unless there are exemptions or restrictions as outlined and defined in Section 1501. The entity's first set of financial statements must show comparative numbers for the previous year as if Part III had always been applied. In addition, the entity must present a statement of financial position on the transition date, which is the beginning of the earliest period for which an organization presents full comparative information. For example, if the first set of financial statements is presented for the year ended December 31, 2012, comparative numbers would be presented for 2011 and an opening statement of financial position would be presented as at January 1, 2011. The entity has an option to not retrospectively adjust when it changes its accounting policies in its first set of financial statements under Part III for certain standards in the following areas: business combinations; fair value for property, plant, and equipment; employee future benefits; cumulative translation differences for self-sustaining foreign operations; financial instruments; and asset retirement obligations. These same elective exemptions are available for private entities transitioning to Part II.

On the other hand, retrospective application is prohibited for some aspects of the standards. The prohibitions include derecognition of financial assets and financial liabilities, hedge accounting, estimates, and non-controlling interests.

Section 3032: Inventories Held by Not-for-Profit Organizations

Except as otherwise provided for in this section, an NFPO applies the section on inventories in Part II. When an NFPO recognizes donations of materials and services, the inventories should initially be recorded at fair value, which is its deemed cost from that point forward. Without this requirement, the inventory would not be recognized because it had no cost to the NFPO.

An NFPO may receive inventory without any cost and may have no intention of ever selling the inventory.

An NFPO may hold inventories whose future economic benefits or service potential are not directly related to their ability to generate net cash flows. These types of inventories may arise when an NFPO distributes certain goods at no charge or for a nominal charge. For example, a food bank would buy food, not to resell it, but to distribute it for free to the homeless. In this case, the future economic benefits or service potential of the inventory for financial reporting purposes is the amount the organization would need to pay to acquire the economic benefits or service potential, if this was necessary to achieve the objectives of the organization. Therefore, an NFPO measures inventories at the lower of cost and current replacement cost (instead of net realizable value), when they are held for distribution at no charge or for a nominal charge or for consumption in the production process of goods to be distributed at no charge or for a nominal charge.

Section 4400: Financial Statement Presentation by Not-for-Profit Organizations

An NFPO must present the following financial statements for external reporting purposes:

An NFPO must present four financial statements.

- Statement of operations
- Statement of financial position
- Statement of changes in net assets
- Statement of cash flows

The names provided here are for descriptive purposes only; an organization can choose the titles it wishes to use. For example, the statement of operations is sometimes called the statement of revenues and expenses, the statement of financial position could be called a balance sheet, and net assets is sometimes referred to as fund balances or accumulated surplus. The statement of operations can be combined with the statement of changes in net assets.

The primary purpose of a statement of operations is to communicate information about changes in the organization's economic resources and obligations for the period. Specifically, this statement provides information about the cost of the organization's service delivery activities for the period and the extent to which these expenses were financed or funded by contributions and other revenue. The information provided in the statement of operations is useful in evaluating the organization's performance during the period, including its ability to continue to provide services, and in assessing how the organization's management has discharged its stewardship responsibilities.

The equity section of the statement of financial position is called "net assets" and must be broken down into three categories (if applicable).

The statement of financial position should show classifications for current assets, non-current assets, current liabilities, and non-current liabilities. Net assets (total assets less total liabilities) must be broken down into the following categories (if applicable):

- Net assets maintained permanently in endowments
- Internally restricted and other externally restricted net assets
- Unrestricted net assets

Prior to 2009, net assets invested in capital assets had to be shown as a separate component of net assets. Starting in 2009, a reporting entity has three options for reporting this item:

- Continue to show it as a separate component of net assets
- Disclose it in the notes to the statements
- Do not present or disclose it separately

Many organizations still present or disclose this item separately because it indicates that this portion of net assets is not available for current use. However, some organizations will not present or disclose the item separately because their users may not fully understand its nature.

Revenues and expenses should be reported on a gross basis when the entity acts as a principal in the transactions.

Information about total gross revenues and expenses is necessary for users to fully understand the organization's operations. The statement of operations will show the revenues and the expenses for the period. Expenses may be classified by object (salaries, rent, utilities), by function (administrative, research, ancillary operations), or by program. An organization should use the method that results in the most meaningful presentation under the circumstances. When an organization has expenses and revenues from the provision of goods or services and acted as a principal in the transactions involved, it recognizes the expenses and the revenues on a gross basis. When it is not acting as a principal in the transactions, it earns the equivalent of a commission or fee or receives the equivalent of a contribution and recognizes revenue for only the net amount received. The following two examples provide guidance in determining whether to recognize revenues and expenses on the gross basis or the net basis.

Example 1 An NFPO engages in a number of fundraising activities, which include a fundraising telethon, a telephone campaign, a direct mail campaign, special events, and a lottery. The organization uses an outside fundraising consultant to conduct the telethon but uses the NFPO's own staff and volunteers in the tele-thon and the telephone campaign. Funds solicited in each of the activities are raised in the name of the organization.

The NFPO is the principal when it receives most of the benefits and/or incurs most of the risks. Even though the organization uses an outside fundraising con-sultant to conduct the telethon, the organization is the principal in the relationship with the donors as the funds are raised in its name and using its staff and volun-teers. The organization has discretion in selecting the outside fundraiser, in estab-lishing the fees to be paid, and in determining the specifications of the telethon. It also has the credit risk if donors to the telethon do not pay according to their pledge. Thus, the organization recognizes the gross fundraising amounts raised in each of the activities as revenue of the organization and the total expenses of each activity, including the fees charged by any outside party, as expenses of the organization.

Example 2   An NFPO is given the net proceeds from an event held by others to benefit the organization, but without having any control over, or responsibility for, the gross amounts of revenues or expenses involved. In this situation, the organiza-tion is not the principal in the fundraising event as it was not involved in organiz-ing the event and did not bear any risks in connection with it. The amount received by the organization is a donation from the organizers. Neither the gross revenues nor the gross expenses of the event are recognized in the organization's financial statements. The net proceeds received are recognized as a contribution. Disclosure of gross revenues and expenses is not required.

The statement of operations does not have a section for other comprehensive income. Similar to a private for-profit entity, foreign exchange adjustments for a self-sustaining foreign operation and the exchange adjustments for a cash flow hedge are given special treatment. These adjustments are recognized directly and accu-mulated separately in the net assets section of the statement of financial position.

> Other comprehensive income does not exist as a separate category on the statement of operations.

The statement of changes in net assets must show changes in each of the three net asset categories required on the statement of financial position. The cash flow statement must segregate changes in cash between operating, investing, and financing activities. Cash flows from operations can be presented using either the direct method or the indirect method.

The 2012 financial statements (excluding footnotes) of the United Way of Ottawa-Carleton presented in Appendix 12A provide an example of an NFPO's financial statements.

THE BASICS OF FUND ACCOUNTING

`L03`

Fund accounting can be and has been used very successfully to keep track of restricted resources and/or programs, and to convey information through the financial statements about the restrictions placed on the organization's resources. The concepts involved can be summarized as follows:

> Fund accounting comprises the collective accounting procedures resulting in a self-balancing set of accounts for each fund established by legal, contractual or voluntary actions of an organization. Elements of a fund can include assets, liabilities, net assets, revenues and expenses (and gains and losses where appropriate). Fund accounting involves an accounting segregation, although not necessarily a physical segregation, of resources. [4400.02]

The following simple example illustrates the use of fund accounting as a means of reporting this form of stewardship.

Fund accounting is often used to convey information about restricted resources.

Example 3   The financial statements of the Helpful Society (HS) at the end of Year 1 are presented in Exhibit 12.1. HS presents two funds in its year-end financial statements. The resources in the *general* fund can be used to carry out the normal activities of the organization, while the resources in the *building* fund, which was established during the current year, are restricted. Each year, the organization raises money through donations and spends the funds raised on programs A, B, and C. During the current year, the general fund's revenues were $7,100 greater than its expenses; as a result, its equity (described as fund balance) increased by that amount. Note that revenues and expenses are measured under the accrual method, so the statement does not show cash inflows and outflows. The assets on hand at the end of the year can be viewed as resources that are spendable. The liabilities at this date are a claim against these resources; therefore, the fund balance

This exhibit illustrates fund accounting. When combined with a policy of non-capitalization of capital assets it becomes a resources-in-and-out form of stewardship reporting.

EXHIBIT 12.1

HELPFUL SOCIETY
STATEMENT OF FINANCIAL POSITION
December 31, Year 1

	General fund	Building fund	Total
Assets			
Cash	$ 17,500	$ 6,000	$ 23,500
Pledges receivable	50,000		50,000
Investments in debt securities	25,000	88,635	113,635
Total	$ 92,500	$ 94,635	$ 187,135
Liabilities and Fund Balance			
Accounts payable and accrued liabilities	$ 60,300		$ 60,300
Fund balance	32,200	$ 94,635	126,835
Total	$ 92,500	$ 94,635	$ 187,135

STATEMENT OF REVENUE AND EXPENSES
AND CHANGES IN FUND BALANCES
for the Year Ended December 31, Year 1

	General fund	Building fund	Total
Revenues			
Contributions	$923,000	$102,000	$1,025,000
Interest	2,700		2,700
Total	925,700	102,000	1,027,700
Expenses			
Program A	625,000		625,000
Program B	190,000		190,000
Program C	100,000		100,000
Fundraising	3,600	6,410	10,010
Miscellaneous		955	955
Total	918,600	7,365	925,965
Excess of revenue over expenses	7,100	94,635	101,735
Fund balance, January 1	25,100	0	25,100
Fund balance, December 31	$ 32,200	$ 94,635	$ 126,835

at the end of the current year represents net resources amounting to $32,200 that is available for spending in future years.

During the current year, a special fundraising campaign was initiated to raise the money necessary to purchase and furnish a building. The building fund's resources on hand at the end of the year, amounting to $94,635, were the result of $102,000 collected during the year, less the fundraising costs and miscellaneous expenses incurred, which amounted to $7,365. The campaign will continue until its goal is reached. At that time, the purchase of the building and furnishings will be recorded as an asset of this fund.

This example was presented to illustrate the basic idea behind financial reporting on a fund basis. In our example, the columnar approach is used to present the two funds. An alternative that gained some prior acceptance was the layered approach, which presented funds one after another, so that the first page would show the operating fund statements, the second page would show the building fund, and so on. The columnar approach is preferred because of a requirement to show totals for each financial statement item for all funds presented.

> Helpful Society presents funds in separate columns for both the statement of financial position and the statement of revenues and expenses, and for changes in fund balances.

A fund basis can be used, but it is not necessary to prepare all statements using this method. For example, the operating statement could be presented on a fund basis while the rest of the statements could be presented on a non-fund basis. An organization that uses fund accounting in its financial statements should provide a brief description of the purpose of each fund reported in the notes to the financial statements.

Section 4410: Contributions—Revenue Recognition   An NFPO can have two **L02** basic types of revenues:

- Contributions
- Other types (investments, the sale of goods and services)

A contribution is a type of revenue that is unique to NFPOs. It is defined as "a non-reciprocal transfer to a not-for-profit organization of cash or other assets or a non-reciprocal settlement or cancellation of its liabilities" (paragraph 4420.02). Non-reciprocal means that the contributor does not directly receive anything for the contribution. Included here are donations of cash, property or services, government grants, pledges, and bequests.

> Contribution revenue is a type of revenue that is unique to NFPOs, because it is non-reciprocal.

Besides receiving contribution revenue, NFPOs may also receive other types of revenue, such as from investments or from the sale of goods and services. These other types of revenue are accounted for in accordance with Part II Section 3400: Revenue. Government funding to an NFPO is typically classified as a contribution, because the government itself does not receive anything from the contribution. When the government is the direct recipient of the good or the service, the receipt from the government is recognized as revenue earned rather than contribution revenue. In the same fashion, payments received from members of an NFPO are classified as either revenues earned or contributions, depending on whether the member does or does not receive goods or services for the amount paid.

The *Handbook* defines three different types of contributions:

- Restricted contributions
- Endowment contributions
- Unrestricted contributions

> NFPOs receive three different types of contributions: restricted, endowment, and unrestricted.

Restricted contributions are subject to *externally imposed* stipulations as to how the funds are to be spent or used. The organization must use the resources in the manner specified by the donor. There may be times when the directors of an organization decide to use certain contributions for certain purposes, but these are considered to be *internally imposed* restrictions and are often referred to as reserves or appropriations. They are reported differently than the restrictions imposed by external parties, mainly because future boards could reverse the designation.

Endowment contributions are a special type of restricted contribution. The donor has specified that the contribution cannot be spent, but must be maintained permanently. Endowment contributions are often invested in high-grade securities. There are many examples of endowments. University scholarships are often funded by the investment income earned on endowment contributions made by donors in prior years. Some well-known private universities, such as Harvard and Stanford, have hundreds of millions of dollars in endowment funds, and use the earnings as their major source of revenue since they do not receive government funding. The Toronto Symphony Orchestra has established an endowment fund as a device to help fund its daily operations. And finally, the Winnipeg Foundation operates with substantial endowment funds. Quite often, restrictions are also placed on how the endowment income can be spent. In other words, investment income can be restricted or unrestricted.

Unrestricted contributions are those that are not restricted or endowment contributions. They can be used for any purposes that are consistent with the goals and objectives of the organization.

Section 4420: Contributions Receivable

Section 4420 provides guidance on how to apply accrual accounting concepts to contributions. It states the following:

A contribution receivable should be recognized as an asset when it meets the following criteria:

(a) The amount to be received can be reasonably estimated

(b) Ultimate collection is reasonably assured [4420.03]

Normally a contribution receivable represents a future inflow of cash, but it could also represent the future receipt of other assets or services valued at fair value. The credit side of the journal entry could be to revenue, using the restricted fund method, or if the deferral method of recording is being used, to deferred revenue for a restricted contribution, or to increase net assets of endowments for an endowment contribution. (The restricted fund and deferral methods are discussed later in this chapter). The section provides additional guidelines for the recording of receivables associated with pledges and bequests.

Because pledges cannot be legally enforced, collectibility is out of the control of the organization. If the organization has the ability to estimate the collectibility based on historical results, it should recognize the pledged amounts as a receivable offset with an allowance for estimated uncollectible amounts. Otherwise, the recognition of pledges should be delayed until the time cash is received. When an allowance for pledges is established, the debit is typically made to contribution revenue rather than to bad debt expense. Since the pledge is not legally binding, it is inappropriate to call the non-payment of a pledge a bad debt expense.

Bequests also pose a problem of uncertainty relating both to the timing of receipt and to the amount to be collected. Wills must be probated and at times are subject

---

Board-created endowments and restrictions are reported differently than external contributions.

Many NFPOs receive a major source of their revenues from endowment earnings.

Pledges are promises to donate cash or other assets to an NFPO, but they are legally unenforceable.

to legal challenges. Because of this extreme uncertainty, bequests are generally not accrued until probation has been completed and the time for appeal has passed.

Bequests are normally not recorded until a will has been probated.

Section 4431: Tangible Capital Assets Held by Not-for-Profit Organizations   In December 2010 when Part III of the *Handbook* was introduced, accounting for capital assets was split into two sections, 4431 and 4432. Prior to the introduction of NFPO standards into the *Handbook* in 1997, NFPOs followed a variety of practices with regard to the financial reporting of their capital assets. Some organizations capitalized all acquisitions and amortized them over their estimated useful lives in the operating statement. Others capitalized them but did not provide amortization. A fairly large number wrote them off in their operating statements in the year of acquisition. In this latter situation, the operating statement showed revenues and expenditures, and from a user perspective reflected the inflow and outflow of spendable resources.

When the AcSB proposed the requirement of capitalization and amortization of all acquisitions, respondents to the exposure drafts voiced strong opposition. The arguments against capitalization were as follows:

There was strong opposition to the proposal that all NFPOs be required to capitalize and amortize acquisitions of capital assets.

- It would change the nature of the operating statement from one that reflects resources spent to one that reflects the cost of resources used.

- Users would not understand the new accounting, having become used to seeing capital asset acquisitions as expenditures.

- As most other assets appearing in a statement of financial position represent spendable resources, the addition of non-spendable resources such as unamortized capital assets would confuse readers.

- Capitalization and amortization would be costly to apply, especially on a retroactive basis.

- Small NFPO financial statement users are interested in seeing only what money has been spent and what money is left over.

The counter-arguments in favour of capitalization were as follows:

- Readers of the financial statements of profit-oriented entities are quite used to seeing capital assets in the statement of financial position and amortization in the operating statement. They are confused when they do not see these items in the financial statements of an NFPO.

- The cash flow statement adequately shows resources spent. The operating statement should reflect resources used.

Section 4431 requires an NFPO to capitalize all tangible capital assets in the statement of financial position and to amortize them as appropriate in the statement of operations. The cost of a purchased capital asset includes all costs incurred to make the asset ready for use. When a capital asset is donated, it is recorded at fair value (if known), and the resultant credit is recorded based on the requirements for contributions, which will be discussed later in this chapter. If the entity paid less than fair value, the asset is recorded at fair value and the difference between fair value and cost is recorded as a contribution. Capital assets of limited useful life are to be amortized on a rational basis over their estimated useful lives. No maximum period of amortization is specified. When an NFPO enters into a lease agreement that would be treated as a capital lease in accordance with Part II Section 3065, the asset is capitalized in accordance with the provisions of

GAAP require large NFPOs to capitalize and amortize their capital assets.

that section. When an asset no longer contributes to the organization's ability to provide services, it should be written down to estimated residual value, with the resulting loss reported as an expense in the statement of operations. Note that this is not the same impairment test as prescribed in Part II Section 3063.

Small NFPOs Section 4431 contains a compromise provision applicable to NFPOs whose two-year average annual revenues in the statement of operations are less than $500,000. Organizations such as these are encouraged to follow the section's recommendations but are exempted from doing so if they disclose the following:

- Accounting policy for capital assets
- Information about capital assets not shown in the statement of financial position
- Amount expensed in the current period if their policy is to expense capital assets when acquired

This leaves a small NFPO the following choices:

- Expensing when acquired
- Capitalizing but not amortizing
- Capitalizing and amortizing

If an NFPO has revenues above $500,000, it is required to capitalize and amortize. If its revenues subsequently fall below $500,000, it is not allowed to change its policy.

If an NFPO has revenues below $500,000, chooses not to capitalize and amortize, and subsequently has revenues above $500,000, then it ceases to be a small NFPO and must capitalize and amortize prospectively. This requirement should be recognized by all small NFPOs that decide to exempt themselves from the section's recommendations, because retroactive restatement can be costly.

Section 4432: Intangible Assets Held by Not-for-Profit Organizations This section was introduced to clarify that Part II Section 3064: Goodwill And Intangible Assets applies to an NFPO's intangible assets. The same requirements as discussed above for tangible capital assets also apply for intangible assets.

Section 4440: Collections Held by Not-for-Profit Organizations Collections are works of art and historical treasures that have been excluded from the definition of capital assets because they meet all of the following criteria:

- Held for public exhibition, education, or research
- Protected, cared for, and preserved
- Subject to organizational policies that require any proceeds from their sale to be used to acquire other items for the collection, or for the direct care of the existing collection

The requirements of Section 4440 allow an NFPO to choose an accounting policy from the following:

- Expense when acquired
- Capitalize but do not amortize
- Capitalize and amortize

*Sidebar notes:*

An exemption from the requirement to capitalize is granted to small NFPOs (those whose two-year average revenues are less than $500,000).

When an NFPO no longer meets the exemption test, it must capitalize and amortize its capital assets and apply the new policy on a retroactive basis.

Collections have been excluded from the definition of capital assets, and NFPOs are allowed three alternative reporting options.

Although collections are usually held by museums or galleries, other organizations may also have items that meet the definition of a collection. For example, an organization's library may include rare books that would be considered to be a collection for purposes of this section. The regular library materials, however, would not usually meet the definition of a collection.

Organizations holding collections act as custodians for the public interest. They undertake to protect and preserve the collection for public exhibition, education, or research. The existence of a policy requiring that any proceeds on the sale of collection items be used to acquire additional items or for the direct care of the collection provides evidence of the organization's commitment to act as custodian of the collection.

NFPOs that have collections are required to include in their disclosures a description of the accounting policies followed with regard to collections, a description of the collection, any significant changes made to the collection during the period, the amount spent on the collection during the period, the proceeds from any sales of collection items, and a statement of how the proceeds were used.

Section 4450: Reporting Controlled and Related Entities by Not-for-Profit Organizations

This section outlines the financial statement presentation and disclosures required when an NFPO has a control, significant influence, joint venture, or economic interest type of relationship with both profit-oriented and NFPOs. The breakdown used is quite similar to that for profit-oriented organizations, but the required financial reporting has some differences.

Control Investments An NFPO can have an investment or relationship that gives it the continuing power to determine the strategic operating, investing, and financing policies of another entity without the cooperation of others. The other entity can be profit-oriented or an NFPO. Control of a profit-oriented organization is normally evidenced by the right to appoint the majority of the board of directors because of ownership of voting shares. Because an NFPO does not issue shares, control of such an entity is normally evidenced by the right to appoint the majority of the board of directors as allowed by that entity's by-laws or articles of incorporation.

> A control investment is one that gives an NFPO control over either profit-oriented organizations or other NFPOs.

Control over NFPOs An example of a not-for-profit control situation is a national organization with local chapters. A large portion of funds raised by the local chapters goes to the national body, and any projects carried out by the local bodies must be approved (and perhaps funded) by the national organization.

The *Handbook*'s reporting requirements are as follows.

An organization should report each controlled NFPO in one of the following ways:

> Consolidation of an NFPO is one of three alternatives allowed. The alternatives apply to each controlled NFPO.

(a) Consolidating the controlled organization in its financial statements.

(b) Providing the disclosure set out in Paragraph 4450.22.

(c) If the controlled organization is one of a large number of individually immaterial organizations, by providing the disclosure set out in Paragraph 4450.26. [4450.14]

Because there is no investment account in the statement of financial position and no shareholders' equity in the others, consolidation is achieved by simply combining the financial statements on a line-by-line basis, and at the same time eliminating any transactions that occurred between the organizations. Accordingly, in the NFP sector, consolidated financial statements have often been referred to as combined financial statements

Since three alternatives are allowed, the management of the organization has to determine the accounting policy to be used. Note that the alternatives listed above are for each controlled entity. This means that if an organization has control over three NFPOs, all of which are material, it could choose to consolidate only one, and provide the required disclosure for the other two, provided that it reports consistently on a year-to-year basis. Later paragraphs further clarify the overall meaning by suggesting that if an NFPO has control over a large number of NFPOs, the decision to consolidate or not should be applied on a group basis. For example, it could establish a policy to consolidate all organizations in Groups A and B and not consolidate the organizations in Group C.

Paragraph 22 requires the disclosure of the totals of all of the assets, liabilities, net assets, revenues, expenses, and cash flows of any controlled NFPOs that are not consolidated. Paragraph 26 requires the disclosure of the reasons that the controlled organizations have been neither consolidated nor included in the disclosure set out in paragraph 4450.22. Possible reasons could include cost–benefit considerations and the decision not to exercise financial control.

A controlled profit-oriented organization can either be consolidated or reported using the equity method.

Control over Profit-Oriented Companies   Section 4450 states an NFPO should report each controlled profit-oriented enterprise in either of the following ways:

(a) Consolidating the controlled enterprise in its financial statements.

(b) Accounting for its investment in the controlled enterprise using the equity method and disclosing total assets, liabilities, and shareholders' equity at the reporting date and revenues, expenses, net income and cash flows for the period.

It should be noted that the requirements here are also applicable to each controlled entity, which could result in some subsidiaries being reported under the equity method and others being consolidated.

A jointly controlled organization can be either proportionately consolidated or reported using the equity method.

Joint Control   This is the contractual right to jointly control an organization with at least one other entity. An interest in a joint venture would be reported by either method:

• Proportionately consolidating the joint venture.
• Reporting the interest using the equity method.

Consistent with the requirements for controlled entities, the alternatives here apply to each joint venture, so that some may be proportionately consolidated and others may not, depending on the accounting policy determined by management. The section also states that if the NFPO's proportionate interest in the joint venture cannot be determined, it should not be considered to be a joint venture in accordance with this section, but might be either a significant influence or a control type of relationship. This seems to indicate that the joint venture would have to be one that issued shares, and thus probably a profit-oriented organization. However, if two or three NFPOs created another NFPO as a joint venture to carry out certain activities, and agreed to the percentage owned by each of the non-profit venturers, then the reporting alternatives outlined here would apply.

Significant Influence   When control is not present, the NFPO may still be able to exercise significant influence over the strategic operating, investing, and financing activities of the other entity. Factors suggesting the presence of significant influence include the ability to place members on the board of directors, the ability to participate in policy making, substantial transactions between the entities, and the sharing of senior personnel. If the significant-influence investment is in a profit-oriented enterprise, it must be accounted for using the equity method. If the significant-influence relationship is with another NFPO, the equity method is not used; instead, full disclosure of the relationship is required. This provision makes sense when one considers that applying the equity method requires using a percentage based on the number of shares held. Because an NFPO does not issue shares, it would be virtually impossible to determine the percentage needed to apply the method.

> A significant-influence investment in a profit-oriented organization is reported using the equity method. A significant-influence investment in another NFPO requires only full disclosure of the relationship.

Economic Interest   An economic interest in another NFPO exists if that organization holds resources for the reporting organization or if the reporting organization is responsible for the other organization's debts. There are varying degrees of economic interest, ranging from control or significant influence to neither of the two. When an organization has an economic interest in another NFPO over which it does not have control or significant influence, the nature and extent of this interest should be disclosed.

> When an organization has an economic interest in another NFPO, the nature and extent of this interest should be disclosed.

An investment in a profit-oriented organization that is not subject to control, significant influence, or joint control, is reported at fair value or using the cost method as per the requirements in the Part II Section 3856: Financial Instruments.

This concludes the discussion of Section 4450. A summary of the various types of investment that an NFPO can have and the reporting requirements for each follows:

Investment	Required reporting
Control of NFPO	Consolidate or disclose
Control of profit entity	Consolidate or equity method
Joint venture	Proportionately consolidate or equity method
Significant influence:	
NFPO	Full disclosure
Profit entity	Equity method
Economic interest	Full disclosure
Other investment:	
Profit entity	Fair value method or cost method or amortized cost method

Section 4460: Disclosure of Related-Party Transactions by Not-for-Profit Organizations
Related parties exist where one party is able to exercise control, joint control, or significant influence over another party. The other party may be either another NFPO or a profit-oriented enterprise. If one NFPO has an economic interest in another NFPO, the two parties are related. A related-party transaction has occurred when there has been a transfer of economic resources or obligations or services between the parties. Unlike Part II Section 3840, which prescribes both measurement and disclosure, this standard prescribes only disclosure for related-party transactions and does not state any requirements related to measurement. The disclosures required here are virtually identical to those required in Part II

> An NFPO must disclose all related-party transactions with another NFPO or a profit-oriented entity.

Section 3840. This section requires that the NFPO should disclose the following information about its transactions with related parties:

(a) A description of the relationship between the transacting parties.

(b) A description of the transaction(s), including those for which no amount has been recorded.

(c) The recorded amount of the transactions classified by financial statement category.

(d) The measurement basis used for recognizing the transaction in the financial statements.

(e) Amounts due to or from related parties and the terms and conditions relating thereto.

(f) Contractual obligations with related parties, separate from other contractual obligations.

(g) Contingencies involving related parties, separate from other contingencies.

Section 4470: Disclosure of Allocated Expenses by Not-for-Profit Organizations

When an organization classifies its expenses by function on the statement of operations, it may need or want to allocate certain expenses to a number of functions to which the expenses relate. For example, fundraising expenses and general support expenses usually contribute to or produce the output of more than one function and are often considered to be directly related to the output of each of those functions. Since aggregate amounts reported for fundraising and general support functions are often of particular significance to financial statement users, this standard requires that the following be disclosed when these two types of expenses are allocated to other functions:

An NFPO must disclose details related to any allocation of fundraising and general support costs to different functions.

- The accounting policy for the allocation of expenses among functions, the nature of the expenses being allocated, and the basis on which such allocations have been made.

- The amounts allocated from functions, and the amounts and the functions to which they have been allocated.

However, this section does not require organizations to classify their expenses by function or to undertake any allocations. Only if it does so is the above disclosure necessary.

ACCOUNTING FOR CONTRIBUTIONS

An NFPO can choose either the deferral method or the restricted fund method to account for contributions.

Part III has defined two methods of accounting for contributions: the *deferral* method and the *restricted fund* method. The deferral method can be used with or without fund accounting. The restricted fund method has to be used in combination with fund accounting.

If the organization wants to present an overall picture of the organization—that is, a set of statements with only one column for each year—it must use the deferral method. If it wants to report on a fund accounting basis—separate columns for different funds—it can choose the deferral method for all funds or the restricted fund method.

With fund accounting, it is easier to present and report on the different restrictions placed on contributions. However, as we will see, the deferral method does a better job of matching revenues to expenses, which makes it easier to see what portion of expenses is financed by contributions and what portion is financed by other sources.

The Deferral Method

The deferral method matches contribution revenues with related expenses. Unrestricted contributions are reported as revenue in the period received or receivable, because there are no particular related expenses associated with them.

The deferral method requires that contribution revenue be matched to expenses.

Endowment contributions are not shown in the operating statement; rather, they are reflected in the statement of changes in net assets. This is because endowment contributions, by definition, will never have related expenses.

Restricted contributions must be matched against related expenses. This matching principle has different implications for different kinds of restricted contributions, as follows:

- Restricted contributions for expenses of future periods are deferred and recognized as revenue in the same periods as the related expenses are incurred.
- The handling of restricted contributions for the acquisition of capital assets depends on whether related expenses are associated with them. If the capital asset is subject to amortization, the related expense is the yearly amortization. The restricted contribution is deferred and recognized as revenue on the same basis as the asset is being amortized. If the capital asset is not subject to amortization (e.g., land), there will be no expenses to match against. In the same manner as for endowment contributions, the restricted capital asset contributions of this type are reflected in the statement of changes in net assets.
- Restricted contributions for expenses of the current period are recognized as revenue in the current period. Matching is achieved, and there is no need for deferral.

Contributions for a depreciable asset are recognized as revenue as the asset is being amortized.

Investment income can be either unrestricted or restricted. Unrestricted investment income is recognized as revenue when it is earned. Restricted investment income has to be recognized in the same manner as restricted contributions. For example, if an endowment contribution states that the purchasing power of the contribution must be preserved, some portion of the income earned must be used to increase the endowment. This portion is treated in exactly the same manner as an endowment contribution, and is reflected in the statement of changes in net assets. Other types of restricted investment income must be deferred and matched against expense in the manner previously discussed. If all investment income is restricted, it is quite possible that all investment income earned in a period will be deferred.

The matching of revenue and expense for an NFPO is the exact opposite to that for a profit-oriented enterprise. With the latter, revenues are recognized and then expenses are matched with those revenues. With an NFPO, restricted revenues are matched to expenses. This means that if contributions have been collected to fund certain expenses and those expenses have yet to be incurred, the contributions are recognized as deferred revenue until a later period, when they can be matched with the expenses.

The Restricted Fund Method

This method requires an NFPO to report a general fund, at least one restricted fund, and, if it has endowments or receives endowment contributions, an endowment fund. The general fund reports all unrestricted revenue and restricted contributions for which no corresponding restricted fund is presented. The fund balance represents net assets that are not subject to externally imposed restrictions. The restricted funds will be used to record externally restricted revenue. Specific requirements are outlined as follows:

- Endowment contributions will be reported as revenue in the endowment fund, and because there are no related expenses associated with endowment contributions, no expenses will appear in the statement of operations of the endowment fund.
- The general fund records all unrestricted contributions and investment income, including unrestricted income from endowment fund investments.
- If some of the endowment fund income is restricted, it is reflected as revenue in the particular restricted fund involved.
- If some of the endowment fund income is permanently restricted, because the purchasing power of the endowment is required to be maintained, it is recorded as revenue of the endowment fund.
- Externally restricted contributions for which there is a corresponding restricted fund are recorded as revenue of the restricted fund when received or receivable.

- If an externally restricted contribution or externally restricted investment income is received for which there is no corresponding restricted fund, the amounts are recorded in the general fund in accordance with the deferral method. In other words, they are recorded as deferred revenue in the general fund and matched with the related expenses in that fund when these expenses are incurred.
- If management decides to impose internal restrictions on general fund unrestricted contributions, the contributions are initially reported as revenue in the general fund. The transfers are reported in the statement of changes in fund balances below the line "excess of revenue over expenses." Note disclosure should clearly indicate the amount of resources shown in restricted funds that have been designated as such by management, because these amounts do not satisfy the *Handbook*'s definition of a contribution.

The excess of revenues over expenses in the general fund represents the increase in unrestricted resources during the period. The fund balance in the general fund shows the unrestricted net assets at the end of the period. A restricted fund shows no deferred revenue. The fund balance of a restricted fund represents the amount of net assets that are restricted for that particular fund's purpose. The fund balance in the endowment fund represents the net assets that have permanent restrictions on them.

Under the restricted fund method, instead of presenting a statement of changes in net assets (as is required under the deferral method of recording contributions), a statement of changes in fund balances is prepared. Because of the requirement to capitalize long-lived assets, capital assets must appear on the statement of financial position of either the general fund or one of the restricted funds (excluding the endowment fund).

This has been a summary of the two methods of accounting for contributions. Before we show these concepts in an extensive illustration, some additional topics must be addressed.

NET ASSETS INVESTED IN CAPITAL ASSETS

The *Handbook* provides an option to report "net assets invested in capital assets" as a separate component of net assets. This amount represents resources spent on and tied up in capital assets and therefore not available for future spending.

The amount shown depends on the method used to account for contributions. If the restricted fund method is used, the amount represents the unamortized portion of *all* capital assets less associated debt, regardless of whether they were purchased from restricted or unrestricted resources. If the deferral method is used, the amount presented represents the unamortized portion of capital assets (net of associated debt) that were purchased with *unrestricted* resources. The following example will illustrate the differences.

Example   At the beginning of the current period, an NFPO purchases equipment costing $5,000 with a useful life of two years. We will assume first that the equipment is acquired from restricted resources, and then from unrestricted resources. We will focus on the equipment transaction only, and the effect of the transaction on the financial statements of the NFPO. In order to do this, we also assume that the organization was formed at the beginning of the period and that the equipment acquisition is the only transaction that has occurred.

The Restricted Fund Method

Purchase from Restricted Resources   Assume that the equipment is purchased from a restricted fund contribution of $5,100. The capital fund records contributions of this nature, as well as the acquisition of capital assets and their subsequent amortization. The journal entries are as follows:

Capital fund

Cash	5,100	
Contribution revenue		5,100
Equipment	5,000	
Cash		5,000
Amortization expense	2,500	
Accumulated amortization		2,500

Because the capital fund did not exist before the start of the period, the financial statements at the end of the period appear as follows:

CAPITAL FUND
OPERATING STATEMENT AND CHANGES IN FUND BALANCE

Contribution revenue	$5,100	The restricted contribution
Amortization expense	2,500	is reported as revenue when
Excess of revenue over expense	2,600	received.
Fund balance—start of period	0	
Fund balance—end of period	$2,600	

STATEMENT OF FINANCIAL POSITION

Cash		$ 100	
Equipment	$5,000		
Accumulated amortization	2,500	2,500	
Total assets		$2,600	
Fund balance			An NFPO can report "net
Invested in capital assets		$2,500	assets invested in capital
Externally restricted funds		100	assets" as a separate
Total fund balance		$2,600	component of net assets.

The unamortized balance of equipment purchased with restricted resources is reflected in the amount of fund balance invested in capital assets.

Note that the fund balance section shows two classifications:

- The $2,500 invested in capital assets represents the unamortized balance of spent resources that have not yet been reflected in the statement of operations as an expense.
- Externally restricted funds of $100 represent resources that can be spent only to acquire capital assets.

As the equipment is amortized on the operating statement, the fund balance itself is reduced, and it is the statement of financial position category "invested in capital assets" that reflects the reduction.

Purchase from Unrestricted Resources   Now assume that the equipment is purchased from unrestricted resources. The general fund receives an unrestricted contribution of $5,100 and uses it to acquire equipment.

The journal entries in the general fund and the capital fund are as follows:

General fund

Cash	5,100	
Contribution revenue		5,100
Transfer to capital fund	5,000	
Cash		5,000

The general fund's operating statement after the transaction shows the following:

GENERAL FUND
STATEMENT OF OPERATIONS AND CHANGES IN FUND BALANCE

Transfers between funds are reported in changes in fund balances, not as revenues and expenses.

Revenues	$5,100
Expenses	0
Excess of revenue over expense	5,100
Fund balance—start of period	0
Transfer to capital fund	(5,000)
Fund balance—end of period	$ 100

STATEMENT OF FINANCIAL POSITION

Cash	$ 100
Total assets	$ 100
Fund balance	
Unrestricted funds	$ 100
Total fund balance	$ 100

The capital fund records the acquisition of the equipment and its amortization with the following entries:

Capital fund

Equipment	5,000	
Transfer from general fund		5,000
Amortization expense	2,500	
Accumulated amortization		2,500

The end-of-period financial statements show the following:

CAPITAL FUND
STATEMENT OF OPERATIONS AND CHANGES IN FUND BALANCE

Amortization expense	$2,500
Excess of revenue over expense	(2,500)
Fund balance—start of period	0
Transfer from general fund	5,000
Fund balance—end of period	$2,500

STATEMENT OF FINANCIAL POSITION

Equipment	$5,000	The unamortized balance of
Accumulated amortization	2,500	equipment purchased with
Total assets	$2,500	unrestricted resources is
Fund balance		also reflected in the amount
Invested in capital assets	$2,500	of fund balance invested in
Total fund balance	$2,500	capital assets.

Note that regardless of the source of resources used to acquire the equipment (restricted or unrestricted), the unamortized balance appears as an asset on the statement of financial position of the capital fund, and the fund balance shows a classification "invested in capital assets" in an amount equal to the asset balance. This is not the case when the deferral method with no fund accounting is used.

The Deferral Method

Purchase from Restricted Resources   Assume that the equipment is purchased from a restricted fund contribution of $5,100. The journal entries to record the contribution, acquisition, and first year's amortization are as follows:

Cash	5,100		Deferred contributions
Deferred contributions—capital assets		5,100	includes unspent resources
			restricted to purchase capital
Equipment	5,000		assets in the future.
Cash		5,000	
Amortization expense	2,500		
Accumulated amortization		2,500	
Deferred contributions—capital assets	2,500		
Contribution revenue		2,500	

Financial statements that reflect these transactions are as follows:

STATEMENT OF OPERATIONS AND CHANGES IN NET ASSETS

Contribution revenue	$2,500
Amortization expense	2,500
Excess of revenue over expenses	0
Net assets—start of period	0
Net assets—end of period	$ 0

STATEMENT OF FINANCIAL POSITION

Cash		$ 100
Equipment	$5,000	
Accumulated amortization	2,500	2,500
Total assets		$2,600
Deferred contributions—capital assets		$2,600
Net Assets		
Unrestricted		0
Total		$2,600

Deferred contributions includes restricted resources that have been spent to acquire capital assets but have not yet been matched to amortization expense.

Deferred contributions of $2,600 includes two components: $100 in unspent resources restricted to future spending on capital assets and $2,500 in restricted resources that has been spent acquiring capital assets, but has not yet been reflected as revenue on the operating statement because there has yet to be an expense to match it against. When amortization occurs, an equal amount is recognized as revenue. Because there is no effect on the "excess of revenue over expense" amount, there is no effect on the equity section "net assets." As the equipment decreases on the asset side due to amortization, the amount "deferred contributions" decreases by the same amount on the liability side. Because this equipment was purchased from restricted resources, there can be no amount shown under "invested in capital assets" in the net assets section.

Purchase from Unrestricted Resources   Assume now that the equipment was purchased from an unrestricted contribution of $5,100. The journal entries to record the events are as follows:

Unrestricted contributions are reported as revenue when received.

Cash	5,100	
Contribution revenue		5,100
Equipment	5,000	
Cash		5,000
Amortization expense	2,500	
Accumulated amortization		2,500

The financial statements that reflect these transactions are as follows:

STATEMENT OF OPERATIONS

Contribution revenue	$5,100
Amortization expense	2,500
Excess of revenue over expenses	$2,600

STATEMENT OF FINANCIAL POSITION

Cash		$ 100
Equipment		5,000
Accumulated amortization		2,500
		2,500
Total assets		$2,600
Net Assets		
Invested in capital assets		$2,500
Unrestricted		100
Total		$2,600

Net assets invested in capital assets represents the unamortized balance of equipment purchased with unrestricted resources.

Note that the statement of operations does not include a reconciliation of opening and ending net assets. A separate statement is usually presented. Because net assets represents total equity, the changes in the classifications of this equity must be shown in the statement as follows:

STATEMENT OF CHANGES IN NET ASSETS

	Invested in capital assets	Unrestricted	Total
Balance—start of period	$ 0	$ 0	$ 0
Excess of revenue over expenses	($2,500)	5,100	2,600
Investment in capital assets	5,000	(5,000)	0
Balance—end of period	$2,500	$ 100	$2,600

Under the deferral method, a statement of changes in net assets is prepared.

The "unrestricted" column represents resources that can be spent for any purpose. The organization received an unrestricted contribution of $5,100 and spent $5,000 on equipment. At the end of the period it has $100 left to spend. The transfer of $5,000 to the category "invested in capital assets" depicts the acquisition of capital assets from unrestricted resources. The operating statement shows an excess of revenue over expenses of $2,600. A $2,500 deduction for the amortization of assets purchased with unrestricted resources was used to arrive at the excess of revenue over expenses. Note that this does not represent resources spent, but rather the cost of services provided by the equipment. By transferring this deduction to "invested in capital assets," the amount of the operating results allocated to unrestricted resources becomes $5,100, which represents the actual inflow of spendable resources, and the amount shown for "invested in capital assets" is equal to the unamortized balance of the equipment purchased from unrestricted resources.

Donated Capital Assets, Materials, and Services

Donated Capital Assets An NFPO is required to record the donation of capital assets at fair value. If fair value cannot be determined, a nominal value will be used. A nominal value could be in the range of $1 to $100 for small NFPOs, and $1,000 and higher for large NFPOs. If an organization receives an unsolicited donation of a capital asset that it has no intention of using, it should be reflected in its financial statements as "other assets" instead of as a capital asset, and a loss or gain should be reflected in the statement of operations when disposal of the asset occurs. The following illustrates the recording of donated capital assets.

Donated capital assets must be recorded at fair value or, if fair value cannot be determined, at a nominal value.

Example A capital asset with a fair value of $10,000 is donated to an NFPO. The initial treatment depends on which of the two methods of recording contributions is being used. If the deferral method is used and the capital asset is subject to amortization (e.g., equipment), the contribution should be deferred and revenue should be recognized later, to match to the amortization expense. The journal entry would be as follows:

Equipment	10,000	
Deferred contributions—capital assets		10,000

A donated depreciable asset is reported as deferred contributions under the deferral method.

Assuming a five-year useful life, in each succeeding year the following entries will be made as the equipment is amortized:

Amortization expense	2,000	
Accumulated amortization		2,000
Deferred contributions—capital assets	2,000	
Contribution revenue		2,000

If the deferral method is being used and the asset is not subject to amortization (e.g., land), the following entry is made:

Land	10,000	
Net assets invested in capital assets		10,000

Because no future expense will be associated with the asset, deferral is not required and the donation of land is reflected in the statement of net assets.

If the restricted fund method is being used, the fair value of the donated capital asset is recorded as revenue in the capital fund as follows:

A donated depreciable asset is reported as contribution revenue under the restricted fund method.

Capital fund

Equipment	10,000	
Contribution revenue—donated equipment		10,000

Donated land will be treated in the same manner, except that the debit will be to land instead of equipment. Small NFPOs that have adopted a policy of non-capitalization of acquisitions of capital assets will still be required to record donated capital assets at fair value. For example, the donation of equipment with a fair value of $10,000 is recorded in the following manner:

Equipment expense	10,000	
Contribution revenue—donated equipment		10,000

Regardless of whether the organization uses the deferral method or the restricted fund method, the entry is the same because the required matching automatically occurs with the entry.

Donated materials and services can be reported if they are needed by the organization.

Donated Materials and Services   The requirements for the reporting of donated materials and services are different from those for donated capital assets. An NFPO has the option of reporting or not reporting donated material and services; however, it can only report these donations if fair value can be determined, if the materials and services would normally be used in the organization's operations and if the NFPO would have been purchased these material and services if they had not been donated.

Section 4410 also makes it clear that the fair value of the services of volunteers is normally not recognized due to the difficulty in determining such values. Furthermore, an organization would probably not record donated materials if it acts as an intermediary for immediate distribution. For example, due to the difficulty of determining fair values and the large number of transactions, a food bank would not normally record the donation of food that it distributes to its clients.

Example   A radio station donated free airtime to help a charity publicize its fundraising campaign. The fair value of the airtime is $5,200, and the policy of the organization is to record the value of donated materials and services. The journal entry is as follows:

Advertising expense	5,200	
Revenue—donated airtime		5,200

If the restricted fund method was being used, this entry would be made in the general fund. If the donation consisted of office supplies rather than airtime, the entry to record the donation under the deferral method would be as follows:

Office supplies (asset)	5,200	
Deferred contribution		5,200

If half of the supplies were used, the entries would be as follows:

Supplies expense	2,600	
Office supplies		2,600
Deferred contribution	2,600	
Contribution revenue		2,600

> Donated materials and services should be reported as contribution revenue when the materials and services are expensed.

The same entries would likely be used under the restricted fund method. Due to the nature of the items donated, the transaction would normally be recorded in the general fund. The deferral method must be used for the general fund.

See Self-Study Problem 1 for a comprehensive problem involving an NFPO. It includes many of the issues we have covered in this chapter so far.

BUDGETARY CONTROL AND ENCUMBRANCES

> **L04**
>
> The actual recording of the budget in the records, along with the use of an encumbrance system, is a device used by NFPOs and governments to control spending.

Budgeting is an essential element of the financial planning, control, and performance evaluation processes for some NFPOs. The budget serves several important purposes:

1. *Expresses the strategic plan.* If, for example, more money is budgeted for research and less for recreational activities, users of the financial statements are made aware of the strategic priorities of the organization.

2. *Serves as an expression of financial intent for the upcoming fiscal year.* The budget presents the financial plan for the NFPO for the upcoming period.

3. *Provides control* because it establishes spending limitations for each activity.

4. *Offers a means of evaluating performance* by allowing a comparison of actual results with the levels found in the budget.

5. *Indicates whether the NFPO anticipates having sufficient revenues to pay for the anticipated expenditures.* In the current economic climate when many NFPOs face declining contributions, the amount and handling of proposed deficits should be of interest to every stakeholder.

Governments and some NFPOs often use a *formal budget recording system* together with an *encumbrance system* as a device to help control spending. Prior to the commencement of a fiscal year, a formal budget is drawn up that shows the budgeted revenues and expenses for the coming year. The usual starting point in the process is a preliminary expense budget based on how the managers of the organization would like to see spending take place. Then a revenue budget is prepared based on the expected results from the revenue-raising activities of the coming year. If this revenue budget is realistic, the next step is to scale down the controllable expenses so that the organization does not plan to have expenses greater than its expected revenues. NFPOs and local governments do not (and in the case of many local governments, are not allowed to) budget for a deficit in any one year unless they have a surplus from prior years. Because both types of organizations raise money each year and then spend it, any deficit spending in a particular year eventually must be offset by surplus spending in later years. Once the budget has been formally passed by the board of directors (or the local government legislative body), the spending for applicable budgeted expenses commences. Often an NFPO's actual expenses turn out to be equal to the amount budgeted, and problems arise when actual revenues are less than budget. Government grants are sometimes reduced, or do not increase as much as was budgeted for, or some fundraising activity is not as successful as was forecast. If this happens over a series of years, the accumulated deficit problem will have to be addressed and the NFPO will have to organize special deficit-reduction fundraising activities in addition to the normal, annual fundraising for operations.

Budgetary Control   If deficits are to be avoided, the managers of NFPOs must have timely information regarding actual results compared with amounts budgeted. This can be accomplished by formally recording the budget in the accounting system.

> Budget accounts can be incorporated in an NFPO's general ledger.

Example   The following is the summarized budget that was approved by the board of directors of an NFPO:

Budgeted revenues (in detail)	$900,000
Budgeted expenses (in detail)	890,000
Budgeted surplus	$ 10,000

If the organization records the budget in its accounting records, the following journal entry is made at the start of the fiscal year:

Estimated revenues (control account)	900,000	
Appropriations (control account)		890,000
Budgetary fund balance		10,000

While it may appear strange to debit an account for budgeted revenues and to credit an account for budgeted expenses, the logic becomes clearer when one considers that budgeted revenues represent *expected* resource inflows and that budgeted expenses (with the exception of amortization) represent *expected* resource outflows. The general ledger accounts used are control accounts to the very detailed subsidiary ledger accounts needed to keep track of actual versus budgeted amounts, particularly in relation to expenses. Spending is often a continuous process, while revenues are received at various times throughout the year. If during the year it appears that actual revenues will be less than budget, it is a difficult task to reduce the budgeted expenses remaining in order to avoid a deficit. It is, however, possible with a system such as this to ensure that actual expenses do not exceed budget. The overall concept of "spending" in this context is based on an accrual system of measurement, not on a cash basis. At the end of the fiscal year the budget accounts are reversed as part of the closing journal entries, and these amounts are not reflected in the organization's external financial statements.

> Budget accounts are used as a control device, and the amounts are not usually reflected in an NFPO's external financial statements.

Encumbrance Accounting   This involves making entries in the accounting records to record the issuance of purchase orders for the acquisition of goods and services from outside suppliers. The amounts recorded are estimates of the actual costs. It is not the normal practice to use encumbrance accounting for employee wage costs, because this particular type of expenditure can be controlled by other means; nor is it normal to use encumbrances for amortization. When the goods and services ordered are actually received, the original encumbrance entry is reversed and the invoiced cost of the goods or services acquired is recorded.

> Encumbrance accounting involves the actual recording of purchase orders at the time of issuance. From a control standpoint, a budget item has been spent at this moment.

Example   Purchase order #3056A is issued for the acquisition of office supplies expected to cost $950. The journal entry to record the purchase order is as follows:

Encumbrances	950	
Estimated commitments[2]		950

When the supplies ordered under purchase order #3056A are received at an invoiced cost of $954, the following journal entries are required:

Estimated commitments	950	
Encumbrances		950
Supplies expense	954	
Accounts payable		954

Control over expenditures is achieved by mandating that the spending of a budgeted amount has occurred when the purchase order is issued, not when the goods are received or paid for. In this example, if the budgeted amount for supplies is $3,000, there is an unspent budget amount of $2,050 after the purchase order is issued, and an unspent amount of $2,046 after the receipt of the actual supplies. The use of encumbrance accounting along with a system of budgetary control prevents the issuing of purchase orders when there are no uncommitted budgeted amounts.

The only accounting problem involved is the financial statement presentation of outstanding purchase orders at the end of a fiscal period. Should the encumbrances be reflected in the operations statement as similar to expenses, and the estimated commitments appear in the statement of financial position as liabilities? In the past, NFPOs have presented these accounts in this manner. Currently, encumbrances are not recognized in the financial statements because they do not meet the definition of a liability. A purchase order is an executory contract under which neither party has performed. No obligation exists until goods are delivered. It follows that outstanding encumbrances should not be reflected as elements of financial statements, but rather should be disclosed in the footnotes to the statements if the amounts are material.[3]

> Amounts for outstanding encumbrances are considered to be executory contracts and, therefore, are not recorded in an NFPO's external financial statements.

COMPREHENSIVE ILLUSTRATION OF THE RESTRICTED FUND METHOD   `L05`

The following example (with 000s omitted) will be used to illustrate the journal entries made for various funds and the annual general-purpose financial statements prepared using the restricted fund method of accounting for contributions.

The Blue Shield Agency is a charitable organization located in a mid-sized Canadian city. The major goal of the organization is to provide food and shelter for the homeless. It operates out of its own premises, and while it has some permanent employees, it also relies heavily on volunteers.

The agency's funds have four sources:

- Government grants are received annually to fund the regular food and shelter operating activities. When the need arises, special government grants are solicited to fund capital asset additions and major renovations.

- Donations are received as a result of public campaigns held each March to raise funds for the current year's operating costs.

- A United Way grant is received each November to help fund the next year's operations.

- Investment income is received from an endowment fund and other investments.

The agency maintains its records in accordance with the restricted fund method of accounting for contributions, and prepares its annual financial statements on this basis. The three funds being used are described below.

The general fund captures the agency's operating activities.

General Fund   This fund is used to record the agency's operating activities. Revenues consist of government operating grants, the proceeds from the annual fundraising campaign, the United Way grant, investment income from the endowment fund, and term deposit interest. Each year, the grant from the United Way is recorded as deferred revenue to be matched against the operating expenses of the year following. Expenses are for the food and shelter programs and for administration costs. An encumbrance system is used to ensure that costs do not exceed budgeted amounts, but the budget itself is not formally recorded in the accounting records. While some donated materials and services are received each year, no record of these donations is made in the ledger accounts. Small-equipment purchases made from this fund are capitalized in the capital fund.

Capital Fund   This fund is used to account for restricted funds raised for building and equipment acquisitions. The capital fund also records the capitalization of buildings and equipment and the amortization taken. Equipment acquisitions made from the general fund are also capitalized in this fund.

Approximately 20 years ago the city donated a building to the agency. While the city retained title to the land on which the building is situated, the agency will not be required to move, and the building will not be torn down, as long as the agency continues with its programs. The value of the donated building was *not* recorded at the time of the donation because it was the organization's policy not to capitalize buildings and equipment. When the current *Handbook* sections became operative several years ago, the organization spent considerable time and money searching past records to determine the cost of capital assets purchased from both restricted and non-restricted contributions and the fair values of capital assets donated. The new *Handbook* sections had to be applied retrospectively, and the following journal entry was made in the capital fund at that time to accomplish this:

The previously unreported capital assets were recorded in the capital fund with an accompanying increase in net assets.

Equipment and furniture	1,100	
Buildings	2,000	
Accumulated amortization		1,200
Fund balance—investment in capital assets		1,900

Endowment Fund   The $500 in this fund was bequeathed to the agency by its founder five years ago. Investment income earned is to be used for operating purposes and is recorded in the general fund.

The statements of financial position of the funds of Blue Shield as at January 1, Year 6 (the start of the next fiscal year), are presented in Exhibit 12.2.

This form of presentation of fund financial statements is called the *multicolumn approach* because each of the fund's financial statements is presented in its own separate column. If fund accounting is used, the *Handbook* requires that totals be shown for each item presented in the statement of financial position and statement of changes in fund balances, so that the "big picture" for the entire organization can be seen. This approach can become very cumbersome if an organization has a large number of funds that need to be presented separately because of all of the restrictions involved. An alternative is to combine the funds into a single set of statements, use the deferral method of accounting for contributions, and provide extensive footnote disclosure of resource restrictions. For the statement of operations, a total column must be presented for general funds, endowment

---

EXHIBIT 12.2

BLUE SHIELD AGENCY
STATEMENT OF FINANCIAL POSITION
January 1, Year 6
(in thousands of dollars)

	General fund	Capital fund	Endowment fund	Total
Current Assets				
Cash and term deposits	$417	$ 62		$ 479
Pledges receivable	490			490
	907	62		969
Investments			$500	500
Capital assets:				
Equipment and furniture		1,482		1,482
Buildings		2,095		2,095
Accumulated amortization		(1,517)		(1,517)
		2,060		2,060
Total assets	$907	$2,122	$500	$3,529
Current Liabilities				
Accounts payable	$613	$ 50		$ 663
Wages payable	70			70
Accrued liabilities	82			82
Deferred revenue	40			40
	805	50		855
Fund Balances				
Investment in capital assets		2,060		2,060
Externally restricted		12	$500	512
Unrestricted	102			102
	102	2,072	500	2,674
Total liabilities and fund balances	$907	$2,122	$500	$3,529

When reporting on a fund basis, the total for each financial statement item must be shown.

Instead of a section for owner's equity, an NFPO's statement of financial position has a section called "fund balances" or "surplus."

funds, and restricted funds. Although it is desirable to show a total for all funds, it is not necessary under the restricted fund method.

Year 6 Events   The year's events are summarized as follows (all dollar amounts are in thousands unless stated otherwise):

(a) The accounts and wages payable and the accrued liabilities at the beginning of the year were paid.

(b) The deferred revenue from Year 5 consisted of the grant from the United Way. An entry was made to recognize this as revenue in Year 6.

(c) The pledges receivable at the beginning of the year were collected in full.

(d) The fundraising campaign was held in March to collect funds for Year 6 operations. Cash of $1,187 was collected, and pledges expected to realize $800 were received. Total fundraising costs were $516, of which $453 was paid in cash, $50 is owed to suppliers, and $13 has been accrued.

(e) During Year 6, the agency announced a plan to construct an addition to its building at an estimated cost of $1,500. The budget includes equipment acquisitions. The addition will be built in two phases, with completion expected in Year 8. At the end of Year 6 the first phase was out for tender, with construction to commence early in Year 7.

   The government announced a grant of $600 in Year 6 to cover the first phase and has remitted $450 of this, with the balance promised in Year 7. The agency spent $103 on equipment near the end of Year 6, of which $91 has been paid and $12 is owed. At the beginning of the year, the agency had $62 on hand from a previous building campaign and an unpaid liability of $50 for capital asset purchases. A public campaign will be conducted next year to raise the balance of the funds needed to complete the project.

(f) Government grants for operating purposes totalled $1,200 in Year 6, of which $910 was received during the year, with the balance expected in January, Year 7.

(g) The agency uses an encumbrance system as a means of controlling expenditures. (Note: Wages of agency employees are not subject to encumbrance because purchase orders are not issued for this type of expenditure.) During the year, orders estimated to total $1,964 were issued for the purchase of goods and services.

(h) Invoices totalling $1,866 were received on purchase orders originally recorded at an estimated cost of $1,870. Suppliers were paid $1,446 on account for these invoices, and the balance owing is still outstanding. The costs were allocated as follows:

Shelter program	$650
Food program	960
Administration	256

(i) The total wage costs, of which $357 was paid and $183 is payable at year-end, were as follows:

Shelter program	$ 90
Food program	150
Administration	300

(j) The United Way grant amounting to $65 was received in December.

(k) Late in the year a prominent supporter donated $50 to be held in endowment, with the income earned to be unrestricted.

(l) The investments in the endowment fund earned interest of $40; a further $14 in interest was received from the term deposits held in the general fund.

(m) Refrigeration equipment costing $3 was purchased with general fund cash.

(n) The Year 6 amortization charges amounted to $150 of which $90 pertains to capital assets that had been donated or purchased with funds restricted for the purchase of capital assets and of which $60 pertains to capital assets that had been purchased with unrestricted funds.

(o) At the end of the year the balances in the encumbrance accounts were closed.

The journal entries required to record these events in each of the three funds are presented next in the order listed:

(a) *General fund*

Accounts payable	613	
Wages payable	70	
Accrued liabilities	82	
Cash		765
Capital fund		
Accounts payable	50	
Cash		50

Accounting records are maintained for each individual fund. Journal entries show the fund being adjusted.

(b) *General fund*

Deferred revenue	40	
Revenue—United Way grant		40

(c) *General fund*

Cash	490	
Pledges receivable		490

(d) *General fund*

Cash	1,187	
Pledges receivable	800	
Revenue—donations		1,987
Expenses—fundraising	516	
Cash		453
Accounts payable		50
Accrued liabilities		13

Contributions and pledges for the current year are reported as revenue in the current year.

(e) *Capital fund*

Cash	450	
Government grant receivable	150	
Revenue—government grant		600
Equipment	103	
Cash		91
Accounts payable		12

Contributions and pledges for a restricted fund are reported as revenue when received/receivable.

(f) *General fund*

Cash	910	
Government grant receivable	290	
Revenue—government grant		1,200

(g) *General fund*
Encumbrances   1,964
    Estimated commitments   1,964

Encumbrances are reversed
when the goods and services
are received.

(h) *General fund*
Estimated commitments   1,870
    Encumbrances   1,870
Expenses—shelter program   650
Expenses—food program   960
Expenses—administration   256
    Cash   1,446
    Accounts payable   420

(i) *General fund*
Expenses—shelter program   90
Expenses—food program   150
Expenses—administration   300
    Cash   357
    Wages payable   183

Contributions for next year's
activities are deferred when
a separate restricted fund
is not established for the
contributions.

(j) *General fund*
Cash   65
    Deferred revenue—United Way   65

(k) *Endowment fund*
Cash   50
    Revenue—contribution   50

(l) *General fund*
Cash   54
    Revenue—investment income   54

(m) *General fund*
Transfer to capital fund   3
    Cash   3

Capital fund
Equipment   3
    Transfer from general fund   3

(n) *Capital fund*
Expenses—amortization   150
    Accumulated amortization   150

(o) *General fund*
Estimated commitments   94
    Encumbrances   94

After these journal entries are posted, financial statements as at December 31, Year 6, can be prepared as shown in Exhibit 12.3. Note that while a fund type of cash flow statement could be prepared, the one in this illustration has been prepared on a non-fund basis, which is in accordance with the *Handbook*'s pronouncements. Letters shown in parentheses represent the journal entries affecting the cash account.

EXHIBIT 12.3

BLUE SHIELD AGENCY
STATEMENT OF FINANCIAL POSITION
December 31, Year 6
(in thousands of dollars)

	General fund	Capital fund	Endowment fund	Total	
Current Assets					The deferral method is used
Cash and term deposits	$ 99	$ 371	$ 50	$ 520	to account for contributions
Pledges receivable	800			800	reported in the general fund.
Government grants receivable	290	150		440	
	1,189	521	50	1,760	
Investments			500	500	
Capital assets:					
Equipment and furniture		1,588		1,588	
Buildings		2,095		2,095	
Accumulated depreciation		(1,667)		(1,667)	
		2,016		2,016	
Total assets	$1,189	$2,537	$550	$4,276	
Current Liabilities					
Accounts payable	$ 470	$ 12		$ 482	
Wages payable	183			183	
Accrued liabilities	13			13	
Deferred revenue	65			65	
	731	12		743	
Fund Balances					Fund balances show the
Investment in capital assets[4]		2,016		2,016	restrictions on the net assets
Externally restricted funds		509	$550	1,059	of the organization.
Unrestricted funds	458			458	
	458	2,525	550	3,533	
Total liabilities and fund balances	$1,189	$2,537	$550	$4,276	

BLUE SHIELD AGENCY
STATEMENT OF REVENUES, EXPENSES, AND
CHANGES IN FUND BALANCES
for the Year Ended December 31, Year 6
(in thousands of dollars)

	General fund	Capital fund	Endowment fund	Total
Revenues				
Government grants	$1,200	$ 600		$1,800
United Way grant	40			40
Contributions	1,987		$ 50	2,037
Investment income	54			54
	3,281	600	50	3,931

(continued)

EXHIBIT 12.3 (continued)	General fund	Capital fund	Endowment fund	Total
Expenses				
Shelter program	740			740
Food program	1,110			1,110
Administration	556			556
Fundraising	516			516
Amortization		150		150
	2,922	150		3,072
Excess of revenue over expenses	359	450	50	859
Interfund transfers	(3)	3		
Fund balances, January 1	102	2,072	500	2,674
Fund balances, December 31	$ 458	$2,525	$550	$3,533

Expenses are classified by function.

BLUE SHIELD AGENCY
CASH FLOW STATEMENT
for the Year Ended December 31, Year 6
(in thousands of dollars)

It is not required to present a cash flow statement on a fund basis.

Cash Flows from Operating Activities	
Cash received from government operating grants **(f)**	$ 910
Cash received from United Way grant **(j)**	65
Cash received from general contributions **(c)**, **(d)**	1,677
Cash received from investment income **(l)**	54
Cash paid to suppliers **(a)**, **(h)**	(2,141)
Cash paid to employees **(a)**, **(i)**	(427)
Cash paid for fundraising **(d)**	(453)
Net cash used in operating activities	(315)
Cash Flows from Investing Activities	
Cash paid for capital asset acquisitions **(a)**, **(e)**, **(m)**	(144)
Net cash used in investing activities	(144)
Cash Flows from Financing Activities	
Contributions of cash for endowment **(k)**	50
Cash received from government grant **(e)**	450
Net cash generated through financing activities	500
Net increase in cash and term deposits	41
Cash and term deposits—January 1	479
Cash and term deposits—December 31	$ 520

The closing entries for each fund are prepared as follows:

Revenues, expenses, and fund transfers are closed to fund balances.

General fund

Revenue—government grant	1,200	
Revenue—United Way grant	40	
Revenue—contributions	1,987	
Revenue—investment income	54	
Expenses—shelter program		740
Expenses—food program		1,110
Expenses—administration		556
Expenses—fundraising		516
Fund balance		359

Fund balance	3	
Transfer to capital fund		3

Capital fund

Revenue—government grant	600	
Expenses—amortization		150
Fund balance		450
Transfer from general fund	3	
Fund balance		3

Endowment fund

Revenue contributions	50	
Fund balance		50

This comprehensive example has illustrated the accounts used and the resulting financial statements under the restricted fund method. The extensive footnote disclosures required by the *Handbook* have not been illustrated.

COMPREHENSIVE ILLUSTRATION OF THE DEFERRAL METHOD

L06

To illustrate the journal entries made and the annual general-purpose financial statements prepared using the deferral method of accounting for contributions, we will use the same basic information as was used in the previous example (with 000s omitted). Although not required, Blue Shield will show "net assets invested in capital assets" as a separate component of net assets.

When the *Handbook*'s current NFPO sections became operative several years ago, the organization spent considerable time and money searching past records to determine the cost of capital assets purchased from both restricted and non-restricted contributions, as well as the fair values of capital assets donated. Because the new *Handbook* had to be applied retrospectively, the following journal entries were made at that time to accomplish this:

Equipment and furniture	1,100	
Accumulated amortization		300
Net assets invested in capital assets		800

> Net assets invested in capital assets represent the portion of unrestricted net assets that is tied up in capital assets and is not available for future spending.

This entry recognized the cost of equipment acquired in past years using unrestricted contributions and the accumulated amortization to date.

Buildings	2,000	
Accumulated amortization		900
Deferred contributions related to capital assets		1,100

> Deferred contributions represent the unamortized amount of capital assets either donated or acquired with restricted contributions.

This entry recorded the fair value of the building donated by the city and the accumulated amortization taken to date. A capital asset donation is treated in the same manner as a contribution restricted for the purchase of a capital asset. As the asset is amortized, a portion of the deferred contribution is recognized as a match against this expense.

The statement of financial position of Blue Shield as at January 1, Year 6 (the start of the next fiscal year), is presented in Exhibit 12.4.

When this statement of financial position is compared to the statement of financial position under the restricted fund method (see Exhibit 12.2), the amounts used on the asset side are fairly obvious. The liability side needs further clarification. The amount in deferred revenue is the United Way grant. The deferred

EXHIBIT 12.4		

BLUE SHIELD AGENCY
STATEMENT OF FINANCIAL POSITION
January 1, Year 6
(in thousands of dollars)

It is quite common to not present separate funds when the entity uses the deferral method.

Current Assets	
Cash and term deposits	$ 479
Pledges receivable	490
	969
Investments	500
Capital assets:	
Equipment and furniture	1,482
Buildings	2,095
Accumulated amortization	(1,517)
	2,060
Total assets	$3,529
Current Liabilities	
Accounts payable	$ 663
Wages payable	70
Accrued liabilities	82
Deferred revenue	40
	855
Long-Term Liabilities	
Deferred contributions related to capital assets	920
Deferred building campaign contributions	12
	932
Total liabilities	1,787
Net Assets	
Net assets invested in capital assets[5]	1,140
Net assets restricted for endowment purposes	500
Unrestricted net assets	102
	1,742
Total liabilities and net assets	$3,529

Net assets invested in capital assets represents the unamortized amount of capital assets purchased from unrestricted contributions.

The deferred contributions distinguish between unspent contributions and the unamortized portion of contributions being matched to amortization expense.

building campaign contributions balance is the externally restricted fund balance from the capital fund, and represents restricted funds received but not spent on capital assets. When this money is spent, an amount will be transferred from this deferred contribution account to the deferred contributions related to capital assets account. The deferred contributions related to capital assets balance represents that portion of the unamortized balance of capital assets that was either donated or purchased from contributions restricted for capital asset purchases. This will be transferred to revenue in future periods as these assets are amortized.

The differences in presentation are as follows:

Restricted fund method:	
Fund balances—investment in capital assets	$2,060
Fund balances—externally restricted	12
	$2,072

Deferral method:		The financial statement
Liability—deferred contributions related to capital assets	$ 920	presentation for
Liability—deferred building campaign contributions	12	contributions is substantially
	932	different under the two
Net assets—net assets invested in capital assets	1,140	different reporting methods.
	$2,072	

The $500 net assets restricted for endowment purposes is the fund balance from the endowment fund and originated from the founder's bequest. Interest earned is not restricted. The unrestricted net asset balance comes from the general fund balance.

Year 6 Events   The year's events for all transactions are the same as were used in the previous example. The journal entries required to record these events are presented next in the order listed.

(a)	Accounts payable	663		Fund accounting is not
	Wages payable	70		applied and journal entries
	Accrued liabilities	82		are not segregated by fund.
	Cash		815	
(b)	Deferred revenue	40		
	Revenue—United Way grant		40	
(c)	Cash	490		
	Pledges receivable		490	
(d)	Cash	1,187		Contributions and pledges
	Pledges receivable	800		for the current year are
	Revenue—donations		1,987	reported as revenue in the
	Expenses—fundraising	516		current year.
	Cash		453	
	Accounts payable		50	
	Accrued liabilities		13	
(e)	Cash	450		Contributions restricted for
	Government grant receivable	150		depreciable capital assets
	Deferred building campaign contributions		600	are reported as deferred
	Equipment	103		contributions.
	Cash		91	
	Accounts payable		12	
	Deferred building campaign contributions	103		
	Deferred contributions—capital assets		103	
(f)	Cash	910		
	Government grant receivable	290		
	Revenue—government grant		1,200	
(g)	Encumbrances	1,964		
	Estimated commitments		1,964	
(h)	Estimated commitments	1,870		
	Encumbrances		1,870	
	Expenses—shelter program	650		
	Expenses—food program	960		
	Expenses—administration	256		
	Cash		1,446	
	Accounts payable		420	

(i)	Expenses—shelter program	90	
	Expenses—food program	150	
	Expenses—administration	300	
	Cash		357
	Wages payable		183

Contributions for next year's activities are deferred until related expenses are recognized.

(j)	Cash	65	
	Deferred revenue—United Way		65

(k)	Cash	50	
	Net assets—endowment		50

Endowment contributions are reported directly in net assets.

(l)	Cash	54	
	Revenue—investment income		54

(m)	Equipment	3	
	Cash		3

Deferred contributions are brought into income as the capital assets are amortized over their useful lives.

(n)	Expenses—amortization	150	
	Accumulated amortization		150
	Deferred contributions—capital assets	90	
	Amortization of deferred contributions		90

(o)	Estimated commitments	94	
	Encumbrances		94

After these journal entries are posted, financial statements as at December 31, Year 6, can be prepared as shown in Exhibit 12.5. The statement of revenue and expenses shows not only unrestricted revenues and expenses but also the restricted revenues recognized during the year as a match to the expenses associated with them (amortization in this case). The $299 excess of revenues over expenses is transferred to the "total" column in the statement of changes in net assets.

The excess of revenues over expenses is split between invested in capital assets and unrestricted in the statement of changes in net assets.

In the statement of changes in net assets, the $60 amortization expense from assets acquired with unrestricted resources is transferred so that it is deducted in the invested in capital assets column, leaving $359 as the amount of operating results allocated to unrestricted resources. The unrestricted resources that were spent on equipment during the period ($3) are shown as a transfer from the unrestricted column to the invested in capital assets column.

An examination of the statement of financial position shows the following equality regarding capital assets purchased from restricted and unrestricted resources:

Deferred contributions—capital assets (restricted)	$ 933
Net assets invested in capital assets (unrestricted)	1,083
Total capital assets (from both sources)	$2,016

If the entity chooses to not present the "net assets invested in capital assets" account separately, the balance from this account would be included in unrestricted net assets. There would not be a separate column for invested in capital assets in the statement of changes in net assets. There would be no need to allocate amounts between the unrestricted column and invested in capital assets column, as described above. The accounting would be simpler but the information value of this account would be lost.

EXHIBIT 12.5

BLUE SHIELD AGENCY
STATEMENT OF FINANCIAL POSITION
December 31, Year 6
(in thousands of dollars)

Current Assets	
Cash and term deposits	$ 520
Pledges receivable	800
Government grants receivable	440
	1,760
Investments	500
Capital assets	
Equipment and furniture	1,588
Buildings	2,095
Accumulated amortization	(1,667)
	2,016
Total assets	$4,276
Current Liabilities	
Accounts payable	$ 482
Wages payable	183
Accrued liabilities	13
Deferred revenue	65
	743
Long-Term Liabilities	
Deferred contributions related to capital assets	933
Deferred building campaign contributions	509
	1,442
Total liabilities	2,185
Net Assets	
Net assets invested in capital assets	1,083
Net assets restricted for endowment purposes	550
Unrestricted net assets	458
	2,091
Total liabilities and net assets	$4,276

The unamortized portion of spent restricted contributions is segregated from the unspent restricted contributions.

The net assets invested in capital assets account does not have to be reported separately; it could be combined with unrestricted net assets.

BLUE SHIELD AGENCY
STATEMENT OF REVENUES AND EXPENSES
for the Year Ended December 31, Year 6
(in thousands of dollars)

Revenues	
Government grants	$1,200
United Way grant	40
Contributions	1,987
Investment income	54
Amortization of deferred contributions	90
	3,371

(continued)

EXHIBIT 12.5   *(continued)*

Expenses

Shelter program	740
Food program	1,110
Administration	556
Fundraising	516
Amortization of capital assets	150
	3,072
Excess of revenues over expenses	$ 299

BLUE SHIELD AGENCY
STATEMENT OF CHANGES IN NET ASSETS
for the Year Ended December 31, Year 6
(in thousands of dollars)

	Invested in capital assets	Restricted for endowment purposes	Unrestricted	Total
Balance, Jan. 1	$1,140	$500	$102	$1,742
Excess of revenues over expenses	(60)		359	299
Endowment contributions		50		50
Investment in capital assets	3		(3)	
Balance, Dec. 31	$1,083	$550	$458	$2,091

The net assets invested in capital assets captures the portion of the unrestricted net assets that is not available for future spending.

BLUE SHIELD AGENCY
CASH FLOW STATEMENT
for the Year Ended December 31, Year 6
(in thousands of dollars)

Cash Flows from Operating Activities

Cash received from government operating grants **(f)**	$ 910
Cash received from United Way grant **(j)**	65
Cash received from general contributions **(c)**, **(d)**	1,677
Cash received from investment income **(l)**	54
Cash paid to suppliers **(a)**, **(h)**	(2,141)
Cash paid to employees **(a)**, **(i)**	(427)
Cash paid for fundraising **(d)**	(453)
Net cash used in operating activities	(315)

Cash Flows from Investing Activities

Cash paid for capital asset acquisitions **(a)**, **(e)**, **(m)**	(144)
Net cash used in investing activities	(144)

Cash Flows from Financing Activities

Contributions of cash for endowment **(k)**	50
Cash received from government grant **(e)**	450
Net cash generated through financing activities	500
Net increase in cash and term deposits	41
Cash and term deposits, Jan. 1	479
Cash and term deposits, Dec. 31	$ 520

The cash flow statement segregates cash flows by operating, investing, and financing activities.

The endowment contribution received during the year does not appear on the operating statement because no expenses will ever appear for the required matching process to occur. Instead, this special restricted resource is shown on the statement of changes in "net assets" as an increase in net assets restricted for endowment. Extensive footnote disclosure is required when statements are prepared using the deferral method, in order to clearly define the amount and nature of restricted and unrestricted resources.

Closing entries as at December 31, Year 6, are presented next.

Revenue—government grant	1,200	
Revenue—United Way grant	40	
Revenue—contributions	1,987	
Revenue—investment income	54	
Expenses—shelter program		740
Expenses—food program		1,110
Expenses—administration		556
Expenses—fundraising		516
Unrestricted net assets		359
To close the unrestricted revenues and expenses		

Revenues and expenses are closed to fund balances.

Unrestricted net assets	3	
Net assets invested in capital assets		3
To transfer the amount of capital assets acquired from unrestricted resources[6]		

Net assets invested in capital assets is updated for changes in capital assets financed by unrestricted resources.

Net assets invested in capital assets	60	
Amortization of deferred contributions	90	
Expenses—amortization		150
To close restricted revenues and the expenses related to capital assets[7]		

ANALYSIS AND INTERPRETATION OF FINANCIAL STATEMENTS

L07

Now that you have prepared journal entries and financial statements for NFPOs, you are now ready to analyze and interpret the financial statements of an NFPO. Let's use the Blue Shield financial statements to calculate and interpret key financial ratios for an NFPO.

Blue Shield operates a 50-bed homeless shelter. It is open 365 days a year but is not necessarily fully occupied every night. For Year 6, the number of person days that the facility was used was 15,000. The following three ratios would typically be used by donors and other users to assess the efficiency and effectiveness of the organization:

The cost per person day or cost per unit of output is a key ratio for many NFPOs.

Name of ratio	Numerator/denominator	What it tells
Cost per person day	Total expenses/Total person days	Efficiency of operations
Debt-to-equity ratio	Total liabilities/Total net assets	Ability to meet obligations
Stewardship ratio	Total revenues/Total expenses	How the entity discharged its stewardship responsibility

The following table presents these three ratios under the two different methods of reporting contributions. The first two columns are taken from Exhibit 12.3 for the restricted fund method and the last column is from Exhibit 12.4 for the deferral method.

	Restricted Fund Method		Deferral Method
Name of Ratio	*General fund*	*All funds*	
Cost per person day	$195	$205	$205
Debt-to-equity ratio	1.60	0.21	1.04
Stewardship ratio	1.12	1.28	1.10

Notice the following from the table above:

- The ratios are significantly different between the two reporting methods. Which method best reflects reality for this organization? Which method would be most useful to the user?

- The ratios are significantly different between the general fund and the total of all funds under the restricted fund method. Which column would the user use in calculating the ratios? Is it useful to have all the columns under the restricted fund method?

- The organization looks most efficient using only the general fund under the restricted fund method. Should one use only the general fund, all funds, or any combination of funds under the restricted fund method?

The debt-to-equity ratio is usually higher under the deferral method because some contributions are reported as deferred contributions, which appears in the liability section of the statement of financial position.

- The solvency of the entity looks much better using all funds under the restricted fund method. Why is there such a big difference between the restricted fund method and the deferral method? Under the restricted fund method, the restricted funds are shown as revenue when received and end up as an addition to net assets. Under the deferral method, many of the contributions are deferred as a long-term liability.

- The stewardship ratio compares revenues to expenses. Some donors would not want to see a high ratio because it implies that the funds were not used as expected. The deferral method matches the contribution revenues to expenses on an accrual basis. Therefore, it is expected that the ratio would be lower under the deferral method.

See Self-Study Problem 2 for a comprehensive problem involving the preparation of a balance sheet under the two methods of reporting contributions. The NFPO uses fund accounting under both methods of reporting contributions.

It is important to note how the NFPO has accounted for donated goods and services. By recording donated goods or services, the bottom line on the statement of operations is usually not affected. However, both revenues and expenses would likely increase. This could have a significant impact on the cost per person day and stewardship ratio.

Disclosure Requirements   The disclosure requirements for NFPOs are quite extensive. Some of those requirements were briefly described throughout the chapter. The following summarizes the main disclosures required in Section 4410 related to revenue from contributions:

The major sources of and accounting policies for contributions must be disclosed.

- Contributions by major sources, including the nature and amount of contributed materials and services recognized in the financial statements.

- The policies followed in accounting for endowment contributions, restricted contributions, and contributed materials and services.

- The nature and amount of changes in deferred contribution balances for the period.
- How and where net investment income earned on resources held for endowment is recognized in the financial statements.

United Way/Centraide Ottawa is a non-profit Ontario corporation and a registered charity. Excerpts from United Way/Centraide Ottawa's 2012 financial statements are provided in Exhibit 12.6. The 2012 financial statement followed Part V of the *Handbook.* Starting in 2013, United Way plans to follow Part III, combined with the relevant sections from Part II.

EXHIBIT 12.6

EXTRACTS (IN PART) FROM UNITED WAY/CENTRAIDE OTTAWA'S 2012 FINANCIAL STATEMENTS

1. Significant accounting policies:

The financial statements have been prepared in accordance with Canadian generally accepted accounting principles and include the following significant accounting policies:

(a) Revenue recognition:

United Way/Centraide Ottawa follows the deferral method of accounting for contributions for not-for-profit organizations.

The United Way uses the deferral method to account for contributions.

Support from the general public consists of pledges and donations relating to the current year's campaign. Pledges receivable are recorded at an estimated realizable value at the time of pledge commitment by individuals and organizations. Funds raised during a campaign, net of related campaign expenses and provisions are used to provide funds for funded programs, other Canadian registered charities and operations in the following fiscal year. Pledges and donations received by the United Way/Centraide Ottawa that are undesignated or are directed from/to an impact area by the donor are recognized as revenue in the year that they are received or pledged. Pledges and donations received by the United Way/Centraide Ottawa that are designated by the donor to funded agencies, charities and other United Ways/Centraides are considered to be restricted by purpose, and are recorded as deferred designated campaign revenue and are recognized as revenue in the year the amount is paid to the designated organization.

Investment revenue earned on restricted endowed investments is recognized as revenue when the related expenditure is incurred. Investment revenue earned on unrestricted investments is recognized in the current year. Contributions to endowment are recorded as direct increases to the endowment net asset balance.

(b) Expense recognition:

Program, fundraising and resource development expenses are recognized in the period incurred. Allocations and designations expenses are recognized in the period paid or in the period that the annual allocation is approved by the Board and the recipient agencies are notified.

(j) Donated services:

Donated services are not recognized because the value of the services is not objectively measurable.

No amounts have been reflected in the financial statements for donated services, since no objective basis is available to measure the value of such services. Nevertheless, a substantial number of volunteers have donated significant amounts of their time in United Way/Centraide programs, services and fundraising campaigns.

Source: Reproduced with permission from United Way/Centraide Ottawa. http://unitedwayottawa.ca/sites/default/files/files/documents/annual-reports/2011-united-way-ottawa-financial-statements-en.pdf]

L08 ## ASPE DIFFERENCES

1. Part II does not contain any standards specifically tailored for NFPOs. However, if the NFPO chooses to follow Part III of the *Handbook*, it must follow the relevant standards in Part II.

2. IFRSs do not contain any standards specifically tailored for NFPOs. If the NFPO chooses to follow IFRSs, it does not apply Part III of the *Handbook*.

SUMMARY

Fourteen sections in Part III of the *Handbook* are specifically dedicated to NFPOs. In addition, NFPOs must follow relevant sections of Part II of the *Handbook*. These *Handbook* sections have dramatically changed the financial reporting of NFPOs over the past 15 years. We have moved from a situation where virtually no authoritative standards existed to one where full and proportionate consolidation of controlled and jointly controlled entities is allowed, and asset capitalization and amortization are required for all but "small" organizations. Rather than mandating a single reporting model, the new standard gives NFPOs the choice between the deferral and restricted fund methods of financial statement presentation and allows them the flexibility to use a mix of both methods if they feel that it will result in a better presentation. While these changes have moved not-for-profit more toward a business approach of reporting and away from the stewardship-of-resources approach that was previously used, not-for-profit reporting is still very distinct, and certainly far more complex than it was before.

Significant Changes in GAAP in the Last Three Years

1. Part III of the *Handbook* was introduced. It contains the 4400 series and five other standards that are unique to NFPOs.

2. For fiscal periods beginning on or after January 1, 2012, private sector NFPOs must adhere to either IFRSs or ASPE combined with Part III of the *Handbook*. Public sector NFPOs must adhere to either IFRSs or the *CICA Public Sector Accounting Handbook* with or without the 4200 series.

Changes Expected in GAAP in the Next Three Years

No significant changes are expected in Part III of the *Handbook* in the next three years.

SELF-STUDY PROBLEM 1

L02, 3   Watrous Housing Corporation (WHC) is a community-sponsored not-for-profit housing organization that was incorporated on September 1, Year 5. Its purpose is to provide residential accommodation for physically disabled adults in the town of Watrous. The nature of WHC's operations and its source of funding are described in Exhibit I. The executive director of WHC has asked for your

NATURE OF OPERATIONS

- In October Year 5, WHC purchased a 15-unit apartment building in downtown Watrous for $750,000. It then spent $250,000 in renovations to upgrade the building to make it accessible for physically disabled adults.
- WHC offers 24-hour non-medical attendant care. Support care services are provided through a combination of staff members and volunteers. The staff members receive a monthly salary. As an inducement to recruit and retain qualified support care workers, each staff member is allowed 15 sick days per year. The employee can bank the sick days not used in any one year. Upon termination or retirement, the employee is paid for banked sick days at the wage rate in effect at that time.
- Rental payments are due the first day of each month and are geared to each tenant's income. Most of the tenants are very good about making their rent payments on time. Some rental payments are received late. On August 31, Year 6, there was $13,000 of unpaid rent.
- WHC plans to install central air conditioning in the building in April Year 7 at an expected cost of $50,000. This expenditure is being financed by a special fundraising drive. By August 31, Year 6, this fundraising drive had raised $20,000 in cash and $15,000 in pledges from citizens in the local community.

SOURCES OF FUNDING

- The cost of acquiring and renovating the apartment building was financed by a $1,000,000 cash donation received from the estate of Mr. Smith who had stipulated that the funds be used for the purchase of a property.
- The provincial government funds approximately 70% of non-medical care and support costs. Claims are made monthly for the previous month's eligible costs.
- WHC depends on outside fundraising efforts, primarily door-to-door canvassing and sponsored bingos, to cover the remaining non-medical care and support costs.

assistance in establishing accounting policies for WHC for its general-purpose, year-end financial statements. The accounting policies should be consistent with Part III combined with relevant sections of Part II of the *CICA Handbook*.

Required:

Identify the major accounting issues, and provide recommendations on the accounting treatment of these issues in WHC's financial statements for the year ended August 31, Year 6. Assume that WHC wants to use fund accounting with two funds, a general fund and a capital fund, and wants to use the deferral method to account for contributions. Also assume that annual revenues exceed $700,000.

SOLUTION TO SELF-STUDY PROBLEM 1

WHC should adopt the following recommendations for the related accounting issues for its year-end financial statements:

- The accrual basis of accounting should be used in order to properly match revenues to expenses.
- The cost of acquiring and renovating the apartment building should be capitalized as an asset in the capital fund.
- The building should be amortized over its useful life. Amortization expense should be reported as an expense of the capital fund.

- The $1,000,000 cash donation from Mr. Smith and the cash received for the planned expenditures on air conditioning equipment should be recorded as deferred contributions in the capital fund. The deferred contributions should be amortized into revenue over the life of the related assets to match to the amortization expense on these assets.
- Salary costs should be expensed as incurred in the general fund.
- The estimated costs of unpaid sick leave should be set up as a liability and as an expense of the general fund on an annual basis.
- The value of the volunteers' time provided for support care services can be set up as revenue and an expense of the general fund, if the amount is measurable and such services would be purchased had the volunteers not provided them.
- The contributions from the provincial government should be accrued as a receivable and revenue of the general fund at the end of each month, based on actual costs incurred during the month.
- The rent from the tenants should be recognized as revenue of the general fund in the month in which it is due. At the end of the year, an allowance should be set up for any doubtful accounts.
- Donations from door-to-door canvassing and proceeds received from bingos should be recognized as revenue of the general fund as the cash is received.
- The pledges received for the planned expenditure on air conditioning equipment should be recorded as pledges receivable and deferred contributions of the capital fund to the extent that the amount to be received can be reasonably estimated and the ultimate collection is reasonably assured. Since this is the first year of operation for WHC, it may not be possible to reasonably estimate the collectibility of the pledges as there is no history for collection of pledges.

SELF-STUDY PROBLEM 2

LO2, 3, 5, 6   Morina Homes is a not-for-profit organization established over forty years ago. It provides care services to seniors in the local community. Fifteen years ago, it raised $2,800,000 of restricted funds to fully fund the purchase of land and to construct and equip a new residence. In Year 4, it undertook a new public campaign to raise funds to replace some of its equipment and expand the home.

Prior to Year 4, the home had only one fund, the general fund. In Year 4, the home set up a separate fund, the capital fund, to account for any new funds restricted for the replacement and expansion of the home. It used the deferral method to account for both funds.

The following are the unclassified statements of financial position for the 2 funds of the Home at December 31, Year 4:

	General FUND	Capital FUND
Cash	$ 20,000	$216,000
Accounts receivable	137,000	
Allowance for doubtful accounts	(17,000)	
Inventory of supplies	14,000	
Investments in marketable securities		284,000
Land	370,000	
Building	1,760,000	
Accumulated amortization of buildings	(528,000)	

(continued)

	General FUND	Capital FUND
Equipment	675,000	
Accumulated amortization of equipment	(540,000)	
Totals	$1,891,000	$500,000
Accounts payable	$ 32,000	
Deferred contributions—building and equipment	1,367,000	
Deferred contributions—future expansion		$500,000
Net assets contributed for land	370,000	
Unrestricted net assets	122,000	
Totals	$1,891,000	$500,000

Additional information for Year 5:

a. Every month, the home bills the provincial government and its residents for home services. The accounts are due in 30 days. Total billings for the year were $1,101,000.

b. Collections of accounts receivable totalled $1,087,000. Accounts receivable written off as uncollectible amounted to $11,000.

c. The estimate of doubtful accounts was 10% of accounts receivable outstanding at December 31, Year 5.

d. The home received $500,000 from the estate of one of its founders. The donor requested that the principal not be spent but invested in government bonds. The interest income from the bonds is restricted for recreational activities, which are accounted for in the general fund.

e. The home received unrestricted donations of $50,000 and interest revenue of $30,000 from the bonds in the endowment fund. The cash received for interest was spent on recreational projects and is included in operating expenses.

f. The home paid the following amounts during the year:

Operating expenses	$1,125,000
Inventory of supplies	60,000
Total	$1,185,000

g. Equipment costing $100,000 was acquired using funds from the capital fund.

h. The accounts payable at the end of Year 4 and Year 5 consisted of the following:

	Year 4	Year 5
Operating expenses	$20,000	$25,000
Inventory of supplies	12,000	15,000
	$32,000	$40,000

No entries affecting accounts payable were made during the year.

i. Supplies on hand at the end of the year were $16,000.

j. Amortization was $44,000 for the building and $51,000 for the equipment, of which $6,000 pertained to equipment purchased by the capital fund. The cost of these capital assets was fully funded by contributions restricted for the purchase of these assets.

k. On December 31, Year 5, the fair value of the marketable securities in the capital fund was $300,000. These securities are being held until the funds are needed for future expansion of the home. The future expansion will not likely occur until Year 8, at the earliest. Any income on these funds is restricted for use in the capital fund. The investment is classified at FVTPL for reporting purposes.

Required:

Prepare a classified statement of financial position for the three funds at December 31, Year 5, assuming that Morina Homes uses the following:

(a) Deferral method combined with fund accounting
(b) Restricted fund method (assume that the change from the deferral method to the restricted fund method is a change in accounting policy and should be applied retrospectively)

SOLUTION TO SELF-STUDY PROBLEM 2

Deferral

(a)

MORINA HOMES
Statement of Financial Position
At December 31, Year 5

	General Fund	Capital Fund	Endowment Fund	Total
Current assets				
Cash (1)	$ 2,000	$116,000		$ 118,000
Accounts receivable (2)	140,000			140,000
Allowance for doubtful accounts (3)	(14,000)			(14,000)
Inventory of supplies (4)	16,000			16,000
	144,000	116,000		260,000
Property, plant & equipment				
Land	370,000			370,000
Building	1,760,000			1,760,000
Accumulated amortization of buildings (6)	(572,000)			(572,000)
Equipment (7)	675,000	100,000		775,000
Accumulated amortization of equipment (8)	(585,000)	(6,000)		(591,000)
	1,648,000	94,000		1,742,000
Long-term investments (5 & 9)		300,000	$500,000	800,000
	$1,792,000	$510,000	$500,000	$2,802,000
Accounts payable (10)	$ 40,000			$ 40,000
Deferred contributions—building and equipment (11)	1,278,000	$ 94,000		1,372,000
Deferred contributions—future expansion (12)		416,000		416,000
Net assets contributed for land (13)	370,000			370,000
Net assets for endowment (14)			$500,000	500,000
Unrestricted net assets (15)	104,000			104,000
	$1,792,000	$510,000	$500,000	$2,802,000

Notes (values in 000's): (letters below refer to letters in additional information in the original question)

1. 20 + (b) 1087 + (e) 50 + (e) 30 − (f) 1185; 216 − (g) 100
2. 137 + (a) 1101 − (b) 1087 − (b) 11
3. 17 − (b) 11 + (c) 8
4. 14 + (f) 60 + (h) 3 − (i) 61
5. 284 + (k) 16
6. 528 + (j) 44
7. 675; 0 + (g) 100
8. 540 + (j) 45; 0 + (j) 6
9. 0 + (d) 500
10. 32 + (h) 8
11. 1,367 − (j) 44 − (j) 51 + (j) 6; (g) 100 − (j) 6
12. 500 − (g) 100 + (k) 16
13. 370

14. 500
15. 122 + (a) 1101 − (c) 8 + (e) 50 + (e) 30 − (f) 1125 − (h) 5 − (i) 61 − (j) (44 + 45) +
    (j) (44 + 45)

Restricted

(b)

MORINA HOMES
Statement of Financial Position
At December 31, Year 5
(Note 1)

	General fund	Capital fund	Endowment fund
Assets			
Current assets			
Cash	$ 2,000	$ 116,000	
Accounts receivable	140,000		
Allowance for doubtful accounts	(14,000)		
Inventory of supplies	16,000		
Investments in marketable securities		300,000	
	144,000	416,000	
Property, plant & equipment			
Land		370,000	
Building		1,760,000	
Accumulated amortization of buildings		(572,000)	
Equipment (2)		775,000	
Accumulated amortization of equipment (3)		(591,000)	
		1,742,000	
Long-term investment in bonds			$500,000
	$144,000	$2,158,000	$500,000
Accounts payable	$ 40,000		
Fund balance (4)	104,000	$2,158,000	$500,000
	$144,000	$2,158,000	$500,000

Notes:
  1. All of the account names and account balances are the same as in Part (a), except for the
     following:
  2. 675 + (g) 100
  3. 540 + (j) 45+ (j) 6
  4. All of the contributions to the capital and endowment funds would have been reported as
     revenue when received and would end up in fund balances. The revenues and expenses
     for the current year also end up in fund balances. There are no deferred contributions in
     the capital and endowment funds.

APPENDIX 12A

SAMPLE FINANCIAL STATEMENTS FOR NOT-FOR-PROFIT ORGANIZATIONS

This appendix contains the 2012 statement of financial position, statement of operations, statement of changes in net assets, and statement of cash flows for United Way/
Centraide Ottawa.[8] This organization brings people together from all parts of its

L06

community to identify, develop, and provide solutions for community needs, helping to ensure that the donations received will go where they are needed most and where they will have the greatest impact. The deferral method of accounting has been used for contributions, and expenses have been recorded using the accrual basis.

UNITED WAY/CENTRAIDE OTTAWA
Statement of Financial Position

March 31	2012	2011
Assets		
Current assets:		
Cash	$ 3,846,133	$ 3,077,972
Pledges receivable	20,417,968	20,529,217
Accounts receivable	1,176,586	1,844,087
Prepaid expenses	84,992	42,292
	25,525,679	25,493,568
Land and building held for sale	–	2,062,227
Long-term assets:		
Investments:		
Endowment	1,866,225	2,496,209
Unrestricted	1,437,094	688,882
	3,303,319	3,185,091
Capital assets	1,110,478	1,358,095
	4,413,797	4,543,186
	$29,939,476	$32,098,981
Liabilities and Net Assets		
Current liabilities:		
Accounts payable and accrued liabilities	$ 2,084,395	$ 2,954,977
Deferred revenue	1,788,208	1,620,629
Deferred designated campaign revenue	12,931,920	12,666,409
Mortgage payable—current	–	100,000
	16,804,523	17,342,015
Long-term liabilities:		
Deferred lease inducement	26,412	29,430
Mortgage payable—long-term	–	1,272,290
Other long-term liabilities	750,000	750,000
	776,412	2,051,720
Net assets:		
Unrestricted	10,391,778	10,034,154
Internally restricted for community services	100,538	174,883
Endowment	1,866,225	2,496,209
	12,358,541	12,705,246
Lease commitments		
Contingency and guarantee		
	$29,939,476	$32,098,981

UNITED WAY/CENTRAIDE OTTAWA
Statement of Operations

Year ended March 31	2012	2011
Revenue:		
Donations	$30,275,207	$30,559,506
Funds transferred from other United Ways/Centraides	1,519,393	1,610,236
Gross campaign revenue	31,794,600	32,169,742
Less: provision for uncollectible pledges	(1,273,992)	(1,220,948)
Recovery of provisioned pledges from prior year campaigns	436,699	1,287,628

	2012	2011
Net campaign revenue	30,957,307	32,236,422
Other revenue	3,177,496	2,291,106
	34,134,803	34,527,528
Fundraising expenses:		
Community campaign	3,657,228	3,357,627
GCWCC	1,481,545	1,323,991
Resource development	453,478	525,149
Recovery of fundraising costs from designated charities	(1,697,890)	(1,475,333)
	3,894,361	3,731,434
Net revenue available for programs	30,240,442	30,796,094
Programs:		
Allocations	10,003,432	10,155,423
Donor directed designations	13,891,599	13,471,820
Grants	1,439,931	695,168
Targeted community investments	532,087	167,500
United Way priority goal investments	4,783,316	5,223,880
	30,650,365	29,713,791
(Deficiency) excess of revenue over expenses	$ (409,923)	$ 1,082,303

UNITED WAY/CENTRAIDE OTTAWA
Statement of Changes in Net Assets

Year ended March 31	2012	2011
Unrestricted:		
Balance, beginning of year	$10,034,154	$ 8,876,851
(Deficiency) excess of revenue over expenses	(409,923)	1,082,303
	9,624,231	9,959,154
Transfer from internally restricted for community services	76,090	75,000
Transfer from endowment	691,457	–
Balance, end of year	$10,391,778	$10,034,154
Internally restricted for community services:		
Balance, beginning of year	$ 174,883	$ 249,883
Contributions	1,745	–
Transfer to unrestricted	(76,090)	(75,000)
Balance, end of year	$ 100,538	$ 174,883
Endowment:		
Balance, beginning of year	$ 2,496,209	$ 2,458,801
Contributions	61,473	37,408
Transfer to unrestricted	(691,457)	–
Balance, end of year	$ 1,866,225	$ 2,496,209
Total net assets	$12,358,541	$12,705,246

UNITED WAY/CENTRAIDE OTTAWA
Statement of Cash Flows

Year ended March 31	2012	2011
Cash provided by (used in):		
Operations:		
(Deficiency) Excess of revenue over expenses	$ (409,923)	$1,082,303
Items not involving cash:		
Amortization of capital assets	311,903	330,713
Amortization of deferred lease inducement	(3,018)	(3,019)
Unrealized loss on unrestricted investments	(65,043)	(33,785)
Loss on sale of land and building held for sale	86,003	–

(continued)

Change in non-cash operating working capital:

Pledges receivable	111,249	(2,198,589)
Accounts receivable	667,501	(170,520)
Prepaid expenses	(42,700)	33,820
Accounts payable and accrued liabilities	(870,582)	792,519
Deferred revenue	167,579	375,457
Deferred designated campaign revenue	265,511	663,139
	218,480	872,038

Investing:

Acquisition of capital assets	(64,286)	(739,135)
Proceeds from sale of land and building held for sale	1,976,224	–
Acquisitions of investments	(53,185)	(154,583)
Contributions to internally restricted for community services	1,745	–
Contributions to endowment	61,473	37,408
	1,921,971	(856,310)

Financing:

Principal payments on mortgage	(1,372,290)	(100,008)
	(1,372,290)	(100,008)
Increase (decrease) in cash	768,161	(84,280)
Cash, beginning of year	3,077,972	3,162,252
Cash, end of year	$3,846,133	$3,077,972

The amount of mortgage interest paid by United Way/Centraide Ottawa was $31,341 (2011— $53,356). The interest is reported as a program expense, which is aligned to the purpose for which the building was originally purchased.

Source: Reproduced with permission from United Way/Centraide Ottawa. http://unitedwayottawa.ca/sites/default/files/files/documents/annual-reports/2011-united-way-ottawa-financial-statements-en.pdf

APPENDIX 12B

ACCOUNTING FOR PUBLIC SECTOR ORGANIZATIONS

The public sector consists of governments, government organizations, and not-for-profit organizations controlled by governments. Governments differ from business organizations in many ways, some of which can be summarized as follows:

Governments differ from business organizations in a number of ways.

- Governments do not exist to make a profit, but rather to provide services.
- While the major source of business revenue comes from the sale of goods or services or both, most of a government's revenue comes from taxation.
- Businesses have to compete, while governments operate in essentially a non-competitive environment.
- Often a major goal of government is the redistribution of wealth. A major goal of a business is the maximization of the wealth of its owners.
- The federal and provincial governments have virtually an unlimited capacity to borrow, constrained only by their ability to raise taxes in order to repay. A business's earning capacity is a major constraining factor in its ability to issue debt.
- While a business purchases capital assets in order to earn a return, a government's capital asset acquisitions are made to provide services.
- A government's budget plan, approved by a legislative process at the start of a fiscal period, attracts considerable attention in the press, as does the eventual

comparison of actual results with those budgeted for originally. Businesses do not normally report their budgets, and their annual results are usually compared with results of prior periods with no mention of the year's budget.

With such differences, it is not surprising that government-reporting models have been quite different from those used by businesses. This was certainly the case 10 or 15 years ago, but lately, changes have been made that have brought government accounting requirements much closer to those required for business, although many differences still exist. This will be more evident when government accounting standards are summarized later in this appendix.

Prior to the 1980s, a comprehensive body of accounting principles for governments did not exist. The CICA was involved only with setting the financial reporting standards for business organizations; no other body had established authoritative standards for governments. The desperate financial condition of some large American cities, which, it was argued, was not adequately reported in their financial statements, became the focus of attention of standard-setting bodies in the United States, soon followed by the CICA in Canada. Before plunging into this area, the CICA created a committee with a mandate to determine what practices were being followed by the federal, provincial, and territorial governments[9] and to recommend needed changes. As a result of the findings and recommendations of this committee, the CICA established the Public Sector Accounting and Auditing Committee (PSAAC) in 1981 and charged it with the development of accounting principles for governments. Before proceeding, PSAAC created a second study group, with a similar mandate to that of the first one, to report on the financial reporting practices of cities, municipalities, towns, and villages.[10] This study group made reference to a previous research study commissioned by the Certified General Accountants Association of Canada[11] and concluded that it would use the CGA study's findings and recommendations as a starting point for its own study. All three research studies came to similar conclusions about government financial reporting practices in general. These conclusions can be summarized by saying *that there was such a diversity of terminology, measurements, and reporting practices being used that comparability among similar government organizations[12] was virtually impossible and that this situation should not be allowed to continue.*

At first the standard-setting process proceeded slowly and only a few statements on accounting and auditing were issued by PSAAC. Then in 1998, the CICA formed the Public Sector Accounting Board (PSAB) and proceeded with the reorganization of the *CICA Handbook* by transferring the auditing recommendations to the assurance section of the *Handbook,* and the creation of a new *Public Sector Accounting Handbook (PSA Handbook).* Previously issued accounting statements were revised and amended as *PSA Handbook* sections.

Prior to 1980, there was much diversity in reporting by government organizations.

The CICA has created a new *Public Sector Accounting Handbook,* which contains the GAAP applicable to federal, provincial, territorial, and local governments.

COMPLIANCE WITH PSAB REPORTING STANDARDS

If a business organization does not follow the *CICA Handbook* in its financial reporting it can suffer substantial penalties, because legislation and security regulations require the *CICA Handbook* to be used. When a new accounting standard is issued, businesses (especially public companies) tend to adopt the new standard immediately. NFPOs also tend to follow the *Handbook* in their financial reporting. Failure to do so could result in a reduction of support, especially in the area of grants from governments and from other NFPOs. Governments, though, are different. They often exhibit tardiness in adopting new standards, and sometimes refuse to adopt certain standards. The reasons for this are as follows:

Some governments in Canada have failed to adopt new government accounting standards for a number of reasons.

- The federal government and each of the provincial and territorial governments prepare their financial reports in accordance with the legislation enacted by each body. The adoption of a new reporting standard often requires an amendment to an act.

- Local governments are created by an act of the legislature of the province or territory in which they are located. Changes in local government reporting often require changes in legislation.

- Legislative changes necessary to adopt new accounting standards do not rank high in the priorities of many governments.

- When auditors report that a government is not following proper accounting practices in its financial statements (an event that often occurs), the press notes the outrage of the opposition parties and the government's denial of any impropriety, and then the matter is forgotten. The general public, which by and large does not understand accounting at all, does not seem to be particularly interested.

- The adoption of certain new standards may be perceived by a government as having the potential to make its financial condition look worse than the government is currently reporting. If so, a change in reporting would not be a high priority.

GAAP FOR GOVERNMENTS

Prior to February 2007, the *PSA Handbook* contained four sections that applied only to federal, provincial, and territorial governments; two sections that applied only to local governments; and a number of specific-item sections that applied to all governments. In 2005, a new model for senior governments was introduced that involved some drastic changes from previous practices. While the old model focused mainly on government spending (the operating statement showed revenues and expenditures), the new model presents a government-cost approach, although it still contains the reporting of government spending. One major change that took place was the requirement that senior governments capitalize their tangible asset acquisitions and amortize them in the statement of operations. In February 2007, an amendment withdrew both the local government sections and any references to federal, provincial, and territorial governments. The *PSA Handbook* presently contains forty-seven sections, including eight sections for NFPOs, and six accounting guidelines. The sections for NFPOs apply only to public sector NFPOs. These sections deal with matters that are unique to not-for-profit organizations or issues where the needs of financial statement users indicate that different requirements from those that apply to governments, other government organizations, or government business enterprises are appropriate. A public sector NFPO can elect to use or not use the 4200 series of the *PSA Handbook*.

All levels of government must follow the *PSA Handbook*. Government business enterprises must follow Part I of the *CICA Handbook*. Other government organizations can either follow Part I of the *CICA Handbook* or the *PSA Handbook*.

The following briefly summarizes the reporting requirement of the standards in the *PSA Handbook*.

Under the new model, five financial statements are required: a statement of financial position, a statement of operations, a statement of remeasurement gains and losses, a statement of change in net debt, and a statement of cash flow.

Statement of Financial Position This statement presents financial assets and then deducts liabilities, with the resultant difference presented as "net debt." Then nonfinancial assets are added or subtracted to arrive at a final line called "accumulated surplus/deficit."

Financial assets include cash and equivalents, receivables, inventories for resale, loans to other governments, available-for-sale investments, and investments in government enterprises. Liabilities include accounts payable and accrued liabilities, pension and employee future-benefit liabilities, deferred revenue, borrowings, and loans from other governments. The net debt position indicates the extent to which the government will have to raise revenues in the future to cover its past spending.

Nonfinancial assets are tangible capital assets, inventories held for consumption or use, and prepaid expenses. Tangible capital assets are assets used by the government to provide services and include land, buildings, equipment, roads, and so on. They *do not* include intangible assets, natural resources, and Crown lands. The accumulated surplus/deficit represents the net recognized economic resources (net assets) of the government, and provides an indicator of the government's ability to provide future services at the end of a fiscal period.

Statement of Operations This statement reports the government's revenues and expenses, other than remeasurement gains and losses for the period, with the difference described as the period's surplus or deficit. This result is added to the accumulated surplus/deficit at the beginning of the period to arrive at the last line, which is called the accumulated surplus/deficit at the end of the period.

Revenues include taxes, non-tax sources (including gains), and transfers from other governments. Revenue for the period should be accrued unless it is impractical to measure. If this is the case the cash basis should be used. Expenses are to be reported by function or major program. Note disclosure should report the breakdown between the major types of expenses such as salaries, debt-servicing costs, amortization of the costs of tangible capital assets, and transfer payments to other governments. A comparison must be made between the actual results for the period and results of the prior period and also with expectations (the budget) at the beginning of the period.

Statement of Remeasurement Gains and Losses This statement should report the remeasurement gains and losses during the period, distinguishing between amounts arising during the period and those reclassified to the statement of operations; any other comprehensive income that arises when a government includes the results of government business enterprises and government business partnerships in its summary financial statements; and the accumulated remeasurement gains and losses at the beginning and end of the period. The remeasurement gains and losses should be segregated between exchange gains and losses on items in the amortized cost category denominated in a foreign currency, and changes in the fair value of (i) derivatives, (ii) portfolio investments in equity instruments that are quoted in an active market, and (iii) financial instruments designated to the fair value category. The accumulated remeasurement gains are reported as a separate category in the accumulated surplus section of the statement of financial position.

A statement showing the period's changes in net debt is required in comparative form with both the budget and the previous period.

Statement of Change in Net Debt   This statement reconciles the net surplus/deficit for the period with the change in net debt for the period by adding back period amortization expense (and other items) and deducting the cost of tangible capital assets and other nonfinancial assets acquired during the period. The change in net debt is then added to the net debt at the beginning of the period to arrive at the net debt at the end of the period.

This statement is designed to provide information about the extent to which expenditures for the period have been met by the period's revenues. An increase in net debt indicates that revenues of future periods will have to be raised to pay for this period's spending. This statement also has to be prepared in comparative form to the budget and the prior period's results.

The cash flow statement shows operating, capital, investing, and financing transactions.

Statement of Cash Flow   This statement reconciles cash and cash equivalents at the beginning of the period with cash and cash equivalents at the end of the period by providing details of receipts and payments in the four categories of operating transactions, capital transactions, investing transactions, and financing transactions. Either the direct or the indirect method can be used to arrive at cash from operations, but the direct method is strongly encouraged because it provides details of cash receipts from a number of categories, and therefore is much more informative than the indirect method. This statement is similar to the statement used by business organizations, except that the latter would report capital asset acquisitions as an investing activity, while this one reports such acquisitions as a separate category.

PS 1300 requires the consolidation of the financial statements of all organizations controlled by the government. Controlled business organizations are not consolidated but rather are reported using the modified equity method.

Section PS 1300, The Financial Reporting Entity   Section PS 1300 states the following:

- The government reporting entity comprises all organizations controlled by the government. An organization is controlled if the government has power over its financial and operating policies and benefits from or is exposed to the results of its operating activities.

- The government statements are prepared by consolidating the statements of the organizations making up the government entity.

- An exception is that government business enterprises are not consolidated on a line-by-line basis but rather reported using the modified equity method. This will reflect the government's share of the business enterprise's profit or loss in the government's operating results on one line in the statement of operations and the government's share of the business enterprise's assets and liabilities on one line on the government's statement of financial position.

- The modified equity method is exactly the same as the equity method described in Chapter 2, except that the business enterprise's accounting principles are not adjusted to conform to the accounting principles used by the government.

SUMMARY

The PSAB has exerted considerable effort on the establishment of a new financial reporting model covering federal, provincial, territorial, and local governments. The resultant standards exhibit significant differences from those required for businesses and NFPOs. Differences will always exist because the operations and user needs of governments, NFPOs, and business organizations are different. While separate standards previously existed for local governments, recent amendments have eliminated any differences so that one set of standards applies to all government organizations.

REVIEW QUESTIONS

Questions, cases, and problems that deal with the appendix material are denoted with an asterisk.

LO1   1. Briefly outline how NFPOs differ from profit-oriented organizations.

LO2   2. The *Handbook* describes revenue that is unique to NFPOs. What is this revenue called, and what characteristic does it have that makes it unique?

LO2   3. Distinguish between unrestricted and restricted contributions of a charitable organization.

LO3   4. Briefly explain the concept of fund accounting.

LO2   5. When and why would a NFPO use replacement cost rather than net realizable value to determine whether or not inventory should be written down?

LO2   6. It is common for an NFPO to receive donated supplies, equipment, and services. Do current accounting standards require the recording of donations of this kind? Explain.

LO2   7. Outline the *Handbook's* requirements for NFPOs with regard to accounting for the capital assets of NFPOs.

LO2   8. What guidelines does the *Handbook* provide for pledges received by an NFPO?

LO2   9. The net assets section of an NFPO's statement of financial position should be divided into three main sections. List the sections, and explain the reasons for each.

LO2   10. How should transfers of resources between funds be presented in fund financial statements? How should they be presented in a single set of non-fund financial statements?

LO2   11. What is the major difference between the capital asset impairment tests used by profit-oriented and NFPOs?

LO2   12. Contrast the revenue recognition and matching concepts that apply to profit-oriented organizations with those that apply to NFPOs.

LO2   13. Outline the financial reporting requirements for an NFPO's investments in other organizations.

LO4   14. Explain the use of budgetary accounting and encumbrances by NFPOs.

LO2   15. Name the two methods of accounting for contributions, and explain how the methods differ from each other.

LO2   16. Is it possible that an organization would be required to use certain aspects of the deferral method even though it reports using the restricted fund method? Explain.

LO2   17. An organization raises funds for purchasing capital assets. Briefly outline how the accounting for such funds raised would differ under the two methods of accounting for contributions.

LO8   18. Explain how Part III of the *Handbook* can or should be used when an NFPO decides to use IFRS for reporting purposes.

LO9   *19. Governments are different from business organizations and NFPOs in many respects and yet in some respect they are similar. Explain.

LO9   *20. Briefly outline how the presentation of assets and liabilities on the statement of financial position of a government differs from the presentation shown on the balance sheet of a typical business enterprise.

CASES

Case 12-1
LO2

Beaucoup Hospital is located near Montreal. A religious organization created the not-for-profit hospital more than 70 years ago to meet the needs of area residents who could not otherwise afford adequate health care. Although the hospital is open to the public in general, its primary mission has always been to provide medical services for the poor.

On December 23, Year 2, a gentleman told the hospital's chief administrative officer the following story: "My mother has been in your hospital since October 30. The doctors have just told me that she will soon be well and can go home. I cannot tell you how relieved I am. The doctors, the nurses, and your entire staff have been just wonderful; my mother could not have gotten better care. She owes her life to your hospital.

"I am from Alberta. Now that my mother is on the road to recovery, I must return immediately to my business. I am in the process of attempting to sell an enormous tract of land. When this acreage is sold, I will receive $15 million in cash. Because of the services that Beaucoup Hospital has provided for my mother, I want to donate $5 million of this money."

The gentlemen proceeded to write this promise on a piece of paper that he dated and signed.

Obviously, all of the hospital's officials were overwhelmed by this individual's generosity. This $5 million gift was 50 times as large as any other gift ever received. However, the controller was concerned about preparing the financial statements for Year 2. "I have a lot of problems with recording this type of donation as an asset. At present, we are having serious cash flow problems; but if we show $5 million in this manner, our normal donors are going to think we have become rich and don't need their support."

Required:

What problems are involved in accounting for the $5 million pledge? How should Beaucoup Hospital report the amount?

Case 12-2
LO2

You have just completed an interview with the newly formed audit committee of the Andrews Street Youth Centre (ASYC). This organization was created to keep neighbourhood youth off the streets by providing recreational facilities where they can meet, exercise, play indoor sports, and hold dances. Since its inception, the organization has managed to survive on the basis of user fees charged to parents whose children use the program. This year the centre received support from a new provincial government program, in the form of an operating grant along with subsidy fees for those parents whose income is considered insufficient to pay the user fee. A local foundation, with a long history in the community and a reputation for honouring its commitments, has also come to the aid of the centre. This outside financial support came with the provision that the centre now present audited financial statements annually.

Your firm is attempting to obtain the audit, as it is a November year-end, and the audit would be completed at a traditionally slow time of year. Many questions were posed during the interview, and the ASYC audit committee has requested a written response to the issues raised. Excerpts from the interview follow:

- "We are looking for financial statements that are understandable to the board. For example, we have heard that we might have to capitalize and depreciate leasehold improvements. We have just completed $20,000 in expenditures to set up a weight room. We don't understand this amortization idea. Will it make us look like we exceeded our operating budget since this budget is based on all expenditures, capital and operating? The government might consider reducing our next operating grant because of this accounting. If you were selected as our auditor, would you have any problem if we simply expensed capital assets as incurred?"

- "The Parent Advisory Group has organized several fundraising events. They raised $250,000 in cash donations. They hired a part-time manager and paid for advertising on a local radio station. The total costs for salaries and advertising were $65,000. The net receipts of $185,000 have been deposited in a separate 'Computer Fund' bank account to allow for the purchase of some PCs. Our financial statements do not reflect this fund. Is that okay with you?"

- "The manager of Sports Supplies Ltd. is a good friend of the centre. This year his company gave us a variety of items, such as exercise and bodybuilding apparatus and some basketball equipment. This is pretty neat stuff and must be worth at least $12,000 to $15,000. The audit committee does not want to record this because they are concerned that if it ends up in revenue our operating grants might be reduced."

- "Certain of the parents have donated goods or their time and would like to receive a tax receipt for the value of these donations. We are not certain whether we will have to reflect these in our financial statements this year. For example,

   1. Jane Barnes provided valuable advice on improved management efficiency. She is a professional consultant and although these consulting fees were not budgeted for, the centre made several changes that resulted in a reduction of administrative costs. Ms. Barnes estimates that her full-rate fee would have been $7,500.

   2. Rick James, who is a qualified Phys. Ed. instructor, has been substituting one day a week at no charge, which reduced our budgeted expenditures by $4,500 this year.

   3. Parents have donated an awful lot of their time to operate fundraising activities (in addition to those involved with the Computer Fund). This time must be worth thousands of dollars."

- "Some of the staff have not been able to take their vacation this year due to scheduling problems. As a result, we will have to pay them vacation pay. These funds will be paid out after the year-end and will likely be covered by next year's operating grant. To keep revenues and expenses matched, we want to record the vacation pay on a cash basis. Would that be okay? Otherwise, we'll record a portion of next year's grant as receivable this year."

- "The local foundation has provided the centre with a $30,000 grant to cover the expenses of a volunteer coordinator for two years. We received an installment of $12,000, but we haven't hired a coordinator yet. The coordinator will be paid on an hourly basis, and the number of hours each month will fluctuate over the next two years depending on the monthly activities."

- "The cost of the fundraising program for the year was $100,000, which includes the salary of one full time employee and the costs of preparing and mailing brochures to past and prospective donors. The brochures provide a summary of the programs at ASYC and some tips and early warnings sign to help parents recognize when their children may be involved with drugs. We are wondering whether these fundraising costs can be classified as educational costs on the statement of operations."

Required:

Prepare a draft of the response that will be sent to the audit committee.

Case 12-3
LO2

You have been recently elected to the position of treasurer on the board of directors for Canoes Are Us, a community-based service and NFPO that provides canoeing lessons and canoe rentals to various community groups.

Canoes Are Us is a large NFPO with annual donations and grants in excess of $2 million. For the past several years, the canoe program has been funded through lesson fees, member contributions, and donations from the community. Canoes Are Us also relies on a large number of volunteers, including volunteers for the solicitation of donations and the performance of routine bookkeeping. Volunteer instructors are allowed to borrow canoes for their personal use for a nominal rental fee of $25 per month, as long as there are spare canoes available.

The board has recently set up a program in conjunction with the local community centre to provide lessons and rentals to various groups of children from low-income families. The municipal government and the lottery commission have announced that they will provide, in total, a one-time grant of $250,000 this year to Canoes Are Us for this initiative. The grant has a number of conditions:

1. $50,000 is to be used to purchase a new truck and trailer to transport the canoes.

2. $150,000 is to be used for the purchase of new canoes and safety equipment.

3. $50,000 is restricted to covering operating costs, such as salaries, advertising, and campaign costs.

4. An external audit by independent auditors must be conducted at the end of the year and the report must be submitted to the municipal government. The books and records of Canoes Are Us were not previously audited.

During a recent fundraising campaign, Canoes Are Us raised $45,000 in cash and received an additional $20,000 in pledges. The pledges are expected to be received by the middle of the next fiscal year. In addition, a local manufacturer has donated a new canoe valued at $2,500 to the program.

The cost of the fundraising program for the year was $20,000, which includes the salary of one part-time employee and the costs of preparing and mailing brochures to past and prospective donors. The brochures describe the programs and services provided at Canoes Are Us and some tips on how to care for a canoe. You are wondering whether these fundraising costs can be classified as educational costs on the statement of operations.

When you review the financial information for Canoes Are Us, you discover that the books and records have been kept on a modified accrual basis, whereby the cash basis is used for inflows but payables are accrued for outflows. Capital expenditures have been expensed in the year of purchase. There is no master list of existing canoes, and, in fact, some of the canoes appear to be in the possession of volunteer instructors on a semi-permanent basis even though the organization has full storage facilities available. The secretary to the board of directors is one of the volunteer instructors who has a canoe in her possession. You have also been advised that several instructors have unpaid rental accounts ranging from $50 to $400 each, and it appears that no serious efforts have been made to collect these accounts.

In discussions with the previous treasurer about how the new grant and other funds are to be used and accounted for, you discover that she is very opposed to any changes in the way that the accounting records are kept and the financial statements are prepared. She says that changes would make it difficult to compare the programs and to understand how the funds are being used. She was very active in setting up the organization and was one of the driving forces behind obtaining the grant for the new program.

Required:

Prepare a memorandum to the board of directors recommending, with supporting explanations, what changes in accounting and reporting are required in order to comply with GAAP and to fulfill the stewardship reporting objective. Assume that the deferral method is used to account for contributions.

(CGA-Canada adapted)

*Case 12-4
LO2

The Sassawinni First Nation is located adjacent to a town in northern Saskatchewan. The Nation is under the jurisdiction of the federal government's Aboriginal Affairs and Northern Development Canada, and for years has received substantial funding from that department. The money has been used mainly to fund housing construction on the reserve and to provide maintenance payments to families that do not have a source of income. The houses are the property of the Sassawinni First Nation, and the band council allocates them to families on the basis of need. In addition to the housing, the band has been able to build a recreational centre, which also contains the band's council chamber and administrative offices.

A few years ago, some council members with an entrepreneurial flair persuaded the Nation's members to build a shopping centre containing a large grocery store and several small specialty stores. The shopping centre is located on reserve land, and the band provided approximately 20% of the financing, with the balance coming from a provincially guaranteed bank loan. The shopping centre operates under the name Great Northern Centre Inc., and the Sassawinni First

Nation owns 100% of its outstanding common shares. The centre has been a financial success, drawing a large proportion of its business from the adjoining town and surrounding agricultural area. Not only has it been a source of employment for First Nation families, but it has also generated enough cash to keep its loan payments current and has recently been able to declare and pay a dividend.

Flushed with its success, the Sassawinni First Nation has submitted to the provincial government a business plan to construct a gambling casino on band property. It will be an incorporated entity and will be under the complete control of the Nation, subject only to provincial government gambling regulations.

Up to the present time, the band has provided stewardship reports to the Department of Indian Affairs and Northern Development that outline the funds received from the federal government and the manner in which they have been spent. Government auditors have verified these statements, but no formal audit reports have been considered necessary. Now, with all of this new business activity taking place, proper audited financial statements will be required for the next fiscal year. You are employed by Fox, Fox, and Jameson, the public accounting firm that is the auditor of Great Northern Centre Inc. Your firm has just been appointed auditor of Sassawinni First Nation, and this will be the firm's first audit of an organization of this nature. Jane Fox, the managing partner in charge of this audit, has asked you to provide her with a written report outlining the specific accounting principles that will be applicable in this case. "I am going to have to catch up quickly," she said. "I am aware that there have been some changes in GAAP recently, but because our firm has not been involved with audits of this nature I have not paid much attention to what has been going on. One of the benefits of hiring new university grads like yourself is that you provide us with up-to-date technical knowledge."

You have just returned from interviewing the band chief, Joe Sullivan. "I am absolutely certain that we are going to get this casino," he said. "The announcement will be made by the premier within two weeks, and I have received information from a knowledgeable insider that we will be on the list of First Nations to be granted casino licences. It will be a financial godsend to our people, employing well over 100 band members and providing us with substantial profits, a portion of which will have to be devoted entirely to accommodations in accordance with the licensing agreement. This will allow us to build more housing for our members, but with all the jobs that we now have, we will probably start charging rent for housing provided to those with jobs. Not only that, we have three permanent employees who have been with us for a while, and council has instructed me to investigate the possibility of providing a pension plan for them as well as for the permanent employees in our business enterprises."

When asked about the band's accounting records, Sullivan responded, "We have a very good bookkeeper, and the government auditor has always complimented her on the accuracy of her records. She provides timely statements showing us how much we have to spend. Our records are all here and go back at least 20 years. I would just as soon carry on the way we have been doing things, but with this new casino we'll have to provide audited financial statements to the two governments—and, of course, to our members."

Required:

Prepare the report requested by your firm's managing partner.

Case 12-5
LO2

Confidence Private is a high school in the historic city of Jeanville. It engages students in a dynamic learning environment and inspires them to become intellectually vibrant, compassionate, and responsible citizens. The private school has been run as an NFPO since its inception 20 years ago.

In an effort to attract sports-minded students from a variety of economic backgrounds, Confidence initiated a fundraising program in July Year 8, to raise $5 million to build a new gymnasium, swimming pool, and fitness centre, and to create an endowment fund for scholarships. The fundraising campaign was a huge success. By May 31, Year 9, the school had received the following contributions:

1. $2.0 million in cash contributions specifically designated for construction and maintenance of the facilities.
2. $3.1 million in cash contributions specifically designated for the scholarship fund.
3. Fitness equipment valued at $0.2 million.

On June 15, Year 9, at the graduation ceremony, the headmaster thanked the parents, students, alumni, and staff for all their support, and officially closed the capital campaign. He provided the following details of the campaign:

- The construction of the facility was nearing completion and would be ready for classes in September Year 9. The final cost for the facility would be approximately $1.9 million.
- The contribution of fitness equipment would more than adequately equip the fitness centre.
- $3.1 million in cash would be invested and managed by a professional investment adviser.

The income earned on the endowment fund would be used to provide scholarships to students. Five students would receive full or partial scholarships in the fall of Year 10. Each year thereafter, it was expected that 25 to 30 students would receive full or partial scholarships to offset the annual tuition fee of $15,000.

You are proud to be an alumnus of Confidence. You attended the graduation ceremony. At the garden reception after the ceremony, you accepted the headmaster's request to help out with the accounting for the capital campaign and related events. He was unsure of whether the school should use the restricted fund or deferral method of accounting for contributions. You agreed to provide a memo in which you would provide recommendations for accounting policies to be applied for the year ended June 30, Year 9, and for future years when the facilities are being used and the scholarships are disbursed.

Required:

Prepare a memo for the headmaster. Explain the rationale for your recommendations and state your assumptions.

(CGA-Canada adapted)

Case 12-6
LO2

In the fall of Year 5, eight wealthy business people from the same ethnic background formed a committee (CKER committee) to obtain a radio licence from the Canadian Radio-Television and Telecommunications Commission (CRTC). Their goal is to start a non-profit, ethnic community radio station for their area. They plan to call the station CKER-FM Ethnic Radio (CKER). It will broadcast music, news and sports from their country of origin, cultural information, ethnic cooking, and other such programs, seven days a week.

The station's capital requirements are to be financed by memberships, donations, and various types of loans. It is expected that on-going operations will be supported by advertising paid for by business people from that ethnic community and by the larger business community targeting that ethnic audience, as well as by donations and memberships.

It is now March Year 6, and the CRTC has announced that hearings will start in one month on a number of broadcasting licence applications, including the CKER committee's application. The CKER committee members are fairly confident about the viability of their proposal; however, they have decided to seek the advice of a professional accounting firm to assist with the endeavour. The CKER committee has engaged Maria & Casano, Chartered Accountants, for the assignment, as three of the five partners of the firm are from the same ethnic community. The partner in charge of the assignment has stated that the firm will donate half its fee for the work.

You, a CA, work for Maria & Casano and have been put in charge of the assignment. You have met with the CKER committee and various volunteers associated with the project. Information gathered on station start-up is contained in Exhibit I. Exhibit II provides other information on the CKER committee's proposal.

EXHIBIT I

INFORMATION ON STATION START-UP

1. Costs to date have totalled $50,000 and are mostly transportation and meeting costs, as well as postage.
    The CKER committee members have paid for these costs personally.

2. To approve the licence application, the CRTC must see written commitments to finance the station's start-up costs and operating losses in the first two years. Remaining costs to obtain the licence, excluding donated legal work, are expected to be about $8,000, and will be paid by CKER committee members.

3. If the CRTC approves the licence application, the CKER committee will immediately set up a non-profit organization and apply to Revenue Canada for charitable status, which it will likely receive.

4. Fairly exhaustive efforts to obtain commercial financing have failed. As a result, four wealthy individuals have volunteered to provide CKER with the financing for the start-up costs. They will each personally borrow $25,000 from financial institutions and give the funds to the station. These individuals expect the loans to be cost free to them as the station will make the interest and principal payments. (Assume that the loan principal is expected to be repaid over a 10-year period and that the rate of interest is 8% annually.)

5. A "Reverse Life-Time Contribution" program will also be instituted. Under this program, a donor will pay the station a capital sum of at least $50,000. The station can do whatever it wants with the funds, but it will repay the donor an equal annual amount calculated as the capital sum divided by 90 years less the individual's age at the time of contribution. Upon the death of the donor, the station will retain the balance of the funds. Currently, a 64-year-old station supporter has committed $78,000, and seven other individuals are considering this method of assisting the station.

6. Initially, the station is to broadcast with a 2,500 watt signal. It is hoped that within three to four years it will be possible to obtain commercial financing for a second transmitter that will boost the power of the signal and the broadcast range.

EXHIBIT II

OTHER INFORMATION ABOUT PLANS FOR STATION

1. The CKER committee has analyzed census and other data to determine the potential market for the station. Engineering studies have mapped out the area that will be covered by the broadcast signal. There are about 1.1 million people in the target listening area. The latest Canadian census shows that 14% of the population comes from the target ethnic group. A number of surveys have shown that, of a given population, nearly 80% listen regularly to the radio. By applying a conservative factor of 50% to these findings, the CKER committee has arrived at a listenership figure of 5.6% or about 62,000 people. The CKER committee has found that about one in five of the businesses in the area are run by members of the ethnic community, many of whom would like a medium for reaching their own people through direct advertising.

2. The amount of time expected to be devoted to commercials per hour is four minutes in Year 1, five minutes in Year 2, and six minutes in Year 3. Advertising cost per minute, discounted to 25% below the current market rate, will be:

Prime time (6 hours a day)	$40
Regular time (10 hours a day)	$30
Off-peak (8 hours a day)	$25

   Advertising time will be sold by sales people whose remuneration will be a 15% commission.

3. Miscellaneous revenue from renting out the recording studio when not in use by CKER could approach $3,000 per month in Year 3 but will start out at about $2,200 per month and will be $2,500 per month in Year 2.

4. At least 120 people have committed to pay a $125 annual membership fee. Membership carries no special privileges other than to be identified as a supporter of the station. Membership is expected to grow by 20% per year.

5. Start-up capital expenditures are as follows: transmission equipment $61,000; broadcast studio equipment $62,000; and production studio equipment $40,000. Administration and other costs, including rent, are expected to total about $1,237,000 per year and will not increase when advertising sales increase.

6. About one-third of the person-hours needed to run the station are expected to come from volunteers.

The partner has asked you to prepare a draft report to the committee members discussing the viability of the proposed radio station over the initial three-year period. Since the committee is fairly confident that they will receive the licence, the partner has also asked you to recommend accounting policies for the transactions that CKER is contemplating.

Required:

Prepare the draft report.

(CICA adapted)

*Case 12-7
LO9

The provincial government (50%) and three private companies (16.67% each) own Access Records Limited (ARL), which commenced operations on April 1, Year 1. The provincial government currently maintains, on a manual basis, all descriptive information on land in the province, such as information on ownership, legal descriptions, etc. ARL's mandate is to computerize this information and to provide additional data not available from the manual system. The conversion of the manual system for several geographical regions of the province commenced on May 1, Year 1, with a targeted completion of all regions by September Year 3. The manual systems for each region will be maintained by ARL until each regional computerized system is operational.

The computer files are to be available to online users; others not online must obtain the information they need by going to designated government offices for hard copies. The prime users are market research firms, publishers of databases, real estate companies, and a variety of individuals and corporations. ARL charges the users a fee based on the information obtained. Computerization will permit additional descriptive information to be added to the database. As a result, user fees will increase as a region is computerized. No other organization provides this information.

In calculating the pre-tax income of ARL, the following items must be taken into account:

- In return for providing the original information, the provincial government receives a royalty for revenue generated from information that was previously available from the manual system. Two of the private companies receive a royalty for revenue generated from any new information that they gather and enter into the database. The computer system automatically identifies charges for previously available information and charges for the new information.
- The three private companies are to receive, for 10 years, a 20% rate of return on the original cost of the computer equipment and technology they were required to provide to ARL. At the end of 10 years, the computer equipment and technology will become the property of ARL.
- One of the three private companies entered into a 10-year agreement to provide the land and building from which ARL operates. It receives a 12% rate of return per year on its investment in the land and building. All operating costs, including repairs and maintenance, property taxes, and necessary improvements, are to be paid by ARL.
- The shareholders of ARL are to receive interest at the rate of prime plus 1% on any funds lent to ARL.

If the private owners, in operating ARL, do not meet certain specified performance standards, the provincial government can acquire their shares at cost.

It is now September Year 1. Your employer, Martin and Partners, Chartered Accountants, has been engaged by ARL as consultant for the fiscal year ending March 31, Year 2. Martin and Partners has been asked to submit a detailed report addressing significant accounting matters.

You obtain the following information:

1. The cash contribution of the four owners totals $40 million. Another $30–50 million will be needed to complete the computerization. ARL will borrow the additional cash from a chartered bank, using ARL's assets as collateral.

2. Most of the total conversion cost of $70–90 million is for the costs of mapping, aerial photography, and computer graphics.

3. At the end of 10 years, the government is entitled to acquire, at fair value, the 50% of the shares that it does not own. The private companies are entitled to a reduced royalty if the provincial government acquires their shares.

4. The user-fee schedule is set by the provincial government.

5. Discounts are offered to volume users.

6. ARL intends to sell its technology to other provinces.

7. The province's auditor is permitted access to ARL's financial records.

Required:

Prepare the report.

(*CICA adapted*)

PROBLEMS

Problem 12-1
LO2, 4, 6

The OPI Care Centre is an NFPO funded by government grants and private donations. It prepares its annual financial statements using the deferral method of accounting for contributions, and it uses only the operations fund to account for all activities. It uses an encumbrance system as a means of controlling expenditures.

The following summarizes some of the transactions made in Year 6:

1. The founding member of OPI contributed $100,000 on the conditions that the principal amount be invested in marketable securities and that only the income earned from the investment is spent on operations.

2. During the year, purchase orders were issued to cover the budgeted cost of $1,400,000 for goods and contracted services.

3. During the year, a public campaign was held to raise funds for daily operations for the current year. Cash of $800,000 was collected, and pledges for an additional $100,000 were received by the end of the year. It is estimated that approximately 95% of these pledges will be collected early in the new year.

4. The provincial government pledged $600,000 for the year to cover operating costs and an additional $1,000,000 to purchase equipment and furniture. All of the grant money was received by the end of the year, except for the last $50,000 to cover operating costs for December.

5. OPI used the $1,000,000 received from the provincial government to purchase equipment and furniture for the care facility. The amortization of these assets amounted to $100,000 for the year. A purchase order had not been issued for this purchase.

6. Invoices totalling $1,450,000 were received for goods and contracted services. Of these invoices, 90% were paid by the end of the fiscal year. Purchase orders in the amount of $1,375,000 had been issued for these services.

Required:

In accordance with the requirements of the *CICA Handbook*, prepare the journal entries necessary to reflect the transactions.

(*CGA-Canada adapted*)

Problem 12-2
LO2, 3, 5

The Perch Falls Minor Hockey Association was established in Perch Falls in January Year 5. Its mandate is to promote recreational hockey in the small community of Perch Falls. With the support of the provincial government, local business people, and many individuals, the association raised sufficient funds to build an indoor hockey arena and it also established an endowment fund for paying travel costs to tournaments on an annual basis.

The following schedule summarizes the cash flows for the year ended December 31, Year 5.

PERCH FALLS MINOR HOCKEY ASSOCIATION
($000s)

	Operating fund	Capital fund	Endowment fund
Cash inflows			
Government grant for operating costs	$ 90		
Government grant for hockey arena		$500	
Corporate donations for hockey arena		460	
Registration fees	50		
Contribution for tournaments			$50
Rental of hockey arena	70		
Interest received			3
	210	960	53
Cash outflows			
Operating expenses	205		
Construction of hockey arena		960	
Purchase of marketable securities			50
Travel costs for tournament			3
	205	960	53
Cash, end of year	$ 5	$ 0	$ 0

Additional Information

- The new hockey arena was completed in late August Year 5. The official opening was held on August 30, with a game between the Perch Falls Old-Timers and the local firefighters. The arena is expected to have a 40-year useful life and no residual value.
- A long-time resident of Perch Falls donated the land on which the arena was built. The land was valued at $100,000. The association gave a donation receipt to the donor.
- A former resident of Perch Falls donated ice-making and ice-cleaning equipment to the association. A receipt for $60,000 was issued for the donation. The equipment has a useful life of 10 years and no residual value.
- The donation for tournaments was contributed on January 1, Year 5, with the condition that the principal amount of $50,000 be invested in 6% corporate bonds. The interest earned on the investment can be used only for travel costs for out-of-town tournaments. All investments in bonds will be held to their maturity date.
- The provincial government pledged $100,000 a year for operating costs. Ninety percent of the grant is advanced throughout the year. Upon receipt of the association's annual report, the government will issue the last 10% of the annual grant to the association.
- Registration fees and rental fees for the hockey arena are received at the beginning of the hockey season and cover the entire season, from September 1, Year 5, to April 30, Year 6.
- At the end of the year, the association owed $7,000 for services received in the month of December.
- The association wants to use the restricted fund method of accounting for contributions and to use three separate funds: operating fund, capital fund, and endowment fund. All capital assets are to be capitalized and amortized, as applicable, over their estimated useful lives.

Required:

Restricted

(a) Prepare a statement of financial position and statement of operations for each of the three funds as at and for the year ended December 31, Year 5.
(b) Assume that 300 children registered with the Association in Year 5. What was the average cost per registered child for Year 5 for running the Association? What costs did you include/exclude and why?

(CGA-Canada adapted)

...ut this NFPO are identical to those described in Problem 2, except that ...ion wants to use the deferral method of accounting for contributions. The centre will continue to use the three separate funds.

Required:

Prepare a statement of financial position and statement of operations for each of the three funds as at and for the year ended December 31, Year 5.

Problem 12-4
LO2, 3, 4, 5, 6

Zak Organization is an NFPO set up for famine relief. It uses the restricted fund method of accounting and has three funds: a general fund, a capital fund (through which it is raising cash to support the purchase of a new administrative building), and an endowment fund. Zak has been operating for 25 years and has a December 31 year-end. Zak's policy with respect to capital assets is to capitalize and amortize the capital assets over their expected useful lives.

On June 30, Year 5, Zak received three donations from a former director:

- $30,000 cash for general famine relief efforts
- $50,000 to be used solely for construction of the new administrative building; of the $50,000, 70% was received in cash, with the remainder promised in February Year 6 (construction is expected to commence in October Year 6)
- $600,000 cash, which was invested on July 1, Year 5, in long-term Government of Canada bonds, with 10% interest to be paid semi-annually on December 31 and June 30; the $600,000 donation was given with the stipulation that it be invested in interest-bearing securities, with the principal to be maintained by Zak, although interest earned on the securities is not restricted

Required:

(a) Briefly explain how each of the three donations should be accounted for using the restricted fund method of accounting. In particular, should each of the donations be recognized as revenue for the year ended December 31, Year 5? If yes, in which fund(s) would the revenue be recognized (including interest earned in fiscal Year 5 on the bonds purchased with the $600,000 donation)? Note: Do not prepare journal entries.
(b) If Zak used the deferral method of accounting instead of the restricted fund method, how would this change the requirements for accounting for the $50,000 and $600,000 donations?
(c) Despite the recent donations from its former director, Zak is increasingly faced with severe budgetary constraints. Zak is considering implementing encumbrance accounting in the coming year.
　(i) Briefly describe the process of encumbrance accounting.
　(ii) Briefly describe how encumbrance accounting might serve as a device to help control spending when it is used in conjunction with a formal budgeting system.

(CGA-Canada adapted)

Problem 12-5
LO2, 4, 6

You have been recruited to act as the treasurer on the board of directors of an NFPO that has had difficulty in recent years controlling its expenditures. The board of directors has very limited accounting experience. The organization, Protect Purple Plants (PPP), is considering implementing an encumbrance accounting system to assist in expenditure control. PPP receives an estimated $800,000 per year in regular contributions from the federal government.

Required:

(a) State *two* advantages and *two* disadvantages of implementing an encumbrance accounting system.

(b) PPP uses the deferral method of accounting for contributions and has no separate fund for restricted contributions. On January 1, Year 6, PPP received its first restricted cash contribution—$120,000 for the purchase and maintenance of land and a greenhouse building for its rare purple plant collection.

   On July 1, Year 6, PPP acquired land and a building for $22,000 and $80,000 cash, respectively. The building has an estimated useful life of 20 years and zero residual value. On December 31, Year 6, the remaining $18,000 cash was paid to KJ Maintenance Ltd. for a three-year maintenance contract that requires KJ personnel to provide maintenance services four days per month until December 31, Year 9. Assuming that encumbrance accounting will *not* be implemented until Year 7, prepare the journal entries for the following dates:

   (i)   January 1, Year 6
   (ii) July 1, Year 6
   (iii) December 31, Year 6

(CGA-Canada adapted)

Problem 12-6
LO2, 6

The Fara Littlebear Society is an NFPO funded by government grants and private donations. It was established in Year 5 by the friends of Fara Littlebear to encourage and promote the work of Native Canadian artists. Fara achieved international recognition for her art depicting images of journey and exploration.

   The society leased a small building in January Year 5. The building contains a small art gallery on the first floor and office space on the second floor. The society spent $83,850 for leasehold improvements. The art gallery opened for public viewing on April 1, Year 5.

   The unadjusted trial balance for the year ended December 31, Year 5, was as follows:

	Debit	Credit
Cash	$ 5,000	
Investment in bonds (Note 1)	80,000	
Artwork (Note 2)	300,000	
Leasehold improvements (Note 3)	83,850	
Government grant—operating costs (Note 6)		$ 90,000
Government grant—restricted for purchase of artwork		150,000
Corporate donations—restricted for purchase of artwork		150,000
Corporate donations—restricted for leasehold improvements		78,000
Individual donations restricted for scholarships (Note 1)		80,000
Interest income		4,000
Revenue from admission fees to art gallery		67,000

(continued)

	Debit	Credit
Rent expense (Note 3)	26,000	
Salaries expense (Note 4)	66,000	
Other expenses	53,150	
Scholarship awarded	5,000	
	$619,000	$619,000

Additional Information

- A wealthy individual donated $80,000 with the condition that the principal be invested in low-risk investments. The principal was invested in long-term bonds, which are expected to be held to maturity. The interest on the bonds is to be used to provide scholarships to aspiring Native artists who wish to study art at a Canadian university or college. The first scholarship of $5,000 was awarded in September Year 5.
- The artwork consists of 20 paintings from a number of Canadian artists. These paintings are expected to be held for at least 10 years. The paintings will likely appreciate in value over the time they are owned by the art gallery.
- The society signed a 5-year lease on the building with an option to renew for one further term of 5 years. The term of the lease commenced on January 1, Year 5. The total rent paid for the year included a deposit of $2,000 for the last month's rent. The leasehold improvements were completed on March 31, Year 5. The office space was occupied by the staff of the society, and the art gallery was opened for business on April 1, Year 5.
- Salaries earned but not yet paid amounted to $5,000 at December 31, Year 5.
- The society received office equipment from a local business person on January 1, Year 5. A donation receipt for $20,000 was given for this contribution. The office equipment has a useful life of five years with no residual value.
- The provincial government provided an operating grant of $100,000 for Year 5, of which $90,000 was received by the end of the year. The remaining $10,000 will be received once the society provides financial statements prepared in accordance with GAAP.
- The society will follow Part III of the *CICA Handbook* and wishes to use the deferral method of accounting for contributions.

Required:

(a) Explain how the matching principle is applied when the deferral method is used to account for restricted contributions.
(b) Prepare a statement of financial position for the society at December 31, Year 5. Show your supporting calculations and state your assumptions. (You can use an assumed number for excess of revenue over expenses to balance your statement of financial position.)

(CGA-Canada adapted)

*Problem 12-7
LO2, 6

The Brown Training Centre is a charitable organization dedicated to providing computer training to unemployed people. Individuals must apply to the centre and indicate why they would like to take the three-month training session. If their application is accepted, they must pay a $200 deposit. The deposit is refunded upon successful completion of the course or is forfeited as a processing fee if the individual does not complete the course.

During the first year of operations in Year 3, 90 individuals were accepted into the course. Of these 90 individuals, 50 completed the course, 10 dropped out, and 30 were still taking the course at the end of the fiscal year.

The centre receives most of its funding from the provincial government. During the year, the government advanced $1,000,000 to cover operating costs. Within two months of the year-end, the centre must provide financial statements prepared in accordance with GAAP. The government will cover all operating costs. The excess of amounts advanced over the amount expended must be carried over and applied to operating costs of the next year. Operating costs to be reimbursed are defined to exclude purchases of capital assets and are to be reduced by the amount of application fees forfeited.

A private company donated computers and office equipment with a fair value of $320,000. The centre was fortunate to receive this donation. Otherwise, it would have had to raise money through other means to purchase these items. The capital assets were put into use as of April 1, Year 3, and have an estimated useful life of three years. The centre uses the straight-line method to amortize its capital assets.

The part-time bookkeeper for the centre prepared the following cash flow statement for the year ended December 31, Year 3:

Cash receipts	
Government grant	$1,000,000
Deposits from course participants	18,000
Total cash receipts	1,018,000
Cash expenditures	
Salaries and benefits	620,000
Administration and supplies	220,000
Rent and utilities	160,000
Refund of deposits	10,000
Total cash disbursements	1,010,000
Cash balance at end of year	$ 8,000

At the end of the year the following costs had been incurred but not yet paid:

Salaries and benefits	$ 8,000
Utilities	6,000

The executive director of the centre has asked you for assistance in preparing the financial statements for the centre for the first year of operations. The deferral method should be used in accounting for the contributions.

Required:

(a) Briefly explain how the accrual basis of accounting is applied when accounting for capital assets for an NFPO.
(b) Prepare the statement of revenues and expenses for the centre for the year ended December 31, Year 3.
(c) Compute the following liabilities on the statement of financial position for the centre at December 31, Year 3:
   (i)   Accrued liabilities
   (ii) Deposits from course participants
   (iii) Deferred contributions

(CGA-Canada adapted)

Problem 12-8
LO2, 3, 4, 5

The Ford Historical Society is an NFPO funded by government grants and private donations. It uses both an operating fund and a capital fund. The capital fund accounts for moneys received and restricted for major capital asset acquisitions. The operating fund is used for all other activities.

The society uses the restricted fund method of accounting for contributions. An encumbrance system is used within the operating fund to ensure that expenditures made in any one year do not exceed the amounts budgeted. Donated materials and services are recorded if such items would have been purchased had they not been received as donations.

The following are some selected activities that took place during the current year:

- Purchase orders in the amount of $500,000 for goods and services were issued during the year.
- Pledges totalling $350,000 were made to the society, of which $150,000 applies to the operations of the following year. It is estimated that 3% of all pledges will be uncollectible.
- Pledges of $310,000 were collected, and pledges totalling $5,000 were written off.
- A government grant of $500,000 for acquisition and renovation of an office building for the society was approved by the government. All of the grant money was received except for the last 10%, which is expected to be received in the first month of the next fiscal year.
- Invoices for all of the goods and services ordered during the year were received. The total cost was $510,000, of which $480,000 was paid for by the end of the year.
- An old office building was acquired and renovated for a cost of $500,000. Amortization expense on the office building was $10,000.
- A local radio station donated free airtime to the society. The society saved the $5,000 it would normally have paid for this airtime.

Required:

Prepare the journal entries required to record these activities, and indicate which fund each journal entry will be recorded in.

(CGA-Canada adapted)

Problem 12-9
LO2, 6

Fairchild Centre is an NFPO funded by government grants and private donations. It was established on January 1, Year 5, to provide counselling services and a drop-in centre for single parents.

On January 1, Year 5, the centre leased an old warehouse in the central part of Smallville for $2,000 per month. It carried out minor renovations in the warehouse to create a large open area for use as a play area for children and three offices for use by the executive director and counsellors. The lease runs from January 1, Year 5, to June 30, Year 7. By that time, the centre hopes to move into new quarters that are more suitable for the activities carried out.

The following schedule summarizes the cash flows for the year ended December 31, Year 5:

Cash inflows	
Government grant for operating costs (Note 1)	$ 50,000
Donations from individuals with no restrictions	63,000
Donations from individuals for rent of warehouse for 2½ years	60,000
Donations from individuals for purchase of land (Note 3)	58,000
	231,000

Cash outflows	
Renovations of warehouse	43,000
Salary of executive director (Note 4)	33,000
Fees paid to counsellors (Note 4)	20,000
Rent paid for 2½ years	60,000
Other operating expenses	24,000
	180,000
Cash, end of year	$ 51,000

Additional Information

- The provincial government agreed to provide an operating grant of $50,000 per year. In addition, the government has pledged to match contributions collected by the centre for the purchase of land for construction of a new complex for the centre. The maximum contribution by the government toward the purchase of land is $100,000.
- The centre has signed an agreement to purchase a property in the downtown area of Smallville for $225,000. There is an old house on the property, which is currently used as a rooming house. The closing date is any time between July 1, Year 6, and December 31, Year 6. The centre plans to demolish the existing house and build a new complex.
- The centre has recently commenced a fundraising program to raise funds to purchase the land and construct a new building. So far, $58,000 has been raised from individuals toward the purchase of the land. In the new year, the centre will focus its efforts to solicit donations from businesses in the area. The provincial government will advance the funds promised under its pledge on the closing date for the purchase of the property.
- All the people working for the centre are volunteers except for the executive director and the counsellors. The executive director receives a salary of $36,000 a year, while the counsellors bill the centre for professional services rendered based on the number of hours they work at the centre. The director has not yet received her salary for the month of December. One of the counsellors received an advance of $1,000 in December Year 5, for work to be performed in January Year 6.
- The centre wishes to use the deferral method of accounting for contributions and to segregate its net assets between restricted and unrestricted. It capitalizes the cost of capital assets and amortizes the capital assets over their useful lives.

Required:

(a) State the assumptions necessary to recognize the pledge contributions from the provincial government, and prepare the journal entry to record the pledge, if applicable.

(b) Prepare a statement of operations for the Fairchild Centre for the year ended December 31, Year 5. Show your supporting calculations and state your assumptions.

(c) Prepare a statement of changes in net assets for the Fairchild Centre for the year ended December 31, Year 5.

(CGA-Canada adapted)

Problem 12-10
LO2, 3, 4, 5

The Far North Centre (the Centre) is an anti-poverty organization funded by contributions from governments and the general public. For a number of years it has been run by a small group of permanent employees with the help of part-timers and dedicated volunteers. It owns its premises, which are in the process of being renovated. The funds for this were obtained through a special capital fund campaign carried out last year. Its main program is the daily provision of meals to the needy. It also distributes clothing, most of which is donated. Operating funds come from government grants, interest earned from endowment investments, and a public campaign held in the latter part of each year to raise funds for the needs of the next fiscal year. The Centre maintains its records in accordance with the restricted fund method of accounting for contributions, and prepares its financial statements using an operating fund, a capital fund (for all activities related to capital assets), and an endowment fund.

The following are the fund trial balances as at January 1, Year 6:

	Debit	Credit
Operating Fund		
Cash	$ 570,500	
Pledges receivable	705,000	
Allowance for uncollectible pledges		$ 30,000
Grants receivable	217,500	
Accounts payable		427,500
Wages payable		137,250
Accrued liabilities		9,750
Deferred revenue		800,000
Fund balance		88,500
	$1,493,000	$1,493,000
Capital Fund		
Cash	$ 287,500	
Grants receivable	112,500	
Land and building	810,250	
Furniture and equipment	491,000	
Accumulated amortization		$ 648,200
Accounts payable		9,000
Investment in capital assets		653,050
Fund balance		391,000
	$1,701,250	$1,701,250
Endowment Fund		
Cash	$ 37,500	
Investments	375,000	
Fund balance		$ 412,500
	$ 412,500	$ 412,500

The following transactions took place in Year 6.

1. The Year 6 budget, the totals of which are summarized below, was recorded.

Budgeted revenues	$2,200,000
Budgeted expenses	2,150,000
Budgeted surplus	$ 50,000

2. The agency uses an encumbrance system in the operating fund as a means of controlling expenditures. During the year, purchase orders for goods and services at an estimated amount of $1,450,000 were issued.

3. $35,000 from endowment fund cash was invested in marketable securities.

4. Office equipment costing $2,500 was purchased with operating fund cash.

5. Invoices totalling $1,375,000 were received on purchase orders originally recorded at an estimated cost of $1,392,000. These invoices were recorded as accounts payable and were allocated 55% to food program, 20% to clothing program, and 25% to administration.

6. The capital fund grants receivable were collected in full, and the $9,000 in accounts payable was paid. During Year 6, building renovations costing $300,000 and equipment purchases of $85,000 were made. Of this cost, 90% was paid, with the balance held back and still owing at year-end.

7. Operating fund accounts payable amounting to $1,560,000 and the wages payable and accrued liabilities at the beginning of the year were all paid.

8. All of the operating fund pledges and grants receivable at the beginning of the year were collected in full.

9. The deferred revenue from the Year 5 fundraising campaign was made up of the following:

Contributions	$1,200,000
Less: Campaign expense	400,000
	$ 800,000

The Centre runs the campaign with its owns people and is fully responsible for all decisions made during the campaign.

10. Government grants for operating purposes totalled $900,000, of which $850,000 was received during the year, with the balance expected early in Year 7.

11. The total wage costs for the year amounted to $400,000, of which $325,000 was paid and $75,000 is payable at year-end. These costs are to be allocated 40% each to the food and clothing programs, with the balance to administration.

12. The campaign to raise funds for next year's operations was held in December. Cash of $500,000 was collected and pledges of $700,000 were received. It is expected that 5% of these pledges will be uncollectible. Total fundraising costs were $322,000, of which $75,000 is still owed to suppliers.

13. An endowment contribution of $8,000 cash was received. In addition, the investments in the endowment fund earned $31,200 in interest.

14. The annual depreciation on the buildings and equipment amounted to $92,000.

15. At the end of the year, the balances in the encumbrance accounts and the budget accounts were closed.

Required:

(a) Prepare the journal entries necessary to reflect the Year 6 events.

(b) For each fund, prepare a Year 6 statement of financial position and statement of operations and changes in fund balance.

(c) Prepare a cash flow statement on a non-fund basis.

(d) Prepare closing entries.

(e) What percentage of Year 6 revenues of the operating fund were spent on program costs and what percentage was spent on administration and fundraising? How will users of these financial statements feel about these percentages?

Problem 12-11
LO2, 3, 4, 6

All facts about this NFPO are identical to those described in Problem 10, except that the deferral method of recording contributions is used for accounting and for external financial reporting. Fund accounting is not used. The Year 6 transactions are also identical to those described in Problem 10.

The organization's statement of financial position on January 1, Year 6, is shown below.

FAR NORTH CENTRE
STATEMENT OF FINANCIAL POSITION
January 1, Year 6

Current Assets	
Cash	$ 895,500
Pledges receivable	705,000
Allowance for uncollectible pledges	(30,000)
Grants receivable	330,000
	1,900,500
Investments	375,000
Capital assets:	
Land and buildings	810,250
Furniture and equipment	491,000
Accumulated depreciation	(648,200)
	653,050
	$2,928,550
Current Liabilities	
Accounts payable	$ 436,500
Wages payable	137,250
Accrued liabilities	9,750
	583,500
Deferred Revenue	
Deferred contributions	800,000
Deferred building campaign contributions	391,000
Deferred contributions related to capital assets	240,500
	1,431,500
Net Assets	
Net assets invested in capital assets	412,550
Net assets restricted for endowment purposes	412,500
Unrestricted net assets	88,500
	913,550
	$2,928,550

Required:

(a) Prepare the journal entries necessary to reflect the Year 6 events.

(b) Prepare a Year 6 statement of financial position, a statement of revenues and expenses, and a statement of changes in net assets for the year.

(c) Prepare a cash flow statement for the year.

(d) Prepare closing entries.

(e) What are fundraising costs as a percent of total revenues for Year 6? What do you think donors to the Centre will think of this percentage?

Problem 12-12
LO2, 3, 4, 6

The William Robertson Society is a charitable organization funded by government grants and private donations. It prepares its annual financial statements using the restricted fund method in accordance with the *CICA Handbook,* and uses both an operating fund and a capital fund.

The operating fund records the regular operating activities of the society. An encumbrance system is used within the fund to ensure that expenditures made in any one year do not exceed the amounts budgeted. It is the policy of the society to record donated materials and services received during the year, if such items would have been purchased had they not been received as donations.

The capital fund accounts for moneys received from special fundraising campaigns conducted when there is a need for major fixed assets acquisitions.

The following are *some* selected events that took place during the current year:

- Pledges for current year's operating costs amounting to $125,000 were received, of which $90,000 was collected in cash.
- Purchase orders were issued during the year as follows:

Office equipment	$ 15,000
Goods and services	100,000

- A grant of $70,000 for this year's operations was announced by the government, of which $55,000 had been received by the society at year-end.
- Employee wages totalled $60,000 for the year. Wages amounting to $2,000 were unpaid at year-end.
- Invoices for all of the goods and services ordered during the year were received. Of the invoiced amounts, 70% was paid. The invoiced amounts were equal to those on the purchase orders.
- The office equipment that was ordered arrived. The invoiced amount of $15,300 was paid in cash, using operating funds.
- A local radio station donated free airtime to the society. The station would normally bill a customer $3,000 for this airtime.
- A prominent citizen made a pledge of $35,000 to help fund the operating expenditures of the next fiscal year.

Required:

Prepare the journal entries required to record these events, and indicate in which fund each journal entry will be recorded.

Problem 12-13
LO2

The Valleytown Senior's Residential Home (Valleytown) engages in palliative care, education, and fundraising programs. The costs of each program include the costs of personnel, premises, and other expenses that are directly related to providing the program. Valleytown also incurs a number of general support expenses that are common to the administration of the organization and each of its programs.

Financial and nonfinancial data for the three programs for the year ended December 31, Year 12 were as follows:

	Palliative	Education	Fundraising
Direct costs	$5,100,000	$1,200,000	$1,400,000
# of employees	45	8	12
# of computer hours	2,000	400	100

Both the education and fundraising programs include the use of the same brochures to further the work of Valleytown. The brochures are designed and intended to achieve a specific educational objective. Included in the fundraising costs above is $200,000 for brochures. Some of the brochures included in direct mail fundraising campaigns are mailed to individuals who have been identified as potential beneficiaries of the educational component of the brochures. Accordingly, 20% of the cost of those brochures is allocated from the fundraising to the education program. The majority of the direct mail campaign expenses remain a cost of the fundraising program.

Valleytown presents its expenses by function on the statement of operations. It allocates certain of its general support expenses by identifying the appropriate basis of allocating each component expense, and applies that basis consistently each year. Corporate governance and general management expenses are not allocated; other general support expenses are allocated on the following bases:

- Human resources department costs—proportionately, on the number of employees working for each program
- Information technology department costs—proportionately, on the number of hours of computer time provided for each of the programs.

The following summarizes the general support costs for the year ended December 31, Year 12:

Corporate governance	$ 300,000
Human resources department	800,000
Information technology department	1,250,000
General management	650,000
	$3,000,000

Required:

(a) Prepare a schedule to allocate an appropriate amount of general support costs and any other costs to the three programs. Then, indicate the percentage of total costs pertaining to the three programs and general support costs.

(b) Write the note to Valleytown's Year 12 financial statements required by Section 4470.08 on the amounts allocated from fundraising and general support functions, and the amounts and the functions to which they have been allocated.

WEB-BASED PROBLEMS

Web Problem 12-1
LO1, 2, 7

Go to the website of the Salvation Army (www.salvationarmy.ca). Answer the following questions based on the 2012 audited financial statements. For each question, indicate where in the financial statements or annual report you found the answer and/or provide a brief explanation. Round percentages to one decimal point and other ratios to two decimal points.

(a) Read the auditor's report. There is a paragraph there that is unique to NFPOs. Explain what message it conveys.

(b) Approximately how much of the organization's fund balances are restricted? What can they be spent on?

(c) How many funds are reported?

(d) Approximately what percentage of the year's revenues was spent on fundraising?

(e) What is its largest single source of revenue?

(f) Has the organization's cash increased or decreased over the past two years? What was a major factor in the change?

(g) Outline what is included in the accounting entity.

(h) Briefly explain the army's amortization policy.

(i) Which method of revenue recognition for contributions is being used?

(j) What is their policy with respect to donated materials and services?

Web Problem 12-2
LO1, 2, 7

Go to the website of the Canadian Cancer Society (www.cancer.ca). Answer as many of the questions from Problem 1 as you can based on the 2012 Canada-wide financial statements. For each question, indicate where in the financial statements or annual report you found the answer and/or provide a brief explanation. (Some questions may not be applicable.)

Web Problem 12-3
LO2, 7

Go to the website of the University of Saskatchewan (www.usask.ca/reporting). Search for the 2012 financial statements and answer the following questions. For each question, indicate where in the financial statements or annual report you found the answer and/or provide a brief explanation. Round percentages to one decimal point and other ratios to two decimal points.

(a) What accounting policy was used for reporting contributions?

(b) What percentage of total revenue came from government grants? Tuition fees? Donations?

(c) What was the ratio of scholarship expense to tuition fee revenue?

(d) Did the university report any pledges receivable and, if so, for how much? What amount is not expected to be collected within one year?

(e) What percentage of total expenses was spent on educating the students, and what was spent on research during the period? List the items you include for each category.

(f) What was the total value of endowment funds at the end of the year? What portion of the endowment funds is designated for scholarships? For research?

(g) What method of reporting was used for investments in the various funds? What was the unrealized gain or loss from these investments during the year and how were these gains or losses reported?

(h) What was the average cost for the university to graduate a student?

 Practise and learn online with Connect

Endnotes

Chapter 1

1 Austria, Belgium, Bulgaria, Cyprus, Czech Republic, Denmark, Estonia, Finland, France, Germany, Greece, Hungary, Ireland, Italy, Latvia, Lithuania, Luxembourg, Malta, Netherlands, Poland, Portugal, Romania, Slovakia, Slovenia, Spain, Sweden, and United Kingdom.

2 The EU countries that have maintained their own currencies are Bulgaria, Czech Republic, Denmark, Estonia, Hungary, Latvia, Poland, Romania, Sweden, and United Kingdom. On the other hand, Andorra, Kosovo, Montenegro, Monaco, San Marino, and Vatican City are not EU members but do officially use the euro as their currency.

3 Ernst & Young, www.ey.com.

Chapter 2

1 The concept of control is discussed in greater detail in Chapter 3.

2 The concept of an acquisition differential is discussed in Chapter 3 and subsequent chapters.

3 Net assets are equal to total assets less total liabilities. Shareholders' equity is equal to net assets. In making this type of calculation, it is often easier to use the amount for shareholders' equity rather than compute the amount for net assets.

Chapter 3

1 Matt Davies, "CMA Management,"*CMA Canada*, June/July 2010, pp. 14–15.

2 An exception to this occurs when the acquiree applies "push-down accounting." This topic is discussed later in this chapter.

3 *Conceptual Framework for Financial Reporting*, paragraph 4.4.

4 It is also possible for a parent to form a less than 100%-owned subsidiary, or for a 100%-owned subsidiary to later issue shares that are not purchased by the parent. In either case, the observations made in this paragraph are basically the same.

5 The net income of the subsidiary earned after the acquisition date would be reduced by the amortization of the acquisition differential, because the asset values in the accounting records of the subsidiary are not the values used for consolidation. This concept will be discussed in Chapter 5.

Chapter 4

1 Carrying amount + (Fair value − Carrying Amount) = Fair value

Chapter 5

1 Some foreign jurisdictions assess tax at the corporate group level.

2 IAS 1: Presentation of Financial Statements requires a statement of changes in equity as part of the complete set of financial statements. It does not require a separate statement of retained earnings. However, the statement of changes in equity does provide reconciliation between the carrying amount of each component of equity at the beginning and the end of the period. Retained earnings is one of those components. In this textbook, we will use the statement of retained earnings as a surrogate for the retained earnings component of the statement of changes in equity.

3 *Indefinite* does not necessarily mean an infinite life, but rather one that extends beyond the foreseeable future.

4 IFRS 8: Operating Segments is discussed in more detail in Chapter 9.

5 LIFO is not acceptable under IFRSs. Unless otherwise noted, we will assume a FIFO cost flow in all examples in the text.

6 This example is adapted from Example 2 of IAS 36: Illustrative Examples.

7 This example is adapted from Example 7a of IAS 36: Illustrative Examples.

8 It should be emphasized again that the elimination entries shown in the working paper are not recorded in the accounting records of either the parent or the subsidiary.

Chapter 6

1 Intercompany losses are not eliminated when the assets are impaired. This situation will be discussed later in this chapter.

2 The use of a contra account is optional. Companies could record the adjustment to fair value directly in the land account. If so, they would lose track of the original cost in the general ledger. The company could use a property, plant, and equipment subledger to track the necessary information.

Chapter 7

1 http://www.suncor.com/pdf/Suncor_financial_statements_2011_en.pdf

2 We will use the straight-line method in the first few illustrations because it is easier to understand. Later in the chapter, we will illustrate the effective-interest method, which is required by IFRSs.

3 The entry for interest revenue or interest expense is usually one entry that incorporates the amortization of the premium or discount on the bonds. In this example, we are showing two separate entries so it is easier to see that the cash amounts are equal and offsetting.

4 We must also reduce the amount of the deferred tax liability that was set up in Year 1 by $30.

5 Reproduced with the permission of BCE Inc. Copyright © 2012. All rights reserved.

6 One could argue that the gain on sale should also be reported in other comprehensive income since it is similar to revaluing the asset to its fair value. However, IAS 16 explicitly states that the gain or loss on derecognition of property, plant, and equipment should be reported in net income.

Chapter 8

1 IAS 7, paragraphs 39 and 40.

2 See the section near the end of Chapter 2 for a further discussion of changes to and from the equity method.

Chapter 9

1 IFRS 10 and 12 were not effective until 2013, when they replaced IAS 27 and SIC 12. Canadian Tire applied IAS 27 and SIC 12 in its 2011 financial statements.

2 Start-up operations may also be operating segments before earning revenues.

Chapter 10

1 http://www.sedar.com/GetFile.do?lang=EN&docClass=5&issuerNo=00001177&fileName=/csfsprod/data127/filings/01867158/00000001/C%3A\clients\Bomb\Ann12\BBD-FS-YE2011-En.pdf.

2 http://www.sedar.com/GetFile.do?lang=EN&docClass=5&issuerNo=00001289&fileName=/csfsprod/data125/filings/01836557/00000001/e%3A\Scotia_FINAL\Annual-Financials_ENG.pdf.

3 See IAS 21, paragraph 16.

4 For example, if the goods are sold to customers in Australia and the selling price of the inventory is A$9,950 on June 30 (assuming that none of the inventory purchased had been sold by year-end), the selling price in Canadian dollars would be $9,443 (A$9,950 × 0.949). Because the translated selling price is greater than the previous translated historical cost of $9,410, a write-down would not be required.

5 See John E. Stewart, "The Challenges of Hedge Accounting."*Journal of Accountancy* (November 1989), pp. 48–56.

6 Accounting for a net investment in a foreign operation will be discussed in Chapter 11.

7 The present value factor for two months at 1% per month is calculated as $1/1.01^2$ or 0.9803.

Chapter 12

1 Hereinafter, all *Handbook* sections referred to will either be found in Part II or Part III unless otherwise noted. The five sections discussed below and the 4400 series appear in Part III, whereas the other sections appear in Part II.

2 An alternative term often used is *reserve for encumbrances.*

3 A similar conclusion was made in a CICA research study. See "Financial Reporting for Non-profit Organizations" (Toronto: CICA, 1980), p. 52.

4 If the entity chooses to not present this account separately, the $2,016 would be included in the other two components of net assets based on whether the capital assets were purchased with restricted or unrestricted resources.

5 If the entity chooses to not present this account separately, the $1,140 would be included in the unrestricted net assets component of net assets.

6 This entry would not be necessary if the entity chose not to present net assets invested in capital assets separately.

7 These two accounts would be closed to unrestricted net assets if the entity chose not to present net assets invested in capital assets separately.

8 For a complete copy of United Way/Centraide Ottawa's financial statements, go to www.unitedwayottawa.ca.

9 "Financial Reporting by Governments," a research study, Toronto: CICA, 1980.

10 "Local Government Financial Reporting," a research study, Toronto: CICA, 1985.

11 A. Beedle, "Accounting for Local Government in Canada: The State of the Art," Vancouver: Canadian Certified General Accountants' Research Foundation, 1981.

12 For example, the provinces of Manitoba and Nova Scotia, and the cities of Vancouver and Montreal.

Credits

Credits

Index

A

accounting (translation) exposure, 615–616, 617, 630

accounting for business combinations
- acquisition method, 99, 100–118
- consolidated financial statements, 106–118
- deferred income tax, 512–517
- investments in subsidiaries, 203–205
- new-entity method, 98–100
- purchase method, 98, 99, 101

accounting for contributions. *See also* contributions; not-for-profit organizations (NFPOs)
- capital fund, 707, 708, 709, 712, 716
- deferral method. *See* deferral method
- endowment contributions, 697–698
- endowment fund, 716, 717–718, 719
- general fund, 716
- net assets invested in capital assets, 706–713
- restricted fund method. *See* restricted fund method

accounting for foreign currency transactions, 561–569
- closing rate, 564–565
- currency perspectives, 561–563
- export transaction, in foreign currency, 566–568
- fair value, 565
- foreign currency–denominated debt, 568–569
- foreign currency–denominated position, 563
- forward rate, 564–565
- historical rate, 564–565, 566, 567, 569
- IAS 21, 562, 563
- import transaction, in foreign currency, 565–566
- monetary items, 563–564
- temporal method. *See* temporal method
- translation, 562, 564–565. *See also* translation of foreign operations

accounting for government/public sector organizations, 740–744

accounting for joint arrangements, 502–503

accounting for not-for-profits. *See* not-for-profit organizations (NFPOs)

Accounting Guideline 15, 494

accounting methods, 26–27

accounting policy. *See also* financial statements, analysis and interpretation of
- financial ratios and, 69–70
- investments measured at fair value, 58–59
- investments not measured at fair value, 59–69

overview, 52–53

professional judgment, 4–5

related IFRSs/ IASs, 54–58

reporting methods and, 53–54. *See also* financial reporting

accounting standards
- convergence, 9–19
- directives and, 10
- control through purchase of shares, 96–97, 108–117
- GAAP and, 19–26
- global capital market and, 6–7
- IFRS/ U.S. GAAP differences, 17–18
- influences on, 8–9
- international accounting, 5–9
- joint arrangements, 502–503

Accounting Standards Board (AcSB), 24

Accounting Standards for Private Enterprises (ASPE). *See* ASPE

accumulated depreciation, 115, 350–354, 361

accumulated other comprehensive income (AOCI), 59, 585

acquisition cost, 64, 69–70, 100–101, 164

acquisition date, 115–116. *See also* consolidation subsequent to acquisition date

acquisition differential
- 100%-owned subsidiaries, subsequent to acquisition date, 215, 216–217, 219–221
- 80%-owned subsidiaries, subsequent to acquisition date, 223, 224, 225
- allocation of, 108–110
- amortization/impairment schedules. *See* amortization and impairment schedules
- annual basis, 214–215
- bargain purchases and, 161
- block acquisitions (step purchases), 427–436
- consolidated cash flow statement, 425
- consolidated income, 206
- deferred income tax, 514–516
- defined, 64
- direct approach, 112–113
- entity theory, 158
- goodwill, 164–165
- indirect shareholdings, 448–453
- integrated foreign operation, 637–640
- inventory, 216
- joint arrangements, 504
- liabilities, assigned to, 231–233
- negative acquisition differential, 162
- negative goodwill, 162–163
- ownership interest, 427, 439–441
- parent company theory, 154
- proprietary theory, 152, 153
- push-down accounting, 113–114

reverse takeover, 128

self-sustaining foreign operation, 640–644

subsidiary, 114

subsidiary and, 164–165, 234

subsidiary with preferred shares, 444, 447–448

working paper approach, 109–110, 111

acquisition method
- acquisition cost, 100–101
- control through purchase of net assets, 96, 103–108
- control through purchase of shares, 96–97, 108–117
- date of acquisition, 100
- depreciable assets, 114–115
- direct approach, 112–113
- goodwill, 102
- identifiable assets, 101–102
- IFRS 3 and, 100
- illustrations, 102–105
- push-down accounting, 113–114
- reverse takeover, 125–126
- status of, 99
- subsidiary formed by parent, 114
- working paper approach, 109–111

acquisitions. *See also* acquisition method; business combinations; ownership changes
- integrated foreign operation, 625–626, 627–632
- self-sustaining foreign operation, 632–636

AcSB, 25

Aecon Group Inc., 68–69

AFS investments, 53, 58–59, 69–70

agency approach, 366, 379

Air Canada, 500

amortization and impairment schedules. *See also* acquisition differential
- 100%-owned subsidiaries, 216–218, 219–221, 222
- 80%-owned subsidiaries, subsequent to acquisition date, 222–225, 228–229
- consolidated financial statements, 206

analysis and interpretation of financial statements. *See* financial statements, analysis and interpretation

ASPE
- *CICA Handbook* and, 24–25
- cost method, 60, 70
- IFRS/ ASPE differences, 28
- intercompany transactions, 312, 382
- investments in associate, 70
- nonstrategic investment, 71

ASPE differences
- business combinations, 119
- consolidation subsequent to acquisition date, 239